CASES AND MATERIALS
ON
INTERNATIONAL LAW

AUSTRALIA
LBC Information Services
Sydney

CANADA AND USA
Carswell
Toronto, Ontario

NEW ZEALAND
Brooker's
Auckland

SINGAPORE AND MALAYSIA
Thomson Information (S.E. Asia)
Singapore

CASES AND MATERIALS ON INTERNATIONAL LAW

By

D. J. HARRIS, LL.M., PH.D.

Professor of Public International Law
University of Nottingham

FIFTH EDITION

LONDON
SWEET & MAXWELL
1998

First Edition (1973)
Second Impression (1976)
Second Edition (1979)
Third Edition (1983)
Second Impression (1986)
Third Impression (1987)
Fourth Impression (1989)
Fifth Impression (1990)
Fourth edition (1991)
Second Impression (1992)
Third Impression (1993)
Fourth Impression (1995)
Fifth Impression (1996)
Fifth edition (1998)
Second Impression (1999)
Third Impression (2000)

Published in 1998 by Sweet and Maxwell Limited
100 Avenue Road
London NW3 3PF
(http://www.sweetandmaxwell.co.uk)

Computerset by Interactive Sciences Ltd, Gloucester
Printed and bound in Great Britain by Clays Ltd, of St Ives

No natural forests were destroyed to make this product;
only farmed timber was used and re-planted.

ISBN 0421 53470 2Hb
0421 53480 XPb

A CIP catalogue record for this book is available
from the British Library.

PREFACE

Much has happened in the years since the last edition of this casebook in 1991. The USSR has disappeared and there has been civil war in the Balkans. The end of the USSR has had repercussions throughout the book and the dissolution of the old Yugoslavia has required much revision of the sections on statehood and recognition in Chapter 4. Events in Bosnia-Hercegovina have lead to the establishment of the International Criminal Tribunal for the former Yugoslavia at The Hague and prompted the addition of a section on Human Rights and Criminal Law in Chapter 9. The same chapter has been revised to take account of the developing jurisprudence and practice of the UN human rights treaty bodies. Sadly, this has meant that the sections on regional human rights treaty arrangements have had to be excluded. Chapter 11 has also been considerably changed to take account of the new lease of life given the Security Council by the end of the Cold War. The Council has expanded its understanding of a threat to the peace and has acted in Iraq, Somalia, Yugoslavia and elsewhere so as to give new meaning to the concept of humanitarian intervention and otherwise to develop its powers. The section on the Gulf War that was included as an Appendix in the last edition has now been integrated into the main text. That section was prepared for the last edition by my colleague, Nigel White, to whom I remain greatly indebted. The section on the Gulf War continues to be largely his.

Other developments on a lesser scale have been taken into account. With the entry into force of the 1982 Law of the Sea Convention, Chapter 7 has been re-arranged and is now based on that treaty instead of the 1958 Law of the Sea Conventions. Chapter 12 has been re-edited to include the Nuclear Weapons and the Genocide Convention cases. Throughout the book, changes have been made that reflect the increase in activity of the I.C.J.

I am very grateful to those people who have made suggestions for improvement. I am also extremely grateful to Robert Cryer who took several weeks off from his studies as a research student in this Department to do an outstanding job of reading the proofs and undertaking research for me.

I have tried to make the book current to July 1997. It has also been possible to include some later information at the proof stage.

Department of Law
University of Nottingham
October 1997   *David Harris*

ACKNOWLEDGEMENTS

Grateful acknowledgement is made to the following authors and publishers for permission to quote from their works:

BOWETT: Reprisals involving Recourse to Armed Force 66 A.J.I.L. 1 (1972). Reprinted by permission of the American Society of International Law

BRIERLY: International Law and Resort to Armed Force. 4 Cam.L.J. 308 (1932). Reprinted by Permission of Cambridge Law Journal

——: The Law of Nations. Edited by Sir Humphrey Waldock (6th ed., 1963). Reprinted with the Permission of Oxford University Press

CRAWFORD: ed., The Rights of Peoples (1988). Reprinted with the Permission of Oxford University Press

DICKINSON: Introductory Comment to the Harvard Research Draft Convention on Jurisdiction with Respect to Crime 29 A.J.I.L.Sup. 443 (1935). Reprinted with the Permission of the American Society of International Law

FITZMAURICE: The Foundations of the Authority of International Law and the Problem of Enforcement (1956) 19 M.L.R. 1

——: The General Principles of International Law Considered from the Standpoint of the Rule of Law 92 Hague Recueil 5 (1957-II). Reprinted by Permission of Kluwer Academic Publishers

——: The Law and Procedure of the International Court of Justice: Treaty Interpretation and Other Treaty Points 28 B.Y.I.L. 1 (1951). Reprinted by Permission. Published by Oxford University for the Royal Institute of International Affairs, London

Some Problems Regarding the Formal Sources of International Law. Symbolae Verzil (1958). Reprinted by Permission of Kluwer Academic Publishers

GROSS: ed., The Future of the International Court of Justice. Reprinted by Permission of Oceana Publications, Inc. Grotius Publications: Extracts from the U.S. Claims Tribunal Reports

HENKIN: How Nations Behave (2nd ed., 1979) pp. 121–127. Reprinted by Permission of Colombia University Press

——: International Law: Politics and Values (1995), pp. 280–283. Reprinted by Permission of Walters Kluwer Academic Publications

McMAHON: Legal Aspects of Outer Space 38 B.Y.I.L. 339 (1962). Reprinted by Permission. Published by Oxford University Press for the Royal Institute of International Affairs, London

McNAIR: The Functions and Differing Legal Character of Treaties 11 B.Y.I.L. 100 (1930). Reprinted by permission. Published by Oxford University Press for the Royal Institute of International Affairs, London

——: The Law of Treaties (2nd ed., 1961), pp. 15–21. Reprinted by permission of Oxford University Press

MORGENTHAU: Politics Among Nations (6th ed., 1963), pp. 312–313. Reprinted by Permission of McGraw-Hill Publishers

OPPENHEIM: Oppenheim's International Law (9th ed., 1992), Vol. 1, paras. 232–235. Reprinted by Permission of Addison Wesley Longman Ltd.

——: Oppenheim's International Law (8th ed., 1955), para. 272. Reprinted by Permission of Addison Wesley Longman Ltd.

PARRY: The Sources and Evidences of International Law (1965), pp. 103–105. Reprinted by Permission

Rosenne: The Law and Practice of the International Court 1965 Vol. 1 pp. 333–334. Reprinted by Permission of Kluwer Academic Publishers

Sloan: General Assembly Resolutions Revisited 58 B.Y.I.L. 39 (1987). Reprinted by Permission of Oxford University Press

Van Hoof: Rethinking the Sources of International Law (1983) pp. 187–189. Reprinted by Permission of Kluwer Academic Publications

Waldock: General Courses on Public International Law 106 Hague Recueil 54 (1962-II). Reprinted by Permission of Walters Kluwer Academic Publishers

While every care has been taken to establish and acknowledge copyright, and contact the copyright owners, the publishers tender their apologies for any accidental infringement. They would be pleased to come to a suitable arrangement with the rightful owners in each case.

CONTENTS

TABLE OF CASES (U.K.)

*[Page references in **bold** type indicate extracts of the case.]*

TABLE OF CASES (International and non-U.K.)

This table includes cases decided by international courts and tribunals and by municipal courts outside the U.K. It also includes international cases and incidents, e.g. the Black Sea Incident, not decided by a court or tribunal.

TABLE OF NATIONAL STATUTES, ETC.

*[Page references in **bold** type indicate extracts of the statute]*

TABLE OF STATUTORY INSTRUMENTS, ETC.

TABLE OF TREATIES

*[Page references in **bold** type indicate extracts of the treaty.]*

TABLE OF OTHER DOCUMENTS

*[Page references in **bold** type indicate extracted material.]*

SECURITY COUNCIL RESOLUTIONS

TABLE OF ABBREVIATIONS

A.A.S.L.	Annals of Air and Space Law
A.B.A.J.	American Bar Association Journal
A.D.	Annual Digest of Public International Law
A.F.D.I.	Annuaire Français de Droit International
A.J.I.L.	American Journal of International Law
A.U.L.R.	American University Law Review
A.Y.I.L.	Australian Yearbook of International Law
Af.J.I.C.L.	African Journal of International and Comparative Law
B.D.I.L.	British Digest of International Law
B.F.S.P.	British and Foreign State Papers
B.P.I.L.	British Practice in International Law
B.U.I.L.J.	Boston University International Law Journal
B.Y.I.L.	British Yearbook of International Law
Brierly	The Law of Nations, 6th ed., 1963
Brooklyn J.I.L.	Brooklyn Journal of International Law
Brownlie	Principles of Public International Law, 4th ed., 1990
C., Cd., Cmd., Cmnd., Cm.	United Kingdom Command Papers
C.L.J.	Cambridge Law Journal
C.L.P.	Current Legal Problems
C.P.U.K.I.L.	Contemporary Practice of the United Kingdom in International Law
C.T.S.	Consolidated Treaty Series
C.W.R.J.I.L.	Case Western Reserve Journal of International Law
C.Y.H.R.	Canadian Yearbook of Human Rights
C.Y.I.L.	Canadian Yearbook of International Law
Cal.L.R.	California Law Review
Cal.West I.L.J.	California Western International Law Journal
Chinese Y.I.L.A.	Chinese Yearbook of International Law and Affairs
Col.H.R.L.R.	Colombia Human Rights Law Review
Col.J.T.L.	Colombia Journal of Transnational Law
Cornell I.L.J.	Cornell International Law Journal
Den.J.I.L.P.	Denver Journal of International Law & Politics
Dick.J.I.L.	Dickinson Journal of International Law
E.C.Bulletin	Official Bulletin of the European Community
E.Ct.H.R.Rep.	European Court of Human Rights Reports
E.H.R.R.	European Human Rights Reports
E.J.I.L.	European Journal of International Law
Encycl.P.I.L.	Encyclopaedia of Public International Law
Fla.St.U.J.Trans.L.P.	Florida State University Journal of Transnational Law and Policy
For.Aff.	Foreign Affairs
G.A.O.R.	General Assembly Official Records
G.A.Resn.	General Assembly Resolution
G.Y.I.L.	German Yearbook of International Law
Ga.J.I.C.L.	Georgia Journal of International and Comparative Law
H.I.L.J.	Harvard International Law Review

H.R.C.	Human Rights Committee
H.R.L.J.	Human Rights Law Journal
H.R.Q.	Human Rights Quarterly
Hackworth	Digest of International Law
Hague Y.I.L.	Hague Yearbook of International Law
Hansard	Debates of the United Kingdom Parliament
Hastings I.C.L.R.	Hastings International and Comparative Law Review
Houston J.I.L.	Houston Journal of International Law
I.C.J.	International Court of Justice
I.C.J.Rep.	International Court of Justice Reports
I.C.L.Q.	International and Comparative Law Quarterly
I.C.S.I.D. Rev-F.I.L.J.	International Centre for the Settlement of International Disputes Review – Foreign Investment Law Journal
I.H.R.R.	International Human Rights Reports
I.J.E.C.L.	International Journal of Estuarine and Coastal Law
I.J.I.L.	Indian Journal of International Law
I.L.C.	International Law Commission
I.L.M.	International Legal Materials
I.L.O.	International Labour Organisation Conventions
I.L.R.	International Law Reports
Ind.J.I.L.	Indian Journal of International Law
Int. Aff.	International Affairs
Int.Arb.	International Arbitration
Int.Conc.	International Conciliation
Int.Lawyer	International Lawyer
Int.Leg.	Hudson, International Legislation, 9 volumes (1931–50)
Int.Org.	International Organisation
Int.Rel.	International Relations
Iran – U.S.C.T.R.	Iran–U.S. Claims Tribunal Reports
Is.L.R.	Israel Law Review
Is.Y.H.R.	Israel Yearbook on Human Rights
J.A.L.C.	Journal of Air Law and Commerce
J.D.I.	Journal du Droit International
J.E.N.R.L.	Journal of Energy and Natural Resources Law
J.W.T.L.	Journal of World Trade Law
J.African L.	Journal of African Law
J.Int.Arb.	Journal of International Arbitration
J.Space L.	Journal of Space Law
Jap.Ann.I.L.	Japanese Annual of International Law
Jur.Rev.	Juridical Review
L.& C.P.	Law and Contemporary Problems
L.N.O.J.	League of Nations Official Journal
L.N.T.S.	League of Nations Treaty Series
L.Q.R.	Law Quarterly Review
Leiden I.J.L.	Leiden International Law Journal
Loyola L.A.I.C.L.J.	Loyola Los Angeles International and Comparative Law Journal
M.L.R.	Modern Law Review
M.U.L.R.	Melbourne University Law Review
McNair	International Law Opinions, 3 vols (1956)
McNair, *Treaties*	The Law of Treaties, 2nd ed., 1961
Mar.Pol.	Marine Policy

Mar.Pol.Rep.	Marine Policy Reports
Mich.J.I.L.	Michigan Journal of International Law
Moore Int.Arb.	International Arbitrations
N.I.L.Q.	Northern Ireland Legal Quarterly
N.I.L.R.	Netherlands International Law Review
N.Q.H.R.	Netherlands Quarterly of Human Rights
N.T.I.R.	Nordisk Tidsskrift for International Ret
N.Y.I.L.	Netherlands Yearbook of International Law
N.Y.U.J.I.L.P.	New York University Journal of International Law and Politics
N.Y.U.L.R.	New York University Law Review
N.Z.L.R.	New Zealand Law Review
N.Z.T.S.	New Zealand Treaty Series
N.Z.U.L.R.	New Zealand Universities Law Review
O.D.I.L.	Ocean Development and International Law
O.Z.O.R.V.	Osterreichische Zeitschrift für öffentliches Recht und Völkerrecht
P.A.U.T.S.	Pan American University Treaty Series
P.C.I.J.	Permanent Court of International Justice
P.L.	Public Law
Palestine Y.I.L.	Palestine Yearbook of International Law
Pol.Y.I.L.	Polish Yearbook of International Law
Proc.A.S.I.L.	Proceedings of the American Society of International Law
R.B.D.I.	Revue Belge de Droit International
R.D.I.S.D.P.	Revue de Droit International, de Sciences Diplomatiques et Politiques
R.G.D.I.P.	Revue Generale de Droit International Public
R.H.D.I.	Revue Hellenique de Droit International
R.I.A.A.	Reports of International Arbitral Awards
Rev.I.C.J.	Review of the International Commission of Jurists
Rev.Int.Studies	Review of International Studies
S.A.	South African Law Reports
S.A.L.J.	South African Law Journal
S.A.Y.I.L.	South African Yearbook of International Law
T.I.L.J.	Texas International Law Journal
Trans.Grot.Soc.	Transactions of the Grotius Society
U.K.M.I.L.	United Kingdom Materials in International Law
U.K.P.I.L.	United Kingdom Practice in International Law
U.K.T.S.	United Kingdom Treaty Series
U.N.C.I.O.	Documents of the United Nations Conference on International Organisation
U.N.T.S.	United Nations Treaty Series
U.S.D.I.L.	United Nations Digest of International Law
U.S.For.Rel.	Foreign Relations of the United States
V.U.W.L.R	Victoria University of Wellington Law Review
Vand.J.T.L.	Vanderbilt Journal of Transnational Law
Virg.J.I.L.	Virginia Journal of International Law
Whiteman	Digest of International Law, 14 vols, (1963–70)
Y.B.E.C.H.R.	Yearbook of the European Convention on Human Rights
Y.B.I.L.C.	Yearbook of the International Law Commission
Y.B.W.A.	Yearbook of World Affairs
Y.S.W.P.O.	Yale Studies in World Political Order
Yale J.I.L.	Yale Journal of International Law

CHAPTER 1

INTRODUCTION[1]

1. INTERNATIONAL LAW AS "LAW"

BRIERLY, THE LAW OF NATIONS

Waldock (6th ed., 1963), pp. 41–42, 68–76

LAW can only exist in a society, and there can be no society without a system of law to regulate the relations of its members with one another. If then we speak of the "law of nations", we are assuming that a "society" of nations exists, and the assumption that the whole of the civilized world constitutes in any real sense a single society or community is one which we are not justified in making without examination. In any case the character of the law of nations is necessarily determined by that of the society within which it operates, and neither can be understood without the other.

The law of nations had its origin among a few kindred nations of western Europe which, despite their frequent quarrels and even despite the religious schism of the sixteenth century, all had and were all conscious of having a common background in the Christian religion and the civilization of Greece and Rome. They were in a real sense a society of nations. But the rise of the modern state system undermined the tradition of the unity of Christendom, and eventually gave rise to those sentiments of exclusive nationalism which are rife in the world today. It is true that side by side with this development there has been an immense growth of the factors that make states mutually dependent on one another. Modern science has given us vastly increased facilities and speed of communications, and modern commerce has created demands for the commodities of other nations which even the extravagances of modern economic

---

[1] In addition to the writings from which passages are printed in this Chapter, see Allott, *Eunomia: New Order for a New World* (1990); Bedjaoui, ed., *International Law: Achievements and Prospects* (1991); Brownlie, (1995–I) 255 Hague Recueil 21; Carty, *The Decay of International Law* (1986); Cassese, *International Law in a Divided World* (1986); Franck, *The Power of Legitimacy Among Nations* (1990); Higgins, *Problems and Process* (1994); Jennings (1958) 34 B.Y.I.L. 334; Koskenniemi, *From Apology to Utopia: The Structure of International Legal Argument* (1986); *id.* (1995) 16 A.Y.I.L. 1; Lissitzyn, *International Law Today and Tomorrow* (1965); McDougal (1953–I) 82 Hague Recueil 133; Merrills, *Anatomy of International Law* (2nd ed., 1981); Mosler, *The International Society as a Legal Community* (1980); Schachter, *International Law in Theory and Practice* (1991); De Visscher, *passim*.

nationalism are not able to stifle. If human affairs were more wisely ordered, and if men were clearer-sighted than they are in seeing their own interests, it might be that this interdependence of the nations would lead to a strengthening of their feelings of community. But their interdependence is mainly in material things, and though material bonds are necessary, they are not enough without a common social consciousness; without that they are as likely to lead to friction as to friendship. Some sentiment of shared responsibility for the conduct of a common life is a necessary element in any society, and the necessary force behind any system of law; and the strength of any legal system is proportionate to the strength of such a sentiment. . . .

It has often been said that international law ought to be classified as a branch of ethics rather than of law. The question is partly one of words, because its solution will clearly depend on the definition of law which we choose to adopt; in any case it does not affect the value of the subject one way or the other, though those who deny the legal character of international law often speak as though "ethical" were a depreciatory epithet. But in fact it is both practically inconvenient and also contrary to the best juristic thought to deny its legal character. It is inconvenient because if international law is nothing but international morality, it is certainly not the whole of international morality, and it is difficult to see how we are to distinguish it from those other admittedly moral standards which we apply in forming our judgments on the conduct of states.[2] Ordinary usage certainly uses two tests in judging the "rightness" of a state's act, a moral test and one which is somehow felt to be independent of morality. Every state habitually commits acts of selfishness which are often gravely injurious to other states, and yet are not contrary to international law; but we do not on that account necessarily judge them to have been "right". It is confusing and pedantic to say that both these tests are moral. Moreover, it is the pedantry of the theorist and not of the practical man; for questions of international law are invariably treated as legal questions by the foreign offices which conduct our international business, and in the courts, national or international, before which they are brought; legal forms and methods are used in diplomatic controversies and in judicial and arbitral proceedings, and authorities and precedents are cited in argument as a matter of course. It is significant too that when a breach of international law is alleged by one party to a controversy, the act impugned is practically never defended by claiming the right of private judgment, which would be the natural defence if the issue concerned the

---

[2] *Ed., e.g.* the legality and morality of refusing economic aid to poor countries (see below, p. 552), or asylum to refugees (see below, p. 530), is to be judged by different standards. And the use of nuclear weapons, which may be thought generally to be immoral, may be lawful in some extreme cases of self defence: *Nuclear Weapons Case*, below, p. 924.

morality of the act, but always by attempting to prove that no rule has been violated. . . . [3]

If, as Sir Frederick Pollock[4] writes, and as probably most competent jurists would today agree, the only essential conditions for the existence of law are the existence of a political community, and the recognition by its members of settled rules binding upon them in that capacity, international law seems on the whole to satisfy these conditions. . . . [5]

The best view is that international law is in fact just a system of customary law, upon which has been erected, almost entirely within the last two generations, a superstructure of "conventional" or treaty-made law, and some of its chief defects are precisely those that the history of law teaches us to expect in a customary system. It is a common mistake to suppose that of these the most conspicuous is the frequency of its violation. Violations of law are rare in all customary systems, and they are so in international law. . . . For the law is normally observed because, as we shall see, the demands that it makes on states are generally not exacting, and on the whole states find it convenient to observe it. . . . But the weakness of the international law lies deeper than any mere question of sanctions. It is not the existence of a police force that makes a system of law strong and respected, but the strength of the law that makes it possible for a police force to be effectively organized. The imperative character of law is felt so strongly and obedience to it has become so much a matter of habit within a highly civilized state that national law has developed a machinery of enforcement which generally works smoothly, though never so smoothly as to make breaches impossible. If the imperative character of international law were equally strongly felt, the institution of definite international sanctions would easily follow.

A customary system of law can never be adequate to the needs of any but a primitive society, and the paradox of the international society is that, whilst on the material side it is far from primitive, and therefore needs a strong and fairly elaborate system of law for the regulation of the clashes to which the material interdependence of different states is constantly giving rise, its spiritual cohesion is, as we have already seen, weak, and as long as that is so the weakness will inevitably be reflected in a weak and primitive system of law.[6]

---

[3] *Ed.* See, *e.g.* the British justification for the invasion of Suez: the Lord Chancellor (Lord Kilmuir), *Hansard*, HL, Vol. 199, col. 1348, and the Argentinian justification for the invasion of the Falkland Islands, below, p. 903.

[4] *First Book of Jurisprudence*, p. 28.

[5] *Ed.* In *The Outlook for International Law* (1944), p. 5, Brierly writes: "The best evidence for the existence of international law is that every actual state recognises that it does exist and that it is itself under obligation to observe it. States may often violate international law, just as individuals often violate municipal law, but no more than individuals do states defend their violations by claiming that they are above the law."

[6] *Ed. cf.* Corbett, *Law in Diplomacy* (1959), pp. 273–274: "What is principally missing is the measure of agreement on supreme common values, the sense of community, loyalty, and mutual tolerance which within the State make compulsory institutions bearable. The reserved domain and the whole legal concept of sovereignty correspond to the fact that

Among the most serious shortcomings of the present system are the rudimentary character of the institutions which exist for the making and the application of the law, and the narrow restrictions on its range. . . . There is no legislature to keep the law abreast of new needs in the international society; no executive power to enforce the law; and although certain administrative bodies have been created, these, though important in themselves, are far from being adequate for the mass of business which ought to be treated today as of international concern. There exist also convenient machinery for the arbitration of disputes and a standing court of justice, but the range of action of these is limited because resort to them is not compulsory.[7]

The restricted range of international law is merely the counterpart of the wide freedom of independent action which states claim in virtue of their sovereignty. . . . Law will never play a really effective part in international relations until it can annex to its own sphere some of the matters which at present lie within the "domestic jurisdictions" of the several states. . . . [8]

It is a natural consequence of the absence of authoritative law-declaring machinery that many of the principles of international law, and even more the detailed application of accepted principles, are uncertain. But on the whole the layman tends to exaggerate this defect. It is not in the nature of any law to provide mathematically certain solutions of problems which may be presented to it; for uncertainty cannot be eliminated from law so long as the possible conjunctions of facts remain infinitely various. Although therefore the difference between international law and the law of a state in this respect is important it is one of degree and not of kind, and it tends to be reduced as the practice of resorting to international courts, which are able to work out the detailed practical implication of general principles, becomes more common.[9] The difficulty of formulating the rules of international law with precision is a necessary

the State remains in the hearts and minds of men the highest center of human authority and chief guardian of the most treasured values . . . the State continues to be for practical purposes the chief end of man. So long as this is so, whatever their covenants or declarations, governments will not assume in practice a position of general subjection to a law of nations."

[7] *Ed.* See below, Chap. 12.

[8] *Ed.* Matters within the "domestic jurisdiction" of a state are matters not regulated by international law so that a state is free to act in its discretion. They are numerous and varied, ranging from the admission of aliens to the regulation of cruelty of cats. Other examples are listed in the *Nicaragua (Merits)* case, para. 205, below, p. 874. The extent of a state's domestic jurisdiction changes with the development of custom and with the treaty obligations it undertakes. For example, the post-1945 international law of human rights—both customary and treaty—greatly limit a state's former freedom to ill-treat their nationals: see Chap. 5. For the concept in the UN Charter, see below, p. 970.

[9] *Ed.* This is optimistic. Although the World Court's docket is now fuller than it has generally been, see below, p. 988, the lack of many cases interpreting the increasing number of "law-making" treaties (see below, p. 46) presents a problem. In municipal law, a new statute that raises questions of interpretation is soon taken to court for a ruling. Unfortunately, that is unlikely to happen in international law, *e.g.* it took over 40 years for

consequence of the kinds of evidence upon which we have to rely in order to establish them. . . .

> Brierly then discusses the international law attitude to the legality of war.[10]

Whether from a review of all these shortcomings we ought to conclude that international law is a failure depends upon what we assume to be its aim. It has not failed to serve the purposes for which states have chosen to use it; in fact it serves these purposes reasonably well . . . the practice of international law proceeds on much the same lines as that of any other kind of law, with the foreign offices taking the place of the private legal adviser[11] and exchanging arguments about the facts and the law, and later, more often than is sometimes supposed, with a hearing before some form of international tribunal. The volume of this work is considerable,[12] but most of it is not sensational. . . . That does not mean that the matters to which it does relate are unimportant in themselves; often they are very important to particular interests or individuals. But it means that international law is performing a useful and indeed a necessary function in international life in enabling states to carry on their day-to-day intercourse along orderly and predictable lines. That is the role for which states have chosen to use it and for that it has proved a serviceable instrument.

Notes

1. *Ubi societas ibi ius.* Is there an international society with a sufficient sense of community to permit one realistically to expect a more than fragmentary system of international law? Or are the attitudes and interests of the world's different geo-political groupings of states too diverse to allow this? An important positive development in this regard has been the end of the Cold War and of the Soviet theory of international law, with its emphasis upon state sovereignty and rejection of bourgeois law.[13] Although some communist states (*e.g.* China,[14] Cuba) remain, the most significant divisions among states are those between developing and developed states, whose economic and other interests differ greatly, and, in some respects, between Islamic states and others.[15]

the I.C.J. to construe Art. 2(4), UN Charter: see the *Nicaragua* case, below, p. 874. An outstanding exception is the European Convention on Human Rights, the meaning of which is gradually being established by the jurisprudence of the Strasbourg authorities.

[10] See below, Chap. 11.

[11] *Ed.* On the role of the Foreign Office legal adviser, see Merillat, ed., *Legal Advisers and Foreign Affairs* (1964), and Vallat, *International Law and the Practitioner* (1966).

[12] *Ed.* The U.K., for example, enters into over 100 treaties each year and requires legal advice and representation in the UN and other international fora.

[13] On the Soviet theory, see Tunkin, *Theory of International Law* (1970), English translation by Butler (1974). On international law after the Cold War, see Henkin, below, p. 19, and Reisman (1993) 87 A.J.I.L. 538.

[14] For the Chinese approach, see Chiu (1987) 28 H.I.L.J. 289, and Chinese Society of International Law, *Selected Articles from the Chinese Yearbook of International Law* (1983).

[15] See Bahar (1992) 33 H.I.L.J. 145. On the problems that shari'a law presents for human rights, see below, p. 627.

A problem of a different kind, namely the continuing reluctance of all states to surrender sovereign powers, is pointed out by De Visscher[16]:

> It is therefore pure illusion to expect from the mere arrangement of inter-State relations the establishment of a community order; this can find a solid foundation only in the development of the true international spirit in men. . . . There will be no international community so long as the political ends of the State overshadow the human ends of power.

Is De Visscher unduly pessimistic? Even if states from different geo-political groupings have widely different interests in some respects and states generally do shrink from surrendering the sovereignty they need to surrender to extend significantly the "range of international law" and permit its enforcement, are there now at least some signs of the recognition by states of more common interests (*e.g.* in environmental protection) and of more accommodation of the human rights of individuals?

2. *The Austinian Handicap.* "Is international law 'law' " is a standard sherry party question. Its sometimes irritating persistence is very largely the responsibility of John Austin, an English jurist of the first part of the nineteenth century and a familiar friend of any student who has taken a course in jurisprudence. He defined laws "properly so-called" as commands and "positive law", which he regarded as the "appropriate matter of jurisprudence", as the commands of a sovereign.[17] A sovereign he defined as a person who received the habitual obedience of the members of an independent political society and who, in turn, did not owe such obedience to any other person. Rules of international law did not qualify as rules of "positive law" by this test and, not being commands of any sort, were placed by Austin in the category of "laws improperly so-called". This uncompromising and unhappily phrased rejection of international law's claim to be law of the same order as municipal law[18] has, to this day, upset international lawyers and placed them on the defensive. Although international law is still not "law" according to Austin's test, most international lawyers would at least dispute that that test is more helpful than certain others (*e.g.* that of Pollock, quoted by Brierly) by which international law could be said to be "law".[19]

3. *The "Law Habit".* No writer would seem to dissent from the view expressed by Brierly that, in terms of the number, as opposed to the political importance, of the occasions on which international law is complied with, it is more honoured in the observance than in the breach. Jessup,[20] for example, takes Brierly's view:

> Wars, breaches of treaties, oppression of the weak by the strong, are the headlines of the daily press and of the history textbooks. The superficial observer has not noted the steady observance of such treaties as that under which letters are carried all over the world at rates fixed by the Universal Postal Union. He ignores the fact that there is scarcely an instance in two hundred years in which an ambassador has been subjected to suit in courts of the country where he is stationed. . . . The superficial observer has not read the hundreds of decisions handed down by international courts called Mixed Claims Commissions, which have awarded money damages duly paid by the

---

[16] De Visscher, pp. 89, 94. See also Mosler, *op. cit.*, p. 1, n. 1, above, pp. 17–47.

[17] See *The Province of Jurisprudence Determined* (1832), Lectures I, V and VI. A recent edition is that edited by Hart in 1954.

[18] This is the term used in international law to refer to the law of a state.

[19] For the view that the question whether international law is "law" is a verbal one not worth bothering with: see Glanville Williams (1945) 22 B.Y.I.L. 146 at 163. See also Hart, *The Concept of Law* (2nd ed., 1994), pp. 214–215.

[20] *A Modern Law of Nations* (1948), pp. 6–8.

defendant states.... He may be unfamiliar with the extent to which international law has been incorporated in national law and has thus secured an enforcement agency through the ordinary governmental machinery of the national states.... One of the wisest and most experienced of them all, John Bassett Moore, has recorded his observation that on the whole international law is as well observed as national law. The Director of the Yale Institute of International Studies has recently remarked that those 'who make light of treaty commitments in general seem to ignore the fact that the vast majority of such engagements are continuously, honestly, and regularly observed even under adverse conditions and at considerable inconvenience to the parties.' ... The record proves that there is a 'law habit' in international relations. It is not immaterial to add that the instances in which judgments of international tribunals have been flouted are so rare that the headline-reader may well place them in the man-bites-dog category.[21]

Although there is clearly some merit to the "law habit" view, might it not, to some extent, be misleading? What has to be emphasised as strongly is that a state can usually flout international law if it wants to and get away with it. How relevant also is a comparison of the number or percentage of violations of municipal and international law? The point about a train robber is that if there is a good case against him and if his whereabouts are known he will be punished. The USSR and the U.S. were not arraigned for intervening unlawfully in Afghanistan in 1979[22] and Grenada in 1983[23] respectively and Israel, though condemned by the UN, has not been brought to book for its annexation of Middle East territory: see below, p. 226. Political and economic considerations may be crucial to the decision of the international community to act. Iraq's invasion of Kuwait, which affected Western oil interests, was rapidly dealt with, but there was no such physical retaliation against Indonesia's invasion of East Timor, see below, p. 119.

But are we asking too much of international law? Are we expecting it to be effective often in disputes in which we would not imagine law to apply, or at least not to be in the forefront, within a state because of the political importance of the problem?

Note also, by way of apology for international law, the following statement. Writing of the North Atlantic Treaty,[24] Katz[25] suggests:

When such a treaty is negotiated and signed, none of the participating states contemplates that its future course under the treaty will be governed exclusively or primarily by technical juridical procedures or patterns of analysis. No participating state considers itself to have acquired a right to demand that the

[21] Nantwi, *The Enforcement of International Judicial Decisions and Arbitral Awards in Public International Law* (1966), Chap. IV, records only a few cases, constituting but a very small proportion of the whole, in which the losing state has not complied with the decision or award. All of the decisions and opinions of the P.C.I.J. were followed; those of the I.C.J. have been less effective: see below, p. 988. World Court jurisdiction is voluntary so that the parties are predisposed (although this is not necessarily true of cases brought under the "optional clause": see below, p. 1002) to accept the ruling made (note that one of the rulings of the I.C.J. not complied with was that against Albania in the *Corfu Channel Case* which had initially been brought before the Court very much against Albania's will: see below, p. 996) and that the percentage of disputes between states referred to the Court is minute.

[22] See below, p. 891.

[23] See below, p. 893.

[24] U.K.T.S. 56 (1949), Cmd. 7789; 34 U.N.T.S. 243; (1949) 43 A.J.I.L., Supp. 159.

[25] *The Relevance of International Adjudication* (1968), pp. 53–54. And see Dean Acheson's comment on the role of law in the Cuban missile crisis, below, p. 901.

course of conduct of the other participating states should be so determined. The relevant procedures are diplomatic, and the relevant intellectual canons are the canons of political thought—with something added. The addition is a sense of law. In the language of lawyers, Article 5 of the North Atlantic Treaty constitutes a formal statement of policy, a formal declaration of purpose or declaration of intent, upon which the participating states are entitled reciprocally to rely subject to the limitations inherent in the nature of such a declaration. Article 5 neither expresses nor was intended to express a contractual obligation in the strict legal sense. It does nevertheless express an obligation. The obligation is diplomatic, reinforced by what I call a sense of law.

MORGENTHAU, POLITICS AMONG NATIONS[26]

(6th ed., 1985), pp. 312–313

The great majority of the rules of international law are generally observed by all nations without actual compulsion, for it is generally in the interest of all nations concerned to honor their obligations under international law. A nation will hesitate to infringe upon the rights of foreign diplomats residing in its capital; for it has an interest, identical with the interests of all other nations, in the universal observance of the rules of international law which extend their protection to its own diplomatic representatives in foreign capitals as well as to the foreign diplomats in its own capital.[27] A nation will likewise be reluctant to disregard its obligations under a commercial treaty, since the benefits that it expects from the execution of the treaty by the other contracting parties are complementary to those anticipated by the latter. It may thus stand to lose more than it would gain by not fulfilling its part of the bargain. This is particularly so in the long run, since a nation that has the reputation of reneging on its commercial obligations will find it hard to conclude commercial treaties beneficial to itself.

Most rules of international law formulate in legal terms such identical or complementary interests. It is for this reason that they generally enforce themselves, as it were, and that there is generally no need for a specific enforcement action. In most cases in which such rules of international law are actually violated despite the underlying community of interests, satisfaction is given to the wronged party either voluntarily or in consequence of adjudication. . . .

Thus the great majority of rules of international law are generally unaffected by the weakness of its system of enforcement, for voluntary compliance prevents the problem of enforcement from arising altogether.

---

[26] See also on sanctions and the enforcement of international law, Damrosch (1994) 8 Ethics and Int. Affairs 59; Doxey (1983) 15 C.W.R.J.I.L. 273; Hufbauer, Schott and Elliott, *Economic Sanctions Reconsidered* (2nd. ed., 1990); Joyner (1995) 16 A.Y.I.L. 241; Leyton-Brown, ed. *The Utility of International Economic Sanctions* (1987); Renwick, *Economic Sanctions* (1981); Rubin (1993) 34 H.I.L.J. 149; Schwebel, ed., *The Effectiveness of International Decisions* (1971); and the Heidelberg Colloquium on the Enforcement of International Obligations, papers printed in (1987) 47 Z.A.O.R.V. 3.

[27] Ed., See, *e.g.* the 1965 U.S. Moscow embassy incident, below, p. 353.

The problem of enforcement becomes acute, however, in that minority of important and generally spectacular cases, particularly important in the context of our discussion, in which compliance with international law and its enforcement have a direct bearing upon the relative power of the nations concerned. In those cases . . . considerations of power rather than of law determine compliance and enforcement.

FITZMAURICE, THE FOUNDATIONS OF THE AUTHORITY OF INTERNATIONAL LAW AND THE PROBLEM OF ENFORCEMENT

(1956) 19 M.L.R. 1

With regard to the actual position concerning the enforceability of the international legal system, there has always been a respectable body of international lawyers that has both considered enforceability to be a necessary characteristic of any system of law, properly so called, and has also believed that international law possessed this characteristic, even if only in a rough and rudimentary form. Oppenheim, for instance, whose treatise may be cited because it constitutes so very much the practitioner's Bible, so to speak, . . . defines law as

> a body of rules for human conduct within a community which, by common consent of this community, shall be enforced by external power [8th ed., p. 10, para. 5].

. . . so great a modernist as Kelsen seems, in one of his latest works, *Principles of International Law*, published in 1952, to incline towards a similar view. He says, on page 5 of this work, that

> . . . law is a coercive order. It provides for socially organised sanctions, and these can be clearly distinguished from a religious order on the one hand and a merely moral order on the other hand. As a coercive order, the law is that specific social technique which consists in the attempt to bring about the desired social conduct of men through the threat of a measure of coercion which is to be taken in case of . . . legally wrong conduct.

Later, on page 14 of the same work, Kelsen points out that in decentralised societies (and the international society is such a society), enforcement of the law is accomplished through the application of the principle of self-help. The legal order leaves the enforcement function to the individuals injured by a delict or illegality. . . .

Eventually—see particularly pages 18–39 of the book—Kelsen appears to reach the conclusion that, judged by these tests, international law is true law because, broadly speaking, it provides sanctions, such as the adoption of reprisals, war, and the use of force generally, and makes the employment of these sanctions lawful as a counter-measure against a legal wrong, but unlawful in all other cases. . . .

Without necessarily subscribing fully to all these views, it can fairly be said that up to a comparatively recent date, war, and the use of force generally, did constitute in some sense a recognised method of enforcing international law; or, more accurately, a means whereby in the last resort a dispute between States as to their rights could be settled. It was a means of settlement or enforcement analogous in the international field to the "blood feud" or "ordeal by battle" or single combat, by which, in a more primitive stage of national societies, disputes between individuals or groups were settled—and it has always been the case, and still is, that the international society tends to reflect national society at an earlier stage of development. . . .

. . . There is no need to retail the steps by which, in the period following on the first world war, up to date, war has, by a series of measures, been divested of its former basic legitimacy. . . .

Now this is, of course, very well, and greatly to be welcomed: no one would wish it otherwise. But it has given rise to one curious and perhaps unforeseen consequence—for in so far as war, or the use of force, was a means, however crude, by which an injured State could assert or defend its legal rights, as the case might be—then the position now is that international law is less enforceable today then it ever has been in the whole of its history—for nothing definite or certain has been put in the place of force as a means of settlement. . . .

It must be concluded that although the international order may have made [through Chapter VII of the U.N. Charter[28]] some attempt at progress in repressing or countering that particular type of illegality that consists in armed aggression or breach of the peace, it has not yet made much progress in the enforcement of international rights and obligations generally, or of international law as such. It now frowns on self-help, without, however, as yet having put anything in its place. It is obvious that such a situation is unsatisfactory. Fortunately, there can be set against it not only the fact that international law has never, in practice, been more than partly dependent for its authority[29] on the possibility of its physical enforcement, but also the principle that no system of law depends, or can, in the last resort, depend for its authority solely on the chances of enforcement. If it did, it could never in practice be enforced. The assumed certainty of enforcement in the national society masks the fact that, in general, the law does not have to be enforced, not so much because it is taken for granted that it would be, but because it commands in practice the general assent or tolerance of the community.

[28] *Ed.* See below, Chap. 11.
[29] *Ed.* The author states elsewhere in the article that "authority" is "a term here used in the sense of prestige."

The real foundation of the authority of international law resides similarly in the fact that the States making up the international society recognise it as binding upon them, and, moreover, as a system that *ipso facto* binds them *as* members of the society, irrespective of their individual wills.

AIR SERVICES AGREEMENT CASE[30]

France v. United States (1978)

Arbitral Tribunal: Riphagen, President; Ehrlich, Reuter. 18 R.I.A.A. 416

By a 1946 bilateral agreement, France and the U.S. provided for civil air flights between their two countries. A 1960 Exchange of Notes between them relating to the 1946 Agreement authorised designated American carriers to fly to Paris from the U.S. west coast via London. In 1978, Pan American Airlines, a designated carrier, announced its resumption of a west coast-London-Paris service, but with a change of gauge in London, passengers transferring from a larger to a smaller plane. France objected that this change of gauge was contrary to the 1946 Agreement, which prohibited changes of gauge within the territory of the two parties, but contained no provision on changes of gauge in the territory of a third state. When, on May 3, 1978, despite further French objection and diplomatic exchanges between the two states, Pan American sought to operate the service, passengers were not allowed to disembark in Paris. Thereafter Pan American suspended its flights. On May 4, the U.S. proposed that the dispute be referred to arbitration. On May 13, France agreed in principle and in July a *compromis* was signed. In the meantime, the U.S., acting contrary to the 1946 Agreement, had, on May 9 taken the first steps in a procedure which led on May 31 to the issue of an order under its C.A.B. Economic Regulations prohibiting flights by French designated carriers to the U.S. west coast from Paris via Montreal so long as the French ban on Pan American flights continued. However, following the signing of the *compromis*, the U.S. ban was not implemented.

The Tribunal decided, by two votes to one, that U.S. carriers were entitled under the 1946 Agreement to operate with a change of gauge in London. The following extract concerns a second question put to the Tribunal, namely whether in international law the U.S. was entitled to take the action that it took immediately prior to the signing of the *compromis*. Neither state was a party to the 1969 Vienna Convention on the Law of Treaties. On this question also the Tribunal decided, unanimously, for the U.S.

Award of the Tribunal

81.　. . . If a situation arises which, in one State's view, results in the violation of an international obligation by another State, the first State is entitled, within the limits set by the general rules of international law pertaining to the use of armed force, to affirm its rights through "countermeasures".

82.　At this point, one could introduce various doctrinal distinctions and adopt a diversified terminology dependent on various criteria, in

[30] See Damrosch (1980) 74 A.J.I.L. 785.

particular whether it is the obligation allegedly breached which is the subject of the counter-measures or whether the latter involve another obligation, and whether or not all the obligations under consideration pertain to the same convention. The Tribunal, however, does not think it necessary to go into these distinctions for the purposes of the present case. Indeed, in the present case, both the alleged violation and the counter-measure directly affect the operation of air services provided for in the Agreement and the Exchange of Notes of 5 April 1960.

83.   It is generally agreed that all counter-measures must, in the first instance, have some degree of equivalence with the alleged breach; this is a well-known rule. . . . It has been observed, generally, that judging the "proportionality" of counter-measures is not an easy task and can at best be accomplished by approximation. In the Tribunal's view, it is essential, in a dispute between States, to take into account not only the injuries suffered by the companies concerned but also the importance of the questions of principle arising from the alleged breach. The Tribunal thinks that it will not suffice, in the present case, to compare the losses suffered by Pan Am on account of the suspension of the projected services with the losses which the French companies would have suffered as a result of the counter-measures; it will also be necessary to take into account the importance of the positions of principle which were taken when the French authorities prohibited changes of gauge in third countries. If the importance of the issue is viewed within the framework of the general air transport policy adopted by the United States Government and implemented by the conclusion of a large number of international agreements with countries other than France, the measures taken by the United States do not appear to be clearly disproportionate when compared to those taken by France. . . .

Notes

1. The *Air Services Agreement* case illustrates one way by which international law may be enforced, namely by self-help. The term "countermeasure",[31] which first made its mark in the *Air Services Agreement* case,[32] has in recent years come to replace the term "reprisal", probably because of the inclusion within the latter term of armed reprisals, which are now illegal. A countermeasure is an illegal[33] act that is rendered lawful as a response to a prior illegal act. According to the *Naulilaa* case,[34] the *locus classicus* on the law of reprisals, the object of a reprisal must be "to effect reparation from the offending state for the offence or a return to legality by the avoidance of further offences" and is only lawful when preceded by an "unsatisfied demand" for reparation, although this latter requirement is not uniformly supported by state practice or writers and may not be appropriate or

---

[31] On countermeasures, see Elagab, *The Legality of Non-Forcible Countermeasures in International Law* (1988) and Zoller, *Peacetime Unilateral Remedies: An Analysis of Countermeasures* (1984).

[32] The term was used in the U.S. pleadings and adopted by the Tribunal.

[33] "Countermeasure" is used in the *Hostages Case*, I.C.J. Rep. 1980, p. 3 at 16, 27 to include *lawful* acts of retorsion also (Iranians deported for immigration infringements).

[34] *Portugal v. Germany* (1928) 2 R.I.A.A. 1012 at 1026. Translation.

possible in some circumstances.[35] The requirement stated in the *Air Services Agreement* case that a countermeasure be in proportion to the prior illegal act in terms of the damage it does is now generally accepted. The retaliatory act, which need not be of the same kind as the prior illegal act, must be directed against the delinquent state, not a third state, although injurious effects for third states may be unavoidable. In the *Cysne* case,[36] in retaliation for a breach by Great Britain of a treaty obligation not to carry certain items as contraband, Germany added further items to the list without authority and sank a Portuguese ship that carried them. Finding against Germany, the Tribunal stated:

> Reprisals are admissible only against the provoking state. Admittedly, legitimate reprisals taken against the offending state may affect the nationals of an innocent state. But that is an indirect and unintentional consequence that the victim state will in practice seek to avoid as far as possible.

Countermeasures involving the use of armed force are prohibited by virtue of Article 2(4), United Nations Charter.[37] The use of economic or political force against the delinquent state is still permitted, as are countermeasures against its nationals (*e.g.* by their arbitrary expulsion). An example of the use of economic force as a countermeasure that would probably still be lawful nearly arose in connection with the *Corfu Channel* case.[38] It would seem that the British Government were prepared to confiscate Albanian assets in the United Kingdom when Albania failed to pay the damages awarded against it by the International Court of Justice in that case but were unable to find any.[39]

The facts of the *Air Services Agreement* case raise the question of the relationship between the general customary international law on countermeasures and the customary international law of treaties[40] which permits the termination or suspension of a treaty in a case of material breach. Although both parties argued their case partly by reference to the customary international law rules on material breach,[41] the Tribunal neither referred to the law of treaties on this point nor considered whether the breach was a material one. It would appear that the general law on countermeasures supplements the law of treaties so that the former permits retaliation in the case of a minor or non-material breach as well as in the case of a material breach, whereas the latter does not. The position in respect of material breaches is less clear. The normal approach would be to regard the *lex specialis* in the customary international law of treaties as replacing the

---

[35] See Malanczuk, in Spinedi and Simma, eds., *United Nations Codification of State Responsibility* (1987), p. 197–214. The I.L.C. described the object of countermeasures as "to inflict punishment or to secure performance": Y.B.I.L.C. 1979, II–2, p. 116.

[36] *Portugal v. Germany* (1928) 2 R.I.A.A. 1052 at 1057. Translation. Footnote omitted. See also Reed (1988) 29 Virg. J.I.L. 175.

[37] See the General Assembly Declaration on Principles of International Law, G.A. Resn. 2625 (XXV), below, Appendix III, which elaborates upon Art. 2(4) and indicates that states "have a duty to refrain from acts of *reprisal* involving the use of force" (emphasis added). Note, however, that in the *Nicaragua Case*, judgment, para. 210, below, p. 876, the I.C.J. left unanswered the question whether proportionate *countermeasures* involving the use of armed force by a victim state would be lawful. On this and the Court's approach to the related question of self-defence, see below, p. 894.

[38] See below, p. 391.

[39] *Hansard*, H.C., Vol. 488, col. 981 (1951).

[40] As to which, see the note to Art. 60, Vienna Convention on the Law of Treaties, below, p. 839.

[41] Neither state was a party to the Vienna Convention and hence were not bound by Art. 60 as a treaty rule.

general law on countermeasures, although the intention of the International Law Commission may have been that the two, different regimes should co-exist.[42]

2. The International Law Commission's Draft Articles on State Responsibility, Part I contain a text on "countermeasures" which reads:

> *Article 30.* Countermeasures in respect of an internationally wrongful act
> The wrongfulness of an act of a State not in conformity with an obligation of that State towards another State is precluded if the act constitutes a measure legitimate under international law against that other State, in consequence of an internationally wrongful act of that other State.[43]

For the purposes of Article 30, "countermeasures" are understood by the Commission to include breaches of treaty obligations justified in accordance with Article 60, Vienna Convention on the Law of Treaties and measures taken by states in pursuance of decisions and recommendations of international organisations.

3. The Tribunal took the view (Award, para. 89) that counter-measures may be taken even though the parties have agreed to arbitration or judicial settlement. This view is not supported by the International Law Commission, which, in its Commentary on Article 30, stated that a condition of the legality of counter-measures is "that there must not be any procedures for peaceful settlement previously agreed upon by the parties".[44] The "unsatisfied demand" requirement in the *Naulilaa* case, which supports the proposition that a state should only take the law into its own hands as a last resort, points in the same direction, as does the idea that good faith requires that a state that has entered into an obligation to arbitrate or seek a judicial settlement should not subvert it, at least by acts that are otherwise illegal.

4. Action available to a state in international law by way of self-help include acts of retorsion as well as countermeasures. Acts of retorsion are acts which, although unfriendly, are, unlike countermeasures, not illegal under international law. The term "retorsion" applies to unfriendly but lawful acts in response to both unlawful and lawful, but unfriendly, acts. Not being unlawful, there is no requirement of proportionality in the case of acts of retorsion.

5. The absence of compulsory international judicial or arbitral remedies and the generally decentralised nature of the international community inevitably mean that self-help is the sanction that is most likely to be available to a state when faced with the breach of an international law obligation owed to it. So far as sanctions organised through the international community are concerned, the main ones are those within the power of the United Nations.[45] They are of limited scope and, insofar as they are exercisable by the Security Council, are subject to the "veto". Friedmann[46] argues that in the "international law of co-operation", which operates in areas in which states participate in activities furthering common state interests through international organisations or otherwise, a sanction of

---

[42] In its Commentary to Art. 60, the I.L.C. stated, in respect of bilateral treaties, that the right to terminate or suspend a treaty that it gave "arises independently of any right of reprisal": Y.B.I.L.C. 1966, II, p. 255.

[43] Y.B.I.L.C. 1980, II–2, p. 33. Art. 30 has been provisionally adopted by the I.L.C. on first reading.

[44] Y.B.I.L.C. 1979, II–2, p. 118, n. 595. Note also the response of the I.C.J. to the U.S. unilateral action to free the Iranian hostages in the *Hostages* case, below, p. 361. Note, however, Damrosch, *loc. cit.* at p. 11, n. 30, above, pp. 802 *et seq.* who argues that a state should not be expected to undertake the expense and delay of arbitration before resorting to countermeasures.

[45] *e.g.* in 1994, the U.K. impounded a Montenegrin owned ship (the *MV Playa*) in the enforcement of UN Security Council sanctions against the former Yugoslavia: see U.K.M.I.L. 1993; (1994) 65 B.Y.I.L. 680. See further on collective UN sanctions, below, Chap. 11.

[46] *The Changing Structure of International Law* (1964), p. 88.

exclusion from the benefits of such activities is available. He gives as an example the power of the World Bank to grant or withhold development funds:

> ... if a borrowing state were to confiscate without compensation and in a discriminatory manner, the property of foreign investors ... it would find itself excluded from participation in further development aid.[47]

As Friedmann suggests, the national interest of the defaulting state in continued participation must be at least as great as that in the course of action that caused it to default for such a sanction to be effective. When Indonesia withdrew from the United Nations in 1965 it left those United Nations specialised agencies from which it "did not have much benefit" but remained a member of the World Health Organisation which was conducting a malaria campaign in Indonesia at the time.[48] Political pressures, such as those at work in the *Certain Expenses* case in the United Nations,[49] may also prevent the application of such sanctions in some cases.

6. An effective way of enforcing international law is through national courts, whose judgments are backed by the power of the state. But not all rules of international law can readily be made the subject of national litigation. For example, the rules of diplomatic and sovereign immunity are commonly applied in national courts, but those prohibiting the use of force are not. Another factor is the extent to which customary international law and self-executing treaties are a part of the law of the land and hence enforceable in the local courts.[50]

7. Of considerable importance in the enforcement of some kinds of international law is the activity of non-governmental organisations (NGOs), such as Greenpeace and Amnesty International. As well as assisting in the development of international law through their participation in international meetings and conferences at which issues are discussed and treaties drafted, NGOs play a role in making information available to the many committees or commissions that enforce treaty obligations (*e.g.* those under environmental or human rights treaties) and in generally bringing pressure to bear upon states to comply with international law.

8. How do the sanctions available in international law differ from those in any developed system of municipal law? What improvements in the former are (i) desirable; (ii) reasonable to expect?[51]

2. THE DEVELOPMENT OF INTERNATIONAL LAW

(i) GENERALLY

Modern international law has its origins in the Europe of the sixteenth and seventeenth centuries. Although communities of states regulated by law had previously existed in Europe (*e.g.* in Greece) and elsewhere (*e.g.* in India) it is, for reasons apparent from subsequent world history, the law created to govern the

---

[47] *ibid.* p. 91. Note that the U.K. Government managed in 1972 to postpone at least consideration of Tanzanian loan proposals by the World Bank on the ground that Tanzania had not paid adequate compensation for British property it had nationalised: *The Times,* January 28, 1972, p. 21.

[48] *The Times,* January 19, 1965, p. 8. This, of course, was a case of voluntary withdrawal, but the attitude might well be adopted in cases of expulsion too.

[49] See below, p. 975.

[50] See below, pp. 74 *et seq.*

[51] See Fisher, *Improving Compliance with International Law* (1981).

diplomatic, commercial, military and other relations of the society of Christian states forming the Europe of that time that provides the basis for the present law. Although the writers[52] who recorded (and, to a large extent, invented) this early "Law of Nations"[53] may have regarded it as having universal application, it was for many generations really no more than the Public Law of Europe. International law was first extended beyond Europe at the end of the eighteenth and at the beginning of the nineteenth centuries to the states that succeeded the rebel European colonies of North and South America respectively. By the mid-nineteenth century, Turkey had been accepted as the first non-Christian subject of international law. By 1914, increasing European penetration into Asia had led to the "admission", though scarcely on terms of equality,[54] of other such subjects, including Persia, China and Japan. It was the advent in 1920 of the League of Nations, membership of which was open to "any" state (Article 1, Covenant), that, as much as any other single event, marked the beginning of the present situation in which international law applies automatically to all states whatever their location or character. Since that time, the community of states has increased dramatically in number to close to 200.

Other changes of great importance too have occurred in the present century. Resort to war has been made illegal and a system of collective enforcement of peace and security has been initiated—though not very successfully[55]—through the United Nations in place of self-help. The change in the balance of interests and values in the world community resulting first from the emergence of Communist states and then from the independence since 1945 of colonial and similar territories has had an effect in shaping or reshaping some international law rules. The demise of Oppenheim's doctrine that "States solely and exclusively are the subject of International Law"[56] is also evident. The growth of public international organisations in particular bears witness to this. If other claimants still have very limited personality, it is nonetheless the case that inter-state treaties are increasingly concerned with the "trans-national" affairs, to use Jessup's terminology,[57] of private individuals and companies. Of great importance is the increase in the subject-matter of international law to cover what Friedmann has called "the international law of co-operation."[58] The development of the international law of human rights and international environmental law are notable examples of this more positive, community-minded kind of law. Science too has had considerable impact. It has added two new territorial areas—outer space and the deep seabed—for which international law rules are required, and it has produced nuclear weapons, which have revised thinking about some existing rules and caused the introduction of new ones.

---

[52] See below, p. 56.

[53] The term "international law" would appear to have been coined later by Bentham (1748–1832).

[54] A system of capitulations, which in some cases lasted well into the present century, commonly applied by which European nationals present in the territory of the capitulating state were subject not to its local law or courts, but were subject instead to their national law administered in the territory of the capitulating state by their national consular courts.

[55] But see the Security Council action against Iraq, below.

[56] Oppenheim (1st ed., 1905), Vol. I, para. 13. Oppenheim, p. 956, now reads, in its 9th ed., Vol. I, p. 16, "States are the principal subjects of international law."

[57] See Jessup, *Transnational Law* (1956), pp. 15–16.

[58] *op. cit*, p. 14, n. 46, pp. 60 *et seq.*

(ii) New States[59]

HENKIN, HOW NATIONS BEHAVE

(2nd ed., 1979), pp. 121–127. Some footnotes omitted

We are frequently reminded that international law was the product of European civilization. . . . One might expect, then, that this law would not survive the decline of Europe's dominance, surely would not govern a society of nations most of which were not European, not Christian, not imperialist, not capitalist, which did not participate in the development of the law, and whose interests were different from those of the nations that shaped the law. In fact, however, international law has survived and would not be unrecognizable to our parents and teachers in the law and in diplomacy. The new nations raised the theoretical difficulties which have long troubled jurists as to why newborn nations should be bound by pre-existing law.[60] Some of those nations spoke and speak suspiciously of white, colonial law and have proclaimed the need for revolutionary transformations. Many indeed have challenged particular principles. But all were eager to enter international society and to accept its law.

The reasons why new nations accepted international law are not difficult to perceive. They came into an established system accepted by all nations, including the revolutionary governments and the many small powers which had supported their struggle for self-determination. Acceptance into that society as an independent equal was the proof and crown of their successful struggle, and international law provided the indispensable framework for living in that society. They adopted traditional forms in international trade and the growing co-operation for welfare of which they have been the principal beneficiaries, and early in their young history they have had to invoke international law in their disputes, among themselves or with others—on the Indus River and in Kashmir, between India and Bangladesh, on the definition of the continental shelf. . . .

The explosion of new states . . . has made it yet more difficult to make new law. It has been long established that law of universal applicability can be made only by universal agreement or acquiescence; the likelihood of general agreement decreases, of course, as the number of nations who must agree increases. New universal customary law, then, may become a rarity. . . . The multilateral convention, then, has become the principal form of general law-making, but already experience suggests that universality (or general acceptance) will be hard to come by. . . . General agreement may be possible only to codify accepted basic principles and

---

[59] See also Anand, ed., *Asian States and the Development of Universal International Law* (1972); Elias, *New Horizons in International Law* (2nd ed. by Ssekandi, 1992); Hague Academy Workshop, *The Future of International Law in a Multicultural World* (1984); Higgins, *Conflict of Interests: International Law in a Divided World* (1965); Kilson, ed., *New States in the Modern World* (1975); Makonnen, *International Law and the New States of Africa* (1983).

[60] *Ed.* See below, p. 104.

practices, or perhaps to adopt some general, imprecise, and ambiguous standards to which time and experience may give some agreed content. ... Regional law and law for other, smaller groupings may be the new law of the future, with universality a distant hope that we must learn not to expect or even desire.

The reluctance to make new law and the difficulties of making it do not apply equally to unmaking or remaking old law. Whatever the theory, new nations can in fact have a sharp impact on the law by collective "massive resistance", especially where older states are reluctant to insist on the old law. ... Customary law cannot long retain validity if a substantial number of states reject it. ...

In several particular respects, however, the new nations, especially as they joined with other developing states and emerged as the Third World, have created new law in their image and interest. The Third World has succeeded where it was united and determined, had the full support of the Communist World, and had some support or sympathy, at least not resistance, among Western powers. They have succeeded in making that new law in the face of the principle of unanimity, by reinterpreting universal agreements (*e.g.* the UN Charter), by overwhelming or silencing or even disregarding remaining opposition, especially through the use of UN resolutions. To date, the changes they have achieved in international law have been limited and special. ...

The success of Third World countries in virtually ending colonialism and racism, their solidarity on economic issues and their ability to extend that solidarity to other issues, on which enough of them feel strongly, have stirred dreams or fears that they might try to eliminate or erode the principle of unanimity in favor of more law-making by majority. Increasingly, they have been encouraged to seek new institutions based essentially on "one state-one vote" and majority rule (*e.g.* the International Sea-bed Authority (see below, p. 475)); to eliminate special voting rights (like the veto in the UN Security Council); to increase the matters subject to majority vote, *e.g.* in UN General Assembly resolutions. They have effectively exploited other procedures, for example, decision by "consensus."[61] The developed majority perhaps originally saw in that change protection against being overwhelmed by top-sided majority votes, but in time the drives for consensus, where the Third World largely agreed, began to weigh heavily on would-be dissenters not to dissent. And resolutions in the United Nations and other multilateral bodies have begun to weigh more heavily in the law-making process.

Notes

1. For instances of the impact of the "new nations" upon international law, see the General Assembly Declaration on the Granting of Independence to Colonial

---

[61] *Ed.* On the attempt at "consensus" in the drafting of the 1982 Convention on the Law of the Sea, see below, p. 370.

Countries and Peoples,[62] the Vienna Convention on the Law of Treaties[63] (which was the first of the "law-making" treaties prepared by the International Law Commission in the drafting of which the "new nations" participated fully) and the 1982 Convention on the Law of the Sea.[64] Note also the impact they have had in the debate over the rules on the treatment of aliens,[65] and the rules concerning the use of force.[66]

HENKIN, INTERNATIONAL LAW: POLITICS AND VALUES

(1995), pp. 280–283

The international system is substantially changed from what it was a half-century ago. Sixty states have become near-200, most of them new states . . . . For a quarter-century they grouped in three "worlds," two of them defined by ideology, the third by non-alignment—by a spirit of "a plague on both your worlds" and by bonds of common colonial history, resentment, poverty. Towards the end of the twentieth century, that configuration of three worlds has vanished: there is no Second World, therefore no Third World. But surely we are not one world. The political system is fluid and its configuration difficult to describe and to character-ize; surely, it is too early for confident prognostications as to what will emerge. . . .

The demise of Communism, the disintegration of the Soviet empire, and the fragmentation of the Soviet Union changed the world order fundamentally. Immediately, dramatically, importantly, it revived the Security Council [which] . . . acted, almost as originally intended, to defeat aggression and restore international peace in the Persian Gulf. It took a broad view of the demands of international peace and security to support humanitarian intervention by various means (including eco-nomic sanctions) in the former Yugoslavia, Haiti, Libya and Cambodia, and by a measure of military intervention to bring food and order in Somalia.[67] . . .

Despite revolution in East and Central Europe, and the resulting changed world order, one ought not anticipate radical change in the law in the decades ahead. The inter-state system will be long with us and therefore inter-state politics and inter-state (international) law. . . . But the international political system is no longer characterized by intense bipo-larism and we have moved into a field of more fluid political forces.

By some measures, the United States is the only super-Power, but others may claim super-Power status by virtue of other indicia, and all

[62] Below, p. 114.
[63] Below, Chap. 10.
[64] Below, Chap. 7.
[65] Below, Chap. 8.
[66] Below, Chap. 11.
[67] *Ed.* Sadly, these promising developments in the early post-Cold War period have proved a false dawn: there is now much less optimism about the role that the Security Council can continue to play: see further, below, Chap. 11.

are exploring hesitatingly, uncertainly, their place and their posture. The former U.S.S.R., now fragmented and in financial difficulties, in search of internal stability and new international roles, is not to be discounted. The Third World will still have the solidarity forged by a common colonial history and common problems of underdevelopment, and its numbers will count, but the significance of being "Third," unaligned, will lessen, and perhaps too its political weight and influence. The system, I expect, will be characterized by divisions that are pragmatic rather than ideological, economic rather than political, and even the common gross distinction between developed and less-developed states will blur and we will recognize a fluid spectrum of degrees of development as some state economies flourish and others falter.

The new array of forces in the system will surely have effect on the content of international law and on compliance with that law. The former U.S.S.R. is not a super-Power, but cooperation rather than confrontation between it and the United States promises new law and better compliance from both of them and in the system at large. Surely, global cold war will not be the obstacle to the development of new law and institutions, for peace and security, human rights,[68] the environment, or to the use and growth and modernization of the International Court of Justice. No other state—China—or groups of states will succeed to the U.S.S.R. role, though China may continue norms and institutions—in human rights, in collective economic-social action, in Security Council intervention.

---

[68] *Ed., e.g.* see the beneficial effect on the working of the UN Human Rights Committee, below, p. 648, n. 59.

CHAPTER 2

THE SOURCES OF INTERNATIONAL LAW

1. GENERALLY[1]

See Article 38(1), Statute of the International Court of Justice[2]

SCHWARZENBERGER, INTERNATIONAL LAW

(3rd ed., 1957), Vol. 1, pp. 26–27. Footnote omitted

THIS paragraph [Art. 38(1)] deals with two different issues. Sub-para-graphs *(a)*–*(c)* are concerned with the pedigree of the rules of inter-national law. In sub-paragraph *(d)*, some of the means for the determination of alleged rules of international law are enumerated.

In order to enable the World Court to apply any asserted rule of international law, it must be shown that it is the product of one, or more, of three law-creating processes: treaties, international customary law or the general principles of law recognised by civilised nations. The sig-nificance of this enumeration lies in its exclusiveness. It rules out other potential law-creating processes such as natural law, moral postulates or the doctrine[3] of international law. Conversely, the court is bound to take into consideration any asserted rule which bears the hall-mark of one of these three law-creating processes. It is immaterial whether such a rule is also claimed as their own by any of the various brands of natural law, has its origin in considerations of humanity, or is postulated by the standards of civilisation.

This interpretation of paragraph 1 of Article 38 is further strengthened by the following paragraph.[4] The power of the Court to decide a case *ex aequo et bono*, that is to say, to ignore rules which are the product of any of the above three law-creating agencies and to substitute itself as a law-creating agency, depends on agreement of the parties to a dispute. In

---

[1] See Danilenko, *Law Making in the International Community* (1993); Fitzmaurice, *Symbolae Verzijl* (1958), p. 153; Jennings, *Cambridge—Tilburg Lectures: 3rd Series* (1983), pp. 3–32; *ibid.*, (1981) 37 *Annuaire Suisse* 59; Parry, *The Sources and Evidences of International Law* (1965); Szasz, in Schachter and Joyner, eds., *United Nations Legal Order* (1995), Vol. 1, Chap. 1; Van Hoof, *Rethinking the Sources of International Law* (1983); Virally, in Sørensen, ed., *Manual of Public International Law* (1968), pp. 116 *et seq.*

[2] Below, Appendix I.

[3] *Ed.* by "doctrine" is meant the views of writers.

[4] *Ed.* Art. 38(2).

other words, such power must itself rest on a rule created by one of the three normal law-creating processes, in this case, a treaty.

In terms of a more conventional terminology, sub-paragraphs (*a*)–(*c*) of paragraph 1 of Article 38 of the Statute of the World Court deal with the three formal sources of international law to which the Court may resort and exclude material sources as such.[5] . . .

By way of contrast to the law-creating processes, sub-paragraph (*d*) of paragraph 1 of Article 38 refers to decisions of judicial institutions and the teachings of the most highly qualified publicists as "subsidiary means for the determination of rules of law." It follows that principal means for the determination of rules of law must exist. In close leaning on this text, these principal and subsidiary means of evidence are called law-determining agencies. Each of these is composed of more or less fallible human beings, and these cannot be taken to be passive agents who merely reflect true international law as it were in a faithful mirror. This term, therefore, is also meant to bring out the unavoidable subjective and formative element which all these agencies have in common. Whereas, in the case of the law-creating processes, the emphasis lies on the forms by which any particular rule of international law is created, in the case of the law-determining agencies it is on how an alleged rule is to be verified.

Notes

1. Article 38 follows the wording of the same Article in the Statute of the Permanent Court of International Justice (which preceded the International Court of Justice as the primary court of the international community[6]), except that the words "whose function is to decide in accordance with international law such disputes as are submitted to it" are inserted in paragraph 1. The original text was drafted in 1920 by an Advisory Committee of Jurists appointed by the League of Nations.[7] Although they were concerned to draft a text relating directly only to the functioning of the P.C.I.J., Article 38 is generally accepted as a correct statement of the sources of international law.[8]

2. *Classification of sources*. The distinction between "formal" and "material" sources to which Schwarzenberger refers was explained by Salmond[9] in the following terms:

> A formal source is that from which a rule of law derives its force and validity. . . . The material sources, on the other hand, are those from which is derived the matter, not the validity of the law. The material source supplies the substance of the rule to which the formal source gives the force and nature of law.

For example, a rule will be legally binding if it meets the requirements of a custom, which is a formal source of international law, and its substance will be

---

[5] *Ed*. For the view that treaties are not a formal source of law, see Fitzmaurice, below, p. 45.

[6] The term World Court is commonly used to refer to each of these Courts.

[7] For a record of the Committee's work, see Permanent Court of International Justice, Advisory Committee of Jurists, *Procés verbaux of the Proceedings of the Committee*, (June 16–July 24, 1920, L.N. Publication, 1920).

[8] On the status of General Assembly resolutions, see below, p. 58.

[9] *Jurisprudence* (7th ed., 1924), para. 44.

indicated by state practice, which is the material source of custom. The term *evidence* is then used in the sense that diplomatic correspondence, for example, is evidence of state practice.

3. *Order of application*.[10] When drafting the original text of Article 38, the Advisory Committee of Jurists considered a proposal that it should state that the sources listed should be considered by the court "in the undermentioned order"[11] (*i.e.* the order (*a*) to (*d*) in which they now appear). Opposing the proposal, M. Ricci-Busatti (Italy) is reported as saying:

> These words were not only superfluous, but they might also suggest the idea that the judge was not authorised to draw upon a certain source, for instance point 3,[12] before having applied conventions and customs mentioned respectively in points 1 and 2. That would be a misinterpretation of the Committee's intentions.[13]

In response, the President of the Committee, Baron Descamps (Belgium), remarked, however, that:

> there was a natural classification. If two States concluded a treaty in which the solution of the dispute could be found, the Court must not apply international custom and neglect the treaty.[14] If a well-known custom exists, there is no occasion to resort to a general principle of law. We shall indicate an order of natural *précellence*, without requiring in a given case the agreement of several sources.[15]

M. Ricci-Busatti held to his opinion. He said:

> if the expression *"ordre successif"* [undermentioned order] only meant that a convention should be considered before, for instance, customary law, it is unnecessary. It is a fundamental principle of law that a special rule goes before general law. This expression also seems to fail to recognise that these various sources may be applied simultaneously, and also that the nature of each source differs.[16]

Agreement with M. Ricci-Busatti was expressed by other members and the statement was omitted.[17]

2. CUSTOM[18]

See the *Lotus* case, below, p. 267, the *Anglo-Norwegian Fisheries* case, below, p. 375 and the *Nicaragua (Merits)* case, below, p. 866. These cases are important to an

---

[10] See Akehurst, (1974–75) 47 B.Y.I.L. 273; Bos (1978) 3 N.I.L.R. 338; Czaplinski and Danilenko (1990) 21 N.Y.I.L. 3.

[11] *loc. cit.*, n. 7 above, p. 344.

[12] *Ed.* General principles of law.

[13] *Ed. ibid.* p. 337.

[14] *Ed.* This must now be read subject to the rules concerning *ius cogens*: see below, p. 835.

[15] *ibid.*

[16] *ibid.*

[17] *ibid.*, p. 338.

[18] See Akehurst (1974–75) 47 B.Y.I.L. 1; Corbett (1925) 6 B.Y.I.L. 20; D'Amato, *The Concept of Custom in International Law* (1971); De Visscher, pp. 144–163; Jenks, *The Prospects of International Adjudication* (1964), Chap. 5; Kopelmanas (1937) 18 B.Y.I.L. 127; Kunz (1953) 47 A.J.I.L. 662; Lauterpacht, *Development*, pp. 368–393; Lowe (1983) 9 Rev. Int. Studies 207; Thirlway, *International Customary Law and Codification* (1972); Wolfke, *Custom in Present International Law* (2nd ed., 1993).

understanding of the nature of custom and the extracts printed later in this book should be read at the same time as those from the cases extracted in this chapter.

ASYLUM CASE[19]

Columbia *v.* Peru

I.C.J. Reports 1950, p. 266

After an unsuccessful rebellion in Peru in 1948, a warrant was issued for the arrest on a criminal charge arising out of the rebellion of one of its leaders, Haya de la Torre, a Peruvian national. He was granted asylum by Colombia in its Peruvian Embassy in Lima. Colombia sought, and Peru refused, a safe conduct to allow Haya de la Torre out of the country. Colombia brought this case against Peru, asking the Court to rule, *inter alia*, that:

> Colombia, as the state granting asylum, is competent to qualify the offence[20] for the purposes of the said asylum.[21]

It argued for such a ruling on the basis of both treaty provisions and "American international law in general". In the following extract, the Court considered the latter basis for the Colombian argument.

Judgment of the Court

The Colombian Government has finally invoked "American international law in general." In addition to the rules arising from agreements which have already been considered, it has relied on an alleged regional or local custom peculiar to Latin-American States.

The Party which relies on a custom of this kind must prove that this custom is established in such a manner that it has become binding on the other Party. The Colombian Government must prove that the rule invoked by it is in accordance with a constant and uniform usage practised by the States in question, and that this usage is the expression of a right appertaining to the State granting asylum and a duty incumbent on the territorial State. This follows from Article 38 of the Statute of the Court, which refers to international custom "as evidence of a general practice accepted as law."

. . . the Colombian Government has referred to a large number of cases in which diplomatic asylum was in fact granted and respected. But it has not shown that the alleged rule of unilateral and definitive qualification was invoked or . . . that it was, apart from conventional stipulations,

---

[19] See Briggs (1951) 45 A.J.I.L. 728.
[20] *i.e.* to characterise the offence—in this case to say whether it was a political offence or not.
[21] I.C.J. Rep. 1950, p. 273.

exercised by the States granting asylum as a right appertaining to them and respected by the territorial State as a duty incumbent on them and not merely for reasons of political expediency. The facts brought to the knowledge of the Court disclose so much uncertainty and contradiction, so much fluctuation and discrepancy in the exercise of diplomatic asylum and in the official views expressed on various occasions, there has been so much inconsistency in the rapid succession of conventions on asylum, ratified by some States and rejected by others, and the practice has been so much influenced by considerations of political expediency in the various cases, that it is not possible to discern in all this any constant and uniform usage, accepted as law, with regard to the alleged rule of uni-lateral and definitive qualification of the offence.

The Court cannot therefore find that the Colombian Government has proved the existence of such a custom. But even if it could be supposed that such a custom existed between certain Latin-American States only, it could not be invoked against Peru which, far from having by its attitude adhered to it, has, on the contrary, repudiated it by refraining from ratifying the Montevideo Conventions of 1933 and 1939, which were the first to include a rule concerning the qualification of the offence in matters of diplomatic asylum.

Notes

1. *General and Local Customs.* As the Court recognised in this case, although Article 38(1)(*b*) refers to "a general" practice, it allows for local (or regional) customs amongst a group of states or just two states[22] in their relations *inter se* as well as for general customs binding upon the international community as a whole. Local customs may supplement or derogate from general customary international law (subject to such rules of *ius cogens* as may exist[23]). A leading Soviet writer, Tunkin,[24] identified socialist international law as a form of local international law which was "coming to replace contemporary general inter-national law" in the relations between socialist states. An example of such law was the Brezhnev Doctrine, which justified intervention by socialist states in the affairs of any one of them to preserve socialism.[25] The Brezhnev Doctrine no longer applies and it is not clear that any other rules of socialist international law remain in the post–USSR era.

The Court's description of custom as a "constant and uniform usage, accepted as law" has been understood by most writers[26] as being applicable to *general* customs (which are by far the more numerous and important) as well as *local* ones.

2. *State Practice.* By "usage" the Court means a usage that is to be found in the practice of states.[27] The International Law Commission included the following in

---

[22] Such a custom was found to exist between India and Portugal in the *Right of Passage* case, below, p. 257.

[23] On *ius cogens*, see below, p. 835.

[24] *Theory of International Law, op. cit.*, p. 5, n. 13, above, p. 444.

[25] *ibid.* p. 433.

[26] But see D'Amato, *op. cit.*, p. 23, n. 18, above, Chap. 8.

[27] On the question whether the practice of other international persons may contribute to the development of custom, see below, p. 143.

a non-exhaustive list[28] of the forms that state practice may take: treaties, decisions of international and national courts, national legislation, diplomatic correspondence, opinions of national legal advisers and the practice of international organisations.[29] Other categories listed by Brownlie[30] are policy statements, press releases, official manuals on legal questions (*e.g.* manuals of military law), executive decisions and practices, orders to naval forces, etc., and comments by governments on drafts produced by the International Law Commission.[31]

In his opinion in the *Anglo-Norwegian Fisheries* case[32] Judge Read said in respect of state practice and with particular reference to the facts of the case before him:

> This cannot be established by citing cases where coastal States have made extensive claims, but have not maintained their claims by the actual assertion of sovereignty over trespassing foreign ships. Such claims may be important as starting points, which, if not challenged, may ripen into historic title in the course of time. The only convincing evidence of State practice is to be found in seizures, where the coastal State asserts its sovereignty over the water in question by arresting a foreign ship and by maintaining its position in the course of diplomatic negotiation and international arbitration.

How far should Judge Read's emphasis upon "action rather than words" be carried? Although acts in support of a claim may be "the only convincing evidence" where the claim is challenged by the acts of another state, abstract statements of a legal position have been recognised as being of value in other cases, as the extract from the *North Sea Continental Shelf* cases below shows. As to the relevance of General Assembly resolutions, see below, p. 58.

On the need to take care in assessing the significance of a state's acts or pronouncements, Brierly[33] states:

> There are multifarious occasions on which persons who act or speak in the name of a state do acts or make declarations which either express or imply some view on a matter of international law. Any such act or declaration may, so far as it goes, be some evidence that a custom, and therefore that a rule of international law, does or does not exist; but of course its value as evidence will be altogether determined by the occasion and the circumstances. States, like individuals, often put forward contentions for the purpose of supporting a particular case which do not necessarily represent their settled or impartial opinion.

Unfortunately,[34] the evidence of state practice is not as available as it should be to permit considered opinions on many questions of customary international law. At present, only the practice of the United States is available in a comprehensive

---

[28] Y.B.I.L.C., 1950, II, pp. 368–372.

[29] "Records of the cumulating practice of international organisations may be regarded as evidence of customary international law with reference to States relations to the organisations": *id.* p. 372.

[30] Brownlie, p. 4.

[31] *cf.* Government reaction to the practice of such bodies as the Human Rights Committee: see below, p. 802.

[32] I.C.J. Rep. 1951, p. 191.

[33] Brierly, p. 4.

[34] Anyone who has spent time sifting through records of state practice may not agree with the use of this word.

form.[35] There are also very useful, but less extensive, digests of British, French, Italian and Swiss practice.[36] The practice of other states is less generally available, although the increasing number of national *Yearbooks* and law reviews on international law with national state practice sections is making recent practice more readily accessible. A lot of evidence of state practice is available to the public at the time that it comes into being in such sources as parliamentary papers, law reports and newspapers. Much of it (for example, diplomatic correspondence and other confidential government papers), is, however, subject to rules such as that in the United Kingdom under which government records are not available to the public until 30 years have elapsed.[37]

NORTH SEA CONTINENTAL SHELF CASES[38]

Federal Republic of Germany *v.* Denmark; Federal Republic of Germany *v.* The Netherlands

I.C.J. Reports 1969, p. 3

A number of bilateral agreements had been made drawing lateral or median lines delimiting the North Sea continental shelves[39] of adjacent and opposite states, including two lateral line agreements between the Netherlands and the Federal Republic of Germany (1964) and Denmark and the Federal Republic of Germany (1965). Each of these last two agreements, however, did no more than draw a dividing line for a short distance from the coast beginning at the point at which the land boundary of the two states concerned was located. Further agreement had proved impossible. Special agreements were concluded between the Netherlands and the Federal Republic of Germany and between Denmark and the Federal Republic of Germany referring the problem to the I.C.J. In each special agreement the question put to the Court was:

---

[35] See the *Digests of International Law*, edited successively by Wharton (3 vols., 1887), Moore (8 vols., 1906), Hackworth (8 vols., 1940–44) and Whiteman (14 vols., 1963–70); the *Digest of United States Practice in International Law* (1973–80); the *Cumulative Digest of United States Practice in International Law 1981–89*; and the A.J.I.L. *Contemporary Practice* sections. There is also the *U.S. Foreign Relations* and *Official Opinions of the Attorney-General of the U.S.* series of documents.

[36] With regard to the U.K., see Parry, ed., *British Digest of International Law* (only Vols. 2b, 5, 6, 7 and 8 of Phase I (1860–1914) published); Smith, *Great Britain and the Law of Nations*, (2 vols., 1932, 1935); McNair, *International Law Opinions* (3 vols., 1956); and E. Lauterpacht, *British Practice in International Law* (B.P.I.L.) (1963–67). The last of these was preceded by *Contemporary Practice of the United Kingdom in the Field of International Law*, which was first published as a series of occasional articles in the I.C.L.Q. covering the years 1956–59 and then published separately in 1962. *United Kingdom Materials in International Law* (U.K.M.I.L.), edited by Marston, published annually (1978–) in the B.Y.I.L. and the *Current Legal Developments* sections in the I.C.L.Q. (1987–) are valuable current sources. The *Digest of the Diplomatic Correspondence of the European States* in the *Fontes Juris Gentium* series includes that of Great Britain for the years 1856–78. There is also the *British and Foreign State Papers* series of documents (terminated 1968). As to France, Italy and Switzerland, see *Répertoire de la pratique française en matière de droit international public* (7 vols., 1962–72); *Italian Practice in International Law* (1971–); and *Répertoire suisse de droit international 1914–1939*, 4 vols.

[37] Public Records Act 1967.

[38] See D'Amato (1970) 64 A.J.I.L. 892; Friedmann (1970) 64 A.J.I.L. 229 and Nelson (1972) 35 M.L.R. 52.

[39] On the law of the continental shelf, see below, p. 455.

What principles and rules of international law are applicable to the delimitation as between the Parties of the areas of the continental shelf in the North Sea which appertain to each of them beyond the partial boundary [already] determined . . . ?

The two cases were joined by the Court. Denmark and the Netherlands argued that the "equidistance-special circumstances principle" in Article 6(2) of the 1958 Geneva Convention on the Continental Shelf[40] applied. The Federal Republic of Germany denied this and proposed "the doctrine of the just and equitable share". The reason for the Federal Republic's opposition to the "equidistance-special circumstances principle" was that the principle has the effect, as the Court pointed out,[41] on a concave coastline such as that shared by the three states concerned of giving the state in the middle—in this case West Germany—a smaller continental shelf than it might otherwise obtain.

The Court rejected the West German proposal. After rejecting also the Danish and Dutch argument that Article 6(2) stated or crystallised customary international law at the time of its adoption, it continued:

Judgment of the Court

70. The Court must now proceed to the last stage in the argument put forward on behalf of Denmark and the Netherlands. This is to the effect that even if there was at the date of the Geneva Convention no rule of customary international law in favour of the equidistance principle, and no such rule was crystallised in Article 6 of the Convention, nevertheless such a rule has come into being since the Convention, partly because of its own impact, partly on the basis of subsequent State practice,—and that this rule, being now a rule of customary international law binding on all States, including therefore the Federal Republic, should be declared applicable to the delimitation of the boundaries between the Parties' respective continental shelf areas in the North Sea.

71. In so far as this contention is based on the view that Article 6 of the Convention has had the influence, and has produced the effect described, it clearly involves treating that Article as a norm-creating provision which has constituted the foundation of, or has generated a rule which, while only conventional or contractual in its origin, has since passed into the general *corpus* of international law, and is now accepted as such by the *opinio juris*, so as to have become binding even for countries which have never, and do not, become parties to the Convention. There is no doubt that this process is a perfectly possible one and does from time to time occur: it constitutes indeed one of the recognised methods by which new rules of customary international law may be formed. At the same time this result is not lightly to be regarded as having been attained.

72. It would in the first place be necessary that the provision con-

---

[40] Below, p. 464.
[41] I.C.J. Rep. 1969, p. 17.

cerned should, at all events potentially, be of a fundamentally norm-creating character such as could be regarded as forming the basis of a general rule of law. Considered *in abstracto* the equidistance principle might be said to fulfil this requirement. Yet in the particular form in which it is embodied in Article 6 of the Geneva Convention, and having regard to the relationship of that Article to other provisions of the Convention, this must be open to some doubt. In the first place, Article 6 is so framed as to put second the obligation to make use of the equidistance method, causing it to come after a primary obligation to effect delimitation by agreement. Such a primary obligation constitutes an unusual preface to what is claimed to be a potential general rule of law. Without attempting to enter into, still less pronounce upon any question of *jus cogens*,[42] it is well understood that, in practice, rules of international law can, by agreement, be derogated from in particular cases, or as between particular parties—but this is not normally the subject of any express provision, as it is in Article 6 of the Geneva Convention. Secondly the part played by the notion of special circumstances relative to the principle of equidistance as embodied in Article 6, and the very considerable, still unresolved controversies as to the exact meaning and scope of this notion, must raise further doubts as to the potentially norm-creating character of the rule. Finally, the faculty of making reservations to Article 6, while it might not of itself prevent the equidistance principle being eventually received as general law, does add considerably to the difficulty of regarding this result as having been brought about (or being potentially possible) on the basis of the Convention: for so long as this faculty continues to exist, and is not the subject of any revision brought about in consequence of a request made under Article 13 of the Convention—of which there is at present no official indication—it is the Convention itself which would, for the reasons already indicated, seem to deny to the provisions of Article 6 the same norm-creating character as, for instance, Articles 1 and 2 possess.

73. With respect to the other elements usually regarded as necessary before a conventional rule can be considered to have become a general rule of international law, it might be that, even without the passage of any considerable period of time, a very widespread and representative participation in the convention might suffice of itself, provided it included that of States whose interests were specially affected. In the present case however, the Court notes that, even if allowance is made for the existence of a number of States to whom participation in the Geneva Convention is not open, or which, by reason for instance of being land-locked States, would have no interest in becoming parties to it, the number of ratifications and accessions so far secured is, though respectable, hardly sufficient. That non-ratification may sometimes be due to factors other than active disapproval of the Convention concerned can hardly constitute a

---

[42] *Ed.* See below, p. 835.

basis on which positive acceptance of its principles can be implied. The reasons are speculative, but the facts remain.

74. As regards the time element, the Court notes that it is over ten years since the Convention was signed, but that it is even now less than five since it came into force in June 1964, and that when the present proceedings were brought it was less than three years, while less than one had elapsed at the time when the respective negotiations between the Federal Republic and the other two Parties for a complete delimitation broke down on the question of the application of the equidistance principle. Although the passage of only a short period of time is not necessarily, or of itself, a bar to the formation of a new rule of customary international law on the basis of what was originally a purely conventional rule, an indispensable requirement would be that within the period in question, short though it might be, State practice, including that of States whose interests are specially affected, should have been both extensive and virtually uniform in the sense of the provision invoked—and should moreover have occurred in such a way as to show a general recognition that a rule of law or legal obligation is involved.

75. The Court must now consider whether State practice in the matter of continental shelf delimitation has, subsequent to the Geneva Convention, been of such a kind as to satisfy this requirement. . . . Some fifteen cases have been cited in the course of the present proceedings, occurring mostly since the signature of the 1958 Geneva Convention, in which continental shelf boundaries have been delimited according to the equidistance principle—in the majority of the cases by agreement, in a few others, unilaterally—or else the delimitation was foreshadowed but has not yet been carried out. . . . even if these various cases constituted more than a very small proportion of those potentially calling for delimitation in the world as a whole, the Court would not think it necessary to enumerate or evaluate them separately, since there are, *a priori*, several grounds which deprive them of weight as precedents in the present context.

76. . . . Over half the States concerned, whether acting unilaterally or conjointly, were or shortly became parties to the Geneva Convention, and were therefore presumably, so far as they were concerned, acting actually or potentially in the application of the Convention. From their action no inference could legitimately be drawn as to the existence of a rule of customary international law in favour of the equidistance principle. As regards those States, on the other hand, which were not, and have not become parties to the Convention, the basis of their action can only be problematical and must remain entirely speculative. Clearly, they were not applying the Convention. But from that no inference could justifiably be drawn that they believed themselves to be applying a mandatory rule of customary international law. There is not a shred of evidence that they did and . . . there is no lack of other reasons for using the equidistance

method, so that acting, or agreeing to act in a certain way, does not of itself demonstrate anything of a juridical nature.

77. The essential point in this connection—and it seems necessary to stress it—is that even if these instances of action by non-parties to the Convention were much more numerous than they in fact are, they would not, even in the aggregate, suffice in themselves to constitute the *opinio juris*—for, in order to achieve this result, two conditions must be fulfilled. Not only must the acts concerned amount to a settled practice, but they must also be such, or be carried out in such a way, as to be evidence of a belief that this practice is rendered obligatory by the existence of a rule of law requiring it. The need for such a belief, *i.e.* the existence of a subjective element, is implicit in the very notion of the *opinio juris sive necessitatis*. The States concerned must therefore feel that they are conforming to what amounts to a legal obligation. The frequency, or even habitual character of the acts is not in itself enough. There are many international acts, *e.g.* in the field of ceremonial and protocol, which are performed almost invariably, but which are motivated only by considerations of courtesy, convenience or tradition, and not by any sense of legal duty.

78. In this respect the Court follows the view adopted by the Permanent Court of International Justice in the *Lotus* case,[43] as stated in the following passage, the principle of which is, by analogy, applicable almost word for word, *mutatis mutandis*, to the present case (P.C.I.J., Series A, No. 10, 1927, at p. 28):

> Even if the rarity of the judicial decisions to be found ... were sufficient to prove ... the circumstance alleged ... it would merely show that States had often, in practice, abstained from instituting criminal proceedings, and not that they recognised themselves as being obliged to do so; for only if such abstention were based on their being conscious of having a duty to abstain would it be possible to speak of an international custom. The alleged fact does not allow one to infer that States have been conscious of having such a duty; on the other hand ... there are other circumstances calculated to show that the contrary is true.

Applying this dictum to the present case, the position is simply that in certain cases—not a great number—the States concerned agreed to draw or did draw the boundaries concerned according to the principle of equidistance. There is no evidence that they so acted because they felt legally compelled to draw them in this way by reason of a rule of customary law obliging them to do so—especially considering that they might have been motivated by other obvious factors. . . .

[43] *Ed.* See below, p. 267.

81. The Court accordingly concludes that if the Geneva Convention was not in its origins or inception declaratory of a mandatory rule of customary international law enjoining the use of the equidistance principle for the delimitation of continental shelf areas between adjacent States neither has its subsequent effect been constitutive of such a rule; and that State practice up-to-date has equally been insufficient for the purpose. . . .

Having thus found that neither of the approaches argued for by the parties was a part of international law, the Court then proceeded to spell out the customary international law principles and rules that did apply "as between States faced with an issue concerning the lateral delimitation of adjacent continental shelves." . . .

85. It emerges from the history of the development of the legal régime of the continental shelf . . . that the essential reason why the equidistance method is not to be regarded as a rule of law is that, if it were to be compulsorily applied in all situations, this would not be consonant with certain basic legal notions which . . . have from the beginning reflected the *opinio juris* in the matter of delimitation; those principles being that delimitation must be the object of agreement between the States concerned, and that such agreement must be arrived at in accordance with equitable principles. . . .

88. . . . Whatever the legal reasoning of a court of justice, its decisions must by definition be just, and therefore in that sense equitable. Nevertheless, when mention is made of a court dispensing justice or declaring the law, what is meant is that the decision finds its objective justification in considerations lying not outside but within the rules, and in this field it is precisely a rule of law that calls for the application of equitable principles. . . . There is consequently no question in this case of any decision *ex aequo et bono*, such as would not be possible under the conditions prescribed by Article 38, paragraph 2, of the Court's Statute. . . .

91. Equity does not necessarily imply equality. There can never be any question of completely refashioning nature, and equity does not require that a State without access to the sea should be allotted an area of continental shelf, any more than there could be a question of rendering the situation of a State with an extensive coastline similar to that of a State with a restricted coastline. Equality is to be reckoned within the same plane, and it is not such natural inequalities as these that equity could remedy. But in the present case there are three States whose North Sea coastlines are in fact comparable in length and which, therefore, have been given broadly equal treatment by nature except that the configuration of one of the coastlines would, if the equidistance method is used, deny to one of these States treatment equal or comparable to that given the other two. Here indeed is a case where, in a theoretical situation of equality within the same order, an inequality is created.

92. It has however been maintained that no one method of delimitation can prevent such results and that all can lead to relative injustices. This argument . . . can only strengthen the view that it is necessary to seek not one method of delimitation but one goal . . . . As the operation of delimiting is a matter of determining areas appertaining to different jurisdictions, it is a truism to say that the determination must be equitable; rather is the problem above all one of defining the means whereby the delimitation can be carried out in such a way as to be recognized as equitable. . . .

101. For these reasons, THE COURT, by eleven votes to six,[44] finds that, in each case,

(A) the use of the equidistance method of delimitation not being obligatory as between the Parties; and

(B) there being no other single method of delimitation the use of which is in all circumstances obligatory;

(C) the principles and rules of international law applicable to the delimitation as between the Parties . . . are as follows:

(1) delimitation is to be effected by agreement in accordance with equitable principles, and taking account of all the relevant circumstances, in such a way as to leave as much as possible to each Party all those parts of the continental shelf that constitute a natural prolongation of its land territory into and under the sea, without encroachment on the natural prolongation of the land territory of the other;

(2) if, in the application of the preceding sub-paragraph, the delimitation leaves to the Parties areas that overlap, these are to be divided between them in agreed proportions or, failing agreement, equally, unless they decide on a régime of joint jurisdiction, user, or exploitation for the zones of overlap or any part of them;

(D) in the course of the negotiations, the factors to be taken into account are to include:

(1) the general configuration of the coasts of the Parties, as well as the presence of any special or unusual features;

(2) so far as known or readily ascertainable, the physical and geological structure, and natural resources, of the continental shelf areas involved;

(3) the element of a reasonable degree of proportionality, which a delimitation carried out in accordance with equitable principles ought to bring about between the extent of the continental shelf

---

[44] The judges in the majority were President Bustamente y Rivero; Judges Sir Gerald Fitzmaurice, Jessup, Sir Muhammad Zafrulla Khan, Padilla Nervo, Forster, Gros, Ammoun, Petrén and Onyeama; Judge *ad hoc* Mosler. Vice-President Koretsky; Judges Tanaka, Morelli, Bengzon and Lachs; Judge *ad hoc* Sørensen dissented.

areas appertaining to the coastal State and the length of its coast measured in the general direction of the coastline, account being taken for this purpose of the effects, actual or prospective, of any other continental shelf delimitations between adjacent States in the same region.[45]

DISSENTING OPINION OF JUDGE TANAKA. To decide whether these two factors [usage and *opinio juris*] in the formative process of a customary law exist or not, is a delicate and difficult matter. The repetition, the number of examples of State practice, the duration of time required for the generation of customary law cannot be mathematically and uniformly decided. Each fact requires to be evaluated relatively according to the different occasions and circumstances. . . . what is important in the matter at issue is not the number or figure of ratifications of and accessions to the Convention or of examples of subsequent State practice, but the meaning which they would imply in the particular circumstances. We cannot evaluate the ratification of the Convention by a large maritime country or the State practice represented by its concluding an agreement on the basis of the equidistance principle, as having exactly the same importance as similar acts by a land-locked country which possesses no particular interest in the delimitation of the continental shelf.

Next, so far as . . . *opinio juris sive necessitatis* is concerned, it is extremely difficult to get evidence of its existence in concrete cases. This factor, relating to international motivation and being of a psychological nature, cannot be ascertained very easily, particularly when diverse legislative and executive organs of a government participate in an internal process of decision-making in respect of ratification or other State acts. There is no other way than to ascertain the existence of *opinio juris* from the fact of the external existence of a certain custom and its necessity felt in the international community, rather than to seek evidence as to the subjective motives for each example of State practice, which is something which is impossible of achievement. . . .

DISSENTING OPINION OF JUDGE LACHS. Delay in the ratification of and accession to multilateral treaties is a well-known phenomenon in contemporary treaty practice . . . experience indicates that in most cases [it is] caused by factors extraneous to the substance and objective of the instrument in question.

. . . [This] indicates that the number of ratifications and accessions cannot, in itself, be considered conclusive with regard to the general acceptance of a given instrument.

In the case of the Convention on the Continental Shelf, there are other elements that must be given their due weight. In particular, thirty-one

---

[45] *Ed.* The parties agreed upon the delimitation of their continental shelves *inter se* on the basis of the Court's judgment by treaties made in 1971: for texts, see *Yearbook of the I.C.J.* 1970–71, pp. 118 *et seq.*

States came into existence during the period between its signature (June 28, 1958) and its entry into force (June 10, 1964), while thirteen other nations have since acceded to independence. Thus the time during which these forty-four States could have completed the necessary procedure enabling them to become parties to the Convention has been rather limited, in some cases very limited. Taking into account the great and urgent problems each of them had to face, one cannot be surprised that many of them did not consider it a matter of priority. This notwithstanding, nine of those States have acceded to the Convention. Twenty-six of the total number of States in existence are moreover land-locked and cannot be considered as having a special and immediate interest in speedy accession to the Convention (only five of them have in fact acceded).

Finally, it is noteworthy that about seventy States are at present engaged in the exploration and exploitation of continental shelf areas.

It is the above analysis which is relevant, not the straight comparison between the total number of States in existence and the number of parties to the Convention. It reveals in fact that the number of parties to the Convention on the Continental Shelf is very impressive, including as it does the majority of States actively engaged in the exploration of continental shelves.

. . . in the world today an essential factor in the formation of a new rule of general international law is to be taken into account: namely that States with different political, economic and legal systems, States of all continents, participate in the process. No more can a general rule of international law be established by the fiat of one or of a few, or—as it was once claimed—by the consensus of European States only. . . .

All this leads to the conclusion that the principles and rules enshrined in the Convention, and in particular the equidistance rule, have been accepted not only by those States which are parties to the Convention on the Continental Shelf, but also by those which have subsequently followed it in agreements, or in their legislation, or have acquiesced in it when faced with legislative acts of other States affecting them. This can be viewed as evidence of a practice widespread enough to satisfy the criteria for a general rule of law.

For to become binding, a rule or principle of international law need not pass the test of universal acceptance. This is reflected in several statements of the Court, *e.g.*: "generally . . . adopted in the practice of States" (*Fisheries, Judgment*, I.C.J. Reports 1951, p. 128). Not all States have . . . an opportunity or possibility of applying a given rule. The evidence should be sought in the behaviour of a great number of States, possibly the majority of States, in any case the great majority of the interested States. . . .

DISSENTING OPINION OF JUDGE AD HOC SØRENSEN. I agree, of course, that one should not lightly reach the conclusion that a convention is binding upon a non-contracting State. But I find it necessary to take account of the fact—to which the Court does not give specific weight—that the Geneva Convention belongs to a particular category of multilateral conventions, namely those which result from the work of the United Nations in the field of codification and progressive development of international law, under Article 13 of the Charter. . . .

According to classic doctrine . . . [the] practice [necessary to establish a rule of customary international law] must have been pursued over a certain length of time. There have even been those who have maintained the necessity of "immemorial usage". In its previous jurisprudence, however, the Court does not seem to have laid down strict requirements as to the duration of the usage or practice which may be accepted as law. In particular, it does not seem to have drawn any conclusion in this respect from the ordinary meaning of the word "custom" when used in other contexts. . . . The possibility has thus been reserved of recognising the rapid emergence of a new rule of customary law based on the recent practice of States. This is particularly important in view of the extremely dynamic process of evolution in which the international community is engaged at the present stage of history.[46] Whether the mainspring of this evolution is to be found in the development of ideas, in social and economic factors, or in new technology, it is characteristic of our time that new problems and circumstances incessantly arise and imperatively call for legal regulation. In situations of this nature, a convention adopted as part of the combined process of codification and progressive development of international law may well constitute, or come to constitute the decisive evidence of generally accepted new rules of international law. The fact that it does not purport simply to be declaratory of existing customary law is immaterial in this context. The convention may serve as an authoritative guide for the practice of States faced with the relevant new legal problems, and its provisions thus become the nucleus around which a new set of generally recognised legal rules may crystallise. The word "custom," with its traditional time connotation, may not even be an adequate expression for the purpose of describing this particular source of law.

. . . The adoption of the Geneva Convention on the Continental Shelf was a very significant element in the process of creating new rules of international law in a field which urgently required legal regulation. . . . No State which has exercised sovereign rights over its continental shelf in conformity with the provisions of the Convention has been met with protests by other States. . . .

---

[46] *Ed.* Judge Lachs took the same view in his Opinion. He gave the following example of the "rapid emergence" of a customary rule: " . . . the first instruments that man sent into outer space traversed the airspace of States and circled above them in outer space, yet the launching States sought no permission nor did the other States protest. This is how the freedom of movement into outer space, and in it, came to be established and recognised as law within a remarkably short period of time" (p. 230).

I do not find it necessary to go into the question of the *opinio juris*. This is a problem of legal doctrine which may cause great difficulties in international adjudication. In view of the manner in which international relations are conducted, there may be numerous cases in which it is practically impossible for one government to produce conclusive evidence of the motives which have prompted the action and policy of other governments. Without going into all aspects of the doctrinal debate on this issue, I wish only to cite the following passage by one of the most qualified commentators on the jurisprudence of the Court. Examining the conditions of the *opinio necessitatis juris* Sir Hersch Lauterpacht writes:

> Unless judicial activity is to result in reducing the legal significance of the most potent source of rules of international law, namely, the conduct of States, it would appear that the accurate principle on the subject consists in regarding all uniform conduct of Governments (or, in appropriate cases, abstention therefrom) as evidencing the *opinio necessitatis juris* except when it is shown that the conduct in question was not accompanied by any such intention. (Sir Hersch Lauterpacht: *The Development of International Law by the International Court*, London 1958, p. 380.)

Applying these considerations to the circumstances of the present cases, I think that the practice of States referred to above may be taken as sufficient evidence of the existence of any necessary *opinio juris*.

In my opinion, the conclusion may therefore safely be drawn that as a result of a continuous process over a quarter of a century, the rules embodied in the Geneva Convention on the Continental Shelf have now attained the status of generally accepted rules of international law.

That being so, it is nevertheless necessary to examine in particular the attitude of the Federal Republic of Germany with regard to the Convention. In the *Fisheries Case* the Court said that the ten-mile rule would in any event "appear to be inapplicable as against Norway inasmuch as she has always opposed any attempt to apply it to the Norwegian coast" (I.C.J. Reports 1951, p. 131). Similarly, it might be argued in the present cases that the Convention on the Continental Shelf would be inapplicable as against the Federal Republic, if she had consistently refused to recognise it as an expression of generally accepted rules of international law and had objected to its applicability as against her. But far from adopting such an attitude, the Federal Republic has gone quite a long way towards recognising the Convention. It is part of the whole picture, though not decisive in itself, that the Federal Republic signed the Convention in 1958, immediately before the time-limit for signature under Article 8. More significant is the fact that the Federal Republic has relied on the Convention for the purpose of asserting her own rights in the continental shelf. . . . This attitude is relevant, not so much in the context of the traditional legal concepts of recognition, acquiescence or estoppel, as in the context of the general process of creating international legal rules of universal applicability. At a decisive stage of this formative process, an interested State, which was not a party to the Convention, formally recorded its view that the Convention was an expression of generally applicable international law. This view being perfectly well founded, that State is not now in a position to escape the authority of the Convention.

It has been asserted that the possibility, made available by Article 12, of entering reservations to certain articles of the Convention, makes it difficult to understand the articles in question as embodying generally accepted rules of international law. . . . In my view, the faculty of making reservations to a treaty provision has no necessary connection with the question whether or not the provision can be considered as expressing a generally recognised rule of law. To substantiate this opinion it may be sufficient to point out that a number of reservations have been made to provisions of the Convention on the High Seas, although this Convention, according to its preamble, is "generally declaratory of established principles of international law." Some of these reservations have been objected to by other contracting States, while other reservations have been tacitly accepted. The acceptance, whether tacit or express, of a reservation made by a contracting party does not have the effect of depriving the Convention as a whole, or the relevant article in particular, of its declaratory character. It only has the effect of establishing a special contractual relationship between the parties concerned within the general framework of the customary law embodied in the Convention. Provided the customary rule does not belong to the category of *jus cogens*, a special contractual relationship of this nature is not invalid as such. Consequently, there is no incompatibility between the faculty of making reservations to certain articles of the Convention on the Continental Shelf and the recognition of that Convention or the particular articles as an expression of generally accepted rules of international law.

Notes

1. *Treaties as a material source of custom. The North Sea Continental Shelf Cases,* which are among the relatively few cases in which the World Court has discussed in any detail the requirements for the existence of a rule of customary international law, were concerned with a question of increasing importance as the process of codifying and developing international law by multilateral treaties continues, namely the role of such treaties as state practice and hence as a material source of customary international law binding upon parties and non-parties alike.[47]

[47] See on this question Baxter (1970–I) 129 Hague Recueil 25; Czaplinski (1989) 38 I.C.L.Q. 151; Charney (1986) 61 Wash. L.R. 971; D'Amato, *op. cit.*, p. 23, n. 18, above, Chap. 5; Jennings, in Wilner, ed., *Jus et Societas: Essays in Tribute to Wolfgang Friedmann* (1979), p. 159; Villiger, *Customary International Law and Treaties* (1985); Weisburd (1988) 21 Vand. J.T.L. 1.

In the Court's opinion, a treaty provision[48] may relate to custom in one of three ways. It may be declaratory of custom at the time that the provision is adopted[49]; it may crystallise custom, as states agree on the provision to be adopted during the treaty drafting process; or the provision may come to be accepted and followed by states as custom in their practice after the treaty's adoption. On the facts of the case, the third possibility was the one most closely examined by the Court. Why, in the opinion of the Court, would Denmark's and the Netherlands' task have been easier if they had been arguing that the rules in Articles 1 or 2 of the Continental Shelf Convention (instead of that in Article 6) had become a part of customary international law? Since states may contract out of a rule of customary international law in their relations *inter se*, should, as the Court suggests (para. 72), it matter whether a treaty rule which is claimed to be a custom is one to which reservations are permitted? Does the Court's judgment indicate whether bilateral (as well as multilateral) treaties may be evidence of state practice? Is it possible that in some cases it may be precisely because the rights and duties set out in a treaty are not a part of customary international law that the parties feel the need to make it?[50]

2. Whereas the question in the *North Sea Continental Shelf Cases* was whether a treaty rule was binding as custom upon a non-party to the treaty, the question in the *Nicaragua Case (Merits)*[51] was whether customary rules applied in the relations between two states when rules covering the same ground existed in treaties to which those states were parties. In that case, Nicaragua claimed that the U.S. had used armed force and intervened in its affairs contrary to international law. The Court accepted that it could not consider U.S. liability under the UN Charter and other multilateral treaties to which the U.S. and Nicaragua were parties. This was because of a U.S. reservation to its acceptance of the Court's jurisdiction that excluded "disputes arising under a multilateral treaty". The question for the Court therefore was whether the customary rules on armed force and intervention continued to bind the parties in parallel with the obligations under the UN Charter and other treaties they had accepted, so that the Court could apply them despite the U.S. reservation. Holding that they did, the Court stated:

> 177 ... The existence of identical rules in international treaty law and customary law has been clearly recognized by the Court in the *North Sea Continental Shelf* cases. To a large extent, those cases turned on the question whether a rule enshrined in a treaty also existed as a customary rule, either because the treaty had merely codified the custom, or caused it to "crystallize", or because it had influenced its subsequent adoption. The Court found that this identity of content in treaty law and in customary international law did not exist in the case of the rule invoked, which appeared in one article of the treaty, but did not suggest that such identity was debarred as a matter of principle: on the contrary, it considered it to be clear that certain other articles of the treaty in question "were ... regarded as reflecting, or as crystallizing, received or at least emergent rules of customary international law" (I.C.J. Reports 1969, p. 39, para. 63). More generally, there are no grounds for holding that when customary international law is comprised of rules identical to those

[48] This includes a provision in a treaty that is not yet in force, or even a draft treaty text. The position is similar to that concerning General Assembly resolutions (see below, p. 58): statements made by states during the drafting process, the agreed treaty text, and later state reaction to the treaty, may be state practice indicative of custom.

[49] The preamble to the High Seas Convention 1958 states that it is "generally declaratory of established principles of international law".

[50] See, on the questions in these last two sentences, the *Lotus Case*, below, p. 267.

[51] I.C.J. Reps. 1986, p. 14 at 94. For further extracts from the Court's judgment, see below, p. 866.

of treaty law, the latter "supervenes" the former, so that the customary international law has no further existence of its own.

178. There are a number of reasons for [this conclusion]... In a legal dispute affecting two States, one of them may argue that the applicability of a treaty rule to its own conduct depends on the other State's conduct in respect of the application of other rules, on other subjects, also included in the same treaty. For example, if a State exercises its right to terminate or suspend the operation of a treaty on the ground of the violation by the other party of a "provision essential to the accomplishment of the object or purpose of the treaty" (in the words of Art. 60, para. 3(*b*), of the Vienna Convention on the Law of Treaties), it is exempted, vis-à-vis the other State, from a rule of treaty-law because of the breach by that other State of a different rule of treaty-law. But if the two rules in question also exist as rules of customary international law, the failure of the one State to apply the one rule does not justify the other State in declining to apply the other rule. Rules which are identical in treaty law and in customary international law are also distinguishable by reference to the methods of interpretation and application. A State may accept a rule contained in a treaty not simply because it favours the application of the rule itself, but also because the treaty establishes what that State regards as desirable institutions or mechanisms to ensure implementation of the rule. Thus, if that rule parallels a rule of customary international law, two rules of the same content are subject to separate treatment as regards the organs competent to verify their implementation, depending on whether they are customary rules or treaty rules. The present dispute illustrates this point.[52]

The situation where the treaty and customary rules are *not* identical, but merely apply in the same field, is an *a fortiori* case for the application of the Court's approach. This was the situation in the *Nicaragua (Merits)* case in respect of the UN Charter and customary rules on self defence: see judgment para. 176, below, p. 867.

3. As well as stating rules on the particular question of the role of treaties as a material source of custom, the Court's judgment in the *North Sea* cases, and those of several of the judges who gave separate opinions, throws light on the nature of customary international law in other respects also. For example, it recognises that there is no precise length of time during which a practice must exist; the position is simply that it must be followed long enough to show that the other requirements of a custom are met.

The Court's approach to the question of the number and kind of states whose practice has to be established is also instructive. It demonstrates that a practice does not have to be followed by all states for it to be the basis of a general custom and that the practice of states with a particular interest in the subject matter is the most relevant (para. 73). As to the practice of the most influential states, in the course of considering whether there was sufficient evidence of state practice to justify the conclusion that the doctrine of the continental shelf was a part of general customary international law, Lauterpacht[53] states:

... assuming here that we are confronted with the creation of new international law by custom, what matters is not so much the number of states participating in its creation and the length of the period within which that change takes place, as the relative importance, in any particular sphere, of

---

[52] Writers are divided on the merits of the Court's approach, with some arguing that the custom is abrogated or suspended while the treaty is in force: see Czaplinski (1989) 38 I.C.L.Q. 151 at 164.

[53] (1950) 27 B.Y.I.L. 376 at 394.

states inaugurating the change. In a matter closely related to the principle of the freedom of the seas the conduct of the two principal maritime Powers —such as Great Britain and the United States—is of special importance. With regard to the continental shelf and submarine areas generally these two states inaugurated the development and their initiative was treated as authoritative almost as a matter of course from the outset.

Which states' practice, if any, should be given particular weight when considering (a) the general customary international law concerning outer space and (b) whether the rule concerning the making of reservations to multilateral treaties has been changed?

In the *Nicaragua (Merits)* case, the ICJ confirmed that when deciding a case on the basis of *general* customary international law, it must discover that law from the practice of states as a whole: it is not sufficient that the states parties to the case have a common view of what that law is.[54]

4. *Opinio juris sive necessitatis.* As the Court indicates in its judgment (para. 77), the second requirement of a custom—acceptance that it is binding in law—is necessary to distinguish it from a rule of international comity,[55] which is a rule based upon a consistent practice in the relations of states which is not accompanied by a feeling of legal obligation. The saluting by a ship at sea of another ship flying a different flag is an example. Another example—which may now have been translated into a rule of customary international law[56]—is the rule by which the goods of a diplomatic agent and his family are immune from customs duty.

As the judgments of Judges Tanaka and Sørensen stress, it is often difficult to discover the necessary *opinio juris* because the reason underlying a state's adoption or acceptance of a particular practice is not clear. In this connection, the suggestion by Judge Sørensen (following Lauterpacht) that *opinio juris* may be presumed to exist if a uniform practice is proven is helpful. The judgment of the Court (para. 78), however, adopts a stricter approach.

Another difficulty with *opinio juris* is that the first states to adopt a new practice are supposed to be acting on the basis that it is binding even as they do so. It was this that Lauterpacht[57] had in mind when he referred to:

the mysterious phenomenon of customary international law which is deemed to be a source of law only on condition that it is in accordance with law.

Would it be correct to say that in the early days of the formation of a new rule the state or states adopting the practice either do not think about whether it is binding or, if they are thinking about its significance in the development of international law, put it forward more as an "offer", which other states can accept or reject, rather than as something which they are convinced is already binding? On this view, the feeling of obligation, if it arises at all, arises only later when there has been general adoption or acceptance of the practice or "offer".

---

[54] *Nicaragua (Merits)* case, judgment para. 184, below, p. 869. This is different from the situation in which the states parties to the case agree (or one of them asserts to the Court's satisfaction) that there is a *local* custom binding on them, in which case there is no need to look to the practice of states generally.

[55] Note that national courts sometimes use the term "international comity" as a synonym for international law: see Akehurst (1972–1973) 46 B.Y.I.L. 145 at 214–216.

[56] See Articles 36 and 37, Vienna Convention on Diplomatic Relations 1961, below, p. 344.

[57] *loc. cit.*, p. 40, n. 53, above, p. 395. See further, Elias (1995) 44 I.C.L.Q. 501 and Maluwa (1994) 6 A.J.I.C.L. 387.

5. What if one state, or just a few states, protest at a practice? Can it, or they, prevent it from establishing a custom? Judge Tanaka, in his dissenting opinion in the *South West Africa Cases, Second Phase*,[58] stated:

> the answer must be in the negative for the reason that Article 38, paragraph 1(*b*), of the Statute does not exclude the possibility of a few dissidents for the purpose of the creation of a customary international law and that the contrary view of a particular State or States would result in the permission of obstruction by veto, which could not have been expected by the legislator who drafted the said Article.

Does the *Anglo-Norwegian Fisheries* case[59] indicate, as Judge Sørensen suggests, that although a dissenting state may not by itself prevent a rule from coming into being, a state will not be bound by the rule if it maintains its dissent throughout the rule's formative period? Would any state, for example, that were to have protested consistently from 1957 (when the first satellite was launched) onwards against the passage of satellites through its airspace, now be bound by any change in the law affecting the upper limit of a state's airspace that may have resulted from the general acquiescence by states in the passage of satellites over their territory? And what was the effect of the consistent opposition by France to any rule prohibiting nuclear tests on the high seas during the 1960s and early 1970s? Is France bound by any such rule that developed?[60] On this question of the "persistent objector", the U.S. *Restatement*[61] reads:

> . . . in principle a state that indicates its dissent from a practice while the law is still in the process of development is not bound by that rule even after it matures. Historically, such dissent and consequent exemption from a principle that became general customary law has been rare.

In the view of some writers,[62] a persistent objector cannot escape being bound by a new rule of customary international law that has the character of *ius cogens*. The concept of *ius cogens* originated in the law of treaties, in which there is a rule prohibiting states from making a treaty by which they derogate from a rule of *ius cogens*, *i.e.* a rule that proscribes conduct that is fundamentally immoral or antisocial.[63] In the view of these writers, the same concept has been transposed into the law on the formation of general custom.[64] For example, Henkin,[65] citing state

---

[58] I.C.J. Rep. 1966, p. 291.

[59] Below, p. 375. See also the final paragraph of the extract from the *Asylum* case quoted above, p. 25.

[60] See below, p. 421. See also the position of developed states in respect of the majority view within the UN on expropriation: see below, p. 550 *et seq.*; and deep sea bed mining, see below, p. 474.

[61] *Restatement of the Foreign Relations Law of the U.S., Third* (1987), Vol. I, para. 102, comment, p. 26. On the persistent objector, see also Charney (1985) 56 B.Y.I.L. 1; Colson (1986) 61 Wash. L.R. 957; Stein (1985) 26 H.I.L.J. 457.

[62] See, *e.g.* Henkin, *International Law: Politics and Values* (1995) p. 39. For a full discussion of the issues, see Charney (1993) 87 A.J.I.L. 529 at 541 and Danilenko, *op. cit.*, p. 21, n. 1, above, chap. 8.

[63] On *ius cogens* in the law of treaties, see below, p. 835. Examples of *ius cogens* rules are those prohibiting genocide and the use of armed force.

[64] Different from this is the position concerning local custom: states may certainly not derogate by local custom from existing general custom that is *ius cogens*.

[65] *loc. cit.*, n. 62. On the prohibition of apartheid and UN sanctions against South Africa, see below, p. 966. For different views as to whether South Africa was a "persistent objector", see Charney, above, p. 539, n. 48.

practice, states that "South Africa's objection to including apartheid as a violation of customary law and of *ius cogens* has been generally disregarded". Cassese,[66] however, argues that the "ultimately *consensual* foundation of international law clearly indicates" that the "persistent objector" can escape *ius cogens* rules as well as others.

6. What is the effect of dissent by a state *after* a custom has been established? Can this by itself affect the application of the custom to the dissenting state? In answering this question, does it matter whether the dissenting state was in existence or not at the time that the custom came into being?[67] Can the dissent of one state bring down a custom if it is coupled with that of others? If so, there is clearly a stage when states leading an assault upon a custom are, although participating in an accepted law-changing process, delinquents.[68] Another intrinsic weakness in the customary international law-making process is that, in some cases, *e.g.* that concerning the breadth of the territorial sea,[69] the change from one rule of customary international law to another is unacceptably slow with an interim period of considerable uncertainty.[70]

7. For the purpose of the formation of rules of customary international law, consent is commonly indicated by state practice not in the form of positive statements or other action approving or following the practice in question, but of acquiescence. This MacGibbon[71] describes as "silence or absence of protest in circumstances which generally call for a positive reaction signifying an objection." For example, if the law concerning airspace has been changed as a result of the use of satellites, the practice of all but the states participating in satellite launching has consisted mostly of acquiescence in this sense. As the *Anglo-Norwegian Fisheries* case[72] shows, acquiescence cannot be established unless a state has actual or constructive knowledge of the claim being made. How strict a standard did the Court apply in that case in finding that the United Kingdom did have knowledge of the Norwegian claims? Would you agree with Johnson's comment that:

> under the Court's formulation, it would seem that ignorance as to another State's legislation on territorial waters, however excusable, can be fatal, and that States may neglect at their own risk, to study each other's statute-books?[73]

8. Some rules of customary international law are often broken. For example, it is not uncommon for states illegally to resort to armed force or to intervene in the affairs of other states[74] and more than one government has tortured its opponents.[75] In such cases, the question must be whether the delinquent and other

---

[66] *International Law in a Divided World* (1986), p. 178. But, on a voluntarist approach (see below, p. 44), might not states have agreed at a more general level to a limitation on the freedom of the persistent objector?

[67] See below, p. 104.

[68] What, for example, was the legal position of Iceland in the late 1950s when it insisted upon a 12-mile exclusive fishing zone off its coasts—something that was questionable then but clearly lawful now (partly because of Iceland's efforts)? What was Iceland's position in the 1970s when it claimed, again to the tune of protest by other states, an exclusive fishing zone of 50 miles (also now clearly lawful)?

[69] See below, p. 373.

[70] See Friedmann, below p. 44.

[71] (1954) 31 B.Y.I.L. 143. See also MacGibbon (1957) 33 B.Y.I.L. 115. On the meaning of protest, see below, p. 212.

[72] See below, p. 375.

[73] (1952) 1 I.C.L.Q. 145 at 166.

[74] See below, Chap. 11.

[75] See below, p. 731.

states continue to recognise the breaches as illegal. In this connection, note that in the *Nicaragua (Merits)* case, para. 186, below, p. 870, the ICJ acknowledged that a practice does not always have to be followed for it to indicate a custom: it is sufficient that any departure from the practice is recognised as illegal.

9. The above materials concerning custom are based upon the voluntarist or consensual theory of the nature of international law, by which states are bound only by that to which they consent. Although this is a theory that presents certain theoretical problems,[76] it remains the one to which the ICJ adheres and one from which, not surprisingly, states do not appear to dissent in their practice. If the theory may involve an element of fiction, it is not easy to find a substitute that is both more intellectually defensible and as serviceable as a working hypothesis.

FRIEDMANN, THE CHANGING STRUCTURE OF INTERNATIONAL LAW

(1964), pp. 121–123. Footnote omitted

Custom, the major instrument of law-making in any primitive society, has been, until recently, the principal source of law-making in international society. . . .

It is an obvious reflection of the radically different character and methods of international relations in our time that custom can no longer be as predominant or important a source of law as it was in the formative period of international law . . . custom is too clumsy and slow moving a criterion to accommodate the evolution of international law in our time, and the difficulties are increased as the number of subjects of the law of nations swells from a small club of Western Powers to 120 or more "sovereign" states. More importantly, custom is an unsuitable vehicle for international "welfare" or "co-operative" law. The latter demands the positive regulation of economic, social, cultural and administrative matters, a regulation that can only be effective by specific formulation and enactment. . . . Even in some of the domains of classical international law, as in the various aspects of the Law of the Sea, multilateral conventions arising out of preparatory work of international legal bodies and international conferences, tend to displace custom.

Yet it would be wrong to dismiss custom too easily as a source of international law of continuing importance, There is today a frequent interplay between the growth or modification of custom, the formulation of such developments by international law, recording bodies, such as the International Law Commission or the International Law Institute, and the eventual "codification" of such custom in a law-making treaty.

[76] See, *e.g.* Charney (1993) 87 A.J.I.L. 529 and Lobo de Souza (1995) 44 I.C.L.Q. 521. Problems commonly pointed to concern (i) the reason why new states are bound by existing customary law; (ii) the question of a *ius cogens* exception to the "persistent objector" rule; and (iii) the "mysterious phenomenon" identified by Lauterpacht, above, p. 41. Note that the voluntarist theory has far fewer problems with treaties as sources than with custom.

Notes

Note also the following comments by De Visscher.[77] On the one hand, he points to a merit of customary international law:

> What gives international custom its special value and its superiority over conventional institutions, in spite of the inherent imprecision of its expression, is the fact that, developing by spontaneous practice, it reflects a deeply felt community of law. Hence the density and stability of its rules.

On the other hand, like Friedmann, he points out a new weakness:

> Malleable as it is, custom can neither establish itself, nor evolve and so remain a source of living law, when, owing to the rapidity with which they follow each other or to their equivocal or contradictory character, State activities cease to crystallise into "a general practice accepted as law". Acceleration of history, and above all diminishing homogeneity in the moral and legal ideas that have long governed the formation of law—such, in their essential elements, are the causes that today curtail the development of customary international law.

3. TREATIES[78]

FITZMAURICE, SOME PROBLEMS REGARDING THE FORMAL SOURCES OF INTERNATIONAL LAW

(1958) Symbolae Verzijl, p. 153. Some footnotes omitted

Considered in themselves, and particularly in their inception, treaties are, formally, a source of obligation rather than a source of law. In their contractual aspect,[79] they are no more a source of law than an ordinary private law contract; which simply creates rights and obligations.... In this connexion, the attempts which have been made to ascribe a law-making character to *all* treaties irrespective of the character of their content or the number of the parties to them, by postulating that some treaties create "particular" international law and others "general", is of extremely dubious validity. There is really no such thing as "particular" international treaty law, though there are particular international treaty rights and obligations. The only "law" that enters into these is derived, not from the treaty creating them—or from any treaty—but from the principle *pacta sunt servanda*—an antecedent general principle of law. The

---

[77] De Visscher, pp. 161–162.

[78] See Jenks, *op. cit.*, p. 23, n. 18, above, pp. 92–98; Jennings, in Wilner, ed., *Jus et Societas: Essays in Tribute to Wolfgang Friedmann* (1979), pp. 159–168; McNair, *Treaties*, Appendix I; Starke (1946) 23 B.Y.I.L. 341.

[79] It may be recalled that in the *Reservations to the Genocide Convention* case, the jointly dissenting Judges (Guerrero, McNair, Read and Hsu Mo), speaking of the so-called "law-making" general multilateral convention, pointed out that the circumstance "that this activity is often described as 'legislative' or 'quasi-legislative', must not obscure the fact that the legal basis of these conventions, and the essential thing that brings them into force, is the common consent of the parties"—(I.C.J. Rep. 1951, p. 32).

law is that the obligation must be carried out, but the obligation is not, in itself, law. . . . A statute is always, *from its inception*, law: a treaty may reflect, or lead to, law but, *particularly* in its inception, is not, as such, "law". . . . True, where it reflects (*e.g.* codifies) existing law, non-parties may conform to the same rules, but they do so by virtue of the rules of general law thus reflected in the treaty, not by virtue of the treaty itself. In that sense, the treaty may be an instrument in which the law is conveniently stated, and evidence of what it is, but it is still not itself the law—it is still formally not a source of law but only evidence of it. Where a treaty is, or rather becomes, a *material* source of law, because the rules it contains come to be generally regarded as representing rules of universal applicability, it will nevertheless be the case that when non-parties apply or conform to these rules, this will be because the rules are or have become rules of general law. . . .

This position is equally true, strictly speaking, of *parties* to the treaty also. If the treaty reflects (codifies) existing law, then, in applying it, the parties merely conform to general law obligations already valid for them. . . .

The position is the same, even as regards parties to a treaty, in those cases where the treaty does not reflect existing law but leads to the emergence of a new general rule of law. Before that occurs, the parties apply the treaty, not as law, but as an obligation *inter se* which antecedent general law respecting treaties compels them to carry out because they have undertaken to do so. If the treaty rule does eventually pass into general law, its formal source *as law* . . . is clearly custom or practice—*i.e.* its adoption into general customary law. The parties, in applying it, are no doubt also (or still) applying the treaty: but, as they would now be bound to apply it even if there were no treaty (or if the treaty, *quâ instrument*, had lapsed or the party concerned had formally "denounced," or given notice of withdrawal from it), its legal basis as *law* is clearly not the treaty, although it retains a treaty basis of *obligation* so far as the parties *inter se* are concerned. . . .

Notes

1. There are now many multilateral treaties to which a large number of states are parties which lay down general rules of conduct for the parties to them.[80] The Vienna Convention on Diplomatic Relations 1961[81] is a good example. They are sometimes referred to as "law-making treaties" or "international legislation." Such terms are probably sufficiently useful to justify their retention even though they are strictly inaccurate. Note also that, in the past at least, the Great Powers have, in effect, legislated for other states by treaty on a number of occasions. Thus

[80] For information as to the parties to multilateral treaties, see Bowman and Harris, *Multilateral Treaties: Index and Current Status* (1984) and annual supplements.

[81] Below, p. 340. The 1949 Red Cross (Geneva) Conventions (188 parties), see below p. 625, and the UN Charter (in respect of its law-making provisions, *e.g.* Art. 2(4), see below, p. 862), are other examples. So are some UN human rights treaties: *e.g.* the 1989 Convention on the Rights of the Child has 191 parties.

the Final Act of the Congress of Vienna 1815, *inter alia*, made Switzerland a neutral state and provided for free navigation on certain international rivers.[82]

2. It scarcely needs adding that whatever dignity treaties may lose by not being "a formal source of law", in practice they are a very, and increasingly, important source of a state's rights and duties.

3. Imagine that State A agrees with State B by treaty that it will hand over to B certain war criminals, including X, if they should enter A. X, a national of State C, enters A as the ambassador of C to A. A hands him over to B. C claims that A has thereby violated a customary international law rule concerning the treatment of diplomatic representatives. Assuming that there is a customary rule concerning the treatment of diplomatic representatives that C can rely on, would A be able to rely on its treaty obligation towards B as a defence to any claim by C? If A had not handed X over, could B have claimed successfully against A for the breach of a treaty obligation? Should a treaty be interpreted as being consistent with customary international law in the absence of clear wording to the contrary?

4. GENERAL PRINCIPLES OF LAW[83]

WALDOCK, GENERAL COURSE ON PUBLIC INTERNATIONAL LAW

(1962–II) 106 Hague Recueil 54. Some footnotes omitted

On one side there are jurists like Verdross,[84] who say that Article 38 has the effect of incorporating "natural law" in international law and even claim that positive rules of international law are invalid if they conflict with natural law. At the other extreme are jurists like Guggenheim,[85] and Tunkin,[86] who maintain that paragraph (c) adds nothing to what is already covered by treaties and custom; for these authorities hold that general principles of national law are part of international law only to the extent that they have been adopted by States in treaties or recognised in State practice. In between stand the majority of jurists. . . . They take the line that general principles recognised in national law constitute a reservoir of principles which an international judge is authorised by Article 38 to apply in an international dispute, if their application appears relevant and appropriate in the different context of inter-State relations.

The *travaux préparatoires* of Article 38 and the decisions of international tribunals support the position taken by the majority. . . .

The Court, it must be admitted, has shown restraint in its recourse to "general principles of national law" as authority for its own pronouncements, although individual judges have been less reluctant to invoke

---

[82] On the juridical nature of such treaties, and of treaties such as the 1959 Antarctic Treaty and also of boundary treaties, see below, p. 825.

[83] See Cheng, *General Principles of Law Applied by International Courts and Tribunals* (1953); Fitzmaurice (1953) 30 B.Y.I.L. 1; Friedmann, *op. cit.*, p. 14, n. 46, above, Chap. 12; H. C. Gutteridge (1952) 38 Trans. Grot. Soc. 125; Jenks, *op. cit.*, p. 23, n. 18, Chap. 6.

[84] See Rec. Acad. 1935, II, pp. 204–206; and R.G.D.I.P., 1938, pp. 44–52.

[85] *Traité de droit international public*, I, p. 152.

[86] Rec. Acad. 1958, III, pp. 25–26.

them as support for their opinions.[87] Even when apparently relying on this source of law, the Court has not infrequently either referred also to customary law or left it ambiguous as to whether it was speaking of a general principle of national or international law.

   ... The main spheres in which these principles have been held to apply have been either the general principles of legal liability and of reparation for breaches of international obligations or the administration of international justice. ... For example, in the *Chorzow Factory Case*[88] the Permanent Court described the principle, that a party cannot take advantage of its own wrong, as a principle "generally accepted in the jurisprudence of international arbitration, as well as by municipal courts"; and at a later stage of the same case[89] the Court said that "it is a general conception of law that every violation of an engagement involves an obligation to make reparation," and it went on to speak of restitution and damages. ...

As to the administration of justice, there are a number of references to "general principles of law" in connection with questions of jurisdiction, procedure, evidence or other aspects of the judicial process. Thus, speaking in the *Corfu Channel Case*[90] of circumstantial evidence, the International Court said: "this indirect evidence is admitted in all systems of law, and its use is recognised by international decisions. ... "

In inter-State relations, however, the Court has shown little disposition to transport into international law substantive doctrines or institutions of national law; as distinct from principles of legal liability and reparation. ...

The correct conclusion, it seems to me, to draw from the practice of the Court may well be that it treats the "common law" which it is authorised to apply under Article 38, paragraphs (b) and (c), very much as a single corpus of law. In this corpus customary law enormously predominates and most of the law applied by the Court falls within it. But paragraph (c) adds to this corpus—very much in the way actually intended by its authors—a flexible element which enables the Court to give greater completeness to customary law and in some limited degree to extend it.

   ... as Lord McNair pointed out in the *South-West Africa Case*,[91] it is never a question of importing into international law private law institutions "lock, stock and barrel", ready made and fully equipped with a set of rules. It is rather a question of finding in the private law institutions indications of legal policy and principles appropriate to the solution of the international problem in hand. It is not the concrete manifestations of a principle in different national systems—which are anyhow likely to

---

[87] *Ed.* See, *e.g.* Judge Lauterpacht's opinion in the *Norwegian Loans* case, below, p. 1008.
[88] (1927) A/9 at 31.
[89] (1928) A/17 at 29.
[90] I.C.J. Rep. 1949, p. 18. Note also the Court's reliance upon "elementary considerations of humanity" in that case: below, p. 496.
[91] I.C.J. Rep. 1950, p. 148.

vary—but the general concept of law underlying them that the international judge is entitled to apply under paragraph (c).

Accordingly, the question arises as to what basic conditions must be satisfied before a principle qualifies to be considered "a general principle of law recognised by civilised nations". The phrase "civilised nations" now has an antiquated look. The intention in using it, clearly, was to leave out of account undeveloped legal systems so that a general principle present in the principal legal systems of the world would not be disqualified from application in international law merely by reason of its absence from, for example, the tribal law of a backward people.... Accordingly, we are quite safe in construing "the general principles of law recognised by civilised nations" as meaning to-day simply the general principles recognised in the legal systems of independent States.

The number of independent States, we know, has doubled since 1920, and is now over one hundred. Does this mean that today a principle has to pass the test of a hundred legal systems and that in this legal tower of Babel no principle will ever be able to qualify for application under paragraph (c)? Two considerations, it is thought, permit us to be reassured on this point.

First, by the accidents of history, some of the principal European systems of law have penetrated over large areas of the globe, mixing in greater or less degree with the indigenous law and often displacing it in just those spheres of law in which we have seen that international law has most readily borrowed from domestic law. In consequence, there is a much larger unity in the fundamental concepts of the legal systems of the world today than there might otherwise have been....

Secondly, it was never intended under paragraph (c) that proof should be furnished of the manifestation of a principle in every known legal system considered to be civilised; and certainly it has never been the practice of the Court or of arbitral tribunals to insist upon proof of the widespread manifestations of a principle or to indulge in elaborate comparative studies of the legal systems of the world. Truth to tell, arbitral tribunals, which usually consist of one, three or five judges, have probably done no more in most cases than take into account their own knowledge of the principles of the systems in which the arbitrators were themselves trained, and these would usually have been Roman law, Common law, or Germanic systems.

Notes

1. In the course of discussion by the Advisory Committee of Jurists on Article 38(1)(c), Lord Phillimore (Great Britain), who, with Mr Root (U.S.), was the author of that provision, pointed out that:

the general principles referred to ... were those which were accepted by all nations *in foro domestico*, such as certain principles of procedure, the principle of good faith, and the principle of *res judicata*, etc.[92]

[92] *loc. cit.*, p. 27, n. 7, above, p. 335.

He later said that by "general principles" he meant "Maxims of law."[93] In the same discussion the President of the Committee, Baron Descamps (Belgium), stated that the draft that became Article 38(1)(c) "was necessary to meet the possibility of a *non liquet*."[94]

2. Fitzmaurice[95] suggests:

A rule answers the question "what": a principle in effect answers the question "why."

Has the World Court followed this distinction in its practice?

3. General principles continue to be identified by international tribunals. For example, in *Sea-Land Service Inc v. Iran*,[96] it was stated that the concept of unjust enrichment is "widely accepted as having been assimilated into the catalogue of general principles of law available to be applied by international tribunals." In the *Barcelona Traction* case,[97] the ICJ relied upon the "lifting the veil" principle, which it found "admitted by municipal law" generally, when deciding that, in exceptional circumstances, the national state of the shareholders of a company could act to protect them in place of the national state of the company.

4. Not all claims to the title of "general principle" have been accepted. In the *South West Africa Cases (Second Phase)*,[98] the International Court of Justice found that the *actio popularis* was known only to certain legal systems and hence was not a general principle. Similarly, the French law of administrative contracts was held in the *Texaco* case[99] to lack sufficient acceptance in other families of legal systems. In the *Abu Dhabi Arbitration*[1] the English law principle of interpretation *expressio unius est exclusio alterius* was held to be a principle "rooted in the good sense and common practice of the generality of civilised nations," but the English rule that grants by a sovereign should be construed against the grantee (which was thought peculiarly English) was not.

5. Consider when reading the cases in these materials whether the Court has taken much advantage of the scope that Article 38(1)(c) gives for judicial legislation.[2] Would it be true to say that the Court has used such "straws" of state practice as it has been able to find to build a custom at least as often as it has relied upon general principles?

THE DIVERSION OF WATER FROM THE MEUSE CASE

Netherlands *v.* Belgium (1937)

P.C.I.J. Reports, Series A/B, No. 70, pp. 76–77

INDIVIDUAL OPINION OF JUDGE HUDSON. What are widely known as principles of equity have long been considered to constitute a part of

---

[93] *ibid.*

[94] *ibid.* p. 336, *i.e.* the possibility that a court or tribunal could not decide a case because of a "gap" in the law. Remarkably, the I.C.J. applied the doctrine of *non liquet* in the *Nuclear Weapons* case, below, p. 924.

[95] (1957–II) 92 Hague Recueil 1 at p. 7.

[96] 6 Iran—U.S.C.T.R. 149 at 168–169 (1984).

[97] I.C.J. Rep. 1970, 6 at 39.

[98] I.C.J. Rep. 1966, 6.

[99] Below, p. 573.

[1] (1952) 1 I.C.L.Q. 247. See also *Seaco v. Iran* (1992) 28 Iran—U.S.C.T.R. 198 at 209 (promissory estoppel not a general principle).

[2] For examples of the greater use to which general principles might be put, see Friedmann, *op. cit.*, p. 14, n. 46, above, Chap. 12.

international law, and as such they have often been applied by international tribunals. . . .

The Court has not been expressly authorised by its Statute to apply equity as distinguished from law. . . . Article 38 of the Statute expressly directs the application of "general principles of law recognised by civilised nations," and in more than one nation principles of equity have an established place in the legal system. The Court's recognition of equity as a part of international law is in no way restricted by the special power conferred upon it "to decide a case *ex aequo et bono,* if the parties agree thereto." . . . It must be concluded, therefore, that under Article 38 of the Statute, if not independently of that Article, the Court has some freedom to consider principles of equity as part of the international law which it must apply.

It would seem to be an important principle of equity that where two parties have assumed an identical or a reciprocal obligation, one party which is engaged in a continuing non-performance of that obligation should not be permitted to take advantage of a similar non-performance of that obligation by the other party. The principle finds expression in the so-called maxims of equity which exercised great influence in the creative period of the development of the Anglo-American law. Some of these maxims are, "Equality is equity"; "He who seeks equity must do equity." It is in line with such maxims that "a court of equity refuses relief to a plaintiff whose conduct in regard to the subject-matter of the litigation has been improper." . . . A very similar principle was received into Roman Law. . . . This conception was the basis of Articles 320 and 322 of the German Civil Code, and even where a code is silent on the point Planiol states the general principle that *"dans tout rapport synallagmatique, chacune des deux parties ne peut exiger la prestation qui lui est due que si elle offre elle-même d'exécuter son obligation."* . . .

Notes[3]

1. In the *River Meuse* case, the Netherlands claimed that Belgium had infringed a treaty obligation by building canals that altered the flow of water in the River Meuse. In the above passage, Judge Hudson was responding to an argument that the Netherlands had lost the right to bring its claim because of similar earlier conduct on its part. Clearly, he understood "principles of equity" as being principles common to national legal systems generally that were a part of international law by virtue of Article 38(1)(c).

2. The I.C.J. has increasingly referred to "equity" in its judgments in recent years. For example, in the *Gulf of Maine* case,[4] it stated that the concepts of acquiescence and estoppel in international law "follow from the fundamental principles of good faith and equity." Note also its reference to "considerations of equity" when seeking to apply the law of diplomatic protection "reasonably" in

---

[3] On equity in international law, see Janis (1983) 9 Brooklyn J.I.L. 7; Jennings (1986) 42 Annuaire Suisse 27; Lapidoth (1987) 22 Israel L.R. 161; E. Lauterpacht, *Aspects of the Administration of International Justice* (1991), Chap. 7; Lowe (1992) 12 A.Y.I.L. 1; Rossi *Equity and International Law* (1993); Van Dijk, in Heere, ed., *International Law and its Sources* (1989), p. 1.

[4] I.C.J. Rep. 1984, p. 246 at 305.

the *Barcelona Traction* case[5]; its incorporation of "equitable principles" into its statement of a rule for the determination of continental shelf boundaries in the *North Sea Continental Shelf* cases[6]; its emphasis on the need to achieve an "equitable result" in that and later maritime boundary cases[7]; and its search for an "equitable solution derived from the applicable law" in the *Fisheries Jurisdiction* cases.[8] In what different ways was the Court using "equity" when applying the sources of law in these cases? As a "general principle of law?" As a concept found in state practice and hence a part of custom? Or in the way that judges often use it, namely to achieve a fair result on the facts when applying a legal rule? Note that maritime boundary cases referred to have been criticised for introducing, through their reliance upon equity, an unduly subjective and uncertain element into international law. Thus in his dissenting opinion in the *Gulf of Maine* case, Judge Gros stated[9]:

> ... equity left, without any objective elements of control, to the wisdom of the judge reminds us that equity was once measured by "the Chancellor's foot"; I doubt that international justice can long survive an equity measured by the judge's eye. When equity is simply a reflection of the judge's perception, the courts which judge in this way part company from those which apply the law.

3. In the United Nations, equity has been referred to in General Assembly resolutions and other documents concerning the New International Economic Order[10] as a part of a "distributive justice" argument favouring the establishment of a new economic order that is more sympathetic to the needs of developing countries. Law-making treaties also now commonly rely upon equity, with the 1982 Law of the Sea Convention[11] being a striking example.[12]

4. *Natural Law* played an important part in the development of international law in its early years. According to the positivist approach, however, it is at best a material source of international law today. The following passage from the *North American Dredging Company* case[13] is a forceful statement of the positivist point of view:

> The law of nature may have been helpful, some three centuries ago, to build up a new law of nations, and the conception of inalienable rights of men and

---

[5] Below, p. 611.

[6] Above, p. 27.

[7] See below, p. 447. In this context, the I.C.J. explained the role of "equity" in international law in the *Continental Shelf* (*Tunisia v. Libya*) case, I.C.J. Rep. 1982, p. 18 at 60, as follows: "the legal concept of equity is a general principle directly applicable as law.... The task of the Court ... is ... to apply equitable principles as part of international law, and to balance up the various considerations which it regards as relevant in order to produce an equitable result. While it is clear that no rigid rules exist as to the exact weight to be attached to each element in the case, this is very far from being an exercise of discretion or conciliation; nor is it an operation of distributive justice." Inequality of natural resources is not relevant: see, *e.g.* the *Land, Island and Maritime Frontier Boundary Dispute* case, I.C.J. Rep. 1992, p. 376.

[8] I.C.J. Rep. 1974, p. 3 at 33. In the *Frontier Dispute Case*, I.C.J. Rep. 1986, p. 555 at 567–568, when determining a land boundary, the I.C.J. had "regard to equity *infra legem*, that is that form of equity which constitutes a method of interpretation of the law in force". *cf.* the *Land, Island and Maritime Frontier Dispute* case, I.C.J. Rep. 1992, p. 351.

[9] I.C.J. Rep. 1984, p. 386. *cf.* Brownlie, (1979–II) 162 Hague Recueil 245 at 287.

[10] See, *e.g.* the preamble to the 1974 Charter of Economic Rights and Duties of States, *loc. cit.*, below p. 526, ("mindful of the need to establish a just and equitable economic and social order.")

[11] See, *e.g.* Arts. 59, 74, 140, below, pp. 449, 451, 472.

[12] See, *e.g.* Art. 74, 1982 Convention, below, 451.

[13] *U.S. v. Mexico* (1926) 4. R.I.A.A. 26.

nations may have exercised a salutary influence, some one hundred and fifty years ago, on the development of modern democracy on both sides of the ocean; but they have failed as a durable foundation of either municipal or international law and cannot be used in the present day as substitutes for positive municipal law, on the one hand, and for positive international law, as recognised by nations and governments through their acts and statements, on the other hand.

Fitzmaurice, however, argues that some general principles of law in the sense of Article 38(1)(c),

> involving inherently necessary principles of natural law, are such as to cause natural law, at any rate in that aspect of it that relates to these principles, to be a formal, not merely a material, source of law.[14]

He gives a number of examples, including the rule *pacta sunt servanda*, and the

> rule that a State or government cannot plead the provisions or deficiencies of its own internal laws or constitution as a ground or excuse for non-compliance with its international obligations.[15]

5. Judicial Decisions

SCHWARZENBERGER, INTERNATIONAL LAW

(3rd ed., 1957), Vol. I pp. 30 et seq. Some footnotes omitted

It may be asked why the views expressed by international judges in their official capacity should carry greater weight than if contained in private studies. The answer certainly cannot be derived in the international field from the principle of *stare decisis*. Nevertheless, it appears advisable not to overestimate the difference between the binding and persuasive authority of judgments. A perusal of the practice of the World Court will reveal remarkable consistency in its judgments. It certainly did not hesitate to refer to, and to quote from, its previous judgments and advisory opinions. Yet the true answer lies first in the greater degree of responsibility and care that the average lawyer shows when he deals in a judicial capacity with real issues as compared with private comments on such issues or the discussion of hypothetical cases. There is a world of difference between practising shooting with dummy ammunition at a wooden target and firing in earnest with live ammunition at a living target. In addition, where a case is argued by experienced counsel from two or more angles, and where the court is composed of members with widely differing legal training and experience, it is more likely that an all-round view of the matter will be taken than where the same topic is turned over by a writer in the isolation of his study or even discussed with colleagues. . . .

[14] *loc. cit.*, p. 21, n. 1, above, p. 174.
[15] *ibid.* pp. 164–165.

Nevertheless, even the World Court is but an element of a law-determining agency[16]—and, be it recalled, of a subsidiary law-determining agency—and, therefore, should not be sacrosanct against sympathetic, but searching criticism. The persuasive character of its judgments and advisory opinions depends on the fullness and cogency of the reasoning offered. It is probably not accidental that the least convincing statements on international law made by the International Court of Justice excel by a remarkable economy of argument. In view of the element of compromise that is the price of any majority decision, this is not surprising. Exactly for this reason, the minority opinions of judges who could not square it with their judicial conscience to join the "compact majority" are especially precious and, in some cases, may constitute evidence of a kind which has at least the same, or even higher, intrinsic value than any particular majority opinion. At this point, the autonomy of the Doctrine of international law must necessarily assert itself. It then becomes the task of a writer to state without fear or favour why he considers any particular judicial pronouncements appear to err, for instance, on the side of either excessive caution or daring.

Municipal courts are not quite in the same category as international courts and tribunals. In the case of the judgments of the courts of some countries it may be justifiable to praise them in the terms in which Chancellor Kent spoke of the decisions of English courts and, especially, of the decisions of the English High Court of Admiralty:

> In the investigation of the rules of the modern law of nations, particularly with regard to the extensive field of maritime capture, reference is generally and freely made to the decisions of the English courts. . . . They contain more intrinsic argument, more full and precise details, more accurate illustrations, and are of more authority than the loose dicta of elementary writers.[17]

Yet there are countries in which the independence of the judiciary from the executive is not so much cherished as in countries in which the rule of law in the Western sense is recognised. Furthermore, the judges of municipal courts are more likely to suffer from subconscious national bias than a body of international judges drawn from all quarters of the globe. It is very much easier for the latter to guard against this most dangerous type of "inarticulate major premise." . . .

Notes

1. For the common lawyer, the most striking feature of the role of international courts and tribunals, and one of which he constantly needs to remind himself, is that cases do not make law. Article 59 of the Statute of the International Court of Justice, for example, provides that "the decision of the Court has no binding force

[16] *Ed.* For the meaning of this term, see above, p. 22.
[17] Kent's *Commentaries on American Law* (1986), Vol. I, pp. 69–70.

except between the parties and in respect of that particular case." In taking this approach, international law follows the civil law tradition. Yet although judgments do not constitute a formal source of law, those of the World Court at least play a larger part in the development of international law than theory might suggest. State practice seldom points so clearly in one direction as to leave the Court no discretion in its formulation of a custom.[18] Quite often it is non-existent, sparse or contradictory so that the Court is thrust into the speculative realm of general principles and analogy to decide a case. In other words, the World Court, as any other international court or tribunal, is by no means the mechanical recorder of law that might be supposed, a fact which becomes important in assessing the contribution of the Court because of the undoubted influence that its pronouncements have on subsequent state practice. The impact of the judgments and opinions in the *Anglo-Norwegian Fisheries*,[19] *Reservations*[20] and *Reparation* cases,[21] for example, bears ample witness to this influence.[22] Note also Judge Azevedo's view in the *Asylum* case[23]:

> It should be remembered . . . that the decision in a particular case has deep repercussions, particularly in international law, because views which have been confirmed by that decision acquire quasi-legislative value, in spite of the legal principle to the effect that the decision has no binding force except between the parties and in respect of that particular case (Statute, Art. 59).

2. International courts and tribunals not only do not make law; they are also not bound by their previous decisions as to the law which they apply. But despite this absence of a doctrine of binding precedent, the World Court, as Schwarzenberger makes clear, does tend to follow or feel the need to distinguish its own jurisprudence.[24] It relies very heavily upon this jurisprudence and only occasionally refers to that of other courts or tribunals.[25] Often the Court will cite only its own case law for a proposition and not bother to refer to state practice supporting it.[26] Other international courts[27] and tribunals[28] that decide more than one case tend

---

[18] For an extreme case where the Court's law-making role would be patent, note the controversy concerning the standard to apply to the treatment of the property of aliens: see below, Chap. 8.

[19] Below, p. 375.

[20] Below, p. 790.

[21] Below, p. 132.

[22] One exceptional instance of a ruling by the Court *not* finding general acceptance is that in the *Lotus* case on criminal jurisdiction in respect of collisions at sea: see below, p. 267. The Court's doctrine of "preferential fishing rights" for coastal states beyond the 12–mile limits in the *Fisheries Jurisdiction (Merits)* cases, I.C.J. Rep. 1974, p. 3, also was not adopted in the 1982 Convention on the Law of the Sea.

[23] I.C.J. Rep. 1950, p. 332.

[24] See, *e.g.* the Court's treatment of its earlier jurisprudence in the *Barcelona Traction* case, below, p. 604, and in the *Certain Phosphate Lands in Nauru* case, I.C.J. Rep. 1992, p. 240 at 259–260. Note in the *Barcelona Traction* case the way in which the Court distinguishes the *Nottebohm* case. Would it in fact be correct to say that the Court was there making use of the distinction between *ratio decidendi* and *obiter dicta*, which does not formally exist in international law?

[25] For references to other tribunals, see the *Land, Island and Maritime Frontier Dispute* case, I.C.J. Rep. 1992, p. 351 at 563 (*Island of Palmas* case, below, p. 190) and the *Jan Mayen* case, I.C.J. Rep. 1993, p. 38 at 67 (*Anglo-French Continental Shelf* case, below, p. 467).

[26] See Kearney, in Gross, ed., *The Future of the International Court of Justice* (1976), Vol. II, p. 610 at 698.

[27] *e.g.* the European Court of Human Rights: see below, Chap. 9.

[28] *e.g.* the Mexican Claims Commissions of the 1920s and 1930s and the U.S.-Iranian Claims Tribunal: see the cases below, Chap. 8.

naturally to build up a consistent jurisprudence too. Although there is no hier-archy of courts, the World Court is indisputably pre-eminent and its judgments and advisory opinions are highly persuasive for other international courts and tribunals.[29] The persuasiveness of the pronouncements of international courts and tribunals apart from the World Court for any other international court or tribunal depends very much, as Schwarzenberger suggests, upon their intrinsic merits.[30]

3. Among the many examples of judicial decisions of municipal courts discuss-ing and applying rules of international law, see the cases below on the recognition of states and governments and on state and diplomatic immunity.[31]

6. WRITERS

PARRY, THE SOURCES AND EVIDENCES OF INTERNATIONAL LAW

(1965), pp. 103–105

In the Court's Statute "the teachings of the most highly qualified pub-licists" are assigned the same subsidiary status, whatever that may be, as judicial decisions. Upon a long view, there would seem to be no legal order wherein the publicist—a peculiar term—has played a greater part than international law. Grotius is the father of the law of nations. And . . . at the beginning of the last century, all States seemed to rely heavily on Vattel. Indeed both the books and the opinions of the nineteenth century seem often to resemble catalogues of the praises of famous men. "Hear also what Hall sayeth. Hear the comfortable words of Oppenheim" is an incantation which persists even into this century.

The credit is to be given to Judge Jessup[32] for finding a truly devastat-ing example of the opposite point of view, that of the Court of Admiralty, expressed in the case of *The Renard*[33] in 1778. . . . The question was how long a prize must be in the captor's hands for the original property in her to be divested. Opposing counsel offered opposing opinions of Grotius and Bynkershoek. And the Court "observed that there was something ridiculous in the decisive way each lawyer, as quoted, had given his opinion. Grotius might as well have laid down, for a rule, twelve hours, as twenty-four; or forty-eight, as twelve. A pedantic man in his closet dictates the law of nations; everybody quotes, and nobody minds him. The usage is plainly as arbitrary as it is uncertain; and who shall decide, when doctors disagree? Bynkershoek, as is natural to every writer or

---

[29] Note, however, the restricted reading in the *Flegenheimer* case, below, p. 596, of the I.C.J.'s judgment in the *Nottebohm* case.

[30] Thus the European Commission of Human Rights—in a binding decision as to admissi-bility—felt itself quite free in the *Nielsen* case, 2 Y.B.E.C.H.R. 412, to disagree with the tribunal in the *Salem* case, below, p. 599.

[31] Below, Chaps. 4 and 6.

[32] *Transnational Law* (1956), p. 11.

[33] Hay & M. 222.

speaker who comes after another, is delighted to contradict Grotius. . . . "

It is difficult not to see truth as well as humour in this. And it is also no doubt true that, as the body of judicial decisions increases, the authority of the commentator is diminished. . . . The literature of international law, to which the majority of the World Court at least pays scant lip-service, possesses evident defects. One of the most frequent charges brought against it is that it displays a great deal of national bias. The charge is probably exaggerated. The fact is that international lawyers are inevitably municipal lawyers first of all. The law, furthermore, is inevitably a somewhat conservative training. The writers of one country thus reflect their national legal tradition and technique rather than any national political viewpoint. . . .

Notes

1. *The current role of writers.* Wolfke,[34] a Polish writer, describes the role of writers today as consisting in the:

> analysis of facts and opinions and in drawing conclusions on binding customary rules and on trends of their evolution. Such conclusions, like all generalisations of this kind, involve unrestricted supplementation by introducing elements lacking and hence, a creative factor. Further, by attracting attention to international practice and appraising it, the writers indirectly influence its further evolution, that is the development of customs.
>
> At present, the influence of doctrine on the formation of international law in general is certainly rather behind-the-scenes and anonymous. To disregard it would, however, be, to say the least, unjustified.

2. *Their earlier role.* The contribution of writers was a much more important one in the formative period of international law. They were largely responsible for establishing the basic idea that there was such a thing as law governing the relations between states. In addition, they exercised a much more creative role in the determination of particular rules of law than would be possible today.[35] Their statements of the law were derived by deduction from natural law principles, by analogy from Roman law, and by generalisation from what state practice they could find, as well as from more bizarre sources such as the writings of Homer. It was after Grotius (1583–1645) that writers became polarised into one of three schools: the "naturalists", of whom Pufendorf (1632–94) is the most well known, who based international law on natural law; the "positivists", such as Bynkershoek (1673–1743), who based it on the consent of states evidenced in state practice; and the "eclectics" or "Grotians", including Vattel (1714–67), who, like Grotius, relied on both. By the nineteenth century, most writers were positivists, reflecting the general change of attitude to natural law thinking. By that time also, as their adoption of positivism ensured, the role of writers had declined to its present state.

3. For a less charitable view of the objectivity of writers than that of Parry, note the following comment by the Arbitrator (Huber) in the *Spanish Zones of Morocco Claims*[36]:

[34] *op. cit.*, p. 23, n. 18, above, p. 77.
[35] Occasionally, a writer may still make an impact upon state practice, *e.g.* idea of the "right to development" emerged first in academic literature: see below, p. 722.
[36] *G.B. v. Spain* (1925) 2 R.I.A.A. 615 at 640. Translation.

It is true that the great majority of writers show a very marked tendency to restrict the responsibility of States. Their doctrines, however, are frequently politically inspired and represent a natural reaction against unjustified intervention in the affairs of certain nations.

7. GENERAL ASSEMBLY RESOLUTIONS[37]

SLOAN, GENERAL ASSEMBLY RESOLUTIONS REVISITED

(1987) 58 B.Y.I.L. 39. Footnotes omitted

There are now over 6,000 resolutions adopted by the General Assembly and forty years of practice on which evaluations may be based. Nevertheless, the legal status of General Assembly resolutions is unresolved and their effects remain controversial. . . .

General Assembly resolutions may . . . be related to customary international law . . . as one of the elements required for the validation of a customary rule . . . [*i.e.*] practice or usage and *opinio juris*. . . .

Unless one takes the extreme, and untenable, position that only physical acts constitute practice, General Assembly resolutions which are collective pronouncements of States must be considered a part of State practice. Dr. Akehurst defines State practice as "any act or statement by a State from which views about customary law can be inferred; it includes physical acts, claims, declarations *in abstracto* (such as General Assembly resolutions), national laws, national judgments and omissions."[38]

State practice may be evidenced either in declarations of general principle or in resolutions dealing with particular cases. The latter, when they involve the application of legal rules and principles, are even more clearly precedents. A condemnatory resolution adopted by 150 States might be compared to 150 diplomatic protests, although the cumulative impact would be different depending on circumstances.

With respect to declarations of general principle it may be objected that practice, to be constitutive of custom, must relate to a specific claim or dispute. It is doubtful if State practice was ever so narrowly confined. In the context of European relations it may have been theoretically possible to attempt such a test, but it is completely impracticable in a community of over 160 States. Nor is such a test supported by a review of the

[37] See Asamoah, *The Legal Significance of the Declarations of the General Assembly of the United Nations* (1966); Bleicher (1969) 63 A.J.I.L. 444; Castaneda, *Legal Effects of UN Resolutions* (1969, English translation by Amoia); Cheng (1965) 5 Ind. J.I.L. 23; Higgins (1970) 64 Proc. A.S.I.L. 37; *ibid.*, (1987) 24 Coexistence 21; Johnson (1955–6) 32 B.Y.I.L. 97; MacGibbon, in Cheng, ed., *International Law: Teaching and Practice* (1982), Chap 2; Schachter (1982–V) 178 Hague Recueil 114; Schwebel (1979) 73 Proc. A.S.I.L. 301; Skubiszewski (1986) 15 Pol. Y.I.L. 135; Sloan, *United Nations General Assembly Resolutions in Our Changing World* (1991), Chap. 2; Tunkin, *Theory of International Law, op. cit.*, p. 5, n. 13, above, pp. 165, 170, 172; *ibid.*, (1987) 24 Coexistence 5; Van Hoof, *op. cit.*, p. 21, n. 1, above, Chap. 10.

[38] *Ed. loc. cit.*, p. 23, n. 18, above, p. 53.

materials which States and tribunals examine in determining a rule of customary international law.

If, as the author suggests, General Assembly resolutions may contribute to custom by providing evidence of state practice, the question arises as to their evidential weight. On this question, Sloan lists the following factors that are to be taken into account:

The terms of the resolution itself are a factor which is rightly accorded considerable weight. Is the resolution drafted in precise legal language? Are the words which it employs mandatory or hortatory? . . .

Intent is widely recognized as a very important factor. . . . The intention of the Assembly may be either expressly stated or implied from the terms of the resolution, or it may be ascertained from extraneous sources such as explanations by the sponsors, statements in the debate, explanations of vote and the circumstances surrounding the adoption of the resolution. . . .

Resolutions that are adopted unanimously, or nearly unanimously, or by a true consensus, (*i.e.* one not accompanied by crippling reservations) carry considerable weight as interpretations of the Charter, statements of law or quasi-judicial determinations. It is normally important that the affirmative votes should include those States whose support may be necessary for effective implementation and States from all economic and legal systems. If, on the other hand, support comes from only certain groups of States, with other groups voting against, this is of course a negative factor.

Commentators differ on the effect of abstentions, some treating them almost as negative votes and others as affirmative votes. It is true that a large proportion of abstentions compared with affirmative votes would show a lack of enthusiasm for the resolution, but the better view is to treat abstentions, as a general rule, as acquiescence. Explanations of abstentions given at the time of voting may be relevant in determining the meaning of an abstention in a particular case. . . .

Another factor relevant to the weight and effect of resolutions is their repetition or recitation in subsequent resolutions. . . . Judge Tanaka [concluded] that an accumulation of resolutions could result in the formation of a rule of a customary international law.[39] . . .

---

[39] *Ed.* In his dissenting opinion in the *South West Africa* cases, I.C.J. Rep. 1966, p. 292, Judge Tanaka stated:

"Of course we cannot admit that individual resolutions, declarations, judgments, decisions, etc. have binding force upon the members of the organization. What is required for customary international law is the repetition of the same practice; accordingly, in this case resolutions, declarations, etc., on the same matter in the same, or diverse, organizations must take place repeatedly. . . . This collective, cumulative and organic process of custom-generation can be characterized as the middle way between legislation by convention and the traditional process of custom making, and can be seen to have an important role from the viewpoint of the development of international law." *cf.* Higgins, in Cheng, ed., *International Law: Teaching and Practice* (1982), *op. cit.*, p. 58, n. 37, above, pp. 27–29.

The repetitive or cumulative factor is considered significant for a number of reasons. In the first place, it demonstrates continuity and distinguishes those resolutions having stable support from those enjoying only an ephemeral majority. It also strengthens their evidential and precedential value and increases expectations of continued interest and support. It mobilizes public opinion and legal thinking, impresses the importance which States attach to the resolution, reinforces claims and confirms a persistent practice. . . .

Another factor emphasized especially by those taking a more traditional approach to General Assembly resolutions is that of State practice or subsequent conduct of States outside the organization. . . .

Some consider that it is the external practice (accompanied by *opinio juris*) alone which creates the law and that the resolution is only the stimulus. . . . On the other hand, such external practice may be considered as only one factor contributing to a normative effect of a resolution. Where the resolution is clearly *de lege ferenda* the first analysis seems best to describe the process. Where, however, the resolution purports to declare existing law the second is preferred. In the latter situation the absence of contrary practice (or confirming practice within the organization) may, in some cases, be sufficient to confirm the normative effect of the resolution. In either event, less practice and certainly less time may be required for the emergence of a rule of law than in the traditional process of custom formation.

Notes

1. United Nations General Assembly resolutions that expressly or impliedly state rules of international law in abstract terms[40] or that apply such rules to particular cases[41] are now an important feature of international relations. Article 38(1), Statute of the I.C.J. was not drafted with them in mind and there is, as Sloan states, uncertainty as to their role in relation to the sources of international law.

---

[40] Examples are the 1960 Declaration on the Granting of Independence to Colonial Territories and Peoples, below, p. 114; the 1962 Resolution on Permanent Sovereignty over Natural Resources, below, p. 549; the 1963 Declaration of Legal Principles Governing Activities of States in the Exploration and Use of Outer Space, *loc. cit.*, p. 248, n. 90, below; the 1965 Declaration on the Inadmissibility of Intervention in the Domestic Affairs of States, below, p. 889; the 1970 Declaration on the Principles of International Law Concerning Friendly Relations among States, below, Appendix III; and the 1970 Declaration of Principles Governing the Sea-Bed, below, p. 469. As to the 1974 Declaration on the Establishment of a New International Economic Order and the 1974 Charter on Economic Rights and Duties of States, see below, p. 550. The following notes are limited to resolutions of the UN General Assembly. Insofar as other inter-governmental organisations of universal membership, (*e.g.* ICAO, UNESCO) adopt non-binding resolutions that state international law rules, the same considerations and arguments as are mentioned in this section apply.

[41] See, *e.g.* the General Assembly resolutions condemning USSR intervention in Afghanistan, below, p. 891, or calling for non-recognition of South African homelands below, p. 110, which are the collective equivalent of individual state protest. Might Security Council condemnations, (*e.g.* of Israeli occupation of territory: see below, p. 226, and U.K. border raids in the Yemen: see, below, p. 916) also be regarded in the same way?

What is clear is that, other than in regard to certain internal matters,[42] General Assembly resolutions are not as such legally binding upon member or non-member states in the manner of legislation enacted by national parliaments. In terms of the sources listed in Article 38(1), although some writers[43] have argued that General Assembly resolutions might be seen as informal treaties or as indicating general principles of law, the most common view—which is that examined by Sloan in the above extract—is that they contribute in some way to the formation of custom.[44]

2. It is generally agreed by writers that General Assembly resolutions may serve as a convenient statement of a custom already established by state practice of the accepted kind (diplomatic notes, etc.), or may at once or gradually cause states to march in step in their practice so as to create one: *cf.* the role of treaties described in the *North Sea Continental Shelf* cases, above, p. 27. But, as Sloan suggests, General Assembly resolutions may also contribute to custom more directly as a form of "collective" state practice.[45] They are the collective equivalent of uni-lateral general statements[46] or, in the context of a particular dispute, "150 diplo-matic protests." The process by which they are adopted ("adopted, unanimously, or nearly unanimously, or by a true consensus" or otherwise) establishes whether the practice is a "general" one. Their repetition in later resolutions[47] goes to the "constancy" and "uniformity" of the practice, as does the conduct of states in conformity with the rules stated in them in their practice outside the General Assembly. As to the requirement of *opinio juris*, this will be evidenced, as Sloan indicates, by the wording of the resolution[48]; by statements made in the General Assembly in debate prior to its adoption or later in explanation of a vote[49]; or by statements made elsewhere.

3. But whatever the opinion of writers, the views of states, who by their practice decide the customary rules on the sources of international law, as to the status and impact of General Assembly resolutions remain crucial. In this connection, the

---

[42] *e.g.* the determination of the UN budget: Art. 17(1), UN Charter. As to the Assembly's power to terminate a League of Nations mandate, see the *Legal Consequences* case, I.C.J. Rep. 1971, p. 16 at 51.

[43] See, *e.g.*, Asamoah, *op. cit.*, p. 58, n. 37, above, pp. 61–62, 70.

[44] Some General Assembly resolutions may be seen as elaborating upon the meaning of treaty provisions in the Charter, (*e.g.* the 1970 Declaration on Principles of International Law, below, Appendix III, elaborates upon the meaning of Art. 2(4) and the Universal Declaration of Human Rights below, p. 630, amplifies the meaning of "human rights" in the UN Charter). This, however, does not solve the problem of classification where such resolutions are also understood to state rules of international law that are binding upon states independently of their treaty obligations: see the *Nicaragua (Merits)* case, below p. 866.

[45] For a different view, see MacGibbon, in Cheng, *op. cit.*, p. 59, n. 39, above, p. 22:
" . . . the kind of State practice which is appropriate to the formation of rules of customary international law is not voting or even making statements in the General Assembly, but what States do and have done 'on the ground' in their relations with other States—not the resolution itself, but actual practice in the sense of the provisions of the resolutions. In other words, it is real State practice in the real world which is required, not the formal conduct of States within the limited and artificial context of the General Assembly."
cf. Thirlway, *op. cit.*, p. 23, n. 18, above, p. 66.

[46] *e.g.* the Truman Proclamation on the Continental Shelf, below, p. 455.

[47] *e.g.* the many resolutions on self-determination cited in the *Western Sahara* case, below, p. 115.

[48] *e.g.* the 1970 Declaration on Principles of International Law, below, Appendix III. See its title and text.

[49] *e.g.* Mrs Roosevelt's statement that the Universal Declaration on Human Rights was not legally binding, below, p. 636.

following careful pronouncement by the U.S. Department of State[50] is significant:

> As a broad statement of U.S. policy in this regard, I think it is fair to state that General Assembly resolutions are regarded as recommendations to Member States of the United Nations.
>
> To the extent, which is exceptional, that such resolutions are meant to be declaratory of international law, are adopted with the support of all members, and are observed by the practice of states, such resolutions are evidence of customary international law on a particular subject matter.

When the question of the role of General Assembly resolutions was considered by states in the General Assembly Sixth Committee in 1974 in the context of a review of the work of the I.C.J., there was general agreement that General Assembly resolutions were not to be seen as a new source of international law, additional to those listed in Article 38. There was, however, acceptance of the idea that they may be evidence of custom. The representative of Mexico[51] went as far as any:

> . . . it was not a question of adding another source of international law to those enumerated in that Article but rather of drawing attention to certain elements of legal interpretation to which the Court must inevitably have recourse when deciding in accordance with international law such disputes as were submitted to it—in strict implementation, of course, of Article 38 of its Statute. The Court unquestionably had to take account of international custom as reflected in the many resolutions and declarations adopted year after year by the General Assembly, whose very reiteration was irrefutable proof of the *diuturnitas* which had traditionally been recognized as one of the constituent elements of international custom. He mentioned by way of example [Resolutions 1514,[52] 2625,[53] and 2749[54]] . . . . Those and many other General Assembly declarations and resolutions of a similar type reflected the desire of Member States to promulgate juridical rules of unquestionable validity to which they all subscribed, in other words, the general *opinio juris*, which was the second traditional element of custom.

The representative of Iraq[55] stated:

> The Court . . . could, without going beyond its Statute, draw from the work of international organisations, especially the General Assembly, which though having only the force of recommendations, reflected the progressive development of the international legal order. Of course such resolutions could not in themselves create law, but they could provide proof of the introduction or abrogation of some of the rules of international law when they were consistent and adopted unanimously or without opposition.

Among representatives of Western states, the representative of Italy[56] stated:

[50.] Letter by Mr Schwebel, Deputy Legal Adviser of the Department of State, 1975 U.S.D.I.L. 85.

[51] G.A.O.R., 29th Sess., A/C.6/SR. 1486, p. 133.

[52] Below, p. 114.

[53] Below, Appendix III.

[54] Below, p. 469.

[55] G.A.O.R., 29th Sess., A/C.6/SR.1467, p. 19.

[56] *id.*, p. 20.

... there now existed new ways of creating law, such as the adoption of general resolutions or declarations by the United Nations, which, though they were not binding *per se*, could spell out and to some extent elaborate existing customary rules or rapidly contribute to the formation of new ones.

More cautiously, the representative of the U.K.[57] stated:

While it was true that General Assembly resolutions might reflect or be evidence of developments in international law, that was not the same as saying that General Assembly resolutions could themselves develop international law. His delegation could not accept the latter proposition.... Even the evidential value of General Assembly resolutions must depend on their circumstances. Many resolutions were of such a nature and had such a content that they could have no relevance to the development of international law.

When assessing these official statements, note the following comment by Sohn[58]:

... there is wide consensus that these declarations [*e.g.* Resolution 2625, Appendix III, below] actually established new rules of international law binding upon all States. This is not treaty-making but a new method of creating customary international law.

... Thus the United Nations has made possible the creation of "instant international law."[59] Many traditional international lawyers have not reconciled themselves yet to this new approach and some legal advisers of Foreign Offices still like to raise doubts about the true nature and effect of such Declarations. But it is quite obvious that most States have found this new procedure quite useful and are willing to apply it whenever they are confronted with important issues of interpreting the basic rules of the Charter of the United Nations or of developing new law for new areas made accessible by modern science and technology. In a rapidly changing world the United Nations has found a method, albeit restricted by the rule of unanimity or quasi-unanimity, to adapt the principles of its Charter and the rules of customary international law to the changing times with an efficiency which even its most optimistic founders did not anticipate.

4. As suggested by Sloan, international courts and tribunals have not doubted that General Assembly resolutions are state practice and hence evidence of custom. Moreover, they have tended to give considerable weight to them as such. Most strikingly, the judgment of the I.C.J. in the *Nicaragua* case[60] relies almost exclusively upon General Assembly resolutions when stating the law on the use of force and intervention, with just a few general references to state practice of a

---

[57] G.A.O.R., 29th Sess., A/C.6/SR. 1492, p. 167.

[58] Bos, ed., *The Present State of International Law and Other Essays* (1973), p. 39, pp. 52–53.

[59] *Ed.* See Cheng (1965) 5 Ind. J.I.L. 23. Cheng invented the now celebrated phrase "instant customary international law" to describe the process by which, in a series of resolutions in the early 1960s, see below, p. 248, the General Assembly had spelt out a new legal regime on outer space. In debate on this new regime, a number of states accepted that General Assembly resolutions had a (not precisely defined) role to play in the development of international law. For example, the U.S. representative stated: "When a General Assembly resolution proclaimed principles of international law ... and was adopted unanimously, it represented the law as generally accepted in the international community:" U.N. Doc. A/AC.105/C.2/SR.20, p. 11.

[60] Below, p. 866. On the Court's approach, see Charney, (1988) 1 Hague Y.I.L. 16 and Charlesworth, 11 A.Y.I.L. 1.

more traditional kind, and the I.C.J.'s opinion in the *Nuclear Weapons Case* (para. 70)[61] follows an approach to the use of General Assembly resolutions which is similar to that of Sloan. Note also the Court's use of General Assembly resolutions on self-determination in the *Western Sahara Case*[62] and the reliance by various arbitral tribunals on General Assembly Resolution 1803 on the rules on expropriation.[63]

8. "Soft Law"[64]

VAN HOOF, RETHINKING THE SOURCES OF INTERNATIONAL LAW

(1983), pp. 187–189. Some footnotes omitted

This brings us to a . . . school of thought which . . . was to a large extent equally prompted by the questions involved in the legal nature of General Assembly resolutions, but its tenets also apply to other documents whose legal status is unclear. . . . authors belonging to this . . . group do not make a black-and-white distinction between law and non-law. After testing a new type of instrument on the basis of the criteria of the traditional sources, they conclude that these instruments cannot be considered as "full-fledged" rules of international law. On the other hand, they stress that these instruments fulfil at least some, if not a great number, of the criteria required for rules to be considered rules of international law and cannot therefore be simply put aside as non-law. In other words, they acknowledge that there exists a considerable "grey area" of "soft-law" between the white space of law and the black territory of non-law. Simultaneously, they make the salient point that the "grey area" may greatly affect the white one and explain, sometimes in considerable detail, in what ways "soft-law" can have legal effects. . . .

The "soft-law" approach is an important asset to the doctrine of international law . . . its main contribution . . . is that it has started to map out the legal implications of legally non-binding instruments, in particular also their relation with full-fledged legal rules. This job . . . is extremely useful, as in international law, because of the lack of a formal organizational structure, "soft-law" rules play a more prominent role than in national legal systems and are likely to do so also in the future.

Notes

1. "Soft law" consists of written instruments that spell out rules of conduct that are not intended to be legally binding, so that they are not subject to the law of

---

[61] Below, p. 924.
[62] Below, p. 115. See also the *Legal Consequences* case, I.C.J. Rep. 1971, p. 16 at 31.
[63] See, *e.g.* the *Texaco* case, below, p. 573, and the *Aminoil Case*, below, p. 578.
[64] See Bothe (1980) 11 N.Y.I.L. 65; Dupuy (1991) 12 Mich. J.I.L. 420; Gruchalla-Wesierski (1984) 30 McGill L.J. 37; Riphagen (1987) 17 V.U.W.L.R. 81; Schachter (1977) 71 A.J.I.L. 296; Seidl-Hohenveldern (1979–II) 163 Hague Recueil 164; Sztucki, in *Festkrift Hjerner* (1990), p. 549; Virally (1970) 16 Annuaire Français 9.

treaties and do not generate the *opinio juris* required for them to be state practice contributing to custom.[65] Not being legally binding, they cannot be enforced in court. Examples of "soft law" include the Helsinki Final Act 1975,[66] the Bonn Declaration on International Terrorism 1978[67]; and the Rio Declaration on Environmental and Development 1992.[68]

2. While it may be paradoxical and confusing to call something "law" when it is *not* law, the concept is nonetheless useful to describe instruments that clearly have an impact on international relations and that may later harden into custom[69] or become the basis of a treaty.[70] And, as Jennings[71] has stated, "recommendations may not make law, but you would hesitate to advise a government that it may, therefore, ignore them, even in a legal argument." Seidl-Hohenveldern[72] suggests that the main value of international "soft law," which is very important in the field of international economic law, is as a device "to overcome a deadlock in relations between states pursuing conflicting ideological and/or economic aims."

3. The concept has, however, been criticised. Sztucki[73] summarises the criticisms as follows:

> *Primo*, the term is inadequate and misleading. There are no two levels or "species" of law—something is law or is not law. *Secundo*, the concept is counterproductive or even dangerous. On the one hand, it creates illusory expectations of (perhaps even insistence on) compliance with what no one is obliged to comply; and on the other hand, it exposes binding legal norms for risks of neglect, and international law as a whole for risks of erosion, by blurring the threshold between what is legally binding and what is not.

9. CODIFICATION AND PROGRESSIVE DEVELOPMENT OF INTERNATIONAL LAW

Notes

The codification of international law has been the subject of public and private action at various levels since the late nineteenth century. Before the First World War notable success was achieved by the Hague Conventions of 1899 and 1907, resulting from the Hague Conferences of the same years, on the laws of war and neutrality. Between the two world wars, the League of Nations sponsored a Codification Conference at The Hague in 1930 which was prepared for in optimistic mood and which examined the law of nationality, territorial waters and state responsibility. It was a great disappointment when agreement proved possible only on certain aspects of the law of nationality.

In 1946, with the major part of international law still to be found in the uncollated practice of states, the General Assembly, acting under Article 13 of the

---

[65] On the related concept of international comity, see above, p. 41.

[66] See below, p. 625. But see the *Nicaragua (Merits)* case, judgment para. 189, below, p. 866, and the *Nuclear Weapons* case, I.C.J. Rep. 1996, p. 924.

[67] See below, p. 299.

[68] (1992) 31 I.L.M. 874.

[69] *e.g.* the Universal Declaration on Human Rights 1948 was "soft law" when it was adopted but has since to some extent hardened into custom: see below, p. 725.

[70] *e.g.* the General Assembly Declaration on Torture 1975, see below, p. 715, n. 12.

[71] *loc. cit.*, p. 21, n. 1, above, p. 14. Although only discussing General Assembly resolutions, which are a major source of "soft law", this comment applied to "soft law" generally.

[72] *loc. cit.*, p. 64, n. 64, above, p. 193.

[73] *loc. cit.*, p. 64, n. 64, above, pp. 550–551.

Charter of the United Nations,[74] established the International Law Commission.[75] The Commission was given the function of promoting the "progressive development" and "codification" of international law. By "progressive development" is meant "the preparation of draft conventions on subjects which have not yet been regulated by international law or in regard to which the law has not yet been sufficiently developed in the practice of States."[76] "Codification" means "the more precise formulation and systematisation of rules of international law in fields where there already has been extensive State practice, precedent and doctrine."[77] Most of the Commission's work now consists of "progressive development" rather than "codification", although the two are closely intertwined.[78]

A number of multilateral conventions now in force are the result of the Commission's work. The established procedure is for the Commission to prepare, on the basis of reports made by a member appointed as special rapporteur, a set of draft articles which are submitted to states for their comments.[79] The United Nations may then decide to call an international conference for the adoption of a convention based on the Commission's draft. For example, the four 1958 Geneva Conventions on the Law of the Sea,[80] the 1961 Vienna Convention on Diplomatic Relations,[81] the 1969 Vienna Convention on the Law of Treaties,[82] the (less successful) 1978 Vienna Convention on Succession of States in Respect of Treaties[83] and, most recently, the 1997 Convention on the Law of the Non–Navigable Uses of International Watercourses[84] all result from the Commission's work. Other recently completed Commission work includes Draft Articles on the Status of the Diplomatic Courier and the Diplomatic Bag[85]; Draft Articles on Jurisdictional Immunities of States and their Property[86]; and a Draft Statute of an International Criminal Court.[87] The first two of these—for which there was never the necessary political consensus—have not been enthusiastically received by states and are unlikely to lead to treaties. The fate of the last remains to be determined. Even though the Commission's work does not lead on to a treaty text, it may nonetheless prove influential in practice.[88] As Lauterpacht[89] stated, the texts

---

[74] Below, Appendix I.

[75] See Briggs, *The International Law Commission* (1965); El Baradei, Franck and Trachtenberg, *The International Law Commission: the Need for a New Direction* (1981); Graefrath (1991) 85 A.J.I.L. 595; McRae (1987) 25 C.Y.I.L. 355; Quentin-Baxter (1987) 17 V.U.W.L.R. 1; Ramcharan, *The International Law Commission* (1977); Rosenne (1960) 36 B.Y.I.L. 104; Sinclair, *The International Law Commission* (1987). A theme in much of this literature is the need to rethink the Commission's role and its working methods.

[76] Article 15, Statute of the I.L.C.

[77] *ibid.*

[78] On their relationship, see the dissenting opinion of Judge *ad hoc* Sørensen in the *North Sea Continental Shelf* cases I.C.J. Rep. 1969, pp. 212–213.

[79] Helpfully, states sometimes submit comments earlier, at the drafting state. Working groups or sub-groups are now used as well as or in place of rapporteurs to speed the Commission's work.

[80] Below, Chap. 7.

[81] *ibid.*

[82] Below, Chap. 10.

[83] See below, p. 128.

[84] UN Doc A/Res/51/229. May 21, 1997. This Convention was adopted following work by the General Assembly Sixth Committee without the need for a diplomatic conference.

[85] See below, p. 356.

[86] See below, p. 335.

[87] See below, p. 752.

[88] For use of the draft Declaration on Rights and Duties of States 1949, see below, p. 71.

[89] "Survey of International Law in Relation to the Work of Codification of the International Law Commission" in E. Lauterpacht, ed., *International Law, Being the Collected Papers of Hersch Lauterpacht* (1970) Vol. 1, p. 445.

prepared by the Commission are, in terms of the rules about sources of international law in Article 38(1)(c), I.C.J. Statute, "at least in the category of writings of the more qualified publicists".

Projects at present under way within the Commission concern state responsibility, international liability for injurious consequences arising out of acts not prohibited by international law, crimes against the peace and security of mankind, the effect of state succession on nationality and reservations to treaties.

The Commission, which meets for three months in the year, is composed now of 34 members, "who shall be persons of recognised competence in international law."[90] Members are elected for five year terms by the General Assembly[91] which "shall bear in mind that . . . in the Commission as a whole representation of the main forms of civilisation and of the principal legal systems of the world should be assured."[92] Members sit as individuals and not as representatives of their Governments. In 1965, one Member wrote:

> Most of the original members of the Commission elected in 1948 were not professional diplomats. . . . Today the Commission is different. Of its present twenty-five members, seventeen [approximately] . . . are professional diplomats, and, of these, seven or eight are Legal Advisers of their respective Foreign Offices, and several others are Legal Advisers of Delegations in New York. This is an interesting development which signifies quite eloquently the raising of the level of official interest in codification and the importance which is now attached on official levels to the preparatory work undertaken by the International Law Commission.[93]

While confirming that "many of its members are high officials in the foreign ministry of their countries and even represent them in the Sixth Committee" of the General Assembly, one recent member has stressed that nonetheless the independent status of members "remains the decisive aspect in determining the nature of the Commission".[94]

It is noticeable that the Commission has not been used in the drafting of a number of important UN sponsored law-making treaties. Thus human rights treaties have mostly been within the jurisdiction of the Charter-based UN Commission on Human Rights[95]; the Committee on Outer Space[96] has been seized with responsibility for treaties on outer space; the 1982 Law of the Sea Convention[97] was the work of UNCLOS III; and recent key environmental treaties derive from other initiatives.[98] The International Law Commission's non-involvement in some of these activities may be partly because of its own reluctance to move beyond areas of traditional international law in which there is a sizeable amount of non-controversial state practice or international caselaw upon which to draw and partly, more recently, because of the reluctance of states—particularly developing states—to leave politically contentious issues involving the progressive development of international law to a body which is not composed of representatives of states.[99]

---

[90] Statute of the I.L.C., Article 2.

[91] *ibid.* Article 3.

[92] *ibid.* Article 8.

[93] Rosenne, *loc. cit.*, p. 66, n. 77 above, p. 188.

[94] Graefrath, *loc. cit*, p. 66, n. 77, above, p. 600, n. 62. The Sixth Committee is the Assembly's legal committee. It debates the Commission's annual reports and is in a position to give guidance to the Commission on the direction that its work should take to have the necessary political backing of states.

[95] See below, p. 628.

[96] See below, p. 251.

[97] See below, p. 369.

[98] See *e.g.* the 1992 Biodiversity Convention, (1992) 31 I.L.M. 882.

[99] See further, El Baradei, Franck and Trachtenberg, *op. cit.*, p. 66, n. 77 above, Chap. 2.

CHAPTER 3

INTERNATIONAL LAW AND MUNICIPAL LAW

1. MONISM AND DUALISM

FITZMAURICE, THE GENERAL PRINCIPLES OF INTERNATIONAL LAW CONSIDERED FROM THE STANDPOINT OF THE RULE OF LAW

(1957–II) 92 Hague Recueil 5 at 70–80. Some footnotes omitted

THIS controversy [between monism and dualism] turns on whether international law and internal law are two separate legal orders, existing independently of one another—and, if so, on what basis it can be said that either is superior to or supreme over the other; or whether they are both part of the same order, one or other of them being supreme over the other *within that order*. The first view is the dualist view, the second monist. . . . [A] radical view of the whole subject may be propounded to the effect that the entire monist-dualist controversy is unreal, artificial and strictly beside the point, because it assumes something that has to exist for there to be any controversy at all—and which in fact does not exist—namely a *common field* in which the two legal orders under discussion both simultaneously have their spheres of activity. . . . For instance . . . it would be idle to start a controversy about whether the English legal system was superior to or supreme over the French or *vice-versa*, because these systems do not pretend to have the same field of application. . . . There is indeed no basis on which it is even possible to start an argument because, although these legal systems may in a certain sense come into conflict in particular cases, thus giving rise to problems of what is called Conflict Law, or Private International Law, each country has its own conflict rules whereby it settles such problems arising before its own Courts. Ultimately therefore, there can be no conflict between any two systems *in the domestic field*, for any apparent conflict is automatically settled by the domestic conflict rules of the forum. Any conflict between them in the international field, that is to say on the inter-governmental plane, would fall to be resolved by international law, because in that field international law is not only supreme, but in effect the only system there is. Domestic law does not, as such, apply at all in the international field. But the supremacy of international law in that field exists, not because of any inherent supremacy of international law as a category over national law as a category, but for other reasons. It is, rather, a supremacy of exactly the same order as the supremacy of French law in France, and of English law in England—*i.e.* a supremacy not arising from *content*, but from the field of operation—not because the law is *French* but because the place, the field, is *France*. The view here suggested is neither dualist nor monist. It is precisely the view put forward in the following passage from Anzilotti,[1] who is often miscalled a dualist in this respect:

> It follows from the same principle that there cannot be conflict between rules belonging to different juridical orders, and, consequently, in particular between international and internal law. To speak of conflict between international law and internal law is as inaccurate as to speak of conflict between the laws of different States: in reality the existence of a conflict between norms belonging to different juridical orders cannot be affirmed except from a standpoint outside both the one and the other.

The logic of this cannot be contraverted, and in actual fact, the necessity for a common field of operation as the basis of any discussion as to the relations between two legal orders, is recognised by modern protagonists of the monist-dualist controversy. This can be seen from the following sentence in an article by a writer of the monist school,[2] reading: "Two normative systems with binding force *in the same field* must form part of the same order"—[italics added]. This may be true, or at least it is capable of discussion, if the two orders in question *are* binding in the same field, but not otherwise. Consider again a sentence such as the following one, taken from one of the most eminent and justly celebrated modern exponents of the positivist-monist view[3]: "International law and national law cannot be mutually different and mutually independent systems . . . if . . . both systems are considered to be valid for the same space and at the same time." Everything here depends of course on the "if"—which surely assumes the very point that has to be proved. What calls for question is precisely the phrase "valid for the same space at the same time." Had this passage said "valid simultaneously for the same class of relations," it would not have been open to question, though only because international and national law do not in fact govern the same set of relations. To say this is not to deny the validity of the monist view, but only its relevance in this particular connexion. Equally, the relevance of the dualist view is

---

[1] *Corso di diritto internazionale*. This passage is translated from the French translation by Gidel, p. 57.

[2] J. G. Starke, "Monism and Dualism in the Theory of International Law" in *British Year Book* (1936), p. 74.

[3] Professor Kelsen, *The Principles of International Law*, Rinehart (1952), p. 404. *Ed.* Now see 2nd ed., 1967, p. 553.

denied.[4] Recognising, as they evidently do, that only relations between legal orders that operate in the same field can usefully and meaningfully be discussed, the protagonists of the monist-dualist controversy seem to be driven to trying to *create* the necessary common field—though it is more particularly the monists who seek to do this, since the dualists can rest quite content with the existence of two orders, provided they operate in separate fields. The endeavour to create a common field takes the form in effect of denying the existence or reality of the State, or reducing it to the sum total of the individuals composing it. For instance, the same eminent authority, evidently aware of the difficulty that must arise unless there is a common field, has suggested the following solution[5]:

> The mutual independence of international and national law is often substantiated by the alleged fact that the two systems regulate different subject matters. National law, it is said, regulates the behaviour of individuals, international law the behaviour of States. We have already shown that the behaviour of States is reducible to the behaviour of individuals representing the State. Thus the alleged difference in subject matter between international and national law cannot be a difference between the kinds of subjects whose behaviour they regulate. . . .

Formally, therefore, international and domestic law as *systems* can never come into conflict. What may occur is something strictly different, namely a conflict of *obligations*, or an inability for the State *on the domestic plane* to act in the manner required by international law. The supremacy of international law in the international field does not in these circumstances entail that the judge in the municipal courts of the State must override local law and apply international law. Whether he does or can do this depends on the local law itself, and on what legislative or administrative steps can be or are taken to deal with the matter. The supremacy of international law in the international field simply means that if nothing can be or is done, the State will, on the international plane, have committed a breach of its international law obligations, for which it will be internationally responsible, and in respect of which it cannot plead the condition of its domestic law by way of absolution. International law does not therefore in any way purport to govern the content of national law in the national field—nor does it need to. It simply says—and this is all it needs to say—that certain things are not valid according to international law, and that if a State in the application of its domestic law acts contrary to international law in these respects, it will commit a breach of its international obligations.

---

[4] If either view were relevant, the monist would seem preferable, but only on the basis that there is a legal order, natural law, behind and above both domestic and international law, which affirms the supremacy of international law. . . .

[5] Kelsen, *op. cit* . . . *ibid. Ed.* Now see 2nd ed., 1967, p. 544.

Notes

Controversy between monism and dualism has taxed and divided international lawyers over many years. It is most relevant when considering whether a national court should apply a rule of international law. Consider when examining the cases in the remainder of this chapter whether the international and municipal courts and tribunals that decided them show any awareness of the monist-dualist controversy.

2. MUNICIPAL LAW IN INTERNATIONAL LAW[6]

DRAFT DECLARATION ON RIGHTS AND DUTIES OF STATES 1949

Y.B.I.L.C. 1949, pp. 286, 288

The Draft Declaration was prepared by the International Law Commission. The United Nations General Assembly noted it and commended it to members and jurists as a "notable and substantial contribution towards the progressive development of international law and its codification": G.A. Resn. 375 (IV), G.A.O.R., 4th Session, *Resolutions*, p. 66 (1949).

Article 13

Every state has the duty to carry out in good faith its obligations arising from treaties and other sources of international law, and it may not invoke provisions in its constitution or its laws as an excuse for failure to perform this duty.

Notes

There is ample judicial and arbitral authority for the rule that a state cannot rely upon its municipal law to avoid its international law obligations. For example, in the *Alabama Claims Arbitration*,[7] the Tribunal rejected the British argument that because its constitutional law was not such as to provide it with the power to interfere with the private construction and sailing of the ships concerned, Great Britain had not violated its obligations as a neutral in the United States Civil War by allowing the construction and sailing to occur:

> . . . the government of Her Britannic Majesty cannot justify itself for a failure in due diligence on the plea of insufficiency of the legal means of action which it possessed.

EXCHANGE OF GREEK AND TURKISH POPULATIONS CASE

Advisory Opinion. P.C.I.J. Reports, Series B, No. 10, p. 20 (1925)

Referring to Article 18 of the Treaty of Lausanne 1923, by which the parties undertook "to introduce in their respective laws such modifications as may be

---

[6] See Ferrari-Bravo, in McDonald and Johnston, eds., *The Structure and Process of International Law* (1983), pp. 715 and 725 and Jenks, *The Prospects of International Adjudication* (1964), Chap. 9.

[7] *U.S. v. G.B.*, Moore, (1872) 1 Int.Arb. 495 at 656.

necessary with a view to ensuring the execution of the present Convention," the Court stated:

Opinion of the Court

This clause ... merely lays stress on a principle which is self-evident, according to which a State which has contracted valid international obligations is bound to make in its legislation such modifications as may be necessary to ensure the fulfilment of the obligations undertaken.

Notes

1. If State A and State B make a treaty by which each agrees to allow the nationals of the other into its territory on terms better than those required by customary international law, and if State A fails to make the necessary changes in its local law to allow the admission of the nationals of State B on the terms agreed, has State A violated international law if no national of State B has tried to obtain, and been refused, admission under the treaty?[8]

2. If, contrary to customary international law, State A claims jurisdiction to board ships on the high seas flying the flag of another state and gives its navy power under its municipal law so to act, does it *thereby* violate international law?[9]

BRAZILIAN LOANS CASE

France *v.* Brazil (1929)

P.C.I.J. Reports, Series A, No. 21, pp. 124–125

The question in this case was one of the interpretation of certain Brazilian Government loans, some bonds of which were held by French nationals. The loans were governed by Brazilian law. The Court ruled that it had jurisdiction under Article 36 of its Statute to decide cases such as the one before it involving disputes between states which turned not upon international law but the interpretation of municipal law. In the following passage the Court considered how it should go about interpreting municipal law when called upon to do so. The Agreement between the parties referring the case to the Court read in part: "In estimating the weight to be attached to any municipal law of either country which may be applicable to the dispute, the Permanent Court of International Justice shall not be bound by the decisions of the respective courts" (Article VI).

Judgment of the Court

Though bound to apply municipal law when circumstances so require, the Court, which is a tribunal of international law, and which, in this capacity, is deemed itself to know what this law is, is not obliged also to know the municipal law of the various countries. All that can be said in

---

[8] See Fitzmaurice, *loc. cit.*, p. 68, above, pp. 89–90; McNair, *Treaties*, p. 100; Schwarzenberger, p. 614.

[9] See Fitzmaurice, *loc. cit.*, n. 8, above.

this respect is that the Court may possibly be obliged to obtain knowledge regarding the municipal law which has to be applied. And this it must do, either by means of evidence furnished it by the Parties or by means of any researches which the Court may think fit to undertake or to cause to be undertaken.

Once the Court has arrived at the conclusion that it is necessary to apply the municipal law of a particular country, there seems no doubt that it must seek to apply it as it would be applied in that country. It would not be applying the municipal law of a country if it were to apply it in a manner different from that in which that law would be applied in the country in which it is in force.

It follows that the Court must pay the utmost regard to the decisions of the municipal courts of a country, for it is with the aid of their jurisprudence that it will be enabled to decide what are the rules which, in actual fact, are applied in the country of the law of which is recognised as applicable in a given case. If the Court were obliged to disregard the decisions of municipal courts, the result would be that it might in certain circumstances apply rules other than those actually applied; this would seem to be contrary to the whole theory on which the application of municipal law is based.

Of course, the Court will endeavour to make a just appreciation of the jurisprudence of municipal courts. If this is uncertain or divided, it will rest with the Court to select the interpretation which it considers most in conformity with the law. . . . As the Court has already observed in the judgment in the case of Serbian loans,[10] it would be a most delicate matter to do so, in a case concerning public policy—a conception the definition of which in any particular country is largely dependant on the opinion prevailing at any given time in such country itself—and in a case where no relevant provisions directly relate to the question at issue. Such are the reasons according to which the Court considers that it must construe Article VI of the Special Agreement to mean that, while the Court is authorised to depart from the jurisprudence of the municipal courts, it remains entirely free to decide that there is no ground for attributing to the municipal law a meaning other than that attributed to it by that jurisprudence.

Notes

1. If a nationalisation statute enacted by State A were alleged to be contrary to international law by State B before an international court or tribunal and if the dispute turned upon the meaning of the compensation provision in the statute, how would the court or tribunal go about interpreting that provision (a) if the statute had not been construed by State A's courts; (b) if it had been construed by them but State B alleged that the court in the case in which this was done had failed to follow a binding precedent that would have led it to a different conclusion?

[10] *Ed.* P.C.I.J. Rep., Series A. No. 20, p. 46 (1929).

2. Note the reliance on the municipal law concept of the company in the *Barcelona Traction Case*.[11]

3. INTERNATIONAL LAW IN MUNICIPAL LAW[12]

(i) THE UNITED KINGDOM[13]

(a) *Customary International Law*

TRIQUET *v.* BATH

(1764) 3 Burr. 1478. Court of King's Bench

In this case, in which the defendant, a domestic servant of the Bavarian Minister to Great Britain, successfully claimed diplomatic immunity, Lord Mansfield discussed the position of international law in English law.

LORD MANSFIELD. This privilege of foreign ministers and their domestic servants depends upon the law of nations. The Act of Parliament of 7 Ann. c. 12,[14] is declaratory of it. . . .

I remember in a case before Lord Talbot, of *Buvot v. Barbuit*[15] upon a motion to discharge the defendant (who was in execution for not performing a decree), "because he was agent of commerce, commissioned by the King of Prussia, and received here as such"; the matter was very elaborately argued at the Bar; and a solemn deliberate opinion given to the Court. These questions arose and were discussed. . . . "What was the rule of decision: the Act of Parliament; or, the law of nations." Lord Talbot declared a clear opinion; "That the law of nations, in its full extent was part of the law of England." . . .

I remember, too, Lord Hardwicke's declaring his opinion to the same effect; and denying that Lord Chief Justice Holt ever had any doubt as to the law of nations being part of the law of England, upon the occasion of the arrest of the Russian Ambassador [which had led to the Act of Anne].

Notes
Although the discussion in the English cases in this section is in terms of English law, the question in issue is one of the public law of the United Kingdom

---

[11] Below, p. 604.
[12] See Cassese (1985–III) 192 Hague Recueil 331; Jacobs and Roberts, eds., *The Effects of Treaties in Domestic Law* (1987); Int. Law Assn., Report of 66th Conference, 1994, p. 326; Morgenstern (1950) 27 B.Y.I.L. 42; Seidl-Hohenveldern (1963) 12 I.C.L.Q. 88; Wildhaber and Breitenmoser (1988) 48 Z.A.O.R.V. 163. On the Japanese position, see Iwasawa (1993) 64 B.Y.I.L. 332.
[13] See Butler (1987) 24 Coexistence 67; Fawcett, *The British Commonwealth in International Law* (1963), Chap. 2; Holdsworth, *Essays in Law and History* (1946) pp. 260–272; Jenks, *op. cit.*, p. 71, n. 6, above, Chap. 13; Lauterpacht (1939) 25 Trans. Grot. Soc. 51; Mann, *Foreign Affairs in English Courts* (1986) Chaps. 5, 6.
[14] *Ed.* Diplomatic Privileges Act 1708.
[15] *Ed.* (1737) Cases t. Talb. 281.

as a whole. *Triquet v. Bath* and *Buvot v. Barbuit* are two of the cases commonly cited in support of the view that United Kingdom law adopts the "incorporation" approach to the reception of customary international law as part of common law, by which customary international law is automatically regarded as a part of municipal law, without the need for a national court decision in each particular case. See also *R. v. Mills*, below, p. 443.

R. v. KEYN

(1876) 2 Ex.D. 63. Court for Crown Cases Reserved

The *Franconia*, a German ship, collided with the *Strathclyde*, a British ship, at a point in the English Channel within three miles of the English coast. The defendant, the German captain of the *Franconia*, was prosecuted at the Central Criminal Court for the manslaughter of a passenger on board the *Strathclyde* who died as a result of the collision. The defendant was found guilty, but the question whether an English court had jurisdiction to try the case was reserved for the Court for Crown Cases Reserved[16] which decided, by seven votes to six, that it did not. The following is an extract from the judgment of Cockburn C.J. who was one of the judges in the majority.

COCKBURN C.J. On board a foreign ship on the high seas, the foreigner is liable to the law of the foreign ship only. It is only when a foreign ship comes into the ports or waters of another state that the ship and those on board become subject to the local law. These are the established rules of the law of nations. They have been adopted into our own municipal law, and must be taken to form part of it.

... Unless, therefore, the accused, Keyn, at the time of the offence of which he has been convicted was committed, was on British territory or on board a British ship, he could not be properly brought to trial under English law, in the absence of express legislation.

On the question whether the three mile belt of sea surrounding Great Britain was British territory in English law, Cockburn C.J. ruled first that it was not such according to "the ancient law of England".[17] He then considered whether it had become such because of a rule of customary international law to that effect. After concluding that the opinions of writers on the width of sea over which jurisdiction could be exercised and on the nature of any such jurisdiction was conflicting, Lord Cockburn continued:

... even if entire unanimity had existed ... the question would still remain, how far the law as stated by the publicists had received the assent of the civilized nations of the world. ... To be binding, the law must have received the assent of the nations who are to be bound by it. This assent may be express, as by treaty or the acknowledged concurrence of governments, or may be implied from established usage. ... Nor, in my opinion, would the clearest proof of unanimous assent on the part of other nations

[16] The case was argued twice. On the first occasion a court of six judges was equally divided.
[17] 2 Ex.D. 174.

be sufficient to authorise the tribunals of this country to apply, without an Act of Parliament, what would practically amount to a new law. In so doing we should be unjustifiably usurping the province of the legislature. The assent of nations is doubtless sufficient to give the power of parliamentary legislation in a matter otherwise within the sphere of international law; but it would be powerless to confer without such legislation a jurisdiction beyond and unknown to the law, such as that now insisted on, a jurisdiction over foreigners in foreign ships on a portion of the high seas.

When I am told that all other nations have assented to such an absolute dominion on the part of the littoral state, over this portion of the sea, as that their ships may be excluded from it, and that, without any open legislation, or notice to them or their subjects, the latter may be held liable to the local law, I ask, first, what proof there is of such assent as here asserted; and, secondly, to what extent has such assent been carried? a question of infinite importance, when, undirected by legislation, we are called upon to apply the law on the strength of such assent. . . .

Cockburn C.J. examined the evidence of treaties and of usage and concluded that in neither case was it clear.

It may well be, I say again, that—after all that has been said and done in this respect—after the instances which have been mentioned of the adoption of the three-mile distance, and the repeated assertion of this doctrine by the writers on public law, a nation which should now deal with this portion of the sea as its own, so as to make foreigners within it subject to its law, for the prevention and punishment of offences, would not be considered as infringing the rights of other nations. But I apprehend that as the ability so to deal with these waters would result, not from any original or inherent right, but, from the acquiescence of other states, some outward manifestation of the national will, in the shape of open practice or municipal legislation, so as to amount, at least constructively, to an occupation of that which was before unappropriated, would be necessary to render the foreigner, not previously amenable to our general law, subject to its control. That such legislation, whether consistent with the general law of nations or not, would be binding on the tribunals of this country—leaving the question of its consistency with international law to be determined between the governments of the respective nations—can of course admit of no doubt. The question is whether such legislation would not, at all events, be necessary to justify our Courts in applying the law of this country to foreigners under entirely novel circumstances in which it has never been applied before.

It is obviously one thing to say that the legislature of a nation may, from the common assent of other nations, have acquired the full right to legislate over a part of that which was before high sea, and as such common to all the world; another and very different thing to say that the law of the local state becomes thereby at once, without anything more, applicable to foreigners within such part, or that, independently of legislation, the Courts of the local state can *proprio vigore* so apply it. The one position does not follow from the other; and it is essential to keep the two things, the power of Parliament to legislate, and the authority of our Courts, without such legislation, to apply the criminal law where it could not have been applied before, altogether distinct, which, it is evident, is not always done. It is unnecessary to the defence, and equally so to the decision of the case, to determine whether Parliament has the right to treat the three-mile zone as part of the realm consistently with international law. That is a matter on which it is for Parliament itself to decide. It is enough for us that it has, so far as to be binding upon us, the power to do so. The question is whether, acting judicially, we can treat the power of Parliament to legislate as making up for the absence of actual legislation. I am clearly of opinion that we cannot, and that it is only in the instances in which foreigners on the seas have been made specifically liable to our law by statutory enactment that the law can be applied to them.

Finally, on the question of the location of the offence, Cockburn C.J. ruled that although the defendant's action had had its effect on board the *Strathclyde*, the offence of manslaughter could not be said to have been committed there so as to give an English court jurisdiction over it.[18]

Pollock B. and Field J. concurred in the judgment of Cockburn C.J. Kelly C.B., Bramwell J.A., Lush J., and Sir Robert Phillimore gave concurring judgments. Lord Coleridge C.J., Brett and Amphlett JJ.A., Grove, Denman, and Lindley JJ., gave dissenting judgments.

Notes

1. *R. v. Keyn* was reversed by the Territorial Waters Jurisdiction Act 1878, the preamble to which reads: "Whereas the rightful jurisdiction of Her Majesty, her heirs and successors, extends *and always has extended* over the open seas adjacent to the coasts of the United Kingdom and of all other parts of Her Majesty's dominions to such a distance as is necessary for the defence and security of such dominions. . . . "[19]

2. Is Cockburn C.J.'s judgment, which is the leading one among those given by the judges in the majority, consistent with the "incorporation" approach to the reception of customary international law? Or does it support the "transformation" approach, according to which only such rules of international law are a part of the municipal law of a state as are actually adopted by a state's courts or legislature in their or its discretion? Did any rule of United Kingdom constitutional law influence Cockburn C.J. in his judgment?[20] Note the following comment on his judgment by Lauterpacht[21]:

> . . . it cannot be said that this judgment amounts to a rejection of the rule that international law is a part of the law of England. Writers seem to forget that the main issue of the controversy in the case was not the question whether a rule

[18] See Beckett (1927) 8 B.Y.I.L. 108.
[19] Italics added.
[20] See Brownlie, p. 45.
[21] *Private Law Sources and Analogies of International Law* (1927), p. 76, footnote. See also *Pianka v. The Queen* [1979] A.C. 107, PC.

of international law can be enforced without an Act of Parliament; what *was* in dispute was the existence and the extent of a rule of international law relating to jurisdiction in territorial waters.

3. Which view of the relationship between international and municipal law (monist, dualist) does the "transformation" approach support?

WEST RAND CENTRAL GOLD MINING CO. *v.* R.

[1905] 2 K.B. 391. King's Bench Division

The South African Republic seized gold, the property of the suppliant, a British company, in a manner allegedly contrary to the law of the Republic. When Great Britain annexed the Republic in 1900, a petition of right was brought against the Crown to recover the gold or compensation for its loss. Upon the Crown's demur, the court rejected the suppliant's contention that a conquering state was liable in international law for the financial obligations of its predecessor. It was therefore not required to rule upon the argument that the alleged rule was a part of English law. Nonetheless, Lord Alverstone, delivering the opinion of the court, made the following comments.

LORD ALVERSTONE C.J. It is quite true that whatever has received the common consent of civilised nations must have received the assent of our country, and that to which we have assented along with other nations in general may properly be called international law, and as such will be acknowledged and applied by our municipal tribunals when legitimate occasion arises for those tribunals to decide questions to which doctrines of international law may be relevant. But any doctrine so invoked must be one really accepted as binding between nations, and the international law sought to be applied must, like anything else, be proved by satisfactory evidence, which must shew either that the particular proposition put forward has been recognised and acted upon by our own country, or that it is of such a nature, and has been so widely and generally accepted, that it can hardly be supposed that any civilised State would repudiate it. . . . *Barbuit's Case*,[22] *Triquet v. Bath*,[23] and *Heathfield v. Chilton*[24] are cases in which the Courts of law have recognised and have given effect to the privilege of ambassadors as established by international law. But the expressions used by Lord Mansfield when dealing with the particular and recognised rule of international law on this subject, that the law of nations forms part of the law of England, ought not to be construed so as to include as part of the law of England opinions of text-writers upon a question as to which there is no evidence that Great Britain has ever assented, and a fortiori if they are contrary to the principles of her laws as declared by her Courts. The cases of *Wolff v. Oxholm*[25] and *Rex v. Keyn*[26]

[22] *Ed., i.e. Buvot v. Barbuit*, above, p. 74, n. 15.
[23] *Ed.* Above, p. 74.
[24] 4 Burr. 2016.
[25] (1817) 6 M. & S. 92.
[26] *Ed.* Above, p. 75.

are only illustrations of the same rule—namely, that questions of international law may arise, and may have to be considered in connection with the administration of municipal law.

Notes

1. What explanation of *R. v. Keyn* does this case support?[27] If a "proposition put forward has been recognised and acted upon by our own country," is this sufficient to establish it as a rule of customary international law for the purpose of its application by an English court? Would it be sufficient to establish it as such for the purpose of its application by an international court or tribunal?

2. Would Lord Alverstone permit the incorporation of a customary rule that was contrary to existing common law? In *Chung Chi Cheung v. The King*,[28] Lord Atkin, delivering the opinion of the Privy Council, stated:

> It must always be remembered that, so far, at any rate, as the Courts of this Country are concerned, international law has no validity save in so far as its principles are accepted and adopted by our own domestic law. There is no external power that imposes its rule upon our own code of substantive law or procedure.
>
> The Courts acknowledge the existence of a body of rules which nations accept amongst themselves. On any judicial issue they seek to ascertain what the relevant rule is, and having found it, they will treat it as incorporated into the domestic law, so far as it is not inconsistent with rules enacted by statutes *or finally declared by* their tribunals.

Lord Atkin then considered and applied the international law rules on state immunity in respect of public ships.

Lord Denning quoted the first sentence of the above passage from Lord Atkin's speech when following the "transformation" approach in *Thakrar v. Secretary of State for the Home Office*.[29] Lord Denning changed his mind in *Trendtex Trading Corp. v. Central Bank of Nigeria*[30] where he adopted the "incorporation" approach. The problem in the *Trendtex* case was whether the doctrine of precedent in English law applies to common law rules that incorporate rules of customary international law so that a change in international law can only be recognised by the English courts as a part of common law within the limits of that doctrine.[31] The majority in that case—Lord Denning M.R. and Shaw L.J.—thought that there was an exception to the doctrine of precedent so that, for example, the Court of Appeal could apply a new rule of international law even though there were Court of Appeal decisions to the contrary based upon the rule's predecessor. Stephenson L.J., dissenting, considered that the Court of Appeal's earlier decisions were binding upon it in the usual way. In *Thai-Europe Tapioca Service Ltd v. Govt of Pakistan*[32] two other members of the Court of Appeal—Lawton and Scarman L.JJ.—had earlier taken the view later taken by Stephenson L.J. in the *Trendtex* case. Scarman L.J. stated:

> I think that it is important to realise that a rule of international law, once incorporated into our law by decisions of a competent court, is not an inference

[27] See Westlake, (1906) 22 L.Q.R. 14.
[28] [1939] A.C. 160 at 167–168. Italics added.
[29] [1974] Q.B. 684, CA.
[30] [1977] Q.B. 529, CA. For the facts, see the extract below p. 331.
[31] See Morgenstern, *loc. cit.*, p. 74, n. 12, above, pp. 80–82.
[32] [1975] 1 W.L.R. 1485.

of fact but a rule of law. It therefore becomes part of our municipal law and the doctrine of *stare decisis* applies as much as to that as to a rule of law with a strictly municipal provenance.[33]

In the *Trendtex*[34] case, Shaw L.J. disagreed:

It is with diffidence that I venture to suggest that there may be a flaw in the reasoning which led to [the *Thai-Europe* Court of Appeal's] conclusion as to the application of the principle of stare decisis. . . . May it not be that the true principle as to the application of international law is that the English courts must at any given time discover what the prevailing international rule is and apply that rule? . . .

What *is* immutable is the principle of English law that the law of nations (not what *was* the law of nations) must be applied in the courts of England. The rule of stare decisis operates to preclude a court from overriding a decision which binds it in regard to a particular rule of (international) law, it does not prevent a court from applying a rule which did not exist when the earlier decision was made if the new rule has had the effect in international law of extinguishing the old rule. . . .

Lawton L.J. [in the *Thai-Europe* case] expressed concern as to the possible prejudice which might result to those engaged in international trade if changes in international law brought about ipso facto corresponding changes in the law of England. But even the law of England changes quite apart from what may be happening to international law. Moreover, changes in rules of international law do not come about abruptly; and changes will not be recognised in an English court without convincing support. Those engaged in world commerce will not be insensible to the incidence of such changes over the years. Lastly there must be a greater risk of confusion if precepts discarded outside England by a majority (or perhaps all) of civilised states are preserved as effective in the English courts in a sort of judicial aspic.

3. *Prize courts*. These constitute a special case. In accordance with international law, prize claims arising out of the capture of ships in war are heard before prize courts. These are courts set up by maritime states, such as the United Kingdom. Although municipal courts, they administer the (customary and treaty) international law of prize. In *The Zamora*,[35] the Judicial Committee of the Privy Council held that a British prize court had to apply that law even though it conflicted with an order in council. Such a court would, however, be bound by a British statute.[36]

MORTENSEN *v.* PETERS

(1906) 8 F. (J.) 93. Court of Justiciary. Scotland

The Fishery Board for Scotland issued a byelaw under the Herring Fishery (Scotland) Act 1889 making it an offence ("no person . . . shall") to fish by beam or otter trawling in the Moray Firth, part of which is more than three miles from the nearest point of land.[37] By the Sea Fisheries Regulation (Scotland) Act 1895, s.10(4), "any person" who fished by beam or otter trawling in contravention of

[33] *ibid*. at 1495.
[34] [1977] Q.B. 578.
[35] [1916] 2 A.C. 77.
[36] *ibid*. at 93.
[37] The Firth as defined by statute was a little over 70 miles wide at its mouth.

that byelaw was subject to a fine or imprisonment. The appellant was a Dane and the master of a Norwegian ship. He was convicted in a Scottish court of the above offence for otter trawling at a place covered by the byelaw but beyond the three mile limit. His appeal against conviction was dismissed unanimously by a full bench of 12 judges.

LORD JUSTICE-GENERAL (LORD DUNEDIN). . . . It is not disputed that if the appellant had been a British subject in a British ship he would have been rightly convicted. . . .

I apprehend that the question is one of construction, and of construction only. In this Court we have nothing to do with the question of whether the Legislature has or has not done what foreign powers may consider a usurpation in a question with them. Neither are we a tribunal sitting to decide whether an Act of the Legislature is *ultra vires* as in contravention of generally acknowledged principles of international law. For us an Act of Parliament duly passed by Lords and Commons and assented to by the King, is supreme, and we are bound to give effect to its terms. The counsel for the appellant advanced the proposition that statutes creating offences must be presumed to apply only (1) to British subjects; and (2) to foreign subjects in British territory; and that short of express enactment their application should not be further extended. The appellant is admittedly not a British subject, which excludes (1); and he further argued that the *locus delicti*, being in the sea beyond the three-mile limit, was not within British territory; and that consequently the appellant was not included in the prohibition of the statute. Viewed as general propositions the two presumptions put forward by the appellant may be taken as correct. This, however, advances the matter but little, for like all presumptions they may be redargued [*i.e.* rebutted], and the question remains whether they have been redargued on this occasion.

The first thing to be noted is that the prohibition here, a breach of which constitutes the offence, is not an absolute prohibition against doing a certain thing, but against doing it in a certain place. Now, when the Legislature, using words of admitted generality—"It shall not be lawful," *etc.*, "Every person who," *etc.*—conditions an offence by territorial limits, it creates, I think, a very strong inference that it is, for the purposes specified, assuming a right to legislate for that territory against all persons whomsoever. This inference seems to me still further strengthened when it is obvious that the remedy to the mischief sought to be obtained by the prohibition would be either defeated or rendered less effective if all persons whosoever were not affected by the enactment. . . .

It is said by the appellant that all this must give way to the consideration that International Law has firmly fixed that a *locus* such as this is beyond the limits of territorial sovereignty, and that consequently it is not to be thought that in such a place the Legislature could seek to affect any but the King's subjects.

It is a trite observation that there is no such thing as a standard of international law extraneous to the domestic law of a kingdom, to which appeal may be made. International law, so far as this Court is concerned, is the body of doctrine regarding the international rights and duties of states which has been adopted and made part of the law of Scotland. Now, can it be said to be clear by the law of Scotland that the *locus* here is beyond what the legislature may assert right to affect by legislation against all whomsoever for the purpose of regulating methods of fishing?

I do not think I need say anything about what is known as the three-mile limit. It may be assumed that within the three miles the territorial sovereignty would be sufficient to cover any such legislation as the present. It is enough to say that that is not a proof of the counter proposition that outside the three miles no such result could be looked for. The *locus* although outside the three-mile limit, is within the bay known as the Moray Firth, and the Moray Firth, says the respondent, is *intra fauces terrae*. Now, I cannot say that there is any definition of what *fauces terrae* exactly are. But there are at least three points which go far to shew that this spot might be considered as lying therein.

1. The dicta of the Scottish institutional writers seem to shew that it would be no usurpation, according to the law of Scotland, so to consider it. . . .

2. The same statute[38] puts forward claims to what are at least analogous places. If attention is paid to the schedule appended to section 6, many places will be found far beyond the three-mile limit—*e.g.* the Firth of Clyde near its mouth. I am not ignoring that it may be said that this in one sense is proving *idem per idem*, but none the less I do not think the fact can be ignored.

3. There are many instances to be found in decided cases where the right of a nation to legislate for waters more or less landlocked or landembraced, although beyond the three-mile limit, has been admitted. . . .

It seems to me therefore, without laying down the proposition that the Moray Firth is for every purpose within the territorial sovereignty, it can at least be clearly said that the appellant cannot make out his proposition that it is inconceivable that the British Legislature should attempt for fishery regulation to legislate against all and sundry in such a place. And if that is so, then I revert to the considerations already stated which as a matter of construction made me think that it did so legislate. . . .

LORD KYLLACHY. . . . This Court is of course not entitled to canvass the power of the Legislature to make the enactment. The only question open is as to its just construction. . . .

Now dealing, first, with the point of construction—the question as to what the statutory enactment means—it may probably be conceded that there is always a certain presumption against the Legislature of a country

[38] *Ed.* Herring Fishery (Scotland) Act 1889.

asserting or assuming the existence of a territorial jurisdiction going clearly beyond limits established by the common consent of nations—that is to say, by international law. . . . But then it is only a presumption, and as such it must always give way to the language used if it is clear, and also to all counter presumptions which may legitimately be had in view in determining, on ordinary principles, the true meaning and intent of the legislation. Express words will of course be conclusive, and so also will plain implication.

The concurring judgments of Lord Johnston and Lord Salvesen are omitted.

Notes

1. Whereas the earlier cases in this section have concerned custom and common law, *Mortensen v. Peters* concerned custom and statutes. In reality the trawler of which the appellant was captain was British financed, controlled and crewed.[39] It had been given a foreign master and registration in the hope of circumventing the Fishery Board's regulations. Shortly after *Mortensen v. Peters*, a number of other successful prosecutions of Norwegian masters of foreign ships occurred. In some cases the convicted men went to prison rather than pay a fine. They were released, however, after protests by Norway. In March, 1907, a Foreign Office spokesman stated in the House of Commons: "The Act of Parliament as interpreted by the High Court of Justiciary is in conflict with international law."[40] In 1909, Parliament tried another approach. It enacted the Trawling in Prohibited Areas Prevention Act which prohibited the landing in the United Kingdom of fish caught contrary to the legislation applied in *Mortensen v. Peters*.

2. Is it possible that Lord Dunedin might have decided the case differently if there had been no argument at all for saying that the Moray Firth was *intra fauces terrae*? If so, why? Because the statute would then have conflicted with the customary international law on freedom of fishing on the high seas, or because of a presumption that Parliament will not legislate contrary to international law?

3. A statute may sometimes incorporate a rule of customary international law by reference. For example, section 7 of the Territorial Waters Jurisdiction Act 1878 defines the "territorial waters of Her Majesty's Dominions" as "such part of the sea . . . as is deemed by international law to be within the territorial sovereignty of Her Majesty."[41]

(b) Treaties[42]

THE PARLEMENT BELGE

(1878–79) 4 P.D. 129. Probate, Divorce and Admiralty Division

SIR ROBERT PHILLIMORE. In the month of February, 1878, the owners of the steam-tug *Daring* served a writ on board the steamship *Parlement Belge* against the owners of that vessel and her freight, in which they claimed the sum of 3500 l. for damage, arising out of a collision which

---

[39] See Fulton, *The Sovereignty of the Sea* (1911), p. 722.
[40] *Hansard*, H.C., Vol. 170, col. 472, March 4, 1907.
[41] See also *Post Office v. Estuary Radio Ltd* [1968] 2 Q.B. 740, CA.
[42] See Mann (1958–59) 44 Trans. Grot. Soc. 29.

occurred between that vessel and the steam-tug *Daring* on the 14th of February 1878, off Dover.

. . . it is in substance contended that this steamship *Parlement Belge* is not amenable to the process of this Court, first, on the ground that she is the property of the King of the Belgians, and at the time of collision was controlled and employed by him. Secondly, that her Majesty the Queen, by a convention with the King of the Belgians,[43] has placed this packet-boat in the category of a public ship of war. . . .

. . . the plaintiffs in this suit have a statutable right of action against the *Parlement Belge*, unless that vessel be of that privileged class which is not amenable to a court of law. . . .

The *Parlement Belge* is a packet conveying certain mails and carrying a considerable commerce, officered, as I have said, by Belgian officers and flying the Belgian pennon.

Upon the whole, I am of opinion that neither upon principle, precedent, nor analogy of general international law, should I be warranted in considering the *Parlement Belge* as belonging to that category of public vessels which are exempt from process of law and all private claims.

I now approach the consideration of the second question. . . .

It is admitted that this convention has not been confirmed by any statute; but it has been contended on the part of the Crown both that it was competent to her Majesty to make this convention, and also to put its provisions into operation without the confirmation of them by parliament. The plaintiffs admit the former, but deny the latter of these propositions.

The power of the Crown to make treaties with foreign states is indisputable.

Blackstone is quoted on the prerogative power to make treaties. . . .

Blackstone must have known very well that there were a class of treaties the provisions of which were inoperative without the confirmation of the legislature; while there were others which operated without such confirmation. The strongest instance of the latter, perhaps, which could be cited is the Declaration of Paris in 1856, by which the Crown in the exercise of its prerogative deprived this country of belligerent rights, which very high authorities in the state and in the law had considered to be of vital importance to it. But this declaration did not affect the private rights of the subject; and the question before me is whether this treaty does affect private rights, and therefore required the sanction of the legislature.

The authority of Chancellor Kent was relied on. That learned writer observes:

[43] *Ed.* A postal convention of 1876.

Treaties of peace, when made by the competent power, are obligatory upon the whole nation. If the treaty requires the payment of money to carry it into effect, and the money cannot be raised but by an Act of the legislature, the treaty is morally obligatory upon the legislature to pass the law, and to refuse it would be a breach of public faith. Kent's Comm. Vol. i. p. 166 (ed. 1873).

And he further observes:

There can be no doubt that the power competent to bind the nation by treaty may alienate the public domain and property by treaty. . . .

If the Crown had power without the authority of parliament by this treaty to order that the *Parlement Belge* should be entitled to all the privileges of a ship of war, then the warrant, which is prayed for against her as a wrong-doer on account of the collision, cannot issue, and the right of the subject, but for this order unquestionable, to recover damages for the injuries done to him by her is extinguished.

This is a use of the treaty-making prerogative of the Crown which I believe to be without precedent, and in principle contrary to the laws of the constitution. Let me consider to what consequences it leads. If the Crown without the authority of parliament, may by process of diplomacy shelter a foreigner from the action of one of her Majesty's subjects who has suffered injury at his hands, I do not see why it might not also give a like privilege of immunity to a number of foreign merchant vessels or to a number of foreign individuals. The law of this country has indeed incorporated those portions of international law which give immunity and privileges to foreign ships of war and foreign ambassadors; but I do not think that it has therefore given the Crown authority to clothe with this immunity foreign vessels, which are really not vessels of war, or foreign persons, who are not really ambassadors.

Let me say one word more in conclusion. Mr. Bowen, in his very able speech, dwelt forcibly upon the wrong which would be done to this packet if, being invited to enter ports of this country with the privileges of a ship of war, she should find them denied to her. I acknowledge the hardship, but the remedy, in my opinion, is not to be found in depriving the British subject without his consent, direct or implied, of his right of action against a wrong-doer, but by the agency of diplomacy, and proper measures of compensation and arrangement, between the Governments of Great Britain and Belgium. I must allow the warrant of arrest to issue.

Notes

1. The decision was reversed by the Court of Appeal[44] on the ground that, contrary to the ruling of Sir Robert Phillimore, the immunity sought was available

[44] (1880) 5 P.D. 197.

at customary international law and hence at common law. The ruling at first instance to the effect that a treaty cannot adversely affect private law rights unless it has been made a part of United Kingdom law by Parliament is still good law. On the question whether individuals may rely in the United Kingdom courts upon provisions in treaties concluded by the United Kingdom as the basis for a claim, see *Rustomjee v. R.*, below, p. 522. The position was explained by Lord Oliver in *Maclaine Watson v. Dept. of Trade*[45] as follows:

> ... as a matter of the constitutional law of the United Kingdom, the royal prerogative, whilst it embraces the making of treaties, does not extend to altering the law or conferring rights on individuals or depriving individuals of rights which they enjoy in domestic law without the intervention of Parliament. Treaties, as it is sometimes expressed, are not self-executing. Quite simply, a treaty is not part of English law unless and until it has been incorporated into the law by legislation. So far as individuals are concerned, it is res inter alios acta from which they cannot derive rights and by which they cannot be deprived of rights or subjected to obligations; and it is outside the purview of the court not only because it is made in the conduct of foreign relations, which are a prerogative of the Crown, but also because, as a source of rights and obligations, it is irrelevant.

2. In *Porter v. Freudenberg*,[46] the Court of Appeal had to consider whether "the old rule (not peculiar to English law, though it has been more prominent in England than elsewhere) that an alien enemy's rights of action are suspended during the war"[47] had been abrogated by the 1907 Hague Convention on Land Warfare. The court ruled, *as a matter of construction of the Convention*, that it had not done so. It is possible to read the judgment as meaning that the Convention *could* have had this effect without statutory implementation as an exercise of the prerogative power if it had been appropriately worded.

ATT.-GEN. FOR CANADA *v.* ATT.-GEN. FOR ONTARIO

[1937] A.C. 326. Judicial Committee of the Privy Council

The Dominion Parliament of Canada legislated to implement certain international labour conventions. On appeal from the Supreme Court of Canada, the Judicial Committee advised that the legislation was *ultra vires* the Dominion Parliament; that legislative competence on the subject concerned vested in the legislatures of the Provinces. The following statement of principle was made by Lord Atkin in the course of delivering the Committee's opinion.

LORD ATKIN. It will be essential to keep in mind the distinction between (1.) the formation, and (2.) the performance, of the obligations constituted by a treaty, using that word as comprising any agreement between two or more sovereign States. Within the British Empire there is a well-established rule that the making of a treaty is an executive act, while the performance of its obligations, if they entail alteration of the existing domestic law, requires legislative action. Unlike some other countries, the stipulations of a treaty duly ratified do not within the Empire, by virtue

---

[45] [1989] 3 All E.R. 523 at 544–545, HL.
[46] [1915] 1 K.B. 857. See McNair (1928) 9 B.Y.I.L. 59.
[47] *ibid*. at 877.

of the treaty alone, have the force of law. If the national executive, the government of the day, decide to incur the obligations of a treaty which involve alteration of law they have to run the risk of obtaining the assent of Parliament to the necessary statute or statutes. To make themselves as secure as possible they will often in such cases before final ratification seek to obtain from Parliament an expression of approval. But it has never been suggested, and it is not the law, that such an expression of approval operates as law, or that in law it precludes the assenting Parliament, or any subsequent Parliament, from refusing to give its sanction to any legislative proposals that may subsequently be brought before it. Parliament, no doubt, as the Chief Justice points out, has a constitutional control over the executive: but it cannot be disputed that the creation of the obligations undertaken in treaties and the assent to their form and quality are the function of the executive alone. Once they are created, while they bind the State as against the other contracting parties, Parliament may refuse to perform them and so leave the State in default.

Notes

On the treaty-making power within the United Kingdom, see below, p. 778.

R. *v.* SECRETARY OF STATE FOR THE HOME DEPARTMENT, EX P. BRIND

[1991] 1 A.C. 696. House of Lords

By Section 29(3), Broadcasting Act 1981, the Home Secretary could "at any time, by notice in writing require the [Independent Broadcasting Authority (IBA)] . . . to refrain from broadcasting any matter or classes of matter specified in the notice." An almost identically worded power was included in Clause 13(4) of the 1981 Licence and Agreement between the Home Secretary and the BBC. Acting under these powers, in 1988 the Home Secretary issued directives to the IBA and the BBC requiring them to refrain from broadcasting on television or radio "words spoken" by any person representing or purporting to represent certain organisations. These organisations were organisations proscribed under the Prevention of Terrorism (Temporary Provisions) Act 1984 or the Northern Ireland (Emergency Provisions) Act 1978 and also Sinn Fein, Republican Sinn Fein and the Ulster Defence Association. The prohibition applied only to the direct speech of such persons. It was permissible to report what they said or to have actors broadcasting their words.

In this case, the applicants, who were journalists and a National Union of Journalists employee, sought judicial review by way of (i) a declaration to the effect that the Home Secretary's directives were *ultra vires* and (ii) *certiorari*, to quash them. Having failed before the Divisional Court and a unanimous Court of Appeal, the applicants appealed to the House of Lords where they relied mainly on the argument that the Home Secretary's discretionary powers under the 1981 Act and the BBC Licence, were exercisable subject to Article 10, European Convention on Human Rights (ECHR). The appeal was dismissed unanimously.

LORD BRIDGE. It is accepted, of course, by the appellants that, like any other treaty obligations which have not been embodied in the law by statute, the Convention is not part of the domestic law, that the courts accordingly have no power to enforce Convention rights directly and that, if domestic legislation conflicts with the Convention, the courts must nevertheless enforce it. But it is already well settled that, in construing any provision in domestic legislation which is ambiguous in the sense that it is capable of a meaning which either conforms to or conflicts with the Convention, the courts will presume that Parliament intended to legislate in conformity with the Convention, not in conflict with it. Hence, it is submitted, when a statute confers upon an administrative authority a discretion capable of being exercised in a way which infringes any basic human right protected by the Convention, it may similarly be presumed that the legislative intention was that the discretion should be exercised within the limitations which the Convention imposes. I confess that I found considerable persuasive force in this submission. But in the end I have been convinced that the logic of it is flawed. When confronted with a simple choice between two possible interpretations of some specific statutory provision, the presumption whereby the courts prefer that which avoids conflict between our domestic legislation and our international treaty obligations is a mere canon of construction which involves no importation of international law into the domestic field. But where Parliament has conferred on the executive an administrative discretion without indicating the precise limits within which it must be exercised, to presume that it must be exercised within Convention limits would be to go far beyond the resolution of an ambiguity. It would be to impute to Parliament an intention not only that the executive should exercise the discretion in conformity with the Convention, but also that the domestic courts should enforce that conformity by the importation into domestic administrative law of the text of the Convention and the jurisprudence of the European Court of Human Rights in the interpretation and application of it. If such a presumption is to apply to the statutory discretion exercised by the Secretary of State under section 29(3) of the Act of 1981 in the instant case, it must also apply to any other statutory discretion exercised by the executive which is capable of involving an infringement of Convention rights. When Parliament has been content for so long to leave those who complain that their Convention rights have been infringed to seek their remedy in Strasbourg, it would be surprising suddenly to find that the judiciary had, without Parliament's aid, the means to incorporate the Convention into such an important area of domestic law and I cannot escape the conclusion that this would be a judicial usurpation of the legislative function. . . .

LORD ACKNER. The Convention which is contained in an international treaty to which the United Kingdom is a party has not yet been incorporated into English domestic law. The appellants accept that it is a constitutional principle that if Parliament has legislated and the words of the statute are clear, the statute must be applied even if its application is in breach of international law. In *Salomon v. Commissioners of Customs & Excise* [1967] 2 Q.B. 116 Diplock L.J. at 143 stated:

> If the terms of the legislation are clear and unambiguous they must be given effect to, whether or not they carry out Her Majesty's treaty obligations.

Much reliance was placed upon the observations of Lord Diplock in *Garland v. British Rail* [1983] 2 A.C. 751 when he said (at 771):

> . . . it is a principle of construction of United Kingdom statutes . . . that the words of a statute passed after the [EEC] Treaty has been signed and dealing with the subject matter of the international obligation of the United Kingdom, are to be construed, if they are reasonably capable of bearing such a meaning, as intended to carry out the obligation, and not to be inconsistent with it.

I did not take the view that Lord Diplock was intending to detract from or modify what he said in *Salomon's* case.

It is well settled that the Convention may be deployed for the purpose of the resolution of an ambiguity in English primary or subordinate legislation. The case of *R. v. Chief Immigration Officer, Heathrow Airport, ex p. Salamat Bibi* [1976] 1 W.L.R. 979 concerned a lady who arrived at London Airport from Pakistan with two small children saying that she was married to a man who was there and who met her. She was refused leave to enter and an application was made for an order of certiorari and also for mandamus on the ground that she ought to have been treated as the wife of the man who met her at the airport. During the course of argument a question arose about the impact of the Convention and in particular Article 8 concerning the right to private and family life and the absence of interference by a public authority with that right.

In his judgment at 984 Lord Denning M.R. said:

> The position as I understand it is that if there is any ambiguity in our statutes, or uncertainty in our law, then these courts can look to the Convention as an aid to clear up the ambiguity and uncertainty . . . but I would dispute altogether that the Convention is part of our law. Treaties and declarations do not become part of our law until they are made law by Parliament. . . .

This decision was . . . most recently followed by the Court of Appeal in *Chundawadra v. Immigration Appeal Tribunal* [1988] Imm. A.R. 161.

Mr Lester contends that section 29(3) is ambiguous or uncertain. He submits that although it contains within its wording no fetter upon the extent of the discretion it gives to the Secretary of State, it is accepted that that discretion is not absolute. There is however no ambiguity in section

29(3). It is not open to two or more different constructions. The limit placed upon the discretion is simply that the power is to be used only for the purposes for which it is was granted by the legislation (the so-called Padfield doctrine) and that it must be exercised reasonably in the Wednesbury sense. No question of the construction of the words of section 29(3) arises, as would be the case if it was alleged to be ambiguous, or its meaning uncertain.

There is yet a further answer to Mr Lester's contention. He claims that the Secretary of State before issuing his directives should have considered not only the Convention (it is accepted that he in fact did so) but that he should have properly construed it and correctly taken it into consideration. It was therefore a relevant, indeed a vital, factor to which he was obliged to have proper regard pursuant to the Wednesbury doctrine, with the result that his failure to do so rendered his decision unlawful. The fallacy of this submission is however plain. If the Secretary of State was obliged to have proper regard to the Convention, *i.e.* to conform with Article 10, this inevitably would result in incorporating the Convention into English domestic law by the back door. It would oblige the Courts to police the operation of the Convention and to ask itself in each case, where there was a challenge, whether the restrictions were "necessary in a democratic society . . . " applying the principles enunciated in the decisions of the European Court of Human Rights. The treaty, not having been incorporated in English law, cannot be a source of rights and obligations and the question—did the Secretary of State act in breach of Article 10—does not therefore arise. . . .

LORDS TEMPLEMAN, ROSKILL and LOWRY delivered concurring speeches.

Notes

1. As stated in the *Brind* case, it is well established in United Kingdom law that a treaty to which the United Kingdom is a party should be referred to and followed in the interpretation of an ambiguous statute, but that, applying a dualist approach, it cannot prevail over a clearly worded statute that contradicts it. In this connection, it is noticeable that Lord Ackner suggested that the passage which he quoted from Lord Diplock's speech in the *Garland Case*, which was made in the special context of EC law, was not intended to depart from the established position and, in particular, was not intended to mean that a judge should go out of his way to find an ambiguity. Note, however, that a treaty provision does not have to be "self-executing" for it to influence the interpretation of an ambiguous statute.

What the *Brind* case is mainly authority for is that a discretionary executive power, whether under a statute or the prerogative and whether exercisable by a lowly immigration officer or a Secretary of State, is not to be interpreted as limited by the ECHR.[48] What reasons do Lords Bridge and Ackner give for not limiting discretionary powers by reference to the ECHR? What distinction is there between limitations that the courts do read into discretionary powers when

---

[48] *cf. R. v. Ministry of Defence, ex p. Smith* [1996] 1 All E.R. 257, CA.

exercising their power of judicial review (*e.g.* the *Wednesbury* "irrationality" limitation) and a limitation that might stem from the ECHR?[49] Are not the former as much limitations upon parliamentary sovereignty as the latter?

2. The ECHR has given rise to a number of cases in which the relationship between treaties and United Kingdom law has been discussed.[50] Although the statements made in these cases are often couched in terms only of the ECHR, there is no logical reason why they should not apply to other treaties too. It may be, however, that the Convention's key role in the debate about the adoption of a "bill of rights" in the "United Kingdom has coloured some judicial pronouncements.

3. A statute may be intended to incorporate a treaty into United Kingdom law or it may co-incidentally apply in an area to which a treaty applies also. In the former case, it is clear that the statute should be interpreted consistently with the treaty (see the *Salomon* case, below, p. 92). The *Brind* case suggests that, in accordance with the presumption that Parliament intends to comply with international law, the same rule applies in a case of co-incidence also—at least where the treaty obligation pre-dates the statute. The same conclusion follows from *Waddington v. Miah*,[51] where Lord Reid, speaking for the whole House of Lords, said (when considering whether an offence created under the Immigration Act 1971 was intended to operate retrospectively) that in view of the Universal Declaration of Human Rights (Article 11)[52] and the ECHR (Article 7) "it is hardly credible that any government department would promote or that Parliament would pass retrospective criminal legislation."

4. A related question is whether the courts should take into account a treaty to which the United Kingdom is a party when applying the common law. Various *dicta* concerning the ECHR are clearly to this effect. For example, Scarman L.J argued in *Ahmad v. Inner London Education Authority*[53] for the use of the ECHR in applying "common law principles" and in *Att.-Gen. v. BBC*[54], as Lord Scarman, he stated that "if the issue should ultimately be . . . a question of legal policy," regard must be had to the same Convention. Similarly, in *Cassell v. Broome*,[55] Lord Kilbrandon stated:

> . . . Since all commercial publication is undertaken for profit, one must be watchful against holding the profit motive to be sufficient to justify punitive damages: to do so would be seriously to hamper what must be regarded, at least since the European Convention [on Human Rights] was ratified, as a constitutional right to free speech.

In *Att. Gen. v. Guardian Newspapers (No. 2)*,[56] Lord Goff, applying the equitable doctrine of breach of confidence, stated that "I conceive it to be my duty, when I am free to do so, to interpret the law in accordance with the obligations of the Crown under this treaty [the ECHR]". However, Sir Robert Megarry, V.-C., suggested a limit in *Malone v. M.P.C.*[57] After holding that the ECHR could not

---

[49] See Jowell (1990) P.L. 149 (on the *Brind* case in the Court of Appeal).

[50] See Cunningham (1994) 43 I.C.L.Q. 537. On the relationship between E.C. law and that of member states, see Lasok and Bridge, *An Introduction to the Law and Institutions of the European Communities* (6th ed., 1994), Chaps. 13–15.

[51] [1974] 1 W.L.R. 683 at 694.

[52] Below, p. 630.

[53] [1978] Q.B. 36 at 48, CA.

[54] [1981] A.C. 303 at 354, HL. Lord Fraser suggested the same "where our domestic law is not firmly settled" (at 352). The ECHR was also referred to as a guide when determining public policy in *Blathwayt v. Baron Cawley* [1976] A.C. 397, HL.

[55] [1972] A.C. 1027 at 1133.

[56] [1990] 1 A.C. 109 at 283, HL.

[57] [1979] Ch. 344 at 379.

directly establish a right to privacy in English law because it had not been incorporated by statute as law in the United Kingdom, the Vice-Chancellor rejected an argument to the effect that it could be used to do so indirectly, by taking it into account when developing the common law:

> I readily accept that if the question before me were one of construing a statute enacted with the purpose of giving effect to obligations imposed by the Convention, the court would readily seek to construe the legislation in a way that would effectuate the Convention rather than frustrate it. However, no relevant legislation of that sort is in existence. It seems to me that where Parliament has abstained from legislating on a point that is plainly suitable for legislation, it is indeed difficult for the court to lay down new rules of common law or equity that will carry out the Crown's treaty obligations, or to discover for the first time that such rules have always existed.

SALOMON v. COMMISSIONERS OF CUSTOMS AND EXCISE

[1967] 2 Q.B. 116. Court of Appeal

The Court was required to interpret an ambiguous provision in the Customs and Excise Act 1952. The Act, drafted in Parliament's own language, was intended to implement the 1950 Convention on the Valuation of Goods for Customs Purposes, a treaty to which a number of European states were parties. The Convention was not included as a Schedule to the Act, or anywhere referred to in it. The question arose whether recourse could be had to the treaty to interpret the statute.

DIPLOCK L.J. Where, by a treaty, Her Majesty's Government undertakes either to introduce domestic legislation to achieve a specified result in the United Kingdom or to secure a specified result which can only be achieved by legislation, the treaty, since in English law it is not self-operating, remains irrelevant to any issue in the English courts until Her Majesty's Government has taken steps by way of legislation to fulfil its treaty obligations. Once the Government has legislated, which it may do in anticipation of the coming into effect of the treaty, as it did in this case, the court must in the first instance construe the legislation, for that is what the court has to apply. If the terms of the legislation are clear and unambiguous, they must be given effect to, whether or not they carry out Her Majesty's treaty obligations, for the sovereign power of the Queen in Parliament extends to breaking treaties (see *Ellerman Lines v. Murray*)[58] . . . and any remedy for such a breach of an international obligation lies in a forum other than Her Majesty's own courts. But if the terms of the legislation are not clear but are reasonably capable of more than one meaning, the treaty itself becomes relevant, for there is a prima facie presumption that Parliament does not intend to act in breach of international law, including therein specific treaty obligations; and if one of the meanings which can reasonably be ascribed to the legislation is

[58] [1931] A.C. 126, HL.

consonant with the treaty obligations and another or others are not, the meaning which is consonant is to be preferred. . . .

It has been argued that the terms of an international convention cannot be consulted to resolve ambiguities or obscurities in a statute unless the statute itself contains either in the enacting part or in the preamble an express reference to the international convention which it is the purpose of the state to implement. The judge seems to have been persuaded that *Ellerman Lines etc. v. Murray etc.* was authority for this proposition. But, with respect, it is not. The statute with which that case was concerned did not refer to the convention. The case is authority only for the proposition for which I have already cited it. . . . I can see no reason in comity or common sense for imposing such a limitation upon the right and duty of the court to consult an international convention to resolve ambiguities and obscurities in a statutory enactment. If from extrinsic evidence it is plain that the enactment was intended to fulfil Her Majesty's Government's obligations under a particular convention, it matters not that there is no express reference to the convention in the statute. One must not presume that Parliament intends to break an international convention merely because it does not say expressly that it is intending to observe it. Of course the court must not merely guess that the statute was intended to give effect to a particular international convention. The extrinsic evidence of the connection must be cogent.

Lord Denning L.J. and Russell L.J. delivered concurring judgments.

Notes

1. On the duty to interpret a statute or Order in Council that is intended to implement a treaty so as to give effect to the treaty if the language of the statute or order allows, see also *Post Office v. Estuary Radio Ltd,*[59] *Benin v. Whimster*[60] and *The Jade.*[61]

2. In *Buchanan v. Babco,*[62] the Carriage of Goods by Road Act 1965, s.1, provided that the English (but not the other, French) authentic text of the multilateral 1956 Convention on the Contract for the International Carriage of Goods by Road, which text was included as a Schedule to the Act, should have the force of law in the United Kingdom. Indicating the rules of interpretation that should apply in the interpretation of the English text of the Convention as a part of English law, Lord Wilberforce[63] stated:

I think that the correct approach is to interpret the English text, which after all is likely to be used by many others than British businessmen, in a normal manner, appropriate for the interpretation of an international convention, unconstrained by technical rules of English law, or by English legal precedent, but on broad principles of general acceptation. . . . Moreover, it is perfectly legitimate . . . to look for assistance, if assistance is needed, to the French

[59] [1968] 2 Q.B. 740, CA.
[60] [1976] Q.B. 297, CA.
[61] [1976] 1 W.L.R. 430 at 436, HL.
[62] [1978] A.C. 141, HL.
[63] *ibid.* at 152.

text. . . . There is no need to impose a preliminary test of ambiguity [before doing so].

3. In *Fothergill v. Monarch Airlines*,[64] Lord Diplock stated that the rules on the interpretation of treaties in the Vienna Convention on the Law of Treaties 1969, which emphasise the purpose of a treaty and permit recourse to its *travaux préparatoires*, should be followed by United Kingdom courts when interpreting a treaty that has been incorporated into United Kingdom law:

> Indeed, in the case of Acts of Parliament giving effect to international conventions concluded after the coming into force of the Vienna Convention on the Law of Treaties (Cmnd. 4140), I think an English court might well be under a constitutional obligation to do so. By ratifying that Convention, Her Majesty's Government has undertaken an international obligation on behalf of the United Kingdom to interpret future treaties in this manner and since under our constitution the function of interpreting the written law is an exercise of judicial power and rests with the courts of justice, that obligation assumed by the United Kingdom falls to be performed by those courts.

In that case, the Carriage by Air Act 1961, s.1, enacted that the 1929 Warsaw Convention for the Unification of Certain Rules regarding Air Transport should have the force of law in the United Kingdom.[65] The two (French and English) authentic texts were scheduled to the Act. Interpreting the word "damage" (*avarie*) in the Convention to include loss of, as well as injury to, goods, the House of Lords held that recourse could be had to the *travaux préparatoires* of the Convention to interpret it. Lord Wilberforce[66] stated:

> These cases [of recourse to *travaux préparatoires*] should be rare, and only where two conditions are fulfilled, first, that the material involved is public and accessible, and, secondly, that the *travaux préparatoires* clearly and indisputably point to a definite legislative intention.

Lord Scarman[67] agreed with Lord Wilberforce and, emphasising the need for uniformity of interpretation, pointed out that the courts of most other states would look to the *travaux préparatoires*. Lord Wilberforce's approach was adopted as *ratio* in *Gatoil International Inc. v. Arkwright-Boston Manufacturers Mutual Insurance Co.*[68]

In *R. v. Secretary of State for the Home Dept., ex p. Sivakumaran*,[69] recourse was had to the *travaux préparatoires* of the 1951 Convention on the Status of Refugees when interpreting a part of the British Immigration Rules that was taken word for word from the Convention. Although not formally incorporated by statute, the Convention had "for all practical purposes," (*per* Lord Keith) been incorporated into United Kingdom law.

[64] [1981] A.C. 251, 283, HL. For criticism of the U.K. courts' use of the Vienna Convention for interpretation, see Gardiner (1995) 44 I.C.L.Q. 629.

[65] *cf.* the Child Abduction and Custody Act 1985, which gives the 1980 Hague Convention on International Child Abduction the force of law. The 1980 Convention is to be interpreted purposively: *Re F. (Minor; abduction)* [1995] 3 All E.R. 641, 645, CA.

[66] *ibid.* at 278. Lord Fraser considered that recourse could not be had to the *travaux* in this case because they had not been sufficiently well published to the persons whose rights were affected: *ibid.* at 287.

[67] *ibid.* at 283.

[68] [1985] A.C. 255, HL.

[69] [1988] 2 A.C. 958, HL.

(ii) THE UNITED STATES[70]

HEAD MONEY CASES: EDYE *v.* ROBERTSON

112 U.S. 580 (1884). U.S. Supreme Court

It was argued in this case that an Act of Congress conflicted with earlier U.S. treaties and that therefore it was invalid. The Court, which was unanimous, found no such conflict on the facts of the case but nonetheless made the following statement of principle.

MR JUSTICE MILLER (FOR THE COURT). A treaty is primarily a compact between independent Nations. . . . But a treaty may also contain provisions which confer certain rights upon the citizens or subjects of one of the Nations residing in the territorial limits of the other, which partake of the nature of municipal law, and which are capable of enforcement as between private parties in the courts of the country. . . . The Constitution of the United States [Article VI] places such provisions as these in the same category as other laws of Congress by its declaration that "This Constitution and the laws made in pursuance thereof, and all treaties made or which shall be made under authority of the United States, shall be the supreme law of the land." A treaty, then, is a law of the land as an Act of Congress is, whenever its provisions prescribe a rule by which the rights of the private citizen or subject may be determined. And when such rights are of a nature to be enforced in a court of justice, that court resorts to the treaty for a rule of decision for the case before it, as it would to a statute.

But even in this aspect of the case, there is nothing in this law which makes it irrepealable or unchangeable. The Constitution gives it no superiority over an Act of Congress in this respect, which may be repealed or modified by an Act of a later date. . . .

In short, we are of opinion that, so far as a treaty is made by the United States with any foreign Nation can become the subject of judicial cognisance in the courts of this country, it is subject to such Acts as Congress may pass for its enforcement, modification or repeal.

SEI FUJII *v.* CALIFORNIA

242 P. 2d 617; 19 I.L.R. 312 (1952). Supreme Court of California

GIBSON C.J. Plaintiff, an alien Japanese . . . appeals from a judgment declaring that certain land purchased by him in 1948 had escheated to the state. There is no treaty between this country and Japan which confers upon plaintiff the right to own land, and the sole question presented on this appeal is the validity of the California alien land law.

[70] See *Restatement of the Foreign Relations Law of the U.S., Third* (1987), Vol. 1, Pt. I, Chap. 2; Henkin (1984) 82 Mich. L.R. 1555; *ibid.* (1986–7) 100 H.L.R. 853.

It is first contended that the land law has been invalidated and superseded by the provisions of the United Nations Charter pledging the
member nations to promote the observance of human rights and fundamental freedoms without distinction as to race. Plaintiff relies on statements in the preamble and in Articles 1, 55 and 56 of the Charter. . . . [71]

It is not disputed that the Charter is a treaty, and our federal Constitution provides that treaties made under the authority of the United States
are part of the supreme law of the land and that the judges in every state
are bound thereby. U.S.Const., art. VI. A treaty, however, does not automatically supersede local laws which are inconsistent with it unless the
treaty provisions are self-executing. In the words of Chief Justice Marshall: A treaty is "to be regarded in courts of justice as equivalent to an act
of the Legislature, whenever it operates of itself, without the aid of any
legislative provision. But when the terms of the stipulation import a
contract—when either of the parties engages to perform a particular act,
the treaty addresses itself to the political, not the judicial department; and
the Legislature must execute the contract, before it can become a rule for
the court." *Foster v. Neilson*, 1829, 2 Pet. 253, 314, 7 L.Ed. 415.

In determining whether a treaty is self-executing courts look to
the intent of the signatory parties as manifested by the language of the
instrument, and if the instrument is uncertain, recourse may be had to the
circumstances surrounding its execution. See *Foster v. Neilson*. . . . In order
for a treaty provision to be operative without the aid of implementing
legislation and to have the force and effect of a statute, it must appear that
the framers of the treaty intended to prescribe a rule that, standing alone,
would be enforceable in the courts. See Head Money Cases [*Edye v.
Robertson*]. . . . [72]

It is clear that the provisions of the preamble and of Article 1 of the
charter which are claimed to be in conflict with the alien land law are not
self-executing. They state general purposes and objectives of the United
Nations Organisation and do not purport to impose legal obligations on
the individual member nations or to create rights in private persons. . . .
Although the member-nations have obligated themselves [in Article 55
and 56] to co-operate with the international organisation in promoting
respect for, and observance of, human rights, it is plain that it was
contemplated that future legislative action by the several nations would
be required to accomplish the declared objectives, and there is nothing to
indicate that these provisions were intended to become rules of law for
the courts of this country upon the ratification of the charter.

The language used in Articles 55 and 56 is not the type customarily
employed in treaties which have been held to be self-executing and to
create rights and duties in individuals. For example, the treaty involved
in *Clark v. Allen*, 331 U.S. 503, 507–508 . . . relating to the rights of a

[71] *Ed.* Below, Appendix I.
[72] *Ed.* Above, p. 95.

national of one country to inherit real property located in another country, specifically provided that "such national shall be allowed a term of three years in which to sell the [property] ... and withdraw the proceeds ... " free from any discriminatory taxation. ... In other instances treaty provisions were enforced without implementing legislation where they prescribed in detail the rules governing rights and obligations of individuals or specifically provided that citizens of one nation shall have the same rights while in the other country as are enjoyed by that country's own citizens. *Bacardi Corp. v. Domenech*, 311 U.S. 150, *Asakura v. City of Seattle*, 265 U.S. 332, 340.

It is significant to note that when the framers of the Charter intended to make certain provisions effective without the aid of implementing legislation they employed language which is clear and definite and manifests that intention. [The Court referred to Articles 104 and 105.[73]] ... In *Curran v. City of New York*, 191 Misc. 229, 77 N.Y.S. 2d 206, 212, these articles were treated as being self-executory.

We are satisfied, however, that the charter provisions relied on by plaintiff were not intended to supersede existing domestic legislation, and we cannot hold that they operate to invalidate the alien land law.[74]

Notes

1. The result of these cases is that "self executing"[75] treaties, or particular treaty provisions, will be treated by American courts as a part of American law and as having the status of a federal statute, so that they are replaced by later, contradictory federal legislation. As to the relationship between "self executing" treaty provisions and later state law, in *Asakura v. City of Seattle*,[76] in which a conflict was alleged (but not found) between a 1911 treaty and a 1921 city ordinance, the U.S. Supreme Court stated: "The rule established by it [the treaty] cannot be rendered nugatory in any part of the United States by municipal ordinances or state laws." In *Johnson v. Browne*,[77] the U.S. Supreme Court, in holding that certain federal statutory provisions had not been repealed by treaty, stated: "Repeals by implication are never favoured, and a later treaty will not be regarded as repealing an earlier statute by implication unless the two are absolutely incompatible and the statute cannot be enforced without antagonising the treaty." In *Cook v. U.S.*,[78] the U.S. Supreme Court noted that "a treaty will not be abrogated or modified by a later [federal] statute unless such purpose on the part of the Congress has been clearly expressed."

[73] *Ed.* Below, Appendix I.
[74] *Ed.* This ruling by the Court, which reversed that of the California Court of Appeals, was unanimous. The Court, nonetheless, decided the case in favour of the plaintiff on another ground.
[75] The decision whether a treaty provision is "self executing" is one for a state's national courts: the criteria relied upon in the *Head Money* case are comparable to those used by national courts in the many other states that make use of the concept of "self executing" treaties. See Buergenthal (1992–IV) 235 Hague Recueil 303 and Jackson (1992) 86 A.J.I.L. 310. On the U.S. approach, see Paust (1988) 82 A.J.I.L. 760, and Vasquez (1995) 89 A.J.I.L. 695.
[76] 265 U.S. 332 at 341 (1924).
[77] 205 U.S. 309 at 321 (1907).
[78] 288 U.S. 102 at 119–120 (1933).

In addition to "treaties", which are made by the President with the advice and consent of the Senate,[79] the U.S. may also enter into "executive agreements" which are made by the President acting alone.[80] Both types of agreements are treaties for the purposes of international law. In *U.S. v. Pink*[81] the Supreme Court stated: "A treaty is a Law of the Land under the supremacy clause (Art. VI, cl. 2) of the Constitution. Such international compacts and agreements as the Litvinoff Assignment [an executive agreement] have a similar dignity." Whereas subsequent federal legislation will override an executive agreement, it is not clear whether an executive agreement will supersede prior federal legislation.[82] In *Territory of Hawaii v. Ho*[83] the Supreme Court of the Territory of Hawaii held that an executive agreement overrode a subsequent inconsistent law of the Territory.

2. As far as customary international law is concerned, the following general statement by Gray J. in *The Paquete Habana*[84] applies:

> International law is part of our law, and must be ascertained and administered by the Courts of Justice of appropriate jurisdiction, as often as questions of right depending upon it are duly presented for their determination. For this purpose, where there is no treaty and no controlling executive or legislative act or judicial decision, resort must be had to the customs and usages of civilised nations . . .

In that case, the U.S. Supreme Court found and applied a customary rule of international law exempting coastal fishing vessels from capture as prize of war. However, in *Garcia-Mir v. Meese*[85] it was held that although the lengthy detention of illegal Cuban immigrants was contrary to customary international law, their detention was not contrary to U.S. law because the Attorney–General's decision to detain them was, in terms of *The Paquete Habana* judgment, a "controlling executive act."

4. THE EXECUTIVE CERTIFICATE

Notes

1. *British practice*.[86] Oppenheim[87] states: "At common law it is the practice of English courts to accept as conclusive statements by or on behalf of the Secretary of State for Foreign and Commonwealth Affairs relating to certain categories of questions of fact in the field of international affairs. In such cases the statement is conclusive even in the face of contrary evidence. . . . The categories of cases on which prerogative statements by the Foreign and Commonwealth Office (or its

---

[79] U.S. Constitution, Art. II, Section 2.
[80] See below, p. 779.
[81] 315 U.S. 203 at 230 (1942).
[82] See *Maria Jeritza Seery v. U.S.*, 127 F. Supp. 601 (1955) (U.S. Court of Claims) (Cert. denied, 359 U.S. 943 (1959)) and *U.S. v. Guy W. Caps Inc.*, 204 F. 2d 655 (1953) (U.S. Court of Appeals, 4th Circuit). See also Erades and Gould, *International Law and Municipal Law in the Netherlands and in the United States* (1961), pp. 388–390 and 459–460.
[83] 41 Hawaii 565 (1957); 26 I.L.R. 557.
[84] 175 U.S. 677 at 700 (1900).
[85] 788 F.2d 1446 (1986). For criticism of the decision, see Henkin (1986) 80 A.J.I.L. 930.
[86] See Lyons (1946) 23 B.Y.I.L. 240; *ibid.* (1952) 29 B.Y.I.L. 227; *ibid.* (1957) 33 B.Y.I.L. 302; Mann, *op. cit.*, p. 741, n. 13 above, Chaps. 2, 3; Warbrick (1986) 35 I.C.L.Q. 138; Wilmshurst (1986) 35 I.C.L.Q. 157.
[87] Oppenheim, Vol. I., p. 1046. Footnotes omitted.

predecessors) have, at common law, been treated as conclusive include: (a) whether a foreign state or government has been recognised by the United Kingdom either *de facto* or *de jure*[88]; (b) whether recognition has been granted to conquest by another State or to other changes of territorial title, and generally, whether certain territory is under the sovereignty of one foreign State or another; (c) the sovereign status of a foreign State or its monarch; (d) the commencement and termination of a state of war against another country; (e) whether a state of war exists with a foreign country or between two foreign countries; (f) the existence of a case for reprisals in maritime war; (g) whether a person is entitled to diplomatic status; (h) the existence or extent of British jurisdiction in a foreign country." However, Foreign Office certificates are not regarded as conclusive in the interpretation of statutes or the construction of documents: see *Re Al-Fin Corporation's Patent*, below, p. 187.

The "practice" of the courts, which has only become established in the present century,[89] has been confirmed by statute in a number of areas of foreign affairs. Thus a Foreign Office certificate is "conclusive evidence" on matters of diplomatic and state immunity under the Diplomatic Privileges Act 1964, section 4, below, p. 362, and the State Immunity Act 1978, section 21, below, p. 327.[90] In *R. v. Secretary of State for Foreign and Commonwealth Affairs, ex p. Trawnik*,[91] it was held that a certificate issued under the State Immunity Act 1978, s.21, is not subject to judicial review on *Wednesbury* principles; it is reviewable only if it constitutes a nullity.

2. In *The Fagernes*,[92] in which the Court of Appeal asked for and received from the Attorney-General a statement on the question whether a point in the Bristol Channel was regarded by the Crown as British territory, Atkin L.J. stated:

> What is the territory of the Crown is a matter of judicial notice. The Court has, therefore, to inform itself from the best material available. . . . Any definite statement from the proper representative of the Crown as to the territory of the Crown must be treated as conclusive.

Lawrence L.J. took the same position. Bankes L.J. was of the opinion that a statement by the Crown was persuasive but not binding. In *Post Office v. Estuary Radio Ltd*,[93] the Court of Appeal followed the approach of Atkin and Lawrence L.JJ.

3. In *Duff Development Co. v. Govt. of Kelantan*[94] Lord Sumner based the conclusive nature of certificates upon the "best evidence" rule and, to a lesser degree, the "one voice" doctrine, *i.e.* the doctrine that the courts and the executive should follow the same approach on matters of foreign affairs. The following statement by Sir Francis Vallat,[95] Legal Adviser to the Foreign Office, suggests another reason why the courts should accept a certificate:

> It is believed that the test of a true certificate is not whether the facts are peculiarly within the knowledge of the Foreign Office or such as the Foreign Office may reasonably be expected to know or which the Foreign Office ought

[88] On certificates concerning the recognition of states and governments, see below, p. 168.
[89] See Lyons (1946) 23 B.Y.I.L. 240.
[90] See also s.1(7) of the Deep Sea Mining (Temporary Provisions) Act 1981. For a fuller list, see Wilmshurst, *loc. cit.*, p. 98, n. 86 above, p. 165.
[91] *The Times*, April 18, 1985 (Q.B.D.). See Warbrick, *loc. cit.*, p. 98, n. 86 above.
[92] [1927] P. 311 at 324. See Edeson (1973) 89 L.Q.R. 364.
[93] [1968] 2 Q.B. 740.
[94] [1924] A.C. 797, HL. The *Duff Development Co. Case* was cited as authority for the conclusive nature of Foreign Office certificates in the *Carl Zeiss Case*, below, p. 176.
[95] *International Law and the Practitioner* (1966), p. 54.

to know in the conduct of its business, but the presence of some element of recognition by Her Majesty's Government.[96] The logic of this position is sound. On matters of pure fact the view of the Foreign Office must be based on the type of evidence normally used to prove facts before a Court, and it is such evidence rather than the certificate that ought in general to be produced before the Court. When, however, it comes to a matter of recognition, there is no source which can state with equal authority what is or is not recognised by the Government.

---

[96] *cf. Spinney v. Royal Ins. Co.* [1980] 1 Lloyd's Rep. 406, QB.

CHAPTER 4

PERSONALITY

1. GENERALLY

O'CONNELL, INTERNATIONAL LAW

(2nd ed., 1970), Vol. I, pp. 80–82

IT is clear that the word "person" is used to refer to one who is a legal actor, but that it is of no assistance in ascertaining who or what is competent to act. Only the rules of law can determine this, and they may select different entities and endow them with different legal functions, so that it is a mistake to suppose that merely by describing an entity as a "person" one is formulating its capacities in law. . . .

The correct questions should be: (a) Do the rules of international law establish that this claimant to capacity has the capacity which it claims? (b) What exactly is the capacity which it claims and which is allowed to it, or in other words, just what sorts of legal relations may this entity enter into? If the claimant to capacity is a novelty there will be, of course, no rule of international law on the subject at all until it appears and asserts itself, whereupon there arises question (c), should the entity be recognised as having the capacity which it claims to have? Recognition here means acquiescence in the claim by the other parties to international actions. . . .

Capacity implies personality, but always it is capacity *to do those particular acts*. Therefore "personality" as a term is only short-hand for the proposition that an entity is endowed by international law with legal capacity. But entity A may have capacity to perform acts X and Y, but not act Z, entity B to perform acts Y and Z but not act X, and entity C to perform all three.

2. STATES[1]

(i) GENERALLY

MONTEVIDEO CONVENTION ON RIGHTS AND DUTIES OF STATES 1933

(1934) 165 L.N.T.S. 19; U.S.T.S. 881; 4 Malloy 4807; 28 A.J.I.L., Supp., 75

Article I

The State as a person of international law should possess the following qualifications: (a) a permanent population; (b) a defined territory; (c) government; and (d) capacity to enter into relations with other States.

Notes

1. For a list of most of the states in the international community, who now total over 190, see the list of members of the United Nations, below Appendix II. Non-member states are Switzerland,[2] the Vatican City[3] and the South Pacific mini-states of Kiribati, Naura, Tonga and Tuvalu.[4] State numbers increased greatly with the dissolution of the USSR and the S.F.R.Y. in the 1990s.[5]

2. The Montevideo Convention was adopted by the 7th International Conference of American States. Fifteen Latin American states and the United States are parties to it. The Convention is commonly accepted as reflecting, in general terms, the requirements of statehood at customary international law. There is some evidence, however, to suggest that these requirements, which are concerned solely with the effectiveness of the entity claiming the rights and duties of a state, have recently been supplemented by others—independence achieved (i) in accordance with the principle of self-determination,[6] and (ii) not in the pursuance of racist policies[7]—of a political or moral character.[8] The term "state" may be given a different meaning for the purposes of a particular treaty.[9] The role of recognition

[1] See Crawford, *The Creation of States in International Law* (1979) and Marek, *Identity and Continuity of States in Public International Law* (2nd ed., 1968).

[2] On the Swiss referendum rejecting UN membership, see Robertson (1988) 12 Fletcher Forum 311.

[3] See below, p. 144.

[4] The European mini-states of Andorra, Liechtenstein, Monaco and San Marino joined the UN in the early 1990s. Andorra was formerly a "fief" under the joint suzerainty of its two co-princes, the President of the French Republic and the Bishop of Urgel (Spain), who were responsible for its international relations. In 1993, it became a state, with the consent of the two co-princes, who remain its head of state. Monaco and San Marino have close treaty relations with France and Italy respectively: see O'Connell, *International Law* (2nd ed., 1970), Vol. I, pp. 290–291. As to Liechtenstein, see below, p. 108.

[5] See below, p. 148.

[6] See the *Southern Rhodesia* case, below, p. 111.

[7] See the *Transkei* case, below, p. 110.

[8] See Crawford, *op. cit.*, p. 102, n. 1, above, pp. 106 and 226. Crawford also suggests that independence obtained by the use of force contrary to Art. 2(4) of the UN Charter may in some cases not give rise to statehood: *ibid.* p. 118; see also, below, p. 112.

[9] On its meaning in the UN Charter, see Higgins, *The Development of International Law through the Political Organs of The United Nations* (1963), pp. 11–57, and Dugard, *Recognition and the United Nations* (1987), pp. 51–111.

by other states in the attainment of international personality by a state is considered below, p. 144.

3. *Population and territory.* There is no lower limit to the size of a state's population and territory. Nauru, for example, has less than 10,000 inhabitants and is only eight square miles in area. The Vatican City has even fewer permanent residents and, whatever domain it may have elsewhere, has less than 100 acres on earth.[10]

There is ample evidence in state practice and in judicial and arbitral decisions to show that to be a state it is not necessary for an entity to have exactly defined or undisputed boundaries, either at the time that it comes into being or subsequently. Israel, for example, is undoubtedly a state although its borders have never been settled.[11] In *Deutsche Continental Gas-Gesellschaft v. Polish State*[12] the German-Polish Mixed Arbitral Tribunal said:

> In order to say that a State exists and can be recognised as such . . . it is enough that . . . [its] territory has a sufficient consistency, even though its boundaries have not yet been accurately delimited.

4. *Government.* One of the preliminary questions which arose in the *Aaland Islands Case* was the date on which Finland became a state. Finland had been a part of the Russian Empire until the Russian Revolution. When the new Soviet Government issued a manifesto proclaiming the right of all peoples within the Russian Empire to self-determination, the Finnish Diet, or Parliament, declared Finland's independence on December 4, 1917. This was recognised by the Soviet Government but there was opposition within Finland by those, including a section of the army, who continued to support the old Russian régime and to reject the idea of independence. As a result, violence broke out and for a time the government of the new state was able to maintain order only with the help of Soviet troops. The Report of the International Committee of Jurists appointed to consider the case reads (in a passage which bears upon "independence" as well as "government" as requirements of statehood):

> In the midst of revolution and anarchy, certain elements essential to the existence of a State, even some elements of fact, were lacking for a fairly considerable period. Political and social life was disorganised; the authorities were not strong enough to assert themselves; civil war was rife; further, the Diet, the legality of which had been disputed by a large section of the people, had been dispersed by the revolutionary party, and the Government had been chased from the capital and forcibly prevented from carrying out its duties; the armed camps and the police were divided into two opposing forces, and Russian troops, and after a time Germans also, took part in the civil war between the inhabitants and between the Red and White Finnish troops. It is, therefore, difficult to say at what exact date the Finnish Republic, in the legal sense of the term, actually became a definitely constituted sovereign State. This certainly did not take place until a stable political organisation had been created, and until the public authorities had become strong enough to assert themselves throughout the territories of the State without the assistance of foreign troops. It would appear that it was in May 1918, that the civil war

---

[10] See further below, p. 144. On "mini" states generally, see Harden, ed., *Small is Dangerous: Micro States in a Macro World* (1985) and Rapaport, Muteba and Therattil, *Small States and Territories: Status and Problems* (1971).

[11] See below, pp. 223 *et seq.*

[12] (1929) 5 A.D. 11 at 15.

ended and that the foreign troops began to leave the country, so that from that time onwards it was possible to re-establish order and normal political and social life, little by little.[13]

State practice suggests that the requirement of a "stable political organisation" in control of the territory does not apply during a civil war in a state that already exists (*e.g.* the Lebanese Civil War 1975–90). A state that currently has problems of effective government is Somalia. Since President Barre's Government was overthrown by guerrillas in 1991, fighting has persisted between rival clan-based militias with different territorial bases. A separate state of Somaliland declared its independence in the north west of Somalia in 1991, but has not gained international recognition. The Djibouti Conference of interested states and parties led to the establishment of an interim Government, but this does not have effective control of Mogadishu, the capital, or the country at large.[14] UN forces were sent into Somalia between 1992 and 1995, but failed to bring the situation under control.[15] Despite these problems, Somalia remains a UN member and continues to be recognised as a state by the international community.

5. An entity is not a state if it declines to be one, as in the case of Taiwan (the Republic of China). Both the Beijing and Taiwan Governments claim to be the one government of the one state of China, with Taiwan as a part of it. This situation developed after the 1949 revolution, following which the defeated Nationalist Government withdrew to Taiwan, *cf.* below, p. 172. In 1972, a joint communiqué[16] was issued by the Governments of the People's Republic and the United States after President Nixon's visit to Beijing in which it was agreed that Taiwan was a part of China and that the question of the government of China was an internal matter, a position from which the Taiwan Government would not dissent. Crawford[17] suggests that Taiwan's "status is that of a consolidated local *de facto* government in a civil war situation" and that, although not a state, it has a "limited status in international law" by which it can make treaties and otherwise commit the state of China in respect of the territory which it effectively controls.

6. It is accepted that a new state is automatically bound by international law upon attaining statehood.[18] Is this because it is deemed to consent to its being so bound? Or is it because there is a rule that says that it shall be so bound? If the latter is the case, why is that rule binding upon it? Is a new state's position different from that of an individual born into a state and automatically subject to its laws?[19]

[13] L.N.O.J., Special Supp. No. 3, p. 3 (1920).

[14] See *Republic of Somalia v. Woodhouse Drake & Carey Suisse S.A.*, below, p. 162.

[15] See below, p. 922.

[16] (1972) 11 I.L.M. 443 at 445. The U.S. continued to recognise the Taiwan Government as the government of the one state of China until 1979, see below, p. 160. The U.K. Government "acknowledge the position of the People's Republic of China . . . that Taiwan is a province of China. We recognise the Government of the People's Republic of China as the sole government of China": Mr Goodlad, Minister of State, FCO, *Hansard*, H.C. Vol. 238, col. 936, (1994).

[17] *op. cit.*, p. 102, n. 1, above, pp. 149–150. See also on the status of Taiwan, Clough (1981) 1 Chinese Y.I.L.A. 17, and Chou, (1986–7) 6 *ibid.* 161. And see the *Luigi Monta of Genoa* and *Reel v. Holder* cases, below, pp. 188 and 189. Taiwan has diplomatic relations with over 30 states, mostly in Africa and Central and South America.

[18] This is subject to any effect that recognition has; see below, p. 144. Although new post-colonial states have objected to particular areas of international law and argue for different rules in those areas, they do not reject the system as a whole.

[19] See Brierly, p. 52; Fitzmaurice, *loc. cit.* p. 21, n. 1, above, pp. 165–167; Kelsen, *Principles of International Law* (2nd ed., 1967), p. 247. See further, below, p. 462.

(ii) INDEPENDENCE

AUSTRO-GERMAN CUSTOMS UNION CASE

Advisory Opinion. P.C.I.J. Reports, Series A/B, No. 41 (1931)

By a Protocol of 1931 Austria and Germany reached preliminary agreement on a customs union establishing free trade between the two states. The proposed union "caused such disturbance in international relations that it is no exaggeration to speak of a European crisis."[20]

Article 88 of the Treaty of Saint-Germain 1919 provided:

> The independence of Austria is inalienable otherwise than with the consent of the Council of the League of Nations. Consequently, Austria undertakes in the absence of the consent of the said Council to abstain from any act which might directly or indirectly or by any means whatever compromise her independence. . . .

A Protocol of 1922 concerning the economic independence of Austria in particular was to the same effect. The Council of the League of Nations asked the P.C.I.J. whether Austria would be acting contrary to these provisions if it went ahead with the proposed union. The Court advised, by eight votes to seven, that the union would be incompatible with the Protocol of 1922. Seven judges who concurred in the Court's opinion (but not a majority of the Court) also thought that it would be contrary to Article 88 of the Treaty of Saint-Germain. The following extracts are limited to the Court's discussion of the nature of independence as applied to states. It has been argued that in its assessment of the situation the Court placed as much emphasis upon the likelihood of a political union occurring as a further, separate step after the establishment of the proposed customs union as it did upon the customs union itself.[21]

Opinion of the Court

. . . irrespective of the definition of the independence of States which may be given by legal doctrine or may be adopted in particular instances in the practice of States, the independence of Austria, according to Article 88 of the Treaty of Saint-Germain, must be understood to mean the continued existence of Austria within her present frontiers as a separate State with sole right of decision in all matters economic, political, financial or other with the result that that independence is violated, as soon as there is any violation there, either in the economic, political, or any other field, these different aspects of independence being in practice one and indivisible . . .

By "alienation", as mentioned in Article 88, must be understood any voluntary act by the Austrian State which would cause it to lose its

[20] Fachiri (1932) 13 B.Y.I.L. 68.
[21] See Borchard (1931) 25 A.J.I.L. 711 at 715.

independence or which would modify its independence in that its sovereign will would be subordinated to the will of another Power or particular group of Powers, or would even be replaced by such will.

SEPARATE OPINION OF JUDGE ANZILOTTI.[22] Independence . . . is really no more than the normal condition of States according to international law; it may also be described as *sovereignty (suprema potestas)*, or *external sovereignty*, by which is meant that the State has over it no other authority than that of international law.

The conception of independence, regarded as the normal characteristic of States as subjects of international law, cannot be better defined than by comparing it with the exceptional and, to some extent, abnormal class of States known as "dependent States". These are States subject to the authority of one or more States. The idea of dependence therefore necessarily implies a relation between a superior State (suzerain, protector, *etc.*) and an inferior or subject State (vassal, *protégé, etc.*); the relation between the State which can legally impose its will and the State which is legally compelled to submit to that will. Where there is no such relation of superiority and subordination, it is impossible to speak of dependence within the meaning of international law.

It follows that the legal conception of independence has nothing to do with a State's subordination to international law or with the numerous and constantly increasing states of *de facto* dependence which characterise the relation of one country to other countries.

It also follows that the restrictions upon a State's liberty, whether arising out of ordinary international law or contractual engagements, do not as such in the least affect its independence. As long as these restrictions do not place the State under the legal authority of another State, the former remains an independent State however extensive and burdensome those obligations may be.

This is obviously the standpoint of the Treaty of Saint-Germain when it proclaims the independence of Austria despite the many serious restrictions it imposes upon her freedom in the economic, military and other spheres. These restrictions do not put Austria under the authority of the other contracting States, which means that Austria is an independent State within the meaning of international law. . . .

Notes
1. When the Montevideo Convention[23] refers to "capacity to enter into relations with other states" as a requirement of statehood it is referring to independence as that term is understood in Judge Anzilotti's opinion, *i.e.* independence in law

[22] Judge Anzilotti was one of the seven judges in the majority who found the proposed union incompatible with Art. 88 of the Treaty of Saint-Germain as well as with the Protocol of 1922.

[23] Above, p. 102.

from the authority of any other state (and hence the capacity under its national law to conduct relations with other states).

2. In the *North Atlantic Coast Fisheries* case,[24] the Permanent Court of Arbitration rejected a United States submission in the following terms: " . . . to hold that the United States, the grantee of the fishing right, has a voice under the treaty granting the right in the preparation of fishing legislation, involves recognition of a right in that country to participate in the internal legislation of Great Britain and her Colonies and to that extent would reduce these countries to a state of dependence." Elsewhere, dealing with the same submission, the Court stated: " . . . the exercise of such a right of consent by the United States would predicate an abandonment of independence in this respect by Great Britain. . . . "[25]

3. By the 1985 Anglo-Irish Agreement,[26] the United Kingdom and Ireland established an Inter-governmental Conference, composed of representatives of the two governments, to deal on a regular basis with political, security and legal matters concerning Northern Ireland and matters of cross-border co-operation. By Article 1, the United Kingdom Government "accept that the Irish Government will put forward [to the Conference] views and proposals on matters relating to Northern Ireland within the field of activity of the Conference in so far as those matters are not the responsibility of a devolved administration in Northern Ireland," but the Irish Government is given no power of decision in respect of Northern Ireland. Article 1 also provides that "[t]here is no derogation from the sovereignty of either the United Kingdom Government or the Irish Government, and each retains responsibility for the decisions and administration of government within its own jurisdiction." Accordingly, the Agreement would not seem to involve "an abandonment of independence" (*North Atlantic Coast Fisheries* case, above).[27]

4. In the *Wimbledon* case[28] the Permanent Court of International Justice stated: "No doubt any convention creating an obligation of this kind places a restriction upon the exercise of the sovereign rights of the State, in the sense that it requires them to be exercised in a certain way. But the right of entering into international engagements is an attribute of State sovereignty."

5. Units within a *federal state* may or may not be allowed by the federal constitution some freedom to conduct their own foreign affairs. If, and to the extent that, they are allowed to do so, such units are regarded by international law as having international personality. For example, the Republics of the former U.S.S.R. were all entitled in law to conduct their own foreign affairs and two of them—Byelorussia (now Belarus) and the Ukraine—to a small extent did so.[29] Such units are not thereby states but international persons *sui generis*.

6. *Protected or dependent states.* These are a dying species which few seem anxious to preserve. In the nineteenth century, European powers sometimes masked a colonial situation by entering into a treaty of protection with an Asian or African state or chieftain, with the degree of sovereignty left with the protected state or tribe being limited, if not totally surrendered. Generally, the protecting state was responsible for the conduct of foreign relations, although precise terms

[24] G.B. v. U.S., Scott *Hague Court Reports* 141 at 170 (1910).
[25] *ibid.* 167.
[26] U.K.T.S. 1 (1985), Cmnd. 9690.
[27] cf. *ex p. Molyneaux* [1986] 1 W.L.R. 331, QBD.
[28] P.C.I.J. Reports, Series A, No. 1, at p. 25 (1923).
[29] See Dolan (1955) 4 I.C.L.Q. 629. Both of the Republics mentioned were original members of the UN, see below, Appendix II. On the apparently comparable position under the Russian Federation Constitution, see Gazzini (1996) 17 H.R.L.J. 93 at 94. See also Art. 32 of the German Basic Law on the treaty-making power of the German *Länder*.

of the arrangement varied from case to case.[30] One remaining example of a protected state is the Indian protected state of Bhutan in the Himalayas.[31] Protected states are to be contrasted with independent states that, for reasons of convenience, freely choose to depute certain sovereign powers to other states. For example, certain of Liechtenstein's foreign relations are conducted for it by Switzerland.[32]

FRENCH INDEMNITY OF 1831

U.S. Claims Commission. Moore, 5 Int.Arb. 4447 at 4472

France paid the U.S. compensation to be distributed among U.S. nationals in respect of certain damage caused during the Napoleonic Wars. Some claims were made that related to injuries apparently caused by Holland and Denmark and the question arose whether France was responsible for them. The report of the U.S. Commission that distributed the compensation was supplemented by notes by Commissioner Kane indicating the general principles upon which the Commission had relied. The following extract from these notes concerns the above question.

1. Holland, after some ten years of political changes, during which though nominally independent she was tributary to all the projects of France, had received in the month of June 1806, a king of the Napoleon family. . . . The form of distinct sovereignties was presented to the public eye; but the energies of the Dutch people were directed more than ever to the advancement of the imperial policy. At last, in the concluding month of 1809, a new crisis approached. At a moment when the finances of Holland were in a state of extreme embarrassment, she was required to destroy her commerce with foreign nations, which formed the principal source of her revenues. Louis ventured to remonstrate. . . . He was reminded in reply, that the country of which he was sovereign was a French conquest, and that "his highest and imprescriptible duties were to the imperial crown;" . . .

The tenth article of the [Franco-Dutch] treaty of 16th March 1810 was as follows: "All merchandize, which has arrived in American vessels in the ports of Holland since the 1st of January 1809, shall be placed under sequestration, and shall belong to France, to be disposed of according to circumstances and to the political relations with the United States." . . .

It was for the value of these cargoes, that reclamations were made before the commissioners. The brief account which has been given of the

---

[30] See the *Nationality Decrees in Tunis and Morocco* case, P.C.I.J. Reps. Series B, No. 4, p. 27 (1923) and the *Rights of Nationals of the U.S. in Morocco* case, I.C. J. Rep. 1952, p. 176. And see Baty (1921–2) 3 B.Y.I.L. 109.

[31] Art. 2, 1949 Treaty of Friendship between India and Bhutan, 157 B.F.S.P. 214, reads: "The Government of India undertakes to exercise no interference in the internal administration of Bhutan. On its part the Government of Bhutan agrees to be guided by the advice of the Government of India in regard to its external relations." Bhutan was admitted to the UN in 1971.

[32] See Kuhn (1987) 61 A.J.I.L. 871. *cf.* the position of Western Samoa, whose foreign relations are conducted by New Zealand: see the 1962 Treaty of Friendship (1962) N.Z.T.S. 5.

political condition of Holland from the year 1809 till it was formally merged in the French empire [in July 1810], sufficiently explains the reason for allowing them. Holland was already a dependent kingdom, and Louis a merely nominal sovereign. The treaty was a form; in substance it was an imperial decree.

2. The spoliations to which Denmark ministered were of a different character. . . .

It may be, that the conduct of King Frederic was dictated by his anxiety to conciliate the favour of the French emperor; or perhaps he was moved by the portion of the spoil which might fall into his hands: we had nothing to do with his motives or his fears. The act was his own: the kingdom of Denmark was then, as now, independent. . . .

This then is the broad distinction between the cases of Holland and Denmark. The former was a nominal, the latter an actual sovereignty. The intervention of one was merely formal, and was exacted by force; the other was the voluntary pander to French avidity.

Notes

1. Independence as a requirement of statehood means, to some extent, factual, as well as legal, independence from other states. Although it is accepted that states may influence the policies and conduct of another state, there may come a point, as this case suggests, where *factual* dependence by one state upon another is so great that it is really no more than a "puppet" state and will not be treated as meeting the requirement of independence. Lauterpacht proposed the following:

> The first condition of statehood is that there must exist a government actually independent of that of any other State. . . . If a community, after having detached itself from the parent State, were to become, legally or actually, a satellite of another State, it would not be fulfilling the primary condition of independence and would not accordingly be entitled to recognition as a State.[33]

He gave "Manchukuo" as an example of an entity that was not a state according to this test. "Manchukuo" came into being after Japan invaded Manchuria, a province of China, in 1931.[34] The following year Japan recognised "Manchukuo" as an independent state. Its territory was that of Manchuria. The League of Nations sent the Lytton Commission to "Manchukuo" to discover the facts. The Commission reported:

> In the "Government of Manchukuo," Japanese officials are prominent and Japanese advisers are attached to all important Departments. Although the Premier and his Ministers are all Chinese, the heads of the various Boards of General Affairs, which, in the organisation of the new State, exercise the greatest measure of actual power, are Japanese. At first they were designated as advisers, but recently those holding the most important posts have been made full Government officials on the same basis as the Chinese. . . . They are doubtless not under the orders of the Tokyo Government, and their policy has

[33] Lauterpacht, *Recognition in International Law* (1948), pp. 26–29.
[34] See 1 Hackworth 333–338.

not always coincided with the official policy either of the Japanese Government or of the Headquarters of the Kwantung Army. But in the case of all-important problems, these officials and advisers, some of whom were able to act more or less independently in the first days of the new organisation, have been constrained more and more to follow the direction of Japanese official authority. This authority, in fact, by reason of the occupation of the country by its troops, by the dependence of the "Manchukuo Government" on those troops for the maintenance of its authority both internally and externally, in consequence, too, of the more and more important role entrusted to the South Manchuria Railway Company in the management of the railways under the jurisdiction of the "Manchukuo Government," and finally by the presence of its consuls, as liaison agents, in the most important urban centres, possesses in every contingency the means of exercising an irresistible pressure.[35]

The Commission did not pronounce upon the specific question whether "Manchukuo" was an independent state. In the light of the Commission's Report, on February 24, 1933, the League of Nations Assembly resolved that "the sovereignty over Manchuria belongs to China."[36] By 1939, only El Salvador, Germany, Hungary, Italy and Japan had recognised "Manchukuo." Manchuria was returned to China after the Second World War. Was it at any time an independent state according to the *Customs Union Case*? Suppose that at the present time an existing state were to come under the influence of another state to such an extent (in a military, economic, or other sense) that the other state could dictate the composition of its Government and its policies? Would that state continue to be independent for the purposes of statehood?[37] Was Czechoslovakia in 1969?[38]

2. In 1976, South Africa, in pursuance of its homelands or bantustan policy, granted independence to the Transkei, the homeland of the Xhosa people. Legal sovereignty over the Transkei was transferred to its new African Government which was in control in law of the internal and external affairs of the Transkei. On October 26, 1976, the United Nations General Assembly, by a vote of 134 to 0, with 1 abstention,

> (i) *Strongly condemns* the establishment of bantustans as designed to consolidate the inhuman policies of *apartheid*, to destroy the territorial integrity of the country, to perpetuate white minority domination and to dispossess the African people of South Africa of their inalienable rights;
>
> (ii) *Rejects* the declaration of "independence" of the Transkei and declares it invalid;
>
> (iii) *Calls upon* all Governments to deny any form of recognition to the so-called independent Transkei and to refrain from having any dealings with the so-called independent Transkei or other bantustans;
>
> (iv) *Requests* all States to take effective measures to prohibit all individuals, corporations and other institutions under their jurisdiction from having any dealings with the so-called independent Transkei or other bantustans.[39]

---

[35] L.N.Doc. C. 663. M 320. 1932, VII.

[36] L.N.O.J. Special Supp. No. 112, p. 75 (1933). On the Stimson Doctrine of Non-Recognition, which was prompted by the "Manchukuo" situation, see below, p. 218.

[37] See the discussion in Marek, *op. cit.*, p. 102, n. 1, above, pp. 162–180. On the relative nature of the independence of states, see Hart, *The Concept of Law* (1961), pp. 215–221.

[38] See below, p. 291.

[39] G.A. Resn. 31/6, G.A.O.R., 31st Session, Supp. 39, p. 10. The U.S. abstained; although agreeing with the recommendation that the Transkei not be recognised, it considered the resolution too strongly worded in other respects. As to the non-recognition of Ciskei, see the *Gur* case, below, p. 183.

No state recognised the Transkei as a state, apart from South Africa.[40] The Transkei and the other homelands no longer exist following the transfer of power in South Africa in the mid-1990s. One interpretation of state practice in the matter is that "the Transkei, as an entity created directly pursuant to a fundamentally illegal policy of *apartheid*" was "for that reason, and irrespective of its degree of formal or actual independence, not a State."[41]

3. In 1965, Southern Rhodesia, a British self-governing colony, declared its independence. The rebel Smith Government sought in this way to continue white rule in Rhodesia. This would inevitably have given way to black majority rule if the normal constitutional progress towards independence had been allowed to take its course. The United Kingdom continued to claim sovereignty and applied economic and political sanctions short of the use of armed force to re-assert its authority. The United Nations Security Council imposed a comprehensive régime of economic sanctions upon the rebel Government and "[called] upon all states not to recognise this illegal racist minority régime."[42] No state recognised Southern Rhodesia as a state. After guerrilla warfare, a political settlement was reached that led to independence in 1980 for Zimbabwe in accordance with the principle of self-determination. Thereupon, Security Council sanctions were terminated. From 1965 onwards, Southern Rhodesia could claim to have met the requirements of statehood in the Montevideo Convention.[43] In terms of the requirement of legal independence, the governing constitution (*i.e.* the one to look to when deciding who has the capacity to enter into relations with other states) is the one that is effective in the state's territory. In the case of Southern Rhodesia, this was the Smith Government's constitution.[44] The Southern Rhodesian case may, however, indicate that an additional requirement of statehood has evolved, namely that independence be achieved in accordance with the principle of self-determination.[45] A difficulty with requirements of statehood such as this, that look beyond legal independence and effective control of territory to moral or political considerations, is that legal rights and duties may become divorced from reality. In the case of Southern Rhodesia, for example, when Smith Government soldiers destroyed guerrilla bases on the Zambian side of the border, who was responsible in international law? The United Kingdom?

4. A case in which the response by the United Nations to a colonial rebellion was strikingly different was that of Portuguese Guinea.[46] PAIGC, a national liberation movement, rebelled against the Portuguese administration and had attained control by armed force over two-thirds of the colony by September 1973 when it declared Guinea-Bissau's independence. In November 1973, while Portuguese troops were still in the field, the General Assembly welcomed "the

---

[40] See Witkin (1977) 18 H.I.L.J. 605.

[41] Crawford, *op. cit.*, p. 102, n. 1, above, p. 226. See also Richardson, 17 Col. J. T. L. 185 (1978). When justifying its non-recognition of another homeland, Bophuthatswana, the U.K. referred to the question of *apartheid*: see below, p. 154.

[42] See below, p. 965. The General Assembly similarly called upon "all states not to recognise any form of independence in Southern Rhodesia without the prior establishment of a government based on majority rule in accordance with General Assembly Resolution 1514 (XX)": G.A. Resn. 2379, G.A.O.R., 26th Sess., Supp. 18, p. 57 (1968); (1968) 7 I.L.M. 1401. The resolution was adopted by 92 votes to 2, with 17 abstentions.

[43] Above, p. 102.

[44] In *R. v. Ndhlovu*, 1968 (4) S.A. 515, the High Court of Rhodesia, Appellate Division, held that the Smith Government's constitution had replaced the British colonial constitution as the valid one, since the Smith Government was in effective control of Southern Rhodesia.

[45] *cf.* Crawford, *op. cit.*, p. 102, n. 1, above, p. 106. On the principle of self-determination, see below, p. 113.

[46] See Rousseau (1974) 78 R.G.D. I.P. 1166.

recent accession to independence of the people of Guinea-Bissau, thereby creating the sovereign State of the Republic of Guinea-Bissau."[47] The Portuguese administration was overthrown by PAIGC in March 1974 and Guinea-Bissau was recognised as a state by 84 states by the end of May. Guinea-Bissau was recommended for UN membership by the Security Council in August 1974,[48] shortly before Portugal formally recognised its independence. Crawford[49] suggests that in cases in which "the metropolitan state forcibly denies self-determination" and where a liberation movement is "supported by the population and controls substantial territory," "if the Guinea-Bissau precedent is regarded as determinative, the situation would appear to be that the principle of self-determination operates as it were to transfer legal sovereignty to the self-determination unit, legitimising recognition of it by other States."

5. What if independence is seized by force by rebels with the assistance of another state contrary to Article 2(4), United Nations Charter or to the principle of non-intervention? As to which, see below, Chap. 11. Crawford[50] suggests:

> Illegality of intervention in aid of independence of a self-determination unit does not then, as a matter of law, impair the status of the local unit. On the other hand, *semble*, where a State illegally intervenes in and foments the secession of part of a metropolitan State, other States are under the same duty of non-recognition as in the case of illegal annexation of territory. An entity created in violation of the rules relating to the use of force in such circumstances will not be regarded as a State.

Indian assistance to Bangladesh, although arguably illegal, did not impair the latter's statehood given that Bangladesh was a unit to which the principle of self-determination applied.[51]

Following the invasion of northern Cyprus by Turkey in 1974[52] 36 per cent of Cyprus, north of a line running through Nicosia and Famagusta, was administered by the Turkish Federated State of Cyprus pending the establishment of an acceptable federal constitution for the one state of Cyprus. In 1983, however, an independent state, called the Turkish Republic of Northern Cyprus, with its own constitution, was declared to have been established in the same area. The United Nations Security Council at once deplored "the purported secession of part of the Republic of Cyprus," resolved that the declaration was "legally invalid," and called upon "all states not to recognise any Cypriot State other than the Republic of Cyprus."[53] The Security Council response supports Crawford's view, supposing that Turkey's intervention in 1974 was illegal and the Turkish Cypriot entity was not a self-determination unit. So does the League of Nations' response to "Manchukuo."[54] Such cases do not often arise in practice; most commonly the occupied territory is annexed.

---

[47] G.A. Resn. 3061 (XXVIII), G.A.O.R., 28th Session, Supp. 30, p. 2.

[48] S.C. Resn. 356 (1974), S.C.O.R., 29th Year, *Resolutions and Decisions*, p. 15.

[49] *op. cit.*, p. 102, n. 1, above, pp. 261–262.

[50] *op. cit.*, p. 102, n. 1 above, p. 118. Footnote omitted. This is one of a list of conclusions that "are to some extent *de lege ferenda*." On the rule as to title to illegally obtained territory, see below, p. 218–219.

[51] *ibid.* p.117. For the facts, see below, p. 892.

[52] On the Turkish invasion of Cyprus, see below, p. 894. See also *Opinion No. 10*, Arbitration Commission, E.C. Conference on Yugoslavia, below, p. 152.

[53] S.C. Resn. 541 (1983), S.C.O.R., 38th Year, *Resolutions and Decisions*, p. 15. *cf.* S.C. Resn. 550 (1984), S.C.O.R., 39th Year, *ibid.* p. 12. No state has recognised the Turkish Republic of Northern Cyprus, except Turkey. See Palmer (1986) 4 Boston U.I.L.J. 423.

[54] On "Manchukuo," see above, p. 109.

(iii) SELF-DETERMINATION[55]

Notes

The principle of self-determination is a controversial one. It has a long history in international relations as a reason for the cession of territory from one state to another and for the use of plebiscites to establish the wishes of the inhabitants in this connection. Under the United Nations Charter, it became the cornerstone of the General Assembly's decolonisation policy of the 1960s and 1970s. The controversy has concerned the principle's status in international law and its meaning. It was not a part of international law before the United Nations Charter.[56] The evidence of the following materials suggests that the point has been reached where the principle has generated a rule of international law[57] by which the political future of a colonial or similar non-independent territory should be determined in accordance with the wishes of its inhabitants, within the limits of the principle of *uti possedetis*.[58] It does not extend to claims for independence by minority groups in a non-colonial context. The principle may, however, have an internal, as well as an external aspect: it may require that government generally have a democratic base, and that minorities be allowed political autonomy.[59] The 1966 International Covenants on Human Rights, common Article 1, below, p. 636 each restate the right to self-determination as a matter of treaty law, although the meaning of the Covenant provisions may differ from that in customary international law.[60] The materials in this section are limited to political self-determination. Economic self-determination is considered in Chapter 8.

[55] See Cassese, *Self-Determination of Peoples* (1995); Emerson (1966) 60 Proc. A.S.I.L. 135; Espiell, *The Right to Self-Determination: Implementation of UN Resolutions*, UN Doc. E/CN.4/Sub.2/390 (1980); Kirgis (1994) 88 A.J.I.L. 304; Koskenniemi (1994) 43 I.C.L.Q. 241; McCorquodale (1994) 43 I.C.L.Q. 857; Müllerson, *International Law, Rights and Politics* (1994), Chap. 2; Pomerance, *Self-Determination in Law and Practice* (1982); Rigo Sureda, *The Evolution of the Right to Self-Determination* (1973); Shaw, *Title to Territory in Africa* (1986), Chap. 3; Tomuschat, ed., *Modern Law of Self-Determination* (1993); Umozurike, *Self-Determination in International Law* (1972).

[56] See the report of the International Committee of Jurists in the *Aaland Islands* case, L.N.O.J., Special Supp. No. 3, p. 5 (1920), and Oppenheim, Vol. I, p. 282.

[57] For the view that it is a rule of *ius cogens*, see Espiell, in Cassese, ed., *UN Law/Fundamental Rights: Two Topics in International Law* (1979), p. 167.

[58] As to compliance with the rule as a requirement of statehood, see above, p. 112. On the legality of the use of force to repress a war of national liberation, *i.e.* one aimed at furthering the principle of self-determination, see below, p. 886.

[59] On internal self-determination, see Cassese, *op. cit.*, p. 113, n. 55, Chap. 5, and Franck (1992) 86 A.J.I.L. 46.

[60] See Cassese *ibid.* and McGoldrick, *The Human Rights Committee* (1991), Chap. 5.

DECLARATION ON THE GRANTING OF INDEPENDENCE TO COLONIAL TERRITORIES AND PEOPLES[61]

G.A. Resn. 1514 (XV). December 14, 1960. G.A.O.R. 15th Sess.,
Supp. 16, p. 66

The General Assembly . . . Declares that:

1. The subjection of peoples to alien subjugation, domination and exploitation constitutes a denial of fundamental human rights, is contrary to the Charter of the United Nations and is an impediment to the promotion of world peace and co-operation;

2. All peoples have the right to self-determination; by virtue of that right they freely determine their political status and freely pursue their economic, social and cultural development;

3. Inadequacy of political, economic, social or education preparedness should never serve as a pretext for delaying independence;

4. All armed action or repressive measures of all kinds directed against dependent peoples shall cease in order to enable them to exercise peacefully and freely their right to complete independence, and the integrity of their national territory shall be respected;

5. Immediate steps shall be taken, in Trust and Non-Self-Governing Territories or all other territories which have not yet attained independence, to transfer all powers to the peoples of those territories, without any conditions or reservations, in accordance with their freely expressed will and desire, without any distinction as to race, creed or colour, in order to enable them to enjoy complete independence and freedom;

6. Any attempt aimed at the partial or total disruption of the national unity and the territorial integrity of a country is incompatible with the Purposes and Principles of the Charter of the United Nations;

7. All States shall observe faithfully and strictly the provisions of the Charter of the United Nations, the Universal Declaration of Human Rights and the present Declaration on the basis of equality, non-interference in the internal affairs of all States, and respect for the sovereign rights of all peoples and their territorial integrity.

---

[61] The resolution was adopted by 89 votes to 0, with nine abstentions. The abstaining states were Australia, Belgium, Dominican Republic, France, Portugal, South Africa, Spain, the U.K. and the U.S.

Notes

1. The 1960 Declaration, which has been the continual point of reference in the General Assembly's decolonisation practice,[62] builds upon Articles 1, 55 and 56 of the Charter[63] and has been supplemented by the 1970 Programme of Action for the Full Implementation of the Declaration[64] and the 1970 Declaration on Principles of International Law.[65]

2. Resolution 1514 does not state that title to colonial and similar non-independent territory that is not in accord with the wishes of its people is invalid. The position is instead that "immediate steps" should be taken to achieve independence in accordance with the principle of self-determination. Resolution 1514 proposes self-determination within existing colonial boundaries (para. 6). The post-colonial states in particular have taken the view that it would be too disruptive of international stability to allow self-determination within those boundaries for minorities (*e.g.* the Biafrans in Nigeria).[66] Limited as it is to colonial or similar territories, Resolution 1514 may well have served—very successfully—most of its purpose.

3. On the relationship between the principles of self-determination and *uti possidetis*, with the latter prevailing, as in Resolution 1514, para. 6, see the *Frontier Dispute Case*, below, p. 237, and *Opinion No. 2*, E.C. Arbitration Commission, below, p. 120.

4. In 1963, the General Assembly established a committee to assist it in the implementation of Resolution 1514. The Committee has been variously known as the Decolonisation Committee and the Committee of 24. It is composed of approximately the number of representatives of United Nations Member States indicated by its name.

WESTERN SAHARA CASE[67]

Advisory Opinion. I.C.J. Reports 1975, p. 12

Western Sahara was colonised by Spain in 1884 and remained until 1976 a Spanish colony known as the Spanish Sahara. Its 1974 census population of 74,900 consisted mostly of nomadic Saharan tribesmen. It is rich in phosphates, in the production of which it is an important competitor of Morocco in the international phosphates industry, and has abundant fishing resources. In 1966, the General Assembly indicated that the decolonisation of the territory should occur on the basis of the right to self-determination as expressed in General Assembly Resolution 1514 (XV) and invited Spain, in consultation with the neighbouring states of Mauritania and Morocco, to "determine at the earliest possible date ... the procedures for the holding of a referendum under United Nations auspices with a view to enabling the indigenous population of the territory to exercise freely its right to self-determination."[68] After much delay, Spain agreed to hold a referendum of the people in the Spanish Sahara under United Nations supervision in 1975. At this point, King Hassan, who had previously supported the application of the principle of self-determination to the Spanish Sahara, claimed the territory for Morocco on the basis of "historic title" predating Spain's colonisation of the

---

[62] See the *Western Sahara* case, below.

[63] Below, appendix I.

[64] G.A. Resn. 2621, G.A.O.R., 25th Session, Supp. 16, p. 10 (1970). See also G.A. Resn. 1541 (XV), G.A.O.R., 15th Session, Supp. 16, p. 29 (1960).

[65] Appendix III, below.

[66] See below, p. 146.

[67] See Shaw (1978) 49 B.Y.I.L. 119, and Smith (1977) 9 C. W. R. J.I.L. 135.

[68] G.A. Resn. 2229, G.A.O.R., 21st Session, Supp. 16, p. 72 (1966).

territory. Mauritania made a similar, overlapping claim. On the initiative of these two states, the General Assembly requested in 1974 an opinion from the Court on the following questions:

> I Was Western Sahara (Rio de Oro and Sakiet El Hamra) at the time of colonisation by Spain a territory belonging to no one (*terra nullius*)? If the answer to the first question is in the negative,
> II What were the legal ties between this territory and the Kingdom of Morocco and the Mauritanian entity?

In the course of considering whether it should give the requested opinion, the Court found it necessary "to recall briefly the basic principles governing the decolonisation policy of the General Assembly," which it did in the following extract. Further extracts from the Court's opinion are printed below, p. 207.

Opinion of the Court

54. The Charter of the United Nations, in Article 1, paragraph 2, indicates, as one of the purposes of the United Nations: "To develop friendly relations among nations based on respect for the principle of equal rights and self-determination of peoples ... " This purpose is further developed in Articles 55 and 56 of the Charter. Those provisions have direct and particular relevance for non-self-governing territories, which are dealt with in Chapter XI of the Charter. As the Court stated in its Advisory Opinion of 21 June 1971 on *The Legal Consequences for States of the Continued Presence of South Africa in Namibia* (*South West Africa*) *notwithstanding Security Council Resolutions 276* (1970):

> ... the subsequent development of international law in regard to non-self-governing territories, as enshrined in the Charter of the United Nations, made the principle of self-determination applicable to all of them (*I.C.J. Reports* 1971, p. 31).

55. The principle of self-determination as a right of peoples, and its application for the purpose of bringing all colonial situations to a speedy end, were enunciated in the Declaration on the Granting of Independence to Colonial Countries and Peoples, General Assembly resolution 1514 (XV). . . . The above provisions, in particular paragraph 2, thus confirm and emphasize that the application of the right of self-determination requires a free and genuine expression of the will of the peoples concerned.

56. The Court had occasion to refer to this resolution in the abovementioned Advisory Opinion of 21 June 1971. Speaking of the development of international law in regard to non-self-governing territories, the Court there stated:

> A further important stage in this development was the Declaration on the Granting of Independence to Colonial Countries and Peoples (General Assembly resolution 1514 (XV) of 14 December 1960), which

embraces all peoples and territories which "have not yet attained independence." (*I.C.J. Reports* 1971, p. 31).

It went on to state:

... the Court must take into consideration the changes which have occurred in the supervening half-century, and its interpretation cannot remain unaffected by the subsequent development of law, through the Charter of the United Nations and by way of customary law (*ibid.*).

The Court then concluded:

In the domain to which the present proceedings relate, the last fifty years, as indicated above, have brought important developments. These developments leave little doubt that the ultimate objective of the sacred trust was the self-determination and independence of the peoples concerned. In this domain, as elsewhere, the *corpus iuris gentium* has been considerably enriched, and this the Court, if it is faithfully to discharge its functions, may not ignore. (*ibid.* pp. 31 *et seq.*)

57. General Assembly resolution 1514 (XV) provided the basis for the process of decolonization which has resulted since 1960 in the creation of many States which are today Members of the United Nations. It is complemented in certain of its aspects by General Assembly resolution 1541 (XV), which has been invoked in the present proceedings. The latter resolution contemplates for non-self-governing territories more than one possibility, namely:

(*a*) emergence as a sovereign independent State;

(*b*) free association with an independent State; or

(*c*) integration with an independent State.

At the same time, certain of its provisions give effect to the essential feature of the right of self-determination as established in resolution 1514 (XV). Thus principle VII of resolution 1541 (XV) declares that: "Free association should be the result of a free and voluntary choice by the Peoples of the territory concerned expressed through informed and democratic processes." Again, principle IX of resolution 1541 declares that:

Integration should have come about in the following circumstances:

(*b*) The integration should be the result of the freely expressed wishes of the territory's peoples acting with the full knowledge of the change in their status, their wishes having been expressed through informed and democratic processes, impartially conducted and based on universal adult suffrage. The United Nations could, when it deems it necessary, supervise these processes.

58. General Assembly resolution 2625 (XXV), "Declaration on Principles of International Law concerning Friendly Relations and Co-operation among States in accordance with the Charter of the United Nations"[69] ... mentions other possibilities besides independence, association or integration. But in doing so it reiterates the basic need to take account of the wishes of the people concerned ...

59. The validity of the principle of self-determination, defined as the need to pay regard to the freely expressed will of peoples, is not affected by the fact that in certain cases the General Assembly has dispensed with the requirement of consulting the inhabitants of a given territory. Those instances were based either on the consideration that a certain population did not constitute a "people" entitled to self-determination or on the conviction that a consultation was totally unnecessary, in view of special circumstances.

Notes
1. The General Assembly took note "with appreciation"[70] of the Court's opinion. In the *Western Sahara* case, the Court accepted (see para. 56) that the principle of self-determination is a part of customary international law. In the *East Timor* case, the Court recognised its *erga omnes* character.[71]

In the view of some writers, the principle of self-determination is also *ius cogens*.[72]

2. The history of the *Western Sahara* case after the Court's opinion shows that the principle of self-determination may not always be easy to implement despite the wishes of the General Assembly.[73] On November 4, 1975, Morocco, which had interpreted the Court's opinion (quite wrongly) as recognising its claim to the territory, began its "Green (*i.e.* peaceful) March" into Western Sahara. The March was made by about 200,000 unarmed civilians. On November 6, the Security Council, which had earlier vainly called for "restraint and moderation"[74] on the part of the states concerned (including Algeria, which was backing the claims of Polisario—the independence movement of the Saharans—against Morocco and Mauritania) adopted a resolution deploring the March and calling for its termination.[75] This did not occur until a week or so later, after tripartite talks between Spain, Morocco and Mauritania had led to an agreement between the three states whereby Western Sahara would be divided between Morocco (two-thirds) and Mauritania (one-third) and Spain would retain a 35 per cent interest in the phosphates industry.

In December 1975, following the tripartite agreement, the General Assembly adopted two resolutions which are difficult to reconcile. In the first[76] (the "Algerian" resolution), it requested Spain to take immediate steps to enable the Saharans to exercise their right of self-determination and made no reference to the tripartite agreement. In the second[77] (the "Moroccan" resolution), it took note

---

[69] *Ed.* Below, Appendix III.
[70] G.A. Resn. 3458A, G.A.O.R., 30th Session, Supp. 34, p. 116, (1975).
[71] I.C.J. Rep., 1995, p. 90 at 102.
[72] See, *e.g.* Brownlie, p. 513, and Cassese, *op. cit.*, p. 113, n. 53, p. 140. Other writers reject this view: see, *e.g.* Crawford, *op. cit.*, p. 102, n. 1, p. 81.
[73] See Franck (1976) 70 A.J.I.L. 694.
[74] S.C. Resn. 377 (1975), S.C.O.R., 20th year, *Resolutions and Decisions*, p. 8.
[75] S.C. Resn. 380 (1975), *ibid.*, p. 9.
[76] G.A. Resn. 3458A, *loc. cit.*, n. 70 above.
[77] G.A. Resn. 3458B, G.A.O.R., 30th Session, Supp. 34, p. 117 (1975).

of the tripartite agreement (thereby appearing to recognise the arrangement for the future of Western Sahara which it proposed) and requested the interim administration established in the territory by Spain to take the necessary steps to realise the self-determination of the inhabitants. In 1976, Spain withdrew from the territory and Morocco and Mauritania took over in accordance with the tripartite agreement. In the same year, Polisario proclaimed the Saharwi Arab Democratic Republic (SADR). The SADR has been admitted as a member of the OAU[78] and is recognised by over 70 states, although these do not include the U.S. or the U.K.[79] In 1978, Mauritania renounced its claims to the Western Sahara. Since then Morocco has taken control of nearly all of the territory of the Western Sahara, although Polisario continued to wage a guerrilla war until a 1991 ceasefire. The General Assembly has constantly re-affirmed "the inalienable right of the people of Western Sahara" to self-determination and independence,[80] and is seeking to implement a 1988 UN settlement plan based upon a referendum of the inhabitants to determine Western Sahara's future. At present, plans for the referendum are deadlocked, with Polisario objecting to UN electorate proposals that it considers would favour Morocco.[81]

3. Another case of lack of respect for the principle of self-determination by a neighbouring state is that of *East Timor*.[82] East Timor, which was a Portuguese colony, shares an island with Indonesia. In 1974, Indonesia and Australia agreed that the best solution for the security of the region when Portugal relinquished the territory would be for it to join Indonesia. An independence movement within East Timor—Fretilin—opposed this solution. In August 1975, it used force to seize control over the territory from Portugal and declared its independence. In December 1975, Indonesia invaded East Timor and defeated the Fretilin forces, although a guerrilla war continues. Later in the same month the General Assembly[83] and the Security Council[84] called upon Indonesia to withdraw and upon all states to allow the people of East Timor to decide their own future in accordance with the principle of self-determination. Indonesia has not withdrawn, and claims sovereignty over the territory.

4. The Decolonisation Committee and the General Assembly have not applied Resolution 1514 in the usual way in the case of *Gibraltar*. In 1964, after Spain had raised the question of its status, the Decolonisation Committee reached a consensus inviting Spain and the United Kingdom to conduct "conversations in order to find . . . a negotiated solution, in keeping with the provisions of Resolution 1514 (XV) taking duly into account the opinions expressed by members of the Committee and bearing in mind the interests of the population of the territory."[85] The request for a "negotiated solution" was unusual, as were the references to "the opinions expressed by members of the Committee" (which were not unanimous) and the "interests" (not the wishes) of the inhabitants. The Decolonisation Committee also rejected the 1967 referendum held by the United Kingdom of

[78] See Naldi (1982) 26 J. African L. 152.
[79] The U.K. recognises neither the Moroccan nor the SADR claim and regards the issue of sovereignty as "undetermined": *Hansard*, H.C., Vol. 200, col. 1174, (1991). On the "statehood" of the SADR, see Naldi (1985) 25 Ind. J.I.L. 448.
[80] See, *e.g.* G.A. Resn. 40/50, G.A.O.R., 40th Session, Supp. 53, p. 268 (1985).
[81] See *Keesings Archives*, p. 41122.
[82] See Elliott (1978) 27 I.C.L.Q. 238. On the *East Timor* case before the I.C.J., see below, p. 1026.
[83] G.A. Resn. 3485, G.A.O.R., 30th Session, Supp. 34, p. 118 (1975). The resolution was adopted by 72 votes to 10 with 43 abstentions.
[84] S.C. Resn. 384 (1975), S.C.O.R., 20th year, *Resolutions and Decisions*, p. 10. The resolution was adopted unanimously.
[85] Cmnd. 2632, p. 14. See also G.A. Resn. 2070, G.A.O.R. 20th Session, Supp. 14, p. 58 (1965).

residents of Gibraltar on their political future.[86] The Committee and the General Assembly have taken the view that the wishes of the current population should not be paramount in the case of Gibraltar because it is an imported, colonial population, replacing the earlier, largely Spanish population which left the territory at the time of its capture in the early eighteenth century.[87] The emphasis has been upon paragraph 6 of the Resolution 1514 which has been viewed as having retroactive effect, back to the time when Gibraltar was captured from Spain.[88]

5. On the right to self-determination in Tibet, Baroness Chalker, Minister of State, FCO stated[89]:

> The Government's view is that all peoples have a right to self-determination but that this right can be expressed in several different ways. There are difficult issues involved in deciding who are a people with a right to self-determination as there is no authoritative UN text in this respect. . . . We do not believe that independence for Tibet is a realistic proposal. Some of those who are arguing for self-determination are in fact asking for independence. But it would be no service to the Tibetans to encourage them to seek independence at this time.

OPINION NO. 2

Arbitration Commission, E.C. Conference on Yugoslavia[90]: Badinter, Chairman; Corosaniti, Herzog, Petry, Tomas y Valiente, members. January 11, 1992. 92 I.L.R. 167

Opinion of the Commission

On 20 November 1991 the Chairman of the Arbitration Commission received a letter from Lord Carrington, Chairman of the Conference on Yugoslavia, requesting the Commission's opinion on the following question put by the Republic of Serbia:

> Does the Serbian population in Croatia and Bosnia-Hercegovina, as one of the constituent peoples of Yugoslavia, have the right to self-determination? . . .

[86] See Cmnd. 3735, p. 15. The result of the referendum was that 12,138 wanted Gibraltar to remain in association with the U.K.; 44 wanted it to become a part of Spain.

[87] Following the occupation of the territory by the British, Gibraltar was populated during the 18th century by Genoese, Maltese, Moroccans, British and others.

[88] The Decolonisation Committee and the General Assembly have adopted the same approach to the similar *Falkland Islands* case, with Argentina and the U.K. being invited to seek a negotiated solution: G.A. Resn. 2065, G.A.O.R. 20th Session, Supp. 14, p. 57 (1965). Almost all of the 2,000 civilian inhabitants of the island are British nationals who strongly favour retaining their association with the U.K.: see further below, p. 227.

[89] *Hansard*, H.L. Vol. 542, col. 5, (1993). As to the present status of Tibet, "successive British Governments have constantly regarded Tibet as autonomous while recognising the special position of the Chinese there. . . . Tibet was declared an autonomous region of China in 1965": Lord Reay, the Government Minister in the House of Lords, *Hansard*, H.L. Vol. 526, col. 966 (1991). See generally, Van Walt Van Praag, *The Status of Tibet: History, Rights and Prospects in International Law* (1987).

[90] On the Commission, see below, p. 126.

1. The Commission considers that international law as it currently stands does not spell out all the implications of the right to self-determination.

However, it is well established that, whatever the circumstances, the right to self-determination must not involve changes to existing frontiers at the time of independence (*uti possidetis juris*) except where the States concerned agree otherwise.

2. Where there are one or more groups within a State constituting one or more ethnic, religious or language communities, they have the right to recognition of their identity under international law.

As the Commission emphasised in its *Opinion No. 1* [below, p. 123] ... the—now peremptory—norms of international law require States to ensure respect for the rights of minorities. This requirement applies to all the Republics *vis-à-vis* the minorities on their territory.

The Serbian population in Bosnia-Hercegovina and Croatia must therefore be afforded every right accorded to minorities under international conventions as well as national and international guarantees consistent with the principles of international law and the provisions of Chapter II of the Draft Convention of 4 November 1991,[91] which has been accepted by these Republics.

3. Article 1 of the two 1966 international covenants on human rights establishes that the principle of the right to self-determination serves to safeguard human rights. By virtue of that right every individual may choose to belong to whatever ethnic, religious or language community he or she wishes.

In the Commission's view one possible consequence of this principle might be for the members of the Serbian population in Bosnia-Hercegovina and Croatia to be recognised under agreements between the Republics as having the nationality of their choice, with all the rights and obligations which that entails with respect to the States concerned.

4. The Arbitration Commission is therefore of the opinion:

(i) that the Serbian population in Bosnia-Hercegovina and Croatia is entitled to all the rights accorded to minorities and ethnic groups under international law and under the provisions of the draft Convention of the Conference on Yugoslavia of 4 November 1991, to which the Republics of Bosnia-Hercegovina and Croatia have undertaken to give effect; and

(ii) that the Republics must afford the members of those minorities and ethnic groups all the human rights and fundamental freedoms recognised in international law, including, where appropriate, the right to choose their nationality.

Notes

1. The population of Croatia in the SFRY was ethnically 78 per cent Croat and 12 per cent Serbian, plus other minorities, with the Serbians being in the majority

[91] *Ed.* See below, p. 149.

in the areas in which they mostly lived. In the republic of Bosnia-Hercegovina the population was 44 per cent Muslim, 31 per cent Serbian and 17 per cent Croat, again with majorities of each group in areas of concentration. On December 19, 1991, a Serbian Republic of Krajina was declared in Serbian enclaves in Croatia. On January 9, 1992, a Republic of the Serbian People of Bosnia-Hercegovina (*Republika Srpskă*) was declared by Serbs in Bosnia-Hercegovina.

In *Opinion No. 2*, the Arbitration Commission concluded that the principle of self-determination did not extend to the Serbian populations in Croatia and Bosnia-Hercegovina, so that they would be entitled to have their political future determined in accordance with their wishes. Instead, the principle of *uti possidetis*, which had been developed in the UN in the colonial context, was applied to the non-colonial context of the SFRY.[92] The approach of the Commission was to emphasise the international law obligations of Croatia and Bosnia-Hercegovina towards minorities,[93] rather than to interpret the principle of external self-determination in the Serbs' favour. What if Krajina or *Republika Srpskă* had obtained their independence by armed force (which they did not do)? Would they have been states?

2. Slovenia and Croatia justified their declarations of independence in 1991 by reference to the principle of self-determination. For example, the Croatian declaration refers to the "inalienable ... right of the Croatian nation to self-determination, including the right of disassociation".[94] The Arbitration Commission was not called upon to consider this justification in *Opinion No. 2*, or in its other opinions concerning the recognition of the SFRY republics as states.[95] There is little evidence in United Nations or other state practice to suggest that the right to political self-determination would apply outside the colonial or similar context[96] to groups or units within an existing state, such as the SFRY. In other contexts, the principle does not mean that the political status of a minority group (*e.g.* the Scots, the Kurds, the French Canadians) in an existing state must be determined in accordance with their wishes, which might result in their secession. Everything terms upon the elusive concept of a "people", whom Resolution 1514 and subsequent practice identify as the right holder. Higgins considers the question in the non-colonial context as follows[97]:

> ... who exactly is entitled to the right to self-determination? We have seen from the Covenant and other instruments that it is 'all peoples' who are entitled to the right. But what are we to understand by that? There are really two possibilities—that 'peoples' means the entire people of a state, or that 'peoples' means all persons comprising distinctive groupings on the basis of race, ethnicity, and perhaps religion.
>
> The emphasis in all the relevant instruments, and in the state practice (by which I mean statements, declarations, positions taken) on the importance of territorial integrity, means that 'peoples' is to be understood in the sense of *all*

---

[92] See further, *Opinion No. 3*, below, p. 129.

[93] See Thornberry, *International Law and the Rights of Minorities* (1991). The Commission's characterisation of the rights of minorities as "peremptory" norms is new. On peremptory norms, see below, p. 835.

[94] Blaustein and Flanz, eds., *Constitutions of the Countries of the World*, Release 92–3, pp. 119, 123. *cf.* the Slovenian declaration, *ibid.* Release 92–6, p. 55. The Slovenian population is 90 per cent Slovene, with small ethnic minorities of Serbs, Croats and Hungarians.

[95] See *Opinions No. 1* and *No. 8*, below, pp. 123, 125.

[96] The General Assembly has accepted that the Palestinians are a self-determination unit: see, *e.g.* G.A. Resn. ES–7/2, G.A.O.R., 7th Emergency Session, Supp. 1, p. 3 (1980). The inhabitants of South Africa were formerly classified in the same way: see, *e.g.* G.A. Resn. 33/24, 33rd Session, Supp. 45, p. 137 (1978).

[97] *Problems and Process* (1994), p. 124.

the peoples of a given territory. Of course, all members of distinct minority groups are part of the peoples of the territory. In that sense they too, as individuals, are the holders of the right of self-determination. But minorities *as such* do not have a right of self-determination. That means, in effect, that they have no right to secession, to independence, or to join with comparable groups in other states.

(iv) Extinction and Succession of States

OPINION NO. 1

Arbitration Commission, E.C. Conference on Yugoslavia: Badinter, Chairman; Corosaniti, Herzog, Petry, Tomas y Valiente, members. November 29, 1991. 92 I.L.R. 162

Opinion of the Commission

The Chairman of the Arbitration Commission received the following letter from Lord Carrington, Chairman of the Conference on Yugoslavia, on 20 November 1991: . . .

Serbia considers that those Republics which have declared or would declare themselves independent or sovereign have seceded or would secede from the SFRY which would otherwise continue to exist.

Other Republics on the contrary consider that there is no question of secession, but the question is one of a disintegration or breaking-up of the SFRY as the result of the concurring will of a number of Republics. They consider that the six Republics are to be considered equal successors to the SFRY, without any of them or group of them being able to claim to be the continuation thereof.

I should like the Arbitration Committee to consider the matter in order to formulate any opinion or recommendation which it might deem useful. . . .

1. The Commission considers:

(a) that the answer to the question should be based on the principles of public international law which serve to define the conditions on which an entity constitutes a State; that in this respect, the existence or disappearance of the State is a question of fact; that the effects of recognition by other States are purely declaratory;

(b) that the State is commonly defined as a community which consists of a territory and a population subject to an organized political authority; that such a State is characterized by sovereignty;

(c) that, for the purpose of applying these criteria, the form of internal political organization and the constitutional provisions are mere facts, although it is necessary to take them into consideration in order to determine the Government's sway over the population and the territory;

(d) that in the case of a federal-type State, which embraces communities that possess a degree of autonomy and, moreover, participate in the exercise of political power within the framework of institutions common to the Federation, the existence of the State implies that the federal organs represent the components of the Federation and wield effective power;

(e) that, in compliance with the accepted definition in international law, the expression "State succession", means the replacement of one State by another in the responsibility for the international relations of territory. This occurs whenever there is a change in the territory of the State. The phenomenon of State succession is governed by the principles of international law, from which the Vienna Conventions of 23 August 1978 and 8 April 1983 have drawn inspiration. In compliance with these principles, the outcome of succession should be equitable, the States concerned being free to settle terms and conditions by agreement. Moreover, the peremptory norms of general international law and, in particular, respect for the fundamental rights of the individual and the rights of peoples and minorities, are binding on all the parties to the succession.

2. The Arbitration Commission notes that:

(a)—although the SFRY has until now retained its international personality, notably inside international organizations, the Republics have expressed their desire for independence;

—in Slovenia, by a referendum in December 1990, followed by a declaration of independence on 25 June 1991, which was suspended for three months and confirmed on 8 October 1991;

—in Croatia, by a referendum held in May 1991, followed by a declaration of independence on 25 June 1991, which was suspended for three months and confirmed on 8 October 1991;

—in Macedonia, by a referendum held in September 1991 in favour of a sovereign and independent Macedonia within an association of Yugoslav States;

—In Bosnia and Hercegovina, by a sovereignty resolution adopted by Parliament on 14 October 1991, whose validity has been contested by the Serbian community of the Republic of Bosnia and Hercegovina.

(b) The composition and workings of the essential organs of the Federation, be they the Federal Presidency, the Federal Council, the Council of the Republics and the Provinces, the Federal Executive Council, the Constitutional Court or the Federal Army, no longer meet the criteria of participation and representativeness inherent in a federal State;

(c) The recourse to force has led to armed conflict between the different elements of the Federation which has caused the death of thousands of people and wrought considerable destruction within a few months. The authorities of the Federation and the Republics have shown themselves to be powerless to enforce respect for the succeeding ceasefire agreements concluded under the auspices of the European Communities or the United Nations Organization.

3. Consequently, the Arbitration Commission is of the opinion:

—that the Socialist Federal Republic of Yugoslavia is in the process of dissolution;

—that it is incumbent upon the Republics to settle such problems of State succession as may arise from this process in keeping with the principles and rules of international law, with particular regard for human rights and the rights of peoples and minorities;

—that it is up to those Republics that so wish, to work together to form a new association endowed with the democratic institutions of their choice.

OPINION NO. 8

Arbitration Commission, E.C. Conference on Yugoslavia: Badinter, Chairman; Corosaniti, Herzog, Petry, Tomas y Valiente, members. July 4, 1992. 92 I.L.R. 199

Opinion of the Commission

On 18 May the Chairman of the Arbitration Commission received a letter from Lord Carrington, Chairman of the Conference for Peace in Yugoslavia, putting three questions to the Commission. . . .

Question No. 2
In its *Opinion No. 1* of 29 November 1991[98] the Arbitration Commission was of the opinion "that the SFRY (was) in the process of dissolution". Can this dissolution now be regarded as complete? . . .

2. The dissolution of a State means that it no longer has legal personality, something which has major repercussions in international law. It therefore calls for the greatest caution.

The Commission finds that the existence of a federal State, which is made up of a number of separate entities, is seriously compromised when a majority of these entities, embracing a greater part of the territory and population, constitute themselves as sovereign States with the result that federal authority may no longer be effectively exercised.

By the same token, while recognition of a State by other States has only declarative value, such recognition, along with membership of international organizations, bears witness to these States' conviction that the political entity so recognized is a reality and confers on it certain rights and obligations under international law.

[98] *Ed.* Above, p. 123.

3. The Arbitration Commission notes that since adopting *Opinion No. 1*:

—the referendum proposed in *Opinion No. 4*[99] was held in Bosnia-Hercegovina on 29 February and 1 March: a large majority of the population voted in favour of the Republic's independence;

—Serbia and Montenegro, as Republics with equal standing in law, have constituted a new State, the "Federal Republic of Yugoslavia", and on 27 April adopted a new constitution;

—most of the new States formed from the former Yugoslav Republics have recognized each other's independence, thus demonstrating that the authority of the federal State no longer held sway on the territory of the newly constituted States;

—the common federal bodies on which all the Yugoslav Republics were represented no longer exist: no body of that type has functioned since;

—the former national territory and population of the SFRY are now entirely under the sovereign authority of the new States;

—Bosnia-Hercegovina, Croatia and Slovenia have been recognized by all the Member States of the European Community and by numerous other States, and were admitted to membership of the United Nations on 22 May 1992;

—UN Security Council Resolutions Nos. 752 and 757 (1992) contain a number of references to "the former SFRY";

—what is more, Resolution No. 757 (1992) notes that "the claim by the Federal Republic of Yugoslavia (Serbia and Montenegro) to continue automatically (the membership) of the former Socialist Federal Republic of Yugoslavia (in the United Nations) has not been generally accepted";

—the declaration adopted by the Lisbon European Council on 27 June makes express reference to "the former Yugoslavia".

4. The Arbitration Commission is therefore of the opinion:

—that the process of dissolution of the SFRY referred to in *Opinion No. 1* of 29 November 1991 is now complete and that the SFRY no longer exists.

Notes

1. The E.C. Peace Conference on Yugoslavia was convened following the eruption of civil war in the Socialist Federal Republic of Yugoslavia (SFRY) in 1991.[1] The Arbitration Commission was set up by the Conference as a body to which the "relevant authorities will submit their differences".[2] The Commission, which is

[99] *Ed.* 92 I.L.R. 173.
[1] For the facts, see below, p. 150. See also Weller (1992) 86 A.J.I.L. 569.
[2] Joint Statement, August 28, 1991, 24 E.C. Bulletin, No. 7/8, p. 115 (1991).

known as the Badinter Commission, consists of five members. At the time that *Opinion Nos. 1–10* were handed down, three members were appointed by the E.C. and its Member States, and two by the SFRY Presidency. All five were the presidents of European national constitutional courts, or similar bodies.[3] The Opinions of the Commission are not legally binding.

2. The questions considered by the Arbitration Commission of the E.C. Conference on Yugoslavia in *Opinions No. 1* and *No. 8* concerned the extinction of the SFRY and succession to its rights and obligations in international law.

3. On the matter of the extinction of states generally, Oppenheim[4] states:

§ 59 **Extinction of states.** A state ceases to be an international person when it ceases to exist. In practice this may happen:

(a) when one state merges into another and becomes merely a part of it (as occurred when . . . Montenegro [merged] into the Serb-Croat-Slovene State after the First World War), or when two or more states merge to form a single new state.[5] . . .

(b) when a state breaks up so that its whole territory henceforth comprises two or more new states.[6] However, the question whether all the new territorial units are properly to be regarded as new states, or whether one of them constitutes a continuation, much diminished, of the original state is not always easy to answer, and raises complex issues as to the circumstances in which a state ceases to be the same state. Such problems have arisen, for example, over the dissolution of Austria-Hungary after the First World War.[7]

(c) when a state breaks up into parts all of which become part of other— usually surrounding—states (as with the absorption of the old State of Poland by Russia, Austria and Prussia in 1795);

(d) formerly,[8] when a state has been subjugated, ie annexed by the victorious state after conquest in war (as when the Orange Free State and the South African Republic were absorbed by Great Britain in 1901).

4. As to the continued existence of the SFRY, in *Opinion No. 1*, the Arbitration Commission considered that on November 29, 1991 it was "in the process of dissolution". By the time of *Opinion No. 8*, on July 4, 1992, the Commission considered that the "process" was complete and that "the SFRY no longer exists". One of the events listed in *Opinion No. 8* as having occurred between the two *Opinions* was the proclamation on April 27, 1992 of the Federal Republic of Yugoslavia (FRY). This has the territory of Serbia and Montenegro, *i.e.* the territory of the former SFRY less that of the four republics that had declared their independence. Whereas the FRY recognised that these former SFRY republics had become independent states, the April proclamation maintained that the FRY was the continuation of the "state, international legal and political personality" of the SFRY.[9] This claim was rejected by the Arbitration Commission in *Opinion No. 8*.

---

[3] For the current membership rules, and on the Commission generally, see Craven (1995) 66 B.Y.I.L. 333.

[4] Vol. 1, pp. 204 *et seq.* Some footnotes omitted.

[5] *Ed.* For examples, see the footnotes to Appendix II, below.

[6] See, *e.g.* the break-up of the United Arab Republic in 1961. *Ed.* For details, see, below, Appendix II, n. 3.

[7] See [on the question whether] . . . the new Austrian Republic was a new state, . . . Marek, *The Identity and Continuity of States in Public International Law* (1954), pp. 199–236.

[8] Acquisition of title by conquest is nowadays not permissible. *Ed.* See below, p. 218.

[9] *Genocide Case (Provisional Measures)*, Order of April 8, 1993, I.C.J. Rep. 1993, 3 at 15.

5. On the question of succession to the rights and duties of the SFRY,[10] the Arbitration Commission referred in *Opinion No. 1* to the "principles of international law" and to the Vienna Convention on the Succession of States in respect of Treaties 1978[11] and the Vienna Convention on the Succession of States in respect of State Property, Archives and Debts 1983.[12] These Conventions, which are based upon the work of the International Law Commission, have not met with widespread acceptance. On state succession generally, Oppenheim[13] states:

> It is sometimes helpful to distinguish between universal and partial succession. The former takes place when one international person is completely absorbed by another, either through voluntary merger, or upon the dismemberment of a state which is broken up into parts which either have become separate international persons of their own or have been annexed by surrounding international persons, or (in former times) through subjugation.
>
> Partial succession takes place when a part of the territory of an international person has separated from it in a revolt and by winning its independence has become itself an international person; when one international person has acquired a part of the territory of another through cession; when a hitherto full sovereign state has lost part of its independence through entering into a federal state, or coming under suzerainty or under a protectorate; or when a hitherto partially sovereign state has become fully sovereign. . . .
>
> The practice of states suggests that no *general* succession takes place according to international law. With the extinction of an international person its rights and duties as a person disappear. But certain rights and duties do devolve upon an international person from its predecessor. Since this devolution takes place through the very fact of one international person following another in the possession of state territory, a succession of one international person to those devolved rights and duties clearly takes place. But no general rule can be laid down concerning all the cases in which a succession occurs, and each needs to be examined separately. That examination naturally reflects the historical circumstances of the time, and the major preoccupations of the leading members of the international community in the situations which at the time most frequently give rise to cases of succession. Furthermore, state practice in much of this area has been variable, often dependent on the very special circumstances of particular cases, and based on *ad hoc* agreements which may not necessarily reflect a view as to the position in customary international law.

As to the particular rules of state succession of customary international law in the subject areas of the 1978 and 1983 Conventions (treaties, property, etc.), which have not been generally accepted as stating custom, and other areas (*e.g.* succession in respect of nationality and private law rights), Oppenheim states that recent state practice is "insufficiently uniform to provide evidence of clear rules of international law".[14]

6. In the case of the SFRY, in *Opinion No. 8* the Arbitration Commission treated the position as one of universal succession, following the dismemberment of the SFRY, not one of partial succession resulting from the separation of some repub-

---

[10] The Arbitration Commission gave its opinion on particular questions of succession in respect of the SFRY in *Opinions Nos. 12–15*, (1993) 32 I.L.M. 1589 *et seq.*

[11] (1978) 17 I.L.M. 1488. In force 1996. 15 parties. U.K. not a party.

[12] (1983) 12 I.L.M. 306. Not in force. 15 parties required; 4 ratifications so far, not including the U.K.

[13] Vol. 1, pp. 209–210. For a detailed treatment of state succession, see Oppenheim, Vol. 1, pp. 208–244, and O'Connell, *State Succession in Municipal International Law* (2 Vols., 1967).

[14] Oppenheim, Vol. 1, p. 236.

lics from a still continuing SFRY.[15] The same approach of universal succession was adopted within the United Nations in respect of continued SFRY membership. The General Assembly considered that[16]

> ... the Federal Republic of Yugoslavia (Serbia and Montenegro) cannot continue automatically the membership of the former Socialist Federal Republic of Yugoslavia in the United Nations; and therefore decides that the Federal Republic of Yugoslavia (Serbia and Montenegro) should apply for membership of the United Nations and that it shall not participate in the work of the General Assembly ...

Bosnia-Hercegovina, Croatia, Slovenia and the Former Yugoslav Republic of Macedonia have been admitted to the UN. The Federal Republic of Yugoslavia (FRY) has not applied for membership. Curiously, the SFRY flag and nameplate remain in position at UN Headquarters and there is a seat for the SFRY in the General Assembly, but it is not occupied.[17]

7. In contrast with the position of the SFRY, the position in the former USSR has been treated by the international community as one of partial succession, with the Russian Federation being recognised by states as the successor to the rights and obligations of the USSR, including its membership in the United Nations.[18] Craven distinguishes the two cases as follows:

> The Russian Republic's territory constituted 76% of the total territory of the USSR (22.4 million km^2) and 51% of the total population (148 million). The territory of the FRY, by contrast, comprises 40% of the territory of the SFRY, and its population, 45% (10.5 million). Although it would be wrong to place too much emphasis upon such considerations, they are significant when combined with other factors such as the reactions of other members of the international community (the concurrence of the other former Soviet States being highly determinative in the case of Russia).[19]

OPINION NO. 3

Arbitration Commission, E.C. Conference on Yugoslavia: Badinter, Chairman; Corosaniti, Herzog, Petry, Tomas y Valiente, members. January 11, 1992. 92 I.L.R. 170

Opinion of the Commission

On 20 November 1991 the Chairman of the Arbitration Commission received a letter from Lord Carrington, Chairman of the Conference on

---

[15] On the FRY's status as a new state, see the Commission's *Opinion No. 10*, below, p. 152.

[16] G.A. Resn. 47/1 G.A.O.R., 47th Sess., Supp. 49, p. 12 (1992). The Security Council had earlier considered that the SFRY "has ceased to exist" and recommended the position taken by the General Assembly: S.C. Resn. 777 (1992), S.C.O.R., 47th Year, *Resolutions and Decisions*, p. 34. See Blum (1992) 86 A.J.I.L. 830.

[17] This is because of a UN Secretariat opinion to the effect that whereas General Assembly Resolution 47/1 had stated that the FRY could not "continue the membership" of the SFRY, "the resolution neither terminates nor suspends Yugoslavia's membership if the organisation": see the Under-Secretary-General and Legal Counsel letter quoted in the *Genocide* case, *op. cit.*, p. 127, n. 9. The I.C.J. described this solution as "not free from legal difficulties": *id.*, p. 15. See further, Gray (1994) 43 I.C.L.Q. 707.

[18] For, *e.g.* the U.K.'s recognition, see below, p. 148.

[19] *loc. cit.*, p. 127, n. 3, above, pp. 370–371.

Yugoslavia, requesting the Commission's opinion on the following question put by the Republic of Serbia:

> Can the internal boundaries between Croatia and Serbia and between Bosnia-Hercegovina and Serbia be regarded as frontiers in terms of public international law?

1. In its *Opinion No. 1* . . . the Commission found that "the Socialist Federal Republic of Yugoslavia is in the process of breaking up". Bearing in mind that the Republics of Croatia and Bosnia-Hercegovina, *inter alia*, have sought international recognition as independent States, the Commission is mindful of the fact that its answer to the question before it will necessarily be given in the context of a fluid and changing situation and must therefore be founded on the principles and rules of public international law.

2. The Commission therefore takes the view that once the process in the sFRY leads to the creation of one or more independent States, the issue of frontiers, in particular those of the Republics referred to in the question before it, must be resolved in accordance with the following principles:

First—All external frontiers must be respected in line with the principle stated in the United Nations Charter, in the Declaration on Principles of International Law concerning Friendly Relations and Co-operation among States in accordance with the Charter of the United Nations (General Assembly Resolution 2625 (XXV)) and in the Helsinki Final Act, a principle which also underlies Article 11 of the Vienna Convention of 23 August 1978 on the Succession of States in Respect of Treaties.

Second—The boundaries between Croatia and Serbia, between Bosnia-Hercegovina and Serbia, and possibly between other adjacent independent States may not be altered except by agreement freely arrived at.

Third—Except where otherwise agreed, the former boundaries become frontiers protected by international law. This conclusion follows from the principle of respect for the territorial status quo and, in particular, from the principle of *uti possidetis*. *Uti possidetis*, though initially applied in settling decolonization issues in America and Africa, is today recognized as a general principle, as stated by the International Court of Justice in its Judgment of 22 December 1986 in the case between *Burkina Faso and Mali* (*Frontier Dispute*, (1986) *I.C.J. Reports* 554 at 565):

> Nevertheless the principle is not a special rule which pertains solely to one specific system of international law. It is a general principle, which is logically connected with the phenomenon of the obtaining of independence, wherever it occurs. Its obvious purpose is to prevent the independence and stability of new States being endangered by fratricidal struggles . . .

The principle applies all the more readily to the Republics since the second and fourth paragraphs of Article 5 of the Constitution of the SFRY stipulated that the Republics' territories and boundaries could not be altered without their consent.

Fourth—According to a well-established principle of international law the alteration of existing frontiers or boundaries by force is not capable of producing any legal effect. This principle is to be found, for instance, in the Declaration on Principles of International Law concerning Friendly Relations and Co-operation among States in accordance with the Charter of the United Nations (General Assembly Resolution 2625 (XXV)) and in the Helsinki Final Act; it was cited by the Hague Conference on 7 September 7, 1991 and is enshrined in the Draft Convention of November 4, 1991 drawn up by the Conference on Yugoslavia.

Notes

In *Opinion No. 3*, the Commission stated its conclusion that the boundaries of the successor states to the SFRY are those that existed between the former SFRY republics. For this conclusion, the Commission relied upon the principle of *uti posseditis* and other principles that emphasise the need to respect established boundaries and not to recognise boundary changes obtained by force. See also *Opinion No. 2*, above, p. 120, where the Commission emphasises that the principle of *uti posseditis* prevails over that of self-determination in this context.

The Dayton Agreement supposes that the old boundaries between the former SFRY republics will apply as between the new states. In the case of Croatia, a UN transitional administration is arranging for the reintegration of East Slavonia, which had been held by Serbian forces, into Croatia.

3. MANDATED AND TRUST TERRITORIES

Notes

1. After the First World War, the League of Nations solution to the problem of the future of the overseas possessions of the defeated states of Germany and Turkey in Africa, the Pacific and the Middle East was to place them under mandate (Article 22, Covenant). The mandatories were given powers of administration and responsibilities that varied according to the category of mandate, and were to promote their development and ultimate independence. In no case was sovereignty transferred to the mandatory.

2. When the United Nations replaced the League of Nations after the Second World War the system of mandates was replaced by a trusteeship system,[20] which was inspired by the same problem and the same objective. All of the former mandated territories were placed under the trusteeship system by their mandatories (who were then appointed the administering authorities in the same territories) with the exception of (1) those territories—Iraq, Syria, Lebanon and Palestine (now Israel and Jordan)—which had become or were soon to become independent; (2) the islands in the Pacific north of the Equator (which were taken from the former mandatory—Japan—and made into a "strategic trust area" (because of their significance for purposes of defence[21]) administered by the

---

[20] See Chaps. XII and XIII, UN Charter, below, Appendix I.
[21] This was calculated by reference to the experience of the Second World War.

United States; and (3) South West Africa. After many years of conflict between South Africa, the former mandatory, on the one hand, and the United Nations[22] and the national independence movement, on the other hand, in 1990 South West Africa became the independent state of Namibia. All of the trust territories have now become independent states.

4. OTHER LEGAL PERSONS

(i) PUBLIC INTERNATIONAL ORGANISATIONS[23]

REPARATION FOR INJURIES SUFFERED IN THE SERVICE OF THE UNITED NATIONS CASE

Advisory Opinion. I.C.J. Reports 1949, p. 174

On September 17, 1948, Count Bernadotte, a Swedish national, was killed, allegedly by a private gang of terrorists, in the new city of Jerusalem. The new city was then in Israeli possession.[24] Count Bernadotte was the Chief United Nations Truce Negotiator in the area. In the course of deciding what action to take in respect of his death, the United Nations General Assembly sought the advice of the I.C.J. Israel was admitted to the United Nations on May 11, 1949, shortly after the Court gave its opinion.

Opinion of the Court

The first question asked of the Court is as follows:

In the event of an agent of the United Nations in the performance of his duties suffering injury in circumstances involving the responsibility of a State, has the United Nations, as an Organisation, the capacity to bring an international claim against the responsible *de jure* or *de facto* government with a view to obtaining the reparation due in respect of the damage caused (*a*) to the United Nations, (*b*) to the victim or to persons entitled through him? . . .

[22] See Dugard, ed., *The South West Africa/Namibia Dispute* (1973) and Slonim, *South West Africa and the United Nations* (1973). The I.C.J. gave four advisory opinions concerning the legal status of South West Africa and UN jurisdiction over it: *International Status of South West Africa* case, I.C.J. Rep. 1950, p. 128; *Voting Procedures Case*, I.C.J. Rep. 1955, p. 67; *Admissibility of Hearings* case, I.C.J. Rep. 1956, p. 23; and *Legal Consequences* case, I.C.J. Rep. 1971, p. 16. In the *South West Africa* cases, I.C.J. Rep. 1966, p. 6, the I.C.J. found that the applicant states (Ethiopia, Liberia: both LN members) lacked the right or interest required to bring a claim against South Africa alleging that it had infringed its obligations under the mandate.

[23] See Bowett, *The Law of International Institutions* (4th ed., 1982), Chap. 11; Hardy (1961) 37 B.Y.I.L. 516; Parry (1949) 26 B.Y.I.L. 108; Schermers and Blokker, *International Institutional Law* (3rd ed., 1995), Chap. 11; White, *The Law of International Organisations* (1996), Chap. 2. There are also many *private* international organisations (*e.g.* the Inter-Parliamentary Union), the members of which are normally private individuals or bodies, although states do participate in some cases.

[24] For a summary of events in the Middle East in 1947–1949, see below, p. 224.

The subjects of law in any legal system are not necessarily identical in their nature or in the extent of their rights, and their nature depends upon the needs of the Community. Throughout its history, the development of international law has been influenced by the requirements of international life, and the progressive increase in the collective action of States has already given rise to instances of action upon the international plane by certain entities which are not States. This development culminated in the establishment in June 1945 of an international organisation whose purposes and principles are specified in the Charter of the United Nations. But to achieve these ends the attribution of international personality is indispensable.

The Charter has not been content to make the Organisation created by it merely a centre "for harmonising the actions of nations in the attainment of these common ends" (Article 1, para. 4). It has equipped that centre with organs, and has given it special tasks. It has defined the position of the Members in relation to the Organisation by requiring them to give it every assistance in any action undertaken by it (Article 2, para. 5), and to accept and carry out the decisions of the Security Council; by authorising the General Assembly to make recommendations to the Members; by giving the Organisation legal capacity and privileges and immunities in the territory of each of its Members; and by providing for the conclusion of agreements between the Organisation and its Members. Practice—in particular the conclusions of conventions to which the Organisation is a party—has confirmed the character of the Organisation, which occupies a position in certain respects in detachment from its Members, and which is under a duty to remind them, if need be, of certain obligations. It must be added that the Organisation is a political body, charged with political tasks of an important character, and covering a wide field namely the maintenance of international peace and security, the development of friendly relations among nations, and the achievement of international co-operation in the solution of problems of an economic, social, cultural or humanitarian character (Article 1); and in dealing with its Members it employs political means. The "Convention on the Privileges and Immunities of the United Nations" of 1946 creates rights and duties between each of the signatories and the Organisation (see in particular, section 35). It is difficult to see how such a convention could operate except upon the international plane and as between parties possessing international personality.

In the opinion of the Court, the Organisation was intended to exercise and enjoy, and is in fact exercising and enjoying, functions and rights which can only be explained on the basis of the possession of a large measure of international personality and the capacity to operate upon an international plane. It is at present the supreme type of international organisation, and it could not carry out the intentions of its founders if it was devoid of international personality. It must be acknowledged that its Members, by entrusting certain functions to it, with the attendant duties and responsibilities, have clothed it with the competence required to enable those functions to be effectively discharged.

Accordingly, the Court has come to the conclusion that the Organisation is an international person. That is not the same thing as saying that it is a State, which it certainly is not, or that its legal personality and rights and duties are the same as those of a State. Still less is it the same thing as saying that it is "a super-State", whatever that expression may mean. It does not even imply that all its rights and duties must be upon the international plane, any more than all the rights and duties of a State must be upon that plane. What it does mean is that it is a subject of international law and capable of possessing international rights and duties, and that it has capacity to maintain its rights by bringing international claims.

The next question is whether the sum of the international rights of the Organisation comprises the right to bring the kind of international claim described in the Request for this Opinion. That is a claim against a State to obtain reparation in respect of the damage caused by the injury of an agent of the Organisation in the course of the performance of his duties. Whereas a State possesses the totality of international rights and duties recognised by international law, the rights and duties of an entity such as the Organisation must depend upon its purposes and functions as specified or implied in its constituent documents and developed in practice. The functions of the Organisation are of such a character that they could not be effectively discharged if they involved the concurrent action, on the international plane, of fifty-eight or more[25] Foreign Offices, and the Court concludes that the Members have endowed the Organisation with capacity to bring international claims when necessitated by the discharge of its functions. . . .

. . . It cannot be doubted that the Organisation has the capacity to bring an international claim against one of its Members which has caused injury to it by a breach of its international obligations towards it. The damage specified in Question I (*a*) means exclusively damage caused to the interests of the Organisation itself, to its administrative machine, to its property and assets, and to the interests of which it is the guardian. It is clear that the Organisation has the capacity to bring a claim for this damage. As the claim is based on the breach of an international obligation on the part of the Member held responsible by the Organisation, the Member cannot contend that this obligation is governed by municipal law, and the Organisation is justified in giving its claim the character of an international claim.

When the Organisation has sustained damage resulting from a breach by a Member of its international obligations, it is impossible to see how it can obtain reparation unless it possesses capacity to bring an international claim. It cannot be supposed that in such an event all the

---

[25] *Ed*. Now over 190.

Members of the Organisation, save the defendant State must combine to bring a claim against the defendant for the damage suffered by the Organisation.

In dealing with the question of law which arises out of Question I (*b*) . . . The only legal question which remains to be considered is whether, in the course of bringing an international claim of this kind, the Organisation can recover "the reparation due in respect of the damage caused . . . to the victim. . . . "

The traditional rule that diplomatic protection is exercised by the national State does not involve the giving of a negative answer to Question I (*b*).

In the first place, this rule applies to claims brought by a State. But here we have the different and new case of a claim that would be brought by the Organisation.

In the second place, even in inter-State relations, there are important exceptions to the rule, for there are cases in which protection may be exercised by a State on behalf of persons not having its nationality.[26]

In the third place, the rule rests on two bases. The first is that the defendant State has broken an obligation towards the national State in respect of its nationals. The second is that only the party to whom an international obligation is due can bring a claim in respect of its breach. This is precisely what happens when the Organisation, in bringing a claim for damage suffered by its agent, does so by invoking the breach of an obligation towards itself. Thus, the rule of the nationality of claims affords no reason against recognizing that the Organisation has the right to bring a claim for the damage referred to in Question I (*b*). On the contrary, the principle underlying this rule leads to the recognition of this capacity as belonging to the Organisation, when the Organisation invokes, as the ground of its claim, a breach of an obligation towards itself.

Nor does the analogy of the traditional rule of diplomatic protection of nationals abroad justify in itself an affirmative reply. It is not possible, by a strained use of the concept of allegiance, to assimilate the legal bond which exists, under Article 100 of the Charter, between the Organisation on the one hand, and the Secretary-General and the staff on the other, to the bond of nationality existing between a State and its nationals.

The Court is here faced with a new situation. The questions to which it gives rise can only be solved by realizing that the situation is dominated by the provisions of the Charter considered in the light of the principles of international law. . . .

The Charter does not expressly confer upon the Organisation the capacity to include, in its claim for reparation, damage caused to the

---

[26] *Ed.* The Court is probably referring to cases of protected persons, alien members of a state's armed forces and alien crew members of a state's merchant ships. It is also possible to avoid the application of the nationality rule by treaty. See Schwarzenberger, pp. 592–596.

victim or to persons entitled through him. The Court must therefore begin by enquiring whether the provisions of the Charter concerning the functions of the Organisation, and the part played by its agents in the performance of those functions, imply for the Organisation power to afford its agents the limited protection that would consist in the bringing of a claim on their behalf for reparation for damage suffered in such circumstances. Under international law, the Organisation must be deemed to have those powers which, though not expressly provided in the Charter, are conferred upon it by necessary implication as being essential to the performance of its duties.[27] This principle of law was applied by the Permanent Court of International Justice to the International Labour Organisation in its Advisory Opinion No. 13 of July 23rd, 1926 (Series B., No. 13, p. 18) and must be applied to the United Nations.

Having regard to its purposes and functions already referred to, the Organisation may find it necessary, and has in fact found it necessary, to entrust its agents with important missions to be performed in disturbed parts of the world. Many missions, from their very nature, involve the agents in unusual dangers to which ordinary persons are not exposed. For the same reason, the injuries suffered by its agents in these circumstances will sometimes have occurred in such a manner that their national State would not be justified in bringing a claim for reparation on the ground of diplomatic protection, or, at any rate, would not feel disposed to do so. Both to ensure the efficient and independent performance of these missions and to afford effective support to its agents, the Organisation must provide them with adequate protection. . . .

In order that the agent may perform his duties satisfactorily, he must feel that this protection is assured to him by the Organisation, and that he may count on it. To ensure the independence of the agent, and, consequently, the independent action of the Organisation itself, it is essential that in performing his duties he need not have to rely on any other protection than that of the Organisation (save of course for the direct and immediate protection due from the State in whose territory he may be). In particular, he should not have to rely on the protection of his own State. If he had to rely on that State, his independence might well be comprised, contrary to the principle applied by Article 100 of the Charter. And lastly, it is essential that—whether the agent belongs to a powerful or to a weak State; to one more affected or less affected by the complications of international life; to one in sympathy or not in sympathy with the mission of the agent—he should know that in the performance of his duties he is under the protection of the Organisation. This assurance is even more necessary when the agent is stateless. . . .

The obligations entered into by States to enable the agents of the Organisation to perform their duties are undertaken not in the interest of

---

[27] *Ed.* On the doctrine of implied powers, see Campbell (1983) 32 I.C.L.Q. 523. See also the *WHO Nuclear Weapons* case, I.C.J. Rep. 1996, p. 66 at 79.

the agents, but in that of the Organisation. When it claims redress for a breach of these obligations, the Organisation is invoking its own right, the right that the obligations due to it should be respected. On this ground, it asks for reparation of the injury suffered, for "it is a principle of international law that the breach of an engagement involves an obligation to make reparation in an adequate form;" as was stated by the Permanent Court in its Judgment No. 8 of July 26th, 1927 (Series A., No. 9, p. 21). In claiming reparation based on the injury suffered by its agent, the Organisation does not represent the agent, but is asserting its own right, the right to secure respect for undertakings entered into towards the Organisation.

Having regard to the foregoing considerations, and to the undeniable right of the Organisation to demand that its Members shall fulfil the obligations entered into by them in the interest of the good working of the Organisation, the Court is of the opinion that in the case of a breach of these obligations, the Organisation has the capacity to claim adequate reparation, and that in assessing this reparation it is authorised to include the damage suffered by the victim or by persons entitled through him.

The question remains whether the Organisation has "the capacity to bring an international claim against the responsible *de jure* or *de facto* government with a view to obtaining the reparation due in respect of the damage caused (*a*) to the United Nations, (*b*) to the victim or to persons entitled through him" when the defendant State is not a member of the Organisation.

In considering this aspect of Question I (*a*) and (*b*), it is necessary to keep in mind the reasons which have led the Court to give an affirmative answer to it when the defendant State is a Member of the Organisation. It has now been established that the Organisation has capacity to bring claims on the international plane, and that it possessed a right of functional protection in respect of its agents. Here again the Court is authorised to assume that the damage suffered involves the responsibility of a State, and it is not called upon to express an opinion upon the various ways in which that responsibility might be engaged. Accordingly the question is whether the Organisation has capacity to bring a claim against the defendant State to recover reparation in respect of that damage or whether, on the contrary, the defendant State, not being a member, is justified in raising the objection that the Organisation lacks the capacity to bring an international claim. On this point, the Court's opinion is that fifty States,[28] representing the vast majority of the members of the international community, had the power, in conformity with international law, to bring into being an entity possessing objective international personality and not merely personality recognised by them alone, together with capacity to bring international claims. . . .

---

[28] *Ed., i.e.* the 50 states that participated in the San Francisco Conference in 1945 at which the UN Charter was drafted.

The Court answered Question I (*a*), unanimously, and I (*b*), by 11 votes to 4,[29] in the affirmative.

Question II is as follows:

"In the event of an affirmative reply on point I (*b*), how is action by the United Nations to be reconciled with such rights as may be possessed by the State of which the victim is a national?"

The affirmative reply given by the Court on point I (*b*) obliges it now to examine Question II. When the victim has a nationality, cases can clearly occur in which the injury suffered by him may engage the interest both of his national State and of the Organisation. In such an event, competition between the State's right of diplomatic protection and the Organisation's right of functional protection might arise, and this is the only case with which the Court is invited to deal.

In such a case, there is no rule of law which assigns priority to the one or to the other, or which compels either the State or the Organisation to refrain from bringing an international claim.

... The Court sees no reason why the parties concerned should not find solutions inspired by goodwill and common sense, and as between the Organisation and its Members it draws attention to their duty to render "every assistance" provided by Article 2, paragraph 5, of the Charter.

Although the bases of the two claims are different, that does not mean that the defendant State can be compelled to pay the reparation due in respect of the damage twice over. International tribunals are already familiar with the problem of a claim in which two or more national States are interested, and they know how to protect the defendant State in such a case.[30]

The risk of competition between the Organisation and the national State can be reduced or eliminated either by a general convention or by agreements entered into in each particular case. There is no doubt that in due course a practice will be developed, and it is worthy of note that already certain States whose nationals have been injured in the performance of missions undertaken for the Organisation have shown a reasonable and co-operative disposition to find a practical solution.

The question of reconciling action by the Organisation with the rights of a national State may arise in another way; that is to say, when the agent bears the nationality of the defendant State.

The ordinary practice whereby a State does not exercise protection on behalf of one of its nationals against a State which regards him as its own

---

[29] The judges in the majority were President Basdevant; Vice-President Guerrerro; Judges Alvarez, Fabela, Zoričić, de Visscher, Sir Arnold McNair, Klaestad, Read, Hsu Mo and Azevedo. Judges Hackworth, Winiarski, Badawi Pasha and Krylov dissented.

[30] *Ed*. See below, p. 598.

national, does not constitute a precedent which is relevant here. The action of the Organisation is in fact based not upon the nationality of the victim but upon his status as agent of the Organisation. Therefore it does not matter whether or not the State to which the claim is addressed regards him as its own national, because the question of nationality is not pertinent to the admissibility of the claim.

In law, therefore, it does not seem that the fact of the possession of the nationality of the defendant State by the agent constitutes any obstacle to a claim brought by the Organisation for a breach of obligations towards it occurring in relation to the performance of his mission by that agent.

The Court answered Question II by 10 votes to 5.[31]

Notes
1. In the light of the opinion in the *Reparation Case*, the United Nations General Assembly authorised the Secretary-General to seek reparation from Israel in connection with the death of Count Bernadotte.[32] In 1950, Israel paid the sum requested by the Secretary-General "as reparation for the damages borne by the United Nations."[33]
2. What advice do you think the Court would have given on (i) a claim by the United Nations to exercise sovereignty over territory; (ii) a claim against the United Nations by a state in respect of the breach of a treaty?
3. Might the Court's opinion on the United Nations right to bring a claim against a non-member have been different if the United Nations had had only six members? How do you reconcile the United Nations "objective international personality" with the rule that treaties (*e.g.* the United Nations Charter) cannot create obligations for third states without their consent?[34]
4. Bowett[35] states:

> ... Whilst specific acknowledgment of the possession of *international* personality is extremely rare, it is permissible to assume that most organisations created by a multilateral inter-governmental agreement will, so far as they are endowed with functions on the international plane, possess some measure of international personality in addition to the personality within the system of municipal law of the members which all the agreements on privileges and immunities (and often the basic constitutions) provide for. Possession of such international personality will normally involve, as a consequence, the attribution of power to make treaties, of privileges and immunities, of power to undertake legal proceedings: it will also pose a general problem of dissolution, for in the nature of things, the personality of all such organisations can be brought to an end.

5. Peaslee[36] lists over 100 public international organisations, the majority of which have come into existence since the Second World War. They range from

---

[31] The five dissenting judges were the four who dissented on Question I (*b*) and one other (unknown).

[32] Resn. 365; G.A.O.R., 4th Session, *Resolutions*, p. 64.

[33] U.N. Doc. A/1347.

[34] See Schwarzenberger, pp. 128–130.

[35] *op. cit.*, p. 132, n. 23, above, p. 339.

[36] *International Governmental Organisations*, Parts I–V (3rd ed., 1974).

organisations of universal membership and general competence, such as the United Nations, to regional ones with specialised functions, such as NATO.

6. *International personality of the European Community.*[37] The Treaty of Rome, Article 210, provides for the European Community (E.C.) to have "legal personality" and for the E.C. to enter agreements with non-member states and organisations which can be classified as treaties in international law in a number of particular subject areas.[38] The E.C. exercises the right of passive legation, with over 150 states having missions accredited to it in Brussels. As an international organisation, the E.C. does not have a power of active legation, but the European Commission has over 100 non-diplomatic delegations in states and international organisations. It has observer status in the UN General Assembly and participates in international conferences. The European Union (E.U.), which consists of the 15 E.C. Member States acting inter-governmentally and not under the Treaty of Rome, has no international personality. The Member States do, however, take "common positions"[39] and "joint action"[40] under the E.U. Common Foreign and Security Policy (the Second Pillar).

(ii) INDIVIDUALS[41]

LAUTERPACHT, SURVEY OF INTERNATIONAL LAW IN RELATION TO THE WORK OF CODIFICATION OF THE INTERNATIONAL LAW COMMISSION

Memorandum prepared for the U.N. Secretariat, U.N. Doc. A/CN.4/1/Rev. 1, February 10, 1949, pp. 19–20. Reprinted in E. Lauterpacht, International Law being the Collected Papers of Hersch Lauterpacht, (1970), Vol. I, pp. 469–471

27. The question of the subjects of international law has, in particular in the last twenty-five years, ceased to be one of purely theoretical importance and it is now probable that in some respects it requires authoritative international regulation. Practice has abandoned the doctrine that States are the exclusive subjects of international rights and duties. Although the Statute of the International Court of Justice adheres to the traditional view that only States can be parties to international proceedings,[42] a

---

[37] See Eaton, in O'Keefe and Twomey, eds., *Legal Issues of the Maastricht Treaty* (1994), p. 215; McGoldrick, *International Relations of the European Union* (1997), Chaps. 2 and 8; and Macleod, Hendry and Hyett, *The External Relations of the European Communities* (1996). The following note is limited to the E.C.; it does not consider the European Coal and Steel Community or EURATOM, which may also make treaties.

[38] These include association agreements (Art. 238) and agreements on commercial policy (Art. 113) and the environment (Art. 130r(4)).

[39] Art. J.2, Treaty of European Union, *e.g.* sanctions against the SFRY: Council Decision 94/336/CFSP [1993] O.J. L165/1.

[40] Art. J.3, *id., e.g.* on the recognition of new states. Note that the power to recognise states remains with the individual Member States, which may act jointly through the E.U. See, *e.g.* the recognition of the republics of the former SFRY, below, p. 149.

[41] See Brownlie (1962) 11 I.C.L.Q. 701; Gormley, *The Procedural Status of the Individual before International and Supranational Tribunals* (1966); Higgins (1978) 4 B.J.I.S. 1; Korowicz (1956) 50 A.J.I.L. 533; Lauterpacht (1947) 63 L.Q.R. 438 and *ibid.* (1948) 64 L.Q.R. 97; Nørgaard, *The Position of the Individual in International Law* (1962).

[42] *Ed.* See below, p. 994.

number of other international instruments have recognised the procedural capacity of the individual. This was the case not only in the provisions of the Treaty of Versailles relating to the jurisdiction of the Mixed Arbitral Tribunals, but also in other treaties such as the Polish-German Convention of 1922 relating to Upper Silesia in which—as was subsequently held by the Upper Silesian Mixed Tribunal—the independent procedural status of individuals as claimants before an international agency was recognised even as against the State of which they were nationals.[43]

28. In the sphere of substantive law, the Permanent Court of International Justice recognised, in the advisory opinion relating to the postal service in Danzig,[44] that there is nothing in international law to prevent individuals from acquiring directly rights under a treaty provided that this is the intention of the contracting parties. A considerable number of decisions of municipal courts tendered subsequently to the advisory opinion of the Permanent Court expressly affirmed that possibility.

29. In the field of customary international law the enjoyment of benefits of international law by individuals as a matter of right followed from the doctrine, accepted by a growing number of countries, that generally recognised rules of the law of nations form part of the law of the land.[45] In the sphere of duties imposed by international law the principle that the obligations of international law bind individuals directly regardless of the law of their State and of any contrary order received from their superiors was proclaimed in the Charter annexed to the Agreement of 8 August 1945, providing for the setting up of the International Military Tribunal at Nürnberg as well as in the Charter of the International Military Tribunal at Tokyo of 19th January 1946.[46] That principle was fully affirmed in the judgment of the Nürnberg Tribunal as flowing from the imperative necessity of making international law effective. The Tribunal said: "Crimes against international law are committed by men, not by abstract entities, and only by punishing individuals who commit such crimes can the provisions of international law be enforced."[47] It was reaffirmed in the resolution of the General Assembly of 11 December, 1946,[48] expressing adherence to the principles of the Nürnberg Charter and Judgment. ...

30. On a different plane the Charter of the Nürnberg Tribunal—and the judgment which followed it—proclaimed the criminality of offences against humanity, *i.e.* of such offences against the fundamental rights of man to life and liberty, even if committed in obedience to the law of the

---

[43] *Ed.* See *Steiner and Gross v. Polish State* (1927–28) 4 A.D. 291.

[44] *Ed.* P.C.I.J.Rep., Series B, No. 11 (1925).

[45] *Ed.* See above, Chap. 3.

[46] *Ed.* See Woetzel, *The Nuremberg Trials in International Law* (1960) and Horwitz, *The Tokyo Trial*, Int. Conc. No. 465 (1950). On the Yugoslav Tribunal, see below, p. 748.

[47] *Ed.* (1947) 41 A.J.I.L. 221.

[48] *Ed.* G.A. Resn. 95(1), G.A.O.R., *Resolutions*, First Session, Part II, p. 188.

State.[49] To that extent, in a different sphere, positive law has recognised the individual as endowed, under international law, with rights the violation of which is a criminal act. The repeated provisions of the Charter of the United Nations in the matter of human rights and fundamental freedoms are directly relevant in this connection.[50]

Notes

1. The "procedural capacity of the individual" has more recently been recognised before the European Court of Justice[51] and in treaties on human rights.[52] The Iran–United States Claims Tribunal may hear claims brought directly by Iranian nationals against the United States and vice versa.[53] As to the arbitration facilities available for companies wishing to bring claims against states under the 1965 Convention on the Settlement of Investment Disputes between States and Nationals of Other States, see below, p. 586. For an example of a treaty imposing duties upon private persons, see the International Convention on Civil Liability for Oil Pollution Damage 1969.[54] Article 1 imposes strict liability for oil pollution on the ship's owner, usually a company.

2. For the most part, however, the individual remains an object, not a subject, of international law whose most important characteristic for international law purposes is his nationality. It is this, for example that determines which state (his national state) may protect him against the extravagances of another (if he is stateless normally no state may do so) and, more ominously, places him within the domestic jurisdiction, and hence the discretionary treatment, of his national state. It is nationality also that decides whether an individual can benefit from treaty guarantees that a state secures for its "nationals".

3. On the juridical nature of some kinds of agreements between states and large companies, see below, p. 578.

(iii) Other Entities

NANNI v. PACE AND THE SOVEREIGN ORDER OF MALTA

(1935–37) 8 A.D. 2. Italian Court of Cassation

The Order, the official title of which is the Sovereign Military Order of St. John of Jerusalem, of Rhodes, and of Malta, was established during the Crusades as a nursing brotherhood and military organisation directed against the Moslems. In 1309, the Order conquered the Island of Rhodes, which it then ruled until 1522 when it was ejected by the Ottoman Empire. In 1530, the Order moved to Malta which had been given to it by Emperor Charles V. This it ruled until 1798 when the island was taken by Napoleon. The Order established its headquarters in Rome in 1834. Since that time it has performed work of a humanitarian character for the poor and the sick. In the present case, which raised the question of the

---

[49] *Ed.* (1947) 41 A.J.I.L. 224.
[50] *Ed.* See below, p. 628.
[51] *Ed.* See, *inter alia*, Art. 173, 1957 Treaty of Rome.
[52] See below, Chap. 9.
[53] See below, p. 987, n. 14.
[54] U.K.T.S. 106 (1975), Cmnd. 6183; 973 U.N.T.S. 3; (1970) 9 I.L.M. 45. In force 1975. 97 parties, including the U.K.

personality of the Order in Italian law, the Court examined its history and status in international law.

Judgment of the Court

With the recognition of the Church and of the Byzantine Empire, the Order established, after the conquest of territory of its own, its independence and sovereignty. . . . The Grand Master was recognised as Sovereign Head of Rhodes with all the attributes of such a position, which included . . . the right of active and passive legation together with the right of negotiating directly with other States and of making conventions and treaties. . . . Such attributes of sovereignty and independence have not ceased, in the case of the Order, at the present day—at least not from the formal point of view in its relations with the Italian State. Nor has its personality in international law come to an end notwithstanding the fact that as a result of the British occupation of Malta such personality cannot be identified with the possession of territory. . . . With regard to this second aspect of the matter it is enough to point out that the modern theory of the subjects of international law recognises a number of collective units whose composition is independent of the nationality of their constituent members and whose scope transcends by virtue of their universal character the territorial confines of any single State. It must be admitted that only States can contribute to the formation of international law as an objective body of rules—States as international entities which are territorially identifiable. This is so because the fulfilment of this latter requirement makes them the principal objects and creators of such rules. But it is impossible to deny to other international collective units a limited capacity of acting internationally within the ambit and the actual exercise of their own functions with the resulting international juridical personality and capacity which is its necessary and natural corollary. In accordance with these doctrines, such personality was never denied to the Holy See even before the Lateran Treaty of February 11, 1929,[55] and it is unanimously conceded to the League of Nations, although it is neither a State, nor a super-State, nor a Confederation of States. It is equally conceded to certain international administrative unions.

Notes

1. The Order maintains diplomatic relations with over 40 states.[56] Is its practice as to, for example, the extent of diplomatic immunity relevant to the formation of customary international law in the way that state practice is? What about the practice of the United Nations with regard, for example, to treaties it has made with states or other public international organisations? Does that contribute to the customary international law of treaties?

[55] *Ed.* See now the 1984 Lateran Treaty (1985) 78 *Acta Apostolicae Sedis* 522.
[56] O'Connell (1976–77) 48 B.Y.I.L. 433. On the Order generally, see Farran (1954) 3 I.C.L.Q. 217 and (1955) 4 I.C.L.Q. 308. The U.K. does not maintain diplomatic relations with the Order.

2. *The Holy See and the Vatican City.* Graham[57] states:

> The view seems to be dominant today . . . that the Holy See does, in fact, enjoy international personality. Furthermore, this personality of the Holy See is distinct from the personality of the State of Vatican City. One is a non-territorial institution, and the other a state. The papacy as a religious organ is a subject of international law and capable of international rights and duties.
>
> . . . The fact that the Holy See is a non-territorial institution is no longer regarded as a reason for denying it international personality. The papacy can act in its own name in the international community. It can enter into legally binding conventions known as concordats. In the world of diplomacy the Pope enjoys the rights of active and passive legation. He can send and receive representatives who are public ministers in the sense of international law.

3. *The Palestine Liberation Movement (PLO).* More than 40 states accord *de jure* or *de facto* diplomatic status to local offices of the PLO.[58] The PLO is a member of the Arab League, the Non-Aligned Movement and the Group of 77.

5. RECOGNITION OF STATES AND GOVERNMENTS[59]

BRIERLY, THE LAW OF NATIONS

Waldock (6th ed., 1963), p. 138

The legal significance of recognition is controversial. According to one view it has a "constitutive" effect; through recognition only and exclusively a state becomes an international person and a subject of international law.[60] But there are serious difficulties in this view. The status of a state recognized by state A but not recognized by state B, and therefore apparently both an "international person" and not an "international person" at the same time, would be a legal curiosity. Perhaps a more substantial difficulty is that the doctrine would oblige us to say that an unrecognized state has neither rights nor duties at international law, and some of the consequences of accepting that conclusion might be startling. We should have to say, for example, that an intervention, otherwise illegal, would not have been illegal in Manchukuo,[61] or that if Manchukuo had been involved in war, she would have been under no legal obligation to respect the rights of neutrals. Non-recognition may certainly make the enforcement of rights and duties more difficult than it

---

[57] *Vatican Diplomacy: a Study of Church and State on the International Plane* (1959), pp. 186, 201. See also Kunz (1952) 46 A.J.I.L. 308.

[58] See the list in U.K.M.I.L. 1982; (1982) 53 B.Y.I.L. 356. On the international personality of national liberation movements generally, see Atlam, in Spinedi and Simma, eds., *United Nations Codification of State Responsibility* (1987), p. 35, pp. 43 *et seq.*

[59] See Blix (1970–II) 130 Hague Recueil 587; Briggs (1949) 43 A.J.I.L. 113; Brownlie (1982) 53 B.Y.I.L. 197; Chen, *The International Law of Recognition* (1951); Dugard, *Recognition and the United Nations* (1987) (states only); Jennings (1967—II) 121 Hague Recueil 323 at 346–368; Lauterpacht, *Recognition in International Law* (1947).

[60] Oppenheim, *International Law* (8th ed., 1955), Vol. 1, para. 71.

[61] *Ed.* see above, p. 109.

would otherwise be, but the practice of states does not support the view
that they have no legal existence before recognition.[62]

The better view is that the granting of recognition to a new state is not
a "constitutive" but a "declaratory" act; it does not bring into legal
existence a state which did not exist before. A state may exist without
being recognized, and if it does exist in fact, then, whether or not it has
been formally recognized by other states, it has a right to be treated by
them *as* a state. The primary function of recognition is to acknowledge as
a fact something which has hitherto been uncertain, namely the independence of the body claiming to be a state, and to declare the recognizing state's readiness to accept the normal consequences of that fact,
namely the usual courtesies of international intercourse. It is true that the
present state of the law makes it possible that different states should act
on different views of the application of the law to the same state of facts.
This does not mean that their differing interpretations are all equally
correct, but only that there exists at present no procedure for determining
which are correct and which are not. The constitutive theory of recognition gains most of its plausibility from the lack of centralized institutions
in the system, and it treats this lack not as an accident due to the stage of
development which the law has so far reached, but as an essential feature
of the system. It is in fact one more relic of absolutist theories of state
sovereignty.

In practice non-recognition does not always imply that the existence of
the unrecognized state is a matter of doubt. States have discovered that
the granting or withholding of recognition can be used to further a
national policy; they have refused it as a mark of disapproval, as nearly
all of them did to Manchukuo; and they have granted it in order to
establish the very independence of which recognition is supposed to be a
mere acknowledgement, as when in 1903 the United States recognized
Panama only three days after it had revolted from Colombia or when in
1948 the United States recognized Israel within a few hours of its proclamation of independence.[63]

Notes

1. The declaratory theory is adopted by most modern writers. It is also supported by arbitral practice. In particular, the *Tinoco Arbitration*, below, p. 160,
suggests that recognition is simply evidence (to be discounted if politically

---

[62] See on this point Jaffé, *Judicial Aspects of Foreign Relations*, p. 98. When Jewish airmen shot
down British aeroplanes over Egypt in January 1949 the British Government at once
informed the government of the Jewish state, which at that time Britain had not recognized, that they would demand compensation.

[63] In regard to the recognition of Israel, Mr W. R. Austin, the representative of the United
States on the Security Council, asserted the political character of the act of recognition in
the most unequivocal terms: "I should regard it as highly improper for me to admit that
any country on earth can question the sovereignty of the United States of America in the
exercise of that high political act of recognition of the *de facto* status of a state. Moreover,
I would not admit here, by implication or by direct answer, that there exists a tribunal of
justice or of any other kind, anywhere, that can pass upon the legality or the validity of
that act of my country" (*New York Times*, May 19, 1948).

biased) that the international law requirements are met. State practice confirms this in the sense that states do not refrain from bringing claims under international law against unrecognised states or governments.[64] The Arbitral Commission of the E.C. Conference on Yugoslavia was of the opinion that recognition of states by other states was "purely declaratory"[65] in effect, although it did "confer certain rights and obligations under international law".[66] An entity that is not recognised by other states will, for example, not have the rights and obligations in the law of state immunity and will have difficulty functioning in the international community if it is not admitted to international organisations. Although the extract from Brierly is expressed in terms only of the recognition of states, it is clear that the declaratory theory applies to the recognition of governments too. The United Kingdom used formerly to take the view that there was a legal duty to grant recognition to a state or government when the necessary requirements were met.[67] This approach, which is not repeated in the 1980 British statement on the recognition of governments, below, p. 155, never found favour with other states.[68] The position would seem to be that recognition is a discretionary act[69] with evidential value in law.

2. On May 30, 1967, Biafra declared its independence of Nigeria, of which it had constituted the Eastern Region. Its war of independence was unsuccessful and Biafra surrendered to the Nigerian Federal Government on January 12, 1970. It is now once again fully a part of Nigeria. Five States—Tanzania, Gabon, Ivory Coast, Zambia and Haiti—recognised it as an independent state during the

[64] See the example given by Brierly, n. 62, above, and the U.S. response to the seizure of the *Pueblo* by North Korea, which the U.S. did not recognise, below, p. 436. In 1957 the U.K. claimed compensation from the unrecognised Taiwan Government for damage done to British vessels by its forces: see C.P.U.K.I.L. 1957 (1957) 6 I.C.L.Q. 507. In 1954, the U.S. claimed under international law against the unrecognised Government of the Chinese People's Republic for the killing of U.S. nationals when a commercial aircraft was shot down by a Chinese military aircraft: see 2 Whiteman 651. Arab states regard Israel as governed by international law although they do not (except for Egypt since 1979) recognise it as a state.

[65] *Opinion No. 1*, above, p. 123.

[66] *Opinion No. 8*, above, p. 125.

[67] See the 1951 Morrison statement of British practice on the recognition of governments, below, p. 157. This statement was influenced by Lauterpacht, *op. cit.*, p. 144, n. 59 above, p. 6, who argued that there was a duty on the part of states to grant recognition in the absence of an international body competent to do so. Lauterpacht also thought that recognition so granted was constitutive. This view was not clearly adopted in the 1951 statement. In 1948, the U.K. adopted a declaratory approach in the UN with respect to the recognition of states: " . . . the existence of a state should not be regarded as depending upon recognition but on whether in fact it fulfils the conditions which create a duty for recognition"; U.N. Doc. A/CN.4/2, p. 53, quoted in Crawford, *op. cit.*, p. 102, n. 1, p. 16.

[68] See, *e.g.* Mr Austin's statement above, n. 63. *cf.* the following statement by the UN Secretariat when considering the question of the representation of members in the UN (U.N. Doc. S/1466; S.C.O.R., 5th Year, Supp. for Jan/May 1950, p. 19): "The recognition of a new state, or a new government of an existing state, is a unilateral act which the recognizing government can grant or withhold. It is true that some legal writers have argued forcibly that when a new government, which comes into power through revolutionary means, enjoys, with a reasonable prospect of permanency, the habitual obedience of the bulk of the population, other states are under a legal duty to recognize it. However, while states may regard it as desirable to follow certain legal principles in according or withholding recognition, the practice of States shows that the act of recognition is still regarded as essentially a political decision, which each state decides in accordance with its own free appreciation of the situation."

[69] *cf. Opinion No. 10*, Arbitration Commission, E.C. Conference on Yugoslavia, below, p. 152.

rebellion, although no state entered into formal diplomatic relations. What effect did these recognitions have in law according to the declaratory and constitutive theories?[70]

3. *Modes of recognition.* Recognition of states or of governments may occur expressly or by implication. There is no precise catalogue of acts that imply recognition.[71] Entry into diplomatic relations clearly implies it, as, normally, does the making of a bilateral treaty arranging for commercial or other relations or support for a state's admission to the United Nations.[72] The crucial question is that of intention. Participation in an international conference with a state or government will not indicate recognition if it is made clear that it is not intended to have this effect. Thus, in 1954, when the Foreign Ministers of France, the United Kingdom, the United States and the USSR proposed the Geneva Conference to discuss Korea and Indochina and invited the Government of the People's Republic of China, the two Koreas and "other interested states", they added: "It is understood that neither the invitation to, nor the holding of, the above mentioned conference shall be deemed to imply diplomatic recognition in any case where it has not already been accorded."[73]

E.C. GUIDELINES ON THE RECOGNITION OF NEW STATES IN EASTERN EUROPE AND IN THE SOVIET UNION

December 16, 1991. U.K.M.I.L. 1991, (1991) 62 B.Y.I.L. 559.

In compliance with the European Council's request, Ministers have assessed developments in Eastern Europe and in the Soviet Union with a view to elaborating an approach regarding relations with new States.

In this connection they adopted the following guidelines on the formal recognition of new States in Eastern Europe and in the Soviet Union:

The Community and its Member States confirm their attachment to the principles of the Helsinki Final Act and the Charter of Paris, in particular the principle of self-determination. They affirm their readiness to recognise, subject to the normal standards of international practice and the political realities in each case, those new States which, following the historic changes in the region, have constituted themselves on a democratic basis, have accepted the appropriate international obligations and have committed themselves in good faith to a peaceful process and to negotiations.

[70] See Ijalaye (1971) 65 A.J.I.L. 551.

[71] Apparently, even the sale of blankets may suffice. In 1962, the question arose of the sale to the Republican Government to the Yemen, which had recently come into being by revolution and which had not been recognised by the British Government, of 50,000 surplus blankets. The Lord Privy Seal stated in Parliament: "We could not sell them to the Yemeni republican authorities without recognizing the republican government": *Hansard*, H.C. Vol. 669, cols. 1253–1254, December 19, 1962; C.P.U.K.I.L. 1962, p. 152.

[72] *e.g.* the U.K.'s support for the UN admission of the Democratic People's Republic of Korea "meant that we also now recognise ... (it) as a state, but we have no plans to establish diplomatic relations": Parliamentary Under-Secretary of State, FCO, *Hansard*, H.C., col. 156, October 16, 1991.

[73] Communiqué on the 1954 Berlin Conference dated February 18, 1954, *Documents on American Foreign Relations* (1954), p. 219.

Therefore, they adopt a common position on the process of recognition of these new States, which requires:

—respect for the provisions of the Charter of the United Nations and the commitments subscribed to in the Final Act of Helsinki and in the Charter of Paris, especially with regard to the rule of law, democracy and human rights;

—guarantees for the rights of ethnic and national groups and minorities in accordance with the commitments subscribed to in the framework of the CSCE:

—respect for the inviolability of all frontiers which can only be changed by peaceful means and by common agreement:

—acceptance of all relevant commitments with regard to disarmament and nuclear non-proliferation as well as to security and regional stability:

—commitment to settle by agreement, including where appropriate by recourse to arbitration, all questions concerning state succession and regional disputes.

The Community and its Member States will not recognise entities which are the result of aggression. They would take account of the effects of recognition on neighbouring States.

The commitment to these principles opens the way to recognition by the Community and its Member States and to the establishment of diplomatic relations. It could be laid down in agreements.

Notes

1. Applying these Guidelines,[74] the E.C. and its Member States recognised as states eleven of the fifteen republics of the former USSR[75] The three Baltic states of Estonia, Latvia and Lithuania that had also been USSR republics were recognised by the E.C. and its Member States before the Guidelines were adopted.[76] The Russian Federation is accepted by the United Kingdom "as the continuing state of the Soviet Union", and hence succeeds to the rights and duties of the former USSR.[77]

The 1991 Guidelines were also applied to the states that emerged from the Socialist Federal Republic of Yugoslavia: see below, p. 149.

2. The Guidelines have in mind the Montevideo Convention requirements of statehood when they refer to "the normal standards of international practice and the political realities in each case".[78] The conditions of respect for the rights of

---

[74] On the Guidelines, see Müllerson, *International Law, Rights and Politics* (1994), Chap. 4; Rich (1993) 4 E.J.I.L. 36; Warbrick (1992) 41 I.C.L.Q. 473.

[75] See the E.C. Ministerial Statement of December 31, 1991, U.K.M.I.L 1993, (1991) 62 B.Y.I.L. 561. Another recognition condition was that those republics that had nuclear weapons on their territory would adhere to the Nuclear Non-Proliferation Treaty: *ibid.* Armenia, Azerbaijan, Belarus, Kazakhstan, Moldova, Turkmenistan, Ukraine and Uzbekistan were recognised in 1991. Georgia, the Kyrgyz Republic and Tajikstan were recognised in 1992 after they had given the required assurances.

[76] See the E.C. Ministerial Declaration of August 27, 1991, (1991) 62 B.Y.I.L. 558. The E.C. acted immediately after the Russian Federation had recognised the Baltic states.

[77] Secretary of State FCO (Mr Hurd), *Hansard*, H.C. Vol. 203, col. 384, January 24, 1994; Minister of State, FCO, *id.*, Vol. 202, W.A. col. 9, January 20, 1992.

[78] The "political realities" are those that answer the question whether the claimant state has a government with effective control over its territory.

minorities, the inviolability of borders, etc., go beyond the legal requirements of statehood in the Montevideo Convention. They were not intended to be additional legal requirements of statehood. Instead they are political conditions,[79] with recognition being used as a force to achieve political objectives.[80] This is a departure from previous statements of United Kingdom practice on the recognition of states, which generally focus on the Montevideo Convention requirements.[81] The title to the Guidelines limits them geographically. No mention was made of them when Eritrea was recognised by the United Kingdom as a state in 1993.[82]

E.C. DECLARATION ON YUGOSLAVIA

December 16, 1991. U.K.M.I.L. 1991, (1991) 62 B.Y.I.L. 559.

The European Community and its Member States discussed the situation in Yugoslavia in the light of their guidelines on the recognition of new States in Eastern Europe and in the Soviet Union. They adopted a common position with regard to the recognition of Yugoslav Republics. In this connection they concluded the following:

The Community and its Member States agree to recognise the independence of all the Yugoslav Republics fulfilling all the conditions set out below. The implementation of this decision will take place on January 15, 1992.

They are therefore inviting all Yugoslav Republics to state by 23 December 23 whether:

—they wish to be recognised as independent
—they accept the commitments contained in the above-mentioned guidelines.
—they accept the provisions laid down in the draft convention[83]— especially those in Chapter II on human rights and rights of national or ethnic groups—under consideration by the Conference on Yugoslavia.
—they continue to support the efforts of the Secretary General and the Security Council of the United Nations, and the continuation of the Conference on Yugoslavia.

[79] But compliance with the principle of self-determination may be a legal requirement of statehood: see the *Southern Rhodesia* case, above, p. 111.

[80] But see *Opinion No. 10*, E.C. Commission, below, p. 152.

[81] The conditions in the Guidelines were a French initiative. Note that some instances of U.K. non-recognition (*e.g.* the non-recognition of East Germany until 1973) have had political overtones.

[82] See the letters sent by the Prime Minister and Foreign and Commonwealth Secretary to the Eritrean Provisional Government on May 14 and 17, 1993, U.K.M.I.L 1993, (1993) 64 B.Y.I.L. 602.

[83] *Ed.* This was an E.C. Conference Draft Convention of November 4, 1991 that proposed terms for the settlement of the Yugoslav crisis. It was never adopted.

The application of those Republics which reply positively will be submitted through the chair of the Conference to the Arbitration Commission for advice before the implementation date. . . .

The Community and its Member States also require a Yugoslav Republic to commit itself, prior to recognition, to adopt constitutional and political guarantees ensuring that it has no territorial claims towards a neighbouring Community State and that it will conduct no hostile propaganda activities versus a neighbouring Community State, including the use of a denomination which implies territorial claims.

Notes

1. The question of the recognition of new states in the Balkans arose out of the disintegration of the Socialist Federal Republic of Yugoslavia (SFRY) which had been established after the Second World War.[84] The SFRY was composed of six republics: Bosnia-Hercegovina, Croatia, Macedonia, Montenegro, Serbia and Slovenia. After the death of President Tito in 1980, tension developed between Serbia and other republics, with Croatia and Slovenia, in particular, complaining of increasing Serbian dominance of the SFRY and seeking greater devolved powers. In June 1991, Croatia and Slovenia declared their independence. Civil war then broke out between the federal army (JNA) and Slovenian and Croatian forces in the territory of the two republics.

Fighting ended in Slovenia in July 1991 when the SFRY presidency ordered the withdrawal of JNA troops from its territory. Fighting continued in Croatia, with the JNA troops being joined by the irregular forces of the Serbian ethnic minority in Croatia. On January 3, 1992, a UN ceasefire was endorsed by Croatia and by Serbian leaders in Belgrade. As part of a UN Security Council peacekeeping plan, a small UN advance force (UNMLO) arrived in Croatia on January 14, to prepare the way for a UN Protection Force (UNPROFOR), which arrived in Croatia in March 1992 with a mandate to secure peace.[85] Sporadic violations of the cease-fire between JNA/ethnic Serbian and Croatian forces continued to occur in parts of Croatia from January until some time after the arrival of UNPROFOR forces.[86]

As regards Bosnia-Hercegovina, fighting broke out on ethnic lines after the February/March 1992 referendum in which Muslims and Croats voted overwhelmingly for independence.[87] Fighting became worse during April 1992 and continued thereafter until the ceasefire prior to the Dayton Agreement in 1995.

2. The E.C. Declaration on Yugoslavia was adopted on the same day as the general E.C. Guidelines on the Recognition of New States in Eastern Europe and in the Soviet Union, above, p. 147, to which the Declaration refers. The Declaration was preceded by *Opinion No. 1* of the Arbitration Commission of the E.C. Conference on Yugoslavia[88] in which the Arbitration Commission expressed the opinion that the SFRY was "in the process of dissolution". It was in the light of this *Opinion* that the E.C. and its Member States took the unusual step in the Declaration of inviting republics within the SFRY to apply for recognition as states. Applications for recognition were made by Croatia and Slovenia, which

---

[84] The SFRY succeeded the Kingdom of the Serbs, Croats and Slovenes, which had been established in 1918 by the merger of provinces of the former Austro-Hungarian Empire (mainly Slovenia, Croatia, Bosnia-Hercegovina) with the Kingdom of the Serbs.

[85] See S.C.Resn 743 (1992), S.C.O.R., 47th Year. *Resolutions and Decisions*, p. 8.

[86] On later developments, see below, p. 922.

[87] On the referendum, see below, p. 151, n. 93.

[88] Above, p. 123. On the Arbitration Commission and the E.C. Conference on Yugoslavia, see above, p. 126.

had already declared their independence, and by Bosnia-Hercegovenia and Macedonia.[89] These applications were referred to the Arbitration Commission, which, on January 11, 1992, expressed the opinion that Slovenia and Macedonia complied with the Guidelines and the Declaration on Yugoslavia, but that Croatia and Bosnia-Hercegovina did not.[90] The Arbitration Commission did not apply the Montevideo Convention requirements on statehood.[91] On January 15, 1992, the E.C. and Member States recognised Slovenia and Croatia.[92] They recognised Bosnia-Hercegovina on April 7, 1992[93] and the Former Yugoslav Republic of Macedonia April 8, 1993.[94]

Was the recognition of Croatia and Bosnia-Hercegovina in accordance with the Montevideo Convention requirements of statehood? The Minister of State, FCO, justified United Kingdom recognition of Croatia as follows[95]:

> The criteria are that a country should have a clearly defined territory with a population; a Government with a prospect of retaining control; and independence in its foreign relations. These criteria are always subject to interpretation in the light of circumstances on the ground. In this case we and our E.C. partners recognised Croatia on the basis of advice from the arbitration commission that Croatia largely fulfilled the guidelines on recognition adopted last December. . . . We also took account of additional undertakings from the Croatian Government on minorities legislation.

The recognition of Bosnia-Hercegovina was justified similarly[96]:

---

[89] Applications were also made, unsuccessfully, by Krajina (a Serbian enclave in Croatia) and Kosovo (a mostly ethnically Albanian autonomous region of Serbia).

[90] *Opinions Nos. 4–7*, 92 I.L.R 173 *et seq.* (1992). Croatia had not incorporated all of the specified human and minorities' rights into its constitution (to protect mostly Croatian Serbs) and Bosnia-Hercegovina had not determined the "will of the people" on independence.

[91] On the Commission's application of the principle of self-determination, see *Opinion No. 2*, above, p. 120.

[92] Germany had already unilaterally recognised Croatia and Slovenia on December 23, 1991. On January 15, 1992, Croatia undertook to comply with all of the obligations in the Draft E.C. Convention on Yugoslavia, and later amended its Constitution, although these amendments did not fully comply with the E.C. Draft Convention: *Observations on Croatian Constitutional Law*, Arbitration Commission, Conference on Yugoslavia, (1992) 92 I.L.R. 209.

[93] This was after Bosnia-Hercegovena had held a referendum in which over 99 per cent of those voting opted for independence. The 31 per cent ethnic Serbian population boycotted the referendum.

[94] Recognition was implied by support by the U.K. and other E.C. states for the Former Yugoslav Republic of Macedonia's UN membership in the General Assembly on that date.

[95] *Hansard*, H.C., Vol. 203, W.A., col. 191, February 5, 1995. The Secretary of State, FCO, (Mr Hurd) later said: "No one could seriously suggest that we could have gone on pretending that the old Yugoslavia still existed . . . the reality was that Croatia existed. Whether it should have been recognised in the autumn, which is what the Germans wanted, or at the end of the year, which is what happened, or a little later, is a matter of dispute . . . " : *id.*, Vol. 259, col. 332. May 3, 1995.

[96] Mr Hogg, FCO Minister of State, H.C. Foreign Affairs Committee, Parliamentary Papers, 1992–3, H.C. Paper 235–iii, p. 88, December 2, 1992. Earlier, he had explained the situation as follows: " . . . if we recognise Bosnia, there will be the substantial risk that the Serbs will fight . . . if we do not recognise Bosnia we will, in a sense, neglect the fact that we encouraged them to hold a referendum to determine their view, and what would be the view of the Croats and the Muslims who clearly want independence . . . It will be extraordinarily difficult to withhold recognition for any extended period": *Hansard*, H.C. Vol. 205, col. 489, March 5, 1992.

I do not think that the recognition of Bosnia is premature, in the sense that a referendum was held within Bosnia which was a sufficient basis for recognition, and Bosnia complied with all the requirements that were established by Mr Badinter and within the E.C. I think that it was a state that we had to recognise, applying ordinary criteria, in the same way that we recognised both Slovenia and Croatia.

As to Macedonia, SFRY forces withdrew from its territory on March 26, 1992. The delay in recognising it until April 1993 was the result of Greek concerns that the intended use of the historic Greek name of "Macedonia"[97] implied designs on Greek territory across the border. After persistent Greek objection, Macedonia was recognised following amendments to its constitution to indicate its absence of territorial ambition and the change of its name to the "Former Yugoslav Republic of Macedonia".[98]

Generally, it would seem that in the search for a settlement of the Yugoslav crisis, the political consequences of recognition or non-recognition, rather than the legal requirements of statehood, played the crucial role in Balkan recognition decisions.[99] Note, however, that *Opinion No. 10* of the E.C. Commission, below, supposes certain legal limits to the recognition of states.

OPINION NO. 10

Arbitration Commission, E.C. Conference on Yugoslavia: Badinter, Chairman; Corosaniti, Herzog, Petry, Tomas y Valiente, members. July 4, 1992. 92 I.L.R. 206.

Opinion of the Commission

On 18 May 1992 the Chairman of the Arbitration Commission received a letter from Lord Carrington, Chairman of the Conference for Peace in Yugoslavia, asking for the Commission's opinion on the following question:

In terms of international law, is the Federal Republic of Yugoslavia a new State calling for recognition by the Member States of the European Community in accordance with the joint statement on Yugoslavia and the Guidelines on the Recognition of new States in Eastern Europe and in the Soviet Union adopted by the Council of the European Communities on 16 December 1991? . . .

[97] The final paragraph of the E.C. Declaration on Yugoslavia, above, p. 149, reflected Greece's concerns in this regard.

[98] See Craven (1995) 15 A.Y.I.L. 1.

[99] *e.g.* Mr Hogg, FCO Minister of State stated: " . . . Croatia does not . . . satisfy the [legal] criteria for recognition, but that . . . is a procedural point . . . The essential question . . . to be addressed is the question of minority rights . . . one of the major levers that we have in order to get people to address fully and properly [this question] . . . is recognition": F.C.A., 1st Report, *Central and Eastern Europe: Problems of the Post-Communist Era*, Vol. II, Minutes of Evidence, H.C. Session 1991–92, p. 59.

1. As the Arbitration Commission found in *Opinion No. 8*,[1] the answer to this question very much depends on that to Question No. 2 from the Chairman of the Conference.

In *Opinion No. 8*, the Arbitration Commission concluded that the dissolution of the Socialist Federal Republic of Yugoslavia ("SFRY") was complete and that none of the resulting entities could claim to be the sole successor to the SFRY.

2. On 27 April this year Montenegro and Serbia decided to establish a new entity bearing the name "Federal Republic of Yugoslavia" and adopted its constitution.

The Arbitration Commission feels that, within the frontiers constituted by the administrative boundaries of Montenegro and Serbia in the SFRY, the new entity meets the criteria of international public law for a State, which were listed in *Opinion No. 1* of 29 November 1991.[2] However, as Resolution 757 (1992) of the UN Security Council points out, "the claim by the Federal Republic of Yugoslavia (Serbia and Montenegro) to continue automatically (the membership) of the former Socialist Federal Republic of Yugoslavia (in the United Nations) has not been generally accepted". As the Arbitration Commission points out in its *Ninth Opinion*,[3] the FRY is actually a new State and could not be the sole successor to the SFRY.

3. This means that the FRY (Serbia and Montenegro) does not *ipso facto* enjoy the recognition enjoyed by the SFRY under completely different circumstances. It is therefore for other States, where appropriate, to recognize the new State.

4. As, however, the Arbitration Commission pointed out in *Opinion No. 1*, while recognition is not a prerequisite for the foundation of a State and is purely declaratory in its impact, it is nonetheless a discretionary act that other States may perform when they choose and in a manner of their own choosing, subject only to compliance with the imperatives of general international law, and particularly those prohibiting the use of force in dealings with other States or guaranteeing the rights of ethnic, religious or linguistic minorities.

Furthermore, the Community and its Member States, in their joint statement of 16 December 1991 on Yugoslavia and the Guidelines, adopted the same day, on the recognition of new States in Eastern Europe and in the Soviet Union, has set out the conditions for the recognition of the Yugoslav republics.

5. Consequently, the opinion of the Arbitration Commission is that:

—the FRY (Serbia and Montenegro) is a new State which cannot be considered the sole successor to the SFRY;

[1] *Ed.* Above, p. 125.
[2] *Ed.* Above, p. 123.
[3] *Ed.* 92 I.L.R. 203.

—its recognition by the Member States of the European Community would be subject to its compliance with the conditions laid down by general international law for such an act and the joint statement and Guidelines of 16 December 1991.

Notes

The E.U. and its Member States have not recognised the FRY as a state. Nor is the FRY a UN member: see above, p. 129. Although *Opinion No. 10* regards recognition as a discretionary act, it supposes certain international law limits to the freedom to recognise states (use of force, rights of minorities).[4]

BRITISH AND U.S. PRACTICE ON THE RECOGNITION OF STATES

Notes

1. *British practice.* In 1986, in response to a question concerning the non-recognition of Bophuthatswana, the Minister of State, Foreign and Commonwealth Office, replied:

> The normal criteria which the Government apply for recognition as a State are that it should have, and seem likely to continue to have, a clearly defined territory with a population, a Government who are able of themselves to exercise effective control of that territory, and independence in their external relations. Other factors, including some United Nations resolutions, may also be relevant.[5]

In a later debate, the Minister of State explained why Bophuthatswana did not qualify:

> Bophuthatswana is a collection of several separate pieces of territory—now six—said to form an independent state. . . . the fragmentation of the territory of Bophuthatswana within South Africa, the pattern of the population and the economic dependence on South Africa more than justify our refusal to recognise Bophuthatswana. One of our criteria is that the territory should be clearly defined, which has not been the case.[6]

In 1988, the Foreign Secretary modified this approach, emphasising *apartheid*[7]:

> Bophuthatswana's fragmentary nature is only one reason why no country thought it right to recognise its independence. That country is financially dependent on South Africa. The very existence of Bophuthatswana is a consequence of apartheid, and I think that that is the principal reason why recognition has not been forthcoming.

[4] As to the precipitate recognition of states on Montevideo Convention grounds, see Oppenheim, Vol. I, p. 143. As to the duty not to recognise the acquisition of statehood by the use of force, see also the *Northern Cyprus* case, above, p. 112.

[5] *Hansard*, H.C., Vol. 102, W.A., col. 977. October 23, 1986; U.K.M.I.L. 1986; (1986) 57 B.Y.I.L. 507. For a relevant UN resolutions, see above, p. 110.

[6] *Hansard*. H.C., Vol. 105, col. 100, November 12, 1986; U.K.M.I.L. 1986; (1986) 57 B.Y.I.L. 507.

[7] *Hansard*, H.C., Vol. 126, col. 760–61, February 3, 1988; U.K.M.I.L. 1988; (1988) 59 B.Y.I.L. 436–37.

Other entities which are not recognised as states by the United Kingdom are the Saharwi Arab Democratic Republic,[8] the Turkish Republic of Northern Cyprus[9] and Taiwan.[10]

2. *U.S. Practice.* In 1976 the United States Department of State stated[11]:

> In the view of the United States, international law does not require a state to recognise another entity as a state; it is a matter for the judgment of each state whether an entity merits recognition as a state. In reaching this judgment, the United States has traditionally looked to the establishment of certain facts. These facts include effective control over a clearly-defined territory and population; and organised governmental administration of that territory; and a capacity to act effectively to conduct foreign relations and to fulfill international obligations. The United States has also taken into account whether the entity in question has attracted the recognition of the international community of states.

BRITISH PRACTICE ON THE RECOGNITION OF GOVERNMENTS[12]

Statement by the Foreign Secretary (Lord Carrington), Hansard, H.L., Vol. 408, cols. 1121–1122. April 28, 1980; U.K.M.I.L. 1980, (1980) 51 B.Y.I.L. 367. cf. the statement by the Lord Privy Seal (Sir Ian Gilmour), ibid. H.C., Vol. 983, cols. 277–279.

... we have conducted a re-examination of British policy and practice concerning the recognition of Governments. This has included a comparison with the practice of our partners and allies. On the basis of this review we have decided that we shall no longer accord recognition to Governments. The British Government recognise States in accordance with common international doctrine.

Where an unconstitutional change of régime takes place in a recognised State, Governments of other States must necessarily consider what dealings, if any, they should have with the new régime, and whether and to what extent it qualifies to be treated as the Government of the State concerned. Many of our partners and allies take the position that they do not recognise Governments and that therefore no question of recognition arises in such cases. By contrast, the policy of successive British Governments has been that we should make and announce a decision formally "recognising" the new Government.

---

[8] See above, p. 119.

[9] See above, p. 112.

[10] Taiwan does not claim to be a state: see above, p. 104. The U.K. Government "acknowledge the position of the People's Republic of China ... that Taiwan is a province of China. We recognise the Government of the People's Republic of China as the sole legal government of China": Mr Goodlad, Minister of State, FCO, *Hansard*, H.C., Vol. 238, col. 936, March 2, 1994.

[11] (1978) 72 A.J.I.L. 337.

[12] See Davidson, (1981) 32 N.I.L.Q. 22; Dixon (1988) 22 Int. Lawyer 555; Symmons [1981] P.L. 249; Talmon (1992) 63 B.Y.I.L. 231; Warbrick (1981) 30 I.C.L.Q. 568.

This practice has sometimes been misunderstood, and, despite explanations to the contrary, our "recognition" interpreted as implying approval. For example, in circumstances where there might be legitimate public concern about the violation of human rights by the new régime, or the manner in which it achieved power, it has not sufficed to say that an announcement of "recognition" is simply a neutral formality.

We have therefore concluded that there are practical advantages in following the policy of many other countries in not according recognition to Governments. Like them, we shall continue to decide the nature of our dealings with régimes which come to power unconstitutionally in the light of our assessment of whether they are able of themselves to exercise effective control of the territory of the State concerned, and seem likely to continue to do so.

Notes

1. This statement is concerned solely with the recognition of new revolutionary governments in existing states. Governments that come into office constitutionally (*e.g.* by election) in existing states require no recognition in international law. New states (and hence their governments) will, as the statement indicates, continue to be recognised expressly, or formally, "in accordance with common international doctrine." The effect of the statement is that the United Kingdom has abandoned the practice of expressly recognising revolutionary governments. The Foreign Secretary's statement and other parliamentary pronouncements say, in keeping with the universal trend towards minimising the role of recognition, that Governments will not be recognised at all. It seems more accurate to regard the move as one from express to implied recognition.[13] The new approach is reminiscent of the Estrada doctrine[14] adopted by Mexico in the 1930s and is in line with the practice of an increasing number of other states, including the United States and E.U. states.[15] Galloway[16] summarises state practice as follows:

> In each region [of the world] the movement is towards de-emphasizing or completely eliminating the recognition issue. However, it is doubtful that the recognition question will be eliminated in the foreseeable future because, in a significant minority of cases, nations consider the political factors strong enough to make an issue of recognition. This desire to de-emphasize recognition in the majority of cases has resulted in the adherence of over thirty states to the Estrada Doctrine, but with the proviso that in certain situations they grant recognition based on political considerations.[17] The desire to de-emphasize recognition also affects the adherence of well over thirty other states to an ad hoc policy based on political considerations in which recognition is usually downplayed and finessed by the euphemism that relations are continuing, or that relations are being resumed. Taken together, the two approaches account for over 75 of the states included in this study.

[13] See, however, the *Woodhouse* case, below, p. 162.
[14] See 2 Whiteman 85.
[15] On U.S. practice, see below, p. 159.
[16] *Recognizing Foreign Governments* (1978), p. 138. See also Peterson (1983) 77 A.J.I.L. 31, who argues that revolutionary governments should continue to be recognised. See also Nomura (1982) 25 Jap. Ann. I.L. 67 and Ando (1985) 28, *ibid.* 29.
[17] *Ed.* See the express U.S. recognition of the Chinese Government in 1979, below, p. 160.

2. The 1980 statement does not basically change the criteria upon which the United Kingdom had previously relied in deciding whether to recognise a government and which will continue to be relied upon when deciding whether to have "dealings" with it. These were stated by the Foreign Secretary (Mr Morrison) in 1951:

> . . . The conditions under international law for the recognition of a new régime as the *de facto* Government of a State are that the new régime has in fact effective control over most of the State's territory and that this control seems likely to continue. The conditions for the recognition of a new régime as the *de jure* Government of a State are that the new régime should not merely have effective control over most of the State's territory, but that it should, in fact, be firmly established. His Majesty's Government consider that recognition should be accorded when the conditions specified by international law are, in fact, fulfilled and that recognition should not be given when these conditions are not fulfilled. The recognition of a Government *de jure* or *de facto* should not depend on whether the character of the régime is such as to command His Majesty's Government's approval.[18]

The effectiveness of a government is, of course, a *sine qua non* of recognition of an entity as the government of a state; recognition of an entity before it has become effective is "precipitate" and intervention in a state's affairs contrary to international law.

3. The 1980 statement differs from that of 1951 in that (i) there is no suggestion of any duty to recognise; (ii) there is no mention of *de jure* and *de facto* governments; and (iii) the words "of themselves" (*i.e.* without outside assistance) are added. The question of the recognition of a government as the *de facto* government only arises where there are two competing governments in being. In most cases, the situation is quickly resolved and the question is simply one of recognising the revolutionary government as the new government if the revolution has succeeded. Even where the struggle continues for some time, the United Kingdom has tended in recent years to wait until matters have sorted themselves out rather than grant interim recognition to a revolutionary movement as the *de facto* government of the territory it controls. Thus in the case of Cambodia in the 1970s, the only step taken was to withdraw recognition from the established government as the *de jure* government and grant it to the revolutionary Pol Pot Government in 1976 once the latter had reached the capital and was in full control. The latter was not recognised as a *de facto* government as it gradually gained control of the countryside. It seems likely that, where two governments remain in being, the United Kingdom will henceforth have "dealings" with only one government, even though another government is in control of a part of the state's territory. The words "of themselves" in the 1980 statement reflect a later stage in the Cambodian case, as does the passage in the statement about the "violation of human rights" and the possibility of misunderstandings. The Pol Pot Government, which had ill-treated the Cambodian population badly, was replaced by force in 1979 by the Heng Samrin Government with the military assistance of Vietnam. In October 1979, the British Government declined to withdraw recognition from the former and to recognise the latter instead. It declined to do so (even though it acknowledged that the latter had "control of the greater part of the territory of Cambodia") for the reason that there was "no other Government which satisfies the criteria for recognition which have been applied by successive British Governments." This would seem to have been a reference to the dependence of the Heng

---

[18] *Hansard*, H.C., Vol. 485, cols. 2410–2411 March 21, 1951. For further evidence of the adoption of an "effectiveness" test in state practice, see Bundu (1978) 27 I.C.L.Q. 18.

Samrin Government upon Vietnamese support. The British Government stressed that its continued recognition of Pol Pot was not to be taken as "approval of . . . the enormity of Pol Pot's human rights violations."[19] By December, the position had changed:

> When we came to power last May, Pol Pot's Government held a dwindling proportion of the territory in Cambodia. Since September that proportion has further dwindled though of course Pol Pot's forces continue to resist. As the House is aware, our normal criteria require us to accord recognition to a Government who enjoy, with a reasonable prospect of permanence, the obedience of the mass of the population and the effective control of much the greater part of the country. . . .
>
> It will therefore come as no surprise to the House if I say that we can no longer regard Pol Pot as leading an effective Government in Cambodia. By the same token, however, the dependence of the so-called Heng Samrin régime on the Vietnamese occupation army is complete; there is no reason to doubt that without the presence of the occupation troops it would be swept away by resurgent Cambodian nationalism. I therefore make it very clear that we emphatically do not recognise any claim by Heng Samrin. Our position is that there is no Government in Cambodia whom we can recognise. This position is shared by the United States and by some of our leading friends in Europe.[20]

4. Despite the United Kingdom's adoption of a "face the facts" approach, it may sometimes have been swayed by politics in its judgment.[21] It was noticeable that the United Kingdom recognised the new Obote Government in Uganda in 1979 while the Tanzanian troops that had brought it to power were still in the country, when at the same time the Heng Samrin Government in Cambodia was refused recognition because of Vietnamese support.[22]

5. In practice, the question of the recognition of governments that have come into being by unconstitutional means in existing states is more common than that of the recognition of new states. As far as the first question is concerned, it is important to distinguish between recognition of a government as the government that can act for a state for international law purposes and entry into diplomatic relations with that government. The latter implies the former, but the former does not require the latter. A not uncommon situation is that in which one government terminates its diplomatic relations with another as an act of retorsion.[23] This by itself does not affect recognition.

---

[19] *Hansard*, H.C., Vol. 972, cols. 31–34; *ibid.* col. 268. October 25, 1979. U.K.M.I.L. 1979, (1979) 50 B.Y.I.L. 296.

[20] *Hansard*, H.C., Vol. 975, col. 723 December 6, 1979. See Warbrick, (1981) 30 I.C.L.Q. 234.

[21] This is true of some of the instances of non-recognition of states cited above, p. 155.

[22] See Symmons, *loc. cit.*, p. 155, n. 12, above, p. 250, referring to a letter by Mr Evan Luard, in *The Guardian*, October 5, 1979.

[23] *e.g.* the U.K. broke off diplomatic relations with Albania as an act of retorsion in 1946 (now restored) and with Libya in 1984 over the Libyan People's Bureau Incident, below, p. 353 (not yet restored). Libya, Iraq and North Korea are the only states recognised by the U.K. with which it has no diplomatic relations. Diplomatic relations with Argentina were broken off between 1982–90 because of the Falklands War. Diplomatic relations were restored in 1990 with Syria (broken off in 1986 because of Syrian involvement in an attempt in London to blow up an El Al airliner) and Iran (broken off in 1989 over the Salman Rushdie Affair).

U.S. PRACTICE ON THE RECOGNITION OF GOVERNMENTS

1977 U.S. Department of State statement, (1977) 77 U.S. Dept. of State Bull. 462; [1977] U.S.D.I.L. 19

... when the revolutionary French Government took power in 1792, Thomas Jefferson, our first Secretary of State, instructed the U.S. envoy in Paris to deal with it because it had been "formed by the will of the nation substantially declared."

Throughout most of the 19th century, the United States recognized stable governments without thereby attempting to confer approval. U.S. recognition policy grew more complex as various Administrations applied differing criteria for recognition and expressed differently the reasons for their decisions. For example, Secretary of State William Seward (1861–69) added as a criterion the government's ability to honour its international obligations; President Rutherford Hayes (1877–81) required a demonstration of popular support for the new government; and President Woodrow Wilson (1913–21) favored using recognition to spread democracy around the world by demanding free elections.

Other criteria have been applied since then. These include the degree of foreign involvement in the government as well as the government's political orientation, attitude toward foreign investment, and treatment of U.S. citizens, corporations, and government representatives.

One result of such complex recognition criteria was to create the impression among other nations that the United States approved of those governments it recognized and disapproved of those from which it withheld recognition. This appearance of approval, in turn, affected our decisions in ways that have not always advanced U.S. interests. In recent years, U.S. practice has been to deemphasize and avoid the use of recognition in cases of changes of governments and to concern ourselves with the question of whether we wish to have diplomatic relations with the new governments.

The Administration's policy is that establishment of relations does not involve approval or disapproval but merely demonstrates a willingness on our part to conduct our affairs with other governments directly.

Notes

1. As the statement indicates, "the United States Government has quietly moved to the Estrada Doctrine" so that "the significance of recognition has faded away."[24] Thus, on the question of the recognition of the Taraki Government in Afghanistan in 1978, the U.S. Government stated that "the question of recognition under the formulation of the last few years doesn't arise *per se*. . . . The important question is not recognition. The question is whether diplomatic relations continue. . . . "[25] On the latter point, it was stated:

[24] Baxter (1978) 72 A.J.I.L. 875 at 876.
[25] Department of State spokesman, May 1, 1978, (1978) 72 A.J.I.L. 879.

"The Government of the United States of America assumes that the Government of the Democratic Republic of Afghanistan will continue to honour and support the existing treaties and international agreements in force between our two states. On that assumption, it is the intention of the U.S. Government . . . to maintain diplomatic relations. . . . "[26]

Note, however, that Governments of the United States and China did expressly agree "to recognise each other and to establish diplomatic relations" as of 1979.[27]

2. On the criterion qualifying a government to be treated as the government of a state, the U.S. would appear to have moved to a simple test of effective control. In 1977, Deputy Secretary of State Christopher[28] stated:

We maintain diplomatic relations with many governments of which we do not necessarily approve. The reality is that, in this day and age, coups and other unscheduled changes of government are not exceptional developments. Withholding diplomatic relations from these régimes, after they have obtained effective control, penalizes us. It means that we forsake much of the chance to influence the attitudes and conduct of a new régime. . . . Isolation may well bring out the worst in the new government.

TINOCO ARBITRATION

Great Britain *v.* Costa Rica (1923)

Sole Arbitrator: William H. Taft, Chief Justice of the United States Supreme Court, 1 R.I.A.A. 369

In 1917, Tinoco ousted the Government of Costa Rica by force. Elections were held and "[f]or a full two years Tinoco and the legislative assembly under him peaceably administered the affairs of the Government of Costa Rica." (*ibid.* p. 379). In 1919, Tinoco was ousted in his turn and the new Government repudiated certain obligations undertaken by the Tinoco Government towards British nationals. In the course of ruling upon the claims brought by Great Britain on the basis of these obligations, the arbitrator discussed the question of recognition.

TAFT C.J. I must hold that from the evidence . . . the Tinoco government was an actual sovereign government.

But it is urged that many leading Powers refused to recognize the Tinoco government, and that recognition by other nations is the chief and best evidence of the birth, existence and continuity of succession of a government. Undoubtedly recognition by other Powers is an important evidential factor in establishing proof of the existence of a government in the society of nations. What are the facts as to this? The Tinoco government was recognized by . . . [20 states]. . . .

---

[26] U.S. Embassy in Kabul statement, May 6, 1978, (1978) 72 A.J.I.L. 879.

[27] Joint Communiqué, U.S. Government and the Government of the People's Republic of China: (1979) 73 A.J.I.L. 277. At the same time, the U.S. withdrew its recognition of the Government of Taiwan as the Government of the one state of China. It also expressly recognised the Angolan Government: (1993) 87 A.J.I.L. 593.

[28] Speech at Occidental College, June 11, 1977, [1977] U.S.D.I.L. p. 18.

The non-recognition by other nations of a government claiming to be a national personality, is usually appropriate evidence that it has not attained the independence and control entitling it by international law to be classed as such. But when recognition *vel non* of a government is by such nations determined by inquiry, not into its *de facto* sovereignty and complete governmental control, but into its illegitimacy or irregularity of origin,[29] their non-recognition loses something of evidential weight on the issue with which those applying the rules of international law are alone concerned. What is true of the non-recognition of the United States in its bearing upon the existence of a *de facto* government under Tinoco for thirty months is probably in a measure true of the non-recognition by her Allies in the European War. Such non-recognition for any reason, however, cannot outweigh the evidence disclosed by this record before me as to the *de facto* character of Tinoco's government, according to the standard set by international law. . . .

It is further objected by Costa Rica that Great Britain by her failure to recognize the Tinoco government is estopped now to urge claims of her subjects dependent upon the acts and contracts of the Tinoco government. . . . The contention here . . . precludes a government which did not recognize a *de facto* government from appearing in an international tribunal in behalf of its nationals to claim any rights based on the acts of such government.

To sustain this view a great number of decisions in English and American courts are cited to the point that a municipal court cannot, in litigation before it, recognize or assume the *de facto* character of a foreign government which the executive department of foreign affairs of the government of which the court is a branch has not recognized. . . . But such cases have no bearing on the point before us. Here the executive of Great Britain takes the position that the Tinoco government which it did not recognize, was nevertheless a *de facto* government that could create rights in British subjects which it now seeks to protect. Of course, as already emphasized, its failure to recognize the *de facto* government can be used against it as evidence to disprove the character it now attributes to that government, but this does not bar it from changing its position. Should a case arise in one of its own courts after it has changed its position doubtless that court would feel it incumbent upon it to note the change in its further rulings.

. . . It may be urged that it would be in the interest of the stability of governments and the orderly adjustment of international relations, and so a proper rule of international law, that a government in recognizing or refusing to recognize a government claiming admission to the society of

---

[29] *Ed.* The Arbitrator is here referring to the "constitutionality" test of recognition introduced as U.S. policy by President Wilson in 1913 which made "the coming into power of a new government by constitutional means a prerequisite of recognition, particularly with respect to the Central American Republics": 2 Whiteman 69. The test was abandoned by 1931.

nations should thereafter be held to an attitude consistent with its deliber-ate conclusion in this issue. Arguments for and against such a rule occur to me; but it suffices to say that I have not been cited to text writers of authority or to decisions of significance indicating a general acquiescence of nations in such a rule. Without this, it cannot be applied here as a principle of international law.

Notes

This case concerned the recognition of governments. On the recognition of states, in *Deutsche Continental Gas-Gesellschaft v. Polish State*[30] the German-Polish Mixed Arbitral Tribunal stated: " . . . according to the opinion rightly admitted by the great majority of writers on international law, the recognition of a State is not constitutive but merely declaratory. The State exists by itself (*par lui-même*) and the recognition is nothing else than a declaration of this existence, recognised by the States from which it emanates."

6. THE EFFECT OF RECOGNITION IN BRITISH COURTS

REPUBLIC OF SOMALIA v. WOODHOUSE DRAKE & CAREY SUISSE S.A.

[1993] Q.B. 54; Queen's Bench Division

In January 1991, the Republic of Somalia bought a cargo of rice for delivery by ship to its capital, Mogadishu. By the time the ship arrived offshore, the Somali Government of President Siad Barre had been overthrown and a civil war was in progress. The captain of the ship decided it was too dangerous to deliver the cargo. By order of the Commercial Court in London, it was sold and the proceeds paid into court. In July 1991, the Djibouti Agreement, following an international conference of interested states and parties, nominated Mr Mahdi as the interim President of Somalia. He appointed Mr Qalib as his Prime Minister. In these proceedings, the question was whether the £2 million in court that belonged to the Republic of Somalia could be paid out to Crossman Block, who were the solicitors acting for the interim government of Mr Qalib.

HOBHOUSE J. The question therefore is whether the interim government is the Government of the Republic of Somalia . . .

The policy of the United Kingdom is now not to confer recognition on governments as opposed to on states . . .

Hobhouse J. then quoted the 1980 Parliamentary Answers, above, p. 155

. . . [Prior to 1980] recognition by Her Majesty's Government was the decisive matter and the courts had no role save to inquire of the executive whether or not it had recognised the government in question.

Some writers appear still to feel that the criterion remains one of recognition by the government of this country, the difference being that,

[30] (1929) 5 A.D. 11 at 13.

whereas before 1980 the government would say expressly whether it recognised the foreign government, now it is to be left to be ascertained as a matter of inference: see Professor J. Crawford ... (1986) 57 B.Y. 405, and the continuing references in *Brownlie, Principles of Public International Law*, 4th ed. (1990) and in (1982) 53 B.Y. 197, 209, to the recognition of governments. Mr Richards [for the Treasury Solicitor] did not seek to support that view and it is clearly contrary to or not adopted in other writings: see, for example, Francis Mann, *Foreign Affairs in English Courts* (1986); C. Warbrick, "The New British Policy on Recognition of Governments" (1981) 30 I.C.L.Q. 568; and indeed the general tenor of Professor Brownlie's work itself. The impracticality of the "inferred recognition" theory as a legal concept for forensic use is obvious and it cannot be thought that that was the intention of Her Majesty's Government in giving the Parliamentary answers. The use of the phrase "left to be inferred" is designed to fulfil a need for information in an international or political, not a judicial, context.

If recognition by Her Majesty's Government is no longer the criterion of the locus standi of a foreign "government" in the English courts and the possession of a legal persona in English law, what criteria is the court to apply? The [1980 Parliamentary] answers do confirm one applicable criterion, namely, whether the relevant régime is able of itself to "exercise effective control of the territory of the state concerned" and is "likely to continue to do so;" and the statement as to what is to be the evidence of the attitude of Her Majesty's Government provides another—to be inferred from the nature of the dealings, if any, that Her Majesty's Government has with it and whether they are on a normal government to government basis. The non-existence of such dealings cannot however be conclusive because their absence may be explained by some extraneous consideration, for example, lack of occasion, the attitude of the régime to human rights, its relationship to another state. As the answers themselves acknowledge, the conduct of governments in their relations with each other may be affected by considerations of policy as well as by considerations of legal characterisation. The courts of this country are now only concerned with the latter consideration. ...

In relation to Somalia and the present litigation, the Foreign and Commonwealth Office has on three occasions responded to inquiries by solicitors ... In the first letter, dated March 4, 1991, reference was made to the fluid and confused situation that had followed upon the successful coup:

Now that opposition forces have overthrown Siad Barre, the single objective which united them has gone. Each movement has its own clan objectives to champion. The United Somali Congress, drawn from the Hawiye Clan and its sub clans, was responsible for the fighting in Mogadishu. It is they who have appointed a new caretaker president and a Government which they claim are interim measures. A separate U.S.C. faction under General Mohamed Farrah Hassan "Aidid," who have the support of the Somali National Movement, do not recognise the new president or government. Neither do the Somali Patriotic Movement or the S.N.M. They argue that the appointments run counter to the U.S.C., S.N.M. and S.P.M. agreement of 2 October 1990. But the faction now in control in Mogadishu was not a party to that agreement.

They also referred to the different factions in control in different parts of the country and said: "The general situation in Somalia continues to be insecure and confused."

On 5 August 1991, the Foreign and Commonwealth Office wrote to Crossman Block confirming that the practice of Her Majesty's Government was to recognise states not governments and that, accordingly, "The question of whether to recognise the purported 'interim government' in Mogadishu thus does not arise for us." They also confirmed that the purported secession of the north western part of the country had not been recognised. They commented: "The 'interim government' does not command nationwide acceptance. We support efforts to establish one that does." They concluded: "In these circumstances, it is very difficult to judge, for the purposes of your case, who is the Government of Somalia." This letter was written after the Djibouti Conference and notwithstanding the communiqué that had been issued at the conclusion of that conference. It is clear that the writer of that letter did not consider that the conference had changed the situation or that any legitimate or other recognisable government had come into existence as a result. . . .

On 20 February 1992 the Foreign and Commonwealth Office wrote again to More Fisher Brown. It reconfirmed that Her Majesty's Government was not concerned with the recognition of governments and had not recognised the purported secession. It continued:

> The comment in [the letter of 5 August 1991] has been somewhat overtaken by subsequent events, in particular fighting between rival elements of the United Somalia Congress which broke out in November 1991 and in which thousands of people have been killed and injured. . . . fighting in Mogadishu has continued . . . The United Kingdom maintains formal contact with all the factions involved, but there have been no dealings on a government to government basis.

It is clear from this letter that Her Majesty's Government does not consider that there is at present any effective government in Somalia. It refers to "factions" and treats the interim government as merely one among a number of factions. . . :

Accordingly, if the question before the court is to be decided on the basis of the attitude adopted by Her Majesty's Government, an order cannot be made in favour of the interim government or Crossman Block. The basis for its attitude is clearly not any disapproval of an established régime but rather that there is no régime which has control, let alone any administrative control which has the requisite element of stable continuity.

Mr Richards submitted that particular weight should be given to these communications. I have difficulty in accepting that submission without some qualification. Once the question for the court becomes one of making its own assessment of the evidence, making findings of fact on all the relevant evidence placed before it and drawing the appropriate legal conclusion, and is no longer a question of simply reflecting government policy, letters from the Foreign and Commonwealth Office become merely part of the evidence in the case. In the present case no problem of admissibility of evidence arises. In so far as the letters make statements about what is happening in the territory of some foreign state, such letters may not be the best evidence; but as regards the question whether Her Majesty's Government has dealings with the foreign government it will almost certainly be the best and only conclusive evidence of that fact. Where Her Majesty's Government is dealing with the foreign government on a normal government to government basis as the government of the relevant foreign state, it is unlikely in the extreme that the inference that the foreign government is the government of that state will be capable of being rebutted and questions of public policy and considerations of the interrelationship of the judicial and executive arms of government may be paramount: see *The Arantzazu Mendi* [1939] A.C. 256, 264 and *Gur Corporation v. Trust Bank of Africa Ltd* [1987] Q.B. 599, 625. But now that the question has ceased to be one of recognition, the theoretical possibility of rebuttal must exist.

There is no decided English authority on the effect of the 1980 answers. *Gur Corporation v. Trust Bank of Africa Ltd* was concerned with a question of the recognition of a state and the competence of a subordinate body within the recognised territory of that state under the laws of that state. The 1980 answers were referred to, p. 619, but were not the basis of the decision. Here no question of the recognition of a state is involved. Nor does this case involve any accredited representative of a foreign state in this country. Different considerations would arise if it did, since it would be contrary to public policy for the court not to recognise as a qualified representative of the head of state of the foreign state the diplomatic representative recognised by Her Majesty's Government. There is no recognised diplomatic representative of the Republic of Somalia to the United Kingdom.

The statements of fact in the letters from the Foreign and Commonwealth Office are confirmed by the other evidence that is before the court concerning the actual situation in Somalia. The interim government is not governing that country and does not exercise administrative or any control over its territory and population[31] ...

The criteria of effective control referred to in the Parliamentary answers are clearly not satisfied. In *The Arantzazu Mendi* [1939] A.C. 256, 264–265, Lord Atkin said:

> By "exercising *de facto* administrative control" or "exercising effective administrative control." I understand exercising all the functions of a sovereign government, in maintaining law and order, instituting and maintaining courts of justice, adopting or imposing laws regulating the relations of the inhabitants of the territory to one another and to the government.

The interim government clearly does not satisfy these criteria; the Republic of Somalia currently has no government. However, there are two other aspects on which counsel for the interim government has relied. These are the recognition of the interim government by some other states and international bodies, and the fact that the interim government was set up by the Djibouti Agreement which resulted from an international conference attended by many international states and bodies.[32]

In evaluating these arguments it is relevant to distinguish between regimes that have been the constitutional and established government of a state and a régime which is seeking to achieve that position either displacing a former government or to fill a vacuum. Since the question is now whether a government *exists*, there is no room for more than one government at a time nor for separate *de jure* and *de facto* governments in respect of the same state. But a loss of control by a constitutional government may not immediately deprive it of its status, whereas an insurgent régime will require to establish control before it can exist as a government.

The argument based on the Djibouti Agreement does not assist the interim government. The Djibouti Agreement was not constitutional. It did not create a *de jure* status for the interim government in Somalia. The interim government was not and did not become the constitutional successor of the Government of President Siad Barre. Accordingly, if the interim government is to be treated as the Government of Somalia, it must be able to show that it is exercising administrative control over the territory of the Republic. That it is not able to do. Accordingly, that argument must fail.

---

[31] *Ed.* Hobhouse J. quoted a report by the Agency for International Development. He had earlier, p. 58, noted that the "interim government has been unable to operate in Mogadishu and Mr Qalib has based himself in a hotel in Riyadh in Saudi Arabia".

[32] *Ed.* The Conference, which was called at Djibouti under the chairmanship of the President of Djibouti, was attended by 16 states, including the United States, the U.S.S.R. and various African and Arab states, but not the U.K.; by international organisations such as the O.A.U. and the EEC; and by representatives of six rival groupings within Somalia.

As regards the argument of international recognition and recognition by the United Nations, though this does not as such involve control of territory or a population, it does correspond to one aspect of statehood. A classic definition of a state is that contained in article 1 of the Montevideo Convention of 1933 as having: "(a) a permanent population; (b) a defined territory; (c) government; and (d) capacity to enter into relations with other states." Whilst illustrating that it is difficult to separate the recognition of a state from the recognition of a government of that state, this definition also shows that part of the function of a government of a state is to have relations with other states. This is also implicit in the reference in the 1980 Parliamentary answers to dealings on a government to government basis.

Accordingly I consider that the degree of international recognition of an alleged government is a relevant factor in assessing whether it exists as the government of a state. But where, as here, the régime exercises virtually no administrative control at all in the territory of the state, international recognition of an unconstitutional regime should not suffice and would, indeed, have to be accounted for by policy considerations rather than legal characterisation; and it is, of course, possible for states to have relations with bodies which are not states or governments of states.

There is evidence from which it appears that the United Nations Organisation considers that there are persons whom it may treat as the representatives of the Republic of Somalia. Resolution 733 started with the words: "Considering the request by Somalia for the Security Council to consider the situation in Somalia." It appears that this request was contained in a letter from Mr Qalib dated December 15, 1991 addressed to the Secretary General to the United Nations and the President of the Security Council. Mr Qalib signed himself as the "Prime Minister of Somalia." ... The text of Resolution 733 was apparently communicated to Mr Mahdi by the Secretary General of the United Nations describing Mr Mahdi as "His Excellency Mr. Ali Mahdi Interim President of Somalia."

This evidence is not wholly satisfactory. The attitude of the United Nations to the interim government could be established in a more direct fashion and more authoritatively. The letter of Mr Hassan suggests something less than a fully recognised status. In any event, membership of an international organisation does not amount to recognition nor does a vote on credentials and representation issues: see Warbrick, 30 I.C.L.Q., 568, 583 citing 1950 UN Doc S/1466. But any apparent acceptance of the interim government by the United Nations and other international organisations and states does not suffice in the present case to demonstrate that the interim government is the Government of the Republic of Somalia. The evidence the other way is too strong.

Accordingly, the factors to be taken into account in deciding whether a government exists as the government of a state are: (a) whether it is the constitutional government of the state; (b) the degree, nature and stability of administrative control, if any, that it of itself exercises over the territory of the state; (c) whether Her Majesty's Government has any dealings with it and if so what is the nature of those dealings; and (d) in marginal cases, the extent of international recognition that it has as the government of the state.

On the evidence before the court the interim government certainly does not qualify having regard to any of the three important factors. Accordingly the court must conclude that Crossman Block does not at present have the authority of the Republic of Somalia to receive and deal with the property of the Republic ... I direct that no part of the sum in court should be paid out to Crossman Block without a further order of the court. ...

Notes

1. Before the 1980 statement, the practice of the British courts when called upon to recognise the law or capacity to act of a foreign state or government was to seek and regard as conclusive a Foreign Office certificate.[33] In this context, recognition was constitutive. The position remains unchanged in respect of the recognition of states. A certificate would still be sought and followed on the facts of the *Carl Zeiss* case, below, p. 176. When asked about the effect of the 1980 statement on legal proceedings concerning new governments, the Foreign Secretary (Lord Carrington) replied:

> In future cases where a new régime comes to power unconstitutionally our attitude on the question whether it qualifies to be treated as a Government, will be left to be inferred from the nature of the dealings, if any, which we may have with it, and in particular on whether we are dealing with it on a normal Government to Government basis.[34]

It is clear from the *Woodhouse* case, and from the *Gur* case, below, p. 183, that the Foreign Office will, if requested, respond to enquiries as to the dealings, if any, the United Kingdom has with a claimant government and comment on the factual situation in the state concerned. However, the *Woodhouse* case decided that indications given by the Foreign Office as to whether "government to government" dealings have taken place with a claimant government are not conclusive. Instead they are just one consideration for the court to take into account when deciding whether "a government exists as the government of a state". Are there good policy reasons for preferring the "one voice" approach instead? If that approach had been followed in the *Woodhouse* case, the Interim Government would have been found not to have been the government of Somalia simply on the basis that the Foreign Office had reported that the United Kingdom did not have dealings with it. Might the *Woodhouse* approach lead to considerable uncertainty in borderline cases, as courts try to apply Hobhouse J.'s list of four factors?[35] Note that the understanding of the Secretary of State (Lord Carrington), above, was clearly that the courts would discover the government's "attitude" and follow it.

[33] See Lord Reid's speech in the *Carl Zeiss* case below, p. 176.
[34] *Hansard*, H.L. Vol. 409, cols. 1097–1098, May 23, 1980; U.K. M.I.L. 1980, (1980) 51 B.Y.I.L. 368.
[35] On these and other points of criticism of the *Woodhouse* approach, see Talmon, *loc. cit.*, p. 155, n. 12, above, pp. 281 *et seq.*

2. It is not clear how the *Woodhouse* approach would apply were the Foreign Office to have dealings with two rival claimant governments that each control part of the territory of the state concerned on the basis that they were the *de jure* and *de facto* governments respectively. There is case law on this situation as it arose under the pre-1980 position: see, *e.g. Haile Selassie v. Cable and Wireless Ltd (No. 2)* [1939] 1 Ch. 182, CA. The Foreign Office has not made this distinction lately.

LUTHER v. SAGOR

[1921] 1 K.B. 456; [1921] 3 K.B. 532. King's Bench Division;
Court of Appeal

In 1920, the defendant company bought a quantity of wood from the new Soviet Government of the USSR. The plaintiff Russian company claimed title to the wood on the ground that it had come from a factory in the USSR that had been owned by it before being nationalised by a 1919 decree of the Soviet Government. The plaintiff argued,[36] that the decree should not be recognised by an English court, *inter alia*, because the Soviet Government had not been recognised by the United Kingdom.

ROCHE J. The attitude proper to be adopted by a Court of this country with regard to foreign governments or powers I understand to be as follows. . . . If a foreign government, or its sovereignty, is not recognized by the Government of this country the Courts of this country either cannot, or at least need not, or ought not, to take notice of, or recognize such foreign government or its sovereignty. This negative proposition is . . . established and recognised by the judgment of Kay J. in *Republic of Peru v. Dreyfus*.[37] . . . In the *City of Berne v. Bank of England*[38] the question at issue was the right of an unrecognized foreign government to maintain a suit, but Lord Eldon's judgment is, I think, an authority for the general proposition I have stated. . . .

This being the law which must guide and direct my decision, I have to consider whether and in what sense the Government represented by M. Krassin in this matter is recognized by His Majesty's Government. . . .

Roche J. then read a letter from the Foreign Office dated November 20, 1920.

Gentlemen,

I am directed by Earl Curzon of Kedleston . . . to inform you that for a certain limited purpose His Majesty's Government has regarded Monsieur Krassin as exempt from the process of the Courts, and also for the like limited purpose His Majesty's Government has assented to the claim that that which Monsieur Krassin represents in this Country is a State Government of Russia, but that beyond these propositions

[36] It also argued that the decree was confiscatory.
[37] 38 Ch.D. at 357, 358 and 359.
[38] 9 Ves. 347.

the Foreign Office has not gone, nor moreover do these expressions of opinion purport to decide difficult, and it may be very special questions of law upon which it may become necessary for the Courts to pronounce. I am to add that His Majesty's Government has never officially recognised the Soviet Government in any way.

It was said on behalf of the defendants that these communications were vague and ambiguous. I should rather say that they were guarded, but as clear as the indeterminate position of affairs in connection with the subject-matter of the communications enabled them to be ... I am not satisfied that His Majesty's Government has recognized the Soviet Government as the Government of a Russian Federative Republic or of any sovereign state or power. I therefore am unable to recognize it, or to hold it has sovereignty, or is able by decree to deprive the plaintiff company of its property.

Roche J. gave judgment for the plaintiffs. The defendants appealed to the Court of Appeal.

Court of Appeal

BANKES L.J. Upon the evidence which was before the learned judge I think that his decision was quite right. . . .

In this Court the appellants asked leave to adduce further evidence . . . It consisted of two letters from the Foreign Office dated respectively April 20 and 22, 1921. The first is . . . in these terms: "I am . . . to inform you that His Majesty's Government recognize the Soviet Government as the *de facto* Government of Russia." The letter of April 22 . . . contains (*inter alia*) the statement that the Provisional Government came into power on March 14, 1917, that it was recognized by His Majesty's Government as the then existing Government of Russia, and that the Constituent Assembly remained in session until December 13, 1917, when it was dispersed by the Soviet authorities.[39] . . .

Under these circumstances the whole aspect of the case is changed, and it becomes necessary to consider matters which were not material in the Court below. The first is a question of law of very considerable importance—namely, what is the effect of the recognition by His Majesty's Government in April, 1921, of the Soviet Government as the *de facto* Government of Russia upon the past acts of that Government, and how far back, if at all, does that recognition extend.

[39] The Provisional Government came into being after the "February Revolution" of 1917, as a result of which the Tsar abdicated. It was led first by Prince Lvov and then by Kerensky. After the "October Revolution" of the same year, the Provisional Government was replaced by the Soviet Government, *i.e.* the Bolshevik Government led by Lenin.

. . . counsel have been unable to refer the Court to any English author-ity. Attention has been called to three cases decided in the Supreme Court of the United States: *Williams v. Bruffy*[40] *Underhill v. Hernandez*[41]; and *Oetjen v. Central Leather Co.*[42] In none of these cases is any distinction attempted to be drawn in argument between the effect of a recognition of a government as a *de facto* government and a recognition of a government as a government *de jure*, nor is any decision given upon that point; nor, except incidentally, is any mention made as to the effect of the recognition of a government upon its past acts. The mention occurs in two passages, one in the judgement of . . . Fuller C.J. in *Underhill v. Hernandez*.[43] He says, in speaking of civil wars: "If the party seeking to dislodge the existing government succeeds, and the independence of the government it has set up is recognized, then the acts of such government from the commence-ment of its existence are regarded as those of an independent nation." . . . On principle the views put forward by these learned judges appear to me to be sound, though there may be cases in which the Courts of a country whose government has recognized the government of some other country as the *de facto* government of that country may have to consider at what stage in its development the government so recognized can, to use the language to which I have already referred of those learned judges, be said to have "commenced its existence." No difficulty of that kind arises in the present case, because, upon the construction which I place upon the communication of the Foreign Office to which I have referred, this Court must treat the Soviet Government, which the Government of this country has now recognized as the *de facto* Government of Russia, as having commenced its existence at a date anterior to any date material to the dispute between the parties to this appeal.

. . . The Government of this country having . . . recognized the Soviet Government as the Government really in possession of the powers of sovereignty in Russia, the acts of that Government must be treated by the Courts of this country with all the respect due to the acts of a duly recognized foreign sovereign state.

. . . From the letter from the Foreign Office addressed to Messrs. Link-later of April 22, 1921, it appears that the Soviet authorities dispersed the then Constituent Assembly on December 13, 1917, from which date I think it must be accepted that the Soviet Government assumed the position of the sovereign Government and purported to act as such.

WARRINGTON L.J. I should have thought that in principle recognition would be retroactive at any rate to such date as our Government accept as that by which the government in question in fact established its authority. It appears from the letter of the Foreign Office dated April 22,

[40] 96 U.S. 176.
[41] 168 U.S. 250.
[42] 246 U.S. 297.
[43] 168 U.S. 253. *Ed.* The other was in the judgment of Field J. in *Williams v. Bruffy.*

1921, that that date is anterior to any of the events material to the present case.

SCRUTTON L.J. delivered a concurring judgment. Appeal allowed.

Notes

Luther v. Sagor establishes that recognition, once given, is retroactive in effect from the time that the recognised government established itself. It also confirms that the British courts will not recognise or enforce the laws or other public acts of an unrecognised government. Similarly, an unrecognised government lacks *locus standi* to bring a suit in a British court: *City of Berne v. Bank of England* (cited by Roche J., above). Nor is it entitled to sovereign immunity. Thus in *The Annette and the Dora*[44] the plaintiffs brought a writ *in rem* for the attachment of ships belonging to them which had been requisitioned by the Provisional Government of Northern Russia in September 1917 and which were allegedly in that Government's possession. In the light of a Foreign Office certificate to the effect that the Provisional Government had not been formally recognised by the British Government, Hill J. held that it could not plead sovereign immunity so as to have the writ set aside.

The above notes are expressed in terms of the pre-1980 rules concerning recognition. If the courts were, under the 1980 statement, to divine and follow the "attitude" of the British Government on the basis of its dealings with the claimant government, the rule in *Luther v. Sagor* would continue to apply.[45] If the approach in the *Woodhouse* case applies instead, does the question of retroactivity arise? Would the courts regard the claimant government as the government of the state concerned, applying Hobhouse J.'s four factors, as soon as it "commenced its existence" (Bankes L.J.).

CIVIL AIR TRANSPORT INC. v. CENTRAL AIR TRANSPORT CORPORATION[46]

[1953] A.C. 70. Judicial Committee of the Privy Council

On October 1, 1949, the Government of the People's Republic of China, which had by then obtained control over most of the Chinese mainland, proclaimed itself the Government of China. Its predecessor, the Nationalist Government, withdrew from the mainland and, on December 9, established its headquarters on the island of Taiwan (Formosa). The United Kingdom Government continued to recognise the Nationalist Government as the *de jure* government of China until midnight on January 5/6, 1950, when it recognised the Government of the People's Republic instead. By September 1949, Nationalist Government employees had flown to Hong Kong 40 aircraft that formed part of the fleet of the respondents, a Chinese state enterprise at that time still under the control of the Nationalist Government. On December 12, 1949, the Nationalist Government sold the aircraft to a United States partnership which resold them to the appellant United States corporation. In the meantime, on November 12, 1949, the respondents and their assets were declared by the People's Republic to be their property. At about the same time, the majority of the respondents' employees in Hong Kong defected from the Nationalist Government and took physical control of the aircraft in Hong Kong for the

---

[44] [1919] P. 105, PD.

[45] The same is true of the decisions in the *Civil Air Transport* and *Gdynia* cases, below, pp. 172 and 175.

[46] See Johnson (1952) 29 B.Y.I.L. 464, and Mann (1953) 16 M.L.R. 226.

People's Republic Government. This they retained in defiance of a Hong Kong court injunction.

In this case, the appellants appealed to the Judicial Committee against a decision of the Appellate Court of Hong Kong dismissing their claim to a declaration that the aircraft were their property and holding instead that the ownership and right to possession of the aircraft were in the People's Republic Government. An Order in Council provided that it would be no bar to jurisdiction in any case concerning the aircraft that a foreign state was impleaded.

LORD SIMON, FOR THE JUDICIAL COMMITTEE. Her Majesty's Government in the United Kingdom is the sovereign government of Hong Kong, and the effect of the above replies [by the Foreign Office to questions on the status of the rival governments] is to establish that, at any rate in the courts of Hong Kong and in the present appeal, the former Nationalist Government must be regarded as the sole *de jure* sovereign government of China up to midnight of January 5–6, 1950; that the present Communist Government was not the *de jure* government until that time; and that, while the Foreign Office, in its answer of March 13, 1950, acknowledged that from October 1, 1949, onwards the *de facto* government of those parts of China in which the Nationalist Government had ceased to be in effective control was the Communist Government, H.M. Government had not announced or communicated their recognition of the Communist Government as the *de facto* government over any part of China before they recognized the Communist Government as the *de jure* government of China on January 5–6, 1950.

. . . the validity of the transaction [for the sale of the aircraft] must be judged as at the date when it was entered into, and not in the light of subsequent events, which might have turned out differently. On December 12, 1949, the Nationalist Government was the *de jure* government of China, of which C.A.T.C. was an organ, and therefore the property in these aeroplanes was in the Nationalist Government. The machines had been moved to Hong Kong two months before, and it was open to their owners to sell them, and thereby to pass the property in them to the purchasers.

. . . At the same time, their Lordships must not be understood to reject the possibility of our courts refusing, in a conceivable case, to recognize the validity of the disposal of State property by a government on the eve of its fall, *e.g.* by a despot, who knows that previous recognition is just being withdrawn, where it is clear that his purpose was to abscond with the proceeds, or to make away with State assets for some private purpose. . . .

Subsequent recognition *de jure* of a new government as the result of successful insurrection can in certain cases annul a sale of goods by a previous government. If the previous government sells goods which belong to it but are situated in territory effectively occupied at the time by insurgent forces acting on behalf of what is already a *de facto* new government, the sale may be valid if the insurgents are afterwards defeated and possession of the goods is regained by the old government. But if the old government never regains the goods and the *de facto* new government becomes recognized by H.M. Government as the *de jure* government, purchasers from the old government will not be held in Her Majesty's courts to have a good title after that recognition.

Primarily, at any rate, retroactivity of recognition operates to validate acts of a *de facto* government which has subsequently become the new *de jure* government, and not to invalidate acts of the previous *de jure* government. It is not necessary to discuss ultimate results in the hypothetical case when before the change in recognition both governments purport to deal with the same goods. The crucial question under this branch of the analysis in the present appeal is whether anything that happened in Hong Kong to these aeroplanes at the instigation of or on behalf of the *de facto* Communist Government before the change of recognition on January 5–6, 1950, is retrospectively validated, so that the title conferred by the contract of December 12, 1949, is extinguished.

It might be too wide a proposition to say that the retroactive effect of *de jure* recognition must in all cases be limited to acts done in territory of the government so recognized, for the case of a ship of the former government taken possession of by insurgents on the high seas and brought into a port which is under the control of the *de facto* government would have to be considered (see *Banco de Bilbao* v. *Sancha*[47]). But the actual question now to be answered concerns chattels in the British colony of Hong Kong which at the time of the sale belonged to the Nationalist Government. Whatever the degree of physical control over these chattels maintained by the defecting ex-employees, this control was in defiance of the injunction granted by the Supreme Court of Hong Kong on November 24. Moreover, if these persons could be regarded as acting on behalf of the *de facto* Communist Government, their action would be a direct infringement of the Representation of Foreign Powers (Control) Ordinance of November 4, 1949, and would be a criminal offence by the law of Hong Kong. This Ordinance provided that no person should "function on behalf of any foreign Power" without the consent of the governor, and "foreign Power" was defined to include "the government whether legal or *de facto* of any foreign State." The governor gave no consent. In such circumstances the action of those who illegally took control of these aeroplanes cannot give ground for the principle of retroactivity.

. . . My opinion therefore upon this aspect of the case is that the Central People's Government could not show any superior title or right to possession; nor can it rely upon any rights arising out of actual possession acquired in the way it was; therefore it had no possession which could bring into effect the doctrine of retroactivity. That doctrine, I think, relates to the acts of a government which has already

---

[47] [1938] 2 K.B. 176.

acquired jurisdiction through possession and cannot include the actual act of taking possession if that act be wrongful. On this point I hold therefore that the ordinary principle of continuity was not displaced by any consideration of retroactivity and that it follows that the Nationalist Government was entitled to possession of and had jurisdiction over the aeroplanes."

Their Lordships agree with the argument and conclusions of Gould J. on this point.

The trial judge attached importance to the announcement of October 1, 1949, the authors of which proclaimed themselves to be the government of China, and to the decree issued on that date purporting in the name of that government to dismiss the ministers of the Nationalist Government. Their Lordships cannot accept the view that this is any reason for saying "that as from October 1, 1949, these aircraft were owned by the Central People's Government." They adopt on this point the opinion of Gould J., who observed: "The purported dismissal on October 1, 1949, of the ministers of the Nationalist Government . . . can only be deemed effective within the territory and as regards assets from time to time in the control of the People's Government. Elsewhere, and so long as the Nationalist Government retained de jure recognition, such a decree could have no effect."

For the above reasons, their Lordships have reached the conclusion that the appeal should be allowed.

Lord Normand, Lord Oaksey, Lord Reid and Sir Lionel Leach also sat in this case.

Notes

1. What if it had been the Government of the People's Republic of China that had purported to sell the aircraft in Hong Kong on December 12? What if, as in the actual case, it were the Nationalist Government, but the aircraft had been in Mainland China on December 12?

2. *Gdynia Ameryka Linie Zeglugowe Spolka Akcyjna v. Boguslawski*[48] concerned the Polish Government in Exile in London during the Second World War. This Government was then recognised by the United Kingdom as the *de jure* government of Poland. Although it had no control over Polish territory during the War, it did have control over that part of the Polish merchant fleet that had avoided capture by Germany. On June 28, 1945, a new communist Provisional Government established itself with *de facto* control of Polish territory. At midnight on July 5–6, 1945, the United Kingdom withdrew its recognition of the London Government and recognised the Provisional Government as the *de jure* government of Poland instead. Just before this, on July 3, the competent Minister of the London Government, Mr K, acting under powers conferred by Polish law not revoked by the Provisional Government, offered certain Polish seamen compensation (to be paid by their employers) should they wish to leave their employment rather than continue to serve under the jurisdiction of the Provisional Government. The two respondents in this case accepted the offer. When their employers, the appellants,

[48] [1953] A.C. 11.

refused to pay, they sought to recover the compensation offered through the English courts. The appellants argued that the recognition by the British Government of the Provisional Government had retroactive effect so that acts of the London Government ceased to have effect in Polish law (which, the House of Lords held, governed the case) from June 28, 1945, when the Provisional Government established itself in Poland. There was consequently, it was argued, no duty on the part of the appellants to make the payments required by Mr K. The argument was rejected and the appeal dismissed unanimously. Lord Reid stated:

> There is ample authority for the proposition that the recognition by the British Government of a new government of a foreign country has at least this effect. It enables and requires the courts of this country to regard as valid not only acts done by the new government after its recognition but also acts done by it before its recognition in so far as those acts related to matters under its control at the time when the acts were done. But there appears to be no English authority which goes beyond that. I do not accept the argument for the appellants that this necessarily or logically involves antedating for all purposes the withdrawal of the recognition of the old government. I do not see anything strange or even difficult in our saying that we still recognize that the old government was the Government of Poland up to midnight of July 5–6 but that we also now accept the validity of certain acts done by the new government before that time and while it was still unrecognized by us. Apart from the distinction between recognition *de jure* and recognition *de facto* which does not affect this case, we cannot recognize two different governments of the same country at the same time, and the British Government did not in fact recognize both the old and the new government at the time. But I do not think that it is inconsistent with this principle to say that the recognition of the new government has certain retroactive effects, but that the recognition of the old government remains effective down to the date when it was in fact withdrawn. I can see that there might be difficulties if the old government had purported before withdrawal of recognition to take some action with regard to matters already under the control of the new government, but that does not arise in this case.[49]

3. On the effect of the *Woodhouse* approach on the *Civil Air Transport* and *Gdynia* cases, see above, pp. 168–169.

CARL ZEISS STIFTUNG v. RAYNER AND KEELER LTD (No. 2)[50]

[1967] 1 A.C. 853. House of Lords

C.Z.S. is a German charitable foundation that makes optical instruments. Under its constitution, it is run by a Special Board. After the First World War, the Board was the Minister of Education of Thuringia, a state within Germany. In 1945, Thuringia became part of the Russian Zone of Occupied Germany. In 1949, the U.S.S.R. handed over government of its Zone to the German Democratic Republic. In 1952, the G.D.R. reorganised its local government and Thuringia ceased to exist. The Special Board of C.Z.S., under the new arrangements, became the Council of Gera.

---

[49] *ibid.* 44–45.
[50] See Greig (1967) 83 L.Q.R. 96; Mann, *Foreign Affairs in English Courts* (1986), pp. 56–57; Richter (1968) 6 M.U.L.R. 448.

In this case, C.Z.S., acting through its new Board, brought a claim in the English courts. In these interlocutory proceedings, the defendants, now the respondents, asked that the claim be dismissed because it had been brought without the proper authority of the appellants. The requested order was denied by Cross J. but granted by the Court of Appeal after an argument based upon recognition had been put to that court for the first time in the case. The argument was that as the United Kingdom had not recognised the G.D.R. the new Special Board, having been created by the G.D.R., could not be recognised by an English court. The House of Lords unanimously reversed the Court of Appeal's ruling on appeal.

LORD REID. If the respondents' argument based on non-recognition is well founded, then it must follow that British courts cannot recognise either the existence of the Council of Gera or the validity of anything done by it, and in particular cannot recognise any authority given by it for the raising of the present action. . . .

In the normal case a law is made either by the sovereign directly or by some body entitled under the constitution of the country to make it or by some person or body to which the sovereign has delegated authority to make it. On the other hand, there are many cases where laws have been made against the will of the sovereign by persons engaged in a rebellion or revolution: then until such persons or the government which they set up have been granted *de facto* recognition by the Government of this country, their laws cannot be recognised by the courts of this country, but after *de facto* recognition such laws will be recognised. So far there is no difficulty. But the present case does not fit neatly into any of these categories. We are considering whether the law of 1952 under which the Council of Gera was set up can be recognised by our courts and therefore we must ascertain what was the situation in East Germany in 1952.

It is a firmly established principle that the question whether a foreign state ruler or government is or is not sovereign is one on which our courts accept as conclusive information provided by Her Majesty's government: no evidence is admissible to contradict that information.[51]

. . . In the present case the Court of Appeal twice received . . . information from the Foreign Secretary. First on September 16, 1964, it was stated: "Her Majesty's Government has not granted any recognition *de jure* or *de facto* to (a) the 'German Democratic Republic' or (b) its 'Government,'" and secondly on November 6, 1964, a further answer was given . . .

In my opinion, this latter answer is decisive on the question which I am now considering and I must therefore quote the relevant question and the relevant parts of the answer or certificate given by the Foreign Secretary. The question was:

What (a) states or (b) governments or (c) authorities (if any) have since July 1, 1945, up to the present date been recognised by Her Majesty's Government as (a) entitled to exercise or (b) exercising

---

[51] *Ed.* Lord Reid cited *Duff Development Co. Ltd v. Kelantan Government* [1924] A.C. 797, HL, as authority. See further on this point, above, p. 99.

governing authority in the area of Germany outside the zones allo-
cated to the Governments of the United Kingdom, the United States of
America and the French Republic by the protocol of September 12,
1944, and the agreement of July 26, 1945, concluded between the
Governments of the said states and the Union of Soviet Socialist
Republics. Has such recognition been *de jure* or *de facto*.

The relevant parts of the certificate are as follows: . . .

(a) From the zone allocated to the Union of Soviet Socialist Republics
Allied forces under the Supreme Allied Commander, General Eisen-
hower, withdrew at or about the end of June, 1945. Since that time and
up to the present date Her Majesty's Government have recognised the
state and Government of the Union of Soviet Socialist Republics as *de
jure* entitled to exercise governing authority in respect of that zone. In
matters affecting Germany as a whole, the states and Governments of
the French Republic, the United Kingdom of Great Britain and Northern Ireland, the United States of America and the Union of Soviet
Socialist Republics were jointly entitled to exercise governing authority. In the period from August 30, 1945, to March 20, 1948, they did
exercise such joint authority through the Control Council for Germany.
Apart from the states, Governments and Control Council aforementioned, Her Majesty's Government have not recognised either *de jure* or
de facto any other authority purporting to exercise governing authority
in or in respect of the zone. Her Majesty's Government, however,
regard the aforementioned Governments as retaining rights and
responsibilities in respect of Germany as a whole. . . .

The purpose of a certificate is to provide information about the status
of foreign governments and states and therefore the statement that since
June, 1945, "Her Majesty's Government have recognised the state and
Government of the Union of Soviet Socialist Republics as *de jure* entitled
to exercise governing authority in respect of that zone" cannot merely
mean that Her Majesty's Government have granted this recognition so as
to leave the courts of this country free to receive evidence as to whether
in fact the U.S.S.R. are still entitled to exercise governing authority there.
The courts of this country are no more entitled to hold that a sovereign,
still recognised by our Government, has ceased in fact to be sovereign *de
jure*, than they are entitled to hold that a government not yet recognised
has acquired sovereign status. So this certificate requires that we must
take it as a fact that the U.S.S.R. have been since 1954 and still are *de jure*
entitled to exercise that governing authority. The certificate makes no
distinction between the period before and the period after the German
Democratic Republic was set up. So we are bound to hold that the setting
up of that Republic made no difference in the right of the U.S.S.R. to
exercise governing authority in the zone. And it must follow from that

that the U.S.S.R. could at any time lawfully bring to an end the German Democratic Republic and its Government and could then resume direct rule of the zone. But that is quite inconsistent with there having in fact been any abdication by the U.S.S.R. of its rights when the German Democratic Republic was set up. . . .

If we are bound to hold that the German Democratic Republic was not in fact set up as a sovereign independent state, the only other possibility is that it was set up as a dependent or subordinate organisation through which the U.S.S.R. is entitled to exercise indirect rule. I do not think that we are concerned to inquire or to know to what extent the U.S.S.R. in fact exercise their right of control. . . .

It was argued that the present case is analogous to cases where subjects of an existing sovereign have rebelled and have succeeded in gaining control of a part of the old sovereign's dominions. When they set up a new government in opposition to the *de jure* sovereign that new government does not and cannot derive any authority or right from the *de jure* sovereign, and our courts must regard its acts and the acts of its organs or officers as nullities until it has established and consolidated its position to such an extent as to warrant our government according *de facto* recognition of it. . . .

Lord Reid referred to *Luther v. Sagor*, above, p. 169, as an example of this situation and approved of the first instance and the Court of Appeal judgments in that case.

But the present case is essentially different. The German Democratic Republic was set up by the U.S.S.R. and it derived its authority and status from the Government of the U.S.S.R. So the only question could be whether or not it was set up as a sovereign state. But the certificate of our Government requires us to hold that it was not set up as a sovereign state because it requires us to hold that the U.S.S.R. remained *de jure* sovereign and therefore did not voluntarily transfer its sovereignty to the Democratic Republic. And, if the Democratic Republic did not become a sovereign state at its inception, there is no suggestion that it has at any subsequent time attempted to deprive the U.S.S.R. of rights which were not granted to it at its inception. The courts of this country must disregard any declarations of the Government of the U.S.S.R. in so far as they conflict with the certificate of Her Majesty's Secretary of State, and we must therefore hold that the U.S.S.R. set up the German Democratic Republic, not as a sovereign state, but as an organisation subordinate to the U.S.S.R. If that is so, then mere declarations by the Government of the Democratic Republic that it is acting as the government of an independent state cannot be regarded as proof that its initial status has been altered, and we must regard the acts of the German Democratic Republic, its government organs and officers as acts done with the consent of the

Government of the U.S.S.R. as the government entitled to exercise governing authority.

It appears to me to be impossible for any *de jure* sovereign governing authority to disclaim responsibility for acts done by subordinate bodies which it has set up and which have not attempted to usurp its sovereignty. So, in my opinion, the courts of this country cannot treat as nullities acts done by or on behalf of the German Democratic Republic. *De facto* recognition is appropriate—and, in my view, is only appropriate —where the new government have usurped power against the will of the *de jure* sovereign. I would think that where a sovereign has granted independence to a dependency any recognition of the new state would be a recognition *de jure*. . . .

I am reinforced in my opinion by a consideration of the consequences which would follow if the view taken by the Court of Appeal were correct. Counsel for the respondents did not dispute that in that case we must not only disregard all new laws and decrees made by the Democratic Republic or its Government, but we must also disregard all executive and judicial acts done by persons appointed by that Government because we must regard their appointments as invalid. The result of that would be far-reaching. Trade with the Eastern Zone of Germany is not discouraged. But the incorporation of every company in East Germany under any new law made by the Democratic Republic or by the official act of any official appointed by its Government would have to be regarded as a nullity, so that any such company could neither sue nor be sued in this country. And any civil marriage under any such new law, or owing its validity to the act of any such official, would also have to be treated as a nullity, so that we should have to regard the children as illegitimate. And the same would apply to divorces and all manner of judicial decisions, whether in family or commercial questions. And that would affect not only status of persons formerly domiciled in East Germany but property in this country the devolution of which depended on East German law.

It was suggested that these consequences might be mitigated if the courts of this country could adopt doctrines which have found some support in the United States of America.[52] . . . In the view which I take of the present case, it is unnecessary to express any opinion whether it would be possible to adopt any similar solutions in this country, if the need should ever arise.

LORD WILBERFORCE. My Lords, if the consequences of non-recognition of the East German "government" were to bring in question the validity of its legislative acts, I should wish seriously to consider whether the invalidity so brought about is total, or whether some mitigation of the severity of this result can be found. As Locke said: "A government without laws is, I suppose, a mystery in politics, inconceivable to human

---

[52] See Lord Wilberforce, below.

capacity and inconsistent with human society," and this must be true of a society—at least a civilised and organised society—such as we know to exist in East Germany. In the United States some glimmerings can be found of the idea that non-recognition cannot be pressed to its ultimate logical limit, and that where private rights, or acts of everyday occurrence, or perfunctory acts of administration are concerned (the scope of these exceptions has never been precisely defined) the courts may, in the interests of justice and common sense, where no consideration of public policy to the contrary has to prevail, give recognition to the actual facts or realities found to exist in the territory in question. These ideas began to take shape on the termination of the Civil War (see *U.S.* v. *Insurance Companies*), and have been developed and reformulated, admittedly as no more than dicta, but dicta by judges of high authority, in later cases. I mention two of these, *Sokoloff* v. *National City Bank* and *Upright* v. *Mercury Business Machines Co. Inc.*, a case which was concerned with a corporate body under East German law. Other references can be found conveniently assembled in Professor D. P. O'Connell's *International Law* (1965), vol. I, pp. 189 *et seq.* No trace of any such doctrine is yet to be found in English law, but equally, in my opinion, there is nothing in those English decisions, in which recognition has been refused to particular acts of non-recognised governments, which would prevent its acceptance or which prescribes the absolute and total invalidity of all laws and acts flowing from unrecognised governments. In view of the conclusion I have reached on the effect to be attributed to non-recognition in this case,[53] it is not necessary here to resort to this doctrine but, for my part, I should wish to regard it as an open question, in English law, in any future case whether and to what extent it can be invoked. . . .

Lords Hodson, Guest and Upjohn delivered concurring speeches.

Notes

1. The decision in the *Carl Zeiss* case is based upon the ingenious but unhappy fiction that the Government of the G.D.R. was acting as the agent of the USSR when legislating to reorganise its local government.[54] Disturbed by the prospects for commercial and private affairs of disregarding all of the legislative and executive acts of a government with which British companies and nationals had substantial dealings (see Lord Reid's speech), the House of Lords seized upon an artificial device that, while doing violence to the concept of agency, at least did not openly undermine the public policy considerations that had led to Foreign Office non-recognition of the G.D.R. The *Carl Zeiss* case has since been followed in the *Gur* case, below, p. 183.

2. The *Carl Zeiss* case is also important for the *obiter dicta* by Lord Wilberforce to the effect that the courts may, in the interests of justice and common sense, be prepared to recognise and enforce an unrecognised government's acts "where private rights, or acts of everyday occurrence, or perfunctory acts are concerned"

---

[53] *Ed.* That the G.D.R. was acting as the agent of the USSR, the *de jure* sovereign.

[54] For criticisms of the decision along these and other lines, see the writings cited on p. 176, n. 50, above and Jennings, *loc. cit.*, p. 144, n. 59, above, p. 361.

—provided that public policy allows. What is not clear, however, is where or how the line will be drawn between recognisable and unrecognisable acts. As Lord Wilberforce states, "the scope of these exceptions has never been precisely defined." One way of avoiding such difficulties of definition would be to see the issue in terms not of recognition but of the "choice of law" rules in the conflict of laws.[55]

3. Lord Wilberforce's view is supported by Sir John Donaldson M.R. *obiter dicta*, in the *Gur* case, below p. 183. Lord Denning M.R. expressed a similar view to that of Lord Wilberforce in *Hesperides Hotels* v. *Aegean Holidays Ltd.*[56] This case concerned two hotels owned by the Greek Cypriot plaintiffs which were being run by Turkish Cypriots with the approval of the Turkish Cypriot administration which has governed the part of Cyprus in which the hotels were located since the armed invasion of Cyprus by Turkey in 1974. The plaintiffs' action in trespass was rejected by the Court of Appeal for lack of jurisdiction on the basis of English conflict of law rules. Addressing the fact that the United Kingdom continues to recognise the pre-invasion constitutional government of Cyprus as the *de jure* government of the whole of Cyprus and does not recognise the Turkish administration *de jure* or *de facto* (and had produced to the court a certificate to this effect), Lord Denning stated *obiter dicta*:

> If it were necessary to [do so] . . . I would unhesitatingly hold that the courts of this country can recognise the laws or acts of a body which is in effective control of a territory even though it has not been recognised by Her Majesty's Government *de jure* or *de facto*: at any rate, in regard to the laws which regulate the day to day affairs of the people, such as their marriages, their divorces, their leases, their occupations, and so forth; and furthermore that the courts can receive evidence of the state of affairs so as to see whether the body is in effective control or not.[57]

See also *Adams* v. *Adams*,[58] in which a divorce decree made by a Rhodesian judge appointed by the unrecognised Smith Government was not recognised by an English court because the decree was not valid under the legal system which continued to be applicable in Southern Rhodesia under United Kingdom law.

Would these problems concerning unrecognised governments (but not states) disappear if the *Woodhouse* approach (see above, p. 162) were followed?

4. The Foreign Corporations Act 1991, s.1(1), also follows Lord Wilberforce's view in providing for the recognition under United Kingdom law of the corporate status of companies established under "the laws of a territory which is not at the time a recognised state", provided that "it appears that the laws of that territory are at that time applied by a settled court system in the territory". This is intended to cover the position of companies incorporated under, for example, the laws of the Turkish Republic of Northern Cyprus and Taiwan.[59]

5. In *Caglar* v. *Billingham*,[60] after referring, *inter alia*, to the *Hesperides* and *Gur* cases, the Special Commissioners of Inland Revenue stated:

[55] See Greig, *loc. cit.*, p. 176, n. 50, above, p. 138.
[56] [1978] Q.B. 205, CA. The matter was not discussed in the House of Lords: [1979] A.C. 508. See Lloyd Jones (1978) 37 C.L.J. 48; Merrills (1979) 28 I.C.L.Q. 523; and Shaw (1978) 94 L.Q.R. 500.
[57] [1978] Q.B. at 218.
[58] [1971] P. 188.
[59] Solicitor-General (Sir Nicholas Lyall), *Hansard*, H.C., Vol. 195, col. 438, July 17, 1991.
[60] 1996 S.T.C. 150 at 171. The question in the case was whether the Turkish Republic of Northern Cyprus was a "foreign state" so that staff at its London office were exempt from U.K. income tax. See also *Polly Peck International plc v. Nadir (No. 2)* [1992] 4 All E.R. 769, CA.

121. The principle we extract from these authorities is that the courts may acknowledge the existence of an unrecognised foreign government in the context of the enforcement of laws relating to commercial obligations or matters of private law between individuals or matters of routine administration such as the registration of births, marriages or deaths. This principle is in line with that adopted in the Foreign Corporations Act 1991. However, the courts will not acknowledge the existence of an unrecognised state if to do so would involve them in acting inconsistently with the foreign policy or diplomatic stance of this country.

122. We are not concerned with commercial obligations or matters of private law or matters of administration but with the construction of an Act of the United Kingdom Parliament. In our view it is a matter of basic public policy that we should not take cognisance of the Turkish Republic of Northern Cyprus as that would involve us in acting inconsistently with the foreign policy and diplomatic stance of this country.

GUR CORPORATION v. TRUST BANK OF AFRICA LTD[61]

[1987] Q.B. 599. Court of Appeal.

The plaintiff Panamanian company contracted with the Republic of Ciskei to build a hospital and two schools. As the contract required, the plaintiffs obtained a guarantee from the defendant bank in favour of the Ciskei Department of Public Works to cover the cost of remedying any building defects. In these proceedings, the plaintiffs sought to recover a sum paid by them to the defendant as security for the guarantee. The defendant joined Ciskei as third parties and Ciskei brought a counterclaim for the money paid as security. Thereupon, Steyn J. raised the preliminary question whether Ciskei had *locus standi* to sue or be sued in the English courts. In the light of two Foreign Office certificates, Steyn J. held that it did not. The Court of Appeal reversed his decision on the ground that the *Carl Zeiss* case applied: the Ciskei Government was acting as the delegate of the *de jure* sovereign, South Africa.

SIR JOHN DONALDSON M.R. The matter came before Steyn J. who ... raised the question of whether it was permissible for the building owners to sue or be sued in the English courts. Let me say at once that the judge was quite right to do so. Although the courts in general, and the Commercial Court in particular, will always do their best to meet the needs and wishes of the litigants, there are certain public policy constraints. So far as is relevant, they are based upon the undesirability, to put it no higher, of the national courts appearing to speak in terms which are not consistent with the nation's foreign policy and diplomatic stance. ...

This decision was greeted with some dismay by all three parties. Probably the most dismayed was the bank and for two somewhat different reasons. The first was that the decision opened up the possibility of judgment being given against the bank in favour of the plaintiffs in this country, without the bank being able to obtain a judgment in their own favour against the Republic of Ciskei, which it could use as a defence if

[61] See Beck (1987) 36 I.C.L.Q. 350; Crawford (1986) 57 B.Y.I.L. 405; Dixon (1988) 22 Int. Lawyer 555; Mann (1987) 36 I.C.L.Q. 348.

sued by Ciskei in the local courts or those of the Republic of South Africa. The second was of more general import. It was that the financial institutions of the City of London which lend money or provide financial services to bodies in a similar position to that of the building owners, and the "Republic of Ciskei" is by no means unique, would have no means of having their rights and obligations determined by the courts of this country.

... the solicitors for the bank wrote to the Foreign and Commonwealth Office on April 10, 1986 on behalf of all parties, asking:

> 1. What recognition, if any, does Her Majesty's Government accord to (1) the "Government of the Republic of Ciskei" and/or (2) the Department of Public Works, Republic of Ciskei"?
> 2. Would it be contrary to the policy or attitudes of Her Majesty's Government for the English courts to recognise either or both of such bodies as (i) contracting parties and (ii) capable of suing or being sued in an English court under such names ...

The answer dated May 1, 1986 was:

> In answer to the first of your questions, ... consistently with the statements made in Parliament in April 1980[62] ... so far as governments are concerned, the attitude of Her Majesty's Government is to be inferred from the nature of its dealings with the regime concerned and in particular whether Her Majesty's Government deals with it on a normal government to government basis. Her Majesty's Government does not recognise the "Republic of Ciskei" as an independent sovereign state, either *de jure* or *de facto*, and does not have any dealings with the "Government of the Republic of Ciskei" or "the Department of Public Works, Republic of Ciskei."
>
> With regard to the second question, it would appear to the Foreign and Commonwealth Office that the capacity to contract and to sue and be sued is a matter for the court to determine having regard to the answer given to the first question and, therefore, that it would not be appropriate for the Foreign and Commonwealth Office to answer the second question.

In a further letter dated May 9, 1986 Messrs. Durrant Piesse asked a further question:

> Which state, if any, does Her Majesty's Government recognise as (a) entitled to exercise or (b) exercising governing authority in respect of the territory in Southern Africa known as Ciskei. Has such recognition been *de jure* or *de facto*?

---

[62] See above, p. 155.

On May 16, 1986 the Foreign and Commonwealth Office answered:

> ... I am therefore instructed to reply that beyond making clear that it has not recognised as independent sovereign States Ciskei or any of the other Homelands established in South Africa Her Majesty's Government has not taken and does not have a formal position as regards the exercise of governing authority over the territory of Ciskei. Her Majesty's Government does not have any dealings with the "Government of the Republic of Ciskei", or with "the Department of Public Works. Republic of Ciskei". Her Majesty's Government has made representations to the South African Government in relation to certain matters occurring in Ciskei and others of the Homelands to which South Africa has purported to grant independence, notably on matters relating to individuals, but has not in general received any positive response from the South African Government.

Sir John Donaldson M.R. next quoted the statement made to Parliament on the recognition of governments in 1980 from which an extract is printed above, p. 155. He then considered the *Carl Zeiss* case, above, p. 176, and said, *inter alia*:

> The House of Lords [in the *Carl Zeiss* case] held that the English courts could take cognizance of the legislative authority of the G.D.R. because, whilst they could not treat it as a sovereign state with legislative powers as such, they could and should treat it as having effective legislative powers on the footing that its legislative acts were those of a subordinate body which the U.S.S.R. had set up to act on its behalf. . . .
>
> Lord Wilberforce . . . reserved for further consideration whether the non-recognition of a government or, I think, a state, would necessarily lead to the English courts treating all its legislative activities as being a nullity or whether, in the interests of justice and common sense, where no consideration of public policy to the contrary has to prevail, it might not be possible to take cognizance of the actual facts or realities found to exist in the territory in question and he instanced private rights, or acts of everyday occurrence or perfunctory acts of administration. I see great force in this reservation, since it is one thing to treat a state or government as being "without the law", but quite another to treat the inhabitants of its territory as "outlaws" who cannot effectively marry, beget legitimate children, purchase goods on credit or undertake countless day-to-day activities having legal consequences. However that is not this case. . . .

Turning to the question whether the present case came within the *Carl Zeiss* decision, Sir John Donaldson M.R. continued:

> There is . . . an apparent contrast between the two certificates when it comes to *entitlement* to exercise governing authority. In each case the certificates are conclusive that the G.D.R. or, as the case may be, the Republic of Ciskei are not recognised as independent sovereign states. It

follows from this that the courts must hold that neither the G.D.R. or its government nor the Republic of Ciskei or its government was in law capable of an executive, administrative or legislative act at the relevant times, unless enabled by some superior authority. In the case of the G.D.R., the certificate pointed expressly to where that superior authority was to be found, namely the sovereign state of the U.S.S.R. The question for our consideration is whether the Ciskei certificates . . . point to any superior authority, of which the courts can take cognizance, as supplying the requisite authority to enable the Government of the Republic of Ciskei to undertake executive, administrative or legislative acts. In reviewing and evaluating that other evidence, we must disregard any declarations or Acts of the Republic of South Africa or of the Republic of Ciskei which conflict with the certificates of the Secretary of State, just as the House of Lords disregarded such declarations by the Government of the U.S.S.R.

. . . We must disregard section 1(1) of the Status of Ciskei Act Act 1981 which declares the Republic of Ciskei to be a sovereign and independent state ceasing to be part of the Republic of South Africa and section 1(2) which declares that the Republic of South Africa will cease to exercise any authority over the territory since this subsection is clearly consequential upon subsection (1). We must also disregard section 1(1) of the Republic of Ciskei Constitution Act 1981. However, we can, and I think must, take cognizance of the remainder of those Acts, notwithstanding that, absent those sections, they may take on a somewhat different character. Thus section 3(1) of the Status of Ciskei Act 1981, which provides:

> The Legislative Assembly of Ciskei . . . may . . . make laws (including a constitution) for the Ciskei in the manner prescribed by the said Act . . . .

becomes a straightforward delegation of legislative power which could be revoked in the same way as it had been conferred, namely by a subsequent legislative Act of the Republic of South Africa.

We also know the constitutional history of the territory of the Ciskei, to which I have already referred, and we can take judicial notice of the fact that the Republic of South Africa is a sovereign state, recognised by Her Majesty's Government, and that it was entitled to exercise sovereignty over the territory of the Ciskei until the passing of the Status of Ciskei Act 1981. If then we disregard section 1 of that Act, as we must, there are no materials from which we could infer that this situation has changed. Indeed, the certified fact that "Her Majesty's Government has made representation to the South African Government in relation to certain matters occurring in Ciskei and others of the Homelands to which South Africa has purported to grant independence" gives rise to a clear inference that Her Majesty's Government regards the Republic of South Africa as continuing to be *entitled* to exercise sovereign authority over the territory. The further certified fact that the Government of the Republic has not in general made any positive response, gives rise only to an inference that the Government of the Republic is not, in general, willing to exercise the authority which it has *de jure*, preferring to leave this to the Government of Ciskei. This is immaterial for, as Lord Reid said [in the *Carl Zeiss* case] no *de jure* governing authority can disclaim responsibility for acts done by subordinate bodies which it has set up and which have not attempted to usurp its authority. There is no evidence whatever that the Republic of Ciskei or its government has attempted to do that.

It follows that in my judgment the legal status of the Republic of Ciskei and its government is indistinguishable from that which obtained in the case of the G.D.R. and its government at the time with which the *Carl Zeiss* case was concerned.

I would therefore allow the appeal and declare that the Government of the Republic of the Ciskei has *locus standi* in the courts of this country as being a subordinate body set up by the Republic of South Africa to act on its behalf.

NOURSE AND GLIDEWELL L.JJ. delivered concurring judgments.

Notes

In this case, the agency approach which was adopted by the House of Lords in the *Carl Zeiss* case to permit the recognition of the acts of an unrecognised government was used by the Court of Appeal to allow such a government *locus standi* in an English court. This facilitated commerce without, on the face of it, contradicting public policy. Might it be, however, that to allow the Ciskei Government *locus standi* was in reality subversive of the public policy (that South Africa's homelands policy should not succeed) that the Foreign Office's refusal to recognise Ciskei was intended to further?[63]

Re AL-FIN CORPORATION'S PATENT[64]

[1970] Ch. 160. Chancery Division

Section 24(1) of the Patents Act 1949 allows a patentee an extension of his patent if he has suffered loss "by reason of hostilities between His Majesty and any foreign state." In this case, the applicants sought an extension under section 24(1) in respect of loss suffered during the Korean War between 1950 and 1953. The Comptroller-General rejected the application partly on the ground that the Korean War did not come within section 24(1) because North Korea, not having been recognised by the United Kingdom, was not a "foreign state". The applicants sought a ruling on this question. The court had before it a letter from the Foreign Office indicating that North Korea was not then recognised as a state.

GRAHAM J. The question depends primarily on the proper construction of section 24, and the difference between the parties may be succinctly stated as follows: Must the section be read as if the words "recognised as such by Her Majesty" were included after the words "any foreign state"

---

[63] See Beck, *loc. cit.*, p. 183, n. 61, above, p. 358.
[64] See Merrills (1971) 20 I.C.L.Q. 476.

in subsection (1), or is it correct to read the section in a broader sense without the necessity for the qualification of recognition? ...

Mr Dillon ... for the applicants ... cited the authority of *Luigi Monta of Genoa v. Cechofracht Co. Ltd* [1956] 2 Q.B. 552. In that case the question was whether the ship had complied with:

> any orders or directions ... given by the government of the nation under whose flag the vessel sails ... or by any other government ... and compliance with any such orders or directions shall not be deemed to be a variation, and delivery in accordance with such orders or directions shall be a fulfilment of the contract voyage and the freight shall be paid accordingly.

The ship was intercepted and ordered by a general who said he came from "the government of Formosa" to discharge her cargo in that country, and did so. On a case stated by the umpire it was held by Sellers J., see pp. 564, 565 and 566, that the question to be decided was very different from a decision on a question of immunity or other question dependent on recognition, and that there was no such rule of law restricting the evidence to be considered to that provided by the Foreign Office, or which precluded the umpire from finding that there was a government in Formosa on all the evidence which was adduced. He held, on p. 564, that:

> the qualities or character required by the body giving the order or on whose behalf it was given or purported to be given must, therefore, include essentially the exercise of full executive and legislative power over an established territory. ...

Although it is true that the *Luigi Monta* case is one dealing with the construction of a clause in a charterparty and Mr MacCrindle [for the respondent comptroller] is entitled to draw some distinction between the construction of such a document and of a statute, nevertheless the general principle must be that the true intention of the document, whether it be a commercial document or a statute, is to be ascertained. ...

... in my judgment, the correct principle is that the word must be construed in its context and given the meaning which it is considered was intended by the legislature.

Applying these principles to section 24, I have no hesitation in holding that the phrase "any foreign state", although of course it includes a foreign state which has been given Foreign Office recognition, is not limited thereto. It must at any rate include a sufficiently defined area of territory over which a foreign government has effective control. Whether or not the state in question satisfies these conditions is a matter primarily of fact in each case. ...

In the present case, apart from paragraph 4 of the Foreign Office Certificate, there is the evidence of Mr Frank in his affidavit of April 24, 1968, which satisfies me, see paragraphs 22 to 25 in particular, that at the relevant time North Korea had a defined territory over which a government had effective control and that His late Majesty was engaged in hostilities with this state albeit his troops were under the command and formed part of the United Nations' forces fighting in the area.

I hold therefore that North Korea was a foreign state within the meaning of section 24. . . .

Notes

1. As this case shows, the English courts, exceptionally are prepared to look beyond the terms of a Foreign Office certificate when interpreting or construing the terms "state" in a statute or document on the basis that their function is to discover the intention of Parliament or the draftsman. In contrast, the courts, as the earlier cases in this section show, accept a Foreign Office certificate as conclusive, when recognising the law or the capacity to act of a foreign state.

2. In *Reel v. Holder*[65] the Court of Appeal held that it was simply concerned with the interpretation of the rules of the IAAF [the International Amateur Athletic Federation] and not "with the international sphere of statehood and sovereignty" when asked to decide whether Taiwan was a "country" within the meaning of the IAAF rules (held that it was). Accordingly, a Foreign Office statement to the effect that Taiwan was not recognised as a state was not in point. *cf. Spinney's Royal Ins. Co.*[66] (certificate not sought on question whether hostilities in Lebanon constituted "civil war" for insurance contract purposes).

3. In *Caglar v. Billingham*,[67] the Special Commissioners of Inland Revenue held that the term "foreign state" in section 321 of the Income and Corporation Taxes Act 1988 referred only to states recognised by the U.K. Government, and hence did not include the Turkish Republic of Northern Cyprus. The Commissioners applied the *Al-Fin* "intention" and "context" principle, but reached a different conclusion on the facts.

---

[65] [1981] 1 W.L.R. 1226 at 1228, CA, *per* Lord Denning M.R.
[66] [1980] 1 Lloyd's Rep. 406, QB.
[67] [1996] S.T.C 150. See Warbrick (1996) 45 I.C.L.Q. 954.

CHAPTER 5

TERRITORY

1. TITLE TO TERRITORY[1]

.(i) OCCUPATION AND PRESCRIPTION

ISLAND OF PALMAS CASE[2]

Netherlands *v.* U.S. (1928)

Permanent Court of Arbitration. Sole Arbitrator:
Huber. 2 R.I.A.A. 829

As a result of the Spanish-American War of 1898, Spain ceded the Philippines to the United States by the Treaty of Paris of that year. In 1906, a United States official visited the island of Palmas (or Miangas), which the United States believed to be a part of the territory ceded to it, and found, to his surprise, a Dutch flag flying there. Palmas lies about 50 miles southeast of Cape San Augustin on the island of Mindanao. It is two miles long and less than a mile wide. In 1928, it had a population of less than 1,000 and was of negligible economic, military or other importance. Nonetheless, the Netherlands and the United States referred the question of sovereignty over the island to arbitration.

Award of the Arbitrator

Sovereignty in the relations between States signifies independence. Independence in regard to a portion of the globe is the right to exercise therein, to the exclusion of any other State, the functions of a State. The development of the national organisation of States during the last few centuries and, as a corollary, the development of international law, have established this principle of the exclusive competence of the State in regard to its own territory in such a way as to make it the point of departure in settling most questions that concern international relations. . . . The fact that the functions of a State can be performed by any State within a given zone is, on the other hand, precisely the characteristic feature of the legal situation pertaining in those parts of the globe which,

[1] See Jennings, *The Acquisition of Territory in International Law* (1963).
[2] See Jessup (1928) 22 A.J.I.L. 735.

like the high seas or lands without a master, cannot or do not yet form the territory of a State.

... If a dispute arises as to the sovereignty over a portion of territory, it is customary to examine which of the States claiming sovereignty possesses a title—cession, conquest, occupation, *etc.*—superior to that which the other State might possibly bring forward against it. However, if the contestation is based on the fact that the other Party has actually displayed sovereignty, it cannot be sufficient to establish the title by which territorial sovereignty was validly acquired at a certain moment; it must also be shown that the territorial sovereignty has continued to exist and did exist at the moment which for the decision of the dispute must be considered as critical. This demonstration consists in the actual display of State activities, such as belongs only to the territorial sovereign.

Titles of acquisition of territorial sovereignty in present-day international law are either based on an act of effective apprehension, such as occupation or conquest, or, like cession, presuppose that the ceding and the cessionary Powers or at least one of them, have the faculty of effectively disposing of the ceded territory. In the same way natural accretion can only be conceived of as an accretion to a portion of territory where there exists an actual sovereignty capable of extending to a spot which falls within its sphere of activity. It seems therefore natural that an element which is essential for the constitution of sovereignty should not be lacking in its continuation. So true is this, that practice, as well as doctrine, recognizes—though under different legal formulae and with certain differences as to the conditions required—that the continuous and peaceful display of territorial sovereignty (peaceful in relation to other States) is as good as a title. The growing insistence with which international law, ever since the middle of the 18th century, has demanded that the occupation shall be effective would be inconceivable, if effectiveness were required only for the act of acquisition and not equally for the maintenance of the right. If the effectiveness has above all been insisted on in regard to occupation, this is because the question rarely arises in connection with territories in which there is already an established order of things. Just as before the rise of international law, boundaries of lands were necessarily determined by the fact that the power of a State was exercised within them, so too, under the reign of international law, the fact of peaceful and continuous display is still one of the most important considerations in establishing boundaries between States.

Territorial sovereignty, as has already been said, involves the exclusive right to display the activities of a State. This right has as corollary a duty: the obligation to protect within the territory the rights of other States, in particular their right to integrity and inviolability in peace and in war, together with the rights which each State may claim for its nationals in foreign territory. Without manifesting its territorial sovereignty in a manner corresponding to circumstances, the State cannot fulfil this duty. ...

Although municipal law, thanks to its complete judicial system, is able to recognize abstract rights of property as existing apart from any material display of them, it has none the less limited their effect by the principles of prescription and the protection of possession. International law, the structure of which is not based on any super-State organisation, cannot be presumed to reduce a right such as territorial sovereignty, with which almost all international relations are bound up, to the category of an abstract right, without concrete manifestations. . . .

Manifestations of territorial sovereignty assume, it is true, different forms, according to conditions of time and place. Although continuous in principle, sovereignty cannot be exercised in fact at every moment on every point of a territory. The intermittence and discontinuity compatible with the maintenance of the right necessarily differ according as inhabited or uninhabited regions are involved, or regions enclosed within territories in which sovereignty is incontestably displayed or again regions accessible from, for instance, the high seas. It is true that neighbouring States may by convention fix limits to their own sovereignty, even in regions such as the interior of scarcely explored continents where such sovereignty is scarcely manifested, and in this way each may prevent the other from any penetration of its territory. The delimitation of Hinterland may also be mentioned in this connection.

If, however, no conventional line of sufficient topographical precision exists or if there are gaps in the frontiers otherwise established, or if a conventional line leaves room for doubt, or if, as, *e.g.* in the case of an island situated in the high seas, the question arises whether a title is valid *erga omnes*, the actual continuous and peaceful display of State functions is in case of dispute the sound and natural criterion of territorial sovereignty. . . .

The *title alleged by the United States of America* as constituting the immediate foundation of its claim is that of *cession*, brought about by the Treaty of Paris, which cession transferred all rights of sovereignty which Spain may have possessed . . . concerning the island of Palmas (or Miangas).

It is evident that Spain could not transfer more rights than she herself possessed . . . the United States bases its claim, as successor of Spain, in the first place on *discovery*. . . .

It is admitted by both sides that international law underwent profound modifications between the end of the Middle Ages and the end of the 19th century, as regards the rights of discovery and acquisition of uninhabited region or regions inhabited by savages or semi-civilized peoples. Both Parties are also agreed that a juridical fact must be appreciated in the light of the law contemporary with it, and not of the law in force at the time when a dispute in regard to it arises or falls to be settled. The effect of discovery by Spain is therefore to be determined by the rules of international law in force in the first half of the 16th century. . . .

If the view most favourable to the American arguments is adopted —with every reservation as to the soundness of such view—that is to say, if we consider as positive law at the period in question the rule that discovery as such, *i.e.* the mere fact of seeing land, without any act, even symbolical, of taking possession, involved *ipso jure* territorial sovereignty and not merely an "inchoate title", a *jus ad rem*, to be completed eventually by an actual and durable taking of possession within a reasonable time, the question arises whether sovereignty yet existed at the critical date, *i.e.* the moment of conclusion and coming into force of the Treaty of Paris.

As regards the question which of different legal systems prevailing at successive periods is to be applied in a particular case (the so-called intertemporal law), a distinction must be made between the creation of rights and the existence of rights. The same principle which subjects the act creative of a right to the law in force at the time the right arises, demands that the existence of right, in other words its continued manifestation, shall follow the conditions required by the evolution of law. International law in the 19th century, having regard to the fact that most parts of the globe were under the sovereignty of States members of the community of nations, and that territories without a master had become relatively few, took account of a tendency already existing and especially developed since the middle of the 18th century, and laid down the principle that occupation, to constitute a claim to territorial sovereignty, must be effective, that is, offer certain guarantees to other States and their nationals. It seems therefore incompatible with this rule of positive law that there should be regions which are neither under the effective sovereignty of a State, nor without a master, but which are reserved for the exclusive influence of one State, in virtue solely of a title of acquisition which is no longer recognized by existing law, even if such a title ever conferred territorial sovereignty. For these reasons, discovery alone, without any subsequent act, cannot, at the present time suffice to prove sovereignty over the Island of Palmas (or Miangas); and in so far as there is no sovereignty, the question of an abandonment properly speaking of sovereignty by one State in order that the sovereignty of another may take its place does not arise.

If on the other hand the view is adopted that discovery does not create a definitive title of sovereignty, but only an "inchoate" title, such a title exists, it is true, without external manifestation. However, according to the view that has prevailed at any rate since the 19th century, an inchoate title of discovery must be completed within a reasonable period by the effective occupation of the region claimed to be discovered. This principle must be applied in the present case, for the reasons given above in regard to the rules determining which of successive legal systems is to be applied (the so-called intertemporal law). Now, no act of occupation nor, except as to a recent period, any exercise of sovereignty at Palmas by Spain has been alleged. But even admitting that the Spanish title still existed as inchoate in 1898 and must be considered as included in the cession under Article III of the Treaty of Paris, an inchoate title could not prevail over the continuous and peaceful display of authority by another State; for such display may prevail even over a prior, definitive title put forward by another State . . .

In the last place [in examining the United States arguments] there remains to be considered *title arising out of contiguity* . . . it is impossible to show the existence of a rule of positive international law to the effect that islands situated outside territorial waters should belong to a State from the mere fact that its territory forms the *terra firma* (nearest continent or island of considerable size). Not only would it seem that there are no precedents sufficiently frequent and sufficiently precise in their bearing to establish such a rule of international law, but the alleged principle itself is by its very nature so uncertain and contested that even Governments of the same State have on different occasions maintained contradictory opinions as to its soundness. The principle of contiguity, in regard to islands, may not be out of place when it is a question of allotting them to one state rather than another, either by agreement between the Parties, or by a decision not necessarily based on law; but as a rule establishing *ipso jure* the presumption of sovereignty in favour of a particular State, this principle would be in conflict with what has been said as to territorial sovereignty and as to the necessary relation between the right to exclude other States from a region and the duty to display therein the activities of a State. Nor is this principle of contiguity admissible as a legal method of deciding questions of territorial sovereignty; for it is wholly lacking in precision and would in its application lead to arbitrary results. This would be especially true in a case such as that of the island in question, which is not relatively close to one single continent, but forms part of a large archipelago in which strict delimitations between the different parts are not naturally obvious.

There lies, however, at the root of the idea of contiguity one point which must be considered also in regard to the Island of Palmas (or Miangas). It has been explained above that in the exercise of territorial sovereignty there are necessarily gaps, intermittence in time and discontinuity in space. This phenomenon will be particularly noticeable in the case of colonial territories, partly uninhabited or as yet partly unsubdued. The fact that a State cannot prove display of sovereignty as regards such a position of territory cannot forthwith be interpreted as showing that sovereignty is inexistent. Each case must be appreciated in accordance with the particular circumstances. . . .

As regards groups of islands, it is possible that a group may under certain circumstances be regarded as in law, a unit, and that the fate of the principal part may involve the rest. Here, however, we must distinguish between, on the one hand, the act of first taking possession, which can hardly extend to every portion of territory, and, on the other hand, the display of sovereignty as a continuous and prolonged manifestation which must make itself felt through the whole territory.

As regards the territory forming the subject of the present dispute, it must be remembered that it is a somewhat isolated island, and therefore a territory clearly delimited and individualised. It is moreover an island permanently inhabited, occupied by a population sufficiently numerous for it to be impossible that acts of administration could be lacking for very long periods. The memoranda of both Parties assert that there is communication by boat and even with native craft between the Island of Palmas (or Miangas) and neighbouring regions. The inability in such a case to indicate any acts of public administration makes it difficult to imagine the actual display of sovereignty, even if the sovereignty be regarded as confined within such narrow limits as would be supposed for a small island inhabited exclusively by natives. . . .

The Court then examined the argument put by the Netherlands.

The Netherlands found their claim to sovereignty essentially on the title of peaceful and continuous display of State authority over the island. Since this title would in international law prevail over a title of acquisition of sovereignty not followed by actual display of State authority, it is necessary to ascertain in the first place, whether the contention of the Netherlands is sufficiently established by evidence, and, if so, for what period of time.

In the opinion of the Arbitrator the Netherlands have succeeded in establishing the following facts:

a. The Island of Palmas (or Miangas) is identical with an island designated by this or a similar name, which has formed, at least since 1700, successively a part of two of the native States of the Island of Sangi (Talautse Isles).

b. These native States were from 1677 onwards connected with the East Indian Company, and thereby with the Netherlands,[3] by contracts of suzerainty, which conferred upon the suzerain such powers as would justify his considering the vassal State as a part of his territory.

c. Acts characteristic of State authority exercised either by the vassal State or by the suzerain Power in regard precisely to the Island of Palmas (or Miangas) have been established as occurring at different epochs between 1700 and 1898, as well as in the period between 1898 and 1906.

---

[3] *Ed.* Elsewhere in his Award the Arbitrator commented on the nature of the acts of the Dutch East India Company as follows: "[They] must, in international law, be entirely assimilated to acts of the Netherlands State itself. From the end of the 16th till the 19th century, companies formed by individuals and engaged in economic pursuits (Chartered Companies), were invested by the State to whom they were subject with public powers for the acquisition and administration of colonies."

The acts of indirect or direct display of Netherlands sovereignty at Palmas (or Miangas), especially in the 18th and early 19th centuries are not numerous, and there are considerable gaps in the evidence of continuous display. But apart from the consideration that the manifestations of sovereignty over a small and distant island, inhabited only by natives, cannot be expected to be frequent, it is not necessary that the display of sovereignty should go back to a very far distant period. It may suffice that such display existed in 1898, and had already existed as continuous and peaceful before that date long enough to enable any Power who might have considered herself as possessing sovereignty over the island, or having a claim to sovereignty, to have, according to local conditions, a reasonable possibility for ascertaining the existence of a state of things contrary to her real or alleged rights.

It is not necessary that the display of sovereignty should be established as having begun at a precise epoch; it suffices that it had existed at the critical period preceding the year 1898. It is quite natural that the establishment of sovereignty may be the outcome of a slow evolution, of a progressive intensification of State control. This is particularly the case, if sovereignty is acquired by the establishment of the suzerainty of a colonial Power over a native State, and in regard to outlying possessions of such a vassal state.

Now the evidence relating to the period after the middle of the 19th century makes it clear that the Netherlands Indian Government considered the island distinctly as a part of its possessions and that, in the years immediately preceding 1898, an intensification of display of sovereignty took place.

Since the moment when the Spaniards, in withdrawing from the Moluccas in 1666, made express reservations as to the maintenance of their sovereign rights, up to the contestation made by the United States in 1906, no contestation or other action whatever or protest against the exercise of territorial rights by the Netherlands over the Talautse (Sangi) Isles and their dependencies (Miangas included) has been recorded. The peaceful character of the display of Netherlands sovereignty for the entire period to which the evidence concerning acts of display relates (1700–1906) must be admitted.

There is moreover no evidence which would establish any act of display of sovereignty over the island by Spain or another Power, such as might counterbalance or annihilate the manifestations of Netherlands sovereignty. As to third Powers, the evidence submitted to the Tribunal does not disclose any trace of such action, at least from the middle of the 17th century onwards. These circumstances, together with the absence of any evidence of a conflict between Spanish and Netherlands authorities during more than two centuries as regards Palmas (or Miangas), are an indirect proof of the exclusive display of Netherlands sovereignty.

This being so, it remains to be considered first whether the display of State authority might not legally be defective and therefore unable to create a valid title of sovereignty, and secondly whether the United States may not put forward a better title to that of the Netherlands.

As to the conditions of acquisition of sovereignty by way of continuous and peaceful display of State authority (so-called prescription), some of which have been discussed in the United States Counter-Memorandum, the following must be said:

The display has been open and public, that is to say that it was in conformity with usages as to exercise of sovereignty over colonial States. A clandestine exercise of State authority over an inhabited territory during a considerable length of time would seem to be impossible. . . .

The conditions of acquisition of sovereignty by the Netherlands are therefore to be considered as fulfilled. It remains now to be seen whether the United States as successors of Spain are in a position to bring forward an equivalent or stronger title. This is to be answered in the negative.

The title of discovery, if it had not been already disposed of by the Treaties of Munster and Utrecht would, under the most favourable and most extensive interpretation, exist only as an inchoate title, as a claim to establish sovereignty by effective occupation. An inchoate title however cannot prevail over a definite title founded on continuous and peaceful display of sovereignty.

The title of contiguity, understood as a basis of territorial sovereignty, has no foundation in international law.

The title of recognition by treaty does not apply, because even if the Sangi States, with the dependency of Miangas, are to be considered as "held and possessed" by Spain in 1648, the rights of Spain to be derived from the Treaty of Munster [1648] would have been superseded by those which were acquired by the Treaty of Utrecht. Now if there is evidence of a state of possession in 1714 concerning the island of Palmas (or Miangas), such evidence is exclusively in favour of the Netherlands. But even if the Treaty of Utrecht could not be taken into consideration, the acquiescence of Spain in the situation created after 1677 would deprive her and her successors of the possibility of still invoking conventional rights at the present time.

The Netherlands title of sovereignty, acquired by continuous and peaceful display of State authority during a long period of time probably going back beyond the year 1700, therefore holds good. . . .

For these reasons the Arbitrator, in conformity with Article I of the Special Agreement of January 23, 1925, decides that: the Island of Palmas (or Miangas) forms in its entirety a part of Netherlands territory.

Notes

1. The Award in the *Palmas Case* is of outstanding importance in the law on the acquisition of title to territory because of its full and scholarly treatment of such basic matters as the nature of territorial sovereignty and because of the emphasis placed upon the effect of a "continuous and peaceful display of State authority." As to the latter, the case indicates very clearly that the state that can show such "a

display of State authority" in the period leading up to the "critical date"[4] (*i.e.* the date on which the location of territorial sovereignty is decisive) can defeat any other claim whatever its basis. It has, however, to be a "peaceful" display of such authority, *i.e.* one without protest by interested states of the sort that prevents prescription, and of sufficient duration to establish a prescriptive title.[5] Thus, a state which exercises continuous and peaceful governmental possession has a title by way of occupation if the territory was previously a *res nullius* and by way of prescription if it was not.[6]

2. *Territorial Sovereignty.*[7] The meaning of territorial sovereignty was discussed by France in its pleadings in the *Nationality Decrees in Tunis and Morocco* case.[8] There M. A. de La Pradelle stated:

> ... territory is neither an object not a substance; it is a framework. What sort of framework? The framework within which the public power is exercised ... territory as such must not be considered, it must be regarded as the external, ostensible sign of the sphere within which the public power of the state is exercised.[9]

3. *Title by Discovery.* On the possibility of obtaining title by discovery, Keller, Lissitzyn and Mann,[10] referring to the years 1400–1800, state:

> Throughout this lengthy period, no state appeared to regard mere discovery, in the sense of "physical" discovery or simple "visual apprehension," as being in any way sufficient *per se* to establish a right of sovereignty over, or a valid title to, *terra nullius*. Furthermore, mere disembarkation upon any portion of such regions—or even extended penetration and exploration therein—was not regarded as sufficient itself to establish such a right or title ... the formal ceremony of taking of possession, the symbolic act, was generally regarded as being wholly sufficient *per se* to establish immediately a right of sovereignty over, or a valid title to, areas so claimed and did not require to be supplemented by the performance of other acts, such as, for example, "effective occupation." A right or title so acquired and established was deemed good against all subsequent claims set up in opposition thereto unless, perhaps, transferred by conquest or treaty, relinquished, abandoned, or successfully opposed by continued occupation on the part of some other state.

4. On the relevance of contiguity (see above, p. 194), see also the *Western Sahara* case, below, p. 207. When the Arbitrator in the *Palmas Case* refers to "the delimitation of Hinterland,"[11] he has the Hinterland doctrine of the period of colonial expansion in mind. The doctrine was expressed as follows by the British Law Officers in 1885:

---

[4] The critical date may change: see the *Land, Island and Maritime Frontier Dispute* case, below, p. 238. On the concept of the critical date, the utility of which has been questioned, see further the *Dubai/Sharjah Boundary Dispute* case, as to which see Bowett (1994) 65 B.Y.I.L. 103 at 111, and Jennings, *op. cit.*, p. 190, n. 1, p. 35.

[5] See below, pp. 212–213.

[6] Prescription will overcome titles based upon occupation, conquest, cession, *etc.*

[7] See Shaw (1982) 13 N.Y.I.L. 61.

[8] P.C.I.J.Rep., Series B, No. 4, (1923).

[9] *ibid.* Series C, No. 2, pp. 106, 108.

[10] *Creation of Rights of Sovereignty through Symbolic Acts 1400–1800* (1938), pp. 148–149.

[11] Above, p. 192.

[T]he general principle is, that if a national has made a settlement it has a right to assume sovereignty over all the adjacent vacant territory, which is necessary to the integrity and security of the Settlement.[12]

5. *Intertemporal Law.* Commenting upon Huber's conception of intertemporal law, Jessup[13] wrote:

Assume that State A in a certain year acquires Island X from State B by a treaty of peace after a war in which A is the victor.[14] Assume Island X is a barren rocky place, uninhabited and desired by A only for strategic reasons to prevent its fortification by another Power. Assume that A holds Island X, but without making direct use of it, for two hundred years. At the end of that time suppose that the development of international morality has so far progressed as to change the previous rule of international law and that the new rule is that no territory may be acquired by a victor from a vanquished at the close of a war. Under the theory of "intertemporal law" as expounded, it would appear that A would no longer have good title to Island X but must secure a new title upon some other basis or in accordance with the new rule. Such a retroactive effect of law would be highly disturbing. Every state would constantly be under the necessity of examining its title to each portion of its territory in order to determine whether a change in the law had necessitated, as it were, a reacquisition.

An extension of the doctrine of intertemporal law from a requirement that title must be valid in accordance with the law in force at the time at which it is claimed to have been established to one by which the validity of title must also be constantly updated as the international law bases for title change would, as Jessup suggests, be extremely disruptive.

6. In the special agreement by which the *Palmas Case* was submitted to arbitration, the arbitrator was instructed to determine whether the island formed "a part of Netherlands territory or of territory belonging to the United States of America." Could he, with these instructions, have decided that the island was *res nullius* or that a third state had title to it? Was his ruling in favour of the Netherlands binding upon third states? In the *Frontier Dispute Case*,[15] the International Court of Justice noted that its determination of the land border between the parties, Burkino Faso and Mali, would not be opposable to Niger, a neighbouring state whose boundaries might be thought to be affected by the determination, because of Article 59, I.C.J. Statute.[16] Is an international judgment or an arbitral award, a further means of acquiring title?[17]

7. The Arbitrator's reliance upon the acts of the Dutch East India Company as evidence of the exercise of authority by the Netherlands makes it relevant to point out the different situation in respect of the acts of individuals unauthorised to act for the state of which they are nationals. In the *Anglo-Norwegian Fisheries Case*, Judge Sir Arnold McNair stated that "the independent activity of private individuals is of little value unless it can be shown that they have acted in pursuance of

[12] 1 McNair 292.

[13] *loc. cit.*, p. 190, n. 2, above, p. 135.

[14] See now Art. 52 of the Vienna Convention on the Law of Treaties 1969, below, p. 831, on treaties the conclusion of which is obtained by armed force.

[15] I.C.J. Rep. 1986, p. 554.

[16] Below, Appendix I.

[17] See Brownlie, pp. 137–138, and the *Land, Island and Maritime Frontier Dispute* case, below, p. 238.

a licence or some other authority received from their Governments or that in some other way their Governments have asserted jurisdiction through them."[18] A somewhat related question arose in the mid-nineteenth century when the Sultan of Borneo ceded Sarawak to Sir James Brooke, a British subject. In 1853, the Law Officers of the Crown were asked by the Foreign Office "whether it would be proper for Her Majesty's Government to recognise Sir James Brooke, as independent ruler or Sovereign of the Foreign State of Sarawak."[19] They replied that this was entirely a question of policy. As a question of *British Constitutional Law,* the report continued, "it is legally competent to Her Majesty to permit one of Her Subjects to assume the Sovereignty of a Foreign state, and to recognize him as such. Without such permission from the Crown, a Subject cannot acquire independent Sovereignty; the latter position being inconsistent with the allegiance which he owes to his own Sovereign. . . . "[20]

CLIPPERTON ISLAND CASE[21]

France *v.* Mexico (1931)

Arbitrator: King Victor Emmanuel III of Italy. (1932) 26 A.J.I.L. 390

Award of the Arbitrator

In fact, we find, in the first place, that on November 17, 1858, Lieutenant Victor Le Coat de Kerwéguen, of the French Navy, commissioner of the French Government, while cruising about one-half mile off Clipperton[22] drew up, on board the commercial vessel *L'Amiral,* an act by which, conformably to the orders which had been given to him by the Minister of Marine, he proclaimed and declared that the sovereignty of the said island beginning from that date belonged in perpetuity to His Majesty the Emperor Napoleon III and to his heirs and successors. During the cruise, careful and minute geographical notes were made; a boat succeeded, after numerous difficulties, in landing some members of the crew; and on the evening of November 20, after a second unsuccessful attempt to reach the shore, the vessel put off without leaving in the island any sign of sovereignty. Lieutenant de Kerwéguen officially notified the accomplishment of his mission to the Consulate of France at Honolulu, which made a like communication to the Government of Hawaii. Moreover, the same consulate had published in English in the journal *The Polynesian,* of Honolulu, on December 8, the declaration by which French sovereignty over Clipperton had already been proclaimed.

Thereafter, until the end of 1887 no positive and apparent act of sovereignty can be recalled either on the part of France or on the part of any

---

[18] I.C.J.Rep. 1951, p. 184.
[19] 1 McNair 21.
[20] *ibid.*
[21] See Dickinson (1933) 27 A.J.I.L. 130.
[22] *Ed.* Clipperton is "a low coral lagoon reef, less than three miles in diameter, situated in the Pacific Ocean . . . some 670 miles south-west of Mexico": Dickinson, *ibid.* p. 131.

other Powers. The island remained without population, at least stable, and no administration was organized there. A concession for the exploitation of guano[23] beds existing there, which had been approved by the Emperor on April 8, 1858, in favor of a certain Mr. Lockart, and which had given rise to the expedition of Lieutenant de Kerwéguen, had not been followed up, nor had its exploitation been undertaken on the part of any other French subjects.

Towards the end of 1897 ... France stated ... that three persons were found in the island collecting guano ... and that they had, on the appearance of the French vessel, raised the American flag. Explanations were demanded on this subject from the United States, which responded that it had not granted any concession to the said company and did not intend to claim any right of sovereignty over Clipperton ...

About a month after this act of surveillance had been accomplished by the French Navy... Mexico, ignoring the occupation claimed by France and considering that Clipperton was territory belonging to her for a long time, sent to the place a gun-boat, *La Democrata*, which action was caused by the report, afterwards acknowledged to be inaccurate, that England had designs upon the island. A detachment of officers and marines landed from the said ship December 13, 1897, and again found the three persons who resided on the island at the time of the preceding arrival of the French ship. It made them lower the American flag and hoist the Mexican flag in its place. Of the three individuals above mentioned, two consented to leave the island, and the third declared his wish to remain there, and in fact remained there until an unknown date. After that the *Democrata* left on December 15.

On January 8, France, having learned of the Mexican expedition, reminded that Power of its rights over Clipperton. ...

According to Mexico, Clipperton Island, which had been given the name of the famous English adventurer who, at the beginning of the 18th century, used it as a place of refuge, was none other than Passion Island ... that this island had been discovered by the Spanish Navy and, by virtue of the law then in force, fixed by the Bull of Alexander VII,[24] had belonged to Spain, and afterwards, from 1836, to Mexico as the successor state of the Spanish state.

But according to the actual state of our knowledge, it has not been proven that this island ... had been actually discovered by the Spanish navigators. ... However, even admitting that the discovery had been made by Spanish subjects, it would be necessary, to establish the contention of Mexico to prove that Spain not only had the right, as a state, to

---

[23] *Ed.* Guano is a fertiliser made from the excrement of sea birds, particularly some that nest on islands off the coast of South America. Its discovery in the nineteenth century led to a sort of "Guano-rush".

[24] *Ed.* This was the Papal Bull *Inter Caetera* of 1493 by which a remarkably generous Pope gave to Spain all land discovered or to be discovered west of a line 100 miles west of the Azores and Cape Verde not in the possession of any Christian king.

incorporate the island in her possessions, but also had effectively exercised the right. But that has not been demonstrated at all. . . .

Consequently, there is ground to admit that, when in November, 1858, France proclaimed her sovereignty over Clipperton, that island was in the legal situation of *territorium nullius*, and, therefore, susceptible of occupation.

The question remains whether France proceeded to an effective occupation, satisfying the conditions required by international law for the validity of this kind of territorial acquisition. In effect, Mexico maintains . . . that the French occupation was not valid, and consequently her own right to occupy the island which must still be considered as *nullius* in 1897.

In whatever concerns this question, there is, first of all, ground to hold as incontestable, the regularity of the act by which France in 1858 made known in a clear and precise manner, her intention to consider the island as her territory.

On the other hand, it is disputed that France took effective possession of the island, and it is maintained that without such a taking of possession of an effective character, the occupation must be considered as null and void.

It is beyond doubt that by immemorial usage having the force of law, besides the *animus occupandi*, the actual, and not the nominal, taking of possession is a necessary condition of occupation. This taking of possession consists in the act, or series of acts, by which the occupying state reduces to its possession the territory in question and takes steps to exercise exclusive authority there. Strictly speaking, and in ordinary cases, that only takes place when the state establishes in the territory itself an organization capable of making its laws respected. But this step is, properly speaking, but a means of procedure to the taking of possession, and, therefore, is not identical with the latter. There may also be cases where it is unnecessary to have recourse to this method. Thus, if a territory, by virtue of the fact that it was completely uninhabited, is, from the first moment when the occupying state makes its appearance there, at the absolute and undisputed disposition of that state, from that moment the taking of possession must be considered as accomplished, and the occupation is thereby complete. . . .

The regularity of the French occupation has also been questioned because the other Powers were not notified of it. But it must be observed that the precise obligation to make such notification is contained in Art. 34 of the Act of Berlin[25] . . . which . . . is not applicable to the present case. There is good reason to think that the notoriety given to the act, by

---

[25] *Ed.* This required a party to the Act that took possession of land on the coast of Africa to notify the other parties that it had done so.

whatever means, sufficed at the time, and that France provoked that notoriety by publishing the said act in the manner above indicated.

It follows from these premises that Clipperton Island was legitimately acquired by France on November 17, 1858. There is no reason to suppose that France has subsequently lost her right by *derelictio*, since she never had the *animus* of abandoning the island, and the fact that she has not exercised her authority there in a positive manner does not imply the forfeiture of an acquisition already definitively perfected.

FOR THESE REASONS, we decide, as arbiter, that the sovereignty over Clipperton Island belongs to France, dating from November 17, 1858.

Notes

1. This is a classic case of obtaining title to *res nullius* by occupation. What amount of authority does it suggest has to be exercised over an uninhabited island to establish possession?

2. In the *Eastern Greenland* case,[26] Norway "officially confirmed" its "taking possession" of Eastern Greenland, an uncolonised part of the island, by a declaration of July 10, 1931. Denmark, which had colonies elsewhere in Greenland and which claimed sovereignty over the whole of the island, asked the Permanent Court of International Justice to declare that the Norwegian declaration was invalid.

Although Denmark had not colonised Eastern Greenland, the Court found sufficient evidence of its claim and of exercise of state authority over the area during many centuries to show that it had established title to it at the "critical date," namely July 10, 1931, when Norway made its claim. In recent history, this evidence consisted from 1814 to 1915 of treaties applying to Greenland as a whole (which showed Denmark's "will and intention to exercise sovereignty"), of the granting of concessions for trading, etc., in Eastern Greenland and of legislation establishing the width of the territorial sea. From 1915 to 1931, it consisted of steps by Denmark to have its title to Greenland recognised by other states as well as various acts of administration and legislation. During both periods, Norwegian expeditions had sometimes wintered in Eastern Greenland and a wireless station and other buildings had been erected. Denmark had protested against the erection of the wireless station. The Court found this evidence sufficient to establish Denmark's sovereignty over the years indicated. Finally, the Court stressed the relative nature of the test to be applied in establishing occupation:

> It is impossible to read the records of the decisions in cases as to territorial sovereignty without observing that in many cases the tribunal has been satisfied with very little in the way of the actual exercise of sovereign rights, provided that the other State could not make out a superior claim. This is particularly true in the case of claims to sovereignty over areas in thinly populated or unsettled countries.[27]

The Court itself added to this jurisprudence by emphasising the absence of any other claim to Greenland prior to 1931.

[26] P.C.I.J.Rep., Series A/B, No. 53 (1933). See the discussion of this case in the *Western Sahara* case, below, p. 207.

[27] P.C.I.J. Rep. Series A/B, No. 53 (1933) p. 46.

MINQUIERS AND ECREHOS CASE[28]

France *v.* U.K.

I.C.J. Reports 1953, p. 47

Judgment of the Court

By Article I of the Special Agreement, signed on December 29th, 1950, the Court is requested:

> to determine whether the sovereignty over the islets and rocks (in so far as they are capable of appropriation) of the Minquiers and Ecrehos groups[29] respectively belongs to the United Kingdom or the French Republic.

Having thus been requested to decide whether these groups belong either to France or to the United Kingdom, the Court has to determine which of the Parties has produced the more convincing proof of title to one or the other of these groups, or to both of them. By the formulation of Article I the Parties have excluded the status of *res nullius* as well as that of *condominium*.

In Article II the Parties have stated their agreement as to the presentation of the Pleadings "without prejudice to any question as to the burden of proof", a question which it is for the Court to decide. Having regard to the position of the Parties, both claiming sovereignty over the same territory, and in view of the formulation of the task of the Court in Article I, and the terms of Article II, the Court is of the opinion that each Party has to prove its alleged title and the facts upon which it relies. . . .

Both Parties contend that they have respectively an ancient or original title to the Ecrehos and the Minquiers, and that their title has always been maintained and was never lost. The present case does not therefore present the characteristics of a dispute concerning the acquisition of sovereignty over *terra nullius*.

The United Kingdom Government derives the ancient title invoked by it from the conquest of England in 1066 by William, Duke of Normandy. By this conquest England became united with the Duchy of Normandy, including the Channel Islands, and this union lasted until 1204 when King Philip Augustus of France drove the Anglo-Norman forces out of Continental Normandy. But his attempts to occupy also the Islands were not successful, except for brief periods when some of them were taken by French forces. On this ground the United Kingdom Government submits the view that all of the Channel Islands, including the Ecrehos and the

---

[28] See Fitzmaurice (1955–56) 32 B.Y.I.L. 20–76; Johnson (1954) 3 I.C.L.Q. 189; Wade (1954) 40 Trans.Grot. Soc. 97.

[29] *Ed.* These are in the English Channel, near Guernsey.

Minquiers, remained, as before, united with England and that this situation of fact was placed on a legal basis by subsequent Treaties concluded between the English and French Kings . . .

The French Government derives the original title invoked by it from the fact that the Dukes of Normandy were the vassals of the Kings of France, and that the Kings of England after 1066, in their capacity as Dukes of Normandy, held the Duchy in fee of the French Kings. . . .

The Court considers it sufficient to state as its view that even if the Kings of France did have an original feudal title also in respect of the Channel Islands, such a title must have lapsed as a consequence of the events of the year 1204 and following years.[30] Such an alleged original feudal title of the Kings of France in respect of the Channel Islands could today produce no legal effect, unless it had been replaced by another title valid according to the law of the time of replacement. What is of decisive importance, in the opinion of the Court, is not indirect presumptions deduced from events in the Middle Ages, but the evidence which relates directly to the possession of the Ecrehos and Minquiers groups. . . .

The Parties have further discussed the question of the selection of a "critical date" for allowing evidence in the present case. The United Kingdom Government submits that, though the Parties have for a long time disagreed as to the sovereignty over the two groups, the dispute did not become "crystallized" before the conclusion of the Special Agreement of December 29th, 1950, and that therefore this date should be considered as the critical date, with the result that all acts before that date must be taken into consideration by the Court. The French Government, on the other hand, contends that the date of the Convention of 1839 should be selected as the critical date, and that all subsequent acts must be excluded from consideration.

At the date of the [fishery] Convention of 1839, no dispute as to the sovereignty over the Ecrehos and Minquiers groups had yet arisen. The Parties had for a considerable time been in disagreement with regard to the exclusive right to fish oysters, but they did not link that question to the question of sovereignty over the Ecrehos and the Minquiers. In such circumstances there is no reason why the conclusion of that Convention should have any effect on the question of allowing or ruling out evidence relating to sovereignty. A dispute as to sovereignty over the groups did not arise before the years 1886 and 1888, when France for the first time claimed sovereignty over the Ecrehos and the Minquiers respectively. But in view of the special circumstances of the present case, subsequent acts should also be considered by the Court, unless the measure in question was taken with a view to improving the legal position of the Party concerned. In many respects activity in regard to these groups had developed gradually long before the dispute as to sovereignty arose, and it has

---

[30] *Ed.* The Duchy of Normandy was dismembered after Anglo-Norman forces had been driven out of Normandy in 1204.

since continued without interruption and in a similar manner. In such circumstances there would be no justification for ruling out all events which during this continued development occurred after the years 1886 and 1888 respectively. . . .

The Court examined evidence of sovereignty in respect of the Ecrehos presented by each party. In the course of considering the evidence produced by the United Kingdom relating to the nineteenth century, the Court stated that it "attaches, in particular, probative value to the acts which relate to the exercise of jurisdiction and local administration and to legislation."[31] The Court concluded unanimously as follows:

The Court, being now called upon to appraise the relative strength of the opposing claims to sovereignty over the Ecrehos in the light of the facts considered above, finds that the Ecrehos group in the beginning of the thirteenth century was considered and treated as an integral part of the fief of the Channel Islands which were held by the English King, and that the group continued to be under the dominion of that King, who in the beginning of the fourteenth century exercised jurisdiction in respect thereof. The Court further finds that British authorities during the greater part of the nineteenth century and in the twentieth century have exercised State functions in respect of the group. The French Government, on the other hand, has not produced evidence showing that it has any valid title to the group. In such circumstances it must be concluded that the sovereignty over the Ecrehos belongs to the United Kingdom.

The Court then examined the evidence relating to the Minquiers group and reached the same conclusion.

For these reasons, the Court, unanimously,[32] finds that the sovereignty over the islets and rocks of the Ecrehos and Minquiers groups, in so far as these islets and rocks are capable of appropriation, belongs to the United Kingdom.

Notes

1. What was the basis for title in this case?
2. Why was the critical date in this case the date of the special agreement submitting it to the Court when it was held to be earlier than this in the *Palmas Case*?
3. Although the pleadings in the case contain lengthy attempts by both parties to trace their title to the islands over many centuries (which must have taken a lot of time and trouble!), the Court decided the case on the basis of recent evidence

---

[31] It referred to the exercise of criminal jurisdiction, the holding of inquests, the collection of taxes and to a British Treasury Warrant of 1875 including the "Ecrehos Rocks" within the Port of Jersey.

[32] The Court consisted of Vice-President (and acting President) Guerrero; President Sir Arnold McNair; Judges Alvarez, Basdevant, Hackworth, Winiarski, Klaestad, Badawi, Read, Hsu Mo, Levi Carneiro and Armand-Ugon.

of the exercise of state authority.[33] Does this confirm the approach taken by the Arbitrator in the *Palmas* case?

WESTERN SAHARA CASE[34]

Advisory Opinion. I.C.J.Reports 1975, p. 12

The background to the request for an opinion in this case and the questions put to the Court are indicated above, p. 116. In the course of argument, Morocco claimed that it had had "legal ties" (see Question II put to the Court) with Western Sahara amounting to sovereignty at the time of its colonisation by Spain in 1884. The following extract concerns the Court's treatment of that claim, prefaced by an extract from the Court's answer to Question I. It ends with the general conclusion to the Court's Opinion.

Opinion of the Court

79. Turning to Question 1 . . . a determination that Western Sahara was a *"terra nullius"* at the time of colonization by Spain would be possible only if it were established that at that time the territory belonged to no one in the sense that it was then open to acquisition through the legal process of "occupation."

80. Whatever differences of opinion there have been among jurists, the State practice of the relevant period [1884] indicates that territories inhabited by tribes or peoples having a social and political organization were not regarded as *terra nullius*. It shows that in the case of such territories the acquisition of sovereignty was not generally considered as effected unilaterally through "occupation" of *terra nullius* by original title but through agreements concluded with local rulers. Such agreements with local rulers, whether or not considered as an actual "cession" of the territory, were regarded as derivative roots of title, and not original titles obtained by occupation of *terra nullius*.

81. In the present instance, the information furnished to the Court shows that at the time of colonization Western Sahara was inhabited by peoples which, if nomadic, were socially and politically organized in tribes and under chiefs competent to represent them. In its Royal Order of 26 December 1884, far from treating the case as one of occupation of *terra nullius*, Spain claimed that the King was taking the Río de Oro under his protection on the basis of agreements which had been entered into with the chiefs of the local tribes: . . .

---

[33] Note, however, that in the *Land, Island and Maritime Frontier Dispute* case, I.C.J. Rep. 1992, p. 351 at pp. 564–565, the Court Chamber stated that in the *Minquiers and Ecrehos* case, the Court did not "simply disregard the ancient titles, and decide on a basis of more recent display of sovereignty". Instead, it was "examining evidence of possession as confirmatory of title".

[34] See Shaw (1978) 49 B.Y.I.L. 119 and Note (1977) 9 C.W.R.J.I.L. 135.

90. [In respect of Question II], Morocco's claim to "legal ties" with Western Sahara at the time of colonization by Spain has been put to the Court as a claim to ties of sovereignty on the ground of an alleged immemorial possession of the territory. . . .

91. In support of this claim Morocco refers to a series of events stretching back to the Arab conquest of North Africa in the seventh century A.D., the evidence of which is, understandably, for the most part taken from historical works. . . . Stressing that during a long period Morocco was the only independent State which existed in the north-west of Africa, it points to the geographical contiguity of Western Sahara to Morocco and the desert character of the territory. In the light of these considerations, it maintains that the historical material suffices to establish Morocco's claim to a title based "upon continued display of authority" [*Eastern Greenland Case*, P.C.I.J. Rep., Ser. A/B, No. 53, p. 43] on the same principles as those applied by the Permanent Court in upholding Denmark's claim to possession of the whole of Greenland [see above p. 203].

92. This method of formulating Morocco's claims to ties of sovereignty with Western Sahara encounters certain difficulties. As the Permanent Court stated in the case concerning the *Legal Status of Eastern Greenland*, a claim to sovereignty based upon continued display of authority involves "two elements each of which must be shown to exist: the intention and will to act as sovereign, and some actual exercise or display of such authority" . . . True, the Permanent Court recognized that in the case of claims to sovereignty over areas of thinly populated or unsettled countries, "very little in the way of actual exercise of sovereign rights" (*ibid.* p. 46) might be sufficient in the absence of a competing claim. But in the present instance, Western Sahara, if somewhat sparsely populated, was a territory across which socially and politically organized tribes were in constant movement and where armed incidents between these tribes were frequent. In the particular circumstances . . . the paucity of evidence of actual display of authority unambiguously relating to Western Sahara renders it difficult to consider the Moroccan claim as on all fours with that of Denmark in the *Eastern Greenland Case*. Nor is the difficulty cured by introducing the argument of geographical unity or contiguity. In fact, the information before the Court shows that the geographical unity of Western Sahara with Morocco is somewhat debatable, which also militates against giving effect to the concept of contiguity. Even if the geographical contiguity of Western Sahara with Morocco could be taken into account in the present connection, it would only make the paucity of evidence of unambiguous display of authority with respect to Western Sahara more difficult to reconcile with Morocco's claim to immemorial possession.

93. In the view of the Court, however, what must be of decisive importance in determining its answer to Question II is not direct inference drawn from events in past history but evidence directly relating to effective display of authority in Western Sahara at the time of its colonization by Spain and in the period immediately preceding that time (*cf.*

Minquiers and Ecrehos, Judgment, I.C.J. Reports 1953, p. 57). As Morocco has also adduced specific evidence relating to the time of colonization and the period preceding it, the Court will now consider that evidence. . . .

The Court then examined this evidence and found that, although there was evidence of *personal* allegiance owed by Saharan tribes to Morocco, there was no *political* authority of the sort associated with sovereignty. The Court also rejected the Moroccan claim that its sovereignty over Western Sahara had been recognised by the international community.

162. The materials and information presented to the Court show the existence at the time of Spanish colonization, of legal ties of allegiance between the Sultan of Morocco and some of the tribes living in the territory of Western Sahara. They equally show the existence of rights, including some rights relating to the land, which constituted legal ties between the Mauritanian entity,[35] as understood by the Court, and the territory of Western Sahara. On the other hand, the Court's conclusion is that the materials and information presented to it do not establish any tie of territorial sovereignty between the territory of Western Sahara and the Kingdom of Morocco or the Mauritanian entity. Thus the Court has not found legal ties of such a nature as might affect the application of resolution 1514 (XV) in the decolonization of Western Sahara and, in particular, of the principle of self-determination through the free and genuine expression of the will of the peoples of the Territory (*cf.* paragraphs 54–59 above[36])

163. For these reasons . . .

THE COURT IS OF OPINION,

with regard to Question I,

unanimously,

that Western Sahara (Río de Oro and Sakiet El Hamra) at the time of colonization by Spain was not a territory belonging to no one (*terra nullius*),

with regard to Question II,

by 14 votes to 2,[37]

that there were legal ties between the territory and the Kingdom of Morocco of the kinds indicated in paragraph 162 of this Opinion,

by 15 votes to 1,[38]

that there were legal ties between this territory and the Mauritanian entity of the kinds indicated in paragraph 162 of this Opinion.

[35] *Ed.* No question of ties amounting to sovereignty in 1884 arose in the case of the "Mauritanian Entity" because it was not then a state.

[36] For these paragraphs of the Court's Judgment, see above, pp. 116–118.

[37] The judges in the majority were President Lachs; Vice-President Ammoun; Judges Forster, Gros, Bengzon, Petrén, Onyeama, Dillard, Ignacio-Pinto, de Castro, Morozov, Jiménez de Aréchaga, Sir Humphrey Waldock and Nagendra Singh. Judge Ruda and Judge *ad hoc* Boni dissented.

[38] Only Judge *ad hoc* Boni dissented.

CHAMIZAL ARBITRATION

U.S. *v.* Mexico (1911)

*International Boundary Commission: La Fleur, Presiding Commissioner;
Mills, U.S. Commissioner; Puga, Mexican Commissioner. (1911) 5 A.J.I.L.
782*

By a treaty of 1848, the Rio Grande was made, for part of its length, the boundary between the United States and Mexico. By 1911, the river had changed its course leaving a tract of land of about 600 acres—the Chamizal Tract—between the old and the new beds of the river on the United States side of the new bed over which both states claimed sovereignty. The Commission decided that the part of the Tract that had resulted from a gradual process of accretion belonged to the United States but that the part of it that had resulted from a flood in 1864 belonged to Mexico. The case was decided on the basis of the relevant treaty provisions; an argument based upon prescription was, however, put by the United States and examined by the Commission in the following passage. The United States Commissioner, who dissented from the Commission's decision, concurred in its treatment of this argument.

Opinion of the Commission

... it is contended that the Republic of Mexico is estopped from asserting the national title over the territory known as "El Chamizal" by reason of the undisturbed, uninterrupted, and unchallenged possession of said territory by the United States of America since the Treaty of Guadaloupe Hidalgo.

Without thinking it necessary to discuss the very controversial question as to whether the right of prescription invoked by the United States is an accepted principle of the law of nations, in the absence of any convention establishing a term of prescription, the commissioners are unanimous in coming to the conclusion that the possession of the United States in the present case was not of such a character as to found a prescriptive title. Upon the evidence adduced it is impossible to hold that the possession of El Chamizal by the United States was undisturbed, uninterrupted and unchallenged from the date of the Treaty of Guadaloupe Hidalgo in 1848 until the year 1895, when, in consequence of the creation of a competent tribunal to decide the question, the Chamizal case was first presented. On the contrary it may be said that the political control exercised by the local and federal governments, have been constantly challenged and questioned by the Republic of Mexico, through its accredited diplomatic agents.... From ... [1867] until the negotiation of the Convention of 1884, a considerable amount of diplomatic correspondence is devoted to the very question and the Convention of 1884 was an endeavour to fix the rights of the two nations with respect to the changes brought about by the action of the waters of the Rio Grande.

The very existence of that convention precludes the United States from acquiring by prescription against the terms of their title and, as has been pointed out above, the two republics have ever since the signing of that convention treated it as a source of all their rights in respect of accretion to the territory on one side or the other of the river.

Another characteristic of possession serving as a foundation for prescription is that it should be peaceable. . . .

It is quite clear from the circumstances . . . that however much the Mexicans may have desired to take physical possession of the district, the result of any attempt to do so would have provoked scenes of violence and the Republic of Mexico can not be blamed for resorting to the milder forms of protest contained in its diplomatic correspondence.

In private law, the interruption of prescription is effected by a suit, but in dealings between nations this is of course impossible unless and until an international tribunal is established for such a purpose. In the present case, the Mexican claim was asserted before the International Boundary Commission within a reasonable time after it commenced to exercise its functions, and prior to that date the Mexican Government had done all that could be reasonably required of it by way of protest against the alleged encroachment.

Under these circumstances the Commissioners have no difficulty in coming to the conclusion that the plea of prescription should be dismissed.

Notes

1. See also the extract from the *Anglo-Norwegian Fisheries* case, below p. 375.
2. In the *Frontier Land* case,[39] Belgium and the Netherlands disputed sovereignty over certain plots of land in the area of the border between them. The Court stated:

> The final contention of the Netherlands is that if sovereignty over the disputed plots was vested in Belgium by virtue of the Boundary Convention [of 1843], acts of sovereignty exercised by the Netherlands since 1843 have established sovereignty in the Netherlands. This is a claim to sovereignty in derogation of title established by treaty. . . . The question for the Court is whether Belgium has lost its sovereignty by non-assertion of its rights and by acquiescence in acts of sovereignty alleged to have been exercised by the Netherlands at different times since 1843.[40]

The Court examined the evidence and concluded that Belgian sovereignty had not been extinguished. The Court here would seem to be accepting that title may be established by prescription. The same conclusion is implicit in the *Palmas* case, above, p. 190. Exceptionally, in the *Right of Passage* case[41] Judge Moreno Quintana, in his dissenting opinion, stated that the reasoning in the majority opinion "implies, by definition, a recognition that territorial sovereignty can be acquired by prescription, a private law institution which I consider finds no place in international law."[42]

[39] I.C.J.Rep. 1959, p. 209. See also the reference to "acquiescence" in the *Land, Island and Maritime Frontier Dispute* case, below, p. 238.
[40] *ibid*. p. 227.
[41] I.C.J.Rep. 1960, p. 6. See the extract below, p. 257.
[42] *ibid*. p. 88.

3. In the *British Guiana v. Venezuela Boundary Arbitration*[43] the arbitrators were instructed by their treaty terms of reference as follows:

Adverse holding or prescription during a period of 50 years shall make a good title.

4. Most writers accept that prescription can be a basis for title. Hall[44] states:

Title by prescription arises out of a long continued possession, where no original source of proprietary right can be shown to exist, or where possession in the first instance being wrongful, the legitimate proprietor has neglected to assert his right, or has been unable to do so.

Johnson[45] states:

"Acquisitive prescription" is the means by which, under international law, legal recognition is given to the right of a state to exercise sovereignty over land or sea territory in cases where that state has, in fact, exercised its authority in a continuous, uninterrupted, and peaceful manner over the area concerned for a sufficient period of time, provided that all other interested and affected states (in the case of land territory the previous possessor, in the case of sea territory neighbouring states and other states whose maritime interests are affected) have acquiesced in this exercise of authority. Such acquiescence is implied in cases where the interested and affected states have failed within a reasonable time to refer the matter to the appropriate international organization or international tribunal or—exceptionally in cases where no such action was possible—have failed to manifest their opposition in a sufficiently positive manner through the instrumentality of diplomatic protests. The length of time required for the establishment of a prescriptive title on the one hand, and the extent of the action required to prevent the establishment of a prescriptive title on the other hand, are invariable matters of fact to be decided by the international tribunal before which the matter is eventually brought for adjudication.

The same writer also states:

... as Verykios[46] ... said, a [diplomatic] protest not followed up by other action becomes in time "academic" and "useless." The other action that was formerly required was forceful opposition of some sort. Since 1919 it was, where possible, reference of the matter to the League of Nations or the Permanent Court of International Justice. Since 1945 it has been, where possible, reference of the matter to the United Nations or to the International Court of Justice ... the advent of this new machinery for settling international disputes has largely altered the role of the protest in the matter of acquisitive prescription. The result is that the diplomatic protest is of reduced significance and is certainly not now the principal method of interrupting prescription. A protest since 1919 can be said to have amounted to no more than a temporary bar.[47]

Brownlie[48] disagrees with the view that "protest must be followed by steps to use available machinery for the settlement of international disputes." He states:

[43] (1899–1900) 92 B.F.S.P. 160.
[44] *International Law* (8th ed., 1924) (Pearce Higgins), p. 143.
[45] (1950) 27 B.Y.I.L. 332 at 353–354.
[46] *Ed. La prescription en droit international* (1934).
[47] *loc. cit.*, n. 45 above, p. 346.
[48] Brownlie, p. 157.

If acquiescence is the crux of the matter (and it is believed that it is) one cannot dictate what its content is to be. . . .

REPORT ON THE FALKLANDS ISLANDS[49]

Fifth Report of the Foreign Affairs Committee of the House of Commons, Session 1983–84, H.C. Papers 268–I, Vol. I, pp. xiv–xvii; Misc. 1 (1985), Cmnd. 9447

15. According to Spanish and Argentine accounts, the Falkland Islands were first discovered by the navigator Esteban Gomez, who sailed with Magellan in 1520. British accounts ascribe the first sighting of the Islands to the mariner John Davis . . . in 1592. It is generally agreed, however, that the first recorded landing was made in 1690 by Captain John Strong RN, who named the Islands after Viscount Falkland, then Treasurer of the Navy, but did not take formal possession in the name of the English Crown.

16. . . . the Islands remained unoccupied until 1764, when the first effective settlement was established by the French at Port Louis on East Falkland. This settlement was subsequently sold to Spain (and renamed Port Soledad) in 1767, and maintained by that country until 1811. Meanwhile, a British landing in 1765 on Saunders Island, a mile off West Falkland, was followed the next year by the establishment of a settlement at Port Egmont [on West Falkland]. The British settlers were expelled by Spanish forces in 1770, returned in 1771 (following an exchange of declarations between the Spanish and British governments), and subsequently withdrawn in 1774, ostensibly on grounds of cost. Although Spanish and Argentine sources claim that the withdrawal of the British settlement was in accordance with face-saving understandings reached by the Spanish and British governments in 1771[50] and implied British recognition of Spanish title, the settlers left behind them the Union flag and a plaque affirming British ownership and possession in the name of King George III.[51] There is no evidence of the Spanish settlement being extended to West Falkland, nor of the British settlement being extended to East Falkland. . . .

17. The Spanish garrison and settlement on East Falkland were withdrawn in 1811, as Spanish rule in southern America collapsed as an

---

[49] On sovereignty over the Falklands, see Anon (1982) Rev. I.C.J., No. 26, p. 26; Beck (1983) 12 Millenium: Jo. Int. Studies 6; Bologna, *id.*, p. 39; Franck (1983) 77 A.J.I.L. 109; Lindsey (1983) 18 Texas I. L.J. 11; Myhre (1983) 12 Millenium: Jo. Int. Studies 29; Goebel, *The Struggle for the Falklands* (1927, rev. ed. 1982); Gustafson, *The Sovereignty Dispute over the Falkland (Malvinas) Islands* (1988); Hassan (1982) 23 Virg. J.I.L. 53; Hoffmann and Hoffmann, *Sovereignty in Dispute: the Falklands/Malvinas* (1984); Perl, *The Falkland Islands Dispute in International Law and Politics* (1983); Lindsey (1983) 18 Texas I.L.J. 11; Pinto (1983) 18 Texas I.L.J. 1; Reisman (1983) 93 Yale L.J. 287; Sanchez (1983) 21 Col. J. T. L. 557. On sovereignty over the Falkland Islands Dependencies, see Symmons (1984) 33 I.C.L.Q. 726.

[50] *e.g.* UN Doc. No. A/37/533.

[51] *Ed.* The Spanish removed the plaque and razed the remaining buildings to the ground.

indirect consequence of the Napoleonic Wars.... [Argentina's] independence was only formally declared ... in July 1816. Meanwhile the Falkland Islands remained unoccupied, save by itinerant sealing and whaling ships, until 1820, when Colonel Daniel Jewett took possession of the Islands in the name of the new Government in Buenos Aires, a fact advertised in the London *Times* in August 1821. Thereafter, the Buenos Aires Government made several attempts to establish occupancy, including the appointment of a Governor, who never actually visited the Islands; in 1823, the granting of land, grazing and fishing rights to Louis Vernet; and in 1829 the appointment of Vernet as Political and Military Commander of the Malvinas, an act which prompted Britain's first formal protest to Argentina, Britain having recognised that country only in 1825.

18. In 1831 Vernet seized three American sailing ships for unlawful sealing in Argentine waters and, in retaliation, the United States corvette *Lexington* sailed to the Islands on the instructions of the U.S. Consul in Buenos Aires and physically destroyed the settlement at Port Soledad, declaring the Islands "free of all government." The following year Argentina (prompting further British protests) appointed yet another Governor, Captain Juan Mestivier, who was murdered by mutinous soldiers soon after his arrival in the Islands. Towards the end of 1832 the British Admiralty issued instructions to Captain Onslow of the sloop *Clio* to "exercise Britain's rights of sovereignty." Captain Onslow arrived at Port Soledad early in January 1833 and, according to British accounts, peacefully persuaded the remainder of the Argentine garrison to leave. According to Argentine accounts, however, the Argentine authorities were "forcibly ousted" by the British troops.[52] The Islands thereafter remained in continuous British possession until April 2, 1982....

19. The Argentine Government formally protested against Britain's occupation of the Islands in 1833, 1834, 1841, 1842 and 1849, in the latter year sending a note to the British Government indicating that, although not intending to protest further in view of Britain's inattention to her protests, Argentine silence should not be interpreted as acquiescence. Argentina again issued formal protests in 1884, 1888 and 1908, thereafter protesting regularly both directly to HM Government and, more recently, indirectly at the United Nations and in other international fora.

20. In 1925 Argentina began to formulate claims to the South Orkney Islands, extending the claim to South Georgia in 1927, the remaining areas of what is now the British Antarctic Territory in 1942, and to the South Sandwich Islands in 1948. Britain sought in 1955 to institute proceedings at the International Court of Justice against both Argentina and Chile concerning their respective claims to sovereignty over the Falkland Island Dependencies and British Antarctic Territory, but neither the Argentine nor the Chilean governments agreed to accept the jurisdiction of the

---

[52] UN Doc. No. A/37/553.

Court. The Islands forming the Dependencies were at no time claimed by Spain, and have at no time, prior to 1982, been occupied by Argentina, with the exception of Southern Thule (in the South Sandwich Group) where Argentina maintained a scientific research station, despite British protests, between 1976 and 1982. Notwithstanding, Argentina has since 1937 made a general reservation of rights in respect of the then existing Dependencies, and has subsequently presented her claim to the Falkland Islands in those terms. . . .

22. We sympathise with our predecessors in the difficulties they faced in seeking to reach conclusions on the respective strengths and weaknesses of the Argentine and United Kingdom claims. **The historical and legal evidence demonstrates such areas of uncertainty that we are unable to reach a categorical conclusion on the legal validity of the historical claims of either country.** It is significant in this context that neither country in modern times has sought to refer the question of sovereignty over the Falkland Island themselves to the International Court of Justice or some other form of legal arbitration. This may be due in part to other considerations, such as doubts about whether any judgment would be honoured by the other side, but almost certainly is evidence also of doubts about the solidarity of their respective legal claims. . . .

23. Like our predecessors, we have no difficulty in concluding that **the claims advanced by Argentina in respect of the Dependencies of South Georgia and the South Sandwich Islands are without legal foundation.** None of these islands was at any time claimed by Spain, and none, apart from Southern Thule, has been at any time occupied by Argentina.

Notes

1. The Falkland Islands, which lie approximately 300 miles off the coast of Argentina, are a Crown Colony in British constitutional law. Sovereignty over them is also claimed by Argentina, which calls them the Malvinas. The small permanent population of about 2,000 persons are mostly descended from British families settled there from the early 19th Century onwards. The Islands' waters contain valuable fishing grounds[53] and may have commercially viable deposits of oil and gas. As to the 1982 Argentinian invasion of the Falklands, see below, p. 902. Diplomatic relations between Argentina and the U.K. were resumed in 1990 without prejudice to the sovereignty claims of either.[54] The two states have since established a South Atlantic Fisheries Commission to conserve fishing stocks and a South West Atlantic Hydrocarbons Commission to promote the development of oil and gas. In 1994, Argentina's Constituent Assembly approved a provision in its new constitution ratifying its claim to sovereignty over the Malvinas.[55]

2. In its response to the Foreign Affairs Committee Report, the British Government expressed its regret at "the Committee's reluctance to reach a categorical

---

[53] As to the Islands' exclusive fishing zone, see below, p. 453, n. 4.

[54] See Evans (1991) 40 I.C.L.Q. 272.

[55] U.K.M.I.L. 1994, (1994) 65 B.Y.I.L. 636. The U.K. expressed its "concern" at this development and was "quite clear about British sovereignty over the Falkland Islands": Secretary of State, FCO (Mr Hurd), UN General Assembly, September 27, 1994, *ibid.*

conclusion on the legal validity of Britain's title to the Islands" and justified the British Government claim as follows[56]:

> Britain's title is derived from early settlement, reinforced by formal claims in the name of the Crown and completed by open, continuous, effective and peaceful possession, occupation and administration of the Islands since 1833 (save for the 10 weeks of forcible Argentine occupation in 1982). The exercise of sovereignty by the United Kingdom over the Falkland Islands has, furthermore, consistently been shown to accord with the wishes of the Islanders, expressed through their democratically elected representatives.

Earlier, the Foreign Secretary had stated in a reply to a letter in 1982:

> "Even leaving aside arguments in our favour based on events before 1833, we have been consistently advised that our title can be soundly based on our possession of the islands from 1833.
> Our case rests on the facts, on prescription and on the principle of self-determination."[57]

With regard to the reference to "events before 1833," would Argentina or the United Kingdom appear to have had the stronger claim to the Falklands before the British action in 1833? Note in this connection the relative nature of the test to be applied when establishing title based upon possession (see the *Eastern Greenland* case, above, p. 203) and the rule that *derelicto* requires an intention to abandon (*Clipperton Island* case, above, p. 200). On the principle of *uti possidetis*, upon which the Argentinian claim to succeed Spain turns, see above, p. 238.

On the United Kingdom's claim to title based upon prescription, Akehurst[58] states:

> A State, in order to acquire title to territory from another State by prescription, must exercise effective control over that territory for a long period. The UK has clearly satisfied this requirement as regards the Falkland Islands. But international lawyers, with very few exceptions, consider that effective control is not enough on its own; it has to be accompanied by acquiescence on the part of the "losing" State. There is some disagreement among international lawyers about the meaning of acquiescence; some say that protests are enough to negative acquiescence, while others say that protests need to be supported by further steps such as breaking off diplomatic relations or offering to refer the dispute to arbitration. This controversy is of little importance as far as the present dispute is concerned, because Argentina's protests against Britain's presence on the Falkland Islands have been accompanied by further steps. In the nineteenth century Argentina offered to refer the dispute to arbitration (but the UK did not accept the offer); later Argentina refused to recognise the British nationality of the islanders and tried to conscript them into the Argentinian army when they visited Argentina; in recent years Argentina has taken the dispute to the UN General Assembly.

[56] *Report on the Falkland Islands*, op. cit., p. 213, above, p. 3.
[57] U.K.M.I.L. 1982, (1983) 54 B.Y.I.L. 461.
[58] H.C. 31–xv, Session 1982–3. House of Commons Foreign Affairs Committee, *Falkland Islands*, Appendices to the Minutes of Evidence, Appendix 12.

The real uncertainty arises from the fact that for long periods (1849–1884, 1888–1908) Argentina remained silent, without protesting or taking other steps to manifest its disapproval of Britain's presence on the Falkland Islands. Normally, in cases of prescription, a State which remains silent for a long time is regarded as acquiescing and therefore as losing its title to the territory in dispute. However, immediately before Argentina fell silent in 1849, she sent a note to the British government in which she said that she did not intend to protest any more because she felt humiliated when Britain paid no attention to her protests; but she added that her silence should not be interpreted as acquiescence. The legal effect of this note is most uncertain. On the one hand Argentina could argue that she was making clear that she did not acquiesce, and that Britain could therefore not acquire title by prescription: on the other hand Britain could argue that protests are the normal way of preserving rights to territory, and that a State which chooses not to protest chooses to deprive itself of the means of preserving its rights, and must therefore be regarded as losing its rights. It is impossible to predict how an international court would decide a case of this sort.

As to the role of the principle of self-determination in deciding the political future of colonial territories generally and as to the approach taken by the UN Decolonisation Committee in applying the principle to the Falklands in particular, see above, pp. 113 and 120, n. 88, respectively. In 1986, 94 per cent of Falklanders voted in a poll to retain their association with the United Kingdom; they did not want independence, nor did they want to merge with Argentina. By virtue of a 1983 amendment to the 1981 British Nationality Act, Falklanders generally are British citizens, with a right of entry to the United Kingdom.

3. Another possible basis for British sovereignty is conquest. This was a recognised basis for title in 1833 and could therefore be relied upon now in accordance with the doctrine of intertemporal law.[59] A claim based upon conquest could not be defeated by the protests made by Argentina. Moreover, conquest can be established "even where there has been no war or even hostilities in the technical sense, where the territory has nevertheless been seized by a display of armed force, as for example the entry of German troops into Austria in 1938."[60] One reason why the United Kingdom does not rely upon conquest might be that Captain Onslow's instructions were "to exercise rights of sovereignty" impliedly already in existence, thus suggesting the absence of the necessary intention to conquer.[61] Another might be the political delicacy of relying upon such an out-dated notion as conquest.

4. A further ground for title might, whatever the quality of Argentinian protest, be general recognition by the international community of the British claim in the period following 1833. For example, the United Kingdom has extended to the Falklands many multilateral treaties to which large numbers of states, including Latin American states, are parties without attracting comment.[62] Similarly, maritime nations have long accepted British authority over Falklands territorial and internal waters.[63]

---

[59] As to which, see above, p. 199.

[60] Jennings, *op. cit.*, p. 190, n. 1, above, p. 53.

[61] Note that the U.K. has made efforts to dispel the "myth" that armed force was used by Captain Onslow's men in 1833. Even so, there would seem to have been a threat of force sufficient for conquest if the necessary *animus* was present.

[62] See, *e.g.* at different times, the 1904 White Slave Traffic Agreement, U.K.T.S. 24, Cd. 2689; 1 L.N.T.S. 83; the 1973 CITES Convention, U.K.T.S. 101, Cmnd. 6647; 993 U.N.T.S. 243; and 25 I.L.O. Conventions. As to general recognition, see below, p. 222.

[63] Only Argentina has protested at the 1986 U.K. declaration of a Falkland Islands exclusive fishing zone. Vessels from more than 12 states have applied to the Falklands for licences.

(ii) CONQUEST

Notes

Conquest was a recognised and important basis for title until the early years
of this century. It is now well established that the "territory of a state shall not
be the object of acquisition by another state resulting from the threat or use of
force" contrary to Article 2(4) United Nations Charter: 1970 Declaration on
Principles of International Law, section on the principle on the use of force,
paragraph 10, below, Appendix II. As the 1928 Briand-Kellogg Pact and the
United Nations Charter have outlawed the use of armed force, see below, pp.
861–862, so the law of conquest has declined in significance to the point where
it provides, under the doctrine of intertemporal law, justification only for the
titles acquired before the force used to obtain them was declared illegal by
customary international law. An interesting question is whether a state that
acts in self-defence to repel armed force used against it contrary to Article 2(4)
can acquire any territory of the aggressor which it occupies during hostilities.
(See, *e.g.* the Middle East situation below, p. 223). Akehurst[64] refers to the
wording of the 1970 Declaration (paragraph referred to above) in support of
the view that it cannot:

> In these words, the Declaration makes a significant distinction between mili-
> tary occupation and acquisition of territory. Military occupation is unlawful
> only if it results from the use of force in contravention of the Charter; *any* threat
> or use of force, whether it is in contravention of the Charter or not, invalidates
> acquisition of territory.

Jennings[65] argues differently for the same conclusion:

> ... the suggestion that the state that does not resort to force unlawfully, *e.g.*
> resorts to war in self defence, may still acquire a title by conquest ... though
> not infrequently heard, is to be regarded with some suspicion. It seems to be
> based upon a curious assumption that, provided a war is lawful in origin, it
> goes on being lawful to whatever lengths it may afterwards be pursued. The
> grave dangers of abuse inherent in any such notion are obvious ... Force used
> in self-defence ... must be proportionate to the threat of immediate danger,
> and when the threat has been averted the plea of self-defence can no longer be
> available ... it would be a curious law of self-defence that permitted the
> defender in the course of his defence to seize and keep the resources and
> territory of the attacker.

THE STIMSON DOCTRINE OF NON-RECOGNITION

1 Hackworth 334

On January 7, 1932, the United States Secretary of State for Foreign Affairs
(Stimson) sent a note to the Japanese and Chinese Governments, from which the
following extract is taken. It was occasioned by the invasion of Manchuria by

---

[64] *A Modern Introduction to International Law* (6th ed., 1987), p. 149. Footnote omitted.
[65] *op cit*, p. 190, n. 1 above, p. 55. Footnote omitted.

Japan and the establishment by the latter of the "puppet state" of "Manchu-kuo."[66]

The American Government deems it to be its duty to notify both the Imperial Japanese Government and the Government of the Chinese Republic that it can not admit the legality of any situation *de facto* nor does it intend to recognize any treaty or agreement entered into between those Governments, or agents thereof, which may impair the treaty rights of the United States or its citizens in China, including those which relate to the sovereignty, the independence, or the territorial and administrative integrity of the Republic of China, or to the international policy relative to China, commonly known as the open-door policy, and that it does not intend to recognize any situation, treaty, or agreement which may be brought about by means contrary to the covenants and obligations of the Pact of Paris of August 27th, 1928, to which treaty both China and Japan, as well as the United States, are parties.

Notes

1. On March 11, 1932, the Assembly of the League of Nations resolved that "it was incumbent upon the Members of the League of Nations not to recognise any situation, treaty or agreement which may be brought about by means contrary to the Covenant of the League of Nations, or the Pact of Paris."[67] This, however, proved the high-water mark of the Stimson Doctrine. It was applied by some states upon the invasion of Ethiopia in 1935 and in response to German and Russian invasions shortly afterwards but is no longer invoked under this name. It has reappeared in the 1970 Declaration on Principles of International Law, Section on the Principle on the Use of Force, paragraph 10, below, Appendix III. Article 11 of the Draft Declaration on Rights and Duties of States[68] similarly reads:

> Every State has the duty to refrain from recognising any territorial acquisition by another State acting in violation of Article 9 [prohibiting resort to war as an instrument of national policy and the threat or use of force contrary to Article 2(4) of the United Nations Charter].[69]

2. On the UN's non-recognition of the territorial consequences of Turkey's invasion of Northern Cyprus in 1974, see above, p. 112.

3. In the *East Timor* case,[70] Australia had agreed with Indonesia by treaty on the allocation of the continental shelf between East Timor and Australia. It acknowledged that by conducting negotiations on the matter, Australia had recognised the incorporation of East Timor into Indonesia.[71] Although it opposed the manner in which this incorporation had been brought about, *i.e.* by the use of force, in the Australian Government's view, "there is no binding international legal obligation

---

[66] See above, p. 109.
[67] L.N.O.J., Special Supp. No. 101, pp. 87, 88 (1932).
[68] Y.B.I.L.C. 1949, II, pp. 286, 288. On the Draft Declaration, see p. 71.
[69] Below, Appendix I.
[70] I.C.J. Rep. 1995, p. 90.
[71] *ibid.*, p. 98.

not to recognise the acquisition of territory that was acquired by force."[72] In his dissenting opinion in the case, Judge Skubiszewski referred to the Stimson doctrine and to Security Council Resolution 384 calling upon "all states to respect the territorial integrity of East Timor" and to allow its inhabitants to exercise their right to self-determination.[73] In his view, recognition of East Timor as a part of Indonesia was contrary to these resolutions and international law: "While recognition of states or government is still a 'free act', it is not so with regard to the irregular acquisition of territory: here the discretionary nature of the act has been changed by the rule on the prohibition of the use of force".[74]

4. On the UN reaction to the 1990 invasion of Kuwait by Iraq, see below, p. 956.

THE INVASION OF GOA[75]

S.C.O.R., 16th Yr, 987th and 988th Meetings, December 18, 1961

On December 17–18, 1961, India invaded the Portuguese territories of Goa, Dañao and Diu on the Indian subcontinent. On December 18, Portugal asked the Security Council of the United Nations "to put a stop to the contemnable act of aggression of the Indian Union, ordering an immediate cease-fire and the withdrawal forthwith from Portuguese territories of Goa, Dañao and Diu of all the invading forces of the Indian Union."[76] A draft resolution rejecting the Portugese complaint was rejected by the Security Council by seven votes to five. A second draft resolution recalling the terms of Articles 2(3), (4) of the Charter and calling both for the immediate ceasefire and for the withdrawal by India of its forces was vetoed by the USSR. The following are extracts from the Security Council debate.

987th Meeting

46. Mr. Jha (India). I have already said that this is a colonial question, in the sense that part of our country is illegally occupied by right of conquest by the Portuguese. The fact that they have occupied it for 450 years is of no consequence because, during nearly 425 or 430 years of that period we really had no chance to do anything because we were under colonial domination ourselves. But during the last fourteen years, from the very day when we became independent, we have not ceased to demand the return of the peoples under illegal domination to their own countrymen, to share their independence, their march forward to their destiny. I would like to put this matter very clearly before the Council:

---

[72] Statement by the Australian Minister for Resources and Energy (Senator Evans), March 20, 1986, quoted by Judge Skubiszewski in his dissenting opinion, *id.*, p. 263. Senator Evans considered the 1970 Declaration on Principles of International Law, below, Appendix III, on this point as "very hotly contested".

[73] For this and the similar General Assembly position, see above, p. 119.

[74] *ibid*, p. 264. *cf.* the dissenting Opinion of Judge Weeramantry, *ibid.*, p. 206. In its majority judgment, the I.C.J. declined jurisdiction in the case because a third party, Indonesia, would be impleaded, so that the non-recognition point was not decided.

[75] See Wright (1962) 56 A.J.I.L. 617.

[76] UN Doc. S/5030.

that Portugal has no sovereign right over this territory. There is no legal frontier—there can be no legal frontier—between India and Goa. And since the whole occupation is illegal as an issue—it started in an illegal manner, it continues to be illegal today and it is even more illegal in the light of resolution 1514 (XV)—there can be no question of aggression against your own frontier, or against your own people, whom you want to keep liberate.

47. That is the situation that we have come to face. If any narrow-minded, legalistic considerations—considerations arising from international law as written by European law writers—should arise, those writers were, after all, brought up on the atmosphere of colonialism. I pay all respect due to Grotius, who is supposed to be the father of international law, and we accept many tenets of international law. They are certainly regulating international life today. But the tenet which says, and which is quoted in support of colonial Powers having sovereign rights over territories which they won by conquest in Asia and Africa is no longer acceptable. It is the European concept and it must die. It is time, in the twentieth century that it died. . . .

72. MR. STEVENSON (UNITED STATES OF AMERICA.) Let it be perfectly clear what is at stake here; it is the question of the use of armed force by one State against another and against its will, an act clearly forbidden by the Charter. We have opposed such action in the past by our closest friends as well as by others. We opposed it in Korea in 1950, in Suez and in Hungary in 1956 and in the Congo in 1960. And we do so again in Goa in 1961. . . .

75. But what is at stake today is not colonialism; it is a bold violation of one of the most basic principles in the United Nations Charter, stated in these words from Article 2, paragraph 4: . . . [77]

76. We realize fully the depths of the differences between India and Portugal concerning the future of Goa. We realize that India maintains that Goa by right should belong to India. Doubtless India would hold, therefore, that its action is aimed at a just end. But, if our Charter means anything, it means that States are obliged to renounce the use of force, are obligated to seek a solution of their differences by peaceful means, are obligated to utilize the procedures of the United Nations when other peaceful means have failed.

988th Meeting

77. MR. JHA (INDIA) . . . We are criticized here by various delegations which say, "Why have you used force? The Charter absolutely prohibits force"; but the Charter itself does not completely eschew force, in the sense that force can be used in self-defence, for the protection of the

[77] *Ed.* below Appendix I.

people of a country—and the people of Goa are as much Indians as the people of any other part of India.[78] We cannot accept any other position.

78. If the use of force is a mockery—and many representatives have said that it is not internationally moral—if that is so, I would say that all freedom movements, all independent countries which have attained freedom through violent movements, should also come in that category. If fighting a colonial Power is immoral I am afraid the existence of many States around this table becomes immoral. The use of force, in all circumstances, is regrettable but so far as the achievement of freedom is concerned, when nothing else is available, I am afraid that it is a very debatable proposition to say that force cannot be used at all. . . .

79 . . . I have said that we accept international law . . . International law is not a static institution. It is developing constantly. If international law would be static, it would be dead driftwood, if it did not respond to the public opinion of the world. And it is responding every day, whether we like it or not General Assembly resolution 1514 (XV),[79] which has been referred to here and elsewhere very frequently, is the embodiment of that great leap forward in the public opinion of the world on these matters. There can be no getting away from that. Just as the process of decolonization is irreversible and irresistible, the embodiment of the principles in resolution 1514 (XV), which has been accepted by virtually every member around this table, is irresistible. One cannot go behind that now. That is the new dictum of international law.

Notes

India remains in control of the territories taken in 1961. Portugal recognised Indian title to them in 1974. Who had title to them between 1961 and 1974 in international law? Is the attitude of Portugal or of other states relevant? On the dispute over the legality of external *material* support for a "people" in *its* war of national liberation, see below p. 886. Jennings,[80] starting with the assumption that a state cannot now obtain title to territory by action contrary to Article 2(4) of the United Nations Charter, suggests the following "general recognition" approach to the sort of problem exemplified by the Goan situation:

> The traditional procedure by which the law is adjusted to fact—by which indeed, the law when occasion requires may seem to embrace illegality—is the procedure of recognition. In the present context recognition is apt not only because title is *ex hypothesi* a matter that concerns States in general, but also because the principal effect of the change in the law concerning force, is to make the use of force itself a matter of concern to States generally and not only to the States immediately involved. This is a reversal of the previous position in regard to the use of force when it could be said that "the validity of the title

[78] *Ed.* According to a 1950 census, of the 650,000 people living in Goa, 800 were European, 316 were of mixed descent and the rest were Indian: *Hansard*, H.C., Vol. 651, col. 1129, December 19, 1961.

[79] Above, p. 114.

[80] *op. cit.*, p. 190, n. 1, above p. 62.

of the subjugating State does not depend upon recognition on the part of other States. Nor is a mere protest of a third State of any legal weight."[81]

SECURITY COUNCIL RESOLUTION ON THE MIDDLE EAST, NOVEMBER 22, 1967[82]

S.C. Resn 242 (XXII), S.C.O.R., 22nd Yr, Resolutions and Decisions 1967, p. 8

The Security Council

Expressing its continuing concern with the grave situation in the Middle East,

Emphasizing the inadmissibility of the acquisition of territory by war and the need to work for a just and lasting peace in which every State in the area can live in security,

Emphasizing further that all Member States in their acceptance of the Charter of the United Nations have undertaken a commitment to act in accordance with Article 2 of the Charter,

1. *Affirms* that the fulfilment of Charter principles requires the establishment of a just and lasting peace in the Middle East which should include the application of both the following principles:

(i) Withdrawal of Israeli armed forces from territories occupied in the recent conflict;

(ii) Termination of all claims or states of belligerency and respect for and acknowledgment of the sovereignty, territorial integrity and political independence of every State in the area and their right to live in peace within secure and recognized boundaries free from threats or acts of force;

2. *Affirms further* the necessity:

(*a*) For guaranteeing freedom of navigation through international waterways in the area;

(*b*) For achieving a just settlement of the refugee problem;

(*c*) For guaranteeing the territorial inviolability and political independence of every State in the area, through measures including the establishment of demilitarized zones;

3. *Requests* the Secretary-General to designate a Special Representative to proceed to the Middle East to establish and maintain contacts with the States concerned in order to promote agreement and assist efforts to achieve a peaceful and accepted settlement in accordance with the provisions of this resolution;

---

[81] Oppenheim, *International Law*, (8th ed.) Vol. 1, p. 573.
[82] See Lapidoth (1992) 26 Israel L.R. 295; Rosenne (1968) 33 L. & C.P. 44; and Shapira (1969) 4 Israel L.R. 229.

4. Requests the Secretary-General to report to the Security Council on the progress of the efforts of the Special Representative as soon as possible.

Notes

1. Resolution 242 (XXII) was made under Chapter VI of the United Nations Charter.[83] It is therefore not binding upon Member States. The term "territories" in paragraph 1(i) was left purposely vague (*some* territories (if so, which)? All?)

2. The history behind Resolution 242 (XXII) may be summarized as follows.[84] In 1947, the United Kingdom gave notice to the United Nations that it was withdrawing forthwith from Palestine, a territory it had administered as mandatory.[85] The General Assembly recommended on November 29, 1947[86] that Palestine should be partitioned into separate Arab and Jewish states subject to provision for economic union. This was acceptable to the Zionists but not to the Palestinian Arabs. On May 14, 1948, Israel unilaterally declared itself an independent state. It was immediately attacked by neighbouring Arab states, whom it defeated. During 1949, armistice agreements were made, with the assistance of the United Nations, between Israel and each of its neighbours. Under these Israel retained considerably more territory than it would have had under the 1947 plan for partition. In 1956, after frequent violations of the armistice agreements on all sides, Israel invaded the Egyptian Sinai Peninsula but later withdrew to the 1949 armistice line on the recommendation of the General Assembly.[87] In the "Six Day War" of June 1967, Israel again invaded the Sinai Peninsula, this time as far as the East Bank of the Suez Canal (including the Gaza Strip) in the West and the Straits of Tiran in the South. It also invaded the West Bank (Jordanian territory); that part of the city of Jerusalem (East Jerusalem)[88] which it had not previously occupied (also Jordanian); and the strategically important Golan Heights in Syria.

Hostilities broke out again in the Yom Kippur War[89] of October 1973. On October 6, Egypt and Syria launched simultaneous attacks upon Israeli forces in the Sinai peninsula and the Golan Heights respectively. When a cease-fire was finally achieved on October 24, Egypt had retaken about 400 square miles of its territory in the Sinai peninsula to the east of the Suez Canal, but had lost about the same amount of territory to Israel on the West Bank. In the Golan Heights area, Syria had been forced back to within 20 miles of Damascus after initial successes.

---

[83] See the U.K. representative (Lord Caradon), UN Doc. No. S/PV. 1379, para. 6. The resolution was adopted unanimously.

[84] See on the international law issues arising out of the Arab-Israeli conflict, Akehurst (1972–3) 5 N.Z.U.L.R. 231; Blum, *Secure Boundaries and Middle East Peace* (1971); Cattan, *Palestine and International Law* (2nd. ed., 1976); Feinberg, *The Arab-Israeli Conflict in International Law* (1970); ibid., *Studies in International Law with Special Reference to the Arab Israeli Conflict* (1979); ibid., (1980) 15 Israel L.R. 160; Gainsborough, *The Arab-Israeli Conflict* (1986); Gerson, *Israel, the West Bank and International Law* (1978); Halderman, ed., *The Middle East Crisis: Test of International Law* (1969); Khouri, *The Arab-Israeli Dilemma* (1968); Moore, ed., *The Arab-Israeli Conflict* (1974–91) 4 vols.; Pogany, *The Security Council and the Arab-Israeli Conflict* (1984); Quigley, *Palestine and Israel: A Challenge to Justice* (1990); Stone, *Israel and Palestine: Assault on the Law of Nations* (1981); Van de Craen (1978–9) 14 R.B.D.I. 500; Wright (1968) 33 L. & C.P. 5.

[85] See above, p. 131.

[86] G.A. Resn. 181 (II), 2 G.A.O.R., *Resolutions 16 Sept–29 Nov 1947*, pp. 131–132.

[87] See Marston (1988) 37 I.C.L.Q. 773 and (1957) Wright 51 A.J.I.L. 257.

[88] On the status of Jerusalem, see Cassese (1986) 3 Palestine Y.I.L. 13; Cattan, *Jerusalem* (1981); Jones (1968) 33 L. & C.P. 169; and E. Lauterpacht., *Jerusalem and the Holy Places* (1968).

[89] The attacks were launched on *Yom Kippur*, the most sacred Jewish holy day. See Rostow (1975) 69 A.J.I.L. 272.

The ceasefire was preceded by Security Council Resolution 338 (1973)[90] which, in addition to calling for a cease-fire, read as follows:

> The Security Council . . .
>   2. Calls upon the parties concerned to start immediately after the cease-fire the implementation of Security Council Resolution 242 (1967) in all of its parts;
>   3. Decides that immediately and concurrently with the cease-fire, negotiations shall start between the parties concerned under appropriate auspices aimed at establishing a just and durable peace in the Middle East.

In 1979, Egypt and Israel made a Treaty of Peace[91] by which Egypt recognised Israel as a state and Israel returned the Sinai Peninsula (but not the Gaza Strip) to Egypt. Israel has since made a peace treaty with Jordan (1994), but not with Syria. By a 1974 Israeli-Syrian disengagement agreement, Israel withdrew from all of the areas taken in the 1973 War and from some of those taken by it in 1967, including part of the Golan Heights. A buffer zone was established which was to be patrolled by the United Nations Disengagement Observation Force (UNDOF).[92] Otherwise attempts to negotiate a full and final settlement of the Arab/Israeli dispute in accordance with Resolutions 242 (1967) and 338 (1973) have been unsuccessful.

A major stumbling block is the question of the Palestinian Arabs, who number approximately 4.9 million.[93] Nearly half of these live in Israel; the remainder live in Israeli-occupied territory or surrounding Arab states. They are represented by the Palestinian Liberation Organisation (PLO). According to the Palestine National Charter 1964 (as affirmed in 1977),[94] they regard Palestine, with the boundaries it had during the British mandate, as "an indivisible territorial unit"[95] and as "the homeland of the Palestinian Arab people."[96] They claim "the legal right to their homeland and have the right to determine their destiny after achieving the liberation of their country in accordance with their wishes and entirely of their own will and accord."[97] To facilitate the establishment of the new state, Jordan has withdrawn from its legal and administrative functions in the West Bank and recognised the PLO's wish to base the new state mainly in what was Jordanian territory.[98]

An historic new stage in the Middle East conflict was reached with the adoption of the 1993 Declaration of Principles on Interim Self-Government Arrangements.[99] The Declaration provides for "interim self-government" for a "transitional period not exceeding five years, leading to a permanent settlement based on Security Resolutions 242 and 338" (Article 1). Under the Declaration, Israel agreed (i) to withdraw from the Gaza Strip and from Jericho in the West Bank and to hand

---

[90] S.C.O.R., 28th Year, *Resolutions and Decisions*, p. 10.

[91] (1979) 18 I.L.M. 362.

[92] On the peacekeeping status of UNDOF, see below, p. 975.

[93] McDowall, *The Palestinians*, Minority Rights Group Report No. 24, 1982, p. 6.

[94] Reprinted in *Keesings Archives*, p. 28385.

[95] Art. 2.

[96] Art. 1. On the principle of self-determination, see above p. 113.

[97] Art. 3.

[98] See *Keesings Archives*, p. 36120.

[99] (1993) 32 I.L.M. 1525. See also the text and summary in *Keesings Archives*, p. 39658. The Declaration, which was signed in Washington, DC, is the result of the Oslo Process. On the Declaration, see Blum (1994) 28 Israel L.R. 210 and Benvenisti (1993) 4 E.J.I.L. 541. On the Israel-PLO Interim Agreement on the West Bank and the Gaza Strip 1995, (1997) 36 I.L.M. 551, which makes detailed provision for the self-government arrangements and for elections in the Gaza Strip and the West Bank, see Giladi (1995) 29 Israel L.R. 506.

them over for Palestinian administration and (ii) to transfer a lesser degree of administrative authority to the Palestinians in the remainder of the occupied territories of the West Bank. No transfer of administration is provided for in respect of Jerusalem. In letters exchanged in connection with the Declaration, Israel agreed to recognise the PLO "as the representative of the Palestinian people" and Mr Arafat, the PLO leader, (i) recognised the right of the state of Israel to exist in peace and security; (ii) undertook that the PLO constitution provision to the contrary would be deleted; and (iii) renounced terrorism.

Israel has handed over the Gaza Strip and the Jericho area, but the transfer of the agreed administrative authority in the rest of the West Bank is as yet incomplete. The powers of administration in the occupied territories are exercised by the Palestinian Interim Self-Government Authority for the Palestinian People in the West Bank and the Gaza Strip (the Council), which was elected by Palestinians in the occupied territories.

Whereas the 1993 Declaration's interim self-government arrangements fall short of statehood for the Palestinian people,[1] the PLO's goal remains the establishment of a Palestinian state. The preamble to the Declaration provides that the "Government of the State of Israel and the Palestinian team, representing the Palestinian people, . . . recognise their mutual and legitimate and political rights". Blum[2] suggests that this and other wording in the Declaration is such that it is "hard to escape the logical conclusion that, by backing mutuality, Israel has in fact, albeit in a roundabout way, implicitly recognised also the right of the Palestinians to a similar status", *i.e.* as a state.

Israel continues to hold much of the territory it gained in 1967, including East Jerusalem, the strategically important parts of the Golan Heights and (but see above) the West Bank. Although no Israeli law mentions annexation, Israeli civilian law has been extended by legislation[3] to East Jerusalem (1967) and the Golan Heights (1981), but not to the West Bank or (formerly) the Gaza Strip. Israel has, however, established (and still retains) settlements in the latter territories. Moreover, a 1980 Basic Law[4] states that "Jerusalem, complete and united, is the capital of Israel." The General Assembly and the Security Council have declared the above laws invalid and have called for the dismantlement of the settlements.[5] The position in international law would seem to be that Israel is in belligerent occupation of all of the territories taken by it in 1967 and that it has the rights and

---

[1] The U.K. Secretary of State, FCO (Mr Hurd) stated that the new Palestinian entity "is not a state and no-one is claiming it is a state": U.K.M.I.L. 1994, (1994) 65 B.Y.I.L. 594.

[2] *loc. cit.*, p. 223, n. 99, above, ibid. Blum quotes Benvenisti, *ibid.*, at p. 544, who argues differently to the same effect: "the consequence of recognising the Palestinian people and its right to govern itself in the West Bank and Gaza is recognition of this people to establish a state in these areas if it so desires."

[3] Jurisdiction and Administration Order No. 1, 1967–5727; Golan Heights Law, 5742–1981. The Israeli Supreme Court has stated that from the date of the 1967 Order, "united Jerusalem became an inseparable part of Israel": *Hanzalis v. Greek Orthodox Patriarchate Court* (1969) 48 I.L.R. 93, 98.

[4] Basic Law: Jerusalem, Capital of Israel, 5740–1980.

[5] See, *e.g.* G.A. Resn. 3215, G.A.O.R., 32nd Session, Supp. 45, p. 41 (1977); S.C. Resr. 478 (1980), S.C.O.R., 35th Year, *Resolutions and Decisions*, p. 14, and S.C. Resn. 497 (1981), S.C.O.R., 36th Year, *Resolutions and Decisions*, p. 6. In Resolution 478, the Council decided "not to recognise the 'basic law' and such other actions by Israel that . . . seek to alter the character and status of Jerusalem."

duties that go with such occupation.[6] As to whether a state that occupies territory in a legitimate exercise of self-defence can continue to occupy or claim sovereignty to it after the attack is repulsed, see above, p. 218.

(iii) CESSION

OPPENHEIM'S INTERNATIONAL LAW

(9th ed., 1992), Vol. I. Edited by Jennings and Watts

§244 . . . Cession of state territory is the transfer of sovereignty over state territory by the owner-state to another state . . . .

Every state as a rule can cede a part of its territory to another state, or by ceding the whole of its territory can even totally merge in another state. To constitute a cession it must be intended that *sovereignty* will pass. Acquisition of governmental powers, even exclusive, without an intention to cede territorial sovereignty, will not suffice.[7] But since certain parts of state territory, as for instance rivers and the maritime belt, are inalienable appurtenances of the land, they cannot be ceded without a piece of land.[8]

Notes

Gibraltar[9] Gibraltar is a British Crown Colony. In 1704, it was captured from Spain by a British/Dutch expedition during the War of Spanish Succession. It was later ceded by Spain to Great Britain after the latter had lost the War. Article X of the Treaty of Utrecht 1714 reads:

> The Catholic King does hereby, for himself, his heirs and successors, yield to the Crown of Great Britain the full and entire property of the town and castle of Gibraltar, together with the port, fortifications, and forts thereunto belonging; and he gives up the said property to be held and enjoyed absolutely with all manner of right for ever, without any exception or impediment whatsoever. . . . [10]

[6] See the 1907 Hague Regulations, U.K.T.S. 9 (1910), Cd. 5030; 1 Bevans 631, and the 1949 Fourth Geneva Red Cross Convention, *loc. cit.*, p. 289, n. 83, below. As to the legality of the Israeli settlements, Art. 49, Fourth Red Cross Convention, reads: "The occupying power shall not . . . transfer parts of its own civilian population into the territory it occupies." The U.K. considers that "all settlements in the occupied territories, including East Jerusalem, are illegal" (Minister of State, FCO, *Hansard*, H.C., Vol. 222, col. 579 April 14, 1993) and regards "Israel's annexation of East Jerusalem as illegal" (*Hansard*, H.C. Vol. 548, col. 27 July 15, 1993).

[7] See *U.S. v. Ushi Shiroma* (1954) I.L.R. 21, p. 82, on the administration of the Ryukyu Islands by the U.S., also Germany after the Second World War. See also *Puccini v. Commissioner-General of the Government of the Territory of Trieste* (1961) I.L.R. 40, p. 43.

[8] This proposition appeared in previous editions of this work, but see McNair, I.C.J. Rep (1951), at p. 160 for a more cautious statement of the position. Doubtless both rivers and the territorial sea are "appurtenant" to land, but both stretches of river and of territorial sea are not infrequently alienated for the purpose of boundary settlements. But see *U.S. v. Angeog* (1961) I.L.R. 32, p. 83, for a decision that a cession of the island of Guam necessarily included its territorial sea. . . .

[9] See Fawcett (1967) 43 Int. Affairs 236.

[10] 28 C.T.S. 325.

In 1963, Spain raised the question of the status of Gibraltar before the United Nations Decolonisation Committee. The following year the Committee reached a consensus by which it invited Spain and the United Kingdom to conduct "conversations in order to find ... a negotiated solution."[11] During the resulting discussions, the following positions were established.[12] Spain argued that Article X granted to Great Britain "a British military base installed in Spain," not sovereignty over the territory of Gibraltar.[13] The United Kingdom disputed this limited reading of Article X.[14] Spain contended that the United Kingdom had no claim to Gibraltar based on conquest because its seizure in 1704 was not in the name of Great Britain but on behalf of a possible King of Spain—the Pretender to the Spanish Crown, Archduke Charles of Austria—and by an allied force, not an exclusively British one.[15] The United Kingdom reserved its opinion on this question.[16] Spain claimed that certain "neutral ground" to the North of the Rock proper was not included in Article X. The United Kingdom denied this and, in the alternative, claimed a prescriptive title:

> "Her Majesty's Government do not accept that the ground between the Gibraltar frontier fence and the foot of the Rock is Spanish sovereign territory. . . . The whole of the territory has in any case been under exclusive British jurisdiction since at least 1838, by which time British sentries were established along the line of the present frontier fence. . . .
> Notwithstanding occasional protests concerned with specific issues such as the construction by Britain of permanent works on the ground, successive Spanish Governments have, in the view of Her Majesty's Government, demonstrated their acquiescence in these developments and forfeited any title which they may at one time have possessed to the area concerned. Nor has the Spanish Government ever sought to have the matter referred to an international tribunal."[17]

Spain denied that a prescriptive title had been established[18]:

> In addition to prescription being a debatable and vague institution, both in judicial decisions and in doctrine ... in order that prescription may produce legal effects it is necessary to take into account the behaviour of both the interested parties; in other words, the indifference or tacit abandonment on the part of one side, and the occupation as owner on the part of the other. And that is something that has certainly not occurred here. The Spanish Government has continually declared that its acts of tolerance did not imply any extension of the concessions made in the Treaty of Utrecht, and the Government of Great Britain has repeatedly assured it that in their actions there was no intention of altering the "status quo ante." Consequently it is not possible to speak to any legitimization of the British presence in part of the neutral ground, by reason of the long series of Spanish protests and refusals which have been made uninterruptedly from 1713 down to the present day.

[11] See above, p. 119.
[12] For a U.K. record of the discussion, see Cmnd. 3131.
[13] *ibid.* p. 8.
[14] *ibid.* p. 53.
[15] *ibid.* p. 8.
[16] *ibid.* p. 53.
[17] *ibid.* p. 62. Does the refusal by Spain to refer the question of title to Gibraltar to the I.C.J., as suggested by the U.K. in 1966, indicate acquiescence? See Fawcett, *loc. cit.*, p. 227, n. 9, above, pp. 240–241.
[18] *ibid.* pp. 27–28.

Spain also claimed sovereignty over Gibraltar's territorial sea. The 1966 (and subsequent) negotiations have proved unsuccessful and the issue remains unresolved. Spain continues to press for the return of Gibraltar, but the United Kingdom continues to refuse.

Is a title based upon a cession made by a defeated state to a victorious state in 1713 still valid? How does the doctrine of inter-temperoral law[19] affect the position? Would such a cession be valid if it were to occur now? On the validity of treaties by which one state cedes territory to another after a war or other use of force contrary to Article 2(4), United Nations Charter, see below, p. 831. What is the relevance of the principle of self-determination?[20]

(iv) Accretion and Avulsion

Notes

A state may also attain sovereignty over new land as a result of natural forces. This may happen slowly (accretion), for example, by the gradual movement of a river bed or suddenly (avulsion), for example, by the creation of an island in territorial waters by volcanic action.[21]

(v) New States

Notes

Which, if any, of the means of acquiring territorial sovereignty considered in the above materials applies or apply when a new state emerges, either by revolution or, as in the case of many former colonial territories since the Second World War, by peaceful means? Do these means apply only to the acquisition of additional territory by an existing state, so that the emergence of a new state is to be considered solely by reference to the criteria of statehood considered in Chapter 4?[22]

2. Polar Regions[23]

(i) Antarctica[24]

NEW ZEALAND'S CLAIM TO THE ROSS DEPENDENCY[25]

1 Hackworth 457

The following correspondence concerned Admiral Byrd's second expedition to the Antarctic in 1934. The United Kingdom learnt that a post office was to be

---

[19] See above, p. 199.
[20] See above, p. 113.
[21] As in the case of Surtsey: see below, p. 389. See further, Oppenheim, Vol. I, pp. 697–698. And see the *Chamizal Arbitration*, above, p. 210.
[22] See Jennings, *op cit.*, p. 190, n. 1 above, pp. 7–9.
[23] See Mouton, (1962–III) 107 Hague Recueil 169.
[24] See Auburn, *Antarctic Law and Politics* (1982); Bush, *Antarctica and International Law* (1982); Grolin (1987) 9 Int. Rel. 39; Hayton (1960) 54 A.J.I.L. 349; Joyner and Chopra, *The Antarctic Legal Regime* (1988); Luard, 1984 For. Aff. 1175; Myhre, *The Antarctic Treaty System: Politics, Law and Diplomacy* (1986); Sahurie, *The International Law of Antarctica* (1992); Triggs, ed., *The Antarctic Treaty Regime* (1987); Various, Symposium: *The International Legal Regime for Antarctica* (1986) 19 Cornell I.L.J. 155.
[25] See Auburn, *The Ross Dependency* (1972).

established at the expedition's base in the Ross Dependency; that special stamps had been issued for use there; and that certain expedition members had been sworn in to act as United States postmasters. The United Kingdom protested that "such acts could not be regarded otherwise than as infringing the British sovereignty and New Zealand administrative rights in the dependency.... " The following exchange then occurred.

Note from the United States Secretary of State to the British Ambassador, November 14, 1934

It is understood that His Majesty's Government in New Zealand bases its claim of sovereignty on the discovery of a portion of the region in question. ... in the light of long established principles of international law, ... I cannot admit that sovereignty accrues from mere discovery unaccompanied by occupancy and use.

Note from the British Ambassador to the United States Secretary of State, December 27, 1934

1. ... The supposition that the British claim to sovereignty over the Ross Dependency is based on discovery alone, and, moreover on the discovery of only a portion of the region, is based on a misapprehension of the facts of the situation.

2. The Dependency was established and placed under New Zealand Administration by an Order in Council of 1923 in which the Dependency's geographical limits were precisely defined. Regulations have been made by the Governor General of New Zealand in respect of the Dependency and the British title has been kept up by the exercise in respect of the Dependency of administrative and governmental powers, *e.g.* as regards the issue of whaling licences and the appointment of a special officer to act as magistrate for the Dependency.

3. As I had the honour to state in my note No. 33 of January 29th last, His Majesty's Government in New Zealand recognize the absence of ordinary postal facilities in the Dependency and desire therefore to facilitate as far as possible the carriage of mail by United States authorities to and from the Byrd Expedition. As regards Mr. Anderson's present mission, they understand that he is carrying letters to which are, or will be, affixed special stamps printed in the United States and that these stamps are to be cancelled and date-stamped on board the Expedition's vessel. They also understand that these stamps are intended to be commemorative of the Byrd Expedition and have been issued as a matter of philatelic interest.

4. In the above circumstances His Majesty's Government in New Zealand have no objection to the proposed visit of Mr. Anderson. They must, however, place it on record that, had his mission appeared to them to be designed as an assertion of United States sovereignty over any part of the

Ross Dependency or as a challenge to British sovereignty therein, they would have been compelled to make a protest.

Notes

1. Antarctica is a land mass covered with ice. At certain points (*e.g.* the Ross Ice Shelf), permanently frozen sea adjoins it. Beyond the land mass and the shelf ice there is a large area of sea that is frozen in some seasons and navigable in others. Official claims to sectors of Antarctica have been made by Argentina, Australia, Chile, France, New Zealand, Norway and the United Kingdom.[26] The only major sector not officially claimed is Marie Byrd Land. Admiral Byrd discovered it and claimed it for the United States, but his claim was not officially adopted. The United States does not recognise the claim of any other state. The claimant states would appear to recognise each others' claims,[27] except that the Argentinian and Chilean sectors overlap with each other, as does each with that of the United Kingdom. In 1955, the United Kingdom instituted proceedings before the International Court of Justice by unilateral application asking the Court to rule on the disputes resulting from this situation between the United Kingdom, on the one hand, and Argentina and Chile, on the other.[28] The applications met with no response from Argentina and Chile and the Court struck them off its list in 1956. Did they nonetheless serve a useful purpose from the standpoint of the United Kingdom?[29] In its applications, the United Kingdom claimed sovereignty over its sector on the basis of "historic British discoveries" followed by "the long-continued and peaceful display of British sovereignty from the date of those discoveries onwards in, and in regard to, the territories concerned."[30]

2. A sector is established by enclosing an area within a line of latitude and two lines of longitude to the point at which the latter lines converge at the South Pole. Thus, applying this method in two stages, the United Kingdom sector, the British Antarctic Territory, consists of "all islands and territories whatsoever which . . . are situated south of the 60th parallel of the south latitude between the 20th degree of west longitude and the 80th degree of west longitude."[31]

ANTARCTIC TREATY 1959[32]

U.K.T.S. 97 (1961), Cmnd. 1535, 402 U.N.T.S. 71; (1960) 54 A.J.I.L. 477

Article 1

1. Antarctica shall be used for peaceful purposes only. There shall be prohibited, *inter alia*, any measures of a military nature, such as the establishment of military bases and fortifications, the carrying out of military manoeuvres, as well as the testing of any type of weapons.

---

[26] For maps of Antarctica with the sectors marked, see the articles by Mouton and Hayton referred to above, n. 23 and n. 24.

[27] See, *e.g.* the implied mutual recognition of claims by France and by Commonwealth states in the exchange of notes of October 25, 1938, Cmd. 5900.

[28] I.C.J. Pleadings, *Antarctica Cases* (*U.K. v. Argentina; U.K. v. Chile*).

[29] On the role of protest, see above, pp. 212–213.

[30] *loc. cit.*, n. 28, above, p. 74.

[31] S.I. 1972 No. 400. Waldock (1948) 25 B.Y.I.L. 311, 328 states that the area "does not seem to have been framed in pursuance of any special sector doctrine. The sector was merely the most convenient geographical definition of the numerous islands and continental territory claimed. . . . "

[32] In force 1961. 45 parties, including the U.K.

2. The present treaty shall not prevent the use of military personnel or equipment for scientific research or for any other peaceful purpose. . . .

Article 4

1. Nothing contained in the present treaty shall be interpreted as:

(*a*) a renunciation by any Contracting Party of previously asserted rights of or claims to territorial sovereignty in Antarctica;

(*b*) a renunciation or diminution by any Contracting Party of any basis of claim to territorial sovereignty in Antarctica which it may have whether as a result of its activities or those of its nationals in Antarctica, or otherwise;

(*c*) prejudicing the position of any Contracting Party as regards its recognition or non-recognition of any other State's right of or claim or basis of claim to territorial sovereignty in Antarctica.

2. No acts or activities taking place while the present treaty is in force shall constitute a basis for asserting, supporting or denying a claim to territorial sovereignty in Antarctica or create any rights of sovereignty in Antarctica. No new claim, or enlargement of an existing claim, to territorial sovereignty in Antarctica shall be asserted while the present treaty is in force.

Article 5

1. Any nuclear explosions in Antarctica and the disposal there of radioactive waste material shall be prohibited. . . .

Article 6

The provisions of the present treaty shall apply to the area south of 60° South Latitude, including all ice shelves, but nothing in the present treaty shall prejudice or in any way affect the rights, or the exercise of the rights, of any state under international law with regard to the high seas within that area.

Article 7

1. In order to promote the objectives and ensure the observance of the provisions of the present treaty, each Contracting Party whose representatives are entitled to participate in the meetings referred to in Article 9 of the treaty shall have the right to designate observers to carry out any inspection provided for by the present article. . . .

Article 8

1. In order to facilitate the exercise of their functions under the present treaty, and without prejudice to the respective positions of the Contracting Parties relating to jurisdiction over all other persons in Antarctica,

observers designated under paragraph 1 of Article 7 and scientific personnel exchanged under subparagraph 1(b) of Article 3 of the treaty, and members of the staffs accompanying any such persons, shall be subject only to the jurisdiction of the Contracting Party of which they are nationals in respect of all acts or omissions occurring while they are in Antarctica for the purpose of exercising their functions.

2. Without prejudice to the provisions of paragraph 1 of this article, and pending the adoption of measures in pursuance of subparagraph 1(e) of Article 9, the Contracting Parties concerned in any case of dispute with regard to the exercise of jurisdiction in Antarctica shall immediately consult together with a view to reaching a mutually acceptable solution.

Notes

1. The Antarctic Treaty's undoubted success stems largely from the "freezing" of territorial claims by Article 4.[33] With the issue of sovereignty defused, Antarctica has experienced scientific co-operation rather than political conflict. Other notable features of the Treaty régime are the demilitarised (Article 1) and "nuclear free" (Article 5) character of Antarctica and the provision for periodic meetings (in fact biennial) of the consultative parties. (Article 9).[34] The Consultative Meetings have adopted over 150 (non-binding) recommendations concerning activities in Antarctica and have led to other important conservation measures, particularly the 1972 Convention for the Conservation of Antarctic Seals[35] and the 1980 Convention for the Conservation of Antarctic Marine Living Resources.[36] The latter establishes a Commission charged with promoting the conservation of marine living resources, primarily krill (a small crustacean).

2. The 1959 Treaty contains no provision on the exploitation of mineral resources. It was intended to fill this gap by the 1988 Convention on the Regulation of Antarctic Mineral Resources Activities.[37] This provided for a permit system by which national operators might exploit minerals subject to stringent environmental safeguards. But the Convention did not enter into force because international opinion favoured a complete ban on mineral exploitation. It was quickly

---

[33] What is the effect of Article 4(2) for states not parties to it? On treaties establishing objective legal regimes, see below, p. 825.

[34] The consultative parties are the 12 named in the Convention preamble (the states with territorial claims, listed above, p. 231, and Belgium, Japan, South Africa, U.S. and the Russian Federation) and the 14 other acceding parties that at present conduct "substantial scientific research activity" in Antarctica (Art. 9(3)).

[35] U.K.T.S. 45 (1978), Cmnd. 7209; 1080 U.N.T.S. 176; 11 I.L.M. 251. In force 1978. 16 parties, including the U.K. Whales are protected by the 1946 International Convention for the Regulation of Whaling, U.K.T.S. 5 (1949), Cmnd. 7604; 161 U.N.T.S. 72, which is not restricted to Antarctica. In force 1948, 38 parties, including the U.K.

[36] U.K.T.S. 48 (1982), Cmnd. 8714; (1980) 19 I.L.M. 841. In force 1982. 27 parties, including the U.K. See Bankes (1981) 19 C.Y.I.L. 303; Frank (1983) 13 O.D.I.L. 291; Gardam (1985) 15 M.U.L.R. 279; Howard (1989) 38 I.C.L.Q. 104.

[37] Misc. 6 (1989), Cm. 634; (1988) 27 I.L.M. 868. Not in force. Ratification by 16 of the 20 drafting conference participants required, including, *inter alia*, all states with territorial claims. No ratifications. See Redgwell (1990) 39 I.C.L.Q. 474; Watts (1990) 39 I.C.L.Q. 169; and Wolfrum, *The Convention on the Regulation of Antarctic Mineral Resource Activity* (1991). On the exploitation of mineral resources generally, see Francioni (1986) 19 Cornell I.L.J. 163; Lagoni (1979) Z.A.O.R.V. 1; Rich (1982) 31 I.C.L.Q. 709; Tetzeli (1987) 10 Hastings I.C.L.R. 525; Visser (1988) 1 Leiden J.I.L. 171.

replaced by the 1991 Protocol on Environmental Protection to the Antarctic Treaty.[38] This designates Antarctica as "a natural reserve, devoted to peace and science" (Article 2), spells out principles and mandatory rules for environmental protection (Article 3, Annexes I–IV)) and establishes a Committee on Environmental Protection (Article 11). The Protocol imposes a ban on mineral resource activity, except for scientific research (Annex V).

3. The 1959 Treaty has no time limit, but a review conference with a view to modification or amendment may be called by a consultative party (Article 12) (none yet). One suggestion is that the present legal régime be replaced by one that regards Antarctica as a part of the "common heritage of mankind."[39] This has been proposed by Malaysia and some other non-aligned countries within the United Nations.[40] Such a régime would make territorial claims to sovereignty inappropriate.

(ii) THE ARCTIC[41]

Notes

1. Two of the states bordering the Arctic Ocean—Canada and the Russian Federation—have made sector claims to land to their north. In 1926, the (then) U.S.S.R. claimed "sovereignty over all territory, discovered or undiscovered, lying in the Arctic Ocean north of the coast of the Soviet Union to the North Pole, between meridian 32° 4' 35" east of Greenwich and meridian 168° 49' 30" west of Greenwich.[42] Canada has also made sector claims to land in the Arctic for many years.[43] Other states bordering the Ocean with less to gain, namely Denmark, Norway and the U.S., have opposed the use of the sector approach.[44] Neither Canada nor the Russian Federation have officially claimed sovereignty over the ice as well. Thus, in 1956, the Canadian Minister of Northern Affairs and National Resources stated[45]:

> We have never subscribed to the sector theory in application to the ice. We are content that our sovereignty exists over all the Arctic Island.

[38] (1991) 30 I.L.M. 1455. Not in force. Ratification by all 26 consultative parties required; ratifications by the U.S., the Russian Federation, Finland and Japan still needed. The U.K. has ratified. See Blay (1992) 86 A.J.I.L. 377. See also the Antarctica Act 1994.

[39] As to which, see below, p. 474.

[40] On the Malaysian initiative, see Hayashi (1986) 19 Cornell I.L.J. 275. The consultative parties, who include members of the main political groupings within the UN, are opposed to this attempt to transfer jurisdiction over Antarctica from states actively involved in the continent's development to UN members generally.

[41] See Boczek (1986) 29 G.Y.I.L. 154; Butler, *Northeast Arctic Passage* (1978); Franck, *Maritime Claims in the Arctic: Canadian and Russian Perspectives* (1993); Pharand, *The Law of the Sea of the Arctic* (1973); *ibid., The Northwest Passage: Arctic Straits* (1984); *ibid., Canada's Arctic Waters in International Law* (1988).

[42] 1 Hackworth 461.

[43] See, *e.g.* the 1956 statement at n. 45 below. Note, however, its recent adoption of a straight baseline approach which may render the sector approach redundant: see below, p. 235.

[44] See 1 Hackworth 463–465.

[45] 1956 Debates, H.C., Canada Vol. 7, p. 6955. See Head (1963) 9 McGill L.J. 200 (1963). More recently Canadian Government spokesmen have claimed that waters in the Canadian sector of the Arctic Ocean, although not Canadian, "have a special undefined status because of the presence of ice and do not qualify as high seas": Pharand, *op. cit.*, n. 41, above p. 175. Whereas USSR writers sometimes claimed sovereignty over the ice, see, *e.g.* Lakhtine (1930) 24 A.J.I.L. 703, at 712, no official claim was made: see Pharand, *op. cit.*, n. 41 above, p. 170.

On the question whether a state may acquire sovereignty over ice by other means, (*e.g.* by occupation), Pharand distinguishes between ice shelves, (*e.g.* those of Ellesmere Island in the Arctic or the Ross Ice Shelf in the Antarctic) and ice islands. As to the former, he states[46]:

> The legal status of ice shelves in international law has never been determined but there appears to be a consensus among interested states that they ought to be considered as land. . . . These huge ice-tongues are partly afloat, but their thickness and quasi-permanency render them much more like land than water . . .

As to ice islands, since they do not satisfy the definition of an island in Article 121, 1982 Law of the Sea Convention, Pharand suggests that the better analogy is with a ship: "The suggestion is that ice islands ought to be considered as ships when occupied [as they may be by research stations] and appropriated."[47]

2. In 1985, Canada drew straight baselines around the outer limits of the islands constituting the Canadian archipelago, claiming the waters on the landward side of the islands, which include Hudson Bay and the various routes of the North West Passage, as internal waters.[48] The baselines were said to indicate the outer limit of Canadian "historic internal waters."[49] By a 1988 U.S.-Canadian Agreement on Arctic Cooperation, the U.S., while objecting to the baselines, agreed to seek Canadian consent before its icebreakers and other vessels navigated the North West Passage.[50]

3. LAND BOUNDARIES[51]

OPPENHEIM'S INTERNATIONAL LAW

(9th ed., 1992), Vol. I. Edited by Jennings and Watts

§ 232 Boundary disputes Boundaries are, for many reasons, of such importance, that disputes relating thereto are relatively frequent. The location of a land boundary line is usually a matter of the correct interpretation of some instrument, by which the boundary has been established. The commonest way of doing this is by a boundary treaty. In other cases an arbitral award or judicial decision can be the final determination, especially where the meaning of a boundary treaty had been disputed.[52]

---

[46] *op. cit.*, p. 234, n. 41. above p. 170.

[47] *ibid.* p. 196. See also Molde (1982) 51 N.T.I.R. 164.

[48] See Pharand (1987) 25 C.Y.I.L. 324.

[49] Statement by the Canadian Secretary of State for External Affairs, quoted by Pharand, *loc. cit.*, n. 48, above, p. 326. *cf.* the earlier Canadian Government statement in (1970) 9 I.L.M. 607, at 613.

[50] See Pharand, *loc. cit.*, p. 234, n. 41, above, p. 327.

[51] See Berntein, *Delimitation of International Boundaries* (1974); Brownlie, *African Boundaries: A Legal and Diplomatic Encyclopaedia* (1979); Prescott, *Boundaries and Frontiers* (1978); Sharma, *International Boundary Disputes and International Law* (1976).

[52] See the *Temple of Preah Vihear Case*, p. 6, I.C.J. Rep. 1962, 34; see also *Aegean Sea Continental Shelf* case (Greece v. Turkey), I.C.J. Rep. 1978, p. 36. The delimitation of land boundaries was the subject-matter of two Advisory Opinions of the P.C.I.J., P.C.I.J., Series B, No. 8 (Poland and Czechoslovakia), and *ibid.* 9 (Albania and the Serb-Croat-Slovene State). . . . For later cases, see the *Frontier Land Case*, I.C.J. Rep. 1959, p. 209; the *King of Spain Award Case*, I.C.J. Rep. 1960, p. 192; the *Rann of Kutch Case*, I.L.M., 7 (1968), p. 633; and see Salmon

In that event, the tribunal will have it in mind that "one of the primary objects" of boundary settlement is "to achieve stability and finality"[53] Sometimes international commissions are specially appointed to settle the boundary lines.[54]

§ 233 Boundary and territorial disputes distinguished   Boundary questions are distinguishable from questions of title to territorial sovereignty[55] ...   As the International Court of Justice said in the *North Sea Continental Shelf* cases, "The appurtenance of a given area, considered as an entirety, in no way governs the precise delimitations of its boundaries, any more than uncertainty as to boundaries can affect territorial rights".[56] A dispute often involves both kinds of argument, however; and the question which is the correct approach may be one of the points at issue.[57] Even in the strictly territorial dispute the boundaries of the disputed territory must be part of the relevant facts, though not disputed. There is also a sense in which a question of title to territory must always be implicitly involved in a pure boundary dispute; except that in this case it is not the fact and mode of acquisition of territorial title that is disputed but the proper interpretation of some instrument, award or adjudication, or course of historical development, that is claimed to have established the boundary of the territory in question.

§ 234 Third states   Boundary questions, as well as questions of territorial title, often concern more than one state for an international boundary dispute is concerned essentially with rights opposable *erga omnes*; as, for example, where the boundaries of three states converge on a tri-point.

in A.F.D.I., 14 (1968), p. 217; the *Encuentro/Palena Case, Argentine-Chile Frontier Case* (1966), I.L.R., 38, p. 19 and I.C.L.Q., 12 (1967), p. 550, and A.J., 12 (1967), 1071 (a dispute between Argentina and Chile) , and Cot, A.F.D.I., 14 (1968), p. 237; the *Beagle Channel Case* (1977), I.L.R., 52, p. 93 (between Argentina and Chile) ... ; see also the *Taba Award* (1988), I.L.R., 80, p. 226, between Egypt and Israel ... I.L.M., 27 (1988), p. 1421, I.L.R., 80, p. 226. ... [; the] Award in the *Dubai-Sharjah* case (1981) (unpublished); the *Burkina Faso and Mali Frontier Dispute*, I.C.J. Rep. 1986, p. 554.

[53] See the *Temple of Preah Vihear Case*, I.C.J. Rep. 1962, p. 34. But for the "relativity" of the principle of finality, see Bardonnet, *op. cit.*, pp. 67–71.

[54] ... The work of a boundary commission was crucial to the *Temple of Preah Vihear Case*, I.C.J. Rep. 1962, p. 6; see also the Award in the *Argentine/Chile Frontier Case* (1967), Cmnd. 7438 and I.L.R., 38, p. 10. See the *Taba Award* (1988), I.L.R., 80, p. 226, where it was held that, "If a boundary line is once demarcated jointly by the parties concerned, the demarcation is considered as an authentic interpretation of the boundary agreement even if deviations may have occurred or if there are some inconsistencies with the maps" (para. 210).

[55] ... Nevertheless, some law is common to both kinds of dispute, *e.g.* the question of the "critical date" (see §273). ...

[56] I.C.J. Rep. 1969, at p. 32; but see also *Burkina Faso and Mali Frontier Dispute*, I.C.J. Rep. 1986, p. 554, para. 17 for a different view.

[57] See, *e.g.* the *Rann of Kutch Case*, I.L.M., 7 (1968), pp. 633 *et seq.* (between India and Pakistan). Also the *Aegean Sea Case*, I.C.J. Rep. 1978, p. 3, para. 84, where the Court said: "it would be difficult to accept the broad proposition that delimitation is entirely extraneous to the notion of territorial status. Any disputed delimitation of a boundary entails some determination of entitlement to the areas to be delimited." ...

When a dispute between two of the states is submitted to a tribunal for settlement, there may therefore also arise questions about the extent of the tribunal's jurisdiction, or, in the International Court of Justice, of intervention under Articles 62 or 63 of the Court's Statute.[58]

Notes

1. Key to the determination of post-colonial boundary disputes is the concept of *uti possidetis juris*, the meaning of which was considered in the *Frontier Dispute* case[59]:

23 . . . The essence of the principle lies in its primary aim of securing respect for the territorial boundaries at the moment when independence is achieved. Such territorial boundaries might be no more than delimitations between different administrative divisions or colonies all subject to the same sovereign. In that case, the application of the principle of *uti possidetis* resulted in administrative boundaries being transformed into international frontiers in the full sense of the term. This is true both of the States which took shape in the regions of South America which were dependent on the Spanish Crown, and of the States Parties to the present case, which took shape within the vast territories of French West Africa. *Uti possidetis*, as a principle which upgraded former administrative delimitations, established during the colonial period, to international frontiers, is therefore a principle of a general kind which is logically connected with this form of decolonization wherever it occurs.

24. The territorial boundaries which have to be respected may also derive from international frontiers which previously divided a colony of one State from a colony of another, or indeed a colonial territory from the territory of an independent State, or one which was under protectorate, but had retained its international personality. There is no doubt that the obligation to respect pre-existing international frontiers in the event of a State succession derives from a general rule of international law whether or not the rule is expressed in the formula *uti possidetis*. . . .

25. However, it may be wondered how the time-hallowed principle has been able to withstand the new approaches to international law as expressed in Africa, where the successive attainment of independence and the emergence of new States have been accompanied by a certain questioning of traditional international law. At first sight this principle conflicts outright with another one, the right of peoples to self-determination. In fact, however, the maintenance of the territorial status quo in Africa is often seen as the wisest course, to preserve what has been achieved by peoples who have struggled for their independence, and to avoid a disruption which would deprive the continent of the gains achieved by much sacrifice. The essential requirement of stability in order to survive, to develop and gradually to consolidate their independence in all fields, has induced African States judiciously to consent to the respecting of colonial frontiers, and to take account of it in the interpretation of the principle of self-determination of peoples.

[58] See I.C.J. Rep. 1984, p. 3, and *ibid*. 1985, p. 13 (Libya/Malta continental shelf and Italy); and specifically on land frontiers and tri-point, see I.C.J. Rep. 1986, p. 554, para. 49.

[59] *Burkina Faso v. Mali* I.C.J. Rep. 1986, p. 554. Court Chamber decision. See Naldi (1987) 36 I.C.L.Q. 893. The principle of *uti possidetis* has not been applied as state practice in post-colonial Africa in every case, as was pointed out by Judge Luchaire (*ibid*., p. 653). He mentioned, *inter alia*, that British Togoland, a trust territory, was merged with the Gold Coast, a British colony, to become the new state of Ghana.

26. Thus the principle of *uti possidetis* has kept its place among the most important legal principles, despite the apparent contradiction which explained its coexistence alongside the new norms . . .

63. . . . the Parties have invoked in support of their respective contentions the "colonial *effectivités*", in other words, the conduct of the administrative authorities as proof of the effective exercise of territorial jurisdiction in the region during the colonial period. . . . The role played in this case by such *effectivités* is complex. Where the act corresponds exactly to law, where effective administration is additional to the *uti possidetis juris*, the only role of *effectivité* is to confirm the exercise of the right derived from a legal title. Where the act does not correspond to the law, where the territory which is the subject of the dispute is effectively administered by a State other than the one possessing the legal title, preference should be given to the holder of the title. In the event that the *effectivité* does not co-exist with any legal title, it must invariably be taken into consideration. Finally, there are cases where the legal title is not capable of showing exactly the territorial expanse to which it relates. The *effectivités* can then play an essential role in showing how the title is interpreted in practice.

On the principle of self-determination, which, as the I.C.J. notes, gives way to that of *uti possidetis*, see above, p. 113. On *uti possidetis* in a non-post colonial context, see *Opinions No. 2 and No. 3*, E.C. Arbitration Commission, above, p. 120, 129.

2. The approach in the *Frontier Dispute* case to the *uti possidetis* was followed by another I.C.J. Chamber in the *Land, Island and Maritime Frontier Dispute* case.[60] In that case, the Chamber also noted that the boundary at the date of independence of states may change as a result of adjudication or the conduct of the parties (treaties, administration, acquiescence):

67. There has also been some argument between the Parties about the "critical date"[61] in relation to this dispute. The principle of *uti possidetis juris* is sometimes stated in almost absolute terms, suggesting that the position at the date of independence is always determinative; in short, that no other critical date can arise. As appears from the discussion above, this cannot be so. A later critical date clearly may arise, for example, either from adjudication or from a boundary treaty. Thus, in the previous Latin American boundary arbitrations it is the award that is now determinative, even though it be based upon a view of the *uti possidetis juris* position. The award's view of the *uti possidetis juris* position prevails and cannot now be questioned juridically, even if it could be questioned historically. So for such a boundary the date of the award has become a new and later critical date. Likewise there can be no question that the parts of the El Salvador/Honduras boundary fixed by the General Treaty of Peace of 1980 now constitute the boundary and 1980 is now the critical date. If the *uti possidetis juris* position can be qualified by adjudication and by treaty, the question then arises whether it can be qualified in other ways, for example, by acquiescence[62] or recognition. There seems to be no reason in principle why these factors should not operate, where there is sufficient evidence to show that the parties have in effect clearly accepted a variation, or at least an interpretation, of the *uti possidetis juris* position.

---

[60] *El Salvador v. Honduras* I.C.J. Rep. 1992, p. 351 at p. 401.
[61] On the concept of the "critical date", see above, p. 198.
[62] As to acquiescence, the Court Chamber noted the relevance of "post independence *effectivités*". If a state administers an area and the other state does not object, this goes to prescription.

3. The boundary between the United Kingdom and France in the Channel Tunnel is at the mid-way point: see section 10 of the Channel Tunnel Act 1987.

4. AIRSPACE[63]

CHICAGO CONVENTION ON INTERNATIONAL CIVIL AVIATION 1944[64]

U.K.T.S. 8 (1953), Cmd. 8742; 15 U.N.T.S. 295

Article 1

The contracting States recognize that every State has complete and exclusive sovereignty over the air space above its territory.

Article 2

For the purposes of this Convention the territory of a State shall be deemed to be the land areas and territorial waters adjacent thereto under the sovereignty, suzerainty, protection or mandate of such State.

Article 3

(*a*) This Convention shall be applicable only to civil aircraft, and shall not be applicable to state aircraft.

(*b*) Aircraft used in military, customs and police services shall be deemed to be state aircraft.

(*c*) No state aircraft of a contracting State shall fly over the territory of another State or land thereon without authorization by special agreement or otherwise, and in accordance with the terms thereof.

(*d*) The contracting States undertake, when issuing regulations for their state aircraft, that they will have due regard for the safety of navigation of civil aircraft.

Article 3 bis

(*a*) The contracting States recognize that every State must refrain from resorting to the use of weapons against civil aircraft in flight and that, in case of interception, the lives of persons on board and the safety of aircraft must not be endangered. This provision shall not be interpreted as modifying in any way the rights and obligations of States set forth in the Charter of the United Nations.

---

[63] See Cheng, *The Law of International Air Transport* (1962); Johnson, *Rights in Air Space* (1965); Naveau, *International Air Transport in a Changing World* (1989); Zylicz, *International Air Transport Law* (1992).

[64] In force 1947. 186 parties, including the U.K.

(*b*) The contracting States recognize that every State, in the exercise of its sovereignty, is entitled to require the landing at some designated airport of a civil aircraft flying above its territory without authority or if there are reasonable grounds to conclude that it is being used for any purpose inconsistent with the aims of this Convention; it may also give such aircraft any other instructions to put an end to such violations. For this purpose, the contracting States may resort to any appropriate means consistent with relevant rules of international law, including the relevant provisions of this Convention, specifically paragraph (*a*) of this Article. Each contracting State agrees to publish its regulations in force regarding the interception of civil aircraft.

(*c*) Every civil aircraft shall comply with an order given in conformity with paragraph (*b*) of this Article. To this end each contracting State shall establish all necessary provisions in its national laws or regulations to make such compliance mandatory for any civil aircraft registered in that State or operated by a person having his principal place of business or permanent residence in that State. Each contracting State shall make any violation of such applicable laws or regulations punishable by severe penalties and shall submit the case to its competent authorities in accordance with its laws or regulations.

(*d*) Each contracting State shall take appropriate measures to prohibit the deliberate use of any civil aircraft registered in that State or operated by an operator who has his principal place of business or permanent residence in that State for any purpose inconsistent with the aims of this Convention. This provision shall not affect paragraph (*a*) or derogate from paragraphs (*b*) and (*c*) of this article.

Article 5

Each contracting State agrees that all aircraft of the other contracting States, being aircraft not engaged in scheduled international air service, shall have the right, subject to the observance of the terms of this Convention, to make flights into or in transit non-stop across its territory and to make stops for non-traffic purposes without the necessity of obtaining prior permission, and subject to the right of the State flown over to require landing. Each contracting State nevertheless reserves the right, for reasons of safety of flight, to require aircraft desiring to proceed over regions which are inaccessible or without adequate air navigation facilities to follow prescribed routes, or to obtain special permission for such flights.

Such aircraft, if engaged in the carriage of passengers, cargo, or mail for remuneration or hire on other than scheduled international air services, shall also, subject to the provisions of Article 7, have the privilege of taking on or discharging passengers, cargo, or mail, subject to the right of any State where such embarkation or discharge takes place to impose such regulations, conditions or limitations as it may consider desirable.

Article 6

No scheduled international air service may be operated over or into the territory of a contracting State, except with the special permission or other authorization of that State, and in accordance with the terms of such permission or authorization.

Article 17

Aircraft have the nationality of the State in which they are registered.

Article 18

An aircraft cannot be validly registered in more than one State, but its registration may be changed from one State to another.

Article 19

The registration or transfer of registration of aircraft in any contracting State shall be made in accordance with its laws and regulations.

Notes

1. Article 1 of the Chicago Convention reflects a rule of customary international law[65] that developed rapidly in the first part of this century. An example of the violation of airspace of great political importance occurred in the *U-2 Incident*.[66] On May 1, 1960, a U-2, a U.S. high altitude reconnaissance aircraft, was shot down at a height of 20,000 metres over Soviet territory. The aeroplane had taken off from Pakistan and was scheduled to land in Finland after taking aerial photographs while over Soviet territory. The USSR protested at the flight. The U.S. did not try to justify its action in terms of international law or protest at the shooting down or of the subsequent trial of the pilot. The lack of protest by the U.S. in this case is consistent with the view that, other than in the case of entry in distress, intentional trespass by military aircraft (with the exception of military *transport* aircraft) may be met by the use of force without warning.[67]

2. Since 1945, trespassing *civil* aircraft have been shot down at the rate of nearly one a year.[68] In 1973, for example, a Libyan Airlines aircraft on a scheduled commercial flight to Cairo was shot down by Israeli fighters after accidentally entering sensitive airspace over Israeli-occupied Sinai. The aircraft had knowingly ignored instructions to land. Israel apologised and paid compensation on an *ex gratia* basis in respect of the resulting loss of 108 lives.[69]

3. Another tragic case was the *Korean Airlines Flight 007 Incident*.[70] In 1983, a Korean Airlines Boeing 747 on a scheduled flight from Alaska to South Korea strayed some 500 kilometres off course over militarily sensitive USSR territory

---

[65] *Nicaragua Case (Merits)*, I.C.J. Rep. 1986, p. 14 at p. 111.
[66] See Lissitzyn (1962) 56 A.J.I.L. 135 and Wright (1960) 54 A.J.I.L. 836.
[67] *cf.* Phelps (1985) 107 Military L.R. 255 at 291.
[68] Richard (1984) 9 A.A.S.L. 147 at 148.
[69] Israel was condemned by the ICAO Council Resolution of June 4, 1973, ICAO Bulletin July 1973, p. 13. See Hughes (1980) 45 J.A.L.C. 595, at 611–12.
[70] See Hassan (1984) 33 I.C.L.Q. 712; Martin (1984) 9 Air Law 138; Morgan (1985) 11 Yale J.I.L. 231; Phelps, n. 67 above; Richard, n. 68 above; Note (1984) 97 H.L.R. 1198.

and was intercepted and then shot down by Soviet military aircraft in darkness in the vicinity of Sakalin Island in USSR airspace north of Japan. All 169 passengers and crew, of 14 different nationalities, were killed. Claims for reparation were lodged with the USSR by states in respect of loss of life and damage to property.[71] An International Civil Aviation Organisation (ICAO) fact-finding investigation report[72] concluded that the aircraft's deviation resulted not from equipment failure or an intention to trespass but from the negligence of the crew who, through "a considerable degree of lack of awareness and attentiveness," never appreciated that the flight was off course. As to the Soviet response, the ICAO investigation, through lack of co-operation by the USSR, lacked the information necessary to assess the adequacy of the measures (of which, the report concluded, the 747 crew were unaware) taken by the Soviet aircraft to intercept the 747 before shooting it down. The report concluded that the USSR authorities, who were conscious of the admitted presence of a U.S. military intelligence aircraft over the high seas in the area, had assumed, without checking by exhaustive visual inspection, that the 747 was an intelligence aircraft and had interpreted a climb by the 747 as evasive action confirming this assumption. Following the report, the ICAO Council condemned the USSR "use of armed force".[73]

In a non-trespass case, the USS Vincennes, a U.S. naval vessel protecting neutral shipping in the Persian Gulf during the Iran-Iraq War, acting in self defence, shot down over the Gulf an Iranian Airlines civil airliner on a scheduled flight with 290 persons on board in the mistaken belief that it was an Iranian military aircraft that was about to attack the USS Vincennes. A claim brought against the U.S. before the I.C.J. was discontinued following a settlement.[74]

4. *Article 3 bis.* A further consequence of the *Korean Airlines Flight 007 Incident* was the adoption by the ICAO Assembly by unanimous vote of Article 3 *bis* of the 1944 ICAO Convention (above). Article 3 *bis* states an almost absolute rule by which weapons must not be used against civil aircraft in flight except where the UN Charter allows this. This would appear to be a reference to the Charter right of self defence (Article 51). Commenting upon this right, the U.K. representative in the ICAO Assembly stated[75]:

> . . . can the use of force in self-defence ever be legitimate? Clearly it could be legitimate if the aircraft is making, or is about to make, an attack or is, for example, dropping paratroops. The aircraft would then in effect be operating as a military aircraft. Lives of persons not on board would be endangered. The State would be entitled to use force against it.

On one view, Article 3 *bis* is stricter than pre-existing custom. This, it is claimed, permitted the use of deadly force as a last resort (*i.e.* when attempts by interception to cause an intruding aircraft to land or to leave had failed) in response to a proportionate national security interest.[76] Supposing this view to be correct, it may be that considerations of humanity and the need for public confidence in the safety of civil airflight have precipitated a new consensus favouring the stricter formulation in Article 3 *bis* as a customary, as well as a treaty, rule.

---

[71] The U.K., for example, claimed £2 million compensation in respect of the deaths of 14 persons entitled to British protection: see U.K.M.I.L. 1985, (1985) 56 B.Y.I.L. 511. For the U.S. claim, see (1984) 78 A.J.I.L. 213. No compensation has been paid.

[72] (1984) 23 I.L.M. 864.

[73] ICAO Council Resolution of March 6, 1984, (1984) 23 I.L.M. 937.

[74] *Aerial Incident of July 3, 1988 Case,* I.C.J. Rep. 1996, p. 9. On the incident, see Linnan (1991) 16 Yale J.I.L. 245.

[75] U.K.M.I.L. 1984, (1984) 55 B.Y.I.L. 591. But see the need for an "armed attack": *Nicaragua Case (Merits),* below, p. 887.

[76] See Hughes, *loc. cit,* p. 241, n. 69 above, p. 619.

The Russian Federation has accepted Article 3 *bis*.[77]

5. In 1952, the ICAO Council defined a "scheduled international air service" (see Article 5 and 6, Chicago Convention) as "a series of flights that possesses all the following characteristics: (a) it passes through the airspace over the territory of more than one State; (b) it is performed by aircraft for the transport of passengers, mail or cargo for remuneration, in such a manner that each flight is open to use by members of the public; (c) it is operated, so as to serve traffic between the same two or more points, either (i) according to a published time-table, or (ii) with flights so regular and frequent that they constitute a recognisably systematic series."[78]

6. Contrast Article 17 of the Chicago Convention with the rules on the nationality of ships.[79] The latter contains a "genuine link" requirement, as in the *Nottebohm* case.[80]

CHICAGO INTERNATIONAL AIR SERVICES TRANSIT AGREEMENT 1944[81]

U.K.T.S. 8 (1953) Cmd. 8742, 171 U.N.T.S. 387

Article 1

1. Each contracting State grants to the other contracting States the following freedoms of the air in respect of scheduled international air services.

(1) The privilege to fly across its territory without landing;

(2) The privilege to land for non-traffic purposes. . . .

Notes

1. The Chicago International Air Services Transit Agreement is known as the "Two Freedoms" Agreement. More ambitious was the Chicago International Air Transport Agreement 1944[82] which guarantees "Five Freedoms" for its parties. These are the two in the "Two Freedoms" Agreement plus the following:

(3) the privilege to put down passengers, mail or cargo taken on in the territory of the State whose nationality the aircraft possesses; (4) The privilege to take on passengers, mail and cargo destined for the territory of the State whose nationality the aircraft possesses; (5) The privilege to take on passengers, mail and cargo destined for the territory of any other contracting State and the privilege to put down passengers, mail and cargo coming from any such territory.[83]

The "Five Freedoms" Agreement has not been widely ratified and, since the withdrawal of the United States in 1947, has not been of great significance.[84]

[77] Not in force. 102 acceptances required; 86 at present, including the U.K.
[78] *Definition of a Scheduled International Air Service*, ICAO Doc. 7278-C/841 (May 10, 1952), p. 3.
[79] See below, p. 424.
[80] See below, p. 588.
[81] In force 1945. 103 parties, including the U.K.
[82] 149 B.F.S.P. 1; 171 U.N.T.S. 387. In force 1945. 11 parties. U.K. not a party.
[83] Art. 5.
[84] See Johnson, *op. cit.*, p. 239, n. 63, above, p. 65.

2. The exclusion of scheduled flights from the multilateral arrangements of the 1944 Chicago Convention (see Article 6) and the failure of the "Five Freedoms" Agreement has led to a network of bilateral and multilateral agreements. It is largely upon the basis of such agreements that international scheduled flights occur.

5. OUTER SPACE[85]

TREATY ON THE PRINCIPLES GOVERNING THE ACTIVITIES OF STATES IN THE EXPLORATION AND USE OF OUTER SPACE, INCLUDING THE MOON AND OTHER CELESTIAL BODIES 1967[86]

U.K.T.S. 10 (1968) Cmnd. 3519; 610 U.N.T.S. 205

Article 1

The exploration and use of outer space, including the moon and other celestial bodies, shall be carried out for the benefit and in the interests of all countries, irrespective of their degree of economic or scientific development, and shall be the province of all mankind.

Outer space, including the moon and other celestial bodies, shall be free for exploration and use by all States without discrimination of any kind, on a basis of equality and in accordance with international law, and there shall be free access to all areas of celestial bodies.

There shall be freedom of scientific investigation in outer space, including the moon and other celestial bodies, and States shall facilitate and encourage international co-operation in such investigation.

Article 2

Outer space, including the moon and other celestial bodies, is not subject to national appropriation by claim of sovereignty, by means of use or occupation, or by any other means.

Article 3

States Parties to the Treaty shall carry on activities in the exploration and use of outer space including the moon and other celestial bodies, in

---

[85] See Andem, *International Legal Problems in the Peaceful Exploration and Use of Outer Space* (1992); Cheng, ed., *The Use of Airspace and Outer Space for all Mankind in the 21st Century* (1995); Christol, *Space Law* (1991); Fawcett, *Outer Space: New Challenges to Law and Policy* (1984); Gorove, *Developments in Space Law: Issues and Policies* (1991); Jasentuligana, ed., *Space Law: Development and Scope* (1992); McDougal, Lasswell and Vlasic, *Law and Public Order in Space* (1963); Matte, *Aerospace Law* (1969); Reijnen, *The United Nations Space Treaties Analysed* (1992); Wadegaonkar, *The Orbit of Space Law* (1984).

[86] In force 1967. 94 parties, including the five Security Council permanent members. For discussion of the treaty, see Darwin (1967) 42 B.Y.I.L. 278; Goedhuis (1968) 15 N.I.L.R. 17; and Cheng (1968) 95 J.D.I. 532.

accordance with international law, including the Charter of the United Nations, in the interest of maintaining international peace and security and promoting international co-operation and understanding.

Article 4

States Parties to the Treaty undertake not to place in orbit around the Earth any objects carrying nuclear weapons or any other kinds of weapons of mass destruction, install such weapons on celestial bodies, or station such weapons in outer space in any other manner.

The moon and other celestial bodies shall be used by all States Parties to the Treaty exclusively for peaceful purposes. The establishment of military bases, installations and fortifications, the testing of any type of weapons and the conduct of military manoeuvres on celestial bodies shall be forbidden. The use of military personnel for scientific research or for any other peaceful purposes shall not be prohibited. The use of any equipment or facility necessary for peaceful exploration of the moon and other celestial bodies shall also not be prohibited.

Article 5

States Parties to the Treaty shall regard astronauts as envoys of mankind in outer space and shall render to them all possible assistance in the event of accident, distress, or emergency landing on the territory of another State Party or on the high seas. When astronauts make such a landing, they shall be safely and promptly returned to the State of registry of their space vehicle.

In carrying on activities in outer space and on celestial bodies, the astronauts of one State Party shall render all possible assistance to the astronauts of other State Parties.

State Parties to the Treaty shall immediately inform the other States Parties to the Treaty or the Secretary-General of the United Nations of any phenomena they discover in outer space, including the moon and other celestial bodies, which could constitute a danger to the life or health of astronauts.

Article 6

States Parties to the Treaty shall bear international responsibility for national activities in outer space, including the moon and other celestial bodies, whether such activities are carried on by governmental agencies or by non-governmental entities, and for assuring that national activities are carried out in conformity with the provisions set forth in the present Treaty. The activities of non-governmental entities in outer space, including the moon and other celestial bodies, shall require authorization and continuing supervision by the appropriate State Party to the Treaty. When activities are carried on in outer space, including the moon and other celestial bodies, by an international organization, responsibility for compliance with this Treaty shall be borne both by the international organization and by the States Parties to the Treaty participating in such organization.

Article 7

Each State Party to the Treaty that launches or procures the launching of an object into outer space, including the moon and other celestial bodies, and each State Party from whose territory or facility an object is launched, is internationally liable for damage to another State Party to the Treaty or to its natural or judicial persons by such object or its component parts on the Earth, in air space or in outer space, including the moon and other celestial bodies.

Article 8

A State Party to the Treaty on whose registry an object launched into outer space is carried shall retain jurisdiction and control over such object, and over any personnel thereof, while in outer space or on a celestial body. Ownership of objects launched into outer space, including objects landed or constructed on a celestial body, and of their component parts, is not affected by their presence in outer space or on a celestial body or by their return to the Earth. Such objects or component parts found beyond the limits of the State Party to the Treaty on whose registry they are carried shall be returned to that State Party, which shall, upon request, furnish identifying data prior to their return.

Article 9

In the exploration and use of outer space, including the moon and other celestial bodies, State Parties to the Treaty shall be guided by the principle of co-operation and mutual assistance and shall conduct all their activities in outer space, including the moon and other celestial bodies, with due regard to the corresponding interests of all other States Parties to the Treaty. States Parties to the Treaty shall pursue studies of outer space, including the moon and other celestial bodies, and conduct exploration of them so as to avoid their harmful contamination and also adverse changes in the environment of the Earth resulting from the introduction of extra terrestrial matter and, where necessary, shall adopt appropriate measures for this purpose. If a State Party to the Treaty has reason to believe that an activity or experiment planned by it or its nationals in outer space, including the moon and other celestial bodies, would cause potentially harmful interference with activities of other States Parties in the peaceful exploration and use of outer space, including the moon and other celestial bodies, it shall undertake appropriate international consultations before proceeding with any such activity or experiment. A State Party to the Treaty which has reason to believe that an activity or experiment planned by another State Party in outer space, including the moon and other celestial bodies, would cause potentially harmful interference with activities in the peaceful exploration and use of outer space, including the moon and other celestial bodies, may request consultation concerning the activity or experiment.

Article 10

In order to promote international co-operation in the exploration and use of outer space, including the moon and other celestial bodies, in conformity with the purposes of this Treaty, the States Parties to the Treaty shall consider on a basis of equality any requests by other States Parties to the Treaty to be afforded an opportunity to observe the flight of space objects launched by those States.

The nature of such an opportunity for observation and the conditions under which it could be afforded shall be determined by agreement between the States concerned.

Article 11

In order to promote international co-operation in the peaceful exploration and use of outer space, States Parties to the Treaty conducting activities in outer space, including the moon and other celestial bodies, agree to inform the Secretary-General of the United Nations as well as the public and the international scientific community, to the greatest extent feasible and practicable, of the nature, conduct, locations and results of such activities. On receiving the said information, the Secretary-General of the United Nations should be prepared to disseminate it immediately and effectively.

Article 12

All stations, installations, equipment and space vehicles on the moon and other celestial bodies shall be open to representatives of other States Parties to the Treaty on a basis of reciprocity. Such representatives shall give reasonable advance notice of a projected visit, in order that appropriate consultations may be held and that maximum precautions may be taken to assure safety and to avoid interference with normal operations in the facility to be visited.

Notes

1. Acting through the United Nations and greatly helped by the common interest of the U.S. and the USSR, the international community was remarkably quick in agreeing upon the basic legal principles governing activities in outer

space.[87] The 1967 Treaty builds upon a number of General Assembly resolutions on space law, particularly Resolutions 1721 (XVI),[88] 1884 (XVIII)[89] and 1962 (XVIII).[90] Resolution 1884 (XVIII) is reproduced in substance in the first paragraph of Article 4 of the Treaty; the various principles stated in the other two resolutions form the basis of Articles 1–3 and 5–9. All three resolutions were adopted unanimously.

2. Note the following criticism of the 1967 Treaty by Fawcett[91]:

> In the Outer Space Treaty we have then a rigidly contractual instrument, in essence a bilateral arrangement between the principal space-users. Apart from its provisions for partial demilitarisation of outer space, tracking and inspection, it does little or nothing to elaborate or secure the principles already set out in General Assembly Resolutions. It may even be that this ill-constructed and precarious instrument is a retrograde step. For in the wise words of Dr. Jenks, written before the conclusion of the Outer Space Treaty[92] "The authority of the Declaration of Legal Principles may be expected to grow with the passage of years. While it is somewhat less than a treaty it must already be regarded as rather more than a statement of custom."
>
> Though Resolution 1962 (XVIII) is for the most part a declaration, not of rules of international law, but of directive principles, it may like other similar General Assembly Resolutions, be regarded as forming part of an international *ordre public*, to which States should strive to make their policies conform. . . .

3. *Article* 2 of the Treaty establishes that territory in outer space, like the high seas, is not subject to sovereignty.[93] It is well known that states have reconnaissance satellites used for military spying purposes; these are not prohibited by Article 4.[94] Does Article 4 prohibit the passage of ballistic missiles through outer space?[95] Article 5 (and to some extent Article 8) is supplemented by the 1968 Agreement on the Rescue of Astronauts, the Return of Astronauts and the Return of Objects launched into Outer Space.[96] Article 6 tackles the problem of imputability[97] in respect of any liability that may arise from space activities. Who is responsible under it for the acts or omissions of any private space activities (*e.g.* by a telecommunications company)?[98] Does the Treaty imagine the possibility of activities by an international organisation, *e.g.* the European Space Agency? On damage resulting from space activities, Article 7 indicates when liability may arise on the part of a state or international organisation responsible under Article 6. It

---

[87] One measure of the importance of a legal régime for outer space is that there are over 5,000 satellites and other objects in outer space.

[88] G.A.O.R., 16th Session, Supp. 17, p. 6 (1961).

[89] G.A.O.R., 18th Session, Supp. 15, p. 13 (1963).

[90] *ibid.* p. 15.

[91] *International Law and the Uses of Outer Space* (1968), pp. 15–16.

[92] *Ed., Space Law* (1965), p. 185.

[93] See Christol (1984) 9 A.A.S.L. 217.

[94] See Goedhuis (1978) 27 I.C.L.Q. 576. The American *Samos* satellites provided Israel with important information about Egyptian military installations in hostilities in the Middle East.

[95] See Darwin, *loc. cit.*, p. 244, n. 86, above, p. 284.

[96] U.K.T.S. 56 (1969), Cmnd. 3997; (1969) 63 A.J.I.L. 382. In force 1968. 86 parties, including the five Security Council permanent members. See Cheng (1969) 23 Y.B.W.A. 185 and Hall (1969) 63 A.J.I.L. 197.

[97] As to imputability generally in international law, see below, p. 499.

[98] See Fawcett, *op. cit.*, p. 244; n. 85, above, pp. 23 *et seq.*

has been supplemented by the 1972 Convention on International Liability for Damages caused by Space Objects, see below, note 5. Article 8 gives the state of registry jurisdiction over space objects and persons on board, but does not indicate the extent to which this is exclusive.[99] The best analogy is with the rules concerning ships.[1]

4. By Resolution 1721 (XVI),[2] the General Assembly called upon "states launching objects into orbit to furnish information promptly to the Committee on the Peaceful Uses of Outer Space . . . for the registration of launching" and requested the Secretary General "to maintain a public registry of the information furnished." This voluntary system has not been wholly satisfactory and has been supplemented, for the parties to it, by the 1975 Convention on Registration of Objects launched into Outer Space.[3] Launching states must register every launch, indicating its purpose on a public register kept by the Secretary General.

5. The 1972 Liability Convention[4] establishes *strict* liability (subject to Article VI) for damage caused by a space object to persons or property on the surface of the earth or to an aircraft in flight (Article II) and *fault* liability for damage to other space objects in flight and to persons in them (Article III). It establishes joint and several liability in the case of a joint launch (Article VI). Local remedies need not be exhausted before a claim is brought (Article XI). A claim in respect of damage to individuals is brought by a national state in the first instance, although the place where the damage occurs or where the individual is a resident may act if the national state fails to do so (Article VIII). If a claim cannot be settled diplomatically, it will be determined by a mixed claims commission established at the request of either party (Article XIV). The compensation due

> shall be determined in accordance with international law, and the principles of justice and equity, in order to provide such reparation in respect of the damage as will restore the person . . . on whose behalf the claim is brought to the condition which would have existed if the damage had not occurred. (Article XII).

No upper limit to the amount of compensation is set. There have been a number of instances recorded of débris or parts of space objects falling to earth. A part of Sputnik IV weighing 20lb that fell on Manitowoc, Wisconsin, in 1962 was handed back to the USSR at a meeting of the United Nations Committee on the Peaceful Uses of Outer Space.[5] In 1969, some Russian débris broke a kitchen window in Southend. In 1978, a malfunctioning Russian satellite, Cosmos 954, powered by a small nuclear reactor weighing about 100lb, broke up over Canada and came down in a remote part of the North-West Territories. Moderate radiation was reported from the débris, although no other damage is known to have occurred.

---

[99] See Czabati, *The Concept of State Jurisdiction in International Space* (1971).

[1] See below, p. 430.

[2] *loc. cit.*, p. 248, n. 88, above.

[3] U.K.T.S. 70 (1978), Cmnd. 7271; 961 U.N.T.S. 187; (1975) 14 I.L.M. 43. In force 1976. 39 parties, including the five Security Council permanent members. See Young (1986) 11 A.A.S.L. 287 who describes the Convention as "moribund."

[4] U.K.T.S. 16 (1974), Cmnd. 5551; 961 U.N.T.S. 187; 10 I.L.M. 965 (1971). In force 1973. 76 parties, including the five Security Council permanent members. See Forkosch, *Outer Space and Legal Liability* (1982); and Hurwitz, *State Liability for Outer Space Activities in Accordance with the 1972 Convention on International Liability for Damage caused by Space Objects* (1992). On the measure of damages, see Alexander (1978) 6 J. Space L. 151 and Foster (1972) 10 C.Y.I.L. 137.

[5] U.N. Doc A/AC. 105/P.V. 15, pp. 33–34 (1962), noted in Lay and Taubenfeld, *The Law Relating to the Activities of Man in Space* (1970), p. 137, where a number of similar incidents are listed.

The USSR agreed to pay C$ 3 million compensation.[6] Damage of a more far-reaching kind, of the sort that may result from experiments conducted in space (for example, affecting the climate or the atmosphere), is the subject of a very limited undertaking in Article XXI.

6. *The Moon Agreement*[7] The 1979 Agreement Governing the Activities of States on the Moon and other Celestial Bodies[8] repeats, clarifies and supplements the 1967 Outer Space Treaty. Most significantly, it deals with the question of natural resources. Article 11 reads:

> 1. The moon[9] and its natural resources are the common heritage of mankind, which finds its expression in the provisions of this Agreement and in particular in paragraph 5 of this article . . .
>
> 2. The moon is not subject to national appropriation by any claim of sovereignty, by means of use or occupation, or by any other means.
>
> 3. Neither the surface nor the subsurface of the moon, nor any part thereof or natural resources in place, shall become property of any State, international intergovernmental or non-governmental organization, national organization or non-governmental entity or of any natural person. The placement of personnel, space vehicles, equipment, facilities, stations and installations on or below the surface of the moon, including structures connected with its surface or subsurface, shall not create a right of ownership over the surface or the subsurface of the moon or any areas thereof. The foregoing provisions are without prejudice to the international régime referred to in paragraph 5 of this article.
>
> 4. States Parties have the right to exploration and use of the moon without discrimination of any kind, on a basis of equality and in accordance with international law and the terms of this Agreement.
>
> 5. States Parties to this Agreement hereby undertake to establish an international régime, including appropriate procedures, to govern the exploitation of the natural resources of the moon as such exploitation is about to become feasible. . . .
>
> 7. The main purposes of the international régime to be established shall include: . . .
>
>> (d) An equitable sharing by all States Parties in the benefits derived from those resources, whereby the interests and needs of the developing countries, as well as the efforts of those countries which have contributed either directly or indirectly to the exploration of the moon, shall be given special consideration.

This adds to the 1967 Treaty by establishing that the natural resources of celestial bodies are, like those of the deep sea-bed, the "common heritage of mankind" and, as such, to be exploited when technical and commercial considerations permit, in accordance with an international régime. Cheng[10] suggests that, although Article 11(5) imposes an obligation to negotiate in good faith to

---

[6] See (1979) 18 I.L.M. 899 and (1981) 20 *ibid.* 689. See also Cohen (1984) 10 Yale J.I.L. 78 and Gorove (1978) 6 J. Space L.141.

[7] See Cheng (1980) 33 C.L.P. 213.

[8] (1979) 18 I.L.M. 1434. In force 1984. 9 parties. None of the Security Council permanent members are parties.

[9] The Convention provisions "relating to the moon shall also apply to other celestial bodies within the solar system, other than the earth": Art. 11(1) Agreement.

[10] *loc. cit.*, n. 7, above, pp. 231–2. On the disagreement concerning a *deep sea-bed* moratorium, see below, p. 471.

establish the proposed international régime, if no such régime can be agreed upon, the Agreement imposes no moratorium upon unilateral exploitation by the contracting parties.

The Agreement clarifies Article 2 of the 1967 Treaty by providing that when carrying out scientific investigations a party has "the right to collect and remove from the moon[11] samples of its minerals and other substances" (Article 6(2)). It also confirms (Article 11(3)) what is implicit in the characterisation of celestial bodies as *res extra commercium* in Article 2 of the 1967 Treaty, namely that private property rights (as well as State sovereignty) may not be acquired over territory or natural resources in outer space, subject, in the case of the latter, to the international régime to be established.

7. The treaties on outer space which have been adopted so far are the work of the United Nations Committee on the Peaceful Uses of Outer Space, a body established in 1958 (then as an *ad hoc* committee) and composed of 61 states. Questions which the Committee has under consideration include the control of remote sensing of the earth (particularly of natural resources) by satellite[12]; the boundary between air and outer space; direct satellite broadcasting[13]; the use of nuclear power sources in outer space; the geostationary orbit; and space debris.[14] After its considerable early achievements, the Committee has lost some of its impetus, with few agreed texts emerging from its deliberations in recent years.

8. In order to ensure compliance with United Kingdom international obligations with regard to the launching and operation of space objects, the Outer Space Act 1986 establishes a system of licensing and registration of space activities by United Kingdom nationals.

McMAHON, LEGAL ASPECTS OF OUTER SPACE

(1962) 38 B.Y.I.L. 339. Some footnotes omitted

One school of thought interprets airspace in terms of aerodynamic lift and maintains that a State may only claim sovereignty over the height up to which aircraft can ascend. Such height would be no more than about 20 miles.[15]

The merits of such a common-sense approach are quite evident. However, it fails to offer a sufficiently precise criterion for drawing the line in

---

[11] See above, n. 9 on the meaning of "moon".

[12] On remote sensing, see Christol (1988) 16 J. Space L. 21; Matte and Desaussure, *Legal Implications of Remote Sensing from Outer Space* (1976); and Okolle, *International Law of Satellite Remote Sensing* (1989). On satellite broadcasting, including direct television broadcasting, see Christol, *op. cit.*, p. 244, n. 85, above, Chap. 12; Gorove, *op. cit.*, p. 244, n. 85, above, p. 390; McWhinney, ed., *The International Law of Communications* (1971); Smith, *Communication via Satellite* (1976).

[13] See Fisher, *Prior Consent to International Direct Satellite Broadcasting* (1990).

[14] See Benko, de Graaff, and Reijnen, *Space Law in the United Nations* (1985).

[15] The height up to which an aircraft ascends would usually be about 12 miles. However, see "Draft Code of Rules on the Exploration and Uses of Outer Space," in *David Davies Memorial Institute of International Studies* (1962), p. 6: "As far as the performance of existing conventional aircraft is a guide to the definition of airspace, the ram jet which makes more efficient use of such air as is available can 'breathe' at greater heights than jet—or piston-engined—aircraft, but 25 miles is probably the outside limit of effective aerodynamic lift."

airspace and is rendered less useful by such hybrid craft as the X-15 which possess characteristics of both aircraft and spacecraft and can attain a height of up to 47 miles. It is also unlikely that States will be content to restrict their claim to sovereignty to 20 miles when they might claim substantially more without unduly interfering with the exploration of outer space by other States.

A number of other writers, invoking what they call the natural principle of interpretation, maintain that airspace is synonymous with atmospheric space and includes any space where air is to be found. As there are traces of air in the atmosphere up to 10,000 miles it would be quite consistent, on the basis of this approach, for States to claim sovereignty up to 10,000 miles. . . .

A third approach, representing an even more exaggerated view than the one above, maintains that State sovereignty extends *usque ad infinitum.* Such a view may be more accurately characterized as *usque ad absurdum.* . . .

One or two writers, proceeding by analogy to the law of the sea, suggest the drawing of several lines rather than one. It has been proposed that a State should exercise full sovereignty up to the height to which aircraft can ascend; that then there should be a second area, of up to 300 miles, designated as a contiguous zone and allowing for a right of transit through this zone for all non-military flight instrumentalities; and that finally there should be outer space, free to all. More recently it has been suggested that there be established a neutral zone between the upper limits of airspace and the lower limits of outer space to be known as "Neutralia" in which the right of innocent passage would be recognized. Such an attempt to divide space up into sectors and zones would seem to be too impractical and artificial to commend itself.

A more sensible approach would seem to be the suggestion that a State should only exercise sovereignty over that area whose boundary is the lowest altitude at which an artificial satellite may be put in orbit at least once around the earth. It would seem that the maximum altitude required to do this would be between 70 and 100 miles. The advantage of such an approach is that it takes cognizance of State practice since the launching of the first sputnik, recognizes the legality of those satellites already in orbit and may easily be reconciled with claims to sovereignty up to the height of aerodynamic lift or even up to 70 miles.

A number of other proposals, suggesting more or less arbitrary criteria, have also been advanced. One may note the suggestion that sovereignty should extend as far out as the subjacent State could exercise effective control; that the boundary should be fixed at an altitude approximating to lift or drag; that the sovereignty ceiling should be the line where an object travelling at 25,000 feet per second loses its aerodynamic lift and centrifugal force takes over (the so-called Karman jurisdiction line which would extend up to about 53 miles); and finally that instead of drawing a demarcation line between airspace and outer space there should only be one doctrine, namely freedom of all-inclusive space subject to agreed restrictions.

Most of the above theories presuppose that a demarcation line must be drawn somewhere in space and the problem is to determine where. However, as an alternative, it has been suggested that States should concentrate on the regulation of activities in space, regardless of the location of those activities. The possibility of such an approach was referred to as early as June 1959 by the United Nations *Ad Hoc* Committee on the Peaceful Uses of Outer Space: "There was also discussion as to whether or not further experience might suggest a different approach, namely, the desirability of basing the legal régime governing outer space activities primarily on the nature and type of particular space activities."[16] Of course, the difficulty here is to reach an agreement concerning those activities which are to be permitted and those which are forbidden; such an agreement will be difficult to reach on account of the almost insuperable technical obstacles in disengaging the civil from the military uses of space vehicles. Secondly, even if such an agreement were reached, it could only be enforced by establishing some form of inspection system. In other words, the whole question merely becomes another facet of the disarmament problem.

Notes

1. The boundary between airspace and outer space has yet to be defined.[17] The question was purposely not dealt with in the seminal General Assembly resolutions and in the 1967 treaty. The Committee on the Peaceful Uses of Outer Space has the question under consideration but has not been able to reach agreement on any particular rule or indeed as to whether a rule is required.[18] The principle of free and equal use of outer space must mean that there is a limit to national sovereignty at some point. It is also significant that states have not protested at the passage of satellites over their territory.[19] This might mean only the acceptance of a right of innocent passage, but this is unlikely.

2. The "perigee" approach, by which the limit of airspace would be the lowest perigee of an orbiting satellite, would appear to be the most likely one to be accepted. It would, in the light of recent studies, probably set the limit at a lower height—between 50 and 60 miles—than that indicated by McMahon.[20]

[16] *Report of the Ad Hoc Committee on the Peaceful Uses of Outer Space*, U.N. Doc. A/4141, July 14, 1959, p. 68.

[17] See the Minister of State, FCO, *Hansard*, H.C., Vol. 546 W.A. 66, July 23, 1993: "There is no universally agreed precise legal, technical or political definition of either the boundaries separating airspace from outer space or of the term outer space itself".

[18] See the 1987 Report of the Committee on the Peaceful Uses of Outer Space, G.A.O.R., 42nd Session, Supp. 20, p. 15. See also Goedhuis (1982–I) 174 Hague Recueil 418.

[19] *cf.* the dissenting opinion of Judge Lachs in the *North Sea Continental Shelf Cases*, above, p. 36, n. 46. And see Fawcett, *op. cit.*, p. 244, n. 85, above, p. 22. For the 1976 Bogota Declaration by which 8 equatorial states claimed exclusive jurisdiction and sovereignty over the geostationary orbit over their territories (about 36,000 km high)—a claim rejected by other states, see Gorove, *op. cit.*, p. 244, n. 85, above, p. 362.

[20] See the UN Secretariat background papers on the subject: U.N.Docs. A/AC.105/C.2/7 and A/AC. 105/C.2/7/Add.1.

6. Rights in Foreign Territory[21]

NORTH ATLANTIC FISHERIES ARBITRATION

U.S. *v.* Great Britain (1910)

Permanent Court of Arbitration: Lammasch; de Savornin Lohman; Gray; Drago; Fitzpatrick. 11 R.I.A.A. 167

By a treaty of 1818, Great Britain and the United States agreed that "the inhabitants of the said United States shall have forever, in common with the subjects of His Britannic Majesty, the liberty to take fish of every kind on that part of the Southern coast of Newfoundland ... [then described]" (Art. 1). A dispute arose over Great Britain's competence under the treaty to regulate fishing by United States nationals exercising the liberty granted by it. In the following passage, the Tribunal considered a United States argument that the liberty amounted to a servitude.

Award of the Tribunal

It is contended by the United States: ...

That the liberties of fishery granted to the United States constitute an International servitude in their favour over the territory of Great Britain, thereby involving a derogation from the sovereignty of Great Britain, the servient State, and therefore Great Britain is deprived, by reason of the grant, of its independent right to regulate the fishery.

The Tribunal is unable to agree with this contention:

(*a*) Because there is no evidence that the doctrine of International servitudes was one with which either American or British Statesmen were conversant in 1818, no English publicists employing the term before 1818, and the mention of it in Mr Gallatin's report being insufficient;

(*b*) Because a servitude in the French law, referred to by Mr. Gallatin, can, since the Code, be only real and cannot be personal (Code Civil, Art. 686);

(*c*) Because a servitude in International law predicates an express grant of a sovereign right and involves an analogy to the relation of a *praedium dominans* and a *praedium serviens*; whereas by the Treaty of 1818 one State grants a liberty to fish, which is not a sovereign right, but a purely economic right, to the inhabitants of another State;

(*d*) Because the doctrine of international servitude in the sense which is now sought to be attributed to it originated in the peculiar and now obsolete conditions prevailing in the Holy Roman Empire of which the *domini terrae* were not fully sovereigns ...

[21] See Reid, *International Servitudes* (1932) and Vali, *Servitudes in International Law* (2nd ed., 1958).

(*e*) Because this doctrine being but little suited to the principle of sovereignty which prevails in States under a system of constitutional government such as Great Britain and the United States, and to the present International relations of Sovereign States, has found little, if any, support from modern publicists. It could therefore in the general interest of the Community of Nations, and of the Parties to this Treaty, be affirmed by this Tribunal only on the express evidence of an International contract;

(*f*) Because even if these liberties of fishery constituted an International servitude, the servitude would derogate from the sovereignty of the servient State only in so far as the exercise of the rights of sovereignty by the servitude State would be contrary to the exercise of the right by the dominant State. Whereas it is evident that, though every regulation of the fishery is to some extent a limitation, as it puts limits to the exercise of the fishery at will, yet such regulations as are reasonable and made for the purpose of securing and preserving the fishery and its exercise for the common benefit, are clearly to be distinguished from those restrictions and "molestations", the annulment of which was the purpose of the American demands formulated by Mr Adams in 1782, and such regulations consequently cannot be held to be inconsistent with a servitude;

(*g*) Because the fishery to which the inhabitants of the United States were admitted in 1783, and again in 1818, was a regulated fishery...

(*h*) Because the fact that Great Britain rarely exercised the right of regulation in the period immediately succeeding 1818 is to be explained by various circumstances and is not evidence of the non-existence of the right;

(*i*) Because the words "in common with British subjects" tend to confirm the opinion that the inhabitants of the United States were admitted to a regulated fishery;

(*j*) Because the statute of Great Britain, 1819, which gives legislative sanction to the Treaty of 1818, provides for the making of "regulations with relation to the taking, drying and curing of fish by inhabitants of the United States in 'common'."

Notes

1. Does the Court's award give any support to the view that international law recognises servitudes or, in English law terms, easement and profits? Does the extract from *The Wimbledon* case, below p. 260? For Brierly,[22] the position is as follows:

Its [a servitude's] essential characteristic is that it is a right *in rem*, that is to say, it is exercisable not only against a particular owner of the servient tenement but against any successor to him in title, and not only by a particular owner of the dominant tenement but also by his successors in title. It is, of course, quite common that a state should acquire rights of one kind or another over the territory of another state, the right, for example, to have an airfield or free port

[22] Brierly, p. 191. See also McNair (1925) 6 B.Y.I.L. 111.

facilities, but ordinarily at least such rights are merely rights *in personam* like any other treaty-created right; they do not in any way resemble servitudes. The test of an international servitude can only be, on the analogy of private law, that the right should be one that will survive a change in the sovereignty of either of the two states concerned in the transaction. There is no real evidence that any such right exists in the international system.

2. In the *Aaland Islands Case*,[23] Sweden argued that the provisions in the General Treaty of Peace of 1856 between France, Great Britain and Russia demilitarising the Islands created a servitude binding upon Finland, which had succeeded Russia as the territorial sovereign.

The International Commission of Jurists which reported on the case stated that "the existence of international servitudes, in the true technical sense of the term, is not generally admitted."[24] Nevertheless, it managed to hold that the demilitar-isation provisions were binding upon Finland:

> The provisions were laid down in European interests. They constituted a special international status relating to military considerations, for the Aaland Islands. It follows that until these provisions are duly replaced by others, every State interested has the right to insist upon compliance with them.[25]

Earlier the Commission had noted:

> ... the Powers have, on many occasions since 1815, and especially at the conclusion of peace treaties, tried to create true objective law, a real political status the effects of which are felt outside the immediate circle of contracting parties.[26]

3. A recent example of one state being granted rights in the territory of another is found in the 1960 Treaty Concerning the Establishment of the Republic of Cyprus[27] between Greece, Turkey and Great Britain, on the one hand, and Cyprus, on the other hand, which permits the present British military bases in Cyprus. Annex B[28] reads:

> The Government of the United Kingdom shall have the right to continue to use, without restriction or interference, the Sites in the territories of the Repub-lic of Cyprus listed in Schedule A. . . .

In 1985, the British Minister of State for the Armed Forces stated: "The base is sovereign British territory as laid down in the 1960 treaty. It has the full rights of sovereignty that we associate with the use of that word."[29]

4. In the nineteenth century, China agreed to lease, while retaining sovereignty, several parts of its territory to Western Powers. For example, in 1898 it agreed by treaty[30] to lease to Great Britain the New Territories on the Chinese mainland adjacent to the island of Hong Kong for a period of 99 years. The island of Hong

---

[23] L.N.O.J., Special Supp. No. 3, p. 3 (1920).
[24] *ibid*. p. 16.
[25] *ibid*. p. 19.
[26] *ibid*. p. 17.
[27] U.K.T.S. 4 (1961), Cmnd. 1252; 382 U.N.T.S. 8.
[28] s.1(1).
[29] *Hansard*, H.C., Vol. 74, col. 161, February 26, 1985; U.K.M.I.L. 1985, (1985) 56 B.Y.I.L. 473.
[30] 90 B.F.S.P. 17.

Kong was a British Crown Colony that was ceded by China to Great Britain by the 1842 Treaty of Nanking[31] after the Opium War. See also the 1860 Treaty of Peking[32] by which China ceded Kowloon on the mainland opposite the island of Hong Kong, to Great Britain. By the 1984 Agreement between China and the United Kingdom,[33] all of the above territories passed or reverted to China in 1997.

RIGHT OF PASSAGE CASE[34]

Portugal *v.* India

I.C.J. Reports 1960, p. 6

Judgment of the Court

In [its] Application the Government of the Portuguese Republic states that the territory of Portugal in the Indian Peninsula is made up of the three districts of Goa, Daman and Diu.[35] It adds that the district of Daman comprises, in addition to its littoral territory, two parcels of territory completely surrounded by the territory of India which constitutes enclaves: Dadra and Nagar-Aveli. It is in respect of the communications between these enclaves and Daman and between each other that the question arises of a right of passage in favour of Portugal through Indian territory, and of a correlative obligation binding upon India. The Application states that in July 1954, contrary to the practice hitherto followed, the Government of India, in pursuance of what the Application calls "the open campaign which it has been carrying on since 1950 for the annexation of Portuguese territories", prevented Portugal from exercising this right of passage. This denial by India having been maintained, it has followed, according to the Application, that the enclaves of Dadra and Nagar-Aveli have been completely cut off from the rest of the Portuguese territory, the Portuguese authorities thus being placed in a position in which it became impossible for them to exercise Portuguese rights of sovereignty there. . . .

Portugal claims a right of passage . . . to the extent necessary for the exercise of its sovereignty over the enclaves, subject to India's right of regulation and control of the passage claimed, and without any immunity in Portugal's favour. It claims further that India is under obligation so to exercise its power of regulation and control as not to prevent the passage necessary for the exercise of Portugal's sovereignty over the enclaves. . . .

[31] 30 B.F.S.P. 389.
[32] 50 B.F.S.P. 10
[33] Misc. 20 (1984), Cmnd. 9352; (1984) 23 I.L.M. 1366. See also the Hong Kong Act 1985. See Mushkat (1987) 10 Houston J.I.L. 1.
[34] See Krenz, *International Enclaves and Rights of Passage* (1961); E. Lauterpacht (1958–59) 44 Trans.Grot.Soc. 313, 352–356; 2 Verzijl 368.
[35] *Ed.* On the subsequent annexation of these territories by India, see above, p. 220.

With regard to Portugal's claim of a right of passage as formulated by it on the basis of local custom, it is objected on behalf of India that no local custom could be established between only two States. It is difficult to see why the number of States between which a local custom may be established on the basis of long practice must necessarily be larger than two. The Court sees no reason why long continued practice between two States accepted by them as regulating their relations should not form the basis of mutual rights and obligations between the two States. . . .

The Court . . . concludes that, with regard to private persons, civil officials and goods in general there existed during the British and post-British periods a constant and uniform practice allowing free passage between Daman and the enclaves. This practice having continued over a period extending beyond a century and a quarter unaffected by the change in regime in respect of the intervening territory which occurred when India became independent, the Court is, in view of all the circumstances of the case, satisfied that that practice was accepted as law by the Parties and has given rise to a right and a correlative obligation. . . .

As regards armed forces, armed police and arms and ammunition, the position is different. . . .

The Court is, therefore, of the view that no right of passage in favour of Portugal involving a correlative obligation on India has been established in respect of armed forces, armed police, and arms and ammunition. The course of dealings established between the Portuguese and the British authorities with respect to the passage of these categories excludes the existence of any such right. The practice that was established shows that, with regard to these categories, it was well understood that passage could take place only by permission of the British authorities. This situation continued during the post-British period.

Portugal also invokes general international custom, as well as the general principles of law recognized by civilized nations, in support of its claim of a right of passage as formulated by it. Having arrived at the conclusion that the course of dealings between the British and Indian authorities on the one hand and the Portuguese on the other established a practice, well understood between the Parties, by virtue of which Portugal had acquired a right of passage in respect of private persons, civil officials and goods in general, the Court does not consider it necessary to examine whether general international custom or the general principles of law recognized by civilized nations may lead to the same result.

As regards armed forces, armed police and arms and ammunition, the finding of the Court that the practice established between the Parties required for passage in respect of these categories the permission of the British or Indian authorities, renders it unnecessary for the Court to determine whether or not, in the absence of the practice that actually prevailed, general international custom or the general principles of law recognized by civilized nations could be relied upon by Portugal in support of its claim to a right of passage in respect of these categories.

The Court is here dealing with a concrete case having special features. Historically the case goes back to a period when, and relates to a region in which, the relations between neighbouring States were not regulated by precisely formulated rules but were governed largely by practice. Where therefore the Court finds a practice clearly established between two States which was accepted by the Parties as governing the relations between them, the Court must attribute decisive effect to that practice for the purpose of determining their specific rights and obligations. Such a particular practice must prevail over any general rules. . . .

Having found that Portugal had in 1954 a right of passage over intervening Indian territory between Daman and the enclaves in respect of private persons, civil officials and goods in general, the Court will proceed to consider whether India has acted contrary to its obligation resulting from Portugal's right of passage in respect of any of these categories. . . .

The events that took place in Dadra on 21–22 July 1954 resulted in the overthrow of Portuguese authority in that enclave. This created tension in the surrounding Indian territory. Thereafter all passage was suspended by India. India contends that this became necessary in view of the abnormal situation which had arisen in Dadra and the tension created in surrounding Indian territory. . . .

In view of the tension then prevailing in intervening Indian territory, the Court is unable to hold that India's refusal of passage to the proposed delegation and its refusal of visas to Portuguese nationals of European origin and to native Indian Portuguese in the employ of the Portuguese Government was action contrary to its obligation resulting from Portugal's right of passage. Portugal's claim of a right of passage is subject to full recognition and exercise of Indian sovereignty over the intervening territory and without any immunity in favour of Portugal. The Court is of the view that India's refusal of passage in those cases was, in the circumstances, covered by its power of regulation and control of the right of passage of Portugal.

For these reasons,

THE COURT, . . . by eleven votes to four,

finds that Portugal had in 1954 a right of passage over intervening Indian territory between the enclaves of Dadra and Nagar-Aveli and the coastal district of Daman and between these enclaves, to the extent necessary for the exercise of Portuguese sovereignty over the enclaves and subject to the regulation and control of India, in respect of private persons, civil officials and goods in general;

by eight votes to seven,

finds that Portugal did not have in 1954 such a right of passage in respect of armed forces, armed police, and arms and ammunition;

by nine votes to six,

finds that India has not acted contrary to its obligations resulting from Portugal's right of passage in respect of private persons, civil officials and goods in general.[36]

Notes

Was the right of passage acknowledged by the Court one that would survive a transfer of title to the territory to which it applied? The Court's judgment was based upon local custom.[37] Does it have any relevance for similar situations, such as that of land-locked states—*e.g.* Lesotho (surrounded entirely by the one state of South Africa) and Austria (surrounded by several states)—that seek access by land to the sea.[38] Writing about freedom of transit across another state's territory generally, Lauterpacht[39] states:

> The operative principle, it is believed, is that States, far from being free to treat the establishment or regulation of routes of transit as a substantial derogation from their sovereignty which they are entirely free to refuse, are bound to act in this matter in the fulfilment of an obligation to the community of which they form a part. It is a principle formulated by Grotius over three hundred years ago in the following words: "Similarly also lands, rivers, and any part of the sea that has become subject to the ownership of a people, ought to be open to those who, for legitimate reasons, have need to cross them; as, for instance, if a people . . . desires to carry on commerce with a distant people. . . . "[40]

> On that view [Grotius's], there exists in customary international law a right to free or innocent passage for purposes of trade, travel and commerce over the territory of all States—a right which derives from the fact of the existence of the international community and which is a direct consequence of the interdependence of States."

THE WIMBLEDON CASE[41]

France, Italy, Japan and the U.K. *v.* Germany (1923)

P.C.I.J. Reports, Series A, No. 1

The Kiel Canal is cut through Germany and links the Baltic and North Seas. Article 380 of the Treaty of Versailles of 1919 reads: "The Kiel Canal and its approaches shall be maintained free and open to the vessels of commerce and of war of all nations at peace with Germany on terms of entire equality." The Court discussed the effect of Article 380 on the legal status of the Canal in the following passage.

---

[36] It is not clear how every judge voted.

[37] On local custom, see above, p. 25.

[38] See the 1982 Convention on the Law of the Sea Art. 90, below, p. 422. See also the 1965 Convention on Transit Trade of Land-Locked States, 597 U.N.T.S. 3; (1965) 4 I.L.M. 957. In force 1967. 36 parties. U.K. not a party. See Fried (1966) 6 I.J.I.L.

[39] E. Lauterpacht, *loc. cit.*, p. 257, n. 34, above, p. 313.

[40] *De Jure Belli ac Pacis*, II, 2, 13, as translated in *Classics of International Law* (1925), pp. 196–197.

[41] On international canals generally, see Baxter, *The Law of International Waterways* (1964), and Lee (1968) 33 L. & C.P. 158.

Judgment of the Court

The Court considers that the terms of Article 380 are categorical and give rise to no doubt. It follows that the canal has ceased to be an internal and national navigable waterway, the use of which by the vessels of states other than the riparian state is left entirely to the discretion of that state, and that it has become an international waterway intended to provide under treaty guarantee easier access to the Baltic for the benefit of all nations of the world. . . .

In order to dispute, in this case, the right of the S.S. "Wimbledon" to free passage through the Kiel Canal under the terms of Article 380, the argument has been urged upon the Court that this right really amounts to a servitude by international law resting upon Germany and that, like all restrictions or limitations upon the exercise of sovereignty, this servitude must be construed as restrictively as possible and confined within its narrowest limits, more especially in the sense that it should not be allowed to affect the rights consequent upon neutrality in an armed conflict. The Court is not called upon to take a definite attitude with regard to the question, which is moreover of a very controversial nature, whether in the domain of international law, there really exist servitudes analogous to the servitudes of private law. Whether the German Government is bound by virtue of a servitude or by virtue of a contractual obligation undertaken towards the Powers entitled to benefit by the terms of the Treaty of Versailles, to allow free access to the Kiel Canal in time of war as in time of peace to the vessels of all nations, the fact remains that Germany had to submit to an important limitation of the exercise of the sovereign rights which no one disputes that she possesses over the Kiel Canal. This fact constitutes a sufficient reason for the restrictive interpretation, in case of doubt, of the clause which produces such a limitation. But the Court feels obliged to stop at the point where the so-called restrictive interpretation would be contrary to the plain terms of the article and would destroy what has been clearly granted.

CONVENTION RESPECTING FREE NAVIGATION OF THE SUEZ CANAL 1888[42]

C. 5623; 79 B.F.S.P. 18; (1909) 3 A.J.I.L. Supp. 123

Article 1

The Suez Maritime Canal shall always be free and open, in time of war as in time of peace, to every vessel of commerce or of war, without distinction of flag.

---

[42] The parties are Austria-Hungary, France, Germany, Great Britain, Italy, the Netherlands, Russia, Spain and the Ottoman Empire.

Consequently, the High Contracting Parties agree not in any way to interfere with the free use of the Canal, in time of war as in time of peace.

The Canal shall never be subjected to the exercise of the right of blockade.

Article 4

The Maritime Canal remaining open in time of war as a free passage, even to the ships of war of belligerents, according to the terms of Article 1 of the present Treaty, the High Contracting Parties agree that no right of war, no act of hostility, nor any act having for its object to obstruct the free navigation of the Canal, shall be committed in the Canal and its ports of access, as well as within a radius of 3 marine miles from those ports, even though the Ottoman Empire should be one of the belligerent Powers. . . .

Article 10

Similarly, the provisions of Articles 4, 5, 7 and 8 shall not interfere with the measures which His Majesty the Sultan and His Highness the Khedive, in the name of His Imperial Majesty, and within the limits of the Firmans granted, might find it necessary to take for securing by their own forces the defence of Egypt and the maintenance of public order.

In case His Imperial Majesty the Sultan, or His Highness the Khedive, should find it necessary to avail themselves of the exceptions for which this Article provides, the Signatory Powers of the Declaration of London shall be notified thereof by the Imperial Ottoman Government.

It is likewise understood that the provisions of the four Articles aforesaid shall in no case occasion any obstacle to the measures which the Imperial Ottoman Government may think necessary to take in order to insure by its own forces the defence of its other possessions situated on the eastern coast of the Red Sea.

Article 11

The measures which shall be taken in the cases provided for by Articles 9 and 10 of the present Treaty shall not interfere with the free use of the Canal. In the same cases, the erection of permanent fortifications contrary to the provisions of Article 8 is prohibited.

Article 14

The High Contracting Parties agree that the engagements resulting from the present Treaty shall not be limited by the duration of the Acts of Concession of the Universal Suez Canal Company.

Notes

1. The Suez Canal was built by the Suez Canal Company in accordance with concession agreements made between the Company and the Sultan of Turkey in the 1850s, at a time when Egypt was a part of the Ottoman Empire. Under the terms of these agreements, the Company was to operate the Canal for ninety-nine years from the time that it opened (1869). At the termination of this period, the Egyptian Government was to "take the place of the company and to enter into full possession of the canal." In July 1956, Egypt nationalised the Suez Canal Company and assumed control of the Canal. In August 1956, a conference of 22 interested states was held in London. A proposal supported by 18 of them called for the "efficient and dependable operation, maintenance and development of the Canal as a free, open and secure international waterway in accordance with the principles of the Convention of 1888."[43] On September 26, 1956, the United States Secretary of State for Foreign Affairs (Mr Dulles) said:

> We believe that the treaty of 1888 internationalises, you might say, the right of use of the canal. It creates a sort of an easement across Egyptian territory, of which we believe the beneficiaries of the treaty as well as the parties to the treaty have the right to make use. And we believe they are also entitled to organise to exercise the right of use and, generally, their rights under the treaty.[44]

In a Declaration made on April 24, 1957, Egypt stated:

> It remains the unaltered policy and firm purpose of the Government of Egypt to respect the terms and the spirit of the Constantinople Convention of 1888 and the rights and obligations arising therefrom. The Government of Egypt will continue to respect, observe and implement them.[45]

2. By the 1977 Panama Canal Treaty[46] between Panama and the United States, sovereignty over the Panama Canal Zone was transferred from the United States to Panama, but the United States will continue to operate and have the right to defend the Canal, with increasing Panamanian involvement, until the termination of the treaty in 1999. Thereupon, Panama will assume full responsibility for the Canal itself. The Canal "shall remain open to peaceful transit by the vessels of all nations on terms of entire equality."[47]

---

[43] 3 Whiteman 1103.

[44] *ibid.* 1102.

[45] (1957) 51 A.J.I.L. 673. On Egypt's acceptance of the I.C.J.'s compulsory jurisdiction concerning Suez Canal disputes, see (1957) 51 A.J.I.L. 675.

[46] (1978) 72 A.J.I.L. 225.

[47] Art. 2 of the 1977 Treaty concerning the Permanent Neutrality and Operation of the Panama Canal, *ibid.* p. 238, which accompanies the main treaty. The canal is declared to be "permanently neutral": Art. 1.

CHAPTER 6

STATE JURISDICTION

1. INTRODUCTORY NOTE[1]

STATE jurisdiction is the power of a state under international law to govern persons and property by its municipal law. It includes both the power to prescribe rules (prescriptive jurisdiction) and the power to enforce them (enforcement jurisdiction). The latter includes both executive and judicial powers of enforcement. Jurisdiction may be concurrent with the jurisdiction of other states or it may be exclusive. It may be civil or criminal. The rules of state jurisdiction identify the persons and the property within the permissible range of a state's law and its procedures for enforcing that law. They are not concerned with the content of a state's law except in so far as it purports to subject a person to it or to prescribe procedures to enforce it. International organisations have jurisdiction in the above sense to a limited extent (*e.g.* over employees).

2. CRIMINAL[2] JURISDICTION

DICKINSON, INTRODUCTORY COMMENT TO THE HARVARD RESEARCH DRAFT CONVENTION ON JURISDICTION WITH RESPECT TO CRIME 1935

(1935) 29 A.J.I.L. Supp. 443

An analysis of modern national codes of penal law and penal procedure, checked against the conclusions of reliable writers and the resolutions of international conferences or learned societies, and supplemented by some exploration of the jurisprudence of national courts, discloses five general principles on which a more or less extensive penal jurisdiction is claimed by states at the present time. These five general principles are: first, the territorial principle, determining jurisdiction by reference to the place

---

[1] See Akehurst (1972–73) 46 B.Y.I.L. 145; Bowett (1982) 53 B.Y.I.L. 1; Jennings (1962) 32 N.T.I.R. 209; *ibid.* (1957) 33 B.Y.I.L. 146; Johnson, in David Davies Memorial Institute of International Studies, *Report of International Law Conference* (1962), p. 32; Mann (1964–I) 111 Hague Recueil 1.

[2] Opinions differ on the extent of civil jurisdiction. Mann suggests that international law requires a "substantial connection" before civil jurisdiction can be exercised: see the extract below, p. 291. Brownlie states that "[e]xcessive and abusive assertion of civil jurisdiction could lead to international responsibility or protests at *ultra vires* acts." He argues that "as civil jurisdiction is ultimately reinforced by procedures of enforcement involving criminal sanctions, there is in principle no great difference between problems

where the offence is committed; second, the nationality principle, determining jurisdiction by reference to the nationality or national character of the person committing the offence; third, the protective principle, determining jurisdiction by reference to the national interest injured by the offence; fourth, the universality principle, determining jurisdiction by reference to the custody of the person committing the offence; and fifth, the passive personality principle, determining jurisdiction by reference to the nationality or national character of the person injured by the offence. Of these five principles, the first is everywhere regarded as of primary importance and of fundamental character. The second is universally accepted, though there are striking differences in the extent to which it is used in the different national systems. The third is claimed by most states, regarded with misgivings in a few, and generally ranked as the basis of an auxiliary competence. The fourth is widely, though by no means universally, accepted as the basis of an auxiliary competence, except for the offence of piracy, with respect to which it is the generally recognized principle of jurisdiction. The fifth, asserted in some form by a considerable number of states and contested by others, is admittedly auxiliary in character and is probably not essential for any state if the ends served are adequately provided for on other principles.

Notes

1. The Harvard Research Draft Convention of 1935 was the product of the unofficial work of a number of American international lawyers. It is not binding upon any state as a treaty and it is not state practice. Nonetheless, both in so far as it is intended to reflect customary international law and in its suggestions *de lege ferenda*, it is of considerable value because of the thorough study of state practice that preceded it. The Draft Convention adopts the first four of the principles listed in the above extract from the Introductory Comment, all of which were thought to be permitted by international law.[3] The passive personality principle, the permissibility of which was thought to be doubtful,[4] was omitted.

Where more than one state has jurisdiction on a basis permitted by international law, it seems that each state is free to exercise prescriptive jurisdiction when it wishes and that priority to exercise enforcement jurisdiction depends solely upon custody. Even a state with territorial jurisdiction, which is the form of jurisdiction the most firmly rooted in state practice, has no prior claim over another state having custody of a person and relying on some extra-territorial

created by assertion of civil and criminal jurisdiction over aliens": Brownlie, p. 299. In contrast, Akehurst states that "[i]n practice, the assumption of jurisdiction by a State does not seem to be subject to any requirement that the defendant or the facts of the case need have any connection with that State; and this practice seems to have met with acquiescence by other States": *loc. cit.*, n. 1, above, p. 176. On the dispute concerning the extraterritorial application of U.S. anti-trust law (which is partly civil), see Jennings (1957) 33 B.Y.I.L. 146; Leigh, in Olmstead, ed., *Extra-territorial Laws and Responses Thereto* (1984), p. 47; Lowe, *Extra-territorial Jurisdiction: An Annotated Collection of Legal Materials* (1983); *ibid.* (1984) 33 I.C.L.Q. 515; Rosenthal and Knighton, *National Laws and International Commerce: The Problem of Extra-territoriality* (1982). On the U.S. Helms-Burton and D'Amato Acts, see Lowe (1997) 46 I.C.L.Q. 378.

[3] (1935) 29 A.J.I.L. Supp. at 480, 519, 556, 563–564.
[4] *ibid.* p. 579.

basis for jurisdiction. Two possible limitations upon a state's freedom to exercise enforcement jurisdiction are suggested by the Harvard Research Draft Convention. The first follows from the idea of double jeopardy. Article 13 of the Harvard Research Draft Convention reads:

> In exercising jurisdiction under this Convention, no state shall prosecute or punish an alien after it is proved that the alien has been prosecuted in another State for a crime requiring proof of substantially the same acts or omissions and has been acquitted on the merits, or has been convicted and undergone the penalty imposed, or having been convicted, has been pardoned.

The Commentary refers to considerable support for such a limitation in municipal law.[5] Article 13 does not protect nationals. On this point, the Commentary reads:

> In the present state of international law . . . it would seem inappropriate for a convention on jurisdiction with respect to crime to incorporate limitations upon a State's authority over its nationals.[6]

Secondly, a somewhat similar problem arises when a person is placed in a position where under the law of State A he is required to do something which he is prohibited from doing under the law of State B. On this, Article 14 of the Harvard Research Draft Convention reads:

> . . . no state shall prosecute or punish an alien for an act which was required of that alien by the law of the place where the alien was at the time of the act or omission.

The Commentary acknowledges that there were "few precedents" in municipal law for Article 14; it was included as "eminently desirable and just."[7] Like Article 13, Article 14 does not apply to nationals.

2. *The Nationality Principle.* The Commentary to the Draft Convention reads:

> The competence of the State to prosecute and punish its nationals on the sole basis of their nationality is based upon the allegiance which the person charged with crime owes to the State of which he is a national. . . . The States which derive their jurisprudence from the civil law assert a competence which is substantially more comprehensive than that exercised by States influenced by the English common law, but all make some use of the principle. . . . The principle that jurisdiction may be founded either upon nationality at the time of the offence or upon nationality at the time of the prosecution appears to be supported by such legislation as has dealt specifically with the question. If international law permits a state to regard the accused as its national, its competence is not impaired or limited by the fact that he is also a national of another State. . . . It is indisputable also that nothing in international law precludes a State from prosecuting and punishing one of its juristic persons for a crime committed outside of its territory.[8]

In United Kingdom law, some of the small number of offences for which a national can be prosecuted for committing abroad can equally be seen as being based upon the idea of protection (*e.g.* treason[9] and offences under the Official

---

[5] *ibid.* pp. 602 *et seq.*
[6] *ibid.* p. 613.
[7] *ibid.* p. 616.
[8] *ibid.* pp. 519 *et seq.*
[9] *R. v. Casement* [1917] 1 K.B. 98.

Secrets Act 1989,[10]) but others (*e.g.* murder and manslaughter,[11] and bigamy[12]) cannot. The nationality principle is also relied upon in English law to give an English court jurisdiction "where any person is charged with having committed any offence . . . if he is a British citizen . . . on board . . . any foreign ship to which he does not belong. . . . "[13]

THE LOTUS CASE

France *v.* Turkey (1927)

P.C.I.J. *Reports, Series A, No. 10*

Judgment of the Court

According to the special agreement, the Court has to decide the following questions:

(1) Has Turkey, contrary to Article 15 of the Convention of Lausanne of July 24th, 1923, respecting conditions of residence and business and jurisdiction, acted in conflict with the principles of international law —and if so, what principles—by instituting, following the collision which occurred on August 2nd, 1926, on the high seas between the French steamer *Lotus* and the Turkish steamer *Boz-Kourt* and upon the arrival of the French steamer at Constantinople—as well as against the captain of the Turkish steamship—joint criminal proceedings in pursuance of Turkish law against M. Demons, officer of the watch on board the *Lotus* at the time of the collision, in consequence of the loss of the *Boz-Kourt* having involved the death of eight Turkish sailors and passengers?[14]

(2) Should the reply be in the affirmative, what pecuniary reparation is due to M. Demons, provided, according to the principles of international law, reparation should be made in similar cases? . . .

3. The prosecution was instituted because the loss of the *Boz-Kourt* involved the death of eight Turkish sailors and passengers. It is clear, in the first place, that this result of the collision constitutes a factor essential for the institution of the criminal proceedings in question; secondly, it

[10] See s.15(1).

[11] Offences against the Person Act 1861, s.9.

[12] Offences against the Person Act 1861, s.57.

[13] Merchant Shipping Act 1995, s.281, which was interpreted (when in the Merchant Shipping Act 1894, s.686(1)) in *R. v. Kelly* [1982] A.C. 665, HL as giving jurisdiction to hear charges under the Criminal Damage Act 1971, which otherwise has no extra-territorial effect, against three U.K. citizens for damage caused by them as passengers on board a Danish North Sea Ferry. See Hirst [1982] Crim.L.R. 496.

[14] *Ed.* M. Demons was a French national. Both accused were convicted.

follows from the statements of the two Parties that no criminal intention has been imputed to either of the officers responsible for navigating the two vessels; it is therefore a case of prosecution for involuntary manslaughter. . . .

. . . Article 15 of the Convention of Lausanne of July 24th, 1923,[15] . . . is as follows:

> Subject to the provisions of Article 16, all questions of jurisdiction shall, as between Turkey and the other contracting Powers, be decided in accordance with the principles of international law.

. . . The French Government contends that the Turkish Courts, in order to have jurisdiction, should be able to point to some title to jurisdiction recognized by international law in favour of Turkey. On the other hand, the Turkish Government takes the view that Article 15 allows Turkey jurisdiction whenever such jurisdiction does not come into conflict with a principle of international law.

The latter view seems to be in conformity with the special agreement itself, No. 1 of which asks the Court to say whether Turkey has acted contrary to the principles of international law and, if so, what principles. . . .

This way of stating the question is also dictated by the very nature and existing conditions of international law.

International law governs relations between independent States. The rules of law binding upon States therefore emanate from their own free will as expressed in conventions or by usages generally accepted as expressing principles of law and established in order to regulate the relations between these co-existing independent communities or with a view to the achievement of common aims. Restrictions upon the independence of States cannot therefore be presumed.

Now the first and foremost restriction imposed by international law upon a State is that—failing the existence of a permissive rule to the contrary—it may not exercise its power in any form in the territory of another State. In this sense jurisdiction is certainly territorial; it cannot be exercised by a State outside its territory except by virtue of a permissive rule derived from international custom or from a convention.[16]

It does not, however, follow that international law prohibits a State from exercising jurisdiction in its own territory, in respect of any case

---

[15] *Ed.* Before the First World War, Turkey had been subject to a régime of capitulations (see p. 16, n. 54, above). The purpose of Article 15 was to recognise that Turkey had become a full and equal member of the international community.

[16] *Ed.* An example of a convention by which each party permits the other parties to exercise jurisdiction within its territory is the NATO Status of Forces Agreement 1951, U.K.T.S. 3 (1955), Cmd. 9363, 199 U.N.T.S. 67, by which each party is permitted to exercise jurisdiction over its forces stationed in the territory of the other parties.

which relates to acts which have taken place abroad, and in which it cannot rely on some permissive rule of international law. Such a view would only be tenable if international law contained a general prohibition to States to extend the application of their laws and the jurisdiction of their courts to persons, property and acts outside their territory, and if, as an exception to this general prohibition, it allowed States to do so in certain specific cases. But this is certainly not the case under international law as it stands at present. Far from laying down a general prohibition to the effect that States may not extend the application of their laws and the jurisdiction of their courts to persons, property and acts outside their territory, it leaves them in this respect a wide measure of discretion which is only limited in certain cases by prohibitive rules. . . .

This discretion left to States by international law explains the great variety of rules which they have been able to adopt without objections or complaints on the part of other States. . . .

. . . Having regard to the terms of Article 15 and to the construction which the Court has just placed upon it, this [the French] contention would apply in regard to civil as well as to criminal cases, and would be applicable on conditions of absolute reciprocity as between Turkey and the other contracting Parties; in practice, it would therefore in many cases result in paralyzing the action of the courts, owing to the impossibility of citing a universally accepted rule on which to support the exercise of their jurisdiction. Nevertheless, it has to be seen whether the foregoing considerations really apply as regards criminal jurisdiction, or whether this jurisdiction is governed by a different principle: this might be the outcome of the close connection which for a long time existed between the conception of supreme criminal jurisdiction and that of a State, and also by the especial importance of criminal jurisdiction from the point of view of the individual.

Though it is true that in all systems of law the principle of the territorial character of criminal law is fundamental, it is equally true that all or nearly all of these systems of law extend their action to offences committed outside the territory of the State which adopts them, and they do so in ways which vary from State to State. The territoriality of criminal law, therefore, is not an absolute principle of international law and by no means coincides with territorial sovereignty.

This situation may be considered from two different standpoints corresponding to the points of view respectively taken up by the Parties. According to one of these standpoints, the principle of freedom, in virtue of which each State may regulate its legislation at its discretion, provided that in so doing it does not come in conflict with a restriction imposed by international law, would also apply as regards law governing the scope of jurisdiction in criminal cases. According to the other standpoint, the exclusively territorial character of law relating to this domain constitutes a principle which, except as otherwise expressly provided, would *ipso facto*, prevent States from extending the criminal jurisdiction of their courts beyond their frontiers; the exceptions in question, which include for instance extra-territorial jurisdiction over nationals and over crimes directed against public safety, would therefore rest on special permissive rules forming part of international law.

Adopting, for the purposes of the argument, the standpoint of the latter of these two systems, it must be recognized that, in the absence of a treaty provision, its correctness depends upon whether there is a custom having the force of law establishing it. The same is true as regards the applicability of this system—assuming it to have been recognized as sound—in the particular case. It follows that, even from this point of view, before ascertaining whether there may be a rule of international law expressly allowing Turkey to prosecute a foreigner for an offence committed by him outside Turkey, it is necessary to begin by establishing both that the system is well-founded and that it is applicable in this particular case. Now, in order to establish the first of these points, one must, as has just been seen, prove the existence of a principle of international law restricting the discretion of States as regards criminal legislation.

Consequently, whichever of the two systems described above be adopted, the same result will be arrived at in this particular case: the necessity of ascertaining whether or not under international law there is a principle which would have prohibited Turkey, in the circumstances of the case before the Court, from prosecuting Lieutenant Demons. . . .

The arguments advanced by the French Government, other than those considered above, are, in substance, the three following:

(1) International law does not allow a State to take proceedings with regard to offences committed by foreigners abroad, simply by reason of the nationality of the victim; and such is the situation in the present case because the offence must be regarded as having been committed on board the French vessel.

(2) International law recognizes the exclusive jurisdiction of the State whose flag is flown as regards everything which occurs on board a ship on the high seas.

(3) Lastly, this principle is especially applicable in a collision case.

As regards the first argument . . . the Court does not think it necessary to consider the contention that a State cannot punish offences committed abroad by a foreigner simply by reason of the nationality of the victim. For this contention only relates to the case where the nationality of the victim is the only criterion on which the criminal jurisdiction of the State is based. Even if that argument were correct generally speaking—and in regard to this the Court reserves its opinion—it could only be used in the present case if international law forbade Turkey to take into consideration the fact that the offence produced its effects on the Turkish vessel and consequently in a place assimilated to Turkish territory in which the application of Turkish criminal law cannot be challenged, even in regard to offences committed there by foreigners. But no such rule of international law exists. No argument has come to the knowledge of the Court from which it could be deduced that States recognize themselves to be under an obligation towards each other only to have regard to the place where the author of the offence happens to be at the time of the offence. On the contrary, it is certain that the courts of many countries, even of countries which have given their criminal legislation a strictly territorial character, interpret criminal law in the sense that offences, the authors of which at the moment of commission are in the territory of another State, are nevertheless to be regarded as having been committed in the national territory, if one of the constituent elements of the offence, and more especially its effects, have taken place there. French courts have, in regard to a variety of situations, given decisions sanctioning this way of interpreting the territorial principle. Again, the Court does not know of any cases in which governments have protested against the fact that the criminal law of some country contained a rule to this effect or that the courts of a country construed their criminal law in this sense. Consequently, once it is admitted that the effects of the offence were produced on the Turkish vessel, it becomes impossible to hold that there is a rule of international law which prohibits Turkey from prosecuting Lieutenant Demons because of the fact that the author of the offence was on board the French ship. Since, as has already been observed, the special agreement does not deal with the provision of Turkish law under which the prosecution was instituted, but only with the question whether the prosecution should be regarded as contrary to the principles of international law, there is no reason preventing the Court from confining itself to observing that, in this case, a prosecution may also be justified from the point of view of the so-called territorial principle.

Nevertheless, even if the Court had to consider whether Article 6 of the Turkish Penal Code[17] was compatible with international law, and if it held that the nationality of the victim did not in all circumstances constitute a sufficient basis for the exercise of criminal jurisdiction by the State of which the victim was a national, the Court would arrive at the same

---

[17] *Ed.* Art. 6 reads:

"Any foreigner who, apart from the cases contemplated by Article 4, commits an offence abroad to the prejudice of Turkey or of a Turkish subject, for which offence Turkish law prescribes a penalty involving loss of freedom for a minimum period of not less than one year, shall be punished in accordance with the Turkish Penal Code provided that he is arrested in Turkey. The penalty shall, however, be reduced by one third and instead of the death penalty, twenty years of penal servitude shall be awarded . . .

If the offence committed injures another foreigner, the guilty person shall be punished at the request of the Minister of Justice, in accordance with the provisions set out in the first paragraph of this article, provided, however, that: (1) the article in question is one for which Turkish law prescribes a penalty involving loss of freedom for a minimum period of three years; (2) there is no extradition treaty or that extradition has not been accepted either by the government of the locality where the guilty person has committed the offence or by the government of his own country."

conclusion for the reasons just set out. For even were Article 6 to be held incompatible with the principles of international law, since the prosecution might have been based on another provision of Turkish law which would not have been contrary to any principle of international law, it follows that it would be impossible to deduce from the mere fact that Article 6 was not in conformity with those principles, that the prosecution itself was contrary to them. The fact that the judicial authorities may have committed an error in their choice of the legal provision applicable to the particular case and compatible with international law only concerns municipal law and can only affect international law in so far as a treaty provision enters into account, or the possibility of a denial of justice arises.

It has been sought to argue that the offence of manslaughter cannot be localized at the spot where the mortal effect is felt; for the effect is not intentional and it cannot be said that there is, in the mind of the delinquent, any culpable intent directed towards the territory where the mortal effect is produced. In reply to this argument it might be observed that the effect is a factor of outstanding importance in offences such as manslaughter, which are punished precisely in consideration of their effects rather than of the subjective intention of the delinquent. But the Court does not feel called upon to consider this question, which is one of the interpretation of Turkish criminal law. It will suffice to observe that no argument has been put forward and nothing has been found from which it would follow that international law has established a rule imposing on States this reading of the conception of the offence of manslaughter.

The second argument put forward by the French Government is the principle that the State whose flag is flown has exclusive jurisdiction over everything which occurs on board a merchant ship on the high seas.

It is certainly true that—apart from certain special cases which are defined by international law—vessels on the high seas are subject to no authority except that of the State whose flag they fly. In virtue of the principle of the freedom of the seas, that is to say, the absence of any territorial sovereignty upon the high seas, no State may exercise any kind of jurisdiction over foreign vessels upon them. Thus, if a war vessel, happening to be at the spot where a collision occurs between a vessel flying its flag and a foreign vessel, were to send on board the latter an officer to make investigations or to take evidence, such an act would undoubtedly be contrary to international law.

But it by no means follows that a State can never in its own territory exercise jurisdiction over acts which have occurred on board a foreign ship on the high seas. A corollary of the principle of the freedom of the seas is that a ship on the high seas is assimilated to the territory of the State of the flag of which it flies, for, just as in its own territory, that State exercises its authority upon it, and no other State may do so. All that can be said is that by virtue of the principle of the freedom of the seas, a ship is placed in the same position as national territory; but there is nothing to support the claim according to which the rights of the State under whose flag the vessel sails may go farther than the rights which it exercises within its territory properly so called. It follows that what occurs on board a vessel on the high seas must be regarded as if it occurred on the territory of the State whose flag the ship flies. If, therefore, a guilty act committed on the high seas produces its effects on a vessel flying another flag or in foreign territory, the same principles must be applied as if the territories of two different States were concerned, and the conclusion must therefore be drawn that there is no rule of international law prohibiting the State to which the ship on which the effects of the offence have taken place belongs, from regarding the offence as having been committed in its territory and prosecuting, accordingly, the delinquent.

This conclusion could only be overcome if it were shown that there was a rule of customary international law which, going further than the principle stated above, established the exclusive jurisdiction of the State whose flag was flown. The French Government has endeavoured to prove the existence of such a rule, having recourse for this purpose to the teachings of publicists, to decisions of municipal and international tribunals, and especially to conventions which, whilst creating exceptions to the principle of the freedom of the seas by permitting the war and police vessels of a State to exercise a more or less extensive control over the merchant vessels of another State, reserve jurisdiction to the courts of the country whose flag is flown by the vessel proceeded against.

In the Court's opinion, the existence of such a rule has not been conclusively proved.

In the first place, as regards teachings of publicists, and apart from the question as to what their value may be from the point of view of establishing the existence of a rule of customary law, it is no doubt true that all or nearly all writers teach that ships on the high seas are subject exclusively to the jurisdiction of the State whose flag they fly. But the important point is the significance attached by them to this principle; now it does not appear that in general, writers bestow upon this principle a scope differing from or wider than that explained above and which is equivalent to saying that the jurisdiction of a State over vessels on the high seas is the same in extent as its jurisdiction in its own territory. On the other hand, there is no lack of writers who, upon a close study of the special question whether a State can prosecute for offences committed on board a foreign ship on the high seas, definitely come to the conclusion that such offences must be regarded as if they had been committed in the territory of the State whose flag the ship flies, and that consequently the general rules of each legal system in regard to offences committed abroad are applicable.

In regard to precedents, it should first be observed that, leaving aside the collision cases which will be alluded to later, none of them relates to offences affecting two ships flying the flags of two different countries, and that consequently they are not of much importance in the case before the

Court. The case of the *Costa Rica Packet*[18] is no exception, for the prauw on which the alleged depredations took place was adrift without flag or crew, and this circumstance certainly influenced, perhaps decisively, the conclusion arrived at by the arbitrator.

On the other hand, there is no lack of cases in which a State has claimed a right to prosecute for an offence, committed on board a foreign ship, which it regarded as punishable under its legislation. Thus Great Britain refused the request of the United States for the extradition of John Anderson, a British seaman who had committed homicide on board an American vessel, stating that she did not dispute the jurisdiction of the United States but that she was entitled to exercise hers concurrently.[19] This case, to which others might be added, is relevant in spite of Anderson's British nationality, in order to show that the principle of exclusive jurisdiction of the country whose flag the vessel flies is not universally accepted.

The cases in which the exclusive jurisdiction of the State whose flag was flown has been recognized would seem rather to have been cases in which the foreign State was interested only by reason of the nationality of the victim, and in which, according to the legislation of that State itself or the practice of its courts, that ground was not regarded as sufficient to authorize prosecution for an offence committed abroad by a foreigner.

Finally, as regards conventions expressly reserving jurisdiction exclusively to the State whose flag is flown, it is not absolutely certain that this stipulation is to be regarded as expressing a general principle of law rather than as corresponding to the extraordinary jurisdiction which these conventions confer on the state-owned ships of a particular country in respect of ships of another country on the high seas. Apart from that, it should be observed that these conventions relate to matters of a particular kind, closely connected with the policing of the seas, such as the slave trade, damage to submarine cables, fisheries, *etc.*, and not to common-law offences. Above all it should be pointed out that the offences contemplated by the conventions in question only concern a single ship; it is impossible therefore to make any deduction from them in regard to matters which concern two ships and consequently the jurisdiction of two different States. . . .

It only remains to examine the third argument advanced by the French Government. . . .

In this connection, the Agent for the French Government has drawn the

---

[18] *Ed. G.B. v. The Netherlands* (1897) Moore, 5 Int.Arb. 4948. Crew from the *Costa Rica Packet*, a British merchant ship, boarded a derelict prauw (a Malayan vessel) on the high seas and took goods (mostly gin and brandy, from which the crew became drunk) from it. When the *Costa Rica Packet* entered a Dutch port in the East Indies, the captain was arrested on charges relating to the seizure of the goods. He was later released without being brought to trial. The Arbitrator (Martens) held that the Netherlands had no jurisdiction to act as it had done—only the flag state of the *Costa Rica Packet* had—and awarded damages against it.

[19] *Ed.* See the official correspondence of 1879 in 1 Moore 932.

Court's attention to the fact that questions of jurisdiction in collision cases, which frequently arise before civil courts, are but rarely encountered in the practice of criminal courts. He deduces from this that, in practice, prosecutions only occur before the courts of the State whose flag is flown and that that circumstance is proof of a tacit consent on the part of States and, consequently, shows what positive international law is in collision cases.

In the Court's opinion, this conclusion is not warranted. Even if the rarity of the judicial decisions to be found among the reported cases were sufficient to prove in point of fact the circumstance alleged by the Agent for the French Government, it would merely show that States had often, in practice, abstained from instituting criminal proceedings, and not that they recognized themselves as being obliged to do so; for only if such abstention were based on their being conscious of having a duty to abstain would it be possible to speak of an international custom. The alleged fact does not allow one to infer that States have been conscious of having such a duty; on the other hand, as will presently be seen, there are other circumstances calculated to show that the contrary is true.

So far as the Court is aware there are no decisions of international tribunals in this matter; but some decisions of municipal courts have been cited. Without pausing to consider the value to be attributed to the judgments of municipal courts in connection with the establishment of the existence of a rule of international law, it will suffice to observe that the decisions quoted sometimes support one view and sometimes the other. . . .

On the other hand, the Court feels called upon to lay stress upon the fact that it does not appear that the States concerned have objected to criminal proceedings in respect of collision cases before the courts of a country other than that the flag of which was flown, or that they have made protests: their conduct does not appear to have differed appreciably from that observed by them in all cases of concurrent jurisdiction. This fact is directly opposed to the existence of a tacit consent on the part of States to the exclusive jurisdiction of the State whose flag is flown, such as the Agent for the French Government has thought it possible to deduce from the infrequency of questions of jurisdiction before criminal courts. It seems hardly probable, and it would not be in accordance with international practice, that the French Government in the *Ortigia v. Oncle-Joseph Case*[20] and the German Government in the *Ekbatana v. West-Hinder Case*[21] would have omitted to protest against the exercise of criminal jurisdiction by the Italian and Belgian Courts, if they had really thought that this was a violation of international law. . . .

The conclusion at which the Court has therefore arrived is that there is no rule of international law in regard to collision cases to the effect that

[20] *Ed.* (1885) 12 J.D.I. 286.
[21] *Ed.* (1914) 41 J.D.I 1327.

criminal proceedings are exclusively within the jurisdiction of the State whose flag is flown. . . .

FOR THESE REASONS. The Court . . . gives by the President's casting vote —the votes being equally divided[22]—judgment to the effect [that the answer to the first question was in the negative].

DISSENTING OPINION OF JUDGE MOORE.[23] . . . the countries by which the claim [to jurisdiction based upon the passive personality principle] has been espoused are said to have adopted the "system of protection."

What, we may ask, is this system? In substance, it means that the citizen of one country, when he visits another country, takes with him for his "protection" the law of his own country and subjects those with whom he comes into contact to the operation of that law. In this way an inhabitant of a great commercial city, in which foreigners congregate, may in the course of an hour unconsciously fall under the operation of a number of foreign criminal codes. This is by no means a fanciful supposition; it is merely an illustration of what is daily occurring, if the "protective" principle is admissible. It is evident that this claim is at variance not only with the principle of the exclusive jurisdiction of a State over its own territory, but also with the equally well-settled principle that a person visiting a foreign country, far from radiating for his protection the jurisdiction of his own country, falls under the dominion of the local law and, except so far as his government may diplomatically intervene in case of a denial of justice, must look to that law for his protection.

No one disputes the right of a State to subject its citizens abroad to the operations of its own penal laws, if it sees fit to do so. This concerns simply the citizen and his own government, and no other government can properly interfere. But the case is fundamentally different where a country claims either that its penal laws apply to other countries and to what takes place wholly within such countries or, if it does not claim this, that it may punish foreigners for alleged violations, even in their own country, of laws to which they were not subject.

In the discussions of the present case, prominence has been given to the case of the editor Cutting, a citizen of the United States, whose release was demanded when he was prosecuted in Mexico, under a statute precisely similar in terms to Article 6 of the Turkish Penal Code, for a libel published in the United States to the detriment of a Mexican. It has been

[22] *Ed.* President Huber; Judges de Bustamante, Oda, Anzilotti, Pessôa; and National Judge Feizi-Daim voted for the Court's judgment. Former President Loder; Vice-President Weiss; and Judges Lord Finlay, Nyholm, Moore and Altimira dissented.

[23] On his reading of the special agreement by which the case was referred to the Court, Judge Moore found it necessary to consider whether Art. 6 of the Turkish Criminal Code, with its reliance on the passive personality (or "protective") principle, was consistent with international law. It was his conclusion on this question that led to his dissent. Note that by "protective principle" the judge means the "passive personality principle" not the protective principle discussed below, p. 288.

intimated that this case was "political," but an examination of the public record (*Foreign Relations of the United States*, 1887, p. 751; *idem*, 1888, II, pp. 1114, 1180) shows that it was discussed by both Governments on purely legal grounds, although in the decision on appeal, by which the prisoner was discharged from custody, his release was justified on grounds of public interest.[24] In its representations to the Mexican Government, the Government of the United States, while maintaining that foreigners could not be "protected in the United States by their national laws," and that the Mexican courts might not, without violating international law, "try a citizen of the United States for an offence committed and consummated in his own country, merely because the person offended happened to be a Mexican," pointed out that it nowhere appeared that the alleged libel "was ever circulated in Mexico so as to constitute the crime of defamation under the Mexican law," or "that any copies were actually found ... in Mexico." The United States thus carefully limited its protest to offences "committed and consummated" within its territory; and, in conformity with this view, it was agreed in the extradition treaty between the two countries of February 22nd, 1889, that except in the case of "embezzlement or criminal malversation of public funds committed within the jurisdiction of either Party by public officers or depositaries," neither Party would "assume jurisdiction in the punishment of crimes committed exclusively within the territory of the other." (Moore, *Digest of International Law*, II pp. 233, 242.)[25]

Notes

1. On the approach of the Court to the question whether France had to prove a limitation upon Turkey's jurisdiction or whether Turkey had to prove a rule giving it jurisdiction, Brierly[26] states:

> ... their reasoning was based on the highly contentious metaphysical proposition of the extreme positivist school that the law emanates from the free will of sovereign independent States, and from this premiss they argued that restrictions on the independence of States cannot be presumed. Neither, it may be said, can the absence of restrictions; for we are not entitled to deduce the law applicable to a specific state of facts from the mere fact of sovereignty or independence. Further, the reasoning of the majority seems to imply that the process by which the international principles of penal jurisdiction have been formed is by the imposition of certain limitations on an originally unlimited competence, and this is surely historically unsound. The original conception of law was personal, and it was only the rise of the modern territorial State that subjected aliens—even when they happened to be resident in a State not their own—to the law of that State. International law did not start as the law of a society of States each of omnicompetent jurisdiction, but of States possessing

---

[24] *Ed.* Cutting had been convicted by the trial court. An appeal court ordered his release because "the offended party... has withdrawn from the action": see U.S.For.Rel., 1887, pp. 766–767.

[25] *Ed.* Mexico regarded itself as justified in using the passive personality principle: see the inclosure to the letter from Mr Romero to Mr Bayard, August 30, 1886, *ibid.* pp. 957 *et seq.*

[26] (1928) 44 L.Q.R. 154 at 155–156.

a personal jurisdiction over their own nationals and later acquiring a territorial jurisdiction over resident non-nationals. If it is alleged that they have now acquired a measure of jurisdiction over non-resident non-nationals, a valid international custom to that effect should surely be established by those who allege it.

2. What does the Court mean when it says that the "territoriality of criminal law . . . is not an absolute principle of international law and by no means coincides with territorial sovereignty?"[27]

3. *The territorial principle.* On the question whether the offence could be said to have been committed on Turkish territory to establish Turkish jurisdiction on a territorial basis, Judge Moore agreed with the Court:

> . . . it appears to be now universally admitted that, where a crime is committed in the territorial jurisdiction of one State as the direct result of the act of a person at the time corporeally present in another State, international law, by reason of the principle of constructive presence of the offender at the place where his act took effect, does not forbid the prosecution of the offender by the former State, should he come within its territorial jurisdiction.[28]

Consistent with this approach, the Harvard Research Draft Convention proposed that a State be allowed territorial jurisdiction when a crime is committed "in whole or in part" within its territory.[29] A crime is committed "in part" within the territory "when any essential constituent element is consummated there."[30] The Commentary to the Draft Convention reads: "The text of the present article conforms to the modern trend by combining the subjective and objective applications of the territorial principle."[31] According to the "subjective application," a crime occurs in a State when it is "commenced within the State but completed or consummated [in the sense of a constituent element occurring] abroad."[32] The "objective" application is to the effect that it does so in the reverse situation.[33] Thus if X, in state A, shoots and kills Y, in state B, an offence is probably committed (depending upon the constituent elements of murder and related offences in the criminal law of the two states) in each state.

As allowed by the rules as to territorial jurisdiction in international law, the Criminal Justice Act 1993, ss.1–2, provides for criminal jurisdiction in respect of listed offences where any act, proof of the commission of which is necessary for a conviction, is committed within the jurisdiction. Section 3(2)(3) of the 1993 Act provides for jurisdiction in respect of extra-territorial conspiracies and attempts in respect of listed offences where the intention is to commit an offence in England, even though no act is committed within the jurisdiction and whether the defendants are British nationals or not.[34] In international law, jurisdiction in these inchoate offence cases may be based on the protective or, possibly, universality principles, depending on the facts. In *D.P.P. v. Doot*,[35] the respondents were aliens convicted of conspiracy to import cannabis resin into the United Kingdom. The

[27] Above, p. 269.
[28] P.C.I.J. Rep., Series A, No. 10, p. 73.
[29] Article 3. See the facts in *R. v. Keyn*, above, p. 75.
[30] (1935) 29 A.J.I.L. Supp. 495.
[31] *ibid.* p. 494. *cf.* Lord Diplock in *Treacy v. D.P.P.* [1971] A.C. 537, HL.
[32] *ibid.* p. 484.
[33] *ibid.* p. 488.
[34] See *Liangsiriprasert v. Govt. of USA* [1991] 1 A.C. 225, PC, and *R. v. Sansom* [1991] 2 Q.B. 130, CA (drug importing conspiracy cases to the same effect). On the 1993 Act and international law jurisdiction rules, see Warbrick (1994) 43 I.C.L.Q. 460.
[35] [1973] A.C. 807, HL.

agreement amounting to the conspiracy had been made abroad before the respondents were arrested in England while in the course of carrying it out. The House of Lords held that the English courts had jurisdiction in the case under English law because the offence continued to occur in England while steps were being taken in concert there to carry out the purpose of the conspiracy.[36] This was so even though the agreement had already been made—and hence the constituent elements of the crime completed—abroad. Referring to the question of jurisdiction in the case according to international law, Lord Wilberforce stated:

> the present case involves "international elements"—the accused are aliens and the conspiracy was initiated abroad—but there can be no question here of any breach of any rules of international law if they are prosecuted in this country. Under the objective territorial principle (I use the terminology of the Harvard Research in International Law) or the principle of universality (for the prevention of the trade in narcotics falls within this description[37]) or both, the courts of this country have a clear right, if not a duty, to prosecute in accordance with our municipal law.

The Court's application of the territorial principle in the *Lotus* case was based upon the view that a ship, like an aircraft, is to be treated as part of a state's territory for jurisdictional purposes.[38] Lord Finlay took a different view in his dissenting opinion. For him, a ship was not "territory"; it was instead a "moving chattel" of a "very special nature" for which the relevant jurisdictional rule was that "[c]riminal jurisdiction for negligence causing a collision is in the courts of the country of the flag, provided that if the offender is of a nationality different from that of his ship, the prosecution may alternatively be in the courts of his own country."[39]

In *R. v. Bates*,[40] the defendant was charged with an offence under the Firearms Act 1937 committed on Rough's Tower, a wartime gun platform on which he was living and located seven miles off the coast of Harwich, then outside United Kingdom territorial waters. The charge was dismissed because "the jurisdiction of the Admiral did not apply to an artificial structure not being a ship and . . . the Firearms Act was intended to operate only within 'the ordinary territorial limits' and on British ships."[41]

4. *The passive personality principle.*[42] This was rejected by all of the six dissenting judges. The Commentary to the Harvard Draft Convention in 1935 lists over twenty States that, in one form or another, made, or proposed to make, use of the "passive personality" principle.[43] It had, however, "been vigorously opposed in Anglo-American countries"[44] and, of the five principles "having substantial support in comtemporary national legislation," it was "the most difficult to justify in theory."[45] The principle was not included in the Draft Convention. What are the objections to it? Why is it less acceptable than jurisdiction based upon the

---

[36] This requirement no longer applies under the 1993 Act: see above.
[37] See below, p. 288.
[38] *cf. R. v. Brixton Prison Governor, ex p. Minervini* [1959] 1 Q.B. 155, QBD (Norwegian ship "territory" on which a crime could be committed in the sense of the British-Norwegian extradition treaty; "territory" in the treaty meant "jurisdiction").
[39] P.C.I.J. Rep., Series A, No. 10, p. 53.
[40] Unreported case before Essex Assizes; summarised in U.K.M.I.L. 1978, (1978) 49 B.Y.I.L. 393.
[41] *ibid.*
[42] See Watson (1993) 28 Texas I.L.J. 2.
[43] (1935) 29 A.J.I.L. Supp. 578.
[44] *ibid.* p. 579.
[45] *ibid.*

nationality of the alleged criminal? Might it be argued that, in some cases at least, the more States that may exercise jurisdiction over an alleged criminal the better in the interest of the administration of justice?[46]

5. The ruling of the Court on the question of jurisdiction in cases of collisions on the high seas is contradicted by the 1982 Law of the Sea Convention.[47] The latter probably now reflects customary international law.

ATTORNEY-GENERAL OF THE GOVERNMENT OF ISRAEL v. EICHMANN[48]

(1961) 36 I.L.R. 5. District Court of Jerusalem

The accused, who had German nationality,[49] was the Head of the Jewish Office of the German Gestapo. He was the administrator in charge of "the final solution"—the policy that led to the extermination of between 4,200,000 and 4,600,000 Jews in Europe.[50] Eichmann was found in Argentina in 1960 by persons who were probably agents of the Israeli Government[51] and abducted to Israel without the knowledge of the Argentinian Government.[52] There he was prosecuted under the Israeli Nazi and Nazi Collaborators (Punishment) Law of 1951 for war crimes, crimes against the Jewish people, the definition of which was modelled upon the definition of genocide in the Genocide Convention 1949,[53] and crimes against humanity.[54] War crimes were punishable under the 1951 Act if "done, during the period of the Second World War, in an enemy country"; other crimes within the Act were punishable if "done, during the period of the Nazi regime, in an enemy country." He was convicted and sentenced to death. His appeal to the Supreme Court of Israel was dismissed.[55] His ashes "were scattered over the Mediterranean waters—lest they defile Jewish soil."[56]

Judgment of the Court

8. Learned defence counsel . . . submits:

(a) that the Israel Law, by imposing punishment for acts done outside the boundaries of the State and before its establishment, against persons who were not Israel citizens, and by a person who acted in the course of

---

[46] The passive personality principle is adopted in the 1963 Tokyo Convention on Offences aboard Aircraft, Art. 4, *loc. cit.*, p. 295, n. 14 below, and the 1984 UN Torture Convention, below, p. 710.

[47] Art. 97, below, p. 427.

[48] See Fawcett (1962) 38 B.Y.I.L. 181; Green (1960) 23 M.L.R. 507; Papadatos, *The Eichmann Trial* (1964); Schwarzenberger (1962) 15 C.L.P. 248; Silving (1961) 55 A.J.I.L. 307.

[49] This at least was claimed by his counsel in Jerusalem: Rosen, ed., *Six Million Accusers* (1962), p. 301. He was born in Germany of German parents and taken to live in Austria as a boy. He entered Argentina with a refugee passport issued by the Red Cross under the false name of Ricardo Klement.

[50] This estimate is that of Reitlinger in *The Final Solution* (1953), Appendix I.

[51] Even supposing they were not, Israel would appear to have adopted their acts.

[52] Note that there was no extradition treaty between Argentina and Israel.

[53] U.K.T.S. 58 (1970), Cmnd. 4421; 78 U.N.T.S. 277; (1951) 45 A.J.I.L. Supp. 7.

[54] These were defined as " . . . any of the following acts: murder, extermination, enslavement, starvation or deportation and other inhumane acts committed against any civilian population, and persecution on national, racial, religious or political grounds."

[55] The Supreme Court Judgment is at (1962) 36 I.L.R. 277. The Supreme Court affirmed the reasoning of the District Court.

[56] Sachar, *A History of the Jews* (1967), p. 467.

duty on behalf of a foreign country ("Act of State") conflicts with international law and exceeds the powers of the Israel Legislature. . . .

10. . . . The law in force in Israel resembles that in force in England in [its application of International Law]. . . .

Our jurisdiction to try this case is based on the Nazi and Nazi Collaborators (Punishment) Law, an enacted Law the provisions of which are unequivocal. The Court has to give effect to a law of the Knesset,[57] and we cannot entertain the contention that this Law conflicts with the principles of international law. . . .

11. We have, however, also considered the sources of international law . . . and have failed to find any foundation for the contention that Israel law is in conflict with the principles of international law. . . .

12. The abhorrent crimes defined in this Law are not crimes under Israel law alone. These crimes, which struck at the whole of mankind and shocked the conscience of nations, are grave offences against the law of nations itself (*delicta juris gentium*).[58] Therefore, so far from international law negating or limiting the jurisdiction of countries with respect to such crimes, international law is, in the absence of an International Court, in need of the judicial and legislative organs of every country to give effect to its criminal interdictions and to bring the criminals to trial. The jurisdiction to try crimes under international law is universal.

13. This universal authority, namely the authority of the *forum deprehensionis* (the court of the country in which the accused is actually held in custody), was already mentioned in the Corpus Juris Civilis (see C.3, 15, *ubi de criminibus agi oportet*) and the towns of northern Italy had already in the Middle Ages followed the practice of trying specific types of dangerous criminals (*banniti, vagabundi, assassini*) who happened to be within their area of jurisdiction, without regard to the place in which the crimes in question were committed. . . . Maritime nations have also since time immemorial acted on the principle of universal jurisdiction in dealing with pirates, whose crime is known in English law, *piracy jure gentium*. . . .

The Court quoted from a number of authors[59] who take the view that "crimes against international law" generally or war crimes in particular give rise to universal jurisdiction. It then considered an objection to its jurisdiction based upon Article 6 of the Genocide Convention 1949[60]:

22. . . . It is clear that Article 6, like all other articles which determine the conventional obligations of the contracting parties, is intended for cases of genocide which will occur in the future after the ratification of the

[57] *Ed.* The Israeli Parliament.
[58] *Ed.* On crimes against international law, see below, p. 738.
[59] These included Hyde, *International Law* (2nd ed., 1947), Vol. I, p. 804, and Cowles (1945) 33 Calif. L. R. 177.
[60] Art. 6 reads: "Persons charged with genocide . . . shall be tried by a competent tribunal of the state in the territory of which the act was committed. . . . ".

treaty or the adherence thereto by the State or States concerned. It cannot be assumed, in the absence of an express provision in the Convention itself, that any of the conventional obligations, including Article 6, will apply to crimes which had been perpetrated in the past. It is of the nature of conventional obligations, as distinct from confirmation of existing principles, that unless another intention is implicit, their application is *ex nunc* and not *ex tunc*. . . . We must . . . draw a clear distinction between the first part of Article I, which lays down that "the Contracting Parties confirm that genocide, whether committed in time of peace or in time of war, is a crime under international law"—a general provision which confirms a principle of customary international law "binding on States, even without any conventional obligation"—and Article 6, which comprises a special provision undertaken by the contracting parties with regard to the trial of crimes that may be committed in the future. Whatever may be the purport of this latter obligation within the meaning of the Convention (and in the event of differences of opinion as to the interpretation thereof, each contracting party may, under Article 9, appeal to the International Court of Justice), it is certain that it constitutes no part of the principles of customary international law, which are also binding outside the conventional application of the Convention.

23. Moreover, even with regard to the conventional application of the Convention, it is not to be assumed that Article 6 is designed to limit the jurisdiction of countries to try crimes of genocide by the principle of territoriality. Without entering into the general question of the limits of municipal criminal jurisdiction, it may be pointed out that no one disputes that customary international law does not prohibit a State from trying its own citizens for offences they have committed abroad. . . . Had Article 6 meant to provide that those accused of genocide shall be tried *only* by "a competent tribunal of the State in the territory of which the act was committed" (or by an "international court" which has not been constituted), then that article would have foiled the very object of the Convention to prevent genocide and inflict punishment therefor. . . .

The Court rejected the defenses of *nullem crimen sine lege, nulla poena sine lege* and "act of state," relying on the reasoning of the International Military Tribunal at Nuremberg.[61]

30. . . . The State of Israel's "right to punish" the accused derives, in our view, from two cumulative sources: a universal source (pertaining to the whole of mankind), which vests the right to prosecute and punish crimes of this order in every State within the family of nations; and a specific or national source, which gives the victim nation the right to try any who assault its existence.

This second foundation of criminal jurisdiction conforms, according to accepted terminology, to the protective principle (*compétence réelle*). In

[61] See the Nuremberg Tribunal Judgment, below, p. 738.

England, which until very recently was considered a country that does not rely on such jurisdiction (see also *Harvard Research in International Law,* "Jurisdiction with respect to Crime," 1935, A.J.I.L., vol. 35 (Suppl.), 544) it was said in *Joyce v. Director of Public Prosecutions* [1946] A.C. 347, 372:

> The second point of appeal . . . was that in any case no English court has jurisdiction to try an alien for a crime committed abroad. . . . There is, I think, a short answer to this point. The statute in question deals with the crime of treason committed within or . . . without the realm: . . . No principle of comity demands that a state should ignore the crime of treason committed against it outside its territory. On the contrary a proper regard for its own security requires that all those who commit that crime, whether they commit it within or without the realm, should be amenable to its laws.[62]

Oppenheim-Lauterpacht, *op. cit.,* vol. 1, S. 147, p. 333, says that the penal jurisdiction of the State includes "crimes injuring its subjects or serious crimes against its own safety." Most European countries go much further than this (see Harvard Research, *loc. cit.,* pp. 546 *et seq.*).

31. Dahm says in his *Zur Problematik des Voelkerstrafrechts* (1956), p. 28, that the protective principle is not confined to those foreign offences that threaten the "vital interests" of the State, and goes on to explain (pp. 38–39) in his reference to the "immanent limitations" of the jurisdiction of the State, a departure from which would constitute an "abuse" of its sovereignty, [that]

> Penal jurisdiction is not a matter for everyone to exercise. It requires a "linking point" (*Anknuepfungspunkte*), a legal connection that links the punisher with the punished. The State may, in so far as international law does not contain rules to the contrary, punish only persons and acts *which concern it more than they concern other States.* . . .

The Court cited other writers in support of the "linking point" doctrine.[63]

33. . . . The "linking point" between Israel and the accused (and for that matter any person accused of a crime against the Jewish people under this Law) is striking in the case of "crime against the Jewish people," a

---

[62] *Ed.* Lord Jowitt L.C. The accused, William Joyce, was charged with treason under the Treason Act 1351 for having made propaganda broadcasts to the U.K. from Germany for the German Government. Although Joyce had spent his adult life in England, the accused was a U.S. citizen born in the U.S. of Irish parents who had emigrated there and become naturalised U.S. nationals. Apart from the "point of appeal" referred to above, it was also contended that the accused did not owe allegiance to the Crown and hence could not be guilty of treason. The House of Lords accepted that allegiance was necessary to the offence but found that the accused, as holder of a British passport in his name still in force at the time of his broadcasts, was entitled to protection by the Crown and, therefore, owed the Crown allegiance. This was so even though the passport had been obtained by fraud. See Lauterpacht (1947) 9 C.L.J. 330.

[63] See also Mann, *loc. cit.,* p. 264, n. 1, above, pp. 49–51.

crime that postulates an intention to exterminate the Jewish people in whole or in part. . . .

34. The connection between the State of Israel and the Jewish people needs no explanation.

35. . . . This crime very deeply concerns the "vital interests" of the State of Israel, and under the "protective principle" this State has the right to punish the criminals. In terms of Dahm's thesis, the acts referred to in this Law of the State of Israel "concern it more than they concern other States," and therefore according also to this author there exists a "linking point." The punishment of Nazi criminals does not derive from the arbitrariness of a country "abusing" its sovereignty but is a legitimate and reasonable exercise of a right of penal jurisdiction.

A people which can be murdered with impunity lives in danger, to say nothing of its "honour and authority" (Grotius). . . .

36. Defence counsel contended that the protective principle cannot apply to this Law because that principle is designed to protect only an existing State, its security and its interests, whereas the State of Israel did not exist at the time of the commission of the said crimes. In his submission the same applies to the principle of "passive personality" which stems from the protective principle, and of which some States have made use through their penal legislation for the protection of their citizens abroad. Counsel pointed out that in the absence of a sovereign Jewish State at the time of the catastrophe the victims of the Nazis were not citizens of the State of Israel when they were murdered.

In our view learned Counsel errs when he examines the protective principle in this retroactive Law according to the time of the commission of the crimes, as is usual in the case of an ordinary law. This Law was enacted in 1950, to be applied to a specified period which had terminated five years before its enactment. The protected interests of the State recognized by the protective principle is in this case the interest existing at the time of the enactment of the Law, and we have already dwelt on the importance of the moral and defensive task which this Law is designed to fulfil in the State of Israel. . . .

39. We should add that the well-known judgment . . . in the *Lotus Case*[64] ruled that the principle of territoriality does not limit the power of a State to try crimes and, moreover, that any argument against such power must point to a specific rule in international law which negates that power. We have followed this principle which, so to speak, shifts the "onus of proof " upon him who pleads against jurisdiction, but have preferred to base ourselves on positive reasons for upholding the jurisdiction of the State of Israel.

40. The second contention of learned defence counsel was that the trial of the accused in Israel following upon his kidnapping in a foreign land,

[64] *Ed.* Above, p. 267.

is in conflict with international law and takes away the jurisdiction of this Court.

... with reference to the circumstances of the arrest of the accused and his transfer to Israel, the Republic of Argentina ... lodged a complaint with the Security Council of the United Nations, which resolved on June 23, 1960, as follows (Doc. S/4349) ... :

The Security Council,

Having examined the complaint that the transfer of Adolf Eichmann to the territory of Israel constitutes a violation of the sovereignty of the Argentine Republic,

Considering that the violation of the sovereignty of a Member State is incompatible with the Charter of the United Nations,

Mindful of the universal condemnation of the persecution of the Jews under the Nazis and of the concern of people in all countries that Eichmann should be brought to appropriate justice for the crimes of which he is accused, ...

1. Declares that acts such as that under consideration, which affect the sovereignty of a Member State and therefore cause international friction, may, if repeated, endanger international peace and security;

2. Requests the Government of Israel to make appropriate reparation in accordance with the Charter of the United Nations and the rules of international law;

3. Expresses the hope that the traditionally friendly . relations between Argentina and Israel will be advanced.

Pursuant to this Resolution the two Governments reached agreement on the settlement of the dispute between them, and on August 3, 1960, issued the following joint communiqué:

The Governments of Argentina and Israel, animated by a desire to give effect to the resolution of the Security Council of June 23, 1960, in so far as the hope was expressed that the traditionally friendly relations between the two countries will be advanced, resolve to regard as closed the incident which arose out of the action taken by citizens of Israel, which infringed the fundamental rights of the State of Argentina.[65] ...

41. It is an established rule of law that a person being tried for an offence against the laws of a State may not oppose his trial by reason of the illegality of his arrest or of the means whereby he was brought within the jurisdiction of that State. The courts in England, the United States and

---

[65] *Ed.* Earlier, Argentina had "requested appropriate reparation for the act, namely the return of Eichmann, for which it set a time limit of one week, and the punishment of those guilty of violating Argentine territory": U.N. Doc. S/4336.

Israel have constantly held that the circumstances of the arrest and the mode of bringing of the accused into the territory of the State have no relevance to his trial, and they have consistently refused in all instances to enter upon an examination of these circumstances. . . .

In *Ex p. Elliott* [1949] 1 All E.R. 373, the Court heard an application for habeas corpus by a British soldier who had deserted his unit in 1946, was arrested in Belgium in 1948 by two British military officers accompanied by two Belgian police officers, was transferred by the British military authorities to England and was there held in custody pending his trial for desertion. Counsel for the applicant pleaded *inter alia*, that the British authorities in Belgium had no power to arrest the applicant and that he was arrested contrary to Belgian law. Lord Goddard dismissed the application, saying in his judgment (at p. 376):

> . . . If a person is arrested abroad and he is brought before a court in this country charged with an offence which that court has jurisdiction to hear, it is no answer for him to say, he being then in lawful custody in this country: "I was arrested contrary to the laws of the State of A or the State of B where I was actually arrested." He is in custody before the court which has jurisdiction to try him. What is it suggested that the court can do? The court cannot dismiss the charge at once without its being heard. He is charged with an offence against English law, the law applicable to the case.

42. That principle is also acknowledged in Palestine case law. . . .

In *Afouneh v. Attorney-General*, Cr.A. 14/42, (1942) 9 P.L.R. 63,[66] the Supreme Court [stated]:

> In our opinion, the law is correctly stated in volume 4 of Moore's *Digest of International Law*, at p. 311 . . . :
> "Where a fugitive is brought back by kidnapping, or by other irregular means, and not under an extradition treaty, he cannot, although an extradition treaty exists between the two countries, set up in answer to the indictment the unlawful manner in which he was brought within the jurisdiction of the court. It belongs exclusively to the government from whose territory he was wrongfully taken to complain of the violation of its rights."[67] . . .

---

[66] *Ed.* (1941–42) 10 A.D. 327 at 328.

[67] *Ed.* Moore relied on *Kerr v. Illinois*, 119 U.S. 436 (1886), as his authority for this proposition. In that case, an agent acting for the state of Illinois went to Peru with a warrant for the extradition of Kerr under the extradition treaty between the U.S. and Peru. At the time, Peru was at war with Chile and most of Peru, including Lima, was in Chilean hands. In this confused situation, the agent approached the Chilean military authorities in Lima and, with their assistance, obtained custody of Kerr and took him back to Illinois. No approach was made to the Peruvian Government, which was still in existence in retreat, and no recourse was had to the extradition treaty. Peru did not protest against the agent's

48. The Anglo-Saxon rule has been accepted by Continental jurists as well. . . . [68]

49. Criticism of English and American case law from the point of view of international law has been levelled by Dickinson, "Jurisdiction Following Seizure or Arrest in Violation of International Law," in (1934) 28 *American Journal of International Law*, 231, and Morgenstern, "Jurisdiction in Seizures Effected in Violation of International Law," in (1952) 29 *British Year Book of International Law*, 265. See also Lauterpacht in (1948) 64 *Law Quarterly Review*, 100, note (14). It is not for us to enter into this controversy between international jurists, but we would draw attention to two important points for this case: (1) the critics admit that the established rule is as summarized above; (2) in the case, before us the controversy is immaterial.

. . . [Dickinson] suggests the following provision, in Harvard Research (p. 653) for which he is responsible, as part of the "Draft Convention on Jurisdiction with Respect to Crime":

> Article 16. Apprehension in Violation of International Law. In exercising jurisdiction under this Convention, no State shall prosecute or punish any person who has been brought within its territory or a place subject to its authority by recourse to measures in violation of international law or international convention *without first obtaining the consent of the State or States whose rights have been violated by such measures.* (Emphasis is ours.)

. . . He proposes this article *de lege ferenda* to ensure "an additional and highly desirable sanction for international law" (p. 624). . . .

50. . . . the question of the violation of international law by the manner in which the accused was brought into the territory of a country arises at the international level, namely, the relations between the two countries concerned alone, and must find its solution at such level. . . .

By the joint decision of the Governments of Argentina and Israel of August 3, 1960 . . . the country whose sovereignty was violated has waived its claims, including the claim for the return of the accused, and

---

action or against Kerr's trial. The U.S. Supreme Court ruled that Kerr's trial was not contrary to the U.S. constitution. For the view that the case involved no violation of Peruvian territorial sovereignty because the Chilean military authorities were competent, in the situation prevailing at the time, to surrender Kerr, see Fairman (1953) 47 A.J.I.L. 678.

[68] *Ed.* See, *e.g.* (after the *Eichmann* case) the decision of the French Court of Cassation (Criminal Chamber) in *Re Argoud* (1964) 45 I.L.R. 90. The accused, a French national, who had been sentenced to death *in absentia* by a French military court for his part in insurrectionist activities and against whom a warrant for arrest was outstanding in respect of subsequent similar conduct, was arrested in Paris after being found there, bound and gagged, following a "tip off". He had been abducted in Munich and brought to Paris by persons who, for the purposes of argument, were taken to be French agents. After noting that the Federal Republic of Germany would have a claim to reparation and that no such claim had been presented, the Court ruled that the illegality of the accused's abduction did not rob it of jurisdiction.

any violation of international law which might have been involved in the "incident" in question has been "cured." According to the principles of international law no doubt can therefore be cast on the jurisdiction of Israel to bring the accused to trial after August 3, 1960. After that date, no cause remained, in respect of a violation of international law, which could have served to support a plea against his trial in Israel.

Notes
1. *Protective principle.* The Harvard Research found that most, if not all, states used this principle to a greater or lesser extent. Great Britain and the United States used it less than most other states.[69] The Commentary to the Harvard Research Draft Convention suggested that use of the protective principle was justifiable as a basis for jurisdiction because of "the inadequacy of most national legislation punishing offences committed within the territory against the security, integrity and independence of foreign states."[70] It also stated:

> In view of the fact that an overwhelming majority of States have enacted such legislation, [*i.e.* legislation relying on the protective principle], it is hardly possible to conclude that such legislation is necessarily in excess of competence as recognised by contemporary international law.[71]

An example of the general acceptance of the protective principle is found in the doctrine of the contiguous zone.[72] Would the principle allow State A to exercise criminal jurisdiction over the officials of State B in respect of their actions in the execution of an unfriendly policy (*e.g.* a trade embargo) of State B towards State A?[73] Who has the final word as to the danger to a state's security, etc.? The state concerned?

2. Was Israel justified in relying on the protective principle to prosecute the accused in the *Eichmann* case for acts committed *before* Israel came into being?[74]

3. *Universality principle.*[75] In addition to *piracy,*[76] the Harvard Research Draft Convention proposes jurisdiction just on the basis of custody in the following situations:

> Article 10:
> (a) When committed in a place not subject to its authority but subject to the authority of another state, if the act or omission which constitutes the crime is also an offence by the law of the place where it was committed, if surrender of the alien for prosecution has been offered to such other state or states and the offer remains unaccepted, and if prosecution is not barred by lapse of time under the law of the place where the crime was committed. The penalty imposed shall in no case be more severe than the penalty prescribed for the

---

[69] For its use in U.K. law, see, *e.g.* the *Joyce* case, above, p. 283; *Molvan v. Att.-Gen. for Palestine* [1948] A.C. 351, PC; the Merchant Shipping Act 1995, s. 137 (shipping casualties: oil pollution prevention powers); and the Criminal Jurisdiction Act 1975 (giving Northern Irish courts jurisdiction over listed offences committed in Ireland across the border).

[70] (1935) 29 A.J.I.L. Supp. 552.

[71] *ibid.* p. 556.

[72] See below, p. 433.

[73] *cf.* Greig, *International Law* (2nd ed., 1976), p. 389.

[74] See (1935) 29 A.J.I.L. Supp. 558.

[75] See Randall (1988) 66 Texas L.R. 785.

[76] See below, p. 432. Piracy remains a real problem in some areas, particularly in South East Asia, South America and East and West Africa.

same act or omission by the law of the place where the crime was committed.

(*b*) When committed in a place not subject to the authority of any state,[77] if the act or omission which constitutes the crime is also an offence by the law of a state of which the alien is a national, if surrender of the alien for prosecution has been offered to the state or states of which he is a national and the offer remains unaccepted, and if prosecution is not barred by lapse of time under the law of a state of which the alien is a national. The penalty imposed shall in no case be more severe than the penalty prescribed for the same act or omission by the law of a state of which the alien is a national.

(*c*) When committed in a place not subject to the authority of any state, if the crime was committed to the injury of the state assuming jurisdiction, or of one of its nationals, or of a corporation or juristic person having its national character.

(*d*) When committed in a place not subject to the authority of any state and the alien is not a national of any state.

The Commentary to the Convention justifies this Article as being necessary to prevent offenders escaping punishment. The Commentary cites the adoption, in some form, of the rule in Article 10(*a*) by a number of states; it could find very little evidence of legislative claims to jurisdictional competence founded upon Article 10(*b*)–(*d*). Does Article 6 of the Turkish Penal Code[78] adopt in part the approach used in Article 10?

On universality jurisdiction in respect of *war crimes*, the *British Manual of Military Law*[79] reads:

> War crimes are crimes *ex jure gentium* and thus triable by the courts of all States. . . . British military courts have jurisdiction outside the United Kingdom over war crimes committed . . . by . . . persons of any nationality. . . . It is not necessary that the victim of the war crime should be a British subject.[80]

The United Nations War Crimes Commission[81] stated:

> . . . the right to punish war crimes . . . is possessed by any independent State whatsoever, just as is the right to punish the offence of piracy.

Is the analogy with piracy a sound one?[82]

Each of the four 1949 Geneva Red Cross Conventions[83] contains the following provision on jurisdiction:

> The High Contracting Parties undertake to enact any legislation necessary to provide effective penal sanctions for persons committing, or ordering to be committed, any of the grave breaches of the present Convention defined in the following Article.
>
> Each High Contracting Party shall be under the obligation to search for persons alleged to have committed, or to have ordered to be committed, such grave breaches and shall bring such persons, regardless of their nationality, before their own courts. . . .

---

[77] *Ed.*, *e.g.* outer space, the high seas (other than on a ship flying the flag of a state), an unoccupied island.

[78] Above, p. 271, n. 17.

[79] Part III, 1958, para. 637.

[80] On war crimes, see Woetzel, *op. cit.*, p. 141, n. 46, above, and below, p. 738.

[81] (1949) 15 *War Crimes Reports* 26.

[82] See Carnegie (1963) 39 B.Y.I.L. 402 at 421.

[83] U.K.T.S. 39 (1958), Cmnd. 550; 75 U.N.T.S. 3.

Each High Contracting Party shall take measures necessary for the suppression of all acts contrary to the provisions of the present Convention other than the grave breaches defined in the following Article.[84]

Universality jurisdiction has also been provided[85] in a number of treaties on matters of general international concern, including drug-trafficking,[86] hi-jacking[87] and the sabotage of aircraft,[88] apartheid,[89] and attacks upon diplomats,[90] the taking of hostages[91] and torture.[92] It is not clear whether any of them state rules of customary international law.

4. In *Yunis v. Yunis*,[93] the defendant and others hijacked a Jordanian airliner at Beirut Airport, with two U.S. nationals and other passengers on board, ultimately blowing it up there. The defendant was arrested by FBI agents on board a yacht in international waters in the Mediterranean. He was convicted in a U.S. court of, *inter alia*, hostage-taking and air piracy and sentenced to 30 years imprisonment. On appeal, it was held that the U.S. courts had jurisdiction under the unambiguous wording of the Hostage Taking Act and Anti-Hijacking Act and that the terms of these statutes prevailed over any customary international law jurisdictional rules to the contrary. The Court of Appeals stated:

Nor is jurisdiction [under the Hostage Taking Act] precluded by norms of customary international law. The district court concluded that two jurisdictional theories of international law, the "universal principle" and the "passive personal principle," supported assertion of U.S. jurisdiction to prosecute Yunis on hijacking and hostage-taking charges.... Under the universal principle, states may prescribe and prosecute "certain offenses recognized by the community of nations as of universal concern, such as piracy, slave trade, attacks on or hijacking of aircraft, genocide, war crimes, and perhaps certain acts of terrorism," even absent any special connection between the state and the offense. *See* RESTATEMENT (THIRD) OF THE FOREIGN RELATIONS LAW OF THE UNITED STATES §§ 404, 423 (1987) ... Under the passive personal principle, a state may punish non-nationals for crimes committed against its nationals outside of its territory, at least where the state has a particularly strong interest in the crime. See ... *United States v. Benitez*, 741 F.2d 1312, 1316 (11th Cir. 1984) (passive personal principle invoked to approve prosecution of Colombian

---

[84] See, *e.g.* Art. 49, Convention I. "Grave offences" include such offences as "extensive destruction and appropriation of property, not justified by military necessity and carried out unlawfully and wantonly" where directed against persons protected by the Conventions concerned: see, *e.g.* Art. 50, Convention I.

[85] But see Bowett, *loc.cit.*, p. 264, n. 1, above, p. 12.

[86] Single Convention on Narcotic Drugs 1961, Art. 36(2)(iv), U.K.T.S. 34 (1965), Cmnd. 2354; 520 U.N.T.S. 204. See Lord Wilberforce in *D.P.P. v. Doot*, above, p. 278. See also the 1988 Convention against Illicit Traffic in Narcotic Drugs, Art. 4(2)(*b*), Misc. 14 (1989), Cm. 804.

[87] Hague Convention for the Suppression of Unlawful Seizure of Aircraft 1970, Art. 4, below, p. 296.

[88] Montreal Convention for the Suppression of Unlawful Acts against the Safety of Civil Aviation 1971, Art. 5, below, p. 302.

[89] Convention on the Suppression and Punishment of the Crime of Apartheid 1973, Art. II–IV, *loc. cit.*, p. 630, n. 41, below.

[90] Convention on the Prevention and Punishment of Crimes against Internationally Protected Persons including Diplomats 1973, Art. 2, *loc. cit.*, p. 546, below.

[91] 1979 International Convention against the Taking of Hostages, Art. 5, *loc. cit.*, p. 300, n. 30, below.

[92] 1984 UN Torture Convention, Art. 5(2), below, p. 711.

[93] (1991) 30 I.L.M. 403, U.S. Ct App. D.C. Circuit.

citizen convicted of shooting U.S. drug agents in Colombia), *cert. denied*, 471 U.S. 1137 (1985).

Relying primarily on the RESTATEMENT, Yunis argues that hostage-taking has not been recognized as a universal crime and that the passive personal principle authorizes assertion of jurisdiction over alleged hostage-takers only where the victims were seized because they were nationals of the prosecuting state. Whatever merit appellant's claims may have as a matter of international law, they cannot prevail before this court . . . Our duty is to enforce the Constitution, and treaties of the United States, not to conform the law of the land to norms of customary international law. . . .

To be sure, courts should hesitate to give penal statutes extraterritorial effect absent a clear congressional directive . . . Similarly, courts will not blind themselves to potential violations of international law where legislative intent is ambiguous. . . . But the statute in question reflects an unmistakable congressional intent, consistent with treaty obligations of the United States, to authorize prosecution of those who take Americans hostage abroad no matter where the offense occurs or where the offender is found. . . .

The Anti-hijacking Act provides for criminal punishment of persons who hijack aircraft operating wholly outside the "special aircraft jurisdiction" of the United States, provided that the hijacker is later "found in the United States." . . .

The district court correctly found that international law does not restrict this statutory jurisdiction to try Yunis on charges of air piracy. . . . Aircraft hijacking may well be one of the few crimes so clearly condemned under the law of nations that states may assert universal jurisdiction to bring offenders to justice, even when the state has no territorial connection to the hijacking and its citizens are not involved. . . . But in any event we are satisfied that the Anti-hijacking Act authorizes assertion of federal jurisdiction to try Yunis regardless of hijacking's status vel non as a universal crime. . . .

5. On the "linking point" doctrine of jurisdiction (see para. 31, Eichmann judgment), note the following suggestion by Mann,[94] who was considering both civil and criminal jurisdiction:

The conclusion, then, is that a State has (legislative) jurisdiction, if its contact with a given set of facts is so close, so substantial, so direct, so weighty, that legislation in respect of them is in harmony with international law and its various aspects (including the practice of States, the principles of non-interference and reciprocity and the demands of inter-dependence). A merely political, economic, commercial or social interest does not in itself constitute a sufficient connection. Whether another State has an equally close or a closer, or perhaps the closest, contact, is not necessarily an irrelevant question, but cannot be decisive where the probability of concurrent jurisdiction is conceded. . . .

It may be said that the test advocated in these pages would substitute vagueness for certainty. This would be formidable criticism if the principles of jurisdiction in fact were at present defined with certainty. . . .

Finally, from the point of view of the progressive evolution of international law it would no doubt be desirable if the principle of exclusivity would come to be accepted for the purpose of jurisdiction, if, in other words, by common consent jurisdiction in respect of a given set of acts were exercised by one State only. Such a development cannot even begin while the doctrine of jurisdiction is embedded in the procrustean law of territoriality. It is, however, likely to be

[94] *loc cit.*, p. 264, n. 1, above, pp. 49–51.

promoted by a doctrine which bases jurisdiction upon closeness of connection.

6. *A fair trial.* It is clear that Eichmann was given a scrupulously fair hearing. Might it nonetheless be argued that, in terms of justice not only being done but being seen to be done, a court other than an Israeli court should have tried Eichmann?[95]

7. *Illegally obtained custody.*[96] In the *Savarkar Case,*[97] an Indian who was being returned to India from Great Britain under the Fugitive Offenders Act 1881 escaped and swam ashore in Marseilles harbour. A French policeman arrested him and handed him over to the British policeman who had come ashore in pursuit. Although the French police in Marseilles had been informed of the presence of Savarkar on board, the French policeman who made the arrest thought that he was handing back a member of the crew who had committed an offence on board. France alleged a violation of its territorial sovereignty and asked for the return of Savarkar to it as restitution. The Permanent Court of Arbitration decided in favour of Great Britain for the following reasons:

> ... it is manifest that the case is not one of recourse to fraud or force in order to obtain possession of a person who had taken refuge in foreign territory, and that there was not, in the circumstances of the arrest and delivery of Savarkar to the British authorities and of his removal to India, anything in the nature of a violation of the sovereignty of France, and that all those who took part in the matter certainly acted in good faith and had no thought of doing anything unlawful ... while admitting that an irregularity was committed by the arrest of Savarkar and by his being handed over to the British police, there is no rule of international law imposing, in circumstances such as those which have been set out above, any obligation on the Power which has in its custody a prisoner, to restore him because of a mistake committed by the foreign agent who delivered him up to that Power.[98]

In the *Lawler Incident,*[99] in 1860, a convict escaped from prison in Gibraltar. He was arrested by a British warder across the border in Spain and taken back to Gibraltar without Spanish consent. The British Law Officers advised:

> A plain breach of international law having occurred, we deem it to be the duty of the State, into whose territory the individual, thus wrongfully deported, was conveyed, to restore the aggrieved State, upon its request to that effect, as far as possible, to its original position.[1]

Fawcett[2] suggests the following limitation upon the duty to return:

> ... it might perhaps be said, in the case of irregular capture and removal for trial of a criminal *jure gentium,* that the State, from which he is taken, may only demand his reconduction if two conditions are satisfied: that that State is the

---

[95] It would seem that one state with territorial jurisdiction, Poland, offered to try Eichmann: Fawcett, *loc. cit.,* p. 280, n. 48, above p. 206.

[96] See Cardozo (1961) 55 A.J.I.L. 127; Evans (1964) 40 B.Y.I.L. 77; O'Higgins (1960) 36 B.Y.I.L. 279.

[97] *France v. G.B.* Scott, Hague Court Reports, p. 275 (1911).

[98] *ibid.* p. 279.

[99] 1 McNair 78.

[1] *ibid.* For an incident in which Canada protested at the kidnapping in Toronto and return to Florida of a fugitive suspect, extradition not having been requested, see (1984) 78 A.J.I.L. 207.

[2] Fawcett, *loc. cit.,* p. 280, n. 48, above, pp. 199–200.

forum conveniens for his trial, and that it declares an intention to put him on trial. If these conditions are not satisfied, then the State must accept reparation in another form, since otherwise the interest of justice would be defeated.

The same author[3] also points out that in the *Corfu Channel Case*,[4] the International Court of Justice allowed evidence to be introduced, and subsequently relied upon that evidence in its judgment, that had been obtained by a British minesweeping exercise which the Court had ruled to be a violation of Albanian territorial sovereignty.

The Jerusalem court cited *ex p. Elliott* as an authority for the proposition that it could exercise jurisdiction over Eichmann although he had been illegally abducted from Argentina. There were a number of inconsistent decisions on this point after the *Elliott* case, but the law has now to an extent been clarified by *R. v. Horseferry Road Magistrates Court, ex p. Bennett*,[5] which reaches the opposite conclusion to that in the *Elliott* case. In the *Bennett* case, a New Zealand national who was wanted for fraud offences committed in England was located in South Africa. After consulting with the Crown Prosecution Service, the English police decided not to seek his extradition under the Extradition Act 1989. However, the defendant was arrested by the South African police and deported to New Zealand, via Taipei. On arrival at Taipei, he was arrested by South African police and flown back to Johannesburg. There he was put, handcuffed, on a plane to Heathrow, where he was arrested and brought to trial. On the question of illegal abduction, Lord Griffiths stated:

> In the present case there is no suggestion that the appellant cannot have a fair trial, nor could it be suggested that it would have been unfair to try him if he had been returned to this country through extradition procedures. If the court is to have the power to interfere with the prosecution in the present circumstances it must be because the judiciary accept a responsibility for the maintenance of the rule of law that embraces a willingness to oversee executive action and to refuse to countenance behaviour that threatens either basic human rights or the rule of law.
>
> My Lords, I have no doubt that the judiciary should accept this responsibility in the field of criminal law. . . . if it comes to the attention of the court that there has been a serious abuse of power it should, in my view, express its disapproval by refusing to act upon it.
>
> . . . Extradition procedures are designed not only to ensure that criminals are returned from one country to another but also to protect the rights of those who are accused of crimes by the requesting country. Thus sufficient evidence has to be produced to show a prima facie case against the accused and the rule of speciality protects the accused from being tried for any crime other than that for which he was extradited. If a practice developed in which the police or prosecuting authorities of this country ignored extradition procedures and secured the return of an accused by a mere request to police colleagues in another country they would be flouting the extradition procedures and depriving the accused of the safeguards built into the extradition process for his benefit. It is to my mind unthinkable that in such circumstances the court should declare itself to be powerless and stand idly by . . .
>
> The courts, of course, have no power to apply direct discipline to the police or the prosecuting authorities, but they can refuse to allow them to take advantage of abuse of power by regarding their behaviour as an abuse of process and thus preventing a prosecution.

[3] *ibid*. p. 201.
[4] Below, p. 391.
[5] [1994] 1 A.C. 42, HL. See Wedgwood (1995) 89 A.J.I.L. 142.

In my view your Lordships should now declare that where process of law is available to return an accused to this country through extradition procedures our courts will refuse to try him if he has been forcibly brought within our jurisdiction in disregard of those procedures by a process to which our own police, prosecuting or other executive authorities have been a knowing party.

If extradition is not available very different considerations will arise on which I express no opinion.

As was pointed out by Lord Oliver, dissenting, the defendant had a civil remedy in respect of his abduction. Note also that, in contrast with the *Eichmann* case, the territorial sovereignty of South Africa, which allegedly colluded rather than protested, was not violated. Should it matter that the offence is one that concerns the security of the state, as in the *Eichmann* case, rather than the enforcement of the ordinary criminal law? Might the *Bennett* approach be the only way of preventing abductions or collusion by state agents?[6]

Approaches in other states vary. In the *Bennett* case, the House of Lords had before it decisions from New Zealand[7] and South African[8] courts ruling against the exercise of jurisdiction in cases of abduction. In contrast, in *U.S. v. Alvarez-Machain*,[9] a Mexican national had been abducted to the U.S. from Mexico by U.S. Drug Enforcement Administration agents to face a charge of murdering another agent of the Administration. Mexico requested his return for trial. Although recognising the abduction as "shocking", the U.S. Supreme Court held that the exercise of criminal jurisdiction in the U.S. was not unconstitutional since there had been no breach of the U.S.-Mexican extradition treaty (which did not prohibit abductions).[10]

3. Hijacking and Sabotage of Aircraft[11]

Note

When hijacking[12] and aircraft sabotage became a problem in the 1960s, it was soon realised that the customary international law rules on criminal jurisdiction did not give states wide enough jurisdiction to deal with offenders and that

---

[6] For other examples of successful abductions, see those by Israel of Mordechai Vanunu (1986) (abducted and convicted for revealing Israeli nuclear secrets) and by France of the terrorist "Carlos the Jackal" (1994) (kidnapped on the street in Sudan for terrorist offences in France).

[7] *R v. Hartley* [1978] 2 N.Z.L.R. 199 (Australian police put him on plane to face murder charge after telephone call from the New Zealand police).

[8] *S. v. Ebrahim*, 1991 (2) S.A. 553, S. African Ct. App. (abduction from Swaziland by South African agents to face treason trial).

[9] (1992) 119 L.Ed. 2d 441. Illegal abduction was also held irrelevant in the *Yunis* case, above, p. 290. In the *Bennett* case, Lord Griffiths distinguished the *Alvarez* case on the ground that it ruled on the question whether criminal jurisdiction, whereas *Bennett* was about the exercise of judicial discretion not to take a case where jurisdiction existed. On the U.S. case law, see Nadelmann (1993) 25 N.Y.U.J.I.P. 813 and Teson (1994) 31 Col.J.T.L. 551.

[10] The *Kerr Case*, above, p. 286, n. 67, was followed.

[11] See, from a large literature, Agrawala, *Aircraft Hijacking and International Law* (1973), Akehurst (1974) 14 Ind. J.I.L. 81; Joyner, *Aerial Hijacking as an International Crime* (1974); McWhinney, ed., *Aerial Piracy and International Law* (1971); Poulantzas (1971) 18 N.I.L.R. 25; Shubber (1968–69) 43 B.Y.I.L. 193; *ibid.* (1973) 22 I.C.L.Q. 687; and White (1971) 6 Rev. I.C.J. 38.

[12] The term "hijacking" comes from the call—"Hi Jack"—used when illegal liquor was seized from bootleggers during prohibition in the U.S.

extradition arrangements were inadequate.[13] The 1963 Tokyo Convention on Offences aboard Aircraft,[14] which is concerned with the long-standing problem of jurisdiction over all crimes aboard aircraft, made some modest improvements. Since then, hijacking and aircraft sabotage have become so urgent a problem that states have taken the time to agree in the 1970 Hague and 1971 Montreal Conventions (below) to more effective, tailor-made rules. Even so, the "political offence" side of most[15] hijackings, as well as the usual considerations of state sovereignty, have prevented the adoption of rules imposing an obligation to exercise jurisdiction in any particular case or to extradite the offender.[16]

HAGUE CONVENTION FOR THE SUPPRESSION OF UNLAWFUL SEIZURE OF AIRCRAFT 1970[17]

U.K.T.S. 39 (1972), Cmnd. 4956; 860 U.N.T.S. 105; (1971) 10 I.L.M. 133

Article 1

Any person who on board an aircraft in flight:

(a) unlawfully, by force or threat thereof, or by any other form of intimidation, seizes, or exercises control of, that aircraft, or attempts to perform any such act, or

(b) is an accomplice of a person who performs or attempts to perform any such act

commits an offence (hereafter referred to as "the offence").

Article 2

Each Contracting State undertakes to make the offence punishable by severe penalties.

Article 3

1. For the purposes of this Convention, an aircraft is considered to be in flight at any time from the moment when all its external doors are closed following embarkation until the moment when any such door is opened for disembarkation. In the case of a forced landing, the flight shall be

---

[13] There is no obligation to extradite in customary international law and most states will not extradite in the absence of bilateral or multilateral extradition treaty obligations governing the case. Extradition treaties normally prohibit the return of political offenders, *i.e.* offenders who commit an offence for a political purpose or who are sought for political reasons (although the definition of a political offence is a matter of debate).

[14] U.K.T.S. 126 (1969), Cmnd. 4230; 704 U.N.T.S. 219. In force 1969. 147 parties including the U.K.

[15] Some hijackings, of course, are purely criminal or crackpot activities.

[16] See, however, the 1977 European Convention on the Suppression of Terrorism, *loc. cit.*, p. 299, n. 23, below.

[17] In force 1971. 151 parties, including the U.K. Hijacking is made an offence in U.K. law by the Hijacking Act 1971.

deemed to continue until the competent authorities take over the responsibility for the aircraft and for persons and property on board.

2. This Convention shall not apply to aircraft used in military, customs or police services.

3. This Convention shall apply only if the place of take-off or the place of actual landing of the aircraft on board which the offence is committed is situated outside the territory of the State other than the State of registration of that aircraft; it shall be immaterial whether the aircraft is engaged in an international or domestic flight. . . .

5. Notwithstanding paragraphs 3 and 4 of this Article, Articles 6, 7, 8 and 10 shall apply whatever the place of take-off or the place of actual landing of the aircraft, if the offender or the alleged offender is found in the territory of a State other than the State of registration of that aircraft.

Article 4

1. Each Contracting State shall take such measures as may be necessary to establish its jurisdiction over the offence and any other act of violence against passengers or crew committed by the alleged offender in connection with the offence, in the following cases:

- (*a*) when the offence is committed on board an aircraft registered in that State;
- (*b*) when the aircraft on board which the offence is committed lands in its territory with the alleged offender still on board;
- (*c*) when the offence is committed on board an aircraft leased without crew to a lessee who has his principal place of business or, if the lessee has no such place of business, his permanent residence, in that State.

2. Each Contracting State shall likewise take such measures as may be necessary to establish its jurisdiction over the offence in the case where the alleged offender is present in its territory and it does not extradite him pursuant to Article 8 to any of the States mentioned in paragraph 1 of this Article.

3. This Convention does not exclude any criminal jurisdiction exercised in accordance with national law.

Article 6

1. Upon being satisfied that the circumstances so warrant, any Contracting State in the territory of which the offender or the alleged offender is present, shall take him into custody or take other measures to ensure his presence. The custody and other measures shall be as provided in the law of that State but may only be continued for such time as is necessary to enable any criminal or extradition proceedings to be instituted.

2. Such State shall immediately make a preliminary enquiry into the facts.

3. Any person in custody pursuant to paragraph 1 of this Article shall be assisted in communicating immediately with the nearest appropriate representative of the State of which he is a national.

4. When a State, pursuant to this Article, has taken a person into custody, it shall immediately notify the State of registration of the aircraft, the State mentioned in Article 4, paragraph 1(c), the State of nationality of the detained person and, if it considers it advisable, any other interested States of the fact that such person is in custody and of the circumstances which warrant his detention. The State which makes the preliminary enquiry contemplated in paragraph 2 of this Article shall promptly report its findings to the said State and shall indicate whether it intends to exercise jurisdiction.

Article 7

The Contracting State in the territory of which the alleged offender is found shall, if it does not extradite him, be obliged, without exception whatsoever and whether or not the offence was committed in its territory, to submit the case to its competent authorities for the purpose of prosecution.

Those authorities shall take their decision in the same manner as in the case of any ordinary offence of a serious nature under the law of that State.

Article 8

1. The offence shall be deemed to be included as an extraditable offence in any extradition treaty existing between Contracting States. Contracting States undertake to include the offence as an extraditable offence in every extradition treaty to be concluded between them.

2. If a Contracting State which makes extradition conditional on the existence of a treaty receives a request for extradition from another Contracting State with which it has no extradition treaty, it may at its option consider this Convention as the legal basis for extradition in respect of the offence. Extradition shall be subject to the other conditions provided by the law of the requested State.

3. Contracting States which do not make extradition conditional on the existence of a treaty shall recognize the offence as an extraditable offence between themselves subject to the conditions provided by the law of the requested State.

4. The offence shall be treated, for the purpose of extradition between Contracting States, as if it had been committed not only in the place in

which it occurred but also in the territories of the States required to establish their jurisdiction in accordance with Article 4, paragraph 1.

Article 9

1. When any of the acts mentioned in Article 1(a) has occurred or is about to occur, Contracting States shall take all appropriate measures to restore control of the aircraft to its lawful commander or to preserve his control of the aircraft.

2. In the cases contemplated by the preceding paragraph, any Contracting State in which the aircraft or its passengers or crew are present shall facilitate the continuation of the journey of the passengers and crew as soon as practicable, and shall without delay return the aircraft and its cargo to the persons lawfully entitled to possession.

Notes

1. Article 1 indicates the "offence" which contracting parties must make a part of their law to comply with the establishment of jurisdiction requirement in Article 4. Prior to the Convention, few states had a separate offence of hijacking; hijackers could only be prosecuted for assault, *etc*. It was understood during the drafting of Article 1 that the "aircraft" hijacked need not be registered in a contracting party for the Convention to apply.[18] The "severe penalties" requirement of Article 2 was introduced when agreement on a minimum sentence proved impossible.[19] The definition of "in flight" in Article 3 is wider and easier to apply than that in the Tokyo Convention. Article 4 requires a state to "establish its jurisdiction" (*i.e.* create the offence of hijacking in its criminal law, *etc*.), but not actually to exercise it. Articles 6 and 7 indicate all that a state has to do in a particular case. "Any other act of violence" in Article 4 would include assault or a killing. There is no order of priority among the grounds for jurisdiction listed in Article 4(1). The third (Article 4(1)(*c*)) was added to meet the "dry leasing" situation, where an aircraft is leased without its crew and where, therefore, the state of registration may have less interest in prosecuting than it normally does.[20] Note the use and extension (beyond nationality) of the passive personality principle in Article 4(1)(*c*).[21] Article 4(2) establishes "universality" jurisdiction for hijacking (but not associated acts of violence) as a "safety net" to catch the person who escapes from, or is allowed to leave, a state with jurisdiction under Article 4(1). In particular, it has to take the person into custody and investigate the matter (Article 6) and then either prosecute, if it would normally do so under its law, or extradite the suspect in accordance with the rules in Article 8 (Article 7).[22] Article 8 makes hijacking an extraditable offence in present and future extradition treaties and practice between contracting parties but does not create an obligation to extradite which does not otherwise exist in such treaties and practice. Thus if hijacking is inserted by Article 8(1) into an existing extradition treaty that (as is

[18] Shubber (1973) 22 I.C.L.Q. 701.
[19] The U.K. Hijacking Act 1971 imposes a life sentence. The U.S. Anti-Hijacking Act 1974 carries a death or life imprisonment sentence where death results from hijacking and a 20-year sentence otherwise.
[20] White, *loc. cit.*, p. 294, n. 11, above, p. 40.
[21] *cf.* Art. 4, Tokyo Convention.
[22] On the duty to extradite or prosecute, see Bassiouni and Wise, *Aut Dedere aut Judicare: The Duty to Extradite or Prosecute in International Law* (1995).

common) allows a state to refuse extradition in the case of a "political offence" or where the offender is its national, the exception will apply to hijacking too.[23]

In 1978, in the Bonn Declaration on International Terrorism,[24] it was agreed that "in cases where a country refuses the extradition or prosecution of those who have hijacked an aircraft and/or does not return such aircraft," action would be taken to cease all flights to and from that country and its airlines.

2. *The Dawson's Field Hijacking.* The most ambitious hijacking to date was probably that in September 1970 when Palestinian arab guerrillas successfully hijacked three civil airliners and forced them to land at the Dawson's Field airstrip in Jordan. The airliners were registered in Switzerland, the United Kingdom and the United States and belonged to Swissair, B.O.A.C., and T.W.A. respectively. The passengers and crew numbered over 400 and were of diverse nationality. The airliners were blown up. The passengers and crew were released in stages after detention for some time, in return for the release of a number of Palestinian arab guerrillas (including Leila Khaled) held by the police in London. The hijackers went their separate ways into various countries. Supposing the states involved were parties to the Hague Convention, which of them would have jurisdiction to arrest and punish the hijackers if the incident were to occur now? Would the Convention apply retroactively to grant jurisdiction now over the incident when it actually occurred?[25]

Another (in)famous hijacking was that leading to the *Entebbe Incident.*[26] Did Uganda have jurisdiction under the Convention there?[27] Supposing it had an extradition treaty with Israel (which was, and is, not the case), would Uganda have been obliged to return the hijackers?

3. Hijacking of aircraft was condemned in 1970 shortly after Dawson's Field by a General Assembly Resolution[28]:

> The General Assembly, . . . recognizing that such acts jeopardize the lives and safety of the passengers and crew and constitute a violation of their human rights, . . .
>
> 1. *Condemns,* without exception whatsoever, all acts of aerial hijacking or other interference with civil air travel, whether originally national or international, through the threat or use of force, and all acts of violence which may be directed against passengers, crew and aircraft engaged in, and air navigation facilities and aeronautical communications used by, civil air transport;
>
> 2. *Calls upon States* to take all appropriate measures to deter, prevent or suppress such acts within their jurisdiction, at every stage of the execution of those acts, and to provide for the prosecution and punishment of persons who perpetrate such acts, in a manner commensurate with the gravity of those crimes, or, without prejudice to the rights and obligations of States under

---

[23] See, however, the 1977 European Convention on the Suppression of Terrorism, U.K.T.S. 93 (1978), Cmnd. 7390; 1137 U.N.T.S. 93. In force 1978. 29 parties, including the U.K. The Convention provides that defined terrorist activities shall not be regarded as political offences so as to prevent extradition. The Suppression of Terrorism Act 1978 brings U.K. extradition law into line with the Convention.

[24] (1978) 17 I.L.M. 1285; U.K.M.I.L. 1978; (1978) 49 B.Y.I.L. 423. The states agreeing to do this were Canada, France, the F.R.G., Italy, Japan, the U.K. and the U.S. On the "soft law" status of the Declaration, see above, p. 65.

[25] On the retroactive operation of treaties, see below, p. 765.

[26] See below, p. 909.

[27] Both Israel and Uganda were parties.

[28] G.A. Resn. 2645, G.A.O.R., 25th Sess, Supp. 28, p. 126; (1970) 9 I.L.M. 1288. The resolution was adopted by 105 votes to 0, with 8 abstentions. See also S.C.Resn. 286, S.C.O.R., 25th Year, (1970) *Resolutions and Decisions,* p. 16.

existing international instruments relating to the matter, for the extradition of such persons for the purpose of their prosecution and punishment;

3. *Declares* that the exploitation of unlawful seizure of aircraft for the purpose of taking hostages is to be condemned;

4. *Declares further* that the unlawful detention of passengers and crew in transit or otherwise engaged in civil air travel is to be condemned as another form of wrongful interference with free and uninterrupted air travel;

5. *Urges* States to the territory of which a hijacked aircraft is diverted to provide for the care and safety of its passengers and crew and to enable them to continue their journey as soon as practicable and to return the aircraft and its cargo to the persons lawfully entitled to possession.

Could it be argued that aerial hijacking has been placed by customary international law on the same footing as piracy on the high seas,[29] *i.e.* it is conduct in respect of which all states may exercise criminal jurisdiction under their law on a universality basis?

4. Similar rules as to jurisdiction have also been included in the 1979 International Convention against the Taking of Hostages,[30] which is aimed at a related form of international terrorism. The Convention offence of "hostage-taking", which each party must incorporate into its law, is defined in Article 1(1):

> Any person who seizes or detains and threatens to kill, to injure or to continue to detain another person . . . in order to compel a third party, namely, a State, an international intergovernmental organization, a natural or juridical person, or a group of persons, to do or abstain from doing any act as an explicit or implicit condition for the release of the hostage commits the offence of taking of hostages . . . within the meaning of this Convention.

Parties must either consider the prosecution of offenders found within their territory or extradite them.

MONTREAL CONVENTION FOR THE SUPPRESSION OF UNLAWFUL ACTS AGAINST THE SAFETY OF CIVIL AVIATION 1971[31]

U.K.T.S. 10 (1974), Cmnd. 5524; (1971) 10 I.L.M. 1151

Article 1

1. Any person commits an offence if he unlawfully and intentionally:

(a) performs an act of violence against a person on board an aircraft in flight if that act is likely to endanger the safety of that aircraft; or

(b) destroys an aircraft in service or causes damage to such an aircraft which renders it incapable of flight or which is likely to endanger its safety in flight; or

---

[29] See below, p. 432.

[30] U.K.T.S. 81 (1983), Cmnd. 9100; (1979) 18 I.L.M. 1456. In force 1983. 78 contracting parties, including the U.K. The U.K. Taking of Hostages Act 1982 gives effect to it. On the Convention, see Shubber (1981) 52 B.Y.I.L. 205. See also the 1973 Convention on the Prevention and Punishment of Crimes against Internationally Protected Persons, below, p. 546.

[31] In force 1973. 151 parties, including the U.K. The U.K. Protection of Aircraft Act 1973 gives effect to it.

(*c*) places or causes to be placed on an aircraft in service, by any means whatsoever, a device or substance which is likely to destroy that aircraft, or to cause damage to it which renders it incapable of flight, or to cause damage to it which is likely to endanger its safety in flight; or

(*d*) destroys or damages air navigation facilities or interferes with their operation, if any such act is likely to endanger the safety of aircraft in flight; or

(*e*) communicates information which he knows to be false, thereby endangering the safety of an aircraft in flight.

[1 *bis*. Any person commits an offence if he unlawfully and intentionally, using any device, substance or weapon:

(*a*) performs an act of violence against a person at an airport serving international civil aviation which causes or is likely to cause serious injury or death; or

(*b*) destroys or seriously damages the facilities of an airport serving international civil aviation or aircraft not in service located thereon or disrupts the services of the airport,

if such an act endangers or is likely to endanger safety at that airport.]
2. Any person also commits an offence if he:

(*a*) attempts to commit any of the offences mentioned in paragraph 1 [or paragraph 1 *bis*] of this Article; or

(*b*) is an accomplice of a person who commits or attempts to commit any such offence.

Article 2

For the purposes of this Convention:

(*a*) an aircraft is considered to be in flight at any time from the moment when all its external doors are closed following embarkation until the moment when any such door is opened for disembarkation; in the case of a forced landing, the flight shall be deemed to continue until the competent authorities take over the responsibility for the aircraft and for persons and property on board;

(*b*) an aircraft is considered to be in service from the beginning of the preflight preparation of the aircraft by ground personnel or by the crew for a specific flight until twenty-four hours after any landing; the period of service shall, in any event, extend for the entire period during which the aircraft is in flight as defined in paragraph (a) of this Article.

Article 3

Each Contracting State undertakes to make the offences mentioned in Article 1 punishable by severe penalties.

Article 4

1. This Convention shall not apply to aircraft used in military, customs or police services.

2. In the cases contemplated in subparagraphs (a), (b), (c) and (e) of paragraph 1 of Article 1, this Convention shall apply, irrespective of whether the aircraft is engaged in an international or domestic flight, only if:

(*a*) the place of take-off or landing, actual or intended, of the aircraft is situated outside the territory of the State of registration of that aircraft; or

(*b*) the offence is committed in the territory of a State other than the State of registration of the aircraft.

3. Notwithstanding paragraph 2 of this Article, in the cases contemplated in subparagraphs (a), (b), (c) and (e) of paragraph 1 of Article 1, this Convention shall also apply if the offender or the alleged offender is found in the territory of a State other than the State of registration of the aircraft.

4. With respect to the States mentioned in Article 9 and in the cases mentioned in subparagraphs (a), (b), (c) and (e) of paragraph 1 of Article 1, this Convention shall not apply if the places referred to in subparagraph (a) of paragraph 2 of this Article are situated within the territory of the same State where that State is one of those referred to in Article 9, unless the offence is committed or the offender or alleged offender is found in the territory of a State other than that State.

5. In the cases contemplated in subparagraph (d) of paragraph 1 of Article 1, this Convention shall apply only if the air navigation facilities are used in international air navigation.

6. The provisions of paragraphs 2, 3, 4 and 5 of this Article shall also apply in the cases contemplated in paragraph 2 of Article 1.

Article 5

1. Each Contracting State shall take such measures as may be necessary to establish its jurisdiction over the offences in the following cases:

(*a*) when the offence is committed in the territory of that State;

(*b*) when the offence is committed against or on board an aircraft registered in that State;

(*c*) when the aircraft on board which the offence is committed lands in
its territory with the alleged offender still on board;

(*d*) when the offence is committed against or on board an aircraft leased
without crew to a lessee who has his principal place of business or,
if the lessee has no such place of business, his permanent residence,
in that State.

2. Each Contracting State shall likewise take such measures as may be
necessary to establish its jurisdiction over the offences mentioned in
Article 1, paragraph 1(a), (b) and (c), and in Article 1, paragraph 2, in so
far as that paragraph relates to those offences, in the case where the
alleged offender is present in its territory and it does not extradite him
pursuant to Article 8 to any of the States mentioned in paragraph 1 of this
Article.

[2 *bis* Each Contracting State shall likewise take such measures as may
be necessary to establish its jurisdiction over the offences mentioned in
Article 1, paragraph 1 *bis* and in Article 1, paragraph 2, in so far as that
paragraph relates to those offences, in the case where the alleged offender
is present in its territory and it does not extradite him pursuant to Article
8 to the State mentioned in paragraph 1(a) of this Article.]

3. This Convention does not exclude any criminal jurisdiction exercised in accordance with national law.

Article 6

1. Upon being satisfied that the circumstances so warrant, any Contracting State in the territory of which the offender or the alleged offender
is present, shall take him into custody or take other measures to ensure
his presence. The custody and other measures shall be as provided in the
law of that State but may only be continued for such time as is necessary
to enable any criminal or extradition proceedings to be instituted.

2. Such State shall immediately make a preliminary enquiry into the
facts.

3. Any person in custody pursuant to paragraph 1 of this Article shall
be assisted in communicating immediately with the nearest appropriate
representative of the State of which he is a national.

4. When a State, pursuant to this Article, has taken a person into
custody, it shall immediately notify the States mentioned in Article 5,
paragraph 1, the State of nationality of the detained person and, if it
considers it advisable, any other interested States of the fact that such
person is in custody and of the circumstances which warrant his detention. The State which makes the preliminary enquiry contemplated in

paragraph 2 of this Article shall promptly report its findings to the said States and shall indicate whether it intends to exercise jurisdiction.

Article 7

The Contracting State in the territory of which the alleged offender is found shall, if it does not extradite him, be obliged, without exception whatsoever and whether or not the offence was committed in its territory, to submit the case to its competent authorities for the purpose of prosecution. Those authorities shall take their decision in the same manner as in the case of any ordinary offence of a serious nature under the law of that State.

Article 8

1. The offences shall be deemed to be included as extraditable offences in any extradition treaty existing between Contracting States. Contracting States undertake to include the offences as extraditable offences in every extradition treaty to be concluded between them.

2. If a Contracting State which makes extradition conditional on the existence of a treaty receives a request for extradition from another Contracting State with which it has no extradition treaty, it may at its option consider this Convention as the legal basis for extradition in respect of the offences. Extradition shall be subject to the other conditions provided by the law of the requested State.

3. Contracting States which do not make extradition conditional on the existence of a treaty shall recognize the offences as extraditable offences between themselves subject to the conditions provided by the law of the requested State.

4. Each of the offences shall be treated, for the purpose of extradition between Contracting States, as if it has been committed not only in the place in which it occurred but also in the territories of the States required to establish their jurisdiction in accordance with Article 5, paragraph 1(b), (c) and (d).

Article 9

The Contracting States which establish joint air transport operating organizations or international operating agencies, which operate aircraft which are subject to joint or international registration shall, by appropriate means, designate for each aircraft the State among them which shall exercise the jurisdiction and have the attributes of the State of registration for the purpose of this Convention and shall give notice thereof to the International Civil Aviation Organization which shall communicate the notice to all States Parties to this Convention.

Article 10

1. Contracting States shall, in accordance with international and national law, endeavour to take all practicable measures for the purpose of preventing the offences mentioned in Article 1. . . .

Article 11

1. Contracting States shall afford one another the greatest measure of assistance in connection with criminal proceedings brought in respect of the offences. The law of the State requested shall apply in all cases.

2. The provisions of paragraph 1 of this Article shall not affect obligations under any other treaty, bilateral or multilateral, which governs or will govern, in whole or in part, mutual assistance in criminal matters.

Article 12

Any Contracting State having reason to believe that one of the offences mentioned in Article 1 will be committed shall, in accordance with its national law, furnish any relevant information in its possession to those States which it believes would be the States mentioned in Article 5, paragraph 1.

Article 14

1. Any dispute between two or more Contracting States concerning the interpretation or application of this Convention which cannot be settled through negotiation, shall, at the request of one of them, be submitted to arbitration. If within six months from the date of the request for arbitration the Parties are unable to agree on the organization of the arbitration, any one of those Parties may refer the dispute to the International Court of Justice by request in conformity with the Statute of the Court.

2. Each State may at the time of signature or ratification of this Convention or accession thereto, declare that it does not consider itself bound by the preceding paragraph. The other Contracting States shall not be bound by the preceding paragraph with respect to any Contracting State having made such a reservation.

3. Any Contracting State having made a reservation in accordance with the preceding paragraph may at any time withdraw this reservation by notification to the Depositary Governments.

Notes

1. The placing of bombs in aircraft and other acts of sabotage endangering both their safety and that of persons on board is a separate problem from hijacking, but one that is related to it in that both are methods used by terrorists. The Montreal Convention tackles it by means of rules as to jurisdiction and extradition similar to those for hijacking in the Hague Convention. The Montreal Convention was amended (Arts 1, 5) by a 1988 Protocol[32] following terrorist attacks at Rome and Vienna airports and brings attacks against people at airports within the Convention for the parties to the Protocol.

[32] Misc. 6 (1988), Cm. 378. In force 1989. 16 parties. U.K. not a party.

2. The duty to prosecute or extradite, with the choice being left to the state in whose territory the alleged offender is, was in issue in the *Lockerbie* case.[33] In 1988, Pan Am Flight 103 from Frankfurt to New York, via London exploded over Lockerbie, Scotland. All 259 passengers and crew were killed, as were 11 persons on the ground. The nationals of 21 states were killed, with two thirds of the dead being U.S. nationals and 66 British. On November 14, 1991, a warrant was issued in Scotland for the arrest of two Libyans who were accused of conspiracy, murder and an offence under the Aviation Security Act 1982. The two accused were believed to be officers in the Libyan Intelligence Services. A similar warrant was issued in the U.S. France also issued arrest warrants against Libyan officials who were accused of being involved in a 1989 explosion of UTA Flight 772 over Niger, killing 192 people. By a November 27, 1991 tripartite declaration, the United Kingdom, the U.S. and France called upon Libya, *inter alia*, (i) to hand over the two Libyans for trial in Scotland or the U.S. and to satisfy the requirements of French justice[34] and (ii) to renounce international terrorism.

Libya's response was not to comply with these requests but to take steps to prosecute the accused in its own courts. Acting in accordance with the Montreal Convention, to which it and the other three states were parties, Libya took the necessary steps to establish its own jurisdiction in the cases and to ensure the presence of the accused in Libya; initiated an inquiry into the facts; and submitted the cases to the competent authorities for the purpose of prosecution. Libya also sought the assistance of the United Kingdom in connection with these proceedings, but the United Kingdom refused to co-operate, insisting instead upon extradition. There was no extradition treaty between Libya and the United Kingdom and Libyan law did not permit the extradition of its nationals.

Following Libya's refusal to accede to their requests, the United Kingdom, the U.S. and France took the case to the UN Security Council, which passed resolutions on January 21, and March 31, 1992, that between them decided that Libya must "provide a full and effective response" to the requests of the three states.[35] In the meantime, on March 3, 1992, Libya took the *Lockerbie* case to the I.C.J.[36] Libya claimed that it had fully complied with its obligations under the Montreal Convention by taking the steps outlined above and that the United Kingdom was in breach of its obligations under that Convention. The case remains pending. Has Libya or the United Kingdom infringed the Montreal Convention? How do Security Council Resolutions 731 and 748 affect the position?

4. STATE IMMUNITY[37]

Notes

The following materials are concerned with the question whether a state can be impleaded before the courts of another state without its consent. There used

---

[33] For literature on the case, see the citations below, p. 1041, n. 78.

[34] France did not demand that the Libyans whom they sought be extradited; French law, like most civil law systems, does not provide for the extradition of nationals.

[35] For resolutions 731 and 748, and the competence of the Security Council to issue them, see below, p. 1041.

[36] See the *Lockerbie Case (Interim Measures)*, I.C.J. Rep. 1992, p. 3. The summary of the facts above is taken partly from the Court's order.

[37] See Badr, *State Immunity: An Analytical and Prognostic View* (1984); Crawford (1983) 54 B.Y.I.L. 75; Johnson (1978) 6 A.Y.I.L. 1; Schreuer, *State Immunity: Some Recent Developments* (1988); Sinclair 113 (1980–II) 167 Hague Recueil; Steinberger, 10 Encycl, P.I.L. 433; Sornarajah (1982) 31 I.C.L.Q. 661; Sucharitkul, *State Immunities and Trading Activities in International Law* (1959); *ibid.*, (1976–I) 149 Hague Recueil 87; *id.*, (1982) 29 N.Y.I.L. 252; Trooboff (1986–V) 200 Hague Recueil 325.

formerly to be a rule of absolute immunity.[38] Since the 1920s, socialist states and others have come to engage in trading activities (acts *iure gestionis*) as well as exercising the public functions traditionally associated with states (acts *iure imperii*). In response, many states moved in their practice to a doctrine of restrictive immunity by which a foreign state is allowed immunity for acts *iure imperii* only. The bulk of this practice consists of municipal court decisions. A 1982 study[39] shows that the courts of the great majority of states in which the matter has been considered in recent years (mostly western states) now favour the doctrine of restrictive immunity. The same study also considers state practice in the form of national legislation and treaties. New legislation, such as the United States Foreign Sovereign Immunities Act 1976[40] and the United Kingdom State Immunity Act 1978, below, p. 321, invariably applies the restrictive immunity doctrine, as do the two main multilateral treaties on the subject, namely the 1926 Brussels Convention for the Unification of Certain Rules relating to the Immunity of State Owned Vessels[41] and the 1972 European Convention on State Immunity.[42] The 1926 Convention places "[s]eagoing vessels owned or operated by States, cargoes owned by them, and cargoes and passengers carried on Government vessels" on the same footing as private vessels (Articles 1 and 2). Article 3 then states the following exception:

> The provisions of the two preceding articles shall not be applicable to ships of war, Government yachts, patrol vessels, hospital ships, auxiliary vessels, supply ships, and other craft owned or operated by a State, and used at the time a cause of action arises exclusively on Governmental and non-commercial service, and such vessels shall not be subject to seizure, attachment or detention by any legal process, nor to judicial proceedings in rem.

The 1972 European Convention allows immunity except in certain listed categories of cases. The extensive bilateral treaty practice strongly supports a restrictive immunity approach as well.

Originally, most of the states that followed the restrictive immunity doctrine were from the west; the Soviet bloc and most developing states (which tended to be socialist) did not. With the demise of the USSR and related developments, only China and a small number of developing states now follow the absolute immunity approach. Although the balance has thus shifted in favour of the restrictive immunity approach, O'Connell's 1970 statement remains correct:

[38] The absolute immunity rule was at its peak in such 1920s common law cases as *The Porto Alexandre* [1920] P. 30, C.A. and *The Pesaro*, 271 U.S. 562 (1926). Civil law jurisprudence has always been more diverse: see Schreuer, *op. cit.*, p. 306, n. 37, above, p.1.

[39] 4th Report on Jurisdictional Immunities of States and their Property, 1982, prepared for the I.L.C. by its Special Rapporteur (Sucharitkul), Y.B.I.L.C. 1982, II–1, p. 199. See also the surveys in Sinclair, *op cit.*, p. 306, n. 37 above, Chap. II, and Badr, *op. cit.*, p. 306, n. 37, above, Chap. III; *Materials on Jurisdictional Immunities of States and their Property*, UN Legislative Series, U.N. Doc. ST/LEG/SER.B/20.

[40] (1976) 15 I.L.M. 1388. See Brower, Bistline and Loomis (1979) 73 A.J.I.L. 200; Delaume (1977) 71 A.J.I.L. 399; Feldman (1985) 35 I.C.L.Q. 302.

[41] Cmnd. 7800; 176 L.N.T.S. 199; Hudson, 3 Int. Leg. 1837. In force 1936. 29 parties to the Convention and to its 1934 Protocol, 176 L.N.T.S. 215; Hudson 6 Int. Leg. 868. The U.K. is a party. 13 states have become parties since 1949. See Thommen, *Legal Status of Government Merchant Ships in International Law* (1962).

[42] U.K.T.S. 74 (1979), Cmnd. 7742; (1972) 11 I.L.M. 470. In force 1976. Eight parties including the U.K. The 1972 Protocol, *ibid.*, has seven parties. In force 1985. The U.K. is not a party to the Protocol. The U.K. Foreign Office has stated that the 1972 Convention reflects "with sufficient accuracy general State practice in the field of sovereign immunity": see Sinclair, *op. cit.*, p. 306, n. 37 above, p. 258, n. 443. On the Convention, see Sinclair (1973) 22 I.C.L.Q. 254, and the Explanatory Report in Cmnd. 5081.

The most that can be said of customary international law is that it enjoins immunity from the judicial process only in respect of governmental activities that pertain to administration, and does not compel it in respect of other activities which are more truly commercial than administrative.[43]

Adoption of the restrictive immunity approach introduces the problem of classifying acts as *iure gestionis* or *iure imperii*. Other problems (which exist whether absolute or restrictive immunity is preferred) lie in deciding (i) which of the many governmental entities (*e.g.* public corporations) that might claim to act for a state qualify for immunity and (ii) whether a state may be indirectly impleaded.

The following materials in this section examine the doctrine of state (or sovereign)[44] immunity largely as it applies in United Kingdom law. Note that, quite apart from the doctrine of state immunity, United Kingdom courts will refrain from adjudicating directly upon the transactions of foreign states. In *Buttes Gas Oil Co. v. Hammer*,[45] applying this doctrine of "non-justiciability," the House of Lords declined to take jurisdiction in a dispute between two oil companies which would have required it to have ruled, *inter alia*, on the boundary between the continental shelves of two Persian Gulf states.

THE SCHOONER EXCHANGE v. McFADDON

7 *Cranch* 116 (1812). U.S. Supreme Court

A French naval vessel put into Philadelphia for repairs after a storm. The libellants, who sought possession of the vessel, claimed that it was in reality the schooner *Exchange*, an American ship which they owned and which had been seized by France on the high seas in 1810 in accordance with a Napoleonic decree. The United States Attorney-General filed a suggestion to the effect that the Court should refuse jurisdiction on the ground of sovereign immunity.

MARSHALL C.J., FOR THE COURT: The jurisdiction of the nation within its own territory is necessarily exclusive and absolute. It is susceptible of no limitation not imposed by itself. . . .

This full and absolute territorial jurisdiction being alike the attribute of every sovereign, and being incapable of conferring extra-territorial power, would not seem to contemplate foreign sovereigns nor their sovereign rights as its objects. One sovereign being in no respect amenable to another, and being bound by obligations of the highest character not to degrade the dignity of his nation, by placing himself or its sovereign rights within the jurisdiction of another, can be supposed to enter a foreign territory only under an express license, or in the confidence that the immunities belonging to his independent sovereign station, though not expressly stipulated, are reserved by implication, and will be extended to him.

---

[43] *International Law*, Vol. II (2nd ed., 1970), p. 841.

[44] These terms tend to be used interchangeably, although, as Sinclair points out, *op. cit.*, p. 507, n. 37, above, p. 197, "[s]overeign immunity in the strict sense of the term should be taken to refer to the immunity which a personal sovereign or Head of State enjoys when present in the territory of another State."

[45] [1982] A.C. 888, HL. The doctrine of state immunity would not have been available on the facts as no state was directly or indirectly implicated.

This perfect equality and absolute independence of sovereigns, and this common interest impelling them to mutual intercourse, and an interchange of good offices with each other, have given rise to a class of cases in which every sovereign is understood to waive the exercise of a part of that complete exclusive territorial jurisdiction, which has been stated to be the attribute of every nation.

1st. One of these is admitted to be the exemption of the person of the sovereign from arrest or detention within a foreign territory. . . .

2nd. A second case, standing on the same principles with the first, is the immunity which all civilised nations allow to foreign ministers. . . .

When private individuals of one nation spread themselves through another as business or caprice may direct, mingling indiscriminately with the inhabitants of that other, or when merchant vessels enter for the purposes of trade, it would be obviously inconvenient and dangerous to society, and would subject the laws to continual infraction, and the government to degradation, if such individuals or merchants did not owe temporary and local allegiance, and were not amenable to the jurisdiction of the country. . . .

But in all respects different is the situation of a public armed ship. She constitutes a part of the military force of her nation; acts under the immediate and direct command of the sovereign; is employed by him in national objects. He has many and powerful motives for preventing those objects from being defeated by the interference of a foreign state. Such interference cannot take place without affecting his power and his dignity. The implied license, therefore, under which such vessel enters a friendly port, may reasonably be construed, and it seems to the court ought to be construed, as containing an exemption from the jurisdiction of the sovereign within whose territory she claims the right of hospitality. . . .

The Court found that the vessel in question was exempt from United States jurisdiction.

Notes

1. The doctrine of state immunity is justified by Marshall C.J. on the basis of the equality, independence, and dignity of states. To the same effect, the maxim *par in parem non habet imperium* (an equal has no authority over an equal) is commonly invoked. Marshall C.J. marries the doctrine with that of the absolute jurisdiction of the territorial sovereign by assuming the latter's implied consent to immunity from its courts' jurisdiction.

2. Although the move away from absolute to restricted immunity is now well established in the practice of many states, state practice does not suggest that sovereign immunity should be abolished altogether. Note, however, that Lord Denning expressed an opinion in *Rahimtoola v. Nizam of Hyderabad*[46] which could be used to support such a development (although Lord Denning did not go so far himself):

[46] [1958] A.C. 379 at 418, PC. See also H. Lauterpacht (1951) 28 B.Y.I.L. 220.

It is more in keeping with the dignity of a foreign sovereign to submit himself to the rule of law than to claim to be above it, and his independence is better ensured by accepting the decisions of courts of acknowledged impartiality than by arbitrarily rejecting their jurisdiction. In all civilised countries there has been a progressive tendency towards making the sovereign liable to be sued in his own courts; notably in England by the Crown Proceedings Act, 1947. Foreign sovereigns should not be in any different position. There is no reason why we should grant to the departments or agencies of foreign Governments an immunity which we do not grant our own, provided always that the matter in dispute arises within the jurisdiction of our courts and is properly cognizable by them.

Contrast these arguments against state immunity, which turn upon fairness to individuals affected by state acts and the idea that no one is above the law, with the arguments in its favour in *The Schooner Exchange*. The latter were developed at a time when (i) immunity meant the personal immunity of a sovereign, not the public immunity of a state, and (ii) state trading, before socialism, was minimal.

I CONGRESO DEL PARTIDO[47]

[1983] 1 A.C. 244. House of Lords

In 1973, Cubazucar, a Cuban state trading enterprise, contracted to sell sugar to a Chilean company. One shipment made under the contract was carried on the *Playa Larga*—a ship flying the Cuban flag, owned by the Cuban Government and operated by Mambisa, a second Cuban state trading enterprise. Such enterprises are legally independent of the Government and not a department of Government under Cuban law; it was not claimed in argument that they attracted sovereign immunity. The cargo was being discharged in Valparaiso when the socialist Allende Government in Chile was overthrown by the right-wing Pinochet Government, of which Cuba disapproved. Thereupon, the *Playa Larga* left Valparaiso on orders from Mambisa (acting on instructions from the Cuban Government) without discharging the remainder of its cargo, which was later sold to someone else in Cuba. A second shipment under the contract was carried on the *Marble Islands*—a ship then flying the Somali flag and owned by a Liechtenstein company which had been chartered by Mambisa for use by Cubazucar. The *Marble Islands*, which was on the high seas on its way to Valparaiso when the *coup d'état* occurred in Chile, was ordered by Mambisa, on Cuban Government instructions, to sail to North Vietnam. During the journey, it became a Cuban ship owned by the Cuban Government. On arrival in Haiphong, the cargo was (i) sold by the master, on behalf of Mambisa, to Alimport, a third Cuban state trading enterprise, and (ii) donated by the latter to the North Vietnamese people. Both of these actions were taken in accordance with Cuban Government instructions.

In this case, the *I Congreso*, another ship owned by the Cuban Government, was arrested in British waters on the application of the plaintiffs, the Chilean owners of the cargoes of the *Playa Larga* and the *Marble Islands*, who had instituted proceedings *in rem* in the English High Court for breach of contract (non-delivery) and in tort (for detinue or conversion). The Cuban Government entered a defence of state immunity. The defence was upheld by Goff J. and by a divided two man Court of Appeal (in which Waller L.J. and Lord Denning M.R. voted for and against immunity respectively). The plaintiffs appealed to the House of Lords. The case was governed by the common law preceding the 1978 Act.

---

[47] See Fox (1982) 98 L.Q.R. 94.

LORD WILBERFORCE. On the basis of these cases [*The Philippine Admiral* [1977] A.C. 373 and *Trendtex Trading Corp. v. Central Bank of Nigeria*, below, p. 331] ... I have no doubt that the "restrictive" doctrine should be applied to the present case.... The issue is as to the limits of the doctrine....

The ... limitation ... under the so called "restrictive theory," arises from the willingness of states to enter into commercial, or other private law, transactions with individuals. It appears to have two main foundations: (a) It is necessary in the interest of justice to individuals having such transactions with states to allow them to bring such transactions before the courts. (b) To require a state to answer a claim based upon such transactions does not involve a challenge to or inquiry into any act of sovereignty or governmental act of that state. It is, in accepted phrases, neither a threat to the dignity of that state, nor any interference with its sovereign functions....

The appellants contend that we have here (I take the case of *Playa Larga* for the present ...) a commercial transaction, *viz.*, a trading vessel, owned by the Republic of Cuba, carrying goods, under normal commercial arrangements. Any claim arising out of this situation is, they assert, a claim of private law, and it is irrelevant that the purpose, for which the act giving rise to the claim was committed, may have been of a political character (sc. briefly, to break off trading relations with a state, Chile, with which Cuba was not friendly)....

In my opinion this argument, though in itself generally acceptable, burkes, or begs, the essential question, which is "what is the relevant act?" It assumes that this is the initial entry into a commercial transaction and that this entry irrevocably confers upon later acts a commercial, or private law, character....

In many cases the process of deciding upon the character of the relevant act presents no difficulty... In *Trendtex* [1977] Q.B. 529, similarly, and the same is true of the acts in issue in other countries relating to the Nigerian cement purchases, the relevant act was simply a breach of a commercial contract and was treated as such, none the less though committed by a state or department of state for reasons of government. The purpose for which the breach was committed could not alter its clear character.[48] Of cases in other jurisdictions one of great clarity is the leading case of the *Claim against the Empire of Iran Case*, 45 I.L.R. 57 decided by the Federal Constitutional Court of the German Federal Republic in 1963. This was a claim for the cost of repairs to the heating

---

[48] In the *Trendtex Case*, Lord Denning M.R. stated: "It was suggested that the original contracts for cement were .... for the building of barracks for the army. On this account it was said that the contracts of purchase were acts of a governmental nature—*iure imperii*. They were like a contract of purchase of boots for the army. But I do not think this should affect the question of immunity. If a government department goes into the market places of the world and buys boots or cement—as a commercial transaction—that government department should be subject to all the rules of the market place. The seller is not concerned with the purpose to which the purchaser intends to put the goods."

system of the Iranian Embassy. The judgment contains the following passage, at 80:

> As a means for determining the distinction between acts jure imperii and jure gestionis one should rather refer to the nature of the state transaction or the resulting legal relationships, and not to the motive or purpose of the state activity. It thus depends upon whether the foreign state has acted in exercise of its sovereign authority, that is in public law, or like a private person, that is in private law.

And later, at 81:

> This court has therefore examined the argument that the conclusion of the contract for repair is to be regarded as a non-sovereign function of the foreign state, and has accepted this proposition as correct. It is obvious that the conclusion of a contract of this kind does not fall within the essential sphere of state authority. It does not depend . . . on whether the conclusion of the contract was necessary for the regular transaction of the embassy's affairs and therefore stood in a recognisable relationship with the sovereign functions of the sending state. Whether a state is entitled to immunity does not depend on the purpose of the function which the foreign state is thereby pursuing.

Clearly a breach of a contract of that character was within the area of private law. . . . These are cases which present no difficulty. The problems with which they were concerned were simply (i) whether it could be said that the relevant contract was concluded for governmental purposes, and (ii) whether it was relevant that governmental motives were advanced for breaching the contract.

In other situations it may not be easy to decide whether the act complained of is within the area of non-immune activity or is an act of sovereignty wholly outside it. The activities of states cannot always be compartmentalised into trading or governmental activities; and what is one to make of a case where a state has, and in the relevant circumstances, clearly displayed, both a commercial interest and a sovereign or governmental interest? To which is the critical action to be attributed?

. . . Under the "restrictive" theory the court has first to characterise the activity into which the defendant state has entered. Having done this, and (assumedly) found it to be of a commercial, or private law, character, it may take the view that contractual breaches, or torts, prima facie fall within the same sphere of activity. It should then be for the defendant state to make a case (*cf. Juan Ysmael*)[49] that the act complained of is outside that sphere, and within that of sovereign action. . . .

The conclusion which emerges is that in considering, under the "restrictive" theory whether state immunity should be granted or not, the

---

[49] *Ed.* See below, p. 329.

court must consider the whole context in which the claim against the state is made, with a view to deciding whether the relevant act(s) upon which the claim is based, should, in that context, be considered as fairly within an area of activity, trading or commercial, or otherwise of a private law character, in which the state has chosen to engage, or whether the relevant act(s) should be considered as having been done outside that area, and within the sphere of governmental or sovereign activity. . . .

(a) *Playa Larga* . . . The appellants are certainly able to show, as a starting point, that this vessel was engaged in trade with the consent, if not with the active participation, of the Republic of Cuba. . . . The question is whether the acts which gave rise to an alleged cause of action were done in the context of the trading relationship, or were done by the government of the Republic of Cuba acting wholly outside the trading relationship and in exercise of the power of the state. . . . In my opinion it must be answered on a broad view of the facts as a whole and not upon narrow issues as to Cuba's possible contractual liability. I do not think that there is any doubt that the decision not to complete unloading at Valparaiso, or to discharge at Callao, was a political decision taken by the government of the Republic of Cuba for political and non-commercial reasons. . . . The change of government in Chile, and the events at Santiago in which the Cuban Embassy was involved, provoked a determination on the part of the government of Cuba to break off and discontinue trading relations with Chile. There may also have been concern for the safety of *Playa Larga* at Valparaiso. . . .

Does this call for characterisation of the act of the Republic of Cuba in withdrawing *Playa Larga* and denying the cargo to its purchasers as done *"jure imperii?"* In my opinion it does not. Everything done by the Republic of Cuba in relation to *Playa Larga* could have been done, and, so far as evidence goes, was done, as owners of the ship: it exercised, and had no need to exercise, sovereign powers. It acted, as any owner of the ship would act, through Mambisa, the managing operators. It invoked no governmental authority. . . .

It may well be that those instructions [to Mambisa] would not have been issued, as they were, if the owner of *Playa Larga* had been anyone but a state: it is almost certainly the case that there was no commercial reason for the decision. But these consequences follow inevitably from the entry of states into the trading field. If immunity were to be granted the moment that any decision taken by the trading state were shown to be not commercially, but politically, inspired, the "restrictive" theory would almost cease to have any content and trading relations as to state-owned ships would become impossible. It is precisely to protect private traders against politically inspired breaches, or wrongs, that the restrictive theory allows states to be brought before a municipal court. It may be too stark to say of a state "once a trader always a trader": but, in order to withdraw its action from the sphere of acts done *jure gestionis*, a state must be able to point to some act clearly done *jure imperii*. Though, with much hesitation, I feel obligated to differ on this issue from the conclusion of the learned judge, I respectfully think that he well put this ultimate test [1978] Q.B. 500, 528:

> ... it is not just that the purpose or motive of the act is to serve the purposes of the state, but that the act is of its own character a governmental act, as opposed to an act which any private citizen can perform.

As to the *Playa Larga*, therefore, I find myself in agreement with Lord Denning M.R. and would allow the appeal.

(b) *Marble Islands* ... I can find no basis on which it can be said that the cargo owners entered into any business relationship with the Republic of Cuba. There can be no doubt, as subsequent events showed, that *Marble Islands* continued to be operated by Mambisa, and though the ownership of *Marble Islands* by the Republic of Cuba is a factor to be considered, what is decisive on the question of immunity is what the Republic of Cuba did as regards the cargo when the ship arrived at Haiphong. ...

The arrangements for the sale of the sugar are then discussed.

The Republic of Cuba never entered into these operations. The captain did not purport to act on its behalf. ... Its actions were confined to directing transfer of the sugar to North Vietnam, and to the enactment of Law No. 1256 [which froze and blocked Chilean assets]. All of this was done in a governmental capacity: any attack upon its actions must call in question its acts as a sovereign state.

... I cannot agree that there was ever any purely commercial obligation upon the Republic of Cuba or any binding commercial obligation: the republic never assumed any such obligation; it never entered the trading area; the cargo owners never entered into a commercial relation with it. I agree that the purpose, above, is not decisive but it may throw some light upon the nature of what was done. The acts of the Republic of Cuba were and remained in their nature purely governmental. The fact is, that if any wrong (contractually or delictually) was done as regards the cargo it was done by Mambisa ... in my opinion ... the acts complained of as regards the Republic of Cuba were acts *jure imperii* and so covered by immunity. I would dismiss the *Marble Islands* appeal.

LORD DIPLOCK.

Although agreeing with Lord Wilberforce that the restrictive immunity doctrine should apply and that no immunity should be allowed in respect of the *Playa Larga*, Lord Diplock disagreed with him in respect of the *Marble Islands*:

The right asserted by the master to discharge and sell the perishable cargo in Haiphong is ... fairly and squarely based on private law (*jus gestionis*), the contractual terms contained in the bills of lading and the Commercial Code in force in Cuba. There is no suggestion that the cargo had been requisitioned by the Cuban government *jure imperii* nor is there any mention of the Law No. 1256. . . .

So all that was done in Haiphong in November to Iansa's sugar laden on *Marble Islands* was done upon the instructions of the Cuban government in purported reliance upon Mambisa's rights in private law (*jus gestionis*) and not upon any *jus imperii* of the Cuban state itself. It was only after the property in the sugar had been purportedly transferred to Alimport under the terms of the sale contract by delivery of the warehouse warrants that the sugar was then handed over by Alimport as a gift by the state of Cuba to the government of Vietnam.

So the legal position of the Cuban government after October 13, 1973, was that it then acquired the ownership of a trading vessel *Marble Islands* then in mid-Pacific engaged in carrying cargo belonging to Iansa upon a voyage which the master claimed was authorised by a power to deviate contained in the bill of lading under which the cargo had been shipped. Mambisa from being demise charterer of *Marble Islands* had become managing operator of the vessel on behalf of the Cuban government, and legal possession of the cargo laden on her passed from Mambisa as former disponent owner to the Cuban government itself which in terms of English law became the "bailee" of Iansa's sugar. Thereafter, as the evidence discloses, everything that was done by the master was done on the express directions of the Cuban government; the Director and Senior Legal Adviser of the Ministry of Merchant Marine and Ports being sent to Haiphong in November to supervise what the master did there and the legal form and nature of the steps he took. . . .

Unless the master's assertions in the documents that the discharge and sale of the cargo was authorised by the bills of lading was right in law, the facts to which I have particularly referred would disclose in English law a prima facie case of conversion of the cargo by the Cuban government as bailee when the master sold and delivered it to Alimport on the instructions of the government in purported exercise of rights under private law. The relevant transaction, *viz.*, the discharge and sale of the cargo to Alimport at Haiphong was, as it seems to me, deliberately treated by the Cuban government as being effected under private law and not in the exercise of any sovereign powers.

For these reasons I for my part would allow the appeal in the case of the *Marble Islands* as well as in the case of the *Playa Larga*.

Lord Edmund Davies delivered a speech agreeing wholly with Lord Wilberforce. Lords Keith and Bridge agreed with the reasoning of Lord Wilberforce. On the facts, they agreed with Lord Diplock that the appeal should also be allowed in respect of the *Marble Islands* as well as the *Playa Larga*. The claim of immunity was therefore disallowed in respect of both ships.

Appeal allowed.

Notes

1. Lord Wilberforce adopted the "nature"/"purpose" of the act distinction in the *Empire of Iran* case above, p. 311, (although his quotation from the trial court judge's judgment in the *I Congreso* case, above, p. 314, suggest that the "purpose" is not totally irrelevant). Lord Wilberforce's "nature" of the act in its context approach has been followed in later British cases: see the *Littrell* and *Kuwait Airways* cases, below, pp. 316 and 318.

2. In this case the House of Lords held, in a contractual context, that the courts must look not only to the nature of the contract, but also to the nature of the breach. If a contract is an act *iure imperii*, there is immunity; if it is an act *iure gestionis*, a defence of immunity may still succeed if the act in breach of contract is an act *iure imperii*. The court, that is, has to consider whether at any stage in the case the state has acted as a sovereign and hence should not be impleaded. The House of Lords unanimously adopted this approach; they disagreed on the facts concerning the *Marble Islands*, the majority considering that the act in breach of contract was an act *iure gestionis* and the minority classifying it as an act *iure imperii*. This would appear to be the first national court case to look beyond the nature of the contract in this way.[50]

3. In 1983, in a case[51] that fell very clearly on the *iure imperii* side of the line, a British Royal Navy Sea Harrier made a forced landing on a Spanish container ship on the high seas when it ran out of fuel. When the harrier was taken into a Spanish port, the British government argued before a Spanish court that under the international law of state immunity the harrier could not "be the object of any kind of insurance or preventive measure for guaranteeing payment of any compensation."[52] The Spanish court ordered the release of the Harrier. The container ship owner was later awarded compensation by way of maritime salvage by a London arbitrator.

LITTRELL v. USA (No. 2)

[1995] 1 W.L.R. 82. Court of Appeal

The plaintiff, a United States soldier stationed in the United Kingdom, brought a claim against the United States Government in tort for negligent medical treatment at an American military hospital at his base. The United States successfully pleaded state immunity before the trial judge. The plaintiff appealed.

HOFFMANN L.J. A claim to state immunity in respect of an action for personal injury would ordinarily fail because section 5 of the State Immunity Act 1978 says in terms that "A state is not immune as respects proceedings in respect of . . . personal injury . . . caused by an act or omission in the United Kingdom." But section 16(2) says that section 5 does not apply to "proceedings relating to anything done by or in relation to the armed forces of a state while present in the United Kingdom . . . " The question must therefore be determined according to the common law. . . .

The question in this case is therefore whether, in accordance with the common law as laid down in *I Congreso del Partido* [1983] 1 A.C. 244, the

---

[50] See Mann (1982) 31 I.C.L.Q. 573.

[51] U.K.M.I.L. 1985, (1985) 56 B.Y.I.L. 462.

[52] *ibid.*, p. 463.

act which forms the basis of the claim was jure imperii or jure gestionis.

Hoffmann L.J. quoted with approval Lord Wilberforce's nature of the act test
and continued:

The context in which the act took place was the maintenance by the
United States of a unit of the United States Air Force in the United
Kingdom. This looks about as imperial an activity as could be imagined.
But it would be facile to regard this context as determinative of the
question. Acts done within that context could range from arrangements
concerning the flights of the bombers—plainly *jure imperii*—to ordering
milk for the base from a local dairy or careless driving by off-duty airmen
on the roads of Suffolk. Both of the latter would seem to me to be jure
gestionis, fairly within an area of private law activity. I do not think that
there is a single test or "bright line" by which cases on either side can be
distinguished. Rather, there are a number of factors which may characterise the act as nearer to or further from the central military activity.

In the present case I think that the most important factors are the
answers to the following questions. First, where did it happen? In cases
in which foreign troops are occupying a defined and self-contained area,
the authorities on customary international law attach importance to
whether or not the act was done within the "lines" or "the rayon [radius]
of the [fortress]" (*Oppenheim, International Law,* vol. 1: Peace, 1st ed. (1905),
p. 483). Secondly, whom did it involve? Acts involving only members of
the visiting force are less likely to be within the jurisdiction of local
municipal courts than acts involving its own citizens as well. Thirdly,
what kind of act was it? Some acts are wholly military in character, some
almost entirely private or commercial and some in between.

In this case, R.A.F. Lakenheath was, in spite of its name and the
presence of an R.A.F. officer for liaison duties, wholly within the control
of the United States Air Force. The act took place at the military hospital
within the base. It involved only United States personnel. And the operation of a military hospital, although no doubt requiring much the same
skills as the operation of a civilian hospital, is a recognised military
activity. If the case had concerned an assault within the base by one
American serviceman on another, I think that under customary international law the English courts would have declined both civil and
criminal jurisdiction. Why should it exercise civil jurisdiction because the
injury was inflicted by negligence? Mr Mendelson said that the reason is
that an assault would have been a disciplinary offence and an assertion of
jurisdiction would have interfered with the foreign sovereign's right to
discipline his own troops. An action for medical negligence, on the other
hand, involves no interference with military matters.

I do not agree. First, the United States engages its troops on the basis of
the doctrine laid down in *Feres v. United States,* 340 U.S. 135, by which it
is immune from suit by servicemen for injuries incident to service. For an

English court to allow visiting United States servicemen to sue their government would clearly be an interference with this aspect of the relationship between the troops and their sovereign. Secondly, the plaintiff's action involves the claim that the treatment which he received in the military hospital fell below the standard which an English court would consider reasonable. In my judgment, however, the standard of medical care which the United States affords its own servicemen is a matter within its own sovereign authority.

In my judgment, therefore, the act of which the plaintiff complains was clearly on the jure imperii side of the line and the judge was right to dismiss the action.

Rose L.J. delivered a judgment to the same effect. Nourse L.J. concurred.

Appeal dismissed.

KUWAIT AIRWAYS CORPN v. IRAQI AIRWAYS CO.

[1995] 1 W.L.R. 1147. House of Lords

Following the invasion of Kuwait by Iraq in August 1990,[53] aircraft belonging to the plaintiffs were transported from Kuwait to Iraq by the first defendants, the Iraqi Airways Co. (I.A.C.), acting under Iraqi Government orders. The plaintiffs were purportedly dissolved by R.C.C. Resolution 369 of the Iraqi Government and their assets transferred to the first defendants. Thereupon, the first defendants treated the aircraft as their own. Four aircraft were destroyed during hostilities; the other six were eventually returned to the plaintiffs. In these proceedings, the plaintiffs, *inter alia*, sought damages resulting from the wrongful interference by the first defendants with the aircraft. The Court of Appeal held that the first defendants were entitled to state immunity: the I.A.C. was a "separate entity" in the sense of section 14 of the State Immunity Act 1978 and the acts in question satisfied the two conditions in section 14. The House of Lords unanimously adopted the approach to the distinction between acts *iure imperii* and *gestioni* found in Lord Wilberforce's speech in the *I Congreso* case and held that the first defendants were a "separate entity" for the purposes of section 14 of the 1978 Act. The following extract concerns the question whether the two conditions for immunity in section 14 were met. The House of Lords rejected the appeal so far as it related to the acts prior to Resolution 369. By three to two, it allowed the appeal in respect of acts occurring thereafter.

LORD GOFF It follows [from the text of section 14] that both conditions have to be satisfied if I.A.C. is to be entitled to immunity. However, as I see it, the central question in the present case is whether the acts performed by I.A.C. to which the proceedings relate were performed in the exercise of sovereign authority, which here means *acta jure imperii* (in the

[53] See further below, p. 956.

sense in which that expression has been adopted by English law from public international law).[54] . . .

It is apparent from Lord Wilberforce's statement or principle that the ultimate test of what constitutes an act *jure imperii* is whether the act in question is of its own character a governmental act, as opposed to an act which any private citizen can perform. It follows that, in the case of acts done by a separate entity, it is not enough that the entity should have acted on the directions of the state, because such an act need not possess the character of a governmental act. To attract immunity under section 14(2), therefore, what is done by the separate entity must be something which possesses that character. . . .

I approach the matter as follows. First, the taking of the aircraft and their removal from Kuwait Airport to Iraq constituted an exercise of governmental power by the State of Iraq. . . . I am of the opinion that I.A.C., in so acting, was acting in the exercise of sovereign authority.

But, as I see the position, the situation changed after R.C.C. Resolution 369 came into effect. Thereafter, as I see it, it cannot be said that I.A.C.'s retention and use of the aircraft as its own constituted acts done in the exercise of sovereign authority. They were acts done by it in consequence of the vesting or purported vesting of the aircraft in it by legislative decree. . . . Then, does it make any difference that, in the present case, the state entity was at an earlier stage involved in the seizure of the property from the former owner in the exercise of sovereign authority? I for my part cannot see that the characterisation as an act *jure imperii* of the earlier involvement by the entity in the act of seizure can, on the facts of the present case, be determinative of the characterisation of the subsequent retention and use of the property by the state entity following the formal vesting of the property in the entity by a legislative act of the state. Indeed, if the Court of Appeal's approach were right, it would lead to the consequence that, however long I.A.C. had been able to keep the aircraft and to use them following the vesting of the aircraft in it by Iraqi legislation, for example by employing them in flights to other countries, it would still have been able to invoke state immunity in the case of a claim by the former owner for damages for wrongful interference with the aircraft in the form of conversion founded solely upon retention of the goods after the Iraqi legislation had taken effect. I cannot think that can be right. Finally I do not think it relevant that (as was very probably the case) the Iraqi government would not have tolerated return of the aircraft by I.A.C. to K.A.C. For the fact remains that I.A.C., in treating the aircraft as its own, was doing so pursuant to the Iraqi legislation which vested the aircraft in I.A.C.; and by so doing it cannot be said to have acted in the exercise of sovereign authority. . . .

---

[54] *Ed.* On the facts of the case, the state would not have been immune under the Act (see ss.3(1)(b), 3(3)(c) and 14(2)(b)) in respect of transactions or activities engaged in "otherwise than in the exercise of sovereign authority".

For these reasons I am satisfied that I.A.C. cannot claim state immunity in respect of the allegations made in paragraphs (c) and (d) of the particulars under paragraph 2 of the point of claim, in so far as they relate to acts alleged to have been performed by I.A.C. after the coming into effect of R.C.C. Resolution 369.

Lords Jauncey and Nicholls concurred. Lords Mustill and Slynn dissented in relation to acts subsequent to Resolution 369. In relation to such acts, Lord Slynn stated:

LORD SLYNN On the facts found by the judge I do not consider that I.A.C. played at any time an independent role. It flew the aircraft out of Kuwait and it used them because Iraq in the exercise of its sovereignty told I.A.C. to do so. The intention, it is accepted, all along was that these aircraft should be seized and used for civil aviation purposes in and from Iraq. The seizure and detention for that purpose was, however, wholly done pursuant to the actions of Iraq in its sovereign capacity. . . .

It remains to consider whether "the circumstances are such that a State . . . would have been so immune:" section 14(2)(*b*). This means as I read it—could Iraq claim sovereign immunity if it or its head of state in his public capacity or the government had done the acts which I.A.C. did? It could not have claimed such immunity if what was done was a "commercial transaction entered into by the State" being for present purposes a transaction or activity into which the state enters or engages otherwise than in the exercise of sovereign authority. If, as I consider, this whole incident is to be regarded as one—*i.e.* the seizure, removal and use of the aircraft—then it is plain that it was being done under sovereign authority and not otherwise. I take the same view if the various stages have to be separated. If Iraq had used Resolution 369 to vest the title to the aircraft in the Minister of Transport and his department had flown the aircraft on civil routes that would have been done as an act of sovereign authority. When the aircraft are vested in I.A.C. and flown by them that is done in the exercise of sovereign authority.

The provision of the Act of 1978 excluding commercial transactions from acts properly seen as the exercise of sovereign authority is derived from decisions of the courts which introduced into the concept of sovereign immunity an exception in order to prevent sovereigns or sovereign states from avoiding foreign courts investigating their activities in what were plainly the sort of commercial transactions which could equally be carried out by other persons. What happened here was totally different. Iraq is not being sued for carelessly flying an aircraft or running a commercial airline in such a way as to cause damage to people or property. It is being sued because of the direct consequences of its act of aggression towards Kuwait, the seizure of K.A.C.'s aircraft and their subsequent detention and use. That is not in any sense the kind of commercial transaction contemplated by the restricted immunity doctrine; it is certainly not within the words in section 3(3)(c) "(whether of a commercial, industrial, financial, professional or other similar character)." I would therefore for my part uphold I.A.C.'s objection to the jurisdiction on this basis.

STATE IMMUNITY ACT 1978[55]

1.—(1) A State is immune from the jurisdiction of the courts of the United Kingdom except as provided in the following provisions of this Part of this Act.

(2) A court shall give effect to the immunity conferred by this section even though the State does not appear in the proceedings in question.

2.—(1) A State is not immune as respects proceedings in respect of which it has submitted to the jurisdiction of the courts of the United Kingdom. . . .

(2) A State may submit after the dispute giving rise to the proceedings has arisen or by a prior written agreement; but a provision in any agreement that it is to be governed by the law of the United Kingdom is not to be regarded as a submission. . . .

3.—(1) A State is not immune as respects proceedings relating to—

(*a*) a commercial transaction entered into by the State; or
(*b*) an obligation of the State which by virtue of a contract (whether a commercial transaction or not) falls to be performed wholly or partly in the United Kingdom.

(2) This section does not apply if the parties to the dispute are States or have otherwise agreed in writing; and subsection (1)(*b*) above does not apply if the contract (not being a commercial transaction) was made in the territory of the State concerned and the obligation in question is governed by its administrative law.

(3) In this section "commercial transaction" means

(*a*) any contract for the supply of goods or services;
(*b*) any loan or other transaction for the provision of finance and any guarantee or indemnity in respect of any such transaction or of any other financial obligation; and

[55] See Bird (1979) 13 *Int. Lawyer* 619; Bowett (1978) 37 C.L.J. 193; Delaume (1979) 73 A.J.I.L. 185; Higgins (1979) 10 N.Y.I.L. 35; Hockl, 48 O.Z.O.R.V. 121; Lewis, *State and Diplomatic Immunity* (3rd. ed., 1990); Mann (1979) 50 B.Y.I.L. 43; Sinclair, *op. cit.*, p. 306, n. 37 above, pp. 257–265; White (1979) 42 M.L.R. 72.

ier transaction or activity (whether of a commercial,
ial, financial, professional or other similar character) into
a State enters or in which it engages otherwise than in the
ercise of sovereign authority;

neither paragraph of subsection (1) above applies to a contract of
employment between a State and an individual.

4.—(1) A State is not immune as respects proceedings relating to a
contract of employment between the State and an individual where the
contract was made in the United Kingdom or the work is to be wholly or
partly performed there. . . .

(2) Subject to subsections (3) and (1) below, this section does not apply
if—

> (*a*) at the time when the proceedings are brought the individual is
> a national of the State concerned[56]; or
> (*b*) at the time when the contract was made the individual was
> neither a national of the United Kingdom nor habitually resi-
> dent there; or
> (*c*) the parties to the contract have otherwise agreed in writing.

(3) Where the work is for an office, agency or establishment maintained
by the State in the United Kingdom for commercial purposes,[57] subsection (2)(*a*) and (*b*) above do not exclude the application of this section
unless the individual was, at the time when the contract was made,
habitually resident in that State.

(4) Subsection (2)(*c*) above does not exclude the application of this
section where the law of the United Kingdom requires the proceedings to
be brought before a court of the United Kingdom. . . .

5. A State is not immune as respects proceedings in respect of—

> (*a*) death or personal injury; or
> (*b*) damage to or loss of tangible property,
>   caused by an act or omission in the United Kingdom.

6.—(1) A State is not immune as respects proceedings relating to—

---

[56] *Ed.* See *Sengupta v. Republic of India* [1983] I.C.R. 221, EAT (Indian national; claim of
immunity would have succeeded under s.4(2)(a)).

[57] *Ed.* The medical office of the Egyptian embassy, whose function was to procure medical
services for Egyptian nationals referred to it by the Egyptian government, was not
maintained for "commercial purposes" within s.4(3): *Arab Republic of Egypt v. Gamal-Eldin*
[1996] 2 All E.R. 237, EAT. So, state immunity prevented an employment law claim by
persons employed by it as drivers. As to contracts of employment generally as an
exception to state immunity in international law, see Fox (1995) 66 B.Y.I.L. 97.

(*a*) any interest of the State in, or its possession or use of, immovable property in the United Kingdom; or

(*b*) any obligation of the State arising out of its interest in, or its possession or use of, any such property.[58]

(2) A State is not immune as respects proceedings relating to any interest of the State in movable or immovable property, being an interest arising by way of succession, gift or bona vacantia.

(3) The fact that a State has or claims an interest in any property shall not preclude any court from exercising in respect of it any jurisdiction relating to the estates of deceased persons or persons of unsound mind or to insolvency,[59] the winding up of companies or the administration of trusts.

(4) A court may entertain proceedings against a person other than a State notwithstanding that the proceedings relate to property—

(*a*) which is in the possession or control of a State; or

(*b*) in which a State claims an interest,

if the State would not have been immune had the proceedings been brought against it or, in a case within paragraph (*b*) above, if the claim is neither admitted nor supported by prima facie evidence.

[A state is not immune as respects proceedings relating to patents, trade marks, designs, plant breeders' rights or copyright (Article 7), its participation in a company, *etc.* (Article 8), or an arbitration agreement (Article 9)]

10.—(1) This section applies to—

(*a*) Admiralty proceedings; and

(*b*) proceedings on any claim which could be made the subject of Admiralty proceedings.

(2) A State is not immune as respects—

---

[58] *Ed.* s.16(1)(*b*) of the 1978 Act, below, p. 326, provides that s.6(1) "does not apply to proceedings concerning a state's title to or its possession of property used for the purposes of a diplomatic mission . . . " In *Intpro Properties Ltd v. Sauvel* [1983] Q.B. 1019, CA, it was held that the private residence of a French diplomatic agent was not "used for the purposes of a diplomatic mission"; even though the agent used it for official social obligations, that was not sufficient for the residence to be regarded as being used for the professional purposes of the mission, which was what s.16(1)(*b*) required. Moreover, s.16(1)(*b*) would not have applied in any event because the claim against the state was for breach of covenant in a lease (preventing access to workmen) and did not concern a question of title or possession. Accordingly, the claim against the defendant state for damages suffered as a result of its breach of covenant could proceed, as s.6 allowed. On a diplomatic immunity point considered in the same case, see below, p. 343, n. 1.

[59] *Ed.* Liquidators were entitled to withhold payments to Iraq of assets deposited in an insolvent London bank by virtue of s.6(3), since the title to the debt owed by the bank to the state was not affected: *Re Rafidain Bank* [1992] B.C.L.C. 301, ChD.

    (*a*) an action in rem against a ship belonging to that State; or

    (*b*) an action in personam for enforcing a claim in connection with
        such a ship,

if, at the time when the cause of action arose, the ship was in use or
intended for use for commercial purposes.[60]

    (3) Where an action in rem is brought against a ship belonging to a State
for enforcing a claim in connection with another ship belonging to that
State, subsection (2)(*a*) above does not apply as respects the first-
mentioned ship unless, at the time when the cause of action relating to the
other ship arose, both ships were in use or intended for use for commercial purposes.[60a]

    (4) A State is not immune as respects—

    (*a*) an action in rem against a cargo belonging to that State if both
        the cargo and the ship carrying it were, at the time when the
        cause of action arose, in use or intended for use for commercial
        purposes[60b]; or

    (*b*) an action in personam for enforcing a claim in connection with
        such a cargo if the ship carrying it was then in use or intended
        for use as aforesaid.

    (5) In the foregoing provisions references to a ship or cargo belonging
to a State include references to a ship or cargo in its possession or control
or in which it claims an interest; and, subject to subsection (4) above,
subsection (2) above applies to property other than a ship as it applies to
a ship.

    (6) Sections 3 to 5 above do not apply to proceedings of the kind
described in subsection (1) above if the State in question is a party to the
Brussels Convention and the claim relates to the operation of a ship owned
or operated by that State, the carriage of cargo or passengers on any such
ship or the carriage of cargo owned by that State on any other ship.

    11. A State is not immune as respects proceedings relating to its liability
for—

    (*a*) value added tax, any duty of customs or excise or any agri-
        cultural levy; or

    (*b*) rates in respect of premises occupied by it for commercial
        purposes.[60c]

    13.—(1) No penalty by way of committal or fine shall be imposed in
respect of any failure or refusal by or on behalf of a State to disclose or

---

[60] *Ed.* s.17(1) states that "commercial purposes" means "purposes of such transactions or
activities as are mentioned in s.3(3)."
[60a] *ibid.*
[60b] *ibid.*
[60c] *ibid.*

produce any document or other information for the purposes of proceedings to which it is a party.

(2) Subject to subsections (3) and (4) below—

(*a*) relief shall not be given against a State by way of injunction or order for specific performance or for the recovery of land or other property; and

(*b*) the property of a State shall not be subject to any process for the enforcement of a judgment or arbitration award or, in an action in rem, for its arrest, detention or sale.

[s.13(3) provides that s.13(2) does not apply if the State consents in writing.]

(4) Subsection 2(*b*) above does not prevent the issue of any process in respect of property which is for the time being in use or intended for use for commercial purposes[60d]; but, in a case not falling within section 10 above, this subsection applies to property of a State party to the European Convention on State Immunity only if—

(*a*) the process is for enforcing a judgment which is final within the meaning of section 18(1)(*b*) below and the State has made a declaration under Article 24 of the Convention; or

(*b*) the process is for enforcing an arbitration award.

(5) The head of a State's diplomatic mission in the United Kingdom, or the person for the time being performing his functions, shall be deemed to have authority to give on behalf of the State any such consent as is mentioned in subsection (3) above and, for the purposes of subsection (4) above, his certificate to the effect that any property is not in use or intended for use by or on behalf of the State for commercial purposes shall be accepted as sufficient evidence of that fact unless the contrary is proved.

14.—(1) The immunities and privileges conferred by this Part of this Act apply to any foreign or commonwealth State other than the United Kingdom; and references to a State include references to—

(*a*) the sovereign or other heads of that State in his public capacity;

(*b*) the government of that State; and

(*c*) any department of that government,

but not to any entity (hereafter referred to as a "separate entity") which is distinct from the executive organs of the government of the State and capable of suing or being sued.

(2) A separate entity is immune from the jurisdiction of the courts of the United Kingdom if, and only if—

[60d] *ibid.*

(*a*) the proceedings relate to anything done by it in the exercise of sovereign authority; and

(*b*) the circumstances are such that a State (or, in the case of proceedings to which section 10 above applies, a State which is not party to the Brussels Convention) would have been so immune.

(3) If a separate entity (not being a State's central bank or other monetary authority) submits to the jurisdiction in respect of proceedings in the case of which it is entitled to immunity by virtue of subsection (2) above, subsections (1) to (4) of section 13 above shall apply to it in respect of those proceedings as if references to a State were references to that entity.

(4) Property of a State's central bank or other monetary authority shall not be regarded for the purposes of subsection (4) of section 13 above as in use or intended for use for commercial purposes[60e]; and where any such bank or authority is a separate entity subsections (1) to (3) of that section shall apply to it as if references to a State were references to the bank or authority.

(5) Section 12 above applies to proceedings against the constituent territories of a federal State; and Her Majesty may by Order in Council provide for the other provisions of this Part of this Act to apply to any such constituent territory specified in the Order as they apply to a State.

(6) Where the provisions of this Part of this Act do not apply to the constituent territory by virtue of any such Order subsections (2) and (3) above shall apply to it as if it were a separate entity.

16.—(1) This Part of this Act does not affect any immunity or privilege conferred by the Diplomatic Privileges Act 1964 or the Consular Relations Act 1968; and—

(*a*) section 4 above does not apply to proceedings concerning the employment of the members of a mission within the meaning of the Convention scheduled to the said Act of 1964[60f] or of the members of consular post within the meaning of the Convention scheduled to the said Act of 1968;

(*b*) section 6(1) above does not apply to proceedings concerning a State's title to or its possession of property used for the purposes of a diplomatic mission.[61]

[60e] *ibid.*

[60f] *Ed.* A British national working as a secretary in a London embassy is a "member of the mission" as a member of its technical or administrative staff within s.16, so that the exception to state immunity in s.4 of the State Immunity Act 1978 in respect of employment did not apply: *Ahmed v. Govt. of the Kingdom of Saudi Arabia* [1996] 2 All E.R. 249, CA. *cf. Arab Republic of Egypt v. Gamal-Eldin* [1996] 2 All E.R. 237, EAT.

[61] Ed. See the *Intpro Properties* case, above, p. 323, n. 58.

(2) This Part of this Act does not apply to proceedings relating to anything done by or in relation to the armed forces of a State while present in the United Kingdom and, in particular, has effect subject to the Visiting Forces Act 1952.

(3) This Part of this Act does not apply to proceedings to which section 17(6) of the Nuclear Installations Act 1965 applies.

(4) This Part of this Act does not apply to criminal proceedings.

(5) This Part of this Act does not apply to any proceedings relating to taxation other than those mentioned in section 11 above.

20.—(1) Subject to the provisions of this section and to any necessary modifications, the Diplomatic Privileges Act 1964[62] shall apply to—

> (*a*) a sovereign or other head of State;
> (*b*) members of his family forming part of his household; and
> (*c*) his private servants,

as it applies to the head of a diplomatic mission, to members of his family forming part of his household and to his private servants.

(2) The immunities and privileges conferred by virtue of subsection (1)(*a*) and (*b*) above shall not be subject to the restrictions by reference to nationality or residence mentioned in Article 37(1) or 38 in Schedule 1 to the said Act of 1964. . . .

(5) This section applies to the sovereign or other head of any State on which immunities and privileges are conferred by Part I of this Act and is without prejudice to the application of that Part to any such sovereign or head of State in his public capacity.

21. A certificate by or on behalf of the Secretary of State shall be conclusive evidence on any question—

> (*a*) whether any country is a State for the purposes of Part I of this Act, whether any territory is a constituent territory of a federal State for those purposes or as to the person or persons to be regarded for those purposes as the head or government of a State; . . . [63]

Notes

1. The Act came into force on November 22, 1978; it does not have retrospective effect.[64] At common law, the British courts had abandoned the doctrine of absolute immunity in *The Philippine Admiral* [1977] A.C. 373, JC (actions *in rem*) and *Trendtex Trading Corpn v. Central Bank of Nigeria* [1977] Q.B. 529, CA (actions in personam), just before the 1978 Act was enacted.

[62] *Ed.* Below, p. 362.
[63] On judicial review of certificates issued under s.21, see the *Trawnik* case, p. 99, above.
[64] s.23. Exceptionally, s.12 (service of process and judgments in default of appearance) applies retrospectively.

2. The Act was introduced partly to permit ratification of the 1926 Brussels Convention and the 1972 European Convention, see above, p. 307, and certain of the complications in its text result from this objective. The Act was also a response to the fear in the City that the United Kingdom would increasingly lose business to other jurisdictions if it did not offer better legal security for persons trading with states.[65] The Act applies to all foreign states, except for the provisions about the recognition of judgments (ss.18–19) which apply only to parties to the 1972 European Convention.

3. The pattern of the Act (like that of the 1972 European Convention), is to provide for general immunity (s.1(1)), subject to a list of exceptions (ss.2–11) which accord with the doctrine of restrictive immunity. As a result, the burden is upon the plaintiff to prove that the case falls within one of the listed exceptions. Although the exceptions in the Act, which are wider than those in the 1972 Convention, are specific to particular contexts (commercial transactions, employment contracts, tort claims, etc.) and are defined in some detail, the Act (like the International Law Commission's Draft Articles, below, p. 335) does not eliminate entirely the general distinction between acts *iure imperii* and acts *iure gestionis* with which the courts have had to grapple at common law since moving to the doctrine of restricted immunity. Thus it will still be necessary in some cases, no doubt with the assistance of common law cases, to interpret the phrase "in the exercise of sovereign authority" when applying section 3(3) in connection with section 3(1)(2) or when interpreting (via s.17) the phrase "commercial purposes" in sections 4(3), 10(3), 11 and 13(4)(5). Would the wording of section 3(3) permit Lord Wilberforce's approach in the *I Congreso del Partido* case, above, p. 310? Can one, that is, look to the nature of the act complained of (the act on breach of contract, of conversion, etc.)? Or must one look only to the nature of the transaction or activity in respect of which it occurs? As to the latter, was there a "commercial transaction" entered into by Cuba in respect of the *Marble Islands* in the *I Congreso del Partido* case? A pre-1978 Act case that would be decided the same way on its facts under the Act was *Planmount Ltd v. Republic of Zaire*.[66] In that case, a builder sued the defendant for the balance of monies due under a contract for repair work done to the official residence of the ambassador of Zaire in London. A defence of state immunity was rejected at common law, Lloyd J. relying upon the *Trendtex* case, below, p. 331. *cf.* the facts of the *Claim against the Empire of Iran*, see above, p. 311. Most of the exceptions in sections 2–11 of the Act are limited by requirements linking the case with the United Kingdom, (*e.g.* the contract to be performed in the United Kingdom: s.3(1)(b)), but this is *not* true of the "commercial transactions" exception in section 3(1)(a), as to which see below, note 5. These requirements are aimed at compliance with the rules limiting the jurisdiction of states in customary international law and hence assisting in the execution of judgments against states that are impleaded. The Act concerns civil proceedings; it does not provide for immunity from criminal liability (*e.g.* for oil pollution).[67]

4. Section 2(2) reverses the rule in *Kahan v. Pakistan Federation* [1951] 2 K.B. 1003, CA by which submission to jurisdiction could only be made before the court and not by prior written agreement. It is quite common for a waiver of immunity to

---

[65] See Lord Hailsham L.C., *Hansard*, H.L., Vol. 389, col. 1502 March 16, 1978.

[66] [1981] 1 All E.R. 1110, QB. In a case under the 1978 Act, a contract for the supply by a British company of the component parts of a super-gun to Iraq was a "commercial transaction" (see s.3(3)(a)) so that the High Court had jurisdiction to make a confiscation order: *Commissioners of Customs and Excise v. Ministry of Industries and Military Manufacturing, Republic of Iraq*, unreported, 1992: see Fox (1994) 43 I.C.L.Q. 193 at 194.

[67] See the Merchant Shipping (Prevention of Oil Pollution) Regulations 1996, Regs. 12, 13, 36, S.I. 1996 No. 2154, which create a criminal offence which may be committed by foreign oil tankers that discharge oil into U.K. waters.

be included in the loan or other financial agreement. A state is deemed to have waived its immunity if it institutes proceedings, or intervenes, or takes any step in the proceedings (s.2(3)).[68]

5. The definition of "commercial transaction" in section 3(3) covers *all* contracts and financial transactions of the kinds listed in section 3(3)(*a*)(*b*); there is no need for the court to consider the difficult question whether they result from the "exercise of sovereign authority." They are, by definition, "commercial transactions." Hence neither the purpose for which the goods or services are wanted nor the fact that the contract or loan is one that could only be made by a governmental entity is relevant. A contract for the supply of cement for an army barracks (*Trendtex* case, below, p. 331) or of military equipment (or of technicians to train soldiers to use it) would come within section 3(3)(*a*). A loan to or by a government would similarly fall within section 3(3)(*b*), as would the letter of credit in the *Trendtex* case. In the case of "any other transaction or activity" in the sense of section 3(3)(*c*), a court will have to decide whether it results from "an exercise of sovereign authority." Mann[69] argues that the word "activity" allows claims in tort to be brought against a state where they do not result from an "exercise of sovereign authority." Thus a claim in libel, such as that in *Krajina v. Tass Agency*, below, p. 332, n. 80, could not be met by a defence of state immunity unless the tort were committed "in the exercise of sovereign authority." For another example of an "activity" that would probably come within section 3(3)(*c*), see the facts of *U.S. v. Dolfus Mieg*, next note. Section 3(1)(*b*) adds to section 3(1)(*a*) by denying immunity in certain non-"commercial transaction" cases in contract. The concurrent or secondary liability of a state under a contract to which it was not a party or the liability of a state as the undisclosed principal of an agent who was a party to a contract would be an "obligation" within section 3(1)(*b*).[70]

6. Section 6(4) deals with one form of indirect impleading, *i.e.* the situation in which proceedings are brought against someone other than the state but which concern property within a state's ownership, possession, or control. A defence of state immunity is allowed in such a case under section 6(4) only if the defence would be available if the proceedings had been brought against the state itself. Under the Act, therefore, the plaintiff would still not have succeeded in respect of the 51 gold bars in *U.S. v. Dolfus Mieg* [1952] A.C. 582, HL. In that case, the plaintiffs claimed, as owners, the return of gold bars deposited by certain Governments with the Bank of England under a contract of bailment, including 51 bars still in the Bank vaults. Although the proceedings were brought against the Bank, a plea of immunity was upheld because the foreign Governments concerned had an immediate right to possession under the contract of bailment and would have been indirectly impleaded had the case gone ahead. Since the bars (which had been taken from the plaintiffs by the German authorities in the Second World War, then recovered by American forces, and finally placed in the possession of the Allied Governments of France, the United Kingdom and the United States, pending restitution proceedings) had undoubtedly been deposited with the Bank by those Governments "in the exercise of sovereign authority," section 3(3)(*c*) would apply so that immunity would now be available to the American and French Governments if sued themselves in a United Kingdom court.

The *prima facie* evidence requirement in an "interest" case inserted at the end of section 6(4) confirms *Juan Ismael and Co. v. Indonesian Govt.* [1955] A.C. 72, HL.

7. *Section 10.* A second form of indirect pleading, which has often been the subject of claim to state immunity at common law, occurs when an action *in rem*

---

[68] For a case of waiver of immunity by an international organisation, see *Standard Charter Bank v. International Tin Council* [1987] 1 W.L.R. 641, QB.

[69] *op. cit.*, p. 321, n. 55, above, p. 52. This is in addition to tort claims allowed by ss.5–6.

[70] *Rayner Ltd v. Dept of Trade* [1989] Ch. 72 at 195 *per* Kerr L.J., CA.

is brought in admiralty proceedings against a ship belonging to a state, *i.e.* in its ownership, possession or control. Under section 10, state immunity does not exist "if, at the time when the cause of action arose, the ship was in use or intended for use for commercial purposes" (s. 10(2)).[71] How would the *I Congreso del Partido* case, above p. 310, have been decided under section 10?

8. Section 13 lists certain procedural privileges which apply even if a state is not entitled to immunity from jurisdiction. Most significantly, in the absence of a state's consent, (i) a *Mareva* injunction[72] is not available to prevent property being taken out of the jurisdiction pending litigation and (ii) a state's property may not be used for the enforcement of a judgment against it unless it is property that is "for the time being in use or intended for use for commercial purposes."[73] As to the latter, consistently with the dignity of states and the need for good international relations, the common law approach had been to apply a rule of absolute immunity from *execution* so that no property of the state could be attached in satisfaction of a judgment against it. The 1978 Act moderates this approach, in line with some (but not all) civil law jurisdictions,[74] so that execution is permitted (in cases of waiver of immunity from jurisdiction or restricted immunity) against property used "for commercial purposes" (s.13(4)). Such execution is not permitted, however, against the property of a party to the 1972 European Convention unless it makes an Article 24 declaration (s.13(4)(a)). The "commercial purposes" exception in section 13(4) was interpreted so as, in effect, to prevent execution against an embassy bank account in *Alcom v. Republic of Colombia*.[75] There it was held that money in an embassy current bank account to pay for the day to day expenses of the Colombian embassy in London was immune from judicial process by virtue of section 13(2)(*b*). Lord Diplock stated[76]:

> Such expenditure will, no doubt, include *some* moneys due under contracts for the supply of goods or services to the mission . . . ; but the account will also be drawn upon to meet many other items of expenditure which fall outside even the extended definition of "commercial purposes" for which section 17(1) and section 3(3) provide. The debt owed by the bank to the foreign sovereign state and represented by the credit balance in the current account kept by the diplomatic mission of that state as a possible subject matter of the enforcement jurisdiction of the court is, however, one and indivisible . . . Unless it can be shown by the judgment creditor who is seeking to attach the credit balance by garnishee proceedings that the bank account was earmarked by the foreign state solely (save for de minimis exceptions) for being drawn upon to settle liabilities incurred in commercial transactions . . . it cannot . . . be sensibly brought within . . . Section 13(4) . . .

On the attachment of ships, see section 10. On the special position of central banks, see below, p. 335.

9. Section 14: see the notes to the *Trendtex* case, below, p. 331.

---

[71] *cf.* the similar lack of immunity in respect of *in rem* proceedings against a ship's cargo: s.10(4). Note also that s.10(2)(*b*) and (4) exclude immunity in actions *in personam* (against the state as third party) in connection with a ship or its cargo where the "commercial purposes" test is met.

[72] See *Mareva Compania Naviera v. International Bulkcarriers* [1975] 2 Lloyd's Rep. 509, CA.

[73] For the meaning of "commercial purposes," see p. 324, n. 60, above.

[74] On immunity from execution in international law, see Crawford (1981) 75 A.J.I.L. 820 and Fox (1985) 34 I.C.L.Q. 115.

[75] [1984] A.C. 580, HL.

[76] *ibid.* at 604. For criticism of the decision, see Crawford (1983) 54 B.Y.I.L. 75. See also Houtte (1986) 19 R.B.D.I. 70.

10. Section 20: The 1978 Act applies to a sovereign or other head of state acting in his *public* capacity. Section 20 provides that such a person in his *private* capacity is, together with his family and servants, entitled to the privileges accorded to the head of a diplomatic mission, *etc.*, under the Diplomatic Privileges Act 1964, below, p. 362. Previously, the position of a sovereign in his personal capacity was regulated by common law.

11. Section 21(a) is consistent with *Duff Development Co. v. Kelantan* [1924] A.C. 797, HL. The statements *obiter dicta* in that case to the effect that if the Foreign Office did not respond to a request for a certificate the courts would have taken their own decision presumably still apply.

12. A claim of immunity under the Act must be decided as a preliminary issue in favour of the plaintiff before the action can proceed on the merits.[77]

TRENDTEX TRADING CORP. v. CENTRAL BANK OF NIGERIA[78]

[1977] Q.B. 529. Court of Appeal

In 1975, the Central Bank of Nigeria issued a letter of credit in favour of the plaintiffs, a Swiss company, for the price of cement to be sold by the plaintiffs to an English company which had secured a contract with the Nigerian Government to supply it with cement for the construction of an army barracks in Nigeria. When, under instructions from the Nigerian Government (which was taking steps to extricate itself from the Nigerian Cement Scandal created by its predecessor Government),[79] the bank refused to honour the letter of credit, the plaintiffs brought an action *in personam* against the bank in the English High Court. The bank successfully claimed sovereign immunity before Donaldson J. The plaintiffs appealed.

LORD DENNING M.R. The Central Bank of Nigeria claims that it cannot be sued in this country on the letter of credit; because it is entitled to sovereign immunity.

... The doctrine grants immunity to a foreign government or its department of state or any body which can be regarded as an "alter ego or organ" of the government.... In some countries the government departments conduct all their business through their own offices—even ordinary commercial dealings—without setting up separate corporations or legal entities. In other countries they set up separate corporations or legal entities which are under the complete control of the department, but which enter into commercial transactions, buying and selling goods, owning and chartering ships, just like any ordinary trading concern. This difference in internal arrangements ought not to affect the availability of immunity in international law. A foreign department of state ought not to

---

[77] *Rayner Ltd v. Dept of Trade* [1989] Ch. 72, CA.
[78] See Markesinis (1977) 36 C.L.J. 211 and White (1977) 26 I.C.L.Q. 674.
[79] Huge quantities of cement had been ordered from different sources—far more than Nigeria needed or the port of Lagos could handle. The new Nigerian Government took steps similar to those taken in this case against suppliers in other cases, leading to comparable court proceedings in the U.S. and the F.R.G.: see (1977) 16 I.L.M. 469. A doctrine of restrictive immunity was applied against the defendant's claim of state immunity in those cases also.

lose its immunity simply because it conducts some of its activities by means of a separate legal entity. It was so held by this court in *Baccus SRL v. Servicio Nacional del Trigo*.[80]

Another problem arises because of the internal laws of many countries which grant immunities and privileges to their own organisations. Some organisations can sue, or be sued, in their courts. Others cannot. In England we have had for centuries special immunities and privileges for "the Crown," a phrase which has been held to cover many governmental departments and many emanations of government departments but not nationalised commercial undertakings: see *Tamlin v. Hannaford*.[81] The phrase "the Crown" is so elastic that under the Crown Proceedings Act 1947, the Treasury has issued a list of government departments covered by the Act. It includes even the Forestry Commission. It cannot be right that international law should grant or refuse absolute immunity, according to the immunities granted internally. I would put on one side, therefore, our cases about the privileges, prerogatives and exceptions of "the Crown."

It is often said that a certificate by the ambassador, saying whether or not an organisation is a department of state, is of much weight, though not decisive: see *Krajina v. Tass Agency*.[82] But even this is not to my mind satisfactory. What is the test which the ambassador is to apply? In the absence of any test, an ambassador may apply the test of control, asking himself: is the organisation under the control of a minister of state? On such a test, he might certify any nationalised undertaking to be a department of state. He might certify that a press agency or an agricultural corporation (which carried out ordinary commercial dealings) was a department of state, simply because it was under the complete control of the government.

I confess that I can think of no satisfactory test except that of looking to the functions and control of the organisation. I do not think that it should depend on the foreign law alone. I would look to all the evidence to see whether the organisation was under government control and exercised governmental functions. That is the way in which we looked at it in *Mellenger v. New Brunswick Development Corpn.* [1971] 1 W.L.R. 604 (C.A.) . . .

At the hearing we were taken through the Act of 1958 under which the Central Bank of Nigeria was established, and the amendments to the Act

[80] [1957] 1 Q.B. 438; [1956] 3 All E.R. 715, CA.
[81] [1950] 1 K.B. 18; [1949] 2 All E.R. 327, CA.
[82] [1949] 2 All E.R. 274, CA. In this case, the plaintiff sought damages for an alleged libel in a newspaper published by the defendant. The latter was described in the Russian statute establishing it as "the central information organ of the USSR" and as enjoying "all the rights of a legal person." The Ambassador of the USSR to the U.K. certified that the defendant was "a department of state of the Soviet State . . . exercising the rights of a legal entity." The Court of Appeal held, unanimously, that the defendant was a department of state and entitled to immunity as such under the doctrine of absolute immunity. The Ambassador's certificate, although not conclusive, had sufficiently established this.

by later decrees. All the relevant provisions were closely examined; and we had the benefit of expert evidence on affidavit which was most helpful.[83] The upshot of it all may be summarised as follows. (1) The Central Bank of Nigeria is a central bank modelled on the Bank of England. (2) It has governmental functions in that it issues legal tender; it safeguards the international value of the currency; and it acts as banker and financial adviser to the government. (3) Its affairs are under a great deal of government control in that the Federal Executive Council may overrule the board of directors on monetary and banking policy and on internal administrative policy. (4) It acts as banker for other banks in Nigeria and abroad, and maintains accounts with other banks. It acts as banker for the states within the Federation, but has few, if any, private customers.

In these circumstances I have found it difficult to decide whether or not the Central Bank of Nigeria should be considered in international law a department of the Federation of Nigeria, even though it is a separate legal entity. But, on the whole, I do not think it should be.

SHAW L.J. Whether a particular organisation is to be accorded the status of a department of government or not must depend on its constitution, its powers and duties and its activities. . . . The bank is, in the first place, a statutory corporation whose personality, powers and legal attributes are determined by the Central Bank of Nigeria Act 1958. . . . Nowhere in that legislation is it called anything but a bank; . . . The 52 sections of the principal Act . . . contain no direct indication that the bank is a department of the government and there are many indications which deny it that status. The very name has a commercial ring. Its powers do not identify it with the government and in some respects preclude identification with the government. . . .

Apart from these matters there is an important practical consideration. . . . Those who contemplate entering into transactions with bodies which may be in a position to claim sovereign immunity are entitled at least to the opportunity of assessing any special risk which may arise. How can they know that such a risk lurks in dealing with a body which assumes a guise and bears a title appropriate to a commercial or financial institution? . . . There is no rule of law which demands this; but where the issue of status trembles on a fine edge, the absence of any positive indication that the body in question was intended to possess sovereign status and its attendant privileges must perforce militate against the view that it enjoys that status or is entitled to those privileges. This is especially the case where the opportunity to define the status of the institution concerned in clear and express terms has existed from the very inception, or indeed conception, of that institution—as in this case.

---

[83] *Ed.* This spoke of the Bank as the agent of the Government and as being under its control; it did not refer to the Bank as a department of government.

... It is clear enough that the bank was the subserving agent of the government in a variety of activities but this is not in my judgment adequate to constitute it as an organ or department of government. I cannot find in the constitution of the bank or in the functions it performs or in the activities it pursues or in all those matters looked at together any compelling or indeed satisfactory basis for the conclusion that it is so related to the Government of Nigeria as to form part of it. Accordingly I would hold that the bank is not entitled to the immunity which it claims. . . .

Notes

1. The appeal was allowed unanimously. Stephenson L.J. agreed with the other two judges on the status of the Bank and that international law had changed to a doctrine of restrictive immunity. Unlike the other two, however, Stephenson L.J. (like the majority in the *Tapioca* case) felt himself bound by precedent to follow the doctrine of absolute immunity.

2. The current rule indicating whose acts are to be treated as state acts attracting immunity is in 1978 Act, section 14, above, p. 325. A department of government under a foreign state's law is entitled to immunity in respect of its acts even though it has a separate legal personality under that law. This is consistent with *Baccus v. S.R.L. Servicio Nacional del Trigo* [1957] 1 Q.B. 438, CA, in which the plaintiff Italian company and the defendants made a contract for the sale of rye which contained an arbitration clause giving jurisdiction over disputes arising under the contract to the English High Court. The plaintiffs initiated proceedings under the clause but the defendants pleaded state immunity on the ground that, although formed as a separate legal person under Spanish law, they were nonetheless a Department of State of the Spanish Government. The Court of Appeal (Jenkins and Parker L.JJ., Singleton L.J. dissenting) upheld this plea in reliance upon affidavit evidence from the Spanish ambassador and a Spanish legal expert to the effect that the defendants were in Spanish law a Department of the Spanish Ministry of Agriculture. Although the same conclusion (that the defendants attracted immunity as a department of government) would be reached under section 14, immunity would nonetheless not be allowed on the facts of the case because the contract was a "commercial transaction": section 3(3)(a).

In the *Trendtex* case, the Court of Appeal looked not only to Nigerian law but also to the functions of the Bank and its relationship with the Government when deciding whether it should be classified as a department of government.[84] Section 14 would seem to limit itself to the first of these considerations. (If so, it is open to the criticism which Lord Denning makes, namely that differences in "internal arrangements ought not to affect the availability of immunity in international law.") State trading agencies of the sort typical of socialist countries would thus qualify as departments of state if they are classified as such under the local law,[85] but not otherwise. The Cuban agencies in the *I Congreso* case above, p. 310, would not qualify. Nor would United Kingdom public corporations such as the Post Office and the Civil Aviation Authority. It seems likely that, when applying section 14, the courts will continue to rely upon expert evidence and the affidavits

---

[84] *cf. Czarnikow Ltd v. Rolimpex* [1979] A.C. 351, HL (Polish state trading organisation with independent legal personality sufficiently free of government control in its commercial activities so as not to be an organ of the Polish Government).

[85] Note, however, the good faith control on claims of state immunity suggested in the *Claim against the Empire of Iran*, (1963) 45 I.L.R. 57, as to which see above, p. 311.

of ambassadors to establish the legal status of an entity as they had done at common law: see the *Trendtex* case, the *Baccus* case and the *Krajina* case.[86]

3. A "separate entity" under section 14 (*i.e.* one that is not a department of state but that is capable of being sued) is not entitled to state immunity unless it is acting "in the exercise of sovereign authority."[87] Here again (as when interpreting section 3(3)(*c*)) the courts will have to develop their own distinction between acts *iure imperii* and acts *iure gestionis*: see above, p. 329. Sinclair[88] suggests that certain of the functions of a body such as the Civil Aviation Authority (*e.g.* the licensing of carriers) might qualify for immunity.

4. Under section 14(5) the "constituent territories of a federal state" do not qualify for immunity under the Act unless and to the extent that an Order in Council is made to the contrary in respect of particular territories.[89] To this extent, the decision in *Mellenger v. New Brunswick Development Corp.* [1971] 1 W.L.R. 604, CA, (Canadian Province of New Brunswick entitled to immunity) is reversed.

5. In the *Trendtex* case, the plaintiffs were granted a *Mareva* injunction ordering that assets held by the bank in a bank account in London remain within the jurisdiction pending the outcome of the case. As a result of section 14(4), such an injunction could not now be granted. The United States Foreign Sovereign Immunities Act 1976, s.1611, contains a similar provision which was justified as follows:

> If execution could be levied on such funds without an explicit waiver, deposit of foreign funds in the U.S. might be discouraged. Moreover, execution against the reserves of foreign states could cause significant foreign relations problems.[90]

Note that section 14(4) means that, unlike other state property, the property of a central bank is not subject to execution *even if it is being used, etc., for commercial purposes*. Section 14(4) also grants central banks the other procedural privileges allowed by section 13, as to which see above, p. 330. These limitations tend to undermine the effectiveness of the restrictive immunity doctrine as applied to central banks.

I.L.C. DRAFT ARTICLES ON JURISDICTIONAL IMMUNITIES OF STATES AND THEIR PROPERTY[91]

Y.B.I.L.C. 1991, Vol. II–2, p. 13; (1991) 30 I.L.M. 1554

Article 2. Use of terms

1. For the purposes of the present articles: . . .

(*b*) "State" means:

---

[86] In the *Kuwait Airways* case, above, p. 318, the status of the I.A.C. as a separate entity was not disputed and no affidavit or certificate was sought. The I.A.C. was owned and controlled by the government of Iraq.

[87] *cf.* the approach of the I.L.C. in respect of state responsibility below, p. 499.

[88] *op. cit.*, p. 306, n. 37, above, p. 259.

[89] Orders have been made for the constituent territories of Austria (S.I. 1979 No. 457) and Germany (S.I. 1993 No. 2809).

[90] Explanatory Memorandum to the Act, quoted in *Hispano Americana Mercantil v. Central Bank of Nigeria* [1979] 2 Lloyd's Rep. 277, CA.

[91] The Draft Articles are based upon the reports of the I.L.C.'s rapporteurs, Mr Sucharitkul and Mr Motoo Ogiso, for which see the references in Y.B.I.L.C. 1991, Vol. II–2, p. 12. On the Draft Articles, see Grieg (1989) 38 I.C.L.Q. 242 at 560; Hess (1993) 4 E.J.I.L. 269; Morris (1989) 17 Denver J.I.L.P. 395; Tomuschat, *Seidl-Hohenveldern Essays* (1993), p. 603. See also the International Law Association's *Revised Draft Articles for a Convention on State Immunity*, Report of the 66th I.L.A. Conference, Buenos Aires (1994), p. 488, and the Institut de droit international's proposals: (1992) 64 *Annuaire de l'Institut de droit international* 388.

(i) the State and its various organs of government;

(ii) constituent units of a federal State;

(iii) political subdivisions of the State which are entitled to perform acts in the exercise of the sovereign authority of the State;

(iv) agencies or instrumentalities of the State and other entities, to the extent that they are entitled to perform acts in the exercise of the sovereign authority of the State;

(v) representatives of the State acting in that capacity;

(c) "commercial transaction" means:

(i) any commercial contract or transaction for the sale of goods or supply of services;

(ii) any contract for a loan or other transaction of a financial nature, including any obligation of guarantee or of indemnity in respect of any such loan or transaction;

(iii) any other contract or transaction of a commercial, industrial, trading or professional nature, but not including a contract of employment of persons.

2. In determining whether a contract or transaction is a "commercial transaction" under paragraph 1(c), reference should be made primarily to the nature of the contract or transaction, but its purpose should also be taken into account if, in the practice of the State which is a party to it, that purpose is relevant to determining the non-commercial character of the contract or transaction.

3. The provisions of paragraphs 1 and 2 regarding the use of terms in the present articles are without prejudice to the use of those terms or to the meanings which may be given to them in other international instruments or in the internal law of any State.

Article 5. State immunity

A State enjoys immunity, in respect of itself and its property, from the jurisdiction of the courts of another State subject to the provisions of the present articles.

Article 10. Commercial transactions

1. If a State engages in a commercial transaction with a foreign natural or juridical person and, by virtue of the applicable rules of private international law, differences relating to the commercial transaction fall within the jurisdiction of a court of another State, the State cannot invoke immunity from that jurisdiction in a proceeding arising out of that commercial transaction.

2. Paragraph 1 does not apply:

(*a*) in the case of a commercial transaction between States; or

(*b*) if the parties to the commercial transaction have expressly agreed otherwise.

3. The immunity from jurisdiction enjoyed by a State shall not be affected with regard to a proceeding which relates to a commercial transaction engaged in by a State enterprise or other entity established by the State which has an independent legal personality and is capable of:

(a) suing or being sued; and

(b) acquiring, owning or possessing and disposing of property, including property which the State has authorized it to operate or manage.

Article 11. Contracts of employment

1. Unless otherwise agreed between the States concerned, a State cannot invoke immunity from jurisdiction before a court of another State which is otherwise competent in a proceeding which relates to a contract of employment between the State and an individual for work performed or to be performed, in whole or in part, in the territory of that other State.

2. Paragraph 1 does not apply if:

(*a*) the employee has been recruited to perform functions closely related to the exercise of governmental authority;

(*b*) the subject of the proceeding is the recruitment, renewal of employment or reinstatement of an individual;

(*c*) the employee was neither a national nor a habitual resident of the State of the forum at the time when the contract of employment was concluded;

(*d*) the employee is a national of the employer State at the time when the proceeding is instituted; or

(*e*) the employer state and the employee have otherwise agreed in writing, subject to any considerations of public policy conferring on the courts of the State of the forum exclusive jurisdiction by reason of the subject-matter of the proceeding.

[Articles 12–15 exclude immunity in cases concerning personal injury or property damage; ownership, possession and use of property; intellectual and industrial property; and participation in companies respectively.]

Article 16. Ships owned or operated by a State

1. Unless otherwise agreed between the States concerned, a State which owns or operates a ship cannot invoke immunity from jurisdiction before a court of another State which is otherwise competent in a proceeding which relates to the operation of that ship, if at the time the cause

of action arose, the ship was used for other than government non-commercial purposes.

2. Paragraph 1 does not apply to warships and naval auxiliaries nor does it apply to other ships owned or operated by a State and used exclusively on government non-commercial service. . . .

4. Unless otherwise agreed between the States concerned, a State cannot invoke immunity from jurisdiction before a court of another State which is otherwise competent in a proceeding which relates to the carriage of cargo on board a ship owned or operated by that State if, at the time the cause of action arose, the ship was used for other than government non-commercial purposes.

5. Paragraph 4 does not apply to any cargo carried on board the ships referred to in paragraph 2 nor does it apply to any cargo owned by a State and used or intended for use exclusively for government non-commercial purposes.

6. States may plead all measures of defence, prescription and limitation of liability which are available to private ships and cargoes and their owners.

7. If in a proceeding there arises a question relating to the government and non-commercial character of a ship owned or operated by a State or cargo owned by a State, a certificate signed by a diplomatic representative or other competent authority of that State and communicated to the court shall serve as evidence of the character of that ship or cargo.

Article 18. *State immunity from measures of constraint*

1. No measures of constraint, such as attachment, arrest and execution, against property of a State may be taken in connection with a proceeding before a court of another State unless and except to the extent that:

(a) the State has expressly consented to the taking of such measures as indicated:

  (i) by international agreement;
  (ii) by an arbitration agreement or in a written contract; or
  (iii) by a declaration before the court or by a written communication after a dispute between the parties has arisen;

(b) the State has allocated or earmarked property for the satisfaction of the claim which is the object of that proceeding; or
(c) the property is specifically in use or intended for use by the State for other than government non-commercial purposes and is in the territory of the State of the forum and has a connection with the claim which is the object of the proceeding or with the agency or instrumentality against which the proceeding was directed.

2. Consent to the exercise of jurisdiction under article 7 shall not imply consent to the taking of measures of constraint under paragraph 1, for which separate consent shall be necessary.

Article 19. *Specific categories of property*

1. The following categories, in particular, of property of a State shall not be considered as property specifically in use or intended for use by the State for other than government non-commercial purposes under paragraph 1(c) of article 18:

(a) property, including any bank account, which is used or intended for use for the purposes of the diplomatic mission of the State or its consular posts, special missions, missions to international organizations, or delegations to organs of international organizations or to international conferences;

(b) property of a military character or used or intended for use for military purposes;

(c) property of the central bank or other monetary authority of the State;

(d) property forming part of the cultural heritage of the State or part of its archives and not placed or intended to be placed on sale;

(e) property forming part of an exhibition of objects of scientific, cultural or historical interest and not placed or intended to be placed on sale.

2. Paragraph 1 is without prejudice to paragraph 1(a) and (b) of article 18.

Notes

1. The Draft Articles, which attempt to achieve a compromise between the absolute and restricted immunity doctrines,[92] follow the pattern of the 1972 European Convention on State Immunity and recent national legislation by stating a general rule of immunity (Article 6) and then listing in some detail exceptions or limitations to it (Articles 11–19). This is a different (and preferable) approach to that found in national court decisions in which an attempt is made to spell out an abstract test distinguishing acts *iure imperii* and acts *iure gestionis* which is then applied in all contexts (commercial transactions, contracts of employment, etc.). Unfortunately, the Draft Articles, like national legislation, do not totally avoid such concepts as "sovereign authority" (see, *e.g.* Article 3, Draft Articles) and "commercial purposes" (see, *e.g.* Articles 18 and 21) so that judicial pronouncements in cases such as the *Empire of Iran* and *I Congreso del Partido* cases would remain to some extent relevant.

2. The Draft Articles have had a mixed reception in the 6th Committee of the General Assembly, with some states insisting on the absolute immunity approach and western states being critical of certain elements of the compromise, *e.g.* the reference to "purpose" as well as "nature" in the test of a "commercial transaction" (s.2(2)). The future of the Draft Articles is uncertain, with states hesitating to

[92] See above, p. 307.

agree to the formal convening of a diplomatic conference (none convened yet) to draft a law making convention based upon them. It may be that the moment for the Draft Articles has passed, with the move towards greater acceptance of the restrictive immunity doctrine causing its supporters to decline a compromise such as that which they represent.

5. DIPLOMATIC IMMUNITY[93]

VIENNA CONVENTION ON DIPLOMATIC RELATIONS 1961[94]

U.K.T.S. 19 (1965), Cmnd. 2565; 500 U.N.T.S. 95; (1961) 55 A.J.I.L. 1064

The States Parties to the present Convention, . . .

Realizing that the purpose of such privileges and immunities is not to benefit individuals but to ensure the efficient performance of the functions of diplomatic missions as representing States,

Affirming that the rules of customary international law should continue to govern questions not expressly regulated by the provisions of the present Convention,

Have agreed as follows:

Article 1

For the purpose of the present Convention, the following expressions shall have the meanings hereunder assigned to them:

(a) the "head of the mission" is the person charged by the sending State with the duty of acting in that capacity;

(b) the "members of the mission" are the head of the mission and the members of the staff of the mission;

(c) the "members of the staff of the mission" are the members of the diplomatic staff, of the administrative and technical staff and of the service staff of the mission;

(d) the "members of the diplomatic staff" are the members of the staff of the mission having diplomatic rank;

(e) a "diplomatic agent" is the head of the mission or a member of the diplomatic staff of the mission;

---

[93] See Brown (1988) 37 I.C.L.Q. 53; Dembinski, *The Modern Law of Diplomacy* (1988), Part IV; Denza, *Diplomatic Law* (1976); Hardy, *Modern Diplomatic Law* (1967); *Satow's Guide to Diplomatic Practice* (5th ed., 1979); Mahmoudi, in *Festskift till Lars Hjerner* (1990), p. 327; Sen, *A Diplomat's Handbook of International Law and Practice* (3rd rev. ed., 1988), Chap. V; Wilson, *Diplomatic Privileges and Immunities* (1967); Young (1964) 40 B.Y.I.L. 141.

[94] In force 1964. 177 parties, including the U.K. See Kerley (1962) 56 A.J.I.L. 88.

(*f*) the "members of the administrative and technical staff" are the members of the staff of the mission employed in the administrative and technical service of the mission[95];

(*g*) the "members of the service staff" are the members of the staff of the mission in the domestic service of the mission[96];

(*h*) a "private servant" is a person who is in the domestic service of a member of the mission and who is not an employee of the sending State;

(*i*) the "premises of the mission" are the buildings or parts of buildings and the land ancillary thereto, irrespective of ownership, used for the purposes of the mission including the residence of the head of the mission.[97]

Article 9

1. The receiving State may at any time and without having to explain its decision, notify the sending State that the head of the mission or any member of the diplomatic staff of the mission is *persona non grata* or that any other member of the staff of the mission is not acceptable. In any such case, the sending State shall, as appropriate, either recall the person concerned or terminate his functions with the mission. A person may be declared *non grata* or not acceptable before arriving in the territory of the receiving State. . . .

Article 22

1. The premises of the mission[98] shall be inviolable. The agents of the receiving State may not enter them, except with the consent of the head of the mission.

2. The receiving State is under a special duty to take all appropriate steps to protect the premises of the mission against any intrusion or damage and to prevent any disturbance of the peace of the mission or impairment of its dignity.

3. The premises of the mission, their furnishings and other property thereon and the means of transport of the mission shall be immune from search, requisition, attachment or execution.

Article 23

[Exemption from taxes on the premises of the mission.]

---

[95] *Ed., e.g.* archivists, clerical and secretarial staff, translators.

[96] *Ed., e.g.* chauffeurs, porters, kitchen staff.

[97] The "premises of the mission" do not include the private residence of a diplomatic agent other than the head of the mission: *Intpro Properties Ltd v. Sauvel* [1983] Q.B. 1019, CA.

[98] Art. 22 only applies to premises that are currently used as the premises of a mission: *Westminster C.C. v. Govt. of Iran* [1986] 1 W.L.R. 979, Ch. D. (premises of Iranian Embassy gutted by fire not within Art. 22).

Article 24

The archives and documents of the mission shall be inviolable at any time and wherever they may be.

Article 25

The receiving State shall accord full facilities for the performance of the functions of the mission.

Article 26

Subject to its laws and regulations concerning zones entry into which is prohibited or regulated for reasons of national security, the receiving State shall ensure to all members of the mission freedom of movement and travel in its territory.

Article 27

1. The receiving State shall permit and protect free communication on the part of the mission for all official purposes. In communicating with the Government and the other missions and consulates of the sending State, wherever situated, the mission may employ all appropriate means, including diplomatic couriers and messages in code or cipher. However, the mission may install and use a wireless transmitter only with the consent of the receiving State.

2. The official correspondence of the mission shall be inviolable. Official correspondence means all correspondence relating to the mission and its functions.

3. The diplomatic bag shall not be opened or detained.

4. The packages constituting the diplomatic bag must bear visible external marks of their character and may contain only diplomatic documents or articles intended for official use. . . .

Article 29

The person of a diplomatic agent shall be inviolable. He shall not be liable to any form of arrest or detention. The receiving State shall treat him with due respect and shall take all appropriate steps to prevent any attack on his person, freedom or dignity.

Article 30

1. The private residence of a diplomatic agent shall enjoy the same inviolability and protection as the premises of the mission.

2. His papers, correspondence and, except as provided in paragraph 3 of Article 31, his property,[99] shall likewise enjoy inviolability.

Article 31

1. A diplomatic agent shall enjoy immunity from the criminal jurisdiction of the receiving State. He shall also enjoy immunity from its civil and administrative jurisdiction, except in the case of:

(a) a real action relating to private immovable property situated in the territory of the receiving State, unless he holds it on behalf of the sending State for the purposes of the mission[1];

(b) an action relating to succession in which the diplomatic agent is involved as executor, administrator, heir or legatee as a private person and not on behalf of the sending State;

(c) an action relating to any professional or commercial activity exercised by the diplomatic agent in the receiving State outside his official functions.

2. A diplomatic agent is not obliged to give evidence as a witness.

3. No measures of execution may be taken in respect of a diplomatic agent except in the cases coming under sub-paragraphs (a), (b) and (c) of paragraph 1 of this Article, and provided that the measures concerned can be taken without infringing the inviolability of his person or of his residence.

4. The immunity of a diplomatic agent from the jurisdiction of the receiving State does not exempt him from the jurisdiction of the sending State.

Article 32

1. The immunity from jurisdiction of diplomatic agents and of persons enjoying immunity under Article 37 may be waived by the sending State.

2. Waiver must always be express.

---

[99] The U.K. takes the view that this does not prevent the towing away of a diplomatic agent's car that is causing an obstruction; wheel-clamping has been discontinued on the basis that it is a penal measure contrary to Art. 31(1), below: *Diplomatic Immunities and Privileges*, Misc. 5 (1985), Cmnd. 9497, p. 26. See also U.K.M.I.L. 1985, (1985) 56 B.Y.I.L. 435.

[1] A "real action," which is a literal translation of the French text of Art. 31 and which is a term not known to English law since the Middle Ages, is an action in which the ownership or possession (as opposed to use) of real property is in issue; hence an action to enforce a covenant under a lease authorising entry to effect repairs does not qualify: *Intpro Properties Ltd v. Sauvel* [1983] Q.B. 1019, CA. In the same case it was held that the private residence of a diplomatic agent other than a head of mission is not held for the "purposes of the mission." For the state immunity aspect of this case (the plaintiff sued both France and its agent), see above, p. 323, n. 58.

3. The initiation of proceedings by a diplomatic agent or by a person enjoying immunity from jurisdiction under Article 37 shall preclude him from invoking immunity from jurisdiction in respect of any counter-claim directly connected with the principal claim.

4. Waiver of immunity from jurisdiction in respect of civil or administrative proceedings shall not be held to imply waiver of immunity in respect of the execution of the judgment, for which a separate waiver shall be necessary.

Article 34

[Exemption from taxation of diplomatic agents.]

Article 36

[Exemption from customs duties for the mission and diplomatic agents and their families.]

Article 37

1. The members of the family of a diplomatic agent forming part of his household shall, if they are not nationals of the receiving State, enjoy the privileges and immunities specified in Articles 29 to 36.

2. Members of the administrative and technical staff of the mission, together with members of their families forming part of their respective households, shall, if they are not nationals of or permanently resident in the receiving State, enjoy the privileges and immunities specified in Articles 29 to 35, except that the immunity from civil administrative jurisdiction of the receiving State specified in paragraph 1 of Article 31 shall not extend to acts performed outside the course of their duties. They shall also enjoy the privileges specified in Article 36, paragraph 1, in respect of articles imported at the time of first installation.

3. Members of the service staff of the mission who are not nationals of or permanently resident in the receiving State shall enjoy immunity in respect of acts performed in the course of their duties, exemption from dues and taxes on the emoluments they receive by reason of their employment and the exemption contained in Article 33 [concerning social security provisions].

4. Private servants of members of the mission shall, if they are not nationals of or permanently resident in the receiving State, be exempt from dues and taxes on the emoluments they receive by reason of their employment. In other respects, they may enjoy privileges and immunities only to the extent admitted by the receiving State. However, the receiving State must exercise its jurisdiction over those persons in such a manner as not to interfere unduly with the performance of the functions of the mission.

Article 38

1. Except insofar as additional privileges and immunities may be granted by the receiving State, a diplomatic agent who is a national of or permanently resident[2] in that State shall enjoy only immunity from jurisdiction, and inviolability, in respect of official acts performed in the exercise of his functions.

2. Other members of the staff of the mission and private servants who are nationals of or permanently resident in the receiving State shall enjoy privileges and immunities only to the extent admitted by the receiving State. However, the receiving State must exercise its jurisdiction over those persons in such a manner as not to interfere unduly with the performance of the functions of the mission.

Article 39

1. Every person entitled to such privileges and immunities shall enjoy them from the moment he enters the territory of the receiving State on proceeding to take up his post or, if already in its territory, from the moment when his appointment is notified to the Ministry of Foreign Affairs or such other ministry as may be agreed.

2. When the functions of a person enjoying privileges and immunities have come to an end, such privileges and immunities shall normally cease at the moment when he leaves the country, or on expiry of a reasonable period in which to do so, but shall subsist until that time, even in case of armed conflict. However, with respect to acts performed by such a person in the exercise of his functions as a member of the mission, immunity shall continue to subsist. . . .

Article 40

1. If a diplomatic agent passes through or is in the territory of a third State, which has granted him a passport visa if such visa was necessary, while proceeding to take up or return to his post, or when returning to his own country, the third State shall accord him inviolability and such other immunities as may be required to ensure his transit or return. The same shall apply in the case of any members of his family enjoying privileges or immunities who are accompanying the diplomatic agent, or travelling separately to join him or to return to their country.

2. In circumstances similar to those specified in paragraph 1 of this Article, third States shall not hinder the passage of members of the

---

[2] The U.K. considers that the test of permanent residence "should normally be whether or not he would be in the United Kingdom but for the requirements of the sending state": 1969 FCO Note to Missions, reprinted in *First Report from the Foreign Affairs Committee*, (1984–85) H.C. 127, p. 14. The Note gives guidance in the application of the test.

administrative and technical or service staff of a mission, and of members of their families, through the territories.

3. Third States shall accord to official correspondence and other official communications in transit, including messages in code or cipher, the same freedom and protection as is accorded by the receiving State. They shall accord to diplomatic couriers, who have been granted a passport visa if such visa was necessary, and diplomatic bags in transit the same inviolability and protection as the receiving State is bound to accord.

4. The obligations of third States under paragraphs 1, 2 and 3 of this Article shall also apply to the persons mentioned respectively in those paragraphs, and to official communications and diplomatic bags, whose presence in the territory of the third State is due to *force majeure*.

Article 41

1. Without prejudice to their privileges and immunities, it is the duty of all persons enjoying such privileges and immunities to respect the laws and regulations of the receiving State. They also have a duty not to interfere in the internal affairs of that State. . . .

3. The premises of the mission must not be used in any manner incompatible with the functions of the mission as laid down in the present Convention or by other rules of general international law or by any special agreements in force between the sending and the receiving State.

Article 45

If diplomatic relations are broken off between two States, or if a mission is permanently or temporarily recalled:

(a) the receiving State must, even in case of armed conflict, respect and protect the premises of the mission, together with its property and archives;

(b) the sending State may entrust the custody of the premises of the mission, together with its property and archives, to a third State acceptable to the receiving State;

(c) the sending State may entrust the protection of its interests and those of its nationals to a third State acceptable to the receiving State.

Article 47

1. In the application of the provisions of the present Convention, the receiving State shall not discriminate as between States.

2. However, discrimination shall not be regarded as taking place:

(a) where the receiving State applies any of the provisions of the present Convention restrictively because of restrictive application of that provision to its mission in the sending State;

(b) where by custom or agreement States extend to each other more favourable treatment than is required by the provisions of the present Convention.

Notes

1. The Convention was adopted at the United Nations Conference on Diplomatic Intercourse and Immunities in Vienna in 1961.[3] The Conference based its work upon Draft Articles prepared by the International Law Commission.[4] Optional Protocols concerning the Acquisition of Nationality[5] and the Compulsory Settlement of Disputes[6] were also adopted. It is not stated in the Convention whether or not it was intended to be declaratory of the customary international law existing in 1961. As far as the law concerning diplomatic immunity is concerned, it is probably correct to regard it as a combination of codification and progressive development. It would seem both to incorporate clearly established rules (see the *U.S. Diplomatic and Consular Staff in Tehran Case*, below, p. 358) and to fill in gaps or to spell out rules where practice was uncertain or inconsistent. Whether the Convention, so far as it engages in progressive development, has yet had sufficient impact upon the attitudes and practice of states to have affected customary international law is impossible to say. What is clear is that its impact upon the legal rights and duties of states has already been great because of the very large number of states that have become parties to it.

The above extracts from the Convention concern the immunity, inviolability and protection afforded to the premises of the mission, to certain property relating to the mission's functioning[7] and to certain persons representing states diplomatically or concerned with such representation.[8] Immunity and inviolability overlap to some extent (see Article 22(1)(3), Vienna Convention for example). The former term is applied mainly to jurisdictional immunity, *i.e.* immunity from the process of the courts, and to immunity from taxes. The latter is concerned mainly with questions of trespass.

The question of abuse of diplomatic immunity has been a frequent theme in recent years. While there has always been concern at the abuse by a small number of individual diplomats of their jurisdictional immunity, the question has become more serious in the light of convincing evidence that a few states use the inviolability of their mission premises and their diplomatic bag to facilitate the commission of acts of violence against their political opponents abroad or to assist terrorists. It is noticeable, however, that even states, such as the United Kingdom, that have expressed concern at these newer forms of abuse would not want, on balance, to limit the immunities and inviolability that exists at present

[3] For the Conference Records, see *U.N. Conference on Diplomatic Intercourse and Immunities, Vienna*, March 2—April 15, 1961. *Official Records*, Vols. I and II, 1962, U.N. Docs.A/ CONF.20/14 and A/CONF.20/14 Add. 1.

[4] Y.B.I.L.C., 1958, II, p. 89.

[5] Misc. 6 (1961), Cmnd. 1368; 500 U.N.T.S. 223. In force 1964. 48 parties. U.K. not a party.

[6] U.K.T.S. 19 (1965), Cmnd. 565; 500 U.N.T.S. 241. In force 1964. 61 parties, including the U.K.

[7] The rules on the availability and immunity of such premises and property are rules of *state*, rather than *diplomatic*, immunity. They are included here for convenience.

[8] In *R. v. Lambeth JJ, ex p. Yusufu* [1985] Crim.L.R. 510, QBD, it was held that a diplomatic agent has diplomatic immunity only from the time that the receiving state accepts him as persona grata, not from the time he is appointed. See Crawford (1985) 56 B.Y.I.L. 328.

because of the value they place upon them to protect their own missions abroad from other kinds of interference with their functioning.[9] Indeed, such new codification proposals as are afoot (*e.g.* the ILC Draft Articles on the Diplomatic Bag, see below, p. 356) are the result of initiatives by states that wish to strengthen diplomatic immunity, not reduce it.

2. *Jurisdictional immunity.* In 1985, there were 45,000 diplomatic agents in London, 15,000 of whom were entitled to full jurisdictional immunity.[10] Article 37(2) of the Convention, on the immunities of administrative and technical staff, was the subject of disagreement at Vienna.[11] Several states have made reservations agreeing to allow the immunity granted by it only on condition of reciprocity and several others have made reservations not accepting it at all; some other states, including the United Kingdom, have deposited objections to reservations of the latter kind.[12] Note that the International Law Commission had appreciated in its Commentary that Article 37(2) would be an example of "progressive development":

> (2) It is the general practice to accord to members of the diplomatic staff of a mission the same privileges and immunities as are enjoyed by heads of mission, and it is not disputed that this is a rule of international law. But beyond this there is no uniformity in the practice of States in deciding which members of the staff of a mission shall enjoy privileges and immunities. Some States include members of the administrative and technical staff among the beneficiaries, and some even include members of the service staff. . . .
>
> (4) In view of the differences in State practice, the Commission had to choose between two courses: either to work on the principle of a bare minimum, and stipulate that any additional rights to be accorded should be decided by bilateral agreement; or to try to establish a general and uniform rule based on what would appear to be necessary and reasonable.
>
> (5) A majority of the Commission favoured the latter course, believing that the rule proposed would represent a progressive step.
>
> (6) The Commission differentiated between members of the administrative and technical staff on the one hand, and members of the service staff on the other.
>
> (7) As regards persons belonging to the administrative and technical staff, it took the view that there were good grounds for granting them the same privileges and immunities as members of the diplomatic staff. . . .
>
> (8) The reasons relied on may be summarized as follows. It is the function of the mission as an organic whole which should be taken into consideration, not the actual work done by each person. Many of the persons belonging to the services in question perform confidential tasks which, for the purposes of the mission's function, may be even more important than the tasks entrusted to some members of the diplomatic staff. An ambassador's secretary or an archivist may be as much the repository of secret or confidential knowledge as members of the diplomatic staff. Such persons equally need protection of the same order against possible pressure by the receiving State.[13]

[9] For the U.K. view, see *Diplomatic Immunities and Privileges, op. cit.,* p. 343, n. 99, above, p. 6. For an argument that immunity should be limited to protect human rights, see Vicuna (1990) 40 I.C.L.Q. 34.

[10] *Diplomatic Immunities and Privileges, op. cit.,* p. 343, n. 99, above, p. 10.

[11] See *op. cit.,* p. 347, n. 3, above, Vol. I, 32nd and 33rd Meetings, pp. 193–201.

[12] For the reservations and objections to them, see *Multilateral Treaties in Respect of which the Secretary-General Performs Depositary Functions,* U.N. Doc. ST/LEG/SER. E/15 pp. 55 *et seq.*

[13] Y.B.I.L.C., 1958, II, pp. 101–102.

Would a "diplomatic agent" who negligently injured a pedestrian while driving his car on holiday in the receiving state be entitled to claim immunity under the Convention in respect of any civil or criminal proceedings arising therefrom? Would a code clerk or a cook employed in an embassy be entitled to do so in the same situation? Would the wife or private employee of any of the above be entitled to do so?[14] Might the nationality or the place of permanent residence of the person claiming immunity in any of the above cases be relevant?

Article 40 of the Convention was interpreted in *R. v. Guildhall Magistrates Court, ex p. Jarrett-Thorpe*.[15] The applicant was the husband of the counsellor to the Sierra Leone Embassy in Rome. His wife travelled to London to buy furnishings for the Rome Embassy. It was intended that the applicant would join her later for the purpose of travelling back to Rome with her and to help with her luggage. It was not intended that he should enter the United Kingdom for any other purpose. When he arrived in the United Kingdom, the applicant received a message to the effect that his wife had already left for Rome. While he was waiting for a flight to Rome the applicant was arrested by the police at Heathrow in connection with criminal proceedings pending against him in London. Lawton J. held that Article 40 applied so that the applicant was entitled to immunity. The court rejected the argument that Article 40 only applied to diplomatic agents and members of their families when they were in transit between the sending state and the receiving state.

3. *Waiver of immunity.* A resolution adopted at Vienna recommended:

> that the sending State should waive the immunity of members of its diplomatic mission in respect of civil claims of persons in the receiving State when this can be done without impeding the performance of the functions of the mission, and that, when immunity is not waived, the sending State should use its best endeavours to bring about a just settlement of the claims.[16]

The following is a 1952 statement of British practice, based upon "the principle that diplomatic immunity is accorded not for the benefit of the individual in question, but for the benefit of the State in whose service he is, in order that he may fulfil his diplomatic duties with the necessary independence":

> ... when a dispute arises between a person living in this country and a person possessing diplomatic immunity here and the dispute cannot be settled directly between the parties, it is commonly reported to the Foreign Office and the Foreign Office then approaches the diplomatic mission concerned with the request that the Head of the Mission will either waive the immunity of the member of his staff so that the dispute can be decided in the ordinary way in the courts or that the matter should be decided by a private arbitration conducted under conditions which are fair to both sides. Such requests are commonly acceded to, and the cases where this approach has not brought about a proper settlement of the matter have generally been cases where, owing to delay, the foreign diplomat in question has already left the country before the matter can be dealt with, a delay which is generally due to a failure of the party who thinks he is injured to approach the Foreign Office promptly. If a case arose where the foreign mission concerned was neither willing to waive immunity nor to persuade the foreign diplomat to accept a reasonable arbitration and the foreign diplomat remained in this country, the Foreign Office would in the circumstances feel obliged, unless there were exceptional

[14] On the status of the family of a diplomatic agent, see O'Keefe (1976) 25 I.C.L.Q. 329.
[15] *The Times*, October 5, 1977, QBD.
[16] U.N. Doc. A/CONF. 20/14, Add. 1, v. 90.

features in the case, to inform the foreign mission concerned that this individual could no longer be accepted as a person holding a diplomatic immunity appointment in this country.

If a person possessing diplomatic immunity is alleged to have committed a criminal offence and there is a prima facie case which, in the ordinary way, would lead to the institution of a prosecution, the Foreign Office approaches the foreign mission concerned and, unless the offence is such that it is considered that an admonition by the Head of the Mission is sufficient, the Foreign Office requests a waiver of immunity in order that the case may be tried, on the footing that, if the immunity is not waived, it may be impossible for the Foreign Secretary to continue to accept the individual concerned as a person possessing diplomatic status in this country.[17]

In 1993, in the United Kingdom there were 29 occasions on which persons claimed diplomatic immunity to avoid arrest or prosecution for serious offences (*i.e.* offences with a possible sentence of six or more months imprisonment). The majority of these concerned shoplifting or drunken driving.[18] 1,941 parking tickets were cancelled.[19]

4. *Inviolability of the premises of the mission*. An amendment[20] to the Convention to require the head of a mission to: "co-operate with the local authorities in case of fire, epidemic or other extreme emergency" was not adopted at Vienna. In the International Law Commission it had been suggested that "[i]t was hardly conceivable that a head of mission would fail to co-operate . . . in an emergency"[21] and that the sanction of declaring him *persona non grata* would be available if he did.[22] In addition, the fear was that "if specific exceptions were made in the Convention this would give . . . a certain power of appreciation to the receiving state which it was thought might . . . be undesirable."[23] Commenting upon an incident in 1929, when French officials entered the Soviet Embassy in Paris after allegations that persons were being detained and might be executed there, Sibert argues that the intervention was consistent with international law:

> because no civilised state could permit a foreign legation to be made a place of imprisonment, or, *a fortiori*, a place of execution.[24]

In the *Sun Yat Sen Incident*,[25] in 1896, a Chinese national who was not in any way connected with the Chinese Embassy in London was kept there against his will. A writ of habeas corpus was refused by Wright J. because he doubted "the propriety of making any order or granting any summons against a foreign

---

[17] Interdepartmental Committee on State Immunities, *Report on Diplomatic Immunity*, Cmnd. 8460, pp. 3–4. The statement still represents British practice.

[18] Foreign Affairs Committee Report, *op. cit.*, p. 345, n. 2, above, p. vi. With regard to drunken driving, a diplomatic agent cannot be required to undergo a blood test or other medical examination, such as a breathalyser test, because of Art. 29: *Hansard*, H.C., Vol. 101, col. 64.

[19] *Hansard*, H.C. Debs., Vol. 554, cols. 5–6. The number of parking tickets has steadily declined (59,625 in 1985).

[20] U.N. Doc. A/CONF. 20/C.I.L.129.

[21] Y.B.I.L.C., 1958, I, 129 (Mr Amado).

[22] *ibid.*, p. 130 (Mr Bartos).

[23] Sir Francis Vallat, Foreign Affairs Committee Report, *op. cit.*, p. 345, n. 2, p. 25.

[24] *Traité de droit international public*, Vol. II, 1951, p.25. Translation.

[25] 1 McNair 85. The person detained gave notice of his plight by placing a slip of paper in a bread roll which he then threw on to the street below through the bars of his window: Viscount Alverstone, *Recollections of Bar and Bench* (1914), pp. 168–169.

legation".[26] The British Government referred to the detention as "an abuse of ... diplomatic privilege" and a "flagrant ... violation of municipal and international law." It added that

> if persisted in or repeated, it would justify the use of whatever measures might be necessary for the liberation of the captive, and a demand for the immediate departure from this country of any persons responsible for his imprisonment.

Denza[27] considers the problem of "abuse" as follows:

> Article 22 thus leaves absolute the inviolability of the premises of the mission. In the last resort however a receiving State which is sufficiently sure of the evidence of abuse which it will find will probably take the risk of acting in breach of the Article if it believes its essential security to be at risk. In 1973 for example the Iraqi Ambassador was called to the Pakistan Ministry of Foreign Affairs and told that arms were being brought into Pakistan under diplomatic immunity and that there was evidence that they were being stored at the Embassy of Iraq. The Ambassador refused permission for a search. In the presence of the Ambassador a raid on the Embassy by armed policemen then took place and huge consignments of arms were found to be stored in crates. The Pakistan Government then sent a strong protest to the Iraq Government, declared that Iraqi Ambassador and an attaché *persona non grata* and recalled their own Ambassador. In this case the forcible entry could be justified *ex post facto* because of the clear breach by Iraq of the duty in paragraph 3 of Article 41 not to use the premises of the mission in any manner incompatible with the functions of the mission. But such an entry could be justified only in an extreme case of abuse.

In the *Libyan People's Bureau Incident*, below, p. 353, in answer to the question whether, following the shooting from the Bureau window, "we had a right to go in immediately in self-defence and seize persons and articles," Sir John Freeland, the Legal Adviser to the British Foreign Office stated[28]:

> I certainly would not exclude the possibility of its being justifiable in a case where, for example, there is continued firing of weapons from the premises of an embassy, where every other method has been tried and has failed to stop that, for it then to be lawful to go into the embassy to stop it ...

How is this consistent with the absolute inviolability rule in Article 22? Could it be argued that since the right of self defence at customary international law is not expressly excluded by Article 22 it is available?[29] Another approach is to regard the shooting as a material breach of the 1961 Convention so that the United

---

[26] 1 McNair 88.

[27] *op. cit.*, p. 340, n. 93, above, p. 84. Footnote omitted.

[28] Foreign Affairs Committee Report, *op. cit.*, p. 345, n. 2, above p. 28. On the issues raised in the Report, see Cameron (1985) 34 I.C.L.Q. 610 and Higgins (1985) 79 A.J.I.L. 641. For the U.K. Government response to the Report, see *Diplomatic Immunities and Privileges, op. cit.*, p. 343, n. 99, above. On the response, see Higgins (1986) 80 A.J.I.L. 135.

[29] See Beaumont (1991) 29 C.Y.I.L. 391; *cf.* Colonel Draper's memorandum, *Diplomatic Immunities and Privileges, op. cit.*, p. 343, n. 99, above, pp. 71–72. Neither Sir John Freeland nor Colonel Draper considered self-defence was available on the facts of the *Libyan People's Bureau Incident* because there was only one round of firing. The persons who left the Bureau on evacuation were searched on the grounds of self-defence in case they were armed: *id.*, p. xxxii.

Kingdom's obligation under Article 22 was, as a state specially affected, suspended (see Article 60(2)(b), Vienna Convention on the Law of Treaties, below, p. 839). The Foreign Affairs Committee, however, pointed out that "the drafting history of the Vienna Convention [on Diplomatic Relations] probably makes this principle inappropriate, especially as a 'remedy' for violation is provided in the form of a severing of diplomatic relations."[30]

The question of *diplomatic asylum*[31] within the premises of a mission was purposely not dealt with in the Convention.[32] Article 41(3) states that the mission should not be used "in any manner incompatible with the functions of the mission," which begs the question. According to British practice at the turn of the century:

> [i]t is in no way necessary for the discharge of an Ambassador's duty that his house should be an asylum for persons charged with crime of any description, and no such privilege can be asserted. . . .

But, according to the same practice, asylum is in fact (although without legal authority) allowed in certain exceptional cases:

> . . . the practice of harbouring political refugees is an objectionable one and should be resorted to only from motives of humanity in cases of instant or imminent personal peril. In such cases the refugee should not be allowed to communicate with his partisans from the shelter of His Majesty's Legation and should be removed the moment he is no longer exposed to summary treatment at the hands of his pursuers.
>
> Protection must, of course, sometimes be afforded to British subjects in time of danger but this is an wholly different matter from harbouring political refugees who are citizens or subjects of the country. In cases where British subjects have committed an offence against the local laws and have sought refuge in His Majesty's Legation they should be given up only to the competent authorities and on satisfactory guarantees being given that they will still receive proper treatment and a fair trial. . . . [33]

The Harvard Research Draft Convention on Diplomatic Privileges and Immunities 1932[34] reads:

> *Article* 6. A sending state shall not permit the premises occupied or used by its mission or by a member of its mission to be used as a place of asylum for fugitives from justice.

Diplomatic asylum is also granted by the U.S. Cardinal Mindszenty, for example, took refuge in the United States Embassy in Budapest after the failure of the

---

[30] *id.*, p. xxix.

[31] See Morgenstern (1948) 25 B.Y.I.L. 236; Porcino (1975–76) 8 N.Y.U.J.I.L.P. 435; Ronning, *Diplomatic Asylum* (1965); Symonides (1986) 15 Pol. Y.I.L. 217.

[32] See Y.B.I.L.C. 1958, II, p. 104.

[33] Sir E. Grey to H.M. Minister in Haiti, May 30, 1913, 7 B.D.I.L. 922. The exception probably covers all cases, whether political or not. The U.K. continues to grant diplomatic asylum on the same basis. Between 1979 and 1984 there were seven cases of foreign citizens seeking sanctuary in British embassies, etc.: *Hansard*, H.C., Vol. 65, col. 813, October 19, 1984.

[34] (1932) 26 A.J.I.L. Suppl. 19.

Hungarian Uprising in 1956 and remained there until 1970 when he was allowed to leave the country to take up residence in Rome.[35] Although the granting of diplomatic asylum has been common practice in Latin American states and is regulated by treaties between them[36] it would not seem that any rules of American customary international law have developed: see the *Asylum* case, above, p. 24. In 1980, following a revolution, Liberian soldiers entered the French Embassy in Monrovia and arrested the son of the former Liberian President who had been granted asylum. France protested against "a blatant and unacceptable violation of the status of diplomatic missions and of international customs.[37] On diplomatic asylum generally, Ronning[38] states:

> The only generalization which seems at all acceptable is that the practice of states in this regard is not based upon any generally recognized *right of asylum* so far as general international law is concerned. Instead, it is a *de facto* result of the fact that international law accords to the various accredited diplomatic officers certain well-recognized immunities from local jurisdiction, such as immunity of their official residences and offices from invasion by local authorities. Humanitarian, political or other motives may lead to the original grant of asylum but once the refugee is inside the legation the territorial state is faced with an insoluble dilemma. Assuming the state of refuge will not surrender the refugee, the territorial state can apprehend him only by violating the immunity of the diplomatic premises or, possibly, by breaking diplomatic relations. The fact is that such extreme measures are considered too high a price to pay for apprehension of the refugee.

5. *Protection of the premises of the mission.* The "special duty" to protect the premises of the mission set out in Article 22 of the Convention is well established in customary international law and is very important at the present time when such premises prove convenient settings for political demonstrations. See the *U.S. Diplomatic and Consular Staff in Iran case*, below, p. 358. See also an incident in 1965 when the United States Embassy in Moscow was attacked by students; the U.S.S.R. expressed regret, indicated stricter measures of protection and agreed to pay compensation for property damage.[39]

In 1984, in the *Libyan People's Bureau Incident*, a demonstration by about 70 Libyan opponents of Colonel Kadhafi's Government was held in St. James Square opposite the Libyan People's Bureau, the Libyan diplomatic mission in London. The demonstration, which the Bureau had unsuccessfully asked the Foreign Office to have banned, was countered by a 20 strong pro-Kadhafi group, the two groups being separated by barriers and a large number of police. During the peaceful demonstration, a burst of automatic gunfire from a Bureau window killed WPC Fletcher and injured 11 demonstrators. The United Kingdom severed diplomatic relations with Libya as a result of the shooting. When the Bureau building was evacuated, it was searched[40] and guns were found. As to whether

---

[35] U.S. policy is "to grant temporary refuge for humanitarian reasons in extreme or exceptional circumstances when the life or safety of a person is put in immediate danger, such as pursuit by a mob": (1981) 75 A.J.I.L. 142.

[36] See, *e.g.* the 1954 Caracas Convention on Diplomatic Asylum, P.A.U.T.S. 18; 161 B.F.S.P. 570. In force 1954. 13 parties.

[37] *Keesings Archives*, p. 30407.

[38] *op. cit.*, p. 352, n. 31, above, p. 22.

[39] 7 Whiteman 387. On state responsibility for the actions of mobs, see below, p. 542.

[40] On the obligation to protect, but not to treat as inviolable, the premises of a mission after diplomatic relations are terminated, see Art. 45, 1961 Convention. As to whether the mission might have been entered prior to its evacuation, see above, p. 351.

the United Kingdom had done sufficient to comply with its "special duty" under Article 22 to protect the Libyan mission, the House of Commons Foreign Affairs Committee stated[41]:

> Our view is that although the "peace of the mission" may not be entirely identical to the Queen's peace, *the receiving state's duty to protect the peace of the mission cannot be given so wide an interpretation as to require the mission to be insulated from expressions of public opinion within the receiving state. Provided always that work at the mission can continue normally, that there is untrammelled access and egress, and that those within the mission are never in fear that the mission might be damaged or its staff injured, the requirements of Article 22 are met.* A breakdown of the public order outside mission premises would put in jeopardy the fulfilling of obligations under Article 22; an orderly expression of opposition to the policies of the sending state cannot of itself do so.

The Committee also referred to the unreported case of *R. v. Roques*[42] (1984) in which anti-apartheid demonstrators who demonstrated, contrary to police orders, on the east pavement of Trafalgar Square, immediately outside the South African embassy, were charged with obstruction of a police officer, the demonstration being in breach of the Diplomatic Privileges Act 1964 (which incorporates Article 22) which it was the police's duty to apply. Dismissing the charges, the magistrates took the view that impairment of the "dignity" of the mission (see Article 22) "required abusive or insulting behaviour, and that political demonstrations do not themselves amount to such."

The duty of protection extends, under Article 30, to the private residence of a diplomatic agent and was interpreted in this context in *Agbor v. Metropolitan Police Commissioner.*[43] There, a dispute arose over the occupation of a flat in a house in London owned by the Nigerian Government and used to house diplomatic agents. Shortly after Biafra purported to secede from Nigeria, a Biafran family managed to gain possession of the flat while its next official tenant was awaited. At the request of the Nigerian Government, the family was evicted by the police. The court was asked in the application before it to allow the family to return to the flat pending a decision by it on the right of possession. The application was granted because the flat was not at the time the residence of a diplomatic agent. Lord Denning added that even if it had been he was

> not at all satisfied that the [Diplomatic Privileges] Act of 1964 gives to the executive any right to evict a person in possession who claims as of right to occupation of the premises. It enables the police to defend the premises against intruders. But not to turn out people who are in possession and claim as of right to be there.[44]

6. *Freedom of communication.* Before the 1961 Convention, "it was certainly accepted international practice, and probably international law," that the receiv-

---

[41] Report, *op. cit.*, p. 345, n. 2, above, p. xvii. Giving evidence to the Committee the Head of the British Diplomatic Service, Sir Antony Acland, stated: "I think the essential thing is that demonstrations should be adequately controlled and policed so that there is no damage done physically or otherwise to the premises of the mission or to the people within that mission. In the case of the tragic St James Square incident there were certainly enough police present": *ibid.*, pp. 21–22. There are 300 demonstrations outside London embassies annually; police practice is to restrict them to the opposite side of the road from the embassy in full compliance with Art. 22: *Diplomatic Immunities and Privileges, op. cit.*, p. 343, n. 99, above p. 17. See also on the incident, Sutton, [1985] P.L. 191.

[42] *ibid.*, p. xvii.

[43] [1969] 1 W.L.R. 703, CA.

[44] *ibid.* at 707. Salmon L.J. agreed, *ibid.* at 710.

ing state had a right of challenge in respect of the diplomatic bag.[45] It could, that is, ask for permission to inspect its contents. The sending state could either allow this to happen, or have the bag returned to its place of origin. Article 27(3) requires that the bag be allowed through without inspection. Reservations to the Convention insisting upon a power of inspection have been made,[46] but have met with protest by some other parties. In the opinion of the United Kingdom Foreign Office, Article 27 does not prohibit electronic scanning of the diplomatic bag or sniffing by dogs.[47] Scanning would seem to be a practice followed by some receiving states, although it "would not necessarily pick up a weapon in a diplomatic bag."[48] In 1985, the United Kingdom Government, which had previously not conducted any scannings, stated that it would "be ready to scan any bag on specific occasions where the grounds for suspicion are sufficiently strong."[49]

In 1984, Mr Dikko, a minister in the overthrown Nigerian Government, was kidnapped in London and found drugged in a crate at Stansted Airport awaiting shipment to Nigeria, where he was wanted on criminal charges.[50] Although labelled "diplomatic baggage," the crate lacked the "visible external marks" required by Article 27(4), 1961 Convention to be a diplomatic bag (in particular, it lacked a seal). Accordingly, there was no breach of Article 27 when customs officials, alerted by medical odours, opened it. The United Kingdom Foreign Secretary stated that even if the crate were a diplomatic bag, "the overriding duty to preserve and protect human life" might have justified its opening in appropriate circumstances.[51] Following the incident, two members of the Nigerian High Commission were expelled and one of the kidnappers, who had unsuccessfully claimed diplomatic immunity,[52] was sentenced to 12 years imprisonment for attempted kidnapping.

Another remarkable incident occurred in 1964 when an Israeli national was found drugged, bound and gagged at Rome airport in a trunk marked "diplomatic mail" that was being sent by the Egyptian mission to Cairo. Italy declared

---

[45] Denza, *op. cit.*, p. 340, n. 93, above, p. 225. The diplomatic bag consists of packages, sacks, or possibly trunks and is usually sent in the custody of a diplomatic courier "who shall be provided with an official document indicating his status and the number of packages constituting the diplomatic bag" (Art. 27(6), Vienna Convention), although it may be entrusted to the safe keeping of the aircraft's captain (Art. 27(7), 1961 Convention). There is no limit on the size or shape of the bag. A USSR lorry was opened for inspection by the West German authorities in 1984 not because of its size or shape but because, being capable of movement, it could not be a bag: Foreign Affairs Committee Report, *op. cit.*, p. 345, n. 2, above, p. xii.

[46] By six Arab states, including Libya. For texts of reservations and objections to them, see U.N. Doc. ST/LEG/ SER. E/15, pp. 55 *et seq.* The U.K. objected to certain of the reservations, but not that by Libya. Accordingly, it could, in accordance with the principle of reciprocity, see below, p. 793, have relied upon the Libyan reservation to have requested the opening (or return unopened) of the Libyan diplomatic bag in the context of the *Libyan People's Bureau Incident*. The decision not to do so was a "political judgment": Foreign Affairs Committee Report, *op. cit.*, p. 345, n. 2, p. xxxii.

[47] Foreign Affairs Committee Report, *op. cit.*, p. 345, n. 2, above pp. xii, 5. Although scanning is regarded by some states as a form of constructive opening, the Foreign Office notes that Art. 27, does not refer to inviolability: *ibid.* Note that scanning "might put at risk sensitive cipher or coding materials contained in the bag:" *ibid.*, p. xiii.

[48] *Hansard*, H.C., Vol. 985, col. 1219, June 2, 1980; U.K.M.I.L. 1980; (1980) 51 B.Y.I.L. 419.

[49] *Diplomatic Immunities and Privileges*, *op. cit.*, p. 343, n. 99, above, p. 21.

[50] For an account of the Dikko Case, see Akinsanya (1985) 34 I.C.L.Q. 602.

[51] Foreign Affairs Committee Report, *op. cit.*, p. 345, n. 2, above, p. xxxiv. Note that the "material breach" remedy of suspension of treaty obligations would not have been available: see below, p. 839.

[52] See *R. v. Lambeth JJ, ex p. Yusufu*, above, p. 347 n. 8.

a First Secretary at the Egyptian Embassy *persona non grata* and expelled two others. The Egyptian Ambassador deplored the incident and claimed ignorance of it.[53]

The status of the diplomatic bag has been considered by the International Law Commission. Its Draft Articles on the Status of the Diplomatic Courier and the Diplomatic Bag not Accompanied by Diplomatic Courier[54] read:

Article 28

1. The diplomatic bag shall be inviolable wherever it may be; it shall not be opened or detained and shall be exempt from examination directly or through electronic or other technical devices.

2. Nevertheless, if the competent authorities of the receiving or the transit State have serious reason to believe that the consular bag contains something other than the correspondence, documents or articles referred to in paragraph 1 of article 25, they may request that the bag be opened in their presence by an authorized representative of the sending State. If this request is refused by the authorities of the sending State, the bag shall be returned to its place of origin.

The Commentary to Article 28 reads

The extent of the principle of inviolability of the diplomatic bag is further clarified by the words "and shall be exempt from examination directly or through electronic or other technical devices." The view prevailed in the Commission that the inclusion of this phrase was necessary as the evolution of technology had created very sophisticated means of examination which might result in the violation of the confidentiality of the bag, means which furthermore were at the disposal of only the most developed States. On the other hand, the paragraph does not extend to an external examination of the bag and of its marks or visible indications of its character as such, to the extent that such an external examination would be conducted for identification purposes only and with a view to ascertaining that a given container claimed to be a diplomatic bag actually bears such a character. The paragraph does not rule out non-intrusive means of examination, such as sniffing dogs, in case of suspicion that the bag is used for the transport of narcotic drugs. . . .

Paragraph 2 applies only to the consular bag *stricto sensu*. It introduces, in connection with the consular bag, a balance between the interests of the sending State in ensuring the protection, safety and confidentiality of the contents of its bag and the security interests of the receiving or transit State.

. . . the Commission has been fully aware that the cases of possible abuses of the bag . . . may extend also to the diplomatic bag *stricto sensu* or to the bags of missions or delegations. Contemporary international practice has witnessed cases of diplomatic bags being used or attempted to be used for the illicit import or export of currency, narcotic drugs,[55] arms or other items, and even for the transport of human beings, which have violated the established rules

---

[53] *Keesings Archives*, p. 20580. In 1980 £500,000 worth of cannabis was found in diplomatic baggage bound for the Moroccan Embassy in London when a crate marked "household effects" split open at Harwich; *The Times*, June 13, 1980. The prohibited import of drugs is the most common abuse of the diplomatic bag in U.K. experience; Foreign Affairs Committee, *op. cit.*, p. 345, n. 2, above, p. 6.

[54] The Draft Articles were finally adopted by the I.L.C. in 1989. For text and commentary, see the Report of the I.L.C. on its 41st Session, G.A.O.R., 44th Sess., Supp. 10, pp. 26 *et seq.*

[55] *ibid.*, pp. 109–10.

regarding the permissible contents of the bag and adversely affected the legitimate interests of the receiving or transit States. The Commission is of the view that while the protection of the diplomatic bag is a fundamental principle for the normal functioning of official communications between States, the implementation of this principle should not provide an opportunity for abuse which may affect the legitimate interests of the receiving or transit States. . . .

In this connection, the Commission considered the possibility of extending to all diplomatic bags the régime of the consular bag as reflected in paragraph 2. Some members, however, were of the view that the establishment of a uniform régime for all bags should be done on the basis of the existing régime for the diplomatic bag *stricto sensu* as reflected in the Convention on Diplomatic Relations, which does not provide the receiving or transit State with the right laid down in paragraph 2. Some intermediate solutions were also considered. In the end and after extensive consideration of the problem, the Commission opted for the present formulation, which maintains the existing régime as contained in the four codification conventions on diplomatic and consular law as a compromise solution capable of ensuring better prospects for a wide adherence by States to the present draft articles.

7. *The basis for diplomatic immunity.* In its Commentary on its Draft Articles the International Law Commission stated:

(1) Among the theories that have exercised an influence on the development of diplomatic privileges and immunities, the Commission will mention the "exterritoriality" theory, according to which the premises of the mission represent a sort of extension of the territory of the sending State; and the "representative character" theory, which bases such privileges and immunities on the idea that the diplomatic mission personifies the sending State.

(2) There is now a third theory which appears to be gaining ground in modern times, namely, the "functional necessity" theory, which justifies privileges and immunities as being necessary to enable the mission to perform its functions.

(3) The Commission was guided by this third theory in solving problems on which practice gave no clear pointers, while also bearing in mind the representative character of the head of the mission and of the mission itself.[56]

In *Radwan v. Radwan*[57] it was held that the Egyptian consulate in London was not a part of the territory of the United Arab Republic so that a divorce obtained there was not obtained "in any country outside the British Isles" for the purposes of the Recognition of Divorces and Legal Separations Act 1971. After reviewing the literature on the subject, which he found rejected the extraterritoriality theory, Cumming-Bruce J. referred to the Vienna Convention:

If it was the view of the high contracting parties that the premises of missions were part of the territory of the sending state, that would undoubtedly be formulated and it would have been quite unnecessary to set out the immunities in the way in which it has been done.[58]

[56] Y.B.I.L.C., 1958, II, pp. 94–95.
[57] [1973] Fam. 24.
[58] *ibid.* at 34.

U.S. DIPLOMATIC AND CONSULAR STAFF IN TEHRAN CASE[59]

U.S. *v.* Iran

I.C.J. Reports 1980, p. 3

On November 4, 1979, several hundred Iranian students and other demonstrators took possession of the U.S. Embassy in Tehran by force. They did so in protest at the admission of the deposed Shah of Iran into the U.S. for medical treatment. The demonstrators were not opposed by the Iranian security forces who "simply disappeared from the scene." U.S. consulates elsewhere in Iran were similarly occupied. The demonstrators were still in occupation when the present judgment was given. They had seized archives and documents and continued to hold 52 U.S. nationals. (Women and black people had been released.) 50 were diplomatic or consular staff; two were private citizens. In an earlier judgment,[60] the Court had indicated interim measures at the request of the U.S. In the present judgment, the Court ruled on the U.S. request for a declaration that Iran had infringed a number of treaties, including the 1961 and 1963 Vienna Conventions on Diplomatic and Consular Relations respectively. It also asked for a declaration calling for the release of the hostages, the evacuation of the Embassy and consulates, the punishment of the persons responsible and the payment of reparation. In April 1980, while the case was pending, U.S. military forces entered Iran by air and landed in a remote desert area in the course of an attempt to rescue the hostages. The attempt was abandoned because of equipment failure. U.S. military personnel were killed in an air collision as the units withdrew. No injury was done to Iranian nationals or property.

Judgment of the Court

The events which are the subject of the United States' claims fall into two phases . . .

57. The first . . . covers the armed attack on the United States Embassy by militants on 4 November 1979.

58. No suggestion has been made that the militants, when they executed their attack on the Embassy, had any form of official status as recognized "agents" or organs of the Iranian State. Their conduct in mounting the attack, overrunning the Embassy and seizing its inmates as hostages cannot, therefore, be regarded as imputable to that State on that basis. . . . Their conduct might be considered as itself directly imputable to the Iranian State only if it were established that, in fact, on the occasion in question the militants acted on behalf of the State, having been charged by some competent organ of the Iranian State to carry out a specific operation. The information before the Court does not, however, suffice to establish with the requisite certainty the existence at that time of such a link. . . .

[59] See Gross (1980) 74 A.J.I.L. 395.
[60] I.C.J.Rep. 1979, p. 7. The Court called for the vacation of the Embassy and other premises; the release of the hostages; and the restoration of full diplomatic protection. In 1979, the Security Council also called upon Iran to release the hostages: S.C. Resn. 457 (1979), S.C.O.R. 24th Year, *Resolutions and Decisions*, p. 24.

59. Previously, it is true, the religious leader of the country, the Aya-tollah Khomeini, had made several public declarations inveighing against the United States as responsible for all his country's problems. . . . In . . . [a November 1, 1979] message the Ayatollah Khomeini had declared that it was "up to the dear pupils, students and theological students to expand with all their might their attacks against the United States and Israel, so they may force the United States to return the deposed and criminal shah. . . . In the view of the Court, however, it would be going too far to interpret such general declarations of the Ayatollah Khomeini to the peo-ple or students of Iran as amounting to an authorization from the State to undertake the specific operation of invading and seizing the United States Embassy. . . .

61. [This] . . . does not mean that Iran is, in consequence, free of any responsibility in regard to those attacks; for its own conduct was in conflict with its international obligations. By a number of provisions of the Vienna Conventions of 1961 and 1963, Iran was placed under the most categorical obligations, as a receiving State, to take appropriate steps to ensure the protection of the United States Embassy and Consulates, their staffs, their archives, their means of communication and the freedom of movement of the members of their staffs. . . .

62. . . . In the view of the Court, the obligations of the Iranian Govern-ment here in question are not merely contractual obligations established by the Vienna Conventions of 1961 and 1963, but also obligations under general international law.

63. The facts . . . establish to the satisfaction of the Court that on 4 November 1979 the Iranian Government failed altogether to take any "appropriate steps" to protect the premises, staff and archives of the United States' mission against attack by the militants, and to take any steps either to prevent this attack or to stop it before it reached its completion. They also show that on 5 November 1979 the Iranian Govern-ment similarly failed to take appropriate steps for the protection of the United States Consulates at Tabriz and Shiraz. In addition they show, in the opinion of the Court, that the failure of the Iranian Government to take such steps was due to more than mere negligence or lack of appro-priate means. . . .

67. This inaction of the Iranian Government by itself constituted clear and serious violation of Iran's obligations to the United States under the provisions of Article 22, paragraph 2, and Articles 24, 25, 26, 27 and 29 of the 1961 Vienna Convention on Diplomatic Relations, and Articles 5 and 36 of the 1963 Vienna Convention on Consular Relations. Similarly, with respect to the attacks of the Consulates at Tabriz and Shiraz, the inaction of the Iranian authorities entailed clear and serious breaches of its obliga-tions under the provisions of several further articles of the 1963 Conven-tion on Consular Relations . . .

69. The second phase of the events . . . comprises the whole series of facts which occurred following the completion of the occupation of the

United States Embassy by the militants, and the seizure of the Consulates at Tabriz and Shiraz. The occupation having taken place and the diplomatic and consular personnel of the United States' mission having been taken hostage, the action required of the Iranian Government by the Vienna Conventions and by general international law was manifest. Its plain duty was at once to make every effort, and to take every appropriate step, to bring these flagrant infringements of the inviolability of the premises, archives and diplomatic and consular staff of the United States Embassy to a speedy end, to restore the Consulates at Tabriz and Shiraz to United States control, and in general to re-establish the status quo and to offer reparation for the damage.

70. No such step was, however, taken by the Iranian authorities. . . .

73. The seal of official government approval was finally set on this situation by a decree issued on 17 November 1979 by the Ayatollah Khomeini. His decree began with the assertion that the American Embassy was "a centre of espionage and conspiracy" and that "those people who hatched plots against our Islamic movement in that place do not enjoy international diplomatic respect." He went on expressly to declare that the premises of the Embassy and the hostages would remain as they were until the United States had handed over the former Shah for trial and returned his property to Iran. . . .

74. . . . The approval given to these facts by the Ayatollah Khomeini and other organs of the Iranian State, and the decision to perpetuate them, translated continuing occupation of the Embassy and detention of the hostages into acts of that State. The militants, authors of the invasion and jailers of the hostages, had now become agents of the Iranian State for whose acts the State itself was internationally responsible. . . .

77. . . . these facts constituted breaches additional to those already committed of [the provisions of the 1961 Convention already infringed, as well as breaches of Article 22(1)(3) of that Convention and of Article 33 of the 1963 Convention.]

91. . . . Wrongfully to deprive human beings of their freedom and to subject them to physical constraint in conditions of hardship is in itself manifestly incompatible with the principles of the Charter of the United Nations, as well as with the fundamental principles enunciated in the Universal Declaration of Human Rights. But what has above all to be emphasized is the extent and seriousness of the conflict between the conduct of the Iranian State and its obligations under the whole corpus of the international rules for which diplomatic and consular law is comprised, rules the fundamental character of which the Court must here again strongly affirm.

92. . . . The frequency with which at the present time the principles of international law governing diplomatic and consular relations are set at naught by individuals or groups of individuals is already deplorable. But this case is unique and of very particular gravity because here it is not only private individuals or groups of individuals that have disregarded

and set at naught the inviolability of a foreign embassy, but the government of the receiving State itself. . . . Such events cannot fail to undermine the edifice of law carefully constructed by mankind over a period of centuries, the maintenance of which is vital for the security and well-being of the complex international community of the present day, to which it is more essential than ever that the rules developed to ensure the ordered progress of relations between its members should be constantly and scrupulously respected.

93. . . . the Court . . . cannot let pass without comment the incursion into the territory of Iran made by United States military units on 24–25 April 1980 . . . No doubt the United States Government may have had understandable preoccupations with respect to the well-being of its nationals held hostage in its Embassy for over five months. No doubt also the United States Government may have had understandable feelings of frustration at Iran's long-continued detention of the hostages, notwithstanding two resolutions of the Security Council as well as the Court's own Order of 15 December 1979 calling expressly for their immediate release. Nevertheless . . . the Court cannot fail to express its concern in regard to the United States' incursion into Iran. . . . the Court was in course of preparing the present judgment adjudicating upon the claims of the United States against Iran when the operation of 24 April 1980 took place. The Court therefore feels bound to observe that an operation undertaken in those circumstances, from whatever motive, is of a kind calculated to undermine respect for the judicial process in international relations and to recall that in paragraph 47, 1 B, of its Order of 15 December 1979 the Court had indicated that no action was to be taken by either party which might aggravate the tension between the two countries.

94. At the same time, however, the Court must point out that neither the question of the legality of the operation of 24 April 1980, under the Charter of the United Nations and under general international law, nor any possible question of responsibility flowing from it, is before the Court.

95. For these reasons, THE COURT, . . . By thirteen votes to two,[61]

Decides that the Islamic Republic of Iran has violated obligations owed by it to the United States of America under international conventions in force between the two countries, as well as under long-established rules of general international law; . . .

Notes

The Court also decided (i) unanimously, that Iran "must immediately take all steps to redress the situation resulting from the events of November 4, 1979," including the release of the hostages and the return of the premises, documents,

---

[61] *Ed.* The judges in the majority were President Sir Humphrey Waldock; Vice-President Elias; Judges Forster, Gros, Lachs, Nagendra Singh, Ruda, Mosler, Oda, Ago, El-Erian, Sette-Camara and Baxter. Judges Morozov and Tarazi dissented.

etc., to the U.S. and (ii) by 12 votes to 3,[62] that Iran was "under an obligation to make reparation" to the U.S. Iran, which declined to participate in the proceedings, did not comply with the Court's judgment in any respect. The hostages were ultimately released in January 1981 as a result of a negotiated settlement with the U.S.

DIPLOMATIC PRIVILEGES ACT 1964

(1964, c. 81)

1. The following provisions of this Act shall, with respect to the matters dealt with therein, have effect in substitution for any previous enactment or rule of law.

2.—(1) Subject to section 3 of this Act, the Articles set out in Schedule 1 to this Act[63] ... shall have the force of law in the United Kingdom ...
(3) For the purposes of Article 32 a waiver by the head of the mission of any State or any person for the time being performing his functions shall be deemed to be a waiver by that State. ...

3.—(1) If it appears to Her Majesty that the privileges and immunities accorded to a mission of Her Majesty in the territory of any State, or to persons connected with that mission, are less than those conferred by this Act on the mission of that State or on persons connected with that mission, Her Majesty may by an Order in Council withdraw such of the privileges and immunities so conferred from the mission of that State or from such persons connected with it as appears to Her Majesty to be proper. ...

4. If in any proceedings any question arises whether or not any person is entitled to any privilege or immunity under this Act a certificate issued by or under the authority of the Secretary of State stating any fact relating to that question shall be conclusive evidence of that fact.

7.—(1) Where any special agreement or arrangement between the Government of any State and the Government of the United Kingdom in force at the commencement of this Act provides for extending—

    (*a*) such immunity from jurisdiction and from arrest or detention, and such inviolability of residence, as are conferred by this Act on a diplomatic agent; or

    (*b*) such exemption from customs duties, taxes and related charges as is conferred by this Act in respect of articles for the personal use of a diplomatic agent;

[62] Judge Lachs joined the dissenting judges.
[63] *Ed.* Articles 1, 22–24, 27–40, Vienna Convention.

to any class of person, or to articles for the personal use of any class of person, connected with the mission of that State, that immunity and inviolability or exemption shall so extend, so long as that agreement or arrangement continues in force. . . .

EMPSON v. SMITH

[1966] 1 Q.B. 426. Court of Appeal

In 1963, the plaintiff brought a county court action against the defendant for breach of a tenancy agreement. The action was stayed after the Ministry of Commonwealth Relations had certified that the defendant was an administrative officer employed by the High Commissioner for Canada.[64] In December 1964, an application by the plaintiff, made in August 1964, to have the stay removed was heard by the County Court, together with an application by the defendant, made in November 1964, to have the writ dismissed as a nullity. By that time the Diplomatic Privileges Act had come into force, on October 1, 1964. The County Court granted the defendant's application. The plaintiff appealed to the Court of Appeal.

DIPLOCK L.J.: [The 1964] Act makes radical amendments in the previously existing law on diplomatic privileges and immunity and in particular draws a distinction between the immunities enjoyed by "members of the diplomatic staff " and "members of the administrative and technical staff " of a mission. Section 4 of that Act provides that a certificate issued by or under the authority of the Secretary of State shall be conclusive evidence of any fact relevant to any person's entitlement to any privilege or immunity. A further certificate dated October 20, 1964, was issued under that Act certifying that the defendant was on October 1, and had continued to be, a member of the administrative and technical staff of the Diplomatic Mission of Canada in the United Kingdom.

When the action was commenced in March 1963, the defendant was entitled under section 1(1)(a) of the Act of 1952 "to the like immunity from suit and legal process as is accorded to members of the official staff of an envoy of a foreign sovereign power." He was thus entitled so long as he remained en poste to complete immunity from civil suit in the United Kingdom, both as respects acts done in his official capacity on behalf of his government and as respects acts done in his private capacity. . . .

If the defendant had applied before the passing of the Diplomatic Privileges Act 1964, to have the plaintiff 's action dismissed there would have been no answer to his application. But he delayed until November, 1964. By that date his right to immunity from civil suit had been curtailed by that Act which applies to the United Kingdom the provisions of

[64] The certificate was issued under the Diplomatic Immunities (Commonwealth Countries and Republic of Ireland) Act 1952, s.1(1), as amended by the Diplomatic Privileges Act 1964, Sched. 2, which gives the missions of the Commonwealth countries listed the same immunities as those of other states.

the Vienna Convention on Diplomatic Relations, 1961, contained in the Schedule to the Act. By the combined effect of Articles 31 and 37 of the Convention as a member of the administrative and technical staff of the mission his immunity from the civil jurisdiction of the courts of the United Kingdom does not extend to acts performed outside the course of his duties. Whether he is entitled to immunity in any particular suit no longer depends solely upon his status but also upon the subject-matter of the suit.

It is elementary law that diplomatic immunity is not immunity from legal liability but immunity from suit. If authority is needed for this it is to be found in *Dickinson v. Del Solar*[65] . . . Statutes relating to diplomatic immunity from civil suit are procedural statutes. The Diplomatic Privileges Act, 1964, is in my view clearly applicable to suits brought after the date on which that statute came into force in respect of acts done before that date. If, therefore, the plaintiff had issued her plaint after October 1, 1964, instead of before, the action could not have been dismissed upon the ground of diplomatic privilege unless and until the court had determined the issue: whether or not the defendant's acts alleged by the plaintiff to constitute her cause of action against him were acts performed outside the course of his duties. It is, to say the least, arguable that acts done by the defendant in relation to his tenancy of his private residence in London were performed by him outside the course of his duties. But this issue is one which can be decided only upon evidence. It has not yet been considered, for the deputy county court judge found it unnecessary to go into it. He dismissed the plaintiff's action upon other grounds. He took the view that "the proceedings were a nullity at the time they were commenced, they are not affected by the 1964 Act which came into operation subsequently."

The deputy county court judge did not refer to section 3 of the Diplomatic Privileges Act, 1708[66] but counsel for the defendant has in this court relied strongly upon it in support of the proposition that Mrs. Empson's plaint was void *ab initio*. The Act of Anne . . . has been repeatedly held to be declaratory of the common law, and must therefore be construed according to the common law of which the law of nations must be deemed a part . . . it was decided in *Re Suarez*[67] that notwithstanding that Act a writ issued in the High Court against an ambassador was not void

---

[65] [1930] 1 K.B. 376, 380. *Ed. cf. Shaw v. Shaw* [1979] Fam. 62, CA: petition for divorce presented by a wife when her husband was a diplomatic agent could not be struck out on the basis of diplomatic immunity after he had ceased to be such.

[66] s.3 reads: "And to prevent the like insolences for the future be it further declared by the authority aforesaid that all writs and processes that shall at any time hereafter be sued forth or prosecuted whereby the person of any ambassador or other publick minister of any foreign prince or state authorized and received as such by her Majesty her heirs or successors or the domestick or domestick servant of any such ambassador or other publick minister may be arrested or imprisoned or his or their goods or chattels may be distrained seized or attached shall be deemed and adjudged to be utterly null and void to all intents constructions and purposes whatsoever."

[67] [1918] 1 Ch. 176.

ab initio. If it were it would, indeed, be impossible for the privilege ever to be waived for, as was decided in *Kahan v. Pakistan Federation*[68] there can be no effective waiver until the court is actually seised of the proceedings. The waiver is an undertaking given not to the other party to the proceedings but to the court itself. It can effectively be given only after the proceedings have commenced. *Kahan's* case was one of state immunity, but it is well settled that diplomatic immunity is governed by the same principles for it is claimed by the head of the mission on behalf of his state.

It follows therefore that until steps were taken to set aside or to dismiss the action the plaintiff's plaint was no nullity: it was a valid plaint. If the defendant had, with the permission of his High Commissioner, appeared to it before October 1, 1964, the procedural bar to the hearing would have been removed. So, too, if the defendant had ceased to be en poste while the plaint was still outstanding the action could then have proceeded against him. I can see no reason in logic or the law of nations why the position should be any different when the procedural bar has been removed by Act of Parliament—particularly when that Act of Parliament gives statutory effect to an international convention, by which sovereign states have mutually waived in part immunities for members of the staff of their foreign missions to which they were formerly entitled by the law of nations.

In holding, in my view, incorrectly, that the proceedings were a nullity at the time they were commenced, the deputy county court judge founded himself upon a passage in the judgment of Lord Parker C.J. in *Reg. v. Madan*[69] in which he referred to the proceedings being "null and void unless and until there is a valid waiver which, as it were, would bring the proceedings to life and give jurisdiction to the court." Lord Parker was clearly not using the words "null and void" in a precise sense for what is null and void is not a phoenix, there are no ashes from which it can be brought to life. In that case he was concerned only with waiver as removing the procedural bar of diplomatic immunity. His words should not be read that *only* waiver can, as it were, bring the proceedings to life. The removal of the procedural bar from any other cause will have the same effect.

I am therefore of opinion that the deputy county court judge was wrong in dismissing the action as he did.[70] . . .

Appeal allowed.

Notes[71]

1. Would the question whether the breach of the tenancy agreement by the defendant was an act "performed outside the course of" his duties have been a

---

[68] [1951] 2 K.B. 1003; [1951] 2 T.L.R. 697, CA.
[69] [1961] 2 Q.B. 1 at 7.
[70] Sellers and Danckwerts L.JJ. delivered concurring judgments.
[71] On the 1964 Act, see Buckley (1965–66) 41 B.Y.I.L. 321.

question of *fact* with which an executive certificate could have dealt and upon which such a certificate would have been conclusive under section 4 of the Diplomatic Privileges Act?

2. *Empson v. Smith* indicates one respect in which the 1964 Act changes the previous English law on diplomatic immunity. Have the following pre-1964 rules also been changed:

   (a) That a diplomatic agent can claim immunity in a civil action for the payment of rates on his private residence?[72]

   (b) That a diplomatic agent can claim immunity in a civil action concerning his private commercial activities?[73]

   (c) That a British subject accredited as a diplomatic agent to a foreign mission in the United Kingdom has immunity from distraint of goods for non-payment of rates unless the contrary has been indicated by the British Government when he is received?[74]

   (d) That immunity can be deemed to have been waived by entry of appearance in an action?[75]

3. In *Engelke v. Musmann*[76] Lord Phillimore, *obiter dicta*, defined an ambassador's family for the purposes of immunity as "his wife and his children if living with him." In *Re C (An Infant)*[77] Harman J., considering whether the son of a person entitled to immunity was himself entitled to it, ruled that the test was whether "he is ordinarily resident with, or is under his father's control."[78] Are these statements consistent with the 1964 Act?

British Foreign Office practice is to treat a diplomat's "family" as "including the spouse and minor children [under 18], and certain other persons in exceptional circumstances." In practice, the "exceptional" cases fall into three categories:

   (a) a person who fulfils the social duties of hostess to the diplomatic agent (for example the sister of an unmarried diplomat or the adult daughter of a widowed diplomat);

   (b) the parent of a diplomat living with him and not engaged in paid employment on a permanent basis; and

   (c) the child of a diplomat living with him who has attained majority but is not engaged in paid employment on a permanent basis. Students are included in this category provided that they reside with the diplomat at least during vacations."[79]

4. *Reciprocity.* Sections 3 and 7 of the 1964 Act follow from Article 47 of the Convention which recognises that immunity may be based upon reciprocity. No orders in council have been made under section 3.[80] The United Kingdom has

[72] *Parkinson v. Potter* (1885) 16 Q.B.D. 152.

[73] *Taylor v. Best* (1854) 14 C.B. 487.

[74] *MacCartney v. Garbutt* (1890) 24 Q.B.D. 368.

[75] *Dickinson v. Del Solar* [1930] 1 K.B. 376.

[76] [1928] A.C. 433.

[77] [1959] 1 Ch. 363.

[78] *ibid.* p. 367.

[79] Denza, *op. cit.*, p. 340, n. 93, above, p. 225.

[80] Foreign Affairs Committee Report, *op. cit.*, p. 350, n. 23, above, p. 6. See, however, the Diplomatic Immunities Restriction Order 1956, S.I. 1956 No. 84, which continued in force by virtue of Diplomatic Privileges Act 1964, s.8(5) and which removes from junior staff and servants of missions personal immunity from suit or legal process to the extent necessary to achieve reciprocity with the treatment given to British members of diplomatic missions in the states concerned: *ibid.*

reciprocal arrangements under section 7(1)(*a*) with three states.[81] The arrangement with the Russian Federation reads in part " . . . members of the staff of Her Majesty's Embassy in Moscow below the rank of attaché (apart from those who are Russian nationals), their wives and families, the personal servants of the Ambassador and servants employed in the Embassy Offices (again, apart from those who are Russian nationals) will henceforth enjoy immunity from personal arrest or other legal process and from the civil and criminal jurisdiction of the Russian courts and inviolability of residence, provided that the corresponding categories of the staff of the Russian Embassy in London continue to enjoy these same immunities."[82] The United Kingdom has arrangements under section 7(1)(*b*) with nine states.[83]

---

[81] Bulgaria, Czechoslavakia and the Russian Federation.

[82] Note from the Foreign Office to the Russian Ambassador in London, April 20, 1956, 1964 B.P.I.L., pp. 226, 227. The arrangements were justified by the British Under Secretary of State for Foreign Affairs as follows: " . . . the threat of legal proceedings, in other words, blackmail, is a weapon which can be and is used to subvert members of diplomatic missions in some countries,"*Hansard*, H.C., Vol. 697, col. 1362, July 1, 1964.

[83] Belgium, Bulgaria, France, Germany, Indonesia, Luxembourg, the Netherlands, Poland, U.S. Lauterpacht suggests that the arrangements made under s.7(1)(*a*) and (*b*) are not regarded as treaties by the parties: 1964 B.P.I.L., p. 226.

CHAPTER 7

THE LAW OF THE SEA

1. INTRODUCTORY NOTE[1]

(i) THE 1958 CONVENTIONS ON THE LAW OF THE SEA

THE law of the sea was the subject of the first completed attempt of the International Law Commission to place a large segment of international law on a multilateral treaty basis. Four Conventions resulting from its work[2] were produced by the first and second Geneva Conferences on the Law of the Sea of 1958[3] and 1960.[4] They are the Geneva Conventions on the Territorial Sea and the Contiguous Zone,[5] on the High Seas,[6] on the Continental Shelf[7] and on Fishing and Conservation of the Living Resources of the High Seas.[8] All four have entered into force and have been ratified by a large, though not overwhelming, number of states.[9]

---

[1] See Bowett, *The Law of the Sea* (1967); Brown, *The International Law of the Sea* (2 vols., 1994); Churchill and Lowe, *The Law of the Sea* (2nd ed., 1988); Colombos, *The International Law of the Sea* (6th ed., 1967); McDougal and Burke, *The Public Order of the Oceans* (1967, reprinted 1987, with new introduction); O'Connell, *The International Law of the Sea* (2 vols., 1982, 1984); B. D. Smith, *State Responsibility and the Marine Environment* (1988). For a helpful bibliographical guide on the law of the sea, see Song (1993) 24 O.D.I.L. 205. It lists, *inter alia*, the many UN publications on the law of the sea (collections of national legislation, analyses of the 1982 Convention, etc.). See also the UN *Law of the Sea Bulletin*, which contains status information about the 1982 Convention and national laws, etc.

[2] In 1956 the Commission submitted to the UN General Assembly 73 *Draft Articles Concerning the Law of the Sea*, together with a Commentary upon them: for the text of the Draft Articles and the Commentary, see Y.B.I.L.C., 1956, II, pp. 256 *et seq.*

[3] See *UN Conference on the Law of the Sea, Geneva*, February 24–April 27, 1958, *Official Records*, Vols. I–VII, UN Doc. A/CONF. 13/37–43. (Referred to in this chapter as *1958 Sea Conference Records*.)

[4] See *2nd UN Conference on the Law of the Sea, Geneva*, March 17–April 26, 1960, *Official Records*, UN Doc. A/CONF. 19/8 and 9. See Dean (1960) 54 A.J.I.L. 751.

[5] U.K.T.S. 3 (1965), Cmnd. 2511; 516 U.N.T.S. 205; (1958) 52 A.J.I.L. 834.

[6] U.K.T.S. 5 (1963), Cmnd. 1929; 450 U.N.T.S. 82; (1958) 52 A.J.I.L. 842.

[7] U.K.T.S. 39 (1964), Cmnd. 2422; 499 U.N.T.S. 311; (1958) 52 A.J.I.L. 858.

[8] U.K.T.S. 39 (1966), Cmnd. 3208; 599 U.N.T.S. 285; (1958) 52 A.J.I.L. 851.

[9] The Territorial Sea Convention entered into force in 1964; there are 51 parties. The High Seas Convention entered into force in 1962; there are 62 parties. The Continental Shelf Convention entered into force in 1964; there are 57 parties. The Fisheries Convention entered into force in 1966; there are 37 parties. The U.K. is a party to all four Conventions. The Conference also adopted an Optional Protocol on the Compulsory Settlement of Disputes, U.K.T.S. 60 (1963), Cmnd. 2112; 450 U.N.T.S. 169; (1958) 52 A.J.I.L. 862. This entered into force in 1962; 37 parties, including the U.K. On the Conventions, see Dean (1958) 52 A.J.I.L. 607; Fitzmaurice (1959) 8 I.C.L.Q. 73; Jessup (1959) 59 Col.L.R. 234; Sørensen, *The Law of the Sea*, Int.Conc., No. 520 (1958).

The High Seas Convention is said in its Preamble to be "generally declaratory of established principles of international law."[10] No such claim is made for any of the other Conventions and it is clear that they are a mixture of "codification" and "progressive development" in the sense of the terms of reference of the International Law Commission.[11] It is often difficult to be sure within which of these two categories a particular rule falls and whether, if within the latter, practice has so developed since its adoption at Geneva that it now states a rule of customary international law. The *North Sea Continental Shelf* cases[12] have shown that it must not be too readily assumed that a treaty provision even in a "law-making" treaty states a rule of customary international law.

Although the Geneva Conventions were a considerable achievement, they were not perfect. In particular, they did not contain a rule on the basic question of the width of the territorial sea or on the related question of the fishing rights, if any, of coastal states beyond their territorial sea. They also have been overtaken by events, both scientific and political. The development of new techniques for underwater exploitation of oil and other mineral resources has made it necessary to reconsider the régime of the continental shelf and to establish a régime for the deep sea-bed. Concern for the conservation of fishing resources and the prevention of pollution has grown and has led to general approval of an approach based upon control by the coastal state over wide areas of the sea adjacent to its coastline. State practice on the width of the territorial sea has changed, again in favour of the coastal state and with consequential problems for innocent passage and overflight. Archipelagic and landlocked states have pressed their claims for better treatment. These, and other considerations, including the fact that most post-colonial states had had no say in the drafting of the Geneva Conventions of 1958,[13] led to the decision to call a Third United Nations Conference on the Law of the Sea (UNCLOS III).[14]

(ii) THE 1982 CONVENTION ON THE LAW OF THE SEA

After nine long years of negotiation,[15] the Conference adopted the 1982 Convention on the Law of the Sea.[16] The 1982 Convention is a remarkable achieve-

---

[10] Note that there are some provisions of the Convention, *e.g.* Art. 15 on piracy (below, p. 432), that are clearly instances of "progressive development" of the law and not "codification."

[11] See above, p. 66.

[12] Above, p. 27.

[13] 86 states participated in the 1958 Conference; over 150 states participated in UNCLOS III.

[14] On the Conference, see Ganz (1977) 26 I.C.L.Q. 1; Oxman (1977) 71 A.J.I.L. 247; Stevenson and Oxman (1974) 68 A.J.I.L. 1; *ibid.* (1975) 69 A.J.I.L. 1 and 763; Oxman (1977) 71 A.J.I.L. 247; *ibid.* (1978) 72 A.J.I.L. 57; *ibid.* (1979) 73 A.J.I.L. 1; *ibid.* (1980) 74 A.J.I.L. 1; *ibid.* (1981) 75 A.J.I.L. 211; *ibid.* (1982) 76 A.J.I.L. 1.

[15] The records of debates and documents of the Conference are published in *Third UN Conference on the Law of the Sea: Official Records*, Vols I–XVII, 1975–84. Referred to in this Chapter as *UNCLOS III Records*, these official records are less useful than the equivalent publications for UNCLOS I and II because most of the drafting at UNCLOS III was done at informal meetings for which there is no official record of debates. See, however, the series of studies being prepared by the UN Office for Ocean Affairs and the Law of the Sea on the legislative history of some of the articles of the Convention, (*e.g.* the 1987 study on the legislative history of Part X on rights of access of land-locked states). For a more extensive set of conference documents, see Platzöder, ed., *Third United Nations Conference on the Law of the Sea*, 18 vols, 1982–1988. For other collections of documents relevant to UNCLOS III, see Lay, Churchill and Nordquist, eds., *New Directions in the Law of the Sea* (11 vols, 1973–81), and Oda, *The International Law of Ocean Development* (2 vols, 1972, 1975), and two looseleaf binders (from 1977). For accounts of UNCLOS III, see Friedheim,

ment. The Convention covers, in its 320 articles and nine annexes, all of the ground of the four 1958 Conventions and quite a lot more. Many of its provisions repeat verbatim or in essence those of the Geneva Conventions. Some contain different or more detailed rules on matters covered by them. Others, most strikingly those on the exclusive economic zone and the deep sea-bed, spell out new legal régimes. The main changes or additions are the acceptance of a 12 mile territorial sea; provision for transit passage through international straits; increased rights for archipelagic and landlocked states; stricter control of marine pollution; further provision for fisheries conservation; acceptance of a 200–mile exclusive economic zone for coastal states; changes in the continental shelf régime; and provision for the development of deep sea-bed mineral resources.[17]

An underlying theme of the Convention is that it should "contribute to the realisation of a just and equitable international economic order which takes into account the interests and needs of mankind as a whole and, in particular, the special interests and needs of developing countries, whether coastal or land-locked" (Preamble). The parts of the Convention in which this theme is most evident are those on the exclusive economic zone, the continental shelf and, above all, the deep sea-bed.

The Convention contains machinery for the settlement of disputes arising under it, including an International Tribunal for the Law of the Sea, with its seat at Hamburg (Article 287 and Annex VI).

The Convention is a remarkable document in that none of its particular provisions were voted upon. Articles were drafted in the working Committees and presented as stating the common, predominant, or accepted view, with the complete text of the Convention seen as an intricate and delicately balanced bargain between the different interests of the participating states. States opposed to provision A were prepared to accept it either in return for the inclusion of provision B or in the interest of an agreed régime for the law of the sea that taken as a whole was acceptable. The intention was that the complete text would be adopted by the same process of consensus too.[18] The thought was that general acceptance of the complete package would increase its chances of ratification and strengthen its claim to be regarded as "instant" customary international law.[19] In the event, this expectation was not realised. At the eleventh hour, the newly elected United States Government asked for time to review the draft text and, when it was unable to obtain all of the changes (almost entirely in respect of the deep sea-bed) that it wanted, requested a vote. The Convention was then adopted, in accordance with traditional Conference practice, by a majority vote.[20]

Dissatisfaction with the deep sea-bed regime in Part XI of the Convention led the U.S. to vote against the adoption of the Convention and, together with the

---

Negotiating the New Ocean Regime (1993) and Sanger, *Ordering the Oceans: The Making of the Law of the Sea* (1986).

[16] UN Doc. A/CONF. 62/122; (1982) 21 I.L.M. 1261. See *Bernaerts' Guide to the Law of the Sea: The 1982 United Nations Convention* (1988) and Noodquist, ed., *United Nations Convention on the Law of the Sea 1982: A Commentary* (Vols I–IV, 1985–93).

[17] On the effect of some of these changes on freedom of the air, see Hailbronner (1983) 77 A.J.I.L. 490.

[18] On the merits of the consensus approach, see Plant (1987) 36 I.C.L.Q. 525.

[19] See Caminos and Molitor (1985) 79 A.J.I.L. 871.

[20] The vote was 130 to four, with 17 abstentions. Israel, Turkey, the U.S., and Venezuela voted against. Seven West European states (Belgium the F.R.G., Italy, Luxembourg, the Netherlands, Spain and the U.K.), eight East European States (Bulgaria, Byelorussia, Czechoslovakia, the G.D.R., Hungary, Poland, Ukraine, and the USSR), Mongolia, and Thailand abstained.

F.R.G. and the U.K., not to become a signatory to it. During the 1980s and early 1990s, the Convention was ratified by developing states, but, because of the deep sea-bed regime, not by developed states. In order to obtain more general ratification of the Convention and to ensure its success, steps were taken within the UN which ultimately led to the adoption of the 1994 New York Implementing Agreement.[21] This amends Part XI to the satisfaction of developed states and has probably secured the future of the 1982 Convention as a generally accepted statement of the law of the sea. The 1982 Convention entered into force in 1994[22] and 119 states are now parties, including many developed states.[23]

It seems likely, even allowing for the *North Sea Continental Shelf Cases*, that state practice will confirm or come to accept many of the particular Convention rules (whether those duplicating or building upon the 1958 Convention or those adding to them) as being binding as custom.[24] But caution is in order since the consensus favouring the inclusion of a particular rule *as a part of the overall package* at UNCLOS III may have masked opposition to the rule taken by itself. A number of provisions in the area of the more traditional law of the sea,[25] as well as the acceptance of compulsory judicial and arbitral settlement, were, for example, concessions by developing states to which acceptance of the (original) deep sea-bed régime was a necessary counterweight.

A package approach to the relationship between the 1982 Convention and custom to that just indicated is suggested by the following remarks of the UNCLOS III President (Mr T. Koh) at the closing ceremony[26]:

> Although the Convention consists of a series of compromises, they form an integral whole. This is why the Convention does not provide for reservations.[27] It is therefore not possible for States to pick what they like and disregard what they do not like. In international law, as in domestic law, rights and duties go hand in hand. It is therefore legally impermissible to claim rights under the Convention without being willing to assume the correlative duties.

On this view, either the whole of the package in the 1982 Convention is likely to be custom or none.[28] The I.C.J., which has found itself almost magnetically drawn to the Convention in a series of cases, mostly on maritime boundaries, has tended not to follow a package approach but, in the more usual way, to assess separately

---

[21] On the Agreement, see below, p. 474.

[22] When the 1982 Convention entered into force, a complicated set of treaty relations resulted, with the 1958 Conventions continuing fully in force for the states parties to them and not parties to the 1982 Convention. The 1958 Conventions also continue to govern states parties to both the 1958 and the 1982 Conventions in their relations with states parties to the 1958 Conventions only. The 1982 Convention replaces completely the 1958 Conventions for the parties to both. See Art. 311, 1982 Convention.

[23] These include Australia, France, Germany, Japan and the U.K. The U.S. is not a party.

[24] See, *e.g.*, the U.S.-USSR statement on innocent passage, below, p. 405. On the relationship between the 1982 Convention and custom, see Bernhardt (1987–V); (1987–V) 205 Hague Receuil 247 (Butler (1988) 12 Mar. Pol. 182; Gamble and Frankowska (1984) 21 San Diego L.R. 491; Larson (1994) 25 O.D.I.L. 75; Lee (1983) 77 A.J.I.L. 541; Macrae (1983) 13 Cal. West I.L.J. 181; Mendelson (1988) 12 Mar. Pol. 192; Sohn (1985) 34 A.U.L.R. 271.

[25] *e.g.* those on the right of transit passage through international straits: see below, p. 410.

[26] *The Law of the Sea: Official Text of the UN Convention on the Law of the Sea* (1983), UN Publication, p. xxxiv. On the "package deal" principle, see also Brown (1984) 2 J.E.N.R.L. 258 at 260.

[27] *Ed.* See Art. 309.

[28] Note, however, that Part XI of the 1982 Convention on the deep sea-bed, which was a crucial part of the bargain for developing states, concerns an issue that is not now as important for them as during UNCLOS III and has, in any event, been revised so as to favour developed states. As a result, the package in the 1982 Convention as a whole now clearly favours developed states.

the status of particular rules or régimes as they arise for consideration. In the *Gulf of Maine Case*,[29] a Chamber of the Court stated:

> Turning lastly to the proceedings of the Third United Nations Conference on the Law of the Sea and the final result of that Conference, the Chamber notes in the first place that the Convention adopted at the end of the Conference has not yet come into force and that a number of States do not appear inclined to ratify it. This, however, in no way detracts from the consensus reached on large portions of the instrument and, above all, cannot invalidate the observation that certain provisions of the Convention concerning the continental shelf and the exclusive economic zone ... were adopted, without any objections ... these provisions, even if in some respects they bear the mark of the compromise surrounding their adoption, may nevertheless be regarded as consonant at present with general international law on the question.

In view of the entry into force of the 1982 Convention and the fact that a majority of states are parties, the materials in the present chapter are based upon it. Its relation with custom and with the rules in the 1958 Conventions is also considered.

2. THE TERRITORIAL SEA[30]

(i) SOVEREIGNTY IN THE TERRITORIAL SEA

CONVENTION ON THE LAW OF THE SEA 1982

UN Doc. A/CONF. 62/122; (1982) 21 I.L.M. 1261

Article 2

1. The sovereignty of a coastal State extends, beyond its land territory and internal waters and, in the case of an archipelagic State, its archipelagic waters, to an adjacent belt of sea, described as the territorial sea.

2. This sovereignty extends to the air space over the territorial sea as well as to its bed and subsoil.

3. The sovereignty over the territorial sea is exercised subject to this Convention and to other rules of international law.

---

[29] I.C.J. Rep. 1984, p. 246 at p. 294. See also *Continental Shelf (Tunisia v. Libya) Case*, I.C.J. Rep. 1982, p. 18 at p. 74 (reference to the Draft 1982 Convention as confirming the definition of the continental shelf) and the *Continental Shelf (Libya v. Malta)* Case, I.C.J. Rep. 1985, p. 13, at p. 30 (" ... the 1982 Convention is of major importance, having been adopted by an overwhelming majority of states; hence it is clearly the duty of the Court ... to consider in what degree any of its relevant provisions are binding upon the Parties as rules of customary international law"). And see the *Nicaragua Case*, I.C.J. Rep. 1986, p. 14, at p. 111 (1982 Convention codifies innocent passage rule).

[30] The term "territorial sea" is interchangeable with "territorial waters".

Notes

1. There can be little doubt that the above rules[31] represent customary international law.[32] The "other rules of international law" referred to in Article 2(3) presumably include both customary rules (*e.g.* concerning the treatment of aliens) and treaty obligations (*e.g.* concerning navigation at sea).

2. In the *Grisbadarna Case*,[33] the Permanent Court of Arbitration held that when certain land territory was ceded to Sweden "the radius of maritime territory constituting an inseparable appurtenance of this land territory must have automatically formed a part of this cession." Judge Sir Arnold McNair, in his dissenting opinion in the *Anglo-Norwegian Fisheries Case*,[34] stated: "International law does not say to a State: 'You are entitled to claim territorial waters if you want them.' No maritime state can refuse them. International law imposes upon a maritime State certain obligations and confers upon it certain rights arising out of the sovereignty which it exercises over its maritime territory."

(ii) WIDTH OF THE TERRITORIAL SEA

CONVENTION ON THE LAW OF THE SEA 1982

UN Doc. A/CONF. 62/122; (1982) 21 I.L.M. 1261

Article 3

Every State has the right to establish the breadth of its territorial sea up to a limit not exceeding 12 nautical miles,[35] measured from baselines determined in accordance with this Convention.

Notes

1. Lack of agreement prevented the inclusion in the 1958 Territorial Sea Convention of a rule on the width of the territorial sea. This absence of agreement reflected the uncertainty which has existed in customary international law for a number of years. It is arguable that at the turn of the century there was a rule of general application, originating for some states and writers in the distance from the coastline that a cannon could fire (and hence protect[36]), by which the territorial sea was three miles in width (the "cannon shot" rule). State practice now does not support such a rule or any other that specifies a single distance as the width of the territorial sea. Most coastal states claim 12 miles. Information available in 1994[37] showed that four states claimed three miles; five claimed from four to six

---

[31] Art. 2 is identical to Arts 1, 2, 1958 Territorial Sea Convention, except for the references to archipelagic states.

[32] On the development of the rule of sovereignty over the seabed of the territorial sea, see Marston (1976–7) 48 B.Y.I.L. 321. On the evolution of British practice, see Marston, *The Marginal Seabed: United Kingdom Legal Practice* (1981).

[33] *Norway v. Sweden*, Scott, *Hague Court Reports* 121 at p. 127 (1909).

[34] I.C.J. Rep. 1951, p. 116 at p. 160. See also above, p. 227, n. 8.

[35] *Ed.* A nautical mile is 1·1508 statute miles.

[36] See the Preamble to the Territorial Waters Jurisdiction Act 1978, above, p. 77.

[37] *Law of the Sea Bulletin, loc. cit.*, p. 368 n. 1, above, No. 25, p. 115.

miles; 120 claimed 12 miles[38] and 16 claimed more than that.[39] Compared with earlier figures,[40] these show a marked swing from three miles to 12 miles as the width most commonly claimed. At UNCLOS III, Ecuador argued for a 200 mile territorial sea but found little support.[41] The 1982 Convention probably states the present customary international law position. Agreement upon a 200 mile exclusive economic zone[42] takes away much of the argument for a territorial sea wider than 12 miles. The validity of claims to territorial seas wider than 12 miles depends upon the response of other states: see the *Anglo-Norwegian Fisheries Case*, below, p. 375.

2. The extension of the territorial sea to 12 miles has important consequences for the right of innocent passage for ships; it also affects aircraft which have no right of innocent passage over the territorial sea.[43] The following factors, referred to by the United States representative at Geneva in 1958, are worth bearing in mind:

> One of the merits of the three mile limit was that it was safest for shipping. Many landmarks still used for visual piloting by small craft were not visible at a range of 12 miles; only 20 per cent of the world's lighthouses had a range exceeding that distance; radar navigation was of only marginal utility beyond 12 miles; and many vessels (which frequently did not wish to enter the territorial sea) did not carry sufficient cable or appropriate equipment to anchor at the depths normally found outside the 12-mile limit. In addition, any extension of the breadth of the territorial sea would mean an increase in the cost of patrolling the larger area.... One further objection to extending the territorial sea was that, in time of war, a neutral State would have greater difficulty in safeguarding the broader belt of territorial waters against the incursions of ships of belligerents.[44]

Note also Judge Sir Gerald Fitzmaurice in his dissenting opinion in the *Fisheries Jurisdiction Case (Jurisdiction)*[45]:

> the territorial sea involves responsibilities as well as rights, which many countries were unable to discharge satisfactorily outside a relatively narrow belt, such as for example policing and maintaining order; buoying and marking channels and reefs, sandbanks and other obstacles; keeping navigable

---

[38] These included most Afro-Asian and Latin American states. Most Western states including Canada, France, Ireland, Japan, the Netherlands, New Zealand, the U.K. and the U.S., also claimed 12 miles, as did China. The U.K. extended its territorial sea from three miles by the Territorial Sea Act 1987. See Churchill (1987) 37 I.C.L.Q. 412. On Germany's extension for reasons of environmental protection of its North Sea territorial sea to, at one point, 16 miles, see Gundling (1986) 1 I.J.E.C.L. 312. The U.S. has protested.

[39] The distances claimed ranged from 20 to 200 miles. 200 miles were claimed by six Latin American states and five African states. It is not clear to what extent these are claims to full territorial sovereignty in all cases. The number of states claiming over 12 miles has recently fallen.

[40] Figures produced by the UN Secretariat for the 1960 Conference showed that 22 states claimed three miles; 18 claimed 4–10 miles; 11 claimed 12 miles; and two claimed more than 12 miles: 4 Whiteman 21. 1973 FAO figures showed 21 claims to three miles and 56 claims to 12 miles.

[41] See *UNCLOS III Records*, Vol. IV, pp. 75–80.

[42] See below, p. 446.

[43] The 1982 Convention right of transit passage through international straits, see below, p. 411, responds to these problems.

[44] *1958 Sea Conference Records*, Vol. III, p. 26.

[45] *UK v. Iceland*. I.C.J. Rep. 1973, p. 28, n. 8. And see Art. 24(2), 1982 Convention, below, p. 399.

channels clear, and giving notice of dangers to navigation; providing rescue services, lighthouses, lightships, bell-buoys, etc.

And see the following comment by the representative of Byelorussia at the 1960 Geneva Conference:

The main objective of the champions of the six-mile limit (the 1960 Canadian/ United States proposal) was to obtain for their naval forces unconditional, so-called legitimate, access to foreign waters close to coasts in which they were interested for strategic or political reasons.[46]

Clearly, if passage through the territorial sea by warships in order to check on a coastal state's security or of demonstrating a state's "presence" as a form of political pressure is not an exercise of the right of innocent passage,[47] the wider the territorial sea the less the sea can be used effectively for such purposes.

(iii) DELIMITATION OF THE TERRITORIAL SEA

ANGLO-NORWEGIAN FISHERIES CASE[48]

U.K. *v.* Norway

I.C.J. Reports 1951, p. 116

A Norwegian Decree of 1935 delimited Norway's "Fishery Zone" (by which was meant its territorial sea) along almost 1,000 miles of coastline north of latitude 66° 28.8' North. The Zone, which the United Kingdom agreed was, as a matter of historic title, four (not three) miles wide, was measured not from the low-water mark at every point along the coast (as is the normal practice) but from straight baselines linking the outermost points of land (sometimes "drying rocks" above water only at low-tide) along it. The preamble to the Decree justified this system on grounds of "well-established national titles of right," "the geographical conditions prevailing on the Norwegian coasts," and "the safeguard of the vital interests of the inhabitants of the northernmost parts of the country." The first of these grounds related to the use of straight baselines in Norwegian decrees of 1869 and 1889 (though for different parts of the coastline totalling only 89 miles) and acquiescence in that use by other states. The "geographic conditions" were that the coastline concerned is deeply indented by *fjords* and *sunds* (sounds) and, for part of its length south of North Cape, is fronted by a fringe of islands and rocks (the *skjærgaard*) that is difficult to separate from the mainland. The third ground is explained in the Court's statement that "[i]n these barren regions the inhabitants of the coastal zone derive their livelihood essentially from fishing." By using straight baselines Norway enclosed waters within its territorial sea that would have been high seas, and hence open to foreign fishing, if it had used the low-water mark line. Several baselines were over 30 miles long; the longest was 44 miles long.[49] In this case, the United Kingdom challenged the legality of Norway's straight baseline system and the choice of certain baselines used in applying it. The question was important for British fishing interests. Norwegian

---

[46] UN Doc. A/CONF. 19/C.1/SR.17, p. 13.
[47] See below, p. 408. On security zones, see below, p. 435.
[48] See Johnson (1952) 1 I.C.L.Q. 145 and Waldock (1951) 28 B.Y.I.L. 114.
[49] For a map showing the baselines, see Waldock, *loc. cit.*, n. 48, above, p. 115.

enforcement of its system had given rise to disputes involving British fishing vessels.

Judgment of the Court

The Court has no difficulty in finding that, for the purpose of measuring the breadth of the territorial sea, it is the low-water mark as opposed to the high-water mark, or the mean between two tides, which has generally been adopted in the practice of States. This criterion is the most favourable to the coastal State and clearly shows the character of territorial waters as appurtenant to the land territory. The Court notes that the Parties agree as to this criterion, but that they differ as to its application.

The Parties also agree that in the case of a low-tide elevation (drying rock) the outer edge at low water of this low-tide elevation may be taken into account as a base-point for calculating the breadth of the territorial sea. . . .

The Court finds itself obliged to decide whether the relevant low-water mark is that of the mainland or of the "skjærgaard." Since the mainland is bordered in its western sector by the "skjærgaard" which constitutes a whole with the mainland, it is the outer line of the "skjærgaard," which must be taken into account in delimiting the belt of Norwegian territorial waters. This solution is dictated by geographic realities.

Three methods have been contemplated to effect the application of the low-water mark rule. The simplest would appear to be the method of the *tracé parallèle*, which consists of drawing the outer limit of the belt of territorial waters by following the coast in all its sinuosities. This method may be applied without difficulty to an ordinary coast, which is not too broken. Where a coast is deeply indented and cut into, as is that of Eastern Finnmark, or where it is bordered by an archipelago such as the "skjærgaard" along the western sector of the coast here in question, the baseline becomes independent of the low-water mark, and can only be determined by means of geometric construction. In such circumstances the line of the low-water mark can no longer be put forward as a rule requiring the coast line to be followed in all its sinuosities. Nor can one characterise as exceptions to the rule the very many derogations which would be necessitated by such a rugged coast; the rule would disappear under the exceptions. Such a coast, viewed as a whole, calls for the application of a different method; that is, the method of baselines which, within reasonable limits, may depart from the physical line of the coast.[50]

It is true that the experts of the Second Sub-Committee of the Second Committee of the 1930 Conference for the codification of international law formulated the low-water mark rule somewhat strictly ("following

---

[50] *Ed.* These last two sentences are a revised translation by the I.C.J. Registry of the authoritative French text: see Y.B.I.L.C., 1956, II, p. 267.

all the sinuosities of the coast"). But they were at the same time obliged to admit many exceptions relating to bays, islands near the coast, groups of islands. In the present case this method of the *tracé parallèle*, which was invoked against Norway in the Memorial, was abandoned in the written Reply, and later in the oral argument of the Agent of the United Kingdom Government. Consequently, it is no longer relevant to the case. "On the other hand," it is said in the Reply, "the *courbe tangente*—or, in English, 'envelopes of arcs of circles'—method is the method which the United Kingdom considers to be the correct one."

The arcs of circles method, which is constantly used for determining the position of a point or object at sea, is a new technique in so far as it is a method for delimiting the territorial sea. This technique was proposed by the United States delegation at the 1930 Conference for the codification of international law. Its purpose is to secure the application of the principle that the belt of territorial waters must follow the line of the coast. It is not obligatory by law, as was admitted by Counsel for the United Kingdom Government in his oral reply. . . .

The principle that the belt of territorial waters must follow the general direction of the coast makes it possible to fix certain criteria valid for any delimitation of the territorial sea; these criteria will be elucidated later. The Court will confine itself at this stage to noting that, in order to apply this principle, several States have deemed it necessary to follow the straight baselines method and that they have not encountered objections of principle by other States. This method consists of selecting appropriate points on the low-water mark and drawing straight lines between them. This has been done, not only in the case of well-defined bays, but also in cases of minor curvatures of the coastline where it was solely a question of giving a simpler form to the belt of territorial waters.

It has been contended, on behalf of the United Kingdom, that Norway may draw straight lines only across bays. The Court is unable to share this view. If the belt of territorial waters must follow the outer line of the "skjærgaard," and if the method of straight baselines must be admitted in certain cases, there is no valid reason to draw them only across bays, as in Eastern Finnmark, and not also to draw them between islands, islets and rocks, across the sea areas separating them, even when such areas do not fall within the conception of a bay. It is sufficient that they should be situated between the island formations of the "skjærgaard," *inter fauces terrarum.*

In the opinion of the United Kingdom Government, Norway is entitled, on historic grounds, to claim as internal waters all fjords and sunds which have the character of a bay. . . .

By "historic waters" are usually meant waters which are treated as internal waters but which would not have that character were it not for the existence of an historic title. . . . In its [the United Kingdom's] opinion Norway can justify the claim that these waters are . . . internal on the ground that she has exercised the necessary jurisdiction over them for a long period without opposition from other States, a kind of *possessio longi temporis*, with the result that her jurisdiction over these waters must now be recognised although it constitutes a derogation from the rules in force. . . . But the United Kingdom Government concedes this only on the basis of historic title; it must therefore be taken that that Government has not abandoned its contention that the 10-mile rule is to be regarded as a rule of international law.

In these circumstances the Court deems it necessary to point out that although the 10-mile rule has been adopted by certain States both in their national law and in their treaties and conventions, and although certain arbitral decisions have applied it as between these States, other States have adopted a different limit. Consequently, the 10-mile rule has not acquired the authority of a general rule of international law.

In any event the 10-mile rule would appear to be inapplicable as against Norway inasmuch as she has always opposed any attempt to apply it to the Norwegian coast.

The Court now comes to the question of the length of the baselines drawn across the waters lying between the various formations of the "skjærgaard." Basing itself on the analogy with the alleged general rule of 10 miles relating to bays, the United Kingdom Government still maintains on this point that the length of straight lines must not exceed 10 miles.

In this connection, the practice of States does not justify the formulation of any general rule of law. The attempts that have been made to subject groups of islands or coastal archipelagoes to conditions analogous to the limitations concerning bays (distance between the islands not exceeding twice the breadth of the territorial waters, or 10 or 12 sea miles), have not got beyond the stage of proposals.

Furthermore, apart from any question of limiting the lines to 10 miles, it may be that several lines can be envisaged. In such cases the coastal State would seem to be in the best position to appraise the local conditions dictating the selection.

Consequently, the Court is unable to share the view of the United Kingdom Government, that "Norway, in the matter of baselines, now claims recognition of an exceptional system." As will be shown later, all that the Court can see therein is the application of general international law to a specific case. . . .

It does not at all follow that, in the absence of rules having the technically precise character alleged by the United Kingdom Government, the delimitation undertaken by the Norwegian Government in 1935 is not subject to certain principles which make it possible to judge as to its validity under international law. The delimitation of sea areas has always an international aspect; it cannot be dependent merely upon the will of the coastal State as expressed in its municipal law. Although it is true that the act of delimitation is necessarily a unilateral act, because only the coastal State is competent to undertake it, the validity of the delimitation with regard to other States depends upon international law.

In this connection, certain basic considerations inherent in the nature of the territorial sea, bring to light certain criteria which, though not entirely precise, can provide courts with an adequate basis for their decisions, which can be adapted to the diverse facts in question.

Among these considerations, some reference must be made to the close dependence of the territorial sea upon the land domain. It is the land which confers upon the coastal State a right to the waters off its coasts. It follows that while such a State must be allowed the latitude necessary in order to be able to adapt its delimitation to practical needs and local requirements, the drawing of baselines must not depart to any appreciable extent from the general direction of the coast.

Another fundamental consideration, of particular importance in this case, is the more or less close relationship existing between certain sea areas and the land formations which divide or surround them. The real question raised in the choice of baselines is in effect whether certain sea areas lying within these lines are sufficiently closely linked to the land domain to be subject to the regime of internal waters. This idea, which is at the basis of the determination of the rules relating to bays, should be liberally applied in the case of a coast, the geographical configuration of which is as unusual as that of Norway.

Finally, there is one consideration not to be overlooked, the scope of which extends beyond purely geographical factors: that of certain economic interests peculiar to a region, the reality and importance of which are clearly evidenced by a long usage.

Norway puts forward the 1935 Decree as the application of a traditional system of delimitation, a system which she claims to be in complete conformity with international law. The Norwegian Government has referred in this connection to an historic title, the meaning of which was made clear by Counsel for Norway at the sitting on October 12, 1951: "The Norwegian Government does not rely upon history to justify exceptional rights, to claim areas of sea which the general law would deny; it invokes history, together with other factors, to justify the way in which it applies the general law." This conception of an historic title is in consonance with the Norwegian Government's understanding of the general rules of international law. In its view, these rules of international law take into account the diversity of facts and, therefore, concede that the drawing of baselines must be adapted to the special conditions obtaining in different regions. In its view, the system of delimitation applied in 1935, a system characterised by the use of straight lines, does not therefore infringe the general law: it is an adaptation rendered necessary by local conditions.

The Court examined the Norwegian system.

The Court . . . finds that this system was consistently applied by Norwegian authorities. . . .

The Court considers that too much importance need not be attached to the few uncertainties or contradictions, real or apparent, which the United Kingdom Government claims to have discovered in Norwegian practice. They may be easily understood in the light of the variety of the facts and conditions prevailing in the long period which has elapsed since 1812, and are not such as to modify the conclusions reached by the Court. . . .

From the standpoint of international law, it is now necessary to consider whether the application of the Norwegian system encountered any opposition from foreign States.

Norway has been in a position to argue without any contradiction that neither the promulgation of her delimitation Decrees in 1869[51] and in 1889, nor their application, gave rise to any opposition on the part of foreign States. Since, moreover, these Decrees constitute, as has been shown above, the application of a well-defined and uniform system, it is indeed this system itself which would reap the benefit of general toleration, the basis of an historical consolidation which would make it enforceable as against all States.

The general toleration of foreign States with regard to the Norwegian practice is an unchallenged fact. For a period of more than 60 years the United Kingdom Government itself in no way contested it. . . . It would appear that it was only in its Memorandum of July 27, 1933, that the United Kingdom made a formal and definite protest on this point.

The United Kingdom Government has argued that the Norwegian system of delimitation was not known to it and that the system therefore lacked the notoriety essential to provide the basis of an historic title enforceable against it. The Court is unable to accept this view. . . .

The notoriety of the facts, the general toleration of the international community, Great Britain's position in the North Sea, her own interest in the question, and her prolonged abstention would in any case warrant Norway's enforcement of her system against the United Kingdom.

The Court is thus led to conclude that the method of straight lines, established in the Norwegian system, was imposed by the peculiar geography of the Norwegian coast; that even before the dispute arose, this method had been consolidated by a constant and sufficiently long practice, in the face of which the attitude of governments bears witness to the fact that they did not consider it to be contrary to international law.

The question now arises whether the Decree of July 12, 1935, which in its preamble is expressed to be an application of this method, conforms to it in its drawing of the baselines, or whether, at certain points, it departs from this method to any considerable extent. . . .

---

[51] *Ed.* France, which had been in dispute with Norway on a related matter, did ask for an explanation of the 1869 Decree. Norway replied, arguing that the enactment was lawful, and France "did not pursue the matter": I.C.J. Rep. 1951, p. 136.

The Norwegian Government admits that the baselines must be drawn in such a way as to respect the general direction of the coast and that they must be drawn in a reasonable manner. . . .

The delimitation of the Lopphavet basin has also been criticised by the United Kingdom. . . . The Lopphavet basin constitutes an ill-defined geographic whole. It cannot be regarded as having the character of a bay. It is made up of an extensive area of water dotted with large islands which are separated by inlets that terminate in the various fjords. The baseline has been challenged on the ground that it does not respect the general direction of the coast.[52] It should be observed that, however justified the rule in question may be, it is devoid of any mathematical precision. In order properly to apply the rule, regard must be had for the relation between the deviation complained of and what, according to the terms of the rule, must be regarded as the *general* direction of the coast. Therefore, one cannot confine oneself to examining one sector of the coast alone, except in a case of manifest abuse. . . . In the case in point, the divergence between the baseline and the land formations is not such that it is a distortion of the general direction of the Norwegian coast.

Even if it were considered that in the sector under review the deviation was too pronounced, it must be pointed out that the Norwegian Government has relied upon an historic title clearly referable to the waters of Lopphavet. . . . The Court considers that, although it is not always clear to what specific areas they apply, the historical data produced . . . lend some weight to the idea of the survival of traditional rights reserved to the inhabitants of the Kingdom over fishing grounds included in the 1935 delimitation, particularly in the case of Lopphavet. Such rights, founded on the vital needs of the population and attested by very ancient and peaceful usage, may legitimately be taken into account in drawing a line which, moreover, appears to the Court to have been kept within the bounds of what is moderate and reasonable. . . .

For these reasons, the Court . . . finds by 10 votes to two[53] that the method employed for the delimitation of the fisheries zone by the Royal Norwegian Decree of July 12, 1935, is not contrary to international law; and by eight votes to four,[54] that the baselines fixed by the said Decree in application of this method are not contrary to international law.

Notes

1. The judgment in the case was greeted with dismay by British commentators who felt that it did not do justice to the not insignificant body of state practice on

[52] *Ed.* The baseline across the Lopphavet basin is 44 miles long. One of the points from which it is drawn is a drying rock 18 miles from the next point, which is also a drying rock.

[53] The judges in the majority were President Basdevant; Vice-President Guerrero; Judges Alvarez, Hackworth, Winiarski, Zoričić, de Visscher, Klaestad, Badawi Pasha and Hsu Mo. The dissenting judges were Judges Sir Arnold McNair and Read. Judge Hackworth voted with the majority on both rulings solely on the basis that Norway had established an historic title.

[54] Judge Hsu Mo joined the dissenting judges. It is not clear who the fourth dissenting judge was.

the questions in issue.[55] Although, as those commentators suggest, it may have been an example of judicial legislation, the judgment has undoubtedly been accepted by states and now almost certainly reflects customary international law on most points.[56]

2. *Measurement of the outer limit of the territorial sea.* The two methods discussed by the Court for finding the outer limit of the territorial sea are the *tracè parallèle and the arcs of circles (courbe tangente)* methods. The former, which is apparently not used in practice,[57] involves drawing a line parallel to the baseline. The line is established by projections the width of the territorial sea from every point along the baseline made outwards in the general direction of the coast. The method is difficult to apply with exactness on any irregular stretch of coastline. With regard to the latter, which Judge Read, disagreeing with the Court, thought was not new but "the way in which the coastline rule has been applied in the international practice of the last century and a half,"[58] Waldock[59] states:

> To apply the rule you take a pair of dividers (compasses) opened to give a three-mile measurement and then draw a three-mile arc either from the land towards the given position at sea or from the position at sea towards the nearest points of land. If the arcs fall short, the position at sea is not within territorial waters. . . . That this was the procedure found in state practice is demonstrated by the fact that very few states indeed ever drew either the outer limit of their territorial waters or their baseline. Without a precise delimitation of territorial waters, the only possible course is to determine the outer limit by taking three-mile arcs from the land. . . . It is nothing but the application to territorial waters of the method used by seamen the world over for measuring distances at sea. . . .

Although easier to apply than the *tracé parallèle* method, the "arcs of circles" method may still lead to awkward pockets of high seas on exceptionally irregular coastlines.[60] It remains the standard method used by mariners in applying the low-water mark baseline, which also remains the baseline used by states along regular coastlines.

3. *Straight baselines.* Did the Court find for Norway because its system for the delimitation of its territorial sea was permitted by customary international law or because, although not permitted by it, Norway had established an historic title?[61] Or both? How long and how irregular does a coastline have to be for the Court's straight baseline approach to be applicable? Is it, where applicable, obligatory or can a state still use the low-water mark method instead? What is the precise relevance of economic factors in the Court's approach? Do they permit a state to be bolder than it might otherwise be in choosing its base points? As far as bays are concerned, might economic factors there too justify a longer closing line than would otherwise be permissible? Does the Court set any upper limit in terms of miles to the length of a straight baseline or of a closing line for a bay?

---

[55] See the articles by Johnson and Waldock cited above, p. 375, n. 48.
[56] Note the different rule in the 1982 Convention, Art. 7(4), below, p. 383, on drying rocks, or low-tide elevations.
[57] Waldock, *loc. cit.*, p. 375, n. 48, above, pp. 134–135.
[58] I.C.J. Rep. 1951, p. 192.
[59] *loc. cit.*, p. 375, n. 48, above, pp. 134–135.
[60] For a proposal made some years ago by the U.S. to prevent such pockets arising, see Boggs (1930) 24 A.J.I.L. 541, at 547 (Fig. 6).
[61] See further on "historic waters," the *Continental Shelf (Tunisia v. Libya)* case, below, p. 388.

CONVENTION ON THE LAW OF THE SEA 1982

UN Doc. A/CONF. 62/122; (1982) 21 I.L.M. 1261

Article 4

The outer limit of the territorial sea is the line every point of which is at a distance from the nearest point of the baseline equal to the breadth of the territorial sea.

Article 5

Except where otherwise provided in this Convention, the normal baseline for measuring the breadth of the territorial sea is the low-water line along the coast as marked on large-scale charts officially recognized by the coastal State.

Article 6

In the case of islands situated on atolls or of islands having fringing reefs, the baseline for measuring the breadth of the territorial sea is the seaward low-water line of the reef, as shown by the appropriate symbol on charts officially recognized by the coastal State.

Article 7

1. In localities where the coastline is deeply indented and cut into, or if there is a fringe of islands along the coast in its immediate vicinity, the method of straight baselines joining appropriate points may be employed in drawing the baseline from which the breadth of the territorial sea is measured.

2. Where because of the presence of a delta and other natural conditions the coastline is highly unstable, the appropriate points may be selected along the furthest seaward extent of the low-water line and, notwithstanding subsequent regression of the low-water line, the straight baselines shall remain effective until changed by the coastal State in accordance with this Convention.

3. The drawing of straight baselines must not depart to any appreciable extent from the general direction of the coast, and the sea areas lying within the lines must be sufficiently closely linked to the land domain to be subject to the régime of internal waters.

4. Straight baselines shall not be drawn to and from low-tide elevations, unless lighthouses or similar installations which are permanently above sea level have been built on them or except in instances where the drawing of baselines to and from such elevations has received general international recognition.

5. Where the method of straight baselines is applicable under paragraph 1, account may be taken, in determining particular baselines, of economic interests peculiar to the region concerned, the reality and the importance of which are clearly evidenced by long usage.

6. The system of straight baselines may not be applied by a State in such a manner as to cut off the territorial sea of another State from the high seas or an exclusive economic zone.

Article 8

1. Except as provided in Part IV,[62] waters on the landward side of the baseline of the territorial sea form part of the internal waters of the State.

2. Where the establishment of a straight baseline in accordance with the method set forth in article 7 has the effect of enclosing as internal waters areas which had not previously been considered as such, a right of innocent passage as provided in this Convention shall exist in those waters.

Article 9

If a river flows directly into the sea, the baseline shall be a straight line across the mouth of the river between points on the low-water line of its banks.

Article 10

1. This article relates only to bays the coasts of which belong to a single State.

2. For the purposes of this Convention, a bay is a well-marked indentation whose penetration is in such proportion to the width of its mouth as to contain land-locked waters and constitute more than a mere curvature of the coast. An indentation shall not, however, be regarded as a bay unless its area is as large as, or larger than, that of the semi-circle whose diameter is a line drawn across the mouth of that indentation.

3. For the purpose of measurement, the area of an indentation is that lying between the low-water mark around the shore of the indentation and a line joining the low-water mark of its natural entrance points. Where, because of the presence of islands, an indentation has more than one mouth, the semi-circle shall be drawn on a line as long as the sum total of the lengths of the lines across the different mouths. Islands within an indentation shall be included as if they were part of the water area of the indentation.

---

[62] *Ed*. Arts. 46–54 on archipelagic states.

4. If the distance between the low-water marks of the natural entrance points of a bay does not exceed 24 nautical miles, a closing line may be drawn between these two low-water marks, and the waters enclosed thereby shall be considered as internal waters.

5. Where the distance between the low-water marks of the natural entrance points of a bay exceeds 24 nautical miles, a straight baseline of 24 nautical miles shall be drawn within the bay in such a manner as to enclose the maximum area of water that is possible with a line of that length.

6. The foregoing provisions do not apply to so-called "historic" bays, or in any case where the system of straight baselines provided for in article 7 is applied.

Article 11

For the purpose of delimiting the territorial sea, the outermost permanent harbour works which form an integral part of the harbour system are regarded as forming part of the coast. Off-shore installations and artificial islands shall not be considered as permanent harbour works.

Article 12

Roadsteads which are normally used for the loading, unloading and anchoring of ships, and which would otherwise be situated wholly or partly outside the outer limit of the territorial sea, are included in the territorial sea.

Article 13

1. A low-tide elevation is a naturally formed area of land which is surrounded by and above water at low tide but submerged at high tide. Where a low-tide elevation is situated wholly or partly at a distance not exceeding the breadth of the territorial sea from the mainland or an island, the low-water line on that elevation may be used as the baseline for measuring the breadth of the territorial sea.

2. Where a low-tide elevation is wholly situated at a distance exceeding the breadth of the territorial sea from the mainland or an island, it has no territorial sea of its own.

Article 14

The coastal State may determine baselines in turn by any of the methods provided for in the foregoing articles to suit different conditions.

Article 15

Where the coasts of two States are opposite or adjacent to each other, neither of the two States is entitled, failing agreement between them to the contrary, to extend its territorial sea beyond the median line every point of which is equidistant from the nearest points on the baselines from which the breadth of the territorial seas of each of the two States is measured. The above provision does not apply, however, where it is necessary by reason of historic title or other special circumstances to delimit the territorial seas of the two States in a way which is at variance therewith.[63]

Article 121

1. An island is a naturally formed area of land, surrounded by water, which is above water at high tide.

2. Except as provided for in paragraph 3, the territorial sea, the contiguous zone, the exclusive economic zone and the continental shelf of an island are determined in accordance with the provisions of this Convention applicable to other land territory.

3. Rocks which cannot sustain human habitation or economic life of their own shall have no exclusive economic zone or continental shelf.

Notes

1. *Baselines*. The 1982 Convention follows the approach of the International Court of Justice in the *Anglo-Norwegian Fisheries* case.[64] It differs only in requiring (Article 7(4)) that low-tide elevations be permanently above sea level to be used as the beginning of a straight baseline[65]; Article 7(6) supplements the judgment. As permitted by Article 7, the United Kingdom now uses straight baselines from Cape Wrath to the Mull of Kintyre on the west coast of Scotland.[66] The result is to enclose as internal waters areas of water between the Outer Hebrides and the mainland which, when a low-water mark baseline was used, were high seas. Because of this result, the right of innocent passage in Article 8(2) applies.

States generally have not been slow to seize the opportunity allowed by straight baselines of, in effect, extending seawards the limits of their territorial sea and other areas of maritime jurisdiction (exclusive economic zone, etc.). At least 40 coastal states now draw straight baselines, not always consistently with the limitations as to their use in Article 7, 1982 Convention.[67] Indeed, Prescott,[68] after analysing state practice, describes Article 7, 1982 Convention as a "dead-letter" and states:

---

[63] For the median line between the U.K. and French territorial seas in the area of the Dover Straits, which are less than 24 miles wide, see the Territorial Sea (Limits) Order 1989, S.I. 1989 No. 482, which implements a 1988 U.K.—France Agreement, Cm. 557.

[64] The 1982 Convention (Arts. 5, 8, 4, 12, 15 and 19) also repeats almost exactly nearly all of the provisions of the 1958 Convention (Arts. 3, 5, 6, 9, 12 and 13 respectively) on baselines. It retains the wording of Art. 4 too (1982 Convention, Art. 7), but adds to the end of Art. 4(4) a new "general recognition" exception (1982 Convention, Art. 7(4)). It also adds an additional paragraph to Art. 4 (1982 Convention, Art. 7(2)) on deltas. The 1982 Convention (Art. 11) similarly retains Art. 8 of the 1958 Convention, but supplements it by an additional final sentence.

[65] On low-tide elevations and straight baselines, see Marston (1972–73) 46 B.Y.I.L. 405.

[66] Territorial Waters Order in Council 1964, Art. 3, S.I. 1965, Part III, s.2, p. 6452A.

[67] See The Geographer, U.S. Department of State, *International Boundary Study, Series A, Limits in the Seas* (separate country pamphlets).

[68] In Blake, ed., *Maritime Boundaries and Ocean Resources* (1987), p. 38, 49.

Because the rules covering baselines in the 1958 and 1982 Conventions are ambiguous and because there is no international authority charged with their supervision there has been widespread abuse of the system. Indeed it would now be possible to draw a straight baseline along any section of coast in the world and cite an existing straight baseline as a precedent.

The abuses he refers to include drawing straight baselines along coasts that are not noticeably irregular or fronted by a fringe of (as opposed to a few) islands. On the use of straight baselines by archipelagic states, see below, p. 389.

Exceptionally, the 1986 Falkland Islands Interim Fishery Zone[69] is measured not from the low-water line or from straight baselines but by drawing a circle 150 miles in circumference from a point on the Islands.

2. *Deltas.* Article 7(2), 1982 Convention has a rule concerning deltas that was not in the 1958 Convention. It would benefit such states as Bangladesh, which suggested it, and Egypt, whose Nile delta is regressing and would be within the "notwithstanding" clause.[70]

3. *Bays.*[71] If an area of water satisfies the requirements of Article 10, 1982 Convention for a bay, it becomes internal waters so that there is no right of innocent passage through it.[72] On the closing line for bays, the Second Sub-Committee of the Second Committee of the 1930 Hague Codification Conference proposed a closing line of 10 miles.[73] In its 1956 Draft Articles, on which the 1958 Territorial Sea Convention was based, the International Law Commission at one stage proposed a closing line of 25 miles, but later reduced it to 15. It explained in its Commentary:

> The proposal to extend the closing line to 25 miles had found little support; a number of Governments stated that, in their view, such an extension was excessive. By a majority, the Commission decided to reduce the 25 miles figure, proposed in 1955, to 15 miles. While appreciating that a line of 10 miles had been recognised by several Governments and established by international conventions, the Commission took account of the fact that the origin of the 10 mile line dates back to a time when the breadth of the territorial sea was much more commonly fixed at three miles than it is now.[74]

The 24 miles rule was inserted in the 1958 Convention at Geneva, and is repeated in Article 10, 1982 Convention.[75] On the relation between the 24–mile rule and customary international law, the following statement in 1963 by the United States Secretary of State on the status of Bristol Bay off the coast of Alaska is of interest:

> Although the Convention is not yet in force . . . it must be regarded in view of its adoption (at Geneva) by a large majority of the States of the world as the best evidence of international law on the subject at the present time. This is particularly so in view of the rejection by the International Court of Justice in the *Anglo-Norwegian Fisheries Case* of the so-called 10-mile rule previously considered as international law by the United States and other countries. . . . -

[69] *Law of the Sea Bulletin, loc. cit.,* p. 368, n. 1, above, No. 9 (1987), p. 19. See Symmons (1987) 37 I.C.L.Q. 283.
[70] See Churchill and Lowe, *op. cit.,* p. 368, n. 1, above, p. 31.
[71] See Bouchez, *The Regime of Bays in International Law* (1964); Strohl, *The International Law of Bays* (1963); Westerman, *The Juridical Bay* (1987).
[72] Art. 10, 1982 Convention is identical to Art. 7, 1958 Convention.
[73] L.N.Doc. C. 351 (b). M. 145 (b). 1930. V, p. 217.
[74] Y.B.I.L.C., 1956, II. p. 269.
[75] *1958 Sea Conference Records,* Vol. III, p. 146.

Since the line drawn ... [across the Bay] is over 162 miles long ... there is no basis in international law ... for Alaska's claim ... unless these waters can be considered an "historic bay."[76]

As to *bays bordered by more than one state*, Colombos[77] states:

There exists a good deal for controversy on the subject, but the correct view is that territorial waters should follow the sinuosities of the coast ... subject to any special agreement. ...

An example of such a bay is the controversial Gulf of Aqaba in the Red Sea which is bordered by the states of Egypt, Israel, Jordan and Saudi Arabia.[78] Neither the 1958 nor the 1982 Conventions govern such bays or historic bays.

Historic bays undoubtedly may exist at customary international law.[79] Thus in the *Land, Island and Maritime Frontier Dispute* case,[80] an I.C.J. Chamber held that the Gulf of Foncesa, which is surrounded by Nicaragua, Honduras and El Salvador and which is about 19 miles across at its mouth, was an historic bay with the three coastal states concerned sharing joint sovereignty over the waters landward of the closing line. In 1974, the U.S. protested at a claim made by Libya that the Gulf of Sirte within a closing line of approximately 300 miles was Libyan internal or territorial waters as a "violation of international law."[81] The Gulf did not "meet the international law standards of past open, notorious and effective exercise of authority, and acquiescence of foreign nations necessary to be regarded historically as Libyan internal or territorial waters."[82] In the *Continental Shelf (Tunisia v. Libya)* case,[83] Tunisia, in the course of developing its continental shelf claim, argued that it had historic rights to the exploitation of fixed fisheries (to catch swimming species) and sponges in the waters off its coastline beyond its territorial sea. After noting that "historic titles," including titles to historic bays, "must enjoy respect and be preserved as they always have been by long usage"; that the juridical régime of "historic waters" had purposely been left for separate, later consideration when the 1958 Convention was being drafted; and that UNCLOS III had not tackled the question either, the Court stated:

It seems clear that the matter continues to be governed by general international law which does not provide for a *single "régime"* for "historic waters" or "historic bays," but only for a particular régime for each of the concrete, recognised cases of "historic waters" or "historic bays." It is clearly the case that, basically, the notion of historic rights or waters and that of the continental shelf are governed by distinct legal régimes in customary international law. The first régime is based on acquisition and occupation, while the second is based on the existence of rights *"ipso facto* and *ab initio."* No doubt both may

---

[76] (1963) 2 I.L.M. 528.

[77] *loc. cit.*, p. 368, n. 1, above, p. 188.

[78] On the right of passage through the Gulf, see below, p. 410.

[79] For examples of claims to historic bays—some contested (*e.g.* Canadian claim to Hudson Bay, contested by U.S.), others accepted (*e.g.* U.S. claim to Delaware Bay), see UN Secretariat Memorandum, *1958 Sea Conference Records*, Vol. I, p. 1.

[80] I.C.J. Rep. 1992, p. 351. See Gioaia (1993) 24 N.Y.I.L. 81. *cf. El Salvador v. Honduras* (1917) 11 A.J.I.L. 674, Central American Court of Justice.

[81] (1974) 68 A.J.I.L. 510.

[82] *ibid. cf.* the U.K. reaction: *Hansard*, H.C., Vol. 91, col. 506, February 13, 1986. In 1981, two Libyan military aircraft were shot down when they attacked U.S. military aircraft engaged in exercises in the disputed area of the Gulf. *cf.* the 1986 Incident, below, p. 913.

[83] I.C.J. Rep. 1982, pp. 73–74.

sometimes coincide in part or in whole, but such coincidence can only be fortuitous ... it may be that Tunisia's historic rights and titles are more nearly related to the concept of the exclusive economic zone, which may be regarded as part of modern international law. ... "

The requirement of "respect" or "acquiescence" points to a distinction between bays that conform to Article 10, 1982 Convention and historic bays, namely that whereas the former are valid irrespective of the response of other states, the latter depend upon consent. Consistent with the Court's comment in the *Tunisia v. Libya Case* that there is no "single régime" for historic bays, there does not appear to be any maximum length for a closing line for such a bay; a line of any length may be accepted by other states.

See also on bays, *Post Office v. Estuary Radio Ltd.*[84]

4. *Islands.*[85] A case of an island being created by natural forces was the creation of Surtsey by volcanic activity in 1963 in Icelandic territorial waters. Would land which is permanently above the sea as a result of dredging operations be an island under the 1982 Convention? Why can a low-tide elevation with a lighthouse built on it be the end of a baseline for measuring the territorial sea (Art. 7(4)) when it cannot be treated as an island under the Convention? Artificial islands, installations and structures are stated by the 1982 Convention not to be islands.[86] Small islands have become more important in recent years because of the possibility of exploiting oil and gas resources in the seabed surrounding them.

The 1982 Convention (Art. 121), which was stated by the Conciliation Commission in the *Jan Mayen* case[87] to "reflect the present status of international law," repeats the definition of an island and the rule about its territorial sea in Article 10, 1958 Territorial Sea Convention, but restricts the circumstances in which it may have an exclusive economic zone of continental shelf, see below, p. 454.

5. *Archipelagos.*[88] In 1957, Indonesia announced that its territorial sea would henceforth be "measured from straight baselines connecting the outermost points of the islands of the Republic of Indonesia."[89] The waters within the baselines would be "national waters subject to the absolute sovereignty of Indonesia," except that the "peaceful passage of foreign vessels would be guaranteed as long as and in so far as it is not contrary to the sovereignty of the Indonesian state or harmful to her security."[90] A number of states, including the United Kingdom,[91] protested. The International Law Commission felt itself unable, for lack of information, to reach any conclusion on the question of a special rule for archipelagos, and there are no provisions on the matter in the 1958 Convention.

---

[84] [1968] 2 Q.B. 740, CA.

[85] See Bowett, *The Legal Régime of Islands in International Law* (1979); Jayewardene, *The Regime of Islands in International Law* (1990); Symmons, *The Maritime Zones of Islands in International Law* (1979); and Symonides (1987) 65 R.D.I. 161.

[86] Art. 60(8), below, p. 449. *cf.* Art. 5(4), Continental Shelf Convention 1958. See also Papadakis, *The International Regime of Artificial Islands* (1977).

[87] (1981) 20 I.L.M. 797, 803.

[88] See Dubner, *The Law of Territorial Waters of Mid-Ocean Archipelagos and Archipelagic States* (1976); Munavvar, *Ocean States: Archipelagic Regimes in the Law of the Sea* (1995); and Rodgers, *Mid-Ocean Archipelagos and International Law* (1981).

[89] 4 Whiteman 284. The Philippines had made a similar announcement in 1955; *ibid.* p. 282. See Sørensen, *Varia Juris Gentium* (1959), p. 315.

[90] 4 Whiteman 284.

[91] See *Hansard*, H.C., Vol. 582, col. 1185, February 19, 1958.

The 1982 Convention contains provisions allowing the use of straight baselines by "mid-ocean" archipelagic states[92] (but not by continental states with "off-lying archipelagos"). These read in part (Art. 47):

1. An archipelagic state may draw straight archipelagic baselines joining the outermost points of the outermost islands and drying reefs of the archipelago provided that within such baselines are included the main islands and an area in which the ratio of the area of the water to the area of the land, including atolls, is between one to one and nine to one.

2. The length of such baselines shall not exceed 100 nautical miles, except that up to three per cent of the total number of baselines enclosing any archipelago may exceed that length, up to a maximum length of 125 nautical miles.

3. The drawing of such baselines shall not depart to any appreciable extent from the general configuration of the archipelago.

The "archipelagic waters" thus enclosed are stated to be within the sovereignty of the archipelagic state (Article 49, 1982 Convention), but are subject to the Convention right of innocent passage (Article 52, 1982 Convention), and to the right of archipelagic sea-lanes passage (Article 53, *ibid.*).[93] The latter is comparable to the right of transit passage through international straits, see below, p. 411, and includes a right of overflight for aircraft.[94] The right of innocent passage is suspendable for security reasons only (Article 52(2)); there is no provision for the right of archipelagic sea-lane passage to be suspended. An archipelagic state must "recognise traditional fishing rights and other legitimate activities of the immediately adjacent neighbouring states" (Article 51(1)) and "respect existing submarine cables" (Article 51(2)). These limitations are more extensive than those upon a coastal state in respect of its territorial sea. Although maritime states were opposed to archipelagic baselines in the 1950s, the rights of passage written into the 1982 Convention would seem to have overcome their doubts; moreover, it has been suggested that the area of exclusive economic zone that results from the use of archipelagic baselines is only 1 or 2 per cent greater than that which would result by the drawing of such zones around each island.[95]

---

[92] Art. 46 reads: "For the purposes of this Convention: (a) 'Archipelagic State' means a State constituted wholly by one or more archipelagos and may include other islands; (b) 'Archipelago' means a group of islands, including parts of islands, interconnecting waters and other natural features which are so closely interrelated with such islands, waters and other natural features form an intrinsic geographical, economic and political entity, or which historically have been regarded as such." As Churchill and Lowe, *op. cit.*, p. 368, n. 1, above, pp. 100–101, state, although this definition might include such island states as Japan and the U.K., the 1:9 rule in Art. 47(1) would prevent them from drawing archipelagic baselines. Excluding such states, there remain 25–35 archipelagic states, of whom 15 (*e.g.* Antigua, Fiji, Papua, Cape Verde, Indonesia and the Philippines) have drawn archipelagic baselines: *ibid.*, pp. 106–107. As to "off-lying archipelagos," (*e.g.* the Canadian Archipelago, around which Canada has now drawn *Anglo-Norwegian Fisheries* case straight baselines: see above, p. 235), see Herman (1985) 23 C.Y.I.L. 172. Note that Denmark has drawn archipelagic baselines around the Faroes and Portugal has done so around the Azores. Is this consistent with the 1982 Convention? See Alexander (1987) 18 O.D.I.L. 333 at 337.

[93] But note that on signing the 1982 Convention, the Philippines made a declaration equating archipelagic waters with internal waters. Australia, the USSR, the Ukranian SSR and the Byelorussian SSR objected: UN Doc. ST/LEG/SER. E/7, pp. 764 *et seq.*

[94] See de Vries Lentsch (1983) 14 N.Y.I.L. 165.

[95] See Hodson and Smith (1976) 3 O.D.I.L. 225 at 244.

(iv) Jurisdiction over Foreign Ships in the Territorial Sea

CORFU CHANNEL CASE (MERITS)

U.K. *v.* Albania

I.C.J. Reports 1949, p. 4

The facts of the case, so far as they concern the Albanian counter-claim, are indicated in the following extract from the Court's judgment. See also the further extract from the judgment below[96] on the United Kingdom's claim for compensation for damage caused by mines to the *Saumarez* and the *Volage* during their passage through the Corfu Channel on October 22, 1946.

Judgment of the Court

In the second part of the Special Agreement, the following question is submitted to the Court:

(2) Has the United Kingdom under international law violated the sovereignty of the Albanian People's Republic by reason of the acts of the Royal Navy in Albanian waters on the 22nd October and on the 12th and 13th November 1946 and is there any duty to give satisfaction? . . .

On May 15, 1946, the British cruisers *Orion* and *Superb*, while passing southward through the North Corfu Channel, were fired at by an Albanian battery in the vicinity of Saranda. . . .

The United Kingdom Government at once protested to the Albanian Government, stating that innocent passage through straits is a right recognised by international law. There ensued a diplomatic correspondence in which the Albanian Government asserted that foreign warships and merchant vessels had no right to pass through Albanian territorial waters without prior notification to, and the permission of, the Albanian authorities. . . .

It was in such circumstances that these two cruisers together with the destroyers *Saumarez* and *Volage* were sent through the North Corfu Strait on . . . [October 22, 1946].

The Court will now consider the Albanian contention that the United Kingdom Government violated Albanian sovereignty by sending the

[96] p. 494.

warships through this Strait without the previous authorisation of the Albanian Government.

It is, in the opinion of the Court, generally recognised and in accordance with international custom that States in time of peace have a right to send their warships through straits used for international navigation between two parts of the high seas without the previous authorisation of a coastal State, provided that the passage is *innocent*. Unless otherwise prescribed in an international convention, there is no right for a coastal State to prohibit such passage through straits in time of peace.

The Albanian Government does not dispute that the North Corfu Channel is a strait in the geographical sense; but it denies that this Channel belongs to the class of international highways through which a right of passage exists, on the grounds that it is only of secondary importance and not even a necessary route between two parts of the high seas, and that it is used almost exclusively for local traffic to and from the ports of Corfu and Saranda.

It may be asked whether the test is to be found in the volume of traffic passing through the Strait or in its greater or lesser importance for international navigation. But in the opinion of the Court the decisive criterion is rather its geographical situation as connecting two parts of the high seas and the fact of its being used for international navigation. Nor can it be decisive that this Strait is not a necessary route between two parts of the high seas, but only an alternative passage between the Ægean and the Adriatic Seas. It has nevertheless been a useful route for international maritime traffic.[97] . . .

One fact of particular importance is that the North Corfu Channel constitutes a frontier between Albania and Greece, that a part of it is wholly within the territorial waters of these States, and that the Strait is of special importance to Greece by reason of the traffic to and from the port of Corfu.

Having regard to these various considerations, the Court has arrived at the conclusion that the North Corfu Channel should be considered as belonging to the class of international highways through which passage cannot be prohibited by a coastal State in time of peace.

On the other hand, it is a fact that the two coastal States did not maintain normal relations, that Greece had made territorial claims precisely with regard to a part of Albanian territory bordering on the Channel, that Greece had declared that she considered herself technically in a state of war with Albania, and that Albania, invoking the danger of Greek incursions, had considered it necessary to take certain measures of vigilance in this region. The Court is of opinion that Albania, in view of these

---

[97] *Ed.* The Court noted that 2884 ships passed through the Channel in one 21–month period, flying seven different flags.

exceptional circumstances, would have been justified in issuing regulations in respect of the passage of warships through the Strait, but not in prohibiting such passage or in subjecting it to the requirement of special authorisation.

For these reasons the Court is unable to accept the Albanian contention that the Government of the United Kingdom has violated Albanian sovereignty by sending the warships through the Strait without having obtained the previous authorisation of the Albanian Government.

In these circumstances, it is unnecessary to consider the more general question, much debated by the Parties, whether States under international law have a right to send warships in time of peace through territorial waters not included in a strait.

The Albanian Government has further contended that the sovereignty of Albania was violated because the passage of the British warships on October 22, 1946, was not an *innocent passage.* . . .

It is shown by the Admiralty telegram of September 21 . . . that the object of sending the warships through the Strait was not only to carry out a passage for purposes of navigation, but also to test Albania's attitude. . . . The legality of this measure taken by the Government of the United Kingdom cannot be disputed, provided that it was carried out in a manner consistent with the requirements of international law. . . . The Government of the United Kingdom was not bound to abstain from exercising its right of passage, which the Albanian Government had illegally denied.

It remains, therefore, to consider whether the *manner* in which the passage was carried out was consistent with the principle of innocent passage and to examine the various contentions of the Albanian Government in so far as they appear to be relevant.

The Court found, contrary to Albania's contention, that the warships were neither in combat formation nor manoeuvering and that there were no soldiers on board.

. . . The guns were . . . "trained fore and aft, which is their normal position at sea in peace time, and were not loaded." . . . In the light of this evidence, the Court cannot accept the Albanian contention that the position of the guns was inconsistent with the rules of innocent passage.

In the . . . telegram of October 26, the Commander-in-Chief reported that the passage "was made with ships at action stations in order that they might be able to retaliate quickly if fired upon again." In view of the firing from the Albanian battery on May 15, this measure of precaution cannot, in itself, be regarded as unreasonable. But four warships—two cruisers and two destroyers—passed in this manner, with crews at action stations, ready to retaliate quickly if fired upon. They passed one after another through this narrow channel, close to the Albanian coast, at a

time of political tension in this region. The intention must have been, not
only to test Albania's attitude, but at the same time to demonstrate such
force that she would abstain from firing again on passing ships. Having
regard, however, to all the circumstances of the case, as described above,
the Court is unable to characterise these measures taken by the United
Kingdom authorities as a violation of Albania's sovereignty.

. . . In a report of the commander of *Volage*, dated October 23, 1946—a
report relating to the passage on the 22nd—it is stated: "The most was
made of the opportunities to study Albanian defences at close
range. . . ."

With regard to the observations of coastal defences made after the
explosions, these were justified by the fact that two ships had just been
blown up and that, in this critical situation, their commanders might fear
that they would be fired on from the coast, as on May 15.

Having thus examined the various contentions of the Albanian Government in so far as they appear to be relevant, the Court has arrived at
the conclusion that the United Kingdom did not violate the sovereignty of
Albania by reason of the acts of the British Navy in Albanian waters on
October 22, 1946.

In addition to the passage of the United Kingdom warships on October
22, 1946, the second question in the Special Agreement relates to the acts
of the Royal Navy in Albanian waters on November 12 and 13, 1946. This
is the minesweeping operation called "Operation Retail." . . .

The United Kingdom Government does not dispute that "Operation
Retail" was carried out against the clearly expressed wish of the Albanian
Government. It recognises that the operation had not the consent of the
international mine clearance organisations, that it could not be justified as
the exercise of a right of innocent passage, and lastly that, in principle,
international law does not allow a State to assemble a large number of
warships in the territorial waters of another State and to carry out mine-
sweeping in those waters. The United Kingdom Government states that
the operation was one of extreme urgency, and that it considered itself
entitled to carry it out without anybody's consent.

. . . the explosions of October 22, 1946, in a channel declared safe for
navigation, and one which the United Kingdom Government, more than
any other government, had reason to consider safe, raised quite a different problem from that of a routine sweep carried out under the orders of
the mine clearance organisations. These explosions were suspicious; they
raised a question of responsibility.

Accordingly, this was the ground on which the United Kingdom Government chose to establish its main line of defence. According to that
Government, the *corpora delicti* must be secured as quickly as possible, for
fear they should be taken away, without leaving traces, by the authors of
the minelaying or by the Albanian authorities. This justification took two
distinct forms in the United Kingdom Government's arguments. It was

presented first as a new and special application of the theory of intervention, by means of which the State intervening would secure possession of evidence in the territory of another State, in order to submit it to an international tribunal and thus facilitate its task.

The Court cannot accept such a line of defence. The Court can only regard the alleged right of intervention as the manifestation of a policy of force, such as has, in the past, given rise to most serious abuses and such as cannot, whatever be the present defects in international organisation, find a place in international law. Intervention is perhaps still less admissible in the particular form it would take here; for, from the nature of things, it would be reserved for the most powerful States, and might easily lead to perverting the administration of international justice itself.

The United Kingdom Agent, in his speech in reply, has further classified "Operation Retail" among methods of self-protection or self-help. The Court cannot accept this defence either. Between independent States, respect for territorial sovereignty is an essential foundation of international relations. The Court recognises that the Albanian Government's complete failure to carry out its duties after the explosions, and the dilatory nature of its diplomatic notes, are extenuating circumstances for the action of the United Kingdom Government. But to ensure respect for international law, of which it is the organ, the Court must declare that the action of the British Navy constituted a violation of Albanian sovereignty.

This declaration is in accordance with the request made by Albania through her Counsel, and is in itself appropriate satisfaction.

The method of carrying out "Operation Retail" has also been criticised by the Albanian Government, the main ground of complaint being that the United Kingdom, on that occasion, made use of an unnecessarily large display of force, out of proportion to the requirements of the sweep. The Court thinks that this criticism is not justified. It does not consider that the action of the British Navy was a demonstration of force for the purpose of exercising political pressure in Albania. The responsible naval commander, who kept his ships at a distance from the coast, cannot be reproached for having employed an important covering force in a region where twice within a few months his ships had been the object of serious outrages.

For these reasons, the Court, . . . by 14 votes to two,[98] gives judgment [for the United Kingdom in respect of the passage on October 22, 1946]

---

[98] The Judges in the majority were Acting President Guerrero; President Basdevant; Judges Alvarez, Fabela, Hackworth, Winiarski, Zoričić, de Visscher, Sir Arnold McNair, Klaestad, Badawi Pasha, Read and Hsu Mo; Judge *ad hoc* Ečer. Judges Krylov and Azevedo dissented.

and, unanimously, gives judgment [for Albania in respect of the mine-sweeping of November 13, 1946].

CONVENTION ON THE LAW OF THE SEA 1982

UN Doc. A/CONF. 62/122; (1982) 21 I.L.M. 1261

Part II

Territorial Sea and Contiguous Zone

Section 3. Innocent passage in the territorial sea

Subsection A. Rules applicable to all ships

Article 17

Subject to this Convention, ships of all States, whether coastal or land-locked enjoy the right of innocent passage through the territorial sea.

Article 18

1. Passage means navigation through the territorial sea for the purpose of:

(a) traversing that sea without entering internal waters or calling at a roadstead or port facility outside internal waters; or
(b) proceeding to or from internal waters or a call at such roadstead or port facility.

2. Passage shall be continuous and expeditious. However, passage includes stopping and anchoring, but only in so far as the same are incidental to ordinary navigation or are rendered necessary by *force majeure* or distress or for the purpose of rendering assistance to persons, ships or aircraft in danger or distress.

Article 19

1. Passage is innocent so long as it is not prejudicial to the peace, good order or security of the coastal State. Such passage shall take place in conformity with this Convention and with other rules of international law.

2. Passage of a foreign ship shall be considered to be prejudicial to the peace, good order or security of the coastal State if in the territorial sea it engages in any of the following activities:

(a) any threat or use of force against the sovereignty, territorial integrity or political independence of the coastal State, or in any other manner in violation of the principles of international law embodied in the Charter of the United Nations;

(b) any exercise or practice with weapons of any kind;

(c) any act aimed at collecting information to the prejudice of the defence or security of the coastal state;

(d) any act of propaganda aimed at affecting the defence or security of the coastal State;

(e) the launching, landing or taking on board of any aircraft;

(f) the launching, landing or taking on board of any military device;

(g) the loading or unloading of any commodity, currency or person contrary to the customs, fiscal, immigration or sanitary laws and regulations of the coastal State;

(h) any act of wilful and serious pollution contrary to this Convention;

(i) any fishing activities;

(j) the carrying out of research or survey activities;

(k) any act aimed at interfering with any systems of communication or any other facilities or installations of the coastal State;

(l) any other activity not having a direct bearing on passage.

Article 20

In the territorial sea, submarines and other underwater vehicles are required to navigate on the surface and to show their flag.

Article 21

1. The coastal State may adopt laws and regulations, in conformity with the provisions of this Convention and other rules of international law, relating to innocent passage through the territorial sea, in respect of all or any of the following:

(a) the safety of navigation and the regulation of maritime traffic;

(b) the protection of navigational aids and facilities and other facilities or installations;

(c) the protection of cables and pipelines;

(d) the conservation of the living resources of the sea;

(e) the prevention of infringement of the fisheries laws and regulations of the coastal State;

(f) the preservation of the environment of the coastal State and the prevention, reduction and control of pollution thereof;

(g) marine scientific research and hydrographic surveys;

(h) the prevention of infringement of the customs, fiscal, immigration or sanitary laws and regulations of the coastal State.

2. Such laws and regulations shall not apply to the design, construction, manning or equipment of foreign ships unless they are giving effect to generally accepted international rules or standards.

3. The coastal State shall give due publicity to all such laws and regulations.

4. Foreign ships exercising the right of innocent passage through the territorial sea shall comply with all such laws and regulations and all generally accepted international regulations relating to the prevention of collisions at sea.

Article 22

1. The coastal State may, where necessary having regard to the safety of navigation, require foreign ships exercising the right of innocent passage through its territorial sea to use such sea lanes and traffic separation schemes as it may designate or prescribe for the regulation of the passage of ships.

2. In particular, tankers, nuclear-powered ships and ships carrying nuclear or other inherently dangerous or noxious substances or materials may be required to confine their passage to such sea lanes.

3. In the designation of sea lanes and the prescription of traffic separation schemes under this article, the coastal State shall take into account:

(a) the recommendations of the competent international organization;
(b) any channels customarily used for international navigation;
(c) the special characteristics of particular ships and channels; and
(d) the density of traffic.

4. The coastal State shall clearly indicate such sea lanes and traffic separation schemes on charts to which due publicity shall be given.

Article 23

Foreign nuclear-powered ships and ships carrying nuclear or other inherently dangerous or noxious substances shall, when exercising the right of innocent passage through the territorial sea, carry documents and observe special precautionary measures established for such ships by international agreements.

Article 24

1. The coastal State shall not hamper the innocent passage of foreign ships through the territorial sea except in accordance with this Convention. In particular, in the application of this Convention or of any laws or regulations adopted in conformity with this Convention, the coastal State shall not:

(a) impose requirements on foreign ships which have the practical effect of denying or impairing the right of innocent passage; or

(b) discriminate in form or in fact against the ships of any State or against ships carrying cargoes to, from or on behalf of any State.

2. The coastal State shall give appropriate publicity to any danger to navigation, of which it has knowledge, within its territorial sea.

Article 25

1. The coastal State may take the necessary steps in its territorial sea to prevent passage which is not innocent.

2. In the case of ships proceeding to internal waters or a call at a port facility outside internal waters, the coastal State also has the right to take the necessary steps to prevent any breach of the conditions to which admission of those ships to internal waters or such a call is subject.

3. The coastal State may, without discrimination in form or in fact among foreign ships, suspend temporarily in specified areas of its territorial sea the innocent passage of foreign ships if such suspension is essential for the protection of its security, including weapons exercises. Such suspension shall take effect only after having been duly published.

Article 26

1. No charge may be levied upon foreign ships by reason only of their passage through the territorial sea.

2. Charges may be levied upon a foreign ship passing through the territorial sea as payment only for specific services rendered to the ship. These charges shall be levied without discrimination.

Subsection B. Rules applicable to merchant ships and government ships operated for commercial purposes

Article 27

1. The criminal jurisdiction of the coastal State should not be exercised on board a foreign ship passing through the territorial sea to arrest any person or to conduct any investigation in connection with any crime committed on board the ship during its passage, save only in the following cases:

(a) if the consequences of the crime extend to the coastal State;

(b) if the crime is of a kind to disturb the peace of the country or the good order of the territorial sea;

(c) if the assistance of the local authorities has been requested by the master of the ship or by a diplomatic agent or consular officer of the flag State; or (*d*) if such measures are necessary for the suppression of illicit traffic in narcotic drugs or psychotropic substances.

2. The above provisions do not affect the right of the coastal State to take any steps authorized by its laws for the purpose of an arrest or investigation on board a foreign ship passing through the territorial sea after leaving internal waters.

3. In the cases provided for in paragraphs 1 and 2, the coastal state shall, if the master so requests, notify a diplomatic agent or consular officer of the flag State before taking any steps, and shall facilitate contact between such agent or officer and the ship's crew. In cases of emergency this notification may be communicated while the measures are being taken.

4. In considering whether or in what manner an arrest should be made, the local authorities shall have due regard to the interests of navigation.

5. Except as provided in Part XII or with respect to violations of laws and regulations adopted in accordance with Part V, the coastal State may not take any steps on board a foreign ship passing through the territorial sea to arrest any person or to conduct any investigation in connection with any crime committed before the ship entered the territorial sea, if the ship, proceeding from a foreign port, is only passing through the territorial sea without entering internal waters.

Article 28

1. The coastal State should not stop or divert a foreign ship passing through the territorial sea for the purpose of exercising civil jurisdiction in relation to a person on board the ship.

2. The coastal State may not levy execution against or arrest the ship for the purpose of any civil proceedings, save only in respect of obligations or liabilities assumed or incurred by the ship itself in the course or for the purpose of its voyage through the waters of the coastal State.

3. Paragraph 2 is without prejudice to the right of the coastal State, in accordance with its laws, to levy execution against or to arrest, for the purpose of any civil proceedings, a foreign ship lying in the territorial sea, or passing through the territorial sea after leaving internal waters.

Subsection C. Rules applicable to warships and other government ship operated for non-commercial purposes

Article 29

For the purposes of this Convention, "warship" means a ship belonging to the armed forces of a state bearing the external marks distinguishing such ships of its nationality, under the command of an officer duly commissioned by the government of the State and whose name appears in the appropriate service list or its equivalent, and manned by a crew which is under regular armed forces discipline.

Article 30

If any warship does not comply with the laws and regulations of the coastal State concerning passage through the territorial sea and disregards any request for compliance therewith which is made to it, the coastal State may require it to leave the territorial sea immediately.

Article 31

The flag State shall bear international responsibility for any loss or damage to the coastal State resulting from the non-compliance by a warship or other government ship operated for non-commercial purposes with the laws and regulations of the coastal State concerning passage through the territorial sea or with the provisions of this Convention or other rules of international law.

Article 32

With such exceptions as are contained in subsection A and in articles 30 and 31, nothing in this Convention affects the immunities of warships and other government ships operated for non-commercial purposes.

Part III

Straits used for International Navigation

Section 1. General provisions

Article 34

1. The régime of passage through straits used for international navigation established in this Part shall not in other respects affect the legal status of the waters forming such straits or the exercise by the States bordering the straits of their sovereignty or jurisdiction over such waters and their air space, bed and subsoil.
2. The sovereignty or jurisdiction of the States bordering the straits is exercised subject to this Part and to other rules of international law.

Article 35

Nothing in this Part affects:

(a) any areas of internal waters within a strait, except where the establishment of a straight baseline in accordance with the method set forth in article 7 has the effect of enclosing as internal waters areas which had not previously been considered as such;

(b) the legal status of the waters beyond the territorial seas of States bordering straits as exclusive economic zones or high seas; or

(c) the legal régime in straits in which passage is regulated in whole or in part by long-standing international conventions in force specifically relating to such straits.

Article 36

This Part does not apply to a strait used for international navigation if there exists through the strait a route through the high seas or through an exclusive economic zone of similar convenience with respect to navigational and hydrographical characteristics; in such routes, the other relevant Parts of this Convention, including the provisions regarding the freedoms of navigation and overflight, apply.

Section 2. Transit passage

Article 37

This section applies to straits which are used for international navigation between one part of the high seas or an exclusive economic zone and another part of the high seas or an exclusive economic zone.

Article 38

1. In straits referred to in article 37, all ships and aircraft enjoy the right of transit passage, which shall not be impeded; except that, if the strait is formed by an island of a State bordering the strait and its mainland, transit passage shall not apply if there exists seaward of the island a route through the high seas or through an exclusive economic zone of similar convenience with respect to navigational and hydrographical characteristics.

2. Transit passage means the exercise in accordance with this Part of the freedom of navigation and overflight solely for the purpose of continuous and expeditious transit of the strait between one part of the high seas or an exclusive economic zone and another part of the high seas or an exclusive economic zone. However, the requirement of continuous and expeditious transit does not preclude passage through the strait for the purpose of entering, leaving or returning from a State bordering the strait, subject to the conditions of entry to that State.

3. Any activity which is not an exercise of the right of transit passage through a strait remains subject to the other applicable provisions of this Convention.

Article 39

1. Ships and aircraft, while exercising the right of transit passage, shall:

(*a*) proceed without delay through or over the strait;
(*b*) refrain from any threat or use of force against the sovereignty, territorial integrity or political independence of States bordering the strait, or in any other manner in violation of the principles of international law embodied in the Charter of the United Nations;
(*c*) refrain from any activities other than those incident to their normal modes of continuous and expeditious transit unless rendered necessary by *force majeure* or by distress;
(*d*) comply with other relevant provisions of this Part.

2. Ships in transit passage shall:

(*a*) comply with generally accepted international regulations, procedures and practices for safety at sea, including the International Regulations for Preventing Collisions at Sea;
(*b*) comply with generally accepted international regulations, procedures and practices for the prevention, reduction and control of pollution from ships.

3. Aircraft in transit passage shall:

(*a*) observe the Rules of the Air established by the International Civil Aviation Organization as they apply to civil aircraft; state aircraft will normally comply with such safety measures and will at all times operate with due regard for the safety of navigation;
(*b*) at all times monitor the radio frequency assigned by the competent internationally designated air traffic control authority or the appropriate international distress radio frequency.

Article 40

During transit passage, foreign ships, including marine scientific research and hydrographic survey ships, may not carry out any research or survey activities without the prior authorization of the States bordering straits.

Article 41

1. In conformity with this Part, States bordering straits may designate sea lanes and prescribe traffic separation schemes for navigation in straits where necessary to promote the safe passage of ships. . . .

Article 42

1. Subject to the provisions of this section, States bordering straits may adopt laws and regulations relating to transit passage through straits, in respect of all or any of the following:

(*a*) the safety of navigation and the regulation of maritime traffic, as provided in article 41;
(*b*) the prevention, reduction and control of pollution, by giving effect to applicable international regulations regarding the discharge of oil, oily wastes and other noxious substances in the strait;
(*c*) with respect to fishing vessels, the prevention of fishing, including the stowage of fishing gear;
(*d*) the loading or unloading of any commodity, currency or person in contravention of the customs, fiscal, immigration or sanitary laws and regulations of States bordering straits.

2. Such laws and regulations shall not discriminate in form or in fact among foreign ships or in their application have the practical effect of denying, hampering or impairing the right of transit passage as defined in this section.

3. States bordering straits shall give due publicity to all such laws and regulations.

4. Foreign ships exercising the right of transit passage shall comply with such laws and regulations.

5. The flag State of a ship or the State or registry of an aircraft entitled to sovereign immunity which acts in a manner contrary to such laws and regulations or other provisions of this Part shall bear international responsibility for any loss or damage which results to States bordering straits.

Article 44

States bordering straits shall not hamper transit passage and shall give appropriate publicity to any danger to navigation or overflight within or over the strait of which they have knowledge. There shall be no suspension of transit passage.

Section 3. Innocent passage

Article 45

1. The régime of innocent passage, in accordance with Part II, section 3,[99] shall apply in straits used for international navigation:

---

[99] *Ed.* Arts. 17–32.

(*a*) excluded from the application of the régime of transit passage under article 38, paragraph 1; or

(*b*) between a part of the high seas or an exclusive economic zone and the territorial sea of a foreign State.

2. There shall be nc suspension of innocent passage through such straits.

JOINT STATEMENT BY THE U.S. AND THE USSR ON UNIFORM INTERPRETATION OF RULES OF INTERNATIONAL LAW GOVERNING INNOCENT PASSAGE 1989[1]

Reprinted in Schachte (1993) 24 O.D.I.L. 179 at 194

1. The relevant rules of international law governing innocent passage of ships in the territorial sea are stated in the 1982 United Nations Convention on the Law of the Sea (Convention of 1982), particularly in Part II, Section 3.

2. All ships, including warships, regardless of cargo, armament or means of propulsion, enjoy the right of innocent passage through the territorial sea in accordance with international law, for which neither prior notification nor authorization is required.

3. Article 19 of the Convention of 1982 sets out in paragraph 2 an exhaustive list of activities that would render passage not innocent. A ship passing through the territorial sea that does not engage in any of those activities is in innocent passage.

4. A coastal State which questions whether the particular passage of a ship through its territorial sea is innocent shall inform the ship of the reason why it questions the innocence of the passage, and provide the ship an opportunity to clarify its intention or correct its conduct in a reasonably short period of time.

5. Ships exercising the right of innocent passage shall comply with all laws and regulations of the coastal State adopted in conformity with relevant rules of international law as reflected in Articles 21, 22, 23 and 25 of the Convention of 1982. These include the laws and regulations requiring ships exercising the right of innocent passage through its territorial sea to use such sea lanes and traffic separation schemes as it may prescribe where needed to protect safety of navigation. In areas where no such sea lanes or traffic separation schemes have been prescribed, ships nevertheless enjoy the right of innocent passage.

6. Such laws and regulations of the coastal State may not have the practical effect of denying or impairing the exercise of the right of innocent passage as set forth in Article 24 of the Convention of 1982.

[1] The Joint Statement was the result of discussions between the U.S. and the USSR over several years and is based upon and interprets the provisions of the 1982 Convention, which the two states consider, "with respect to traditional uses of the oceans, generally constitute international law and practice".

7. If a warship engages in conduct which violates such laws or regulations or renders its passage not innocent and does not take corrective action upon request, the coastal state may require it to leave the territorial sea, as set forth in Article 30 of the Convention of 1982. In such case the warship shall do so immediately.

8. Without prejudice to the exercise of rights of coastal and flag states, all differences which may arise regarding a particular case of passage of ships through the territorial sea shall be settled through diplomatic channels or other agreed means.

Notes

1. *Vessels entitled to innocent passage.*[2] In 1896, the British Law Officers referred to "an accepted principle of international law that the innocent passage of *merchant vessels* for the purposes of navigation should be permitted through territorial waters."[3] With regard to *warships*,[4] in the *Corfu Channel* case the Court held that they had a right of innocent passage through international straits in the territorial sea but did not consider their position beyond that. In 1956, the International Law Commission proposed a Draft Article which permitted coastal states to make the passage of warships "subject to previous authorisation or notification."[5] In its Commentary, the Commission stated that since "a number of States do require previous notification or authorisation" it could not "dispute the right of States to take such a measure."[6] At Geneva, the Draft Article, which was intended to precede that which became Article 23 of the 1958 Convention,[7] was rejected without a replacement text being inserted.[8] In this situation, is there a right of innocent passage for warships under the Territorial Sea Convention? Note the wording, "all ships" preceding Article 14[9] and the reference to "submarines" in it. When ratifying the 1958 Convention, the USSR made the following declaration in respect of Article 23: "The . . . [USSR] considers that the coastal state has the right to establish procedures for the authorisation of the passage of foreign warships through its territorial waters."[10] In contrast, in 1967 the British Foreign Secretary, in response to the question "what steps are being taken to prevent the

---

[2] On innocent passage generally, see Brown, *Passage through the Territorial Sea, Straits used for International Navigation, and Archipelagos* (1974) and Lee (1961) 55 A.J.I.L. 77.

[3] 1 McNair 343. Italics added.

[4] The definition of "warship" in Art. 29, 1982 Convention (above, p. 400), which is repeated from Art. 8(2), 1958 High Seas Convention, is based upon Arts. 3 and 4, Hague Convention on the Conversion of Merchantships into Warships 1907, U.K.T.S. 11 (1910), Cd. 5115; (1908) 2 A.J.I.L. Supp. 1933. On the regime of warships in the 1982 Convention, see Lowe (1986) 10 Mar. Pol. 171 and Oxman (1984) 24 Virg. J.I.L. 809.

[5] Art. 24, I.L.C. Draft Articles.

[6] Y.B.I.L.C., 1956, II, p. 277.

[7] This is now Art. 30, 1982 Convention, with the word "immediately" added.

[8] An amendment to the Commission's text to omit "authorisation or" was carried by the Plenary Session by 45 votes to 27, with six abstentions. The text as thus amended was then voted on as a whole and failed to obtain the necessary two-thirds majority (the vote was 43 in favour, 24 against, with 12 abstentions): *1958 Sea Conference Records*, Vol. II, pp. 67–68.

[9] This is now Art. 19, 1982 Convention.

[10] UN Doc. ST/LEG/SER. E/7, p. 731. Similar declarations were made by a number of other East European states and by Colombia; Some states objected, including Australia and Thailand who refer to one or more of the declarations as reservations; *ibid.* pp. 730–31.

deliberate violation of British territorial waters off Gibraltar by Spanish warships?" stated in Parliament:

> Under international law Spanish and other warships enjoy the right of innocent passage through Gibraltar's territorial sea. Exercise of this right is subject to compliance with the local regulations and with normal navigational practice.[11]

The 1982 Convention also contains no provision expressly allowing or denying a right of innocent passage for warships. Several attempts were made to add a provision requiring prior notification and authorisation, but it proved impossible to obtain the necessary consensus,[12] most states preferring not to press a delicate question.[13] Like the 1958 Convention, the 1982 Convention has a heading "all ships" before the articles on innocent passage and requires "submarines" to navigate on the surface.[14]

The balance of state practice on the question of a right of innocent passage for warships was greatly changed in 1989, when in the U.S.–USSR Joint Statement, above, p. 405, the USSR accepted that there was such a right.[15] But the position remains unresolved; writing in 1990, Kwiatowska[16] notes that the position taken in the Joint Statement

> is not shared by a relatively large number of over 40 coastal states, as evidenced by national legislation and declarations made by these states upon signing and ratifying the 1982 . . . Convention. These states consist of 4 Eastern European states, 5 Western European states, 32 developing states (including Brazil, China, and India), as well as Albania, Malta, and Yugoslavia, all of which . . . presently claim a right to control entry of warships into their territorial seas by means of prior notification, authorization, or limitations on number of warships present at any one time. . . . This practice, to which the pre-*glasnost* Soviet position . . . importantly contributed, appears irreversible.

2. *Passage through internal waters.*[17] There is no right of innocent passage through *internal* waters.[18] As to entry into a state's ports, in *Saudi Arabia v. Aramco*,[19] the arbitrator stated: "According to a great principle of public international law, the

---

[11] *Hansard*, H.C., Vol. 754, col. 20 November 13, 1967; B.P.I.L. 1967, p. 95. The U.K. interprets the 1958 and the 1982 Conventions as allowing innocent passage for warships: *Hansard*, H.L., Vol. 388, cols. 846–847 February 1, 1978; UKM.I.L. 1978 (1978) 49 B.Y.I.L. 395.

[12] See Oxman (1981) 75 A.J.I.L. 235. The 1982 Convention took the text of the 1958 Convention as its starting point.

[13] Several states (Cape Verde, Democratic Yemen, Iran, Romania, Sao Tomé, Sudan) made declarations upon signature or ratification of the 1982 Convention to the effect that authorisation of warship passage may be required: UN Doc. ST/LEG/SER.E./15, pp. 822 *et seq.* Others (Albania, China, Pakistan) made similar statements at UNCLOS III: *UNCLOS III Records*, Vol. XVI, pp. 155 *et seq.* Note that certain of these pronouncements (*e.g.* that by Sao Tomé) can be read, *quaere* unintentionally, as reservations to the Convention rather than mere interpretative declarations.

[14] Art. 20, 1982 Convention, which adds "other underwater vehicles" to submarines for this purpose.

[15] See Juda (1990) 21 O.D.I.L. 111.

[16] (1990) 21 O.D.I.L. 447. *cf.* the list of states requiring authorisation in Froman (1984) 21 San Diego L.R. 630 at 652.

[17] See Degan (1986) 17 N.Y.I.L. 3.

[18] *cf.* Colombos, *op. cit.*, p. 368, n. 1, above p. 176.

[19] (1963) 27 I.L.R. 117 at 212.

ports of every state must be open to foreign vessels and can only be closed when the vital interests of the state so require." O'Connell,[20] however, states:

> ... it is questionable whether the rule of international law to which he [the arbitrator] referred is a rule that ports must be open to trade, or the corollary of a different rule of international law which forbids discrimination among foreign ships using ports. . . . If a country chooses to close its ports altogether that would seem to be an act of sovereignty; but if it opens them, it must open them . . . arguably . . . to all-comers, on a non-discriminatory basis.

In the *Nicaragua (Merits)* case,[21] the I.C.J. stated that "by virtue of its sovereignty . . . a coastal state may regulate access to its ports."

3. *Meaning of passage.* Passage is defined in Article 18, 1982 Convention.[22] In the *Nicaragua* case,[23] the I.C.J. stated that "in order to enjoy access to ports, foreign vessels possess a customary right of innocent passage in territorial waters for the purposes of entering or leaving internal waters . . . "

Is the right of innocent passage in Article 18, 1982 Convention, the same in scope as that applied by the Court in the *Corfu Channel* case?[24] Were the British warships that swept the Corfu Channel for mines on November 13, 1946, engaged in "passage" in the sense of Article 18? Were those that earlier went through the Channel on October 22, 1946, to test Albanian reaction?[25]

4. *Innocence of passage.* After adopting a general definition of "innocent" in Article 19(1), the 1982 Convention adds a long list of prejudicial activities in Article 19(2).[26] This list was regarded as "exhaustive" in the U.S.–USSR Joint Statement, above, p. 405. Was the passage of British warships through the Corfu Channel on October 22, 1946, "innocent" according to Article 19? Would it have been if they had been taking arms to a third state which was then at war with Albania?[27] Suppose a merchant ship of State A wishes to pass through the territorial sea of State B at a time when the nationals of State B are inclined to demonstrate against State A. Could State B exclude the ship if it feared demonstrations against it? Would it matter whether the captain of the ship knew that demonstrations were likely to occur? Article 20 requires submarines (warships or otherwise) to navigate on the surface and to show their flag. It is not stated that non-compliance with this requirement renders passage non-innocent. O'Connell suggests that "[w]hile it is possible . . . for a submerged submarine to be in innocent passage . . . this is a matter for evaluation . . . of . . . the submarine's behaviour, and the chances of its not being in innocent passage are high."[28]

---

[20] *op. cit.*, p. 368, n. 1, above, Vol. II, p. 848. *cf.* Lowe (1977) 14 San Diego L.R. 597. It is generally accepted that warships have no right to enter a foreign port. On New Zealand's exclusion of U.S. warships carrying nuclear weapons contrary, in the U.S. view, to the 1951 ANZUS Pact (1952) 46 A.J.I.L. Supp. 93, see Woodliffe (1986) 35 I.C.L.Q. 730.

[21] I.C.J. Rep. 1986, p. 14 at p. 111.

[22] *cf.* Art. 14(2)(3), 1958 Territorial Sea Convention.

[23] I.C.J. Rep. 1986, p. 14 at p. 111. The Court states that Art. 18(1)(b) "does no more than codify customary international law."

[24] Although that case was only concerned with the innocent passage of warships through international straits, it seems permissible to regard the Court's understanding of the nature of innocent passage as of general application.

[25] Is the distinction between motive and intention for the purpose of *mens rea* in criminal law helpful here?

[26] Above, p. 396. Art. 14, 1958 Convention has a general obligation, but no list.

[27] Non-innocent passage is expressly limited in Art. 19(2) to conduct *in* the territorial sea: contrast Art. 14, 1958 Convention.

[28] *op. cit.*, p. 368, n. 1, above, p. 297. The suggestion concerned the same provision as submarines in Art. 14(6), 1958 Convention. On USSR submarines in Swedish waters, see below, p. 410, n. 35.

The passage of nuclear powered ships and ships carrying nuclear substances (presumably including nuclear weapons) is regulated by Article 23, 1982 Convention but is not non-innocent in itself.[29] In the 1982 Convention, "fishing activities" render passage non-innocent (Article 19(2)(i)), but non-compliance with fishing regulations generally does not.

If compliance by a foreign ship with the requirements of the right of innocent passage is not clear, upon whom is the burden of proof? The coastal state? Or the state claiming a right of passage for its ships? O'Connell[30] suggests:

> The Draft Convention (1980), by linking innocence explicitly with the list of subject-matters within coastal State competence, could have the effect of reversing the presumption of innocence. If passage is innocent until the commission of a prejudicial act, the burden of proving non-innocence could logically rest on the coastal State, which should be required to establish the fact and its prejudicial implications. But if no overt act need be committed for passage to be non-innocent then logically the burden of proving innocence would tend to shift to the ship.

5. *Laws governing passage.* Articles 21–24, 1982 Convention contains much more detailed provisions on the laws and regulations that a coastal State may make governing passage, than the equivalent Article 17, 1958 Territorial Sea Convention.

Article 21, 1982 Convention must be read in the context of a difference of opinion between common law and civil law states on the extent of the prescriptive (legislative) jurisdiction of coastal states over foreign ships passing through their territorial sea.[31]

The common law view is that, since the territorial sea is sovereign territory, coastal states have an unlimited power to legislate on civil and criminal law matters for all ships that venture therein,[32] although as a matter of comity they will exercise self-restraint.

The civil law view, which is influenced by the fact that, for jurisdictional purposes, a ship is the territory of the flag state, is that coastal states have only such prescriptive jurisdiction as states generally agree, and that agreement exists only in respect of matters that are of their nature related to passage. Since it lists only such matters, it might be inferred from the text of Article 21 that it favours the civil law view so that, for example, a coastal state may legislate to prevent dangerous navigation by a ship in innocent passage, but not the murder of crew members on board.

As to the duty to give publicity to dangers to navigation (Article 24(2), 1982 Convention), there is a customary international law duty to warn of mines: see the *Corfu Channel Case*, above, p. 391.

6. *Enforcement powers in respect of non-innocent passage.* Article 25(1), 1982 Convention, authorises a coastal state to "take the necessary steps" to prevent non-

---

[29] See, however, the declarations by Egypt and Yemen upon signature or ratification of the 1982 Convention requiring authorisation of passage: UN Doc. ST/LEG/SER.E/15, pp. 822 *et seq.*

[30] *op. cit.,* p. 368, n. 1, above, p. 273. *Footnote omitted.*

[31] See the Report of the Sub-committee (M. Schücking, *Rapporteur*) of the L.N. Committee of Experts for the Progressive Codification of International Law, L.N. Doc. C. 44.M.21. 1926, V, section XII. See also O'Connell, *op. cit.,* p. 368, n. 1, above, Vol. II, Chap. 19. *cf.* the similar difference of opinion as to enforcement jurisdiction in the territorial sea: see below, p. 413.

[32] See, *e.g.* the Territorial Waters Jurisdiction Act 1878, following the decision in *R. v. Keyn*, above, p. 76.

innocent passage.[33] Such steps may include the use of reasonable force as a last resort,[34] even against warships since "entry of a warship for purposes other than the purpose of innocent passage is an intrusion upon national territory and may be repelled just as a military intrusion on land may be."[35]

Non-innocent passage may involve a breach of the coastal state's criminal law so as to bring the power of arrest in Article 27, 1982 Convention, discussed below, p. 413, into play if the ship is a merchant ship or a government ship operated for commercial purposes.

7. *Passage through international straits.*[36] In the *Corfu Channel* case, the I.C.J. recognised that at customary international law the right of innocent passage cannot be suspended on grounds of security in a part of the territorial sea that is an international strait used for navigation from one part of the high seas to another, as it can in other parts of the territorial sea. This rule, which underlines the importance placed upon access to the high seas, was extended by Article 16(4), 1958 Convention, to straits which lead from the high seas into the territorial sea of a state. This extension is repeated in Art. 45, 1982 Convention. An important example of such straits are the Straits of Tiran in the Red Sea. These lead into the Gulf of Aqaba, which is about 17 miles wide at its widest point and which is bordered by Egypt, Israel, Jordan and Saudi Arabia. Given the claims to a 12 mile territorial sea of both Egypt and Saudi Arabia, which border the Gulf at its mouth and along most of its length, all of the Gulf is territorial sea.[37] Accordingly, whereas the *Corfu Channel* case does not recognise an unrestricted right of innocent passage for ships bound for Israel or Jordan, at the end of the Gulf, Article 16(4) does. While Israel is a party to the Territorial Sea Convention, the other three states are not; the reverse is true of the 1982 Convention. In 1967, the decision of the United Arab Republic (now Egypt) to prevent Israeli and other ships carrying strategic material to Israel from passing through the Straits of Tiran was the *casus belli* of the "Six Day War." At the time of the closure, the British Prime Minister was reported as saying: "It is the view of Her Majesty's Government . . . that the Straits of Tiran must be regarded as an international waterway through which the vessels of all nations have a right of passage."[38] The Security Council Resolution of November 22, 1967,[39] setting out a basis for the settlement of the Arab-Israeli conflict, refers to the need to guarantee "freedom of navigation through inter-

---

[33] Art. 25 repeats verbatim Art. 16(1), 1958 Convention.

[34] On the "reasonable force" rule, see the *I'm Alone* case, below, p. 437.

[35] O'Connell, *op. cit.*, p. 368, n. 1, above. Vol. I, p. 297. Accordingly, the legality of the use of depth charges by Sweden to cause submerged USSR submarines suspected of non-innocent passage in Swedish internal and territorial waters to come to the surface could not be "ruled out": *ibid.* See also on Sweden's action, Sadurska (1984) 10 Yale J.I.L. 34. And see the Swedish declaration on signature of the 1982 Convention: UN Doc. ST/LEG/SER.E/15, p. 839.

[36] See Brown, *loc. cit.*, p. 406, n. 2, above; Bordunov (1988) 12 Mar. Pol. 219; Bruel, *International Straits* (1947), 2 vols.; Burke and Deleo (1983) 9 Y.S.W.P.O. 389; Caminos (1987–V) 205 Hague Recueil 9; Frank (1982) 3 N.Y.J.I.C.L. 243; Koh, *Straits in International Navigation: Contemporary Issues* (1982); Grunawalt (1987) 18 O.D.I.L. 445; Moore (1980) 74 A.J.I.L. 77; Nandan and Anderson (1989) 60 B.Y.I.L. 159; Reisman (1989) 60 B.Y.I.L. 48; Schachte (1993) 24 O.D.I.L. 179; Schachte and Bernhardt (1993) 33 Virg.J.I.L. 527. For particular straits, see the books in the *International Straits of the World Series*, edited by Mangone and published by Nijthoff.

[37] The water-line across the Straits of Tiran is about seven miles long. It is interrupted by the island of Tiran which is about three miles from the Egyptian side of the Straits and four miles from the Saudi Arabian side. The only navigable channel is on the Egyptian side of the island. See Gross (1959) 53 A.J.I.L. 564; *ibid.* (1968) 33 L. & C.P. 125; Johnson (1968) 31 M.L.R. 153; Selak (1958) 52 A.J.I.L. 660.

[38] UN Doc. 5/PV 1342, p. 20, May 23, 1967.

[39] Above, p. 223.

national waterways in the area." By the 1979 Treaty of Peace between Egypt and Israel,[40] it is provided:

> The Parties consider the Strait of Tiran and the Gulf of Aqaba to be international waterways open to all nations for unimpeded and non-suspendable freedom of navigation and overflight. The Parties will respect each other's right to navigation and overflight for access to either country through the Straits of Tiran and the Gulf of Aqaba.

Passage through a number of other straits is also guaranteed in varying degrees by particular treaty régimes. For example, passage through the Bosphorus and the Dardanelles is fully guaranteed for merchant ships by the 1936 Treaty of Montreux.[41]

8. *The right of transit passage.* The question of passage through international straits has become more important as states have widened their territorial seas. The English Channel and the Straits of Gibraltar, for example, are not more than 24 miles wide at their narrowest points.[42] Responding to Western concern at this encroachment upon freedom of the high seas, the 1982 Convention contains provisions allowing a new right of *transit passage* through an international strait within the territorial sea of one or more coastal states.

The right of *transit passage* in the 1982 Convention has no counterpart in the 1958 Convention. The wording "used for international navigation" in Article 37 of the 1982 Convention follows the wording of the judgment in the *Corfu Channel* case (and that of 1958 Convention, Art. 16(4)). The right of transit passage does not apply (i) to a strait through which there exists "a route through the high seas or through an exclusive economic zone of similar convenience with respect to navigational and hydrographical characteristics" (Article 36); (ii) in the "island" situation described in Article 38(1)[43]; and (iii) to straits between a part of the high seas or an exclusive economic zone and the territorial sea of a foreign state (like the Straits of Tiran: see Article 37). In (ii) and (iii), the ordinary right of innocent passage through the territorial sea applies, except that, as in the case of international straits in the 1958 Convention, that right cannot be suspended (1982 Convention, Article 45).[44]

The right of *transit passage* through international straits is more generous than the right of innocent passage through other parts of the territorial sea in both the

---

[40] Art. 5(2), (1979) 18 I.L.M. 362. See El Baradei (1982) 76 A.J.I.L. 532 and Lapidoth (1983) 77 *ibid*. 84.

[41] U.K.T.S. 30 (1937), Cmd. 5551; (1937) 173 L.N.T.S. 213, 31 A.J.I.L. Supp. 1. In force 1936. 12 parties, including Turkey, the U.K. and the USSR but not the U.S. The Treaty's restrictions on the passage of warships (Art. 8–22) are not now being strictly observed: see Froman (1977) 14 San Diego L.R. 681. For the British view (not shared by Turkey) that the passage of aircraft carriers is prohibited, see *Hansard*, H.L. Vol. 472, col. 498, March 10, 1986. See generally, Rozakis and Stagos, *The Turkish Straits* (1987).

[42] There are over 100 straits less than 24 miles in width: see Ganz, *loc. cit.*, p. 369, n. 14, above, p. 7.

[43] On the "routes of similar convenience" exception in Arts. 36 and 38(1), see Alexander (1987) 18 O.D.I.L. 479. The exception in Art. 38(1) was introduced "in response to Italy's concern over the status of the Strait of Messina": *ibid*. p. 484.

[44] The 1982 provisions on the right of transit and innocent passage through international straits do not affect "the legal régime in straits in which passage is regulated in whole or in part by long-standing international conventions in force specifically relating to such straits" (Art. 35(c), 1982 Convention). See, *e.g.* the Treaty of Montreux, above, n. 41.

1958 and 1982 Conventions.[45] It expressly allows passage by aircraft including, it seems, military aircraft—"all . . . aircraft" (Article 38(1))[46]; "state aircraft" (Article 39(3))—and it appears to allow underwater transit by submarines (no provision comparable to 1982 Convention, Art. 20, above, p. 397, on innocent passage). There are also fewer Convention restrictions on conduct during passage (see Articles 39–41) and less power is given to the coastal state to regulate passage (see Articles 41, 42) than is the case with innocent passage. The right of transit passage probably allows passage by warships,[47] as in the case of the previously established customary international law right of innocent passage through international straits (*Corfu Channel* case).

The United Kingdom, which is not a signatory to the 1982 Convention, regards the right of transit passage as already stating customary law. In the debate on the bill extending British territorial waters to 12 miles, a Government spokesman stated[48]:

> International law and practice have now developed to the point where, if the United Kingdom extends to 12 miles, we should afford to others the essential rights in some internationally important straits for which there is no alternative route; namely, the Straits of Dover, the North Channel lying between Scotland and Northern Ireland, and the passage between Shetland and Orkney. These rights, which are widely recognised as necessary, include: a right of unimpeded passage through such straits for merchant vessels and warships; a right of overflight; the right of submarines to pass through the straits submerged; and appropriate safeguards for the security and other interests of the coastal state.
>
> In other straits used for international navigation, such as the Pentland Firth south of Orkney and the passage between the Scilly Isles and the mainland of Cornwall, as in other parts of the territorial sea, a right of innocent passage will continue to exist in accordance with the practice of states.

The "right of unimpeded transit passage" through the Dover Straits is recognised by the 1988 Anglo-French Joint Declaration.[49]

9. *Civil and criminal jurisdiction over foreign merchant ships in the territorial sea.* This is provided for in Articles 27 and 28, 1982 Convention, which follow Articles 19 and 20, 1958 Convention respectively very closely. According to some commentators, the use of the word "should", as opposed to "may", in Article 19(1), 1958 Convention, and now Article 27, 1982 Convention, indicates that the rule it contains is one of comity and not of law.[50] The International Law Commission had

---

[45] Although the reason for this is that the right of transit passage was prompted by the extension of the territorial sea into waters in which freedom of the high seas formerly applied, the right applies over the whole of the territorial sea, even within three miles of the coast.

[46] Note that there is no provision equivalent to Arts. 27–28, 1982 Convention (Arts. 19–20, 1958 Convention) on innocent passage on the question of enforcement jurisdiction during transit passage. See Shearer (1986) 35 I.C.L.Q. 320 at 332, who concludes that it does not exist.

[47] On the passage of warships through the straits of Hormuz, see Mahmoudi (1991) 15 Mar. Pol. 338.

[48] *Hansard*, H.L., Vol. 484, col. 382 February 5, 1987. *cf.* the U.S. recognition of the "right of transit passage" in a note concerning passage through the Persian Gulf: (1984) 78 A.J.I.L. 884.

[49] Cm. 557 (1989), p. 4.

[50] See Fitzmaurice, *loc. cit.*, p. 368, n. 9, above, p. 104, and Lee (1961) 55 A.J.I.L. 77 at 83–86, but see McDougal and Burke, *loc. cit.*, p. 368, n. 1, above, p. 300. The French text, which, like the English, is one of five authentic texts, uses "devrait."

proposed "may."[51] The wording was changed at Geneva on the suggestion of the United States, which explained its suggestion as follows:

> It was the practice of most states not to arrest or conduct criminal investigations on board foreign ships passing through their territorial waters save in the instances mentioned in sub-paragraphs *a*, *b* and *c*, but the declaration in the Commissions text that "A State may not take any steps . . . " was a departure from the doctrine of international law that the coastal State had unlimited criminal jurisdiction within its territorial seas.[52]

The United States also successfully proposed the use of "should" in place of "may" in Article 20, 1958 Convention, now Article 28, 1982 Convention, for the same reason.[53] Note, however, that in both cases the United States full proposal was "should, generally." The word "generally" was deleted in the First Committee in respect of Article 20[54] and in the Plenary Meetings in respect of Article 19.[55] At least one delegate opposing that word would seem to have thought that its exclusion had the effect of confirming that a coastal state *"could* not stop a ship for the purpose of exercising its *civil* jurisdiction in respect of an individual on board."[56] This uncertainty is parallelled by a difference in state practice between common law and civil law states. Generally, common law states follow the rules in the 1958 and 1982 Conventions in practice as rules of comity whereas civil law states regard them as binding in law.[57] Articles 27 and 28, 1982 Convention, following Articles 19 and 20, 1958 Convention, give enforcement jurisdiction only in respect of merchant ships and government ships used for commercial purposes; warships and government ships used for non-commercial purposes are immune from enforcement jurisdiction for non-compliance with the local law, except[58] that measures may be taken to remove them from the territorial sea.[59]

In *Pianka v. The Queen*,[60] the appellants, United States citizens, had been given clearance to head from a Jamaican port to Montego Bay in Jamaica in their United States registered motor boat. The next night they were discovered in Jamaican territorial waters with a large quantity of the drug ganja on board. Their appeal in these proceedings against conviction by a Jamaican court, *inter alia*, for illegal possession of the drug in Jamaican territorial waters was unsuccessful. A part of their defence was that their arrest conflicted with Article 19 of the 1958 Convention (which had been incorporated by statute into Jamaican law). The Jamaican Court of Appeal rejected this defence[61]:

---

[51] Y.B.I.L.C., 1956, II, p. 274.
[52] *1958 Sea Conference Records*, Vol. III, p. 81.
[53] *ibid*. p. 82.
[54] *ibid*. p. 125.
[55] *ibid*. Vol. I, p. 66.
[56] M. Petrén (Sweden), *ibid*. p. 125. Italics added. He was discussing Art. 20, in particular.
[57] *cf*. the difference of opinion as to prescriptive jurisdiction, see above, p. 409, and as to jurisdiction in ports, see below, p. 418.
[58] See the heading to Part I, Section III, Subsection B and Arts. 21 and 22, 1958 Convention and the heading to Part I, Section 3, Subsection B and Art. 32, 1982 Convention.
[59] Art. 23, 1958 Convention and Art. 30, 1982 Convention. These provisions apply only to warships. There is a lacuna in respect of government ships operated for non-commercial purposes, which constitute an *a fortiori* case. The flag state of a warship or a government ship operated for non-commercial purposes is responsible for damage resulting from a breach of the local law: Art. 31, 1982 Convention. As to permissible enforcement action against a warship engaged in non-innocent passage, see above, p. 410.
[60] [1979] A.C. 107, PC.
[61] (1975) 24 W.L.R. 285 at 292–293.

... even if the 'Star Baby' was not bound for Montego Bay ... but rather was
making for the high seas this was not in right of innocent passage through the
territorial sea for the appellants had received into their possession while on the
territorial sea a dangerous drug, the possession and conveyance of which were
prohibited under the criminal law ... of Jamaica, and its receipt and conveyance by the appellants in that event was prejudicial to the good order of
Jamaica. The consequences of the crime, therefore, extended to Jamaica and
additionally was such as to disturb the good order of the territorial sea. That
being so, and these being within the exceptions contained in art. 19, there was
no contravention of art. 19 in seeking to invoke the criminal jurisdiction of the
court.

The Privy Council upheld the Court of Appeal judgment on the application of
Article 19, adding only that "these provisions [of that Article] should receive a
liberal construction" and that the case could have been dealt with under Article
19(1)(*d*)[62] because Jamaica was a party to the 1961 Single Convention on Narcotic
Drugs[63] which covers ganja.

In *The David*,[64] the facts were that *The David*, a Panamanian merchant ship, was
arrested in 1925 in the territorial sea of the Panama Canal Zone, within the
territorial jurisdiction of the United States, in connection with civil proceedings
against it concerning a collision that had occurred in 1923. The United States-
Panama General Claims Commission rejected Panama's claim that the arrest had
been contrary to international law. It said:

> There is no clear pre-ponderance of authority to the effect that such vessels
> [foreign merchant vessels] when passing through territorial waters are exempt
> from civil arrest. In the absence of such authority, the Commission cannot say
> that a country may not under the rules of international law, assert the right to
> arrest on civil process merchant ships passing through its territorial
> waters.[65]

The Panamanian Commissioner (Alfaro), dissenting, stated:

> It is proper to point out also that the claimant does not maintain that absolute
> immunity exists from the jurisdiction of the littoral authorities; that it does not
> allege, for example, lack of jurisdiction in the case of an offence committed
> within territorial waters in the course of innocent passage, although some
> writers deny jurisdiction even in such cases. The claimant also accepts that the
> ship is obliged to comply with orders and maritime regulations which contrib-
> ute to the safety of navigation, or that are of a sanitary or police character. The
> claimant maintains only that in case of a civil action growing out of a collision
> occurring previously beyond the jurisdiction of the littoral authorities, the
> latter were without jurisdiction later to interfere with the passage of the same
> ship by means of a civil suit not affecting in any way territorial sovereign
> interests.[66]

Presumably "the consequences of the crime extend to the coastal state" (Article
28(1)(a), 1982 Convention) in such cases as smuggling, illegal immigration, pollution and violations of security laws. Would it do so just because the perpetrator

[62] *cf*. Art. 27(1)(d), 1982 Convention.
[63] *loc. cit.*, p. 290, n. 86, above.
[64] (1933) 6 R.I.A.A. 382.
[65] *ibid*. p. 384.
[66] *ibid*. p. 386.

or the victim "of the crime" (which presumably refers to a crime under the law of the coastal state) on board a foreign ship is a national of the coastal state? The International Law Commission's draft of Article 19(1)(a), 1958 Convention[67] read "beyond the ship." It was changed to "to the coastal state" at Geneva. Does the wording finally adopted exclude the coastal state's jurisdiction in cases of collisions between two ships neither of which is flying its flag?[68] What if the effect, as in some cases of pollution, is felt only in the territorial sea and not on land or in inland waters? On the meaning of the terms "peace" and "good order", see the cases on jurisdiction over foreign ships in internal waters immediately below. Are the limitations upon the coastal state's jurisdiction in Articles 28 and 29, 1982 Convention limitations upon executive enforcement jurisdiction only? Would, for example, a prosecution under the Territorial Waters Jurisdiction Act 1878 in the circumstances of *R. v. Keyn* be prohibited by Article 28 of the 1982 Convention?[69]

(v) JURISDICTION OVER FOREIGN SHIPS IN INTERNAL WATERS[70]

R. v. ANDERSON

(1868) 11 Cox's Criminal Cases 198. Court of Criminal Appeal

The defendant, a United States national, was found guilty by the Central Criminal Court of manslaughter on board a British merchant ship of which he was a crew member. The offence was committed on the River Garonne in France some 300 yards from shore when the ship was on its way to Bordeaux. The defendant appealed on the ground that the Court had lacked jurisdiction to try him.

BOVILL C.J.: There is no doubt that the place where the offence was committed was within the territory of France, and that the prisoner was therefore subject to the laws of France, which the local authorities of that realm might have enforced if so minded; but at the same time, in point of law, the offence was also committed within British territory, for the prisoner was a seaman on board a merchant vessel, which, as to her crew and master, must be taken to have been at the time under the protection of the British flag, and, therefore, also amenable to the provisions of the British law. It is true that the prisoner was an American citizen, but he had with his own consent embarked on board a British vessel as one of the crew. Although the prisoner was subject to the American jurisprudence as an American citizen, and to the law of France as having committed an offence within the territory of France, yet he must also be considered as subject to the jurisdiction of British law, which extends to the protection of British vessels, though in ports belonging to another country. From the passage in the treatise of Ortolan[71] . . . it appears that, with regard to

---

[67] Now Art. 28(1)(a), 1982 Convention.
[68] See McDougal and Burke, *loc. cit.*, p. 368, n. 1, above, p. 300.
[69] See above, p. 75.
[70] See Charteris (1920–21) 1 B.Y.I.L. 45; Degan (1986) 17 N.Y.I.L. 3; Francioni (1975) 1 It. Y.I.L. 27; Jessup, *The Law of Territorial Waters and Maritime Jurisdiction* (1927), pp. 144–194. On entry into foreign ports, see above, p. 407.
[71] *Règles internationales et diplomatie de la mer* (4th ed., 1864), Vol. I, pp. 269–271.

offences committed on board of foreign vessels within the French territory, the French nation will not assert their police law unless invoked by
the master of the vessel, or unless the offence leads to a disturbance of the
peace of the port. . . . The place where the offence was committed was in
a navigable part of the river below bridge, and where the tide ebbs and
flows, and great ships do lie and hover. An offence committed at such a
place, according to the authorities, is within the Admiralty jurisdiction,
and it is the same as if the offence had been committed on the high seas.
On the whole I come to the conclusion that the prisoner was amenable to
the British law, and that the conviction was right.

BYLES J.: I am of the same opinion. . . . A British ship is, for the purposes
of this question, like a floating island; and, when a crime is committed on
board a British ship, it is within the jurisdiction of the Admiralty Court,
and therefore of the Central Criminal Court, and the offender is as
amenable to British law as if he had stood on the Isle of Wight and
committed the crime. . . .

Channel B. and Lush J. delivered concurring judgments.

WILDENHUS'S CASE

120 U.S. 1 (1887). US Supreme Court

W., a Belgian crew member of a Belgian merchant ship, was found guilty by an
American state court of the murder of another Belgian crew member on board the
ship when it was docked in the port of Jersey City, New Jersey. It was argued in
this application for habeas corpus that, under a consular convention of 1880
between Belgium and the United States, the United States court had lacked
jurisdiction. The application was rejected by the United States Supreme Court.

WAITE C.J.: It is part of the law of civilised nations that when a merchant vessel of one country enters the ports of another for the purposes
of trade, it subjects itself to the law of the place to which it goes, unless
by treaty or otherwise the two countries have come to some different
understanding or agreement. . . . As the owner has voluntarily taken his
vessel for his own private purposes to a place within the dominion of a
government other than his own, and from which he seeks protection
during his stay, he owes that government such allegiance for the time
being as is due for the protection to which he becomes entitled.

From experience, however, it was found long ago that it would be
beneficial to commerce if the local government would abstain from interfering with the internal discipline of the ship and the general regulation
of the rights and duties of the officers and crew towards the vessel or
among themselves. And so by comity it came to be generally understood
among civilised nations that all matters of discipline and all things done
on board which affected only the vessel or those belonging to her, and did
not involve the peace or dignity of the country, or the tranquillity of the

port, should be left by the local government to be dealt with by the authorities of the nation to which the vessel belonged as the laws of that nation or the interests of its commerce should require. But if crimes are committed on board of a character to disturb the peace and tranquillity of the country to which the vessel has been brought, the offenders have never by comity or usage been entitled to any exemption from the operation of the local laws for their punishment, if the local tribunals see fit to assert their authority. Such being the general public law on this subject, treaties and conventions have been entered into by nations having commercial intercourse, the purpose of which was to settle and define the rights and duties of the contracting parties with respect to each other in these particulars, and thus prevent the inconvenience that might arise from attempts to exercise conflicting jurisdictions. . . .

The Treaty [now before the Court] is part of the supreme law of the United States, and has the same force and effect in New Jersey that it is entitled to elsewhere. If it gives the Consul of Belgium exclusive jurisdiction over the offence which it is alleged has been committed within the territory of New Jersey, we see no reason why he may not enforce his rights under the Treaty by writ of *habeas corpus* in any proper court of the United States. This being the case, the only important question left for our determination is whether the thing which has been done—the disorder that has arisen—on board this vessel is of a nature to disturb the public peace, or, as some writers term it, the "public repose" of the people who look to the State of New Jersey for their protection. If the thing done—"the disorder," as it is called in the Treaty—is of a character to affect those on shore or in the port when it becomes known, the fact that only those on the ship saw it when it was done, is a matter of no moment. Those who are not on the vessel pay no special attention to the mere disputes or quarrels of the seamen while on board, whether they occur under deck or above. Neither do they as a rule care for anything done on board which relates only to the discipline of the ship, or to the preservation of order and authority. Not so, however, with crimes which from their gravity awaken a public interest as soon as they become known, and especially those of a character which every civilised nation considers itself bound to provide a severe punishment for when committed within its own jurisdiction. In such cases inquiry is certain to be instituted at once to ascertain how or why the thing was done, and the popular excitement rises or falls as the news spreads and the facts become known. It is not alone the publicity of the act, or the noise and clamour which attends it, that fixes the nature of the crime, but the act itself. If that is of a character to awaken public interest when it becomes known, it is a "disorder" the nature of which is to affect the community at large, and consequently to invoke the power of the local government whose peoples have been disturbed by what was done. The very nature of such an act is to disturb the quiet of a peaceful community, and to create, in the language of the Treaty, a "disorder" which will "disturb tranquillity and public order on shore or in the port." The principle which governs the whole matter is this: Disorders which disturb only the peace of the ship or those on board are to be dealt with exclusively by the sovereignty of the home of the ship, but those which disturb the public peace may be suppressed, and, if need be, the offenders punished by the proper authorities of the local jurisdiction. It may not be easy at all times to determine to which of the two jurisdictions a particular act of disorder belongs. Much will undoubtedly depend on the attending circumstances of the particular case, but all must concede that felonious homicide is a subject for the local jurisdiction, and that if the proper authorities are proceeding with the case in a regular way the consul has no right to interfere to prevent it. That, according to the petition for the *habeas corpus*, is this case.

Notes

1. *Wildenhus's* case adopts the common law view as to a coastal state's enforcement jurisdiction over crimes committed by foreign ships in international water, namely that the coastal state may in law exercise jurisdiction in all criminal matters but that as a matter of comity it should not do so unless the crime disturbs its "peace or tranquillity."[72] The civil law view is that this is a limitation of international law, not comity.[73] It would appear generally agreed that the coastal state's enforcement jurisdiction in civil matters is unrestricted.[74]

2. In the *Eisler* case,[75] in 1949, Eisler was arrested and taken off a Polish ship at Southampton for extradition to the United States. Poland protested "on the ground that Eisler was a political refugee entitled under international law to asylum and protection under the Polish flag, and that a state's jurisdiction over territorial and national waters did not entitle the state to arrest persons on board a foreign vessel for the purpose of extradition to a third state."[76] The British Government is reported as rejecting Poland's argument for the following reason:

> it would mean . . . that States could grant to persons on board their merchant or passenger ships in foreign ports or waters the same asylum that a State can grant to persons on its territory. It was, however, quite contrary to the practice of States to recognise any principle of asylum in connexion with merchant ships, and the Polish Government had refused it in the case of offences committed by persons who subsequently went on board a foreign ship in a Polish port. The absence of any right to grant asylum on board merchant ships sprang from a universally recognised principle of international law that a merchant ship in the ports or roadsteads of another country falls under the jurisdiction of the coastal State.[77]

---

[72] See the 1929 *Harvard Draft Convention on Territorial Waters*, Art. 18 and Commentary thereto, (1929) 23 A.J.I.L. Sp. Supp. 243 at 307, and the 1929 Report of the Sub-committee (M. Schücking, *rapporteur*) of the L.N. Committee of Experts for the Progressive Codification of International law, L.N. Doc. C.44. M.21. 1926. V, Section XI.

[73] *ibid. cf.* the common law/civil law difference of approach to legislative jurisdiction in the territorial sea: above, pp. 409 and 413.

[74] *ibid.*

[75] Jennings (1949) 26 B.Y.I.L. 468.

[76] *ibid.*

[77] *The Times*, June 9, 1949, p. 3. See also the *Medvid* case (1986) 80 A.J.I.L. 622.

What if the Polish ship in question had been stopped for the purpose of arresting Eisler while it was passing through British territorial waters?

3. On criminal jurisdiction over foreign warships in port, see *The Schooner Exchange v. McFaddon.*[78]

In 1977, while H.M.S. *Danae* was in Rio de Janeiro on a goodwill visit, some junior ratings invited Ronald Biggs, the Great Train Robber and a United Kingdom citizen, on board. When it was discovered who he was, Mr Biggs was asked to leave the ship. Later the question was asked in Parliament why he had not been arrested. The following Government explanation was given:

> Since Mr Biggs did not commit an offence while on board HMS "Danae" the only powers under which he could have been arrested would have been the powers of "citizen's arrest" under the provisions of the Criminal Law Act 1967. The relevant provisions of this Act, however, apply only to England and Wales.
>
> Whilst one of Her Majesty's ships in a foreign port has extra-territoriality —that is, it is immune from local jurisdiction and enforcement of local laws—it is not correct to regard it as floating United Kingdom territory, and all laws of the United Kingdom do not necessarily apply to all persons on board that ship. The relevant provisions of the Criminal Law Act are such an example.[79]

3. THE HIGH SEAS

(i) FREEDOM OF THE HIGH SEAS

CONVENTION ON THE LAW OF THE SEA 1982

UN Doc. A/CONF. 62/122; (1982) 21 I.L.M. 1261

Article 86

The provisions of this Part apply to all parts of the sea that are not included in the exclusive economic zone, in the territorial sea or in the internal waters of a State, or in the archipelagic waters of an archipelagic State. This article does not entail any abridgement of the freedoms enjoyed by all States in the exclusive economic zone in accordance with article 58.

Article 87

1. The high seas are open to all States, whether coastal or land-locked. Freedom of the high seas is exercised under the conditions laid down by this Convention and by other rules of international law. It comprises, *inter alia*, both for coastal and land-locked States:

(*a*) freedom of navigation;

[78] Above, p. 308.
[79] *Hansard*, H.C., Vol. 930, col. 450, April 29, 1977.

(*b*) freedom of overflight;

(*c*) freedom to lay submarine cables and pipelines, subject to Part VI[80];

(*d*) freedom to construct artificial islands and other installations permitted under international law, subject to Part VI[80];

(*e*) freedom of fishing, subject to the conditions laid down in section 2;

(*f*) freedom of scientific research, subject to Parts VI[81] and XIII.[82]

2. These freedoms shall be exercised by all States with due regard for the interests of other States in their exercise of the freedom of the high seas, and also with due regard for the rights under this Convention with respect to activities in the Area.

Article 88

The high seas shall be reserved for peaceful purposes.

Article 89

No State may validly purport to subject any part of the high seas to its sovereignty.

Notes

1. *Freedom of the high seas.* Article 86, 1982 Convention takes into account the emergence of the concept of the exclusive economic zone and the new provisions as to archipelagic states. Whereas under the equivalent Article 1, 1958 High Seas Convention, the high seas begin where the territorial sea ends, the 1982 Convention concept of the high seas is a more limited one, applying only beyond the limit of the exclusive economic zone.

2. Other freedoms additional to those in Article 87, 1982 Convention, include the freedom to use the high seas for weapon testing and naval exercises. To this should be added the freedom to observe the naval exercises of other states. Whiteman records:

> When a Soviet "electronics ship," supposedly operating as a Soviet trawler, cruised through a Polaris submarine test area off Long Island in April 1960 . . . Rear Admiral Charles C. Kirkpatrick . . . emphasised at a Pentagon news conference that, since the ship was in international waters at all times, the Soviet ship remained unmolested . . . "We are a legal people and abide by international law," he said . . . As reported, it was explained by an officer present that the Soviet ship with its electronic gear could monitor radio information for "hundreds of miles."[83]

States sometimes use the high seas to make a show of strength off the coast of other states. The 1982 Convention limits the use of the high seas to "peaceful

---

[80] *Ed.* Arts. 76–85 (on the continental shelf).
[81] *Ed.* Arts. 116–120 (on conservation and management of the living resources).
[82] *Ed.* Arts. 238–265 (on marine scientific research).
[83] 4 Whiteman, 516–517.

purposes" (Article 88). The United Kingdom Government takes the view that rocket and other weapons testing on the high seas does not contravene this provision.[84]

In 1954, radiation from hydrogen bomb tests conducted by the United States on the high seas in the area of the Eniwetok Atoll in the Trust Territory then administered by the United States[85] caused the death of a Japanese fisherman and caused injury to other Japanese fishermen, to some inhabitants of the Rongelap Atoll within the Territory and to some United States nationals.[86] The tests took place in a danger zone, within which shipping was advised not to go, of 50,000 square miles. Both the Japanese fishing vessel concerned and the Rongelap Atoll were outside this zone. They were affected because the force of the explosion had been miscalculated and because of a sudden change of wind. The United States gave medical and other assistance and paid monetary compensation. In the case of the Japanese nationals, the compensation, which was for personal injuries and for economic loss resulting from the contamination of Japanese fishing catches, was expressly stated to be *ex gratia*. At the time of a later test series in 1958, the United States took the following legal position:

> The high seas have long been used by the nations of the world for naval manoeuvres, weapons tests, and other matters of this kind. Such measures no doubt result in some inconvenience to other users of the high seas but they are not proscribed by international law.[87]

When plans for the 1958 United States tests were announced, Japan stated that it was "greatly concerned" and expressed the view that "the United States Government has the responsibility of compensating for economic losses that may be caused by the establishment of a danger zone and for all losses and damages that may be inflicted on Japan and the Japanese people as a result of the nuclear tests."[88] Japan did not refer expressly to international law. On July 2, 1958, a United States national entered the danger zone in a yacht as a protest. He was prosecuted under United States law applying to United States nationals only. Could the United States have legislated to have excluded an alien? Could the national state of an alien injured by radiation in a danger zone successfully claim compensation under international law if the alien (a) deliberately ignores the warning or (b) is unaware of it?

An amendment to what became Article 2 of the High Seas Convention[89] proposed by the USSR, which was conducting most of its nuclear tests in Siberia,[90] to make nuclear testing on the high seas a violation of the Convention was not voted upon at Geneva; instead the Conference adopted the proposal of India that the matter should be referred to the General Assembly "for appropriate action."[91] In 1963, the Nuclear Test Ban Treaty[92] was signed and came into force. This prohibits the testing of nuclear weapons, *inter alia*, on the high seas. France,

---

[84] *Hansard*, H.L., Vol. 388, col. 842, February 1, 1978; UKM.I.L. 1978, (1978) 49 B.Y.I.L. 397.

[85] See above, p. 131.

[86] See generally 4 Whiteman 553 *et seq.* See also McDougal and Schlei (1955) 64 Yale L.J. 648 ("for" the legality of the tests) and Margolis (1955) 64 Yale L.J. 629 ("against" their legality).

[87] 4 Whiteman 595.

[88] *ibid.* pp. 585–586.

[89] See now Art. 87, 1982 Convention.

[90] But some were conducted in the Barents Sea: *ibid.* p. 574.

[91] Resolution on Nuclear Tests on the High Seas, *1958 Sea Conference Records*, Vol. II, p. 24, p. 101 (text).

[92] U.K.T.S. 3 (1964), Cmnd. 2245; 480 U.N.T.S. 43. In force 1963. 122 parties, including the U.K.

which is not a party to the Treaty, continued to conduct tests in the South Pacific until 1973 when it completed its final series of tests in the atmosphere.[93] The 1972 and 1973 tests were the subject of protests by several states and led to the *Nuclear Tests Cases*.[94] These were brought by Australia and New Zealand against France. The cases were taken off the Court's list without a decision being given on the merits when France announced that it would not conduct further tests after 1973; despite argument to the contrary by the applicant states, the Court found that their claims no longer had any object.[95] The applicants had asked the Court for a declaration that the carrying out of further nuclear tests in the South Pacific was not consistent with international law.[96]

In order to develop its long range missiles, the United States found it necessary to arrange for test sites in the territory of other states[97] in the Atlantic area and to fire the missiles over the high seas. One writer records:

> None of the missiles ... carry warheads, atomic or otherwise; they are loaded with concrete blocks instead. A missile weighing many tons can, however, do considerable damage ... accidents can occur, as in the case of the errant flight of a Snark into the wilds of Brazil in December 1956. ... Thus far no official complaints from other governments, comparable to those voiced in and out of the United Nations with respect to the nuclear weapons testing, have apparently been made to the government of the United States. ... [98]

2. *Land-locked states.* Article 90, 1982 Convention[99] contains the right of land-locked states (of which there are over 30) to have ships flying their flag. In addition, the 1982 Convention has other detailed provisions on the transit trade of land-locked states and their access to the high seas which are stronger than their equivalent in the 1958 High Seas Convention (Article 3).[1]

(ii) NATIONALITY OF SHIPS

CONVENTION ON THE LAW OF THE SEA 1982

UN Doc. A/CONF. 62/122; (1982) 21 I.L.M. 1261

Article 90

Every State, whether coastal or land-locked, has the right to sail ships flying its flag on the high seas.

---

[93] For a discussion of the legality of these tests, see Mercer (1968) N.Z.L.J. 405–408, 418–421 and Swan (1973–74) 9 M.U.L.R. 296.

[94] I.C.J. Rep. 1974, p. 253 (*Australia v. France*); I.C.J. Rep. 1974, p. 457 (*New Zealand v. France*).

[95] See below, p. 774. France began testing again in 1981. The I.C.J. dismissed a request by New Zealand to examine the situation in connection with the French 1995 tests: I.C.J. Rep. 1995, p. 288.

[96] This was specifically the Australian request; for the similar New Zealand request, see I.C.J. Rep. 1974, p. 460.

[97] The U.K., for example, agreed to a U.S. base in the Bahamas. See generally 4 Whiteman 619–623.

[98] Reiff, *The United States and the Treaty Law of the Sea* (1959), p. 371.

[99] Below, p. 422. *cf.* Art. 4, 1958 High Seas Convention.

[1] Arts 124–132, 1982 Convention. See Caflisch (1978) 49 B.Y.I.L. 71; Menefee (1992) 23 Cal.West.I.L.J. 1; Sinjela, *Land-Locked States and the UNCLOS Regime* (1983); Sulaiman (1984) 10 S.A.Y.I.L. 144; Vasciannie, *Land-Locked and Geographically Disadvantaged States in the International Law of the Sea* (1990); Wani (1982) 22 Virg.J.I.L. 627. As to the rights of land-locked states in the exclusive economic zone, see Art. 69, 1982 Convention. See also the 1965 Convention on Transit Trade of Land-Locked States, and Art. 3, 1958 High Seas Convention.

Article 91

1. Every State shall fix the conditions for the grant of its nationality to ships, for the registration of ships in its territory, and for the right to fly its flag. Ships have the nationality of the State whose flag they are entitled to fly. There must exist a genuine link between the State and the ship.

2. Every State shall issue to ships to which it has granted the right to fly its flag documents to that effect.

Article 92

1. Ships shall sail under the flag of one State only and, save in exceptional cases expressly provided for in international treaties or in this Convention, shall be subject to its exclusive jurisdiction on the high seas. A ship may not change its flag during a voyage or while in a port of call, save in the case of a real transfer of ownership or change of registry.

2. A ship which sails under the flags of two or more States, using them according to convenience, may be assimilated to a ship without nationality.

Article 94

1. Every State shall effectively exercise its jurisdiction and control in administrative, technical and social matters over ships flying its flag.

2. In particular every State shall:

(a) maintain a register of ships containing the names and particulars of ships flying its flag, except those which are excluded from generally accepted international regulations on account of their small size; and

(b) assume jurisdiction under its internal law over each ship flying its flag and its master, officers and crew in respect of administrative, technical and social matters concerning the ship.

3. Every State shall take such measures for ships flying its flag as are necessary to ensure safety at sea with regard, *inter alia*, to:

(a) the construction, equipment and seaworthiness of ships;

(b) the manning of ships, labour conditions and the training of crews, taking into account the applicable international instruments;

(c) the use of signals, the maintenance of communications and the prevention of collisions.

4. Such measures shall include those necessary to ensure:

(a) that each ship, before registration and thereafter at appropriate intervals, is surveyed by a qualified surveyor of ships, and has on board such charts, nautical publications and navigational equipment and instruments as are appropriate for the safe navigation of the ship;

(b) that each ship is in the charge of a master and officers who possess appropriate qualifications, in particular in seamanship, navigation, communications and marine engineering, and that the crew is appropriate in qualification and numbers for the type, size, machinery and equipment of the ship;

(c) that the master, officers and, to the extent appropriate, the crew are fully conversant with and required to observe the applicable international regulations concerning the safety of life at sea, the prevention of collisions, the prevention, reduction and control of marine pollution, and the maintenance of communications by radio.

5. In taking the measures called for in paragraphs 3 and 4 each State is required to conform to generally accepted international regulations, procedures and practices and to take any steps which may be necessary to secure their observance.

6. A State which has clear grounds to believe that proper jurisdiction and control with respect to a ship have not been exercised may report the facts to the flag State. Upon receiving such a report, the flag State shall investigate the matter and, if appropriate, take any action necessary to remedy the situation.

7. Each State shall cause an inquiry to be held by or before a suitably qualified person or persons into every marine casualty or incident of navigation on the high seas involving a ship flying its flag and causing loss of life or serious injury to nationals of another State or serious damage to ships or installations of another State or to the marine environment. The flag State and the other State shall co-operate in the conduct of any inquiry held by that other State into any such marine casualty or incident of navigation.

Notes
1. Ships are deemed to have a nationality for international law purposes.[2] Normally, a ship is registered under the law of a particular state and is then, under that state's law, both entitled to fly its flag and deemed to have its nationality. Before the *Nottebohm* case,[3] a ship's nationality thus accorded by a state by its unilateral decision was accepted in international law as being that of the ship for international law purposes such as jurisdiction and state responsibility.[4] As a result of the *Nottebohm* case, concerning the nationality of individuals for the purpose of diplomatic protection in international law, the International Law Commission inserted a "genuine link" requirement in its Draft Articles and the requirement was adopted at Geneva in Article 5 of the High Seas Convention, and is now included in Article 91, 1982 Convention.[5]

[2] See Myers, *The Nationality of Ships* (1967).
[3] See below, p. 588.
[4] See Watts (1957) 33 B.Y.I.L. 52.
[5] For criticism of Art. 5 because of the uncertainty, and hence the threat of instability, that it introduces into the law, see McDougal and Burke, *op. cit.*, p. 368, n. 1, above, Chap. 8.

2. The introduction of the "genuine link" requirement was prompted by the advent of "flags of convenience" or "open registry" states. Of these, Sørenson[6] writes:

> Owners register their ships in such countries for various reasons. Taxation is very low, or practically non-existent. Operating costs are lower because the legislation and collective agreements on wages, labour conditions, and social security of the traditionally maritime countries do not apply. Lack of adequate administrative machinery, especially inspection services, means that the countries concerned are unable to enforce effectively such laws and regulations as they may have enacted with respect to safety standards, accommodation and protection of crews, and so forth.

The leading "flags of convenience" states are Liberia and Panama, each of which has more registered tonnage (much of it Greek or U.S. beneficially owned) than the leading maritime powers.[7]

3. The reasons for concern about "flags of convenience" are (i) the abuse of the concept of nationality involved in a ship having a state's nationality for international law purposes regardless of the nationality of its owner, operator or crew; (ii) the reputation of the "flags of convenience" states for failing to enforce health and safety standards; and (iii) the fact that "the expansion of open-registry fleets has adversely affected the development and competitiveness of fleets of countries which do not offer open-registry facilities, including those of developing countries."[8] This last, economic reason led UNCTAD to sponsor the 1986 UN Convention on Conditions for Registration of Ships.[9] This requires a party to have a "competent and adequate national maritime administration" which must, *inter alia*, ensure that ships flying its flag comply with international rules concerning the safety of ships and marine pollution. A party must also (i) include in its register of shipping information identifying those owning and managing its ships and hence accountable for them; (ii) ensure that its nationals participate to a required degree in *either* the ownership *or* the manning of its ships; and (iii) ensure that those responsible for the management of its ships are able to meet operational financial obligations. These requirements are additional to those in Article 5, 1958 High Seas Convention and add an extra dimension to the concept of a genuine link. They nonetheless represent a compromise between the interests of developed and developing states, the Group of 77 states having argued, *inter alia*, for *both* ownership *and* manning obligations in the 1986 Convention.

4. The "genuine link" question did not attract much attention at UNCLOS III. The text of Article 5, 1958 Convention is retained in the 1982 Convention (Article 91(1)), and the concept of a "genuine link" is left undefined. However, Article 94, 1982 Convention imposes, in some detail, duties on the flag state in respect of "administrative, technical and social matters" and safety at sea.

5. Whether the "genuine link" requirement is a part of customary international law is unclear. The *travaux préparatoires* of the 1986 Registration Convention shows widespread support for it. However, Liberia—which like Panama, the other leading "flag of convenience" state, is not a party to the 1958 High Seas

---

[6] *loc. cit.*, p. 368, n. 9, pp. 202–203. See generally Bozcek, *Flags of Convenience* (1962) and Osieke (1979) 73 A.J.I.L. 604.

[7] For 1985 world tonnage figures, see (1986) 26 I.L.M. 1246.

[8] 1978 Resolution of an *ad hoc* intergovernmental working group of the UNCTAD Committee on Shipping, quoted in Marston (1986) 20 J.W.T.L. 576.

[9] (1987) 26 I.L.M. 1236. Not in force. The Convention requires 40 parties with 25 per cent of the world's tonnage to enter into force. 11 parties. The U.K. is not a party. On the Convention generally, see Bettink (1987) 18 N.Y.I.L. 69; Egiyan (1988) 12 Mar. Pol. 314; Marston, *loc. cit.*, n. 8, above.

Convention or the 1982 Convention—has asserted that "[a]ny limitation on the rights of states to determine the conditions under which vessels should be accepted on national shipping registers would be contrary to customary international law."[10] There are also different views on the part of the Group of 77 and western states as to what a "genuine link" is.

6. In its advisory opinion in the *IMCO* case,[11] the International Court of Justice advised that the term "largest ship-owning nations" in the IMCO Constitution (Article 28(*a*)) referred to registered tonnage and not beneficially owned tonnage. On this basis, it advised that Liberia and Panama should have been elected to membership of the Maritime Safety Committee of IMCO. The Court limited itself to the particular issue of treaty interpretation before it and did not consider the question of the nationality of ships and flags of convenience generally.

7. A different kind of "flag of convenience" emerged in the context of the Iran-Iraq War, in response to the danger to shipping in the Persian Gulf,[12] when Kuwaiti tankers were re-registered under the U.K. and U.S. flags to benefit from the protection of the U.K. and U.S. naval presence in the Gulf.[13]

8. A ship is not prohibited from sailing without a flag. If it does so, however, it is, for the purpose of protection at least, treated as the equivalent of a stateless person. Thus, in *Naim Molvan v. Att.-Gen. for Palestine*,[14] the Judicial Committee of the Privy Council stated,

> No question of comity nor of any breach of international law can arise if there is no State under whose flag the vessel sails.... having no [flag] ... the *Asya* could not claim the protection of any State nor could any State claim that any principle of international law was broken by her seizure.

Nonetheless the State of which the owner of a ship without a flag was a national could intervene on the ground of injury to a national's property.[15]

(iii) JURISDICTION ON THE HIGH SEAS[16]

CONVENTION ON THE LAW OF THE SEA 1982

UN Doc. A/CONF. 62/122; (1982) 21 I.L.M. 1261

Article 95

Warships[17] on the high seas have complete immunity from the jurisdiction of any State other than the flag State.

Article 96

Ships owned or operated by a State and used only on government non-commercial service shall, on the high seas, have complete immunity from the jurisdiction of any State other than the flag State.

[10] UN Doc. TD/RS/CONF/15, pp. 7–8, quoted in Marston, *loc. cit.*, p. 425, n. 8, above, p. 578.
[11] I.C.J. Rep. 1960, p. 150.
[12] As to the War, see below, p. 899.
[13] See Gray (1988) 37 I.C.L.Q. 420 at 424.
[14] [1948] A.C. 351 at 369–370.
[15] See below, Chap. 8.
[16] See Van Zwanenberg (1961) 10 I.C.L.Q. 785.
[17] *Ed.* For the definition of a "warship", see Art. 29, 1982 Convention, above, p. 400.

Article 97

1. In the event of a collision or any other incident of navigation concerning a ship on the high seas, involving the penal or disciplinary responsibility of the master or of any other person in the service of the ship, no penal or disciplinary proceedings may be instituted against such person except before the judicial or administrative authorities either of the flag State or of the State of which such person is a national.

2. In disciplinary matters, the State which has issued a master's certificate or a certificate of competence or licence shall alone be competent, after due legal process, to pronounce the withdrawal of such certificates, even if the holder is not a national of the State which issued them.

3. No arrest or detention of the ship, even as a measure of investigation, shall be ordered by any authorities other than those of the flag State.

Article 98

1. Every State shall require the master of a ship flying its flag, in so far as he can do so without serious danger to the ship, the crew or the passengers:

(a) to render assistance to any person found at sea in danger of being lost;

(b) to proceed with all possible speed to the rescue of persons in distress, if informed of their need of assistance, in so far as such action may reasonably be expected of him;

(c) after a collision, to render assistance to the other ship, its crew and its passengers and, where possible, to inform the other ship of the name of his own ship, its port of registry and the nearest port at which it will call.

2. Every coastal State shall promote the establishment, operation and maintenance of an adequate and effective search and rescue service regarding safety on and over the sea and, where circumstances so require, by way of mutual regional arrangements co-operate with neighbouring States for this purpose.

Article 99

Every State shall take effective measures to prevent and punish the transport of slaves in ships authorized to fly its flag and to prevent the unlawful use of its flag for that purpose. Any slave taking refuge on board any ship, whatever its flag, shall *ipso facto* be free.

Article 100

All States shall co-operate to the fullest possible extent in the repression of piracy on the high seas or in any other place outside the jurisdiction of any State.

Article 101

Piracy consists of any of the following acts:

(a) any illegal acts of violence or detention, or any act of depredation, committed for private ends by the crew or the passengers of a private ship or a private aircraft, and directed:
  (i) on the high seas against another ship or aircraft, or against persons or property on board such ship or aircraft;
  (ii) against a ship, aircraft, persons or property in a place outside the jurisdiction of any State;
(b) any act of voluntary participation in the operation of a ship or of an aircraft with knowledge of facts making it a pirate ship or aircraft;
(c) any act of inciting or of intentionally facilitating an act described in sub-paragraph (a) or (b).

Article 102

The acts of piracy, as defined in Article 101, committed by a warship, government ship or government aircraft whose crew has mutinied and taken control of the ship or aircraft are assimilated to acts committed by a private ship or aircraft.

Article 103

A ship or aircraft is considered a pirate ship or aircraft if it is intended by the persons in dominant control to be used for the purpose of committing one of the acts referred to in Article 101. The same applies if the ship or aircraft has been used to commit any such act, so long as it remains under the control of the persons guilty of that act.

Article 104

A ship or aircraft may retain its nationality although it has become a pirate ship or aircraft. The retention or loss of nationality is determined by the law of the State from which such nationality was derived.

Article 105

On the high seas, or in any other place outside the jurisdiction of any State, every State may seize a pirate ship or aircraft, or a ship or aircraft taken by piracy and under the control of pirates, and arrest the persons and seize the property on board. The courts of the State which carried out the seizure may decide upon the penalties to be imposed, and may also determine the action to be taken with regard to the ships, aircraft or property, subject to the rights of third parties acting in good faith.

Article 106

Where the seizure of a ship or aircraft on suspicion of piracy has been effected without adequate grounds, the State making the seizure shall be liable to the State the nationality of which is possessed by the ship or aircraft for any loss or damage caused by the seizure.

Article 107

A seizure on account of piracy may be carried out only by warships or military aircraft, or other ships or aircraft clearly marked and identifiable as being on government service and authorized to that effect.

Article 108

1. All States shall co-operate in the suppression of illicit traffic in narcotic drugs and psychotropic substances engaged in by ships on the high seas contrary to international conventions.

2. Any State which has reasonable grounds for believing that a ship flying its flag is engaged in illicit traffic in narcotic drugs or psychotropic substances may request the co-operation of other States to suppress such traffic.

Article 109

1. All States shall co-operate in the suppression of unauthorized broadcasting from the high seas.

2. For the purposes of this Convention, "unauthorized broadcasting" means the transmission of sound radio or television broadcasts from a ship or installation on the high seas intended for reception by the general public contrary to international regulations, but excluding the transmission of distress calls.

3. Any person engaged in unauthorized broadcasting may be prosecuted before the court of:

(a) the flag State of the ship;
(b) the State of registry of the installation;
(c) the State of which the person is a national;
(d) any State where the transmissions can be received; or
(e) any State where authorized radio communication is suffering interference.

4. On the high seas, a State having jurisdiction in accordance with paragraph 3 may, in conformity with Article 110, arrest any person or ship engaged in unauthorized broadcasting and seize the broadcasting apparatus.

Article 110

1. Except where acts of interference derive from powers conferred by treaty, a warship which encounters on the high seas a foreign ship, other than a ship entitled to complete immunity in accordance with Articles 95 and 96, is not justified in boarding it unless there is reasonable ground for suspecting that;

(*a*) the ship is engaged in piracy;
(*b*) the ship is engaged in the slave trade;
(*c*) the ship is engaged in unauthorized broadcasting and the flag State of the warship has jurisdiction under Article 109;
(*d*) the ship is without nationality; or
(*e*) though flying a foreign flag or refusing to show its flag, the ship is, in reality, of the same nationality as the warship.

2. In the cases provided for in paragraph 1, the warship may proceed to verify the ship's right to fly its flag. To this end, it may send a boat under the command of an officer to the suspected ship. If suspicion remains after the documents have been checked, it may proceed to a further examination on board the ship, which must be carried out with all possible consideration.

3. If the suspicions prove to be unfounded, and provided that the ship boarded has not committed any act justifying them, it shall be compensated for any loss or damage that may have been sustained.

4. These provisions apply *mutatis mutandis* to military aircraft.

5. These provisions also apply to any other duly authorized ships or aircraft clearly marked and identifiable as being on government service.

Notes
1. The basic principle of customary international law that "vessels on the high seas are subject to no authority except that of the State whose flag they fly" is stated and elaborated upon by the Permanent Court of International Justice in the *Lotus* case.[18] Articles 95 and 96, 1982 Convention[19] contain rules on the immunity of warships and other state ships not used for commercial purposes. Some exceptions to the exclusive administrative jurisdiction of the flag state on the high seas exist. Smith comments on them as follows:

---

[18] See above, p. 267.
[19] These are identical to Arts. 8(1) and 9, 1958 High Seas Convention.

The right of any ship to fly a particular flag must obviously be subject to verification by proper authority, and from this it follows that warships have a general right to verify the nationality of any merchant ship, which they may meet on the high seas. This "right of approach" (*vérification du pavillon* or *reconnaissance*) is the only qualification under customary law of the general principle which forbids any interference in time of peace with ships of another nationality upon the high seas. Any other act of interference (apart from the repression of piracy) must be justified under powers conferred by treaty. Provided that the merchant vessel responds by showing her flag the captain of the warship is not justified in boarding her or taking any further action, unless there is reasonable ground for suspecting that she is engaged in piracy or some other improper activity . . . In the past the question of the right of approach has been the subject of some controversy and has occasionally given rise to friction. Under modern conditions the general use of wireless and other developments have made the matter one of very small importance.[20]

Slavery is not mentioned by Smith and it would seem that, subject to the effect of Article 110, 1982 Convention, customary international law gives no powers over foreign ships on the high seas in respect of it.[21] The 1982 Convention adds to the list of situations in which a right of visit is permitted by Article 22, High Seas Convention, cases in which there are reasonable grounds to suspect that the ship is operating a private radio station or is without a nationality (Article 110(1)(c), (d)). The 1982 Convention (Article 110(4), (5)) also allows the right of visit to be carried out *mutatis mutandis* by "military aircraft" and by "any other duly authorised ships or aircraft clearly marked and identifiable as being on government service." On the coastal state's right to visit ships in the exclusive economic zone under Article 73, 1982 Convention, see below, p. 451. Other customary international law powers exist under the doctrines of hot pursuit[22] and the contiguous zone[23] and, possibly, for the purpose of self-defence[24] or to deal with marine casualties threatening pollution.[25] As far as treaty exceptions are concerned, treaty powers of jurisdiction exist for the parties *inter se* in respect, *inter alia*, of fishing practices and conservation[26] and of interference with submarine cables.[27] The severe penalty in Article 110(3), 1982 Convention, which probably reflects customary international law,[28] was thought by the International Law Commission to be "justified in order to prevent the right of visit being abused."[29]

2. *Penal Jurisdiction in Collisions*. Article 97, 1982 Convention, which conflicts with the decision in the *Lotus Case*,[30] probably states the customary international law rule.

---

[20] *The Law and Custom of the Sea* (3rd ed., 1959), pp. 64–65.

[21] See Colombos, *loc. cit.*, p. 368, n. 1, above, pp. 457–463. On the uncertain position under the treaties on slavery, see Gutteridge (1957) 6 I.C.L.Q. 449.

[22] See below, p. 437.

[23] See below, p. 433.

[24] See below, p. 901.

[25] See Smith, *op. cit.*, p. 368, n. 1, pp. 221–222.

[26] See, *e.g.* Canada-U.S. Convention for the Preservation of the Halibut Fishery of the North Pacific Ocean and the Bering Sea 1953, Art. II, U.S.T.I.A.S. 2900.

[27] See, *e.g.* Convention for the Protection of Submarine Cables 1884, Article X, 75 B.F.S.P. 356; 2 Malloy 1949.

[28] See Smith, *op. cit.*, n. 20, above, p. 65.

[29] Y.B.I.L.C., 1956, II, p. 284.

[30] See above, p. 267. Essentially the same rule as that in Art. 97 is included in the Brussels Convention on Penal Jurisdiction in Matters of Collision 1952, Art. 1, U.K.T.S. 47 (1960); Cmnd. 1128; 429 U.N.T.S. 233; (1959) 53 A.J.I.L. 536. Art. 97 reproduces verbatim Art. 11, 1958 High Seas Convention.

3. *Piracy*.[31] Articles 100–107, 1982 Convention repeat the rules on piracy in Articles 14–21, 1958 High Seas Convention. There is doubt as to the customary international law definition of piracy *jure gentium*. Oppenheim[32] writes:

> Piracy, in its original and strict meaning, is every unauthorised act of violence committed by a private vessel on the high seas against another vessel with intent to plunder (*animo furandi*) . . . Piracy *jure gentium* is to be distinguished from some acts which particular municipal laws may denominate as piracy, "and which therefore are not of universal cognizance, so as to be punishable by all nations". There has been dispute as to what other possible cases, which are not covered by the original conception, may be treated as piracy. Earlier editions of the present work offered a definition which really covers all such acts as are in practice treated as piratical: *every unauthorised act of violence against persons or goods committed on the open sea either by a private vessel against another vessel or by the mutinous crew or passengers against their own vessel.*
>
> Nowadays, however, the definition of piracy *jure gentium* in Article 15 of the Geneva Convention on the High Seas 1958, based as it was on the work of the International Law Commission, and now confirmed and repeated word for word in the Convention on the Law of the Sea 1982, must be regarded as having great authority.

Article 101, 1982 Convention requires two ships, but not an intent to plunder; any "private ends" are sufficient. The precise role of piracy *jure gentium* is also uncertain. According to one view, piracy is a crime under international law in respect of which all states are allowed jurisdiction.[33] According to another view, there is no international crime of piracy; instead international law authorises states to exercise criminal jurisdiction under their municipal law on a universality basis in respect of acts which come within the definition of *piracy jure gentium*.[34] A state may define piracy differently in its municipal law (*e.g.* the United Kingdom includes slave trading on the high seas[35] and acts committed in the territorial sea[36]) from piracy *jure gentium*. It will, however, have the special jurisdiction allowed by international law only in respect of acts amounting to piracy *jure gentium*.

In its Commentary on its Draft Articles, the International Law Commission states that by "place outside the jurisdiction of any state" in what is now Article 100, 1982 Convention, it "had chiefly in mind acts committed by a ship or aircraft on an island constituting *terra nullius* or on the shores of an unoccupied territory.[37] The extension of the crime to cover aircraft is an instance of "progressive development" of the law. Article 101 does not cover the hijacking of aircraft by the passengers or crew of the hijacked aircraft.

In the *Santa Maria Incident*,[38] in 1961, a Portuguese passenger vessel called the *Santa Maria* was seized in the Atlantic on the high seas by armed men who had boarded it as passengers. One member of the crew was killed and others injured. The men were supporters of General Delgado, a political opponent of President Salazar of Portugal. The ship was eventually handed over to Brazil and returned

---

[31] See Birnie (1987) 11 Mar. Pol. 163; Dubner, *The Law of International Sea Piracy* (1980); Johnson (1957) 43 Trans.Grot.Soc. 63; and Symposium articles in (1990–91) 21 Cal.W.I.L.J. 104.

[32] Oppenheim, Vol. I, pp. 746–747. *Footnotes omitted.*

[33] See, *e.g.* 2 Moore 951. On international crimes, see below, p. 738.

[34] See, *e.g.* Schwarzenberger (1950) 3 C.L.P. 263.

[35] Slave Trade Act 1824, s.9. And see *Cameron v. H.M. Advocate* (1871) S.C. 50.

[36] *Athens Maritime Enterprises Corpn. v. Hellenic Mutual War Risks Assn Ltd* [1983] Q.B. 647.

[37] Y.B.I.L.C., 1956, II, p. 282.

[38] 4 Whiteman 665.

to Portugal. The men were given political asylum by Brazil. Were they pirates?[39]

In a similar incident in 1985, the *Achille Lauro*,[40] an Italian liner, was seized in Port Said beyond the limit of Egyptian territorial waters by PLO hijackers on board as passengers. The crew and passengers were held hostage and a Jewish U.S. national among the passengers was killed when demands for the release of Palestinian prisoners held by Israel were not met. Later, an Egyptian civil aircraft carrying the hijackers to Tunis was intercepted by a U.S. military aircraft over the high seas in the Mediterranean and forced to land in Italy. The hijackers were handed over to the Italian authorities and convicted of terrorist offences in the Italian courts. In response to the *Achille Lauro* Incident, the 1988 IMO Convention on the Suppression of Unlawful Acts against the Safety of Maritime Navigation[41] was adopted. This, *inter alia*, makes it an offence to seize control of a ship by the use or threat of force where the ship "is navigating . . . through . . . waters beyond the limit of the territorial sea." (Articles 3–4). In accordance with the now familiar pattern as to jurisdiction, the parties are obliged to consider prosecution of, or whether to extradite, offenders found on their territory.

4. *Pirate Radio Stations*.[42] Article 109, 1982 Convention gives wide powers of enforcement jurisdiction over pirate radio stations on the high seas. See also the European Agreement for the Prevention of Broadcasting from Stations outside National Waters 1965[43] which permits the exercise of criminal jurisdiction but does not give a right to visit.

(iv) THE CONTIGUOUS ZONE[44]

CONVENTION ON THE LAW OF THE SEA 1982

UN Doc. A/CONF. 62/122; (1982) 21 I.L.M. 1261

Article 33

1. In a zone contiguous to its territorial sea, described as the contiguous zone, the coastal State may exercise the control necessary to:

(a) prevent infringement of its customs, fiscal, immigration or sanitary laws and regulations within its territory or territorial sea;

---

[39] See Franck (1961) 36 N.Y.U.L.R. 839, reprinted in Mueller and Wise, *International Criminal Law* (1965), p. 218, and Green (1961) 37 B.Y.I.L. 496.

[40] See Green, in Dinstein, ed., *International Law in a Time of Perplexity: Essays in Honour of Shabtai Rosenne* (1989), p. 249; Halberstam (1988) 82 A.J.I.L. 269; Paust (1987) 20 Vand. J.T.L. 235; note (1986) 26 Virg. J.I.L. 723.

[41] (1988) 27 I.L.M. 668. In force 1992. 23 parties, including the U.K. The Convention was accompanied by a 1988 Protocol for the Suppression of Unlawful Acts against the Safety of Fixed Platforms Located on the Continental Shelf, *ibid.*, p. 685. In force 1992. 21 parties, including the U.K. See Freestone (1988) 3 I.J.E.C.L. 305.

[42] See Hunnings (1965) 14 I.C.L.Q. 410; Van Panhuys and Van Emde Boas (1966) 60 A.J.I.L. 303; Woodliffe (1986) 1 I.J.E.C.L. 402.

[43] E.T.S. No. 53; 634 U.N.T.S. 239; U.K.T.S. 1 (1968), Cmnd. 1497. In force 1967. 17 parties, including the U.K.

[44] See Fitzmaurice, *loc. cit.*, p. 368, n. 9, above, p. 108; Lowe (1981) 52 B.Y.I.L. 109; Oda (1962) 11 I.C.L.Q. 131.

(b) punish infringement of the above laws and regulations committed within its territory or territorial sea.

2. The contiguous zone may not extend beyond 24 nautical miles from the baselines from which the breadth of the territorial sea is measured.

Notes
1. The 1982 Convention (Article 33) retains the contiguous zone and gives coastal states the same powers as they have under Article 24, 1958 Territorial Sea Convention, except that the contiguous zone can be used to control traffic in archeological and historical objects found at sea by virtue of Article 303(2), 1982 Convention:

> In order to control traffic in such objects, the coastal state may, in applying article 33, presume that their removal from the sea-bed in the zone referred to in that article without its approval would result in an infringement within its territory or territorial sea of the laws and regulations referred to in that article.

The zone may, however, extend to 24 miles from the territorial sea baseline, instead of 12 miles which is the 1958 Convention limit. In the 12 miles beyond the limit of a 12 miles territorial sea, therefore, a coastal state may exercise powers that are additional to those (applying to different kinds of activities) that exist under the exclusive economic zone régime in the 1982 Convention.[45]

2. The International Law Commission's Commentary on its Draft Articles reads:

> (1) International law accords States the right to exercise preventative or protective control for certain purposes over a belt of the high seas contiguous to their territorial sea. It is of course, understood that this power of control does not change the legal status of the waters over which it is exercised. These waters are and remain a part of the high seas and are not subject to the sovereignty of the coastal State, which can exercise over them only such rights as are conferred on it by the present draft or are derived from international treaties.

> (2) Many States have adopted the principle that in the contiguous zone the coastal State may exercise customs control in order to prevent attempted infringements of its customs and fiscal regulations within its territory or territorial sea, and to punish infringements of those regulations committed within its territory or territorial sea. The Commission considered that it would be impossible to deny to States the exercise of such rights.

> (3) Although the number of States which claim rights over the contiguous zone for the purpose of applying sanitary regulations is fairly small, the Commission considers that, in view of the connexion between customs and sanitary regulations, such rights should also be recognised for sanitary regulations.

> (4) The Commission did not recognise special security rights in the contiguous zone. It considered that the extreme vagueness of the term "security" would open the way for abuses and that the granting of such rights was not necessary. The enforcement of customs and sanitary regulations will be sufficient in most cases to safeguard the security of the State. In so far as measures of self-defence against an imminent and direct threat to the security of the State

---

[45] See below, p. 446. The contiguous zone and the exclusive economic zone physically overlap.

are concerned, the Commission refers to the general principles of international law and the Charter of the United Nations.

(5) Nor was the Commission willing to recognise any exclusive rights of the coastal State to engage in fishing in the contiguous zone. The Preparatory Committee of the Hague Codification Conference found, in 1930, that the replies from Governments offered no prospect of an agreement to extend the exclusive fishing rights of the coastal State beyond the territorial sea. The Commission considered that in that respect the position has not changed.[46]

A proposal at Geneva to add "and violations of security" to Article 24(1)(a), 1958 Convention was defeated.[47] A number of states have nonetheless established security zones, apparently without protest from other states.[48] On the right of self-defence, see below. Note in this connection the practice of some states of having an aircraft carrier or other warship stationed offshore on the high seas as a "reminder" to a coastal state of its interest in events taking place within it. On the use of spy ships, see note 4, below. The reference to immigration regulations was added at Geneva. The International Law Commission had thought it unsupported by state practice and otherwise undesirable.[49] It also thought that the reference to sanitary regulations would cover immigration so far as the latter related to questions of public health.[50]

In *U.S. v. Fishing Vessel Taiyo Maru No. 28*,[51] in which a Japanese ship was found fishing illegally in the United States exclusive fishing zone nine miles offshore and beyond the United States territorial sea limit, it was held that the list of purposes in Article 24 for which a contiguous zone may be established is not exhaustive[52]:

Article 24 . . . is permissive, rather than restrictive. It provides that a coastal state "may" establish a contiguous zone for the purposes of enforcing its customs, fiscal, immigration or sanitary regulations. Although Article 24 only affirmatively recognises the right of a coastal state to create a contiguous zone for one of the four enumerated purposes, nothing in the Article precludes the establishment of such a zone for other purposes, including the enforcement of domestic fisheries law.

3. Article 33(1)(b), which gives enforcement jurisdiction to the coastal state after an offence has been committed in its territory or territorial sea, clearly must be read as giving a power of arrest. Does Article 33(1)(a), which applies before an offence is committed, do so too? Shearer states[53]:

Since laws on the substantive subjects of customs, fiscal, immigration and sanitary matters cannot be applied to the contiguous zone, it follows that an offence cannot be committed until the boundary of territorial waters is crossed by inward-bound ships. "Control" therefore must be limited to such measures as inspections and warnings, and cannot include arrest or forcible taking into port. It is arguable, however, and probably sustainable on the history of the British Hovering Acts and similar legislation elsewhere, that a coastal State

[46] Y.B.I.L.C., 1956, II, pp. 294–295.
[47] *1958 Sea Conference Records*, Vol. II, p. 40. See also *ibid.* p. 117.
[48] See Churchill and Lowe, *op. cit.*, p. 368, n. 1. above, p. 117, and Appendix, who list 11 states with security zones.
[49] Y.B.I.L.C. 1956, II, pp. 76–78.
[50] *ibid.*
[51] 395 F.Supp. 413 (D.Me. 1975). See Fidell (1976) 70 A.J.I.L. 95.
[52] 395 F.Supp. 419.
[53] (1986) 35 I.C.L.Q. 320 at 330. For other views, see Fitzmaurice, *loc. cit.*, p. 368, n. 9, above, pp. 113–115 and McDougal and Burke, *op. cit.*, p. 368, n. 1, above, pp. 621–630.

might lawfully legislate to make it an offence to hover or to trans-ship dutiable cargoes in the contiguous zone and to carry out an arrest there because these activities are within the connotations of "prevention."[54]

4. On January 23, 1968, the *Pueblo*, a U.S. "Navy intelligence collection auxiliary ship," was ordered to heave to by North Korean patrol ships off the coast of North Korea.[55] It was boarded and escorted into Wonsan. In December 1968, the crew of the *Pueblo* were returned to the U.S. after detention without trial and after the U.S. had signed a document indicating that the *Pueblo* had been spying in North Korean territorial waters.[56] The body of the crew member who had died after being injured in the struggle during the capture of the *Pueblo* was also returned. Earlier, in February 1968, Secretary of State Rusk had sent this telegram to all U.S. diplomatic posts:

> The ship was seized slightly more than 15 miles from the nearest land, Ung Do Island, which lies slightly seaward of a straight line across the mouth of Wonsan Bay. The geographic situation of Wonsan Bay is such as to warrant treating the bay as internal waters. The outer limits of the territorial waters would, therefore, be measured from a straight line across the mouth of Wonsan Bay or from Ung Do Island, to the extent measurement from the island increases the area within the territorial sea. . . .
>
> The United States Government has no official information concerning breadth of territorial sea claimed by North Korea, but we assume it claims 12 miles in line with claims of most other communist countries and in view of the position it took in the 1953 armistice talks. . . .
>
> The *Pueblo* was a commissioned vessel of the United States Navy and therefore entitled to the immunities recognised by article eight of the 1958 convention on the high seas.[57] Absolute immunity from any jurisdiction other than that of the flag state is, of course, the traditional rule of international law, and the fact that North Korea is not a party to the 1958 convention is irrelevant.
>
> The United States Government recognises only the three-mile limit, North Korea has never alleged that the *Pueblo* was within three miles of the North Korean coast. Thus from the United States view of international law even if the Pueblo had been at the position alleged by North Korea (7·1 miles offshore), it would still have been on the high seas. Nonetheless, the Pueblo was under orders to stay at least 13 miles from North Korea, *i.e.* at least one mile beyond waters presumably claimed by North Korea.
>
> Even if the *Pueblo* had been in the territorial waters of North Korea, its seizure would have been improper. On numerous occasions similar Soviet ships have intruded into United States territorial waters; we have warned them to leave and, when appropriate, have submitted protest through diplomatic channels. In the absence of immediate threat of armed attack (the *Pueblo* was armed with only two machine guns), escorting foreign naval vessels out of territorial waters is the strongest action a coastal state should take. The seizure of foreign war ships or other attacks upon them are much too dangerous and provocative acts to be permitted by international law. This restriction on the use of force by a coastal state is set forth in article 23 of the 1958

---

[54] O'Connell, *op. cit.*, p. 368, n. 1, above, . . . Vol II, at p. 1060.
[55] For the facts, see *Keesings Archives*, p. 23120A. See also Butler (1969) 63 Proc.A.S.I.L. 7 and Rubin (1969) 18 I.C.L.Q. 961.
[56] See (1969) 8 I.L.M. 199. This admission was later retracted; *ibid.*
[57] *Ed.* Or Art. 8, see above, p. 406, n. 4.

convention on the territorial sea, which authorises, as the sole remedy, requiring a war ship to leave the territorial sea.[58]

Had North Korea violated international law? Had the U.S.?

5. In 1994, 43 states claimed 24 mile contiguous zones; another eight states claimed such a zone less than 24 miles in width; and Syria claimed a 41 mile zone.[59] The U.K. does not claim a contiguous zone. Would the exercise of any powers justified by Article 33 be regarded as lawful in U.K. law by a British court without legislation?[60]

(v) Hot Pursuit[61]

THE I'M ALONE[62]

Canada *v.* United States

Interim and Final Reports of a Joint Commission. 1933 and 1935. (1935) 3 R.I.A.A. 1609; 29 A.J.I.L. 326

In 1929, the *I'm Alone*, a British schooner registered in Canada was ordered to heave to by the *Wolcott*, a United States coastguard vessel, on suspicion of smuggling liquor at the time of prohibition in the United States when, according to the United States, she was 10 miles off the Louisiana coast. She fled and was pursued by the *Wolcott* and, after the *Wolcott's* gun had jammed, by the *Dexter*, a second United States coastguard vessel. The *Dexter* and the *Wolcott* caught up with the *I'm Alone* more than 200 miles off the coast of the United States. When the *I'm Alone* refused to heave to, she was fired upon by the *Dexter* and sunk. The gunfire was aimed first above the water line. Later it was aimed below it. The boatswain died and the schooner's cargo was lost. The United States justified its action under the 1924 Convention between the United States and Great Britain by which the latter agreed "to raise no objection to the boarding of private vessels under the British flag outside the limits of territorial waters by the authorities of the United States" in order to check liquor smuggling. The power was not to be "exercised at a greater distance from the coast of the United States than can be traversed in one hour by the vessel suspected. . . . " Certain questions were put to two Commissioners appointed under the 1924 Convention.

Joint Interim Report of the Commissioners

The first question is whether the Commissioners may enquire into the beneficial or ultimate ownership of the *I'm Alone* or of the shares of the corporation that owned the ship. If the Commissioners are authorised to make this enquiry, a further question arises as to the effect of indirect ownership and control by citizens of the United States upon the Claim;

---

[58] (1968) 62 A.J.I.L. 756.

[59] Syria claims a 35 mile territorial sea. For these figures, see *Law of the Sea Bulletin, loc. cit.,* p. 368, n. 1, above, No. 25, p. 104.

[60] See *R. v. Keyn,* above, p. 75.

[61] See Allen (1989) 20 O.D.I.L. 309; Poulantzas, *The Right of Hot Pursuit in International Law* (1969) and Williams (1939) 20 B.Y.I.L. 83.

[62] See Fitzmaurice (1936) 17 B.Y.I.L. 82; and Reuland (1993) 33 Virg.J.I.L. 556.

viz., whether it would be an answer to the Claim under the Convention, or whether it would go to mitigation of damages, or whether it would merely be a circumstance that should actuate the claimant Government in refraining from pressing the claim, in whole or in part. . . .

The Commissioners think they may enquire into the beneficial or ultimate ownership of the *I'm Alone* and of the shares of the corporation owning the ship; as well as into the management and control of the ship and the venture in which it was engaged; and that this may be done as a basis for considering the recommendations which they shall make. But the Commissioners reserve for further consideration the extent to which, if at all, the facts of such ownership, management and control may effect particular branches or phases of the claim presented.

The second question relates to the right of hot pursuit. Further, it has two aspects, and it is based upon the assumption that the averments in the Answer [of the United States] with regard to the location and speed of the *I'm Alone* are true. The question in its first aspect is whether the Government of the United States under the Convention has the right of hot pursuit where the offending vessel is within an hour's sailing distance of the shore at the commencement of the pursuit and beyond that distance at its termination. The question in its second aspect is whether the Government of the United States has the right of hot pursuit of a vessel when the pursuit commenced within the distance of 12 miles established by the revenue laws of the United States and was terminated on the high seas beyond that distance . . .

As respects the question in its first aspect . . . the Commissioners are as yet not in agreement as to the proper answer, nor have they reached a final disagreement on the matter. The Commissioners, therefore, suggest that the proceeding go forward. . . .

The question in its second aspect need not be answered because the Government of the United States has now withdrawn so much of its answer as led to the propounding of that aspect of the question.

The third question is based upon the assumption that the United States Government had the right of hot pursuit in the circumstances and was entitled to exercise the rights under Article II of the Convention at the time when the *Dexter* joined the *Wolcott* in the pursuit of the *I'm Alone*. It is also based upon the assumption that the averments set forth in paragraph eight of the Answer are true. The question is whether, in the circumstances, the Government of the United States was legally justified in sinking the *I'm Alone*. . . .

On the assumptions stated in the question, the United States might, consistently with the Convention, use necessary and reasonable force for the purpose of effecting the objects of boarding, searching, seizing and bringing into port the suspected vessel; and if sinking should occur incidentally, as a result of the exercise of necessary and reasonable force for such purpose, the pursuing vessel might be entirely blameless. But the Commissioners think that, in the circumstances stated in paragraph eight of the Answer, the admittedly intentional sinking of the suspected vessel was not justified by anything in the Convention. . . .

Joint Final Report of the Commissioners

By their interim report the Commissioners found that the sinking of the vessel was not justified by anything in the Convention. The Commission now add that it could not be justified by any principle of international law. . . .

We find as a fact that, from September, 1928, down to the date when she was sunk, the *I'm Alone*, although a British ship of Canadian registry, was *de facto* owned, controlled, and at the critical times, managed, and her movements directed and her cargo dealt with and disposed of, by a group of persons acting in concert who were entirely, or nearly so, citizens of the United States, and who employed her for the purposes mentioned.[63] The possibility that one of the group may not have been of United States nationality we regard as of no importance in the circumstances of this case.

The Commissioners consider that, in view of the facts, no compensation ought to be paid in respect of the loss of the ship or the cargo.

The act of sinking the ship, however, by officers of the United States Coast Guard, was as we have already indicated, an unlawful act; and the Commissioners consider that the United States ought formally to acknowledge its illegality, and to apologise to His Majesty's Canadian Government therefor; and further, that as a material amend in respect of the wrong the United States should pay the sum of $25,000 to His Majesty's Canadian Government; and they recommend accordingly.

The Commissioners have had under consideration the compensation which ought to be paid by the United States to His Majesty's Canadian Government for the benefit of the captain and members of the crew, none of whom was a party to the illegal conspiracy to smuggle liquor into the United States and sell the same there. The Commissioners recommend that [a further sum of approximately $25,000] compensation be paid [under this heading]. . . .

Notes
McNair states:

> [The British Law Officers] have repeatedly affirmed the right of "hot pursuit" of a ship which has committed an offence within territorial waters. The pursuit must be hot, that is, immediate, and it may even begin when the offending ship has reached the high seas.[64]

On this last point, McNair quotes an Opinion of 1891 as follows:

[63] *Ed.* They were in fact led by one Hogan, a notorious New York gangster who was subsequently imprisoned under the U.S. liquor laws.
[64] 1 McNair 253.

In order to justify a seizure beyond the territorial waters it is necessary that the pursuit should have been undertaken immediately on the commission of the offence. In most cases it is obvious that such pursuit will, in fact, have been begun within the territorial waters. But cases may occur in which, though the offence was committed just within the limits of the territorial waters, the offender passed these limits before the pursuing vessel actually started in pursuit. It is a question of fact in each case whether the pursuit can fairly be described as immediate. If it were, a seizure in the open sea would not be unlawful, because, during the brief period that elapsed before the pursuing vessel got actually under way, the offender succeeded in passing out of the territorial water.[65]

On the degree of force that may be used to make an arrest, the Law Officers advised in 1852:

We conceive the use of fire-arms in the case in question to have been wholly unjustifiable; a Cruizer can almost always capture a boat without having recourse to Arms, and we are of opinion that firing in such a case could (if at all) be justified only where resistance was threatened or offered or where escape would otherwise have been imminent and that then it should have been such as to disable the boat without, if it can be avoided, risking life.[66]

The Preparatory Committee of the Hague Codification Conference 1930 stated:

With one exception, all the replies [of Governments] . . . recognise that a state is entitled to continue on the high seas a pursuit begun within its territorial waters. The only differences of opinion are as to whether the entry of the ship pursued into the territorial waters of another country merely suspends the pursuit or puts an end to it.[67]

CONVENTION ON THE LAW OF THE SEA 1982

UN Doc. A/CONF. 62/122; (1982) 21 I.L.M. 1261

Article 111

1. The hot pursuit of a foreign ship may be undertaken when the competent authorities of the coastal State have good reason to believe that the ship has violated the laws and regulations of that State. Such pursuit must be commenced when the foreign ship or one of its boats is within the internal waters, the archipelagic waters, the territorial sea or the contiguous zone of the pursuing State, and may only be continued outside the territorial sea or the contiguous zone if the pursuit has not been interrupted. It is not necessary that, at the time when the foreign ship within the territorial sea or the contiguous zone receives the order to stop, the ship giving the order should likewise be within the territorial sea or the contiguous zone. If the foreign ship is within a contiguous zone, as

---

[65] *ibid.* p. 255.
[66] *ibid.* pp. 253–254.
[67] L.N.Doc. C.74, M.39, 1939 V, p. 96.

defined in Article 33, the pursuit may only be undertaken if there has been a violation of the rights for the protection of which the zone was established.

2. The right of hot pursuit shall apply *mutatis mutandis* to violations in the exclusive economic zone or on the continental shelf, including safety zones around continental shelf installations, of the laws and regulations of the coastal State applicable in accordance with this Convention to the exclusive economic zone or the continental shelf, including such safety zones.

3. The right of hot pursuit ceases as soon as the ship pursued enters the territorial sea of its own State or of a third State.

4. Hot pursuit is not deemed to have begun unless the pursuing ship has satisfied itself by such practicable means as may be available that the ship pursued or one of its boats or other craft working as a team and using the ship pursued as a mother ship is within the limits of the territorial sea, or, as the case may be, within the contiguous zone or the exclusive economic zone or above the continental shelf. The pursuit may only be commenced after a visual or auditory signal to stop has been given at a distance which enables it to be seen or heard by the foreign ship.

5. The right of hot pursuit may be exercised only by warships or military aircraft, or other ships or aircraft clearly marked and identifiable as being on government service and authorized to that effect.

6. Where hot pursuit is effected by an aircraft:

(*a*) the provisions of paragraphs 1 to 4 shall apply *mutatis mutandis*;
(*b*) the aircraft giving the order to stop must itself actively pursue the ship until a ship or another aircraft of the coastal State, summoned by the aircraft, arrives to take over the pursuit, unless the aircraft is itself able to arrest the ship. It does not suffice to justify an arrest outside the territorial sea that the ship was merely sighted by the aircraft as an offender or suspected offender, if it was not both ordered to stop and pursued by the aircraft itself or other aircraft or ships which continue the pursuit without interruption.

7. The release of a ship arrested within the jurisdiction of a State and escorted to a port of that State for the purposes of an inquiry before the competent authorities may not be claimed solely on the ground that the ship, in the course of its voyage, was escorted across a portion of the exclusive economic zone or the high seas, if the circumstances rendered this necessary.

8. Where a ship has been stopped or arrested outside the territorial sea in circumstances which do not justify the exercise of the right of hot pursuit, it shall be compensated for any loss or damage that may have been thereby sustained.

Notes

1. The 1982 Convention repeats Article 23, High Seas Convention with alterations to allow for the right of hot pursuit in cases of violations of the coastal state's law and regulations applicable to the exclusive economic zone or continental shelf where the violations occur in or on those places (Article 111(2)). It also permits hot pursuit where the ship is in archipelagic waters (Article 111(1)). In the 1982 Convention, "other ships or aircraft" in government service must be "clearly marked and identifiable" as such, as well as "authorised", to exercise the right of hot pursuit.

2. Does "ship" in Article 111(1) include warship?[68] Can the hot pursuit of a ship be undertaken under the Convention when the violation of the local law has occurred not in the current passage but on some previous one? Can it be undertaken under the Convention where a violation is not by the ship but by a crew member or passenger on board? Note that a signal to stop made by radio is not sufficient for the purpose of Article 111(4). The International Law Commission stated:

> To prevent abuse, the Commission declined to admit orders given by wireless, as these could be given at any distance.[69]

This, it would seem, prevents a "signal" being given by radio after a ship has been detected by radar and hence may allow a ship which itself has radar sufficient time after detecting a coastguard or similar vessel by radar to escape to a place where hot pursuit cannot begin before a "signal" beginning it can be given.[70] See now, however, *R. v. Mills*, below, p. 443, which supposes that custom has changed.

3. In *U.S. v. Fishing Vessel Taiyo Maru No. 28*,[71] a Japanese ship found fishing illegally nine miles offshore in the U.S. exclusive fishing zone was pursued by United States coastguard vessels and seized some 68 miles off land on the high seas. The Court held that "neither the language nor the history of the [1958] Conventions shows that the signatory parties intended to limit the right of a coastal state to . . . conduct hot pursuit from . . . [an exclusive fishing] zone." See now the right of hot pursuit in respect of the exclusive economic zone (next note). For those states, like the United Kingdom, that have an EFZ but not an EEZ, the above case remains relevant.

4. Neither the 1958 High Seas Convention nor the 1982 Convention contain any rule about the use of force to effect arrest, either in the particular context of hot pursuit or generally. The "necessary and reasonable force" rule in the *I'm Alone Case* can probably be taken to state the position in customary international law, both in respect of arrests following hot pursuit and other lawful arrests at sea as well.

In *The Red Crusader Case*,[72] a Danish fisheries inspection vessel arrested a Scottish trawler, *The Red Crusader*, off the Faroes and ordered it to proceed to the Faroes for trial for fishing in an area in which this was prohibited by a Danish–U.K. treaty. After obeying for a while, *The Red Crusader*, with Danish crew from the fisheries inspection vessel stationed on board, sought to escape. Thereupon, the Danish vessel fired warning shots close to *The Red Crusader* and ordered it to stop. When these warnings were not heeded, *The Red Crusader* was fired upon directly with solid shot and damaged (but not sunk). All of the firing occurred in

---

[68] See Art. 95, 1982 Convention, above, p. 426.

[69] Y.B.I.L.C., 1956, II, p. 285.

[70] See the U.S. Coastguard memorandum, July 1957, 4 Whiteman 683 at 685.

[71] *loc. cit.*, p. 435, above, p. 419. See Sisco (1977) 14 San Diego L.R. 656.

[72] (1962) 35 I.L.R. 485. Following the Commission of Enquiry Report, the purpose of which was to establish the facts, a mutual waiver of claims for compensation for trawler damage and of criminal charges was agreed: *ibid.*, p. 500.

Faroese territorial waters. In its Report, an Anglo-Danish Commission of Enquiry found:

> In opening fire at 03.22 hours up to 03.53 hours, the Commanding Officer of the *Niels Ebbesen* exceeded legitimate use of armed force on two counts: (a) firing without warning of solid gun-shot; (b) creating danger to human life on board the Red Crusader without proved necessity, by the effective firing at the *Red Crusader* after 03.40 hours.
>
> The escape of the *Red Crusader* in flagrant violation of the order received and obeyed, the seclusion on board the trawler of an officer and rating of the crew of *Niels Ebbesen*, and Skipper Wood's refusal to stop may explain some resentment on the part of Captain Sølling. Those circumstances, however, cannot justify such violent action.
>
> The Commission is of the opinion that other means should have been attempted, which, if duly persisted in, might have finally persuaded Skipper Wood to stop and revert to the normal procedure which he himself had previously followed.

R. v. MILLS[73]

1995, Croydon Crown Court. Unreported. Transcript supplied by H.M.
Customs and Excise, Solicitor's Office

The *Poseidon* was a diving support vessel registered in the Caribbean state of St Vincent. On the high seas, some 100 miles west of the U.K. from 10.25 am to 14.40 pm on November 10, 1993, it transferred to the *Delvan*, a British registered fishing vessel which had sailed out from Cork in Ireland for this purpose, part of a cargo of cannabis valued at £24 million, which the *Poseidon* had transported from Morocco. It was planned that the *Delvan* would land the cannabis illegally in the U.K. The transfer was observed by radar by *HMS Avenger*, a British naval vessel close by on the high seas. After the transfer, the *Poseidon* moved further out into the Atlantic, shadowed by *HMS Avenger*. The *Delvan*, under surveillance by the *Seeker*, a U.K. customs cutter, sailed slowly up the Channel and landed at 21.00 p.m. on November 12, in Littlehampton, where those involved were arrested. Thereupon, at 23.15 p.m. the same night, *HMS Avenger* was instructed by London to arrest the *Poseidon*, but the arrest was delayed overnight for practical reasons. After attempts to communicate with the *Poseidon* by radio at 7.33 a.m. on November 13 proved unsuccessful, the *Poseidon* was boarded by helicopter and control of it was established by 8.00 a.m. The arrest was effected in international waters in the Atlantic, the *Poseidon* having remained in such waters all the while. The crew members, none of whom were United Kingdom nationals, were arrested and charged with conspiracy to import cannabis into the United Kingdom.

The defendants applied to stay the criminal proceedings against them on grounds of abuse of process. They based their application on the contention that they had been arrested on the high seas in breach of international law. In reply, the Crown argued that the Court had no jurisdiction to hear the application, *inter alia*, because the Geneva Convention on the High Seas 1958, upon which the defendants relied, was a treaty and as such was not a part of United Kingdom law. The Crown Court ruled that it had jurisdiction because the High Seas Convention "codified existing principles of international law"[74] which principles "had been

---

[73] See Gilmore (1995) 44 I.C.L.Q. 949.
[74] More particularly, Devonshire J. stated: "The right of 'hot pursuit' under which the *Poseidon* was arrested is a power conferred by the general principles of international law of which the Geneva Convention was merely declaratory".

incorporated in the Common Law of England". In the following extract, the Court went on to decide whether the arrest had been lawful under the customary international law doctrine of hot pursuit. Devonshire J. first considered whether the *Poseidon* was constructively present in British waters.

DEVONSHIRE J. This [constructive presence] arises when the pursued ship is working as a team with another ship—not being one of its boats—which is itself within territorial waters. It is described in article 23(3) of the Convention in the following words:

> . . . the ship pursued or one of its boats or other craft working as a team and using the ship pursued as a mother ship . . .

The Doctrine was . . . upheld by the Nova Scotia Supreme Court in *R. v. Sunila and Solayman*. In that case a tran-shipment of 13.4 tons of cannabis resin had taken place within territorial waters and the mother ship had returned to the high seas. She was arrested in international waters after the daughter ship had arrived in port and completed her importation.

All the cases to which I have referred above were cases in which the daughter ship had come from the shore of the pursuing State and returned to those shores. The defendants submit these circumstances were not present in this instant case . . . In my judgement the location of the port of departure of the daughter ship is irrelevant. It is clear to me that the policy consideration behind doctrine is the prevention of the commission of crimes in the territorial waters of the state which exercises the right to hot pursuit. That consideration would be defeated if the point of departure was relevant, mother ships hovering outside territorial waters could never be arrested if the daughter ship departed from a different jurisdiction to her ultimate destination. . . .

The defendants submitted that hot pursuit should have commenced immediately the *Delvan* entered United Kingdom Territorial Waters at 0130 on 11 November. Article 23 in the Convention is silent on the time at which the pursuit must commence. . . .

Poulantzas in "The Right of Hot Pursuit in International Law" published in 1969 said:

> The right of hot pursuit represents a traditional limitation to the freedom of the high seas and should only be used for exceptional and urgent circumstances which necessitate very quick action on the part of the coastal state. If the period of time between committing an infringement by a foreign vessel and the commencement of the pursuit is not short, then the right of hot pursuit cannot any longer be justified under international law. . . . However, the element of immediacy should not be interpreted *stricto sensu*, but in a broader sense. . . .

It is necessary to consider also the historic justification for both immediacy and continuity of pursuit. Before the installation in ships of modern tracking devices it was essential that the pursuing vessel maintained contact with the offending ship to be able to demonstrate that it had not arrested an innocent vessel exercising its right to navigate freely on the high seas. Similar considerations applied historically to the exercise on land of the right of "fresh pursuit", the sheriff's officers needed to be able to prove that they had arrested the true offender. Those practical considerations do not apply today when modern and accurate tracking devices are available at sea. The undisputed evidence shows that the identity and position of the *Poseidon* was known at all times to *HMS Avenger*. . . .

In this instant case the delay in commencing the pursuit of the *Poseidon* until after the arrival of the *Delvan* in Littlehampton and the completion of the importation does not, in my judgement, mean that the right of hot pursuit was lost. The decision to delay was made for justifiable reasons and, as the *Poseidon* had been under effective surveillance since the time of the tran-shipment, there was no risk of the arrest of an innocent vessel. The offence in this case is conspiracy to evade the ban on the importation of drugs or to supply drugs. . . . the offence of conspiracy was not necessarily complete until the drugs landed in Littlehampton.[75] It was therefore arguable that the right to hot pursuit had not arisen until that time. In my judgement Mr Delahunty was entitled to delay the issue of order for arrest of the *Poseidon* until the drugs had been landed in the United Kingdom at 2130.

There followed a delay until first light on the 13th November. For the reasons which I have given earlier I am satisfied the commander of the Naval Forces was justified, having regard to all the ambient conditions, sea state and light, to delay the commencement of the hot pursuit until then. . . .

Article 23(3) provides [as a condition] . . . precedent to the commencement of hot pursuit; . . .

(b) the giving of a visual or auditory signal to stop at a distance which enables it to be seen or heard.

The signal to stop ensures that the offending ship is aware that it has been detected, identified and is being ordered to heave to for boarding. The pursuing vessel is entitled to open fire if its order is not complied with . . . A signal will go some way to prevent unnecessary damage or injury. . . .

The defendants argue that a signal sent by radio did not comply with the condition precedent in article 23(3). . . .

It is clear from Poulantzas at 204 that both the Hague Codification Conference of 1930 and the Geneva Conference of 1958 accepted that signals by radio should not be regarded as lawful for the commencement

---

[75] *Ed*. But see now the Criminal Justice Act 1993, s.3, above, p. 278.

of the pursuit. It was thought that this exclusion was justified to prevent abuse from radio signals sent from a considerable distance. He accepted that wireless could be used by the pursuing ship in order to be assured that the auditory or visual signals had been understood. . . .

Craig Allen said[76]:

> . . . Most modern publicists agree that enforcing craft should be permitted to give the initial signal by radio, even before the pursuing vessel comes within sight. Where it is clear by the offending vessel's acknowledgement or otherwise that the vessel received and understood a signal to stop given by radio, such a signal meets the underlying policy goal of providing adequate notice to the vessel.

Modern technology has moved on since 1958 and the law must take account of those changes. Mr Montalto told me that VHF radio is now the standard method of communication between vessels at sea which are required by International Radio Regulations to keep a watch on Channel 16. I hold that the messages sent by this medium comply with the preconditions of the Convention to the exercise of the right of hot pursuit.

I hold that the *Poseidon* was properly arrested in international waters under the terms of the Geneva Convention and in accordance with the provisions of the international law of the sea. For these reasons I disallowed the defendants application to stay the indictment on the grounds of abuse of process.

4. THE EXCLUSIVE ECONOMIC ZONE[77]

The exclusive economic zone has its roots in the concept of the exclusive fishing zone and the doctrine of the continental shelf. It combines and develops the two. The emergence of the concept of the exclusive fishing zone and its translation into the exclusive economic zone is considered in the following materials. The doctrine of the continental shelf is considered separately in section 5.

The exclusive fishing zone is a zone of the sea adjacent to a coastal state's territorial sea within which the coastal state has exclusive jurisdiction over fishing. The concept can be traced to the (then) extravagant 200-mile claims of certain Latin American states in the late 1940s to protect whaling and other fishing interests.[78] These were the subject of protest and were not thought to be lawful.[79] Then, as now, such claims were motivated by a genuine concern for conservation (international action not proving effective) as well as other national considerations. A turning point came with the failure of the 1958 Conference on the Law of

[76.] *Ed.* (1989) 20 O.D.I.L. 309.

[77] See Attard, *The Exclusive Economic Zone in International Law* (1987); Charney (1985) 15 O.D.I.L. 233; Extavour, *The Exclusive Economic Zone* (2nd ed., 1981); Juda (1986) 16 O.D.I.L. 1; Koh (1988) 30 Malaya L.R. 1; Phillips (1977) 26 I.C.L.Q. 585; Pharand, ed., *The Continental Shelf and the Exclusive Economic Zone* (1993); Smith, *Exclusive Economic Claims: An Analysis and Primary Documents* (1986); Symonides (1985) 14 Pol. Y.I.L. 43.

[78] See Hollick (1977) 71 A.J.I.L. 494.

[79] See Kunz (1956) 50 A.J.I.L. 828.

the Sea and the supplementary 1960 Conference to agree upon a wider territorial sea than the traditional three-mile sea or upon fishing jurisdiction for coastal states beyond their territorial sea.[80] The majority view in 1958 was that, in the absence of agreement to the contrary, fishing beyond the limit of a lawful territorial sea was open to all states in accordance with "freedom of fishing" on the high seas. Unilateral action by Iceland and other states in the years that followed led gradually to an acceptance of a 12-mile[81] exclusive fishing zone,[82] the legality of which was recognised in the *Fisheries Jurisdiction (Merits)* cases.[83] Thereafter, claims became more ambitious so that by 1978 23 states claimed 200 miles exclusive fishing zones and another 38 claimed exclusive economic zones.[84] Indicative of the speed of events is the fact that the United Kingdom, which had fought a "war" over Iceland's claim to a 200–mile exclusive fishing zone just 12 months previously, claimed its own 200–mile exclusive fishing zone as of 1977.[85] By 1994, the point had been reached where 84 states, from all political groupings, claimed 200–mile exclusive economic zones, without protest from other states.[86]

CONVENTION ON THE LAW OF THE SEA 1982

UN Doc. A/CONF. 62/122; (1982) 21 I.L.M. 1261

Article 55

The exclusive economic zone is an area beyond and adjacent to the territorial sea, subject to the specific legal régime established in this Part [Part V], under which the rights and jurisdiction of the coastal State and the rights and freedoms of other States are governed by the relevant provisions of this Convention.

Article 56

1. In the exclusive economic zone, the coastal State has:

(a) sovereign rights for the purpose of exploring and exploiting, conserving and managing the natural resources, whether living or non-

---

[80] See 4 Whiteman 91–137.

[81] *i.e.* 12 miles as measured from the same baselines as those used for the territorial sea.

[82] A 1967 survey showed that exclusive fishing zones (mostly for 12 miles) were claimed by 33 states, including the U.K. (Fishery Limits Act 1964): *Limits and Status of the Territorial Sea, Exclusive Zone, Fisheries Conservation Zones and the Continental Shelf*, FAO Legislative Series No. 8, 1969, as revised. Other states had achieved the same result by claiming a 12-mile territorial sea. Most coastal states making such claims allowed other states to fish, permanently or for a phasing-out period, in the areas claimed where they could show that their fishermen had long done so.

[83] I.C.J. Rep. 1974, p. 3 (*U.K. v. Iceland*); *ibid.*, p. 175 (*F.R.G. v. Iceland*). But the I.C.J. ruled that Iceland's 1971 claim to a 50–mile exclusive fishing zone was illegal.

[84] FAO figures published in Nordquist and Simmons, *op. cit.*, p. 368, n. 1, above, Vol X, p. 472.

[85] Fishery Limits Act 1976. The Act allows certain states to fish within the 200-mile limit and in accordance with the Fishery Limits Act 1964. These include EC states and the Russian Federation.

[86] *Law of the Sea Bulletin, loc. cit.*, p. 368, n. 1, No. 25, p. 104.

living, of the waters superjacent to the sea-bed and of the sea-bed
and subsoil, and with regard to other activities for the economic
exploitation and exploration of the zone, such as the production of
energy from the water, currents and winds;

(b) jurisdiction as provided for in the relevant provisions of this Convention with regard to:

(i) the establishment and use of artificial islands, installations and
structures;
(ii) marine scientific research;
(iii) the protection and preservation of the marine environment;

(c) other rights and duties provided for in this Convention.

2. In exercising its rights and performing its duties under this Convention in the exclusive economic zone, the coastal State shall have due
regard to the rights and duties of other States and shall act in a manner
compatible with the provisions of this Convention.

3. The rights set out in this article with respect to the sea-bed and
subsoil shall be exercised in accordance with Part VI [on the continental
shelf].

Article 57

The exclusive economic zone shall not extend beyond 200 nautical miles
from the baselines from which the breadth of the territorial sea is
measured.

Article 58

1. In the exclusive economic zone, all States, whether coastal or land-
locked, enjoy, subject to the relevant provisions of this Convention, the
freedoms referred to in article 87[87] of navigation and overflight and of the
laying of submarine cables and pipelines, and other internationally lawful uses of the sea related to these freedoms, such as those associated with
the operation of ships, aircraft and submarine cables and pipelines, and
compatible with the other provisions of this Convention.

2. Article 88 to 115 and other pertinent rules of international law apply
to the exclusive economic zone in so far as they are not incompatible with
this Part [Part V].

3. In exercising their rights and performing their duties under this
Convention in the exclusive economic zone, States shall have due regard
to the rights and duties of the coastal State and shall comply with the laws
and regulations adopted by the coastal State in accordance with the

[87] See above, p. 419.

provisions of this Convention and other rules of international law in so far as they are not incompatible with this Part.

Article 59

In cases where this Convention does not attribute rights or jurisdiction to the coastal State or to other States within the exclusive economic zone, and a conflict arises between the interests of the coastal State and any other State or States, the conflict should be resolved on the basis of equity and in the light of all the relevant circumstances, taking into account the respective importance of the interests involved to the parties as well as to the international community as a whole.

Article 60

1. In the exclusive economic zone, the coastal State shall have the exclusive right to construct and to authorise and regulate the construction, operation and use of:

(a) artificial islands;
(b) installations and structures for the purposes provided for in article 56 and other economic purposes;
(c) installations and structures which may interfere with the exercise of the rights of the coastal State in the zone.

2. The coastal State shall have exclusive jurisdiction over such artificial islands, installations and structures, including jurisdiction with regard to customs, fiscal, health, safety and immigration laws and regulations. . . .

7. Artificial islands, installations and structures and the safety zones around them may not be established where interference may be caused to the use of recognised sea lanes essential to international navigation.

8. Artificial islands, installations and structures do not possess the status of islands. They have no territorial sea of their own, and their presence does not affect the delimitation of the territorial sea, the exclusive economic zone or the continental shelf.

Article 61

1. The coastal State shall determine the allowable catch of the living resources in its exclusive economic zone.

2. The coastal State, taking into account the best scientific evidence available to it, shall ensure through proper conservation and management measures that the maintenance of the living resources in the exclusive economic zone is not endangered by over-exploitation. As appropriate, the coastal State and competent international organisations, whether subregional, regional, or global, shall co-operate to this end.

3. Such measures shall also be designed to maintain or restore populations of harvested species at levels which can produce the maximum sustainable yield, as qualified by relevant environmental and economic factors, including the economic needs of coastal fishing communities and the special requirements of developing states, and taking into account fishing patterns, the interdependence of stocks and any generally recommended international minimum standards, whether subregional, regional or global. . . .

Article 62

1. The coastal State shall promote the objective of optimum utilisation of the living resources in the exclusive economic zone without prejudice to Article 61.

2. The coastal State shall determine its capacity to harvest the living resources of the exclusive economic zone. Where the coastal State does not have the capacity to harvest the entire allowable catch, it shall, through agreements or other arrangements and pursuant to the terms, conditions, laws and regulations referred to in paragraph 4, give other States access to the surplus of the allowable catch, having particular regard to the provisions of Articles 69 and 70,[88] especially in relation to the developing states mentioned therein.

3. In giving access to other States to its exclusive economic zone under this article, the coastal State shall take into account all relevant factors, including, *inter alia*, the significance of the living resources of the area to the economy of the coastal State concerned and its other national interests, the provisions of Articles 69 and 70,[88] the requirements of developing countries in the subregion or region in harvesting part of the surplus and the need to minimise economic dislocation in States whose nationals have habitually fished in the zone or which have made substantial efforts in research and identification of stocks.

4. Nationals of other States fishing in the exclusive economic zone shall comply with the conservation measures and with the other terms and conditions established in the regulations of the coastal State. . . .

[Articles 64–67 make special provision for highly migratory species (*e.g.* tuna, swordfish), marine mammals (*e.g.* whales, seals), anadromous stocks (*e.g.* salmon), and catadromous species (*e.g.* eels)]

Article 68

This Part [Articles 55–75] does not apply to sedentary species as defined in Article 77, paragraph 4.

---

[88] *Ed.* On the rights of land-locked states and states "with special geographical characteristics" (who together constituted about one third of the states at UNCLOS III). The latter are defined in 1982 Convention, Art. 70(2).

Article 73

1. The coastal State may, in the exercise of its sovereign rights to explore, exploit, conserve and manage the living resources in the exclusive economic zone, take such measures, including boarding, inspection, arrest and judicial proceedings, as may be necessary to ensure compliance with the laws and regulations adopted by it in conformity with this Convention.

2. Arrested vessels and their crews shall be promptly released upon the posting of reasonable bond or other security.

3. Coastal State penalties for violations of fisheries laws and regulations in the exclusive economic zone may not include imprisonment, in the absence of agreements to the contrary by the States concerned, or any other form of corporal punishment.

4. In cases of arrest or detention of foreign vessels the coastal State shall promptly notify the flag State, through appropriate channels, of the action taken and of any penalties subsequently imposed.

Article 74

1. The delimitation of the exclusive economic zone between States with opposite or adjacent coasts shall be effected by agreement on the basis of international law, as referred to in Article 38 of the Statute of the International Court of Justice, in order to achieve an equitable solution.

2. If no agreement can be reached within a reasonable period of time, the States concerned shall resort to the procedures provided for in Part XV [on the settlement of disputes].[89]

3. Pending agreement as provided for in paragraph 1, the States concerned, in a spirit of understanding and co-operation, shall make every effort to enter into provisional arrangements of a practical nature and, during this transitional period, not to jeopardise or hamper the reaching of the final agreement. Such arrangements shall be without prejudice to the final delimitation. . . .

Notes

1. It is clear that the international community allows coastal states a 200–mile exclusive economic zone. A consensus to this effect quickly emerged at UNCLOS III and provision is accordingly made for such a zone in the 1982 Convention. In the *Continental Shelf* (*Libya v. Malta*) case,[90] the International Court of Justice observed that "the institution of the exclusive economic zone . . . is shown by the practice of states to have become part of customary law." What is not clear is whether the whole of the 1982 Convention régime on the exclusive economic zone

[89] See below, p. 476. For the approach adopted by international courts and tribunals in resolving maritime boundary disputes in the absence of agreement, see below, p. 463.
[90] I.C.J. Rep. 1985, p. 13 at p. 33. Earlier in the *Continental Shelf* (*Tunisia v. Libya*) case, I.C.J. Rep. 1982, p. 18 at p. 74, the Court had stated that the zone "may be regarded as part of modern international law." *cf.* the *Gulf of Maine* case, extract above, p. 372.

may be considered as custom or only parts of it.[91] Churchill and Lowe,[92] after concluding that a state may claim a 200–mile exclusive economic zone, state:

> What is much less certain is whether the coastal State's fishery management duties set out in articles 61 and 62 have become part of customary law. Relatively few States' national legislation refers to these duties. This may be, not because the duties are not accepted, but because these duties are not considered as an appropriate matter for legislation, since they relate to administrative practices. On the other hand, the duties may be too vague and insufficiently of a "norm-creating character" to pass into customary law.

2. The 1982 Convention intentionally refrains from describing the exclusive economic zone as a part of the high seas. The zone is treated instead as an intermediate area of sea between the high seas and the territorial sea with a distinct régime of its own. This régime accords the coastal state (i) sovereign rights of exploitation of zone resources and (ii) ancillary and other powers of exclusive jurisdiction, notably in respect of marine research and the control of pollution (1982 Convention, Article 56). Although the position of the coastal state in an area previously regarded as being fully subject to the "freedom of the high seas" is thus greatly strengthened, it falls far short of sovereignty. In particular, states generally may continue to exercise within the zone freedom of navigation and overflight and other freedoms[93] not covered by Article 56, 1982 Convention that form part of the established concept of "freedom of the high seas" (Article 58). To this large extent, the 1982 Convention does not revert to Selden's idea of the closed sea in respect of the zone.[94] Foreign ships in passage are, however, subject to the coastal state's enforcement jurisdiction in respect of illegal fishing (Article 73) and the control of pollution (Article 220). An unresolved question is whether foreign warships, which enjoy freedom of navigation through the exclusive economic zone, may conduct naval exercises therein, as they can on the high seas.[95] Several states[96] made declarations when signing the 1982 Convention to the effect that such exercises were not permitted by it. A number of other uses of the economic zone are not regulated by the 1982 Convention. Examples given by Churchill and Lowe[97] are "the emplacement of underwater listening devices for submarines, . . . the recovery of historic wrecks beyond the contiguous zone . . . and jurisdiction over buoys used for pure scientific research." In the case of such

[91] *cf.* the distinction drawn in the *North Sea Continental Shelf* cases, above, p. 27, between Arts. 1 and 2 and Art. 6, Continental Shelf Convention.

[92] *op. cit.,* p. 368, n. 1, above, p. 233.

[93] See those listed in Art. 87, 1982 Convention, above, p. 419. On freedom of navigation in the EEZ, see Burke (1983) 20 San Diego L.R. 595 and Robertson (1984) 24 Virg. J.I.L. 865.

[94] See Ganz, *loc. cit.,* p. 369, n. 14, above, p. 53. Selden was a 17th-century English lawyer who argued unsuccessfully that the seas might be subjected to territorial sovereignty. The opposing view of Grotius, propounded when the Netherlands was the dominant maritime power, prevailed.

[95] The UNCLOS III President (Mr Koh) has stated that there was a general understanding at UNCLOS III that military activities in the EEZ would not require coastal state permission: in Van Dyke, ed., *Consensus and Confrontation: the U.S. and the Law of the Sea Convention* (1985), pp. 303–304.

[96] Brazil, Cape Verde, Uruguay: UN Doc. ST/LEG/SER. E/15, p. 822, *et seq.* Italy made a contrary declaration: *ibid.* Cape Verde and Uruguay stated that naval exercises are "non-peaceful" uses of the EEZ which are prohibited without the coastal state's consent. Note (i) that although there is no express prohibition of "non-peaceful" uses of the EEZ, there is such a prohibition in respect of the high seas (Article 87), and presumably therefore an implied one in respect of the EEZ, but (ii) that naval exercises on the high seas are thought to be lawful: see above, p. 420.

[97] *op. cit.,* p. 368, n. 1, p. 144.

unregulated uses, any conflict between a coastal and other state "should be resolved on the basis of equity," etc. (Article 59).

3. Well over 90 per cent of the world's annual catch of fish is harvested within 200 miles of land.[98] Accordingly, the exclusive fishing rights given to the coastal state in the EEZ by Article 56 are economically very valuable.[99] The obligations placed upon the coastal state to conserve fisheries (Article 61) are matched by rights of exploitation that make little concession to the interests of other states. The coastal state is entitled under Article 62 to reserve all of the allowable catch for its fishermen if they are capable of exploiting it. The access of fishermen of other states, including landlocked and geographically disadvantaged states (Article 69), to the surplus (Article 62(3)) depends on "agreements or other arrangements" (Article 62(2)). Disputes concerning a coastal state's rights over fisheries within its exclusive economic zone are not subject to compulsory arbitration or adjudication; *extreme* cases are subject to compulsory but non-binding conciliation (Article 297(3)). The consequent absence of binding, third-party procedures makes it difficult to enforce conservation and other limitations on a coastal state's fishing rights.[1] Note also its wide powers of enforcement jurisdiction (boarding, arrest, etc.) over foreign ships suspected of illegal fishing (Article 73).

4. The coastal state's rights to exploit continental shelf, (*i.e.* sea-bed and subsoil) resources in its exclusive economic zone are exercised in accordance with the separate régime for the continental shelf in Part VI (Articles 76–85) of the 1982 Convention, below, p. 455.[2] Some of the rules in Part VI are identical to those in the exclusive economic zone régime in Part V.[3] But the exploitation of shelf resources, including sedentary species (see Article 68), within the 200–mile limit is not subject to the conservation and sharing restrictions that apply under the exclusive economic zone régime (Articles 61–62) applicable to fish.

5. *Exclusive Fishing Zones.* In 1994, 15 states, including the United Kingdom, claimed 200–mile exclusive fishing zones, but not exclusive economic zones.[4] Such EFZ claims, although much wider than the 12 miles EFZ's recognised as valid in the *Fisheries Jurisdiction Cases (Merits)*[5] in 1974, have not met with protest and are clearly permissible in customary international law. If a 200-mile exclusive economic zone is lawful, then *a fortiori* an equivalent fishing zone is lawful too. However, it is not clear precisely what this entails. Whereas there is in the 1982 Convention a detailed régime in respect of conservation, access to fisheries,

[98] Gulland (1979) 22 *Oceanus* 36.

[99] On the EEZ fishing regime generally, see Burke (1984) 63 Oregon L.R. 73; Dahmani, *The Fisheries Régime of the Exclusive Economic Zone* (1987); Ulfstein (1983) 52 N.T.I.R. 3.

[1] Before the EEZ evolved, the standard medium for fisheries conservation was the international fisheries commission, (*e.g.* the North Atlantic Salmon Conservation Organisation). The limitations of such commissions are that states are generally unwilling to give them sufficient legislative or enforcement powers. The problem with reliance upon coastal states for conservation is that fish move inconveniently from one maritime zone to another and that not all states take their obligations to control fishermen seriously. See Juda (1987) 18 O.D.I.L. 305.

[2] Art. 56(3), 1982 Convention. Although inelegantly drafted, a separate continental shelf régime was necessary to provide for (i) states that have a continental shelf but not an exclusive economic zone and (ii) states with a continental shelf beyond the 200–mile limit of the exclusive economic zone. The U.K. is an example of both kinds of states.

[3] The same rules apply in respect of artificial structures, etc. (Arts. 60 and 80), the delimitation of boundaries (Arts. 74 and 83) and the publishing of charts (Arts. 75 and 84).

[4] *Law of the Sea Bulletin, loc. cit.*, p. 368, n. 1, above, No. 25. p. 104. Three states claimed narrower fishing zones. In addition the EEC has adopted a 200–mile exclusive fishing zone *vis-à-vis* third states. In 1983, it agreed upon a fishing policy for its members *inter se*: see Gutteridge (1978) 49 B.Y.I.L. 202. On the U.K. 150–mile Falkland Islands fishing zone, see Churchill (1988) 12 Mar. Pol. 343.

[5] *loc. cit.*, p. 447, n. 83, above.

enforcement jurisdiction, etc., in respect of fishing within the exclusive economic zone, the 1982 Convention has no separate régime in respect of exclusive fishing zones that could apply to parties to the Convention as treaty rules or to states generally as custom. It would be surprising, however, if the same regime did not apply as a matter of custom to fishing in the same waters, whether the waters were classified as an exclusive economic or fishing zone.

The United Kingdom, now a party to the 1982 Convention, explained its decision not to replace its EFZ and continental shelf (within its first 200 miles) by an EEZ as follows[6]:

> We see no point at present in creating one in order to secure resources. The United Kingdom already has a fishery zone extending to a maximum of 200 nautical miles and, since rights over our continental shelf (which extends well beyond 200 miles) are inherent and do not have to be proclaimed, there would be no advantage to the United Kingdom in declaring such a zone.

An exclusive economic zone does, nonetheless, bring with it certain other benefits, particularly (i) Article 56 jurisdiction in respect of marine research and pollution control and (ii) clearly defined enforcement jurisdiction in respect of illegal fishing (Article 73). Such a zone might, however, also bring additional conservation and "access to foreign fishermen" obligations, unless the rules in Articles 61 and 62 come to be accepted as applicable equally to EEZs and EFZs.

6. *Islands*. The 1982 Convention (Article 121(3)) provides that an island may have an exclusive economic zone or a continental shelf with the following exceptions: "Rocks which cannot sustain human habitation or economic life of their own shall have no exclusive economic zone or continental shelf."[7] In the *Jan Mayen Case*,[8] the Conciliation Commission stated that Article 121 "reflects the present status of international law." The meaning of "economic life" is obscure. An island such as Rockall[9] would not qualify for an exclusive economic zone under Article 121(3).[10] Such an island close to the mainland may, however, be taken into account when drawing baselines for an exclusive economic zone or

---

[6] *Hansard*, H.L., Vol. 473, col. 46, April 7, 1986.

[7] Such rocks do have a territorial sea under the 1982 Convention, as under the Territorial Sea Convention, if they come within the definition of an island common to both texts: see above, p. 389.

[8] (1981) 20 I.L.M. 797 at 803.

[9] Rockall is a bare, uninhabitable rock that rises 70 feet out of the North East Atlantic 170 miles from the nearest Scottish island of St Kilda and over 200 miles from Ireland. It was annexed by the U.K. in 1955 and made a part of Scotland for legal purposes by the Island of Rockall Act 1972. British sovereignty over Rockall is not disputed.

[10] On the unresolved dispute between Denmark (in respect of the Faroes), and the U.K. arising out of their overlapping exclusive economic and fishing zone and continental shelf claims in the North East Atlantic, see Brown (1978) 2 Mar. Pol. 191 at 275; Symmons, *op. cit.*, p. 389, n. 85, above (see index); *ibid.* (1986) 35 I.C.L.Q. 344. Some of the overlap results from U.K. reliance upon Rockall. Referring to the 1982 Convention, Denmark protested at the U.K.'s use of Rockall as a baseline for its 1977 200 mile exclusive fishing zone: see the Danish press release in U.K.M.I.L. 1985, (1985) 56 B.Y.I.L. 491. The huge, 52,000 square miles continental shelf around Rockall claimed by the U.K. in 1974, S.I. 1974 No. 1489, against which Ireland (see now the U.K.–Irish Agreement, U.K.T.S. 1 (1988), Cm. 535) and Denmark protested, was originally explained as being generated by Rockall as well as being a natural prolongation of Scotland: see Symmons, *op. cit.* p. 135; since the 1982 Convention, the U.K. has relied on the latter ground only: see the 1985 FCO statement, U.K.M.I.L. 1994 (1994) 65 B.Y.I.L. 655.

continental shelf.[11] France has declared a 200-mile EEZ around Clipperton Island.[12] Is that consistent with Article 121(3)?

7. The EEZ régime was seen as one of the vehicles in the 1982 Convention for achieving a new international economic order that would redress the economic balance in the interest of developing states.[13] According to Wijkman,[14] however, it is unlikely to have this result. Writing in 1982, he states:

> The draft Convention would redistribute income from long distance fishing fleets and other foreign fishermen to those states with long coasts bordering on rich fishing grounds. The richest fishing grounds, like the richest countries, are located in the temperate zones, and three-quarters of the world catch is taken from waters off the developed countries. . . . About one-third of the catch in developing countries' waters is taken by non-local fishermen, and these are largely from developed countries.
>
> . . . a total of at least 1·2 billion dollars annually is to be redistributed to coastal states, and of this the developed countries would enjoy the major part. Developing coastal countries do gain somewhat at the expense of the developed. The major losers are long-distance fishing fleets and those fishermen who historically have fished in waters that now are declared "foreign."
>
> Whether this redistribution of income is fair is a matter of opinion. Coastal countries claim ownership of the fishing stocks by right of proximity. Less fortunately located nations stress that this resource, too, should be part of the common heritage in which they have a share. Undeniably, the proposed treaty fails to compensate those fishing nations that lose historical rights, and favours currently rich coastal countries over poor ones, and coastal states over others.

8. *Boundaries between exclusive economic zones.* This question, which is dealt with in Article 74, 1982 Convention, is considered in connection with continental shelf boundaries, below, p. 463.

5. THE CONTINENTAL SHELF[15]

THE TRUMAN PROCLAMATION ON THE CONTINENTAL SHELF 1945

4 Whiteman 756

Whereas the Government of the United States of America, aware of the long range world-wide need for new sources of petroleum and other minerals, holds the view that efforts to discover and make available new supplies of these resources should be encouraged; and. . . .

---

[11] See the *Anglo-French Continental Shelf* case (1978) Misc. 15, Cmnd. 7438; (1979) 18 I.L.M. 397, 434: 54 I.L.R. 6 (use of the Eddystone Rocks).
[12] See Van Dyke and Brooks (1983) 12 O.D.I.L. 265. On Clipperton Island, see above, p. 200.
[13] See above, p. 370.
[14] (1982) 16 J.W.T.L. 27.
[15] See Anderson (1988) 6 J.E.N.R.L. 95; Brown, *Sea-bed Energy and Minerals: the International Legal Regime* (1993), Vol. I.

Whereas recognised jurisdiction over these resources is required in the interest of their conservation and prudent utilisation when and as development is undertaken; and

Whereas it is the view of the Government of the United States that the exercise of jurisdiction over the natural resources of the subsoil and sea bed of the continental shelf by the contiguous nation is reasonable and just, since the effectiveness of measures to utilise or conserve these resources would be contingent upon cooperation and protection from the shore, since the continental shelf may be regarded as an extension of the land mass of the coastal nation and thus naturally appurtenant to it, since these resources frequently form a seaward extension of a pool or deposit lying within the territory, and since self-protection compels the coastal nation to keep close watch over activities off its shores which are of the nature necessary for utilisation of these resources:

Now therefore, I, Harry S. Truman, President of the United States of America, do hereby proclaim the following policy of the United States of America with respect to the natural resources of the subsoil and sea bed of the continental shelf.

Having concern for the urgency of conserving and prudently utilising its natural resources, the Government of the United States regards the natural resources of the subsoil and sea bed of the continental shelf beneath the high seas but contiguous to the coasts of the United States as appertaining to the United States, subject to its jurisdiction and control. In cases where the continental shelf extends to the shores of another state, or is shared with an adjacent state, the boundary shall be determined by the United States and the state concerned in accordance with equitable principles. The character as high seas of the waters above the continental shelf and the right to their free and unimpeded navigation are in no way thus affected.

Notes
1. The Truman Proclamation, which was the first of its kind, was quickly followed by similar declarations made by other states. By 1945, it had become technically possible to drill for oil and other mineral resources in the seabed from the sea and the Truman Proclamation was aimed at filling a gap in international law on the legal rights and duties of states arising from that possibility.
2. Geomorphologically, the continental shelf is the gently sloping platform of submerged land surrounding the continents and islands. Normally it extends to a depth of approximately 200 metres or 100 fathoms[16] at which point the seabed falls away sharply. In some places it continues beyond a depth of 200 metres. It varies in width from less than five miles (off the coast of California, for example), to 750 miles (below the Barents Sea). The continental shelf west of the United Kingdom has an outer limit at a depth of about 200 metres and extends to about 300 miles off Land's End. Shelves occupy about 7·5 per cent of the total ocean area.

[16] This was the depth that the U.S. had in mind in the Truman Proclamation.

3. The status of the continental shelf doctrine in customary international law was considered by the Arbitrator, Lord Asquith, in the *Abu Dhabi Arbitration* in 1951.[17] In the light of the declarations then in existence, he concluded:

... there are in this field so many ragged ends and unfilled blanks, so much that is merely tentative and exploratory, that in no form can the doctrine claim as yet to have assumed hitherto the hard lineaments or the definitive status of an established rule of international law.

CONVENTION ON THE LAW OF THE SEA 1982

UN Doc. A/CONF. 62/122; (1982) 21 I.L.M. 1261

Article 76

1. The continental shelf of a coastal State comprises the sea-bed and subsoil of the submarine areas that extend beyond its territorial sea throughout the natural prolongation of its land territory to the outer edge of the continental margin, or to a distance of 200 nautical miles from the baselines from which the breadth of the territorial sea is measured where the outer edge of the continental margin does not extend up to that distance.

2. The continental shelf of a coastal State shall not extend beyond the limits provided for in paragraphs 4 to 6.

3. The continental margin comprises the submerged prolongation of the land mass of the coastal State, and consists of the sea-bed and subsoil of the shelf, the slope and the rise. It does not include the deep ocean floor with its oceanic ridges or the subsoil thereof.

4. (a) For the purposes of this Convention, the coastal State shall establish the outer edge of the continental margin wherever the margin extends beyond 200 nautical miles from the baselines from which the breadth of the territorial sea is measured, by either:

(i) a line delineated in accordance with paragraph 7 by reference to the outermost fixed points at each of which the thickness of sedimentary rocks is at least 1 per cent of the shortest distance from such point to the foot of the continental slope; or

(ii) a line delineated in accordance with paragraph 7 by reference to fixed points not more than 60 nautical miles from the foot of the continental slope.

---

[17] (1952) 1 I.C.L.Q. 247; (1951) 18 I.L.R. 144. See now, however, the *North Sea Continental Shelf Cases*, above, p. 27.

(b) In the absence of evidence to the contrary, the foot of the continental slope shall be determined as the point of maximum
change in the gradient at its base.

5. The fixed points comprising the line of the outer limits of the
continental shelf on the sea-bed, drawn in accordance with paragraph
4(a)(i) and (ii), either shall not exceed 350 nautical miles from the baselines from which the breadth of the territorial sea is measured or shall not
exceed 100 nautical miles from the 2,500 metre isobath, which is a line
connecting the depth of 2,500 metres.

6. Notwithstanding the provisions of paragraph 5, on submarine
ridges, the outer limit of the continental shelf shall not exceed 350 nautical
miles from the baselines from which the breadth of the territorial sea is
measured. This paragraph does not apply to submarine elevations that
are natural components of the continental margin, such as its plateaux,
rises, caps, banks and spurs.

7. The coastal State shall delineate the outer limits of its continental
shelf, where that shelf extends beyond 200 nautical miles from the baselines from which the breadth of the territorial sea is measured, by straight
lines not exceeding 60 nautical miles in length, connecting fixed points,
defined by co-ordinates of latitude and longitude.

8. Information on the limits of the continental shelf beyond 200 nautical miles from the baselines from which the breadth of the territorial sea
is measured shall be submitted by the coastal State to the Commission on
the Limits of the Continental Shelf set up under Annex II on the basis of
equitable geographical representation. The Commission shall make recommendations to coastal States on matters related to the establishment of
the outer limits of their continental shelf. The limits of the shelf established by a coastal State on the basis of these recommendations shall be
final and binding.

9. The coastal State shall deposit with the Secretary-General of the
United Nations charts and relevant information, including geodetic data,
permanently describing the outer limits of its continental shelf. The
Secretary-General shall give due publicity thereto.

10. The provisions of this article are without prejudice to the question
of delimitation of the continental shelf between States with opposite or
adjacent coasts.

Article 77

1. The coastal State exercises over the continental shelf sovereign rights
for the purpose of exploring it and exploiting its natural resources.

2. The rights referred to in paragraph 1 are exclusive in the sense that
if the coastal State does not explore the continental shelf or exploit its
natural resources, no one may undertake these activities without the
express consent of the coastal State.

3. The rights of the coastal State over the continental shelf do not depend on occupation, effective or notional, or on any express proclamation.

4. The natural resources referred to in this Part consist of the mineral and other non-living resources of the sea-bed and subsoil together with living organisms belonging to sedentary species, that is to say, organisms which, at the harvestable stage, either are immobile on or under the sea-bed or are unable to move except in constant physical contact with the sea-bed or the subsoil.

Article 78

1. The rights of the coastal State over the continental shelf do not affect the legal status of the superjacent waters or of the air space above those waters.

2. The exercise of the rights of the coastal State over the continental shelf must not infringe or result in any unjustifiable interference with navigation and other rights and freedoms of other States as provided for in this Convention.

Article 79

1. All States are entitled to lay submarine cables and pipelines on the continental shelf, in accordance with the provisions of this article.

2. Subject to its right to take reasonable measures for the exploration of the continental shelf, the exploitation of its natural resources and the prevention, reduction and control of pollution from pipelines, the coastal State may not impede the laying or maintenance of such cables or pipelines.

3. The delineation of the course for the laying of such pipelines on the continental shelf is subject to the consent of the coastal State.

4. Nothing in this Part affects the right of the coastal State to establish conditions for cables or pipelines entering its territory or territorial sea, or its jurisdiction over cables and pipelines constructed or used in connection with the exploration of its continental shelf or exploitation of its resources or the operations of artificial islands, installations and structures under its jurisdiction.

5. When laying submarine cables or pipelines, States shall have due regard to cables or pipelines already in position. In particular, possibilities of repairing existing cables or pipelines shall not be prejudiced.

Article 80

Article 60 applies *mutatis mutandis* to artificial islands, installations and structures on the continental shelf.

Article 81

The coastal State shall have the exclusive right to authorize and regulate drilling on the continental shelf for all purposes.

Article 82

1. The coastal State shall make payments or contributions in kind in respect of the exploitation of the non-living resources of the continental shelf beyond 200 nautical miles from the baselines from which the breadth of the territorial sea is measured.

2. The payments and contributions shall be made annually with respect to all production at a site after the first five years of production at that site. For the sixth year, the rate of payment or contribution shall be 1 per cent of the value or volume of production at the site. The rate shall increase by 1 per cent for each subsequent year until the twelfth year and shall . remain at 7 per cent thereafter. Production does not include resources used in connection with exploitation.

3. A developing State which is a net importer of a mineral resource produced from its continental shelf is exempt from making such payments or contributions in respect of that mineral resource.

4. The payments or contributions shall be made through the Authority, which shall distribute them to States Parties to this Convention, on the basis of equitable sharing criteria, taking into account the interests and needs of developing States, particularly the least developed and the land-locked among them.

Article 83

1. The delimitation of the continental shelf between States with opposite or adjacent coasts shall be effected by agreement on the basis of international law, as referred to in Article 38 of the Statute of the International Court of Justice, in order to achieve an equitable solution.

2. If no agreement can be reached within a reasonable period of time, the States concerned shall resort to the procedures provided for in Part XV [on the settlement of disputes: see below, p. 476].

3. Pending agreement as provided for in paragraph 1, the States concerned, in a spirit of understanding and co-operation, shall make every effort to enter into provisional arrangements of a practical nature and, during this transitional period, not to jeopardize or hamper the reaching of the final agreement. Such arrangements shall be without prejudice to the final delimitation. . . .

Article 84

1. Subject to this Part, the outer limit lines of the continental shelf and the lines of delimitation drawn in accordance with article 83 shall be shown on charts of a scale or scales adequate for ascertaining their

position. Where appropriate, lists of geographical co-ordinates of points, specifying the geodetic datum, may be substituted for such outer limit lines or lines of delimitation.

2. The coastal State shall give due publicity to such charts or lists of geographical co-ordinates and shall deposit a copy of each such chart or list with the Secretary-General of the United Nations and, in the case of those showing the outer limit lines of the continental shelf, with the Secretary-General of the Authority.

Article 85

This Part does not prejudice the right of the coastal State to exploit the subsoil by means of tunnelling, irrespective of the depth of water above the subsoil.

Notes

1. The legal definition of the continental shelf in Article 96, 1982 Convention, differs from that in Article 1, 1958 Continental Shelf Convention, which reads:

> For the purpose of these articles, the term "continental shelf" is used as referring (a) to the seabed and subsoil of the submarine areas adjacent to the coast but outside the area of the territorial sea, to a depth of 200 metres or, beyond that limit, to where the depth of the superjacent waters admits of the exploitation of the natural resources of the said areas; (b) to the seabed and subsoil of similar submarine areas adjacent to the coasts of islands.

Under Article 76(3), 1982 Convention, the continental shelf extends to the outer edge of the "continental margin", which includes the shelf itself and "the slope and the rise" beyond it.[18] The "continental slope" is the steep slope with which the shelf proper terminates; the "continental rise" is the less sharply sloping area between the "slope" and the deep seabed. Unlike the 1958 Convention, the 1982 Convention does not define the shelf in terms of "exploitability." It also differs in providing that the shelf extends a distance of 200 miles from the coast whether it reaches that distance in nature or not. The 1982 Convention retains an advantage, however, for the naturally favoured state in that the shelf extends beyond that distance in law to the "outer edge" of the continental shelf *if* geomorphologically that point is more than 200 miles out. This was an advantage which such states have under the 1958 Convention and which they were not prepared to surrender; its inclusion was for them an essential part of the package in the 1982 Convention. Even so, the advantage is limited in two respects. First, no shelf may in law extend more than 350 miles from the territorial sea baseline or, beyond that (subject to Article 76(6), the "2500 metres depth plus 100 miles" limit set in Article 76(5). Article 76(6) concerns the role of submarine ridges that geomorphologically are not "natural components of the continental margin" but rise from the deep seabed. The shallower depths that these cause cannot be used to extend the "margin" into an area that is really a part of the deep seabed.[19] Second, Article

---

[18] See Kwiatkowska (1991) 22 O.D.I.L. 153. On the customary international law status of the 1982 Convention régime, see the *Gulf of Maine* case, above, p. 372. Article 76 was assumed to state custom in the *St Pierre and Miguelon* case (1992) 31 I.L.M. 1149. See *contra* the dissenting opinion of Mr Weil as to Art. 76(4)–(9).

[19] For further details on the rules for the drawing of outer limits beyond 200 miles, see Art. 76(7), 1982 Convention, above, p. 458. A state must submit details of a "beyond 200 mile" claim to the Commission on the Limits of the Continental Shelf for its "recommendations": see Art. 76(8).

82(1) of the 1982 Convention provides that a state shall make "payments or contributions in kind" in respect of the exploitation of shelf resources more than 200 miles from its coast. These payments or contributions go to the International Sea-bed Authority for distribution "on the basis of equitable sharing criteria, taking into account the interests and needs of developing states, particularly the least developed and the land-locked among them." (Article 82(4)). Payments commence after five years of production and increase from 1 per cent to 7 per cent in the following years (Article 82(2)).

2. In other respects, the 1982 Convention mostly follows the 1958 Convention. Articles 2, 3, 4 and 7 of the latter are repeated in Articles 77, 78(1), 79(2) and 87 respectively of the former.[20]

3. As noted above, p. 453, the continental shelf régime in Part VI of the 1982 Convention (Articles 76–85) applies to shelf resources of states that have made an exclusive economic zone claim (Article 56(3)) as well as states that have not done so. It also applies to the continental shelf resources that any state has beyond the 200 mile limit.

4. *Islands.* As noted earlier,[21] islands have a continental shelf in the 1982 Convention unless they are just "rocks which cannot sustain human habitation or economic life of their own."[22]

5. *No territorial sovereignty.* Article 77, 1982 Convention gives only limited rights to the coastal state in the continental shelf, not sovereignty.[23] The Truman Proclamation and most others had not claimed sovereignty. In contrast, the claims of some Latin American states are to "national sovereignty."[24]

6. *Living resources.* The phrase "living organisms belonging to the sedentary species" in Article 77(4), 1982 Convention was said at Geneva[25] to include, *inter alia*, "coral, sponges, oysters, including pearl oysters, pearl shell, the sacred chank of India and Ceylon, the trocus and plants."[26] It probably also includes clams[27] and scallops. It excludes bottom fish, shrimps, prawns and, probably, octopuses. Crabs and lobsters have caused problems. The United Kingdom position has been expressed as follows:

> . . . lobsters swim and crabs do not. Therefore, crabs are within the Convention, and lobsters are not.[28]

---

[20] The rules concerning artificial structures, etc., in Art. 5 of the 1958 Convention re-appear (by virtue of Art. 80 of the 1982 Convention) with modification in Art. 60 of the 1982 Convention, above, p. 449, although there is no full equivalent of Art. 5(1) of the 1958 Convention. Art. 6 of the 1958 Convention is replaced by a different rule in Art. 83 of the 1982 Convention.

[21] p. 389.

[22] 1982 Convention, Art. 121(3).

[23] *cf.* Art. 2, 1958 Continental Shelf Convention.

[24] See the claims made by Chile and Peru in 1947: 4 Whiteman 794–799. Such claims have been the subject of protests: *ibid.*

[25] *i.e.* during the adoption of the same wording in Art. 2(4), 1958 Continental Shelf Convention.

[26] Mr Bailey (Australia), *1958 Sea Conference Records*, Vol. VI, p. 57. See Scott (1992) 41 I.C.L.Q. 788.

[27] This is the U.S. view: 4 Whiteman 863.

[28] *Hansard*, H.C., Vol. 688, col. 277, January 28, 1964; 1964 B.P.I.L. 58–59 (but see the attitude taken by the U.K. on lobster fishing off the Bahamas: 4 Whiteman 863). The U.S. distinguishes between lobsters and crabs in the same way; 4 Whiteman 863. Zoologically, this clear cut distinction between lobsters and crabs is an oversimplification. France stated that it understood Art. 2(4) to exclude all crustacea except for one kind of crab (*le crabe anatife*) when it ratified the Convention: see Hartingh (1965) 11 *Annuaire Français* 725.

The intention of at least one of the states sponsoring the text adopted was, however, to exclude all crustacea, including crabs.[29] In 1963, a dispute occurred between France and Brazil over the fishing of crawfish (*langoustes*) by Breton fishermen on the Brazilian continental shelf. It would seem that adult crawfish normally stay in rock holes or clamber about, but will swim if pursued. It is interesting that, although neither France nor Brazil were then parties to the Convention, both relied on their (differing) interpretations of Article 2(4), 1958 Convention to support their claims in respect of freedom to fish for the crawfish.[30]

The inclusion in the 1958 and 1982 Conventions of living resources as well as mineral resources was probably an instance of "progressive development" rather than "codification." The Truman Proclamation is clearly concerned with mineral resources only and the customary international law position before the Convention was probably that claims to exploit living resources, such as pearls, sponges and oysters had to be based upon occupation.[31]

7. *Maritime boundaries.*[32] This is a matter that has generated much litigation because of the important economic consequences. The early cases concerned just continental shelf delimitations, and for convenience the question of maritime boundaries generally is considered here. More recently, some cases have concerned the boundaries between both continental shelves and exclusive fishery zones,[33] either treated as a single maritime boundary[34] or as separate boundaries for the individual maritime areas concerned.[35] Most cases have involved the application of customary international law, because not all of the states concerned have been parties to the 1958 or 1982 Conventions; but some have been decided on the basis of the 1958 Continental Shelf Convention[36] (not the 1982 Convention yet). In one sense, the position has been simplified because the I.C.J. and arbitral tribunals have applied the same general approach in customary and treaty law cases, regarding the achievement of an equitable result according to law (*infra legem*) as the overriding consideration in each. At the same time, it has been complicated by the practice of deciding cases in a common law way, with different considerations (equidistance, natural prolongation, proportionality, adjacent/opposite states) being emphasised on the particular facts. These have been geographic, geomorphological or similar facts; economic and social (*e.g.* population) circumstances have, at least overtly, not been taken into account.

With regard to *continental shelf* delimitations, Article 83, 1982 Convention, above, p. 460, differs from the 1958 Continental Shelf Convention in requiring the

---

[29] See Mr Bailey, Australia, *loc. cit.*, n. 26, above.

[30] A compromise was reached in 1964 allowing a limited number of French boats to fish for crawfish for the following five years. See Goldie, in Alexander, ed., *The Law of the Sea* (1967), pp. 286–287. See also Azzam (1964) 13 I.C.L.Q. 1453. Zoologically, the crawfish, although sometimes known as the rock lobster, is not a lobster at all. On the U.S.–Japanese dispute over the king crab, see 4 Whiteman 864.

[31] Young (1961) 55 A.J.I.L. 359 at 360–362. See the Tunisian claim to historic rights in the *Continental Shelf (Tunisia v. Libya)* case, extract above, p. 388.

[32] See Charney and Alexander, eds., *International Maritime Boundaries* (2 Vols, 1993); Charney (1994) 88 A.J.I.L. 227; Evans, *Relevant Circumstances and Maritime Delimitations* (1989); *id.* (1993) 64 B.Y.I.L. 283; Jagota, *Maritime Boundary* (1985); Johnston, *The Theory and History of Ocean Boundary-Making* (1988); Tanja, *The Legal Delimitation of International Maritime Boundaries* (1990); Thirlway (1994) 65 B.Y.I.L. 2; Weil, *The Law of Maritime Delimitation: Reflections* (1989).

[33] Or some other combination of maritime areas: see the *Guinea-Guinea Bissau* case, below, p. 465.

[34] The *Gulf of Maine* and *St Pierre and Miquelon* cases, below, pp. 465 and 465, n. 45.

[35] The *Jan Mayen* case, I.C.J. Rep. 1993, p. 38.

[36] The *Anglo-French Continental Shelf Case*, below, p. 467, and the *Jan Mayen* case (in part).

states concerned (i) to reach agreement on the basis of international law "in order to achieve an equitable solution" and (ii), in the absence of agreement, to have recourse to the 1982 Convention dispute settlement procedures. Under Article 6(2), 1958 Convention, states are free to make such agreements as they wish; in the absence of agreement, an equidistance rule applies. Article 6(2) reads:

> 1. Where the same continental shelf is adjacent to the territories of two or more states whose coasts are opposite each other, the boundary of the continental shelf appertaining to such states shall be determined by agreement between them. In the absence of agreement, and unless another boundary line is justified by special circumstances, the boundary is the median line, every point of which is equidistant from the nearest points of the baselines from which the breadth of the territorial sea of each state is measured.
>
> 2. Where the same continental shelf is adjacent to the territories of two adjacent states, the boundary of the continental shelf shall be determined by agreement between them. In the absence of agreement, and unless another boundary line is justified by special circumstances, the boundary shall be determined by application of the principle of equidistance from the nearest points of the baselines from which the breadth of the territorial sea of each state is measured.
>
> 3. In delimiting the boundaries of the continental shelf, any lines which are drawn in accordance with the principles set out in paragraphs 1 and 2 of this article should be defined with reference to charts and geographical features as they exist at a particular date, and reference should be made to fixed permanent identifiable points on the land.

In the *North Sea Continental Shelf* cases, the International Court of Justice ruled that Article 6(2) of the 1958 Continental Shelf Convention did not represent customary international law at least as far as lateral line delimitations between adjacent states (as opposed to median line delimitations between opposite states) were concerned. The Court then stated the customary rules that did apply, emphasising above all the need to achieve an equitable result.[37] It took the same approach when applying custom in the *Continental Shelf (Tunisia v. Libya)* case[38]:

> ... the Court considers that it is bound to decide the case on the basis of equitable principles ... It is, however, the result which is predominant; the principles are subordinate to the goal. The equitableness of a principle must be

---

[37] See the passage from the judgment quoted pp. 32–34 above.

[38] I.C.J. Rep. 1982, p. 18 at p. 59. See Brown (1983) 7 Mar. Pol. 142; Feldman (1983) 77 A.J.I.L. 219; Herman (1984) 33 I.C.L.Q. 825; Hodgson (1984) 16 C.W.R.J.I.L. 1. Neither Tunisia nor Libya was a party to the Continental Shelf Convention. The Court confirmed its "equitable result" approach in the *Gulf of Maine* case, I.C.J. Rep. 1984, p. 246 at p. 300, and the *Continental Shelf (Libya v. Malta)* case, I.C.J. Rep. 1985, p. 13 at pp. 30–31. For the Court's understanding of "equity" as justice according to law, see the extract from its *Tunisia v. Libya* judgment, above, p. 52, n. 7. In accordance with the view expressed in that extract that its role was not to achieve "distributive justice," the Court rejected a Tunisian argument based in part upon its relative poverty *vis-à-vis* Libya: such economic consideration could not be taken into account: I.C.J. Rep. 1982, p. 77. Likewise, a Maltese argument based upon its absence of land-based energy resources was unsuccessful in the *Libya v. Malta* case, I.C.J. Rep. 1985, p. 41; while the 1982 LOSC concept of the EEZ does make special provision for developing states, this related not to boundaries, the Court noted, but to the fruits of resource exploitation. Similarly, the Court emphasised that "there is no question of refashioning nature"; to the contrary, a principle of proportionality between coastline length and shelf size applies: *ibid.*, p. 39.

assessed in the light of its usefulness for the purpose of arriving at an equitable result.

In the same case, the Court emphasised that "each continental shelf case in dispute should be considered and judged on its own merits, having regard to its peculiar circumstances," and that, consequently "no attempt should be made . . . to overconceptualise the application of the principles and rules relating to the continental shelf."[39] Applying this approach to the facts before it, the Court decided not to make use of the equidistance rule. The same rule was rejected as inappropriate in the *Guinea-Guinea Bissau Arbitration*[40] in the geographic context of the West African coast; as the middle state in a concave coastline (with Guinea Bissau and Sierra Leone on either side), Guinea would have suffered inequitably from its use.[41] On the facts of the *Continental Shelf* (*Libya v. Malta*) case,[42] however, the International Court of Justice placed great reliance upon the equidistance rule in the case of opposite states.[43] Applying custom, its approach in that case was first to draw a line every point of which was equidistant from the coast of the two opposite states concerned and then to make adjustments in the light of relevant circumstances and factors to achieve an equitable result. The circumstances and factors in that case were:

(1) the general configuration of the coasts of the Parties, their oppositeness, and their relationship to each other within the general geographical context[44];
(2) the disparity in the lengths of the relevant coasts of the Parties and the distance between them;
(3) the need to avoid in the delimitation any excessive disproportion between the extent of the continental shelf areas appertaining to the coastal State and the length of the relevant part of its coast, measured in the general direction of the coastlines.[45]

In the *North Sea* case, the Court placed much emphasis upon the "natural prolongation" factor. Commenting upon this in the *Tunisia v. Libya* case, the Court indicated that this was a factor that, while important, was subservient to the overall need to satisfy equitable principles and, in any event, might, as on the

---

[39] *ibid.*
[40] (1985) 77 I.L.R. 635. Neither state was a party to the 1958 Continental Shelf Convention, so that custom was applied.
[41] *cf.* the I.C.J.'s response to the F.R.G.'s similar geographic position in the *North Sea Cases*, above, p. 27.
[42] I.C.J. Rep. 1985, p. 13 at p. 57. See McDorman (1986) 24 C.Y.I.L. 335 and Wlosowicz (1985) 44 C.L.J. 341. *cf.* the factors listed by the I.C.J. in the *North Sea* cases, above, p. 33–34. Note that the Court's two stage approach (the drawing of an equidistance line followed by corrections to it to achieve equity) is commended by Weil, *op. cit.*, p. 463, n. 32, above, pp. 279–288, as the approach that should generally be followed.
[43] Equidistance was also emphasised in the context of opposite states in the *Jan Mayen* case. In boundary agreements made in state practice, "equidistance easily exceeds all of the other methods of maritime boundary delimitation in frequency of use": Charney (1994) 88 A.J.I.L. 227 at 245.
[44] *cf.* the tribunal's consideration of West African coastal geography generally in the *Guinea-Guinea Bissau Arbitration*.
[45] The proportionality between the ratio of coastline and of allocated maritime area was also an important factor in the *St Pierre and Miquelon* case (1992) 31 I.L.M. 1149. On this case, see Evans (1994) 43 I.C.L.Q. 678; Marston (1993) 17 Mar. Pol. 155; and Charney (1994) 88 A.J.I.L. 227. When determining proportionality, the choice of the relevant area of coastline for ratio purposes is crucial and can be difficult to make where the geography is complicated.

facts of the *Tunisia v. Libya* case, not be helpful in a particular geological situation.[46] In the *Libya v. Malta* case,[47] the Court further discounted the "natural prolongation" factor in all cases within the 200–mile limit:

> Since the development of the law enables a State to claim that the continental shelf appertaining to it extends up to as far as 200 miles from its coast, whatever the geological characteristics of the corresponding sea–bed and subsoil, there is no reason to ascribe any role to geological or geophysical factors within that distance either in verifying the legal title of the States concerned or in proceeding to a delimitation as between their claims.

Accordingly, the Court rejected a Libyan argument relying upon a "rift zone" which it contended was the natural boundary between the two continental shelves.

Whereas most of the cases considered above have concerned continental shelf delimitations only, in the *Gulf of Maine* case,[48] in the first case of its kind, a Chamber of the International Court of Justice was called upon to determine the "single maritime boundary" between the continental shelves and exclusive fishing zones between Canada and the United States in the Gulf of Maine.[49] The Chamber stated that when drawing a single maritime boundary (i) the objective must be, as it is when delimiting boundaries between continental shelves alone, to achieve an equitable result and (ii) "it is necessary to . . . rule out the application of any criterion found to be typically and exclusively bound up with the particular characteristics of" the continental shelf or the water column above it, or which leads to preferential treatment for either of them.[50] With this in mind, the Chamber decided that it should emphasise the geography of the coastal situation, with a view to achieving "an equal distribution of the areas where the maritime projections of the coasts of the states between which delimitation is to be effected converge and overlap"[51]—the result being tempered, however, in order to achieve an equitable result, by considerations such as whether the principle of proportionality between length of coastline and size of zone is respected and whether the location of islands may have distorted the outcome.[52] Another feature of the case was that both states were parties to the 1958 Continental Shelf Convention. The Chamber held that Article 6(2) of that Convention, which would have applied to the boundary of the continental shelf, but not of the exclusive fishing zone (there was no treaty provision applicable to the latter), does not apply when the issue is the determination of a single maritime boundary. To rule otherwise would "make the maritime water mass overlying the continental shelf a mere accessory of that shelf."[53]

---

[46] In that case, the area of shelf in issue was the "natural prolongation" of a land mass common to both states. On the continued relevance of the "natural prolongation" factor, see Lloyd (1991) 3 A.J.I.C.L. 558.

[47] I.C.J. Rep. 1985, p. 35.

[48] I.C.J. Rep. 1984, p. 246. See Clain (1985) 25 Virg.J.I.L. 521; Collins and Rogoff (1986) 38 Maine L.R. 1.; Cooper (1986) 16 O.D.I.L. 59; McRae (1981) 19 C.Y.I.L. 287; Schneider (1985) 79 A.J.I.L. 539.

[49] On single maritime boundaries, see Legault and Hankey 79 (1985) A.J.I.L. 961 and Sharma (1987) 2 I.J.E.C.L. 203.

[50] I.C.J. Rep. 1984, p. 300.

[51] *ibid.* p. 327.

[52] *cf.* the Chamber's two stage approach (a line based on "equal distribution," then corrections to achieve "equity") with that of the I.C.J. in *Libya v. Malta*: see above, n. 42.

[53] I.C.J. Rep. 1984, p. 301.

In the *Anglo-French Continental Shelf* case,[54] the Court of Arbitration was asked to delimit the continental shelves of the United Kingdom and France in the English Channel (West of Selsey Bill) and in the South Western Approaches. In contrast with the International Court of Justice cases discussed above, the case was decided on the basis of the Continental Shelf Convention, Article 6(2),[55] to which both states were parties. In interpreting that provision, the Court of Arbitration observed:

> 68. Article 6 . . . does not formulate the equidistance principle and "special circumstances" as two separate rules. The rule there stated in each of the two cases is a single one, a combined equidistance-special circumstances rule. . . .
>
> 70. The Court does not overlook that under Article 6 the equidistance principle ultimately possesses an obligatory force which it does not have in the same measure under the rules of customary law; for Article 6 makes the application of the equidistance principle a matter of treaty obligation for Parties to the Convention. But the combined character of the equidistance-special circumstances rule means that the obligation to apply the equidistance principle is always one qualified by the condition "unless another boundary line is justified by special circumstances." . . . In short, the role of the "special circumstances" condition in Article 6 is to ensure an equitable delimitation; and the combined "equidistance-special circumstances rule," in effect, gives particular expression to a general norm that, failing agreement, the boundary between States abutting on the same continental shelf is to be determined on equitable principles. . . .
>
> 97. In short, this Court considers that the appropriateness of the equidistance method or any other method for the purpose of effecting an equitable delimitation is a function or reflection of the geographical and other relevant circumstances of each particular case. The choice of the method or methods of delimitation in any given case, whether under the 1958 Convention or customary law, has therefore to be determined in the light of those circumstances and of the fundamental norm that the delimitation must be in accordance with equitable principles. Furthermore, in appreciating the appropriateness of the equidistance method as a means of achieving an equitable solution, regard must be had to the difference between a "lateral" boundary between "adjacent" States and a "medium" boundary between "opposite" States.[56]

In the last analysis, therefore, both the 1958 Convention rule and customary international law require an equitable solution—which is also the objective stated in Article 83(1), 1982 Convention. The difficulty with such an approach is, as Bowett points out,[57] that, since different states will have different views of what equity requires, it reduces the chances of settling boundary disputes without litigation.

A particularly difficult problem of boundary delimitation occurs where one state has territory on the "wrong" side of the putative line. The *Anglo-French*

---

[54] (1979) 18 I.L.M. 397, including both the 1977 Award and the 1978 interpretative decision. The Court of Arbitration was composed of Castren, President; Briggs, Gros, Ustor and Waldock. See Bowett (1978) 49 B.Y.I.L. 1; Brown (1979) 33 Y.B.W.A. 304; Colson (1978) 72 A.J.I.L. 95; *ibid.* (1979) 73 A.J.I.L. 112. On U.K. maritime delimitations generally, see Anderson (1988) 12 Mar. Pol. 231.

[55] The Court held that Art. 6(2) applied to the dispute subject to the French reservations to it.

[56] (1979) 18 I.L.M. 421 at 426–427.

[57] *loc. cit.*, n. 54, above, p. 6. On the resulting uncertainty, see Judge Gros in the *Gulf of Maine Case*, quoted above, p. 52. For a case in which the line drawn would not have been predicted by many, see the *St Pierre and Miquelon* case (1992) 31 I.L.M. 1149.

Continental Shelf Case had to consider the effect of the Scilly and Channel Islands on the boundary between the United Kingdom and French shelves. In the case of the former, "[w]hat equity calls for is an appropriate abatement of the disproportionate effects" of a full application (favouring the United Kingdom) of the equidistance method. Taking a lead from examples of state practice "in which only partial effect has been given to offshore islands situated outside the territorial sea of the mainland," the Court accorded a "half effect" to the Scilly Islands.[58] The Channel Islands presented the problem of islands on the wrong side of the median line and "wholly detached geographically from the United Kingdom."[59] The solution adopted by the Court, in its search for a "more equitable balance" than would have resulted from the arguments put by either party, was to give the Channel Islands a continental shelf of 12 miles from its territorial sea baselines as an enclave within the French continental shelf. In the *Jan Mayen Case*,[60] the Conciliation Commission noted that in state practice where both coastal states have islands along their coasts, examples are found where a "trade off" takes place by ignoring the islands on each side of the line when drawing the boundary "line."

8. Provision is made by the Continental Shelf Act 1964 for the granting of licences for the exploration and exploitation of oil and natural gas in the United Kingdom continental shelf.

9. *Tunnelling.* The 1982 Convention does not affect tunnelling through the subsoil of the continental shelf from the territory of the coastal state (see Article 85).[61] Colombos suggests that "the subsoil under the bed of the sea may be considered capable of occupation" and that it would "be unreasonable to withhold recognition of the right of a State to drive mines or build tunnels in the subsoil, even when they extend considerably beyond the three-mile limit of territorial waters, provided that they do not affect or endanger the surface of the sea."[62] He also suggests that "in the case of a tunnel between two different States, the territorial property and jurisdiction of that part of the tunnel which runs under the bed of the high seas would have to be regulated by agreement between the two States chiefly concerned."[63] Tunnelling for mining purposes beyond the three-mile limit has occurred in Cornwall, for example, under the Cornwall Submarine Mines Act 1858. Section 2 states that "all mines and minerals lying below low-water mark under the open sea adjacent to, but not being part of the county of Cornwall, are vested in Her Majesty the Queen in right of her Crown as part of the soil and territorial possession of the Crown." The Channel Tunnel Act 1987, s.10, which was enacted when the United Kingdom claimed only a three-mile territorial sea (so that a part of the Straits of Dover was high seas) provides that the Channel "tunnel system as far as the frontier . . . shall, as it becomes occupied by . . . the concessionaires working from England . . . be incorporated into England."[64]

10. In 1994, 80 states had made continental shelf claims; 40 of these were to a depth of 200 metres and beyond that where exploitable; 22 were 200 miles wide plus the continental margin beyond that; the others varied: *Law of the Sea Bulletin*, No 25, p. 117. Many of these states also had EEZ claims.

---

[58] (1979) 18 I.L.M. 455.
[59] *ibid.* p. 444.
[60] (1981) 20 I.L.M. 797 at 824.
[61] *cf.* Art. 7, 1958 Continental Shelf Convention.
[62] *op. cit.*, p. 368, n. 1, above, p. 69.
[63] *ibid.*
[64] On the Channel Tunnel, see further above, p. 239.

6. THE DEEP SEA-BED[65]

DECLARATION OF PRINCIPLES GOVERNING THE SEA-BED
AND THE OCEAN FLOOR, AND THE SUBSOIL THEREOF,
BEYOND THE LIMITS OF NATIONAL JURISDICTION[66]

G.A.Res 2749 (XXV), December 17, 1970. (1971) 10 I.L.M. 220

The General Assembly...

Affirming that there is an area of the sea-bed and the ocean floor, and the subsoil thereof, beyond the limits of national jurisdiction, the precise limits of which are yet to be determined,

Recognising that the existing legal régime of the high seas does not provide substantive rules for regulating the exploration of the aforesaid area and the exploitation of its resources, ...

Solemnly declares that:

1. The sea-bed and ocean floor, and the subsoil thereof, beyond the limits of national jurisdiction (hereinafter referred to as the area), as well as the resources of the area, are the common heritage of mankind.

2. The area shall not be subject to appropriation by any means by States or persons, natural or juridical, and no State shall claim or exercise sovereignty or sovereign rights over any part thereof.

3. No State or person, natural or juridical, shall claim, exercise or acquire rights with respect to the area or its resources incompatible with the international régime to be established and the principles of this Declaration.

4. All activities regarding the exploration and exploitation of the resources of the area and other related activities shall be governed by the international régime to be established.

5. The area shall be open to use exclusively for peaceful purposes by all States whether coastal or land-locked, without discrimination, in accordance with the international régime to be established.

6. States shall act in the area in accordance with the applicable principles and rules of international law including the Charter of the United Nations and the [1970] Declaration on Principles of International Law concerning Friendly Relations and Co-operation among States [below, Appendix III] in the interests of maintaining international peace and security and promoting international co-operation and mutual understanding.

7. The exploration of the area and the exploitation of its resources shall be carried out for the benefit of mankind as a whole, irrespective of the

---

[65] See Andrassy, *International Law and the Resources of the Sea* (1970); Brown *op. cit.*, p. 368, n. 1, above, Vol. 1, Chap. 17; Mahmoudi, *The Law of Deep Sea-Bed Mining* (1987); Meese (1986) 17 O.D.I.L. 131; Paolillo (1984–IV) 188 Hague Recueil 135; Post, *Deepsea Mining and the Law of the Sea* (1983); Young (1968) 62 A.J.I.L. 641.

[66] The resolution was adopted by 104 votes to 0, with 14 abstentions.

geographical location of States, whether land-locked or coastal, and taking into particular consideration the interests and needs of the developing countries.

8. The area shall be reserved exclusively for peaceful purposes, without prejudice to any measures which have been or may be agreed upon in the context of international negotiations undertaken in the field of disarmament and which may be applicable to a broader area. One or more international agreements shall be concluded as soon as possible in order to implement effectively this principle and to constitute a step towards the exclusion of the sea-bed, the ocean floor and the subsoil thereof from the arms race.

9. On the basis of the principles of this Declaration, an international régime applying to the area and its resources and including appropriate international machinery to give effect to its provisions shall be established by an international treaty of a universal character, generally agreed upon. The régime shall, *inter alia*, provide for the orderly and safe development and rational management of the area and its resources and for expanding opportunities in the use thereof and ensure the equitable sharing by States in the benefits derived therefrom, taking into particular consideration the interests and needs of the developing countries, whether land-locked or coastal.

Notes

1. The 1970 Declaration was prompted primarily by the wish to establish rules governing the exploitation[67] of the mineral resources of the deep sea-bed which is now a practicable (though expensive) proposition. Interest centres upon:

> ... the hard minerals found in the so-called manganese nodules. The nodules themselves are strange potato-shaped little pieces of rock scattered over thousands of square miles of sea-bed, under 12,000 to 20,000 feet of water. They contain a score or more of minerals, but the ones of greatest value, taking into account their relative percentage in the ore, are manganese, copper, nickel and cobalt.[68]

Manganese nodules are to be found in the Pacific, Atlantic, and Indian Oceans and elsewhere in the seas of the world. Most attention would seem to be concentrated on an area of the sea-bed of the North Pacific, between the United States mainland and Hawaii. During the drafting of the 1982 Convention, a number of international consortia composed of companies from developed states made substantial investments in research and development with a view to beginning production when this proved economically worthwhile, and a stable legal régime prevailed. But investment has since been severely cut back as the market price of deep sea-bed minerals has declined and the high cost of underwater mining has been confirmed. There seems little prospect of such mining in the foreseeable future.

2. The United Nations has had the question of the legal régime of the deep sea-bed under discussion since 1967. It was not long before the analogy with "freedom of fishing" on the high seas, with each state controlling its own nationals,

---

[67] Unless otherwise apparent, this term is used in this section to include exploration also.
[68] Ely (1976) 10 Int. Lawyer 537.

was abandoned (but see now the U.K. Deep Sea Mining (Temporary Provisions) Act 1981 and similar legislation) in favour of the idea of an international régime. Even developed states preferred the security that a limited international régime would offer their national undertakings[69] to the hazards of a "free for all." In 1969, the General Assembly, by a majority,[70] declared a moratorium on sea-bed exploitation "beyond the limits of national jurisdiction" pending the establishment of an international régime. Similarly, the 1970 Declaration rules out the possibility of a "free for all" and indicates some principles upon which an international régime should be based.[71] Above all, it establishes, in a text that attracted no dissent, the principle that the resources of the deep sea-bed are "the common heritage of mankind." They are, that is, to be used to benefit all states, not just those with the technology and capital to recover them. The understanding in 1970 was that a share of the profits from deep sea-bed mining should, in accordance with this principle, be distributed among developing states. The emergence of a new area in which there were no vested interests was seen to offer a good opportunity of progress towards a more equitable international economic order. What the 1970 Declaration did not do was to indicate whether the mining should be done by national undertakings under the aegis of an international body or by the international body itself. This, and other details, could only be formulated in a Convention.

CONVENTION ON THE LAW OF THE SEA 1982

UN Doc. A/CONF. 62/122; (1982) 21 I.L.M. 1261

Article 135

Neither this Part [XI] nor any rights granted or exercised pursuant thereto shall affect the legal status of the waters superjacent to the Area[72] or that of the air space above those waters.

Article 136

The Area and its resources[73] are the common heritage of mankind.

Article 137

1. No state shall claim or exercise sovereignty or sovereign rights over any part of the Area or its resources, nor shall any State or natural or

---

[69] This term is used to include public and private undertakings at the national level, including consortia of companies of different nationalities.

[70] G.A. Resn. 2574D (XXIV), G.A.O.R., 24th Session, Supp. 30 (1969). The Resolution was adopted by 62 votes to 28, with 28 abstentions.

[71] On the impact of the Declaration upon custom, see Brown (1983) 20 San Diego L.R. 521.

[72] *Ed.* The "area" is the "sea-bed and ocean floor and subsoil thereof beyond the limits of national jurisdiction" (1982 Convention, Art. 1(1)), *i.e.* the area beyond the edge of the "continental margin": see above, p. 461.

[73] *Ed.* 1982 Convention, Art. 133, reads: "For the purposes of this Part: (a) 'resources' means all solid, liquid or gaseous mineral resources *in situ* in the Area at or beneath the sea-bed, including polymetallic nodules; (b) resources, when recovered from the Area, are referred to as 'minerals.' " The definition of "resources" is very generally phrased to allow for the future discovery in commercial quantities of resources other than "polymetallic" (or manganese) nodules.

juridical person appropriate any part thereof. No such claim or exercise of sovereignty or sovereign rights nor such appropriation shall be recognised.

2. All rights in the resources of the Area are vested in mankind as a whole, on whose behalf the Authority shall act. These resources are not subject to alienation. The minerals recovered from the Area, however, may only be alienated in accordance with this Part and the rules, regulations and procedures of the Authority.

3. No State or natural or juridical person shall claim, acquire or exercise rights with respect to the minerals recovered from the Area except in accordance with this Part. Otherwise, no such claim, acquisition or exercise of such rights shall be recognised. . . .

Article 140

1. Activities in the Area shall . . . be carried out for the benefit of mankind as a whole, irrespective of the geographical location of States, whether coastal or land-locked, and taking into particular consideration the interests and needs of developing States and of peoples who have not attained full independence or other self-governing status recognised by the United Nations in accordance with General Assembly 1514 (XV)[74] and other relevant General Assembly resolutions.

2. The Authority shall provide for the equitable sharing of financial and other economic benefits derived from activities in the Area through any appropriate mechanism, on a non-discriminatory basis, in accordance with article 160, paragraph 2(f)(i).[75]

Article 141

The Area shall be open to use exclusively for peaceful purposes by all States, whether coastal or land-locked, without discrimination and without prejudice to the other provisions of this Part. . . .

Article 150

Activities in the Area shall . . . be carried out in such a manner as to foster healthy development of the world economy and balanced growth of international trade, and to promote international co-operation for the over-all development of all countries, especially developing States, and with a view to ensuring:

(a) the development of the resources of the Area;

---

[74] *Ed.* Above, p. 114.
[75] *Ed.* This gives the Authority power to make regulations for "equitable sharing," "taking into particular consideration the interests and needs of developing states and peoples who have not attained full independence or other self-governing status."

(b) orderly, safe and rational management of the resources of the Area . . .

(d) participation in revenues by the Authority and the transfer of technology to the Enterprise and developing States as provided for in this Convention; . . .

(f) the promotion of just and stable prices remunerative to producers and fair to consumers for minerals derived both from the Area and from other sources, and the promotion of long-term equilibrium between supply and demand;

(g) the enhancement of opportunities for all States Parties, irrespective of their social and economic systems or geographical location, to participate in the development of the resources of the Area and the prevention of monopolization of activities in the Area;

(h) the protection of developing countries from adverse effects on their economies or on their export earnings resulting from a reduction in the price of an affected mineral, or in the volume of exports of that mineral, to the extent that such reduction is caused by activities in the Area . . .

(i) the development of the common heritage for the benefit of mankind as a whole . . .

Article 153

1. Activities in the Area shall be organised, carried out and controlled by the Authority on behalf of mankind as a whole in accordance with this article as well as other relevant provisions of this Part and the relevant Annexes, and the rules, regulations and procedures of the Authority.

2. Activities in the Area shall be carried out: . . .

(a) by the Enterprise, and

(b) in association with the Authority by States Parties, or state enterprises or natural or juridical persons which possess the nationality of States Parties or are effectively controlled by them or their nationals, when sponsored by such States, or any group of the foregoing which meets the requirements provided in this Part and in Annex III. . . .

Notes

1. Part XI (Articles 133–191), 1982 Convention, established the "international regime" on the deep sea-bed referred to in the 1970 Declaration (above). Unfortunately, it proved not to be acceptable to the U.S. and other developed states, who declined to sign and/or ratify the 1982 Convention because of it.[76] Although enough developing states had ratified the Convention to bring it into force in 1994, these states lacked the financial capacity to fund both the deep sea-bed regime in Part XI of the Convention and other institutions created by the 1982

[76] See above, p. 370.

Convention.[77] Anticipating this and other threats to the success of the 1982 Convention regime as a whole caused by the non-involvement in it of developed states, the UN took steps[78] in the early 1990s to facilitate their acceptance of the 1982 Convention, resulting in the 1994 New York Agreement Relating to the Implementation of Part XI.[79] In effect, the Agreement modifies Part XI in such a way as to meet the objections of developed states to the Convention's original deep sea-bed regime. Developing states were willing to accept this mainly because changed economic circumstances have meant that the exploitation of deep sea-bed mineral resources, with resulting payments for them (see Articles 140(2) and 160(2)(f)(i), 1982 Convention), is unlikely in the foreseeable future[80] and because of the financial need to involve developed states in the 1982 Convention generally.[81]

The 1994 Agreement entered into force in 1996[82] and Part XI of the 1982 Convention is in its early stages of implementation in accordance with its terms. The following notes on Part XI take account of the changes made by the 1994 Agreement.

2. The Convention adopts the idea of the 1970 Declaration that the deep sea-bed and its resources are "the common heritage of mankind"[83] not open to claims of sovereignty or sovereign rights. This was not controversial. The problem was to take the matter further and to devise a system for the exploitation of resources that was both consistent with this idea and met the demands of developed and developing states alike. Developing states pressed for a system by which exploitation would be conducted by an international body—the Authority (see below)—and not by states or national undertakings. Developed states preferred the idea by which exploitation would be by states or national undertakings subject to a system of registration or, at most, licensing. The system of "parallel access" adopted in the Convention is a compromise between the two approaches, although one that, in the original text of Part XI, leans mostly towards the approach of the developing states. Under Article 153 of the 1982 Convention,

---

[77] These are the International Tribunal for the Law of the Sea and the Commission on the Limits of the Continental Shelf.

[78] See Anderson (1993) 42 I.C.L.Q. 654; *ibid.* (1994) 43 I.C.L.Q. 886; *ibid.* (1995) 44 I.C.L.Q. 313.

[79] (1994) 33 I.L.M. 1309. See Brown (1995) 19 Mar. Pol. 5; Oxman (1994) 88 A.J.I.L. 687; Platzöder, ed., *The 1994 United Nations Convention on the Law of the Sea* (1995); *id.* (1993) 4 E.J.I.L. 390; and Sohn (1994) 88 A.J.I.L. 696. The Agreement and Part XI "shall be interpreted and applied together as a single instrument" and in the event "of any inconsistency... the provisions of the agreement shall prevail": Art. 2, 1994 Agreement.

[80] These minerals now command lower prices with the development of artificial substitutes and for other reasons.

[81] Other factors which strengthened the hand of developed states were the disintegration of the USSR; the reduction in the political power of developing states in the UN; and the world-wide move from state to private enterprise: see de Marffy-Mantuano (1995) 89 A.J.I.L. 825.

[82] There are 78 parties, including the U.K. States that become parties to the 1982 Convention after the Agreement entered into force on July 28, 1994 thereby become parties to the Agreement also; parties to the 1982 Convention prior to that date became parties to the Agreement by signing it by July 28, 1995: Gen. Ass. Resn. 48/263 (1994) 33 I.L.M. 1309. On this ingenious application of the law concerning the acceptance of treaties, see de Marffy-Mantuano, *loc. cit.* at n. 81, above. However, there are some pre-July 28, 1994 Convention parties, including some who abstained in the voting on Resn. 48/263, that did not sign the 1994 Agreement within the 12 month period and have not otherwise become parties to it.

[83] On the concept of the "common heritage of mankind", see Larshan and Brennan (1983) 21 Col. J.T.L. 305; Goldie (1983) 10 Syracuse J.I.L.C. 69; Joyner (1986) 35 I.C.L.Q. 190; Kiss (1985) 40 Int. Jo. 423; Schmidt, *Common Heritage or Common Burden?* (1989); Van Hoof (1986) 7 Grotiana 49; White (1982) 14 C.W.R.J.I.L. 509; Wolfrum (1983) 43 Z.A.O.R.V. 312.

control of all sea-bed activities is placed in the hands of the Authority, which may exploit resources itself or contract with a national undertaking[84] to do so. Under the 1994 Agreement, the Enterprise, acting for the Authority, "shall conduct its initial deep sea-bed operations through joint ventures" with national undertakings, not by itself, and must act in accordance with "sound commercial principles" when doing so.[85] The original Part XI contains provisions for the setting of production levels (to protect land-based producers) and for the transfer to technology by national undertakings to the Enterprise and to developing countries. The 1994 Agreement states that these provisions shall not apply.[86] These changes made by the 1994 Agreement clearly reflect the wishes and interests of developed states.

Other changes made by the 1994 Agreement respond to the financial concerns of developed states. The "cost effectiveness" principle and other new rules governing the operation of the Authority[87] and the establishment of a finance Committee to oversee the budget[88] reduce the financial contributions due from Convention parties, as will the fact that the Enterprise will remain largely inactive until deep sea mining occurs. Also, as noted, the Enterprise must operate in accordance with commercial principles and initially will operate through joint ventures funded by private sector consortia, not by states through the Authority.

3. The Convention (Articles 156–168) provides for an independent International Sea-Bed Authority, with its seat in Jamaica, which has overall responsibility for the deep sea-bed regime. The Authority was established in 1994 following the entry into force of the 1982 Convention.[89] In addition, there is a separate body called the Enterprise, which is responsible for the actual conduct of deep sea-bed operations for the Authority. The Authority has two political organs, the Assembly and the Council. The Assembly, of which all Convention parties are members, is the policy-making body. It takes decisions by a two thirds majority. Under the 1994 Agreement, decisions by the Assembly on matters in respect of which the Council has competence must be taken on the recommendation of the Council.[90]

The Council, which is composed of 36 members elected by the Assembly to represent various interest groups, is the executive body. Under the 1994 Agreement, a seat on the Council is guaranteed for "the state, on the date of entry into force of the Convention having the largest economy in terms of domestic gross

---

[84] Only national undertakings that meet the (i) nationality or control and (ii) sponsorship requirements of Art. 153(2)(b) and Annex III of the 1982 Convention (linking the undertaking enterprise with a Convention party) are eligible for a contract. Art. 4(2) of Annex III makes particular provision for partnerships or consortia from more than one state.

[85] Annex, s. 2, para. 2. The Enterprise will not be able to operate independently until the Council has established the governing rules: *ibid*. Prospecting, as opposed to exploitation, needs no contract and may be carried out by more than one prospector in the same area simultaneously: Art. 2, Annex III, 1982 Convention.

[86] Annex, s. 6, para. 7, and s. 5, para. 2. Production is to occur instead on the basis of "sound commercial principles" and the provisions of the GATT (Section 6, para. 1); developing states that suffer serious adverse effects on their export earnings or economies are to be compensated from the proceeds of mining (S. 7). The Enterprise and developing states are to obtain technology on commercial terms on the open market; if they are unable to do so, the Authority may "request" the assistance of contractors or their sponsoring state, subject to "the effective protection of intellectual property rights": Annex, s. 5, para. 1.

[87] Annex, s. 1.

[88] Annex, s. 9.

[89] For documents on the Preparatory Committee for the Sea-bed Authority, see Platzöder, ed., *The Law of the Sea: Documents 1983–9* (13 Vols., 1983).

[90] Annex, s. 3, paras. 1, 4.

national product"[91] namely the United States. Under the 1994 Agreement, decisions by the Council on questions of substance are taken by a two-thirds majority, provided that they are not opposed by a majority in any one of the Council chambers.[92] These chambers, composed of groupings of states with specified interests, are provided for by the 1994 Agreement and some of them will be controlled by the developed states.

The amendments made by the 1994 Agreement to the original Part XI provisions on decision making that are indicated above, which increase the power of the Council at the expense of the Assembly and the influence in the Council of developed states, again follow the wishes and interests of that group of states.

4. Another criticism of the original Part XI regime was the absence of any protection for pre-Convention investment in exploration. This problem was tackled by Resolution II of the Final Act of UNCLOS III.[93] This permits the registration of states and national undertakings that have spent $30 million on seabed activities as "pioneer" investors. As such, they have priority over other applicants in the allocation of exploitation contracts.

5. *The reciprocating states régime.* Following its rejection of the 1982 Convention régime for the deep sea-bed, the United States enacted the Deep Sea-bed Hard Mineral Resources Act 1980,[94] by which the United States may issue licences to exploit deep sea-bed resources. Similar legislation has since been enacted by the United Kingdom and a number of other developed states.[95] This legislation remains in force for the present; the United Kingdom Act will be repealed upon acceptance of the 1982 Convention.

7. SETTLEMENT OF DISPUTES

CONVENTION ON THE LAW OF THE SEA 1982

UN Doc. A/CONF. 62/122; (1982) 21 I.L.M. 1261

Article 286

Subject to section 3 [Articles 297–299], any dispute concerning the interpretation or application of this Convention shall, where no settlement has been reached by recourse to section 1,[96] be submitted at the request of any party to the dispute to the court or tribunal having jurisdiction under this section.

---

[91] *ibid.* para. 15(a).

[92] *ibid.* para. 5.

[93] Reprinted in Brown, *op. cit.*, p. 368, n. 1, above, Vol. 2, p. 343. See Kimball (1986) 17 O.D.I.L. 367, and Larson (1986) 17 O.D.I.L. 271. There are 18, mostly developed, state pioneer investors. They include the U.K. and the U.S. The four western consortia (involving companies of Belgian, Canadian, French, German, Italian, Japanese, Dutch, British and U.S. nationality) that are eligible have not applied for registration.

[94] (1980) 19 I.L.M. 1003.

[95] The FRG (1981) 20 I.L.M. 393; France (1982) 21 I.L.M. 808; the USSR (1982) 21 I.L.M. 551; Japan (1983) 22 I.L.M. 102; and Italy (1985) 24 I.L.M. 983.

[96] *Ed.* Section 1 (Arts. 279–285) provides for the settlement of disputes by the peaceful means listed in Art. 33, UN Charter, other than judicial settlement or arbitration.

Article 287

1. When signing, ratifying or acceding to this Convention or at any time thereafter, a State shall be free to choose, by means of a written declaration, one or more of the following means for the settlement of disputes concerning the interpretation or application of this Convention:

(a) the International Tribunal for the Law of the Sea established in accordance with Annex VI:
(b) the International Court of Justice;
(c) an arbitral tribunal constituted in accordance with Annex VII;
(d) a special arbitral tribunal constituted in accordance with Annex VIII for one or more of the categories of disputes specified therein [*i.e.* fisheries, marine environment, marine scientific research and navigation, including pollution from vessels and dumping].

2. A declaration made under paragraph 1 shall not affect or be affected by the obligation of a State Party to accept the jurisdiction of the Sea-Bed Disputes Chamber of the International Tribunal for the Law of the Sea to the extent and in the manner provided for in Part XI, section 5 [concerning the deep sea-bed].

3. A State Party, which is a party to a dispute not covered by a declaration in force, shall be deemed to have accepted arbitration in accordance with Annex VII.

4. If the parties to a dispute have accepted the same procedure for the settlement of the dispute, it may be submitted only to that procedure, unless the parties otherwise agree.

5. If the parties to a dispute have not accepted the same procedure for the settlement of the dispute, it may be submitted only to arbitration in accordance with Annex VII, unless the parties otherwise agree.

6. A declaration made under paragraph 1 shall remain in force until three months after notice of revocation has been deposited with the Secretary-General of the United Nations.

7. A new declaration, a notice of revocation or the expiry of a declaration does not in any way affect proceedings pending before a court or tribunal having jurisdiction under this article, unless the parties otherwise agree.

8. Declarations and notices referred to in this article shall be deposited with the Secretary-General of the United Nations, who shall transmit copies thereof to the States Parties.

Article 288

1. A court or tribunal referred to in article 287 shall have jurisdiction over any dispute concerning the interpretation or application of this Convention which is submitted to it in accordance with this Part.

2. A court or tribunal referred to in article 287 shall also have jurisdiction over any dispute concerning the interpretation or application of an international agreement related to the purposes of this Convention, which is submitted to it in accordance with the agreement.

3. The Sea-Bed Disputes Chamber of the International Tribunal for the Law of the Sea established in accordance with Annex VI, and any other chamber or arbitral tribunal referred to in Part XI, section 5, shall have jurisdiction in any matter which is submitted to it in accordance therewith.

4. In the event of a dispute as to whether a court or tribunal has jurisdiction, the matter shall be settled by decision of that court or tribunal.

Article 291

1. All the dispute settlement procedures specified in this Part shall be open to States Parties.

2. The dispute settlement procedures specified in this Part shall be open to entities other than States Parties only as specifically provided for in this Convention.

Article 293

1. A court or tribunal having jurisdiction under this section shall apply this Convention and other rules of international law not incompatible with this Convention.

2. Paragraph 1 does not prejudice the power of the court or tribunal having jurisdiction under this section to decide a case *ex aequo et bono*, if the parties so agree.

Article 295

Any dispute between States Parties concerning the interpretation or application of this Convention may be submitted to the procedures provided for in this section only after local remedies have been exhausted where this is required by international law.

Article 296

1. Any decision rendered by a court or tribunal having jurisdiction under this section shall be final and shall be complied with by all the parties to the dispute.

2. Any such decision shall have no binding force except between the parties and in respect of that particular dispute.

Article 297

1. Disputes concerning the interpretation or application of this Convention with regard to the exercise by a coastal State of its sovereign

rights or jurisdiction provided for in this Convention shall be subject to the procedures provided for in section 2 [Articles 286–296] in the following cases:

1. (a) when it is alleged that a coastal State has acted in contravention of the provisions of this Convention in regard to the freedoms and rights of navigation, overflight or the laying of submarine cables and pipelines, or in regard to other internationally lawful uses of the sea specified in article 58 [above, p. 448];

    (b) when it is alleged that a State in exercising the aforementioned freedoms, rights or uses has acted in contravention of this Convention or of laws or regulations adopted by the coastal State in conformity with this Convention and other rules of international law not incompatible with this Convention; or

    (c) when it is alleged that a coastal State has acted in contravention of specified international rules and standards for the protection and preservation of the marine environment which are applicable to the coastal State and which have been established by this Convention or through a competent international organization or diplomatic conference in accordance with this Convention.

2. (a) Disputes concerning the interpretation or application of the provisions of this Convention with regard to marine scientific research shall be settled in accordance with section 2, except that the coastal State shall not be obliged to accept the submission to such settlement of any dispute arising out of:

    (i) the exercise by the coastal State of a right or discretion in accordance with article 246 [marine scientific research in the EEZ and on the continental shelf]; or

    (ii) a decision by the coastal State to order suspension or cessation of a research project in accordance with article 253 [marine scientific research in the deep sea-bed area].

    (b) A dispute arising from an allegation by the researching State that with respect to a specific project the coastal state is not exercising its rights under articles 246 and 253 in a manner compatible with this Convention shall be submitted, at the request of either party, to conciliation under Annex V, section 2, provided that the conciliation commission shall not call in question the exercise by the coastal State of its discretion to designate specific areas as referred to in article 246, paragraph 6, or of its discretion to withhold consent in accordance with article 246, paragraph 5.

3. (a) Disputes concerning the interpretation or application of the provisions of this Convention with regard to fisheries shall be settled in accordance with section 2, except that the coastal State shall not be obliged to accept the submission to such settlement of any dispute relating to its sovereign rights with respect to the living resources in the exclusive economic zone or their exercise,

including its discretionary powers for determining the allowable catch, its harvesting capacity, the allocation of surpluses to other States and the terms and conditions established in its conservation and management laws and regulations.

(b) Where no settlement has been reached by recourse to section 1 of this Part, a dispute shall be submitted to conciliation under Annex V, section 2, at the request of any party to the dispute, when it is alleged that:

(i) a coastal State has manifestly failed to comply with its obligations to ensure through proper conservation and management measures that the maintenance of the living resources in the exclusive economic zone is not seriously endangered;

(ii) a coastal state has arbitrarily refused to determine, at the request of another State, the allowable catch and its capacity to harvest living resources with respect to stocks which that other State is interested in fishing; or

(iii) a coastal State has arbitrarily refused to allocate to any State, under articles 62 [above, p. 450], 69 and 70 [on the rights of land-locked and geographically disadvantaged states respectively] and under the terms and conditions established by the coastal State consistent with this Convention, the whole or part of the surplus it has declared to exist.

(c) In no case shall the conciliation commission substitute its discretion for that of the coastal State.

(d) The report of the conciliation commission shall be communicated to the appropriate international organizations.

(e) In negotiating agreements pursuant to articles 69 and 70, States Parties, unless they otherwise agree, shall include a clause on measures which they shall take in order to minimize the possibility of a disagreement concerning the interpretation or application of the agreement, and on how they should proceed if a disagreement nevertheless arises.

Article 298

1. When signing, ratifying or acceding to this Convention or at any time thereafter, a State may, without prejudice to the obligations arising under section 1, declare in writing that it does not accept any one or more of the procedures provided for in section 2 with respect to one or more of the following categories of disputes:

(a) (i) disputes concerning the interpretation or application of articles 15, 74 and 83 relating to sea boundary delimitations, or those involving historic bays or titles, provided that a State having made such a declaration shall, when such a dispute arises subsequent to the entry into force of this Convention and where no agreement within a reasonable period of time is reached in negotiations between the parties, at the request of any party to the dispute, accept submission of the matter to conciliation under Annex V, section 2; and provided further that any dispute that necessarily involves the concurrent consideration of any unsettled dispute concerning sovereign or other rights over continental or insular land territory shall be excluded from such submission;

  (ii) after the conciliation commission has presented its report, which shall state the reasons on which it is based, the parties shall negotiate an agreement on the basis of that report; if these negotiations do not result in an agreement, the parties shall, by mutual consent, submit the question to one of the procedures provided for in section 2, unless the parties otherwise agree;

  (iii) this subparagraph does not apply to any sea boundary dispute finally settled by an arrangement between the parties, or to any such dispute which is to be settled in accordance with a bilateral or multilateral agreement binding upon those parties;

(*b*)   disputes concerning military activities, including military activities by government vessels and aircraft engaged in non-commercial service, and disputes concerning law enforcement activities in regard to the exercise of sovereign rights or jurisdiction excluded from the jurisdiction of a court or tribunal under article 297, paragraph 2 or 3;

(*c*)   disputes in respect of which the Security Council of the United Nations is exercising the functions assigned to it by the Charter of the United Nations, unless the Security Council decides to remove the matter from its agenda or calls upon the parties to settle it by the means provided for in this Convention.

2. A State Party which has made a declaration under paragraph 1 may at any time withdraw it, or agree to submit a dispute excluded by such declaration to any procedure specified in this Convention.

3. A State Party which has made a declaration under paragraph 1 shall not be entitled to submit any dispute falling within the excepted category of disputes to any procedure in this Convention as against another State Party, without the consent of that party.

4. If one of the State Parties has made a declaration under paragraph 1(a), any other State Party may submit any dispute falling within an excepted category against the declarant party to the procedure specified in such declaration.

5. A new declaration, or the withdrawal of a declaration, does not in any way affect proceedings pending before a court or tribunal in accordance with this article, unless the parties otherwise agree.

6. Declarations and notices of withdrawal of declarations under this article shall be deposited with the Secretary-General of the United Nations, who shall transmit copies thereof to the States Parties.

Article 299

1. A dispute excluded under article 297 or excepted by a declaration made under article 298 from the dispute settlement procedures provided for in section 2 may be submitted to such procedures only by agreement of the parties to the dispute.

2. Nothing in this section impairs the right of the parties to the dispute to agree to some other procedure for the settlement of such dispute or to reach an amicable settlement.

Notes

1. The 1982 Convention is notable for the provision it makes for the settlement of disputes by judicial settlement or arbitration if negotiation, conciliation or other means of peacefully settling disputes listed in Article 33, UN Charter are unsuccessful.[97] A considerable achievement is the provision for the *compulsory* judicial settlement or arbitration of most kinds of disputes that may arise under the Convention, at the request of just one of the parties to the dispute (Article 286). Exceptionally, some kinds of disputes concerning the exercise by a coastal state of its sovereign rights, powers, and jurisdiction are not subject to compulsory jurisdiction (Article 297). In addition a contracting state or party may make a declaration excluding certain other kinds of disputes (territorial sea, continental shelf, exclusive economic zone boundary disputes; disputes concerning military activities; and disputes before the Security Council) from compulsory jurisdiction (Article 298). The 1958 Conventions make no such provision; the Optional Protocol that accompanies these Conventions is all that drafting Conferences normally achieve. Since many of the 1982 Convention rules contain *lacunae*[98] or, inevitably, are generally phrased,[99] and since some state practice is of doubtful consistency with them,[1] the availability of judicial or arbitral proceedings offers an exceptional opportunity to clarify the law and resolve disputes between the parties.

Under Article 287, a party may make a declaration by which it indicates its acceptance of the jurisdiction of one or more of the newly created International Tribunal for the Law of the Sea, the I.C.J. or an arbitral tribunal constituted in accordance with Annexes VII or VIII. The effect of the Law of the Sea Tribunal's having parallel jurisdiction with the I.C.J., whose cases often concern maritime boundaries or other law of the sea matters, has raised the question whether the result will be lack of consistency of case law on the law of the sea. 18 Convention parties have made declarations for the purposes of Article 287 which indicate

---

[97] See Adede, *The System for Settlement of Disputes under the United Nations Convention on the Law of the Sea* (1987); Birnie, in Butler, ed., *The Law of the Sea and International Shipping* (1985), p. 39; Carnegie (1979) 28 I.C.L.Q. 669; Charney (1990) 90 A.J.I.L. 69; Gaertner (1982) 19 San Diego L.R. 577; Gamble (1991) 9 B.U.I.L.J. 39; Jaenicke (1983) 43 Z.A.O.R.V. 813; Janis (1992) 16 Mar. Pol. 102; Oda, in Makarczk, ed., *Essays in Honour of Judge Manfred Lachs* (1985), p. 646; Riphagen, in Rozakis and Stephanou, eds., *The New Law of the Sea* (1983), p. 281.

[98] *e.g.* on innocent passage for warships: see above, p. 406.

[99] *e.g.* the "routes" of similar convenience" exception to the right of transit passage: see above p. 411.

[1] *e.g.* on the use of straight baselines: see above, p. 386.

their choice of forum for the settlement of disputes. Among various combinations of choice, some have nominated either the Law of the Sea Tribunal (three) or the I.C.J. (four) as their only choice; others have nominated the Tribunal (six) or the I.C.J. (two) as their first or equal first choice; several have nominated an arbitral tribunal as their second or only choice.[2]

2. The judges of the International Tribunal for the Law of the Sea have been elected and the Tribunal, which has its seat in Hamburg, awaits its first case.

[2] UN Doc. ST/L.E.G./SER. E/15, p. 822 *et seq.*

CHAPTER 8

STATE RESPONSIBILITY

1. INTRODUCTORY NOTE

IN any legal system there must be liability for failure to observe obligations imposed by its rules. Such liability is known in international law as *responsibility.* The materials in this chapter directly concern the responsibility of states. Other international persons are, of course, responsible for violating their obligations also.

In municipal law, a division is made between civil and criminal liability and, within the former, between liability in contract and in tort. From a different standpoint, liability is based upon intentional or negligent conduct or arises without fault at all. There are also rules about such matters as imputability (*e.g.* rules about the liability of employers for the *ultra vires* actions of their employees), remedies and *locus standi*. Some of these divisions and rules exist in international law, but, as will be apparent from the extracts in section 2 of this chapter, the theory of state responsibility is not very well developed.

The International Law Commission, after earlier uncompleted work that linked questions of responsibility generally with responsibility for the treatment of aliens in particular, has now adopted a different approach and is limiting itself for the time being to the codification of the rules concerning responsibility generally.[1] It is possible that, when its Draft Articles are finally adopted[2] they will form the basis of a law-making treaty, although it should be noted that they have been much criticised and contain controversial provisions, such as that (Article 19) on the criminal responsibility of states.[3]

Responsibility arises for the breach of any obligation owed under international law. A state is responsible, for example, if it fails to honour a treaty, if it violates the territorial sovereignty of another state, if it damages the territory or property of another state, if it employs armed force against another state, if it injures the diplomatic representatives of another state, or if it mistreats the nationals of another state. For some writers the term state responsibility has been used only in connection with the last of these examples. Although it is not used in this limited sense here, the only particular category of state responsibility dealt with in this chapter, in section 3, is, in fact, the treatment of aliens. Materials on other categories of responsibility are included elsewhere.

---

[1] For criticism of this approach see Lillich (1978–III) 161 Hague Recueil 329 at 373 *et seq.*

[2] In 1996, the I.L.C. provisionally adopted its Draft Articles on first reading: for the text see the I.L.C.'s 1996 Report, G.A.O.R, 51st Sess., Supp. 10, p. 125. The I.L.C. will reconsider the Draft Articles on a second and final reading once governments have made their written comments on them. On Arts. 1–35 (Pt. I), see Rosenne, ed., *The International Law Commission's Draft Articles on State Responsibility* (1991).

[3] See, *e.g.* Allott (1988) 29 H.I.L.J. 1 and Gray (1985) 56 B.Y.I.L. 25.

2. THE THEORY OF RESPONSIBILITY[4]

(i) ITS EXISTENCE[5]

I.L.C. DRAFT ARTICLES ON STATE RESPONSIBILITY

I.L.C.'s 1996 Report, G.A.O.R., 51st Sess., Supp. 10, p. 125

Article 1

Every internationally wrongful act of a State entails the international responsibility of that State.

Article 2

Every State is subject to the possibility of being held to have committed an internationally wrongful act entailing its international responsibility.

Article 3

There is an internationally wrongful act of a State when:

(*a*) conduct consisting of an action or omission is attributable[6] to the State under international law; and

(*b*) that conduct constitutes a breach of an international obligation of the State.

Article 4

An act of a State may only be characterized as internationally wrongful by international law. Such characterization cannot be affected by the characterization of the same act as lawful by internal law.

---

[4] See Brownlie, *State Responsibility* (Part I, 1983); Borchard (1929) 1 Z.A.O.R.V. 223; Cheng, *General Principles of Law as Applied by International Courts and Tribunals* (1953), Chaps. 6–10; Eagleton, *The Responsibility of States in International Law* (1928); Garcia Amador (1958–II) 94 Hague Recueil 365; Thirlway (1995) 66 B.Y.I.L. 1 at 38. Among textbooks, see, in particular, Brownlie, Chap. 20 and Schwarzenberger, Chaps. 31–36. See also the reports of the I.L.C. Special Rapporteurs on state responsibility, Ago, Riphagen and Arangio Ruiz, printed in the volumes of the Y.B.I.L.C. from 1969 onwards.

[5] In addition to the following extracts, see also those in subsection (v) on "Reparation", below, p. 514, and the extract from the *Corfu Channel* case, below p. 494.

[6] *Ed., i.e.* "imputable" in the terminology used in this Chap.

Notes

1. As the International Law Commission's Commentary to the Draft Articles states, the principle in Article 1 is "one of the principles most strongly upheld by State practice and judicial decisions and most deeply rooted in the doctrine of international law."[7] In the *Chorzów Factory (Indemnity) (Merits)* case,[8] the P.C.I.J. commented:

> . . . it is a principle of international law, and even a general conception of law, that any breach of an engagement involves an obligation to make reparation. In Judgment No. 8[9] . . . the Court has already said that reparation is the indispensable complement of a failure to apply a convention, and there is no necessity for this to be stated in the convention itself.

If two states join together in injuring a third state (*e.g.* by the activities of a joint military force[10]), they will be jointly liable.[11]

2. Article 2 is intended to make it clear that all states are responsible in law for their illegal acts; there are no exceptions based upon lack of capacity (as, for example, in the case of infants in municipal law). In particular, there is no exception for new states:

> States establish themselves as equal members of the international community as soon as they achieve an independent and sovereign existence. If it is the prerogative of sovereignty to be able to assert its rights, the counterpart of that prerogative is the duty to discharge its obligations.[12]

3. Article 3 separates, in (a) and (b), what the Commission refers to as the "subjective" and "objective" elements of any internationally wrongful act. Article 3 does not list resulting damage as a requirement of a wrongful act; the breach of the obligation is itself sufficient.[13]

4. Elsewhere in its Draft Articles, the Commission defines the defences that a state may generally rely upon to deny responsibility. These are consent, countermeasures, force majeure, distress, necessity and self defence (Articles 29–34 respectively).[14] The Commission also states that responsibility does not arise if the obligation is not in force for the state at the time of its act (Article 18) or if local remedies are not exhausted (Article 22).[15]

5. A state is responsible for the wrongful acts of another state in which it is implicated, either by giving that other state aid or assistance (Article 27) or by exercising control over or coercing it (Article 28).[16]

---

[7] Y.B.I.L.C., 1973, II, p. 173.

[8] P.C.I.J. Rep., Ser. A. No. 17, (1928) p. 29.

[9] *Chorzów Factory Case (Jurisdiction), ibid.* No. 9, p. 21.

[10] As in the *Samoan Claims Arbitration, Germany v. U.K. and U.S* (1902) 9 R.I.A.A. 15.

[11] See Noyes and Smith (1988) 13 Yale J.I.L. 225. The question of joint and severable responsibility was raised, but not decided, in the *Phosphate Lands in Nauru Case (Preliminary Objections),* I.C.J. Rep. 1992, p. 249 at p. 258.

[12] Y.B.I.L.C., 1973, II, p. 177.

[13] See Schwarzenberger, pp. 653, 658, and Thirlway (1995) 66 B.Y.I.L. 1 at 65. See also Tanzi, in Spinedi and Simma, eds., *UN Codification of State Responsibility* (1987).

[14] On the Draft Articles on countermeasures and self defence, see Alland, in Spinedi and Simma, above, p. 143, and Malanczuk, *ibid.,* p. 197.

[15] For the text of Art. 22, see below. p. 617.

[16] See Quigley (1986) 57 B.Y.I.L. 77.

(ii) CIVIL AND CRIMINAL RESPONSIBILITY

I.L.C. DRAFT ARTICLES ON STATE RESPONSIBILITY

I.L.C.'s 1996 Report, G.A.O.R., 51st Sess., Supp. 10, p. 125.

Article 19

1. An act of a State which constitutes a breach of an international obligation is an internationally wrongful act, regardless of the subject-matter of the obligation breached.

2. An internationally wrongful act which results from the breach by a State of an international obligation so essential for the protection of fundamental interests of the international community that its breach is recognized as a crime by that community as a whole, constitutes an international crime.

3. Subject to paragraph 2, and on the basis of the rules of international law in force, an international crime may result, *inter alia*, from:

(*a*) a serious breach of an international obligation of essential importance for maintenance or international peace and security, such as that prohibiting aggression;

(*b*) a serious breach of an international obligation of essential importance for safeguarding the right of self-determination of peoples, such as that prohibiting the establishment or maintenance by force of colonial domination;

(*c*) a serious breach on a widespread scale of an international obligation of essential importance for safeguarding the human being, such as those prohibiting slavery, genocide, *apartheid*;

(*d*) a serious breach of an international obligation of essential importance for the safeguarding and preservation of the human environment, such as those prohibiting massive pollution of the atmosphere or of the seas.

4. Any internationally wrongful act which is not an international crime in accordance with paragraph 2, constitutes an international delict.

Notes

1. The Draft Articles distinguish between civil and criminal liability on the part of states in international law. As far as *civil* (or delictual) liability is concerned, international law does not separate contractual and tortious liability. The breach of a treaty obligation is subject to the same rules on the burden of proof and reparation as a violation of a customary rule of international law. Some writers[17] refer to a breach of any international law obligation as an "international tort." When used in this sense, the term "tort" clearly has a wider meaning than it has at common law.

---

[17] See, *e.g.* Schwarzenberger, pp. 581–582.

2. The question whether states may be *criminally* liable has long been the subject of debate.[18] In reaching the conclusion that they can, the International Law Commission commented on state practice as follows:

> It seems undeniable that today's unanimous and prompt condemnation of any direct attack on international peace and security is paralleled by almost universal disapproval on the part of States towards certain other activities. Contemporary international law has reached the point of condemning outright the practice of certain States in forcibly keeping other peoples under colonial domination or forcibly imposing international régimes based on discrimination and the most absolute racial segregation, in imperilling human life and dignity in other ways, or in so acting as gravely to endanger the preservation and conservation of the human environment. The international community as a whole, and not merely one or other of its members, now considers that such acts violate principles formally embodied in the Charter and, even outside the scope of the Charter, principles which are now so deeply rooted in the conscience of mankind that they have become particularly essential rules of general international law. There are enough manifestations of the views of States to warrant the conclusion that in the general opinion, some of these act genuinely constitute "international crimes," that is to say, international wrongs which are more serious than others and which as such, should entail more severe legal consequences ... in adopting the designation "international crime," the Commission intends only to refer to "crimes" of the State, to acts attributable to the State as such. Once again it wishes to sound a warning against any confusion between the expression "international crime" as used in this article and similar expressions, such as "crime under international law," "war crime," "crime against peace," "crime against humanity," etc., which are used in a number of conventions and international instruments to designate certain heinous individual crimes, for which those instruments require States to punish the guilty persons adequately, in accordance with the rules of their internal law.[19]

The International Law Commission was influenced in its decision to provide for a separate régime of criminal liability by the International Court of Justice's development of the concept of "obligations *erga omnes*" in the *Barcelona Traction* case.[20] The Commentary to Article 19 reads[21]:

> This passage [in the *Barcelona Traction Case*] has been the subject of differing interpretations; but it seems undeniable that the Court intended by such affirmations to draw a fundamental distinction between international obligations and hence between the acts committed in breach of them. ... In the Court's opinion, there are in fact a number, albeit a small one, of international obligations which, by reason of the importance of their subject-matter for the international community as a whole, are—unlike the others—obligations in whose fulfillment all States have a legal interest. It follows, according to the Court, that the responsibility engaged by the breach of these obligations is engaged not only in regard to the State which was the direct victim of the

---

[18] See Brownlie, *International Law and the Use of Force by States* (1963), p. 154; Oppenheim, Vol. I, p. 533; Schwarzenberger (1950) 3 C.L.P. 263.

[19] Y.B.I.L.C., 1976, II (Part II), pp. 109, 119. On Art. 19, Draft Articles, see Gilbert (1990) 39 I.C.L.Q. 345; Green (1981) 11 Israel Y.H.R. 9; Marek (1978–9) 14 R.B.D.I. 460; Mohr, in Spinedi and Simma, p. 486, n. 13, above, p. 115; Quigley (1988) 66 R.D.I. 117; Ten Napel (1988) 1 Leiden J.I.L. 149.

[20] Paras 33–4, judgment, below, p. 605.

[21] Y.B.I.L.C., 1976, II (Part Two), p. 99.

breach; it is also engaged in regard to all the other members of the international community, so that, in the event of a breach of these obligations, every State must be considered justified in invoking—probably through judicial channels—the responsibility of the State committing the internationally wrongful act.

Note, however, that the *Barcelona Traction* case does not mention criminal liability: the Court's idea is that the breach of an *erga omnes* obligation is a breach of a civil obligation owed to each and every state and that any state or group of states may accordingly take up their case, by diplomatic protest, followed where appropriate or possible, by judicial or arbitral proceedings or some other form of pacific settlement.[22] The *Barcelona Traction* case does not envisage intervention by force.[23] In terms of reparation, although a claim to compensation by a state that has not directly suffered damage would not be appropriate where the state was protecting its own nationals or other national interests, a state in breach of an *erga omnes* obligation might be called upon to compensate individuals (or to release them, etc).

On the inter-relationship between the concepts of international crimes, obligations *erga omnes* and rules of *ius cogens*, see below, p. 835.

3. In 1976, in the Sixth Committee of the General Assembly (the Legal Committee), Article 19 met with a generally favourable response from developing and East European states.[24] The reaction of Western states was more cautious, with most speaking against the idea of criminal responsibility.[25] The United Kingdom, which reserved its position,[26] stated that:

> "[a]lthough there was growing evidence of the existence of such a distinction between civil and criminal responsibility based on the importance attached by the international community as a whole to certain international obligations of a fundamental nature, the difficulty lay in defining such international obligations and assessing the consequences of such a distinction."[27]

Later, in 1994, when the consequences of an international crime were under consideration within the I.L.C., a minority of members expressed doubts as to whether the Draft Articles should provide for criminal liability on the part of states at all. Rosenstock, the United States member and one of the doubters, summarises their position as follows[28]:

> One group of members of the Commission argued that the inclusion of the notion of crimes by states in Article 19 of part I of the Commission's draft was a mistake that should not be compounded by attempting to elaborate the consequences of such a "crime" as distinguished from the consequences of a delict. Those who took this position argued, inter alia, that there was no basis in state practice for the notion of "crimes" by states and that the notion seemed to suggest the idea of collective punishment or other like penal sanctions, both

---

[22] In the *South West Africa (Second Phase)* cases, I.C.J. Rep. 1966, p. 47, the I.C.J. decided that an "actio popularis, or right resident in any member of the community to take legal action in vindication of a public interest ... is not known to international law". The Court would appear in effect to have changed its position in the *Barcelona Traction* case.

[23] On a right to humanitarian intervention, see below, p. 917.

[24] See, *e.g.* G.A.O.R., 31st Sess., 1976, A/C.6/SR 29, p. 6 (India) and *id.*, A/C.6/SR 26, pp. 7–8.

[25] See, *e.g.* G.A.O.R. 31st Sess., 1976, A/C.6/SR 26, p. 4 (France).

[26] G.A.O.R., 37th Sess., 1982, A/C.6/SR 48, p. 6.

[27] G.A.O.R., 31th Sess., 1976, A/C.6/SR 18, para. 35.

[28] (1995) 89 A.J.I.L. 390 at 393. Footnote omitted.

of which were unacceptable. Those holding this view argued that the recognition of *erga omnes* obligations did not imply the existence of a qualitatively different form of responsibility. They noted that the early and middle 1970s, when the Commission decided to include the notion of crimes by states in the draft, had been an era of agitation propaganda stemming from the Cold War, anti-colonialism and North-South tensions and that the wisdom of this decision needed to be reconsidered. Questions were also raised as to the adequacy of the definition contained in Article 19 of part I. Some of those who questioned the need or utility of including the notion of crimes by states suggested that it might be better to consider a continuum within a single regime of responsibility extending from minor breaches to serious ones and that the distinction should be quantitative, not qualitative.

In view of these doubts and those of some states, it is not certain that the concept of criminal responsibility will be retained in the final text of the Draft Articles. Even if it is, it would appear at present not to have general acceptance among states.

4. Article 19 does not state the legal consequences of an international crime. These are indicated in Part II of the Draft Articles:

Article 40

. . .

3. In addition, "injured State" means, if the internationally wrongful act constitutes an international crime, all other States.

Article 51

An international crime entails all the legal consequences of any other internationally wrongful act and, in addition, such further consequences as are set out in articles 52 and 53.

Article 52

Where an internationally wrongful act of a State is an international crime:

(a) an injured State's entitlement to obtain restitution in kind is not subject to the limitations set out in subparagraphs (c) and (d) of article 43 (below p. 517);

(b) an injured State's entitlement to obtain satisfaction is not subject to the restriction in paragraph 3 of article 45 (below, p. 517).

Article 53

An international crime committed by a State entails an obligation for every other State:

(a) not to recognize as lawful the situation created by the crime;

(b) not to render aid or assistance to the State which has committed the crime in maintaining the situation so created;

(c) to cooperate with other States in carrying out the obligations under subparagraphs (a) and (b); and

(d) to cooperate with other States in the application of measures designed to eliminate the consequences of the crime.

Article 53 focuses mainly on collective sanctions, imposing obligations on all other states in their dealings with the criminal state. These are not onerous. The Draft Articles make no mention of collectively imposed fines or the imprisonment of state officials or of the use of force against the delinquent state, all of which would clearly be unacceptable. Article 52 preserves, with some modifications, the right to reparation of a state that is directly injured.

(iii) THE BASIS FOR RESPONSIBILITY: RISK OR FAULT?[29]

Note

The question considered in this subsection is whether responsibility results from the commission of the prohibited act alone or whether it arises only when this is accompanied by some degree of intention or negligence on the part of the actor. In other words, is there strict liability or must some degree of blameworthiness be attributable to the actor? The first possibility is called the "risk" or "objective" theory of responsibility; the second, the "fault" or "subjective" theory. With regard to the latter, the Roman law terms *dolus*, referring to intentional conduct, and *culpa*, referring to negligent conduct, are sometimes used. It will be apparent from the following extracts in this sub-section from international judicial and arbitral practice[30] that authority can be found supporting either theory, although strict liability of states is more common. As in municipal law, it seems likely that the need for intention or negligence varies from one area of responsibility to another. State practice on this theoretical question is, so far as it is available, of little help.

HOME MISSIONARY SOCIETY CLAIM

U.S. *v.* Great Britain (1920)

American and British Claims Arbitration: Fromageot, President; Anderson, American Arbitrator; Fitzpatrick, British Arbitrator. 6 R.I.A.A. 42

Award of the Tribunal

In 1898 the collection of a tax newly imposed [by Great Britain] on the natives of the Protectorate [of Sierra Leone] and known as the "hut tax" was the signal for a serious and widespread revolt in the Ronietta district. The revolt broke out on April 27 and lasted for several days. . . .

In the course of the rebellion all [the claimant's] . . . missions were attacked, and either destroyed or damaged, and some of the missionaries were murdered. . . .

The contention of the United States Government before this Tribunal is that the revolt was the result of the imposition and attempted collection of the "hut tax"; that it was within the knowledge of the British Government that this tax was the object of deep native resentment; that in the

---

[29] See Lauterpacht, *Private Law Sources and Analogies of International Law* (1927), pp. 135–143, and Pisillo-Mazzeschi (1992) 35 G.Y.I.L. 9.

[30] See also the *Neer Claim*, below, p. 522, and the *Tippetts* case, below, p. 556, and the *Asian Agricultural Products Ltd* case, below, p. 543.

face of the native danger the British Government wholly failed to take proper steps for the maintenance of order and the protection of life and property; that the loss of life and damage to property was the result of this neglect and failure of duty, and therefore that it is liable to pay compensation.

Now, even assuming that the "hut tax" was the effective cause of the native rebellion, it was in itself a fiscal measure in accordance not only with general usage in colonial administration, but also with the usual practice in African countries. . . .

It was a measure to which the British Government was perfectly entitled to resort in the legitimate exercise of its sovereignty, if it was required. . . .

Further, though it may be true that some difficulty might have been foreseen, there was nothing to suggest that it would be more serious than is usual and inevitable in a semi-barbarous and only partially colonized protectorate, and certainly nothing to lead to any apprehension of widespread revolt.

It is a well-established principle of international law that no government can be held responsible for the act of rebellious bodies of men committed in violation of its authority, where it is itself guilty of no breach of good faith, or of no negligence in suppressing insurrection. (Moore's *International Law Digest*, vol. VI, p. 956; VII, p. 957; Moore's *Arbitrations*, pp. 2991–92; British answer, p. 1).

The good faith of the British Government cannot be questioned, and as to the conditions prevailing in the Protectorate there is no evidence to support the contention that it failed in its duty to afford adequate protection for life and property. . . .

The Tribunal decides that this claim must be dismissed.

CAIRE CLAIM

France *v.* Mexico (1929)

French-Mexican Claims Commission: Verzijl, Presiding Commissioner;
Ayguesparsse, French Commissioner; Gonzalez Roa, Mexican Commissioner.
5 R.I.A.A. 516. Translation

Caire, a French national, was killed in Mexico by Mexican soldiers after they had demanded money from him.

Verzijl, Presiding Commissioner

(4) Responsibility of Mexico for actions of individual military personnel, acting without orders or against the wishes of their commanding officers and independently of the needs and aims of the revolution. . . .

In approaching the examination of the questions indicated under 4 in the light of the general principles I have just outlined, I should like to make clear first of all that I am interpreting the said principles in accordance with the doctrine of the "objective responsibility" of the State, that is, the responsibility for the acts of the officials or organs of a State, which may devolve upon it even in the absence of any "fault" of its own. It is widely known that theoretical conceptions in this sphere have advanced a great deal in recent times, and that the innovating work of Dionisio Anzilotti in particular has paved the way for new ideas, which no longer rank the responsibility of the State for the acts of its officials as subordinate to the question of the "fault" attaching to the State itself. Without going into the question of whether these new ideas, which are perhaps too absolute, may require some modifications in the direction proposed by Dr. Karl Strupp,[31] I can say that I regard them as perfectly correct in that they tend to impute to the State, in international affairs, the responsibility for all the acts committed by its officials or organs which constitute offences from the point of view of the law of nations, whether the official or organ in question has acted within or exceeded the limits of his competence. "It is generally agreed," as M. Bourquin has rightly said, "that acts committed by the officials and agents of a State entail the international responsibility of that State, even if the perpetrator did not have specific authorisation. This responsibility does not find its justification in general principles—I mean those principles regulating the judicial organisation of the State. The act of an official is only judicially established as an act of State if such an act lies within the official's sphere of competence. The act of an official operating beyond his competence is not an act of State. It should not in principle, therefore, affect the responsibility of the State. If it is accepted in international law that the position is different, it is for reasons peculiar to the mechanism of international life; it is because it is felt that international relations would become too difficult, too complicated and too insecure if foreign States were obliged to take into account the often complex judicial arrangements that regulate competence in the international affairs of a State. From this it is immediately clear that in the hypothesis under consideration the international responsibility of the State is purely *objective* in character, and that it rests on an idea of *guarantee*, in which the subjective notion of fault plays no part."

But in order to be able to admit this so-called objective responsibility of the State for acts committed by its officials or organs outside their competence, they must have acted at least to all appearances as competent officials or organs, or they must have used powers or methods appropriate to their official capacity. . . .

If the principles stated above are applied to the present case, and if it is taken into account that the perpetrators of the murder of M. J.-B. Caire

---

[31] In his work *Das Volkerrechtliche Delikt*, pp. 48 *et seq*. Strupp makes express exception for "Unterlassungsdelikte", that is, for the offences of a State consisting, not of some positive act or its organs or officials, but of an omission on their part.

were military personnel occupying the ranks of "mayor" and "capitán primero" aided by a few privates, it is found that the conditions of responsibility formulated above are completely fulfilled. The officers in question, whatever their previous record, consistently conducted themselves as officers in the brigade of the *Villista* general, Tomás Urbina; in this capacity they began by exacting the remittance of certain sums of money; they continued by having the victim taken to a barracks of the occupying troops; and it was clearly because of the refusal of M. Caire to meet their repeated demands that they finally shot him. Under these circumstances, there remains no doubt that, even if they are to be regarded as having acted outside their competence, which is by no means certain, and even if their superior officers issued a counter-order, these two officers have involved the responsibility of the State, in view of the fact that they acted in their capacity of officers and used the means placed at their disposition by virtue of that capacity.

On these grounds, I have no hesitation in stating that, in accordance with the most authoritative doctrine supported by numerous arbitral awards, the events of 11 December 1914, which led to the death of M. J.-B. Caire, fall within the category of acts for which international responsibility devolves upon the State to which the perpetrators of the injury are amenable.

CORFU CHANNEL CASE (MERITS)[32]

U.K. *v.* Albania

I.C.J. Reports 1949, p. 4

Judgment of the Court

On October 22, 1946, a squadron of British warships, the cruisers *Mauritius* and *Leander* and the destroyers *Saumarez* and *Volage*, left the port of Corfu and proceeded northwards through a channel previously swept for mines in the North Corfu Strait. . . . Outside the Bay of Saranda, *Saumarez* struck a mine and was heavily damaged. . . . Whilst towing the damaged ship, *Volage* struck a mine and was much damaged. . . .

Three weeks later, on November 13th, the North Corfu Channel was swept by British minesweepers and twenty-two mines were cut. . . .

In October, 1944, the North Corfu Channel was swept by the British Navy and no mines were found in the Channel thus swept. . . . In January

---

[32] See 2 Verzijl 22. For the part of the Court's judgment dealing with Albania's counter-claim, see above, p. 391.

and February, 1945, the Channel was check-swept by the British Navy with negative results. . . . It was in this swept Channel that the minefield was discovered on November 13, 1946.

. . . the mining of *Saumarez* and *Volage* occurred in Albanian territorial waters, just at the place in the swept Channel where the minefield was found. . . .

Such are the facts upon which the Court must, in order to reply to the first question of the Special Agreement, give judgment as to Albania's responsibility for the explosions on October 22, 1946, and for the damage and loss of human life which resulted, and for the compensation, if any, due in respect of such damage and loss.

. . . the main position of the United Kingdom is to be found in its submission No. 2: that the minefield which caused the explosions was laid between May 15, 1946, and October 22, 1946, by or with the connivance of the Albanian Government. . . .

In fact, although the United Kingdom Government never abandoned its contention that Albania herself laid the mines, very little attempt was made by the Government to demonstrate this point. . . .

In these circumstances, the Court need pay no further attention to this matter.

The Court now comes to the second alternative argument of the United Kingdom Government, namely that the minefield was laid with the connivance of the Albanian Government. According to this argument, the minelaying operation was carried out by two Yugoslav warships at a date prior to October 22, but very near that date. This would imply collusion between the Albanian and the Yugoslav Governments, consisting either of a request by the Albanian Government to the Yugoslav Government for assistance, or of acquiescence by the Albanian authorities in the laying of the mines. . . .

The Court found that there was insufficient evidence to establish connivance.

Finally, the United Kingdom Government put forward the argument that, whoever the authors of the minelaying were, it could not have been done without the Albanian Government's knowledge.

It is clear that knowledge of the minelaying cannot be imputed to the Albanian Government by reason merely of the fact that a minefield discovered in Albanian territorial waters caused the explosions of which the British warships were the victims. It is true, as international practice shows, that a State on whose territory or in whose waters an act contrary to international law has occurred, may be called upon to give an explanation. It is also true that that State cannot evade such a request by limiting itself to a reply that it is ignorant of the circumstances of the act and of its authors. The state may, up to a certain point, be bound to supply particulars of the use made by it of the means of information and inquiry at its disposal. But it cannot be concluded from the mere fact of the control

exercised by a State over its territory and waters that that State necessarily knew, or ought to have known, of any unlawful act perpetrated
therein, nor yet that it necessarily knew, or should have known, the
authors. This fact, by itself and apart from other circumstances, neither
involves *prima facie* responsibility nor shifts the burden of proof.

On the other hand, the fact of this exclusive territorial control exercised
by a State within its frontiers has a bearing upon the methods of proof
available to establish the knowledge of that State as to such events. By
reason of this exclusive control, the other State, the victim of a breach of
international law, is often unable to furnish direct proof of facts giving
rise to responsibility. Such a State should be allowed a more liberal
recourse to inferences of fact and circumstantial evidence. This indirect
evidence is admitted in all systems of law, and its use is recognized by
international decisions. It must be regarded as of special weight when it
is based on a series of facts linked together and leading logically to a
single conclusion.

The Court must examine therefore whether it has been established by
means of indirect evidence that Albania has knowledge of minelaying in
her territorial waters independently of any connivance on her part in this
operation. The proof may be drawn from inferences of fact, provided that
they leave *no room* for reasonable doubt. . . .

From all facts and observations mentioned above, the court draws the
conclusion that the laying of the minefield which caused the explosions
on October 22, 1946, could not have been accomplished without the
knowledge of the Albanian Government.

The obligations resulting for Albania from this knowledge are not
disputed between the parties. Counsel for the Albanian Government
expressly recognized that [*translation*] "if Albania had been informed of
the operation before the incidents of October 22, and in time to warn the
British vessels and shipping in general of the existence of mines in the
Corfu Channel, her responsibility would be involved. . . . "

The obligations incumbent upon the Albanian authorities consisted in
notifying for the benefit of shipping in general, the existence of a minefield in Albanian territorial waters and in warning the approaching British warships of the imminent danger to which the minefield exposed
them. Such obligations are based not on the Hague Convention of 1907,
No. VIII, which is applicable in time of war, but on certain general and
well-recognised principles, namely: elementary considerations of humanity, even more exacting in peace than in war; the principle of freedom of
maritime communication; and every State's obligation not to allow knowingly its territory to be used for acts contrary to the rights of other
States.

In fact, Albania neither notified the existence of the minefield, nor
warned the British warships of the danger they were approaching.

But Albania's obligation to notify shipping of the existence of mines in
her waters depends on her having obtained knowledge of that fact in

sufficient time before October 22; and the duty of the Albanian coastal authorities to warn the British ships depends on the time that elapsed between the moment that these ships were reported and the moment of the first explosion.

On this subject, the Court makes the following observations. As has already been stated, the parties agree that the mines were recently laid. It must be concluded that the minelaying, whatever may have been its exact date, was done at a time when there was a close Albanian surveillance over the Strait. If it be supposed that it took place at the last possible moment, *i.e.* in the night of October 21st–22nd, the only conclusion to be drawn would be that a general notification to the shipping of all States before the time of the explosions would have been difficult, perhaps even impossible. But this would certainly not have prevented the Albanian authorities from taking, as they should have done, all necessary steps immediately to warn ships near the danger zone. When on October 22nd about 13.00 hours the British warships were reported by the look-out post at St. George's Monastery to the Commander of the Coastal Defences as approaching Cape Long, it was perfectly possible for the Albanian authorities to use the interval of almost two hours that elapsed before the explosion affecting *Saumarez* (14.53 hours or 14.55 hours) to warn the vessels of the danger into which they were running.

In fact, nothing was attempted by the Albanian authorities to prevent the disaster. These grave omissions involve the international responsibility of Albania. . . .

For these reasons, the Court, on the first question put by the Special Agreement of March 25, 1948, by eleven votes to five,[33] gives judgment that the People's Republic of Albania is responsible under international law for the explosions which occurred on October 22, 1946, in Albanian waters, and for the damage and loss of human life which resulted therefrom.[34]

DISSENTING OPINION OF JUDGE KRYLOV. [Having found that it was not proven that Albania had connived in laying the mines or had knowledge of their presence, Judge Krylov continued:]

But it is perhaps the case that the Albanian authorities *ought to* have seen or heard the minelaying operation?

To answer that question in the affirmative would, in my opinion, be to found Albania's responsibility on the notion of *culpa*.

I employ this term, subject to a reservation. I consider that the terms of Roman law and of contemporary civil and criminal law may be used in international law, but with a certain flexibility and without making too subtle distinctions. There is no need to transfer the distinctions which we

---

[33] Judge Zoričić, Winiarski, Badawi, Krylov and Judge *ad hoc* Ečer dissented.

[34] The duty to make reparation for this responsibility was also acknowledged and damages were awarded in a separate judgment: *Corfu Channel Case* (*Assessment of Compensation*), I.C.J. Rep. 1949, p. 244.

sometimes meet in certain systems of municipal law into the system of international law.

Is it then possible to found the international responsibility of Albania on the notion of *culpa*? Can it be argued that Albania failed to exercise the diligence required by international law to prevent the laying of mines in the Corfu Channel? Can it be asserted that international law involves an obligation for a coastal state to prevent the laying of mines in its territorial waters? I do not think so. However perfectly the coastal watch of a coastal State may be organized, the clandestine laying of mines cannot be considered impossible, especially, one might add, in peace time when the coastal guards are not in a state of instant readiness. But the history of maritime war provides plenty of examples of clandestine minelaying.

Here I have an observation to make. The responsibility of a State in consequence of an international delinquency presupposes, at the very least, *culpa* on the part of that State. One cannot found the international responsibility of a State on the argument that, the act of which the State is accused took place in its territory—terrestrial, maritime, or aerial territory. One cannot transfer the theory of risk, which is developed in the municipal law of some States into the domain of international law. In order to found the responsibility of the States recourse must be had to the notion of *culpa*. I refer to the famous English author, Oppenheim. In his work on international law, he writes that the conception of international delinquency presumes that the State acted "wilfully and maliciously," or in cases of acts of omission "with culpable negligence" (Vol. 1, para. 154). Mr. Lauterpacht, the editor of the 7th edition (1948), adds that one can discern among modern authors a definite tendency to reject the theory of absolute responsibility and to found the responsibility of States on the notion of *culpa* (p. 311).

In view of the foregoing and owing to the inadequacy of the evidence produced by the British, I am unable to reach the conclusion that Albania was responsible for the explosions which took place on October 22, 1946, in Albanian waters. One cannot condemn a State on the basis of probabilities. To establish international responsibility, one must have clear and indisputable facts. In the present case these facts are absent.

DISSENTING OPINION OF JUDGE AZEVEDO. The notion of *culpa* is always changing and undergoing a slow process of evolution; moving away from the classical elements of imprudence and negligence, it tends to draw nearer to the system of objective responsibility; and this has led certain present-day authors to deny that *culpa* is definitely separate, in regard to a theory based solely on risk.

Notes

1. Would Albania have been responsible if it had not known of the mines? What if it had known of them and had done its best to warn the British ships in time but had failed to make contact, perhaps because of fog or failure of radio communications?

2. Do the cases in this subsection support Strupp's view[35] that responsibility is subjective in the case of an omission, but objective in other cases?[36]

3. Are these reasons that make strict liability more acceptable in international law than it is in municipal law?[37]

(iv) IMPUTABILITY[38]

(a) *Generally*

I.L.C. DRAFT ARTICLES ON STATE RESPONSIBILITY

I.L.C.'s 1996 Report, G.A.O.R., 51st Sess., Supp. 10, p. 125

Article 5

For the purposes of the present articles, conduct of any State organ having that status under the internal law of that State shall be considered as an act of the State concerned under international law, provided that organ was acting in that capacity in the case in question.

Article 6

The conduct of an organ of the State shall be considered as an act of that State under international law, whether that organ belongs to the constituent, legislative, executive, judicial or other power, whether its functions are of an international or an internal character and whether it holds a superior or a subordinate position in the organization of the State.

Article 7

1. The conduct of an organ of a territorial governmental entity within a State shall also be considered as an act of that State under international law, provided that organ was acting in that capacity in the case in question.

2. The conduct of an organ of an entity which is not part of the formal structure of the State or a territorial governmental entity, but which is empowered by the internal law of that State to exercise elements of the governmental authority, shall also be considered as an act of the State under international law, provided that organ was acting in that capacity in the case in question.

---

[35] See above, n. 31.

[36] See also the *ELSI Case* I.C.J. Rep. 1989, p. 14 at p. 65 (duty to protect alien property not absolute). On the liability of states for omissions, see Christenson (1991) 12 Mich. J.I.L. 312.

[37] See Brownlie, p. 423.

[38] See Starke (1938) 19 B.Y.I.L 104, and Christenson, in Lillich, ed., *International Law of State Responsibility for Injuries to Aliens* (1983), p. 321.

Article 8

The conduct of a person or a group of persons shall also be considered as an act of the State under international law if

(*a*) it is established that such person or group of persons was in fact acting on behalf of that State; or
(*b*) such person or group of persons was in fact exercising elements of the governmental authority in the absence of the official authorities and in circumstances which justified the exercise of those elements of authority.

Article 9

The conduct of an organ which has been placed at the disposal of a State by another State or by an international organization shall be considered as an act of the former State under international law, if that organ was acting in the exercise of elements of the governmental authority of the State at whose disposal it has been placed.

Notes

1. Article 5 states a well established rule. Article 6 indicates that responsibility is not excluded in the case of low level officials. Similarly, in the *Massey Case*,[39] Commissioner Nielsen stated:

> To attempt by some broad classification to make a distinction between some "minor" or "petty" officials and other kinds of officials must obviously at times involve practical difficulties. Irrespective of the propriety of attempting to make any such distinction at all, it would seem that in reaching conclusions in any given case with respect to responsibility for acts of public servants, the most important considerations of which account must be taken are the character of the acts alleged to have resulted in injury to persons or to property, or the nature of functions performed whenever a question is raised as to their proper discharge.

2. A "territorial government entity" in Article 7 includes a local government organ and the government of a unit within a federal state. The rule in Article 7(2)

> ... stems from, and is designed to cover, ... the tendency within State communities, to set up more and more ... "entities" ... which are required under internal law to perform certain tasks in the interest of the community but which possess, in the eyes of the law, an organisation and a personality of their own, separate from those of the state. Among these various "entities"—whatever the régime by which they are governed—there are some whose particular characteristic is that the internal legal system confers upon them, to a greater or lesser extent, the exercise of certain elements of the governmental authority, usually of a regulatory or executive nature. The fact that an entity can be

---

[39] *U.S. v. Mexico*, (1927) 4 R.I.A.A. 155 at 157. Van Vollenhoven, Presiding Commissioner, concurred.

classified as public or private according to the criteria of a given legal system, the existence of a greater or lesser State participation in its capital or, more generally, in the ownership of its assets, and the fact that it is not subject to State control, or that it is subject to such control to a greater or lesser extent, and so on, do not emerge as decisive criteria for the purposes of attribution or non-attribution to the State of the conduct of its organs. The Commission has come to the conclusion that the most appropriate solution is to refer to the real common feature which these entities have: namely that they are empowered, if only exceptionally and to a limited extent, to exercise specified functions which are akin to those normally exercised by its organs of the State. Thus, for example, the conduct of an organ of a railway company to which certain police powers have been granted will be regarded as an act of State under international law if it falls within the exercise of those powers.[40]

3. Article 8 covers different kinds of *de facto* state acts. Article 8(a) covers, first, the conduct of private individuals or groups of private individuals who, while remaining such, are employed as auxiliaries in the police or armed forces or sent as "volunteers" to neighboring countries, and, second, the acts of persons employed to carry out certain missions in foreign territory.[41] The Commentary gives the acts of the crew in the *Zafiro Case*[42] and of the abductors in the *Eichmann*[43] and *Argoud*[44] Cases as examples of these two kinds of acts respectively. See also the *United States Diplomatic and Consular Staff in Tehran Case*, above, p. 358, and *Yeager v. Iran*, below, p. 503.

In *Schering Corp. v. Iran*,[45] the claimant argued that allegedly expropriatory acts of the Workers Council of Schering Iran, the claimant's Iranian subsidiary company, were attributable to Iran. The Iran-U.S. Claims Tribunal rejected this argument, finding that, although brought into being by the state, Workers Councils had as their role the protection of workers' interests; they were not intended "to function as part of the State machinery" and hence were not organs of state (*cf.* Article 6, I.L.C. Draft Articles). In addition they did not "in fact" act on behalf of the state (*cf.* Article 8, *id.*), there being no evidence that "there was any governmental influence over the election of the members of the Council, that any governmental orders, directives or recommendations were issued to the Council or that it acted under instructions of any governmental body." The same Tribunal has looked to see whether there has been government influence "in fact" when considering whether acts by private, commercial Iranian companies engaged the responsibility of the state. In *Foremost Tehran Inc. v. Iran*,[46] it was held that a decision by such a company not to pay dividends to shareholders, who included the claimant American company, was attributable to the state because it had been influenced by Government representatives on the board of directors who were seeking to implement government policy in respect of foreigners. In *Flexi-Van Leasing Inc. v. Iran*,[47] however, allegedly expropriatory breaches of contract by a private Iranian company that was admittedly under the control of the Iranian Government were not attributable to the state since it had not been established

---

[40] Commentary, Y.B.I.L.C., 1974, II, (Part One), pp. 281–282. *cf.* the problem which arises in respect of state immunity, above, p. 334.

[41] *ibid.* p. 283.

[42] Below, p. 509.

[43] Above, p. 280.

[44] Above, p. 287, n. 68.

[45] (1984) 5 Iran-U.S.C.T.R. 361 at 370.

[46] (1986) 10 Iran-U.S.C.T.R. 228.

[47] (1986) 12 Iran-U.S.C.T.R. 335 at 349. *cf. International Technical Products Corp. v. Iran*, (1985) 9 Iran-U.S.C.T.R. 206.

that the company "had acted under orders ... from ... the Government when it did not pay rentals ... "

Article 8(b) covers acts by private persons acting on their own initiative at a time of emergency for the defence of the realm or during a natural disaster.

4. The Commentary to Article 9 reads:

> As examples of situations in which application of the rule stated in article 9 might be entertained, reference was made in the Commission to the case in which certain conduct is engaged in by a detachment of police placed at the disposal of another State to deal with internal disturbances; by a section of the health service or some other unit placed under the orders of another country to assist in overcoming an epidemic or the consequences of a natural disaster; by officials of a State or of an international organization appointed by another State to administer in its territory a public service which its own officials are unable, in certain circumstances, to administer; by judicial organs appointed in particular cases to act as judicial organs of another State; and so on. Specific instances were cited: for example, that of the United Kingdom Privy Council acting as the highest court of appeals for New Zealand and that of judicial organs of Nigeria appointed to serve also as Chief Justices of Botswana and Uganda and as President of the Court of Appeal of the Gambia. It was pointed out that Nigeria has also placed some of its civil servants at the disposal of other African States to take temporary charge of organizing the civil service of the beneficiary State.[48]

The Commission considered that the acts of the armed contingents of one state stationed in another state or employed in military operations there would not be covered.

5. A state is responsible for the acts of its security services. In a case involving state responsibility for the conduct of government agents abroad, in the *Rainbow Warrior Case*,[49] a Greenpeace vessel was blown up in Auckland Harbour by French secret service agents as it was leaving to protest against French nuclear tests in the Pacific. The two agents were convicted of offences under New Zealand criminal law and each sentenced to ten years imprisonment. Following negotiations, the two states referred all issues arising out of the incident, which involved a clear violation of territorial sovereignty, to the UN Secretary-General for arbitration, the award to be "equitable and principled." After written pleadings, the Secretary-General, without giving reasons, ruled that France should formally apologise to New Zealand for "the violation of its sovereignty and its rights under international law" and should pay US$ 7 million to New Zealand "as compensation for all the damages it has suffered," which would appear to have included compensation for moral damage, as New Zealand requested, as well as for material damage. The ruling also required New Zealand to transfer the secret agents to French custody, to be kept by France in "a French military facility on an isolated island outside of Europe [in fact in the Pacific] for a period of three years."

6. In 1984, a number of Libyans were convicted in British courts and/or deported from the United Kingdom following bomb attacks on Libyan opponents of the Libyan Government. The British Foreign Secretary informed Libya that the

---

[48] *op. cit.*, p. 501, n. 40, above, p. 288.
[49] (1987) 26 I.L.M. 1346. See Davidson (1991) 40 I.C.L.Q. 446; Pugh (1987) 36 I.C.L.Q. 655; and Wexler (1987) 5 Boston U.I.L.J. 389.

use of British territory for such attacks was "totally unacceptable."[50] In what circumstances would Libya be liable in international law for these attacks?

YEAGER v. IRAN

U.S. v. Iran (1987)

Iran—U.S. Claims Tribunal. Chamber One: Bockstiegel, Chairman; Mostafavi, Holtzmann, Members.
17 Iran–U.S.C.T.R. 92

The claimant, an American national, was employed by BHI, an American company, in Iran. On February 13, 1979, two days after the Islamic Revolutionary Government took office, "revolutionary guards" came to his apartment and, after giving him 30 minutes to pack, took the claimant to the Hilton Hotel where he was detained by guards for several days. The claimant was then flown out of Iran as part of an evacuation operation. In response to a claim of expulsion contrary to customary international law, Iran argued that the conduct of the "guards" was not attributable to it.

Award of the Tribunal

39. . . . Many of Ayatollah Khomeini's supporters were organised in local revolutionary committees, so-called Komitehs, which . . . served as local security forces in the immediate aftermath of the revolution. It is reported that they made arrests, confiscated property, and took people to prison. . . . While there were complaints about a lack of discipline among the numerous Komitehs, Ayatollah Khomeini [the leader of the revolution] stood behind them. . . . Soon after the Revolution, the Komitehs . . . obtained a firm position within the State structure and were eventually conferred a permanent place in the State budget. . . .

42. The question then arises whether the acts at issue are attributable to Iran under international law. While there is some doubt as to whether revolutionary "Komitehs" or "Guards" can be considered "organs" of the Government of Iran, since they were not formally recognized during the period relevant to this Case, attributability of acts to the State is not limited to acts of organs formally recognized under internal law. Otherwise a State could avoid responsibility under international law merely by invoking its internal law. It is generally accepted in international law that a State is also responsible for acts of persons, if it is established that those persons were in fact acting on behalf of the State. *See* ILC-Draft Article 8(a). An act is attributable even if a person or group of persons was in fact merely exercising elements of governmental authority in the absence of the official authorities and in circumstances which justified the exercise of those elements of authority. *See* ILC-Draft Article 8(b).

---

[50] *Keesings Archives*, p. 33004.

43. The Tribunal finds sufficient evidence in the record to establish a presumption that revolutionary "Komitehs" or "Guards" after 11 February 1979 were acting in fact on behalf of the new Government, or at least exercised elements of governmental authority in the absence of official authorities, in operations of which the new Government must have had knowledge and to which it did not specifically object.[51] Under those circumstances, and for the kind of measures involved here, the Respondent has the burden of coming forward with evidence showing that members of "Komitehs" or "Guards" were in fact *not* acting on its behalf, or were not exercising elements of government authority, or that it would not control them.

44. The Tribunal is convinced that the evacuation of BHI employees, subsequent to 12 February 1979, was controlled by revolutionary "Komitehs" or "Guards" loyal to the new Government . . . and that an operation of this size and nature was known to the new Government. Under those circumstances, the Respondent has failed, in the Tribunal's view, to offer satisfactory evidence that these "Komitehs" or "Guards" did not act in fact on behalf of the new Government, or that they did not exercise elements of government authority. Rather, the evidence suggests that the new Government, despite occasional complaints about a lack of discipline, stood behind them. The Tribunal is persuaded, therefore, that the revolutionary "Komitehs" or "Guards" involved in this Case, were acting "for" Iran.

45. Nor has the Respondent established that it could not control the revolutionary "Komitehs" or "Guards" in this operation. . . . On the basis of the evidence in this case, therefore, the Tribunal finds the acts of the two men who took the claimant to the Hilton Hotel attributable to Iran.

The Tribunal unanimously found the expulsion to be unlawful and awarded the claimant compensation for the loss of personal property left behind in Iran and his loss of salary.[52]

(b) *Liability for ultra vires acts*[53]

I.L.C. DRAFT ARTICLES ON STATE RESPONSIBILITY

I.L.C.'s 1996 Report, G.A.O.R., 51st Sess., Supp. 10, p. 125.

Article 10

The conduct of an organ of a State, of a territorial governmental entity empowered to exercise elements of the governmental authority, such

---

[51] Ed. cf. *William L. Pereira Associates*, (1984) 5 Iran-U.S.C.T.R 198.
[52] cf. *Leach v. Iran* (1989) 23 Iran-U.S.C.T.R. 233.
[53] See Przetacznik, (1983) 61 R.D.I.S.D.P. 67, 129, and *id.* (1989) 1 Sri Lankan J.I.L. 151.

organ having acted in that capacity, shall be considered as an act of the State under international law even if, in the particular case, the organ exceeded its competence according to international law or contravened instructions concerning its activity.

Notes

1. The Commentary to Article 10 gives the following reason for the rule:

> In the opinion of the Commission there is no need to reopen the discussion on the basic criterion which has been affirmed in diplomatic practice and in the decisions of international tribunals in this century, *i.e.* the criterion of the attribution to the State, as a subject of international law, of the acts and omissions of its organs which have acted in that capacity, even when they have contravened the provisions of municipal law concerning their activity. This criterion is based on the need for clarity and security in international relations which seems to be the dominant theme in modern international life. In international law, the State must recognize that it acts whenever persons or groups of persons whom it has instructed to act in its name in a given area of activity appear to be acting effectively in its name. Even when in so doing those persons or groups exceed the formal limits of their competence according to municipal law or contravene the provisions of that law or of administrative ordinances or internal instructions issued by their superiors, they are nevertheless acting, even though improperly, within the scope of the discharge of their functions. The State cannot take refuge behind the notion that, according to the provisions of its legal system, those actions or omissions ought not to have occurred or ought to have taken a different form. They have nevertheless occurred and the State is therefore obliged to assume responsibility for them and to bear the consequences provided for in international law.[54]

2. Article 10 does not limit responsibility to cases of apparent exercise of authority (so that a state would not be liable where it is manifest that the action is *ultra vires*). There are instances of state practice and arbitral decisions supporting such a limitation. In correspondence in the *American Bible Society* case in 1885 the United States Secretary of State (Bayard) wrote:

> ... it is a rule of international law that sovereigns are not liable ... for damages to a foreigner when arising from the misconduct of agents acting out of the range not only of their real but of their apparent authority.[55]

See also the *Caire* case, above, p. 492. The Commission rejected this limitation:

> In justification of this conclusion it has been argued that if the lack of competence of the organ was manifest at the time when the organ acted, the injured party could and should have been aware of it, and, in consequence, been able to prevent the illicit act from taking place. ... On the other hand, in the majority of cases at least, the fact of knowing that the organ engaging in unlawful conduct is either exceeding its competence, or contravening its instructions, will not enable the victim of such conduct to escape its harmful consequences. We are, then, faced with a dilemma. Either we simply include the limitation ruling out attribution to the State of the conduct of organs acting in situations "manifestly" outside their competence, in which case we run the

[54] Y.B.I.L.C., 1975, II, p. 67.
[55] 6 Moore 743.

unpardonable risk of presenting the State with an easy loophole in particularly serious cases where its international responsibility ought to be affirmed; we formulate the limitation in question in the way proposed by several writers, who maintain that conduct of an organ acting outside its competence should not be attributable to the State if the organ's lack of competence was so manifest that the injured party ought to have been aware of it and could, *ipso facto, have avoided the injury*. But then we finish up by reducing the applicability of the limitation to such a small number of cases that, in the end, it would only weaken unnecessarily the force of the basic rule which it is essential to confirm in the most positive fashion. In conclusion, the Commission is of the opinion that, however worded, the limitation to exclude from qualification as acts of the State the actions of organs in situations of "manifest" lack of competence has no place in the rule defined in the present article.[56]

One of the "writers" to whom the Commission refers is Meron,[57] who proposes responsibility for:

1. An act committed within the scope of the official's apparent authority.

2. An act committed outside the scope of the official's apparent authority, if the commission of the act was made possible through means put at the official's disposal by the state. However, a state is not responsible if the alien could, in consequence of the apparent lack of authority of the official, avoid the damage.

UNION BRIDGE COMPANY CLAIM

U.S. *v.* Great Britain (1924)

American and British Claims Arbitration: Fromageot, President; Olds, American arbitrator; Mitchell-Innes, British arbitrator.
6 R.I.A.A. 138

In 1899, shortly after the outbreak of war between Great Britain and the Orange Free State, the claimant company delivered material to Port Elizabeth under contract with the Government of the latter state. It claimed damages arising out of the removal of the material from Port Elizabeth to Bloemfontein without its consent by an agent of the British Government and its subsequent sale.

Award of the Tribunal

The material continued to lie at Port Elizabeth till August 1901, when . . . it was forwarded by the order of Mr. W. H. Harrison, the Storekeeper of the Cape Government Railways at Port Elizabeth, by rail to . . . Bloemfontein. . . . In our view the result of the evidence is that Mr. Harrison purported to act upon instructions given to him, shortly after the outbreak of war, when he was storekeeper at East London, to forward all bridge material intended for the Orange Free State railways, to the

---

[56] Y.B.I.L.C., 1975, II, p. 69.
[57] (1957) 33 B.Y.I.L. 85 at 113.

Imperial Military Railways, Bloemfontein. . . . In so forwarding this material, therefore, he made two mistakes, inasmuch as it (1) was neutral property; and (2) was intended for a road, and not a railway bridge. . . .

The consignment of the material to Bloemfontein was a wrongful interference with neutral property. It was certainly within the scope of Mr. Harrison's duty as Railway Storekeeper to forward material by rail, and he did so under instructions which fix liability on His Britannic Majesty's Government.

That liability is not affected either by the fact that he did so under a mistake as to the character and ownership of the material or that it was a time of pressure and confusion caused by war, or by the fact, which, on the evidence, must be admitted, that there was no intention on the part of the British authorities to appropriate the material in question. . . .

Note
Would the United Kingdom have been liable if Mr Harrison had taken the materials home to build an ornamental bridge for himself in his garden?

YOUMANS CLAIM

U.S. *v.* Mexico (1926)

U.S.–Mexican General Claims Commission: Van Vollenhoven, Presiding Commissioner; Fernández McGregor, Mexican Commissioner; Nielsen, U.S. Commissioner. 4 R.I.A.A. 110

A mob gathered around a house in Mexico within which were 3 U.S. nationals. The local mayor was called.

Opinion of the Commission

The Mayor promptly went to the house, but was unable to quieten the mob. He then returned to his office and ordered José Maria Mora, *Jefe de la Tropa de la Seguridad Pública,* who held the rank of Lieutenant in the forces of the State of Michoacán, to proceed with troops to quell the riot and put an end to the attack upon the Americans. The troops, on arriving at the scene of the riot, instead of dispersing the mob, opened fire on the house, as a consequence of which Arnold was killed. . . . Connelly and Youmans were forced to leave, and as they did so they were killed by the troops and members of the mob. . . .

11. The claim made by the United States is predicated [*inter alia*] on the failure of the Mexican Government to exercise due diligence to protect the father of the claimant from the fury of the mob at whose hands he was killed. . . . In connection with the contention with respect to the failure of the authorities to protect Youmans from the acts of the mob, particular emphasis is laid on the participation of soldiers which is asserted to be in

itself a ground of liability. On behalf of the respondent Government it is contended that . . . even if it were assumed that the soldiers were guilty of such participation, the Mexican Government should not be held responsible for the wrongful acts of ten soldiers and one officer of the State of Michoacán, who, after having been ordered by the highest official in the locality to protect American citizens, instead of carrying out orders given then acted in violation of them in consequence of which the Americans were killed. . . .

13. With respect to the question of responsibility for the acts of soldiers there are citations in the Mexican Government's brief of extracts from a discussion of a subcommittee of the League of Nations Committee of Experts for the Progressive Codification of International Law.[58] The passage quoted, which deals with the responsibility of a State for illegal acts of officials resulting in damages to foreigners, begins with a statement relative to the acts of an official accomplished "outside the scope of his competency, that is to say, if he has exceeded his powers." An illegal act of this kind, it is stated in the quotation, is one that cannot be imputed to the State. Apart from the question whether the acts of officials referred to in this discussion have any relation to the rule of international law with regard to responsibility for acts of soldiers, it seems clear that the passage to which particular attention is called in the Mexican Government's brief is concerned solely with the question of the authority of an officer as defined by domestic law to act for his Government with reference to some particular subject. Clearly it is not intended by the rule asserted to say that no wrongful act of an official acting in the discharge of duties entrusted to him can impose responsibility on a Government under international law because any such wrongful act must be considered to be "outside the scope of his competency." If this were the meaning intended by the rule it would follow that no wrongful acts committed by an official could be considered as acts for which his Government could be held liable. We do not consider that any of these passages from the discussion of the subcommittee quoted in the Mexican brief are at variance with the view which we take that the action of the troops in participating in the murder at Angangueo imposed a direct responsibility on the Government of Mexico.

14. Citation is also made in the Mexican brief to an opinion rendered by Umpire Lieber in which effect is evidently given to the well-recognized rule of international law that a Government is not responsible for malicious acts of soldiers committed in their private capacity. Awards have repeatedly been rendered for wrongful acts of soldiers acting under the command of an officer. . . . Certain cases coming before the international tribunals may have revealed some uncertainty whether the acts of soldiers should properly be regarded as private acts for which there was no

---

[58] *Ed.* The reference is to the report of the sub-committee, which is reprinted in (1926) 20 A.J.I.L. Sp. Supp. 176.

liability on the State, or acts for which the State should be held responsible. But we do not consider that the participation of the soldiers in the murder at Angangueo can be regarded as acts of soldiers committed in their private capacity when it is clear that at the time of the commission of these acts the men were on duty under the immediate supervision and in the presence of a commanding officer. Soldiers inflicting personal injuries or committing wanton destruction or looting always act in disobedience of some rules laid down by superior authority. There could be no liability whatever for such misdeeds if the view were taken that any acts committed by soldiers in contravention of instructions must always be considered as personal acts.

The Commission awarded compensation.

Notes

1. Would there have been liability under (i) the I.L.C. or (ii) Meron's approach?

2. To what extent might liability for *ultra vires* acts depend upon the character of the act?[59] Might there, for example, be particularly strict liability for the *ultra vires* acts of soldiers as opposed to civil servants?

3. Are the rules concerning responsibility for *ultra vires* acts based upon fault or risk?

ZAFIRO CLAIM

Great Britain *v.* U.S. (1925)

American and British Claims Arbitration: Nerincx, President; Pound, American Arbitrator; Fitzpatrick, British Arbitrator.
6 R.I.A.A. 160

The case arose out of looting during the Spanish-American War of 1898 at Cavite in the Philippines. The *Zafiro* was a privately owned ship, with a Chinese crew. It was being used during the war by the United States as a supply ship, with its master and crew being placed under the command of a United States naval officer.

Award of the Tribunal

It is well settled that we must distinguish between soldiers or sailors under the command of officers, on the one hand, and, on the other hand, bodies of straggling and marauding soldiers not under the command of an officer, or marauding sailors not under command or control of officers. Hayden's case, 3 Moore, International Arbitrations, 2985; case of Terry and Angus, Id. 2993; Mexican Claims, Id. 2996–7. These cases draw a very

---

[59] See Brownlie, p. 435; Schwarzenberger, pp. 615–617.

clear line between what is done by order or in the presence of an officer and what is done without the order or presence of an officer. But it is not necessary that an officer be on the very spot. . . .

In the case before us, we think the officers were not actually present at the houses when the looting was done. . . . After the matter was drawn to the attention of the naval officers, the vessel was searched and the articles found on board were returned to the claimants. But the damage had been done. Moreover, Captain Whitton's statement that he "stopped anything he saw coming on board" gives the impression that he did not stop with sufficient promptitude the taking of things on land before they could come on board, after he found that plundering was going on. Without regard to this point, however, we feel that there was no effective control of the Chinese crew at the time when the real damage took place. When the *Zafiro* was tied up alongside the company's wharf, where the houses were, the naval officer and the merchant captain went off to look at the Spanish batteries, leaving the crew in charge of the first mate. The latter gave half of the crew leave to go ashore. Captain Whitton says significantly: "You know what Chinese are, especially these times." To let this crew go ashore where these houses were, with no one in charge of them, at a time when plunder and pillage were certain—and plunder and pillage by the Filipinos had been observed by all the officers—seems to us to have been highly culpable.

It was said in argument that a government is not responsible for what its sailors do when on shore leave. But we cannot agree that letting this Chinese crew go ashore uncontrolled at the time and place in question was like allowing shore leave to sailors in a policed port where social order is maintained by the ordinary agencies of government. Here the Spaniards had evacuated Cavite, and no one was in control except as the Navy controlled its own men. The nature of the crew, the absence of a régime of civil or military control ashore, and the situation of the neutral property, were circumstances calling for diligence on the part of those in charge of the Chinese crew to see to it that they were under control when they went ashore in a body. . . .

We think it clear that not all of the damage was done by the Chinese crew of the *Zafiro*. The evidence indicates that an unascertainable part was done by Filipino insurgents, and makes it likely that some part was done by the Chinese employees of the company. But we do not consider that the burden is on Great Britain to prove exactly what items of damage are chargeable to the *Zafiro*. As the Chinese crew of the *Zafiro* are shown to have participated to a substantial extent and the part chargeable to unknown wrongdoers cannot be identified, we are constrained to hold the United States liable for the whole.

In view, however, of our finding that a considerable, though unascertainable, part of the damage is not chargeable to the Chinese crew of the *Zafiro*, we hold that interest on the claims should not be allowed.

(c) *Absence of Liability for the Acts of Private Persons, Organs of Other States, and International Organisations*

I.L.C. DRAFT ARTICLES ON STATE RESPONSIBILITY

I.L.C.'s 1996 Report, G.A.O.R., 51st Sess., Supp. 10, p. 125.

Article 11

1. The conduct of a person or a group of persons not acting on behalf of the State shall not be considered as an act of the State under international law.

2. Paragraph 1 is without prejudice to the attribution to the State of any other conduct which is related to that of the persons or groups of persons referred to in that paragraph and which is to be considered as an act of the State by virtue of article 5 to 10. [above, pp. 499–500, 505]

Article 12

1. The conduct of an organ of a State acting in that capacity, which takes place in the territory of another State or in any other territory under its jurisdiction, shall not be considered as an act of the latter State under international law.

2. Paragraph 1 is without prejudice to the attribution to a State of any other conduct which is related to that referred to in that paragraph and which is to be considered as an act of that State by virtue of articles 5 to 10.

Article 13

The conduct of an organ of an international organization acting in that capacity shall not be considered as an act of a State under international law by reason only of the fact that such conduct has taken place in the territory under its jurisdiction.

(d) *Liability for the Acts of Insurrectionaries*

I.L.C. DRAFT ARTICLES ON STATE RESPONSIBILITY

I.L.C.'s 1996 Report, G.A.O.R., 51st Sess., Supp. 10, p. 125.

Article 14

1. The conduct of an organ of an insurrectional movement, which is established in the territory of a State or in any other territory under its administration, shall not be considered as an act of that State under international law.

2. Paragraph 1 is without prejudice to the attribution to a State of any other conduct which is related to that of the organ of the insurrectional

movement and which is to be considered as an act of that State by virtue of articles 5 to 10. [above, pp. 499–500, 505]

3. Similarly, paragraph 1 is without prejudice to the attribution of the conduct of the organ of the insurrectional movement to that movement in any case in which such attribution may be made under international law.

Article 15

1. The act of an insurrectional movement which becomes the new government of a State shall be considered as an act of that State. However, such attribution shall be without prejudice to the attribution to that State of conduct which would have been previously considered as an act of the State by virtue of articles 5 to 10.

2. The act of an insurrectional movement whose action results in the formation of a new State in part of the territory of a pre-existing State or in a territory under its administration shall be considered as an act of the new State.

Note[60]

Articles 14 and 15, Draft Articles apply to national liberation movements as well as to other "insurrectional movements." The Commentary to Article 15 reads[61]:

> The Commission considered that no distinction should be made, for the purposes of this article, between different categories of insurrectional movements on the basis of any international "legitimacy" or any illegality in respect of their establishment as the government, despite the possible importance of such distinctions in other contexts. From the standpoint of the formulation of rules of law governing State responsibility, it would be extremely dangerous to introduce concepts which might exonerate a new government or a new State from all responsibility by reason of the fact that it derived from an insurrectional movement characterized as "illegitimate" or from an insurrectional movement which had attained power as the result of internationally wrongful actions.

SHORT *v*. IRAN

U.S. *v*. Iran (1987)

Iran-U.S. Claims Tribunal. Chamber Three: Virally, Chairman; Brower, Ansari, Members. 16 Iran-U.S.C.T.R. 76

The claimant, an American national, was employed by Lockheed, an American company, in Iran. On February 8, 1979, three days before the Islamic Revolutionary Government took office, the claimant was evacuated from Iran on company orders because of the deteriorating situation. The claimant sought compensation for salary and other losses resulting from his alleged expulsion contrary to international law.

---

[60] See Akehurst (1968–69) 43 B.Y.I.L. 49.
[61] Y.B.I.L.C., 1975, II (Part Two), p. 105. *cf.* the Commentary to Art. 14, *ibid.* p. 92. See Atlam, in Spinedi and Simma, *loc. cit.*, p. 486, n. 13, above, p. 35, and Gayim, (1985) 54 N.T.I.R. 85.

Award of the Tribunal

33. Where a revolution leads to the establishment of a new government the State is held responsible for the acts of the overthrown government insofar as the latter maintained control of the situation. The successor government is also held responsible for the acts imputable to the revolutionary movement which established it, even if those acts occurred prior to its establishment, as a consequence of the continuity existing between the new organization of the State and the organization of the revolutionary movement. *See* Draft Articles on State Responsibility, *supra*, Commentary on Article 15, paras. 3 and 4 . . .

34. The Claimant relies on acts committed by revolutionaries. . . . He is unable, however, to identify any agent of the revolutionary movement, the actions of which compelled him to leave Iran.[62] The acts of supporters of a revolution [as opposed to its *agents*] cannot be attributed to the government following the success of the revolution just as the acts of supporters of an existing government are not attributable to the government. This was clearly recalled by the International Court of Justice in *United States Diplomatic and Consular Staff in Tehran* (United States *v.* Iran), 1980 I.C.J. 3, 29, para. 58 [above, p. 358] . . .

35. The Claimant . . . [relies] on the declarations made by the leader of the Revolution, Ayatollah Khomeini. . . . While these statements are of anti-foreign and in particular anti-American sentiment, the Tribunal notes that these pronouncements were of a general nature and did not specify that Americans should be expelled *en masse*. On this issue also it is worthwhile to quote the International Court of Justice in the judgment [para. 59] just referred to [above, p. 359] . . . Similarly, it cannot be said that the declarations referred to by the Claimant amounted to an authorization to revolutionaries to act in such a way that the Claimant should be forced to leave Iran forthwith. Nor is there any evidence that any action prompted by such statements was the cause of the Claimant's decision to leave Iran. In these circumstances, the Tribunal is of the view that the Claimant has failed to prove that his departure from Iran can be imputed to the wrongful conduct of Iran. The claim is therefore dismissed.[63]

Notes

1. The lack of responsibility of a state for the acts of revolutionaries, other than in the case where they have become the government, was explained by the Umpire (Ralston) in the *Sambaggio* case,[64] in which a claim by an Italian national for compensation for damage caused by unsuccessful revolutionaries in Venezuela was rejected:

> Governments are responsible, as a general principle, for the acts of those they control. But the very existence of a flagrant revolution presupposes that a

---

[62] *Ed.* The claimant alleged hostility from his landlord and of being watched by a man in the street.

[63] *Ed.* Brower, U.S. arbitrator, dissented.

[64] *Italy v. Venezuela*, (1903) 10 R.I.A.A. 499.

certain set of men have gone temporarily or permanently beyond the power of the authorities; and unless it clearly appears that the government has failed to use promptly and with appropriate force its constituted authority, it cannot reasonably be said that it should be responsible for a condition of affairs created without its volition. When we bear in mind that for six months previous to the taking complained of in the present case a bloody and determined revolution demanding the entire resources of the Government to quell it had been raging throughout the larger part of Venezuela, it can not be determined generally that there was such neglect on the part of the Government as to charge it with the offences of the revolutionists whose acts are now in question.

We find ourselves therefore obliged to conclude, from the standpoint of general principle, that, save under the exceptional circumstances indicated, the Government should not be held responsible for the acts of revolutionists because—

1. Revolutionists are not the agents of government, and a natural responsibility does not exist.
2. Their acts are committed to destroy the government, and no one should be held responsible for the acts of an enemy attempting his life.
3. The revolutionists were beyond governmental control, and the Government can not be held responsible for injuries committed by those who have escaped its restraint.[65]

2. The rule of non-liability in the *Sambaggio* case applies not only to revolutions in the traditional *coup d'etat* sense, but also to terrorist activities such as those of the IRA and PLO kind. Such terrorist activity has led to treaties providing for jurisdiction over terrorists[66]; no state is liable for their activities in the absence of complicity to the point where international responsibility is engaged. See in this connection the *Nicaragua* cases (*Merits*), below, p. 866, on the question of U.S. liability for the acts of the *contras*. However, a state does have a duty to protect aliens from the acts of terrorists or revolutionaries as an aspect of its general duty to protect them.[67]

(v) REPARATION[68]

CHORZÓW FACTORY CASE (INDEMNITY) (MERITS)

Germany *v.* Poland (1928)

P.C.I.J. Reports, Series A, No. 17, pp. 46–48

The case concerned the expropriation by Poland of a factory at Chorzów contrary, as the Court had held,[69] to the Geneva Convention of 1922 between Germany and Poland on Upper Silesia. In this judgment the Court ruled upon a claim by Germany for an indemnity for the damage caused by the illegal expropriation.

---

[65] *ibid.* p. 513. *cf.* the *Gelbtrunk Claim, U.S. v. Salvador,* 1902 U.S. For. Rel. 876 at 877–878. See also the *Home Missionary Society Claim,* above, p. 491.

[66] See the 1977 European Convention on the Suppression of Terrorism, *loc. cit.,* p. 299, ·ι. 23, above, and the Hague and Montreal Conventions, above, pp. 295 and 300.

[67] See the *Asian Agricultural Products Ltd* case, below, p. 543.

[68] See Mann (1978) 48 B.Y.I.L. 1, and Gray, *Judicial Remedies in International Law* (1987).

[69] *Certain German Interests in Polish Upper Silesia Case,* P.C.I.J. Rep., Ser. A, No. 7 (1926).

Judgment of the Court

The action of Poland which the Court has judged to be contrary to the Geneva Convention is not an expropriation—to render which lawful only the payment of fair compensation would have been wanting; it is a seizure of property, rights and interests which could not be expropriated even against compensation, save under the exceptional conditions fixed by Article 7 of the said Convention. . . .

It follows that the compensation due to the German Government is not necessarily limited to the value of the undertaking at the moment of dispossession, plus interest to the day of payment. This limitation would only be admissible if the Polish Government had had the right to expropriate, and if its wrongful act consisted merely in not having paid to the two Companies the just price of what was expropriated; in the present case, such a limitation might result in placing Germany and the interests protected by the Geneva Convention, on behalf of which interests the German Government is acting, in a situation more unfavourable than that in which Germany and these interests would have been if Poland had respected the said Convention. Such a consequence would not only be unjust, but also and above all incompatible with the aim of Article 6 and following articles of the Convention—that is to say, the prohibition, in principle, of the liquidation of the property, rights and interests of German nationals and of companies controlled by German nationals in Upper Silesia—since it would be tantamount to rendering lawful liquidation and unlawful dispossession indistinguishable in so far as their financial results are concerned.

The essential principle contained in the actual notion of an illegal act—a principle which seems to be established by international practice and in particular by the decisions of arbitral tribunals—is that reparation must, as far as possible, wipe out all the consequences of the illegal act and re-establish the situation which would, in all probability, have existed if that act had not been committed. Restitution in kind, or, if this is not possible, payment of a sum corresponding to the value which a restitution in kind would bear; the award, if need be, of damages for loss sustained which would not be covered by restitution in kind or payment in place of it—such are the principles which should serve to determine the amount of compensation due for an act contrary to international law.

This conclusion particularly applies as regards the Geneva Convention, the object of which is to provide for the maintenance of economic life in Upper Silesia on the basis of respect for the *status quo*. The dispossession of an industrial undertaking—the expropriation of which is prohibited by the Geneva Convention—then involves the obligation to restore the undertaking and, if this be not possible, to pay its value at the time of the indemnification, which value is designed to take the place of restitution which has become impossible. To this obligation, in virtue of the general principles of international law, must be added that of compensating loss sustained as the result of the seizure. The impossibility, on which the Parties are agreed, of restoring the Chorzów factory could therefore have no other effect but that of substituting payment of the value of the undertaking for restitution; it would not be in conformity either with the principles of law or with the wish of the Parties to infer from that agreement that the question of compensation must henceforth be dealt with as though an expropriation properly so called was involved.

I.L.C. DRAFT ARTICLES ON STATE RESPONSIBILITY

I.L.C.'s 1996 Report, G.A.O.R., 51st Sess., Supp. 10, p. 125.

Article 41

A State whose conduct constitutes an internationally wrongful act having a continuing character is under the obligation to cease that conduct, without prejudice to the responsibility it has already incurred.

Article 42

1. The injured State is entitled to obtain from the State which has committed an internationally wrongful act full reparation in the form of restitution in kind, compensation, satisfaction and assurances and guarantees of non-repetition, either singly or in combination.

2. In the determination of reparation, account shall be taken of the negligence or the wilful act or omission of:

(*a*) the injured State; or
(*b*) a national of that State on whose behalf the claim is brought;

which contributed to the damage.

3. In no case shall reparation result in depriving the population of a State of its own means of subsistence.

4. The State which has committed the internationally wrongful act may not invoke the provisions of its internal law as justification for the failure to provide full reparation.

Article 43

The injured State is entitled to obtain from the State which has committed an internationally wrongful act restitution in kind, that is, the re-establishment of the situation which existed before the wrongful act was committed, provided and to the extent that restitution in kind:

(*a*) is not materially impossible;
(*b*) would not involve a breach of an obligation arising from a peremptory norm of general international law;

(c) would not involve a burden out of all proportion to the benefit which the injured State would gain from obtaining restitution in kind instead of compensation; or

(d) would not seriously jeopardize the political independence or economic stability of the State which has committed the internationally wrongful act, whereas the injured State would not be similarly affected if it did not obtain restitution in kind.

Article 44

1. The injured State is entitled to obtain from the State which has committed an internationally wrongful act compensation for the damage caused by that act, if and to the extent that the damage is not made good by restitution in kind.

2. For the purposes of the present article, compensation covers any economically assessable damage sustained by the injured State, and may include interest and, where appropriate, loss of profits.

Article 45

1. The injured State is entitled to obtain from the State which has committed an internationally wrongful act satisfaction for the damage, in particular moral damage, caused by that act, if and to the extent necessary to provide full reparation.

2. Satisfaction may take the form of one or more of the following:

(a) an apology;

(b) nominal damages;

(c) in cases of gross infringement of the rights of the injured State, damages reflecting the gravity of the infringement;

(d) in cases where the internationally wrongful act arose from the serious misconduct of officials or from criminal conduct of officials or private parties, disciplinary action against, or punishment of, those responsible.

3. The right of the injured State to obtain satisfaction does not justify demands which would impair the dignity of the State which has committed the internationally wrongful act.

Article 46

The injured State is entitled, where appropriate, to obtain from the State which has committed an internationally wrongful act assurances or guarantees of non-repetition of the wrongful act.

Notes

1. On the cessation of wrongful conduct, the Commentary to Article 41 reads[70]:

[70] Y.B.I.L.C., 1993, II (Part Two), p. 58. Footnotes omitted.

(7) . . . cessation is not part of reparation. It is targeted towards the wrongful conduct *per se*, irrespective of its consequences. . . .

(8) The difficulty in isolating cessation from reparation is compounded by the fact that in practice the result of cessation may be indistinguishable from that of one specific form of reparation, namely restitution in kind. Reference is made here to cases involving the liberation of persons or the restitution of objects or premises. Such measures are often cited as examples of reparation in the form of restitution in kind. In fact, they aim at stopping the breach. . . .

(10) . . . Instances of a continuing wrongful act are provided in paragraph (21) of the commentary to [Draft] article 18 as follows: "The maintenance in force of a law which the State is internationally required to repeal or, conversely, failure to pass a law which it is internationally required to enact; unjustified occupation of the territory of another State; unlawful blockade of foreign coasts or ports, etc." In the same context, the Commission also referred to the *De Becker* case[71] in which the European Commission on Human Rights held that the loss of the right to work as a journalist as a result of a judgement which had preceded the entry into force of the Convention . . . constituted a continuing violation with respect to which the claimant rightly considered himself to be the victim of a violation of his freedom of expression under article 10 of the Convention.

2. The forms that reparation may take are indicated in Article 42, Draft Articles. Of these, "restitution in kind", or *restitutio in integrum*, has priority. The Commentary to Article 43 reads[72]:

> The logical and temporal primacy of restitution in kind is confirmed first of all by practice, not only by the application of the rule by PCIJ in the *Chorzów Factory* case but also in the cases in which States or arbitral bodies have moved to reparation by equivalent only after the more or less explicit *constat* that, for one reason or another, *restitutio* could not be effected.

An example of restitution in kind is found in the *Martini* case.[73] There the Tribunal ruled that proceedings in a case in the Venezuelan courts that was lost by the claimant company had been "manifestly unjust" and decided that "the Venezuelan Government is bound to recognise, by way of reparation, the annulment of the financial obligations imposed" by the Venezuelan courts on the claimant company. See also the *Temple* case,[74] in which Thailand was ordered to return to Cambodia religious objects it had taken illegally from a temple in Cambodia. Brownlie[75] states that "it would seem that territorial disputes may be settled by specific restitution, although the declaratory form of the judgments of the International Court masks the element of restitution."

3. "Restitution in kind," however, is exceptional.[76] Much more common as a means of "wiping out the consequences of the illegal act" is the award of monetary compensation (see Article 44). Rules about the award of such compensation in international law are far from clear.[77] Examples of approaches taken by international tribunals to the question of monetary compensation for material

---

[71] *Ed*. E.Ct.H.R. Rep., Ser. A, No. 4 (1962).

[72] Y.B.I.L.C., 1993, II (Part Two), p. 62.

[73] *Italy v. Venezuela*, (1930) 2 R.I.A.A. 975 at 1002. Translation.

[74] I.C.J. Rep. 1962, p. 6. See also the remedy sought by France in the *Savarkar* case, above, p. 292, and the advice given by the Law Officers in the *Lawler Incident*, above, p. 292.

[75] Brownlie, p. 463.

[76] It was awarded in the *Texaco* case, see below, p. 548.

[77] See Brownlie, *op. cit.*, p. 485, n. 4, pp. 222–234, and Gray, *op. cit.*, p. 515, n. 68, above (see table of contents). See also the survey in the I.L.C.'s commentary to Article 44, Y.B.I.L.C., 1993, II (Part Two), p. 67.

injury to property interests and for injury to the person in cases concerning the treatment of aliens are found in Section 3 of this chapter.

Monetary compensation has been awarded for non-material damage. In the *I'm Alone* case, for example, the Commissioners recommended the payment by the United States of $25,000 "as a material amend in respect of the wrong" committed by the United States in sinking the *I'm Alone*.[78] The compensation was related to the indignity suffered by Canada by the unlawful sinking of a ship registered in Montreal; it was not related to the value of the ship or its cargo.

4. An illustration of one form that satisfaction (see Article 45) may take is found in the *Borchgrave* case.[79] There, in a case in which a Belgian national working at the Belgian Embassy in Madrid was found dead on the roadside in Spain in 1936, the Court listed the reparation sought by Belgium in diplomatic proceedings with Spain as follows: "In consequence, proceeding on the principles of international law relating to the responsibility of States, the Belgian Government demanded as reparation: (1) an expression of the Spanish Government's excuses and regrets; (2) transfer of the corpse to the port of embarcation with military honours; (3) the payment of an indemnity of one million Belgian francs in favour of the persons entitled; and (4) just punishment of the guilty." The forms of reparation listed under (1), (2) and (4) are clearly forms of satisfaction.[80] A declaration by a court or tribunal that a state has acted illegally may itself be sufficient satisfaction in some cases.[81]

5. Article 46 adds as a final form of reparation the obtaining of assurances or guarantees of non-repetition. The Commentary[82] states:

> (1) . . . assurances and guarantees of non-repetition . . . have a preventative rather than a remedial function. They furthermore presuppose a risk of repetition of the wrongful act. . . .
>
> (2) A request for safeguards against repetition suggests that the injured State is seeking to obtain from the offender something additional to and different from mere reparation, the re-establishment of the pre-existing situation being considered insufficient. For example, following demonstrations against the United States Embassy in Moscow in February 1965 (less than three months after those of November 1964), the President of the United States affirmed that: "The United States Government must insist that its diplomatic establishments and personnel be given the protection which is required by international law and custom and which is necessary for the conduct of diplomatic relations between States. Expressions of regret and compensation are no substitute for adequate protection". . . .
>
> (5) . . . it appears that assurances and guarantees of non-repetition are a *sui generis* remedy to be distinguished from satisfaction and other forms of compensation. The text adopted by the Commission . . . recognizes that the wrongdoing State is under an obligation to provide such guarantees subject to a demand from the injured State and when circumstances so warrant. Circumstances to be taken into consideration include the existence of a real risk of repetition and the seriousness of the injury suffered by the claimant State as a result of the wrongful act. The phrase "where appropriate" makes it clear that it will be for the judge (or other third party called upon to apply the rule) to determine if the conditions for the granting of what the Commission considers as an exceptional remedy are met and also to deny abusive claims which would impair the dignity of the wrongdoing State.

---

[78] See above, p. 437.
[79] P.C.I.J. Rep., Ser. A/B, No. 72 (1937) p. 165.
[80] Note also the apology recommended in the *I'm Alone* case, above, p. 437.
[81] See the *Corfu Channel* case, above, p. 391 (on Albania's counter-claim).
[82] Y.B.I.L.C. 1993, II (Part Two), pp. 81–82.

3. The Treatment of Aliens[83]

(i) Introductory Note

The treatment of aliens (or, more accurately, the treatment of the nationals of other states) is as controversial a subject as any in international law. The controversy stems from a difference of approach between those states that consider that there is an "international minimum standard" of treatment which must be accorded to aliens by all states irrespective of how they treat their own nationals and those that argue that aliens may only insist upon "national treatment," *i.e.* treatment equal to that given by the state concerned to its own nationals.[84] Generally speaking, developed states follow the "international minimum standard" approach while the developing states favour "national treatment."[85] At the turn of the century, the latter states consisted mainly of Latin American states; more recently they have been joined by most of the post-colonial Afro-Asian states. The former USSR rejected the "international minimum standard" approach also. The support for both points of view makes it difficult to determine many of the rules of international law in this area.

Whether an "international minimum standard" or a "national treatment" rule applies, it is commonly agreed by states that international law does not control their treatment of aliens in every area of activity. Whereas, on either basis, states are limited in their treatment of aliens in the areas indicated in the materials in this section, in certain other areas states may at customary international law treat aliens *qua* aliens[86] in their discretion. For example, aliens may be, and commonly are, restricted in the ownership of property, participation in public life and the taking of employment. In the United Kingdom, an alien may not own a British ship, vote in a parliamentary election, or hold any office under the Crown.[87]

(ii) An Injury to the State

MAVROMATTIS PALESTINE CONCESSIONS CASE (JURISDICTION)

Greece *v.* U.K. (1924)

P.C.I.J. Reports, Series A, No. 2, p. 12

Judgment of the Court

In the case of the Mavromattis concessions it is true that the dispute was at first between a private person and a State—*i.e.* between M. Mavromattis and Great Britain. Subsequently, the Greek Government took

---

[83] See Amerasinghe, *State Responsibility for Injuries to Aliens* (1967); Borchard, *The Diplomatic Protection of Citizens Abroad* (1915); Dunn, *The Protection of Nationals* (1932); Eagleton, *The Responsibility of States in International Law* (1928); Freeman, *The International Responsibility of States for Denial of Justice* (1938); Jessup, *A Modern Law of Nations* (1946), Chap. V; Lillich, ed., *International Law of State Responsibility for Injuries to Aliens* (1983); Parry, (1956–II) 90 Hague Recueil 653.

[84] On the position of stateless persons, see below, p. 596.

[85] On the approach now adopted by developing states in the particular case of expropriation, see below, p. 548.

[86] Aliens may, as individuals, have some protection at customary international law and by treaty on a human rights basis: see below, Chap. 9.

[87] Wade and Bradley, *Constitutional and Administrative Law* (11th ed., 1993), pp. 436–437.

up the case. The dispute then entered upon a new phase; it entered the domain of international law, and became a dispute between two States.

... It is an elementary principle of international law that a State is entitled to protect its subjects, when injured by acts contrary to international law committed by another State, from whom they have been unable to obtain satisfaction through the ordinary channels. By taking up the case of one of its subjects and by resorting to diplomatic action or international judicial proceedings on his behalf, a State is in reality asserting its own rights—its right to ensure, in the person of its subjects, respect for the rules of international law.

The question, therefore, whether the present dispute originates in an injury to a private interest, which in point of fact is the case in many international disputes, is irrelevant from this standpoint. Once a State has taken up a case on behalf of one of its subjects before an international tribunal, in the eyes of the latter the State is sole claimant.

ADMINISTRATIVE DECISION No. V

U.S. *v.* Germany (1924)

Mixed Claims Commission: Parker, Umpire; Anderson, American Commissioner; Kiesselbalch, German Commissioner. (1924) 7 R.I.A.A. 119

Opinion of the Umpire

Ordinarily a nation will not espouse a claim on behalf of its national against another national unless requested so to do by such national. When on such request a claim is espoused, the nation's absolute right to control it is necessarily exclusive. In exercising such control it is governed not only by the interest of the particular claimant but by the larger interests of the whole people of the nation and must exercise an untrammelled discretion in determining when and how the claim will be presented and pressed, or withdrawn or compromised, and the private owner will be bound by the action taken. Even if payment is made to the espousing nation in pursuance of an award, it has complete control over the fund so paid to and held by it and may, to prevent fraud, correct a mistake, or protect the national honour, at its election return the fund to the nation paying it or otherwise dispose of it. . . .

The Umpire agrees with the American Commissioner that the *control* of the United States over claims espoused by it before this Commission is complete. But the generally accepted theory formulated by Vattel, which makes the injury to the national an injury to the nation and internationally therefore the claim a national claim which may and should be espoused by the nation injured, must not be permitted to obscure the realities or blind us to the fact that the ultimate object of asserting the claim is to provide reparation for the private claimant. . . .

Notes

1. Is a state obliged to take up a national's case?[88] Who decides on what terms to settle the case (if this question arises) if it does? Exceptionally, treaties may allow individuals to bring claims against the parties to them.[89] Why should not customary international law allow them to bring claims against states in at least some cases?

2. A state is not obliged by international law to hand over to a claimant compensation received in his case; the question is one of municipal law. As far as English law is concerned, in *Rustomjee v. The Queen*,[90] Lush J. stated:

> No doubt a duty arose as soon as the money was received to distribute that money amongst the persons towards whose losses it was paid by the Emperor of China; but then the distribution when made would be, not the act of an agent accounting to a principal, but the act of the sovereign in dispensing justice to her subjects. For any omission of that duty the sovereign cannot be held responsible.

The case concerned moneys paid to Great Britain by China by treaty as compensation for damage suffered by British nationals in China. Similarly, in United Kingdom law the Crown owes no legal duty to provide protection so that failure to obtain the release of a British citizen is not actionable in the British courts.[91]

3. Consider whether, despite the theory that the injury is to the state and not to its national, the cases in this Section suggest that in practice tribunals commonly assess compensation by reference to the injury suffered by the latter.

(iii) INTERNATIONAL MINIMUM STANDARD OR NATIONAL TREATMENT?

NEER CLAIM

U.S. *v.* Mexico (1926)

U.S.-Mexican General Claims Commission: for the Commissioners, see above, p. 507. 4 R.I.A.A. 60

In this case the United States claimed that Mexico had failed to exercise due diligence in finding and prosecuting the murderer of a United States national. In the course of rejecting the claim, the Commission indicated the standard that it would have to apply. The Commission was unanimous.

Opinion of the Commission

The Commission recognises the difficulty of devising a general formula for determining the boundary between an international delinquency of this type and an unsatisfactory use of power included in national sovereignty.... Without attempting to announce a precise formula, it is in the

---

[88] Alleging U.S. failure to take up the cases of nationals against Saudi Arabia, see Young (1992–1993) 16 Hastings I.C.L.R. 663.

[89] See above, p. 141.

[90] (1876) 1 Q.B.D. 487 at 497. See also *Civilian War Claimants' Association Ltd v. The King* [1932] A.C. 14, HL.

[91] *Mutasa v. Att.-Gen.* [1980] Q.B. 114.

opinion of the Commission possible . . . to hold (first) that the propriety of governmental acts should be put to the test of international standards, and (second) that the treatment of an alien, in order to constitute an international delinquency, should amount to an outrage, to bad faith, to wilful neglect of duty, or to an insufficiency of governmental action so far short of international standards that every reasonable and impartial man would readily recognize its insufficiency. Whether the insufficiency proceeds from deficient execution of an intelligent law or from the fact that the laws of the country do not empower the authorities to measure up to international standards is immaterial.

Notes

1. The great majority of arbitration awards are like that in the *Neer Claim* in supporting the view that international law requires states to treat aliens according to an "international minimum standard." In the *Chevreau* case,[92] for instance, in which France claimed on behalf of a French national in respect of his arrest and treatment in detention by Great Britain, the Arbitrator (Beichmann) said: "The detained man must be treated in a manner fitting his station, and which conforms to the standard habitually practised among civilized nations."[93] More recently the tribunal in the *Asian Agricultural Products Ltd* case[94] applied the " 'due diligence' obligation under the *minimum standard* of customary international law". The majority of arbitrators in such awards tend to be from developed states.

2. How persuasive is the argument that an alien who visits, takes up residence in, or does business in a foreign state must take conditions as he finds them?

PREPARATORY STUDY CONCERNING A DRAFT DECLARATION ON RIGHTS AND DUTIES OF STATES

Memorandum submitted by the UN Secretary-General, U.N.Doc. A/CN. 4/2, p. 71, 1949

Early discussion in the International Law Commission on a Draft Declaration on Rights and Duties of States was based upon a Panamanian draft upon which governments were asked to comment. Article 7 of that draft reads in part: "Foreigners may not claim rights different from, or more extensive than, those enjoyed by nationals." The following is the response by the United Kingdom Government to that Article. The sentence was finally omitted from the Commission's Draft Declaration on the separate ground that the question should be dealt with in the course of codifying the law of state responsibility.

The second sentence of this article is not in accord with existing international law, as His Majesty's Government apprehend it. There is much international authority for the existence of a minimum international

---

[92] *France v. Great Britain*, (1931) 2 R.I.A.A. 1113. English translation in (1933) 27 A.J.I.L. 153.

[93] (1933) 27 A.J.I.L. at 160. See also the extracts from the *Roberts Claim*, below, p. 535. On the other hand, see, in the context of the protection of resident aliens against injury in war, revolution, etc., the *Sambaggio* case, above, p. 513.

[94] (1990) 30 I.L.M. 577 at 608. See also the Court Chamber ("minimum international standard") in the *ELSI* case, I.C.J. Rep. 1989, p. 14.

standard, with which States are obliged to comply in their treatment of foreigners, whether or not they do so in the treatment of their nationals. If, and in so far as international law develops so as to limit the domestic jurisdiction of States in the treatment of their nationals to such an extent that every treatment of a national, which falls below the international standard, is a breach of international law (and therefore a matter on which other States may intervene), then the existing principle of international law with regard to the "international standard" will apply to both nationals and foreigners. Unless and until that position is reached, His Majesty's Government consider that the doctrine of the minimum international standard, with regard to the treatment of foreigners, remains part of international law and that agreement to abolish that doctrine will not be attained.

Notes

1. At the Hague Codification Conference in 1930 the following text on the particular question of injury to aliens at the hands of private persons was rejected by 23 votes to 17:

> A state is only responsible for damage caused by private persons to the persons or property of foreigners if it has manifestly failed to take such preventive or punitive measures as in the circumstances might reasonably be expected of it had the persons injured been its own nationals.

A text on the same question favouring an international minimum standard was then adopted by 21 votes to 17.[95] On the other hand, Article 9 of the 1933 Montevideo Convention on Rights and Duties of States,[96] which would still represent the view of most developing states, reads in part:

> Nationals and foreigners are under the same protection of the law and the national authorities and the foreigners may not claim rights other or more extensive than those of the nationals.

2. For a robust, Victorian statement favouring the international minimum standard in the administration of justice, note that of Lord Palmerston (Foreign Secretary) in 1850:

> We shall be told, perhaps, as we have already been told, that if the people of the country are liable to have heavy stones placed upon their breasts, and police officers to dance upon them; if they are liable to have their heads tied to their knees, and to be left for hours in that state; or to be swung like a pendulum and to be bastinadoed as they swing, foreigners have no right to be better treated than the natives, and have no business to complain if the same things are practised upon them. We may be told this, but this is not my opinion, nor do I believe it is the opinion of any reasonable man.[97]

---

[95] See Hackworth, (1930) 24 A.J.I.L. 500 at pp. 513–514.

[96] *loc. cit.*, p. 102, above. There are 16 parties to the Convention, including the U.S. See, however, the U.S. reservation, 4 Malloy 4810.

[97] H.C.Debs., 3rd Series, CXII, Col. 387; 6 B.D.I.L. 290.

3. In 1957, the International Law Commission debated the Second Report on State Responsibility of its Special Rapporteur (Garcia Amador).[98] The Rapporteur proposed in his Report the following draft article:

> *Article* 5.1. The State is under a duty to ensure to aliens the enjoyment of the same civil rights, and to make available to them the same individual guarantees as are enjoyed by its nationals. These rights and guarantees shall not, however, in any case be less than the "fundamental human rights" recognized and defined in contemporary international instruments.

This ambitious proposal would, in a sense, have married the international minimum standard and national treatment approaches. Its human right basis, which would have made substantial inroads upon the domestic jurisdiction of states, was too far out of line with state practice to have had any real hope of approval. Despite redrafting, it was felt to be impracticable for purposes of codification and not pursued further. Since then the Commission has changed its approach and, as indicated earlier,[99] is concentrating upon the codification of the general principles of responsibility.

Nonetheless, it is possible that the general post-1945 development of international human rights law, which protects aliens and nationals alike, may in effect lead the law of state responsibility for the treatment of aliens back to Garcia Amador's approach, although this is as yet to be confirmed by state practice.[1] That the law of state responsibility for aliens is not made redundant by the emergence of international human rights law follows from the difficulties in enforcing customary human rights law[2] and the less than perfect remedies and universal acceptance of human rights treaties. For the time being at least, the possibility of diplomatic protection by one's national state is a valuable alternative and supplement to such guarantees and procedures under international human rights law as may exist.

(iv) ADMISSION AND EXPULSION[3]

REPORT ON ADMISSION TO LOUISIANA

Report by J. Dodson, Queen's Advocate, to the Foreign Secretary, August 4, 1843. 2 McNair 105

... the purport of the Act in question [a Louisiana State Statute] is to prohibit free persons of colour from entering the State of Louisiana by

---

[98] Y.B.I.L.C., 1957, II, p. 104. The debate was a famous one, in which nationals from developing and developed states put different points of view most forcefully: *ibid.* Vol. I, pp. 155 *et seq.*

[99] See above, p. 484.

[1] For another approach, see the General Assembly's 1985 *Declaration on the Human Rights of Individuals who are not Nationals of the Country in which They Live*, G.A. Resn. 40/144, G.A.O.R., 40th Sess., Supp. 53, p. 252 (1985). This is limited and tailored to the human rights of aliens (*e.g.* provisions concerning the right to transfer assets home), and was a response to the ill-treatment of aliens in Amin's Uganda in the late 1970s. It has not proved significant in practice. On the Declaration, see Lillich and Neff (1978) 21 G.Y.I.L. 97 and Lillich, *The Human Rights of Aliens in Contemporary International Law* (1984), pp. 55–56.

[2] See below, p. 725.

[3] See Dowty, *Closed Borders* (1987); Goodwin-Gill, *International Law and the Movement of Persons between States* (1978); Plender, *International Migration Law* (2nd ed., 1988); Pellonpää, *Expulsion in International Law* (1984).

sea, and of punishing them with great severity in case of their arrival within the territory contrary to the tenor of this inhospitable law.

The provisions of this extraordinary and illiberal Act are calculated to operate with peculiar harshness as regards the free coloured subjects of Her Majesty; and I therefore think that Her Majesty's Government would be justified in making a representation against it, in the shape of a remonstrance to the Government of the United States. Whether Her Majesty's Government would have a right to go further and insist upon the repeal of this specimen of Louisianian legislation, may be a matter not altogether free from doubt, but upon the best consideration I have been able to give the subject, I incline to think that Great Britain does not possess such right. It cannot be denied that every independent State or nation is entitled to admit or exclude from its territories the subjects and citizens of foreign States, unless it has entered into any engagement by treaty on the subject, in which case the treaty must of course prescribe the rule to be observed.

Note

In *Att.-Gen. for Canada v. Cain*,[4] the Judicial Committee of the Privy Council said:

> One of the rights possessed by the supreme power in every State is the right to refuse to permit an alien to enter that State, to annex what conditions it pleases to the permission to enter it, and to expel or deport from the State, at pleasure, even a friendly alien, especially if it considers his presence in the State opposed to its peace, order, and good government, or to its social or material interests.

RANKIN *v.* IRAN

U.S. *v.* Iran (1987)

Iran-U.S. Claims Tribunal. Chamber Two: Briner, Chairman; Aldrich, Bahrami, Members. 17 Iran-U.S.C.T.R. 135

The claimant was an American national employed by BHI, an American company, in Iran at the time of the fall of the Shah's Government and its replacement by the Islamic Revolutionary Government in February 1979. On February 12, the day after the new Government took office, the claimant, who was still under contract to work for BHI in Iran, requested and was granted BHI permission to be evacuated from the country with other BHI employees whom BHI had arranged to be repatriated. In this case, he claimed compensation for loss of salary and abandoned personal property resulting from his alleged expulsion from Iran contrary to international law.

[4] [1906] A.C. 542 at 546.

Award of the Tribunal

22. According to the practice of States, the writings of scholars, the decisions of international tribunals, and bilateral treaty provisions such as those contained in the [1955] Treaty of Amity... between Iran and the United States... , international law imposes certain restraints on the circumstances and the manner in which a State may expel aliens from its territory. A claimant alleging expulsion has the burden of proving the wrongfulness of the expelling State's action, in other words that it was arbitrary, discriminatory, or in breach of the expelling State's obligations. These restraints have usually been considered in the context of specific measures directed against an individual emanating directly from the State or legally attributable to it. However, these general principles apply equally to a situation in which, while there is no law, regulation, or directive which forces the individual alien to leave, his or her continued presence in the host country is made impossible because of conditions generated by wrongful acts of the State or attributable to it. . . .

30 . . . a. A distinction must be made between the period prior to February 1979 and thereafter, when the Ayatollah Khomeini returned to Iran from exile and the new Islamic Government replaced that of the Shah.

b. During the earlier period, the leaders of the Revolution fostered anti-American attitudes. . . . However, the evidence before us is inadequate to show that in the period prior to February 1979 there existed a general expulsion policy towards foreigners. The thrust of the Revolutionary Movement was then aimed at the overthrow of the regime of the Shah. . . .

d. However, when the Ayatollah Khomeini returned to Iran on February 1, 1979, he was reported to have called for the departure of all foreigners. Shortly thereafter, the newly-formed Government began to take action to cancel contracts with non-Iranian persons and companies and to implement a policy to lessen the influence of foreigners in Iran and cause the departure of, among others, most Americans.

e. The implementation of this policy could, in general terms, be violative of both procedural and substantive limitations on a State's right to expel aliens from its territory, as found in the provisions of the Treaty of Amity and in customary international law.[5] However, it . . . is necessary to examine the circumstances of each departure and to identify the general and specific acts relied on and evidenced to determine how they affected or motivated at that time the individual who now is alleging expulsion and whether such acts are attributable to Iran (*See* Articles 5–10, Draft Articles on State Responsibility...). In this regard the Tribunal

---

[5] *e.g.* by expelling an alien who had a continued right to residence in Iran or by depriving an alien of a reasonable opportunity to protect his property interests prior to his expulsion.

notes the significance of the general turmoil and disorder which ensued after the return of Ayatollah Khomeini as competing groups vied for power in the revolutionary environment which existed in Iran at that time. The Tribunal considers this a factor which could have caused an individual's decision to leave and which could not be attributed to the State or its agents or organs. . . .

39. [Having reviewed the evidence] . . . . the Tribunal finds that the Claimant has not satisfied the burden of proving that the implementation of the new policy of the Respondent . . . was a substantial causal factor in his departure from Iran. Neither has the Claimant satisfied the burden of proving that his decision to leave was caused by specific acts or omissions of or attributable to the Respondent. Rather, the turmoil and generally chaotic conditions associated with this crucial stage of the Revolution would appear to have been the motivating factor in the Claimant's decision to leave.

Claim dismissed

Note

For other claims before the Iran-U.S. Claims Tribunal acknowledging the possibility of "constructive expulsion," see *Yeager v. Iran*, above, p. 503, and *Short v. Iran* above, p. 513. The requirements were expressed as follows by Chamber Three of the Tribunal in *International Technical Products Corp. v. Iran*[6]:

> Such cases would seem to presuppose at least (1) that the circumstances in the country of residence are such that the alien cannot reasonably be regarded as having any real choice, and (2) that behind the events or acts leading to the departure there is an intention of having the alien ejected and these acts, moreover, are attributable to the State in accordance with principles of state responsibility.

DR BREGER'S CASE

Letter of December 15, 1961, from the U.S. Department of State to a Congressman. 8 Whiteman 861

As to Dr Breger's expulsion from the Island of Rhodes in 1938, it may be pointed out that under generally accepted principles of international law, a state may expel an alien whenever it wishes, provided it does not carry out the expulsion in an arbitrary manner, such as by using unnecessary force to effect the expulsion or by otherwise mistreating the alien or by refusing to allow the alien a reasonable opportunity to safeguard property. In view of Dr Breger's statement to the effect that he was ordered by the Italian authorities to leave the Island of Rhodes within six months, it appears doubtful that international liability of the Italian Government

---

[6] (1985) 9 Iran-U.S.C.T.R. 18. On the Iranian "constructive expulsion" cases, see Cove, (1987–8) 11 Fordham I.L.J. 802.

could be based on the ground that he was not given enough time to safeguard his property.

Notes

1. In *Yeager v. Iran*,[7] the Tribunal awarded compensation to an American expelled from Iran who "was given only 30 minutes to pack a few personal belongings without advance notice" on the basis that customary international law recognised "that a state must give the foreigner to be expelled sufficient time to wind up his affairs."

Goodwin-Gill[8] suggests that there are substantive as well as procedural limitations upon the power to expel aliens:

> State practice accepts that expulsion is justified:
>
> (a) for entry in breach of law;
> (b) for breach of the conditions of admission;
> (c) for involvement in criminal activities;
> (d) in the light of political and security considerations.
>
> In determining whether its interests are adversely affected by the continuing presence of the alien, or whether there is a threat to "ordre public," the expelling State enjoys under international law a fairly wide margin of appreciation.
>
> "Ordre public" remains a "general legal conception," the content of which is determined by law. Whether or not reasons of "ordre public" exist is open to impartial adjudication in the light of the prescribed function of expulsion and of the international obligations which each State owes.
>
> The principle of good faith and the requirement of justification, or "reasonable cause," demand that due consideration be given to the interests of the individual, including his basic human rights, his family, property, and other connections with the State of residence, and his legitimate expectations. These must be weighed against the competing claims of "ordre public."

2. On the expulsion of refugees, see the 1951 Convention relating to the Status of Refugees.[9] Although there is no duty to admit a refugee, contracting parties "shall not expel a refugee lawfully in their territory save on grounds of national security or public order" (Article 32(1)). Further, a refugee, whether lawfully or unlawfully present, must not be returned "to the frontiers of territories where his life or freedom would be threatened on account of his race, religion, nationality,

---

[7] 17 Iran-U.S.C.T.R. 92 (1987) p. 106. See also the extract from the case, above, p. 503.

[8] *Op. cit.*, p. 526, n. 3, above, p. 262. As to procedure, he suggests that the expulsion must be in accordance with the local law and not arbitrary: *ibid.* p. 263.

[9] U.K.T.S. 39 (1954), Cmd. 9171; 189 U.N.T.S. 150. In force 1954. 128 parties, including the U.K. See also the 1967 Protocol, U.K.T.S. 15 (1969), Cmnd. 3906, 606 U.N.T.S. 267, to which there are 128 parties, including the U.K. A refugee is defined, Art. 1A(2), as amended by the 1967 Protocol, as a person who "owing to well-founded fear of being persecuted for reasons of race, religion, nationality, membership of a particular social group or political opinion, is outside the country of his nationality and is unable or, owing to such fear, is unwilling to avail himself of the protection of that country, or who, not having a nationality and being outside the country of his former habitual residence is unable or, owing to such fear, is unwilling to return to it." In *R. v. S.S. for the Home Dept, ex p. Sivakumaran* [1988] A.C. 958, HL, it was held that a "well founded fear of persecution" meant a reasonable degree of likelihood of persecution, objectively determined.

membership of a particular social group or political opinion." (Art. 33(1)).[10] It is arguable that the Convention now states rules of customary international law.[11]

3. With regard to the deportation of stateless persons, British practice has been expressed as follows:

> H.M. Government observe the principle that an alien should not be deported except to the country of which he is a national. Accordingly, it is not the practice to deport stateless aliens resident in the United Kingdom.[12]

4. The admission and expulsion of aliens is regulated by a number of bilateral and multilateral treaties. The 1962 Anglo-Japanese Treaty of Commerce, Establishment and Navigation,[13] for example, reads:

> Nationals of one High Contracting Party shall be accorded, with respect to entry into, residence in and departure from any territory of the other, treatment not less favourable than that accorded to the nationals of any other foreign country.

See also the European Convention on Establishment 1955.[14] The European Communities allow freedom of movement for employment for nationals of member states.[15] Human rights treaties contain guarantees concerning the expulsion of aliens.[16]

5. In a press release dated May 21, 1951,[17] the United States Department of State expressed its concern "over the continued denial by Chinese Communist authorities of exit permits to certain Americans, including a number of Shanghai businessmen, some of whom have been endeavouring for over a year to leave China." It continued: "Arbitrary refusal to permit aliens to depart from a country is of course a violation of the elementary principles of international law and practice."

6. Whereas a state may exclude aliens in its discretion, it is obliged to admit its own nationals who have been expelled from another state, at least where they have nowhere else to go.[18] When Kenya and Uganda became independent, some East African Asians chose (as, exceptionally, the constitutional arrangements for independence allowed them to do) to remain citizens of the United Kingdom and Colonies or British protected persons[19] and not to take the nationality of the newly independent state. This possibility was provided because of the fears of such persons for the treatment that they would receive within the new states; it was understood that as United Kingdom citizens or protected persons they would have a right of entry into the United Kingdom if need be. By the Commonwealth Immigrants Act 1968 (now the Immigration Act 1971), United Kingdom citizens

---

[10] This is unless he is reasonably suspected of being a security risk or, having been finally convicted of a particularly serious crime, constitutes a danger to the community: Art. 33(2).

[11] See Goodwin-Gill, *op. cit.*, p. 525, n. 3, above, p. 141.

[12] L.N.O.J. 1934, p. 373. This remains British practice.

[13] U.K.T.S. 17 (1963), Cmnd. 1979, Art. 3(1).

[14] U.K.T.S. 1 (1971), Cmnd. 453; 529 U.N.T.S. 141. In force 1965. 12 parties, including the U.K.

[15] See Hartley, *E.E.C. Immigration Law* (1978), and Wyatt and Dashwood, *European Community Law* (3rd ed., 1993), Chap. 9.

[16] See, *e.g.* Art. 13, I.C.C.P.R., below, p. 614.

[17] 8 Whiteman 874.

[18] Although the admission, etc., of nationals does not properly come within this section, it is considered here for convenience.

[19] On British citizenship see below, p. 595.

and British protected persons who did not, mainly by birth or ancestry, have certain defined ties with the United Kingdom lost their right of entry into the United Kingdom in United Kingdom law and were made the subject of a system of controlled entry. In consequence, a large number of East African Asians who *voluntarily* left Kenya and Uganda after the 1968 Act came into force were refused entry. When, in 1972, Uganda *expelled* all East African Asians who were not Ugandan nationals, the United Kingdom acknowledged and acted upon an international law obligation to admit them. The Lord Chancellor (Lord Hailsham) stated:

> If I may now turn to the position in international law more generally, the Attorney General, acting in his capacity as the professional legal advisor to the Government, and not, as quite improperly suggested, instigated by his polit-ical colleagues, advised us that in international law a State is under a duty as between other States to accept in its territories those of its nationals who have nowhere else to go. If a citizen of the United Kingdom is expelled, as I think illegally from Uganda, and is not accepted for settlement elsewhere, we could be required by any State where he then was to accept him.[20]

Was the refusal to admit East African Asians who had *voluntarily* left Kenya and Uganda a breach of customary international law? In *Van Duyn v. Home Office*,[21] the European Court of Justice stated that "it is a principle of international law . . . that a State is precluded from refusing to its own nationals the right of entry or residence."[22] To whom is the resulting duty owed? All states?[23]

7. On the *expulsion* of nationals, Weis states:

> As between national and State of nationality the question of the right of sojourn is not a question of international law. It may, however, become a question bearing on the relations between States. The expulsion of nationals forces other States to admit aliens, but, according to the accepted principles of international law, the admission of aliens is in the discretion of each State. . . . It follows that the expulsion of a national may only be carried out with the consent of the State to whose territory he is to be expelled, and that the State of nationality is under a duty towards other States to receive its nationals back on its territory.[24]

See also Article 13 of the Universal Declaration of Human Rights 1948,[25] and Article 12 of the International Covenant on Civil and Political Rights 1966.[26]

8. The right of "[e]veryone to be free to leave any country, including his own," subject to public order, etc., limitations is recognised on a human rights basis (for

---

[20] *Hansard*, H.L., Vol. 335, col. 497. But see Lord Denning M.R., in *R. v. Immigration Officer, ex p. Thakrar*, CA [1974] Q.B. 684 (no duty to admit British subjects expelled *en masse* from a British overseas territory). See Akehurst (1975) 38 M.L.R. 72 and Sharma and Wooldridge (1974) 23 I.C.L.Q. 397. See also the *East African Asians Cases*, (1973) 3 E.H.R.R. 76.

[21] [1974] E.C.R. 1337. The statement was made in the context of freedom of movement for employment, not expulsion from another state.

[22] *cf.* Art. 13, U.D.H.R., below, p. 632; Art. 12(4), I.C.C.P.R., below, p. 641.

[23] See Goodwin-Gill, *op. cit.*, p. 525, n. 3, above, p. 137.

[24] *Nationality and Statelessness in International Law* (2nd ed., 1979), pp. 45–46. Footnote omitted.

[25] Below, p. 632.

[26] Below, p. 640.

nationals and aliens) in international human rights treaties[27] and, although diffi-cult to enforce, may be protected by customary international law too.[28] Departure from a state's territory will in most cases be dependent upon the possession of a passport.[29] In 1976, the British Government withdrew the passports of United Kingdom citizens who had fought as mercenaries in the Angolan war of inde-pendence. "The Foreign Office said that these will not be returned, and that future applications will be refused unless the men sign a declaration they will not work as mercenaries."[30]

(v) The Administration of Justice

HAGUE CODIFICATION CONFERENCE: THE BRITISH GOVERNMENT'S REPLY

L.N.Doc. C. 75, M. 69, 1929. V, pp. 44, 49

In preparation for the Hague Codification Conference of 1930, governments were asked by the Conference Preparatory Committee to reply to certain "Points" on state responsibility. The following is the British reply to Point IV on "acts relating to the operation of tribunals."

Courts capable of administering justice effectively for the protection and enforcement of the rights of private persons constitute a necessary part of the machinery of a State.

1. The State is responsible if it refuses to give foreigners access to these courts for the protection and enforcement of their rights.

2. If the decision of the courts are inconsistent with the treaty obliga-tions or international duties of the State, the State is responsible.

3. A State is responsible if it is established that there has been uncon-scionable delay on the part of the courts.

4. If the courts of justice established by a State give erroneous decisions which can be shown to be prompted by ill will against foreigners as such, or as nationals of a particular country, the State is responsible. It has failed to organise courts of justice capable of administering justice effectively for the protection and enforcement of the rights of such foreigners and is bound to make reparation.

5. The State is not responsible merely because a decision given in the courts is erroneous. But an erroneous decision on the part of a court of justice may engage the responsibility of the State if it is:

---

[27] See, *e.g.* Art. 12(2), I.C.C.P.R., below, p. 640. See also Art. 13, U.D.H.R., below, p. 632.

[28] On the right to leave and return, see Dinstein (1974) 4 Is. Y.H.R. 266; Hannum, *The Right to Leave and Return in International Law and Practice* (1987); Higgins (1974) 4 Is. Y.H.R. 275; Ingles, *Study of Discrimination in Respect of the Right of Everyone to Leave any Country, etc.,* UN Doc. E/CN.4/Sub.2/229/Rev. 1 (1963); Jagerskold, in Henkin, ed., *The International Bill of Rights* (1981), Chap. 7; and Torovsky (1962–63) 4 J.I.C.J. 63.

[29] On the law concerning passports, see Turack, *The Passport in International Law* (1972). On the U.K. position, see Williams (1974) 23 I.C.L.Q. 642.

[30] *The Times*, February 20, 1976.

(*a*) so erroneous that no properly constituted court could honestly have arrived at such a decision;

(*b*) due to corruption;

(*c*) due to pressure from the executive organs of the Government;

(*d*) caused by procedure so faulty as to exclude all reasonable hope of just decisions.

The above enumeration is not intended to be exhaustive.

Notes

As stated above, an erroneous decision of a municipal court in interpreting its own municipal law is not by itself a violation of international law. See, for example, the Law Officers' Report in *Mr Lindsay's* case:

> There is no evidence of any corrupt judicial proceeding. The Judge may have been wrong in his law, the jury inconsistent in their finding of facts—I should rather incline to the opinion, as at present advised, that such was the case; but such untoward incidents in the administration of justice are not confined to the Courts of Portugal, or even unknown to those of this country. It is to be hoped that these miscarriages as to law and facts, if such they be, will be corrected by the Court of Appeal to which Mr. Lindsay has resorted.
>
> ... there is at present no adequate ground for any interference, strictly speaking, on the part of Her Majesty's Government; ... [31]

POPE CASE

8 Whiteman 709

This extract is from a 1958 United States Department of State Memorandum on "Legal Problems Involved in the Detention and Trial of Allan L. Pope in Indonesia." Pope, an American national, was tried by an Indonesian tribunal for offences arising out of acts committed while he was employed by rebels against the Indonesian Government. He was represented at his trial by an Indonesian lawyer chosen by the Indonesian Government and accepted by him. He was found guilty and sentenced to death.

... The right to the assistance of counsel ... has been considered to be one of the fundamental rights protected by an international standard. The derivative or corollary implications of this right are a subject of difference among States. Some of these implications, though, seem clearly necessary for effective exercise of the right to the assistance of counsel. For example, this right implies the assistance of a diligent and effective counsel capable of conducting an adequate defense. Similarly, the right of the accused to counsel should include the opportunity of securing counsel of his choice, where the accused has the financial capability to make such a choice. The right to counsel also implies the right that his counsel should be in a position to prepare adequately a defense and to insure fair conduct of the

[31] (1862) 6 B.D.I.L. 289.

trial. This should mean that at some point the accused's counsel has a right to access to his client prior to the trial and the opportunity to confer privately with him.

As a necessary implication of the right to the assistance of counsel, the United States has maintained that its nationals are entitled to the opportunity of choosing their own counsel in foreign courts, while the United States has secured this right to all persons in American courts. The choice of counsel, however, is not an unrestricted one, but is subject to a reasonable exercise of the police power by a State in prescribing the qualifications for the appearance of counsel in its courts. In terms of his procedural rights under international law, an alien is not entitled to demand the assistance of counsel, foreign or national, who otherwise would not be entitled to appear in the courts of that country. . . . The more difficult question is the point at which an alien prisoner is entitled to the assistance of counsel during pre-trial detention. In all countries, even the United States,[32] there is a certain period of time during which the authorities are permitted to question a prisoner without allowing him the assistance of counsel. At some point, however, denial of the assistance of counsel during pre-trial detention prejudices the right to make an effective defense and enjoy the advocacy of counsel at trial, as all defense efforts require some preparation. Thus, at the point where the reasonable objectives of a foreign government in investigating the crime have been completed, the United States would appear to be justified in requesting that its nationals be permitted the assistance of counsel, so that an adequate period of time is provided for preparation of a defense. . . .

The United States has maintained that private communication with its nationals is essential to their effective protection. The purpose of a visit by a consular or diplomatic officer is to determine whether an alien prisoner is receiving decent, sanitary, and humane treatment during his detention and the investigation of his alleged crime. Frequently prisoners are unwilling to complain of maltreatment in the presence of their captors. Likewise, a visit from American authorities provides an alien prisoner with an opportunity to enjoy or safeguard other procedural rights protected by international law, such as the right to the assistance of counsel for his defense.

Notes
With regard to communication with a consular officer, it was stated in the *Chevreau Claim*[33] that in customary international law:

> [i]n cases of arrest . . . the arrested person . . . [must be] given an opportunity . . . to communicate with the consul of his country if he requests it.

---

[32] *Ed.* But now see *Miranda v. Arizona*, 384 U.S. 436 (1966).
[33] *France v. Great Britain* (1931) 2 R.I.A.A. 1113 at 1123. Translation in (1933) 27 A.J.I.L. 153 at 160.

In the *Firth* case, Mrs Firth, a British subject employed by the British Embassy in Warsaw, was arrested in 1949 on espionage charges. Poland, acting in accordance with Polish law applicable to all Polish and foreign defendants alike, refused to allow the British consul access to her until five days before the trial. The United Kingdom protested against "this violation of international usage."[34]

ROBERTS CLAIM

U.S. *v.* Mexico (1926)

U.S.-Mexican General Claims Commission: for the Commissioners, see above, p. 507. 4 R.I.A.A. 77

Opinion of the Commission

1. This claim is presented by the United States of America on behalf of Harry Roberts, an American citizen who, it is alleged in the Memorial, was arbitrarily and illegally arrested by Mexican authorities, who held him prisoner for a long time in contravention of Mexican law and subjected him to cruel and inhumane treatment throughout the entire period of confinement. . . .

6. The Commission is not called upon to reach a conclusion whether Roberts committed the crime with which he was charged.[35] The determination of that question rested with the Mexican judiciary, and it is distinct from the question whether the Mexican authorities had just cause to arrest Roberts and to bring him to trial. Aliens of course are obliged to submit to proceedings properly instituted against them in conformity with local laws. In the light of the evidence presented in the case the Commission is of the opinion that the Mexican authorities had ample grounds to suspect that Harry Roberts had committed a crime and to proceed against him as they did. The Commission therefore holds that the claim is not substantiated with respect to the charge of illegal arrest.

7. In order to pass upon the complaint with reference to an excessive period of imprisonment, it is necessary to consider whether the proceedings instituted against Roberts while he was incarcerated exceeded reasonable limits within which an alien charged with crime may be held in custody pending the investigation of the charge against him. Clearly there is no definite standard prescribed by international law by which such limits may be fixed. Doubtless an examination of local laws fixing a maximum length of time within which a person charged with crime may be held without being brought to trial may be useful in determining whether detention has been unreasonable in a given case. The Mexican Constitution of 1917, provides by its Article 20, section 8, that a person

---

[34] *Hansard,* H.C., Vol. 467, col. 30, July 11, 1949; 8 Whiteman 881.
[35] *Ed.* The crime was "assault upon a house." It was alleged that Roberts had, with other armed men, surrounded a house with a view to committing a crime therein.

accused of crime "must be judged within four months if he is accused of a crime the maximum penalty for which may not exceed two years' imprisonment, and within one year if the maximum penalty is greater." From the judicial records presented by the Mexican Agent it clearly appears that there was a failure of compliance with this constitutional provision, since the proceedings were instituted on May 17, 1922, and that Roberts had not been brought to trial on December 16, 1923, the date when he was released. It was contended by the Mexican Agency that the delay was due to the fact that the accused repeatedly refused to name counsel to defend him, and that as a result of such refusal on his part proceedings were to his advantage suspended in order that he might obtain satisfactory counsel to defend him. We do not consider that this contention is sound. There is evidence in the record that Roberts constantly requested the American Consul at Tampico to take steps to expedite the trial. . . . It was the duty of the Mexican Judge under Article 20, section 9, of the Mexican Constitution to appoint counsel to act for Roberts from the time of the institution of the proceedings against him. The Commission is of the opinion that preliminary proceedings could have been completed before the lapse of a year after the arrest of Roberts. Even though it may have been necessary to make use of rogatory letters to obtain the testimony of witnesses in different localities, it would seem that that could have been accomplished at least within six or seven months from the time of the arrest. In any event, it is evident in the light of provisions of Mexican law that Roberts was unlawfully held a prisoner without trial for at least seven months. . . . The Commission holds that an indemnity is due on the ground of unreasonably long detention.

8. With respect to the charge of ill-treatment of Roberts, it appears from evidence submitted by the American Agency that the jail in which he was kept was a room thirty-five feet long and twenty-feet wide with stone walls, earthen floor, straw roof, a single window, a single door and no sanitary accommodations, all the prisoners depositing their excrement in a barrel kept in a corner of the room; that thirty or forty men were at times thrown together in this single room; that the prisoners were given no facilities to clean themselves; that the room contained no furniture except that which the prisoners were able to obtain by their own means; that they were afforded no opportunity to take physical exercise; and that the food given them was scarce, unclean, and of the coarsest kind. The Mexican Agency did not present evidence disproving that such conditions existed in the jail. It was stated by the Agency that Roberts was accorded the same treatment as that given to all other persons, and with respect to the food Roberts received, it was observed in the Answer that he was given "the food that was believed necessary, and within the means of the municipality." All of the details given by Roberts in testimony which accompanies the Memorial with respect to the conditions of the jail are corroborated by a statement of the American Consul at Tampico who visited the jail. Facts with respect to equality of treatment of

aliens and nationals may be important in determining the merits of a complaint of mistreatment of an alien. But such equality is not the ultimate test of the propriety of the acts of authorities in the light of international law. That test is, broadly speaking, whether aliens are treated in accordance with ordinary standards of civilization. We do not hesitate to say that the treatment of Roberts was such as to warrant an indemnity on the ground of cruel and inhumane imprisonment.

JANES CLAIM[36]

U.S. *v.* Mexico (1926)

U.S.-Mexican General Claims Commission for the Commissioners, see above, p. 507. 4 R.I.A.A. 82

Opinion of the Commission

1. Claim is made by the United States of America in this case for losses and damages amounting to $25,000.00, which it is alleged in the Memorial were "suffered on account of the murder, on or about July 10, 1918, at a mine near El Tigre, Sonora, Mexico, of Byron Everett Janes," an American citizen. The claim is presented, as stated in the Memorial, "on behalf of [the deceased's wife and children] . . .

17. Carbajal, the person who killed Janes, was well known in the community where the killing took place. Numerous persons witnessed the deed. The slayer, after killing his victim, left on foot. There is evidence that a Mexican police magistrate was informed of the shooting within five minutes after it took place. The official records with regard to the action taken to apprehend and punish the slayer speak for themselves. Eight years have elapsed since the murder, and it does not appear from the records that Carbajal has been apprehended at this time. Our conclusions to the effect that the Mexican authorities did not take proper steps to apprehend and punish the slayer of Janes is based on the record before us consisting of evidence produced by both Governments. . . .

26. Giving careful consideration to all elements involved, the Commission holds that an amount of $12,000, without interest, is not excessive as satisfaction for the personal damage caused the claimants by the non-apprehension and non-punishment of the murderer of Janes.

Note
See also the *Noyes Claim*, below, p. 542.

See also the *Noyes Claim*, below, p. 542.

---

[36] See Brierly (1928) 9 B.Y.I.L. 42.

(vi) Detention and Physical Injury to the Person or to Property

QUINTANILLA CLAIM

Mexico *v.* U.S. (1926)

U.S.-Mexican General Claims Commission: for the Commissioners, see above p. 507. 4 R.I.A.A. 101

Opinion of the Commission

1. This claim is presented by the United Mexican States against the United States in behalf of F. Quintanilla and M. I. Perez de Quintanilla, Mexican nationals, father and mother of Alejo Quintanilla, a young man, who was killed on or about July 16, 1922, not far from Edinburg, Hidalgo County, Texas, USA. On July 15, 1922, about 5 p.m., said Alejo Quintanilla in a lonely spot had lassoed a girl of fourteen years, Agnes Casey, who was on horseback, and thrown her from the horse; she screamed, and the young Mexican fled. She told the occurrence to her father, Tom Casey with whom Quintanilla had been employed some time before; the father the next morning went to lodge his complaint with the authorities, first to Edinburg (the County seat), where he did not find the sheriff, and then to Donna, where he found the deputy sheriff, one Sam A. Bernard. According to the record, this deputy sheriff with three other men, whose names are not mentioned, went to Quintanilla's house, took him from it, and the deputy sheriff with one Walter Weaver placed him in a motor car and drove with him, first to Casey's house, where they put on a new tire, and then in the direction of Edinburg to take him to the county jail. On July 18, 1922, about noon, Quintanilla's corpse was found near the side of this road, some three miles from Edinburg, traces showing that he had been taken there in a motor car. Bernard and Weaver were accused by the Mexican Consul at Hidalgo, Texas, and were accordingly arrested, but released on bail; Bernard's appointment as a deputy sheriff was cancelled by his sheriff on July 22, 1922. The public prosecutor made investigations and submitted the case to the Grand Jury, but the Grand Jury deferred it from 1922 to 1923, from 1923 to 1924, and never took action upon it. . . .

2. It appears from the record that Quintanilla was taken into custody on July 16, 1922, by a deputy sheriff of the State of Texas, to put him at the disposal of the judicial officers; it is left uncertain whether this official was provided with any authorization to take Quintanilla from his house and arrest him. The United States Government never reported what this deputy sheriff did with Quintanilla after he had taken him under custody. The young man apparently never reached the county jail. The deputy sheriff may have changed his mind and set him at liberty, and after that Quintanilla may have been murdered by an unknown person. An enemy

of Quintanilla may have come up and taken him from the car. The companion of the deputy sheriff, who was not an official, may have killed Quintanilla; or the two custodians may have acted in self-defence. The United States Government has been silent on all of this. The only thing the record clearly shows is that Quintanilla was taken into custody by a State official, and that he never was delivered to any jail. The first question before this Commission, therefore, is whether under international law these circumstances present a case for which a Government must be held liable.

3. The Commission does not hesitate to answer in the affirmative. The most notable parallel in international law relates to war prisoners, hostages, and interned members of a belligerent army and navy. . . . The case before this Commission is analogous. A foreigner is taken into custody by a state official. It would go too far to hold that the Government is liable for everything which may befall him. But it has to account for him. The Government can be held liable if it is proven that it has treated him cruelly, harshly, unlawfully; so much the more it is liable if it can say only that it took him into custody—either in jail or in some other place and form—and that it ignores what happened to him.

4. The question then arises whether this duty to account for a man in Governmental custody is modified by the fact that the custodian himself is accused of having killed his prisoner and, as an accused, can not be made to testify against himself. The two things clearly are separate. If the Government is obligated to state what happened to the man in its custody, its officials are bound to inform their Governments. It might be that the custodians themselves perish in a calamity together with the men in their custody, and therefore can not furnish any information. But if they are alive, and are silent, the Government has to bear the consequences. The Commission holds, therefore, that under international law . . . the respondent Government is liable for the damages originating in this act of a State official and resulting in injustice.

Notes

1. In the *Turner Claim*,[37] the United States-Mexican General Claims Commission, in finding Mexico responsible for the death of a United States national who became ill while detained contrary to Mexican law in a Mexican jail pending trial, said:

> Though there is no convincing proof that his death was caused by his treatment in prison, there can be no doubt but that, if at liberty, he would have been able to take better measures for restoring his health than he could do either in prison, or in a prison hospital. If having a man in custody obligates a government to account for him, having a man in *illegal* custody doubtless renders a

---

[37] *U.S. v. Mexico* (1927) 4 R.I.A.A. 278 at 281.

government liable for dangers and disasters which would not have been his share, or in a less degree, if he had been at liberty.

2. As the above cases suppose, a state is liable for the arbitary killing of aliens. Note in this connection that on February 14, 1989, Ayatollah Khomeini, Iran's spiritual leader, issued a fatwa saying that Salmon Rushdie and his publishers were "sentenced to death", because of the publication of the book *Satanic Verses*, which was grossly offensive to Moslems, and calling on all Moslems to "execute them wherever they find them".[38] The fatwa has been reaffirmed by the Iranian Government.[39] It has been condemned by the United Kingdom as a "serious violation of international law and an outrageous infringement of his [Rushdie's] fundamental rights as a British citizen".[40]

THE OELSNER AND SELLERS CASE

8 Whiteman 880

On July 31, 1949, two American students on a bicycling holiday in Europe accidentally entered the Soviet Zone of Germany. They were arrested and detained for eight weeks, including two weeks in solitary confinement, before being released. They were not charged with any offence. The following is an extract from a United States note of October 9, 1949, to the USSR.

... two American students, in Europe as tourists, whose identity and harmless purposes could never have been long in doubt, have been treated as criminals, subject to long incarceration, and not allowed to communicate with their families or their government. This treatment the United States Government finds to be in shocking contravention to the most elementary standards of international decency. The reaction of the Soviet authorities to the incursion of a pair of youthful bicyclists is the more astonishing as they can scarcely have been considered to be a serious threat to the security of the ample Soviet occupation army in Germany. . . .

The Government of the United States raises the most energetic protest against such actions by the Soviet authorities in Germany, and expects that those Soviet officials who are responsible for these acts will be punished. The Government of the United States further insists that the elementary rights of its citizens be observed in the future in accordance with the international comity which governs the conduct of all civilized states.

---

[38] *Keesings Archives*, p. 36450.

[39] *e.g.* by President Rafsanjani in 1993, *ibid.* p. 39293.

[40] Lord Henley, Parliamentary Under-secretary of State, Department of Employment, *Hansard*, H.L., Vol. 555, col. 1514, June 13, 1994; U.K.M.I.L. 1994, 65 B.Y.I.L. 585 (1994). The E.U. has condemned the fatwa as contrary to international law also: see the *Statement by Spain in the General Assembly*, 3rd Committee for the E.U., U.K.M.I.L. 1995, (1995) 66 B.Y.I.L. 616.

HARVARD DRAFT CONVENTION ON THE INTERNATIONAL RESPONSIBILITY OF STATES FOR INJURIES TO ALIENS 1961

(1961) 55 A.J.I.L. 548

Article 9

1. Deliberate destruction of or damage to the property of an alien is wrongful, unless it was required by circumstances of urgent necessity not reasonably admitting of any other course of action.

2. A destruction of the property of an alien resulting from the judgment of a competent tribunal or from the action of the competent authorities of the State in the maintenance of public order, health, or morality shall not be considered wrongful, provided there has not been:

(a) a clear and discriminatory violation of the law of the State concerned;

(b) a violation of any provision of Articles 6 to 8 of this Convention;

(c) an unreasonable departure from the principles of justice recognized by the principal legal systems of the world; or

(d) an abuse of the powers specified in this paragraph for the purpose of depriving an alien of his property.

Notes

1. The Harvard Draft Convention is, like its predecessors,[41] an unofficial document prepared under the auspices of the Harvard Law School. The purpose of the draft Convention "is to codify with some particularity the standards established by international law for the protection of aliens and thereby to obviate, as far as possible, the necessity of looking to customary international law."[42] In some respects, it engages in "progressive development" rather than "codification" (in the terminology of the International Law Commission).

2. The explanatory note to Article 9 reads:

The Convention distinguishes a destruction of property or the damaging of property from an uncompensated taking of property or the deprivation of the use or enjoyment of property.[43] ... Examples of destruction of or damage to property which would be wrongful under this Article would be: the deliberate burning by the police of a car owned by an alien; or physical damage to mercantile premises owned by an alien enterprise resulting from the intentional acts of employees of the State, whether such persons were acting under orders of higher authority or on their own initiative but within the scope of their function.

There is excepted from the scope of wrongful destruction of or damage to property such action as was required by circumstances of urgent necessity. The classic example of such destruction or damage is the tearing down of buildings

---

[41] See, *e.g.* the 1935 Harvard Draft Convention on Jurisdiction with Respect to Crime, above, p. 264.

[42] (1961) 55 A.J.I.L. 547. The two *rapporteurs* were Professors Sohn and Baxter.

[43] *Ed.* The latter is dealt with in Art. 10, Draft Convention, see below, p. 556.

in order to prevent the spread of fire. The destruction of property in actual combat operations during an international conflict or the destruction or damaging of property of an alien in order to interdict its use by the enemy typify legitimate destruction of property in time of war.[44]

(vii) PROTECTION OF ALIENS

NOYES CLAIM

U.S. *v.* Panama (1933)

General Claims Arbitration: Van Heeckeren, Presiding Commissioner; Root, U.S. Commissioner; Alfaro, Panamanian Commissioner. 6 R.I.A.A. 308

Opinion of the Commission

In this case a claim is made against the Republic of Panama by the United States of America on behalf of Walter A. Noyes, who was born, and has ever remained, an American citizen. The sum of $1,683 is claimed as an indemnity for the personal injuries and property losses sustained by Mr. Noyes through the attacks made upon him on June 19, 1927, in, and in the neighborhood of, the village of Juan Diaz, situated not far from Panama City. The claim is based upon an alleged failure to provide to the claimant adequate police protection, to exercise due diligence in the maintenance of order and to take adequate measures to apprehend and punish the aggressors. . . .

The village of Juan Diaz has only a small population, but on June 19, 1927, several hundreds of adherents of the party then in control of the Government had gathered there for a meeting. The police on the spot had not been increased for the occasion; it consisted of the usual three policemen stationed there. In the course of the day the authorities in Panama City learned that the crowd in Juan Diaz had become unruly under the influence of liquor. The chief of the police, General Pretelt, thereupon drove thither with reinforcements. . . .

At about 3.00 p.m. the claimant passed through the village in his automobile, on his return to Panama City from a trip to the Tapia River bridge. In the center of the village a crowd blocked the road and Mr. Noyes stopped and sounded his horn, whereupon the crowd slowly opened. Whilst he was progressing very slowly through it, he had to stop again, because somebody lurched against the car and fell upon the running-board. Thereupon members of the crowd smashed the windows of the car and attacked Mr. Noyes, who was stabbed in the wrist and hurt by fragments of glass. A police officer who had been giving orders that gangway should be made for the automobile, but who had not before been able to reach the car, then sprang upon the running-board and

[44] (1961) 55 A.J.I.L. 551–552.

remained there, protecting the claimant and urging him to get away as quickly as possible. He remained with Mr. Noyes, until the latter had got clear of the crowd. At some distance from Juan Diaz the claimant was further attacked by members of the same crowd, who pursued him in a bus and who forced him to drive his car off the road and into a ditch. He was then rescued by General Pretelt who, having come from the opposite direction, had, after reaching the plaza of the village, returned upon his way in order to protect Mr. Noyes against his pursuers.

The facts related above show that in both instances the police most actively protected the claimant against his assailants and that in the second instance the protection was due to the fact, that the authorities sent reinforcements from Panama City upon learning that the conditions in Juan Diaz rendered assistance necessary. The contention of the American Agent however is, that the Panamanian Government incurred a liability under international law, because its officials had not taken the precaution of increasing for that day the police force at Juan Diaz, although they knew some time in advance that the meeting would assemble there.

The mere fact that an alien has suffered at the hands of private persons an aggression, which could have been averted by the presence of a sufficient police force on the spot, does not make a government liable for damages under international law. There must be shown special circumstances from which the responsibility of the authorities arises: either their behavior in connection with the particular occurrence, or a general failure to comply with their duty to maintain order, to prevent crimes or to prosecute and punish criminals.

There were no such circumstances in the present case. Accordingly a lack of protection has not been established. . . .

The claim is disallowed.

Notes

See also the *Janes Case*, above, p. 537.

ASIAN AGRICULTURAL PRODUCTS LTD *v.* SRI LANKA[45]

I.C.S.I.D. Tribunal, 1990. Tribunal Members: El-Kosheri, President; Goldman'
Asante, Members. (1991) 30 I.L.M. 577

This case was brought by a British company against Sri Lanka before a Tribunal established under the Convention for the Settlement of Investment Disputes 1965, see below, p. 585, to which both Sri Lanka and the United Kingdom were parties, on the basis of the consent given by Article 8, Sri-Lanka-U.K. Bilateral Investment Treaty 1980.

The company claimed compensation for the destruction of its Sri Lankan farm. On the facts, the Tribunal found that at the relevant time in 1987 the farm was in

[45] See Boloro (1992) 18 S.A.Y.I.L. 105.

an area that was largely under the control of Tamil Tiger rebels and that the farm management had offered to dismiss farm staff thought by the Government to be in league with them. The Tribunal was unable to establish whether the destruction of the farm was the result of rebel action or the work of Government security forces seeking to destroy a rebel base. Having established that the state's duty to protect aliens and their property in customary international law involved due diligence,[46] not absolute or strict liability, the Tribunal then considered the responsibility of a state in the context of rebel or terrorist activity:

Final Award

72. It is a generally accepted rule of International Law, clearly stated in international arbitral awards and in the writings of the doctrinal authorities, that:

(i) —A State on whose territory an insurrection occurs is not responsible for loss or damage sustained by foreign investors unless it can be shown that the Government of that state failed to provide the standard of protection required, either by treaty, or under general customary law, as the case may be[47]; and

(ii) —Failure to provide the standard of protection required entails the state's international responsibility for losses suffered, regardless of whether the damages occurred during an insurgents' offensive act or resulting [sic] from governmental counter-insurgency activities.

73. The long established arbitral case law was adequately expressed by Max Huber, the *Rapporteur* in the *Spanish Zone of Morocco* claims (1923), in the following terms:

The principle of non-responsibility in no way excludes the duty to exercise a certain degree of vigilance. If a state is not responsible for the revolutionary events themselves, it may nevertheless be responsible, for what its authorities do or do not do to ward off the consequences, within the limits of possibility" (Translation from the French original text reported by Cheng, in his *General Principles* ... p. 229).

Furthermore, the famous arbitrator indicated that the "degree of vigilance" required in providing the necessary protection and security would differ according to the circumstances. In the absence of any higher standard provided for by Treaty, the general international law standard was stated to reflect the "degree of security reasonably expected". ...

76. ... Furthermore, "there is an extensive and consistent state practice supporting the duty to exercise due diligence" (Brownlie, *System of the Law of Nations, State Responsibility—Part I*, Oxford, 1986, p. 162). ...

---

[46] On this standard, see above, p. 523. The Tribunal held that the applicable law was the 1980 Bilateral Treaty, supplemented by international and Sri Lankan law. The 1980 Treaty guaranteed foreign investment "full protection and security" and compensation on "most favoured nation" terms in respect of insurrection loss. In its award, the Tribunal examined customary international law in the course of applying these Treaty guarantees.

[47] *Ed.* See the *Sambaggio* case, above, p. 513.

After reviewing all categories of precedents, including more recent international judicial case law, the learned Oxford University Professor ... [also noted] "a sliding scale of liability related to the standard of due diligence" (*State Responsibility, op. cit.*, p. 162 and p. 168). ...

77. A number of other contemporary international law authorities noticed the "sliding scale", from the old "subjective" criteria that takes into consideration the relatively limited existing possibilities of local authorities in a given context, towards an "objective" standard of vigilance in assessing the required degree of protection and security with regard to what should be legitimately expected to be secured for foreign investors by a reasonably well organized modern State. ...

According to modern doctrine, the violation of international law entailing the State's responsibility has to be considered constituted by "the mere lack or want of diligence", without any need to establish malice or negligence . . . .

The Tribunal then applied the "due diligence" rule to the facts.

In the light of said uncontested evidence [that the farm management had offered to dismiss staff suspected by the Government], the Tribunal is of the opinion that reasonably the Government should have at least tried to use such peaceful available high level channel of communication in order to get any suspect elements excluded from the farm's staff. This would have been essential to minimize the risks of killings and destruction when planning to undertake a vast military counter-insurgency operation in that area for regaining lost control.

The Tribunal notes in this respect that the failure to resort to such precautionary measures acquires more significance when taking into consideration that such measures fall within the normal exercise of governmental inherent powers—as a public authority—entitled to order undesirable persons out from security sensitive areas. The failure became particularly serious when the highest executive officer of the Company reconfirmed just ten days before his willingness to comply with any governmental requests in this respect.

Accordingly, the Tribunal considers that the Respondent through said inaction and omission violated its due diligence obligation which requires undertaking all possible measures that could be reasonably expected to prevent the eventual occurrence of killings and property destructions.

Notes

Mr Asante dissented from the Tribunal's award in favour of the company on the matter of the application of the "due diligence" rule[48]:

The precautionary measure envisaged by the majority opinion would have been a reasonable police measure if the situation to be addressed were no more

[48] (1991) 30 I.L.M. 652. On the duty to protect aliens against terrorists, see Lillich and Paxman (1976–7) 16 Am. U.L.R. 217.

than an ordinary case of civil disorder. However, in the face of a major insurrection launched by well-armed insurgents engaged in a sophisticated guerrilla warfare against Government forces, it ... does not seem feasible or reasonable to expect the Government to take such a step when launching a sensitive security operation against powerful insurgents who had infiltrated the entire Batticaloa area.

1973 CONVENTION ON THE PREVENTION AND PUNISHMENT OF CRIMES AGAINST INTERNATIONALLY PROTECTED PERSONS INCLUDING DIPLOMATIC AGENTS[49]

U.K.T.S. 3 (1980), Cmnd. 7765; 1035 U.N.T.S. 167; (1974) 13 I.L.M. 42

Article 2

1. The intentional commission of:

(*a*) a murder, kidnapping or other attack upon the person or liberty of an internationally protected person;
(*b*) a violent attack upon the official premises, the private accommodation or the means of transport of an internationally protected person likely to endanger his person or liberty;
(*c*) a threat to commit any such attack;
(*d*) an attempt to commit any such attack; and
(*e*) an act constituting participation as an accomplice in any such attack

shall be made by each State Party a crime under its internal law.

2. Each State Party shall make these crimes punishable by appropriate penalties which take into account their grave nature.

3. Paragraphs 1 and 2 of this article in no way derogate from the obligations of States Parties under international law to take all appropriate measures to prevent other attacks on the person, freedom or dignity of an internationally protected person.

Article 3

1. Each State Party shall take such measures as may be necessary to establish its jurisdiction over the crimes set forth in article 2 in the following cases:

(*a*) when the crime is committed in the territory of that State or on board a ship or aircraft registered in that State;

---

[49] In force 1977. 71 parties, including the U.K. See the Internationally Protected Persons Act 1978. See Rozakis (1974) 23 I.C.L.Q. 32 and Wood, *ibid.* p. 791.

(b) when the alleged offender is a national of that State;

(c) when the crime is committed against an internationally protected person as defined in article 1 who enjoys his status as such by virtue of functions which he exercises on behalf of that State.

Each State Party shall likewise take such measures as may be necessary to establish its jurisdiction over these crimes in cases where the alleged offender is present in its territory and it does not extradite him pursuant to article 8 to any of the States mentioned in paragraph 1 of this article.

3. This Convention does not exclude any criminal jurisdiction exercised in accordance with internal law.

Notes[50]

1. An "internationally protected person" includes heads of state and their accompanying families and any representative or official of a State or any official who, at the time when and in the place where a crime against him, his official premises, his private accommodation or his means of transport is committed, is entitled pursuant to international law to special protection from any attack on his person, freedom or dignity, as well as members of his family forming part of his household. (Article 20, 1973 Convention).

2. On the special duty to protect the premises of diplomatic missions and agents, see above, p. 353.

3. In the *Mallen* case,[51] where a Mexican consul had been injured by a private person in Texas, the United States-Mexican General Claims Commission stated:

> The question has been raised whether consuls are entitled to a "special protection" for their persons. The answer depends upon the meaning given these two words. If they should indicate that, apart from prerogatives extended to consuls either by treaty or by unwritten law, the Government of their temporary residence is bound to grant them other prerogatives not enjoyed by common residents (be it citizens or aliens), the answer is in the negative. But if "special protection" means that in executing the laws of the country, especially those concerning police and penal law, the Government should realize that foreign Governments are sensitive regarding the treatment accorded their representatives, and that therefore the Government of the consul's residence should exercise greater vigilance in respect to their security and safety, the answer as evidently shall be in the affirmative. . . . In this second sense it was rightly stated by the Committee of Jurists appointed by the League of Nations on the Corfu difficulties, in a report adopted on March 13, 1924: "The recognized public character of a foreigner and the circumstances in which he is present in its territory, entail upon the State a corresponding duty of special vigilance on his behalf." (1924) 18 A.J.I.L. 543.

4. On April 2, 1970, the West German Ambassador to Guatemala, Count von Spreti, was kidnapped in Guatemala City by the "Revolutionary Armed Forces,"

---

[50] See generally, Hevener, ed., *Diplomacy in a Dangerous World* (1986) and Przetacznik, *Protection of Officials of Foreign States according to International Law* (1983).

[51] *U.S. v. Mexico* (1927) 4 R.I.A.A. 173.

an extreme left-wing guerrilla organisation. The organisation demanded the
release of certain prisoners. Despite West German appeals, the Guatemalan Government refused the demand and Count von Spreti was found murdered on April
5. The West German Government withdrew its *charge d'affaires* from Guatemala in
protest. It is reported as saying that the Guatemalan Government had "shown
itself unable to give accredited diplomatic representatives necessary security."[52]
Had Guatemala violated international law? Note that earlier in 1970 the Guatemalan Government had released other prisoners in response to other kidnappings.

5. See also the UN Convention on the Safety of UN and Associated Personnel
1994.[53]

(viii) EXPROPRIATION[54]

Notes

Expropriation, or the compulsory taking of private property by the state, is a
phenomenon that became especially important in international law with the
spread of socialism and the emergence of the post-colonial state. If the typical
nineteenth century case was the occasional taking of the property of a single
foreigner in the context of a particular project or dispute, more recently it has been
the general expropriation by law of enterprises with a view to their public
management in the national interest. It is normally in this last context that the
twentieth century term "nationalisation" is used. Whereas expropriation and
nationalisation are sometimes treated as separate concepts, the view taken in the
following pages is that the latter is a species of the former. Unfortunately, the
political differences between capitalist and communist or socialist states coupled
with the economic differences between developed and developing states have led
to a situation in which there has been little agreement on the rules on expropriation, as the following extracts show. Whereas it is generally agreed that expropriation may occur, developed states suggest that it must take place in accordance
with an "international minimum standard" set by international law while developing states deny that this is so. In their opinion, the circumstances and conditions of expropriation are matters to be left largely to the expropriating state to
regulate in its discretion under its law. However, as the comment by Walde,
below, p. 552, suggests these divisions are becoming less sharp.

---

[52] *Keesings Archives*, p. 23906.
[53] UN Doc. A/49/742; (1995) 34 I.L.M. 482. Not in force. 9 parties, not including the U.K. 22
parties required.
[54] Among the extensive literature, see Akinsanya, *The Expropriation of Multinational Property
in the Third World* (1980); Asante (1988) 37 I.C.L.Q. 588; Brownlie, (1979–I) 162 Hague
Recueil 255; Dolzer (1981) 75 A.J.I.L. 553; Fatouros, *Government Guarantees to Foreign
Investors* (1962); Friedmann, *Expropriation in International Law* (1953); Higgins, (1982–III)
176 Hague Recueil 259; Hossain and Chowdhury, eds., *Permanent Sovereignty over Natural
Resources in International Law* (1984); Jain, *Nationalisation of Foreign Property* (1983); Jimenez
de Aréchega (1978) 11 N.Y.U.J.I.L.P. 179; Katzarov, *The Theory of Nationalisation* (1964);
Lillich, ed., *The Valuation of Nationalised Property in International Law*, 4 vols. (1972–1987);
Norton (1991) 85 A.J.I.L. 474; Pellonpää and Fitzmaurice (1988) 19 N.Y.I.L. 53; Sornarajah,
The Pursuit of Nationalised Property (1986); *id., The International Law on Foreign Investment*
(1994); Verwey, and Schrijver (1984) 15 N.Y.I.L. 3; Weston, in Lillich, ed., *International Law
of State Responsibility for Injuries to Aliens* (1983), p. 89; White, *Nationalisation of Foreign
Property* (1961); Wortley, *Expropriation in Public International Law* (1959). The U.S. *Restatement, 3d, Foreign Relations Law of the U.S.* (1987), Vol 2, para. 712, contains an excellent
treatment of the subject.

RESOLUTION ON PERMANENT SOVEREIGNTY OVER NATURAL RESOURCES 1962[55]

G.A. Res. 1803 (XVII), G.A.O.R., 17th Sess., Supp. 17, p. 15

The General Assembly

Declares that:

1. The rights of peoples and nations to permanent sovereignty over their natural wealth and resources must be exercised in the interest of their national development and of the well-being of the people of the State concerned; . . .

3. In cases where authorization is granted, the capital imported and the earnings on that capital shall be governed by the terms thereof, by the national legislation in force, and by international law. The profits derived must be shared in the proportions freely agreed upon, in each case, between the investors and the recipient State, due care being taken to ensure that there is no impairment, for any reason, of that State's sovereignty over its natural wealth and resources;

4. Nationalization, expropriation or requisitioning shall be based on grounds or reasons of public utility, security or the national interest which are recognized as overriding purely individual or private interests, both domestic and foreign. In such cases the owner shall be paid appropriate compensation in accordance with the rules in force in the State taking such measures in the exercise of its sovereignty and in accordance with international law. In any case where the question of compensation gives rise to a controversy, the national jurisdiction of the State taking such measures shall be exhausted. However, upon agreement by sovereign States and other parties concerned, settlement of the dispute should be made through arbitration or international adjudication; . . .

8. Foreign investment agreements freely entered into by, or between, sovereign States shall be observed in good faith; States and international organizations shall strictly and conscientiously respect the sovereignty of peoples and nations over their natural wealth and resources in accordance with the Charter and the principles set forth in the present resolution.

Notes

1. The resolution was adopted by 87 votes to 2, with 12 abstentions. France and South Africa voted against it; the Soviet bloc, Burma, Cuba and Ghana abstained.

2. Resolution 1803 has been accepted in a number of arbitration awards as reflecting customary international law.[56] It recognises the right to expropriate

---

[55] See Gess (1964) 13 I.C.L.Q. 398 and O'Keefe (1974) 8 J.W.T.L. 239.
[56] See, *e.g.* the *Texaco* case, below, p. 573; the *Aminoil Case,* below p. 578; the *Amoco* case, below, p. 558; and the *Sedco* case *(Second Interlocutory Award)* (1986) 10 Iran-U.S. C.T.R. 180 at 198.

foreign property. That there is such a right is common ground among states generally, with developed, as well as developing, states availing themselves of it.[57] The Resolution's public purpose ("public utility," etc.) and compensation requirements are considered later, as is its lack of a "non-discrimination" guarantee.

CHARTER OF ECONOMIC RIGHTS AND DUTIES OF STATES 1974[58]

G.A. Res. 3281 (XXIX). (1975) 14 I.L.M. 251

Article 2

1. Every State has and shall freely exercise full permanent sovereignty, . . . including possession, use and disposal, over all its wealth, natural resources and economic activities.

2. Each State has the right:

(a) To regulate and exercise authority over foreign investment within its national jurisdiction in accordance with its laws and regulations and in conformity with its national objectives and priorities. No State shall be compelled to grant preferential treatment to foreign investment;

(b) To regulate and supervise the activities of transnational corporations within its national jurisdiction and take measures to ensure that such activities comply with its laws, rules and regulations and conform with its economic and social policies. . . .

(c) To nationalize, expropriate or transfer ownership of foreign property in which case appropriate compensation should be paid by the State adopting such measures, taking into account its relevant laws and regulations and all circumstances that the State considers pertinent. In any case where the question of compensation gives rise to a

---

[57] On the 1982 French nationalisations, see Borde and Eggleston (1982) 68 A.B.A.J. 422.

[58] The Charter was adopted by 120 votes to six, with 10 abstentions. The states voting against were Belgium, Denmark, the F.R.G., Luxembourg, the U.K. and the U.S. The abstaining states were Austria, Canada, France, Ireland, Israel, Italy, Japan, the Netherlands, Norway, and Spain. A separate vote was taken on Art. 2(2)(c). The majority in favour of it was 104 to 16, with six abstentions. The votes against were by the six states that later voted against the Charter as a whole and by nine of the 10 states that later abstained on the Charter as whole plus Sweden (instead of Israel). The six states that abstained on Art. 2(2)(c) were Australia, Barbados, Finland, Israel, New Zealand and Portugal. An amendment to Art. 2(2)(c) which would have replaced the present wording by "to nationalise, expropriate, or requisition foreign property for a public purpose, provided that just compensation in the light of all the relevant circumstances shall be paid" was proposed by a group of western states in the Second Committee: UN Doc. A/C.2/L.1404 (1974). It was defeated by 87 votes to 19, with 11 abstentions. On the Charter, see Brower and Tepe (1975) 9 Int. Lawyer 295; De Waart (1977) 24 N.I.L.R. 304; Fatouros and Meagher (1980) 12 N.Y.U.J.I.L.P. 653; Jain (1979) 19 Ind. J.I.L. 544; McWhinney (1976) 14 C.Y.I.L. 57; Weston (1981) 75 A.J.I.L. 437; White (1975) 24 I.C.L.Q. 542.

controversy, it shall be settled under the domestic law of the nationalizing State and by its tribunals, unless it is freely and mutually
agreed by all States concerned that other peaceful means be sought
on the basis of the sovereign equality of States and in accordance
with the principle of free choice of means.

Notes

1. The Charter was prepared by the United Nations Conference on Trade and
Development (UNCTAD), an organ of the General Assembly whose function is
primarily "to promote international trade . . . particularly trade between countries
at different stages of development, between developing countries and between
countries with different systems of economic and social organisation."[59] The
Charter sets out economic rights and duties of states over the whole spectrum of
international trade, including the right to engage without discrimination in international trade; the right to participate fully in the international decision-making
process in the solution of world economic, financial and monetary problems; and
the duty to co-operate in the expansion of world trade. Only the Article on
expropriation is printed above.

2. The Charter was preceded by General Assembly Resolution 3171 (XXVIII)[60]
of 1973 and by the Declaration on the Establishment of a New International
Economic Order 1974[61] which follow the same pattern on expropriation. In
Resolution 3171 (XXVIII), the Assembly:

Affirms that the application of the principle of nationalization carried out by
States as an expression of their sovereignty in order to safeguard their natural
resources, implies that each State is entitled to determine the amount of
possible compensation and the mode of payment, and that any disputes which
might arise should be settled in accordance with the national legislation of
each State carrying out such measures.

The 1974 Declaration contains a similar provision. Para. (4)(*e*) states the principle
of:

Full permanent sovereignty of every State over its natural resources and
economic activities. In order to safeguard these resources, each State is entitled
to exercise effective control over them and their exploitation with means
suitable to its own situation, including the right to nationalization or transfer
of ownership to its nationals, this right being an expression of the full permanent sovereignty of the State. No State may be subjected to economic, political
or any other type of coercion to prevent the free and full exercise of this
inalienable right.

3. Clearly, the 1974 Charter favours the view of developing states—much more
so than the earlier Resolution 1803. It does not mention any public purpose

[59] G.A. Resn. 1995, G.A.O.R., 19th Sess., Supp. 15, p. 1. (1964).
[60] G.A.O.R., 28th Sess., Supp. 30, p. 52 (1973), (1974) 68 A.J.I.L. 381. The Resolution was
adopted by 108 votes to one, with 16 abstentions. The vote on para. 3 was 86 to 11, with
28 abstentions. The states voting against were, predictably, 11 of the developed states that
later voted against or abstained in respect of Art. 2(2)(*c*), Charter of Economic Rights and
Duties of States, above, including the U.K. and the U.S. The 28 abstaining states consisted
of such states also and some developing states as well.
[61] G.A. Resn. 3201 (S-VI), (1974) 13 I.L.M. 715. The Declaration was adopted without a vote.
The F.R.G., France, Japan, the U.K. and the U.S. made reservations to it: *ibid.* pp. 744 *et seq.*
(1974).

limitation upon the power to expropriate and the compensation provision contradicts developed states' views. These points are taken up later. What should be emphasised for the moment is that the Charter's value as a statement of custom is doubtful. In the *Texaco Case*, below, p. 573, the arbitrator considered that Article 2 was put forward *de lege ferenda* and not as a statement of current law. In any event, he considered that the opposition to it was of sufficient size and significance to deny it the status of custom. Other arbitration awards have drawn the same distinction between Resolution 1803 and the 1974 Charter, taking the view that the latter is not reflective of custom.[62]

Brownlie states:[63]

> It is fairly clear that the Charter does not purport to be a declaration of pre-existing principles and overall it has a strong programmatic, political and didactic flavour. Nonetheless, there can be little doubt that Article 2, paragraph 2(c), is regarded by many States as an emergent principle, a statement of presently applicable rules.

The New International Economic Order (NIEO) has had very little success in causing developed states to alter their ways generally and in establishing a new consensus on the international law of expropriation in particular. Moreover, since its adoption, the attitudes of developing countries have changed so that the NIEO is no longer central to their approach. Commenting on the present situation, Walde states[64]:

> This paper has followed the comprehensive onslaught of the Third World [through the NIEO] on a world economic system dominated in law, in institutions and in key concepts by Western countries. This onslaught can be explained by decolonisation and by the alliance among developing countries keen to have economic emancipation follow political association with the socialist countries competing with Western capitalism. An often historically rooted view of the State as the proper guardian and director of economic development propelled a very statist view of how economic development should be brought about, and in its wake an exaggerated concept of national sovereignty, seen as a defense against the overwhelming economic power of multinational companies and the Western school of international law protecting them.
>   Within the space of twenty years, this dominant paradigm of international economic relations has changed dramatically. On many issues one can see in fact a complete reversal—from statism to market liberalism, from nationalisation to privatisation, from foreign investment restriction to deregulated open-door policies. The failure of high expectations for the State-driven model of economic development, the collapse of communism and the emergence of new commercially-oriented middle-classes challenging the NIEO-focussed State classes in developing countries have contributed to this complete change of paradigm.

---

[62] See the arbitration awards referred to in n. 56 above. But in the *Liamco* case, the arbitrator concluded that Resolution 1803 and the 1974 Charter "if not a unanimous source of law", were both "evidence of the recent dominant trend of international opinion concerning the sovereign right of states over their natural resources": (1981) 20 I.L.M. 53.

[63] *loc. cit.*, p. 548, n. 54, above, p. 268.

[64] Al-Nauimi and Meese, eds., *International Legal Issues Arising under the United Nations Decade of International Law* (1995), p. 1301, p. 1335.

STARRETT HOUSING CORP. *v.* IRAN
(INTERLOCUTORY AWARD)

U.S. *v.* Iran (1983)

Iran-U.S. Claims Tribunal.[65] *Chamber One: Lagergren, Chairman; Kashani, Holtzmann, Members. 4 Iran-U.S.C.T.R. 122; (1984) 23 I.L.M. 1090*

In 1974, the claimant American company, operating through Shah Goli, an Iranian subsidiary company, entered into an agreement with an Iranian development bank to buy land in Iran and build houses upon it. The project was proceeding on schedule when their harassment during the 1979 revolution caused the withdrawal of most of the American and other foreign personnel working on it. This, coupled with general revolutionary disruption and government intervention (*e.g.* by making Shah Goli forgo contractual payments under duress and freezing its bank account), caused the project to fall behind schedule and Shah Goli to be in financial difficulties. In this situation, in January 1980, the Iranian Government, acting under a July 1979 decree, placed Shah Goli under the control of a temporary manager. The claimants sought compensation for the expropriation of their property rights in the project and in Shah Goli. In this interlocutory award, the Tribunal determined that there had been a "taking" of the claimant's property and appointed experts to evaluate the loss.

Award of the Tribunal

It is undisputed in this case that the Government of Iran did not issue any law or decree according to which the Zomorod Project or Shah Goli expressly was nationalized or expropriated. However, it is recognized in international law that measures taken by a State can interfere with property rights to such an extent that these rights are rendered so useless that they must be deemed to have been expropriated, even though the State does not purport to have expropriated them and the legal title to the property formally remains with the original owner.

... There can be little doubt that at least at the end of January 1980 the claimants had been deprived of the effective use, control and benefits of their property rights in Shah Goli. By that time the Ministry of Housing had appointed Mr Erfan as Temporary Manager of Shah Goli to direct all further activities in connection with the Project on behalf of the Government.... As a result of these measures the Claimants could no longer exercise their rights to manage Shah Goli and were deprived of their possibilities of effective use and control of it.

It has, however, to be borne in mind that assumption of control over property by a government does not automatically and immediately justify a conclusion that the property has been taken by the government, thus requiring compensation under international law. In this case it

[65] On the Iran-U.S. Claims Tribunal, see below, p. 987. On expropriation, see Mouri, *The International Law of Expropriation as Reflected in the Work of the Iran-U.S. Claims Tribunal* (1994).

cannot be disregarded that Starrett has been requested to resume the Project. The Government of Iran argues that it would have been possible for Starrett to appoint managers from any country other than the United States, but the evidence does not in other respects indicate on what conditions Starrett has been afforded any possibility to resume the Project. The completion of the Project was dependent upon a large number of American construction supervisors and subcontractors whom it would have been necessary to replace and the right freely to select management, supervisors and subcontractors is an essential element of the right to manage a project. Further, given the contents of the [January 1980] Construction Completion Bill it must be taken for granted that Starrett can only resume the Project subject to the provisions of that Bill, which entail far-reaching restrictions in the right of former owners to manage housing projects. Indeed, the language of that bill seems to indicate that the right to manage such projects ultimately rests with the Ministry of Housing and Bank Maskan. . . .

There is an allegation that Starrett abandoned the Project for economic reasons. The Tribunal does not go into this issue because it is notorious that at least after November 4, 1979, the date when the hostage crisis began, all American companies with projects in Iran were forced to leave their projects and had to evacuate their personnel. Therefore, at least as regards the situation subsequent to that date the Government of Iran cannot possibly rely on any withdrawal of personnel as a justification for the appointment of a new manager. In fact, the evidence shows that Starrett maintained staff in Iran longer than most other American companies, obviously in an attempt to secure future possibilities to complete the Project.

However, in this case the Claimants assert that [before January 1980] the effects of what is referred to as "virulent anti-American and other policies and actions of the Revolutionary Group and the Islamic Republic"—both before and after the establishment of the new Government —rendered it impossible for Starrett to continue operations at the Project and that this amounted to an unlawful expropriation under general principles of international law . . .

There is no reason to doubt that the events in Iran prior to January 1980 to which the Claimants refer, seriously hampered their possibilities to proceed with the construction work and eventually paralysed the Project. But investors in Iran, like investors in all other countries, have to assume a risk that the country might experience strikes, lock-outs, disturbances, changes of the economic and political system and even revolution. That any of these risks materialized does not necessarily mean that property rights affected by such events can be deemed to have been taken. A revolution as such does not entitle investors to compensation under international law. . . . the Tribunal does not find that any of these events individually or taken together can be said to amount to a taking of the Claimants' contractual rights and shares. . . .

The next question for the Tribunal is to determine the exact nature of the property rights that were taken. The Claimants contend that it was neither the land and the buildings only nor their shares in Shah Goli that were taken. The Claimants assert that the expropriated rights comprised the assets and contractual rights and the other property of, in the first instance, Shah Goli as a controlled subsidiary of Starrett Housing. The Claimants define the principal assets of Shah Goli as the buildings and the principal contractual rights as including the rights to complete the Project and to earn reasonable profits which Starrett anticipated, and to recover the funds which it loaned and which were used to build the Project.

There is nothing unique in the Claimants' position in this regard. They rely on precedents in international law in which cases measures of expropriation or taking, primarily aimed at physical property, have been deemed to comprise also rights of a contractual nature closely related to the physical property. In this case it appears from the very nature of the measures taken by the Government of Iran in January 1980 that these measures were aimed at the taking of Shah Goli. The Tribunal holds that the property interest taken by the Government of Iran must be deemed to comprise the physical property as well as the right to manage the Project and to complete the construction in accordance with the Basic Project Agreement and related agreements, and to deliver the apartments and collect the proceeds of the sale as provided in the Apartment Purchase Agreements.

Mr Holtzmann, U.S. arbitrator, filed a concurring opinion. Mr Kashani, Iranian arbitrator, dissented but would not appear to have filed an opinion.

Notes

1. The *Starrett* case considers the meaning of a *taking* of property,[66] a question not addressed in General Assembly Resolution 1803 or the 1974 Charter. A taking may be effected by the transfer of title by law, as in the typical case of nationalisation or of the expropriation for example, of land, to build a road. The physical seizure of property may suffice,[67] as may its transfer under duress[68] or by confiscatory taxation.[69] However, "[i]t is an accepted principle of international law that a state is not liable for economic injury which is a consequence of bona fide "regulation" within the accepted police power of states."[70] Accordingly,

---

[66] See Christie (1962) 38 B.Y.I.L. 307 and, on the U.S.-Iran Claims Tribunal case law, Aldrich (1994) 88 A.J.I.L. 585.

[67] See *Daley v. Iran* (1988) 18 Iran-U.S.C.T.R. 232 (car seized by Revolutionary Guards) and *Dames and Moore v. Iran* (1983) 4 *id.* 212 at 223 ("The unilateral taking of possession of property [in that case field laboratory equipment] and the denial of its use to the rightful owners may amount to an expropriation even without a formal decree regarding title to the property").

[68] *American Bell International Inc. v. Iran* (1984) 6 Iran-U.S.C.T.R. 74 (threats of "serious personal consequences" for company representative).

[69] *e.g.* in 1964, the U.K. Government characterised a Burmese profits tax of 99 per cent as "de facto expropriation without compensation": 1964 B.P.I.L. 202.

[70] *Sedco Inc. v. N.I.O.C. (First Interlocutory Award)* (1985) 9 Iran-U.S.C.T.R. 248 at 275.

economic measures such as non-confiscatory taxation, exchange control regulation and currency revaluation do not normally result in expropriation. In addition, the forfeiture of property as a criminal sanction is in principle lawful.

The kind of taking illustrated by the *Starrett* case is the taking of the "effective use" of property, variously also known as indirect, "creeping" or "constructive" expropriation.[71] In *Tippetts v. TAMS–ATTA*,[72] the Iran-U.S. Claims Tribunal suggested that "constructive expropriation" occurs when "events demonstrate that the owner was deprived of fundamental rights of ownership and it appears that this deprivation is not merely ephemeral." In the same case, the Tribunal took the view that an objective theory of state responsibility applies[73];

> The intent of the government is less important than the effects of the measures on the owner, and the form of the measures of control or interference is less important than the reality of their impact.

"Constructive expropriation" is also considered in the Explanatory Note to the 1961 Harvard Draft Convention, Article 10[74]:

> There are a variety of methods by which an alien natural or juridical person may have the use or enjoyment of his property limited by State action, even to the extent of the State's forcing the alien to dispose of his property at a price representing only a fraction of what its value would be had not the alien's use of it been subjected to interference by the State.[75]
>
> ... A State may make it impossible for an alien to operate a factory which he owns by blocking the entrances on the professed ground of maintaining order. It may, through its labor legislation and labor courts, designedly set the wages of local employees of the enterprise at a prohibitively high level. If technical personnel are needed from outside the country, entry visas may be denied them. Essential replacement parts or machinery may be refused entrance, or allocations of foreign exchange may deliberately be denied with the purpose of making it impossible to import the requisite machinery. Any one of these measures ... could make it impossible for the alien owner to use or enjoy his property. More direct interferences may also be imagined. The alien may simply be forbidden to employ a certain portion of a building which he occupies, either on a wholly arbitrary basis or on the authority of some asserted requirement of the local law. A government, while leaving ownership of an enterprise in the alien owner, might appoint conservators, managers, or inspectors who might interfere with the free use by the alien of its premises and its facilities. Or, simply by forbidding an alien to sell his property, a government could effectively deprive that property of its value.
>
> Whether an interference with the use, enjoyment, or disposal of property constitutes a "taking" or a "taking of use" will be dependent upon the

---

[71] *cf. United Painting Co. Inc. v. Iran* (1989) 23 Iran-U.S.C.T.R. 351. See Dolzer (1986) 1 I.C.S.I.D. Rev.-F.I.L.J. 4; Vagts (1978) 72 A.J.I.L. 17; Weston (1975–6) 16 Virg. J.I.L. 103.

[72] (1985) 6 Iran-U.S.C.T.R. 219 at 225.

[73] *ibid.*, p. 226. *cf.* the *Starrett* case, above, p. 553.

[74] (1961) 55 A.J.I.L. 558–59.

[75] *Ed.* On the forced sale of foreign owned commercial enterprises to nationals under West African indigenisation programmes, see Akinsanya, *Economic Independence and Indigenisation of Private Foreign Investments: the Experience of Nigeria and Ghana* (1982) and Beveridge (1991) 40 I.C.L.Q. 302.

duration of the interference.[76] Although a restriction on the use of property may purport to be temporary, there obviously comes a stage at which an objective observer would conclude that there is no immediate prospect that the owner will be able to resume the enjoyment of his property. Considerable latitude has been left to the adjudicator of the claim to determine what period of interference is unreasonable and when the taking therefore ceases to be temporary.

The unreasonableness of an interference with the use, enjoyment, or disposal of property must be determined in conformity with the general principles of law recognized by the principal legal systems of the world.

The following instance of British practice is of interest in this connection. In 1964, the Indonesian Government took the following action against British commercial interests:

> Under Presidential Decree No. 6 of 1964, dated November 26, 1964, all British owned commercial interests in Indonesia, including estates, industrial enterprises and commercial agencies, were placed under complete and direct Indonesian management and control. This comprehensive Decree, however, was only the culminating point of a series of discriminatory measures introduced by the Indonesian authorities in the months following September 16, 1963, the day on which Malaysia came into being. . . .
>
> The control exercised over British interests initially varied from complete take-over, as in the case of the firm called Pemanukan and Tjiasem Lands who ran 21 rubber and tea estates in Java, to small security teams posted at manufacturing enterprises. The differences in approach and timing, as well as in the degree of harassment and take-over were due to the varying circumstances of each firm, the labour pressure brought against them, the personalities involved, the capacity of the British staff to resist take-over attempts, and the emotional or economic significance of the interests attacked.[77]

In a note[78] to the Indonesian Government dated July 20, 1965, the British Government stated:

> . . . in view of the complete inability of British enterprises and plantations to exercise and enjoy any of their rights of ownership in relation to their properties in Indonesia, Her Majesty's Government have concluded that the Indonesian Government have expropriated this property.

2. The *Starrett Case* also examines what is property for the purpose of expropriation. The 1961 Harvard Draft Convention defines it as comprising "all movable and immovable property, whether tangible or intangible, including industrial, literary, and artistic property, as well as rights and interests in any property" (Article 10(7)). The definition excludes contractual rights; these are regarded as

---

[76] In the *ELSI Case*, I.C.J. Rep. 1989, p. 14 at p. 71, a Court Chamber held that the requisition of a firm's plant and machinery that was for a limited period of six months and was subject to administrative appeal was not by itself a "significant deprivation" of the firm's property so as to amount to a "taking". On the case, see Hamrock (1992) 27 Tex.I.L.J. 837, and Murphy (1991) 18 Yale J.I.L. 291.

[77] 1964 B.P.I.L., 194–195. *cf.* Judge Sir Gerald Fitzmaurice's assessment of the facts in the *Barcelona Traction Case*, *loc. cit.*, p. 604, below, p. 106 ("disguised expropriation"). See also Judge Gros, *ibid.* p. 274.

[78] *ibid.* p. 200.

being subject to a different rule. But in the *Anglo-Iranian Oil Co.* case, the claimant United Kingdom Government argued[79]:

> The Government of the United Kingdom does not consider it necessary to elaborate the proposition that rights acquired by foreign nationals by virtue of concessionary contracts are property rights and that as such they are entitled to the same protection as international law grants to the property rights of foreigners.

Note also that in the *Shufeldt Claim*, the Arbitrator, in awarding compensation for the premature termination by Guatemala by legislative decree of a concession contract for the exploitation of chicle, stated:

> There cannot be any doubt that property rights are created under and by virtue of a contract.[80]

This view is confirmed by the jurisprudence of the Iran-U.S. Claims Tribunal. Although the *Starrett* case extends only to contract rights which are "closely related" to physical property which has also been expropriated, the *Amoco International Finance Corp.* case[81] is not so limited.

AMOCO INTERNATIONAL FINANCE CORP. *v.* IRAN

U.S. *v.* Iran (1987)

Iran–U.S. Claims Tribunal. Chamber Three: Virally, Chairman; Brower, Ansari, members. 15 Iran–U.S.C.T.R. 189.
Footnote omitted.

The claimant Swiss company, a wholly owned subsidiary of Standard Oil, a U.S. company, entered into a 1966 joint venture agreement (the Khemco Agreement) with NPC, an Iranian company controlled by the Iranian Government, to form Khemco, an Iranian company jointly owned and managed by the contracting companies, to process and sell Iranian natural gas, each contracting company having a 50 per cent stake in Khemco's profits. In 1980, the Khemco Agreement, which by its terms was valid for 35 years, was declared null and void by the Iranian Government following the 1979 Iranian revolution and in implementation of Iranian legislation (the 1980 Single Article Act) that was intended to complete the nationalisation of the Iranian Oil Industry. The claimant sought compensation for the loss of its interests in Khemco arising under the Khemco Agreement as a result of the 1980 nationalisation.

Award of the Tribunal

108 . . . Expropriation, which can be defined as a compulsory transfer of property rights, may extend to any right which can be the object of a

---

[79] *Anglo-Iranian Oil Co.* case (1951) I.C.J. Pleadings, p. 83. The U.K. took the generally accepted view that a state can only expropriate an alien's property that is within its territory: *ibid.* p. 81.

[80] *U.S. v. Guatemala* (1930) 2 R.I.A.A. 1083, at 1097.

[81] Award, para. 108, below, p. 558, *cf. Mobil Oil Iran Inc. v. Iran* (1987) 16 Iran-U.S.C.T.R. 3 at 25 ("the expropriation . . . of contractual rights").

commercial transaction, *i.e.* freely sold and bought, and thus has a monetary value. It is because Amoco's interests under the Khemco Agreement have such an economic value that the nullification of those interests by the Single Article Act can be considered as a nationalisation . . .

113 . . . A leading expression of these rules [of customary international law on expropriation] is the judgment . . . in the *Case Concerning Certain German Interests in Polish Upper Silesia* . . . , 1926 P.C.I.J., Ser. A, No. 7 . . . As reflected in this case, the principles of international law generally accepted some sixty years ago in regard to the treatment of foreigners recognized very few exceptions to the principle of respect for vested rights. The Court listed among such exceptions only "expropriation for reasons of public utility, judicial liquidation and similar measures." *Id.* at 22. A very important evolution in the law has taken place since then, with the progressive recognition of the right of States to nationalize foreign property for a public purpose. This right is today unanimously accepted, even by States which reject the principle of permanent sovereignty over natural resources, considered by a majority of States as the legal foundation of such a right.

114. The importance of this evolution derives from the fact that nationalization is generally defined as the transfer of an economic activity from private ownership to the public sector. It is realized through expropriation of the assets of an enterprise or of its capital stock, with a view to maintaining such enterprise as a going concern under State control. Modern nationalization often brings into State ownership a number of enterprises of the same kind and may even be applied to all enterprises in a particular industry. It may result, therefore, in a taking of private property of much greater magnitude than the traditional expropriation for reasons of public utility, and is also of a very different nature, since it is always linked to determined political choices. For these reasons, and because it applies to going concerns, taken as such, modern nationalization raises specific legal problems, notably in relation to the issue of compensation.

The Tribunal then considered the particular grounds upon which the claimant argued that the nationalisation was unlawful in international law, including grounds of discrimination and absence of public purpose considered below. A claim that the expropriation was in breach of "stabilisation clauses" in the contract was rejected, *inter alia*, because these did not bind Iran because it was not a party to the contract.

139. In support of its contention that the expropriation was discriminatory, the Claimant relies on the fact that, in another of NPC's joint ventures, the Japanese share of a consortium [IJPC] . . . was not expropriated. In contrast, all American interests in petrochemical joint ventures with NPC were expropriated. . . .

140. Discrimination is widely held as prohibited by customary international law in the field of expropriation. . . . the Respondents recognize

that a discriminatory expropriation is wrongful, but deny that the expropriation was discriminatory in the instant case.

141. The Respondents assert that the Single Article Act applied to the entire oil industry, irrespective of the nationality of the foreign companies involved in this industry. In the event, it was applied to non-United States corporations as well as United States corporations. Therefore, it can not be held to be discriminatory. That the Special Commission did not include the contract with IJPC among those which were nullified, the Respondents submit, was an exception due to specific circumstances. They mention specifically the fact that the operation of the IJPC joint venture was not closely linked with other contracts relating to the exploitation of oil fields, whereas the operation of the Khemco plant was linked to the supply of gas from the oil fields operated jointly by Amoco and NIOC pursuant to the JSA. Furthermore, the Respondents emphasize that IJPC was not yet an operational concern at the relevant time, a point that was confirmed by the Claimant.

142. The Tribunal finds it difficult, in the absence of any other evidence, to draw the conclusion that the expropriation of a concern was discriminatory only from the fact that another concern in the same economic branch was not expropriated. Reasons specific to the non-expropriated enterprise, or to the expropriated one, or to both, may justify such a difference of treatment. Furthermore, as observed by the arbitral tribunal in *Kuwait v. American Independent Oil Company (AMINOIL)*[82] . . . a coherent policy of nationalization can reasonably be operated gradually in successive stages. In the present Case, the peculiarities discussed by the Parties can explain why IJPC was not treated in the same manner as Khemco. The Tribunal declines to find that Khemco's expropriation was discriminatory. . . .

145. A precise definition of the "public purpose" for which an expropriation may be lawfully decided has neither been agreed upon in international law nor even suggested. It is clear that, as a result of the modern acceptance of the right to nationalize, this term is broadly interpreted, and that States, in practice, are granted extensive discretion. An expropriation, the only purpose of which would have been to avoid contractual obligations of the State or of an entity controlled by it, could not, nevertheless be considered as lawful under international law. *See* AMINOIL, para.

---

[82] *Ed.* Rejecting the claimant's argument that the nationalisation measure in issue was invalid because it related only to the claimant's concession, the *Aminoil* Tribunal did "not see why a Government that is pursuing a coherent policy of nationalisation should not have been entitled to do so progressively, . . . in step with the development of the necessary administrative and technical availabilities": below, para. 86. In the *Aminoil Case*, the Tribunal found good reasons why, 90 per cent of the oil industry having already been nationalised, only the claimant, of the two remaining concessionaires, was nationalised in 1977. These were that the other concession was for offshore operations, requiring special expertise that Kuwait lacked, and was a concession granted jointly with Saudi Arabia: *id.*, para. 87.

109.[83] . . . Such an expropriation, indeed, would be contrary to the principle of good faith and to accept it as lawful would run counter to the well-settled rule that a State has the right to commit itself by contract to foreign corporations. *Id*. para. 90, [below, p. 579] . . . . It is also generally accepted that a State has no right to expropriate a foreign concern only for financial purposes. It must, however, be observed that, in recent practice and mostly in the oil industry, States have admitted expressly. . . that they were nationalizing foreign properties primarily in order to obtain a greater share, or even the totality, of the revenues drawn from the exploitation of a national natural resource, which, according to them, should accrue to the development of the country. Such a purpose has not generally been denounced as unlawful and illegitimate.

146. . . . It cannot be doubted that the Single Article Act was adopted for a clear public purpose, namely to complete the nationalization of the oil industry in Iran initiated by the 1951 Nationalization of the Iranian Oil Industry Act, with a view to implementing one of the main economic and political objectives of the new Islamic Government. The decision of the Special Commission relative to Khemco was taken in apparent conformity with the Single Article Act. Even if financial considerations were considered in the adoption of such a decision—which would have been only natural, but which has not been evidenced—this fact would not be sufficient, in the opinion of the Tribunal, to prove that this decision was not taken for a public purpose. . . .

192. For the reasons set forth above, the Tribunal finds that Amoco's rights and interests under the Khemco Agreement, including its shares in Khemco, were lawfully expropriated by Iran . . . . The next issue, therefore, relates to the rules to be applied in determining the compensation to be paid in such a circumstance.

191. . . . the leading case in this context is [the *Chorzów Factory Case*, above, p. 515]. In spite of the fact that it is nearly sixty years old, this judgment is widely regarded as the most authoritative exposition of the principles applicable in this field, and is still valid today. . . .

192. . . . the first principle established by the Court is that a clear distinction must be made between lawful and unlawful expropriations, since the rules applicable to the compensation to be paid by the expropriating State differ according to the legal characterization of the taking. *Id*. at 46–47. Such a principle has been recently and expressly confirmed by the celebrated AMINOIL case [below, p.553] . . . .

193. According to the Court in the *Chorzów Factory Case* an obligation of reparation of all the damages sustained by the owner of expropriated property arises from an unlawful expropriation [as on the facts in the

---

[83] *Ed.* para. 109 reads: " . . . it can be conceded in its [Aminoil's] favour that a nationalisation whose alleged justification lies *solely* in the advantages to be derived from putting a term to a contractual dispute would not be regular."

Chorzów Factory Case]. The rules of international law relating to international responsibility of States apply in such a case. They provide for *restitutio in integrum*: restitution in kind or, if impossible, its monetary equivalent. If need be, "damages for loss sustained which would not be covered by restitution" should also be awarded. *See Chorzów Factory, supra*, at 47 [printed above, p.490]. On the other hand, a lawful expropriation must give rise to "the payment of fair compensation," *id.* at 46, or of "the just price of what was expropriated." *Id.* at 47. . . .

197. Obviously the value of an expropriated enterprise does not vary according to the lawfulness or the unlawfulness of the taking . . . . In the traditional language of international law it equates the *damnum emergens*, which must be compensated in any case. . . . The difference is that if the taking is lawful the value of the undertaking at the time of the dispossession is the measure and the limit of the compensation, while if it is unlawful, this value is, or may be, only a part of the reparation to be paid. In any event, even in case of unlawful expropriation the damage actually sustained is the measure of the reparation, and there is no indication that "punitive damages" could be considered.

198. What can be added to the value of the enterprise in order to meet the requirements of *restitutio?* An answer to this question can be found in the formulation of the questions on which an expert inquiry was arranged by the Court. *See Chorzów Factory, supra*, at 51. . . .

200. . . . The clear implication is that . . . the compensation would include the two elements: the value of the undertaking at the date of the expropriation, plus the profits which would have been earned after this date, had the taking not occurred, until the date of the judgment. Equally clear is the consequence to be drawn from this finding: that this lost profit was not included in the valuation of the enterprise as of the date of the taking. Otherwise, there would be double recovery.

201. Of paramount interest is the list of the components enumerated by the Court as included in the value of the undertaking. They appertain to three categories: corporeal properties (lands, buildings, equipment, stocks), contractual rights (supply and delivery contracts) and other intangible valuables (processes, goodwill and "future prospects"). Using today's vocabulary, this would mean "going concern value," which is not a new concept after all. Only one component relates to the future: "future prospects" . . .

203. . . . "future prospects" does not equal lost profit (*lucrum cessans*). Those are two different concepts. The first one clearly refers to the fact that the undertaking was a "going concern" which had demonstrated a certain ability to earn revenues and was, therefore, to be considered as keeping such ability for the future: this is an element of its value at the time of the taking. The second relates to the amount of the earnings hypothetically accrued from the date of the taking to the date of the expert opinion, had the enterprise remained in the hands of its former owner. . . .

205. It is relevant to note that, even for the purpose of *restitutio*, the Court takes into consideration *lucrum cessans* (in the meaning previously defined) only for a limited and rather short period of time. Furthermore, the quantification of *lucrum cessans* implies no projection into the future, since it finds its *dies ad quem* at the date of the judgment.

206. The case law developed since the judgment of the Court has generally followed the principles set forth in this judgment, at least on the distinction between lawful and unlawful expropriation. It is particularly remarkable that all the awards which adopted the standard of *restitutio* relate to expropriation found unlawful.... [84]

217. For the purpose of valuing the compensation due in case of the lawful expropriation of an asset, market value, apparently, is the most commendable standard, since it is also the most objective and the most easily ascertained when a market exists for identical or similar assets....

219. Market value, on the other hand, is an ambiguous concept, to say the least..., when an open market does not exist for the expropriated asset or for goods identical or comparable to it....

220.... The Tribunal is therefore of the view that the... choice between all the available methods must rather be made in view of the purpose to be attained, in order to avoid arbitrary results and to arrive at an equitable compensation in conformity with the applicable legal standards....

226. This conclusion is fully in conformity with the practice of international arbitral tribunals, which, in considering lawful expropriation, have consistently tried to determine according to the law, by all the available means, often using several methods, the appropriate compensation to be paid in the circumstances of each case.... *See, e.g.* LIAMCO, *supra,* at 146–51, 62 I.L.R. at 208–10; AMINOIL, *supra,* paras. 146–49, 153, 21 *Int'l Legal Mat'ls* at 1033–35.

The tribunal then considered and rejected the discounted cash flow (DCF) and net book value methods of valuation proposed by the U.S. and Iran respectively and continued:

262. In the instant Case... the Claimant was deprived of its contractual rights under the Khemco Agreement, and the compensation due relates to these rights. It is not disputed, however, that the value of such rights equals the value of the shares owned by Amoco in the joint stock company incorporated pursuant to the Khemco Agreement....

263. Khemco was a going concern at the time of the expropriation.... Going concern value, accordingly, is the measure of compensation in this case.

[84] *Ed.* The tribunal refers, *inter alia,* to the *Lighthouses Arbitration,* (1956) 23 I.L.R. 299; *Sapphire Int. Petroleums v. NIOC,* (1967) 35 I.L.R. 136; the *BP Case,* below, p. 573; the *Texaco* case, below, p. 548; and the *AGIP* case, (1982) 21 I.L.M. 726.

264. Going concern value encompasses not only the physical and financial assets of the undertaking, but also the intangible valuables which contribute to its earning power, such as contractual rights (supply and delivery contracts, patent licences and so on), as well as goodwill and commercial prospects. Although those assets are closely linked to the profitability of the concern, they cannot and must not be confused with the financial capitalization of the revenues which might be generated by such a concern after the transfer of property resulting from the expropriation (*lucrum cessans*). . . .

341. For the foregoing reasons, the Tribunal awards as follows:

(a) The shareholding interest of Amoco International S.A. in Kharg Chemical Company Limited was lawfully expropriated by the Government of the Islamic Republic of Iran as of 24 December 1980,

(b) The Government of the Islamic Republic of Iran shall pay to the Claimant . . . a compensation measured at fifty per cent . . . of the going concern value of Khemco . . . as of 31 July 1979,[85] without the addition of future lost profits beyond such value. . . .

Judge Brower, the U.S. arbitrator, filed a concurring opinion.[86] The signature of Mr Ansari, the Iranian Arbitrator, was accompanied by the words: "Concurring opinion in part, Dissenting opinion in part."

Notes

1. *Public purpose.* The *Amoco* case supports the view adopted in most international judicial and arbitral decisions[87] that, to be lawful, an expropriation must have a public purpose. Exceptionally, in the *Liamco* case,[88] the arbitrator held that, although there was a requirement of non-discrimination, as to which, see below, p. 565, there was no separate public purpose requirement in international law, at least in the case of *nationalisation*:

As to the contention that the said measures were politically motivated and not in pursuance of a legitimate public purpose, it is the general opinion in international theory that the public utility principle is not a necessary requisite for the legality of a nationalisation. This principle was mentioned by Grotius and other later publicists, but now there is no international authority, from a judicial or any other source, to support its application to nationalisation. . . .

---

[85] *Ed.* The date chosen for the valuation of the expropriated property was that on which measures depriving the claimant of its rights in the management of Khemco were effective, not the later date when the process of expropriation was completed [24 December 1980].

[86] Although concurring, Judge Brower disagreed with the Tribunal's reasoning in several respects. He considered, *inter alia*, that the expropriation was unlawful under customary international law because insufficient guarantees of compensation had been given at the time of the taking and that the Tribunal had misinterpreted the *Chorzów Factory* case when concluding that it excluded lost profits from the compensation due for a lawful expropriation.

[87] Other Iran–U.S. Claims Tribunal cases are to the same effect. See, *e.g.* the *INA* case (1985) 8 Iran–U.S.C.T.R. 373 at 378. *cf.* the *Certain German Interests* case, extract in the *Amoco* case, above, p. 558; the *Aminoil* case, below, p. 578; and the *BP* case, below, p. 565.

[88] (1981) 20 I.L.M. 1 at 58–59. The sole arbitrator was Dr Mahamssani, a Lebanese lawyer.

However, political motivation may take the shape of discrimination as a result of political retaliation. . . .

It is clear and undisputed that non-discrimination is a requisite for the validity of a lawful nationalisation. This is a rule well established in international legal theory and practice (V. White . . . [*op. cit.* at p. 524, n. 50, above] pp. 119 *et. seq.*). Therefore, a purely discriminatory nationalisation is illegal and wrongful.

The *Liamco* case was very similar on its facts to the *Texaco* case, below, p. 573, with a United States oil company complaining of Libya's nationalisation of property contrary to the terms of an oil concession contract. The company claimed in part that the nationalisation (i) had been effected as "part of an overall program of political retaliation against those nations including the United States whose politics were contrary to those of the new Libyan regime" and (ii) was discriminatory against "selected foreign companies." After examining evidence of Libyan policy and practice, the arbitrator concluded that the nationalisation was not discriminatory because "Libya's motive for nationalisation was its desire to preserve the ownership of its oil. . . . The political motive [complained of] was not the predominant motive for nationalisation, and . . . such motive per se does not constitute a sufficient proof of a purely discriminatory measure."[89]

The *Liamco* case is not in accord with General Assembly Resolution 1803, which affirms the need for a public purpose. Although the 1974 Declaration on Economic Rights and Duties of States, adopting the view of developing states, makes no mention of such a requirement, it probably does not reflect present customary law in this respect.[90] However, although a public purpose may be necessary, the *Amoco* case suggests that this is a requirement that is easily satisfied, by virtue, in effect, of a wide "margin of appreciation" doctrine.[91] The *Amoco* case does, nonetheless, give examples (Award, para. 145) of situations in which the requirement might not be complied with, and the *BP* case[92] may indicate another. In that case, in 1971, Libya had nationalised the property, rights and assets under an oil concession contract of British Petroleum, a British company in which the British Government then held 49 per cent of the shares. The British Government protested to Libya that its action infringed international law for the following reasons[93]:

An act of nationalisation is not legitimate in international law unless it satisfies the following requirements:

---

[89] *ibid.* n. 60. Note that in the *Texaco* case, allegations of political motivation for the nationalisations were not examined; it was neither thought necessary nor, in Libya's absence, appropriate to do so.

[90] On the *de lege ferenda* character of the 1974 Declaration, see above, p. 552.

[91] See also the *American International Group* case, (1983) 4 Iran–U.S.C.T.R. 96 at 105, which supposes that the burden of proof is upon the owner to show that there is no valid public purpose.

[92] (1974) 53 I.L.R. 297.

[93] *id.* p. 317. *cf.* the terms of the official U.S. protest at one of several 1973 Libyan nationalisations, which it thought to be motivated by political opposition to U.S. policies in the Middle East and U.S. protest at the Arab oil boycott: "Under established principles of international law, measures taken against the rights and property of foreign nationals which are arbitrary, discriminatory, or based on considerations of political reprisal and economic coercion are invalid and not entitled to recognition by other states": quoted in Von Mehren and Kourides (1981) 75 A.J.I.L. 476 at 486.

(i) it must be for a public purpose related to the internal needs of the taking State[94]; and

(ii) it must be followed by the payment of prompt, adequate and effective compensation.

Nationalisation measures which are arbitrary or discriminatory or which are motivated by considerations of a political nature unrelated to the internal well being of the taking state are, by a reference to those principles, illegal and invalid.

In the *BP* case, the nationalisation was not accompanied by that of property held by other foreign oil companies under concession contracts (or even property held by British Petroleum itself under other concessions). The reason for the nationalisation was the refusal of the United Kingdom shortly before the nationalisation to intervene to prevent Iran from forcibly occupying the Tunb Islands in the Persian Gulf.[95] The islands were the territory of the trucial state of Ras Al-Khaymah (now within the United Arab Emirates) which at the time of the occupation was still a state entitled by treaty to protection from the United Kingdom. The treaty of protection expired the day following the occupation. The dispute was referred to arbitration by British Petroleum under the contract.[96] The sole arbitrator held[97]:

> The BP Nationalisation Law, and the actions taken thereunder by the Respondent, do constitute a fundamental breach of the BP Concession as they amount to a total repudiation of the agreement and the obligations of the Respondent thereunder, and, on the basis of rules of applicable systems of law too elementary and voluminous to require or permit citation, the Tribunal so holds. Further, the taking by the Respondent of the property, rights and interests of the Claimant clearly violates public international law as it was made for purely extraneous political reasons and was arbitrary and discriminatory in character. Nearly two years have now passed since the nationalisation, and the fact that no offer of compensation has been made indicates that the taking was also confiscatory.

In 1979, Nigeria expropriated BP assets because it was continuing to supply oil to South Africa contrary to Nigerian policy on trade with South Africa.[98] Would this motive render the expropriation illegal according to the *BP* case?

2. *Non-discrimination.* The *Aramco* case also suggests that non-discrimination is a condition of a lawful expropriation.[99] However, the tribunal recognises (para. 142) that it is not an absolute requirement; discrimination that is reasonably related to the public purpose that underlies the expropriation is not illegal.

---

[94] *Ed.* Italics added. The limitation "related to the internal needs" of the taking state is used in U.K. bilateral investment protection treaties: see, *e.g.* Art. 5(1), 1989 U.K.–Guyana, below, p. 572, n. 31.

[95] Libya justified the nationalisation thus in the Security Council: S.C.O.R. 1610th Meeting, p. 20, December 9, 1971.

[96] Libya declined to appoint an arbitrator or otherwise participate in the proceedings so that a sole arbitrator (Largergren, a Swedish national) was appointed. Although the *BP* case does not refer expressly to a "public purpose" requirement, the references to expropriations that are "arbitrary" and "for purely extraneous political reasons" imply one.

[97] 53 I.L.R. 329.

[98] *Keesings Archives*, p. 29902.

[99] Other Iran–U.S. Claims Tribunal cases are to the same effect: see, *e.g.* the *American International Group Case, loc. cit.*, p. 565, n. 91, above. *cf.* the *BP* case, above, p. 565; the *Liamco* case, above, p. 564; and the *Aminoil* case, below, p. 578.

Neither General Assembly Resolution 1803 nor the 1974 Declaration on Economic Rights and Duties of States mention non-discrimination. Developed states continue to insist that discrimination against or between foreigners vitiates an expropriation. See, *e.g.* the United Kingdom and United States protests against the Libyan nationalisations, above, pp. 565–566. Earlier, in the *Anglo-Iranian Oil Co.* case,[1] the United Kingdom submitted that a "measure of expropriation or nationalisation . . . becomes unlawful in international law, if in effect it is exclusively or primarily directed against foreigners as such, and it cannot be shown that, but for the measure of expropriation or nationalisation, public interests of vital importance would suffer." On the basis of the above submission, the United Kingdom challenged the legality of the Iranian Oil Nationalisation Act 1951. That Act "resolved that the oil industry throughout all parts of the country, without exception, be nationalised. . . . " In fact, the "oil industry" consisted only of the Anglo-Iranian Oil Co.[2] When can a state nationalise an industry that is wholly owned by foreign interests consistently with the British submission in the *Anglo-Iranian Oil Co.* case? Baade[3] argues that against a non-discrimination requirement:

> Since states are free to decide with whom to trade, they must also be free to decide with whom to stop dealing—subject, of course, to as yet unexpired treaty obligations. . . . Discrimination can be dictated by a number of reasons: preferences based on consideration of foreign policy, military alliances, and the like; ethnic or cultural preferences or aversions; retaliation; or, more importantly for present purposes, decolonization in fact as well as in law. Independence would seem an empty gesture or even a cruel hoax to many a new country if it were prevented from singling out the key investments of the former colonial power for nationalization. There is no support in law or reason for the proposition that a taking that meets other relevant tests of legality is illegal under international law merely because it is discriminatory.

Does the non-discrimination requirement spelt out in the *Amoco* case meet Baade's objections? Pellonpää and Fitzmaurice[4] suggest that, as formulated in that case, the requirement is not a difficult one to meet:

> Justification is probably quite easily available in so far as distinctions, made between foreigners as a class on the one hand, and the State and its nationals on the other, are concerned, and specific reasons may also justify differential treatment of various classes of foreigners. In similarity to the condition of public purpose, the State's assertion that such reasons exist creates a strong presumption of the correctness of such an assertion. Thus, while both the public purpose and non-discrimination requirements are well established, a certain shift in favour of the State's economic sovereignty appears to be discernible in the way they are interpreted today.

3. *Expropriation contrary to a treaty obligation.* This clearly engages responsibility, as illustrated in the *Chorzów Factory* case (*Indemnity*) (*Merits*).[5]

---

[1] *Anglo-Iranian Oil Co.* case, I.C.J. Pleadings, p. 81.
[2] A small concession owned partly by a Russian company was understood to have stopped working.
[3] In Miller & Stanger, eds., *Essays on Expropriations* (1967), p. 24. Footnotes omitted.
[4] *loc. cit.*, p. 548, n. 54, above, p. 67.
[5] See the extract from the judgment, above, p. 514. On expropriation in breach of an "internationalised contract", see below, p. 578.

4. *Compensation for a lawful expropriation.*[6] As stated in the *Amoco* case, the rules on the compensation to be paid for a lawful expropriation are "the object of heated controversies" (Award para. 117), with fundamental disagreement between developed and developing states. The long-standing view of developed states was expressed in a note from the United States Secretary of State Hull to the Mexican Government in 1940 on the expropriation by Mexico of foreign oil interests:

> ... the right to expropriate property is coupled with and conditioned on the obligation to make adequate, effective and prompt compensation. The legality of an expropriation is in fact dependent upon the observance of this requirement.[7]

Some indication of the United Kingdom's understanding of the meaning of the terms used in the Hull formula is found in its memorial in the *Anglo-Iranian Oil Co.* case[8]:

> ... it is clear that the nationalisation of the property of foreigners, even if not unlawful on any other ground, becomes an unlawful confiscation unless provision is made for compensation which is adequate, prompt and effective. By "adequate" compensation is meant "the value of the undertaking at the moment of dispossession, plus interest to the day of [payment]"—*per* the Permanent Court of International Justice in the *Chorzów Factory (Claim for Indemnity) (Merits)* case, Series A, No. 17 ... There have, in fact, been pronouncements that prompt compensation means immediate payment in cash. Thus, in the arbitration between the United States and Norway relating to the requisitioning of contracts for the building of ships in the United States, it was held: "The Tribunal is of opinion that full compensation should have been paid ... at the latest on the day of the effective taking" (Scott, *Hague Court Reports*, Second Series (1932) at 77). The Government of the United Kingdom is, however, prepared to admit that deferred payment may be interpreted as satisfying the requirement of payment in accordance with the rules of international law if:
>   (a) the total amount to be paid is fixed promptly;
>   (b) allowance for interest for late payment is made;
>   (c) the guarantees that the future payments will in fact be made are satisfactory, so that the person to be compensated may, if he so desires, raise the full sum at once on the security of the future payments. ...

The third requirement is summed up in the word "effective" and means that the recipient of the compensation must be able to make use of it. He must, for instance, be able, if he wishes, to use it to set up a new enterprise to replace the one that has been expropriated or to use it for such other purposes as he wishes.

---

[6] See Claggett, in Lillich, *op. cit.*, p. 548, n. 54, above, Vol. 4, p. 31; Francioni (1975) 24 I.C.L.Q. 255; Gann (1985) 23 Col. J.T.L. 615; Mavroidis (1992) 45 R.H.D.I. 69; Mendelson (1985) 79 A.J.I.L. 414; Muller (1981) 19 Col.J.T.L. 35; Murphy (1993) 110 S.A.L.J. 79; Schachter (1984) 78 A.J.I.L. 121 and (1985) 79 A.J.I.L. 420; Westberg (1993) 8 For.Invest.L.J. 1 and (1990) 5 I.C.S.I.D. Rev-For.Invest.L.J. 256.

[7] 3 Hackworth 662. More recently, the U.S. Restatement stated that the "Executive Branch and the Congress of the United States have held resolutely to the view that international law requires compensation that is 'prompt, adequate and effective' ": *Third Restatement of U.S. Foreign Relations Law*, Vol. 2, (1987), para. 712, reporters' notes, p. 207. By "adequate," the U.S. means "fair market value," which in the case of an enterprise is its "going concern" value: U.S. Department of State Legal Adviser's Memorandum, (1983) 22 I.L.M. 1406 at 1407, n. 42. There is no express mention of "lost profits".

[8] *Anglo-Iranian Oil Co.* case, I.C.J. Pleadings, pp. 105–106. The word "payment" in the above quotation is substituted for "judgment", which is found, mistakenly, in the pleadings.

Monetary compensation which is in blocked currency is not effective because, where the person to be compensated is a foreigner, he is not in a position to use it or to obtain the benefit of it. The compensation therefore must be freely transferrable from the country paying it and, so far as that country's restrictions are concerned, convertible into other currencies.

Developed states still keep to the Hull compensation formula (which appears in various permutations) and condition the legality of an expropriation upon the payment of compensation complying with it.[9] See, *e.g.* the United Kingdom protest in the *BP* case, above, p. 565. When Resolution 1803 was being debated, the United States repeatedly said that it understood "appropriate compensation" (para. 4) as incorporating the "international minimum standard" of the Hull formula.[10] In truth, the use of such a general and undefined phrase probably was an exercise in evasion. It is significant that the following amendment[11] to para. 4 proposed by the USSR, although defeated, received 28 votes.[12]

The question of compensation to the owners shall in such cases be decided in accordance with the national law of the country taking these measures in the exercise of its sovereignty.

If the 1974 Charter, which is generally taken to present the views of developing states, takes a very different stance on compensation from that in the Hull formula, it does not, in the opinion of Jimenez de Aréchaga,[13] a former I.C.J. President and Argentinian international lawyer, assert that the question of compensation ceases to be regulated by international law at all:

The *travaux préparatoires* of the Charter... show that... paragraph 2(*c*) is not based on a position which denies the existence of any obligation to pay compensation. This position, originally adopted by the working group which drafted the Charter, was abandoned during discussion.... The text as finally adopted not only imposes the duty to pay "appropriate compensation"... it also provides that such compensation shall be determined by "taking into account... all circumstances that the State considers pertinent."...

Thus, it is clear that the basic features of Article 2, paragraph 2(*c*)—the recognition of an international duty to pay compensation and the determination of the amount due in light of the particular circumstances of each case—are rooted in equitable considerations....

However, this interpretation of the Charter provision has been widely criticized, especially by writers from industrialized countries. The main criticism... is "the absence of any references in Article 2 to the applicability of international law to the treatment of foreign investment."... [14] Other critics have concluded that the only obligation "is to grant such compensation, if any, as it is subjectively thought to be 'appropriate,' considering only local law and 'circumstances,' to which international law is not necessarily 'pertinent.' "[15]

... It is true that Article 2, paragraph 2(*c*) does not include the provision of ...

---

[9] This last point is important for the question whether restitution can be claimed.

[10] See, *e.g.* UN Doc. A/C.2/SR. 835, para. 10.

[11] UN Doc. A/C.2/L670.

[12] The full vote was 28 to 39, with 21 abstentions: UN Doc. A/C.2/SR.858, para. 41.

[13] (1978) 11 N.Y.U.J.I.L.P. 179 at 183–187. Some footnotes omitted. *cf.* Brownlie, 162 Hague Recueil 255 at 268–269 (1979–I).

[14] Statement by the delegate of Canada, 29 U.N.G.A.O.R., C.2 (1649th Mtg.) 446, UN Doc.A/C.2/SR. 1649 (1974).

[15] Browner and Tepe (1975) 9 Int. Lawyer 295 at 305.

Resolution 1803 requiring . . . the payment of appropriate compensation " . . . *in accordance with international law."* . . .

Article 2 of the Charter also refers to the application by the expropriating State of its laws and regulations and to its appreciation of all pertinent circumstances. It is perfectly legitimate to accept this determination as the one to be made in the first instance since under the local remedies rule national law and local remedies must be applied and exhausted. But the requirement of Article 2, paragraph 2(c) for the payment of an "appropriate compensation" remains.

Thus, if a nationalizing State, in application of its laws and in its appreciation of the circumstances, were to offer compensation which was not considered "appropriate" by the other interested State (and not just by the individual party), the subjective determination by the host State would not be final. The State of nationality of the expropriated owner would become authorized under the existing rules of international law to take up the case of its national and to make a claim on its behalf, based on the host State's non-compliance with the international duty to pay "appropriate compensation."

Supposing that the Hull formula did at one time state a customary rule of compensation of general application, it no longer does so in the absence of support by states as a whole. The problem is that the view of developing states, as indicated in Article 2(2)(c), 1974 Charter, p. 550, above, has, by the same token, by no means replaced it. This creates difficulties for international arbitral tribunals, which have struggled to find a middle way.

The 1974 Charter has found little favour in international arbitral awards.[16] Nor has the Western "prompt, adequate and effective" compensation standard been adopted. Instead tribunals have recently been attracted by the "appropriate compensation" rule upon which states generally were able to agree in Resolution 1803. It was used, for example, in the *Aminoil* case,[17] and in the *Amoco* case and other Iran–United States Claims Tribunal cases. The problem is to know what "appropriate compensation" means.[18] Adopted in Resolution 1803 to achieve the appearance of agreement, "appropriate compensation" was used in the *Aminoil* case as a standard that permitted by its generality a flexible and equitable response to the legitimate expectations of the parties, taking into account, on the facts of that case, such considerations as the presence of a stabilisation clause[19] and the history of the particular investment.[20] Its interpretation by the Iran–United States Claims Tribunal has varied according to the views of the particular chairman of the Chamber of the Tribunal concerned. For the most part, "appropriate compensation" has been understood by the Tribunal in a way that approximates more closely to the views of Western states than to those of developing states. In the *Sola Tiles* case,[21] Bocksteigel, Chairman of Chamber One, having settled on the "appropriate compensation" formula as having achieved "widespread use in recent years", interpreted it as the equivalent of "adequate" compensation and regarded Resolution 1803, which incorporated the "appropriate

---

[16] They have generally questioned its standing as evidence of custom: see above, p. 552.

[17] Below, p. 578.

[18] There has been little consideration by tribunals of, in terms of the Hull formula, the "promptness" or "effectiveness" of compensation; the discussion has concentrated almost entirely upon its amount.

[19] As to stabilisation clauses, see below, p. 584.

[20] Note that most of the cases concern the expropriation of enterprises. Where what is taken is the private property of an individual, (*e.g.* his car), fewer complications arise.

[21] (1987) 14 Iran–U.S.C.T.R. 223. *cf.* the *American International Group* case, (1983) 4 *ibid.* 96 ("the former owner of the nationalised property is normally entitled to compensation for the value of the property taken", in that case regarded as the "going concern" value).

compensation" formula, as intending "no break with prevailing customary law". "Appropriate compensation" was, however, to be determined in the light of the particular circumstances of the case so that if, as on the facts of the *Sola Tiles* case, a company's prospects were poor, no compensation should be awarded for its going concern value. In the *Amoco* case, Virally, Chairman of Chamber Three, understood that the payment, in the normal case, of the market value of an enterprise in the application of the *damnum emergens* approach in the *Chorzow Factory* case to be in accord with the "appropriate compensation" standard.

However, in the *INA* case,[22] in a separate opinion, Lagergren, an earlier Chairman of Chamber One, adopted a more flexible approach, drawing a distinction between "large-scale nationalisations" and other lawful expropriations:

> I conclude from the foregoing that an application of current principles of international law, as encapsulated in the "appropriate compensation" formula, would in a case of lawful large-scale nationalisations in a state undergoing a process of radical economic restructuring normally require the "fair market value" standard to be discounted in taking account of "all circumstances." However, such discounting may, of course, never be such as to bring the compensation below a point which would lead to "unjust enrichment" of the expropriating state. It might also be added that the discounting often will be greater in a situation where the investor has enjoyed the profits of his capital outlay over a long period of time, but less, or none, in the case of a recent investor, such as INA.

But Lagergren also raised the question whether the standard of "appropriate compensation" with the above meaning may have replaced the Hull formula for other lawful expropriations too[23]:

> Whether this standard is more correctly characterised as an exception to a still subsisting—though admittedly shrinking—Hull doctrine, or as evidence of a more general tendency towards the wholesale displacement of that doctrine as the repository of the *opinio juris*, is still the subject of debate. But the latter view appears by now to have achieved a rather solid basis in arbitral decisions and in writings.

As important as the *standard* of compensation (full, partial) is the *method of valuation* of the expropriated property.[24] How does the "going concern" value applied in the *Amoco* case differ from the "net book" claimed by the respondent? Might recovery for "future prospects" as allowed in the *Amoco* case to some extent mitigate the lack of compensation for lost profits?

On the question whether, as claimed by developed states,[25] the payment of the required compensation is a condition of the legality of an expropriation, the jurisprudence of the Iran–U.S. Claims Tribunal suggests that it is not. For example, in the *INA* case,[26] the Tribunal distinguished between the public purpose

---

[22] (1985) 8 Iran–U.S.C.T.R. 373 at 390. *cf. Lithgow v. U.K.*, Eur. Ct. H.R. Rep, Ser. A, No. 102, para. 121 (1986).

[23] *ibid.* p. 387. But see the *Sedco* case (*Second Interlocutory Award*), (1986) 10 Iran–U.S.C.T.R. 180 at 187 in which it was noted that the view of writers, upon which no opinion was expressed, that custom no longer required full compensation was limited mostly to "large-scale nationalisation, *e.g.* of an entire industry or natural resource;" in the case of a "discrete expropriation of alien property," it was not disputed that full compensation was required.

[24] See Lillich, *op. cit.*, p. 548, n. 54, above.

[25] See above, p. 569.

[26] *loc. cit.*, p. 571, n. 22, above, p. 378. See also the *American International Group* case, *loc. cit.*, p. 565, n. 91, above.

requirement, non-compliance with which renders an expropriation "*per se* unlawful," and the requirement to pay compensation in the case of a "lawful expropriation." The inference is that if compensation is not paid as required, the position is simply that the obligation to pay it continues, with interest to the time of payment; the rules as to reparation for an illegal act[27] do not apply. There may, however, be a duty to make sufficient provision for the payment of compensation at the time of the expropriation.[28] Judge Brower, an American arbitrator, while doubting that the payment of compensation was a condition of legality, stated in his separate opinion in the *Sedco (Second Interlocutory Award)* case[29]:

> If . . . no provision for compensation is made contemporaneously with the taking, or one is made which clearly cannot produce the required compensation, or unreasonably insufficient compensation is paid at the time of taking, it would seem appropriate to deem the taking itself wrongful.

5. *Lump sum settlement agreements and bilateral investment protection agreements.* In lump sum settlement agreements, as to which, see below, p. 585, the sum paid consistently falls short of "adequate compensation" in the sense of the Hull formula. Many such bilateral agreements have been made since World War II and it has been argued that they constitute state practice indicative of the customary international law on compensation for a lawful expropriation.[30] A similar argument can be made in respect of bilateral investment protection agreements, although to the contrary effect, since they generally require compensation according to the Hull formula.[31] The value of both kinds of evidence of state practice was considered in the *Sedco (Second Interlocutory Award)* case[32]:

> Assessment of the present state of customary law on this subject on the basis of the conduct of States in actual practice is difficult, *inter alia*, because of the questionable evidentiary value for customary international law of much of the practice available. This is particularly true in regard to "lump sum" agreements between States (a practice often claimed to support the position of less than full compensation), as well as to compensation settlements negotiated between States and foreign companies. Both types of agreements can be so greatly inspired by non-judicial considerations—*e.g.* resumption of diplomatic or trading relations—that it is extremely difficult to draw from them conclusions as to *opinio juris, i.e.* the determination that the content of such settlements was thought by the States involved to be required by international law. The International Court of Justice[33] and international arbitral tribunals[34] have cast serious doubts on the value of such settlements as evidence of custom. . . . The bilateral investment treaty practice of States, which much more often than not reflects the traditional international law standard of compensation for

---

[27] See below, p. 573.

[28] See Pellonpää and Fitzmaurice, *loc. cit.*, p. 548, n. 54 above, p. 69.

[29] (1986) 10 Iran-U.S. C.T.R. 180 at 204, n. 39.

[30] See, *e.g.* Lillich and Weston (1988) 82 A.J.I.L. 69.

[31] See, *e.g.* Art. 5(1), 1989 U.K.–Guyana Agreement, Cm 909. On U.K. bilateral investment promotion and protection agreements, of which there are 39, see Denza and Brooks (1987) 36 I.C.L.Q. 908 and Warbrick, *ibid.*, p. 929. More generally, see Dolzer and Stevens, *Bilateral Investment Treaties* (1995).

[32] (1986) 10 Iran–U.S. C.T.R. 180 at 184–185.

[33] See, *e.g. Barcelona Traction (Belg. v. Spain)*, I.C.J. Rep. 1970, p. 3 at p. 40 . . . *Ed.* The I.C.J. there states: "Far from evidencing any norm as to the classes of beneficiaries of compensation, such arrangements are *sui generis* and provide no guide in the present case."

[34] See, *e.g.* [the *Aminoil* case *loc. cit.*, p. 578, below] . . . paras. 156–157 . . . .

expropriation, more nearly constitutes an accurate measure of the High Contracting Parties' views as to customary international law, but also carries with it some of the same evidentiary limitations as lump sum agreements. Both kinds of agreements involve in some degree bargaining in a context to which *"opinio juris* seems a stranger."[35]

6. *Reparation for an illegal expropriation.* The *Amoco* case follows the *Chorzów Factory* and *Aminoil* cases in recognising that in a case of illegal expropriation the ordinary rules of state responsibility apply.[36] Restitution was awarded in the *Texaco* case, although the claimant eventually accepted compensation. Restitution will seldom be possible where an enterprise is expropriated. As to compensation, the *Amoco* case follows the *Chorzów Factory* case in supposing that damages by way of reparation for any illegal expropriation may include lost profits, although apparently only to the time of judgment. If the intention is to place the claimant in the position that existed before expropriation, why, in the case of an enterprise with the prospect of doing business into the foreseeable future, should directly attributable lost profits be limited to those accruing at the date of the judgment? Should punitive damages be available in an appropriate case of illegal expropriation?[37]

TEXACO *v.* LIBYA[38]

Texaco Overseas Petroleum Co. and California Asiatic Oil Co. v. Libya (1977)
53 I.L.R. 389; (1978) 17 I.L.M. 1

In 1973 and 1974, Libya nationalised all of the properties, rights, assets and interests of the two claimant United States companies under certain concession contracts made between Libya and the claimants for the exploitation of oil in Libya. Each contract (clause 16) provided that "the contractual rights expressly created by this concession shall not be altered except by mutual consent of the parties." Each indicated the law of the contract (clause 28):

> This concession shall be governed by and interpreted in accordance with the principles of the law of Libya common to the principles of international law and in the absence of such common principles then by and in accordance with the general principles of law, including such of those principles as may have been applied by international tribunals.

The contracts provided for the reference of any dispute arising under them to "two arbitrators, one of whom shall be appointed by each such party, and an Umpire who shall be appointed by the Arbitrators" (*ibid.*). In the event of either party failing to appoint an arbitrator, a sole arbitrator was to be appointed by the

---

[35] *Aminoil [Case]* . . . at para. 157.
[36] For these rules, see above, p. 515.
[37] See the *Amoco* case, para. 197, above, and Arbitrator Brower in *Sedco v. Iran (Second Interlocutory Award)*, (1986) 10 Iran–U.S. C.T.R. 180 at 205. On punitive damages, see Gray, *op. cit.*, p. 515, n. 68, pp. 26–28.
[38] See Bowett (1978) 37 C.L.J. 5; Fatouros (1980) 74 A.J.I.L. 134; Greenwood (1982) 53 B.Y.I.L. 27; Von Mehren and Kourides, *loc. cit.*, p. 565, n. 93 above; Varma (1979) 18 Col. J.T.L. 259; White (1981) 30 I.C.L.Q. 1. See also Benton (1974) 11 Houston L.R. 924. On international contracts generally, see Asante (1979) 28 I.C.L.Q. 401; Friedmann, *op. cit.*, p. 548, n. 54 above, pp. 200–210; Hyde (1962–I) 105 Hague Recueil 267; Lalive (1964) 13 I.C.L.Q. 987; McNair (1957) 33 B.Y.I.L. 1; Mann (1959) 35 B.Y.I.L. 34; Schwebel (1959) 53 Proc. A.S.I.L. 266.

President of the I.C.J. (*ibid.*). In this case, Professor Dupuy, a French international lawyer, was appointed as a sole arbitrator after Libya had failed to act. Libya did not participate in the proceedings at any stage, except by way of memorandum to the President of the I.C.J. objecting to the proceedings.

The arbitrator held that the concessions were "internationalised" contracts and that the law applying to them was that chosen by the parties in clause 28. In the following extract, the arbitrator indicates more fully when a contract between a state and an alien may be characterised as an "internationalised" one, and what the consequences of such a characterisation are. He then considers whether the contracts are binding under the applicable law and whether the Libyan nationalisation measures in breach of the contracts can be justified on other grounds.

Award of the arbitrator

40. The internationalisation of contracts entered into between States and foreign private persons can result in various ways . . .

42. International arbitration case law confirms that the reference to the general principles of law [in its proper law clause] is always regarded to be a sufficient criterion for the internationalisation of a contract.[39]

44. . . . Another process for the internationalisation of a contract consists in inserting a clause providing that possible differences which may arise in respect of the interpretation and the performance of the contract shall be submitted to arbitration.

. . . It is . . . unquestionable that the reference to international arbitration is sufficient to internationalise a contract, in other words, to situate it within a specific legal order—the order of the international law of contracts.

45. . . . A third element of the internationalisation of the contracts in dispute results from the fact that it takes on a dimension of a new category of agreements between States and private persons: economic development agreements. . . .

Several elements characterise these agreements: in the first place, their subject matter is particularly broad: they are not concerned only with an isolated purchase or performance, but tend to bring to developing countries investments and technical assistance. . . . Thus, they assume a real importance in the development of the country where they are performed. . . .

In the second place, the long duration of these contracts implies close co-operation between the State and the contracting party and requires permanent installations as well as the acceptance of extensive responsibilities by the investor.

Finally, because of the purpose of the co-operation in which the contracting party must participate with the State and the magnitude of the investments to which it agreed, the contractual nature of this type of

[39] *Ed.* The arbitrator cited the following cases: the *Lena Goldfields Arbitration* (1930) 5 A.D. 3, 426; the *Abu Dhabi Arbitration, loc. cit.,* p. 457, n. 17, above; the *Qatar* case (1953) 20 I.L.R. 534; and the *Sapphire* case (1963) 35 I.L.R. 136. See also the *Aramco* case (1963) 27 I.L.R. 117.

agreement is reinforced. . . . This investor must in particular be protected against legislative uncertainties, that is to say the risks of the municipal law of the host country being modified, or against any government measures which would lead to an abrogation or rescission of the contract. Hence, the insertion, as in the present case, of so-called stabilisation clauses: these clauses tend to remove all or part of the agreement from the internal law and to provide for its correlative submission to *sui generis* rules . . . or to a system which is properly an international law system. . . .

47. . . . stating that a contract between a State and a private person falls within the international legal order means that for the purposes of interpretation and performance of the contract, it should be recognized that a private contracting party has specific international capacities. But, unlike a State, the private person has only a limited capacity and his quality as a subject of international law does enable him only to invoke, in the field of international law, the rights which he derives from the contract.

The arbitrator next applied the law of the contracts in clause 28 and held that the concessions were binding. This was because both Libyan and international law accepted that contracts were binding (*pacta sunt servanda*).

53. The Tribunal must now rule on the point whether . . . the defendant Government has, or has not, breached its obligations arising from the contracts it executed. For this purpose, this Tribunal should examine the various reasons which could be envisaged in order to justify the defendant Government's behaviour. . . .

After rejecting the possibility that Libya could be excused from its obligations in accordance with the law applicable to administrative contracts (so that the obligations could be altered or terminated unilaterally by the state),[40] the arbitrator considered an argument based upon "the concept of sovereignty and the nature of measures of nationalisation."

61. . . . It is clear from an international point of view that it is not possible to criticize a nationalisation measure concerning nationals of the State concerned, or any measure affecting aliens in respect of whom the State concerned has made no particular commitment to guarantee and maintain their position. On the assumption that the nationalising State has concluded with a foreign company a contract which stems from the municipal law of that State and is completely governed by that law the resolution of the new situation created by nationalisation will be subject to the legal and administrative provisions then in force.

62. But the case is totally different where the State has concluded with a foreign contracting party an internationalised agreement. . . .

---

[40] The arbitrator held that (i) the concessions were not administrative contracts under Libyan law and (ii) the theory of administrative contracts was not a part of international law. French in origin, it was not a general principle of law found in all of the main kinds of legal systems.

71.... the recognition by international law of the right to nationalise is not sufficient ground to empower a State to disregard its commitments, because the same law also recognises the power of a State to commit itself internationally, especially by accepting the inclusion of stabilisation clauses in a contract entered into with a foreign private party....

73. Thus, in respect of the international law of contracts, a nationalisation cannot prevail over an internationalised contract, containing stabilisation clauses, entered into between a State and a foreign private company....

The arbitrator then considered, thirdly and finally, whether "resolution concerning natural resources and wealth adopted by the General Assembly" justified Libya's conduct.

87.... On the basis of the circumstances of adoption ... and by expressing an *opinio juris communis*, Resolution 1803 (XVII)[41] seems to this Tribunal to reflect the state of customary law existing in this field.... The consensus by a majority of States belonging to the various representative groups indicates without the slightest doubt universal recognition of the rules therein incorporated, *i.e.* with respect to nationalisation and compensation the use of the rules in force in the nationalising State, but all this in conformity with international law.

88. While Resolution 1803 (XVII) appears to a large extent as the expression of a real general will, this is not at all the case with respect to the other Resolutions mentioned above.[42] ... In particular, as regards the Charter of Economic Rights and Duties of States, several factors contribute to denying legal value to those provisions of the document which are of interest in the instant case.

—In the first place, Article 2 of this Charter must be analysed as a political rather than as a legal declaration concerned with the ideological strategy of development and, as such, supported only by non-industrialised States.

—In the second place, this Tribunal notes that in the draft submitted by the Group of 77 to the Second Commission ... the General Assembly was invited to adopt the Charter "as a first measure of codification and progressive development" within the field of the international law of development. However, because of the opposition of several States, this description was deleted from the text submitted to the vote of the Assembly....

The absence of any connection between the procedure of compensation and international law and the subjection of this procedure solely to municipal law cannot be regarded by this Tribunal except as a *de lege ferenda* formulation, which even appears *contra legem* in the eyes of many

[41] *Ed.* Above, p. 549.
[42] *Ed.* Resolutions 3171, 3201, and 3281, above, pp. 550–551.

developed countries.[43] Similarly, several developing countries, although having voted favorably on the Charter of Economic Rights and Duties of States as a whole, in explaining their votes regretted the absence of any reference to international law....

90. The argument of the Libyan Government ... is also negated by a complete analysis of the whole text of the Charter of Economic Rights and Duties of States.

Analysing the scope of these various provisions, Ambassador Castañeda, who chaired the Working Group charged with drawing up the Charter of Economic Rights and Duties of States, formally stated that the principle of performance in good faith of international obligations laid down in Chapter I(j) of the Charter applies to all matters governed by it, including, in particular, matters referred to in Article 2. Following his analysis, this particularly competent and eminent scholar concluded as follows[44]:

> The Charter accepts that international law may operate as a factor limiting the freedom of the State should foreign interests be affected, even though Article 2 does not state this explicitly. This stems legally from the provisions included in other Articles of the Charter which should be interpreted and applied jointly with those of Article 2.

The arbitrator, having found no justification for Libya's acts, held that the appropriate remedy was *restitutio in integrum*, as claimed by the concessionaires, so that Libya was "legally bound to perform" the contracts. In fact, the claimants subsequently accepted an offer of compensation in full settlement of their claim.[45]

Notes

Most contracts between states and aliens are governed by municipal law —normally, but not always,[46] the municipal law of the contracting states.[47] Nonetheless, some—particularly concession contracts for the exploitation of natural resources—are governed by other legal rules indicated usually in a choice of law clause in the contract. The contract in the *Texaco* case—(which is also known as the *Topco* case) was typical of the latter kind of contract.

[43] *Ed.* Earlier, the arbitrator had examined the voting record of the 1974 Charter and similar resolutions and concluded that they "were supported by a majority of states but not by any of the developed countries with market economies which carry on the largest part of international trade" (para. 86).

[44] *Ed.* 20 *Annuaire Français* 31 at 54 (1974). Translation in Award. Chapter I(j) reads "Economic as well as political and other relations among States shall be governed, *inter alia*, by the following principles ... (j) Fulfillment in good faith of international obligations." Art. 32(2), 1974 Charter states that "[i]n their interpretation and application, the provisions of the present Charter are interrelated and each provision should be construed in the context of other provisions."

[45] See (1978) 17 I.L.M. 2.

[46] See, *e.g. R. v. International Trustee for the Protection of Bondholders Aktiengesellschaft* [1937] A.C. 500, HL.

[47] On the question whether the breach by a state of a contract between it and an alien that is governed by municipal law is contrary to international law, see Jennings (1961) 37 B.Y.I.L. 156 and Mann (1960) 54 A.J.I.L. 572. On the position where such a breach is by way of nationalisation, see the *Texaco* case, para. 61, above.

According to a theory developed by some Western writers[48] and adopted in the *Texaco* case, such a contract may qualify as an "internationalised contract" or "economic development agreement" with the result that the contracting state is deemed to have surrendered the power to expropriate contrary to its terms, by virtue of the contract's "stabilisation clauses." This theory is questioned by other Western writers[49] and is strongly contested in the developing world.[50] For a different approach, see the *Aminoil* case, below.

AMINOIL CASE[51]

Kuwait *v.* American Independent Oil Co. (1982)

Arbitration Tribunal: Reuter, President; Sultan, Fitzmaurice, members.
21 I.L.M. 976

In 1948, Aminoil, an American company, was granted by Kuwait an oil concession of 60 years duration. In 1977, Kuwait terminated the concession by Decree Law No. 124 and transferred to itself the company's concession assets against compensation to be assessed by a Kuwaiti "Compensation Committee." Aminoil declined to co-operate with the Committee, contesting instead the legality of the Decree Law. The parties referred the case to arbitration under a special Arbitration Agreement which provided in Article III(2):

> The law governing the substantive issues between the Parties shall be determined by the Tribunal, having regard to the quality of the Parties, the transnational character of their relations and the principles of law and practice prevailing in the modern world.

Interpreting Article III(2), the Tribunal decided that it was required to apply Kuwaiti law, of which international law—with its rules governing the legality of an expropriation—formed a part. The Tribunal rejected Aminoil's claim that the nationalisation did not satisfy the international law requirements, the existence of which the Tribunal did not question, that it be for a public purpose and non-discriminatory. The Tribunal then, in the following extracts, considered whether the nationalisation was contrary to international law because it was inconsistent with the stabilisation clauses in the contract and discussed the compensation that was payable in respect of what it held to be a lawful taking.

Award of the Tribunal

88. . . . Nevertheless, Aminoil's concessionary contract contained specific provisions in the light of which it may be queried whether the nationalisation was in truth lawful. . . . The relevant part of *Article 1 of 1948* provided that:

---

[48] See, *e.g.* recently, Schwebel, in *International Law at the Time of its Codification: Essays in Honour of Robert Ago* (1989), Vol. 3, p. 401, and Curtis (1988) 29 H. I.L.J. 317.

[49] See, *e.g.* Bowett (1988) 69 B.Y.I.L. 49, 51.

[50] See, *e.g.* Jimenez de Aréchaga, *loc. cit.*, p. 548, n. 54, above.

[51] See Mann (1983) 54 B.Y.I.L. 213; Marston, (1983) 17 J.W.T.L. 177; Redfern (1984) 55 B.Y.I.L. 65, Teson (1984) 24 Virg. J.I.L. 323; Tschanz (1984) 18 Int. Lawyer 245, Young and Owen, in Lillich, ed., *Valuation of Nationalised Property in International Law* (1987), Vol. 4, p. 3.

"The period of this Agreement shall be sixty (60) years from the date of signature."

Article 17 of 1948 provided as follows:

"The Shaikh shall not by general or special legislation or by administrative measures or by any other act whatever annul this Agreement except as provided in Article 11. No alteration shall be made in the terms of this Agreement by either the Shaikh or the Company except in the event of the Shaikh and the Company jointly agreeing that it is desirable in the interest of both parties to make certain alterations, deletions or additions to this Agreement."

Finally, ... [as amended in 1961] *Article 11*, after indicating in a first paragraph (A) certain events (not here relevant) in which the Ruler of Kuwait would be entitled to terminate the Concession, went on in a second paragraph (B) to state

"(B) Save as aforesaid this Agreement shall not be terminated before the expiration of the period specified in Article 1 thereof except by surrender as provided in Article 12 or if the Company shall be in default under the arbitration provisions of Article 18."

These clauses combined, but especially Article 17, constituted what are sometimes called the "stabilisation" clauses of the contract. A straightforward and direct reading of them can lead to the conclusion that they prohibit any nationalisation. ...

90. [In contrast, Kuwait] ... claimed that permanent sovereignty over natural resources has become an imperative rule of *jus cogens* prohibiting States from affording, by contract or by treaty, guarantees of any kind against the exercise of the public authority in regard to all matters relating to natural riches. This contention lacks all foundation. Even if Assembly Resolution 1803 [above, p. 549] ... is to be regarded, by reason of the circumstance of its adoption, as reflecting the then state of international law, such is not the case with subsequent resolutions which have not had the same degree of authority. Even if some of their provisions can be regarded as codifying rules that reflect international practice, it would not be possible from this to deduce the existence of a rule of international law prohibiting a State from undertaking not to proceed to a nationalisation during a limited period of time. It may indeed well be eminently useful that "host" States should, if they so desire, be able to pledge themselves not to nationalise given foreign undertakings within a limited period; and no rule of public international law prevents them from doing so. ...

95. ... contractual limitations on the State's right to nationalise are juridically possible, but what that would involve would be a particularly

serious undertaking which would have to be expressly stipulated for, and be within the regulations governing the conclusion of State contracts; and it is to be expected that it should cover only a relatively limited period. In the present case however, the existence of such a stipulation would have to be presumed as being covered by the general language of the stabilisation clauses, and over the whole period of an especially long concession since it extended to 60 years. A limitation on the sovereign rights of the State is all the less to be presumed where the concessionaire is in any event in possession of important guarantees regarding its essential interests in the shape of a legal right to eventual compensation.

96. Such is the case here,—for if the Tribunal thus holds that it cannot interpret Articles 17 and . . . revised 11 as absolutely forbidding nationalisation, it is nevertheless the fact that these provisions are far from having lost all their value and efficacy on that account since, by impliedly requiring that nationalisation shall not have any confiscatory character, they re-inforce the necessity for a proper indemnification as a condition of it.

97. There is another aspect of the matter which has weighed with the Tribunal. While attributing its full value to the fundamental principle of *pacta sunt servanda*, the Tribunal has felt obliged to recognize that the contract of Concession has undergone great changes since 1948: changes conceded—often unwillingly, but conceded nevertheless—by the Company. These changes have . . . been the consequence of . . . a profound and general transformation in the terms of oil concessions that occurred in the Middle-East, and later throughout the world. . . . They were introduced into the contractual relations between the Government and Aminoil through the play of Article 9 [*i.e.* by textual amendment], or else as the result of at least tacit acceptances by the Company. . . .

98. This Concession—in its origin a mining concession granted by a State whose institutions were still incomplete and directed to narrow patrimonial ends—became one of the essential instruments in the economic and social progress of a national community in full process of development. This transformation, progressively achieved, took place at first by means of successive increases in the financial levies going to the State, and then through the growing influence of the State in the economic and technical management of the undertaking . . . and the regulation of works and investment programmes. The contract of Concession thus changed its character and became one of those contracts in regard to which, in most legal systems, the State, while remaining bound to respect the contractual equilibrium, enjoys special advantages. . . .

100. The faculty of nationalising the Concession could not thenceforward be excluded in relation to the régime of the undertaking as it resulted from the sum total of the considerations relevant to its functioning. . . .

102. The Tribunal thus arrives at the conclusion that the "take-over" of Aminoil's enterprise was not, in 1977, inconsistent with the contract of

concession, provided always that the nationalisation did not possess any confiscatory character. . . .

The Tribunal then considered the compensation due for what was a lawful taking:

143. The most general formulation of the rules applicable for a lawful nationalisation was contained in the United Nations General Assembly Resolution No 1803 (XVII) of December 14, 1962, on Permanent Sovereignty over Natural Resources, Article 4 [above, p. 549] . . .

This text which obtained a unanimous vote in the General Assembly, codifies positive principles, recognised by the Constitution and Law of Kuwait, that have not been contested in the present proceedings. It calls for a concrete interpretation of the term "appropriate compensation." Other disputes have long since turned upon different terms such as "fair," "just," "equitable," not to speak of "adequate," "effective," "'prompt," etc. There are indeed, several tendencies, all appealing to the same principle, one of which however reduces compensation almost to the status of a symbol, and the other of which assimilates the compensation due for a legitimate take-over to that due in respect of an illegitimate one. These tendencies were in mutual opposition in the United Nations when the Resolutions following No 1803 were voted, none of which obtained unanimous acceptance, and some of which, such as the Charter of the Economic Rights and Duties of States, have been the subject of divergent interpretations.

144. The Tribunal considers that the determination of the amount of an award of "appropriate" compensation is better carried out by means of an enquiry into all the circumstances relevant to the particular concrete case, than through abstract theoretical discussion. Moreover the Charter of the Economic Rights and Duties of States, even in its most disputed clause (Article 2, paragraph 2c) [above, p. 550]—and the one that occasioned reservations on the part of the industrialized States—recommended taking account of "all circumstances" in order to determine the amount of compensation—which does not in any way exclude a substantial indemnity.[52]

145. Careful consideration of the circumstances proper to each case sometimes enables certain difficulties to be set aside. Thus the opposition manifested by some States to any but the most incomplete compensation may be explicable on the basis that their object is to do away with foreign

[52] As stated by the United States Court of Appeals for the Second Circuit in *Banco Nacional de Cuba v. Chase Manhattan Bank*, (August 4, 1981). "It may well be the consensus of nations that full compensation need not be paid 'in all circumstances' . . . and that requiring an expropriating state to pay 'appropriate compensation'—even considering the lack of precise definition of that term,—would come closest to reflecting what international law requires. But the adoption of an 'appropriate compensation' requirement would not exclude the possibility that in some cases full compensation would be appropriate."

investments entirely, because they do not welcome foreign capital and are even less favourable to investing abroad themselves. . . .

146. . . . In this respect it is not disputed that Kuwait is a country favouring foreign investment, and itself an important investor abroad. . . . The Tribunal will therefore confine itself to registering that in the case of the present dispute there is no room for rules of compensation that would make nonsense of foreign investment. . . .

148. Both Parties to the present litigation have invoked the notion of "legitimate expectations" for deciding on compensation. That formula is well-advised, and justifiably brings to mind the fact that, with reference to every long-term contract, especially such as involve an important investment, there must necessarily be economic calculations, and the weighing-up of rights and obligations, of chances and risks, constituting the contractual equilibrium. . . .

149. For assessment of that equilibrium itself, and of the legitimate expectations to which it gives rise . . . it is not only a question of the original text; there are also the amendments, the interpretations, and the behaviour manifested along the course of its existence, that indicate (often fortuitously) how the legitimate expectations of the Parties are to be seen, and sometimes seen as becoming modified according to the circumstances. . . .

158. The Tribunal now comes to the basis on which the evaluation of the legitimate expectations of Aminoil must proceed. . . .

159. To start with . . . whereas the contract of concession did not forbid nationalisation, the stabilisation clauses inserted in it . . . were nevertheless not devoid of all consequence, for they prohibited any measures that would have had a confiscatory character. These clauses created for the concessionaire a legitimate expectation that must be taken into account. . . .

160. But above all, account must be taken of the position of Aminoil in its relations with the Government of Kuwait. From the time when its rate of production reached a satisfactory level, Aminoil was in the position of an undertaking whose aim was to obtain a "reasonable rate of return" and not speculative profits which, in practice, it never did realise. . . .

161. . . . over the years, Aminoil had come to accept the principle of a moderate estimate of profits, and . . . it was this that constituted its legitimate expectations . . .

164. Having thus described the place occupied by the notion of a reasonable rate of return in the indemnification of Aminoil, the Tribunal must now indicate what principles are, in its view, valid for determining the compensation due in respect of the Company's assets. As the Tribunal has stated earlier, it considers it to be just and reasonable to take some measure of account of all the elements of an undertaking. This leads to a separate appraisal of the value, on the one hand of the undertaking itself, as a source of profit, and on the other of the totality of the assets, and adding together the results obtained. . . .

178. *Amounts due to Aminoil—*

(1) These are made up of the values of the various components of the undertaking separately considered, and of the undertaking itself considered as an organic totality—or going concern—therefore as a unified whole, the value of which is greater than that of its component parts, and which must also take account of the legitimate expectations of the owners. These principles remain good even if the undertaking was due to revert, free of cost, to the concessionary Authority in another 30 years, the profits having been restricted to a reasonable level.

(2) As regards the evaluation of the different concrete components that constitute the undertaking, the Joint Report furnishes acceptable indications concerning the assets other than fixed assets. But as regards the fixed assets, the "net book value" used as a basis merely gives a formal accounting figure which, in the present case, cannot be considered adequate.

(3) For the purposes of the present *case*, and *for the fixed assets*, it is a depreciated replacement value that seems appropriate. In consequence, taking that basis for the fixed assets, taking the order of value indicated in the Joint Report for the non-fixed assets, and taking into account the legitimate expectations of the concessionaire, the Tribunal comes to the conclusion that, at the date of 19 September, 1977, a sum estimated at $206,041,000 represented the reasonably appraised value of what constituted the object of the takeover. . . .

179. For these reasons,

THE TRIBUNAL, unanimously, having regard to all of the above mentioned considerations,

AWARDS to Aminoil,

THE SUM OF ONE HUNDRED AND SEVENTY NINE MILLION, SEVEN HUNDRED AND FIFTY THOUSAND, SEVEN HUNDRED AND SIXTY FOUR UNITED STATES DOLLARS[53]

Separate Opinion of Sir Gerald Fitzmaurice[54]

21. The Award however holds that, despite their unambiguous language, these provisions did not operate to prevent an eventual nationalisation by unilateral legislative act—or at least, that whatever the original position, they had ceased to do so by the date of the take-over in 1977—(this is probably the vital point in the reasoning). . . .

23. I know of no general legal principle . . . which would require something to be expressly stated rather than left to be implied from representative language clearly covering it according to normal canons of

---

[53] *Ed.* This final figure allows for certain Aminoil debts.

[54] Sir Gerald Fitzmaurice agreed with the operative section (*dispositif*) of the tribunal's award (which is limited to the amount of compensation due to Aminoil) and so did not dissent.

interpretation; or rather, and more correctly, which would prohibit something from being inferred from such language *merely because* it was not expressly stated.

24. There is absolutely nothing in the stabilization clauses to warrant the view that they were intended to be confined in the manner suggested —*i.e.* to the case of confiscatory measures only. . . .

25. In my opinion, so far was it from being the case that the Parties in 1948 had not got the eventuality of an ultimate nationalisation in mind, that I feel confident that, at least on Aminoil's side, it was precisely one of the principal contingencies foreseen as possible. The language of Article 17, though general, smacks strongly of it. . . .

26. It is an illusion to suppose that monetary compensation alone, even on a generous scale, necessarily removes the confiscatory element from a take-over, whether called nationalisation or something else. It is like paying compensation to a man who has lost his leg. Unfortunately it does not restore the leg. When a company such as Aminoil procures the insertion in its Concession of a clause like Article 17, its aim is not to obtain money if the Article is breached, but to guarantee if possible that it is not breached. . . .

28. . . . [with regard to the "evolution" argument in paras. 97–100 Award], the argument seems to me to break down in one crucial respect: whatever changes were consented to by the Company, and whatever the quality of that consent, they were changes that were to take place within the framework of a *continuing* Concession—not of one that was to come, and did come, to an end without any such consent, but by the sole will of the other Party. It was change, not termination that Aminoil agreed to. . . .

30. In consequence, . . . although the nationalisation of Aminoil's undertaking may otherwise have been perfectly lawful, considered simply in its aspect of being an act of the State, it was nevertheless irreconcilable with the stabilization clauses of a Concession that was still in force at the moment of the take-over.

Notes

1. *Stabilisation clauses.*[55] The *Aminoil* case makes no mention of the theory of internationalised contracts that was at the heart of the award in the *Texaco* case, above, p. 573. It does accept that a state may surrender its power to expropriate property by agreeing to a stabilisation clause in a contract—but only if (as is unlikely) the clause is expressly and specifically to this effect.[56] Note, however, Sir Gerald Fitzmaurice's more *Texaco*-like view. Although other arbitrations have followed or are consistent with the *Texaco* case in supposing that a generally worded stabilisation clause may prevent expropriation,[57] the more balanced view

[55] See Garcia-Amador (1993) 2 Fla.St.U.J. Trans.L.P. 23, and Paasivirta (1989) 60 B.Y.I.L. 315. See also Mariruzzaman (1992) 9 J.Int.Arb. 141.

[56] *cf.* the *Amoco* case, *loc. cit.*, p. 558, above, para. 179.

[57] See *Revere Copper Inc. v. OPIC*, (1978) 17 I.L.M. 1321 and *AGIP v. Congo* (1982) 21 *ibid.* 726. See also the concurring opinion of Arbitrator Brower in *Mobil v. Iran*, (1987) 16 Iran–U.S. C.T.R. 3 at 64–68.

in the *Aminoil* case seems likely to prevail. The fact that expropriation runs counter to a stabilisation clause may, however, be relevant to the determination of "appropriate compensation."

A study of practice in the late 1960s and 1970s shows that, because of the increased bargaining power of producer states, the majority of oil contracts then made were governed by the law of the contracting state and subject to the jurisdiction of its courts.[58] To the extent that this practice continues, the role of stabilisation clauses is likely to decline.

2. *Compensation.* The *Aminoil* case is a notable example of the increasing use by tribunals of the "appropriate compensation" formula in Resolution 1803 as the standard of compensation required by international law. See further on compensation, above, p. 568.

(ix) Procedures for Settling Disputes

Notes

1. Since 1945, mixed claims commissions, from the extensive jurisprudence of which most of the cases in this Chapter are taken, have been replaced[59] as the predominant means of settling disputes concerning the treatment of aliens by the "lump sum settlement" agreement.[60] By such agreements, one state agrees by treaty to pay another a "lump sum" in full satisfaction of outstanding claims by the nationals of the latter against the former.[61] The latter then arranges itself for the distribution of the settlement sum, typically by a national claims commission which normally adjudicates upon claims in accordance with international law. Settlements between the United Kingdom and East European states arising out of the nationalisations of the late 1940s, for example, have been reached in this way, the "lump sum" being distributed by the Foreign Compensation Commission.[62] Such settlements are invariably of a compromise character so that claims are not fully met.[63]

2. In addition to national compensation commissions, there is also the UN Compensation Commission, which was established by the Security Council[64] to decide claims by governments and individuals against Iraq for direct loss or damage arising out of its 1990 invasion of Kuwait. The Commission, which is based in Geneva, has available to it a fund consisting of the proceeds of Iraqi oil sales. It has already taken decisions awarding compensation in some of the huge number of claims that it has received.

3. In respect of investment disputes, available methods of settlement have been supplemented by the Convention on the Settlement of Investment Disputes between States and Nationals of Other States 1965.[65] This establishes an International Centre for the Settlement of Investment Disputes (in Washington D.C.).

---

[58] See Kuusi, *The Host State and the Transnational Corporation* (1979), pp. 140–145.

[59] But see the Iran–U.S. Claims Tribunal: below, p. 987.

[60] See Lillich, *International Claims: Their Adjudication by National Commissions* (1962); Lillich and Weston, *International Claims: Their Settlement by Lump Sum Agreements*, 2 Vols. (1975); *ibid.*, *International Claims: Contemporary European Practice* (1982); Weston, *International Claims: Post-war French Practice* (1971).

[61] As to value of such agreements as evidence of state practice, see above, p. 572.

[62] On British practice generally, see Lillich, *International Claims: Post-war British Practice* (1967). On the Foreign Compensation Commission, see Magnus, (1988) 37 I.C.L.Q. 975.

[63] See Lillich (1962), above, pp. 133–139.

[64] Resn. 687, S.C.Resns. and Decns. 1991, p. 11; (1991) 30 I.L.M. 846. See Crook (1993) 87 A.J.I.L. 144, and Graefrath (1995) 55 Z.A.O.R. 1.

[65] U.K.T.S. 25 (1967), Cmnd. 3255; 575 U.N.T.S. 159; (1965) 4 I.L.M. 532. In force 1966. 92 parties. These include France, the U.K. and the U.S. among developed states and most African and some Asian and Latin American developing states.

Conciliation and arbitration facilities are available through the Centre to settle cases between contracting parties and companies of the nationality of a contracting party where both sides consent.[66]

(x) Nationality of Claims[67]

(a) *The General Rule*

PANEVEZYS-SALDUTISKIS CASE[68]

Estonia *v.* Lithuania (1939)

P.C.I.J. Reports, Series A/B, No. 76

Judgment of the Court

... In taking up the case of one of its nationals, by resorting to diplomatic action or international judicial proceedings on his behalf, a State is in reality asserting its own right, the right to ensure in the person of its nationals respect for the rules of international law. This rule is necessarily limited to intervention on behalf of its own nationals because, in the absence of a special agreement, it is the bond of nationality between the State and the individual which alone confers upon the State the right of diplomatic protection, and it is as a part of the function of diplomatic protection that the right to take up a claim and to ensure respect for the rules of international law must be envisaged. Where the injury was done to the national of some other State, no claim to which such injury may give rise falls within the scope of the diplomatic protection which a State is entitled to afford nor can it give rise to a claim which that State is entitled to espouse.

1930 HAGUE CONVENTION ON CERTAIN QUESTIONS RELATING TO THE CONFLICT OF NATIONALITY LAWS[69]

179 L.N.T.S. 89

Article 1

It is for each State to determine under its own law who are its nationals. This law shall be recognised by other States in so far as it is consistent

---

[66] See Rodley, (1966) 4 C.Y.I.L. 43; Schwarzenberger, *Foreign Investments and International Law* (1969), Chap. 9; Starke, in Starke, ed., *The Protection and Encouragement of Private Foreign Investment* (1966), Chap. 1; Amerasinghe, (1977) 11 *Int. Lawyer* 45; Baker and Ryans (1976) 10 J.W.T.L. 65; O'Keefe (1980) 34 Y.B.W.A. 286; Sutherland (1979) 28 I.C.L.Q. 367; Tupman (1986) 35 I.C.L.Q. 813.

[67] See Donner, *The Regulation of Nationality in International Law* (2nd ed., 1994), Chap. 2. Hurst (1926) 7 B.Y.I.L. 163; Joseph, *Nationality and Diplomatic Protection: The Commonwealth of Nations* (1969); Leigh (1971) 20 I.C.L.Q. 453; Sinclair (1950) 27 B.Y.I.L. 124.

[68] See also the *Barcelona Traction* case, below, p. 604.

[69] In force 1937. 20 parties, including the U.K.

with international conventions, international custom, and the principles of law generally recognised with regard to nationality....

Article 2

Any question as to whether a person possesses the nationality of a particular State shall be determined in accordance with the law of that State.

Article 3

Subject to the provisions of the present Convention, a person having two or more nationalities may be regarded as its national by each of the States whose nationality he possesses.

Article 4

A State may not afford diplomatic protection to one of its nationals against a State whose nationality such person also possesses.

Article 5

Within a third State, a person having more than one nationality shall be treated as if he had only one. Without prejudice to the application of its law in matters of personal status and of any conventions in force, a third State shall, of the nationalities which any such person possesses, recognise exclusively in its territory either the nationality of the country in which he is habitually and principally resident, or the nationality of the country with which in the circumstances he appears to be in fact most closely connected.

Notes

1. In the *Nationality Decrees in Tunis and Morocco* case,[70] the Permanent Court of International Justice stated:

> Thus, in the present state of international law, questions of nationality are ... in principle within the reserved domain [of a state's domestic jurisdiction].

2. The *British Digest of International Law*[71] states:

> There is today a strong current of international legal thinking to the effect that, apart from the case of concessions of territory or in very special circumstances, international recognition need not be accorded to the nationality of a State conferred on the recipient *not at his request or without his consent,* unless, by both parentage and permanent domicile, he has a genuine connexion with that State. (*cf. Weis, Nationality and Statelessness in International Law* (1956),

[70] P.C.I.J. Rep., Ser. B, No. 4, p. 24 (1923).
[71] 5 B.D.I.L. 25. Italics added.

pp. 110–113; Jones, *British Nationality Law and Practice* (1947), p. 15; Fitzmaurice, *Recueil des Cours*, 1957, II, pp. 198–201).

NOTTEBOHM CASE[72]

Liechtenstein *v.* Guatemala

I.C.J. Reports 1955, p. 4

Judgment of the Court

By the application filed on December 17, 1951, the Government of Liechtenstein instituted proceedings before the Court in which it claimed restitution and compensation on the ground that the Government of Guatemala had "acted towards the person and property of Mr. Friedrich Nottebohm, a citizen of Liechtenstein, in a manner contrary to international law."[73] In its Counter-Memorial, the Government of Guatemala contended that this claim was inadmissible on a number of grounds, and one of its objections to the admissibility of the claim related to the nationality of the person for whose protection Liechtenstein had seised the Court . . . .

Guatemala has referred to a well-established principle of international law, which it expressed in Counter-Memorial, where it is stated that "it is the bond of nationality between the State and the individual which alone confers upon the State the right of diplomatic protection." . . .

Nottebohm was born at Hamburg on September 16, 1881. He was German by birth, and still possessed German nationality when, in October 1939, he applied for naturalization in Liechtenstein.

In 1905 he went to Guatemala. He took up residence there and made that country the headquarters of his business activities . . . . After 1905 he sometimes went to Germany on business and to other countries for holidays. He continued to have business connections in Germany. He paid a few visits to a brother who had lived in Liechtenstein since 1931. Some of his other brothers, relatives and friends were in Germany, others in Guatemala. He himself continued to have his fixed abode in Guatemala until 1943, that is to say, until the occurrence of the events which constitute the basis of the present dispute. . . .

The Liechtenstein Law of January 4, 1934, lays down the conditions for the naturalization of foreigners. . . . The Law specifies certain mandatory requirements, namely, that the applicant for naturalization should prove:

---

[72] See Jones (1956) 5 I.C.L.Q. 230; Kunz (1960) 54 A.J.I.L. 536; 2 Verzijl 210.
[73] *Ed*. The Court was asked to "adjudge and declare that the Government of Guatemala in arresting, detaining, expelling and refusing to re–admit Mr Nottebohm and in seizing and retaining his property without compensation acted in breach of their obligations under international law": I.C.J.Rep. 1955, pp. 6–7.

(1) "that the acceptance into the Home Corporation (*Heimatverband*) of a Liechtenstein commune has been promised to him in case of acquisition of the nationality of the State (2) that he will lose his former nationality as a result of naturalization, although this requirement may be waived under stated conditions. It further makes naturalization conditional upon compliance with the requirement of residence for at least three years in the territory of the Principality, although it is provided that "this requirement can be dispensed with in circumstances deserving special consideration and by way of exception." In addition, the applicant for naturalization is required to submit a number of documents, such as . . ., if he is not a resident in the Principality, proof that he has concluded an agreement with the Revenue authorities . . . . The Law further provides for the payment by the applicant of a naturalization fee . . . .

On October 9, 1939, Nottebohm, "resident in Guatemala since 1905 (at present residing as a visitor with his brother, Hermann Nottebohm, in Vaduz)," applied for admission as a national of Liechtenstein . . . . He sought dispensation from the condition of three years' residence as prescribed by law, without indicating the special circumstances warranting such waiver . . . .

Lastly, he requested "that naturalization proceedings be initiated and concluded before the Government of the Principality and before the Commune of Mauren without delay . . . .

A certificate of nationality has . . . been produced . . . to the effect that Nottebohm was naturalized by Supreme Resolution of the Reigning Prince dated October 13, 1939.

Having obtained a Liechtenstein passport, Nottebohm had it visaed by the Consul General of Guatemala in Zurich on December 1, 1939, and returned to Guatemala at the beginning of 1940, where he resumed his former business activities . . . .

In order to decide upon the admissibility of the Application, the Court must ascertain whether the nationality conferred on Nottebohm by Liechtenstein by means of a naturalization which took place in the circumstances which have been described, can be validly invoked as against Guatemala, whether it bestows upon Liechtenstein a sufficient title to the exercise of protection in respect of Nottebohm as against Guatemala and therefore entitles it to seise the Court of a claim relating to him. In this connection, Counsel for Liechtenstein said: "the essential question is whether Mr. Nottebohm, having acquired the nationality of Liechtenstein, that acquisition of nationality is one which must be recognised by other States." This formulation is accurate, subject to the twofold reservation that, in the first place, what is involved is not recognition for all purposes but merely for the purposes of the admissibility of the Application, and, secondly, that what is involved is not recognition by all States but only by Guatemala.

The Court does not propose to go beyond the limited scope of the question which it has to decide, namely whether the nationality conferred on Nottebohm can be relied upon as against Guatemala in justification of the proceedings instituted before the Court . . . .

In order to establish that the Application must be held to be admissible, Liechtenstein has argued that Guatemala formerly recognized the naturalization which it now challenges and cannot therefore be heard to put forward a contention which is inconsistent with its former attitude. . . .

The Court considered and rejected this contention on the evidence. It dismissed part of the evidence as irrelevant because it referred to "the control of aliens in Guatemala and not to the exercise of diplomatic protection."

It is for Liechtenstein, as it is for every sovereign State, to settle by its own legislation the rules relating to the acquisition of its nationality, and to confer that nationality by naturalization granted by its own organs in accordance with that legislation. It is not necessary to determine whether international law imposes any limitations on its freedom of decision in this domain. Furthermore, nationality has its most immediate, its most far-reaching and, for most people, its only effects within the legal system of the State conferring it. Nationality serves above all to determine that the person upon whom it is conferred enjoys the rights and is bound by the obligations which the law of the State in question grants to or imposes on its nationals. This is implied in the wider concept that nationality is within the domestic jurisdiction of the State.

But the issue which the Court must decide is not one which pertains to the legal system of Liechtenstein. It does not depend on the law or on the decision of Liechtenstein whether that State is entitled to exercise its protection in the case under consideration. To exercise protection, to apply to the Court, is to place oneself on the plane of international law. It is international law which determines whether a State is entitled to exercise protection and to seise the Court . . . .

International practice provides many examples of acts performed by States in the exercise of their domestic jurisdiction which do not necessarily or automatically have international effect, which are not necessarily and automatically binding on other States or which are binding on them only subject to certain conditions: this is the case, for instance, of a judgment given by the competent court of a State which it is sought to invoke in another State . . . .

International arbitrators have decided . . . numerous cases of dual nationality, where the question arose with regard to the exercise of protection. They have given their preference to the real and effective nationality, that which accorded with the facts, that based on stronger factual ties between the person concerned and one of the States whose nationality is involved. Different factors are taken into consideration, and their importance will vary from one case to the next: the habitual residence of the individual concerned is an important factor, but there are other factors such as the centre of his interests, his family ties, his participation in public life, attachment shown by him for a given country and inculcated in his children, etc.

Similarly, the courts of third States, when they have before them an individual whom two other States hold to be their national, seek to resolve the conflict by having recourse to international criteria and their prevailing tendency is to prefer the real and effective nationality.

The same tendency prevails in the writings of publicists and in practice. This notion is inherent in the provisions of Article 3, paragraph 2, of the Statute of the Court.[74] National laws reflect this tendency when, *inter alia*, they make naturalization dependent on conditions indicating the existence of a link, which may vary in their purpose or in their nature but which are essentially concerned with this idea. The Liechtenstein Law of January 4, 1934, is a good example.

The practice of certain States which refrain from exercising protection in favour of a naturalized person when the latter has in fact, by his prolonged absence, severed his links with what is no longer for him anything but his nominal country, manifests the view of these States that, in order to be capable of being invoked against another State, nationality must correspond with the factual situation. A similar view is manifested in the relevant provisions of the bilateral nationality treaties concluded between the United States of America and other States since 1868, such as those sometimes referred to as the Bancroft Treaties, and in the Pan-American Convention, signed at Rio de Janeiro on August 13, 1906, on the status of naturalized citizens who resume residence in their country of origin.

The character thus recognized on the international level as pertaining to nationality is in no way inconsistent with the fact that international law leaves it to each State to lay down the rules governing the grant of its own nationality. The reason for this is that the diversity of demographic conditions has thus far made it impossible for any general agreement to be reached on the rules relating to nationality, although the latter by its very nature affects international relations. It has been considered that the best way of making such rules accord with the varying demographic conditions in different countries is to leave the fixing of such rules to the competence of each State. On the other hand, a State cannot claim that the rules it has thus laid down are entitled to recognition by another State unless it has acted in conformity with this general aim of making the legal bond of nationality accord with the individual's genuine connection with the State which assumes the defence of its citizens by means of protection as against other States.

The requirement that such a concordance must exist is to be found in the studies carried on in the course of the last thirty years upon the initiative and under the auspices of the League of Nations and the United

[74] *Ed.* Below, Appendix I.

Nations. It explains the provisions which the Conference for the Codification of International Law, held at The Hague in 1930, inserted in Article I of the Convention relating to the Conflict of Nationality Laws . . . .[75] In the same spirit, Article 5 of the Convention refers to criteria of the individual's genuine connections for the purpose of resolving questions of dual nationality which arise in third States.

According to the practice of States, to arbitral and judicial decisions and to the opinions of writers, nationality is a legal bond having as its basis a social fact of attachment, a genuine connection of existence, interests and sentiments, together with the existence of reciprocal rights and duties. It may be said to constitute the juridical expression of the fact that the individual upon whom it is conferred, either directly by the law or as the result of an act of the authorities, is in fact more closely connected with the population of the State conferring nationality than with that of any other State. Conferred by a State, it only entitles that State to exercise protection *vis-à-vis* another State, if it constitutes a translation into juridical terms of the individual's connection with the State which has made him its national.

Diplomatic protection and protection by means of international juridical proceedings constitute measures for the defence of the rights of the State. . . .

Since this is the character which nationality must present when it is invoked to furnish the State which has granted it with a title to the exercise of protection and to the institution of international judicial proceedings, the Court must ascertain whether the nationality granted to Nottebohm by means of naturalization is of this character or, in other words, whether the factual connection between Nottebohm and Liechtenstein in the period preceding, contemporaneous with and following his naturalization appears to be sufficiently close, so preponderant in relation to any connection which may have existed between him and any other State, that it is possible to regard the nationality conferred upon him as real and effective, as the exact juridical expression of a social fact of a connection which existed previously or came into existence thereafter.

Naturalization is not a matter to be taken lightly. To seek and to obtain it is not something that happens frequently, in the life of a human being. It involves his breaking of a bond of allegiance and his establishment of a new bond of allegiance. It may have far-reaching consequences and involve profound changes in the destiny of the individual who obtains it. It concerns him personally, and to consider it only from the point of view of its repercussions with regard to his property would be to misunderstand its profound significance. In order to appraise its international effect, it is impossible to disregard the circumstances in which it was conferred, the serious character which attaches to it, the real and effective,

---

[75] *Ed.* Above, p. 587.

and not merely the verbal preference of the individual seeking it for the country which grants it to him.

At the time of his naturalization does Nottebohm appear to have been more closely attached by his tradition, his establishment, his interests, his activities, his family ties, his intentions for the near future to Liechtenstein than to any other State? . . .

The essential facts are as follows:

At the date when he applied for naturalization Nottebohm had been a German national from the time of his birth. He had always retained his connections with members of his family who had remained in Germany and he had always had business connections with that country. His country had been at war for more than a month, and there is nothing to indicate that the application for naturalization then made by Nottebohm was motivated by any desire to dissociate himself from the Government of his country.

He had been settled in Guatemala for 34 years. He had carried on his activities there. It was the main seat of his interests. He returned there shortly after his naturalization, and it remained the centre of his interests and of his business activities. He stayed there until his removal as a result of war measures in 1943. He subsequently attempted to return there, and he now complains of Guatemala's refusal to admit him. There, too, were several members of his family who sought to safeguard his interests.

In contrast, his actual connections with Liechtenstein were extremely tenuous. No settled abode, no prolonged residence in that country at the time of his application for naturalization: the application indicates that he was paying a visit there and confirms the transient character of this visit by its request that the naturalization proceedings should be initiated and concluded without delay. No intention of settling there was shown at that time or realized in the ensuing weeks, months or years—on the contrary, he returned to Guatemala very shortly after his naturalization and showed every intention of remaining there. If Nottebohm went to Liechtenstein in 1946, this was because of the refusal of Guatemala to admit him. No indication is given of the grounds warranting the waiver of the condition of residence, required by the 1934 Nationality Law, which waiver was implicitly granted to him. There is no allegation of any economic interest or of any activities exercised or to be exercised in Liechtenstein and no manifestation of any intention whatsoever to transfer all or some of his interests and business activities to Liechtenstein. It is unnecessary in this connection to attribute much importance to the promise to pay the taxes levied at the time of his naturalization. The only links to be discovered between the Principality and Nottebohm are the short sojourns already referred to and the presence in Vaduz of one of his brothers: but his brother's presence is referred to in his application for naturalization only as a reference to his good conduct. Furthermore, other members of his family have asserted Nottebohm's desire to spend his old age in Guatemala.

These facts clearly establish, on the one hand, the absence of any bond of attachment between Nottebohm and Liechtenstein and, on the other hand, the existence of a long-standing and close connection between him and Guatemala, a link which his naturalization in no way weakened. That naturalization was not based on any real prior connection with Liechtenstein, nor did it in any way alter the manner of life of the person upon whom it was conferred in exceptional circumstances of speed and accommodation. In both respects, it was lacking in the genuineness requisite to an act of such importance, if it is to be entitled to be respected by a State in the position of Guatemala. It was granted without regard to the concept of nationality adopted in international relations.

Naturalization was asked for not so much for the purpose of obtaining a legal recognition of Nottebohm's membership in fact in the population of Liechtenstein, as it was to enable him to substitute for his status as a national of a belligerent State that of a national of a neutral State, with the sole aim of thus coming within the protection of Liechtenstein but not of becoming wedded to its traditions, its interests, its way of life or of assuming the obligations—other than fiscal obligations—and exercising the rights pertaining to the status thus acquired.

Guatemala is under no obligation to recognise a nationality granted in such circumstances. Liechtenstein consequently is not entitled to extend its protection to Nottebohm *vis-à-vis* Guatemala and its claim must, for this reason, be held to be inadmissible . . . .

For these reasons, THE COURT, by eleven votes to three,[76] Holds that the claim submitted by the Government of the Principality of Liechtenstein is inadmissible.

Notes

1. Nottebohm had lost his German nationality upon taking that of Liechtenstein. What state could have protected him against Guatemala in accordance with the "genuine connection" requirement insisted upon by the Court? Could Liechtenstein have protected Nottebohm against any state? Could Guatemala ever have protected him?

2. How important do you think it was in the *Nottebohm* case that Nottebohm's nationality was a "nationality of convenience?" Suppose he had been a Liechtenstein national by birth who had emigrated to Guatemala?

3. Should there be a "genuine connection" requirement, or should international law allow a state to protect any of its nationals without question? The Court supported its "genuine connection" requirement largely by reference to practice concerning dual nationality. Might that be a special case? Note that the requirement had an immediate impact upon the rule concerning the nationality of ships in the 1958 High Seas Convention.[77]

---

[76] The judges in the majority were President Hackworth; Vice-President Badawi; Judges Basdevant, Zoričić, Hsu Mo, Armand-Ugon, Kojevnikov, Sir Muhammad Zafrulla Khan, Moreno Quintana and Cordova; Judge *ad hoc* Garcia Bauer. Judges Klaestad and Read and Judge *ad hoc* Guggenheim dissented.

[77] See above, p. 424.

4. The Rules regarding International Claims issued by the British Foreign and Commonwealth Office in 1985,[78] which state the rules applying when a United Kingdom national seeks the protection of the British Government, make no mention of a "genuine connection" requirement. They read in part:

Rule I

Her Majesty's Government will not take up the claim unless the claimant is a United Kingdom national and was so at the date of the injury.

Comment

International law requires that for a claim to be sustainable, the claimant must be a national of the state which is presenting the claim both at the time when the injury occurred and continuously thereafter up to the date of formal presentation of the claim. In practice however it has hitherto been sufficient to prove nationality at the date of injury and of presentation of the claim.
The term "United Kingdom national" includes:
  (a) individuals who fall into one of the following categories under the British Nationality Act 1981 (or one of the corresponding categories under earlier legislation):
     British citizens
     British Dependent Territories citizens
     British Overseas citizens
     British subjects under Part IV of the Act
     British Protected Persons
  (b) companies incorporated under the law of the United Kingdom or of any territory for which the United Kingdom is internationally responsible.

Rule II

Where the claimant has become or ceases to be a United Kingdom national after the date of the injury, Her Majesty's Government may in an appropriate case take up his claim in concert with the Government of the country of his former or subsequent nationality.

Rule IX

HMG will not take up a claim if there has been undue delay in its presentation to them unless the delay results from causes outside the control of the claimant, but no time limits are fixed and they are subject to equitable rather than legal definition.

Rule XI

Where the prospective claimant has died since the date of the injury to him or his property, his personal representatives may seek to obtain relief or compensation for the injury on behalf of his estate. Such a claim is not to be confused with a claim by a dependant of a deceased person for damages for his death.

---

[78] (1988) 37 I.C.L.Q. 1006.

Comment

Where the personal representatives are of a different nationality from that of the original claimant, the rules set out above would probably be applied as if it were a single claimant who had changed his national status.

Why should international law require that the claimant be a national at the time of the injury and when the claim is formally presented?

5. As to the exceptional cases in which a state may protect a person who is not its national, see above, p. 135, n. 26.

6. The position of stateless persons was indicated in the *Dickson Car Wheel Company* case:

> A State . . . does not commit an international delinquency in inflicting an injury upon an individual lacking nationality, and consequently, no State is empowered to intervene or complain on his behalf either before or after the injury.[79]

FLEGENHEIMER CLAIM

Italian-United States Conciliation Commission: Sauser-Hall, Matturri, Sorrentino. (1958) 25 I.L.R. 91

Under the 1947 Peace Treaty between the Allied Powers and Italy, claims could be brought against Italy on behalf of "United Nations nationals" in certain cases arising out of the Second World War concerning property rights. In this case, brought by the United States, the Commission found that the claimant was not a United States national and hence not a "United Nations national" within the meaning of the Peace Treaty. The claim was therefore not admissible. Although its decision was based upon this finding, the Commission did consider an Italian argument that assumed that the claimant was a United States national and relied upon the absence of a "genuine connection" of the kind required by the *Nottebohm* case. Note that the claimant was not a national of any other state. He had been a national of Germany, but had forfeited his German nationality in 1940 under German law.

Opinion of the Commission

The Commission is of the opinion that it is doubtful that the International Court of Justice intended to establish a rule of general international law in requiring, in the *Nottebohm* case, that there must exist an effective link between the person and the State in order that the latter may exercise its right of diplomatic protection in behalf of the former. The Court itself restricted the scope of its Decision by affirming that the

---

[79] *U.S. v. Mexico* (1931) 4 R.I.A.A. 669 at 678.

acquisition of nationality in a State must be recognized by all other States,

> subject to the twofold reservation that, in the first place, what is involved is not recognition for all purposes but merely for the purposes of the admissibility of the Application, and, secondly, that what is involved is not recognition by all States but only by Guatemala.

The Court further clarified its thought by affirming:

> The Court does not propose to go beyond the limited scope of the question which it has to decide, namely, whether the nationality conferred on Nottebohm can be relied upon as against Guatemala in justification of the proceedings instituted before the Court. (*I.C.J. Reports*, 1955, p. 17.)

The Court has thus distinctly affirmed the relative nature of its decision, cannot be opposed to the Government of the United States in this dispute.

The theory of effective or active nationality was established, in the Law of Nations, and above all in international private law, for the purpose of settling conflicts between two national States, or two national laws, regarding persons simultaneously vested with both nationalities, in order to decide which of them is to be dominant, whether that described as nominal, based on legal provisions of a given legal system, or that described as effective or active, equally based on legal provisions of another legal system, but confirmed by elements of fact (domicile, participation in the political life, the center of family and business interests, etc.) . . . .

Application thereof was made in cases of dual nationality, like the *Canevaro* case[80] . . .

The Commission referred also to the 1930 Hague Convention.[81]

The theory of effective or active nationality was nevertheless limited in its application by the principle of the unopposability of the nationality of a third State, which, in an international dispute caused by a person with multiple nationalities, permits the dismissal of the nationality of the third State, even when it should be considered as predominant in the light of the circumstances; this was the decision rendered on June 8, 1932, by the

---

[80] *Ed.* See below.
[81] See above, p. 587.

Arbitral Tribunal in the *Salem* case,[82] disputed between the United States and Egypt, when this latter country invoked the Persian nationality which the claimant possessed, besides Egyptian nationality, to obtain a rejection of the claim of the United States . . . .

But when a person is vested with only one nationality, which is attributed to him or her either *jure sanguinis* or *jure soli*, or by a valid naturalization entailing the positive loss of the former nationality, the theory of effective nationality cannot be applied without the risk of causing confusion. It lacks a sufficiently positive basis to be applied to a nationality which finds support in a state law. There does not in fact exist any criterion of proven effectiveness for disclosing the effectiveness of a bond with a political collectivity, and the persons by the thousands who, because of the facility of travel in the modern world, possess the positive legal nationality of a State, but live in foreign States where they are domiciled and where their family and business center is located, would be exposed to non-recognition, at the international level, of the nationality with which they are undeniably vested by virtue of the laws of their national State, if this doctrine were to be generalized.

(b) *Protection in Cases of Dual Nationality*

CANEVARO CASE

Italy *v.* Peru (1912)

Permanent Court of Arbitration: Renault, Fusinato, Calderon. 11 R.I.A.A. 397. Translation in (1912) 6 A.J.I.L. 746

The Tribunal was asked whether Italy could claim on behalf of Canevaro, who had Italian nationality by descent from an Italian father and Peruvian nationality by birth in Peru.

Award of the Tribunal

And whereas, as a matter of fact, Raphael Canevaro has on several occasions acted as a Peruvian citizen, both by running as a candidate for the Senate, where none are admitted except Peruvian citizens and where he went to defend his election, and also especially by accepting the office of Consul General of the Netherlands, after soliciting the authorization of the Peruvian Government and then of the Peruvian Congress;

And whereas, under these circumstances, whatever Raphael Canevaro's status may be in Italy with respect to his nationality, the Government of Peru has a right to consider him as a Peruvian citizen and to deny his status as an Italian claimant.

---

[82] *Ed.* See below, p. 599.

SALEM CASE

Egypt *v.* U.S. (1932)

Arbitral Tribunal: Simons; Nielsen, American member; Badawi, Egyptian member. 2 R.I.A.A. 1161

Award of the Tribunal[83]

The principle of the so-called "effective nationality" the Egyptian Government referred to does not seem to be sufficiently established in international law. It was used in the famous *Canevaro* case; but the decision of the Arbitral Tribunal appointed at that time has remained isolated. In spite of the *Canevaro* case, the practice of several governments, for instance the German, is that if two powers are both entitled by international law to treat a person as their national, neither of these powers can raise a claim against the other in the name of such person (Borchard, 1. c., p. 588). Accordingly the Egyptian Government need not refer to the rule of "effective nationality" to oppose the American claim if they can only bring evidence that Salem was an Egyptian subject and that he acquired the American nationality without the express consent of the Egyptian Government.

. . . In the opinion of the Arbitral Court the Egyptian Government is unable to bring such evidence. Indeed from the circumstances it must be assumed that Salem was not an Egyptian subject but a Persian subject when he acquired American nationality. . . .

It is beside the point to ask whether Salem lost his Persian nationality or not by the acquisition of American nationality. . . . Whatever may be the true interpretation, the Egyptian Government cannot set forth against the United States the eventual continuation of the Persian nationality of George Salem; the rule of international law being that in a case of dual nationality a third power is not entitled to contest the claim of one of the two powers whose national is interested in the case by referring to the nationality of the other power.

Note
Could Italy have brought its claim against Peru in the *Canevaro* case according to the Tribunal in the *Salem* case? Could Peru have claimed against Italy?

MERGÉ CLAIM

Italian-United States Conciliation Commission: Yanguas Messia, Matturri, Sorentino. (1955) 22 I.L.R. 443

As in the *Flegenheimer Claim* (above, p. 596), the United States brought this claim under the 1947 Italian Peace Treaty. In this case the problem was that the claimant

---

[83] Nielsen dissenting.

was of both United States and Italian nationality. Having determined that the treaty, which permitted claims on behalf of "United Nations nationals," who included United States nationals, contained no provisions governing the case of dual nationality, the Commission decided that the question whether the United States could bring the claim against Italy must be decided according to "the general principles of international law."

Opinion of the Commission

(1) The rules of the Hague Convention of 1930[84] and the customary law manifested in international precedents and in the legal writings of the authors attest the existence and the practice of two principles in the problem of diplomatic protection in dual nationality cases. The first of these, specifically referring to the scope of diplomatic protection, as a question of public international law, is based on the sovereign equality of the States in the matter of nationality and bars protection in behalf of those who are simultaneously also nationals of the defendant State. The second of the principles had its origin in *private* international law, in those cases, that is, in which the courts of a third State had to resolve a conflict of nationality law. Thus, the principle of effective nationality was created with relation to the individual. But decisions and legal writings, because of its evident justice, quickly transported it to the sphere of *public* international law.

(2) It is not a question of adopting one nationality to the exclusion of the other. Even less when it is recognized by both Parties that the claimant possesses the two nationalities. The problem to be explained is, simply, that of determining whether diplomatic protection can be exercised in such cases.

(3) ... The Commission is of the opinion that no irreconcilable opposition between the two principles exists; in fact, to the contrary, it believes that they complement each other reciprocally. The principle according to which a State cannot protect one of its nationals against a State which also considers him its national and the principle of effective, in the sense of dominant, nationality, have both been accepted by the Hague Convention (Articles 4 and 5) and by the International Court of Justice (Advisory Opinion of April 11, 1949,[85] and the *Nottebohm* decision of April 6, 1955). If these two principles were irreconcilable, the acceptance of both by the Hague Convention and by the International Court of Justice would be incomprehensible ... .

(5) The principle, based on the sovereign equality of States, which excludes diplomatic protection in the case of dual nationality, must yield before the principle of effective nationality whenever such nationality is that of the claiming State. But it must not yield when such predominance is not proved, because the first of these two principles is generally

[84] *Ed.* See above, p. 586.
[85] *Ed. Reparation* case, above p. 132.

recognized and may constitute a criterion of practical application for the elimination of any possible uncertainty.

(6) The question of dual nationality obviously arises only in cases where the claimant was in possession of both nationalities at the time the damage occurred and during the whole of the period comprised between the date of the Armistice (September 3, 1943) and the date of the coming into force of the Treaty of Peace (September 15, 1947). In view of the principles accepted, it is considered that the Government of the United States of America shall be entitled to protect its nationals before this Commission in cases of dual nationality, United States and Italian, whenever the United States nationality is the effective nationality. In order to establish the prevalence of the United States nationality in individual cases, habitual residence can be one of the criteria of evaluation, but not the only one. The conduct of the individual in his economic, social, political, civic and family life, as well as the closer and more effective bond with one of the two States must also be considered.

The Commission applied this test to the facts before it and found that the claimant failed to satisfy it.

Notes

The Rules regarding International Claims issued by the British Foreign and Commonwealth Office in 1985[86] read:

Rule III

Where the claimant is a dual national, Her Majesty's Government may take up his claim (although in certain circumstances it may be appropriate for Her Majesty's Government to do so jointly with the other government entitled to do so). Her Majesty's Government will not normally take up his claim as a United Kingdom national if the respondent state is the state of his second nationality, but may do so if the respondent state has, in the circumstances which gave rise to the injury, treated the claimant as a United Kingdom national.

IRAN–UNITED STATES No. A/18

Iran-US Claims Tribunal. Full Tribunal. (1984) 5 Iran-U.S.C.T.R. 251

A large number of claims having been brought against Iran by dual Iranian-U.S. nationals, the full tribunal was called upon to decide whether it had jurisdiction to hear such claims. Finding the text of the Iranian-U.S. Claims Settlement Declaration (one of the Algiers Declarations) insufficiently clear, the Tribunal examined the position in customary international law. The Tribunal first considered the impact of the 1930 Hague Convention, above, p. 586.

---

[86] *loc. cit.*, p. 595, n. 78, above.

Decision of the Tribunal

Article 4 of the [Hague] Convention . . . must be interpreted very cautiously. Not only is it more than 50 years old and found in a treaty to which only 20 States are parties, but great changes have occurred since then in the concept of diplomatic protection. . . . This concept continues to be in a process of transformation, and it is necessary to distinguish between different types of protection, whether consular or claims-related.

Moreover, the negotiating history of Article 4 of the Hague Convention suggests that its application is doubtful in a case, such as the present one, where a dual national, by himself, brings before an international tribunal his own claim against one of the States whose nationality he possesses. Such a proposal was made during the Conference, but it was rejected. . . .

Another reason why the applicability of Article 4 to the claims of dual nationals before this Tribunal is debatable is that it applies by its own terms solely to "diplomatic protection" by a State. While this Tribunal is clearly an international tribunal established by treaty and while some of its cases involve disputes between the two Governments and involve the interpretation and application of public international law, most disputes (including all of those brought by dual nationals) involve a private party on one side and a Government or Government-controlled entity on the other, and many involve primarily issues of municipal law and general principles of law. In such cases it is the rights of the claimant, not of his nation, that are to be determined by the Tribunal. This should be contrasted with the situation of espousal of claims in international law. . . .

In this field, there is a considerable number of relevant judicial and arbitral decisions, most of them prior to the Second World War, supplemented and interpreted by the writing of scholars. The writing of at least one scholar, Professor E. M. Borchard,[87] apparently had a considerable . . . influence on the . . . 1930 Convention . . . . In fact, the precedents on which Borchard relied did not generally support his conclusion [adopted in Article 4], and the Parties in the present case have acknowledged that the law prior to 1930 was uncertain. . . . The Tribunal . . . is satisfied that, whatever the state of the law prior to 1945, the better rule at the time the Algiers Declarations were concluded and today is the rule of dominant and effective nationality.

The two most important decisions on the subject in the years following the Second World War have had a decisive effect. . . .

While *Nottebohm* itself did not involve a claim against a State of which Nottebohm was a national, it demonstrated the acceptance and approval by the International Court of Justice of the search for the real and effective nationality based on the facts of a case, instead of an approach relying on

---

[87] *Ed. See* Borchard, *The Diplomatic Protection of Citizens Abroad* (1927), p. 588.

more formalistic criteria. The effects of the *Nottebohm* decision have radiated throughout the international law of nationality.

A few months later . . . the Italian-United States Conciliation Commission . . . decided in the *Mergé Case* that the principle " . . . based on the sovereign equality of States, which excludes diplomatic protection in the case of dual nationality, must yield before the principle of effective nationality whenever such nationality is that of the claiming State." . . .

Support for the principles applied in these cases is shared by some of the most competent international lawyers. . . . [88]

This trend toward modification of the Hague Convention rule of nonresponsibility by search for the dominant and effective nationality is scarcely surprising as it is consistent with the contemporaneous development of international law to accord legal protections to individuals, even against the State of which they are nationals. . . .

For the reasons stated above, the Tribunal holds that it has jurisdiction over claims against Iran by dual Iran-United States nationals when the dominant and effective nationality of the claimant during the relevant period from the date the claim arose until 19 January 1981 was that of the United States. In determining the dominant and effective nationality, the Tribunal will consider all relevant factors, including habitual residence, center of interests, family ties, participation in public life and other evidence of attachment.

Note

The Tribunal's decision was taken by 6 votes to 3, with the 3 Iranian national arbitrators dissenting. One of the tribunal chamber cases that led to the matter being referred to the full tribunal was *Esphahanian v. Bank Tejarat*.[89] There the effective nationality test was applied to the facts in the following passage from the Chamber's award:

Esphahanian's contacts with the United States[90] were long and consistent. He has resided in the United States since 1946. He served in the United States armed forces. He became an American citizen in 1958. He is married to an American woman, and they have two children who are American, speak no Farsi and have been educated solely in American schools. . . . He bought four residences in the United States between 1957 and 1979. Since becoming a citizen of the United States, Esphahanian has paid United States taxes and has voted in United States elections, even during the years 1970–78 when he was outside the United States most of the year.

Esphahanian's contacts with Iran since he went to the United States to study have been significant, but much more limited. Aside from contact with relatives still living in Iran, he has made many visits to Iran, has retained his Iranian passport, and most important, had his principal residence there for approximately nine months of each of the years 1970–77 where his family lived

---

[88] The Tribunal refers, *inter alia*, to Brownlie, p. 399; Donner, *op. cit.*, p. 586, n. 67, above, p. 95; and Leigh (1971) 20 I.C.L.Q. 453.

[89] (1983) 2 Iran–U.S. C.T.R. 157.

[90] *Ed.* The claimant was born in Iran of Iranian descent and lived there until he left at the age of 17 to study in the U.S.

while the children attended the American school in Tehran. The evidence presented shows that his American employer required him to divide his time among a number of countries in the Middle East and paid all of his and his family's living expenses. In effect, he operated out of Iran and spent only about one-third of his time there. The evidence also shows that the family returned to the United States each year for the summer months and, thus, maintained a secondary residence there. Esphahanian paid (or his employer paid for him) taxes to Iran on that part of his salary attributable to his work in Iran, whereas his US taxes were based on his total salary.

In this connection, the Tribunal is troubled by the evidence that Esphahanian was the nominal owner of a number of shares of stock in the Iran Marine Industrial Co. The beneficial owner was SEDCO [the claimant's employer], and it is possible, if not certain, that Esphahanian was made SEDCO'S nominee because he had Iranian nationality and could be used to disguise the true extent of SEDCO'S ownership. This is the kind of use of a second nationality that may cause the Tribunal to deny a claim, but in this case there is no evidence that his allowing his employer to use him as its nominee shareholder was a substantial part of his job. Thus, it does not seem that the Claimant used that subterfuge in a significant way to obtain benefits available only to Iranian nationals for which he is now claiming.

On the basis of these facts, the Tribunal concludes that Esphahanian's dominant and effective nationality at all relevant times has been that of the United States, and the funds at issue in the present claim are related primarily to his American nationality, not his Iranian nationality. With the exceptions of his use of an Iranian passport to enter and leave Iran[91] and his nominal ownership of stock on behalf of his employer, all of his actions relevant to this claim could have been done by a non-Iranian.

The Chamber then made an award in favour of the claimant for the amount due to him on a dishonoured cheque.

(c) *Protection of Companies and Shareholders*

BARCELONA TRACTION, LIGHT AND POWER CO. CASE[92]

Belgium *v.* Spain

I.C.J. Reports 1970, p. 3

The company concerned was established under Canadian law in 1911 in connection with the development of electricity supplies in Spain. In 1948, it was declared bankrupt by a Spanish court and, at about the same time, other steps were taken by Spanish authorities injuring it. Canada intervened on its behalf to begin with but later withdrew. At all relevant times, 88 per cent of the shares in the company were, Belgium claimed, owned by Belgian nationals. Belgium brought this claim in respect of the injury to its nationals who were shareholders resulting from the injury to the company. Spain objected that since the injury was to the company,

---

[91] *Ed.* With respect to the claimant's use of an Iranian passport, the Tribunal noted that "the laws of Iran in effect forced such use" since he would not have been admitted to Iran on a U.S. passport. It also noted that if the claimant had renounced his Iranian nationality, he would have only been allowed one further visit to Iran to settle his affairs.

[92] See Briggs (1971) 65 A.J.I.L. 327; Higgins (1971) 11 Virg. J.I.L. 327; Lillich (1971) 65 A.J.I.L. 522; Staker (1990) 61 B.Y.I.L. 155.

not the shareholders, Belgium lacked *locus standi* to bring the claim. In a judgment in 1964,[93] the Court joined this preliminary objection to the merits.

Judgment of the Court

33. When a State admits into its territory foreign investments or foreign nationals, whether natural or juristic persons, it is bound to extend to them the protection of the law and assumes obligations concerning the treatment to be afforded them. These obligations, however, are neither absolute nor unqualified. In particular, an essential distinction should be drawn between the obligations of a State towards the international community as a whole, and those arising *vis-à-vis* another State in the field of diplomatic protection. By their very nature the former are the concern of all States. In view of the importance of the rights involved, all States can be held to have a legal interest in their protection; they are obligations *erga omnes*.

34. Such obligations derive, for example, in contemporary international law, from the outlawing of acts of aggression, and of genocide, as also from the principles and rules concerning basic rights of the human person including protection from slavery and racial discrimination. Some of the corresponding rights of protection have entered into the body of general international law (*Reservations to the Convention on the Prevention and Punishment of the Crime of Genocide, Advisory Opinion, I.C.J. Reports* 1951, p. 23); others are conferred by international instruments of a universal or quasi-universal character.

35. Obligations the performance of which is the subject of diplomatic protection are not of the same category. It cannot be held, when one such obligation in particular is in question, in a specific case, that all States have a legal interest in its observance. In order to bring a claim in respect of the breach of such an obligation, a State must first establish its right to do so, for the rules on the subject rest on two suppositions:

> The first is that the defendant State had broken an obligation towards the national State in respect of its nationals. The second is that only the party to whom an international obligation is due can bring a claim in respect of its breach. (*Reparation for Injuries Suffered in the Service of the United Nations, Advisory Opinion, I.C.J. Reports* 1949, pp. 181–182).

In the present case it is therefore essential to establish whether the losses allegedly suffered by Belgian shareholders in Barcelona Traction were the consequence of the violation of obligations of which they were the beneficiaries. In other words: has a right of Belgium been violated on account of its nationals' having suffered infringement of their rights as shareholders in a company not of Belgian nationality?

[93] I.C.J. Rep. 1964, p. 6.

36. Thus it is the existence or absence of a right, belonging to Belgium and recognized as such by international law, which is decisive for the problem of Belgium's capacity. . . .

38. In this field international law is called upon to recognize institutions of municipal law that have an important and extensive role in the international field. . . .

41. . . . The concept and structure of the [limited liability] company are founded on and determined by a firm distinction between the separate entity of the company and that of the shareholder, each with a distinct set of rights. The separation of property rights as between company and shareholder is an important manifestation of this distinction. So long as the company is in existence the shareholder has no right to the corporate assets. . . .

44. Notwithstanding the separate corporate personality, a wrong done to the company frequently causes prejudice to its shareholders. But the mere fact that damage is sustained by both company and shareholder does not imply that both are entitled to claim compensation. . . . Thus whenever a shareholder's interests are harmed by an act done to the company, it is to the latter that he must look to institute appropriate action; for although two separate entities may have suffered from the same wrong, it is only one entity whose rights have been infringed. . . .

47. The situation is different if the act complained of is aimed at the direct rights of the shareholder as such. It is well known that there are rights which municipal law confers upon the latter distinct from those of the company, including the right to any declared dividend, the right to attend and vote at general meetings, the right to share in the residual assets of the company on liquidation. Whenever one of his direct rights is infringed, the shareholder has an independent right of action. . . .

48. The Belgian Government claims that shareholders of Belgian nationality suffered damage in consequence of unlawful acts of the Spanish authorities and, in particular, that the Barcelona Traction shares, though they did not cease to exist, were emptied of all real economic content. It accordingly contends that the shareholders had an independent right to redress, notwithstanding the fact that the acts complained of were directed against the company as such. Thus the legal issue is reducible to the question of whether it is legitimate to identify an attack on company rights, resulting in damage to shareholders, with the violation of their direct rights. . . .

50. In turning now to the international legal aspects of the case, the Court must, as already indicated, start from the fact that the present case essentially involves factors derived from municipal law—the distinction and the community between the company and the shareholder—which the Parties, however widely their interpretations may differ, each take as the point of departure of their reasoning. If the Court were to decide the case in disregard of the relevant institutions of municipal law it would, without justification, invite serious legal difficulties. It would lose touch

with reality, for there are no corresponding institutions of international law to which the Court could resort. Thus the Court has, as indicated, not only to take cognizance of municipal law but also to refer to it. It is to rules generally accepted by municipal legal systems which recognize the limited company whose capital is represented by shares, and not to the municipal law of a particular State, that international law refers. In referring to such rules, the Court cannot modify, still less deform them.

51. On the international plane, the Belgian Government has advanced the proposition that it is inadmissible to deny the shareholder's national State a right of diplomatic protection merely on the ground that another State possesses a corresponding right in respect of the company itself. In strict logic and law this formulation of the Belgian claim to *jus standi* assumes the existence of the very right that requires demonstration. In fact the Belgian Government has repeatedly stressed that there exists no rule of international law which would deny the national State of the shareholders the right of diplomatic protection for the purpose of seeking redress pursuant to unlawful acts committed by another State against the company in which they hold shares. This, by emphasizing the absence of any express denial of the right, conversely implies the admission that there is no rule of international law which expressly confers such a right on the shareholders' national State.

52. International law may not, in some fields, provide specific rules in particular cases. In the concrete situation, the company against which allegedly unlawful acts were directed is expressly vested with a right, whereas no such right is specifically provided for the shareholder in respect of those acts. Thus the position of the company rests on a positive rule of both municipal and international law. As to the shareholder, while he has certain rights expressly provided for him by municipal law . . . , appeal can, in the circumstances of the present case, only be made to the silence of international law. Such silence scarcely admits of interpretation in favour of the shareholder.

53. It is quite true, as was recalled in the course of oral argument in the present case, that concurrent claims are not excluded in the case of a person who, having entered the service of an international organization and retained his nationality, enjoys simultaneously the right to be protected by his national State and the right to be protected by the organization to which he belongs. This however is a case of one person in possession of two separate bases of protection, each of which is valid (*Reparation for Injuries Suffered in the Service of the United Nations, Advisory Opinion, I.C.J. Reports* 1949, p. 185). There is no analogy between such a situation and that of foreign shareholders in a company which has been the victim of a violation of international law which has caused them damage. . . .

55. The Court will now examine other grounds on which it is conceivable that the submission by the Belgian Government of a claim on behalf of shareholders in Barcelona Traction may be justified. . . .

The Court then refers to municipal law again and the practice of "lifting the veil" for some purposes to take account of the identity of persons behind the company.

58. In accordance with the principle expounded above, the process of lifting the veil, being an exceptional one admitted by municipal law in respect of an institution of its own making, is equally admissible to play a similar role in international law. It follows that on the international plane also there may in principle be special circumstances which justify the lifting of the veil in the interest of shareholders. . . .

64. . . . In this connection two particular situations must be studied: the case of the company having ceased to exist and the case of the company's national State lacking capacity to take action on its behalf.

65. As regards the first of these possibilities the Court observes that . . . Barcelona Traction has lost all its assets in Spain, and was placed in receivership in Canada, a receiver and manager having been appointed. It is common ground that from the economic viewpoint the company has been entirely paralyzed. . . .

66. It cannot however, be contended that the corporate entity of the company has ceased to exist, or that it has lost its capacity to take corporate action. . . . It has not become incapable in law of defending its own rights and the interests of the shareholders. In particular, a precarious financial situation cannot be equated with the demise of the corporate entity, which is the hypothesis under consideration: the company's status in law is alone relevant, and not its economic condition, nor even the possibility of its being "practically defunct"—a description on which argument has been based but which lacks all legal precision. Only in the event of the legal demise of the company are the shareholders deprived of the possibility of a remedy available through the company; it is only if they became deprived of all such possibility that an independent right of action for them and their government could arise.

67. In the present case, Barcelona Traction is in receivership in the country of incorporation. Far from implying the demise of the entity or of its rights, this much rather denotes that those rights are preserved for so long as no liquidation has ensued. Though in receivership, the company continues to exist. Moreover, it is a matter of public record that the company's shares were quoted on the stock-market at a recent date.

68. . . . The Court is thus not confronted with the first hypothesis contemplated in paragraph 64, and need not pronounce upon it.

69. The Court will now turn to the second possibility, that of the lack of capacity of the company's national State to act on its behalf. The first question which must be asked here is whether Canada—the third apex of the triangular relationship—is, in law, the national State of Barcelona Traction.

70. In allocating corporate entities to States for purposes of diplomatic protection, international law is based, but only to a limited extent, on an

analogy with the rules governing the nationality of individuals. The traditional rule attributes the right of diplomatic protection of a corporate entity to the State under the laws of which it is incorporated and in whose territory it has its registered office. These two criteria have been confirmed by long practice and by numerous international instruments. This notwithstanding, further or different links are at times said to be required in order that a right of diplomatic protection should exist. Indeed, it has been the practice of some States to give a company incorporated under their law diplomatic protection solely when it has its seat (*siège social*) or management or centre of control in their territory, or when a majority or a substantial proportion of the shares has been owned by nationals of the State concerned. Only then, it has been held, does there exist between the corporation and the State in question a genuine connection of the kind familiar from other branches of international law. However, in the particular field of the diplomatic protection of corporate entities, no absolute test of the "genuine connection" has found general acceptance. Such tests as have been applied are of a relative nature, and sometimes links with one State have had to be weighed against those with another. In this connection reference has been made to the *Nottebohm* case.[94] . . . However, given both the legal and factual aspects of protection in the present case the Court is of the opinion that there can be no analogy with the issues raised or the decision given in that case.

71. In the present case, it is not disputed that the company was incorporated in Canada and has its registered office in that country. The incorporation of the company under the law of Canada was an act of free choice. Not only did the founders of the company seek its corporation under Canadian law but it has remained under that law for a period of over 50 years. It has maintained in Canada its registered office, its accounts and its share registers. Board meetings were held there for many years; it has been listed in the records of the Canadian tax authorities. Thus a close and permanent connection has been established, fortified by the passage of over half a century. This connection is in no way weakened by the fact that the company engaged from the very outset in commercial activities outside Canada, for that was its declared object. Barcelona Traction's links with Canada are thus manifold.

72. Furthermore, the Canadian nationality of the company has received general recognition. Prior to the institution of proceedings before the Court, three other governments apart from that of Canada (those of the United Kingdom, the United States and Belgium) made representations concerning the treatment accorded to Barcelona Traction by the Spanish authorities. The United Kingdom Government intervened on behalf of bondholders and of shareholders. Several representations were also made by the United States Government, but not on behalf of the Barcelona Traction company as such. . . .

---

[94] *Ed.* See above, p. 588.

73. Both Governments acted at certain stages in close co-operation with the Canadian Government. . . .

74. As to the Belgian Government, its earlier action was also undertaken in close co-operation with the Canadian Government. The Belgian Government admitted the Canadian character of the company in the course of the present proceedings. It explicity stated that Barcelona Traction was a company of neither Spanish nor Belgian nationality but a Canadian company incorporated in Canada. The Belgian Government has even conceded that it was not concerned with the injury suffered by Barcelona Traction itself, since that was Canada's affair. . . .

76. In sum, the record shows that from 1948 onwards the Canadian Government made to the Spanish Government numerous representations which cannot be viewed otherwise than as the exercise of diplomatic protection in respect of the Barcelona Traction company. Therefore this was not a case where diplomatic protection was refused or remained in the sphere of fiction. It is also clear that over the whole period of its diplomatic activity the Canadian Government proceeded in full knowledge of the Belgian attitude and activity.

77. It is true that at a certain point the Canadian Government ceased to act on behalf of Barcelona Traction, for reasons which have not been fully revealed, though a statement made in a letter of July 19, 1955 by the Canadian Secretary of State for External Affairs suggests that it felt the matter should be settled by means of private negotiations.[95] The Canadian Government has nonetheless retained its capacity to exercise diplomatic protection; no legal impediment has prevented it from doing so: no fact has arisen to render this protection impossible. It has discontinued its action of its own free will.

78. The Court would here observe that, within the limits prescribed by international law, a State may exercise diplomatic protection by whatever means and to whatever extent it thinks fit, for it is its own right that the State is asserting. Should the natural or legal persons on whose behalf it is acting consider that their rights are not adequately protected, they have no remedy in international law. All they can do is to resort to municipal law, if means are available, with a view to furthering their cause or obtaining redress. The municipal legislator may lay upon the State an obligation to protect its citizens abroad, and may also confer upon the national a right to demand the performance of that obligation, and clothe the right with corresponding sanctions. However, all these questions remain within the province of municipal law and do not affect the position internationally.

---

[95] *Ed.* "By late 1951 the Canadian Secretary of State for External Affairs told the Spanish Consul in Canada that 'Canadian interests in this case are so slight that it is of little interest to us' ": *Barcelona Traction Case (Preliminary Objections)*, Separate Opinion of Judge Wellington Koo, I.C.J. Rep. 1964, pp. 61–62.

79. The State must be viewed as the sole judge to decide whether its protection will be granted, to what extent it is granted, and when it will cease. It remains in this respect a discretionary power the exercise of which may be determined by considerations of a political or other nature, unrelated to the particular case. Since the claim of the State is not identical with that of the individual or corporate person whose cause is espoused, the State enjoys complete freedom of action. Whatever the reasons for any change of attitude, the fact cannot in itself constitute a justification for the exercise of diplomatic protection by another government, unless there is some independent and otherwise valid ground for that. . . .

81. The cessation by the Canadian Government of the diplomatic protection of Barcelona Traction cannot, then, be interpreted to mean that there is no remedy against the Spanish Government for the damage done by the allegedly unlawful acts of the Spanish authorities. . . . Therefore there is no substance in the argument that for the Belgian Government to bring a claim before the Court represented the only possibility of obtaining redress for the damage suffered by Barcelona Traction and, through it, by its shareholders. . . .

83. The Canadian Government's right of protection in respect of the Barcelona Traction company remains unaffected by the present proceedings. The Spanish Government has never challenged the Canadian nationality of the company, either in the diplomatic correspondence with the Canadian Government or before the Court. Moreover it has unreservedly recognized Canada as the national State of Barcelona Traction in both written pleadings and oral statements made in the course of the present proceedings. Consequently, the Court considers that the Spanish Government has not questioned Canada's right to protect the company. . . .

92. Since the general rule on the subject does not entitle the Belgian Government to put forward a claim in the case, the question remains to be considered whether nonetheless, as the Belgian Government has contended during the proceedings, considerations of equity do not require that it be held to possess a right of protection . . . a theory has been developed to the effect that the State of the shareholders has a right of diplomatic protection when the State whose responsibility is invoked is the national State of the company. Whatever the validity of this theory may be, it is certainly not applicable to the present case, since Spain is not the national State of Barcelona Traction.

93. On the other hand, the Court considers that, in the field of diplomatic protection as in all other fields of international law, it is necessary that the law be applied reasonably. It has been suggested that if in a given case it is not possible to apply the general rule that the right of diplomatic protection of a company belongs to its national State, considerations of equity might call for the possibility of protection of the shareholders in question by their own national State. This hypothesis does not correspond to the circumstances of the present case.

94. In view, however, of the discretionary nature of diplomatic protection, considerations of equity cannot require more than the possibility for some protector State to intervene, whether it be the national State of the company, by virtue of the general rule mentioned above, or, in a secondary capacity, the national State of the shareholders who claim protection. In this connection, account should also be taken of the practical effects of deducing from considerations of equity any broader right of protection for the national State of the shareholders. It must first of all be observed that it would be difficult on an equitable basis to make distinctions according to any quantitative test: it would seem that the owner of 1 per cent and the owner of 90 per cent of the share-capital should have the same possibility of enjoying the benefit of diplomatic protection. The protector State may, of course, be disinclined to take up the case of a single small shareholder, but it could scarcely be denied the right to do so in the name of equitable considerations. In that field, protection by the national State of the shareholders can hardly be graduated according to the absolute or relative size of the shareholding involved. . . .

96. The Court considers that the adoption of the theory of diplomatic protection of shareholders as such, by opening the door of competing diplomatic claims, could create an atmosphere of confusion and insecurity in international economic relations. The danger would be all the greater inasmuch as the shares of companies whose activity is international are widely scattered and frequently change hands. It might perhaps be claimed that, if the right of protection belonging to the national States of the shareholders were considered as only secondary to that of the national State of the company, there would be less danger of difficulties of the kind contemplated. However, the Court must state that the essence of a secondary right is that it only comes into existence at the time when the original right ceases to exist. As the right of protection vested in the national State of the company cannot be regarded as extinguished because it is not exercised, it is not possible to accept the proposition that in case of its non-exercise the national States of the shareholders have a right of protection secondary to that of the national State of the company. Furthermore, study of factual situations in which this theory might possibly be applied gives rise to the following observations.

97. The situations in which foreign shareholders in a company wish to have recourse to diplomatic protection by their own national State may vary. It may happen that the national State of the company simply refuses to grant it its diplomatic protection, or that it begins to exercise it (as in the present case) but does not pursue its action to the end. It may also happen that the national State of the company and the State which has committed a violation of international law with regard to the company arrive at a settlement of the matter, by agreeing on compensation for the company, but that the foreign shareholders find the compensation insufficient. Now, as a matter of principle, it would be difficult to draw a distinction between these three cases so far as the protection of foreign

shareholders by their national State is concerned, since in each case they may have suffered real damage. Furthermore, the national State of the company is perfectly free to decide how far it is appropriate for it to protect the company, and is not bound to make public the reasons for its decision. To reconcile this discretionary power of the company's national State with a right of protection falling to the shareholders' national State would be particularly difficult when the former State has concluded, with the State which has contravened international law with regard to the company, an agreement granting the company compensation which the foreign shareholders find inadequate. If, after such a settlement, the national State of the foreign shareholders could in its turn put forward a claim based on the same facts, this would be likely to introduce into the negotiation of this kind of agreement a lack of security which would be contrary to the stability which it is the object of international law to establish in international relations.

98. It is quite true, as recalled in paragraph 53, that international law recognizes parallel rights of protection in the case of a person in the service of an international organization. Nor is the possibility excluded of concurrent claims being made on behalf of persons having dual nationality, although in that case lack of a genuine link with one of the two States may be set up against the exercise by that State of the right of protection. It must be observed, however, that in these two types of situation the number of possible protectors is necessarily very small, and their identity normally not difficult to determine. In this respect such cases of dual protection are markedly different from the claims to which recognition of a general right of protection of foreign shareholders by their various national States might give rise.

99. It should also be observed that the promoters of a company whose operations will be international must take into account the fact that States have, with regard to their nationals, a discretionary power to grant diplomatic protection or to refuse it. When establishing a company in a foreign country, its promoters are normally impelled by particular considerations; it is often a question of tax or other advantages offered by the host State. It does not seem to be in any way inequitable that the advantages thus obtained should be balanced by the risks arising from the fact that the protection of the company and hence of its shareholders is thus entrusted to a State other than the national State of the shareholders.

100. In the present case, it is clear from what has been said above that Barcelona Traction was never reduced to a position of impotence such that it could not have approached its national State, Canada, to ask for its diplomatic protection, and that, as far as appeared to the Court, there was nothing to prevent Canada from continuing to grant its diplomatic protection to Barcelona Traction if it had considered that it should do so.

101. For the above reasons, the Court is not of the opinion that, in the particular circumstances of the present case, *jus standi* is conferred on the Belgian Government by considerations of equity. . . .

103. Accordingly, the Court rejects the Belgian Government's claim by fifteen votes to one, twelve votes of the majority being based on the reasons set out in the present Judgment.[96]

Notes

1. *The Protection of Companies*.[97] The Barcelona Traction Company continued legally in existence, although it did not trade, until 1980 when it was dissolved under Canadian law. It would seem to have been understood by states before the *Nottebohm* case that they could protect any company having their nationality according to their law. In 1911, for example, when it became known that the Government of Siam, in interpreting a treaty between Siam and the United Kingdom guaranteeing "British subjects" national treatment in respect of land in Siam, was of a mind to treat British companies, to which the treaty undoubtedly extended, differently from other British subjects because non-British interests were incorporating British companies in order to take advantage of its terms, the Foreign Office responded in the following terms: "The Siamese Government could not be permitted to maintain that a company, duly incorporated as British, was really foreign and that His Majesty's Government had no right to protect it."[98] Is this attitude supported by the *Barcelona Traction* case? Note that the Rules regarding International Claims[99] issued by the British Foreign and Commonwealth Office after that case read:

Rule IV

Her Majesty's Government may take up the claim of a corporation or other juridical person which is created and regulated by the law of the United Kingdom or of any territory for which Her Majesty's Government are internationally responsible.

Comment

This rule rests on the principle that a juridical person (such as a company, corporation or other association having a legal personality distinct from its members), has the nationality of that country whose law has formally created it, which regulates its constitution and under whose law it can be wound up or dissolved. This principle was endorsed by the International Court of Justice in the *Barcelona Traction* case (*Belgium v. Spain*) in 1970. Certain states determine nationality of a corporation by different tests: the place of central administration (*siège social*) or the place of effective control (to determine which, the residence of the majority of shareholders as well as of the directors may be taken into account). The International Court however said that not one of these tests of "genuine connexion" has found general international acceptance.

In determining whether to exercise its right of protection, Her Majesty's Government may consider whether the company has in fact a real and substantial connexion with the United Kingdom.

---

[96] The judges in the majority were President Bustamante y Rivero; Vice-President Koretsky; Judges Sir Gerald Fitzmaurice, Tanaka, Jessup, Morelli, Padilla Nervo, Forster, Gros, Ammoun, Bengzon, Petrén, Lachs and Onyeama; Judge *ad hoc* Armand-Ugon. The dissenting judge was Judge *ad hoc* Riphagen. The three judges in the majority who did not concur in the reasoning of the Court were Judges Tanaka, Jessup and Gros.

[97] See Beckett (1931) 17 Trans.Grot.Soc. 175 and Harris (1969) 18 I.C.L.Q. 275.

[98] (1911) 5 B.D.I.L. 510 at 511.

[99] *loc. cit.*, p. 595, n. 78, above.

2. *Protection of Shareholders.*[1] Do you find the reasons given by the Court for rejecting the argument for a secondary power of protection on the part of the national state of shareholders in a foreign company when the national state of the company will not act convincing? Should the case be regarded as indicating one situation in which the general rule of protection in international law, leaving the interests of individuals as a discretionary matter in the hands of their national state, can lead to injustice? The Court suggests in its judgment (para. 99) that the promoters of companies should take into account the risk of non-protection as well as considerations such as tax advantage. Is the Court also suggesting that persons thinking of investing in foreign companies should bear in mind the same factor?

In 1925, in the *Romano-Americana* case,[2] the United States sought compensation from the United Kingdom for the destruction in 1916 of the assets in Roumania of a Roumanian subsidiary company of an American parent company. The assets had been destroyed by "the Roumanian authorities with the collaboration of certain British Officers acting under instructions from the British Government"[3] to prevent them coming into the hands of the enemy. In denying responsibility, the United Kingdom argued: " . . . it will be found upon examination that the cases in which the right of a Government to intervene on behalf of the shareholders of such a corporation for the purpose of establishing a claim against another Government, has been admitted, are few in number and exhibit certain marked characteristics, none of which are present in the case now under consideration. Cases of this kind fall generally speaking into two cases: (1) where the action of the Government against whom the claim is made has, in law or in fact, put an end to the Company's existence, or by confiscating its property, has compelled it to suspend operations; (2) where by special agreement between the two Governments a right to compensation has been accorded to the shareholders. . . . The first class, so far from being an exception to the general rule, is in fact an example of its application; for it is not until a company has ceased to have an active existence or has gone into liquidation that the interest of its shareholders ceases to be merely the right to share in the company's profits and becomes a right to share in its actual surplus assets."[4] The United States later discontinued its claim against the United Kingdom and took up its case against Roumania, which eventually agreed to pay compensation. Is the British argument consistent with the Court's judgment?[5]

In 1938, in the *Mexican Eagle Co.* case,[6] Mexico expropriated the assets of an oil company registered in Mexico the shares in which were almost entirely foreign owned. When Mexico protested at British intervention on behalf of the substantial British interests in the company, the United Kingdom replied: "If the doctrine were admitted that a government can first make the operation of foreign interests in its territories depend upon their incorporation under local law, and then plead such incorporation as the justification for rejecting foreign diplomatic intervention, it is clear that the means would never be wanting whereby foreign governments could be prevented from exercising their undoubted right under

---

[1] See Jones (1949) 26 B.Y.I.L. 225.
[2] 5 Hackworth 840.
[3] *ibid.* p. 841.
[4] *ibid.* p. 843.
[5] Note also that in 1889, in the *Delagoa Bay* case, the U.K. and the U.S. successfully intervened to protect Anglo-American shareholders in a Portuguese company on the ground that the Portuguese company was "practically defunct": (1888–89) B.F.S.P. 691. Was *this* consistent with the Court's judgment?
[6] Cmd. 5758, p. 9.

international law to protect the commercial interests of their nationals abroad."
Eventually arrangements for the payment of compensation were made. Does the
Court's judgment leave open the possibility that the British argument here would
be acceptable to it? See para. 92, judgment. Note that several of the judges
delivering separate, concurring opinions express the view that a state could
protect its shareholders in a foreign company where the defendant state is the
national state of the company.[7]

The Rules regarding International Claims[8] issued by the British Foreign and
Commonwealth Office after the *Barcelona Traction* case read:

Rule V

Where a United Kingdom national has an interest, as a shareholder or otherwise, in a company incorporated in another state, and that company is injured
by the acts of a third state, Her Majesty's Government may normally take up
his claim only in concert with the government of the state in which the
company is incorporated. Exceptionally, as where the company is defunct,
there may be independent intervention.

Rule VI

Where a United Kingdom national has an interest, as a shareholder or otherwise, in a company incorporated in another state and of which it is therefore
a national, and that state injures the company, Her Majesty's Government may
intervene to protect the interests of that United Kingdom national.

Comment

In some cases the state of incorporation of a company does not possess the
primary national interest in the company. A company may be created for
reasons of legal or economic advantage under the law of one state though
nearly all the capital is owned by nationals of another. In such circumstances,
the state in which the company is incorporated may have little interest in
protecting it, while the state to which the nationals who own the capital belong
has considerable interest in so doing. In the *Barcelona Traction* case the International Court of Justice denied the existence under customary international
law of an inherent right for the national state of shareholders in a foreign
company to exercise diplomatic protection. However, the majority of the Court
accepted the existence of a right to protect shareholders in the two cases
described in Rules V and VI (when the company is defunct, and where the
state in which the company is incorporated, although theoretically the legal
protector of the company, itself causes injury to the company).

Where the capital in a foreign company is owned in various proportions by
nationals of several states, including the United Kingdom, it is unusual for Her
Majesty's Government to make representations unless the states whose nationals hold the bulk of the capital will support them in making representations.

---

[7] Judge Sir Gerald Fitzmaurice, I.C.J. Rep 1970, p. 73; Judge Tanaka, *ibid.*, p. 134; and Judge
Jessup, *ibid.* at p. 192. Judge Sir Gerald Fitzmaurice draws no distinction between enforced
and voluntary local incorporations; Judge Jessup notes that the equities are particularly
strong in the former case. Judge Tanaka does not refer to the point.
[8] *loc. cit.*, p. 595, n. 78, above.

(xi) Exhaustion of Local Remedies[9]

I.L.C. DRAFT ARTICLES ON STATE RESPONSIBILITY

I.L.C.'s 1996 Report, G.A.O.R., 51st Sess., Supp. 10, p. 125.

Article 22

When the conduct of a State has created a situation not in conformity with the result required of it by an international obligation concerning the treatment to be accorded to aliens, whether natural or juridical persons, but the obligation allows that this or an equivalent result may nevertheless be achieved by subsequent conduct of the State, there is a breach of the obligation only if the aliens concerned have exhausted the effective local remedies available to them without obtaining the treatment called for by the obligation or, where that is not possible, an equivalent treatment.

AMBATIELOS ARBITRATION

Greece *v.* U.K. (1956)

Commission of Arbitration: Alfaro, President; Bagge, Bourquin, Spiropoulos, Thesiger. 12 R.I.A.A. 83; (1956) 23 I.L.R. 306

In 1919, Ambatielos, a Greek national, agreed to buy a number of ships from the United Kingdom. On the British side, negotiations were conducted by a Major Laing. In this arbitration, Greece brought claims on behalf of Ambatielos arising out of the contract. The claims were rejected by the Tribunal, *inter alia*, on the ground of non-exhaustion of local remedies.

Award of the Commission

The rule thus invoked by the United Kingdom Government is well established in international law. Nor is its existence contested by the Greek Government. It means that the State against which an international action is brought for injuries suffered by private individuals has the right to resist such an action if the persons alleged to have been injured have not first exhausted all the remedies available to them under the municipal law of that State. The defendant State has the right to demand that full advantage shall have been taken of all local remedies before the matters

---

[9] See Amerasinghe, *Local Remedies in International Law* (1990); Head (1967) 5 C.Y.I.L. 142; Law, *The Local Remedies Rule in International Law* (1961); Meron (1959) 35 B.Y.I.L. 83; Mummery (1964) 58 A.J.I.L. 389; Trinidade, *The Exhaustion of Local Remedies in International Law* (1983). On the question whether local remedies need to be exhausted before a claim that a human rights obligation has been infringed is brought, see Meron, *Human Rights and Humanitarian Norms as Customary Law* (1989), pp. 171–182.

in dispute are taken on the international level by the State of which the persons alleged to have been injured are nationals.

In order to contend successfully that international proceedings are inadmissible, the defendant State must prove the existence, in its system of internal law, of remedies which have not been used. The views expressed by writers and in judicial precedents, however, coincide in that the existence of remedies which are obviously ineffective is held not to be sufficient to justify the application of the rule. Remedies which could not rectify the situation cannot be relied upon by the defendant State as precluding an international action.

The Greek Government contends that in the present case the remedies which English law offered to Mr. Ambatielos were ineffective and that, accordingly, the rule is not applicable.

The ineffectiveness of local remedies may result clearly from the municipal law itself. That is the case, for example, when a Court of Appeal is not competent to reconsider the judgment given by a Court of first instance on matters of fact, and when, failing such reconsideration, no redress can be obtained. . . .

Furthermore, however, it is generally considered that the ineffectiveness of available remedies, without being legally certain, may also result from circumstances which do not permit any hope of redress to be placed in the use of those remedies. But in a case of that kind it is essential that such remedies, if they had been resorted to, would have proved to be *obviously futile*. . . .

If the rule of exhaustion of local remedies is relied upon against the action of the claimant State, what is the test to be applied by an international tribunal for the purpose of determining the applicability of the rule?

As the arbitrator ruled in the *Finnish Vessels* Case of May 9, 1934,[10] the only possible test is to assume the truth of the facts on which the claimant State bases its claim. . . .

In the Ambatielos Case, failure to use certain means of appeal is . . . relied upon by the United Kingdom Government, but reliance is also placed on the failure of Mr. Ambatielos to adduce before Mr. Justice Hill evidence which it is now said would have been essential to establish his claims. There is no doubt that the exhaustion of local remedies requires the use of the means of procedure which are essential to redress the situation complained of by the person who is alleged to have been injured. . . .

The rule requires that "local remedies" shall have been exhausted before an international action can be brought. These "local remedies" include not only reference to the courts and tribunals, but also the use of

---

[10] See below, p. 621.

the procedural facilities which municipal law makes available to litigants before such courts and tribunals. It is the whole systems of legal protection, as provided by municipal law, which must have been put to the test before a State, as the protector of its nationals, can prosecute the claim on the international plane. . . .

It is clear, however, that [this view] . . . cannot be strained too far. Taken literally, it would imply that the fact of having neglected to make use of some means of procedure—even one which is not important to the defence of the action—would suffice to allow a defendant State to claim that local remedies have not been exhausted, and that, therefore, an international action cannot be brought. This would confer on the rule of the prior exhaustion of local remedies a scope which is unacceptable.

In the view of the Commission the non-utilisation of certain means of procedure can be accepted as constituting a gap in the exhaustion of local remedies only if the use of these means of procedure were essential to establish the claimant's case before the municipal courts. . . .

As regards Claim A [for compensation for breach of contract], the questions of the non-exhaustion of local remedies thus raised are:

(1) In the 1922 proceedings Mr. Ambatielos failed to call (as he could have done) the witnesses who, as he now says, were essential to establish his case. . . .

It is not possible for the Commission to decide on the evidence before it the question whether the case would have been decided in favour of Mr. Ambatielos if Major Laing had been heard as a witness. The Commission has not heard the witnesses called before Mr. Justice Hill and cannot solely on the documentary evidence put before the Commission form an opinion whether the testimony of Major Laing would have been successful in establishing the claim of Mr. Ambatielos before Mr. Justice Hill. The Commission cannot put itself in the position of Mr. Justice Hill in this respect.

The test as regards the question whether the testimony of Major Laing was essential must therefore be what the claimant Government in this respect has contended, viz. that the testimony of Major Laing would have had the effect of establishing the claim put forward by Mr. Ambatielos before Mr. Justice Hill.

Under English Law Mr. Ambatielos was not precluded from calling Major Laing as a witness.

In so far as concerns Claim A, the failure of Mr. Ambatielos to call Major Laing as a witness at the hearing before Mr. Justice Hill must therefore be held to amount to non-exhaustion of the local remedy available to him in the proceedings before Mr. Justice Hill.

It may be that the decision of Mr. Ambatielos not to call Major Laing as a witness, with the result that he did not exhaust local remedies, was dictated by reasons of expediency—quite understandable in themselves —in putting his case before Mr. Justice Hill. This, however, is not the question to be determined. The Commission is not concerned with the question as to whether he was right or wrong in acting as he did. He took his decision at his own risk.

(2) The second question as to non-exhaustion raised by the United Kingdom Government is the failure of Mr. Ambatielos to make use of or exhaust his appellate rights. . . .

Ambatielos instituted appeal proceedings in the Court of Appeal but did not continue with them after that Court had refused him leave to call Major Laing in evidence before it. He did not appeal against the Court of Appeal's decision on this question.

The refusal of the Court of Appeal to give leave to adduce the evidence of Major Laing did not, of course, in itself prevent this general appeal from being proceeded with.

The Greek Government argues by way of explanation that to proceed with the general appeal once the decision of the Court of Appeal not to admit the Laing evidence had been given would have been futile because the Laing evidence was essential to enable the Court to arrive at a decision favourable to Mr. Ambatielos.

The reason why Mr. Ambatielos was not allowed to call Major Laing in the Court of Appeal was, in the words of Lord Justice Scrutton, that "One of the principal rules which this Court adopts is that it will not give leave to adduce further evidence which might have been adduced with reasonable care at the trial of the action."

Accordingly, the failure of Mr. Ambatielos to exhaust the local remedy before Mr. Justice Hill, by not calling Major Laing as a witness, is the reason why it was futile for him to prosecute his appeal.

It would be wrong to hold that a party who, by failing to exhaust his opportunities in the Court of first instance, has caused an appeal to become futile should be allowed to rely on this fact in order to rid himself of the rule of exhaustion of local remedies.

It may be added that Mr. Ambatielos did not submit to the Court of Appeal any argument suggesting, or any evidence to show, that any illegal or improper manoeuvres by his opponents had prevented him from calling Major Laing or producing any documents.

In so far as concerns the appeal to the House of Lords, it is of course unlikely that that Court would have differed from the decision of the Court of Appeal, refusing to allow Major Laing to be called as a witness in the latter Court. If it is held that such an appeal would *not* have been obviously futile, the failure of Mr. Ambatielos to appeal to the House of Lords must be regarded as a failure to exhaust local remedies. If, on the other hand, it is held that an appeal to the House of Lords *would* have been obviously futile, Mr. Ambatielos must likewise be held to have lost his hope of a successful appeal, by reason of his failure to call Major Laing.

Arbitrators Alfaro and Spiropoulos dissented from the Commission's ruling on the question of local remedies.

Notes

1. Is there any indication in the arbitrators' award or in Article 22, I.L.C. Draft Articles on State Responsibility, above, whether responsibility arises only upon the unsuccessful exhaustion of local remedies or whether it arises instead before and independently of their exhaustion upon the commission of the act being questioned?[11] The answer to this question has practical significance in connection with the rule concerning the nationality of claims that requires the claimant to have been a national of the state acting for him at the time that the claim arises and when the claim is brought.

2. In the *Aerial Incident of 27 July 1955* case,[12] Israel argued, correctly it is believed, as follows: " . . . it is universally recognised that the rule regarding exhaustion of local remedies is inapplicable to a case of a direct injury caused by one State to another. . . . The rule . . . applies solely to the case of so-called diplomatic protection. . . . " Any extension of the application of the rule to cover, for example, a case of violation of territorial sovereignty would conflict with the principle *par in parem non habet imperium, non habet jurisdictionem.*

3. *Kinds of Remedies.* The 1961 Harvard Draft Convention on the International Responsibility of States for Injuries to Aliens calls upon a claimant to employ "all administrative, arbitral, or judicial remedies" available to him.[13] The European Commission of Human Rights has ruled that an appeal for clemency is not a remedy for the purposes of the rule.[14] In the *Salem* case,[15] Egypt argued that local remedies had not been exhausted because the claimant had available "the right to *recours en requête civile* against the decision of the Mixed Court of Appeal at Alexandria. . . . "[16] The Tribunal rejected the argument because "the *recours en requête civile* is no regular legal remedy but intends to re-open a process which has already been closed by a judgment of last resort."[17] It continued: "As a rule it is sufficient if the claimant has brought his suit up to the highest instance of the national judiciary."[18] In the *Nielsen* case[19] the European Commission of Human Rights expressly disagreed and ruled that the extraordinary remedy in the case before it—recourse to the Danish Special Court of Revision—had to be exhausted to satisfy the rule.

Would the British Parliamentary Commissioner[20] be a local remedy for the purposes of the rule?

4. *Effective Remedies.* In the *Finnish Ships Arbitration,*[21] the arbitrator was asked to decide whether the local remedies rule had been exhausted by Finland in seeking compensation from Great Britain for the use by the latter of Finnish ships requisitioned during the First World War. Finland had sought compensation before the Admiralty Transport Arbitration Board but had been unsuccessful because the Arbitration Board had found as a fact that, although used during the War by Great Britain, the ships had been requisitioned by or on behalf of Russia (which then had sovereignty over Finland) and not, as required by the British legislation concerning compensation, by Great Britain. The Arbitrator ruled that

---

[11] See Fawcett (1954) 31 B.Y.I.L. 452.

[12] *Aerial Incident of 27 July 1955* case, I.C.J. Pleadings, pp. 530–531 *cf.* Read (1963) I.C.Y.I.L. 203 at 207, 208.

[13] Draft Art. 19, (1961) 55 A.J.I.L. 577.

[14] Application 458/59, (1960) 3 Y.B.E.C.H.R. 234.

[15] *Egypt v. U.S.,* (1932) 2 R.I.A.A. 1161.

[16] *ibid.* p. 1177.

[17] *ibid.* p. 1189.

[18] *ibid.*

[19] (1958–59) 2 Y.B.E.C.H.R. 413 at 436. And see the *Second Cyprus* case, *ibid.* p. 186.

[20] See Wade and Bradley, *Constitutional and Administrative Law* (11th ed., 1993), pp. 661–670.

[21] *Finland v. Great Britain,* (1934) 3 R.I.A.A. 1479.

Finland's failure to appeal to the Court of Appeal did not mean that it had not exhausted local remedies. Such an appeal would have been "obviously futile" because the Court of Appeal could not have reversed the Board's crucial finding of fact; it could only have considered questions of law. In the *Panevezys-Saldutiskis Railway* case,[22] the P.C.I.J. said: "There can be no need to resort to the municipal court if ... the result must be a repetition of a decision already given." Since 1966, the House of Lords has been free to reverse its own decisions where "the interests of justice so require."[23] Does this mean that an alien should now always take his case to the House of Lords to satisfy the local remedies rule?[24]

In the *El Oro Mining and Railway Co.* case,[25] the British-Mexican Claims Commission took jurisdiction despite the presence of a "Calvo" clause.[26] The claimant went to the local courts, but the case was undecided after nine years. The Commission was of the opinion that "nine years by far exceeds the limit of the most liberal allowance that may be made."[27] There was, as a result, a denial of justice that excused the claimant company from its obligation not to resort to the Commission. It is arguable that such a delay in deciding a case would render a remedy ineffective for the purposes of the exhaustion of local remedies rule.

In the *Robert E. Brown* case,[28] the Tribunal rejected a claim of non-exhaustion of local remedies by reference to "the frequently quoted language of an American Secretary of State: 'A claimant in a foreign State is not required to exhaust justice in such State when there is no justice to exhaust.' " The Tribunal found this to be so in the case before it: "All three branches of the Government [of the South African Republic] conspired to ruin his [the claimant's] enterprise. ... The judiciary, at first recalcitrant, was at length reduced to submission and brought into line with a determined policy of the Executive. ... "

Should the absence of counsel, the right to cross examine, etc.—*i.e.* other aspects of a fair trial as spelt out in the "international minimum standard" (which, according to one view, applies to the treatment of aliens)—also excuse a claimant from the need to exhaust local remedies?

The Rules regarding International Claims issued by the British Foreign and Commonwealth Office[29] in 1971 read:

Rule VII

Her Majesty's Government will not normally take over and formally espouse a claim of a United Kingdom national against another state until all the legal remedies, if any, available to him in the state concerned have been exhausted.

---

[22] P.C.I.J. Rep., Ser. A/B, No. 76, p. 18 (1939). *cf.* the *Vagrancy* cases, Eur. Court H.R., Ser. A, Vol. 12. Judgment of June 18, 1971.

[23] *Practice Statement* [1966] 1 W.L.R. 1234.

[24] On the position under the European Convention on Human Rights, see Harris, O'Boyle and Warbrick, *The Law of the European Convention on Human Rights* (1995), p. 610. Note that the defence of Act of State will still be available against him in some cases, thus preventing any claim in the British courts: see Wade and Bradley, *op. cit.*, p. 621, n. 20, above, p. 330.

[25] G.B. v. Mexico, (1931) 5 R.I.A.A. 191.

[26] A "Calvo" clause is a clause in a contract between a state and an alien whereby the latter agrees to resort to local remedies only and not invoke the protection of the state of which it is a national. Calvo was an Argentinian international lawyer. See Shea, *The Calvo Clause* (1955).

[27] *ibid.* p. 198.

[28] U.S. v. G.B., (1923) 6 R.I.A.A. 120 at 129.

[29] *loc. cit.*, p. 595, n. 78, above.

Comment

Failure to exhaust any local remedies will not constitute a bar to a claim if it is clearly established that in the circumstances of the case an appeal to a higher municipal tribunal would have had no effect. Nor is a claimant against another state required to exhaust justice in that state where there is no justice to exhaust.

Rule VIII

If, in exhausting any municipal remedies the claimant has met with prejudice or obstruction, which are a denial of justice, Her Majesty's Government may intervene on his behalf to secure redress of injustice.

5. Note that the requirement of the exhaustion of local remedies is sometimes dispensed with by treaty. For example, claims heard by the United States-Mexican General Claims Commission, extracts from some of which are included in this chapter, did not have to satisfy the rule.[30] In the *ELSI* case[31] it was held that such an "important principle of customary international law" could not be held to have been "tacitly dispensed with"; the treaty text must be clearly to this effect.

---

[30] See Art. V, U.S.-Mexican General Claims Convention 1923, 4 R.I.A.A., p. 11.
[31] I.C.J. Rep. 1989, p. 15 at p. 42.

CHAPTER 9

HUMAN RIGHTS

1. INTRODUCTION[1]

INTERNATIONAL law rules framed in terms of the protection of human rights against state interference are very largely a post-1945 phenomenon. Before then individuals were seen mostly as aliens and nationals, not as individuals. Some protection was afforded to them as aliens,[2] but the treatment of nationals was regarded as being within the domestic jurisdiction of sovereign states. By the nineteenth century, most writers recognised an exception in the case of humanitarian intervention, although state practice shows that intervention by a state on that ground was usually justified on other grounds at the same time.[3] After the First World War, efforts were made to protect minority groups by treaty,[4] but no protection of individuals generally was attempted. Events in Europe in the 1930s and in the Second World War focused attention upon this wider question and the guarantee of human rights became one of the purposes for which the Allied Powers fought.[5] It was therefore no surprise when the realisation and protection of human rights became one of the purposes of the United Nations[6] and when the Charter imposed obligations upon members to this end.[7] The Charter was followed by the Universal Declaration of Human Rights 1948[8] and a series of multilateral treaties concluded through the United Nations. At a regional level, the European Convention on Human Rights 1950,[9] the European Social Charter

---

[1] On the international law of human rights generally, see Cassese, *Human Rights in a Changing World* (1989); Donnelly, *International Human Rights* (1993); Dominguez, Rodley, Wood and Falk, *Enhancing Global Human Rights* (1979); Dowrick, ed., *Human Rights* (1979); Hannum, ed., *Guide to International Human Rights Practice* (2nd. ed., 1992); Lauterpacht, *International Law and Human Rights* (1950); Henkin and Hargrove, *Human Rights: An Agenda for the Next Century* (1994); Luard, ed., *The International Protection of Human Rights* (1967); McDougal, Lasswell and Chen, *Human Rights and World Public Order* (1980); Mahoney and Mahoney, eds., *Human Rights in the Twenty-First Century* (1993); Meron, ed., *Human Rights in International Law* (1984); *ibid. Human Rights Lawmaking in the UN* (1986); Robertson and Merrills, *Human Rights in the World* (4th ed., 1996); Sieghart, *The Lawful Rights of Mankind* (1985); *ibid. The International Law of Human Rights* (1983); Steiner and Alston, *International Human Rights in Context* (1996); Vasak and Alston, eds., *The International Dimensions of Human Rights* (1982).
[2] See above, Chap. 8.
[3] On humanitarian intervention, see below, p. 917.
[4] See Oppenheim, Vol. I, p. 973.
[5] See the UN Declaration of January 1, 1942: (1942) 36 A.J.I.L., Supp. 191.
[6] UN Charter, Art. 1, below, Appendix I.
[7] *ibid.* Arts. 55–56.
[8] See below, p. 630.
[9] U.K.T.S. 71 (1953), 213 U.N.T.S. 221. In force 1953. 35 parties, including the U.K. See Harris, O'Boyle and Warbrick, *The Law of the European Convention on Human Rights* (1995) and Van Dijk and Van Hoof, *Theory and Practice of the European Convention on Human Rights* (2nd ed., 1990).

1961,[10] the American Convention on Human Rights 1969[11] and the African Charter on Human Rights and Peoples' Rights 1981[12] have been adopted; all four are now in force. There are also International Labour Conventions that contain human rights guarantees,[13] and the four Geneva "Red Cross" Conventions of 1949.[14] The Human Dimension of the Final Act of the Conference on Security and Co-operation in Europe 1975 (the Helsinki Declaration)[15] and later OSCE texts and developments are also relevant.

The following two sections concern, firstly, the action taken at a universal level to protect human rights within the United Nations, mainly by the UN Commission on Human Rights through the adoption and implementation of treaties and by other means and, secondly, the protection of human rights in customary international law.

Writers commonly refer to human rights as belonging to one of three generations. The "first generation" consists of those civil and political rights that derive from the natural rights philosophy of Locke, Rousseau and others and that have traditionally been given priority by Western states. The "second generation" are those economic, social and cultural rights that attained recognition in the twentieth century with the advent of socialism. Although there is jurisprudential debate[16] and scepticism on the part of some Western states[17] as to the human rights character of "second generation" human rights, the Universal Declaration on Human Rights catalogues rights within both generations as human rights, and the International Covenants on Civil and Political Rights and on Economic, Social and Cultural Rights impose legal obligations in respect of each. Moreover, the premise underlying all United Nations human rights texts is that civil and political rights and economic, social and cultural rights are of equal priority, with the realisation of the two groups of rights being interdependent. The idea of a "third generation" of human rights emerged as recently as the 1970s and is supported predominantly by developing states. It is the idea that in addition to the individual rights of the first two "generations," there are collective, group

---

[10] U.K.T.S. 38 (1965), Cmnd. 2643; 529 U.N.T.S. 89. In force 1965. 21 parties, including the U.K. See Harris, *The European Social Charter* (1984).

[11] P.A.U.T.S. 36; (1970) 9 I.L.M. 673. In force 1978. 25 parties. See Buergenthal and Shelton, eds., *Protecting Human Rights in the Americas* (4th ed., 1995); Davidson, *The Inter-American Human Rights System* (1997); and Harris and Livingstone, eds., *The Inter-American System of Human Rights* (1998).

[12] (1982) 21 I.L.M. 59. In force 1986. 50 parties. See D'Sa (1985) 29 J.Afr.L. 72; Gittleman (1982) 22 V.J.I.L. 667; Rembe, *The System of Protection of Human Rights under the African Charter on Human and Peoples Rights* (1991).

[13] See Jenks, *Human Rights and International Labour Standards* (1960); *ibid. Social Justice in the Law of Nations* (1970); and Samson, in Matscher, ed., *The Implementation of Economic and Social Rights* (1991), p. 123.

[14] See Cassese, ed., *The New Humanitarian Law of Armed Conflict* (1980); Delissen and Tanja, eds., *Humanitarian Law of Armed Conflict: Challenges Ahead: Essays in Honour of Frits Kalshoven* (1991); McCoubrey, *International Humanitarian Law* (1990); Meyer, ed., *Armed Conflict and the New Law* (1989); Roberts and Guelff, eds., *Documents on the Laws of War* (2nd. ed., 1989). Each Convention has 188 parties, including the U.K. See also the 1977 Protocols I and II to the Geneva Conventions, Misc. 19 (1977), Cmnd. 6927; 1125 U.N.T.S. 609. In force 1978. 131 (Protocol I) and 121 (Protocol II) parties. The U.K. is not a party.

[15] (1975) 14 I.L.M. 1292. The declaration is not binding in law: see Russell (1976) 70 A.J.I.L. 242. On the OSCE and human rights, see Brett (1996) 18 H.R.Q. 668.

[16] See, *e.g.* Cranston, *What are Human Rights* (1973); McFarlane, *The Theory and Practice of Human Rights* (1985); Raphael, ed., *Political Thought and the Rights of Man* (1967); Vincent, *Human Rights and International Relations* (1986).

[17] During the Reagan Presidency, the U.S. took the view that such rights were "societal goals" rather than human rights: see the U.S. statement in UN Doc.A/40/C.3/36, p. 5 (1985).

rights, such as the right to self-determination and the right to development, that may properly qualify as human rights.

The evolution of the international law of human rights has been one of the more remarkable features of the development of international law since 1945. Whereas progress has so far been made mainly through treaties, the customary international law of human rights is in the process of evolution too. However, it remains uncertain how far customary law extends beyond some fundamental civil and political rights and who in law holds or may enforce the resulting substantive legal rights. As to human rights treaties, many states have accepted an increasing number of universal or regional human rights treaties protecting either human rights generally, or one "generation" of human rights or just one particular right. Such treaties typically provide for bodies to monitor compliance, although the powers of enforcement granted to them vary greatly, ranging from the competence of a court to take a legally binding decision following an individual petition[18] to that of a committee to make only non-binding general comments or recommendations after the examination of national reports.[19] Nonetheless all such supervisory bodies contribute in their functioning to the meaning of the rights their treaties guarantee and to the corpus of practice applying international human rights standards.

HIGGINS, PROBLEMS AND PROCESS: INTERNATIONAL LAW AND HOW WE USE IT

1994, pp. 96–97

It is sometimes suggested that there can be no fully universal concept of human rights, for it is necessary to take into account the diverse cultures and political systems of the world.[20] In my view this is a point advanced mostly by states, and by liberal scholars anxious not to impose the Western view of things on others. It is rarely advanced by the oppressed, who are only too anxious to benefit from perceived universal standards. The non-universal, relativist view of human rights is in fact a very state-centred view and loses sight of the fact that human rights are *human* rights and not dependent on the fact that states, or groupings of states, may behave differently from each other so far as their politics, economic policy, and culture are concerned. I believe, profoundly, in the universality of the human spirit. Individuals everywhere want the same essential things: to have sufficient food and shelter; to be able to speak freely; to practise their own religion or to abstain from religious belief; to feel that their person is not threatened by the state; to know that they will

---

[18] *e.g.* the European and American Courts of Human Rights.
[19] *e.g.* the Committee on Economic, Social and Cultural Rights.
[20] On this see, *inter alia*, I. Nguema, "Human Rights Perspective in Africa" (1990) 11 H.R.L.J. 261; D. Donoho, "Relativism Versus Universalism in Human Rights: The Search for Meaningful Standards" (1991) 27 *Stanford Law Journal* 345; H. Gros Espiel, "The Evolving Concept of Human Rights: Western Socialist and Third World Approaches", in B. Ramcharan (ed.), *Human Rights Thirty Years after the Universal Declaration* (1979), 41 ff.

not be tortured, or detained without charge, and that, if charged, they will have a fair trial. I believe there is nothing in these aspirations that is dependent upon culture, or religion or stage of development. They are as keenly felt by the African tribesman as by the European city-dweller, by the inhabitant of a Latin American shanty-town as by the resident of a Manhattan apartment.

Notes

1. Ahead of the Vienna World Conference on Human Rights 1993, Asian states adopted the Bangkok Declaration 1993[21] which challenged what was perceived as the western concept of human rights. The Declaration stressed the need to consider human rights in their national and regional contexts and emphasised the principles of respect for national sovereignty and non-interference in the international affairs of states. However, the universality of human rights and its place beyond the limits of domestic jurisdiction were reaffirmed by the Vienna Declaration and Programme of Action on Human Rights 1993[22] that was adopted by the Vienna World Conference:

1. The World Conference on Human Rights reaffirms the solemn commitment of all States to fulfil their obligations to promote universal respect for, and observance and protection of, all human rights and fundamental freedoms for all in accordance with the Charter of the United Nations, other instruments relating to human rights, and international law. The universal nature of these rights and freedoms is beyond question. . . .
4. The promotion and protection of all human rights and fundamental freedoms must be considered as a priority objective of the United Nations in accordance with its purposes and principles, in particular the purpose of international cooperation. In the framework of these purposes and principles, the promotion and protection of all human rights is a legitimate concern of the international community. . . .
5. All human rights are universal, indivisible and interdependent and interrelated. The international community must treat human rights globally in a fair and equal manner, on the same footing, and with the same emphasis. While the significance of national and regional particularities and various historical, cultural and religious backgrounds must be borne in mind, it is the duty of States, regardless of their political, economic and cultural systems, to promote and protect all human rights and fundamental freedoms.

2. Whereas no one argues that states may torture or arbitrarily detain or kill individuals, there are some contexts in which religious and other cultural differences do disclose genuine disagreement.[23] In some Islamic states, apostacy and adultery are capital criminal offences.[24] Discrimination against women in respect of property and marital rights have led certain Islamic states to make reservations to key provisions of the 1979 Convention on the Elimination of Discrimination

---

[21] (1993) 14 H.R.L.J. 370.
[22] (1994) 1–1 I.H.R.R. 240.
[23] See further on cultural relativism, Renteln, *International Human Rights: Universalism versus Relativism* (1990).
[24] See below, p. 660.

against Women.[25] Catholic states may take a different view from others about abortion and the right to life of the unborn child. Female genital mutilation is widely practised in African and other states.[26] On a different kind of issue, the extent to which the press is free from legal censorship varies widely between states. Is this last example a matter of cultural diversity or the determination of some governments to control political opposition?

Does corporal punishment present a problem of cultural diversity? In 1994, despite President Clintion's intervention and much public outcry in the U.S., a criminal judicial sentence of four strokes of the cane for vandalising cars by spray paint was carried out against an American youth of 18 years.[27] In *Tyrer v. U.K.*,[28] three strokes of the birch as a penalty for assault were held to be inhuman and degrading punishment in breach of Article 3, European Convention on Human Rights. Interpreting Article 7, ICCPR, the Human Rights Committee has stated that it is infringed by "corporal punishment, including excessive chastisement ordered as a punishment for a crime": General Comment 20, below, p. 665.

2. ACTION THROUGH THE UNITED NATIONS[29]

Note

Articles 55 and 56, UN Charter impose upon the United Nations and its members legal obligations to "promote" respect for and observance of human rights. United Nations action under Article 55 is centred largely on the UN Commission on Human Rights, which was established by ECOSOC under Article 68, UN Charter. The Commission has 54 member states, with membership being distributed by convention among the various UN political blocs.[30] Accordingly, the Commission is a highly political animal, with its initiatives and priorities reflecting bloc interests as well as the human rights merits of each case. Over the years, the balance of power within the Commission, and hence its agenda, has fluctuated, with Western states (emphasising civil and political rights) holding sway early on, Third World states (concerned with racial discrimination and self-determination) prevailing from 1967 to 1980, and the West recovering ground, through effective caucusing, since then.

The Commission's work has taken three distinct forms: standard-setting, promotional activities, monitoring and enforcement, with each predominating for a time. The first decade saw a concentration on standard-setting, with the drafting of the Universal Declaration of Human Rights and the Covenants, the latter being completed in the Commission by the mid-1950s. Then less ambitious, promotional activities (advisory services, regional seminars, fellowships) became the order of the day. As of the late 1960s, the emphasis has shifted again, attention

---

[25] *e.g.* Egypt has made a reservation to Art. 16 "concerning the equality of men and women in all matters relating to marriage and family relations" in so far as it runs counter to the "Islamic Sharia's provisions whereby women are accorded rights subject to those of their spouses so as to ensure a just balance between them": UN Doc. ST/LEG/Ser.E/15, p. 171.

[26] See *Harmful and Traditional Practices Affecting the Health of Women and Children*, UN Human Rights Fact Sheet No. 23, p. 7.

[27] *Keesings Archives*, p. 40013.

[28] E. Court H.R. Rep A 28 (1978).

[29] See Alston, *The United Nations and Human Rights* (1992); Humphrey, *Human Rights and the United Nations* (1984); and Meron, *Human Rights Lawmaking in the UN* (1986).

[30] In 1996, membership was distributed as follows: 15 African States, 13 Asian states; 11 Latin American states; 5 East European states; and 10 West European and other states.

turning to the monitoring and enforcement of the standards that had been set.[31] This has occurred through the establishment within the Commission of procedures to consider allegations of human rights violations by particular states and by the more recent addition of a thematic approach.[32]

As to allegations against particular states, in 1967, ECOSOC Resolution 1235[33] authorised the Commission to "examine information relevant to gross violations of human rights" and to "make a thorough study of situations which reveal a consistent pattern of violations of human rights." Resolution 1235 has provided the basis for the Commission's now well established *public* procedure for the investigation of allegations of human rights violations by particular states. The Commission appoints a Working Group or Special Rapporteur to examine the allegations made against a state and to report on the situation in a public document that is then discussed at public Commission meetings. The examination of the resulting "country reports" is a large part of the Commission's work.

Since 1970, the public procedure under Resolution 1235, the use of which results normally from a state initiative, has been complemented by a confidential procedure established under ECOSOC Resolution 1503[34] which authorises the consideration of communications from individuals or Non-Governmental Organisations (NGOs). Until then, the practice had been to file without comment the many thousands of petitions received by the United Nations annually alleging breaches of human rights. By Resolution 1503, ECOSOC authorised the Commission's Sub-Commission on Prevention of Discrimination and Protection of Minorities (a body of 26 independent experts[35]) to examine in private communications received by the UN Secretary-General with a view to referring to the Commission "situations which appear to reveal a consistent pattern of gross and reliably attested violations of human rights." If a situation is referred to it under Resolution 1503, the Commission may decide to appoint an ad hoc committee to conduct an investigation "which shall be undertaken only with the express consent of the state concerned." In the light of the report of any such ad hoc committee, the Commission may submit a "report and recommendations" to ECOSOC. All action under Resolution 1503 "shall remain confidential until such time as the Commission may decide to make recommendations to ECOSOC". Although a large number of states have been the subject of the Resolution 1503 procedure, it has proved to be only a qualified success. The confidential nature of the proceedings has been a handicap, as evidenced by the fact that states have sometimes preferred to have allegations against them considered under the Resolution 1503 procedure rather than risk the publicity attendant upon the public Resolution 1235 procedure. Situations that have been referred by the Sub-Commission to the Commission under Resolution 1503 have not always been considered on their merits, as bloc politics have intervened.

With regard to the thematic approach, as of the 1980s, the Commission has established Working Groups on Enforced or Involuntary Disappearances and Arbitrary Detention and Special Rapporteurs on Summary or Arbitrary Executions, Torture, Religious Intolerance, Mercenaries, the Sale of Children, the Right to Freedom of Opinion and Expression, Contemporary Forms of Racism and Toxic Wastes. The Working Groups and Special Rapporteurs prepare public

---

[31] See Tolley, *The UN Commission on Human Rights* (1987), Chap. 6. This is a change of emphasis only; standard setting and promotional activities continue in parallel.

[32] See Nowak (1991) 22 N.Y.I.L. 39.

[33] E.S.C.O.R., 42nd Sess., Supp. 1 (1967).

[34] E.S.C.O.R., 48th Sess., Supp. 1A (1970).

[35] In practice, there is a spectrum of independence, with some members having a close connection with their national government, but with others being fully independent: see Tolley, above, pp. 166–167.

reports which monitor state practice in their areas of concern and provide the basis for discussion within the Commission at public meetings. The thematic approach has meant not so much that the Working Group or Rapporteur consider questions in the abstract, but that they call attention to possible human rights violations in all states in respect of which evidence accumulates, not just one state that may have been singled out by the Commission.

Whereas the Commission's monitoring and enforcement work of the kinds described is undoubtedly worthwhile in the sense that it results in reports evidencing state conduct and requires states to defend themselves at Commission sessions, there are limits to its value. Although attention may be focused beneficially on situations of real concern for human rights, politics clearly influence the choice and treatment of particular cases. There are also no mandatory powers to hear witnesses or to enter territory to conduct investigations. Where infringements of human rights are found, the Commission's powers are restricted to persuasion, public criticism[36] and, in the most serious cases, attempts at isolation of the offending state[37]; there are no legally binding sanctions available.

At the very least, however, as a result to a large extent of the Commission's work, the idea that the treatment of a state's own nationals is a matter within its domestic jurisdiction has been abandoned. The practice of the Commission shows clearly the acceptance by states, as they respond without question to allegations against them, that the protection of human rights is now within the domain of international law.

A recent development was the establishment in 1993 of the post of UN High Commissioner for Human Rights, as a result of the Vienna World Conference on Human Rights. The Commissioner's responsibilities are very generally phrased and remain to be defined in practice. They include the following[38]:

(a) To promote and protect the effective enjoyment by all of all civil, cultural, economic, political and social rights;

(b) To carry out the tasks assigned to him/her by the competent bodies of the United Nations system in the field of human rights and to make recommendations to them with a view to improving the promotion and protection of all human rights; . . .

(f) To play an active role in removing the current obstacles and in meeting the challenges to the full realization of all human rights and in preventing the continuation of human rights violations throughout the world, as reflected in the Vienna Declaration and Programme of Action;

The materials in the remainder of this section are concerned with some of the human rights treaties, declarations, etc., adopted by the United Nations. Other UN human rights treaties include the 1948 Genocide Convention[39]; the 1951 Convention relating to the Status of Refugees[40]; the 1973 Convention on the Crime of Apartheid[41]; the 1979 Convention on the Elimination of Discrimination against

---

[36] But note the confidential nature of the Resolution 1503 procedure.

[37] See Tolley, above, pp. 67–70.

[38] G.A. Resolution 48/141, G.A.O.R., Supp. 49, p. 261. See Clapham (1994) 5 E.J.I.L. 557. See also the annual reports of the Commissioner in G.A.O.R., Supp. 36. The first Commissioner was Mr Ayala Lasso, an Ecuadorian diplomat. He was succeeded in 1997 by Mrs Mary Robinson, former President of Ireland.

[39] Below, p. 745.

[40] U.K.T.S. 39 (1954), Cmnd. 9171; 189 U.N.T.S. 150. In force 1954. 128 parties, including the U.K.

[41] (1974) 13 I.L.M. 50. In force 1976. 100 parties. The UK is not a party.

Women[42]; the 1989 Convention on the Rights of the Child[43]; and the 1990 Convention on the Protection of the Rights of Migrant Workers.[44]

UNIVERSAL DECLARATION OF HUMAN RIGHTS 1948

G.A. Resolution 217A (III), G.A.O.R., 3rd Sess., Part I, Resns, p. 71

THE GENERAL ASSEMBLY proclaims
THIS UNIVERSAL DECLARATION OF HUMAN RIGHTS as a common standard of achievement for all peoples and all nations, to the end that every individual and every organ of society, keeping this Declaration constantly in mind, shall strive by teaching and education to promote respect for these rights and freedoms and by progressive measures, national and international, to secure their universal and effective recognition and observance, both among the peoples of Member States themselves and among the peoples of territories under their jurisdiction.

Article 1

All human beings are born free and equal in dignity and rights. They are endowed with reason and conscience and should act towards one another in a spirit of brotherhood.

Article 2

Everyone is entitled to all the rights and freedoms set forth in this Declaration, without distinction of any kind, such as race, colour, sex, language, religion, political or other opinion, national or social origin, property, birth or other status. Furthermore, no distinction shall be made on the basis of the political, jurisdictional or international status of the country or territory to which a person belongs, whether it be independent, trust, non-self-governing or under any other limitation of sovereignty.

Article 3

Everyone has the right of life, liberty and security of person.

Article 4

No one shall be held in slavery or servitude; slavery and the slave trade shall be prohibited in all their forms.

Article 5

No one shall be subjected to torture or to cruel, inhuman or degrading treatment or punishment.

[42] Misc. 1 (1982), Cmnd. 8444; (1980) 19 I.L.M. 33. In force 1981. 154 parties, including the U.K.
[43] (1989) 28 I.L.M. 1448. In force 1990. 191 parties, including the U.K.
[44] (1991) 30 I.L.M. 1521. Not in force. 20 parties required. 8 so far. The U.K. is not a signatory.

Article 6

Everyone has the right to recognition everywhere as a person before the law.

Article 7

All are equal before the law and are entitled without any discrimination to equal protection of the law. All are entitled to equal protection against any discrimination in violation of this Declaration and against any incitement to such discrimination.

Article 8

Everyone has the right to an effective remedy by the competent national tribunals for acts violating the fundamental rights granted him by the constitution or by law.

Article 9

No one shall be subjected to arbitrary arrest, detention or exile.

Article 10

Everyone is entitled in full equality to a fair and public hearing by an independent and impartial tribunal, in the determination of his rights and obligations and of any criminal charge against him.

Article 11

1. Everyone charged with a penal offence has the right to be presumed innocent until proved guilty according to law in a public trial at which he has had all the guarantees necessary for his defence.

2. No one shall be held guilty of any penal offence on account of any act or omission which did not constitute a penal offence, under national or international law, at the time when it was committed. Nor shall a heavier penalty be imposed than the one that was applicable at the time the penal offence was committed.

Article 12

No one shall be subjected to arbitrary interference with his privacy, family, home or correspondence, nor to attacks upon his honour and reputation. Everyone has the right to the protection of the law against such interference or attacks.

Article 13

1. Everyone has the right to freedom of movement and residence within the borders of each state.

2. Everyone has the right to leave any country, including his own, and to return to his country.

Article 14

1. Everyone has the right to seek and to enjoy in other countries asylum from persecution.

2. This right may not be invoked in the case of prosecutions genuinely arising from non-political crimes or from acts contrary to the purposes and principles of the United Nations.

Article 15

1. Everyone has the right to a nationality.

2. No one shall be arbitrarily deprived of his nationality nor denied the right to change his nationality.

Article 16

1. Men and women of full age, without limitation due to race, nationality or religion, have the right to marry and to found a family. They are entitled to equal rights as to marriage, during marriage and at its dissolution.

2. Marriage shall be entered into only with the free and full consent of the intending spouses.

3. The family is the natural and fundamental group unit of society and is entitled to protection by society and the State.

Article 17

1. Everyone has the right to own property alone as well as in association with others.

2. No one shall be arbitrarily deprived of his property.

Article 18

Everyone has the right to freedom of thought, conscience and religion; this right includes freedom to change his religion or belief, and freedom, either alone or in community with others and in public or private, to manifest his religion or belief in teaching, practice, worship and observance.

Article 19

Everyone has the right to freedom of opinion and expression; this right includes freedom to hold opinions without interference and to seek, receive and impart information and ideas through any media and regardless of frontiers.

Article 20

1. Everyone has the right to freedom of peaceful assembly and association.

2. No one may be compelled to belong to an association.

Article 21

1. Everyone has the right to take part in the government of his country, directly or through freely chosen representatives.

2. Everyone has the right of equal access to public service in his country.

3. The will of the people shall be the basis of the authority of government; this will shall be expressed in periodic and genuine elections which shall be by universal and equal suffrage and shall be held by secret vote or by equivalent free voting procedures.

Article 22

Everyone, as a member of society, has the right to social security and is entitled to realisation through national effort and international co-operation and in accordance with the organisation and resources of each State, of the economic, social and cultural rights indispensable for his dignity and the free development of his personality.

Article 23

1. Everyone has the right to work, to free choice of employment, to just and favourable conditions of work and to protection against unemployment.

2. Everyone, without any discrimination, has the right to equal pay for equal work.

3. Everyone who works has the right to just and favourable remuneration ensuring for himself and his family an existence worthy of human dignity, and supplemented, if necessary, by other means of social protection.

4. Everyone has the right to form and to join trade unions for the protection of his interests.

Article 24

Everyone has the right to rest and leisure including reasonable limitation of working hours and periodic holidays with pay.

Article 25

Everyone has the right to a standard of living adequate for the health and well-being of himself and of his family, including food, clothing, housing and medical care and necessary social services, and the right to security in the event of unemployment, sickness, disability, widowhood, old age or other lack of livelihood in circumstances beyond his control.

2. Motherhood and childhood are entitled to special care and assistance. All children, whether born in or out of wedlock, shall enjoy the same social protection.

Article 26

1. Everyone has the right to education. Education shall be free, at least in the elementary and fundamental stages. Elementary education shall be compulsory. Technical and professional education shall be made generally available and higher education shall be equally accessible to all on the basis of merit.

2. Education shall be directed to the full development of the human personality and to the strengthening of respect for human rights and fundamental freedoms. It shall promote understanding, tolerance and friendship among all nations, racial or religious groups, and shall further the activities of the United Nations for the maintenance of peace.

3. Parents have a prior right to choose the kind of education that shall be given to their children.

Article 27

1. Everyone has the right freely to participate in the cultural life of the community, to enjoy the arts and to share in scientific advancement and its benefits.

2. Everyone has the right to protection of the moral and material interests resulting from any scientific, literary or artistic production of which he is the author.

Article 28

Everyone is entitled to a social and international order in which the rights and freedoms set forth in the Declaration can be fully realised.

Article 29

1. Everyone has duties to the community in which alone the free and full development of his personality is possible.

2. In the exercise of his rights and freedoms, everyone shall be subject only to such limitations as are determined by law solely for the purpose of securing due recognition and respect for the rights and freedoms of others and of meeting the just requirements of morality, public order and the general welfare in a democratic society.

3. These rights and freedoms may in no case be exercised contrary to the purposes and principles of the United Nations.

Article 30

Nothing in this Declaration may be interpreted as implying for any State, group or person any right to engage in any activity or to perform any act aimed at the destruction of any of the rights and freedoms set forth herein.

Notes

One of the first steps taken by the United Nations was the adoption by the General Assembly of the Universal Declaration of Human Rights, by 48 votes to none, with eight abstentions.[45] The Declaration contains a comprehensive list of civil, political, economic, social and cultural rights. According to Mrs Eleanor Roosevelt, United States representative to the General Assembly and Chairman of the United Nations Commission on Human Rights during the drafting of the Declaration, it "is not, and does not purport to be a statement of law or of legal obligation"; it is instead, she continued, "a common standard of achievement for all peoples of all nations."[46] Despite this, the Declaration has undoubtedly had considerable impact in shaping subsequent treaties on human rights, and has been relied upon extensively by persons putting forward claims for fair treatment in terms of human rights; it has also had some impact upon the content of the constitutions of new states and upon decisions of municipal courts.[47] The status of the Declaration as a source of rules of customary international law was considered in the *Filartiga* case.[48]

INTERNATIONAL COVENANT ON CIVIL AND POLITICAL RIGHTS 1966[49]

999 U.N.T.S. 171; U.K.T.S. 6 (1977), Cmnd. 6702; (1967) 61 A.J.I.L. 870

Article 1

1. All people have the right of self-determination. By virtue of that right they freely determine their political status and freely pursue their economic, social and cultural development.

2. All peoples may, for their own ends, freely dispose of their natural wealth and resources without prejudice to any obligations arising out of international economic co-operation, based upon the principle of mutual benefit, and international law. In no case may a people be deprived of its own means of subsistence.

---

[45] The abstaining states were, Byelorussian SSR, Czechoslovakia, Poland, Saudi Arabia, South Africa, Ukrainian SSR, USSR and Yugoslavia.

[46] (1948) 19 *US Dept. of State Bull.* 751.

[47] See *Measures taken within the United Nations in the field of Human Rights* UN Doc. A/CONF. 32/5, pp. 28–30.

[48] Below, p. 731.

[49] In force 1976. 136 parties, including the U.K. See McGoldrick, *The Human Rights Committee* (1991) and Nowak, *UN Covenant on Civil and Political Rights: CCPR Commentary* (1993).

3. The States Parties to the present Covenant, including those having responsibility for the administration of Non-Self-Governing and Trust Territories, shall promote the realisation of the right of self-determination, and shall respect that right, in conformity with the provisions of the Charter of the United Nations.

Article 2

1. Each State Party to the present Covenant undertakes to respect and to ensure to all individuals within its territory and subject to its jurisdiction the rights recognised in the present Covenant, without distinction of any kind, such as race, colour, sex, language, religion, political or other opinion, national or social origin, property, birth or other status.

2. Where not already provided for by existing legislative or other measures, each State Party to the present Covenant undertakes to take the necessary steps, in accordance with its constitutional processes and with the provisions of the present Covenant, to adopt such legislative or other measures as may be necessary to give effect to the rights recognised in the present Covenant.

3. Each State Party to the present Covenant undertakes:

(a) To ensure that any person whose rights or freedoms as herein recognized are violated shall have an effective remedy, notwithstanding that the violation has been committed by persons acting in an official capacity;

(b) To ensure that any person claiming such a remedy shall have his right thereto determined by competent judicial, administrative or legislative authorities, or by any other competent authority provided for by the legal system of the State, and to develop the possibilities of judicial remedy;

(c) To ensure that the competent authorities shall enforce such remedies when granted.

Article 3

The States Parties to the present Covenant undertake to ensure the equal right of men and women to the enjoyment of all civil and political rights set forth in the present Covenant.

Article 4

1. In time of public emergency which threatens the life of the nation and the existence of which is officially proclaimed, the States Parties to the present Covenant may take measures derogating from their obligations under the present Covenant to the extent strictly required by the exigencies of the situation, provided that such measures are not inconsistent with their other obligations under international law and do not

involve discrimination solely on the ground of race, colour, sex, language, religion or social origin.

2. No derogation from articles 6, 7, 8 (paragraphs 1 and 2), 11, 15, 16 and 18 may be made under this provision.

3. Any State Party to the present Covenant availing itself of the right of derogation shall immediately inform the other States Parties to the present Covenant, through the intermediary of the Secretary-General of the United Nations, of the provisions from which it has derogated and of the reasons by which it was actuated. A further communication shall be made, through the same intermediary, on the date on which it terminates such derogation.

Article 5

1. Nothing in the present Covenant may be interpreted as implying for any State, group or person any right to engage in any activity or perform any act aimed at the destruction of any of the rights and freedoms recognised herein or at their limitation to a greater extent than is provided for in the present Covenant.

2. There shall be no restriction upon or derogation from any of the fundamental human rights recognised or existing in any State Party to the present Covenant pursuant to law, conventions, regulations or custom on the pretext that the present Covenant does not recognise such rights or that it recognises them to a lesser extent.

Article 6

1. Every human being has the inherent right to life. This right shall be protected by law. No one shall be arbitrarily deprived of his life.

2. In countries which have not abolished the death penalty, sentence of death may be imposed only for the most serious crimes in accordance with the law in force at the time of the commission of the crime and not contrary to the provisions of the present Covenant and to the Convention on the Prevention and Punishment of the Crime of Genocide. This penalty can only be carried out pursuant to a final judgment rendered by a competent court.

3. When deprivation of life constitutes the crime of genocide, it is understood that nothing in this article shall authorise any State Party to the present Covenant to derogate in any way from any obligation assumed under the provisions of the Convention on the Prevention and Punishment of the Crime of Genocide.

4. Anyone sentenced to death shall have the right to seek pardon or commutation of the sentence. Amnesty, pardon or commutation of the sentence of death may be granted in all cases.

5. Sentence of death shall not be imposed for crimes committed by persons below 18 years of age and shall not be carried out on pregnant women.

6. Nothing in this article shall be invoked to delay or to prevent the abolition of capital punishment by any State Party to the present Covenant.

Article 7

No one shall be subjected to torture or to cruel, inhuman or degrading treatment or punishment. In particular, no one shall be subjected without his free consent to medical or scientific experimentation.

Article 8

1. No one shall be held in slavery; slavery and the slave-trade in all their forms shall be prohibited.

2. No one shall be held in servitude.

3. (a) No one shall be required to perform forced or compulsory labour;

   (b) Paragraph 3(a) shall not be held to preclude, in countries where imprisonment with hard labour may be imposed as a punishment for a crime, the performance of hard labour in pursuance of a sentence to such punishment by a competent court;

   (c) For the purpose of this paragraph the term "forced or compulsory labour" shall not include:

      (i) Any work or service, not referred to in subparagraph (b), normally required of a person who is under detention in consequence of a lawful order of a court, or of a person during conditional release from such detention;

      (ii) Any service of a military character and, in countries where conscientious objection is recognised, any national service required by law of conscientious objectors;

      (iii) Any service exacted in cases of emergency or calamity threatening the life or well-being of the community;

      (iv) Any work or service which forms part of normal civil obligations.

Article 9

1. Everyone has the right to liberty and security of person. No one shall be subjected to arbitrary arrest or detention. No one shall be deprived of his liberty except on such grounds and in accordance with such procedure as are established by law.

2. Anyone who is arrested shall be informed, at the time of arrest, of the reasons for his arrest and shall be promptly informed of any charges against him.

3. Anyone arrested or detained on a criminal charge shall be brought promptly before a judge or other officer authorised by law to exercise judicial power and shall be entitled to trial within a reasonable time or to release. It shall not be the general rule that persons awaiting trial shall be detained in custody, but release may be subject to guarantees to appear for trial, at any other stage of the judicial proceedings, and, should occasion arise, for execution of the judgment.

4. Anyone who is deprived of his liberty by arrest or detention shall be entitled to take proceedings before a court, in order that that court may decide without delay on the lawfulness of his detention and order his release if the detention is not lawful.

5. Anyone who has been the victim of unlawful arrest or detention shall have an enforceable right to compensation.

Article 10

1. All persons deprived of their liberty shall be treated with humanity and with respect for the inherent dignity of the human person.

2. (*a*) Accused persons shall, save in exceptional circumstances, be segregated from convicted persons and shall be subject to separate treatment appropriate to their status as unconvicted persons;

   (*b*) Accused juvenile persons shall be separated from adults and brought as speedily as possible for adjudication.

3. The penitentiary system shall comprise treatment of prisoners the essential aim of which shall be their reformation and social rehabilitation. Juvenile offenders shall be segregated from adults and be accorded treatment appropriate to their age and legal status.

Article 11

No one shall be imprisoned merely on the ground of inability to fulfil a contractual obligation.

Article 12

1. Everyone lawfully within the territory of a State shall, within that territory, have the right to liberty of movement and freedom to choose his residence.

2. Everyone shall be free to leave any country, including his own.

3. The above-mentioned rights shall not be subject to any restrictions except those which are provided by law, are necessary to protect national

security, public order (*ordre public*), public health or morals or the rights and freedoms of others, and are consistent with the other rights recognised in the present Covenant.

4. No one shall be arbitrarily deprived of the right to enter his own country.

Article 13

An alien lawfully in the territory of a State Party to the present Covenant may be expelled therefrom only in pursuance of a decision reached in accordance with law and shall, except where compelling reasons of national security otherwise require, be allowed to submit the reasons against his expulsion and to have his case reviewed by, and be represented for the purpose before, the competent authority or a person or persons especially designated by the competent authority.

Article 14

1. All persons shall be equal before the courts and tribunals. In the determination of any criminal charge against him, or of his rights and obligations in a suit of law, everyone shall be entitled to a fair and public hearing of a competent, independent and impartial tribunal established by law. The Press and the public may be excluded from all or part of a trial for reasons of morals, public order (*ordre public*) or national security in a democratic society, or where the interest of the private lives of the parties so requires, or the extent strictly necessary in the opinion of the court in special circumstances where publicity would prejudice the interests of justice; but any judgment rendered in a criminal case or in a suit at law shall be made public except where the interest of juvenile persons otherwise requires or the proceedings concern matrimonial disputes or the guardianship of children.

2. Everyone charged with a criminal offence shall have the right to be presumed innocent until proved guilty according to law.

3. In the determination of any criminal charge against him, everyone shall be entitled to the following minimum guarantees, in full equality:

(*a*) To be informed promptly and in detail in a language which he understands of the nature and cause of the charge against him;
(*b*) To have adequate time and facilities for the preparation of his defence and to communicate with counsel of his own choosing;
(*c*) To be tried without undue delay;
(*d*) To be tried in his presence, and to defend himself in person or through legal assistance of his own choosing; to be informed, if he does not have legal assistance, of this right; and to have legal assistance assigned to him, in any case where the interests of justice so require, and without payment by him in any such case if he does not have sufficient means to pay for it;

(*e*) To examine, or have examined, the witnesses against him and to obtain the attendance and examination of witnesses on his behalf under the same conditions as witnesses against him;

(*f*) To have the free assistance of an interpreter if he cannot understand or speak the language used in court;

(*g*) Not to be compelled to testify against himself or to confess guilt.

4. In the case of juvenile persons, the procedure shall be such as will take account of their age and the desirability of promoting their rehabilitation.

5. Everyone convicted of a crime shall have the right to his conviction and sentence being reviewed by a higher tribunal according to law.

6. When a person has by a final decision been convicted of a criminal offence and when subsequently his conviction has been reversed or he has been pardoned on the ground that a new or newly discovered fact shows conclusively that there has been a miscarriage of justice, the person who has suffered punishment as a result of such conviction shall be compensated according to law, unless it is proved that the non-disclosure of the unknown fact in time is wholly or partly attributable to him.

7. No one shall be liable to be tried or punished again for an offence for which he has already been finally convicted or acquitted in accordance with the law and penal procedure of each country.

Article 15

1. No one shall be held guilty of any criminal offence on account of any act or omission which did not constitute a criminal offence, under national or international law, at the time when it was committed. Nor shall a heavier penalty be imposed than the one that was applicable at the time when the criminal offence was committed. If, subsequent to the commission of the offence, provision is made by law for imposition of a lighter penalty, the offender shall benefit thereby.

2. Nothing in this article shall prejudice the trial and punishment of any person for any act or omission which, at the time when it was committed, was criminal according to the general principles of law recognised by the community of nations.

Article 16

Everyone shall have the right to recognition everywhere as a person before the law.

Article 17

1. No one shall be subjected to arbitrary or unlawful interference with his privacy, family, home or correspondence, nor to unlawful attacks on his honour and reputation.

2. Everyone has the right to the protection of the law against such interference or attacks.

Article 18

1. Everyone shall have the right to freedom of thought, conscience and religion. This right shall include freedom to have or adopt a religion or belief of his choice, and freedom, either individually or in community with others and in public or private, to manifest his religion or belief in worship, observance, practice and teaching.

2. No one shall be subject to coercion which would impair his freedom to have or to adopt a religion or belief of his choice.

3. Freedom to manifest one's religion or beliefs may be subject only to such limitations as are prescribed by law and are necessary to protect public safety, order, health, or morals or the fundamental rights and freedoms of others.

4. The States Parties to the present Covenant undertake to have respect for the liberty of parents and, when applicable, legal guardians to ensure the religious and moral education of their children in conformity with their own convictions.

Article 19

1. Everyone shall have the right to hold opinions without interference.

2. Everyone shall have the right to freedom of expression; this right shall include freedom to seek, receive and impart information and ideas of all kinds, regardless of frontiers, either orally, in writing or in print, in the form of art, or through any other media of his choice.

3. The exercise of the rights provided for in paragraph 2 of this article carries with it special duties and responsibilities. It may therefore be subject to certain restrictions, but these shall only be such as are provided by law and are necessary:

(*a*) For respect of the rights or reputations of others;
(*b*) For the protection of national security or of public order (*ordre public*), or of public health or morals.

Article 20

1. Any propaganda for war shall be prohibited by law.

2. Any advocacy of national, racial or religious hatred that constitutes incitement to discrimination, hostility or violence shall be prohibited by law.

Article 21

The right of peaceful assembly shall be recognised. No restrictions may be placed on the exercise of this right other than those imposed in conformity with the law and which are necessary in a democratic society in the interests of national security or public safety, public order (*ordre public*), the protection of public health or morals or the protection of the rights and freedoms of others.

Article 22

1. Everyone shall have the right to freedom of association with others, including the right to form and join trade unions for the protection of his interests.

2. No restrictions may be placed on the exercise of this right other than those which are prescribed by law and which are necessary in a democratic society in the interests of national security or public safety, public order (*ordre public*), the protection of public health or morals or the protection of the rights and freedoms of others. This article shall not prevent the imposition of lawful restrictions on members of the armed forces and of the police in their exercise of this right.

3. Nothing in this article shall authorise States Parties to the International Labour Organisation Convention of 1948 concerning Freedom of Association and Protection of the Right to Organize to take legislative measures which would prejudice, or to apply the law in such a manner as to prejudice, the guarantees provided for in that Convention.

Article 23

1. The family is the natural and fundamental group unit of society and is entitled to protection by society and the State.

2. The right of men and women of marriageable age to marry and to found a family shall be recognised.

3. No marriage shall be entered into without the free and full consent of the intending spouses.

4. State Parties to the present Covenant shall take appropriate steps to ensure equality of rights and responsibilities of spouses as to marriage, during marriage and at its dissolution. In the case of dissolution, provision shall be made for the necessary protection of any children.

Article 24

1. Every child shall have, without any discrimination as to race, colour, sex, language, religion, national or social origin, property or birth, the right to such measures of protection as are required by his status as a minor, on the part of his family, society and the State.

2. Every child shall be registered immediately after birth and shall have a name.

3. Every child has the right to acquire a nationality.

Article 25

Every citizen shall have the right and the opportunity, without any of the distinctions mentioned in article 2 and without unreasonable restrictions:

(*a*) To take part in the conduct of public affairs, directly or through freely chosen representatives;

(*b*) To vote and to be elected at genuine periodic elections which shall be by universal and equal suffrage and shall be held by secret ballot, guaranteeing the free expression of the will of the electors;

(*c*) To have access, on general terms of equality, to public service in his country.

Article 26

All persons are equal before the law and are entitled without any discrimination to the equal protection of the law. In this respect, the law shall prohibit any discrimination and guarantee to all persons equal and effective protection against discrimination on any ground such as race, colour, sex, language, religion, political or other opinion, national or social origin, property, birth or other status.

Article 27

In those States in which ethnic, religious or linguistic minorities exist, persons belonging to such minorities shall not be denied the right, in community with the other members of their group, to enjoy their own culture, to profess and practice their own religion, or to use their own language.

Article 47

Nothing in the present Covenant shall be interpreted as impairing the inherent right of all peoples to enjoy and utilise fully and freely their natural wealth and resources.

Article 50

The provisions of the present Covenant shall extend to all parts of federal States without any limitations or exceptions.

SECOND OPTIONAL PROTOCOL TO THE INTERNATIONAL COVENANT ON CIVIL AND POLITICAL RIGHTS, AIMING AT THE ABOLITION OF THE DEATH PENALTY 1989[50]

Annex to G.A. Resolution 44/128.

Article 1

1. No one within the jurisdiction of a State Party to the present Optional Protocol shall be executed.
2. Each State party shall take all necessary measures to abolish the death penalty within its jurisdiction.

Article 2

1. No reservation is admissible to the present Protocol, except for a reservation made at the time of ratification or accession that provides for the application of the death penalty in time of war pursuant to a conviction for a most serious crime of a military nature committed during wartime.
2. The State Party making such a reservation shall at the time of ratification or accession communicate to the Secretary-General of the United Nations the relevant provisions of its national legislation applicable during wartime.
3. The State Party having made such a reservation shall notify the Secretary-General of the United National of any beginning or ending of a state of war applicable to its territory.

Article 3

The States Parties to the present protocol shall include in the reports they submit to the Human Rights Committee, in accordance with article 40 of the Covenant, information on the measures that they have adopted to give effect to the present Protocol.

Article 4

With respect to the States Parties to the Covenant that have made a declaration under article 41, the competence of the Human Rights Committee to receive and consider communications when a State Party claims that another State Party is not fulfilling its obligations shall extend to the provisions of the present protocol, unless the State Party concerned has made a statement to the contrary at the moment of ratification or accession.

---

[50] In force 1991. 29 parties, not including the U.K.

Article 5

With respect to the States Parties to the (First) Optional Protocol to the International Covenant on Civil and Political Rights adopted on December 16, 1966, the competence of the Human Rights Committee to receive and consider communications from individuals subject to its jurisdiction shall extend to the provisions of the present Protocol, unless the State party concerned has made a statement to the contrary at the moment of ratification or accession.

Article 6

1. The provisions of the present Protocol shall apply as additional provisions to the Covenant.

2. Without prejudice to the possibility of a reservation under article 2 of the present Protocol, the right guaranteed in article 1, paragraph 1, of the present Protocol shall not be subject to any derogation under article 4 of the Covenant.

Article 9

The provisions of the present Protocol shall extend to all parts of federal States without any limitations or exceptions.

Notes

1. The Universal Declaration has been followed by a series of treaties adopted within the United Nations. Chief among these are the two 1966 International Covenants on Civil and Political Rights (ICCPR) and on Economic, Social and Cultural Rights (ICESCR) (below, p. 689).

2. The system of implementation of the ICCPR centres upon the Human Rights Committee.[51] This consists of 18 members elected from among the nationals of the contracting parties.[52] In the election, "consideration shall be given to equitable geographic distribution of membership and to the representation of the different forms of civilisation and of the principal legal systems" (Article 31(2), ICCPR) The members are independent experts; they do not represent their governments. They are nearly all lawyers. Despite Article 31(2), at present the Committee has a membership that does not accurately reflect the spread of states parties, being disproportionately Western.[53]

3. The parties to the Covenant "undertake to submit periodic reports on the measures they have adopted which give effect to the rights recognised herein and

---

[51] On the Committee, see Harris, in Harris and Joseph, eds., *The International Covenant on Civil and Political Rights and United Kingdom Law* (1995), pp. 1–41, and Opsahl, in Alston, ed., *The United Nations and Human Rights* (1992), Chap. 10. See also Schmidt (1992) 41 I.C.L.Q. 645.

[52] Article 28. Members, who serve part-time, are elected for four year terms.

[53] In 1997, the Committee was composed of nationals of the following states: European states: Finland, France, Germany, Italy, Slovenia, the U.K.; other Western states: Australia, Canada, the U.S.; Latin American and Caribbean states: Chile, Costa Rica, Ecuador, Jamaica, Venezuela; Asian states: India, Japan; Middle Eastern states: Israel; African states: Egypt.

on the progress made in the enjoyment of those rights" (Article 40(1)).[54] The
Committee has decided that, after a state's initial report, subsequent reports shall
be submitted at five–yearly intervals.[55] The Committee has experienced the same
problems of unsubmitted, late and inadequate reports as other international bodies
that operate reporting systems to monitor international human rights treaty
obligations.[56] Its practice is to consider reports at public hearings to which the state
whose report is being discussed is invited to send representatives to introduce the
report and respond to questions. So far only one state has refused to do so.[57] The
exchanges have generally been courteous, with the Committee emphasising that
its role is to achieve "constructive dialogue" in order to define the obligations in the
Covenant and to encourage compliance rather than to criticise.[58]

An important matter is the information that the Committee may have recourse
to when considering a state's report. Given that national reports inevitably present the government point of view, the question arises whether the Committee
may rely upon information from specialised agencies (particularly the ILO and
UNESCO) that operate in areas covered by the ICCPR and from NGOs, such as
Amnesty International and the International Commission of Jurists. The Committee has decided that specialised agencies should not be invited to comment on
states' reports; they may, however, submit information to individual members of
the Committee who are free to use it as they think fit. It is now established
practice for individual members to receive information from NGOs which they
commonly rely upon when questioning state representatives. Information provided by NGOs plays a very large part in the work of the Committee.

Having completed its examination of national reports, the HRC "shall transmit . . . such general comments as it may consider appropriate . . . to the States
Parties" to the ICCPR (Article 40(4)). It is by reference to this duty that the
Committee now completes its consideration of national reports by adopting
Concluding Comments on the state's human rights record.[59] On the basis of the
same duty, the Committee also adopts General Comments that are not specific to
particular states.

So far the General Comments made by the Committee have concerned the
reporting process (*e.g.* on the kind of information required) and the Committee's
interpretation of the Covenant guarantee. General Comments of the latter kind
have varied a great deal, with the Second General Comment on the right to life
(Article 6), see below, p. 655, for example, including a controversial statement

---

[54] On the reporting system, see Fischer (1982) 76 A.J.I.L. 142; Jhabvala (1984) 6 H.R.Q. 81; and
Joseph (1995) 13 N.Q.H.R. 5.
[55] G.A.O.R., 36th Sess., Supp. 40, Annex V (1981).
[56] In its 1996 Report, G.A.O.R., 51st Sess., Supp. 40, Annex IV, the Committee noted that four
initial reports (from Gabon, Niger, St Vincent and Sudan) and 21 subsequent reports due
in 1987 or earlier had not been submitted.
[57] In 1983, the report of Guinea was considered in the absence of a government representative after much delay: see Nowak, *op. cit.*, p. 647, n. 51 above, p. 563. In 1981, in General
Comment 2, para. 4, the HRC noted that government representatives were not of uniformly high quality and urged parties to ensure that their delegations were well-qualified
and well-briefed.
[58] For a notable exception, see the hearing of the first Iranian report which the Iranian
representative described as "a political inquisition"; S.R. 368, para. 58. The 1994 hearing
of the Egyptian report, S.R. 1244–7, was brought to life—hearings can seem less than
exciting to the outside observer—by persistent questioning that led to some unexpectedly
frank answers on issues such as the superiority of shari'a law over the ICCPR and the
treatment of the Baha'i.
[59] This practice dates from 1992, following the end of the Cold War. Earlier, East European
members had opposed such a practice, so that the Committee, which operates by consensus, did not make collective comments on particular states. The Comments review a
state's human rights record and may identify a breach of the Covenant by it.

about nuclear weapons, and others containing either little more than a wordy restatement of the relevant text (*e.g.* the General Comment on freedom of speech (Article 19)),[60] or useful elaboration upon its meaning (*e.g.* the General Comment on freedom from torture (Article 7), below, p. 665). General Comments are being increasingly supplemented as interpretations of the ICCPR by Committee "views" expressed in Optional Protocol cases (see below) in which the concept of consensus is not so predominant.

4. The Covenant also provides in Article 41 for an optional system of *state* applications.[61] A contracting party *may*, on condition of reciprocity, accept the right of the other contracting parties to bring a claim to the Committee alleging a violation of the Covenant by it. So far 40 parties (including the United Kingdom) have accepted it. A claim cannot be lodged unless a prescribed process of negotiation between the two parties has been completed without success. If satisfied that local remedies have been exhausted, the Committee "shall make available its good offices." The Committee must, within 12 months, submit a report indicating the facts and the solution reached or, if no solution has been reached, indicating just the facts and attaching to its reports the submission of the two parties. If no solution is reached, the Committee "may, with the prior consent of the States Parties concerned," appoint an *ad hoc* Conciliation Commission. If such a Commission is used by the parties and no settlement is reached through it, the Commission must make a report stating the facts and indicating "its views on the possibilities of an amicable settlement." The Report of the Commission is not binding. No state applications have been brought so far.

5. 89 of the parties to the ICCPR are parties also to its 1966 First Protocol (the Optional Protocol).[62] By this, a party

> recognises the competence of the Committee to receive and consider communications from individuals subject to its jurisdiction who claim to be victims of a violation by that State Party of any of the rights set forth in the Covenant. (Article 1).[63]

Aumeeruddy-Cziffra v. Mauritius (the Mauritian Women case)[64] is the leading case on the meaning of "victim". There the Committee stated:

> 9.2 . . . A person can only claim to be a victim in the sense of article 1 of the Optional Protocol if he or she is actually affected. It is a matter of degree how concretely this requirement should be taken. However, no individual can in the abstract, by way of an *actio popularis*, challenge a law or practice claimed to be contrary to the Covenant. If the law or practice has not already been concretely applied to the detriment of that individual, it must in any event be applicable in such a way that the alleged victim's risk of being affected is more than a theoretical possibility.

---

[60] H.R.C. Report, G.A.O.R. 38th Sess., Supp. 40, p. 109 (1983). Freedom of speech has been an area in which the UN has found it difficult to make progress because of differences of approach on the part of Western and other states.

[61] See Leckie (1988) 10 H.R.Q. 249.

[62] Misc. 4 (1976), Cmnd. 3320; (1967) 61 A.J.I.L. 887; 999 U.N.T.S. 302. The U.K. is not a party. It takes the view that an individual has a sufficient remedy through the European Convention on Human Rights. On the Committee's practice under the Optional Protocol, see Davidson (1991) 4 Canterbury L.R. 337; de Zayas, Möller and Opsahl, [1986] C.Y.H.R. 101 (same article in (1985) 28 G.Y.I.L. 9); and Ghandi (1986) 57 B.Y.I.L. 201.

[63] The Committee may also hear claims under the 1966 Protocol that arise under the 1989 Second Optional Protocol: see Art. 5 of the latter, above, p. 647.

[64] (1981) 1 Selected Decisions H.R.C. 67.

On the fact of that case, women whose husbands were at risk of deportation because their residence permits might be withdrawn at any time were considered "victims", but unmarried women were not.[65]

The overlap between the Protocol and petition systems under other human rights treaties is the subject of a rule by which the Committee may not consider a communication unless the "same matter is not being examined under another procedure of international investigation or settlement."[66] Thus an application pending at Strasbourg[67] or before the Inter-American Commission on Human Rights[68] is excluded. The Committee has, however, held that where the conduct of a state has resulted in more than one alleged victim, it may receive a communication from one of the victims even though the same conduct is the subject of a pending petition submitted elsewhere by another victim.[69] Consideration of communications under Resolution 1503[70] and country studies by the Inter-American Commission on Human Rights or the ILO Freedom of Association Committee do not relate to the "same matter"[71] as an individual communication under the Optional Protocol and so do not exclude the Committee's jurisdiction. The Committee's competence is also subject to other admissibility requirements, including the exhaustion of local remedies (Article 5(2)(*b*)). There is no time limit on the bringing of a claim. Legal aid is not available in the preparation or presentation of a communication.

6. The Committee considers both the admissibility and the merits of communications in private on the basis of written statements or explanations by the complainant and the defendant state. There is no provision for oral hearings. The Committee has discussed the possibility of inviting the complainant and the defendant state to participate in oral hearings, which would undoubtedly assist in the elucidation of the facts and the consideration of legal argument.[72]

7. The Committee's early jurisprudence was dominated by cases against Uruguay in which the then Government, which was accused of gross ill-treatment of political opponents, did not co-operate fully with the Committee, often failing to respond to requests for information.[73] It was in this context that the Committee established its rules concerning the burden of proof. In *Bleier v. Uruguay*,[74] in

---

[65] See also the *Toonen* case, below, p. 675, and *Hertzberg v. Finland* (1982) 1 Selected Decisions H.R.C. 124, where persons whose conduct was inhibited by laws which created the threat of prosecution were "victims" even though they had not been prosecuted.

[66] Art. 5(2)(*a*), First Optional Protocol. The Human Rights Committee will consider a claim "if it has been withdrawn from or is no longer being examined under... [another] procedure at the time that the Committee reaches a decision on the admissibility" of it: H.R.C. Report, G.A.O.R., 33rd Sess., Supp. 40, p. 100 (1978).

[67] *D.F. v. Sweden* (1985) 2 Selected Decisions H.R.C., p. 55. The Committee may consider a case the examination of which at Strasbourg has been completed, unless the state concerned has made a reservation to its acceptance of the Optional Protocol excluding such cases; see, *e.g. Valentjin v. France* (1997) 4 I.H.R.R. 273.

[68] *Millàn v. Uruguay,* (1980) 1 Selected Decisions H.R.C. 52.

[69] *Fanali v. Italy,* (1983) 2 Selected Decisions H.R.C. 99.

[70] *A v. S.,* (1978) 1 Selected Decisions H.R.C. 17.

[71] *Baboeram v. Suriname,* (1985) 2 Selected Decisions H.R.C. 172.

[72] See Tomuschat (1980) 1 H.R.L.J. 249 at 354, a former Committee member, who notes the inadequacy of written proceedings, but points to the burden that oral proceedings would add for a hard-pressed, part-time body. Note that at present cases can take four years to complete.

[73] The Uruguayan Government that accepted the Optional Protocol in 1970 was overthrown by a revolutionary Government whose acts resulted in the numerous cases against Uruguay. In 1984 that Government was itself overthrown and replaced the following year by an elected Government which has been commended for its co-operation with the Committee: *Conteris v. Uruguay,* (1985) 2 Selected Decisions H.R.C. 168 at 171.

[74] (1982) 1 Selected Decisions H.R.C. 109 at 112.

which Uruguay's denial that a disappeared person was in its custody was contradicted by other evidence, the Committee stated:

> 13.3 With regard to the burden of proof, this cannot rest alone on the author of the communication, especially considering that the author and the State Party do not always have equal access to the evidence and that frequently the State Party alone has access to relevant information. It is implicit in Article 4(2) of the Optional Protocol that the State Party has the duty to investigate in good faith all allegations of violation of the Covenant made against it and its authorities, especially when such allegations are corroborated by evidence submitted by the author of the communication, and to furnish to the Committee the information available to it. In cases where the author has submitted to the Committee allegations supported by substantial witness testimony, as in this case, and where further clarification of the case depends on information exclusively in the hands of the State Party, the Committee may consider such allegations as substantiated in the absence of satisfactory evidence and explanations to the contrary submitted by the State Party.

The Committee continues to decide cases on the basis of the author's uncontested, but substantiated allegations, sometimes in situations where the state cannot be said to have exclusive access to any relevant evidence in the sense of the *Bleier* case but where the state simply refuses to respond.[75]

8. The Committee may suggest interim measures "to avoid irreparable damage to the victim,"[76] as it did when it successfully requested a stay of execution of the death penalty in *Pratt and Morgan v. Jamaica*.[77] States do not always comply with requests. In *Ashley v. Trinidad*,[78] a sentence of capital punishment was carried out in a pending case despite the Committee's request to the contrary.

9. The Committee is required to formulate its "views" on the question whether a breach has occurred and to send them to the defendant state and the complainant (Article 5(4)). In deciding on its "views" (and when taking decision as to admissibility), the Committee "strives to reach its decisions by consensus, without resorting to voting. However, . . . members can append their individual opinions to the Committee's decisions of a final nature."[79] The Committee's "views" are not legally binding and there is no provision for a court or any other body to take binding decisions. The Committee has explained its functions and powers as follows[80]:

> . . . the Committee is neither a court nor a body with a quasi-judicial mandate, like the organs created under another international Human Rights instrument, the European Convention on Human Rights . . . Still, the Committee applies the provisions of the Covenant and of the Optional Protocol in a judicial spirit and performs functions similar to those of the European Commission of Human Rights, in as much as the consideration of applications from individuals is concerned. Its decisions on the merits (of a communication) are, in principle, comparable to the reports of the European Commission, non-binding recommendations. The two systems differ, however, in that the Optional Protocol does not provide explicitly for friendly settlement between the parties, and, more importantly, in that the Committee has no power to hand down

---

[75] See, *e.g. Reid v. Jamaica* (1995) 2 I.H.R.R. 57.
[76] Rule 86, H.R.C. Rules of Procedure, G.A.O.R., 32nd Sess., Supp. 44, Annex II (1977).
[77] See below, p. 666.
[78] H.R.C. Report, G.A.O.R., 49th Sess., Supp. 40, Vol. I, p. 70 (1994).
[79] H.R.C. Report, G.A.O.R., 44th Sess., Supp. 40, p. 14 (1989).
[80] (1990) 2 Selected Decisions H.R.C. 1–2.

binding decisions as does the European Court of Human Rights. States parties to the Optional Protocol endeavour to observe the Committee's views, but in case of non-compliance the Optional Protocol does not provide for an enforcement mechanism or for sanctions.

Although its "views" are not legally binding, the Committee has received information from some defendant states indicating that they have taken, or are in the process of taking, action in response to findings against them.[81] But in many cases, states have not implemented the Committee's views. As a result, the Committee has appointed a "special rapporteur for the follow up on views"[82] to monitor the situation and list states that have not responded to requests for information.

10. By 1996, 591 communications, naming 28 defendant states, had been registered. The Committee had adopted views on the merits in 120 of these cases, in 93 of which breaches had been found. 85 cases had been declared inadmissible. The remainder were pending or had been withdrawn. The number of petitions is likely to increase as more states become parties to the Protocol and the Committee's jurisprudence becomes better known. Applications against state parties to the European and American Conventions are, however, likely to remain relatively low in number given the substantial overlap between the guarantees in the ICCPR and these regional conventions and the binding nature of Court decisions within the two regional convention systems.[83]

GUERRERO *v.* COLOMBIA

(1982) 1 Selected Decisions H.R.C. 112

In this case, the Colombian police raided a house in which it was thought that a kidnap victim was being detained. The victim was not found, but the police hid in the house awaiting the arrival of the suspected kidnappers. Seven persons, who were never proved to have been connected with the kidnapping, were shot without warning as they arrived at intervals at the house. The police action was justified by the government on the basis of Legislative Decree No. 0070 which, for so long as "the national territory is in a state of siege," provided the police with a defence to any criminal charge arising out of acts committed "in the course of operations planned with the object of preventing and curbing kidnapping."

Views of the Committee

13.1 . . . The right enshrined in [Article 6] . . . is the supreme right of the human being. It follows that the deprivation of life by the authorities of the State is a matter of the utmost gravity. This follows from the article as

[81] See *Aumeeruddy-Cziffra v. Mauritius* (1981) 1 Selected Decisions H.R.C. 67; *Lovelace v. Canada*, below, p. 684; and *Vuolanne v. Finland*, below, p. 669. In 1984, Uruguay sent the Committee a list of detainees who had been released, including two in whose cases the Committee had found breaches of the Covenant: see H.R.C. Report, G.A.O.R., 39th Sess., Supp. 40, p. 126 (1984). The Committee had also learnt unofficially of the release of three other such detainees: *ibid.*

[82] H.R.C. Report, G.A.O.R., 45th Sess., Supp. 40, Vol. II, Annex XI (1990). On the follow-up Procedure, see the Committee's submission to the 1993 Vienna World Conference on Human Rights ("Follow-up on Views, etc.") (1994) 1–2 I.H.R.R. 345, and de Zayas (1991) 47 I.C.J. Rev. 28.

[83] Note, however, that the Optional Protocol does not impose a time limit on the bringing of cases, whereas the two American and European Conventions have a six–month time limit.

a whole and in particular is the reason why paragraph 2 of the article lays down that the death penalty may be imposed only for the most serious crimes. The requirements that the right shall be protected by law and that no one shall be arbitrarily deprived of his life mean that the law must strictly control and limit the circumstances in which a person may be deprived of his life by the authorities of a State.

13.2 In the present case it is evident from the fact that seven persons lost their lives as a result of the deliberate action of the police that the deprivation of life was intentional. Moreover, the police action was apparently taken without warning to the victims and without giving them any opportunity to surrender to the police patrol or to offer any explanation of their presence or intentions. There is no evidence that the action of the police was necessary in their own defence or that of others, or that it was necessary to effect the arrest or prevent the escape of the persons concerned. Moreover, the victims were no more than suspects of the kidnapping which had occurred some days earlier and their killing by the police deprived them of all the protections of due process of law laid down by the Covenant. In the case of Mrs. María Fanny Suárez de Guerrero, the forensic report showed that she had been shot several times after she had already died from a heart attack. There can be no reasonable doubt that her death was caused by the police patrol.

13.3 For these reasons it is the Committee's view that the action of the police resulting in the death of Mrs. María Fanny Suárez de Guerrero was disproportionate to the requirements of law enforcement in the circumstances of the case and that she was arbitrarily deprived of her life contrary to article 6(1). . . . Inasmuch as the police action was made justifiable as a matter of Colombian law by Legislative Decree No. 0070 . . . , the right to life was not adequately protected by the law of Colombia as required by article 6(1). . . .

15. The Committee is accordingly of the view that the State Party should take the necessary measures to compensate the husband of Mrs. María Fanny Suárez de Guerrero for the death of his wife and to ensure that the right to life is duly protected by amending the law.

Notes

1. The *Guerrero* case (sometimes referred to as the *Camargo* case) stresses the pre-eminent importance of the right to life and imposes strict standards for the taking of life by the state.[84] The Committee gives some indication of the meaning of a taking of life that is "arbitrary" contrary to Article 6(1). The fact that it is

---

[84] *cf.* para. 4, H.R.C. First General Comment on Art. 6, H.R.C. Report, G.A.O.R., 37th Sess., Supp. 40, p. 93 (1982). *cf.* also *Baboeram v. Suriname*, (1985) 2 Selected Decisions H.R.C. 172, in which 15 prominent Surinamese citizens associated with attempts to introduce democracy into Suriname were taken from their homes at night by the military and killed. The Government claimed that they had been killed trying to escape following an attempted coup. In view of evidence provided by the authors of the communications of injuries to the bodies that were not consistent with this explanation and in the absence of any medical reports from the Government to the contrary, the Committee concluded that "the victims were arbitrarily deprived of their lives" contrary to Art. 6(1).

lawful under national law is not such as to prevent it from being "arbitrary." The self defence, arrest and prevention of escape justifications that the Committee implies are acceptable are ones commonly allowed in national law and expressly permitted (on a basis of absolute necessity) by the European Convention on Human Rights, Article 2.

2. An important problem concerning the right to life is that of "disappeared persons". In its First General Comment on Article 6,[85] the Committee commented on this problem as follows:

> 4. States parties should also take specific and effective measures to prevent the disappearance of individuals, something which unfortunately has become all too frequent and leads too often to arbitrary deprivation of life. Furthermore, States should establish effective facilities and procedures to investigate thoroughly cases of missing and disappeared persons in circumstances which may involve a violation of the right to life.

In *Bleir v. Uruguay*,[86] in which the defendant state's denial that a disappeared person was in its custody was contradicted by other evidence, the Committee, applying its burden of proof rule, see above, p. 650, stated:

> 13.4 The Committee finds that the disappearance of Eduardo Bleier in October 1975 does not alone establish that he was arrested by Uruguayan authorities. But, the allegation that he was so arrested and detained is confirmed (i) by the information, unexplained and substantially unrefuted by the State party, that Eduardo Bleier's name was on a list of prisoners read out once a week at an army unit in Montevideo where his family delivered clothing for him and received his dirty clothing until the summer of 1976, and (ii) by the testimony of other prisoners that they saw him in Uruguayan detention centres. Also there are the reports of several eyewitnesses that Eduardo Bleier was subjected to severe torture while in detention.
>
> 14. It is therefore the Committee's view that the information before it reveals breaches of articles 7, 9 and 10(1) of the International Covenant on Civil and Political Rights and that there are serious reasons to believe that the ultimate violation of article 6 has been perpetrated by the Uruguayan authorities.
>
> 15. As regards the latter point the Human Rights Committee urges the Uruguayan Government to reconsider its position in this case and to take effective steps (i) to establish what has happened to Eduardo Bleier since October 1975; to bring to justice any persons found to be responsible for his death, disappearance or ill-treatment; and to pay compensation to him or his family for any injury which he has suffered; and (ii) to ensure that similar violations do not occur in the future.

3. The Committee has considered several cases in which individuals have died after being taken into custody but in which the defendant state has denied that death was attributable to its agents. In *Herrera Rubio v. Colombia*,[87] the author's parents were taken from their home by "individuals wearing military uniforms, identifying themselves as members of the counter-guerilla." After the parents had

---

[85] See previous note.

[86] (1982) 1 Selected Decisions H.R.C. 109 at 112. For other more recent cases of disappearances resulting in findings of breaches of Arts. 6, 7 and 9, see *Mojica v. Dominican Rep.* (1995) 2 I.H.R.R. 86; *Bautista de Arellana v. Colombia* (1996) 3 I.H.R.R. 315; and *Celis Laureano v. Peru* (1997) 4 I.H.R.R. 54.

[87] (1985) 2 Selected Decisions H.R.C. 192. *cf. Barbato v. Uruguay, ibid.*, p. 112 (1982) and *Miango v. Zaire, ibid.*, p. 219 (1987). See also *Burrell v. Jamaica* (1997) 4 I.H.R.R. 350.

later been found dead, a state investigation "established that no member of the armed forces had taken part in the killings." The Committee stated[88]:

> 10.3. Whereas the Committee considers that there is reason to believe, in the light of the author's allegations, that Colombian military persons bear responsibility for the deaths of José Herrera and Emma Rubio de Herrera, no conclusive evidence has been produced to establish the identity of the murderers. In this connection the Committee refers to its general comment No. 6 (16) concerning article 6 of the Covenant, [para. 4, note 2 above] . . . The Committee has duly noted the State Party's submissions concerning the investigations carried out in this case, which, however, appear to have been inadequate in the light of the State Party's obligations under article 2 of the Covenant . . .
> 11. The Human Rights Committee, . . . is of the view that the facts as found by the Committee disclose violations of the Covenant with respect to:
> Article 6, because the State Party failed to take appropriate measures to prevent the disappearance and subsequent killings of José Herrera and Emma Rubio de Herrera and to investigate effectively the responsibility for their murders; . . .

4. In its First General Comment on Article 6, the Committee noted the link between non-compliance with the international law rules prohibiting resort to armed force and the loss of innocent lives. The matter was taken up again in the Second General Comment[89] on Article 6, in which the Committee focused on the dangers of nuclear weapons:

> 4. . . . It is evident that the designing, testing, manufacture, possession and deployment of nuclear weapons are among the greatest threats to the right to life which confront mankind today. This threat is compounded by the danger that the actual use of such weapons may be brought about, not only in the event of war, but even through human or mechanical error or failure. . . .
> 6. The production, testing, possession, deployment and use of nuclear weapons should be prohibited and recognised as crimes against humanity.
> 7. The Committee accordingly, in the interest of mankind, calls upon all States whether parties to the Covenant or not, to take urgent steps, unilaterally and by agreement, to rid the world of this menace.

The Committee does not now refer to this Second General Comment and may be taken to have accepted that it went too far.

5. In its First General Comment on Article 6, the Committee also interpreted Article 6 in such a way as to impose a positive obligation upon states, of the kind more normally associated with the protection of economic, social and cultural rights[90]:

> 5. Moreover, the Committee has noted that the right to life has been too often narrowly interpreted. The expression "inherent right to life" cannot properly be understood in a restrictive manner, and the protection of this right requires that States adopt positive measures. In this connection, the Committee considers that it would be desirable for States Parties to take all possible measures

---

[88] *ibid.*, p. 195. *cf.* the obligation upon a state to account for an alien in its custody under the law of state responsibility: See the *Quintanilla* case, above, p. 538.

[89] G.A.O.R., 40th Sess., Supp. 40, p. 162 (1985). Para. 6 of the General Comment was the subject of criticism by some states in the General Assembly Third Committee: see G.A.O.R., 39th Sess., A/C.3/SR 46, 48–51 (1984).

[90] *loc. cit.*, p. 653, n. 84, above.

to reduce infant mortality and to increase life expectancy, especially in adopting measures to eliminate malnutrition and epidemics.

NG *v.* CANADA

(1994) 1–2 I.H.R.R. 161

In 1985, the author, a British subject resident in the U.S., was convicted in Canada of offences following the shooting a security guard. In 1990, he was extradited to stand trial in California for kidnapping and 12 murders. After reviewing the facts, the Canadian Minister of Justice decided not to exercise his power under the extradition treaty to obtain an assurance, as a condition of extradition, that the death penalty would not be imposed. The author claimed, in his 1991 communication to the HRC that his extradition was in breach, *inter alia*, of Articles 6 and 7, ICCPR. He had not been tried in California by the time the HRC's views were adopted.

Views of the Committee

14.2 If a State party extradites a person within its jurisdiction in such circumstances that as a result there is a real risk that his or her rights under the Covenant will be violated in another jurisdiction, the State party itself may be in violation of the Covenant.

15.1 With regard to a possible violation by Canada of article 6 of the Covenant by its decision to extradite Mr. Ng, two related questions arise:

(a) Did the requirement under article 6, paragraph 1, to protect the right to life prohibit Canada from exposing a person within its jurisdiction to the real risk (i.e. a necessary and forseeable consequence) of being sentenced to death and losing his life in circumstances incompatible with article 6 of the Covenant as a consequence of extradition to the United States?

(b) Did the fact that Canada had abolished capital punishment except for certain military offences require Canada to refuse extradition or request assurances from the United States, as it was entitled to do under article 6 of the Extradition Treaty, that the death penalty would not be imposed against Mr. Ng? . . .

15.3 . . . Among the requirements of article 6, paragraph 2, is that capital punishment be imposed only for the most serious crimes, under circumstances not contrary to the Covenant and other instruments, and that it be carried out pursuant to a final judgment rendered by a competent court. The Committee notes that Mr. Ng was extradited to stand trial on 19 criminal charges, including 12 counts of murder. If sentenced to death, that sentence, based on the information which the Committee has before it, would be based on a conviction of guilt in respect of very serious crimes. He was over eighteen years when the crimes of which he stands accused were committed. Finally, while the author has claimed before the Supreme Court of Canada and before the Committee that his right to a fair trial would not be guaranteed in the judicial process in California, because of racial bias in the jury selection process and in the imposition of the death penalty, these claims have been advanced in respect of purely hypothetical events, and nothing in the file supports the contention that the author's trial in the Calaveras County Court would not meet the requirements of article 14 of the Covenant.

15.4 Moreover, the Committee observes that Mr. Ng was extradited to the United States after extensive proceedings in the Canadian courts, which reviewed all the charges and the evidence available against the author. In the circumstances, the Committee concludes that Canada's obligations under article 6, paragraph 1, did not require it to refuse Mr. Ng's extradition.

15.5 The Committee notes that Canada has itself, except for certain categories of military offences, abolished capital punishment; it is not, however, a party to the Second Optional Protocol to the Covenant [above, p. 646]. As to issue (b) in paragraph 15.1 above, ... the Committee observes that abolition of capital punishment does not release Canada of its obligations under extradition treaties. However, it should be expected that, when exercising a permitted discretion under an extradition treaty (namely, whether or not to seek assurances that the death penalty would not be imposed) a State party which itself abandoned capital punishment gives serious consideration to its own chosen policy. The Committee notes, however, that Canada has indicated that the possibility to seek assurances would normally be exercised where special circumstances existed; in the present case, this possibility was considered and rejected.

15.6 While States must be mindful of their obligation to protect the right to life when exercising their discretion in the application of extradition treaties, the Committee does not find that the terms of article 6 of the Covenant necessarily require Canada to refuse to extradite or to seek assurances. The Committee notes that the extradition of Mr. Ng would have violated Canada's obligations under article 6 of the Covenant, if the decision to extradite without assurances had been taken summarily or arbitrarily. The evidence before the Committee reveals, however, that the Minister of Justice reached his decision after hearing extensive arguments in favour of seeking assurances. The Committee further takes note of the reasons advanced by the Minister of Justice, in his letter dated 26 October 1989 addressed to Mr. Ng's counsel, in particular, the absence of exceptional circumstances, the availability of due process and of appeal against conviction, and the importance of not providing a safe haven for those accused for murder.

15.7 In the light of the above, the Committee concludes that Mr. Ng is not a victim of a violation by Canada of article 6 of the Covenant. ...

16.1 In determining whether, in a particular case, the imposition of capital punishment constitutes a violation of article 7, the Committee will have regard to the relevant personal factors regarding the author, the specific conditions of detention on death row, and whether the proposed method of execution is particularly abhorrent. In the instant case, it is contented that execution by gas asphyxiation is contrary to internationally accepted standards of humane treatment, and that it amounts to treatment in violation of article 7 of the Covenant. The Committee begins by noting that whereas article 6, paragraph 2, allows for the imposition of the death penalty under certain limited circumstances, any method of execution provided for by law must be designed in such a way as to avoid conflict with article 7.

16.2 The Committee is aware that, by definition, every execution of a sentence of death may be considered to constitute cruel and inhuman treatment within the meaning of article 7 of the Covenant; on the other hand, article 6, paragraph 2, permits the imposition of capital punishment for the most serious crimes. Nonetheless, the Committee reaffirms, as it did in its General Comment 20[44] on article 7 of the Covenant (CCPR/C/21Add.3, paragraph 6) that, when imposing capital punishment, the execution of the sentence " . . . must be carried out in such a way as to cause the least possible physical and mental suffering".

16.3 In the present case, the author has provided detailed information that execution by gas asphyxiation may cause prolonged suffering and agony and does not result in death as swiftly as possible, as asphyxiation by cyanide gas may take over 10 minutes. The State party had the opportunity to refute these allegations on the facts; it has failed to do so. Rather, the State party has confined itself to arguing that in the absence of a norm of international law which expressly prohibits asphyxiation by cyanide gas, "it would be interfering to an unwarranted degree with the internal laws and practices of the United States to refuse to extradite a fugitive to face the possible imposition of the death penalty by cyanide gas asphyxiation".

16.4 In the instant case and on the basis of the information before it, the Committee concludes that execution by gas asphyxiation, should the death penalty be imposed on the author, would not meet the test of "least possible physical and mental suffering", and constitutes cruel and inhuman treatment, in violation of article 7 of the Covenant. Accordingly, Canada which could reasonably foresee that Mr. Ng, if sentenced to death, would be executed in a way that amounts to a violation of article 7, failed to comply with its obligations under the Covenant, by extraditing Mr. Ng without having sought and received assurances that he would not be executed.

16.5 The Committee need not pronounce itself on the compatibility, with article 7, of methods of execution other than that which is at issue in this case.

17. The Human Rights Committee, acting under article 5, paragraph 4, of the International Covenant on Civil and Political Rights, is of the view that the facts as found by the Committee reveal a violation by Canada of article 7 of the Covenant.

18. The Human Rights Committee requests the State party to make such representations as might still be possible to avoid the imposition of the death penalty and appeals to the State party to ensure that a similar situation does not arise in the future.

Dissenting Opinion of Messrs Mavrommatis and Sadi

We do not believe that, on the basis of the material before us, execution by gas asphyxiation could constitute cruel and inhuman treatment within the meaning of article 7 of the Covenant. A method of execution such as death by stoning, which is intended to and actually inflicts prolonged pain and suffering, is contrary to article 7.

Every known method of judicial execution in use today, including execution by lethal injection, has come under criticism for causing prolonged pain or the necessity to have the process repeated. We do not believe that the Committee should look into such details in respect of execution such as whether acute pain of limited duration or less pain of longer duration is preferable and could be a criterion for a finding of violation of the Covenant.

Dissenting Opinion of Mr. Ando

In the view of the Committee . . . (paragraph 16.3) . . . the swiftness of death seems to be the very criterion by which the Committee has concluded that execution by gas asphyxiation violates article 7.

In many of the States parties to the Covenant where death penalty has not been abolished, other methods of execution such as hanging, shooting, electrocution or injection of certain materials are used. Some of them may take a longer time and others shorter than gas asphyxiation, but I wonder if, irrespective of the kind and degree of suffering inflicted on the executed, all those methods that may take over ten minutes are in violation of article 7 and all others that take less are in conformity with it. In other words I consider that the criteria of permissible suffering under article 7 should not solely depend on the swiftness of death.

The phrase "least possible physical and mental suffering" comes from the Committee's General Comment 20 on article 7, which states that the death penalty must be carried out in such a way as to cause the least possible physical and mental suffering. This statement, in fact, implies that there is no method of execution which does not cause any physical or mental suffering and that every method of execution is bound to cause some suffering.

However, I must admit that it is impossible for me to specify which kind of suffering is permitted under article 7 and what degree of suffering is not permitted under the same article. I am totally incapable of indicating any absolute criterion as to the scope of suffering permissible under article 7. What I can say is that article 7 prohibits any method of execution which is *intended for* prolonging suffering of the executed or causing unnecessary pain to him or her. As I do not believe that gas asphyxiation is so intended, I cannot concur with the Committee's view that execution by gas asphyxiation violates article 7 of the Covenant.

Notes

1. With regard to the death penalty, the Committee's First General Comment on Article 6 reads[91]:

> 6. While it follows from article 6(2) to (6) that States Parties are not obliged to abolish the death penalty totally, they are obliged to limit its use and, in particular, to abolish it for other than the "most serious crimes." Accordingly, they ought to consider reviewing their criminal laws in this light and, in any event, are obliged to restrict the application of the death penalty to the "most serious crimes." The article also refers generally to abolition in terms which strongly suggest (paras. 2(2) and (6)) that abolition is desirable. The Committee concludes that all measures of abolition should be considered as progress in the enjoyment of the right to life within the meaning of article 40, and should as such be reported to the Committee. The Committee notes that a number of States have already abolished the death penalty or suspended its application. Nevertheless, States' reports show that progress made towards abolishing or limiting the application of the death penalty is quite inadequate.
>
> 7. The Committee is of the opinion that the expression "most serious crimes" must be read restrictively to mean that the death penalty should be a quite exceptional measure. It also follows from the express terms of article 6 that it can only be imposed in accordance with the law in force at the time of the commission of the crime and not contrary to the Covenant. The procedural guarantees therein prescribed must be observed, including the right to a fair hearing by an independent tribunal, the presumption of innocence, the minimum guarantees for the defence, and the right to review by a higher tribunal. These rights are applicable in addition to the particular right to seek pardon or commutation of the sentence.

As to "procedural guarantees", in *Mbenge v. Zaire*,[92] having found breaches of the fair trial guarantees in Article 14(3)(a)(b)(d) and (e), the Committee concluded that as a result of these findings "the death sentences pronounced against the author . . . were imposed contrary to the provisions of the Covenant, and therefore in violation of Article 6(2)."

Under the Second Optional Protocol to the Covenant, above, p. 646, the parties thereto undertake not to execute persons and to take all the necessary measures to abolish the death penalty.

2. 90 states retain the death penalty.[93] It exists for political offences (*e.g.* treason[94]), military offences (*e.g.* mutiny), terrorist offences (*e.g.* hijacking), drug trafficking offences, ordinary offences (*e.g.* murder, kidnapping), economic offences (*e.g.* public corruption) and rape. Some Islamic states make apostacy,

---

[91] *loc. cit.*, p. 653, n. 84.

[92] (1983) 2 Selected Decisions H.R.C. 76 at 79. *cf. Pratt and Morgan v. Jamaica* below, p. 666.

[93] Hood, *The Death Penalty: A World Wide Perspective* (2nd ed., 1996), p. 9. See generally, Schabas, *The Abolition of the Death Penalty in International Law* (1993), and Naldi (1991) 38 N.I.L.R. 373.

[94] Treason and piracy with violence are capital offences in the U.K., although no execution, or conviction, has occurred since the late 1940s.

adultery, sodomy, drinking liquor, sex between a muslim and a non-muslim capital offences.[95] Are these all "the most serious crimes"? Consistently with the U.S. Constitution, some U.S. states make juveniles of 16 or 17 liable for the death penalty; the U.S. made a reservation[96] when ratifying the ICCPR to safeguard this position in view of Article 6(5).

3. In the *Ng* case, five members of the Committee[97] dissented from its finding that Article 6 had not been infringed, mostly for the reason that it prohibited Canada from reintroducing the death penalty, both indirectly (by extradition) and directly.

4. In two other death penalty cases involving extradition by Canada to the United States, no breach of the ICCPR were found. In *Kindler v. Canada*,[98] the author had been convicted of murder in the U.S. and the death penalty recommended by the jury when he escaped to Canada. In *Cox v. Canada*,[99] the author was wanted for trial on capital murder charges. On Article 6, the Committee's reasoning in both cases was the same as that in *Ng*. On Article 7, there were no personal factors or special prison conditions in either case that indicated a breach. In the *Cox* case, the Committee held that, in contrast with gas asphyxiation, execution by lethal injection of cyanide was not a breach of Article 7.[1] Are such fine distinctions defensible? Would you agree with the different approach to Article 7 in death penalty cases in the dissenting opinions of Messrs Mavrommatis, Sadi and Ando?

5. The Human Rights Committee has long taken the view that detention for a long period of time on death row does not *per se* amount to a breach of Article 7 or Article 10 (concerning the treatment of prisoners); there have to be further "compelling circumstances". In *Barrett and Sutcliffe v. Jamaica*,[2] the Committee justified this view as follows:

> The Committee . . . reiterates that prolonged judicial proceedings do not *per se* constitute cruel, inhuman and degrading treatment, even if they may be a source of mental strain and tension for detained persons. This also applies to appeal and review proceedings in cases involving capital punishment, although an assessment of the particular circumstances of each case would be called for. In States whose judicial system provides for a review of criminal convictions and sentences, an element of delay between the lawful imposition of a sentence of death and the exhaustion of available remedies is inherent in the review of the sentence; thus, even prolonged periods of detention under a severe custodial regime on death row cannot generally be considered to constitute cruel, inhuman or degrading treatment if the convicted person is merely availing himself of appellate remedies.

Aware of the Committee's view, in *Pratt v. Att.-Gen. of Jamaica*,[3] the Privy Council took a different stance. In its opinion, "in any case in which execution is to take

---

[95] See the survey in Hood, above, Chap. 2.

[96] See UN Doc. ST/LEG/SER.E/15, p. 130.

[97] Messrs Aguillar, Lallah, Pocar and Wennergren, and Mme Chanet.

[98] (1994) 1–2 I.H.R.R. 98.

[99] (1995) 2 I.H.R.R. 307.

[1] Lethal injection was the method in the *Kindler* case also, but the Committee did not rule expressly on this point in that case since the author did not argue it.

[2] H.R.C. Report, G.A.O.R., 47th Sess., Supp. 40, p. 246 at p. 250 (1992). Mme Chanet, dissenting, preferred the approach of the European Court of Human Rights in *Soering v. U.K.* E.Ct.H.R.Rep., Ser. A, No. 161, para. 105 (1989), that no allowance should be made to the benefit of the state for the fact that the delay was caused by the convicted person exercising a right of appeal, because it is "part of human nature that the person will cling to life by exploiting those safeguards to the full".

[3] [1994] 2 A.C. 1 at 35.

place more than five years after sentence there will be strong grounds for believing that the delay is such as to constitute 'inhuman or degrading punishment or other treatment'."

Partly in answer to the Privy Council's opinion, in *Johnson v. Jamaica*,[4] the Committee gave other reasons for its view:

> 8.3 . . . we must examine the implications of holding the length of detention on death row, *per se*, to be in violation of articles 7 and 10. The first, and most serious, implication is that if a State party executes a condemned prisoner after he has spent a certain period of time on death row, it will not be in violation of its obligations under the Covenant, whereas if it refrains from doing so, it will violate the Covenant. An interpretation of the Covenant leading to this result cannot be consistent with the Covenant's object and purpose. The above implication cannot be avoided by refraining from determining a definite period of detention on death row, after which there will be a presumption that detention on death row constitutes cruel and inhuman punishment. Setting a cut-off date certainly exacerbates the problem and gives the State party a clear deadline for executing a person if it is to avoid violating its obligations under the Covenant. However, this implication is not a function of fixing the maximum permissible period of detention on death row, but of making the time factor, *per se*, the determining one. If the maximum acceptable period is left open, States parties which seek to avoid overstepping the deadline will be tempted to look to the decisions of the Committee in previous cases so as to determine what length of detention on death row the Committee has found permissible in the past.
>
> 8.4 The second implication of making the time factor *per se* the determining one, *i.e.* the factor that turns detention on death row into a violation of the Covenant, is that it conveys a message to States parties retaining the death penalty that they should carry out a capital sentence as expeditiously as possible after it was imposed. This is not a message the Committee would wish to convey to States parties. Life on death row, harsh as it may be, is preferable to death. Furthermore, experience shows that delays in carrying out the death penalty can be the necessary consequence of several factors, many of which may be attributable to the State party. Sometimes a moratorium is placed on executions while the whole question of the death penalty is under review. At other times the executive branch of government delays executions even though it is not feasible politically to abolish the death penalty. The Committee would wish to avoid adopting a line of jurisprudence which weakens the influence of factors that may very well lessen the number of prisoners actually executed. It should be stressed that by adopting the approach that prolonged detention on death row cannot, *per se*, be regarded as cruel and inhuman treatment or punishment under the Covenant, the Committee does not wish to convey the impression that keeping condemned prisoners on death row for many years is an acceptable way of treating them. It is not. However, the cruelty of the death row phenomenon is first and foremost a function of the permissibility of capital punishment under the Covenant. This situation has unfortunate consequences.
>
> 8.5 Finally, to hold that prolonged detention on death row does not, *per se*, constitute a violation of articles 7 and 10, does not imply that other circumstances connected with detention on death row may not turn that detention

---

[4] (1997) 4 I.H.R.R. 21 at 27.

into cruel, inhuman and degrading treatment or punishment. The jurisprudence of the Committee has been that where compelling circumstances of the detention are substantiated, that detention may constitute a violation of the Covenant. This jurisprudence should be maintained in future cases.

In the *Johnson* case, the author had been on death row for 11 years. The Committee found no breach of Articles 7 and 10, there being "no compelling circumstances, over and above the length of the detention on death row".

ESTRELLA *v.* URUGUAY

(1983) 2 Selected Decisions H.R.C. 93

The author, an Argentinian national, was a professional pianist living in Uruguay. He was officially informed that, as a Peronist, he was regarded as an opponent of the Uruguayan Government and his concerts and teaching were cancelled. While he was preparing to leave Uruguay, the author was arrested and taken to a place of detention with others.

Views of the Committee

1.6. The author claims that in that place, the four of them were subjected to torture:

> The tortures consisted of electric shocks, beatings with rubber truncheons, punches and kicks, hanging us up with our hands tied behind our backs, pushing us into water until we were nearly asphyxiated, making us stand with legs apart and arms raised for up to 20 hours, and psychological torture. The latter consisted chiefly in threats of torture or violence to relatives or friends, or of dispatch to Argentina to be executed, in threats of making us witness the torture of friends, and in inducing in us a state of hallucination in which we thought we could see and hear things which were not real. In my own case, their point of concentration was my hands. For hours upon end, they put me through a mock amputation with an electric saw, telling me, "we are going to do the same to you as Victor Jara."[5] Amongst the effects from which I suffered as a result were a loss of sensitivity in both arms and hands for 11 months, discomfort that still persists in the right thumb, and severe pain in the knees. I reported the fact to a number of military medical officers in the barracks and in the "Libertad" prison.

The author alleges that he was interrogated for the purpose of forcing him to admit that he had been involved in plans to carry out armed operations in Uruguay and Argentina. . . .

1.10. In the second part of his communication . . . the author gives a detailed description of [prison conditions at Libertad prison, to which he was transferred]. He states, in particular, that five floors of the prison are

---

[5] A well-known Chilean singer and guitarist who was found dead with his hands badly broken at the end of a September 1973 concert in a stadium in Santiago, Chile.

divided into very small cells; that two detainees share each cell (except on
the second floor, which is reserved for detainees held in solitary confinement); that these cells are so small that "when one detainee walks, the
other has to sit"; that detainees are usually kept in their cells 23 hours per
day, that they are not allowed to lie on their beds from 6.30 a.m. to 9 p.m.
or to do any exercise and that they are allowed to go into the open air for
only one hour per day, provided that they have not been punished. . . .

1.11. The author states that the reasons for punishment at Libertad
prison are endless (for example, for walking without having their hands
behind their back; for looking directly at a prison guard; for trying to
share food or clothes . . .).

1.12. The author maintains that in fact a policy of arbitrary sanctions is
continually applied for the purpose of generating moments of hope
followed by frustration. He alleges that the whole system at Libertad is
aimed at destroying the detainees' physical and psychological balance,
that detainees are continuously kept in a state of anxiety, uncertainty and
tension. . . . He claims that many detainees are psychologically ill . . . Up
to three times a day during alarms, detainees have to lie down on the
floor wherever they are, face downward, hands over their heads and any
movement could mean being shot by a prison guard. Shooting exercises
are carried out in the prison yard and the dummy targets wear exactly the
same uniforms as the prisoners. The author also maintains that even
Sunday masses were discontinued in 1975 for being moments shared by
most detainees. . . .

8.1. The Human Rights Committee has considered the present communication in the light of all information made available to it by the parties
as provided in article 5(1) of the Optional Protocol. The Committee bases
its views on the following facts, which, in the absence of any substantive
clarifications from the State Party, are unrefuted. . . .

8.3. On December 15, 1977, at a time when the author was about to
leave Uruguay, he and his friend, Luis Bracony, were kidnapped at his
home in Montevideo by some 15 strongly armed individuals in civilian
clothes. They were brought blindfolded to a place where . . . the author
was subjected to severe physical and psychological torture, including the
threat that the author's hands would be cut off by an electric saw, in an
effort to force him to admit subversive activities. This ill-treatment had
lasting effects, particularly to his arms and hands.

8.4. On December 23, 1977, the author was transferred to a military
barracks, probably of Batallón 13, where he continued to be subjected to
ill-treatment. In particular, he was threatened with death and he was
denied medical attention. On January 20, 1978 he was taken to Libertad
prison. He spent the first 10 days in solitary confinement in a cell which
was a kind of cage in a section known as "La Isla." He remained imprisoned at Libertad until February 13, 1980.

8.5. At Libertad prison the author was subjected to continued ill-
treatment and to arbitrary punishments including 30 days in solitary

confinement in a punishment cell and seven months without mail or recreation and subjected to harassment and searches. . . .

9.1. On the basis of the detailed information submitted by the author . . ., the Committee is in a position to conclude that the conditions of imprisonment to which Miguel Angel Estrella was subjected at Libertad prison were inhuman. In this connection, the Committee recalls its consideration of other communications . . . which confirm the existence of a practice of inhuman treatment at Libertad.

10. The Human Rights Committee . . . is of the view that the facts, as found by the Committee, disclose violations of the . . . Covenant in particular of:

Article 7, because Miguel Angel Estrella was subjected to torture during the first days of his detention (December 15–23, 1977);

Article 10(1), because he was detained under inhuman prison conditions; . . .

11. The Committee, accordingly, is of the opinion that the State party is under an obligation to provide the victim with effective remedies, including compensation, for the violations he has suffered and to take steps to ensure that similar violations do not occur in the future.

Notes

1. The *Estrella* case is one of many that have alleged torture or other ill-treatment contrary to Article 7. Commenting on the scope of Article 7, the Committee stated in General Comment 20[6]:

2. . . . the scope of protection required goes far beyond torture as normally understood. It may not be necessary to draw sharp distinctions between the various prohibited forms of treatment or punishment. These distinctions depend on the kind, purpose and severity of the particular treatment. In the view of the Committee the prohibition must extend to corporal punishment, including excessive chastisement as an educational or disciplinary measure. Even such a measure as solitary confinement may, according to the circumstances, and especially when the person is kept incommunicado, be contrary to this article. Moreover, the article clearly protects not only persons arrested or imprisoned, but also pupils and patients in educational and medical institutions. Finally, it is also the duty of public authorities to ensure protection by the law against such treatment even when committed by persons acting outside or without any official authority. For all persons deprived of their liberty, the prohibition of treatment contrary to article 7 is supplemented by the positive requirement of article 10(1) of the Covenant that they shall be treated with humanity and with respect for the inherent dignity of the human person.

3. In particular, the prohibition extends to medical or scientific experimentation without the free consent of the person concerned. The Committee . . . takes the view that at least in countries where science and medicine are highly developed, and even for peoples and areas outside their borders if affected by their experiments, more attention should be given to the possible need and means to ensure the observance of this provision. Special protection in regard to such experiments is necessary in the case of persons not capable of giving their consent.

[6] H.R.C. Report, G.A.O.R., 37th Sess., Supp. 40, pp. 94–95 (1982); (1994) 1–2 I.H.R.R. 26.

In fact, most cases have involved allegations of physical ill-treatment of the kind found to have been inflicted in the *Estrella* case or of inhuman conditions of detention or lack of medical treatment in prison. The Committee's general approach to the assessment of prison conditions was stated and applied in *Mukong v. Cameroon*[7]:

> 9.3 As to the conditions of detention in general, the Committee observes that certain minimum standards regarding the conditions of detention must be observed regardless of a State party's level of development. These include, in accordance with Rules 10, 12, 17, 19 and 20 of the *U.N. Standard Minimum Rules for the Treatment of Prisoners*,[8] minimum floor space and cubic content of air for each prisoner, adequate sanitary facilities, clothing which shall be in no manner degrading or humiliating, provision of a separate bed, and provision of food of nutritional value adequate for health and strength. It should be noted that these are *minimum* requirements which the Committee considers should always be observed, even if economic or budgetary considerations may make compliance with these obligations difficult. It transpires from the file that these requirements were not met during the author's detention in the summer of 1988 and in February/March 1990.
>
> 9.4 The Committee further notes that quite apart from the general conditions of detention, the author has been singled out for exceptionally harsh and degrading treatment. Thus, he was kept detained *incommunicado*, was threatened with torture and death and intimidated, deprived of food, and kept locked in his cell for several days on end without the possibility of recreation. In this context, the Committee recalls its General Comment 20[44] which recommends that States parties should make provision against *incommunicado* detention and notes that total isolation of a detained or imprisoned person may amount to acts prohibited by article 7. In view of the above, the Committee finds that Mr. Mukong has been subjected to cruel, inhuman and degrading treatment, in violation of article 7 of the Covenant.

Note that the Committee makes no allowance for a state's economic circumstances.

The infliction of mental suffering may be sufficient to infringe Article 7. In the death penalty case of *Pratt and Morgan v. Jamaica*,[9] the Committee stated:

> 13.7 The second issue under article 7 concerns the issue of warrants for execution and the notification of the stay of execution. The issue of a warrant for execution necessarily causes intense anguish to the individual concerned. In the authors' case, death warrants were issued twice by the Governor General, first on February 13, 1987 and again on February 23, 1988. It is uncontested that the decision to grant a first stay of execution, taken at noon

---

[7] (1995) 2 I.H.R.R. 131.

[8] *Ed.* Printed in *Human Rights: A Compilation of International Instruments*, Vol. I, Pt. I, UN Publication, 1993, p. 243.

[9] H.R.C. Report, G.A.O.R., 44th Sess., Supp. 40, p. 222 at 230 (1989). The Committee also accepted that in a death penalty case "undue delay" in proceedings in breach of Art. 14(3)(c) might be "cruel, inhuman and degrading treatment" contrary to Art. 7, although this was not established on the facts of the *Pratt and Morgan* case. *cf. Quinteros v. Uruguay,* (1983) 2 Selected Decisions H.R.C. 138 at 142, in which a daughter was arrested and held incommunicado: "The Committee understands the anguish and stress caused to the mother by the disappearance of her daughter and by the continuing uncertainty concerning her fate and whereabouts. The author has the right to know what has happened to her daughter. In these respects, she too is a victim of the violations of the Covenant suffered by her daughter in particular of Art. 7."

on February 23, 1987, was not notified to the authors until 45 minutes before the scheduled time of the execution on February 24, 1987. The Committee considers that a delay of close to 20 hours from the time the stay of execution was granted to the time the authors were removed from their death cell constitutes cruel and inhuman treatment within the meaning of article 7.

Although the Committee has not adopted any abstract definition of "torture" in its jurisprudence, it is probable that the definition in the 1984 UN Torture Convention, below, p. 710, applies.[10] As the General Comment indicates, the Committee has not been concerned to distinguish between "torture" and other forms of conduct contrary to Article 7. This is surprising in view of the effect of a finding of "torture" on a state's reputation. Nor, in cases in which the victim is in detention, has the Committee sought to draw an exact line between breaches of Articles 7 and 10. Prison conditions are generally dealt with under Article 10, but Article 7 is sometimes invoked as well. In the *Estrella* case, prison conditions which the Committee described as "inhuman" were found to be contrary to Article 10, not Article 7, with no consideration being given to the boundary or overlap between the two.
As the Committee stated in *Vuolanne v. Finland*[11]:

the assessment of what constitutes inhuman or degrading treatment falling within the meaning of article 7 depends on all the circumstances of the case, such as the duration and manner of the treatment, its physical or mental effects as well as the sex, age and state of health of the victim.

For treatment or a punishment to be degrading, a threshold level of humiliation or debasement must be reached. In the *Vuolanne* case, the Committee stated that "for punishment to be degrading, the humiliation or debasement must exceed a particular level and must, in any event, entail other elements beyond the mere fact of deprivation." The Committee has expressed regret that "corporal punishment may still be permitted in certain circumstances in independent schools" in the United Kingdom,[12] presumably on the basis that it is inhuman or degrading.
2. Consistent with its concern at the number of Optional Protocol cases in which a violation of Article 7 has been found, the Committee indicated in its General Comment that states are required by Article 7 to do more than just make torture, etc., illegal and gave some indication of what administrative steps a state might take to comply with the ICCPR[13]:

The Committee notes that it is not sufficient for the implementation of this article to prohibit such treatment or punishment or to make it a crime. Most States have penal provisions which are applicable to cases of torture or similar practices. Because such cases nevertheless occur, it follows from article 7, read together with article 2 of the Covenant, that States must ensure an effective protection through some machinery of control. Complaints about ill-treatment must be investigated effectively by competent authorities. Those found guilty must be held responsible, and the alleged victims must themselves have effective remedies at their disposal, including the right to obtain compensation. Among the safeguards which may make control effective are provisions

---

[10] Note that the UN Torture Convention does not control private acts or "lawful sanctions."
[11] H.R.C. Report, G.A.O.R., 44th Sess., Supp. 40, p. 249 (1989).
[12] 1995 Concluding Comments on the U.K. Report (1996) 3 I.H.R.R. 181 at 183.
[13] *loc. cit.*, p. 665, n. 6, above.

against detention incommunicado, granting, without prejudice to the investigation, persons such as doctors, lawyers and family members access to the detainees; provisions requiring that detainees should be held in places that are publicly recognised and that their names and places of detention should be entered in a central register available to persons concerned, such as relatives; provisions making confessions or other evidence obtained through torture or other treatment contrary to article 7 inadmissible in court; and measures of training and instruction of law enforcement officials not to apply such treatment.

MUKONG *v.* CAMEROON

(1995) 2 I.H.R.R. 131

The author was a journalist who had long advocated multi-party democracy in the one party state of Cameroon. He was arrested in 1988 following a BBC broadcast in which he criticised the President of Cameroon and the Government. The reason for the arrest was that his remarks were subversive contrary to an Ordinance under which he was later charged with an offence. He was re-arrested in 1990 following a public meeting in which he advocated multi-party democracy. The Committee found that the conditions of his detention infringed Article 7, ICCPR (see above, p. 666) and that the limitation on his freedom of speech was in breach of Article 19 (see below, p. 679). The following extract concerns the meaning of "arbitrary" in Article 9(1) and the permissible public interest reasons for detaining an accused on remand.

Views of the Committee

9.8 The Committee notes that the State party has dismissed the author's claim under article 9 by indicating that he was arrested and detained in application of the rules of criminal procedure, and that the police detention and preliminary enquiries by the examining magistrate were compatible with article 9. It remains however to be determined whether other factors may render an otherwise lawful arrest and lawful detention "arbitrary" within the meaning of article 9. The drafting history of article 9, paragraph 1, confirms that "arbitrariness" is not to be equated with "against the law", but must be interpreted more broadly to include elements of inappropriateness, injustice, lack of predictability and due process of law. As the Committee has observed on a previous occasion, this means that remand in custody pursuant to lawful arrest must not only be lawful but reasonable in all the circumstances. Remand in custody must further be necessary in all the circumstances, for example to prevent flight, interference with evidence or the recurrence of crime. In the present case, the State party has not shown that any of these factors was present. It has merely contended that the author's arrest and detention were clearly justified by reference to article 19, paragraph 3, *i.e.* permissible restrictions on the author's freedom of expression. . . . the Committee finds that the author's detention in 1988–1989 and 1990 was neither reasonable not necessary in the circumstances of the case, and thus in violation of article 9, paragraph 1, of the Covenant.

Notes

1. There have been many cases brought under Article 9 in which the arrested person had been given no reason for arrest, had no judicial remedy available to challenge the legality of his detention and was eventually released without being charged. *Carballal v. Uruguay*[14] is one of a number of such cases involving multiple breaches of Article 9. The uncontested facts were:

> Leopoldo Buffo Carballal was arrested on January 4, 1976 and held incommunicado for more than five months, much of the time tied and blindfolded, in several places of detention. Recourse to *habeas corpus* was not available to him. He was brought before a military judge on May 5, 1976 and again on June 28, or July 28, 1976, when an order was issued for his release. He was, however, kept in detention until January 26, 1977.

The Committee found breaches of Article 9 as follows:

> Article 9(1), because he was not released until approximately six or seven months after an order for his release was issued by the military court;
> Article 9(2), because he was not informed of the charges brought against him;
> Article 9(3), because he was not brought before a judge until four months after he was detained and 44 days after the Covenant entered into force for Uruguay;
> Article 9(4), because recourse to *habeas corpus* was not available to him;

2. The Committee has commented that "promptly" in Article 9(3) means that "delays must not exceed a few days".[15] The 44-day delay in the *Carballal* case was well in excess of this. In *Grant v. Jamaica*,[16] the author was not brought "promptly" before a judge when this did not happen in the seven days following his arrest.

Whether a detained person is tried "within a reasonable time" (Article 9(3)) depends on the facts of each case; a period of four years and four months was not "reasonable" when there were no "special circumstances".[17]

3. Article 9(4), which applies to detention for any reason (criminal suspect, mentally disordered, deportation, etc.) is the *habeas corpus* provision of the Covenant. In *Voulanne v. Finland*,[18] the Committee found a breach where a soldier was arrested for a military disciplinary charge:

> The Committee does not accept the contention of the State Party that the request for review before a superior military officer according to the Law on Military Disciplinary Procedure currently in effect in Finland is comparable to judicial scrutiny of an appeal and that the officials ordering detention act in a judicial or quasi-judicial manner. The procedure followed in the case of Mr. Vuolanne did not have a judicial character, and the supervisory military officer who upheld the decision of July 17, 1987 against Mr. Vuolanne cannot be deemed to be a "court" within the meaning of article 9, paragraph 4; therefore,

---

[14] (1981) 1 Selected Decisions H.R.C. 63 at 64–65.
[15] H.R.C. Report, G.A.O.R., 37th Sess., Supp. 40, p. 95 (1982).
[16] (1997) 4 I.H.R.R. 42.
[17] *Kone v. Senegal* (1995) 2 I.H.R.R. 279. A period of 30 months between arrest and the beginning of the trial was a breach of Article 9(3) on the facts: *Douglas v. Jamaica* (1997) 4 I.H.R.R. 387. So was four years between an appeal court decision ordering retrial and the retrial starting: *Shalto v. Trinidad* (1995) 2 I.H.R.R. 568.
[18] H.R.C. Report, G.A.O.R., 44th Sess., Supp. 40, p. 249 (1989).

the obligations laid down therein have not been complied with by the authorities of the State Party. . . .

There have been breaches of Article 9(4) where a detained person has not been
brought before a "court" for a lengthy period of time.[19]

Y.L. *v.* CANADA

(1986) 2 Selected Decisions H.R.C. 28

The author of the communication was dismissed from the Canadian army
because of mental illness. His application to the Canadian Pension Commission
for a disability pension was rejected since his disability did not result from
military service. An appeal to the Pension Review Board was unsuccessful. The
author claimed that, contrary to Article 14, ICCPR he had been denied access to
his medical file; that he had not been allowed to attend the Board hearing; and
that the Board, being composed of civil servants, was not an "independent and
impartial tribunal." The H.R.C. first found it necessary to consider whether
Article 14 applied to the case. Before taking its decision on this point, the H.R.C.
put questions to the defendant state, eliciting that "within the Canadian legal
system the relationship between a member of the armed forces and the Crown
was classified as a matter of public law."

Decision as to Admissibility

9.1. With regard to the alleged violation of the guarantees of "a fair and
public hearing by a competent, independent and impartial tribunal established by law," contained in article 14, paragraph 1, of the Covenant, it is
correct to state that those guarantees are limited to criminal proceedings
and to any "suit at law." The latter expression is formulated differently in
the various language texts of the Covenant and each and every one of
those texts is, under article 53, equally authentic.

9.2. The *travaux préparatoires* do not resolve the apparent discrepancy in
the various language texts. In the view of the Committee, the concept of
a "suit at law" or its equivalent in the other language texts is based on the
nature of the right in question rather than on the status of one of the
parties (governmental, parastatal or autonomous statutory entities), or
else on the particular forum in which individual legal systems may
provide that the right in question is to be adjudicated upon, especially in
common law systems where there is no inherent difference between
public law and private law, and where the courts normally exercise
control over the proceedings either at first instance or on appeal specifically provided by statute or else by way of judicial review. In this regard,
each communication must be examined in the light of its particular
features.

---

[19] See, *e.g. Torres v. Finland*, H.R.C. Report, G.A.O.R. 45th Sess., Supp. 40, p. 96 (1990) (seven
days too long).

9.3. In the present communication, the right to a fair hearing in relation to the claim for a pension by the author must be looked at globally, irrespective of the different steps which the author had to take in order to have his claim for a pension finally adjudicated.

9.4. The Committee notes that the author pursued his claim successively before the Canadian Pension Commission, an Entitlement Board of the Commission and, finally, the Pension Review Board. It is clear from the observations made by the State Party on the author's communication that the Canadian legal system subjects the proceedings in those various bodies to judicial supervision and control, because the Federal Court Act does provide the possibility of *judicial review* in unsuccessful claims of this nature. It would be hazardous to speculate on whether that Court would or would not have, first, quashed the decision of the Board on the grounds advanced by the author and, secondly, directed the Board to give the author a fair hearing on his claim. The fact that the author was not advised that he could have resorted to judicial review is irrelevant in determining the question whether the claim of the author was of a kind subject to judicial supervision and control. It has not been claimed by the author that this remedy would not have complied with the guarantees provided in article 14, paragraph 1, of the Covenant. Nor has he claimed that this remedy would not have availed in correcting whatever deficiencies may have marked the hearing of his case before the lower jurisdictions, including any grievance that he may have had regarding the denial of access to his medical file.

9.5. In the view of the Committee, therefore, it would appear that the Canadian legal system does contain provisions in the Federal Court Act to ensure to the author the right to a fair hearing in the situation. Consequently, his basic allegations do not reveal the possibility of any breach of the Covenant.

10. The Committee, therefore concludes that the author has no claim under article 2 of the Optional Protocol and decides:

The communication is inadmissible.

Individual Opinion of Messrs. Graefrath, Pocar and Tomuschat

1. We concur in the view expressed by the majority of the Committee that the communication is inadmissible. But we do not share the reasons on which that view is based.

2. The majority view stresses in paragraph 9.4 that the Canadian legal system, in accordance with article 14, paragraph 1, of the Covenant, provides sufficient protection for a claim of the kind pursued by the author, because an appeal could be made to the Federal Court of Appeal. However, the availability of this legal remedy cannot be held against the author. In the letter by which the Pension Review Board informed the author of its decision as being final and enforceable, no mention was made of the possibility of such an appeal to a judicial body. Moreover, the

lawyers who acted for the author and who are civil servants specifically appointed to represent claimants before the Pension Review Board did not advise the author accordingly. Under these circumstances, Canada is estopped from asserting that either, procedurally, the author has failed to exhaust local remedies or that, substantively, the requisite guarantees under article 14, paragraph 1, of the Covenant have been complied with.

3. However, the dispute between the author and Canada does not come within the purview of article 14, paragraph 1, of the Covenant. The guarantees therein contained apply to the determination both of any criminal charge and of rights and obligations in a suit at law. Whereas this phrase in its English and Russian versions refers to proceedings, the French and the Spanish texts rely on the nature of the right or obligation which constitutes the subject-matter of the proceedings concerned. In the circumstances of the present case, there is no need to clarify the common meaning to be given to the different terms used in the various languages which, under article 53 of the Covenant, are equally authentic. It is quite clear from the submissions of both the State Party and the author that in Canada the relationship between a soldier, whether in active service or retired, and the Crown has many specific features, differing essentially from a labour contract under Canadian law. In addition, it has emerged that the Pension Review Board is an administrative body functioning within the executive branch of the Government of Canada, lacking the quality of a court. Thus, in the present case, neither of the two criteria which would appear to determine conjunctively the scope of article 14, paragraph 1, of the Covenant is met. It must be concluded, therefore that proceedings before the Pension Review Board, initiated with a view to claiming pension rights, cannot be challenged by contending that the requirements of a fair hearing as laid down in article 14, paragraph 1, of the Covenant have been violated.

Notes

1. *Y.L. v. Canada* considers the field of application of the right to a fair trial guarantee in Article 14 in non-criminal cases. The Committee adopts a two-part test to decide whether a case comes within Article 14 in such cases. First, it looks to the "nature of the right," with the determination of private law rights being within Article 14, but not the determination of public law rights (*i.e.* rights that an individual has in his relations with the state). Secondly, if a case does not involve the determination of a private law right, it will, nonetheless, involve a "suit at law," if, in the legal system concerned, it can be determined on the merits before a court of law or the executive decision determining the public law right in question is subject to judicial review.[20] On what basis did the Committee declare the application in *Y.L. v. Canada* inadmissible? That the case did not reveal a "suit at law" according to either part of the Committee's test? Or that a tribunal (the Federal Court of Appeal) with a power of judicial review capable of acting on the

[20] Seemingly on this basis, Art. 14 has been applied to judicial proceedings in cases involving the dismissal of civil servants (*Casanovas v. France* (1995) 2 I.H.R.R. 119) and their social security rights (*Pons v. Spain* (1996) 3 I.H.R.R. 325).

author's allegations of breaches of Article 14 was available and had not been used? Do you prefer the Committee's reasoning or that in the joint individual opinion?

2. A number of cases have raised other points under Article 14(1). In *Avellanal v. Peru*[21] a married woman who owned two apartment blocks was unable to bring a claim in the courts for arrears of rent because, under Peruvian law, "when a woman is married only the husband is entitled to represent matrimonial property before the Courts." The Committee found this to be in a breach of the "equal before the courts" guarantee in Article 14(1). In *Robinson v. Jamaica*,[22] the failure of the trial judge "to order an adjournment to allow the author to have legal representation, when several adjournments had already been ordered when the prosecution's witnesses were unavailable or unready," was in breach of Article 14(1) "due to inequality of arms between the parties." In *Morael v. France*,[23] the Committee stated that the undefined "fair hearing" guarantee in Article 14(1) in non-criminal cases included, *inter alia*, "equality of arms, preclusion of *ex officio reformation in pejus* (*ex officio* correction worsening of an earlier verdict), and expeditious procedure." The general "public hearing" and "judgment ... made public" requirements for criminal and non-criminal trials alike have been infringed in a number of cases, particularly before military courts. For example, in *Pietraroia v. Uruguay*,[24] the victim "was sentenced to 12 years' imprisonment, in a closed trial, conducted in writing and without his presence ... and the judgment of the court was not made public."

3. The guarantees in Article 14(2) onwards apply to criminal cases only. With regard to the presumption of innocence (Article 14(2)), the Committee has noted that it applies not only in the courtroom; there is a "duty for all public authorities to refrain from prejudging the outcome of a trial."[25]

4. Article 14(3). Violations of the right to communicate with counsel (Article 14(3)(b)) have been found in a number of cases. For example, in *Wight v. Madagascar*,[26] there was a breach "because during a 10-month period ... while criminal charges against him were being investigated and determined ... [the victim] was kept incommunicado without access to legal counsel." The Committee has also commented upon Article 14(3) (b) as follows[27]:

> What is "adequate time" depends on the circumstances of each case, but the facilities must include access to documents and other evidence which the accused requires to prepare his case.... Furthermore, this subparagraph requires counsel to communicate with the accused in conditions giving full respect for the confidentiality of their communications. Lawyers should be able to counsel and to represent their clients in accordance with their established professional standards and judgment without any restrictions, influences, pressures or undue interference from any quarter.

The guarantee of trial "without undue delay" in Article 14(3)(c) has brought to light criminal cases lasting many years, often with the accused detained pending

---

[21] H.R.C. Report, G.A.O.R., 44th Sess., Supp. 40, p. 196 (1989).

[22] *ibid.* 241 at 245 (1989).

[23] *ibid.*, p. 210 (1989). *cf. Fei v. Colombia* (1995) 2 I.H.R.R. 583. Special expedition is needed in child custody cases: *ibid.*

[24] (1981) 1 Selected Decisions H.R.C. 76 at 79.

[25] General Comment on Art. 14, G.A.O.R., 39th Sess., Supp. 40, p. 143 (1984). This would apply, *e.g.* to the police.

[26] (1985) 2 Selected Decisions H.R.C. 151 at 154. *cf. Kelly v. Jamaica* (1997) 4 I.H.R.R. 334.

[27] General Comment on Art. 14, above.

trial. For example, in *Solorzano v. Venezuela*[28] the accused was arrested in February 1977 and his detention ordered by a military court on charges of having joined in armed rebellion. The case was still pending in December 1984 when proceedings against the accused were dismissed by legislative decree, more than seven years after they had begun. During the whole of this time the accused was detained in conditions that the Committee found to be in breach of Article 10, ICCPR. The guarantee of trial "without undue delay" applies to appeal proceedings as well as the trial.[29] Thus it was infringed in *Pinkney v. Canada*[30] when the victim's appeal was delayed because it took two and a half years for the transcript of the trial to be produced as a result of admitted "administrative mishaps in the Official Reporter's Office." In *Pratt and Morgan v. Jamaica*[31] a breach of Article 14(3)(c) was found in a death penalty case when the Jamaican Court of Appeal took 45 months between the dismissal of the appeal and the delivery of a written judgment because of an oversight. The Committee noted that Article 14(3)(c) and (5) "are to be read together, so that the right to review of conviction and sentence must be made available without undue delay."

As to the right to counsel in Article 14(3)(c), the Committee has held that "the interests of justice" require that counsel always be available in capital punishment cases.[32] They also demand that the lawyer of an accused who has been sentenced to death should consult with his client if he is minded to argue on appeal that the appeal has no merits.[33] In several cases, the Committee has found breaches of Article 14(3)(d) where an accused has been "forced to agree to *ex officio* legal counsel" and not allowed to appoint their own.[34]

The right to free legal aid was considered in *O.F. v. Norway*[35] in which it was found that "the interests of justice" did not require the defendant state to provide free legal aid in a case in which the accused was convicted of two petty offences and sentenced to a fine of NKr 1000 or 10 days imprisonment.

In *Burgos v. Uruguay*,[36] Article 14(3)(g) was infringed when the accused was forced, as a result of conduct that the Committee found to be torture contrary to Article 7 ICCPR, "to sign false testimony against himself and that this testimony was used in the trial against him."

On the right of the accused to "be tried in his presence," in *Mbenge v. Zaire*,[37] in which the victim was twice sentenced to death in his absence, the Committee commented upon permissibility and consequences of trial *in absentia* as follows:

> ... Article 14 cannot be construed as invariably rendering proceedings *in absentia* inadmissible irrespective of the reasons for the accused person's absence. Indeed, proceedings *in absentia* are in some circumstances (for

---

[28] (1986) 2 Selected Decisions H.R.C. 183. *cf., e.g. Bolanos v. Ecuador*, H.R.C. Report, G.A.O.R., 44th Sess., Supp. 40, p. 246 (1989) (six years for murder trial, accused in detention, case still pending). For a case of "undue delay" in civil proceedings, contrary to the "fair hearing" guarantee in Art. 14(1), see *Hermoza v. Peru*, G.A.O.R., 44th Sess., Supp. 40, p. 200 (1989) (administrative and judicial review proceedings—the administrative proceedings being a necessary preliminary to the judicial proceedings—to consider the dismissal of a policeman for insulting a superior lasted over 10 years).

[29] General Comment on Art. 7, para. 10, *loc. cit.*, p. 665, n. 6, above.

[30] (1981) 1 Selected Decisions H.R.C. 95.

[31] *loc. cit.*, p. 666, n. 9 above.

[32] See, *e.g. Wright and Harvey v. Jamaica* (1996) 3 I.H.R.R. 309.

[33] *Kelly v. Jamaica* (1997) 4 I.H.R.R. 334.

[34] See, *e.g. Burgos v. Uruguay* (1981) 1 Selected Decisions H.R.C. 88.

[35] (1984) 2 Selected Decisions H.R.C. 44.

[36] *loc. cit.*, n. 34, above, at 90. *cf. Johnson v. Jamaica* (1997) 4 I.H.R.R. 21 and *Zelaya Blanco v. Nicaragua* (1995) 2 I.H.R.R. 123.

[37] (1983) 2 Selected Decisions H.R.C. 76 at 78. Breach of Art. 14(3)(a)(b)(c)(e) found on facts because insufficient steps had been taken to inform the accused of his trial.

instance, when the accused person, although informed of the proceedings sufficiently in advance, declines to exercise his right to be present) permissible in the interest of the proper administration of justice. Nevertheless, the effective exercise of the rights under Article 14 presupposes that the necessary steps should be taken to inform the accused beforehand about the proceedings against him (art. 14(3)(a)). Judgment *in absentia* requires that, notwithstanding the absence of the accused, all due notification has been made to inform him of the date and place of his trial and to request his attendance. Otherwise, the accused, in particular, is not given adequate time and facilities for the preparation of his defence (art. 14(3)(b)), cannot defend himself through legal assistance of his own choosing (art. 14(3)(d)) nor does he have the opportunity to examine, or have examined, the witnesses against him and to obtain the attendance and examination of witnesses on his behalf (art. 14(3)(e)).

5. In its General Comment on Article 14, *loc. cit.*, p. 673, n. 25, above, the Committee expressed its concern at the administration of justice by military or special courts:

Para. 4. The Committee notes the existence, in many countries, of military or special courts which try civilians. This could present serious problems as far as the equitable, impartial and independent administration of justice is concerned. Quite often the reason for the establishment of such courts is to enable exceptional procedures to be applied which do not comply with normal standards of justice. While the Covenant does not prohibit such categories of courts, nevertheless the conditions which it lays down clearly indicate that the trying of civilians by such courts should be very exceptional and take place under conditions which genuinely afford the full guarantees stipulated in Article 14.

TOONEN *v.* AUSTRALIA[38]

(1994) 1–3 I.H.R.R. 97

The author alleged that sections of the Tasmanian Criminal Code that made private homosexual conduct a criminal offence were in breach of Articles 17 and 26, ICCPR. Although the author had not been prosecuted and the police had not brought any prosecutions for several years, the Committee considered that the author was a "victim" competent to bring the communication. This was because the "threat of enforcement (he was a gay rights activist and a practising homosexual) and the pervasive impact of the continued existence of these provisions on administrative practices and public opinion had affected him and continued to affect him personally." Whereas the state of Tasmania argued that there was no breach of Article 17, ICCPR, the Australian Federal Government (the "state party" referred to in para. 8.4, H.R.C. Views, below) accepted that there was. The H.R.C. did not consider the claim under Article 26.

Views of the Committee

8.2 Inasmuch as article 17 is concerned, it is undisputed that adult consensual sexual activity in private is covered by the concept of "privacy", and that Mr. Toonen is actually and currently affected by the

[38] Joseph (1994) 13 U.Tas.L.R. 392.

continued existence of the Tasmanian laws. The Committee considers that Sections 122(a), (c) and 123 of the Tasmanian Criminal Code "interfere" with the author's privacy, even if these provisions have not been enforced for a decade. In this context, it notes that the policy of the Department of Public Prosecutions not to initiate criminal proceedings in respect of private homosexual conduct does not amount to a guarantee that no actions will be brought against homosexuals in the future, particularly in the light of undisputed statements of the Director of Public Prosecutions of Tasmania in 1988 and those of members of the Tasmanian Parliament. The continued existence of the challenged provisions therefore continuously and directly "interferes" with the author's privacy.

8.3 The prohibition against private homosexual behaviour is provided for by law, namely, Sections 122 and 123 of the Tasmanian Criminal Code. As to whether it may be deemed arbitrary, the Committee recalls that pursuant to its General Comment 16[32] on article 17, the "introduction of the concept of arbitrariness is intended to guarantee that even interference provided for by the law should be in accordance with the provisions, aims and objectives of the Covenant and should be, in any event, reasonable in the circumstances". The Committee interprets the requirements of reasonableness to imply that any interference with privacy must be proportional to the end sought and be necessary in the circumstances of any given case.

8.4 While the State party acknowledges that the impugned provisions constitute an arbitrary interference with Mr. Toonen's privacy, the Tasmanian authorities submit that the challenged laws are justified on public health and moral grounds, as they are intended in part to prevent the spread of HIV/AIDS in Tasmania, and because, in the absence of specific limitation clauses in article 17, moral issues must be deemed a matter for domestic decision.

8.5 As far as the public health argument of the Tasmanian authorities is concerned, the Committee notes that the criminalization of homosexual practices cannot be considered a reasonable means or proportionate measure to achieve the aim of preventing the spread of HIV/AIDS. The Australian Government observes that statutes criminalizing homosexual activity tend to impede public health programmes "by driving underground many of the people at the risk of infection". Criminalization of homosexual activity thus would appear to run counter to the implementation of effective education programmes in respect of the HIV/AIDS prevention. Secondly, the Committee notes that no link has been shown between the continued criminalization of homosexual activity and the effective control of the spread of the HIV/AIDS virus.

8.6 The Committee cannot accept either that for the purposes of article 17 of the Covenant, moral issues are exclusively a matter of domestic concern, as this would open the door to withdrawing from the Committee's scrutiny a potentially large number of statutes interfering with privacy. It further notes that, with the exception of Tasmania, all laws criminalizing homosexuality have been repealed throughout Australia and that, even in Tasmania, it is apparent that there is no consensus as to whether Sections 122 and 123 should not also be repealed. Considering further that these provisions are not currently enforced, which implies that they are not deemed essential to the protection of morals in Tasmania, the Committee concludes that the provisions do not meet the "reasonableness" test in the circumstances of the case, and that they arbitrarily interfere with Mr. Toonen's right under article 17, paragraph 1. . . .

9. The Human Rights Committee, acting under article 5, paragraph 4, of the Optional Protocol to the International Covenant on Civil and Political Rights, is of the view that the facts before it reveal a violation of articles 17, paragraph 1, *juncto* 2, paragraph 1, of the Covenant.

10. Under article 2(3)(a) of the Covenant, the author, victim of a violation of articles 17, paragraphs 1, *juncto* 2, paragraph 1, of the Covenant, is entitled to a remedy. In the opinion of the Committee, an effective remedy would be the repeal of Sections 122(a), (c) and 123 of the Tasmanian Criminal Code.

Notes

1. Criminal laws prohibiting homosexual acts are actively enforced in some states. Would a conviction in such a state be in breach of Article 17, or might it be justified as being for the enforcement of that state's public morals?

2. Another aspect of privacy protected by Article 17 is the choice of one's name. In *Coeriel and Aurik v. Netherlands*,[39] the applicants' claim that they should be allowed to change their surnames was successful:

> 10.3 . . . The Committee considers that the notion of privacy refers to the sphere of a person's life in which he or she can freely express his or her identity, be it by entering into relationships with others or alone. The Committee is of the view that a person's surname constitutes an important component of one's identity and that the protection against arbitrary or unlawful interference with one's privacy includes the protection against arbitrary or unlawful interference with the right to choose and change one's own name. For instance, if a State were to compel all foreigners to change their surnames, this would constitute interference in contravention of article 17. The question arises whether the refusal of the authorities to recognize a change of surname is also beyond the threshold of permissible interference within the meaning of article 17. . . .
>
> 10.4 The Committee notes that the circumstances in which a change of surname will be recognised are defined narrowly in the [official Dutch] Guidelines and that the exercise of discretion in other cases is restricted to exceptional cases. The Committee recalls its General Comment on article 17, in which it observed that the notion of arbitrariness "is intended to guarantee that even interference provided for by law should be in accordance with the provisions, aims and objectives of the Covenant and should be, in any event, reasonable in the particular circumstances". Thus, the request to have one's change of name recognised can only be refused on grounds that are reasonable in the specific circumstances of the case.

---

[39] (1995) 2 I.H.R.R. 297. An application under the European Convention on Human Rights on the same facts had earlier been declared inadmissible.

10.5 In the present case, the author's request for recognition of the change of their first names to Hindu names in order to pursue their religious studies had been granted in 1986. The State party based its refusal of the request also to change their surnames on the grounds that the authors had not shown that the changes sought were essential to pursue their studies, that the names had religious connotations and that they were not "Dutch sounding". The Committee finds the grounds for so limiting the authors' rights under article 17 not to be reasonable. In the circumstances of the instant case the refusal of the authors' request was therefore arbitrary within the meaning of article 17, paragraph 1, of the Covenant.

FAURISSON *v.* FRANCE

(1996) 4 I.H.R.R. 444

The Gayssot Act 1990 made it a criminal offence to challenge the correctness of the conviction of war criminals at Nuremberg for crimes against humanity. As a result of an interview published in a French magazine in which he repeated his view that there were no homicidal gas chambers for the extermination of jews in Nazi concentration camps, the author, who was a professor of literature, was convicted of a criminal offence under this Act. The author alleged, *inter alia*, a breach of Article 19, ICCPR.

Views of the Committee

9.2 The Committee takes note of public debates in France, including negative comments made by French parliamentarians on the Gayssot Act, as well as of arguments put forward in other, mainly European, countries which support and oppose the introduction of similar legislations.

9.3 Although it does not contest that the application of the terms of the Gayssot Act, which, in their effect, make it a criminal offence to challenge the conclusions and the verdict of the International Military Tribunal at Nuremberg, may lead, under different conditions than the facts of the instant case, to decisions or measures incompatible with the Covenant, the Committee is not called upon to criticize in the abstract laws enacted by States parties. . . .

9.4 Any restriction on the right of freedom of expression must cumulatively meet the following conditions: it must be provided by law, it must address one of the aims set out in paragraph 3(a) and (b) of article 19, and must be necessary to achieve a legitimate purpose.

9.5 The restriction on the author's freedom of expression was indeed provided by law *i.e.* the Act of 13 July 1990. It is the constant jurisprudence of the Committee that the restrictive law itself must be in compliance with the provisions of the Covenant. In this regard the Committee concludes, on the basis of the reading of the judgment of the 17th *Chambre correctionnelle du Tribunal de grande instance de Paris* that the finding of the author's guilt was based on his following two statements: " . . . I have excellent reasons not to believe in the policy of extermination of Jews or in the magic gas chambers . . . I wish to see that 100 per cent of the French citizens realize that the myth of the gas chambers is a dishonest fabrication". His conviction therefore did not encroach upon his right to hold and express an opinion in general, rather the court convicted Mr. Faurisson for having violated the rights and reputation of others. For these reasons the Committee is satisfied that the Gayssot Act, as read, interpreted and applied to the author's case by the French courts, is in compliance with the provisions of the Covenant.

9.6 To assess whether the restrictions placed on the author's freedom of expression by his criminal conviction were applied for the purposes provided for by the Covenant, the Committee begins by noting, as it did in its General Comment 10 [on Article 19] that the rights for the protection of which restrictions on the freedom of expression are permitted by article 19, paragraph 3, may relate to the interests of other persons or to those of the *community as a whole*. Since the statements made by the author, read in their full context, were of such a nature as to raise or strengthen anti-semitic feelings, the restriction served the respect of the Jewish community to live free from fear of an atmosphere of anti-semitism. The Committee therefore concludes that the restriction of the author's freedom of expression was permissible under article 19, paragraph 3(a), of the Covenant.

9.7 Lastly the Committee needs to consider whether the restriction of the author's freedom of expression was necessary. The Committee noted the State party's argument contending that the introduction of the Gayssot Act was intended to serve the struggle against racism and anti-semitism. It also noted the statement of a member of the French Government, the then Minister of Justice, which characterized the denial of the existence of the Holocaust as the principal vehicle for anti-semitism. In the absence in the material before it of any argument undermining the validity of the State party's position as to the necessity of the restriction, the Committee is satisfied that the restriction of Mr. Faurisson's freedom of expression was necessary within the meaning of article 19, paragraph 3, of the Covenant.

10. The Human Rights Committee, acting under article 5, paragraph 4, of the Optional Protocol to the International Covenant on Civil and Political Rights, is of the view that the facts as found by the Committee do not reveal a violation by France of article 19, paragraph 3, of the Covenant.

Notes

1. In *Mukong v. Cameroon*,[40] a journalist had been detained because of his advocacy of political views contrary to those of the Government. Rejecting the Government's argument that this restriction upon freedom of expression could be justified under Article 19(3) in terms of national security and/or public order, the Committee stated:

---

[40] For further facts of the case, see above, p. 668.

9.7 . . . Any restriction of the freedom of expression pursuant to paragraph 3 of article 19 must cumulatively meet the following conditions: it must be provided for by law, it must address one of the aims enumerated in paragraph 3(a) and (b) of article 19, and must be necessary to achieve the legitimate purpose. The State party has indirectly justified its actions on grounds of national security and/or public order, by arguing that the author's right to freedom of expression was exercised without regard to the country's political context and continued struggle for unity. While the State party has indicated that the restrictions on the author's freedom of expression were provided for by law, it must still be determined whether the measures taken against the author were necessary for the safeguard of national security and/or public order. The Committee considers that it was not necessary to safeguard an alleged vulnerable state of national unity by subjecting the author to arrest, continued detention and treatment in violation of article 17. It further considers that the legitimate objective of safeguarding and indeed strengthening national unity under difficult political circumstances cannot be achieved by attempting to muzzle advocacy of multi-party democracy, democratic tenets and human rights; in this regard, the question of deciding which measures might meet the "necessity" test in such situations does not arise. In the circumstances of the author's case, the Committee concludes that there has been a violation of article 19 of the Covenant.

It is noticeable that in this case, the Committee made its own objective assessment of the needs of national security and public order in Cameroon. In contrast, under the European Convention on Human Rights, the Strasbourg Commission and Court, while making the final determination, allows states a certain measure of discretion, or "margin of appreciation", when assessing whether a particular restriction upon human rights can be justified as being in the interest of, for example, national security or public morals.[41] The Committee has decided not to adopt a "margin of appreciation" approach when interpreting the Covenant generally. In *Lansmann v. Finland*,[42] the Committee expressly rejected a state argument that it should apply a "a margin of appreciation" when deciding whether quarrying that allegedly interfered with the rights of the Sami to engage in reindeer husbandry was in breach of their minority rights under Article 27, Covenant. Should it apply a "margin of appreciation", perhaps on the basis that states have local knowledge and responsibilities? Or does such a doctrine run the risk of abuse by states?

2. In *Singer v. Canada*,[43] the author, whose business clientele were mostly anglophonic, claimed that Quebec legislation requiring that all outdoor advertising be in French, not in English, was in breach of Article 19. Ruling in his favour, the Committee "concluded that a State party to the Covenant may choose one or more official languages, but it may not exclude, outside the spheres of public life, the freedom to express oneself in a language of one's choice".

---

[41] No "margin of appreciation" was referred to by the Committee in the *Toonen* case, above, p. 675, in a public morals case. Under the European Convention a wide "margin of appreciation is generally allowed in public morality cases because of the differences around Europe on such matters as obscenity legislation": see Harris, O'Boyle and Warbrick, *The Law of the European Convention on Human Rights* (1995), p. 15.

[42] (1995) 2 I.H.R.R. 287. The Committee did apply a "margin of appreciation" in a public morals context in the early case of *Hertzberg v. Finland* (1982) 1 Selected Decisions H.R.C. 124, but has not done so since.

[43] (1995) 2 I.H.R.R. 149 at 156. The requirement had been repealed by the time the Committee adopted its views.

BROEKS *v.* NETHERLANDS

(1987) 2 Selected Decisions H.R.C. 196

The author was dismissed from her employment as a nurse because of illness. Under Dutch social security law, in order to receive unemployment benefit beyond a certain period, she had, as a married woman, to show that she was the "breadwinner," a condition which did not apply to a married man. The author claimed that this discrimination was in breach of Article 26, ICCPR.

Views of the Committee

12.1. The State Party contends that there is considerable overlapping of the provisions of article 26 with the provisions of article 2 of the International Covenant on Economic, Social and Cultural Rights. The Committee is of the view that the International Covenant on Civil and Political Rights would still apply even if a particular subject-matter is referred to or covered in other international instruments. . . . Notwithstanding the interrelated drafting history of the two Covenants, it remains necessary for the Committee to apply fully the terms of the International Covenant on Civil and Political Rights. The Committee observes in this connection that the provisions of article 2 of the International Covenant on Economic, Social and Cultural Rights do not detract from the full application of article 26 of the International Covenant on Civil and Political Rights.

12.2. The Committee has also examined the contention of the State Party that article 26 of the International Covenant on Civil and Political Rights cannot be invoked in respect of a right which is specifically provided for under article 9 of the International Covenant on Economic, Social and Cultural Rights (social security, including social insurance). . . . The discussions, at the time of drafting, concerning the question whether the scope of article 26 extended to rights not otherwise guaranteed by the Covenant, were inconclusive and cannot alter the conclusion arrived at by the ordinary means of interpretation referred to in paragraph 12.3 below.

12.3. For the purpose of determining the scope of article 26, the Committee has taken into account the "ordinary meaning" of each element of the article in its context and in the light of its object and purpose (art. 31 of the Vienna Convention on the Law of Treaties). The Committee begins by noting that article 26 does not merely duplicate the guarantees already provided for in article 2. It derives from the principle of equal protection of the law without discrimination, as contained in article 7 of the Universal Declaration of Human Rights, which prohibits discrimination in law or in practice in any field regulated and protected by public authorities. Article 26 is thus concerned with the obligations imposed on States in regard to their legislation and the application thereof.

12.4. Although article 26 requires that legislation should prohibit discrimination, it does not of itself contain any obligation with respect to the matters that may be provided for by legislation. Thus it does not, for example, require any State to enact legislation to provide for social security. However, when such legislation is adopted in the exercise of a State's sovereign power, then such legislation must comply with article 26 of the Covenant.

12.5. The Committee observes in this connection that what is at issue is not whether or not social security should be progressively established in the Netherlands, but whether the legislation providing for social security violates the prohibition against discrimination contained in article 26 of the International Covenant on Civil and Political Rights and the guarantee given therein to all persons regarding equal and effective protection against discrimination.

13. The right to equality before the law and to equal protection of the law without any discrimination does not make all differences of treatment discriminatory. A differentiation based on reasonable and objective criteria does not amount to prohibited discrimination within the meaning of article 26.

14. It therefore remains for the Committee to determine whether the differentiation in Netherlands law at the time in question and as applied to Mrs. Broeks constituted discrimination within the meaning of article 26. The Committee notes that in Netherlands law the provisions of articles 84 and 85 of the Netherlands Civil Code impose equal rights and obligations on both spouses with regard to their joint income. Under section 13, subsection 1(1), of the Unemployment Benefits Act (WWV), a married woman, in order to receive WWV benefits, had to prove that she was a "breadwinner"—a condition that did not apply to married men. Thus a differentiation which appears on one level to be one of status is in fact one of sex, placing married women at a disadvantage compared with married men. Such a differentiation is not reasonable; and this seems to have been effectively acknowledged even by the State Party by the enactment of a change in the law on April 29, 1985, with retroactive effect to December 23, 1984. . . .

15. The circumstances in which Mrs. Broeks found herself at the material time and the application of the then valid Netherlands law made her a victim of a violation, based on sex, of article 26 of the International Covenant on Civil and Political Rights, because she was denied a social security benefit on an equal footing with men.

16. The Committee notes that the State Party had not intended to discriminate against women and further notes with appreciation that the discriminatory provisions in the law applied to Mrs. Broeks have, subsequently, been eliminated. Although the State Party has thus taken the necessary measures to put an end to the kind of discrimination suffered by Mrs. Broeks at the time complained of, the Committee is of the view that the State Party should offer Mrs. Broeks an appropriate remedy.

Notes

1. The *Broeks* case confirms that Article 26 prohibits discrimination in any area of law, not just in areas relating to rights protected in the ICCPR. It is thus an exact equivalent of the "equal protection" clause in the 14th Amendment of the United States Constitution and much wider in scope than Article 14, ECHR, which has only the latter meaning. One consequence is that, as on the facts of the *Broeks* case, discrimination in areas of law covered by rights within the ICESCR may be the subject of an Optional Clause communication in so far as the claim is one of sexual, racial, etc., inequality in the guarantee of the right concerned. Although Article 2(2), ICESR, provides a non-discrimination guarantee which might well mean that, for example, on the facts of the *Broeks* case, there was a breach of the ICESCR (Article 2 read with Article 9), no remedy would exist under the ICESCR for the victim since the ICESCR only provides for a system of reports.

2. The *Broeks* case establishes that Article 26 does not prohibit "differentiation based upon reasonable and objective criteria." In *Danning v. Netherlands*,[44] in which a social security benefit for an unemployed disabled person was higher for a married man than, as in the case of the victim, for a person co-habiting without being married, the Committee found that there were "reasonable and objective criteria" for the discrimination and hence no breach of Article 26:

> The Committee observes, in this connection, that the decision to enter into a legal status by marriage, which provides, in Netherlands law, both for certain benefits and for certain duties and responsibilities, lies entirely with the cohabiting persons. By choosing not to enter into marriage, Mr. Danning and his cohabitant have not, in law, assumed the full extent of the duties and responsibilities incumbent on married couples. Consequently, Mr. Danning does not receive the full benefits provided for in Netherlands law for married couples. The Committee concludes that the differentiation complained of by Mr. Danning does not constitute discrimination in the sense of article 26 of the Covenant.

The Committee's jurisprudence in this area has worried states[45] and there are signs that the Committee may be having second thoughts, with some members taking the view that economic and social rights can be realised only progressively.[46]

3. Article 26 has been found to be infringed in other contexts also. A breach of Article 26, as well as of Articles 3 and 14(1), was found in *Avellanal v. Peru*,[47] in which a married woman was not allowed to sue in respect of matrimonial property. There was also a breach of Article 26 when a law provided for the restitution of property confiscated from persons fleeing from Czechoslovakia under the former communist Government only to Czech citizens resident in the Czech Republic.[48]

---

[44] (1987) 2 Selected Decisions H.R.C. 205. A breach of Art. 26 was found in *Zwaan-de Vries v. Netherlands* (1987) 2 Selected Decisions H.R.C. 209 (another social security "breadwinner" case); *Gueye v. France*, H.R.C. Report, G.A.O.R., 44th Sess., Supp. 40, p. 189 at p. 194 (1989) (army pensions); and *Sprenger v. Austria*, H.R.C. Report, G.A.O.R., 47th Sess., Supp. 40, p. 319 (1992) (public health insurance).

[45] Germany made a reservation intended to exclude such Art. 26 cases when it ratified the First Optional Protocol: for the text, see ST/LEG/SER.E/15, p. 160.

[46] See Schmidt, in Harris and Joseph, eds., *The International Covenant on Civil and Political Rights and United Kingdom Law* (1995), p. 637.

[47] *loc. cit.*, p. 673, n. 21, above.

[48] *Simunek v. Czech Republic* (1996) 3 I.H.R.R. 28. *Cf: Adam v. Czech Republic* (1997) 4 I.H.R.R. 379.

LOVELACE *v.* CANADA[49]

(1981) 2 Selected Decisions 28

The author was a Maliseet Indian who, under the Indian Act, had lost her rights and status as an Indian following her marriage to a non-Indian. As a result, she was, *inter alia*, no longer entitled to live on the Tobique Indian Reserve where she had lived with her parents. Consequently, she was unable to return there to settle after her divorce. The author claimed that this situation was in breach of Article 27, ICCPR.

Views of the Committee

13.2. . . . . It has to be considered whether Sandra Lovelace, because she is denied the legal right to reside on the Tobique Reserve, has by that fact been denied the right guaranteed by article 27 to persons belonging to minorities, to enjoy their own culture and to use their own language in community with other members of their group.

14. The rights under article 27 of the Covenant have to be secured to "persons belonging" to the minority. At present Sandra Lovelace does not qualify as an Indian under Canadian legislation. However, the Indian Act deals primarily with a number of privileges which, as stated above, do not as such come within the scope of the Covenant. Protection under the Indian Act and protection under article 27 of the Covenant therefore have to be distinguished. Persons who are born and brought up on a reserve, who have kept ties with their community and wish to maintain these ties must normally be considered as belonging to that minority within the meaning of the Covenant. Since Sandra Lovelace is ethnically a Maliseet Indian and has only been absent from her home reserve for a few years during the existence of her marriage, she is, in the opinion of the Committee, entitled to be regarded as "belonging" to this minority and to claim the benefits of article 27 of the Covenant. The question whether these benefits have been denied to her, depends on how far they extend.

15. The right to live on a reserve is not as such guaranteed by article 27 of the Covenant. Moreover, the Indian Act does not interfere directly with the functions which are expressly mentioned in that article. However, in the opinion of the Committee the right of Sandra Lovelace to access to her native culture and language "in community with the other members" of her group, has in fact been, and continues to be interfered with, because there is no place outside the Tobique Reserve where such a community exists. On the other hand, not every interference can be regarded as a denial of rights within the meaning of article 27. Restrictions on the right to residence, by way of national legislation, cannot be ruled out under article 27 of the Covenant. This also follows from the restrictions to article 12(1) of the Covenant set out in article 12(3). The Committee recognises

[49] See Bayefsky (1982) 20 C.Y.I.L. 244.

the need to define the category of persons entitled to live on a reserve, for such purposes as those explained by the Government regarding protection of its resources and preservation of the identity of its people. However, the obligations which the Government has since undertaken under the Covenant must also be taken into account.

16. In this respect, the Committee is of the view that statutory restrictions affecting the right to residence on a reserve of a person belonging to the minority concerned, must have both a reasonable and objective justification and be consistent with the other provisions of the Covenant, read as a whole. Article 27 must be construed and applied in the light of the other provisions mentioned above, such as articles 12, 17 and 23 in so far as they may be relevant to the particular case, and also the provisions against discrimination, such as articles 2, 3 and 26, as the case may be. It is not necessary, however, to determine in any general manner which restrictions may be justified under the Covenant, in particular as a result of marriage, because the circumstances are special in the present case.

17. The case of Sandra Lovelace should be considered in the light of the fact that her marriage to a non-Indian has broken up. It is natural that in such a situation she wishes to return to the environment in which she was born, particularly as after the dissolution of her marriage her main cultural attachment again was to the Maliseet band. Whatever may be the merits of the Indian Act in other respects, it does not seem to the Committee that to deny Sandra Lovelace the right to reside on the reserve is reasonable, or necessary to preserve the identity of the tribe. The Committee therefore concludes that to prevent her recognition as belonging to the band is an unjustifiable denial of her rights under article 27 of the Covenant, read in the context of the other provisions referred to.

18. In view of this finding, the Committee does not consider it necessary to examine whether the same facts also show separate breaches of the other rights invoked. The specific rights most directly applicable to her situation are those under article 27 of the Covenant. The rights to choose one's residence (article 12), and the rights aimed at protecting family life and children (articles 17, 23 and 24) are only indirectly at stake in the present case. . . .

19. Accordingly, the Human Rights Committee, . . . is of the view that the facts of the present case which established that Sandra Lovelace has been denied the legal right to reside on the Tobique Reserve, disclose a breach by Canada of article 27 of the Covenant.

Individual Opinion of Mr. Bouriri

In the Lovelace case, not only article 27 but also articles 2 (para. 1), 3, 23 (paras. 1 and 4) and 26 of the Covenant have been breached, for some of the provisions of the Indian Act are discriminatory, particularly as between men and women. The Act is still in force and, even though the Lovelace case arose before the date on which the Covenant became applicable in Canada, Mrs. Lovelace is still suffering from the adverse discriminatory effects of the Act in matters other than that covered by article 27.

Notes

1. Section 12 of the Indian Act discriminated against the victim on sexual grounds also; Indian men who married non-Indian women were not affected. However, having decided that there was a breach of Article 27, the Committee found it unnecessary to consider the victim's claim of sexual discrimination contrary to Article 26.

2. Canada informed the Committee that steps were being taken to amend the Indian Act in accordance with the Committee's views.[50]

3. In *Kitok v. Sweden*,[51] the author was a Swedish citizen and a member of the Sami people who was, as a result of a Swedish statute, denied the right to breed reindeer, an immemorial custom of the Sami community. Under the statute, reindeer breeding was restricted to members of Sami villages, membership of which was determined by the Sami people themselves. The applicant, like most Sami, was not a village member. With some hesitation, the Committee found that there was no breach of Article 27. The Committee stated:

> 9.1 The main question before the Committee is whether the author of the communication is the victim of a violation of article 27 of the Covenant because, as he alleges, he is arbitrarily denied immemorial rights granted to the Sami community, in particular, the right to membership of the Sami community and the right to carry out reindeer husbandry. . . .
>
> 9.2 The regulation of an economic activity is normally a matter for the State alone. However, where that activity is an essential element in the culture of an ethnic community, its application to an individual may fall under article 27 . . .
>
> 9.5 According to the State Party, the purposes of the Reindeer Husbandry Act are to restrict the number of reindeer breeders for economic and ecological reasons and to secure the preservation and well-being of the Sami minority. Both parties agree that effective measures are required to ensure the future of reindeer breeding and the livelihood of those for whom reindeer farming is the primary source of income. The method selected by the State Party to secure these objectives is the limitation of the right to engage in reindeer breeding to members of the Sami villages. The Committee is of the opinion that all these objectives and measures are reasonable and consistent with article 27 of the Covenant.
>
> 9.6 The Committee has none the less had grave doubts as to whether certain provisions of the Reindeer Husbandry Act, and their application to the author, are compatible with article 27 . . .
>
> 9.7 . . . The Act provides certain criteria for participation in the life of an ethnic minority whereby a person who is ethnically a Sami can be held not to be a Sami for the purposes of the Act. The Committee has been concerned that the ignoring of objective ethnic criteria in determining membership of a minority, and the application to Mr. Kitok of the designated rules, may have been disproportionate to the legitimate ends sought by the legislation. It has further

[50] 2 Selected Decisions H.R.C. 224.
[51] H.R.C. Report, G.A.O.R., 44th Sess., Supp. 40, p. 271 at pp. 228–30 (1989). For other indigenous peoples cases under Article 27, see *Lansmann v. Finland* (1995) 2 I.H.R.R. 287; *ibid.* (1997) 4 I.H.R.R. 405; and *Ominyak and Lubicon Lake Band v. Canada*, H.R.C. Report, G.A.O.R., 45th Sess., Supp. 40, Vol. II, p. 1 (1990).

noted that Mr. Kitok has always retained some links with the Sami community, always living on Sami lands and seeking to return to full-time reindeer farming as soon as it became financially possible, in his particular circumstances, for him to do so.

9.8 In resolving this problem, in which there is an apparent conflict between the legislation, which seems to protect the rights of the minority as a whole, and its application to a single member of that minority, the Committee has been guided by the *ratio decidendi* in the Lovelace case ... namely, that a restriction upon the right of an individual member of a minority must be shown to have a reasonable and objective justification and to be necessary for the continued viability and welfare of the minority as a whole. After a careful review of all the elements involved in this case, the Committee is of the view that there is no violation of article 27 by the State Party. In this context, the Committee notes that Mr. Kitok is permitted, albeit not as of right, to graze and farm his reindeer, to hunt and to fish.

SILVA *v.* URUGUAY

(1981) 1 Selected Decisions H.R.C. 65

The authors alleged breaches of Article 25, ICCPR because they were banned by a 1976 executive decree from engaging in "any activity of a political nature, including the right to vote, for a term of 15 years." The authors, who were professors, an accountant and an engineer, had been candidates for elective office for political groups which had since been banned by decree. The defendant state relied unsuccessfully on a notice of derogation made under Article 4.

Views of the Committee

According to article 4(1) of the Covenant, the States Parties may take measures derogating from their obligations under that instrument in a situation of public emergency which threatens the life of the nation and the existence of which has been formally proclaimed. Even in such circumstances, derogations are only permissible to the extent strictly required by the exigencies of the situation. In its note of June 28, 1979 to the Secretary-General of the United Nations[52] ... which was designed to comply with the formal requirements laid down in article 4(3) of the Covenant, the Government of Uruguay has made reference to an emergency situation in the country which was legally acknowledged in a number of "Institutional Acts." However, no factual details were given at that time. The note confined itself to stating that the existence of the emergency situation was "a matter of universal knowledge"; no attempt was made to indicate the nature and the scope of the derogations actually resorted to with regard to the rights guaranteed by the Covenant, or to show that such derogations were strictly necessary.

Although the sovereign right of a State Party to declare a state of emergency is not questioned, yet, in the specific context of the present

[52] *Ed.* Text in UN Doc. ST/LEG/SER.E/15, p. 155.

communication, the Human Rights Committee is of the opinion that a State, by merely invoking the existence of exceptional circumstances, cannot evade the obligations which it has undertaken by ratifying the Covenant. Although the substantive right to take derogatory measures may not depend on a formal notification being made pursuant to article 4(3) of the Covenant, the State Party concerned is duty-bound to give a sufficiently detailed account of the relevant facts when it invokes article 4(1) of the Covenant in proceedings under the Optional Protocol. It is the function of the Human Rights Committee, acting under the Optional Protocol, to see to it that States Parties live up to their commitments under the Covenant. In order to discharge this function and to assess whether a situation of the kind described in article 4(1) of the Covenant exists in the country concerned, it needs full and comprehensive information. If the respondent Government does not furnish the required justification itself, as it is required to do under article 4(2) of the Optional Protocol and article 4(3) of the Covenant, the Human Rights Committee cannot conclude that valid reasons exist to legitimise a departure from the normal legal régime prescribed by the Covenant.

The Committee considered the merits of the claims and found breaches of Article 25.

Notes

1. Article 4 permits a state to derogate from its obligations under the Covenant in time of "public emergency" in the circumstances and subject to the conditions indicated in Article 4(1).[53] Derogation is not permitted in respect of certain basic rights identified in Article 4(2) which were not in issue in the *Silva* case. Did the Committee take the view that non-compliance with the notification requirement would invalidate a derogation that was consistent with Article 4(1)? What would Uruguay had to have done to satisfy the Committee under Article 4(1)?

2. Since the ICCPR entered into force, 22 states have submitted to the UN Secretary General notices of derogation, some of which have since been terminated.[54] The current 1989 United Kingdom notice[55] in respect of Northern Ireland reads:

> The Government of the United Kingdom have [previously] found it necessary to take and continue [various measures], derogating in certain respects from obligations under Article 9 of the International Covenant on Civil and Political Rights.
>
> On November 14, 1989 the Home Secretary announced that the Government had concluded that a satisfactory procedure for the review of detention of terrorist suspects involving the judiciary had not been identified and that the derogation notified under Article 4 of the Covenant would therefore remain in place for as long as circumstances require.

[53] See De Zayas, in Premont, Stenersen and Oseredczuk, eds., *Non-Derogable Rights and States of Emergency* (1996), p. 225, and Oraa, *Human Rights in States of Emergency in International Law* (1992).

[54] UN Doc. ST/LEG/SER.E/15, pp. 137 *et seq.*

[55] *ibid.* p. 155.

3. Trinidad and Tobago has made a reservation to the Covenant reserving the right "not to apply in full" Article 4(2).[56] This reservation which permits derogation from a non-derogable provision, has been objected to as being contrary to the object and purpose of the Covenant.[57]

INTERNATIONAL COVENANT ON ECONOMIC, SOCIAL AND CULTURAL RIGHTS 1966[58]

993 U.N.T.S. 3; U.K.T.S. 6 (1977), Cmnd. 6702; (1967) 6 I.L.M. 360

Article 1

Identical to Article 1, ICCPR, above, p. 636

Article 2

1. Each State Party to the present Covenant undertakes to take steps, individually and through international assistance and co-operation, especially economic and technical, to the maximum of its available resources, with a view to achieving progressively the full realisation of the rights recognised in the present Covenant by all appropriate means, including particularly the adoption of legislative measures.

2. The States Parties to the present Covenant undertake to guarantee that the rights enunciated in the present Covenant will be exercised without discrimination of any kind as to race, colour, sex, language, religion, political or other opinion, national or social origin, property, birth or other status.

3. Developing countries, with due regard to human rights and their national economy, may determine to what extent they would guarantee the economic rights recognised in the present Covenant to non-nationals.

Article 3

The States Parties to the present Covenant undertake to ensure the equal right of men and women to the enjoyment of all economic, social and cultural rights set forth in the present Covenant.

---

[56] *ibid.* p. 128.
[57] Objections by Germany and the Netherlands: *ibid.* p. 132. Note also the French reservation to Art. 4(1): *ibid.* p. 132.
[58] In force 1976. 135 parties, including the U.K. See Alston and Quinn (1987) 9 H.R.Q. 156; Craven, *The International Covenant on Economic, Social and Cultural Rights* (1995); *id.* (1993) 40 N.I.L.R. 367; Henkaerts, in Trindade, ed., *The Modern World of Human Rights: Essays in Honour of Thomas Buergenthal* (1996), p. 267; Simma, in Matscher, ed., *The Implementation of Economic and Social Rights* (1991), p. 75. See also the 1986 Limburg Principles on the Implementation of the International Covenant on Economic, Social and Cultural Rights and Commentaries thereto: (1987) 9 H.R.Q. 121.

Article 4

The States Parties to the present Covenant recognise that, in the enjoyment of those rights provided by the State in conformity with the present Covenant, the State may subject such rights only to such limitations as are determined by law only in so far as this may be compatible with the nature of these rights and solely for the purpose of promoting the general welfare in a democratic society.

Article 5

1. Nothing in the present Covenant may be interpreted as implying for any State, group or person any right to engage in any activity or to perform any act aimed at the destruction of any of the rights or freedoms recognised herein, or at their limitation to a greater extent than is provided for in the present Covenant.

2. No restriction upon or derogation from any of the fundamental human rights recognised or existing in any country in virtue of law, conventions, regulations or custom shall be admitted on the pretext that the present Covenant does not recognise such rights or that it recognises them to a lesser extent.

Article 6

1. The States Parties to the present Covenant recognise the right to work, which includes the right of everyone to the opportunity to gain his living by work which he freely chooses or accepts, and will take appropriate steps to safeguard this right.

2. The steps to be taken by a State Party to the present Covenant to achieve the full realisation of this right shall include technical and vocational guidance and training programmes, policies and techniques to achieve steady economic, social and cultural development and full and productive employment under conditions safeguarding fundamental political and economic freedoms to the individual.

Article 7

The States Parties to the present Covenant recognise the right of everyone to the enjoyment of just and favourable conditions of work, which ensure, in particular:

(a) Remuneration which provides all workers, as a minimum, with:
   (i) Fair wages and equal remuneration for work of equal value without distinction of any kind, in particular women being guaranteed conditions of work not inferior to those enjoyed by men, with equal pay for equal work;
   (ii) A decent living for themselves and their families in accordance with the provisions of the present Covenant;

(b) Safe and healthy working conditions;

(c) Equal opportunity for everyone to be promoted in his employment to an appropriate higher level, subject to no considerations other than those of seniority and competence;

(d) Rest, leisure and reasonable limitation of working hours and periodic holidays with pay, as well as remuneration for public holidays.

Article 8

1. The States Parties to the present Covenant undertake to ensure:

(a) The right of everyone to form trade unions and join the trade union of his choice, subject only to the rules of the organisation concerned, for the promotion and protection of his economic and social interests. No restrictions may be placed on the exercise of this right other than those prescribed by law and which are necessary in a democratic society in the interests of national security or public order or for the protection of the rights and freedoms of others;

(b) The right of trade unions to establish national federations or confederations and the right of the latter to form or join international trade-union organisations;

(c) The right of trade unions to function freely subject to no limitations other than those prescribed by law and which are necessary in a democratic society in the interests of national security or public order or for the protection of the rights and freedoms of others;

(d) The right to strike, provided that it is exercised in conformity with the laws of the particular country.

2. This article shall not prevent the imposition of lawful restrictions on the exercise of these rights by members of the armed forces or of the police or of the administration of the State.

3. Nothing in this article shall authorise States Parties to the International Labour Organization Convention of 1948 concerning Freedom of Association and Protection of the Right to Organize to take legislative measures which would prejudice, or apply the law in such a manner as would prejudice, the guarantees provided for in that Convention.

Article 9

The States Parties to the present Covenant recognise the right of everyone to social security, including social insurance.

Article 10

The States Parties to the present Covenant recognise that:

1. The widest possible protection and assistance should be accorded to the family, which is the natural and fundamental group unit of society,

particularly for its establishment and while it is responsible for the care and education of dependent children. Marriage must be entered into with the free consent of the intending spouses.

2. Special protection should be accorded to mothers during a reasonable period before and after childbirth. During such period working mothers should be accorded paid leave or leave with adequate social security benefits.

3. Special measures of protection and assistance should be taken on behalf of all children and young persons without any discrimination for reasons of parentage or other conditions. Children and young persons should be protected from economic and social exploitation. Their employment in work harmful to their morals or health or dangerous to life or likely to hamper their normal development should be punishable by law. States should also set age limits below which the paid employment of child labour should be prohibited and punishable by law.

Article 11

1. The States Parties to the present Covenant recognise the right of everyone to an adequate standard of living for himself and his family, including adequate food, clothing and housing, and to the continuous improvement of living conditions. The States Parties will take appropriate steps to ensure the realisation of this right, recognising to this effect the essential importance of international co-operation based on free consent.

2. The States Parties to the present Covenant, recognising the fundamental right of everyone to be free from hunger, shall take, individually and through international co-operation, the measures, including specific programmes, which are needed:
  (a) To improve methods of production, conservation and distribution of food by making full use of technical and scientific knowledge by disseminating knowledge of the principles of nutrition and by developing or reforming agrarian systems in such a way as to achieve the most efficient development and utilisation of natural resources;
  (b) Taking into account the problems of both food-importing and food-exporting countries, to ensure an equitable distribution of world food supplies in relation to need.

Article 12

1. The States Parties to the present Covenant recognise the right of everyone to the enjoyment of the highest attainable standard of physical and mental health.

2. The steps to be taken by the States Parties to the present Covenant to achieve the full realisation of this right shall include those necessary for:

(*a*) The provision for the reduction of the stillbirth-rate and of infant mortality and for the healthy development of the child;

(*b*) The improvement of all aspects of environmental and industrial hygiene;

(*c*) The prevention, treatment and control of epidemic, endemic, occupational and other diseases;

(*d*) The creation of conditions which would assure to all medical service and medical attention in the event of sickness.

Article 13

1. The States Parties to the present Covenant recognise the right of everyone to education. They agree that education shall be directed to the full development of the human personality and the sense of its dignity, and shall strengthen the respect for human rights and fundamental freedoms. They further agree that education shall enable all persons to participate effectively in a free society, promote understanding, tolerance and friendship among all nations and all racial, ethnic or religious groups, and further the activities of the United Nations for the maintenance of peace.

2. The States Parties to the present Covenant recognise that, with a view to achieving the full realisation of this right:

(*a*) Primary education shall be compulsory and available free to all;

(*b*) Secondary education in its different forms, including technical and vocational secondary education, shall be made generally available and accessible to all by every appropriate means, and in particular by the progressive introduction of free education;

(*c*) Higher education shall be made equally accessible to all, on the basis of capacity, by every appropriate means, and in particular by the progressive introduction of free education;

(*d*) Fundamental education shall be encouraged or intensified as far as possible for those persons who have not received or completed the whole period of their primary education;

(*e*) The development of a system of schools at all levels shall be actively pursued, an adequate fellowship system shall be established, and the material conditions of teaching staff shall be continuously improved.

3. The States Parties to the present Covenant undertake to have respect for the liberty of parents and, when applicable, legal guardians, to choose for their children schools, other than those established by the public authorities, which conform to such minimum educational standards as may be laid down or approved by the State and to ensure the religious

and moral education of their children in conformity with their own convictions.

4. No part of this article shall be construed so as to interfere with the liberty of individuals and bodies to establish and direct educational institutions, subject always to the observance of the principles set forth in paragraph 1 of this article and to the requirement that the education given in such institutions shall conform to such minimum standards as may be laid down by the State.

Article 14

Each State Party to the present Covenant which, at the time of becoming a Party, has not been able to secure in its metropolitan territory or other territories under its jurisdiction compulsory primary education, free of charge, undertakes, within two years, to work out and adopt a detailed plan of action for the progressive implementation, within a reasonable number of years, to be fixed in the plan, of the principle of compulsory education free of charge for all.

Article 15

1. The States Parties to the present Covenant recognise the right of everyone:
   (*a*) To take part in cultural life;
   (*b*) To enjoy the benefits of scientific progress and its applications;
   (*c*) To benefit from the protection of the moral and material interests resulting from any scientific, literary or artistic production of which he is the author.

2. The steps to be taken by the States Parties to the present Covenant to achieve the full realisation of this right shall include those necessary for the conservation, the development and the diffusion of science and culture.

3. The States Parties to the present Covenant undertake to respect the freedom indispensable for scientific research and creative activity.

4. The States Parties to the present Covenant recognise the benefits to be derived from the encouragement and development of international contacts and co-operation in the scientific and cultural fields.

Article 23

The States Parties to the present Covenant agree that international action for the achievement of the rights recognised in the present Covenant includes such methods as the conclusion of conventions, the adoption of recommendations, the furnishing of technical assistance and the holding of regional meetings and technical meetings for the purpose of consultation and study organised in conjunction with the Governments concerned.

Article 25

Identical to Article 47, ICCPR, above, p. 645

Article 28

The provisions of the present Covenant shall extend to all parts of federal States without any limitations or exceptions.

Notes

1. The ICESCR protects "second generation" human rights, as to which see above, p. 625. After early attempts to include both "first" and "second" generation rights in one document, it was decided to guarantee civil and political rights and economic, social and cultural rights in two separate Covenants. This was because there were seen to be differences in the nature of the legal obligations and the systems of supervision that could be imposed.[59] As to the former, the obligations appropriate to civil and political rights, (*e.g.* not to torture) were typically negative and capable of immediate implementation by all states, whereas those suitable for economic, social and cultural rights, (*e.g.* to provide adequate housing) were mostly positive and susceptible only of progressive and differential compliance as each state's economy permitted.[60] As to remedies, it was thought to follow from the differing nature of the obligations described above that whereas breaches of civil and political rights could properly be challenged through a system of petitions, the essentially programmatic and conditional nature of economic, social and cultural rights obligations made them "non-justiciable," so that only a system of reports was possible.

2. The basic obligation which parties undertake in Article 2(1), ICESCR to "take steps . . . to achieve progressively the full realisation of the rights recognised in the Covenants contrasts with the equivalent obligation in Article 2, ICCPR, to "respect and ensure" at once the civil and political rights guaranteed by that Covenant. There are, however, some obligations of immediate effect for all parties to the ICESCR. See, in particular, the undertakings to "guarantee" and "ensure" non-discrimination and equal treatment respectively (Articles 2(2) and (3))[61] and to "ensure" trade union rights (Article 8). States also agree to "respect," and hence not interfere with, parental choice of schools (Article 13(3)) and scientific freedom (Article 15(3)). The obligation to "take steps" is itself an immediate one, as well as being a continuing or dynamic one, with an unceasing expectation of incremental progress within the limits of the economy. Moreover, to the extent that an article in the Covenant guaranteeing a particular right details the steps to be taken, the

---

[59] For contrasting views as to the validity of these differences, see Bossuyt (1975) 8 H.R.J. 783; Van Boven, in Vasak and Alston, eds., *The International Dimension of Human Rights* (1982), Vol. I, Chap. 3; Van Hoof, in Alston and Tomasevski, eds., *The Right to Food* (1984), p. 97; Vierdag (1978) 9 N.Y.I.L. 69.

[60] Although this analysis is helpful as a generalisation, there are civil and political rights that require positive action and money, (*e.g.* the right to a fair trial supposes court buildings and legal aid) and some economic, social and cultural rights, (*e.g.* the right to form a trade union) call only for non-intervention by states. Moreover, civil and political rights may, although theoretically capable of immediate implementation, require a change in "societal structures" or attitudes, which takes time: see Alston and Quinn, *loc. cit.*, p. 689, n. 58 above, p. 172.

[61] On Arts. 2(2) and (3), see Klerk (1987) 9 H.R.Q. 250. On the Art. 2(3) exception open to developing states, see Dankwa, *ibid.*, 230.

obligation in respect of that right becomes an "obligation of conduct," not one of "result."[62]

The Committee on Economic, Social and Cultural Rights in its Third General Comment on the Nature of States Parties' Obligations (Article 2(1))[63] commented as follows on the questions of "justiciability" and the judicial enforcement in national courts of obligations in the Covenant as "self-executing" treaty provisions:

> 5. Among the measures which might be considered appropriate [see Article 2(1)], in addition to legislation, is the provision of judicial remedies with respect to rights which may, in accordance with the national legal system, be considered justiciable. The Committee notes, for example, that the enjoyment of the rights recognized, *without discrimination*, will often be appropriately promoted, in part, through the provision of judicial or other effective remedies. . . . In addition, there are a number of other provisions, including articles 3, 7(a)(i), 8, 10(3), 13(2)(a), 13(3), 13(4) and 15(3) which would seem to be capable of immediate application by judicial and other organs in many national legal systems. Any suggestion that the provisions indicated are inherently non-self-executing would seem to be difficult to sustain.

When a state is determining the amount of "available resources" that it has to devote to the realisation of ICESCR rights, does it have a complete discretion as to how it allocates its gross national product between, for example, the right to social security and national defence?[64] The Limburg Principles read[65]:

> 28. In the use of the available resources due priority shall be given to the realisation of rights recognised in the Covenant, mindful of the need to assure to everyone the satisfaction of subsistence requirements as well as the provision of essential services.

Alston and Quinn suggest[66]:

> The discretion to which a state is entitled is, however, not unlimited, and its position is clearly not immune from scrutiny by the international body charged with responsibility for supervising States Parties' compliance with their treaty obligations. While the Covenant itself is, inevitably, devoid of specific allocational benchmarks, there is presumably a process requirement by which states might be requested to show that adequate consideration has been given to the possible resources available to satisfy each of the Covenant's requirements, even if the effort was ultimately unsuccessful. If a state is unable to do so then it fails to meet its obligation of conduct to ensure a principled policy-making process—one reflecting a sense of the importance of the relevant rights.

As to "appropriate means," legislation, although singled out in Article 2(1) as particularly important, is neither required nor in every case sufficient. Exceptionally, repealing legislation may be necessary where existing legislation is contrary

---

[62] On "obligations of conduct" (to do or not do something specified at once) and "result" (to take undefined action to achieve a required result), see Goodwin-Gill, in Alston and Tomasevski, eds., *op. cit.*, p. 696, n. 60 above, p. 111.

[63] UN Doc. E/C/ 12/1990/CRP.5/ Add. 4, pp. 3–4.

[64] On "maximum available resources" see Robertson (1994) 16 H.R.Q. 693.

[65] *loc. cit.*, p. 689, n. 58, above.

[66] *ibid.*, pp. 180–181.

to an ICESCR obligation (see, *e.g.* Article 2(2)). Realisation of a right in the sense of Article 2(1), however, means realisation in fact, so that legislation requiring, for example, "fair wages" (Article 7(*a*)(i)) may not be necessary if these can be achieved, for example, by collective agreements between employers and trades unions.

With regard to "international assistance and co-operation," does Article 2(1) impose an obligation on developed states to assist developing states to realise economic, social and cultural rights? See also Articles 11 and 23.

3. Primary responsibility for the implementation of the ICESCR is placed on the UN Economic and Social Council (ECOSOC) (Articles 16–22). Originally, ECOSOC delegated this responsibility to a Working Group composed of government representatives. Partly because of its representative character, the Working Group was not a success. With effect from 1987, it was replaced by the Committee on Economic, Social and Cultural Rights (CESCR), which has similarities with the ICCPR Human Rights Committee.[67] The CESCR is composed of 18 members elected by the ICESCR parties, with "due consideration" being "given to equitable geographic distribution and to the representation of different forms of social and legal systems."[68] As with the Human Rights Committee, members are independent experts who do not represent their national governments. Most have a legal background.

4. Each party must submit "reports on the measures which they have adopted and the progress made in achieving the observance of the rights recognised" in the ICESCR (Article 16(1)). Following an initial report, parties must submit reports for consideration by the CESCR every five years.[69] Many reports have been submitted late or not at all. In 1996, 143 reports were overdue, with 29 parties not having submitted any of the initial or subsequent reports required of them.[70] As with the Human Rights Committee, there is little that the CESCR can do except remind such parties of their reporting obligations or publish the names or express criticism of defaulting states. The CESCR examines reports at public hearings to which reporting states are invited to send representatives to introduce their reports and answer questions. The CESCR has made good progress in ensuring the availability of information from sources other than national reports to assist it in their examination. Specialised agencies, particularly the ILO, UNESCO and WHO, are "called upon to submit reports on the progress made" by reporting states "in achieving the observance of the provisions of the Covenant falling within the scope of their activities."[71] Most significantly, NGOs having UN consultative status may submit written statements to the CESCR.[72]

Following its consideration of a state's report, the Committee adopts Concluding Observations in which it reviews a state's performance.[73] These both praise

---

[67] On the CESCR see Alston (1987) 9 H.R.Q. 332 and Alston and Simma (1987) 81 A.J.I.L. 747 and (1988) 82 A.J.I.L. 603.

[68] ECOSOC Resolution 1985/17, para. (b).

[69] Art. 17, ICESCR. The requirement of quinquennial reports on all of the rights in the ICESCR was introduced in 1988: ECOSOC Resolution 88/4, E/C.12/1988/4, p. 58. Earlier, parties had reported every three years on one of three groups of rights for second and later reports.

[70] See CESCR Report, ESCOR, Supp. 3, Annex I (1990).

[71] Rule 69, CESCR Provisional Rules of Procedure, UN Doc. E/C.12/1990/4.

[72] ECOSOC Resolution 1987/5, para. 6.

[73] The Covenant or ECOSOC Resolution basis for this power is unclear: see Craven, *op. cit.* p. 689, n. 58, above, p. 87. No party has objected to the Committee's practice, which is comparable to that of other human rights treaty bodies: see, *e.g.* the Human Rights Committee, above, p. 648.

and criticise a state's record, and have, so far only in a few cases, contained findings of non-compliance with the Covenant. The CESCR may also prepare General Comments based on the various articles and provisions of the Covenant with a view to assisting States Parties in fulfilling their reporting obligations.[74] This power is modelled on that of the ICCPR Human Rights Committee and, *inter alia*, authorises the CESCR to spell out its interpretation of particular provisions of the ICESCR.[75]

5. Implementation of the ICESCR is based exclusively upon national reports; in contrast with the ICCPR, there is no right of state or individual petition. This was thought to follow from the generally progressive character of the obligations in the ICESCR, which in turn were considered to result from the nature of economic, social and cultural rights. Is there any reason why the obligations in the ICESCR that are immediate, rather than progressive, in kind (see above, note 2) should not be treated as "justiciable"? Note that remedies are available for the enforcement of economic and social rights in national courts and tribunals. Note also the *Broeks* case, above, p. 681, and the *Yilmaz Dogan* case, below, p. 707. With regard to the progressive obligations in the ICESCR, (*e.g.* to "take steps" to realise the right to work by the provision of vocational guidance: Articles 2(1) and 6(1)(2)), if these are, as would appear, legal obligations compliance with which the CESCR may assess when examining national reports, why can they not equally be the subject of a system of petitions? If, that is, appropriate and differential standards of achievement or endeavour may be established and applied when examining reports, why should this not be so when considering petitions from individuals or groups, (*e.g.* trade unions or social rights NGOs)? How relevant to the decision not to allow a right of petition in the ICESCR might it have been that the states then most likely to accept a system of petitions were the ones that emphasised economic, social and cultural rights least?[76]

6. On the relative merits of report and petition systems for the implementation of international human rights guarantees, note the following comments[77]:

> There are advantages to . . . a [report] system. . . . There is no need to wait upon the chance of a petition being brought by a person with the *locus standi*, knowledge, time, inclination, and, possibly, funds to do so; the initiative lies with the supervisory organs. . . . In contrast, every part of the law and practice of the contracting parties . . . is examined automatically [in each reporting period]. But there are disadvantages too. . . . The [supervisory body] may not discover how a law or practice actually operates without the sort of information that appears from the facts of particular cases and that emerges from the sharpness of conflict in adversary proceedings. . . . There is also the fact that a finding against a state in favour of a particular individual . . . is likely to make a much greater impact upon public opinion than an abstract ruling upon the

---

[74] ECOSOC Resolution 1987/5; Rule 65, CESCR Provisional Rules of Procedure. Three General Comments of this kind have been made: on "Reporting by States Parties", CESCR Report, ESCOR, Supp. 4, Annex III (1989); on "International Technical Assistance" (Art. 22), CESCR Report, ESCOR, Supp. 3, Annex IV (1990); and on "The Nature of States Parties Obligations" (Art. 2(1)) *loc. cit.*, p. 696, n. 63, above.

[75] The following have been adopted: General Comments on the Right to Adequate Housing (No. 4), UN Doc. E/1992/3, Annex III; Persons with Disabilities (No. 5) (1995) 2 I.H.R.R. 261; and the Rights of Older Persons (No. 6) (1996) 3 I.H.R.R. 252.

[76] In 1996, the CESCR approved and referred to ECOSOC a draft protocol to the Covenant permitting individual petitions: CESCR Report, E.S.C.O.R., Supp. 2, p. 64 (1996).

[77] Harris, *The European Social Charter* (1984), pp. 267–268.

question of compliance. Above all, from the standpoint of the individual whose rights are directly or indirectly in issue, there is no substitute for a remedy directly available to him.

If a choice is to be made, it is likely that a system of petitions is the more effective ... it not only provides a remedy for the particular individual who brings the petition, but in most cases it will ... cause the law or practice in question to be changed to the advantage of all ... more speedily and more certainly than a report system.

INTERNATIONAL CONVENTION ON THE ELIMINATION OF ALL FORMS OF RACIAL DISCRIMINATION 1966[78]

U.K.T.S. 77 (1969), Cmnd. 4108; 60 U.N.T.S. 195; (1966) 60 A.J.I.L. 650; (1966) 5 I.L.M. 352

Article 1

1. In this Convention, the term "racial discrimination" shall mean any distinction, exclusion, restriction or preference based on race, colour, descent, or national or ethnic origin which has the purpose or effect of nullifying or impairing the recognition, enjoyment or exercise, on an equal footing, of human rights and fundamental freedoms in the political, economic, social, cultural or any other field of public life.

2. This Convention shall not apply to distinctions, exclusions, restrictions or preferences made by a State Party to this Convention between citizens and non-citizens.

3. Nothing in this Convention may be interpreted as affecting in any way the legal provisions of States Parties concerning nationality, citizenship or naturalisation, provided that such provisions do not discriminate against any particular nationality.

4. Special measures taken for the sole purpose of securing adequate advancement of certain racial or ethnic groups or individuals requiring such protection as may be necessary in order to ensure such groups or individuals equal enjoyment or exercise of human rights and fundamental freedoms shall not be deemed racial discrimination, provided, however, that such measures do not, as a consequence, lead to the maintenance of separate rights for different racial groups and that they shall not be continued after the objectives for which they were taken have been achieved.

---

[78] In force 1969. 148 parties, including the U.K. See Banton, *International Action against Racial Discrimination* (1996); Cholewinski, 69 R.D.I. 157; Buergenthal (1977) 12 T.I.L.J. 187; Lerner, *The UN Convention on the Elimination of all Forms of Racial Discrimination* (2nd. ed., 1980); Meron (1985) 79 A.J.I.L. 283; Partsch (1979) 14 T.I.L.J. 191; Schwelb (1966) 15 I.C.L.Q. 996.

Article 2

1. States Parties condemn racial discrimination and undertake to pursue by all appropriate means and without delay a policy of eliminating racial discrimination in all its forms and promoting understanding among all races, and, to this end:

(a) Each State Party undertakes to engage in no act or practice of racial discrimination against persons, groups of persons or institutions and to ensure that all public authorities and public institutions, national and local, shall act in conformity with this obligation;

(b) Each State Party undertakes not to sponsor, defend or support racial discrimination by any persons or organisations;

(c) Each State Party shall take effective measures to review governmental, national and local policies, and to amend, rescind or nullify any laws and regulations which have the effect of creating or perpetuating racial discrimination wherever it exists;

(d) Each State Party shall prohibit and bring to an end, by all appropriate means, including legislation as required by circumstances, racial discrimination by any persons, group or organisation;

(e) Each State Party undertakes to encourage, where appropriate, integrationist multi-racial organisations and movements and other means of eliminating barriers between races, and to discourage anything which tends to strengthen racial division.

2. States Parties shall, when the circumstances so warrant, take, in the social, economic, cultural and other fields, special and concrete measures to ensure the adequate development and protection of certain racial groups or individuals belonging to them, for the purpose of guaranteeing them the full and equal enjoyment of human rights and fundamental freedoms. These measures shall in no case entail as a consequence the maintenance of unequal or separate rights for different racial groups after the objectives for which they were taken have been achieved.

Article 3

States Parties particularly condemn racial segregation and *apartheid* and undertake to prevent, prohibit and eradicate all practices of this nature in territories under their jurisdiction.

Article 4

State Parties condemn all propaganda and all organisations which are based on ideas or theories of superiority of one race or group of persons of one colour or ethnic origin, or which attempt to justify or promote racial hatred and discrimination in any form, and undertake to adopt immediate and positive measures designed to eradicate all incitement to, or acts of, such discrimination and, to this end, with due regard to the principles embodied in the Universal Declaration of Human Rights and the rights expressly set forth in Article 5 of this Convention, *inter alia*:

(a) Shall declare an offence punishable by law all dissemination of ideas based on racial superiority or hatred, incitement to racial discrimination, as well as all acts of violence or incitement to such acts against any race or group of persons of another colour or ethnic origin, and also the provision of any assistance to racist activities including the financing thereof;

(b) Shall declare illegal and prohibit organisations, and also organised and all other propaganda activities, which promote and incite racial discrimination, and shall recognise participation in such organisations or activities as an offence punishable by law;

(c) Shall not permit public authorities or public institutions, national or local, to promote or incite racial discrimination.

Article 5

In compliance with the fundamental obligations laid down in Article 2 of this Convention, States Parties undertake to prohibit and to eliminate racial discrimination in all its forms and to guarantee the right of everyone, without distinction as to race, colour, or national or ethnic origin, to equality before the law, notably in the enjoyment of the following rights:

(a) The right to equal treatment before the tribunals and all other organs administering justice;

(b) The right to security of person and protection by the State against violence or bodily harm, whether inflicted by government officials or by any individual, group or institution;

(c) Political rights, in particular the rights to participate in elections—to vote and to stand for election—on the basis of universal and equal suffrage, to take part in the Government as well as in the conduct of public affairs at any level and to have equal access to public service;

(d) Other civil rights, in particular:

(i) The right to freedom of movement and residence within the border of the State;

(ii) The right to leave any country, including one's own, and to return to one's country;

(iii) The right to nationality;

(iv) The right to marriage and choice of spouse;

(v) The right to own property alone as well as in association with others;

(vi) The right to inherit;

(vii) The right to freedom of thought, conscience and religion;

(viii) The right to freedom of opinion and expression;

(ix) The right to freedom of peaceful assembly and association;
  (e) Economic, social and cultural rights, in particular:
    (i) The rights to work, to free choice of employment, to just and favourable conditions of work, to protection against unemployment, to equal pay for equal work, to just and favourable remuneration;
    (ii) The right to form and join trade unions;
    (iii) The right to housing;
    (iv) The right to public health, medical care, social security and social services;
    (v) The right to education and training;
    (vi) The right to equal participation in cultural activities;
  (f) The right of access to any place or service intended for use by the general public, such as transport, hotels, restaurants, cafés, theatres and parks.

Article 6

States Parties shall assure to everyone within their jurisdiction effective protection and remedies, through the competent national tribunals and other State institutions, against any acts of racial discrimination which violate his human rights and fundamental freedoms contrary to this Convention, as well as the right to seek from such tribunals just and adequate reparation or satisfaction for any damage suffered as a result of such discrimination.

Article 7

States Parties undertake to adopt immediate and effective measures, particularly in the fields of teaching, education, culture and information, with a view to combating prejudices which lead to racial discrimination and to promoting understanding, tolerance and friendship among nations and racial or ethnical groups, as well as to propagating the purposes and principles of the Charter of the United Nations, the Universal Declaration of Human Rights, the United Nations Declaration on the Elimination of All Forms of Racial Discrimination, and this Convention.

Notes
1. The Convention on the Elimination of All Forms of Racial Discrimination (RDC) was the first of the new generation of United Nations human rights treaties to be concluded and has been widely accepted. Prompted initially by a resurgence of anti-semitism in 1959–60, the driving force that secured its early adoption was the determination of developing states to outlaw discrimination based on colour.

2. The definition of "racial discrimination" in Article 1, although wide, does not include discrimination on grounds of religion[79] or nationality.[80] Discrimination based on "descent" includes discrimination against members of a caste.[81] Discrimination on "ethnic origins" covers discrimination against Jews[82] and probably sikhs and gypsies.[83] On the limiting effect of the words "public life" in Art. 1(1), see below, note 7.

3. For discrimination to be "racial discrimination" in the sense of Article 1, it must have the "purpose or effect" of impairing the enjoyment, etc., of a person's "human rights." "Human rights" in Article 1 were understood to include—without being limited to—all of the rights in the Universal Declaration of Human Rights,[84] so that discrimination in most areas of conduct comes within the Convention. Article 1 would appear to prohibit indirect discrimination (*i.e.* discrimination resulting from conduct that is not intended to discriminate, but nonetheless has this "effect"). Within limits, it excludes "affirmative action" (*i.e.* discrimination in favour of a racial group on the ground that it would be in the public interest to redress the consequences of discrimination from which members of the group have previously suffered) by excluding such action from the definition of "racial discrimination" (Article 1(4)).[85]

4. Article 2, RDC, requires parties, *inter alia*, to ensure that their public authorities do not engage in "racial discrimination" (Article 2(1)(*a*)) and to prohibit and act administratively against private "racial discrimination" (Article 2(1)(*d*)). It also *requires* "affirmative action" "when circumstances so warrant" (Article 2(2)).

5. Article 3 is understood by the Committee on the Elimination of Racial Discrimination (CERD) as meaning that a party must not merely condemn racial segregation and apartheid; it must also not have diplomatic, economic or other relations with a state that practises them.[86] Article 3 has not been significant in practice with the change of government in South Africa.

6. The meaning of Article 4 has been the subject of disagreement, with some Western states again being at odds with CERD, this time because of the tension between CERD's interpretation of Article 4 and the freedoms of speech and

---

[79] Religious discrimination is dealt with by separate UN action: see the 1981 General Assembly Declaration on the Elimination of All Forms of Intolerance and of Discrimination based on Religion or Belief, G.A.O.R., 36th Sess., Supp. 51, p. 171 (1981). There is no UN treaty on what is a contentious subject, one difficulty being that different religions have different approaches to the toleration of others.

[80] "National origins" concerns a person's ancestors or place of birth, not his current nationality. Art. 1(2) permits discrimination against aliens, even if it amounts to indirect racial discrimination. Art. 1(3) allows discrimination on racial grounds when, for example, granting nationality or discriminating between naturalised and other nationals. Schwelb, *loc. cit.*, p. 699, n. 76, above, p. 1008, suggests that, because of Art. 1(3), Art. 5(*d*)(iii) "is probably limited to prohibiting the deprivation of nationals of their nationality on racial grounds."

[81] The word "descent" was introduced at the suggestion of India: UN Docs. A/C.3L.1216 and L.1238.

[82] Although an attempt to refer to anti-semitism expressly was defeated, there is no doubt that it was intended to be within the general wording of Art. 1: see Schwelb, *ibid.* pp. 1011–1015.

[83] The same term has been so interpreted in the U.K. Race Relations Act 1976: see Bailey, Harris and Jones, *Civil Liberties: Cases and Materials* (4th ed. 1995), Chap. 10.

[84] See Schwelb, *loc. cit.*, p. 699, n. 76, above at p. 1004, who points out that some rights in Art. 5 (see Arts. 5(*d*)(vi), and 5(*f*)) are not in the Universal Declaration.

[85] See Meron, *loc. cit.*, p. 699, n. 76, above at p. 296.

[86] General Recommendation III (1972), *loc. cit.*, p. 706, n. 99, below, Annex V.

association.[87] The main problem concerns freedom of speech and the requirement in Article 4(a) that a party make it a criminal offence to "disseminate" ideas based on racial superiority, irrespective of intention or their likely effect. The GFR, for example, "reached the conclusion that dissemination of opinions of racial superiority should be punishable if it was intended to create racial discrimination or hatred,"[88] but not otherwise. United Kingdom law, while not now requiring specific intent, makes the dissemination of such ideas an offence if the words used are "threatening, abusive or insulting" and if the stirring up of racial hatred is intended or if "having regard to all the circumstances racial hatred is likely to be stirred up."[89] Both states have relied upon the "due regard" provision in Article 4, which, it can be argued, must have some meaning. CERD, however, has questioned both states' law.[90] A CERD Report on Article 4 reads[91]:

225. Another factor hindering the full application of article 4 of the Convention is the interpretation that implementation of that article might impair or jeopardise freedom of opinion and expression and of peaceful assembly and association. This is the extreme position. Midway lies the proposition that a "balance" has to be struck between article 4(*a*) and freedom of speech, and between article 4(*b*) and freedom of association. The weight of opinion inclines to the view that the rights of free speech and of free association are not absolute, but subject to limitations. . . .

231. Even in societies most zealous of safeguarding the right of free speech, there are laws against defamation and sedition. Laws against incitement to racial discrimination or hatred are certainly no less necessary to protect public order or the rights of others. The majority of the Committee is convinced that the same applies without distinction to the dissemination of ideas based on racial superiority. . . .

235. The legislation of some State parties subject the "dissemination of ideas based on racial superiority or hatred" or "incitement to racial discrimination" to certain conditions, for example that the dissemination or incitement must be intentional, or must have certain objectives such as "to stir up hatred," or that they be "threatening, abusive or insulting," or accompanied by "mocking,

---

[87] Several Western states have made reservations or interpretative statements: see UN Doc. ST/LEG/SER.E/15, pp. 95 *et seq.* The U.K. text reads: "It interprets article 4 as requiring a party to the Convention to adopt further legislative measures in the fields covered by sub-paragraphs (a), (b) and (c) of that article only in so far as it may consider with due regard to the principles embodied in the Universal Declaration of Human Rights and the rights expressly set forth in article 5 of the Convention (in particular the right to freedom of opinion and expression and the right to freedom of peaceful assembly and association) that some legislative addition to or variation of existing law and practice in those fields is necessary for the attainment of the end specified in the earlier part of article 4." As to whether the U.K. text is a reservation or a "mere interpretative statement," see the *Belilos* case, below, p. 794. (Note that it is described as an "interpretative statement" and accompanied by a "reservation" on a different matter). If the latter, it does not protect the U.K. from a different interpretation by CERD; *cf.* Ingles, *Positive Measures Designed to Eradicate all Incitement to, or Acts of, Racial Discrimination,* UN Doc. CERD/2 p. 35 (1986).

[88] CERD Report, G.A.O.R., 32nd Sess., Supp. 18, para. 87 (1977).

[89] s.18, Public Order Act 1986. Specific intent to stir up racial hatred had been *required* by the Race Relations Act 1965, s.6, which had been criticised by CERD. As to whether Art. 4 applies to speech in private as well as in public places, see Meron, *loc. cit.,* p. 699, n. 48, above, p. 302.

[90] See CERD Report, G.A.O.R., 34th Sess., Supp. 18, para. 350 (1979) (GFR) and *ibid.* 33rd Sess., Supp. 18, para. 389 (1978) (U.K.).

[91] Ingles, *loc. cit.,* n. 87, above, pp. 37–39 (1986). See also the CERD statement in CERD Report, G.A.O.R., 42nd Sess., Supp. 18, p. 89 (1987).

slander, insult, threat or other means." Obviously, these conditions are restrictive and ignore the fact that article 4(*a*) of the Convention declares punishable the mere act of dissemination or incitement, without any conditions.

The disagreement as to the meaning of Article 4 raises the larger question (which concerns all human rights treaties with supervisory organs) as to who has the authority to interpret the RDC. While this ultimately vests in the States Parties (who may not agree), any ruling by the I.C.J. in a case referred to it under Article 22[92] is very likely to be accepted. On the role of CERD in the absence of any Court reference, Meron[93] states:

> While the Committee has not been given general competence to interpret the Convention, as a treaty organ, the Committee may be competent to interpret the Convention insofar as is required for the performance of the Committee's functions. Such an interpretation *per se* is not binding on state parties, but it affects their reporting obligations and their internal and external behaviour. It shapes the practice of states in applying the Convention and may establish and reflect their agreement regarding its interpretation. Whether a particular interpretation or decision by the Committee serves such a function can, of course, be determined only *in concerto*.

7. Article 5, RDC requires parties to guarantee "equality before the law" in the enjoyment of a long list of human rights, including economic, social and cultural rights as well as civil and political rights. Read with the general obligations imposed upon parties by Article 2, Article 5 requires states to act to control private discrimination in, for example, employment (Articles 5(*c*) and 5(*e*)(i)), housing (Article 5(*e*)(iii)) and access to places of public resort (Article 5(*f*)). Is a state obliged to have adequate laws and policing to prevent or punish private racial attacks (see Article 5(*b*))? There is an inconsistency between the wording of Articles 1 and 5, which were drafted at different times, in that whereas the former defines racial discrimination, and hence the ambit of the RDC, in terms of lack of equal realisation of human rights in fields of "public life," the latter contains no such limitation and lists, moreover, rights (see, *e.g.* Articles 5(*d*) (iv) (vi) and (f)) that are essentially a matter of private life. The principle of "intimate and personal relations" that has been applied in national law might be applied here so that, for example, a small bed and breakfast establishment might be regarded, by virtue of the "public life" limitation in Article 1, as not falling within Article 5(*f*), but other places of public accommodation would.[94] Such an interpretation would, consistently with the purpose of the RDC and the clear wording of the specific provisions of Article 5, considerably limit the effect of the "public life" limitation of Article 1.

8. The system of enforcement of the RDC is based upon the Committee for the Elimination of Racial Discrimination (CERD), which consists of 18 members elected by the parties from among their nationals, bearing in mind the need for "equitable geographic distribution" and "the representation of the different forms of civilisation and of the principle legal systems" (Article 8). CERD was the first

---

[92] Art. 22 provides for the reference to the I.C.J. of any "dispute between two or more States Parties with respect to the interpretation or application" of the RDC "at the request of any of the parties to the dispute." Art. 22 was the subject of considerable disagreement and over 20 states have made reservations excluding the Court's jurisdiction. The U.K. has not done so.

[93] *loc. cit.*, p. 699, n. 78, above, p. 285. Footnote omitted. See also CERD Report, G.A.O.R., 28th Sess., Supp. 18, para. 46 (1973).

[94] *cf.* Meron, *ibid.* p. 294, who points out that some CERD members have questioned states about such matters as rental of private accommodation: *ibid.* p. 293.

supervisory committee to be established under a UN human rights treaty. As in the case of the two Covenant Committees, its members are independent experts. Most have legal or diplomatic backgrounds.

9. The parties to the RDC must submit to CERD biennial reports on its implementation. In fact, CERD has decided that "comprehensive reports" need be submitted only every four years, with "brief updating reports" being sufficient "on each intervening occasion."[95] The reason for this is that CERD has experienced the same problem of unsubmitted or late reports as the Covenant Committees and yet, at the same time, has accumulated a large backlog of reports for consideration.[96] The backlog of CERD work is attributable partly to financial difficulties which have caused the cancellation of one of CERD's two annual sessions for several years. Whereas the Covenant committees are paid for wholly out of UN funds, the RDC parties are responsible for the expenses of CERD members (Article 8(6)) and a number of parties have not paid their contributions.[97] CERD examines national reports at public hearings to which parties are invited to send representatives to introduce their reports and answer questions. CERD was the first UN human rights treaty committee to adopt this practice, which is not provided for in the RDC (or in any UN human rights treaty). Although representation is not legally required, most, though not all, parties send representatives.[98]

Article 9(2), RDC, reads:

2. The Committee shall report annually through the Secretary-General, to the General Assembly of the United Nations on its activities and may make suggestions and general recommendations based on the examination of the reports and information received from the States Parties. Such suggestions and general recommendations shall be reported to the General Assembly together with comments, if any, from States Parties.

Commenting on its power to make "suggestions and general recommendations" in the light of the RDC *travaux préparatoires*, CERD stated[99]:

117. It would appear, then, that by retaining the word "suggestions" and keeping it free of qualification as to generality or specificity, the authors of the Convention wanted to avoid language that might have inhibited the Committee from adopting "suggestions" relating to particular cases. On the other hand, by retaining the qualification "general" in relation to the "recommendations" which the Committee may make, the Third Committee appears to have

[95] CERD Report, G.A.O.R. 43rd Sess., Supp. 18, p. 6 (1988). On the RDC reporting system, see Gomez del Pardo (1985) 7 H.R.Q. 492.

[96] In 1995, "358 reports expected from 122 states parties before that date had not yet been received": *ibid.*, 49th Sess., Supp. 18, p. 95 (1995). Some reports were 10 years overdue, including three initial reports. Most of the missing reports were from developing countries that commonly lack the administrative resources to compile and submit such documents promptly.

[97] By a 1992 amendment to Art. 8(7), UN Doc. CERD/sp/45, the UN will pay for CERD member emoluments. Not in force. Acceptance by 2/3rd parties required. 21 so far.

[98] In 1995, 4 (Chad, Maldives, Niger, Tonga) out of 28 states whose reports were considered did not send representatives: CERD Report, 43rd Sess., Supp. 18, p. 6 (1988).

[99] *CERD and the Progress Made Towards the Achievement of the Objectives of the International Convention on the Elimination of All Forms of Racial Discrimination*, UN Doc. CERD/1 p. 13. *cf.* Rule 67(3), CERD Rules of Procedure ("If the Committee determines that some of the obligations of that state ... have not been discharged, it may make suggestions and general recommendations ... ").

intended that the competence of the Committee to "recommend" was to be exercised only in situations of general relevance.

So far, CERD has made a number of "general recommendations," which mostly contain requests for information in national reports or interpretations of the Convention.[1] It also adopts concluding observations on national reports.

Although the wording of Article 9(2) indicates that a "general recommendation" or "suggestion" must be "based upon the examination of the reports and information received from the States Parties," CERD has adopted the practice of "allowing members to use any information they might have as experts," which may include information from NGOs, when questioning states representatives and otherwise considering reports.[2] Likewise, it has been established that ILO and UNESCO representatives may be invited to attend its meetings and that information submitted by the ILO and UNESCO concerning relevant ILO or UNESCO conventions shall be made available to CERD members.[3] As with the Covenant Committees, the availability of sources of information from other than national reports is crucial to CERD's functioning.

10. There is provision in the RDC for a *compulsory* system of interstate claims (Article 11) but so far no state has made an application. Any application brought by a state is referred by CERD to the other state for comment (*ibid.*) If this does not lead to a satisfactory negotiated outcome, either state may refer the matter back to CERD which is then competent to conduct a fact-finding inquiry and to appoint an ad hoc Conciliation Commission (Article 13). The findings and recommendation that result from this process are not binding upon the states concerned.

11. CERD is also competent (Article 15) to receive copies of petitions from inhabitants of Trust and Non-Self-Governing Territories subject to Resolution 1514, see above, p. 114, via the Committee of 24, see above, p. 115, but no such petitions have been received. There are now few territories to which Resolution 1514 applies and petitions under Article 15 are unlikely to be forthcoming.

YILMAZ-DOGAN *v.* NETHERLANDS

C.E.R.D. Report, G.A.O.R., 43rd Sess., Supp. 18, p. 59 (1988)

The petitioner's employer sought permission from the District Labour Exchange to terminate her contract of employment at a time when the petitioner, a Turkish national, was pregnant. Permission was refused because under Article 1639(*h*) (4), Netherlands Civil Code, employment could not be terminated during pregnancy. The employer took his request to the local Sub-District Court, which granted it. In a letter to the Court supporting his case, the employer stated:

> When a Netherlands girl marries and has a baby, she stops working. Our foreign women workers, on the other hand, take the child to neighbours or family and at the slightest set-back disappear on sick-leave under the terms of

---

[1] For the text of the first five General Recommendations, see *ibid.* Annex V. For later ones, see the CERD annual reports to the General Assembly (1972).

[2] Chairman's statement, CERD Report, G.A.O.R., 27th Sess., Supp. 18, p. 11 (1972). The statement, which did not represent a unanimous view within the Committee, followed a UN Office of Legal Affairs opinion that Art. 9(2) did not apply to CERD's "preliminary consideration of reports": 1972 UN Juridical Yearbook 163 at p. 164.

[3] CERD Decision 2(VI), CERD Report, G.A.O.R., 27th Sess., Supp. 18, p. 40.

the Sickness Act. They repeat that endlessly. Since we all must do our utmost to avoid going under, we cannot afford such goings-on.

Following her dismissal, the petitioner requested the Prosecutor at the District Court to prosecute her former employer for offences under ss.137 and 429, Netherlands Penal Code which prohibit the dissemination of ideas involving racial superiority, etc., and which had been enacted to comply with Article 4, RDC. The Prosecutor having declined to act, the petitioner complained to the Court of Appeal under Article 12, Netherlands Code of Criminal Procedure, requesting it to order a prosecution. The Court of Appeal refused, stating that although the employer's remarks were "unfortunate and objectionable," it "could not be determined that the defendant by raising the issue of differences between foreign and Netherlands women workers with regard to absenteeism owing to childbirth and illness intended to discriminate by race, or that his remarks resulted in racial discrimination." The petitioner alleged a breach of Article (5)(e)(i), RDC because, *inter alia*, the Sub-District Court had terminated her contract of employment on the basis of reasons in the employer's request that were racially discriminatory. In reply, the defendant state contended:

... the decision of the ... [Sub-District] Court does not, in any way, justify the conclusion that the Court accepted the reasons put forth by the employer. In reaching its decision to dissolve the contract between the petitioner and her employer, the Court merely considered the case in the light of the relevant rules of civil law and civil procedure; it refrained from referring to the petitioner's national or ethnic origin.

The petitioner also claimed breaches of Articles 4 and 6, RDC.

Opinion of the Committee

9.2 The main issue before the Committee are (a) whether the State party failed to meet its obligation, under article 5(e)(i), to guarantee equality before the law in respect of the right to work and protection against unemployment, and (b) whether articles 4 and 6 impose on States parties an obligation to initiate criminal proceedings in cases of alleged racial discrimination and to provide for an appeal mechanism in cases of such discrimination.

9.3 With respect to the alleged violation of article 5(e)(i), the Committee notes that the final decision as to the dismissal of the petitioner was the decision of the Sub-District Court of September 29, 1982, which was based on article 1639w (2) of the Netherlands Civil Code. The Committee notes that this decision does not address the alleged discrimination in the employer's letter of July 19, 1982, which requested the termination of the petitioner's employment contract. After careful examination, the Committee considers that the petitioner's dismissal was the result of a failure to take into account all the circumstances of the case. Consequently, her right to work under article 5(e)(i) was not protected.

9.4 Concerning the alleged violation of articles 4 and 6, the Committee has noted the petitioner's claim that these provisions require the State party actively to prosecute cases of alleged racial discrimination and to provide victims of such discrimination with the opportunity of judicial review of a judgment in their case. The Committee observes that the freedom to prosecute criminal offences—commonly known as the expediency principle—is governed by considerations of public policy and notes that the Convention cannot be interpreted as challenging the raison d'être of that principle. Notwithstanding, it should be applied in each case of alleged racial discrimination, in the light of the guarantees laid down in the Convention. In the case of Mrs. Yilmaz-Dogan, the Committee concludes that the prosecutor acted in accordance with these criteria. Furthermore, the State Party has shown that the application of the expediency principle is subjected to, and has indeed in the present case been subject to, judicial review, since a decision *not* to prosecute may be, and was reviewed in this case, by the Court of Appeal, pursuant to article 12 of the Netherlands Code of Criminal Procedure. In the Committee's opinion, this mechanism of judicial review is compatible with article 4 of the Convention; contrary to the petitioner's affirmation, it does not render meaningless the protection afforded by sections 137c to e and 429 *ter* and *quater* of the Netherlands Penal Code.[4] Concerning the petitioner's inability to have the Sub-District Court's decision pronouncing the termination of her employment contract reviewed by a higher tribunal, the Committee observes that the terms of article 6 do not impose upon States Parties the duty to institute a mechanism of sequential remedies, up to and including the Supreme Court level, in cases of alleged racial discrimination.

10. The Committee on the Elimination of Racial Discrimination, acting under article 14, paragraph 7, of the Convention, is of the opinion that the information as submitted by the parties sustains the claim that the petitioner was not afforded protection in respect of her right to work. The Committee suggests that the State Party take this into account and recommends that it ascertain whether Mrs. Yilmaz-Dogan is now gainfully employed and, if not, that it use its good offices to secure alternative employment for her and/or to provide her with such other relief as may be considered equitable.

Notes

1. The *Yilmaz-Dogan* case derives from Article 14, RDC, which provides for an optional system of individual communications "from individuals or groups of individuals within . . . a party's jurisdiction claiming to be victims of a violation . . . of any of the rights set forth in the Convention."[5] A petitioner must exhaust local remedies and bring his case within six months. The RDC does not state that a communication may not be brought if it is pending before another international body, such as the H.R.C. Having heard evidence and argument presented by both sides in the form of written proceedings, CERD "shall forward

[4] *Ed.* For the text of ss.137 (c)(d)(e) and 429 ter, see Ingles, *loc. cit.*, p. 704, n. 87, above, p. 9.

[5] 23 parties have made declarations accepting the right of individuals to petition against them. The U.K. has not, for reasons comparable to those applicable to the ICCPR right of petition (see p. 649, n. 62, above), it is also concerned about the effect of Art. 4, RDC.

its suggestions and recommendations, if any, to the state party concerned and to the petitioner." (Article 14(7)(*b*)). CERD has no power to take a legally binding decision. It has so far decided only five cases, including the *Yilmaz-Dogan* case.[6]

2. In response to CERD's opinion, which was not binding, the Dutch government paid the petitioner approximately £3000 compensation. Is it clear from CERD's brief opinion on what basis the Netherlands had infringed Article 5(*e*)(*i*)? Because one of its public authorities—the Sub-District Court—had adopted the employer's discriminatory motive? Or because it had failed to control private discriminatory conduct? Or for some other reason? Was the discrimination, which on its face was on grounds of nationality, "racial discrimination" within Article 1, RDC? With regard to the claims under Articles 4 and 6, the *Yilmaz-Dogan* case accepts *sub silentio* that such claims may be made under Article 14 (which refers to breaches of "the rights set forth"), as well as claims alleging a breach of Article 5. Would there have been a breach of the ICCPR or the ICESCR on the facts of the *Yilmaz-Dogan* case? See Articles 2(3) of each Covenant, Article 26, ICCPR and Article 6, ICESCR. Note that the ICESCR provides no right of petition.

CONVENTION AGAINST TORTURE AND OTHER CRUEL, INHUMAN OR DEGRADING TREATMENT OR PUNISHMENT 1984[7]

Misc. 12 (1985), Cmnd. 9593; (1984) 23 I.L.M. 1027 and (1985) 24 I.L.M. 535

Article 1

1. For the purposes of this Convention, the term "torture" means any act by which severe pain or suffering, whether physical or mental, is intentionally inflicted on a person for such purposes as obtaining from him or a third person information or a confession, punishing him for an act he or a third person has committed or is suspected of having committed, or intimidating or coercing him or a third person, or for any reason based on discrimination of any kind, when such pain or suffering is inflicted by or at the instigation of or with the consent or acquiescence of a public official or other person acting in an official capacity. It does not include pain or suffering arising only from, inherent in or incidental to lawful sanctions.

2. This article is without prejudice to any international instrument or national legislation which does or may contain provisions of wider application.

---

[6] The only other case in which a breach was found was *L.K. v. Netherlands* (1994) 1–1 I.H.R.R. 32 (breaches of Arts. 4 and 6: incitement to racial hatred, ineffective protection).

[7] In force 1987. 101 parties, including the U.K. See Boulesbaa (1986) 4 Dick. J.I.L. 185; *ibid.*, (1990) 12 H.R.Q. 53; Burgers and Danelius, *The UN Convention against Torture* (1988); Skupinski, (1986) 15 Pol. Y.I.L. 183; Voyame, in Cassese, ed., *The International Fight against Torture* (1991), p. 43.

Article 2

1. Each State Party shall take effective legislative administrative, judicial or other measures to prevent acts of torture in any territory under its jurisdiction.

2. No exceptional circumstances whatsoever, whether a state of war or a threat of war, internal political instability or any other public emergency, may be invoked as a justification of torture.

3. An order from a superior officer or a public authority may not be invoked as a justification of torture.

Article 3

1. No State Party shall expel, return (*"refouler"*) or extradite a person to another State where there are substantial grounds for believing that he would be in danger of being subjected to torture.

2. For the purpose of determining whether there are such grounds, the competent authorities shall take into account all relevant considerations including, where applicable, the existence in the State concerned of a consistent pattern of gross, flagrant or mass violations of human rights.

Article 4

1. Each State Party shall ensure that all acts of torture are offences under its criminal law. The same shall apply to an attempt to commit torture and to an act by any person which constitutes complicity or participation in torture.

2. Each State Party shall make these offences punishable by appropriate penalties which take into account their grave nature.

Article 5

1. Each State Party shall take such measures as may be necessary to establish its jurisdiction over the offences referred to in article 4 in the following cases[8]:

  (*a*) When the offences are committed in any territory under its jurisdiction or on board a ship or aircraft registered in that State;
  (*b*) When the alleged offender is a national of that State;
  (*c*) When the victim is a national of that State if that State considers it appropriate.

2. Each State Party shall likewise take such measures as may be necessary to establish its jurisdiction over such offences in cases where the alleged offender is present in any territory under its jurisdiction and it

[8] *Ed.* See, *e.g.* in the U.K., s.134 of the Criminal Justice Act 1988, below, p. 738.

does not extradite him pursuant to article 8 to any of the States mentioned in paragraph 1 of this article.

3. This Convention does not exclude any criminal jurisdiction exercised in accordance with internal law.

Article 6

1. Upon being satisfied, after an examination of information available to it, that the circumstances so warrant, any State Party in whose territory a person alleged to have committed any offence referred to in article 4 is present shall take him into custody or take other legal measures to ensure his presence. The custody and other legal measures shall be as provided in the law of that State but may be continued only for such time as is necessary to enable any criminal or extradition proceedings to be instituted.

2. Such State shall immediately make a preliminary inquiry into the facts.

3. Any person in custody pursuant to paragraph 1 of this article shall be assisted in communicating immediately with the nearest appropriate representative of the State of which he is a national, or, if he is a stateless person, with the representative of the State where he usually resides.

4. When a State, pursuant to this article, has taken a person into custody, it shall immediately notify the States referred to in article 5, paragraph 1, of the fact that such person is in custody and of the circumstances which warrant his detention. The State which makes the preliminary inquiry contemplated in paragraph 2 of this article shall promptly report its findings to the said States and shall indicate whether it intends to exercise jurisdiction.

Article 7

1. The State Party in the territory under whose jurisdiction a person alleged to have committed any offence referred to in article 4 is found shall in the cases contemplated in article 5, if it does not extradite him, submit the case to its competent authorities for the purpose of prosecution.

2. These authorities shall take their decision in the same manner as in the case of any ordinary offence of a serious nature under the law of that State. In the cases referred to in article 5, paragraph 2, the standards of evidence required for prosecution and conviction shall in no way be less stringent than those which apply in the cases referred to in article 5, paragraph 1.

3. Any person regarding whom proceedings are brought in connection with any of the offences referred to in article 4 shall be guaranteed fair treatment at all stages of the proceedings.

Article 8

1. The offences referred to in article 4 shall be deemed to be included as extraditable offences in any extradition treaty existing between States Parties. States Parties undertake to include such offences as extraditable offences in every extradition treaty to be concluded between them.

2. If a State Party which makes extradition conditional on the existence of a treaty receives a request for extradition from another State Party with which it has no extradition treaty, it may consider this Convention as the legal basis for extradition in respect of such offences. Extradition shall be subject to the other conditions provided by the law of the requested State.

3. States Parties which do not make extradition conditional on the existence of a treaty shall recognise such offences as extraditable offences between themselves subject to the conditions provided by the law of the requested State.

4. Such offences shall be treated, for the purpose of extradition between States Parties, as if they had been committed not only in the place in which they occurred but also in the territories of the States required to establish their jurisdiction in accordance with article 5, paragraph 1.

Article 9

1. States Parties shall afford one another the greatest measure of assistance in connection with criminal proceedings brought in respect of any of the offences referred to in article 4, including the supply of all evidence at their disposal necessary for the proceedings.

2. States Parties shall carry out their obligations under paragraph 1 of this article in conformity with any treaties on mutual judicial assistance that may exist between them.

Article 10

1. Each State Party shall ensure that education and information regarding the prohibition against torture are fully included in the training of law enforcement personnel, civil or military, medical personnel, public officials and other persons who may be involved in the custody, interrogation or treatment of any individual subjected to any form of arrest, detention or imprisonment.

2. Each state Party shall include this prohibition in the rules or instructions issued in regard to the duties and functions of any such person.

Article 11

Each State Party shall keep under systematic review interrogation rules, instructions, methods and practices as well as arrangements for the custody and treatment of persons subjected to any form of arrest, detention or imprisonment in any territory under its jurisdiction, with a view to preventing any cases of torture.

Article 12

Each State Party shall ensure that its competent authorities proceed to a prompt and impartial investigation, wherever there is reasonable ground to believe that an act of torture has been committed in any territory under its jurisdiction.[9]

Article 13

Each State Party shall ensure that any individual who alleges he has been subjected to torture in any territory under its jurisdiction has the right to complain to, and to have his case promptly and impartially examined by, its competent authorities. Steps shall be taken to ensure that the complainant and witnesses are protected against all ill-treatment or intimidation as a consequence of his complaint or any evidence given.

Article 14

1. Each State Party shall ensure in its legal system that the victim of an act of torture obtains redress and has an enforceable right to fair and adequate compensation, including the means for as full rehabilitation as possible. In the event of the death of the victim as a result of an act of torture, his dependants shall be entitled to compensation.

2. Nothing in this article shall affect any right of the victim or other persons to compensation which may exist under national law.

Article 15

Each State Party shall ensure that any statement which is established to have been made as a result of torture shall not be invoked as evidence in any proceedings, except against a person accused of torture as evidence that the statement was made.

Article 16

1. Each State Party shall undertake to prevent in any territory under its jurisdiction other acts of cruel, inhuman or degrading treatment or punishment which do not amount to torture as defined in article 1, when such

---

[9] *Ed.* A period of 15 months before an investigation of an allegation of torture was instituted was a breach of the obligation in Art. 12 to conduct a "prompt" investigation: *Qani Halimi-Nedzibi v. Austria* (1994) 2 I.H.R.R. 190.

acts are committed by or at the instigation of or with the consent or acquiescence of a public official or other person acting in an official capacity. In particular, the obligations contained in articles 10, 11, 12 and 13 shall apply with the substitution for references to torture of references to other forms of cruel, inhuman or degrading treatment or punishment.

2. The provisions of this Convention are without prejudice to the provisions of any other international instrument or national law which prohibits cruel, inhuman or degrading treatment or punishment or which relates to extradition or expulsion.

Notes

1. For the parties to it, the UN Convention on Torture adds to the customary international law prohibition on torture, see below, p. 725, by requiring them to facilitate the punishment of torture through their municipal law. The Convention also provides further international procedures for the investigation and condemnation of torture, thus adding to the obligations and enforcement mechanisms in the ICCPR, see above, p. 636, and other, regional human rights treaties concerning torture.[10]

2. The definition of "torture" in Article 1 covers the infliction of pain or suffering by persons acting for or with the acquiescence of the state; it does not extend to wholly private acts.[11] It is limited to the intentional infliction of pain or suffering for a listed or similar purpose; it also excludes pain or suffering inflicted as a "lawful sanction."[12] Whereas the unintentional infliction of pain or suffering or its imposition as a lawful sanction may come within the Convention as "cruel, inhuman or degrading treatment or punishment" (Article 16), the distinction between "torture" and these other forms of proscribed conduct is important in that certain provisions of the Convention apply only to "torture": see Article 16(1), above, and the Article 20 procedure described below. What amounts to "severe pain or suffering" will need to be established by CAT in its practice. Elsewhere it has been accepted that the effect of ill-treatment is relative to the age and other personal circumstances of the victim and that suffering not severe enough to constitute "torture" may nonetheless be "inhuman treatment," etc.[13] Is domestic violence or rape "torture" or "cruel, inhuman or degrading treatment" within the Convention.[14]

3. Articles 4–8 follow a familiar pattern[15] by which the parties agree to make torture an offence in their criminal law and, subject to prosecutorial discretion, to prosecute or extradite an alleged offender. Significantly, the Convention grounds

---

[10] See the European Convention on Human Rights, Art. 3; the American Convention on Human Rights, Art. 5; the African Charter on Human and Peoples' Rights, Art. 5; the 1987 European Convention on Torture, E.T.S. 126; Misc. 5 (1988), Cm. 339; and the 1985 Inter-American Convention on Torture, 25 I.L.M. 519.

[11] See Sharvit (1993) 23 Israel Y.H.R. 147.

[12] The UN Declaration on the Protection of All Persons from Being Subjected to Torture and Other Cruel, Inhuman or Degrading Treatment or Punishment, G.A. Resn. 3452, G.A.O.R., 30th Sess., Supp. 34, p. 91 (1975), upon which the UN Convention is largely based, excludes pain and suffering caused by lawful sanctions "to the extent consistent with the UN Standard Minimum Rules for the Treatment of Prisoners," UN Doc. A/CONF/6/1, Annex I (1957), as amended in 1977 (See ECOSOC Resn. 2076 (LXII); reprinted in Rodley, *The Treatment of Prisoners in International Law* (1987), Annex 3).

[13] See especially *Ireland v. UK*, Eur. Court H.R., Series A, Vol. 3 (1978).

[14] On domestic violence as torture, see Copelon (1994) 25 Col. H.R.L.R. 291.

[15] See, *e.g.* the 1970 Hague Convention on the Unlawful Seizure of Aircraft, above, p. 295.

for criminal jurisdiction include universality jurisdiction; it is sufficient that "the alleged offender is present" in its territory for the Convention to apply (Article 5(2)).

4. The Convention establishes the Committee against Torture (CAT) to supervise its implementation (Article 17). CAT consists of 10 experts "of high moral standing and recognised competence in the field of human rights" who serve in their "personal capacity"; they are not government representatives (Article 17(1)).[16] Members are elected by States Parties to the Convention from among their nationals, "consideration being given to equitable geographical distribution and to the usefulness of the participation of some persons having legal experience" (Article 19(2)(3)). Parties are encouraged to nominate members of the ICCPR Human Rights Committee, given the overlap between Article 7, ICCPR and the Convention. As with the RDC Convention, see above, p. 699, States Parties, not the UN, are responsible for the expenses of the members of the Committee. Uniquely among UN human rights treaties, States Parties are also responsible for the other expenses of CAT and of States Parties' meetings (Article 18(5)).

5. Parties must submit to CAT initial "reports on the measures they have taken to give effect to their undertakings under" the Convention and "thereafter submit supplementary reports every four years on any new measures taken and such other reports as the Committee may request" (Article 19(1)). CAT has adopted the now standard procedure of inviting parties to introduce their reports and respond to questions during public hearings at which national reports are considered. Following the examination of a report, CAT "may make such general comments on the report as it may consider appropriate and shall forward these to the State Party concerned" (Article 19(3)). Exercising this power, CAT adopts Conclusions and Recommendations on each state's report, which are published in CAT's annual report (Article 19(4)).

6. A potentially valuable new mechanism for bringing to light the existence of a practice of torture is the provision in Article 20 by which CAT may examine in co-operation with the party concerned "reliable information" containing "well-founded indications" that torture—not inhuman treatment, etc.—"is being systematically practised" in that party's territory. The Article 20 procedure, which has similarities with that under ECOSOC Resolution 1503, above, p. 629, is available namely all Convention parties that do not opt out of it.[17] CAT's examination of a case may, with the state's consent, include a visit to the territory of the state concerned. Having conducted its examination, CAT must transmit its "findings to the State Party concerned together with any comments or suggestions which seem appropriate" (Article 20(4)). The procedure is confidential, except that following its completion CAT may include a "summary account" of the results in its annual report, which is published (Article 20(5)).[18] Such publicity is the only sanction available should CAT find the existence of a "systematic practice" of torture.

7. In addition to the Article 20 "systematic practice" procedure, the Convention also provides for optional state and individual petition procedures. Under Article 21, a party may, on condition of reciprocity, make a declaration accepting the right

---

[16] The members are Burns (Canada); Camara (Senegal); Dipanda Mouelle (Cameroon); Gonzales-Poblete (Chile); Iliopoulos-Strangas (Greece); Pikis (Cyprus); Regmi (Nepal); Sørensen (Denmark); Yakovlev (Russian Federation); Zupančič (Slovenia). Members, who serve part-time, are elected for four years.

[17] 10 parties have made opting out declarations. The U.K. has not done so.

[18] See the "summary accounts" concerning Turkey (1993), (1997) 4 I.H.R.R. 227, and Egypt (1996), *id.* 235 (systematic practice of torture found in both cases).

of another party to raise a matter before CAT alleging a breach of the party's "obligations under the Convention." The procedure is similar to that under Article 41, ICCPR, above, p. 649. A matter may only be referred to CAT if a prescribed process of negotiations between the parties has been unsuccessful. Having determined that local remedies have been exhausted, CAT must make available its good offices, which may include the establishment of an *ad hoc* conciliation commission, with a view to achieving a friendly settlement. CAT must, within 12 months, submit to the parties a report indicating the facts and the solution reached if a friendly settlement is achieved. If no such settlement is reached, CAT must confine its report to a brief statement of the facts.[19]

8. Article 22 provides for an optional system of individual petitions, which is closely modelled on that under the ICCPR Optional Protocol, above p. 649. A party may make a declaration recognising the competence of CAT to consider communications "from or on behalf of individuals subject to its jurisdiction who claim to be victims of a violation" by it of "the provisions of the Convention" (Article 22(1)).[20] Communications alleging cruel, inhuman or degrading treatment or punishment as well as torture are thus admissible. CAT may only consider a communication if the "same matter has not been, and is not being, examined under another procedure of international investigation or settlement" (Article 22(5)(*b*)). This excludes, for example, cases concerning torture, etc., examined under the ICCPR Optional Protocol or the European or American Conventions on Human Rights; it does not rule out a communication concerning a matter examined under ECOSOC Resolution 1503, above, p. 629. Other admissibility requirements include the exhaustion of local remedies (Article 22(5)(*b*)). There is no time limit for the bringing of a case. A departure from the ICCPR Optional Protocol procedure is that CAT may consider a communication "in the light of all information made available to it by or on behalf of the individual and by the State Party concerned" (Article 22(4)). It is thus not limited to the consideration of written submissions and may, in particular, hear witnesses. When CAT has completed its examination of a communication, it "shall forward its views to the State Party concerned and to the individual" (Article 22(7)). These "views" are not binding in law.

ALAN *v.* SWITZERLAND

UN Doc. CAT/C/16/D/41/1996; (1997) 4 I.H.R.R. 66

The author was a Turkish citizen and had been an active member of KAWA, an outlawed kurdish marxist-leninist organisation in Turkey. He was detained for periods of days in 1981 and 1983 and claimed to have been tortured then. In 1984, he was sentenced by a military tribunal to two–and–a–half years' imprisonment and 10 months' internal exile for assisting KAWA militants. Upon his release, he was arrested several times in 1988 and 1989 and allegedly tortured. In 1990, after having his house searched by the police, he decided to seek asylum in Switzerland, leaving Turkey on a false passport. A medical report and scars on his body

---

[19] 37 parties, including the U.K., have made Art. 21 declarations. No cases have yet been referred to CAT.

[20] 35 parties have made Art. 22 declarations. The U.K. has not done so. CAT has adopted views on seven individual petition cases.

supported his claims of torture. The Swiss Federal Refugee Office rejected the author's asylum claim in view of factual inconsistencies in it. The author claimed a breach of Article 3, UN Torture Convention.

Views of the Committee

11.2 Pursuant to paragraph 1 of article 3, the Committee must decide whether there are substantial grounds for believing that Mr. Alan would be in danger of being subject to torture upon return to Turkey. In reaching this conclusion, the Committee must take into account all relevant considerations, pursuant to paragraph 2 of article 3, including the existence of a consistent pattern of gross, flagrant or mass violations of human rights. The aim of the determination, however, is to establish whether the individual concerned would be *personally* at risk of being subjected to torture in the country to which he would return. It follows that the existence of a consistent pattern of gross, flagrant or mass violations of human rights in a country does not as such constitute a sufficient ground for determining that a person would be in danger of being subjected to torture upon his return to that country; specific grounds must exist that indicate that the individual concerned would be personally at risk. Similarly, the absence of a consistent pattern of gross violations of human rights does not mean that a person cannot be considered to be in danger of being subjected to torture in his specific circumstances.

11.3 In the instant case, the Committee considers that the author's [Kurdish] ethnic background, his alleged political affiliation, his history of detention, and his internal exile should all be taken into account when determining whether he would be in danger of being subjected to torture upon his return. The State party has pointed to contradictions and inconsistencies in the author's story, but the Committee considers that complete accuracy is seldom to be expected by victims of torture and that such inconsistencies as may exist in the author's presentation of the facts are not material and do not raise doubts about the general veracity of the author's claims.

11.4 The Committee has noted the State party's argument that the author has invoked the general situation of Kurds in Turkey to substantiate his fears of torture, but that he has failed to demonstrate that he personally risks to be subject to torture. The Committee has also noted the State party's statement that, according to information collected by its embassy in Ankara, the author is no longer sought by the police and that no prohibition of a passport is in force for him. On the other hand, the author's counsel has stated that, according to the author's wife, his house in Izmir had been under constant surveillance by the police, also after his departure, and that, in January 1995, the police questioned his former neighbours about the author. Furthermore, since the author left, his brother has been arrested on more than one occasion and his native village was demolished. As regards the State party's argument that the author could find a safe area elsewhere in Turkey, the Committee notes that the author already had to leave his native area, that Izmir did not prove secure for him either, and that, since there are indications that the police are looking for him, it is not likely that a "safe" area for him exists in Turkey. In the circumstances, the Committee finds that the author has sufficiently substantiated that he personally is at risk of being subjected to torture if returned to Turkey.

11.5 Finally, the Committee has taken note of the State party's argument that Turkey is a party to the Convention against Torture and has recognized the Committee's competence under article 22 of the Convention to receive and examine individual communications. The Committee regretfully notes, however, that practice of torture is still systematic in Turkey, as attested to in the Committee's findings in its inquiry under article 20 of the Convention. The Committee observes that the main aim and purpose of the Convention is to *prevent* torture, not to redress torture once it has occurred, and finds that the fact that Turkey is a party to the Convention and has recognized the Committee's competence under article 22, does not, in the circumstances of the instant case, constitute a sufficient guarantee for the author's security.

11.6 The Committee concludes that the expulsion or return of the author to Turkey in the prevailing circumstances would constitute a violation of article 3 of the Convention against Torture and Other Cruel, Inhuman or Degrading Treatment or Punishment.

12. In the light of the above, the Committee is of the view that, in the prevailing circumstances, the State party has an obligation to refrain from forcibly returning Ismail Alan to Turkey.

Notes

1. The *Alan* case is one of several cases in which the author's application for asylum had been refused by the defendant state but in which CAT found that his return to another state would be a breach of the obligation in Article 3(1) not to return a person to a state where he faces a real risk of torture.[21] The other cases involved states which were not parties to the Torture Convention, so that the author would not have been protected by the Convention on his return. In the *Alan* case, CAT held that this was not a necessary part of its reasoning in those cases.

The *Alan* and the other cases demonstrate that Article 3 is a valuable supplement to Article 33(1), 1951 Refugee Convention, by which parties to the Refugee Convention—who included all of the returning states in the above Article 3 cases—undertake not to "expel or return ('refouler') a refugee[22] to the frontiers of territories where his life or freedom would be threatened on account of his race,

---

[21] See also *Mutombo v. Switzerland* (1994) 1–3 I.H.R.R. 122; *Khan v. Canada* (1995) 2 I.H.R.R. 337; *Muzonzo v. Sweden* (1997) 4 I.H.R.R. 78.
[22] *Ed.* In all of the above CAT cases, the returning state had rejected the author's claim to be a refugee.

religion, nationality, membership of a particular social group or political opinion."

DECLARATION ON THE RIGHT TO DEVELOPMENT 1986

G.A. Resolution 41/128, G.A.O.R., 41st Sess., Supp. 53, p. 186 (1986)

Article 1

1. The right to development is an inalienable human right by virtue of
which every human person and all peoples are entitled to participate in,
contribute to and enjoy economic, social, cultural and political development, in which all human rights and fundamental freedoms can be fully
realised.

2. The human right to development also implies the full realisation of
the right of peoples to self-determination, which includes, subject to
relevant provisions of both International Covenants on Human Rights,
the exercise of their inalienable right to full sovereignty over all their
natural wealth and resources.

Article 2

1. The human person is the central subject of development and should
be the active participant and beneficiary of the right to development.

2. All human beings have a responsibility for development, individually and collectively, taking into account the need for full respect of their
human rights and fundamental freedoms as well as their duties to the
community, which alone can ensure the free and complete fulfilment of
the human being, and they should therefore promote and protect an
appropriate political, social and economic order for development.

3. States have the right and the duty to formulate appropriate national
development policies that aim at the constant improvement of the well-
being of the entire population and of all individuals, on the basis of their
active, free and meaningful participation in development and in the fair
distribution of the benefits resulting therefrom.

Article 3

1. States have the primary responsibility for the creation of national and
international conditions favourable to the realisation of the right to
development.

2. The realisation of the right to development requires full respect for
the principles of international law concerning friendly relations and
co-operation among States in accordance with the Charter of the United
Nations.

3. States have the duty to co-operate with each other in ensuring
development and eliminating obstacles to development. States should

fulfil their rights and duties in such a manner as to promote a new international economic order based on sovereign equality, interdependence, mutual interest and co-operation among all States, as well as to encourage the observance and realisation of human rights.

Article 4

1. States have the duty to take steps, individually and collectively, to formulate international development policies with a view to facilitating the full realisation of the right to development.

2. Sustained action is required to promote more rapid development of developing countries. As a complement to the efforts of developing countries effective international co-operation is essential in providing these countries with appropriate means and facilities to foster their comprehensive development.

Article 5

States shall take resolute steps to eliminate the massive and flagrant violations of the human rights of peoples and human beings affected by situations such as those resulting from *apartheid*, all forms of racism and racial discrimination, colonialism, foreign domination and occupation, aggression, foreign interference and threats against national sovereignty, national unity and territorial integrity, threats of war and refusal to recognise the fundamental right of peoples to self-determination.

Article 6

1. All States should co-operate with a view to promoting, encouraging and strengthening universal respect for and observance of all human rights and fundamental freedoms for all without any distinction as to race, sex, language and religion.

2. All human rights and fundamental freedoms are indivisible and interdependent; equal attention and urgent consideration should be given to the implementation, promotion and protection of civil, political, economic, social and cultural rights.

3. States should take steps to eliminate obstacles to development resulting from failure to observe civil and political rights as well as economic, social and cultural rights.

Article 7

All States should promote the establishment, maintenance and strengthening of international peace and security and, to that end, should do their utmost to achieve general and complete disarmament under effective international control as well as to ensure that the resources released by effective disarmament measures are used for comprehensive development, in particular that of the developing countries.

Article 8

1. States should undertake, at the national level, all necessary measures for the realisation of the right to development and shall ensure, *inter alia*, equality of opportunity for all in their access to basic resources, education, health services, food, housing, employment and the fair distribution of income. Effective measures should be undertaken to ensure that women have an active role in the development process. Appropriate economic and social reforms should be made with a view to eradicating all social injustices.

2. States should encourage popular participation in all spheres as an important factor in development and in the full realisation of all human rights.

Article 9

1. All the aspects of the right to development set forth in this Declaration are indivisible and interdependent and each of them should be considered in the context of the whole.

2. Nothing in this Declaration shall be construed as being contrary to the purposes and principles of the United Nations, or as implying that any State, group or person has a right to engage in any activity or to perform any act aimed at the violation of the rights set forth in the Universal Declaration of Human Rights and in the International Covenants on Human Rights.

Article 10

Steps should be taken to ensure the full exercise and progressive enhancement of the right to development, including the formulation, adoption and implementation of policy, legislative and other measures at the national and international levels.

Notes

1. The right to development is a controversial but important example of a claimed "third generation" or "solidarity" human right. Such rights, the theory of which dates only from the 1970s, are collective, group rights, in contrast with the individual rights of the first and second "generations."[23] The most well established example of such a right is the right to self-determination, above, p. 114. Other candidates are the freedom of groups from genocide and the various peoples' rights, such as the right to the environment and the right to peace, found in the African Charter on Human Rights and Peoples' Rights. Some Western states

---

[23] On "third generation" human rights, see Alston (1982) 29 N.I.L.R. 307; Crawford, ed., *The Rights of Peoples* (1988); Marks (1981) 33 Rutgers L.R. 435; Sanders (1991) 13 H.R.Q. 368.

and commentators have been sceptical of such rights as human rights. Sieghart,[24] for example, states:

> Apart from being new, what these rights have in common is that it is sometimes difficult to see how they can be vested in, or exercised by, individuals. According to the classical theory, only the rights of human individuals can be 'human' rights; any rights belonging to entities of some other kind (such as states, churches, corporations, trade unions, and so forth) may be highly desirable, accepted, valid, and even enforceable—but, whatever else they may be, they cannot be *human* rights.

A balanced view is expressed by Crawford,[25] who concludes that "peoples' rights should be regarded as a sub-category of human rights":

> One does not have to accept the view that international human rights are a closed category to regard some of the suggestions for the elaboration of 'solidarity rights' as mere novelties.... The excessive generality and the disregard for content demonstrated in some of the elaborations of new rights not only raise questions about individual proposals, but reflect badly on the notion of a 'third generation' of rights as such. Their relation to existing human rights is also problematic.
>
> Despite these difficulties, there is no doubt that the issues posed in the debate over peoples' rights are important ones.... Can the legitimate interests of groups be sufficiently protected by recognition of the individual right to associate? Should individual rights, including the right to opt out of groups or communities, prevail over the interests of those groups or communities? Is development better thought of as a human right, and if so, should that right be treated as an individual or communal one?
>
> ... [In conclusion] there are good grounds for accepting the category of peoples' rights in international law. There is at least one incontrovertible case of a peoples' right, the right of self-determination. A second example, the principle of permanent sovereignty over natural resources, is also widely recognised. There may be other examples, although most are in the course of development rather than fully fledged rights. In view of the increasingly widespread reference to peoples' rights, in the African Charter of Human and Peoples Rights, in General Assembly resolutions, and also in the literature, the category should be regarded as an established one.
>
> To say this does not imply that the category 'peoples' rights' requires that the term 'peoples' should have the same meaning for the purposes of all rights accepted as falling within the category, that peoples as distinct from individuals are necessarily the bearers of the rights in question, or that peoples are 'subjects' of international law in the orthodox sense, any more than human beings are subjects of international law notwithstanding the recognition that the category 'human rights' is an international law category with a distinct content. But recognition of the category does imply, first, that peoples' rights are distinct from the rights of States or governments ... and secondly, that the peoples in whom a particular right is vested are not inherently or necessarily represented by States or by the governments of States for that purpose. In particular cases, governments may be agents through which rights can be

---

[24] *The Lawful Rights of Mankind* (1986), p. 161.
[25] *op. cit.*, n. 23, above, pp. 159–166 and (second extract) pp. 65–66. Footnotes omitted.

vindicated. But they will be acting in a secondary capacity, rather than as the holders of the right. . . .

With regard to the right to development in particular, Crawford states:

> Notwithstanding its scanty recognition in international human rights treaties, the notion of a right to development as a human or peoples' right is very much at the centre of the debate about peoples' rights . . . The right to development is, outside specific contexts and specific instruments (e.g. relating to development aid, or the distribution of benefits in the law of the sea regime), less well integrated into the body of international practice than the notion of permanent sovereignty. So far as other States are concerned, the notion that 'peoples' have a right to development does not appear to differ from the proposition that States have such a right. So far, the assessment of one leading African international lawyer seems accurate [Umozurike, (1983) 77 A.J.I.L. 902 at 907:
>
> The right to development . . . appears not to have attained the definitive status of rule of law despite its powerful advocates. Its inclusion in the African Charter will be as effective as the Charter itself. The negative duty not to impede the development of States may go down well; the positive duty to aid such development, in the absence of specific accords, is a higher level of commitment that still rests on non legal considerations.

2. As the 1970s plan for a New International Economic Order, see above, p. 550, lost momentum, efforts to alleviate third world economic problems turned to the idea of "development" as a human right,[26] resulting ultimately in the 1986 Declaration. Unfortunately, attempts to attract the support of developed states generally for the Declaration were both unsuccessful and the cause of a puzzling, compromise text. The resulting uncertainty as to both the meaning of the Declaration and whether it was intended to state law, argue against regarding the Declaration as evidence that the right to development is a part of present customary international law.[27]

3. Does the Declaration see the right as an individual or a peoples' right, or both? What obligations does it impose upon a state to realise the right? Must it, in particular, ensure that a state's assets are used to achieve economic or social justice, as opposed, for example, to the vainglory of its leaders? Does the Declaration require that developed states give economic assistance to developing states, or does it just call for co-operation between all states? May a state restrict civil or political rights (*e.g.* freedom of speech, the right to vote or freedom to join a trade

---

[26] The idea had first been suggested by M'baye (1972) 5 H.R.J. 528. On the right to development, see Bartsch (1991) 13 H.R.Q. 322; Bedjaoui, in Snyder and Slinn, eds., *International Law of Development* (1987), p. 117; Brietzke (1985) 15 Cal. W.I.L.J. 560; Brownlie, *The Human Right to Development*, Commonwealth Secretariat Study (1989); De Waart, Peters and Denters, eds., *International Law and Development* (1988) (articles by Turk, Bulajic, Kenig-Witkowska and De Waart); Donnelly (1985) 15 Cal. West.I.L.J. 473; Dupuy, ed., *The Right to Development at the International Level*, Hague Academy Workshop (1980); Ferrero, *The New International Economic Order and the Protection of Human Rights*, UN Doc. E/CN.4/Sub.2/1983/24/Rev. 1; Gros Espiell (1981) 16 T.I.L.J. 189; I.C.J. Conference Report, *Development, Human Rights and the Rule of Law* (1981); Koojimans (1990) 37 N.I.L.R. 315; Mestagh (1981) 28 N.I.L.R. 30; Nanda (1985) 13 Denver J.I.L.P. 141; Rich, in Crawford, *op. cit.*, p. 722, n. 23, above, p. 39; Van Boven, I.C.J. Rev. No. 28, p. 49 (1982); *The Right to Development as a Human Right*, UN Doc. E/CN/.4/1334 (1979).

[27] The Declaration was not adopted by consensus, but by a vote of 146 to one (the U.S.), with eight abstentions (including the G.F.R., Japan and the U.K.).

union) in order to further economic progress and hence the implementation of the right to development? Is realisation of the right to development different from realisation of all of an individual's first and second generation rights?

4. A Working Group on the Right to Development has been established by the UN Commission on Human Rights to try to revitalise the idea of the right to development, which has failed to make progress beyond the adoption of the 1986 Declaration. See the Report of the Working Group on the Right to Development on its fourth session, 1995, UN Doc. E/CN.4/1996/10.

3. CUSTOMARY INTERNATIONAL LAW[28]

RESTATEMENT OF THE LAW: THIRD RESTATEMENT OF U.S. FOREIGN RELATIONS LAW[29]

Vol. 2 (1987), p. 165

§ 702. Customary international law of human rights

A state violates international law if, as a matter of state policy, it practices, encourages, or condones

(a) genocide,

(b) slavery or slave trade,

(c) the murder or causing the disappearance of individuals,

(d) torture or other cruel, inhuman, or degrading treatment or punishment,

(e) prolonged arbitrary detention,

(f) systematic racial discrimination, or

(g) a consistent pattern of gross violations of internationally recognised human rights.

Comment: ...

f. Murder as state policy and capital punishment. Under this section, it is a violation of international law for a state to kill an individual other than as lawful punishment pursuant to conviction in accordance with due process of law, or as necessary under exigent circumstances, for example by police officials in line of duty in defence of themselves or of other innocent persons, or to prevent serious crime.

Capital punishment, imposed pursuant to conviction in accordance with due process of law, has not been recognised as a violation of the customary law of human rights. It may, however, constitute cruel or inhuman punishment under clause (d) if grossly disproportionate to the crime. Compare Article 6 of the Covenant on Civil and Political Rights. ...

---

[28] See the excellent Colloquium papers in (1995–96) 25 Ga. J.I.C.L. 1.

[29] The *Restatement* is a private document prepared by a team of U.S. international lawyers; it does not necessarily represent U.S. Government views.

j. Systematic religious discrimination. The United Nations Charter (Articles 1, 13, 55) links religious discrimination with racial discrimination and treats them alike; to the extent that racial discrimination violates the Charter religious discrimination does also. Religious discrimination is also treated identically with racial discrimination in the principal covenants and in the constitutions and laws of many states. There is as yet no convention on the elimination of religious discrimination, and there has been no concerted attack on such discrimination comparable to that on *apartheid*, but there is a strong case that systematic discrimination on grounds of religion as a matter of state policy is also a violation of customary law. . . .

k. Right to property. The Universal Declaration of Human Rights includes the right to own and not to be arbitrarily deprived of property. . . . There is, however, wide disagreement among states as to the scope and content of that right, which weighs against the conclusion that a human right to property generally has become a principle of customary law. . . .

l. Gender discrimination. The United Nations Charter (Article 1(3)) and the Universal Declaration of Human Rights (Article 2) prohibit discrimination in respect of human rights on various grounds, including sex. Discrimination on the basis of sex in respect of recognised rights is prohibited by a number of international agreements, including the Covenant on Civil and Political Rights, the Covenant on Economic, Social and Cultural Rights, and more generally by the Convention on the Elimination of All Forms of Discrimination Against Women. . . . Gender-based discrimination is still practised in many states in varying degrees, but freedom from gender discrimination as state policy, in many matters, may already be a principle of customary international law. . . .

m. Consistent pattern of gross violations of human rights. The acts enumerated in clauses (a) to (f) are violations of customary law even if the practice is not consistent, or not part of a "pattern," and those acts are inherently "gross" violations of human rights. Clause (g) includes other infringements of recognised human rights that are not violations of customary law when committed singly or sporadically. . . : they become violations of customary law if the state is guilty of a "consistent pattern of gross violations" as state policy. A violation is gross if it is particularly shocking because of the importance of the right or the gravity of the violation. All the rights proclaimed in the Universal Declaration and protected by the principal International Covenants . . . are internationally recognised human rights, but some rights are fundamental and intrinsic to human dignity. Consistent patterns of violation of such rights as state policy may be deemed "gross" *ipso facto*. These include, for example, systematic harassment, invasions of the privacy of the home, arbitrary arrest and detention (even if not prolonged); denial of fair trial in criminal cases; grossly disproportionate punishment; denial of freedom to leave a country; denial of the right to return to one's country; mass uprooting of a country's population; denial of freedom of conscience and religion; denial of personality before the law; denial of basic privacy such as the right to marry and raise a family; and invidious racial or religious discrimination. . . .

n. Customary law of human rights and jus cogens. Not all human rights norms are peremptory norms (*jus cogens*), but those in clauses (a) to (f) of this section are, and an international agreement that violates them is void. . . .

o. Responsibility to all states (erga omnes). Violations of the rules stated in this section are violations of obligations to all other states and any state may invoke the ordinary remedies available to a state when its rights under customary law are violated. . . .

Reporters' Notes

1. *Customary law of human rights.* This section adopts the view that customary international law prohibits the particular human rights violations indicated, if the violations are state policy. This view is accepted by virtually all states; with the exception of the Republic of South Africa in respect of *apartheid*, no state claims the right to commit the practices set forth in this section as state policy, and few, if any, would deny that they are violations of international law. Other rights may already have become customary law and international law may develop to include additional rights. It has been argued that customary international law is already more comprehensive than here indicated and forbids violation of any of the rights set forth in the Universal Declaration. See . . . McDougal, Lasswell, and Chen, Human Rights and World Public Order 273–74, 325–27 (1980); . . .

The practice of states has established the principles of this section in customary law, as indicated in the following notes. Clauses (a) through (e) (and perhaps (f)) also reflect general principles common to the major legal systems that may have been absorbed into international law.

2. *State responsibility for private violations of rights.* Under customary law, the state is responsible for the acts enumerated in this section when committed by its officials as state policy, or, when committed by private persons, if they were encouraged or condoned as state policy. By contrast, under the Covenant on Civil and Political Rights, a state is required not only to respect but also to "ensure" the rights recognised by the Covenant, suggesting an obligation to act to prevent their violation whether by officials or by private persons. See Art. 2. . . .

3. *Genocide.* The term was not coined until later, but genocide was in fact considered a "crime against humanity" in the indictments brought under the Nuremberg Charter, the principles of which were affirmed by the United Nations General Assembly in a resolution . . . In another resolution adopted at the same time, the General Assembly declared genocide an international crime. G.A. Res. 96, 1. G.A.O.R. UN Doc. A/64/Add 1, at 188. The Convention on the Prevention and Punishment

of the Crime of Genocide was the first human rights agreement concluded under United Nations auspices. . . .

Draft articles on state responsibility provisionally adopted by the International Law Commission would (in Article 19) declare "a serious breach on a widespread scale of an international obligation of essential importance for safeguarding the human being, such as . . . genocide," to be an international crime. . . .

4. *Slavery and slave trade.* Slavery and slave trade are forbidden by international law, both as a matter of customary law and as general principles common to major legal systems. Slavery is outlawed by the constitutions or laws of virtually all states. . . . A convention to outlaw slavery was concluded . . . in 1926,[30] and one on forced labour in 1930.[31] The Universal Declaration of Human Rights declares that slavery and the slave trade shall be prohibited in all their forms. Art. 4. Slavery has been condemned and declared illegal by unanimous resolutions of the United Nations and other international bodies. . . . The report of the International Law Commission, . . . cites slavery as example of an international crime. Slavery and slave trade are also offences subject to universal jurisdiction to prescribe and adjudicate. . . .

5. *Torture or other cruel, inhuman or degrading treatment or punishment.* Torture as well as other cruel, inhuman, or degrading treatment or punishment, when practiced as state policy, are violations of customary international law. The prohibition on torture at least, may also have been absorbed into international law as a general principle common to major legal systems. The prohibition is included in all comprehensive international instruments. . . . Universal Declaration of Human Rights, Art. 5 . . . the International Covenant on Civil and Political Rights, Art. 7; the European Convention on Human Rights, Art. 3; the American Convention on Human Rights, Art. 5; the African Charter of Human and Peoples' Rights, Art. 5. . . . Official torture is also barred by the constitutions or laws of states generally. . . . The difference between torture and cruel, inhuman, or degrading treatment or punishment "derives principally from a difference in the intensity of the suffering inflicted." Ireland v. United Kingdom, 25 Pub. Eur. Ct. Hum. Rts., ser. A. para. 167 (1978).

6. *Prolonged arbitrary detention.* Arbitrary detention is cited as a violation of international law in all comprehensive international human rights instruments, *e.g.*, the Universal Declaration, Art. 9; the International Covenant on Civil and Political Rights, Art. 9; the European Convention, Art. 5; the American Convention, Art. 7; the African Convention, Art. 6. . . .

7. *Systematic racial discrimination.* Numerous United Nations resolutions have declared *apartheid* to be a violation of international law. The

---

[30] *Ed.* Slavery Convention 1926, U.K.T.S. 16 (1927), Cmd 2910; 60 L.N.T.S. 253. In force 1927. 108 parties, including the U.K.
[31] *Ed.* Forced Labour Convention 1930, Cmd. 3693; 39 U.N.T.S. 55. In force 1932. 132 parties, including the U.K.

General Assembly has adopted the International Convention on the Suppression and Punishment of the Crime of *Apartheid*. . . . The International Court of Justice has declared *apartheid* to be "a flagrant violation of the purposes and principles of the Charter." See the advisory opinion, Legal Consequences for States of the Continued Presence of South Africa in Namibia, [1971] I.C.J. Rep. 3, 57. *Apartheid* is listed as an example of an international crime in the draft articles provisionally approved by the International Law Commission. . . .

§ 703. Remedies for violation of human rights obligations

. . .

(2) Any state may pursue international remedies against any other state for a violation of the customary international law of human rights. . . .

(3) An individual victim of a violation of a human rights agreement may pursue any remedy provided by that agreement or by other applicable international agreements.

Comment:

a. Remedies for violation of international human rights obligations. Under international law, a breach of an international obligation, whether deriving from customary law or from international agreement, gives rise to international remedies against the violating state. These remedies include the right to make an international claim; to resort to the International Court of Justice or other international tribunal to whose jurisdiction the complaining and responding states have submitted; and in some circumstances to some measures of self-help. . . .

b. Remedies for violation of customary law of human rights. Since the obligations of the customary law of human rights are *erga omnes* (obligations to all states), any state may pursue remedies for their violation, even if the individual victims were not nationals of the complaining state and the violation did not affect any other particular interest of that state. . . .

c. Remedies of individual victims. In general, individuals do not have direct international remedies against a state violating their human rights except where such remedies are provided by international agreement. . . . Whether they have a remedy under the law of a state depends on that state's law. . . . International human rights agreements generally require a state party to provide such remedies. See, *e.g.*, International Covenant on Civil and Political Rights, Article 2(3). . . .

Reporters' Notes . . .

3. . . . In the *Barcelona Traction* case, [above, p. 604] . . . the International Court of Justice seemed to distinguish diplomatic protection in general, including protection for ordinary violations of human rights, which is available only for nationals of the complaining state . . . from

protection against violations of the "basic rights of the human person" set forth in this section, as to which "all States can be held to have a legal interest in their protection."

Notes

1. Commenting on the *U.S. Restatement*, Meron states[32]:

> . . . I believe that it is, perhaps, somewhat too cautious . . . The right of self-determination, which the I.C.J. has recognised as customary, could safely have been added.[33] Among other customary human rights, or general principles of law, I would include the right to humane treatment of detainees, stated in Article 10 of the Political Covenant. There is little doubt that the prohibition of retroactive penal measures (which is non-derogable in the Political Covenant and in both the American and the European Conventions on Human Rights) stated in Article 15 of the Political Covenant is a norm of customary international law. I believe that at least the core of a number of the due process guarantees stated in Article 14 of the Covenant have a strong claim to customary law status.
>
> . . . A somewhat different enumeration of customary rights prepared by Professor Lillich mentions the right to equality before the law and to non-discrimination, as stated in Article 7 of the Universal Declaration, as probably customary law, as well as the right of the individual to leave any country and to return to his own country.[34]
>
> Other scholars would list as customary the principle of non-refoulement in the context of Article 3 of the [UN Torture] Convention . . . some economic, social and cultural or 'second generation' rights, and possibly even some solidarity or 'third generation' rights.[35] Such economic rights as have been recognised by the internal laws of most states (*e.g.* as a result of ratifications of ILO's international labour conventions) may have matured into general international law as general principles of law recognised by civilised nations.

2. What is the theory underlying the international law of human rights? Is the prohibition of, for example, torture a part of *customary* international law? Or a rule of international law as a "general principle of law" (Article 38(1)(c))? In either case, states are subject to the resulting legal obligation, but who is the holder of the substantive right and who has the procedural right to enforce it? Does the Restatement or the Court in the *Barcelona Traction* case, paras. 33–34, judgment, above, p. 605, suppose that the individual is a subject of international law so that he or she has these legal rights, although enforceable perhaps only by states as agents?[36] Or is he or she just the third party beneficiary of an obligation which each state owes to all other states (*erga omnes*), for example, not to torture individuals?

---

[32] *Human Rights and Humanitarian Norms as Customary Law* (1989), pp. 95–8. Some footnotes omitted.

[33] . . . Perhaps this right has not been included because of its "collective" or "group-"—rather than individual—character. (However, the prohibition of genocide, which is listed in the Restatement, is also a "collective" right.) . . .

[34] Lillich, "Civil Rights", in 1 Human Rights in International Law 115, 133, 151 (T. Meron ed. 1984).

[35] . . . The General Assembly has declared that the right to development is "an inalienable human right." Declaration on the Right to Development, Art. 1, . . .

[36] See Crawford, above, p. 723.

FILARTIGA v. PENA-IRALA[37]

*630 F. 2d 876 (1980); (1980) 19 I.L.M. 966. U.S. Circuit Court
of Appeals, 2nd Circuit*

The plaintiffs, a father and daughter, were Paraguayan citizens who entered the United States in 1978 and applied for political asylum there. Shortly after their arrival, they learnt of the illegal presence in the United States of the defendant, who was a Paraguayan citizen and the former head of police in Asuncion, Paraguay. The plaintiffs brought civil proceedings for damages in a United States federal district court alleging that he had wrongfully caused the death of their son and brother (also a Paraguayan citizen) in Paraguay in 1976 by torture in retaliation for the father's political opposition to the Paraguayan Government. The cause of action was stated as arising under "wrongful death statutes; the United Nations Charter; the Universal Declaration of Human Rights; the United Nations Declaration against Torture; the American Declaration of the Rights and Duties of Man; and other pertinent declarations, documents and practices constituting the customary international law of human rights and the law of nations." It was claimed that the court had jurisdiction under the United States Judiciary Act 1789 (28 U.S.C. § 1350) which establishes original federal district court jurisdiction over "all causes where an alien sues for a tort ... [committed] in violation of the law of nations." In this judgment for the Court of Appeals, the plaintiffs appeal against the District Court ruling that it did not have jurisdiction to hear the case was considered.

KAUFMAN, CIRCUIT JUDGE ... A threshold question on the jurisdictional issue is whether the conduct alleged violates the law of nations. In light of the universal condemnation of torture in numerous international agreements, and the renunciation of torture as an instrument of official policy by virtually all of the nations of the world (in principle if not in practice), we find that an act of torture committed by a state official against one held in detention violates established norms of the international law of human rights. and hence the law of nations. ...

The United Nations Charter ... [Preamble, and Articles 55 and 56] makes it clear that in this modern age a state's treatment of its own citizens is a matter of international concern.

... although there is no universal agreement as to the precise extent of the "human rights and fundamental freedoms" guaranteed to all by the Charter, there is at present no dissent from the view that the guarantees include, at a bare minimum, the right to be free from torture. This prohibition has become part of customary international law, as evidenced and defined by the Universal Declaration of Human Rights ... which states, in plainest of terms, "no one shall be subjected to torture." The General Assembly has declared that the Charter precepts embodied in this Universal Declaration "constitute basic principles of international law." G.A. Res. 2635 (XXV) (Oct. 24, 1970).[38]

---

[37] See Blum and Steinhardt (1981) 22 H.I.L.J. 53; D'Zurilla (1981) 56 Tul. L.R. 186; Holt (1990) 20 Ga.J.I.C.L. 543; the articles in (1981) 10 Ga.J.I.C.L. 305 *et seq.*; and the case notes in (1981) 75 A.J.I.L. 149 and (1981) 67 Virg. L.R. 1379.

[38] *Ed.* Below Appendix III. Does Resolution 2625 really declare this?

Particularly relevant is the [1975] Declaration on the Protection of All Persons from Being Subjected to Torture.[39] . . . This Declaration, like the Declaration of Human Rights before it, was adopted without dissent by the General Assembly. . . .

These UN declarations are significant because they specify with great precision the obligations of member nations under the Charter. . . . it has been observed that the Universal Declaration of Human Rights "no longer fits into the dichotomy of 'binding treaty' against 'non-binding pronouncement,' but is rather an authoritative statement of the international community." E. Schwelb, *Human Rights and the International Community* 70 (1964). Thus a Declaration creates an expectation of adherence, and "insofar as the expectation is gradually justified by State practice, a declaration may by custom become recognised as laying down rules binding upon the States." 34 UN ESCOR, *supra*. Indeed, several commentators have concluded that the Universal Declaration has become, *in toto*, a part of binding, customary international law. Nayar, . . . [19 Harv. Int. L.J. 813] at 816–17; Waldock, "Human Rights in Contemporary International Law and the Significance of the European Convention," *Int'l & Comp. L.Q.*, Supp. Publ. No. 11 at 15 (1965).

Turning to the act of torture, we have little difficulty discerning its universal renunciation in the modern usage and practice of nations. . . . The international consensus surrounding torture has found expression in numerous international treaties and accords, *e.g. American Convention on Human Rights*, Art. 5, . . . ; . . . European Convention for the Protection of Human Rights and Fundamental Freedoms, Art. 3. The substance of these international agreements is reflected in modern municipal—*i.e.* national—law as well. Although torture was once a routine concomitant of criminal interrogations in many nations, during the modern and hopefully more enlightened era it has been universally renounced. According to one survey, torture is prohibited, expressly or implicitly, by the constitutions of over fifty-five nations, including both the United States and Paraguay.

. . . United States diplomatic contacts confirm the universal abhorrence with which torture is viewed:

In exchanges between United States embassies and all foreign states with which the United States maintains relations, it has been the Department of State's general experience that no government has asserted a right to torture its own nationals. Where reports of torture elicit some credence, a state usually responds by denial or, less frequently, by asserting that the conduct was unauthorised or constituted rough treatment short of torture.

---

[39] *Ed.* Above, p. 715, n. 12.

Memorandum of the United States as *Amicus Curiae* at 16, n. 34.

Having examined the sources from which customary international law is derived—the usage of nations, judicial opinions and the works of jurists—we conclude that official torture is now prohibited by the law of nations. The prohibition is clear and unambiguous, and admits of no distinction between treatment of aliens and citizens.

The Court then held that the District Court did have jurisdiction under the 1789 Act to hear the case.

Notes

1. The Court of Appeals did not rule upon the question whether the claim should be dismissed on the ground of *forum non conveniens*. The defendant was allowed to return to Paraguay before the Court of Appeal's judgment. In later proceedings, the federal district court gave judgment against him in default. Each plaintiff was awarded $5 million punitive damages.[40]

2. The Alien Tort Act 1790 is invoked in cases where the violation of international law occurs abroad; violations that take place on United States territory give rise to jurisdiction in tort, etc., under other more familiar rules.[41] The *Filartiga* case has been followed by others in which large amounts of damage have also been awarded.[42] The Alien Tort Act gives jurisdiction only in cases where claims are brought by aliens.[43] The Torture Victim Protection Act 1991 extends the jurisdiction of American courts to torture[44] claims brought by United States nationals. The *Filartiga* case ruled that "official" torture, *i.e.* torture by a person acting for the state, was in violation of international law. In *Tadic v. Karadžić*,[45] it was held that genocide and war crimes committed by private persons were violations of international law. The Court held that private acts of torture or summary execution were not in violation of the law of nations, except to the extent that they were committed "in pursuit of genocide and war crimes". The case concerned a claim brought against the President of the "Bosnian-Serb entity" (Republica-Srpksá[46]) in the state of Bosnia concerning of "genocide, rape, forced prostitution and impregnation, torture and other cruel, inhuman and degrading treatment, assault and battery, sex and ethnic inequality, summary execution and wrongful death". The case was referred back to the District Court for further proceedings in accordance with this jurisdictional ruling.

3. Although a breakthrough, the *Filartiga* case has its limitations. It is dependent upon a defendant being within the jurisdiction[47] and having assets there against which a judgment may be enforced. The damages in the *Filartiga* case and

---

[40] 577 F. Supp. 860 (1984).

[41] See, *e.g. Letellier v. Chile*, 488 F. Supp. 665 D.D.C. (1980) (tort claim for the car bomb death in Washington D.C. of political opponents of the Chilean Government by its agents).

[42] Several cases have been brought successfully against former President Marcos for the torture and murder of Filipinos under his regime: see, *inter alia*, *Re Estate of Marcos*, 25 F. 3d 1467 (9th Cir. 1992). See also *Abebe-Jiri v. Newego*, U.S.D.Ct.N.D.Ga. August 19, 1993 (Ethiopian Government torturer); and *Paul v. Avril*, 812 F. Supp. 207 (S.D. Fla. 1993) (Haitian presidential adviser responsible for acts of torture).

[43] See 28 U.S.C. § 1350 quoted above, p. 731.

[44] The 1991 Act applies only to torture. The Alien Tort Act remains the basis for jurisdiction in claims brought by aliens for other international law violations, whether to do with human rights or not.

[45] 70 F. 2d 232 (2d Cir. 1995). See Posner (1996) 90 A.J.I.L. 655.

[46] As to which, see above, p. 122.

[47] In the *Karadžić* case, a writ was served on the defendant in New York when he visited the United Nations. He then left the jurisdiction.

similar cases have not been paid. State immunity has prevented these limitations from being sidestepped by bringing the claim against the state for which the human rights violator is acting, instead of the violator himself.[48] Nonetheless, *Filartiga* judgments meet the very real need of the victims of human rights violations and their families to have the truth objectively established and the responsibility of the violators publically pronounced. Such satisfaction and vindication may well be more important to them than any award of compensation. *Filartiga* judgments also may prevent the United States from being used as a place of refuge by human rights violators and may influence United States Government policies.

AL ADSANI *v.* GOVERNMENT OF KUWAIT

Court of Appeal. March 12, 1995. Unreported

The plaintiff, who held British and Kuwaiti nationality, came into the possession in Kuwait of video tapes that contained sexual scenes, the contents of which then became common knowledge, much to the embarrassment of the second defendant. In retaliation, on May 2, 1991, the plaintiff was taken by the second, third and fourth defendants, who were all members of the Kuwaiti royal family, to a state security prison where he was allegedly beaten by security guards. It was accepted by the Court, for the purposes of these proceedings, that any such beatings were the vicarious responsibility of the first defendant, the Government of Kuwait. On May 7, 1991, he was again abducted by the second, third and fourth defendants and taken to a royal palace where he was put in a swimming pool that had several corpses in it and placed in a cell where a mattress was set alight, causing him severe burns. It was not alleged that the first defendant was responsible for the acts on May 7th. The plaintiff then moved to England for hospital treatment for his burns. On being discharged from hospital, he went to live in his mother's London flat, where he received anonymous telephone calls with "threats of dire consequences if he continued to publicise his case in the Western media and pursued it through the courts" (Stuart-Smith J.). The plaintiff claimed that the calls were made by agents of the first defendant and that they hindered his recovery and caused him suffering. In support of these claims, the plaintiff relied upon two conversations between the Kuwaiti ambassador in London and the plaintiff and his brother in which threats were allegedly made against the plaintiff, although the Ambassador denied this.

In these proceedings, the plaintiff appealed against a judgment of Mantell J. holding that the first defendant was entitled to state immunity in respect of the plaintiff's claims in tort against it for the personal injuries caused by the beatings by the security guards in Kuwait and by the threats made in England.

STUART-SMITH L.J. Jurisdiction of the English Courts in respect of foreign States is governed by the State Immunity Act 1978. Section 1(1) provides:

(1) A state is immune from the jurisdiction of the courts of the United Kingdom except as provided in the following provisions of this Part of this Act. . . .

---

[48] See the *Al Adsani* case, below, and the American cases quoted there.

The only relevant exception is section 5, which provides:

A State is not immune as respects proceedings in respect of—
  (a) death or personal injury; or
  (b) damage or loss of tangible property,
caused by an act or omission in the United Kingdom.

It is plain that the events in Kuwait do not fall within the exception in section 5, and the express words of section 1 provide immunity to the First Defendant. Despite this, in what Mr. McDonald, Q.C. for the Plaintiff acknowledges is a bold submission, he contends that that section must be read subject to the implication that the State is only granted immunity if it is acting within the Law of Nations. So that the section reads: "A state *acting within the Law of Nations* is immune from jurisdiction except as provided . . . "

In international law, torture is a violation of a fundamental human right, it is a crime and a tort for which the victim should be compensated. . . .

Stuart-Smith L.J. cited the 1975 General Assembly Declaration on Torture, see above, p. 715, n. 12; the European Convention on Human Rights 1950, Art. 3; and the UN Torture Convention, Arts. 1, 2, 4, above, p. 710.

The argument is . . . that international law against torture is so fundamental that it is a *jus cogens*, or compelling law, which overrides all other principles of international law, including the well-established principles of sovereign immunity. . . .

It is inconceivable, it seems to me, that the draughtsman, who must have been well aware of the various international agreements about torture, intended section 1 to be subject to an overriding qualification.

Moreover, authority in the United States at the highest level is completely contrary to Mr. MacDonald's submission. In *Argentine Republic v. Amerada Hess Shipping Corporation* 488 U.S. 428 Supreme Court 1989, the United States Supreme Court had to consider the provisions of the Foreign State Immunities Act 1976, which in all material respects for present purposes is the same as State Immunity Act 1978. The action concerned a claim arising out of damage suffered by an oil tanker when attacked by Argentine military aircraft during the Falklands War. Jurisdiction was claimed in the United States District Court on the basis that the attack was in violation of the Law of Nations. In so claiming, the plaintiff was met with the provisions of the Act which provided no exceptions relevant to the facts of the case. A similar argument to that which is advanced by Mr. MacDonald was rejected by the Court. Rehnquist C.J., delivering the judgment of the court, said at page 7:

From Congress's decision to deny immunity to foreign states in the class of cases just mentioned, we draw the plain implication that immunity is granted in those cases involving alleged violations of international law that do not come within one of the FSIA's exceptions.

That reasoning was applied by the U.S. Court of Appeal for the 9th Circuit in *Siderman de Blake v. Republic of Argentina* 965 F (2d) 699 (1992). Jose Siderman claimed that he had been tortured by the Argentine Military Officials, for whom the State were responsible. . . . Fletcher J., giving the judgment of the court, said:

> While we agree with the Sidermans that official acts of torture of the sort they allege Argentina to have committed constitute a jus cogens violation, we conclude that Amerada Hess forecloses their attempt to posit a basis for jurisdiction not expressly countenanced by the FSIA.

At page 56 he said this: . . .

> Unfortunately, we do not write on a clean slate. We deal not only with customary international law, but with an affirmative Act of Congress, the FSIA. We must interpret the FSIA through the prism of Amerada Hess. Nothing in the text or legislative history of the FSIA explicitly addresses the effect violations of jus cogens might have on the FSIA's cloak of immunity.

Mr. MacDonald submits that we should not follow the highly persuasive judgments of the American Courts. I cannot agree.

A moment's reflection is enough to show that the practical consequences of the Plaintiff's submission would be dire. The Courts in the United Kingdom are open to all who seek their help, whether they are British citizens or not. A vast number of people come to this country each year seeking refuge and asylum, and many of these allege that they have been tortured in the country whence they came. Some of these claims are no doubt justified, others are more doubtful. Those who are presently charged with the responsibility for deciding whether applicants are genuine refugees have a difficult enough task, but at least they know much of the background and surrounding circumstances against which the claim is made. The Court would be in no such position. The foreign state would be unlikely to submit to the jurisdiction of the United Kingdom Court, and in its absence the Court would have no means of testing the claim or making a just determination.

I have no doubt the Judge was right to hold that the First Defendant is entitled to immunity in respect of the events alleged to have taken place in Kuwait.

Turning to the acts committed in England, the Judge said that he was satisfied that threats had been made, that they occurred within the United

Kingdom and that personal injury had resulted from them. He added that this claim came as something of a postscript in the Plaintiff's main case and he entertained the suspicion, which I share, that this relatively minor head of claim may have been introduced simply to overcome problems of service and jurisdiction. But he was not satisfied that the threats emanated from a person or persons acting at the behest of the Government of Kuwait, or for whom the Government of Kuwait is otherwise vicariously responsible.

It is common ground that the onus is upon the Plaintiff to satisfy the Court on the balance of probability that the threats do so emanate . . . While it is perfectly possible that those anonymous threats came from the First Defendant, it is equally likely, indeed I think more likely, that they came from the Second, Third or Fourth Defendants, who demonstrated without doubt their readiness to take the law into their own hands in Kuwait and subject the Plaintiff to extreme and life-threatening assaults.

It is accepted by the Plaintiff, as I understand it, that nothing said by the Ambassador amounted to a threat to the Plaintiff's life or limb. The warning that he gave was quite open. As the Judge commented, he did not "hide behind the cloak of anonymity". I do not think that any adverse inference can be drawn from those conversations. . . .

For these reasons, I agree with the Judge that the Plaintiff does not establish jurisdiction against the First Defendant in relation to the threats in England. I would dismiss the appeal.

WARD L.J. delivered a concurring judgment. BUCKLEY J. concurred.

Notes

1. In deciding that no exception could be read into section 1 of the State Immunity Act 1978, the Court of Appeal adopted the same approach as the American courts in the *Hess* and *Siderman* cases quoted by Stuart-Smith L.J. In another American case, an argument that the doctrine of sovereign immunity did not apply was unsuccessful. In *Saudi Arabia v. Nelson*,[49] when the plaintiff persisted in reporting safety defects at a state hospital in Saudi Arabia at which he was employed, he was detained and tortured by the police. His claim against Saudi Arabia in an American court for personal injuries was dismissed on grounds of state immunity. The plaintiff's argument that his claim was based upon his employment at a hospital and for that reason fell within the "commercial activity" exception in the Foreign State Immunities Act 1976 failed. Souter J., for the Supreme Court, stated that the "conduct boils down to abuse of the power of its police by the Saudi Government, and however monstrous such abuse undoubtedly may be, a foreign state's exercise of the power of its police has long been understood for the purpose of the restrictive theory as peculiarly sovereign in nature". Note that even if state immunity is not established, a state may still be immune from the execution of judgments against it: see above, p. 330.

[49] (1993) 123 L. Ed. 47 at 61.

2. Are the policy arguments (see the refugee/asylum example) given by Stuart-Smith L.J. convincing?[50] Might another reason in the Court of Appeal's mind have been that it could be inappropriate for the British courts to act in cases where the executive is not inclined to do so internationally?

3. With the leave of the High Court[51] the plaintiff served a writ in Kuwait on the second, third and fourth defendants in a claim in tort for personal injuries and obtained a default judgment in the High Court against them. In the absence of an equivalent to the Alien Tort Act 1790, the United Kingdom courts do not have *civil* jurisdiction over acts of torture committed entirely abroad, such as those in Kuwait in the *Al Adsani* case.

4. There is, however, *criminal* jurisdiction over individuals for official torture committed in the United Kingdom or elsewhere under section 134 of the Criminal Justice Act 1988, which reads in part:

> (1) A public official or person acting in an official capacity, whatever his nationality, commits the offence of torture if in the United Kingdom or elsewhere he intentionally inflicts severe pain or suffering on another in the performance or purported performance of his official duties.
>
> (2) A person not falling within subsection (1) above commits the offence of torture, whatever his nationality, if—
>
> (a) in the United Kingdom or elsewhere he intentionally inflicts severe pain or suffering on another at the instigation or with the consent or acquiescence—
>
> (i) of a public official; or
>
> (ii) of a person acting in an official capacity; and
>
> (b) the official or other person is performing or purporting to perform his official duties when he instigates the commission of the offence or consents to or acquiesces in it.

Section 134 provides for prosecution in the United Kingdom with the consent of the Attorney-General, or extradition.

4. HUMAN RIGHTS AND INTERNATIONAL CRIMINAL LAW[52]

JUDGMENT OF THE NUREMBERG INTERNATIONAL MILITARY TRIBUNAL[53]

1946. (1947) 41 A.J.I.L. 172

On August 8, 1946, the Governments of France, the United Kingdom, the United States and the USSR, "acting in the interests of all the United Nations and by their representatives duly authorized thereto," signed in London an Agreement for the

---

[50] See Marks (1997) 57 C.L.J. 8. Arguing that priority for sovereign immunity over human rights is out of date, see Bianchi, in Conforti and Francioni, eds., *Enforcing International Human Rights in Domestic Courts* (1997), Chap. 17. On diplomatic immunity and human rights, see Vicuna (1991) 40 I.C.L.Q. 34.

[51] Leave to serve a writ out of the jurisdiction may be given by the High Court for a tort action where "the damage was sustained, or resulted from an act committed, within the jurisdiction": R.S.C., Ord. 11, r. 1(1)(f).

[52] On the criminal responsibility of *states* in international law, see above, p. 487.

[53] See Goodhart (1946) 58 *Juridical Review* 1; Wright (1947) 41 A.J.I.L. 38; Woetzel, *The Nuremberg Trials in International Law* (1960).

Establishment of an International Military Tribunal.[54] The Tribunal was "for the trial of war criminals whose offences have no particular geographical location."[55] It was to operate in accordance with a Charter annexed to the Agreement. The Tribunal was composed of four members, one appointed by each of the signatory governments. The members were Lawrence L.J., President; Biddle, Nikitchenko and de Vabres. The alternate members were Birkett J., Parker, Volchov and Falco.

Judgment of the Tribunal

The individual defendants are indicted under Article 6 of the Charter, which is as follows:

Article 6. The Tribunal established by the Agreement referred to in Article 1 hereof for the trial and punishment of the major war criminals of the European Axis countries shall have the power to try and punish persons who, acting in the interests of the European Axis countries whether as individuals or as members of organizations, committed any of the following crimes:

The following acts, or any of them, are crimes coming within the jurisdiction of the Tribunal for which there shall be individual responsibility:

(a) Crimes Against Peace: namely, planning, preparation, initiation or waging of a war of aggression, or a war in violation of international treaties, agreements or assurances, or participation in a common plan or conspiracy for the accomplishment of any of the foregoing:

(b) War Crimes: namely, violations of the laws or customs of war. Such violations shall include, but not be limited to, murder, ill-treatment or deportation to slave labor or for any other purpose of civilian population of or in occupied territory, murder or ill-treatment of prisoners of war or persons on the seas, killing of hostages, plunder of public or private property, wanton destruction of cities, towns or villages, or devastation not justified by military necessity:

(c) Crimes Against Humanity: namely, murder, extermination, enslavement, deportation, and other inhumane acts committed against any civilian population, before or during the war, or persecutions on political, racial, or religious grounds in execution of or in connection with any crime within the jurisdiction of the Tribunal whether or not in violation of the domestic law of the country where perpetrated.

Leaders, organizers, instigators, and accomplices, participating in the formulation or execution of a common plan or conspiracy to

[54] U.K.T.S. 4 (1945), Cmd. 6671; 5 U.N.T.S. 251; (1945) 39 A.J.I.L. Supp. 257.
[55] *ibid.* Art. 2.

commit any of the foregoing crimes are responsible for all acts performed by any persons in execution of such plan.

The Law of the Charter

The jurisdiction of the Tribunal is defined in the Agreement and Charter, and the crimes coming within the jurisdiction of the Tribunal, for which there shall be individual responsibility, are set out in Article 6. The law of the Charter is decisive, and binding upon the Tribunal.

The making of the Charter was the exercise of the sovereign legislative power by the countries to which the German Reich unconditionally surrendered; and the undoubted right of these countries to legislate for the occupied territories has been recognized by the civilized world. The Charter is not an arbitrary exercise of power on the part of the victorious Nations, but in the view of the Tribunal, as will be shown, it is the expression of international law existing at the time of its creation; and to that extent is itself a contribution to international law.

The Signatory Powers created this Tribunal, defined the law it was to administer, and made regulations for the proper conduct of the Trial. In doing so, they have done together what any one of them might have done singly; for it is not to be doubted that any nation has the right to set up special courts to administer law. With regard to the constitution of the Court, all that the defendants are entitled to ask is to receive a fair trial on the facts and law.

The Charter makes the planning or waging of a war of aggression or a war in violation of international treaties a crime; and it is therefore not strictly necessary to consider whether and to what extent aggressive war was a crime before the execution of the London Agreement. But in view of the great importance of the questions of law involved, the Tribunal has heard full argument from the Prosecution and the Defense, and will express its view on the matter.

It was urged on behalf of the defendants that a fundamental principle of all law—international and domestic—is that there can be no punishment of crime without a pre-existing law. "*Nullum crimen sine lege, nulla poena sine lege.*" It was submitted that *ex post facto* punishment is abhorrent to the law of all civilized nations, that no sovereign power had made aggressive war a crime at the time that the alleged criminal acts were committed, that no statute had defined aggressive war, that no penalty had been fixed for its commission, and no court had been created to try and punish offenders.

In the first place, it is to be observed that the maxim *nullum crimen sine lege* is not a limitation of sovereignty, but is in general a principle of justice. To assert that it is unjust to punish those who in defiance of treaties and assurances have attacked neighboring states without warning is obviously untrue, for in such circumstances the attacker must know that he is doing wrong, and so far from it being unjust to punish him, it would be unjust if his wrong were allowed to go unpunished. Occupying the positions they did in the Government of Germany, the defendants or at least some of them must have known of the treaties signed by Germany, outlawing recourse to war for the settlement of international disputes, they must have known that they were acting in defiance of all international law when in complete deliberation they carried out their designs of invasion and aggression. On this view of the case alone, it would appear that the maxim has no application to the present facts.

This view is strongly reinforced by a consideration of the state of international law in 1939, so far as aggressive war is concerned. The General Treaty for the Renunciation of War of 27 August 1928, more generally known as the Pact of Paris or the Kellogg-Briand Pact, was binding on 63 nations, including Germany, Italy and Japan at the outbreak of war in 1939.... In the opinion of the Tribunal, the solemn renunciation of war as an instrument of national policy necessarily involves the proposition that such a war is illegal in international law; and that those who plan and wage such a war, with its inevitable and terrible consequences, are committing a crime in so doing.... But it is argued that the Pact does not expressly enact that such wars are crimes, or set up courts to try those who make such wars. To that extent the same is true with regard to the laws of war contained in the Hague Convention. The Hague Convention of 1907 prohibited resort to certain methods of waging war.... Many of these prohibitions had been enforced long before the date of the Convention; but since 1907 they have certainly been crimes, punishable as offenses against the law of war; yet the Hague Convention nowhere designates such practices as criminal, nor is any sentence prescribed, nor any mention made of a court to try and punish offenders. For many years past, however, military tribunals have tried and punished individuals guilty of violating the rules of land warfare laid down by this Convention....

It was submitted that international law is concerned with the actions of sovereign States, and provides no punishment for individuals; and further, that where the act in question is an act of State, those who carry it out are not personally responsible, but are protected by the doctrine of the sovereignty of the State. In the opinion of the Tribunal, both these submissions must be rejected. That international law imposes duties and liabilities upon individuals as well as upon States has long been recognized. In the recent case of *Ex Parte Quirin* (1942 317 U.S. 1), before the Supreme Court of the United States, persons were charged during the war with landing in the United States for purposes of spying and sabotage. The late Chief Justice Stone, speaking for the Court, said:

> From the very beginning of its history this Court has applied the law of war as including that part of the law of nations which prescribes for the conduct of war, the status, rights, and duties of enemy nations as well as enemy individuals.

He went on to give a list of cases tried by the Courts, where individual offenders were charged with offenses against the laws of nations, and particularly the laws of war. Many other authorities could be cited, but enough has been said to show that individuals can be punished for violations of international law. Crimes against international law are committed by men, not by abstract entities, and only by punishing individuals who commit such crimes can the provisions of international law be enforced. . . .

It was also submitted on behalf of most of these defendants that in doing what they did they were acting under the orders of Hitler, and therefore cannot be held responsible for the acts committed by them in carrying out these orders. The Charter specifically provides in Article 8:

> The fact that the Defendant acted pursuant to order of his Government or of a superior shall not free him from responsibility, but may be considered in mitigation of punishment.

The provisions of this article are in conformity with the law of all nations. That a soldier was ordered to kill or torture in violation of the international law of war has never been recognized as a defense to such acts of brutality, though, as the Charter here provides, the order may be urged in mitigation of the punishment. The true test, which is found in varying degrees in the criminal law of most nations, is not the existence of the order, but whether moral choice was in fact possible.

The Law as to the Common Plan or Conspiracy

In the previous recital of the facts relating to aggressive war, it is clear that planning and preparation had been carried out in the most systematic way at every stage of history.

Planning and preparation are essential to the making of war. In the opinion of the Tribunal aggressive war is a crime under international law. The Charter defines this offense as planning, preparation, initiation, or waging of a war of aggression "or participation in a Common Plan or Conspiracy for the accomplishment . . . of the foregoing." . . .

The "Common Plan or Conspiracy" charged in the Indictment covers 25 years, from the formation of the Nazi Party in 1919 to the end of the war in 1945. . . .

The Prosecution says, in effect, that any significant participation in the affairs of the Nazi Party or Government is evidence of a participation in a conspiracy that is in itself criminal. Conspiracy is not defined in the Charter. But in the opinion of the Tribunal the conspiracy must be clearly outlined in its criminal purpose. It must not be too far removed from the time of decision and of action. The planning, to be criminal, must not rest merely on the declarations of a party program, such as are found in the

25 points of the Nazi Party, announced in 1920, or the political affirmations expressed in *Mein Kampf* in later years. The Tribunal must examine whether a concrete plan to wage war existed, and determine the participants in that concrete plan. . . .

In the opinion of the Tribunal, the evidence establishes the common planning to prepare and wage war by certain of the defendants. . . .

War Crimes and Crimes against Humanity

The evidence relating to War Crimes has been overwhelming . . .

. . . Prisoners of war were ill-treated and tortured and murdered, not only in defiance of the well-established rules of international law, but in complete disregard of the elementary dictates of humanity. Civilian populations in occupied territories suffered the same fate. Whole populations were deported to Germany for the purposes of slave labor upon defense works, armament production, and similar tasks connected with the war effort. Hostages were taken in very large numbers from the civilian populations in all the occupied countries, and were shot as suited the German purposes. Public and private property was systematically plundered and pillaged in order to enlarge the resources of Germany at the expense of the rest of Europe. Cities and towns and villages were wantonly destroyed without military justification or necessity. . . .

The Tribunal is of course bound by the Charter, in the definition which it gives both of War Crimes and Crimes against Humanity. With respect to War Crimes, however, as has already been pointed out, the crimes defined by Article 6, Section (b), of the Charter were already recognized as War Crimes under international law. They were covered by Articles 46, 50, 52, and 56 of the Hague Convention of 1907, and Articles 2, 3, 4, 46, and 51 of the Geneva Convention of 1929. That violation of these provisions constituted crimes for which the guilty individuals were punishable is too well settled to admit of argument. . . .

With regard to Crimes against Humanity there is no doubt whatever that political opponents were murdered in Germany before the war, and that many of them were kept in concentration camps in circumstances of great horror and cruelty. The policy of terror was certainly carried out on a vast scale, and in many cases was organized and systematic. The policy of persecution, repression, and murder of civilians in Germany before the war of 1939, who were likely to be hostile to the Government, was most ruthlessly carried out. The persecution of Jews during the same period is established beyond all doubt. To constitute Crimes against Humanity, the acts relied on before the outbreak of war must have been in execution of, or in connection with, any crime within the jurisdiction of the Tribunal. The Tribunal is of the opinion that revolting and horrible as many of these crimes were, it has not been satisfactorily proved that they were done in execution of, or in connection with, any such crime. The Tribunal therefore cannot make a general declaration that the acts before 1939 were

Crimes against Humanity within the meaning of the Charter, but from the beginning of the war in 1939 War Crimes were committed on a vast scale, which were also Crimes against Humanity; and insofar as the inhumane acts charged in the Indictments, and committed after the beginning of the war, did not constitute War Crimes, they were all committed in execution of, or in connection with, the aggressive war, and therefore constituted Crimes against Humanity.

The Accused Oranizations

[The Tribunal then considered the nature of the responsibility of the German organisations that were indicted:]

A criminal organization is analogous to a criminal conspiracy in that the essence of both is co-operation for criminal purposes. There must be a group bound together and organized for a common purpose. The group must be formed or used in connection with the commission of crimes denounced by the Charter. Since the declaration with respect to the organizations and groups will, as has been pointed out, fix the criminality of its members, that definition should exclude persons who had no knowledge of the criminal purposes or acts of the organization and those who were drafted by the State for membership, unless they were personally implicated in the commission of acts declared criminal by Article 6 of the Charter as members of the organization. Membership alone is not enough to come within the scope of these declarations.

Notes

1. After dealing with these general questions in the above part of its judgment, the Tribunal proceeded to review the cases of each of the indicted individuals and organisations. Of the twenty-two individuals indicted, three were acquitted; the remainder were found guilty on one or more of the counts in the indictment, which was based upon Article 6 of the Tribunal's Charter. Of those found guilty, twelve (including Goering, Von Ribbentrop, Keitel, Streicher and Bormann) were sentenced to death[56]; three (including Hess) were sentenced to life imprisonment; and four were sentenced to periods of ten to twenty years' imprisonment. Of the six organisations indicted, three were declared criminal, including the Gestapo and the SS. The Soviet judge dissented on some of the acquittals and on the refusal of the Tribunal to pass a death sentence on Hess.

2. *Did* the case infringe the principle *nullum crimen sine lege*? Consider the position with regard to crimes against humanity (which was the only offence of which Streicher, for example, was found guilty) in particular. With regard to the defence of superior orders,[57] what does the Tribunal mean when it says that the "true test . . . is . . . whether moral choice was in fact possible"? Could it be argued that the Tribunal violated the principle *nemo judex in sua propria causa*? or that the trial was invalid because war criminals on the Allied side were not tried also?

---

[56] Goering committed suicide before the sentence could be carried out. Borman was tried *in absentia* (a fair trial?).

[57] See Dinstein, "The Defence of 'Obedience to Superior Orders'" International Law (1965).

3. Was the Tribunal an international tribunal or was it a municipal court established in Germany by the governments jointly exercising sovereignty therein for the time being?

4. In 1946, the General Assembly of the United Nations resolved that it "affirms the principles of international law recognised by the Charter of the Nurnberg Tribunal and the judgment of the Tribunal".[58] The Nuremberg Principles were later formulated by the International Law Commission[59] on the instruction of the General Assembly. The Commission understood its task as not requiring it to "express any appreciation of these principles as principles of international law but merely to formulate them". In 1963, the Lord Chancellor stated in Parliament that the United Kingdom took the view that the Nuremberg Principles "are generally accepted among states and have the status of customary international law."[60]

5. The Japanese war leaders were tried by a similar tribunal—the International Tribunal for the Far East.[61] Other war crimes tribunals established by the Allied Powers tried lesser offenders.[62]

6. The Convention on the Non-applicability of Statutory Limitations to War Crimes and Crimes against Humanity 1968[63] achieves what its title suggests for parties to it. Article IV reads:

> The States Parties to the present Convention undertake to adopt, in accordance with their respective constitutional processes, any legislative or other measures necessary to ensure that statutory or other limitations shall not apply to the prosecution and punishment of the crimes referred to in articles I and II of this Convention and that, where they exist, such limitations shall be abolished.

7. In 1971, the United Nations General Assembly reaffirmed that *apartheid* is a crime against humanity.[64] The International Convention on the Suppression and Punishment of the Crime of Apartheid 1973, Article 1, states the same.[65]

CONVENTION ON THE PREVENTION AND PUNISHMENT OF THE CRIME OF GENOCIDE 1948[66]

U.K.T.S. 58 (1970), Cmnd. 4421; 78 U.N.T.S. 277; (1951) 45 A.J.I.L. Supp. 6

The *Contracting Parties*,

Having considered the declaration made by the General Assembly of the United Nations in its resolution 96 (I) dated 11 December 1946 that

---

[58] G.A. Res. 95 (I), G.A.O.R., Resolutions, 1st Sess. Part II, p. 188.

[59] They are printed in Y.B.I.L.C., 1950, II, p. 195.

[60] *Hansard*, H.L., Vol. 253, col. 831, December 2, 1963; B.P.I.L. 1963, p. 212.

[61] See Horwitz, *The Tokyo Trial, Int. Conc. No. 465* (1950).

[62] See Taylor, *Nuremberg Trials: War Crimes and International Law, Int. Conc. No. 450* (1949).

[63] (1969) 8 I.L.M. 68. In force 1977. 43 parties; U.K. not a party. See Miller (1971) 65 A.J.I.L. 476. The War Crimes Act 1991 gives U.K. courts universality jurisdiction for war crimes in Germany or German occupied territory in World War II. No successful prosecutions yet.

[64] G.A. Res. 2784 (XXVI). The resolution was adopted by 93 votes to 5, with 15 abstentions.

[65] *loc. cit.*, p. 630, n. 41, above.

[66] The Convention was adopted unanimously by the General Assembly on December 9, 1948. It entered into force on January 13, 1951. 122 contracting parties, including the U.K. The offence in Art. 2 was made an offence in English law by the Genocide Act 1969. See Kunz (1949) 43 A.J.I.L. 738; Lemkin (1947) 41 A.J.I.L. 145; Robinson, *The Genocide Convention. A Commentary* (1960).

genocide is a crime under international law, contrary to the spirit and aims of the United Nations and condemned by the civilized world;

Recognizing that at all periods of history genocide has inflicted great losses on humanity; and

Being convinced that, in order to liberate mankind from such an odious scourge, international co-operation is required;

Hereby agree as hereinafter provided:

Article I

The Contracting Parties confirm that genocide, whether committed in time of peace or in time of war, is a crime under international law which they undertake to prevent and punish.

Article II

In the present Convention, genocide means any of the following acts committed with intent to destroy, in whole or in part, a national, ethnical, racial or religious group, as such:

- (*a*) Killing members of the group;
- (*b*) Causing serious bodily or mental harm to members of the group;
- (*c*) Deliberately inflicting on the group conditions of life calculated to bring about its physical destruction in whole or in part;
- (*d*) Imposing measures intended to prevent births within the group;
- (*e*) Forcibly transferring children of the group to another group.

Article III

The following acts shall be punishable:

- (*a*) Genocide;
- (*b*) Conspiracy to commit genocide;
- (*c*) Direct and public incitement to commit genocide;
- (*d*) Attempt to commit genocide;
- (*e*) Complicity in genocide.

Article IV

Persons committing genocide or any of the other acts enumerated in Article III shall be punished, whether they are constitutionally responsible rulers, public officials or private individuals.

Article V

The Contracting Parties undertake to enact, in accordance with their respective Constitutions, the necessary legislation to give effect to the provisions of the present Convention and, in particular, to provide effective penalties for persons guilty of genocide or any of the other acts enumerated in Article III.

Article VI

Persons charged with genocide or any of the other acts enumerated in Article III shall be tried by a competent tribunal of the State in the territory of which the act was committed, or by such international penal tribunal as may have jurisdiction with respect to those Contracting Parties which shall have accepted its jurisdiction.

Article VII

Genocide and the other acts enumerated in Article III shall not be considered as political crimes for the purpose of extradition.

Article IX

Disputes between the Contracting Parties relating to the interpretation, application or fulfilment of the present Convention, including those relating to the responsibility of a State for genocide or any of the other acts enumerated in Article III, shall be submitted to the International Court of Justice at the request of any of the parties to the dispute.

Notes

1. The term "genocide" was coined by Lemkin, a private individual whose efforts played a large part in prompting the United Nations work on genocide.

2. Is the offence of genocide defined in the Convention the same in scope as that of crimes against humanity in the Charter of the Nuremberg International Military Tribunal? Does the Convention cover cultural genocide? Note how vague the concept of "complicity in genocide" is.

3. There is as yet no permanent "international penal tribunal" with jurisdiction to try persons for genocide or any other international crime.[67] In this situation, how satisfactory is Article VI? Shouldn't there be universal jurisdiction to try persons for genocide?[68]

4. The Convention probably reflects customary international law.[69] Note that it was adopted unanimously in the General Assembly and that Resolution 96 (I) of the General Assembly upon which it was based was adopted unanimously too. Note also the *Barcelona Traction* case.[70]

5. A large number of parties have made reservations not accepting the rule of compulsory jurisdiction in Art. IX of the Convention, including most of the

---

[67] For the proposal for a permanent international criminal court, see below, p. 752.
[68] Note the approach of the court in the *Eichmann* case, above, p. 280.
[69] See the *Reservations* case I.C.J. Rep. 1951, p. 15 and above p. 725.
[70] See above, p. 604, in paras. 33, 34.

former Soviet bloc.[71] Several states, including the United Kingdom, have objected to such reservations.[72]

STATUTE OF THE INTERNATIONAL CRIMINAL TRIBUNAL FOR THE FORMER YUGOSLAVIA

Annex to Security Council Resolution 827. (1993) 32 I.L.M. 1203; (1993) 2 I.H.R.R. 510

Article 1

The International Tribunal shall have the power to prosecute persons responsible for serious violations of international humanitarian law committed in the territory of the former Yugoslavia since 1991 in accordance with the provisions of the present Statute.

Article 2

The International Tribunal shall have the power to prosecute persons committing or ordering to be committed grave breaches of the Geneva Conventions of 12 August 1949, namely the following acts against persons or property protected under the provisions of the relevant Geneva Convention:

(a) wilful killing;
(b) torture or inhuman treatment, including biological experiments;
(c) wilfully causing great suffering or serious injury to body or health;
(d) extensive destruction and appropriation of property, not justified by military necessity and carried out unlawfully and wantonly;
(e) compelling a prisoner of war or a civilian to serve in the forces of a hostile power;
(f) wilfully depriving a prisoner of war or a civilian of the rights of fair and regular trial;
(g) unlawful deportation or transfer or unlawful confinement of a civilian;
(h) taking civilians as hostages.

Article 3

The International Tribunal shall have the power to prosecute persons violating the laws or customs of war. Such violations shall include, but not be limited to:

---

[71] See UN Doc. ST/LEG/SER.E/15, pp. 86–88.
[72] *ibid.* pp. 89–91.

(a) employment of poisonous weapons or other weapons calculated to cause unnecessary suffering;
(b) wanton destruction of cities, towns or villages, or devastation not justified by military necessity;
(c) attack, or bombardment, by whatever means, of undefended towns, villages, dwellings, or buildings;
(d) seizure of, destruction or wilful damage done to institutions dedicated to religion, charity and education, the arts and sciences, historic monuments and works of art and science;
(e) plunder of public or private property.

Article 4

1. The International Tribunal shall have the power to prosecute persons committing genocide as defined in paragraph 2 of this article or of committing any of the other acts enumerated in paragraph 3 of this article.

2. Genocide means any of the following acts committed with intent to destroy, in whole or in part, a national, ethnical, racial or religious group, as such:

(a) killing members of the group;
(b) causing serious bodily or mental harm to members of the group;
(c) deliberately inflicting on the group conditions of life calculated to bring about its physical destruction in whole or in part;
(d) imposing measures intended to prevent births within the group;
(e) forcibly transferring children of the group to another group.

3. The following acts shall be punishable:

(a) genocide;
(b) conspiracy to commit genocide;
(c) direct and public incitement to commit genocide;
(d) attempt to commit genocide;
(e) complicity in genocide.

Article 5

The International Tribunal shall have the power to prosecute persons responsible for the following crimes when committed in armed conflict, whether international or internal in character, and directed against any civilian population:

(a) murder;
(b) extermination;
(c) enslavement;

(d) deportation;
(e) imprisonment;
(f) torture;
(g) rape;
(h) persecutions on political, racial and religious grounds;
(i) other inhumane acts.

Article 6

The International Tribunal shall have jurisdiction over natural persons pursuant to the provisions of the present Statute.

Article 7

1. A person who planned, instigated, ordered, committed or otherwise aided and abetted in the planning, preparation or execution of a crime referred to in articles 2 to 5 of the present Statute, shall be individually responsible for the crime.

2. The official position of any accused person, whether as Head of State or Government or as a responsible Government official, shall not relieve such person of criminal responsibility nor mitigate punishment.

3. The fact that any of the acts referred to in articles 2 to 5 of the present Statute was committed by a subordinate does not relieve his superior of criminal responsibility if he knew or had reason to know that the subordinate was about to commit such acts or had done so and the superior failed to take the necessary and reasonable measures to prevent such acts or to punish the perpetrators thereof.

4. The fact that an accused person acted pursuant to an order of a Government or of a superior shall not relieve him of criminal responsibility, but may be considered in mitigation of punishment if the International Tribunal determines that justice so requires.

Article 8

The territorial jurisdiction of the International Tribunal shall extend to the territory of the former Socialist Federal Republic of Yugoslavia, including its land surface, airspace and territorial waters. The temporal jurisdiction of the International Tribunal shall extend to a period beginning on 1 January 1991.

Article 9

1. The International Tribunal and national courts shall have concurrent jurisdiction to prosecute persons for serious violations of international humanitarian law committed in the territory of the former Yugoslavia since 1 January 1991.

2. The International Tribunal shall have primacy over national courts. At any stage of the procedure, the International Tribunal may formally request national courts to defer to the competence of the International Tribunal in accordance with the present Statute and the Rules of Procedure and Evidence of the International Tribunal.

Article 10

1. No person shall be tried before a national court for acts constituting serious violations of international humanitarian law under the present Statute, for which he or she has already been tried by the International Tribunal.

2. A person who has been tried by a national court for acts constituting serious violations of international humanitarian law may be subsequently tried by the International Tribunal only if:

(a) the act for which he or she was tried was characterized as an ordinary crime; or
(b) the national court proceedings were not impartial or independent, were designed to shield the accused from international criminal responsibility, or the case was not diligently prosecuted.

3. In considering the penalty to be imposed on a person convicted of a crime under the present Statute, the International Tribunal shall take into account the extent to which any penalty imposed by a national court on the same person for the same act has already been served.

Article 21

1. All persons shall be equal before the International Tribunal.

2. In the determination of charges against him, the accused shall be entitled to a fair and public hearing, subject to article 22 of the Statute.

3. The accused shall be presumed innocent until proved guilty according to the provisions of the present Statute.

4. In the determination of any charge against the accused pursuant to the present Statute, the accused shall be entitled to the following minimum guarantees, in full equality:

(a) to be informed promptly and in detail in a language which he understands of the nature and cause of the charge against him;
(b) to have adequate time and facilities for the preparation of his defence and to communicate with counsel of his own choosing;
(c) to be tried without undue delay;
(d) to be tried in his presence, and to defend himself in person or through legal assistance of his own choosing; to be informed, if he does not have legal assistance, of this right; and to have legal assistance assigned to him, in any case where the interests of justice

so require, and without payment by him in any such case if he does not have sufficient means to pay for it;

(e) to examine, or have examined, the witnesses against him and to obtain the attendance and examination of witnesses on his behalf under the same conditions as witnesses against him;

(f) to have the free assistance of an interpreter if he cannot understand or speak the language used in the International Tribunal;

(g) not to be compelled to testify against himself or to confess guilt.

Article 22

The International Tribunal shall provide in its rules of procedure and evidence for the protection of victims and witnesses. Such protection measures shall include, but shall not be limited to, the conduct of in camera proceedings and the protection of the victim's identity.

Article 24

1. The penalty imposed by the Trial Chamber shall be limited to imprisonment. In determining the terms of imprisonment, the Trial Chambers shall have recourse to the general practice regarding prison sentences in the courts of the former Yugoslavia.

Notes

1. The International Criminal Tribunal for the former Yugoslavia was established as an *ad hoc* response to the events during the conflict in the territory of the former Yugoslavia. It has issued over 50 indictments against alleged war criminals, including Mr Karadžić, the political leader of Bosnian Serbs. So far two accused persons, Erdemovic, who pleaded guilty, and Tadic have been convicted and sentenced to terms of imprisonment. Ten other cases of persons in the detention of the Tribunal at The Hague are being processed.

2. The Security Council has also established an International Tribunal for Rwanda[73] that has comparable jurisdiction to that of the Yugoslav Tribunal. It has several thousand accused are in custody in Rwanda.

3. The Yugoslav and Rwanda Tribunals are *ad hoc* bodies founded upon the insecure base of Security Council resolutions. Work is being done to establish a permanent tribunal on a treaty basis. In 1994, the International Law Commission adopted a Draft Statute for an International Criminal Court.[74] The General Assembly has since convened a diplomatic conference in Rome in 1998 for the adoption of a treaty, in the form of a Statute, to establish a permanent court. A UN Preparatory Committee meets periodically to prepare for the Rome Conference

---

[73] S.C. Res. 955; (1994) 33 I.L.M. 1600. See Akhavem (1996) 90 A.J.I.L. 501 and Schraga and Zacklin (1996) 7 E.J.I.L. 501.

[74] (1994) 33 I.L.M. 253. See Crawford (1995) 89 A.J.I.L. 404. On the General Assembly Sixth Committee's consideration of the I.L.C. Draft, see Morris and Bourloyannis-Vrailas (1996) 90 A.J.I.L. 491.

and is developing its own draft Statute, building upon the International Law Commission's text.[75]

PROSECUTOR *v.* TADIC (JURISDICTION)

International Criminal Tribunal for the Former Yugoslavia, Appeals Chamber: Judge Cassese, presiding, Judges Li, Deschênes, Abi-Saab and Sidhwa

(1996) 35 I.L.M. 35; (1996) 3 I.H.R.R. 578

This was an interlocutory appeal by the defendant against the judgment of the Trial Chamber in which the Chamber held that the Tribunal had jurisdiction to hear the case. The appellant appealed on the following grounds: the unlawful establishment of the Tribunal; its unjustified primacy over competent domestic courts; and the lack of subject-matter jurisdiction. In the following extract, the Tribunal begins by confirming, on the basis of the "compétence de la compétence" doctrine, to consider the first ground of appeal.

Decision of the Appeals Chamber

18. This power, known as the principle of *"Kompetenz-Kompetenz"* in German or *"la compétence de la compétence"* in French, is part, and indeed a major part, of the incidental or inherent jurisdiction of any judicial or arbitral tribunal, consisting of its "jurisdiction to determine its own jurisdiction". It is a necessary component in the exercise of the judicial function and does not need to be expressly provided for in the constitutive documents of those tribunals, although this is often done (see, *e.g.*, Statute of the International Court of Justice, Art. 36, para. 6). . . .

20. . . . There is no question, of course, of the International Tribunal acting as a constitutional tribunal, reviewing the acts of the other organs of the United Nations, particularly those of the Security Council, its own "creator". It was not established for that purpose, as is clear from the definition of the ambit of its "primary" or "substantive" jurisdiction in Articles 1 to 5 of its Statute.

But this is beside the point. The question before the Appeals Chamber is whether the International Tribunal, in exercising this "incidental" jurisdiction, can examine the legality of its establishment by the Security Council, solely for the purpose of ascertaining its own "primary" jurisdiction over the case before it. . . .

21. . . . The same sort of examination was undertaken by the International Court of Justice, *inter alia*, in its advisory opinion on the *Effect of Awards Case*:

---

[75] For an account of the work of PREPCOM, see Hall (1997) 91 A.J.I.L. 177.

"[T]he legal power of the General Assembly to establish a tribunal competent to render judgements binding on the United Nations has been challenged. Accordingly, it is necessary to consider whether the General Assembly has been given this power by the Charter." (Effect of Awards, at 56.)

Obviously, the wider the discretion of the Security Council under the Charter of the United Nations, the narrower the scope for the International Tribunal to review its actions, even as a matter of incidental jurisdiction. Nevertheless, this does not mean that the power disappears altogether, particularly in cases where there might be a manifest contradiction with the Principles and Purposes of the Charter.

22. In conclusion, the Appeals Chamber finds that the International Tribunal has jurisdiction to examine the plea against its jurisdiction based on the invalidity of its establishment by the Security Council. . . .

26. Many arguments have been put forward by Appellant in support of the contention that the establishment of the International Tribunal is invalid under the Charter of the United Nations or that it was not duly established by law. . . .

28. . . . It is clear from this text [of Article 39, Charter] that the Security Council plays a pivotal role and exercises a very wide discretion under this Article. But this does not mean that its powers are unlimited. The Security Council is an organ of an international organization, established by a treaty which serves as a constitutional framework for that organization. The Security Council is thus subjected to certain constitutional limitations, however broad its powers under the constitution may be. Those powers cannot, in any case, go beyond the limits of the jurisdiction of the Organization at large, not to mention other specific limitations or those which may derive from the internal division of power within the Organization. In any case, neither the text nor the spirit of the Charter conceives of the Security Council as *legibus solutus* (unbound by law).

In particular, Article 24, after declaring, in paragraph 1, that the Members of the United Nations "confer on the Security Council primary responsibility for the maintenance of international peace and security" . . . provides . . . in paragraph 2, that:

"In discharging these duties the Security Council shall act in accordance with the Purposes and Principles of the United Nations. The specific powers granted to the Security Council for the discharge of these duties are laid down in Chapters VI, VII, VIII, and XII." (Id., Art. 24(2).)

The Charter thus speaks the language of specific powers, not of absolute fiat.

29. . . . The Security Council plays the central role in the application of both parts of . . . Article [39]. It is the Security Council that makes the

determination that there exists one of the situations justifying the use of the "exceptional powers" of Chapter VII. And it is also the Security Council that chooses the reaction to such a situation: it either makes recommendations (i.e., opts not to use the exceptional powers but to continue to operate under Chapter VI) or decides to use the exceptional powers by ordering measures to be taken in accordance with Articles 41 and 42 with a view to maintaining or restoring international peace and security.

The situations justifying resort to the powers provided for in Chapter VII are a "threat to the peace", a "breach of the peace" or an "act of aggression". While the "act of aggression" is more amenable to a legal determination, the "threat to the peace" is more of a political concept. But the determination that there exists such a threat is not a totally unfettered discretion, as it has to remain, at the very least, within the limits of the Purposes and Principles of the Charter.

30. It is not necessary for the purposes of the present decision to examine any further the question of the limits of the discretion of the Security Council in determining the existence of a "threat to the peace", for two reasons.

The first is that an armed conflict (or a series of armed conflicts) has been taking place in the territory of the former Yugoslavia since long before the decision of the Security Council to establish this International Tribunal. If it is considered an international armed conflict, there is no doubt that it falls within the literal sense of the words "breach of the peace" (between the parties or, at the very least, as a "threat to the peace" of others).

But even if it were considered merely as an "internal armed conflict", it would still constitute a "threat to the peace" according to the settled practice of the Security Council and the common understanding of the United Nations membership in general. Indeed, the practice of the Security Council is rich with cases of civil war or internal strife which it classified as a "threat to the peace" and dealt with under Chapter VII, with the encouragement or even at the behest of the General Assembly, such as the Congo crisis at the beginning of the 1960s and more recently, Liberia and Somalia. It can thus be said that there is a common understanding, manifested by the "subsequent practice" of the membership of the United Nations at large, that the "threat to the peace" of Article 39 may include, as one of its species, internal armed conflicts. . . .

The second reason was that the appellant no longer contested the point.

32. As with the determination of the existence of a threat to the peace, a breach of the peace or an act of aggression, the Security Council has a very wide margin of discretion under Article 39 to choose the appropriate course of action and to evaluate the suitability of the measures chosen, as

well as their potential contribution to the restoration or maintenance of peace. But here again, this discretion is not unfettered; moreover, it is limited to the measures provided for in Articles 41 and 42. . . .

In its resolution 827, the Security Council considers that "in the particular circumstances of the former Yugoslavia", the establishment of the International Tribunal "would contribute to the restoration and maintenance of peace" and indicates that, in establishing it, the Security Council was acting under Chapter VII (S.C. Res. 827, U.N. Doc. S/RES/827 (1993)). However, it did not specify a particular Article as a basis for this action. . . .

33. The establishment of an international criminal tribunal is not expressly mentioned among the enforcement measures provided for in Chapter VII, and more particularly in Articles 41 and 42.

Obviously, the establishment of the International Tribunal is not a measure under Article 42, as these are measures of a military nature, implying the use of armed force. Nor can it be considered a "provisional measure" under Article 40. . . .

34. *Prima facie*, the International Tribunal matches perfectly the description in Article 41 of "measures not involving the use of force". . . .

That the examples [in Article 41] do not suggest judicial measures goes some way towards the other argument that the Article does not contemplate institutional measures implemented directly by the United Nations through one of its organs but, as the given examples suggest, only action by Member States, such as economic sanctions (though possibly coordinated through an organ of the Organization). However, as mentioned above, nothing in the Article suggests the limitation of the measures to those implemented by States. The Article only prescribes what these measures cannot be. Beyond that it does not say or suggest what they have to be. Moreover, even a simple literal analysis of the Article shows that the first phrase of the first sentence carries a very general prescription which can accommodate both institutional and Member State action. The second phrase can be read as referring particularly to one species of this very large category of measures referred to in the first phrase, but not necessarily the only one, namely, measures undertaken directly by States. It is also clear that the second sentence, starting with "These [measures]" not "Those [measures]", refers to the species mentioned in the second phrase rather than to the "genus" referred to in the first phrase of this sentence.

36. Logically, if the Organization can undertake measures which have to be implemented through the intermediary of its Members, it can *a fortiori* undertake measures which it can implement directly via its organs, if it happens to have the resources to do so. It is only for want of such resources that the United Nations has to act through its Members. But it is of the essence of "collective measures" that they are collectively undertaken. Action by Member States on behalf of the Organization is but a poor substitute *faute de mieux*, or a "second best" for want of the first.

This is also the pattern of Article 42 on measures involving the use of armed force.

In sum, the establishment of the International Tribunal falls squarely within the powers of the Security Council under Article 41. . . .

37. The argument that the Security Council, not being endowed with judicial powers, cannot establish a subsidiary organ possessed of such powers is untenable: it results from a fundamental misunderstanding of the constitutional set-up of the Charter.

Plainly, the Security Council is not a judicial organ and is not provided with judicial powers (though it may incidentally perform certain quasi-judicial activities such as effecting determinations or findings). The principal function of the Security Council is the maintenance of international peace and security, in the discharge of which the Security Council exercises both decision-making and executive powers.

38. The establishment of the International Tribunal by the Security Council does not signify, however, that the Security Council has delegated to it some of its own functions or the exercise of some of its own powers. Nor does it mean, in reverse, that the Security Council was usurping for itself part of a judicial function which does not belong to it but to other organs of the United Nations according to the Charter. The Security Council has resorted to the establishment of a judicial organ in the form of an international criminal tribunal as an instrument for the exercise of its own principal function of maintenance of peace and security, *i.e.*, as a measure contributing to the restoration and maintenance of peace in the former Yugoslavia. . . .

39. The third argument is directed against the discretionary power of the Security Council in evaluating the appropriateness of the chosen measure and its effectiveness in achieving its objective, the restoration of peace.

Article 39 leaves the choice of means and their evaluation to the Security Council, which enjoys wide discretionary powers in this regard; and it could not have been otherwise, as such a choice involves political evaluation of highly complex and dynamic situations. It would be a total misconception of what are the criteria of legality and validity in law to test the legality of such measures *ex post facto* by their success or failure to achieve their ends (in the present case, the restoration of peace in the former Yugoslavia, in quest of which the establishment of the International Tribunal is but one of many measures adopted by the Security Council).

40. For the aforementioned reasons, the Appeals Chamber considers that the International Tribunal has been lawfully established as a measure under Chapter VII of the Charter. . . .

The Tribunal referred to the "fair trial" guarantees in Article 14, ICCPR and Article 6, ECHR, which both contain such a requirement.

43. Indeed, there are three possible interpretations of the term "established by law". First, as Appellant argues, "established by law" could mean established by a legislature. Appellant claims that the International Tribunal is the product of a "mere executive order" and not of a "decision making process under democratic control, necessary to create a judicial organisation in a democratic society".

It is clearly impossible to classify the organs of the United Nations into the above-discussed divisions which exist in the national law of States. Indeed, Appellant has agreed that the constitutional structure of the United Nations does not follow the division of powers often found in national constitutions. Consequently the separation of powers element of the requirement that a tribunal be "established by law" finds no application in an international law setting. The aforementioned principle can only impose an obligation on States concerning the functioning of their own national systems.

44. A second possible interpretation is that the words "established by law" refer to establishment of international courts by a body which, though not a Parliament, has a limited power to take binding decisions. In our view, one such body is the Security Council when, acting under Chapter VII of the United Nations Charter, it makes decisions binding by virtue of Article 25 of the Charter.

According to Appellant, however, there must be something more for a tribunal to be "established by law". Appellant takes the position that, given the differences between the United Nations system and national division of powers, discussed above, the conclusion must be that the United Nations system is not capable of creating the International Tribunal unless there is an amendment to the United Nations Charter. We disagree. It does not follow from the fact that the United Nations has no legislature that the Security Council is not empowered to set up this International Tribunal if it is acting pursuant to an authority found within its constitution, the United Nations Charter. As set out above (paras. 28–40) we are of the view that the Security Council was endowed with the power to create this International Tribunal as a measure under Chapter VII in the light of its determination that there here exists a threat to the peace. . . .

45. The third possible interpretation of the requirement that the International Tribunal be "established by law" is that its establishment must be in accordance with the rule of law. This appears to be the most sensible and most likely meaning of the term in the context of international law. For a tribunal such as this one to be established according to the rule of law, it must be established in accordance with the proper international standards; it must provide all the guarantees of fairness, justice and even-handedness, in full conformity with internationally recognized human rights instruments. . . .

46. An examination of the Statute of the International Tribunal, and of the Rules of Procedure and Evidence adopted pursuant to that Statute

leads to the conclusion that it has been established in accordance with the rule of law. The fair trial guarantees in Article 14 of the International Covenant on Civil and Political Rights have been adopted almost verbatim in Article 21 of the Statute. Other fair trial guarantees appear in the Statute and the Rules of Procedure and Evidence. For example, Article 13, paragraph 1, of the Statute ensures the high moral character, impartiality, integrity and competence of the Judges of the International Tribunal, while various other provisions in the Rules ensure equality of arms and fair trial.

47. In conclusion, the Appeals Chamber finds that the International Tribunal has been established in accordance with the appropriate procedures under the United Nations Charter and provides all the necessary safeguards of a fair trial. It is thus "established by law".

48. The first ground of Appeal: unlawful establishment of the International Tribunal, is accordingly dismissed. . . .

49. The second ground of appeal attacks the primacy of the International Tribunal over national courts.

50. This primacy is established by Article 9 of the Statute of the International Tribunal. . . .

58. . . . Indeed, when an international tribunal such as the present one is created, it must be endowed with primacy over national courts. Otherwise, human nature being what it is, there would be a perennial danger of international crimes being characterised as "ordinary crimes" (Statute of the International Tribunal, art. 10, para. 2(2)), or proceedings being "designed to shield the accused", or cases not being diligently prosecuted (Statute of the International Tribunal, art. 10, para. 2(b)).

If not effectively countered by the principle of primacy, any one of those stratagems might be used to defeat the very purpose of the creation of an international criminal jurisdiction, to the benefit of the very people whom it has been designed to prosecute.

59. The principle of primacy of this International Tribunal over national courts must be affirmed; the more so since it is confined within the strict limits of Articles 9 and 10 of the Statute and Rules 9 and 10 of the Rules of Procedure of the International Tribunal. . . .

61. Appellant argues that he has a right to be tried by his national courts under his national laws.

No one has questioned that right of Appellant. The problem is elsewhere: is that right exclusive? Does it prevent Appellant from being tried—and having an equally fair trial (see Statute of the International Tribunal, art. 21)—before an international tribunal? . . .

62. As a matter of fact—and of law—the principle advocated by Appellant aims at one very specific goal: to avoid the creation of special or extraordinary courts designed to try political offences in times of social unrest without guarantees of a fair trial.

This principle is not breached by the transfer of jurisdiction to an international tribunal created by the Security Council acting on behalf of the community of nations. No rights of accused are thereby infringed or threatened; quite to the contrary, they are all specifically spelt out and protected under the Statute of the International Tribunal. No accused can complain. True, he will be removed from his "natural" national forum; but he will be brought before a tribunal at least equally fair, more distanced from the facts of the case and taking a broader view of the matter.

Furthermore, one cannot but rejoice at the thought that, universal jurisdiction being nowadays acknowledged in the case of international crimes, a person suspected of such offences may finally be brought before an international judicial body for a dispassionate consideration of his indictment by impartial, independent and disinterested judges coming, as it happens here, from all continents of the world.

63. The objection founded on the theory of *jus de non evocando* was considered by the Trial Chamber which disposed of it in the following terms:

"Reference was also made to the *jus de non evocando*, a feature of a number of national constitutions. But that principle, if it requires that an accused be tried by the regularly established courts and not by some special tribunal set up for that particular purpose, has no application when what is in issue is the exercise by the Security Council, acting under Chapter VII, of the powers conferred upon it by the Charter of the United Nations. Of course, this involves some surrender of sovereignty by the member nations of the United Nations but that is precisely what was achieved by the adoption of the Charter." (Decision at Trial, at para. 37.)

No new objections were raised before the Appeals Chamber, which is satisfied with concurring, on this particular point, with the views expressed by the Trial Chamber.

64. For these reasons the Appeals Chamber concludes that Appellant's second ground of appeal, contesting the primacy of the International Tribunal, is ill-founded and must be dismissed. . . .

65. Appellant's third ground of appeal is the claim that the International Tribunal lacks subject-matter jurisdiction over the crimes alleged.

The Tribunal first considered and rejected the appellant's contention that there was no armed conflict, whether national or international, at the time and place that his alleged offences were committed. The tribunal then considered whether Articles 2, 3 and 5 were limited in scope to international armed conflict, as the appellant claimed. Having examined the nature of the conflict in the former Yugoslavia and the intention of the Security Council, it concluded:

77. On the basis of the foregoing, we conclude that the conflicts in the former Yugoslavia have both internal and international aspects, that the

members of the Security Council clearly had both aspects of the conflicts in mind when they adopted the Statute of the International Tribunal, and that they intended to empower the International Tribunal to adjudicate violations of humanitarian law that occurred in either context. To the extent possible under existing international law, the Statute should therefore be construed to give effect to that purpose. . . .

Examining the terms of Articles 2 and 3, the Tribunal concluded (i) that the wording "grave breaches" limited Article 2 to offences committed in international armed conflict, but that Article 3 extended to internal conflicts also. On Article 3, the Tribunal stated:

91. Article 3 thus confers on the International Tribunal jurisdiction over *any* serious offence against international humanitarian law not covered by Article 2, 4 or 5. Article 3 is a fundamental provision laying down that any "serious violation of international humanitarian law" must be prosecuted by the International Tribunal. In other words, Article 3 functions as a residual clause designed to ensure that no serious violation of international humanitarian law is taken away from the jurisdiction of the International Tribunal. Article 3 aims to make such jurisdiction watertight and inescapable. . . .

94. The Appeals Chamber deems it fitting to specify the conditions to be fulfilled for Article 3 to become applicable. The following requirements must be met for an offence to be subject to prosecution before the International Tribunal under Article 3:

(i) the violation must constitute an infringement of a rule of international humanitarian law;
(ii) the rule must be customary in nature or, if it belongs to treaty law, the required conditions must be met (see below, para. 143);
(iii) the violation must be "serious", that is to say, it must constitute a breach of a rule protecting important values, and the breach must involve grave consequences for the victim. Thus, for instance, the fact of a combatant simply appropriating a loaf of bread in an occupied village would not amount to a "serious violation of international humanitarian law" although it may be regarded as falling foul of the basic principle laid down in Article 46, paragraph 1, of the Hague Regulations (and the corresponding rule of customary international law) whereby "private property must be respected" by any army occupying an enemy territory;
(iv) the violation of the rule must entail, under customary or conventional law, the individual criminal responsibility of the person breaching the rule.

It follows that it does not matter whether the "serious violation" has occurred within the context of an international or an internal armed conflict, as long as the requirements set out above are met. . . .

With regard to the requirement of individual responsibility, the Tribunal stated:

128. Even if customary international law includes certain basic principles applicable to both internal and international armed conflicts, Appellant argues that such prohibitions do not entail individual criminal responsibility when breaches are committed in internal armed conflicts; these provisions cannot, therefore, fall within the scope of the International Tribunal's jurisdiction. It is true that, for example, common Article 3 of the Geneva Conventions contains no explicit reference to criminal liability for violation of its provisions. Faced with similar claims with respect to the various agreements and conventions that formed the basis of its jurisdiction, the International Military Tribunal at Nuremberg [see above, p. 738] concluded that a finding of individual criminal responsibility is not barred by the absence of treaty provisions on punishment of breaches. . . .

The Nuremberg Tribunal considered a number of factors relevant to its conclusion that the authors of particular prohibitions incur individual responsibility: the clear and unequivocal recognition of the rules of warfare in international law and State practice indicating an intention to criminalize the prohibition, including statements by government officials and international organizations, as well as punishment of violations by national courts and military tribunals. . . .

129. Applying the foregoing criteria to the violations at issue here, we have no doubt that they entail individual criminal responsibility, regardless of whether they are committed in internal or international armed conflicts. Principles and rules of humanitarian law reflect "elementary considerations of humanity" widely recognized as the mandatory minimum for conduct in armed conflicts of any kind. No one can doubt the gravity of the acts at issue, nor the interest of the international community in their prohibition.

130. Furthermore, many elements of international practice show that States intend to criminalize serious breaches of customary rules and principles on internal conflicts. As mentioned above, during the Nigerian Civil War, both members of the Federal Army and rebels were brought before Nigerian courts and tried for violations of principles of international humanitarian law (see paras. 106 and 125). . . .

The Tribunal then cited examples of national military law (in Germany, the U.K., the U.S., New Zealand, etc.) under which breaches of common Article 3 engaged individual criminal liability.

133. Of great relevance to the formation of *opinio juris* to the effect that violations of general international humanitarian law governing internal armed conflicts entail the criminal responsibility of those committing or ordering those violations are certain resolutions unanimously adopted by the Security Council. Thus, for instance, in two resolutions on Somalia,

where a civil strife was under way, the Security Council unanimously condemned breaches of humanitarian law and stated that the authors of such breaches or those who had ordered their commission would be held "individually responsible" for them. (See S.C. Res. 794 (3 December 1992); S.C. Res. 814 (26 March 1993).)

134. All of these factors confirm that customary international law imposes criminal liability for serious violations of common Article 3, as supplemented by other general principles and rules on the protection of victims of internal armed conflict, and for breaching certain fundamental principles and rules regarding means and methods of combat in civil strife.

135. It should be added that, in so far as it applies to offences committed in the former Yugoslavia, the notion that serious violations of international humanitarian law governing internal armed conflicts entail individual criminal responsibility is also fully warranted from the point of view of substantive justice and equity. . . . such violations were punishable under the Criminal Code of the Socialist Federal Republic of Yugoslavia and the law implementing the two Additional Protocols of 1977. The same violations have been made punishable in the Republic of Bosnia and Herzegovina by virtue of the decree-law of 11 April 1992. Nationals of the former Yugoslavia as well as, at present, those of Bosnia-Herzegovina were therefore aware, or should have been aware, that they were amenable to the jurisdiction of their national criminal courts in cases of violation of international humanitarian law. . . .

137. In the light of the intent of the Security Council and the logical and systematic interpretation of Article 3 as well as customary international law, the Appeals Chamber concludes that, under Article 3, the International Tribunal has jurisdiction over the acts alleged in the indictment, regardless of whether they occurred within an internal or international armed conflict. Thus, to the extent that Appellant's challenge to jurisdiction under Article 3 is based on the nature of the underlying conflict, the motion must be denied.

138. Article 5 of the Statute confers jurisdiction over crimes against humanity... As noted by the Secretary-General in his Report on the Statute [of the Tribunal (1993) 32 I.L.M. 1159], crimes against humanity were first recognized in the trials of war criminals following World War II. (Report of the Secretary-General, at para. 47.) The offence was defined in Article 6, paragraph 2(c) of the Nuremberg Charter and subsequently affirmed in the 1948 General Assembly Resolution affirming the Nuremberg principles.

141. It is by now a settled rule of customary international law that crimes against humanity do not require a connection to international armed conflict. Indeed, as the Prosecutor points out, customary international law may not require a connection between crimes against humanity and any conflict at all. Thus, by requiring that crimes against humanity be committed in either internal or international armed conflict,

the Security Council may have defined the crime in Article 5 more narrowly than necessary under customary international law. There is no question, however, that the definition of crimes against humanity adopted by the Security Council in Article 5 comports with the principle of *nullum crimen sine lege*.

142. We conclude, therefore, that Article 5 may be invoked as a basis of jurisdiction over crimes committed in either internal or international armed conflicts. . . . Therefore, the Appellant's challenge to the jurisdiction of the International Tribunal under Article 5 must be dismissed.

The Appeals Chamber decided that (i) the Tribunal was empowered to pronounce on the plea challenging the legality of its establishment of the Tribunal (four votes to one, Judge Li dissenting); (ii) the plea was dismissed (unanimously); (iii) the challenge to the primacy of the Tribunal over national courts was dismissed (unanimously); (iv) the Tribunal had subject-matter jurisdiction over the case (four votes to one, Judge Sidhwa dissenting). Accordingly, the jurisdiction of the Tribunal in the case was affirmed and the appeal dismissed.

Note[76]
Tadic was later convicted on counts involving grave breaches of the Geneva Conventions (Article 2, Tribunal Statute), violations of the laws and customs of war (Article 3, Tribunal Statute) and crimes against humanity (Article 5, Tribunal Statute).[77] He was sentenced to life imprisonment.

---

[76] On the ICTY, see Bassiouni and Hanikos, The Law of the International Criminal Tribunal for Former Yugoslavia (1996); Greenwood (1993) 69 Int. Affairs 641; Harris and Scharf An Insider's Guide to the International Criminal Tribunal for Former Yugoslavia (1995); O'Brien (1993) 87 A.J.I.L. 639; Shraga and Zachlin (1993) 5 E.J.I.L. 360. On the Tadic jurisdictional appeal, see Aldrich (1996) 90 A.J.I.L. 64; Alvarec (1996) 7 E.J.I.L. 265; Rowe (1996) 45 I.C.L.Q. 691.

[77] Proscutor v. Tadic (1997) 4 I.H.R.R. 645; (1997) I.L.M. 908.

CHAPTER 10

THE LAW OF TREATIES

1. INTRODUCTORY NOTE[1]

THE special importance of the law of treaties in international law scarcely needs emphasis. The treaty is the ubiquitous instrument through which all kinds of international transactions are conducted. It is also the closest analogy to legislation that international law has to offer. Although being challenged in this latter role by the General Assembly resolution, the multilateral treaty remains the best medium available at the moment for imposing binding rules of precision and details in the new areas into which international law is expanding[2] and for codifying, clarifying and supplementing the customary law already in existence in more familiar settings.

Given the extent to which treaties have long been woven into the fabric of international law, it is more than a little disappointing to find that the law governing them is in no happier a position than that of most other areas of customary international law. Whereas some rules are clear, a high proportion of them are not. In this situation, the adoption of the Vienna Convention on the Law of Treaties[3] in 1969 was particularly welcome. Like a number of other law–making treaties, it is based upon Draft Articles, supplemented by an invaluable Commentary, produced by the International Law Commission.[4] Like those Conventions also, it is a compound of codification and of progressive development of customary international law.

Although the Convention does not have retroactive effect,[5] the materials in this chapter are moulded around it. This is so because of the great impact that the

---

[1] See Detter, *Essays on the Law of Treaties* (1967); Elias, *The Modern Law of Treaties* (1974); Reuter, *Introduction to the Law of Treaties* (2nd ed., 1995, trans. and revisd by Mico and Haggenmacher); Rosenne, *Developments in the Law of Treaties 1945–1986* (1989); Sinclair, *The Vienna Convention on the Law of Treaties* (2nd ed., 1984); and McNair, *Treaties*. The last of these is the classic work on the subject.

[2] *e.g.* human rights law and environmental law.

[3] U.K.T.S. 58 (1980), Cmnd. 7964; 1155 U.N.T.S. 331; (1969) 8 I.L.M. 679; (1969) 63 A.J.I.L. 875. In force 1980. 81 parties, including the U.K. The Convention was adopted on May 22, 1969, by the United Nations Conference on the Law of Treaties held at Vienna in two sessions in 1968 and 1969. See *UN Conference on the Law of Treaties, First and Second Session 1968 and 1969, Official Records*, UN Docs. A/Conf. 39/11 and Add 1. These are referred to in this chapter as *Treaty Conference Records*, 1968, 1969.

[4] For the text of the Draft Articles and the Commentary, see Y.B.I.L.C., 1966, II, pp. 177–274; (1967) 61 A.J.I.L. 263–463. Also of great value are the reports presented to the I.L.C. by its four Special Rapporteurs, who were, in chronological order, Brierly, Lauterpacht, Fitzmaurice and Waldock. The reports are printed in the *Yearbooks* of the I.L.C. on the Vienna Conference and Convention, see Kearney and Dalton (1970) 64 A.J.I.L. 495; Rosenne, *The Law of Treaties: A Guide to the Legislative History of the Vienna Convention* (1970); Sinclair (1970) 19 I.C.L.Q. 47. See also Rosenne (1966) 41 Wash. L.R. 261.

[5] Art. 4 of the Convention reads: "Without prejudice to the application of any rules set forth in the present Convention to which treaties would be subject under international law independently of the Convention, the Convention applies only to treaties which are

Convention, which was adopted by 79 votes to 1, with 19 abstentions,[6] has been in reinforcing and advancing customary international law.[7] Most of the law of treaties is "lawyers' law" over which the political interests of states do not clash. In this situation, and although certain doctrinal legal disputes (*e.g.* that on treaty interpretation) exist and some difficult issues (*e.g.* the law of reservations and material breach) are glossed over, the common interest of states in having a coherent, detailed and workable set of rules for their day-to-day international transactions has enhanced the attractiveness of the rules conveniently set out in the Convention. Less certain is the effect of the solutions offered by the Convention to the relatively few politically controversial questions concerning the substantive rules of the law of treaties (*e.g.* that concerning the doctrine of "unequal treaties") although the idea of *ius cogens* has now taken root.

2. General Considerations

McNAIR, THE FUNCTIONS AND DIFFERING LEGAL CHARACTER OF TREATIES

(1930) 11 B.Y.I.L. 100. Footnotes omitted

The internal laws of the modern state provide its members with a variety of legal instruments for the regulation of life within that community: the contract; the conveyance or assignment of immovable or movable property, which may be made for valuable consideration or may be a gift or an exchange; the gratuitous promise clothed in a particular form; the charter or private Act of Parliament creating a corporation; legislation, which may be constituent, such as a written constitution, fragmentary or complete, or may be declaratory of existing law, or create a new law, or codify

concluded by States after the entry into force of the present Convention with regard to such States." On Art. 4, see McDade (1986) 35 I.C.L.Q. 499. On the law of treaties governing the relations between parties and non-parties to the Vienna Convention, see Vierdag (1982) 76 A.J.I.L. 779.

[6] *Treaty Conference Records*, 1969, pp. 206–207. France dissented. It objected to the provisions on *ius cogens* and the procedures providing for the settlement of disputes: *ibid.* p. 203. A lot of the abstentions were by members of the Soviet bloc who objected to the failure of the Convention to adopt the principle of universality of participation in multilateral law-making treaties. They felt that all states should be entitled to participate in such treaties: *ibid.* pp. 204–208. The Soviet bloc was concerned, for example, with the position of East Germany, Mainland China, North Korea and North Vietnam, which were not invited to Vienna. The Vienna Convention itself is open "for signature by all States, Members of the United Nations or of any of the specialised agencies or of the International Atomic Energy Agency or parties to the Statute of the International Court of Justice, and by any other state invited by the General Assembly of the United Nations to become a party to the Convention . . . " (Convention, Art. 81). Some other abstentions were based on the inadequacy of the procedures providing for the settlement of disputes: *ibid.*

[7] Note the reliance placed upon the Convention by the I.C.J. in the *Legal Consequences* case, see below, p. 843; the *Fisheries Jurisdiction Cases*, below, p. 847; and the *Maritime Delimitation and Territorial Questions* case (Qatar v. Bahrain), I.C.J. Rep. 1995, p. 6 at p. 18; and by the Law Officers of the Crown in 1971 in connection with the Simonstown Agreements. The law officers stated that the "rules of international law for the interpretation of treaties have recently been declared in the Vienna Convention . . . ": Cmnd. 4589, p. 5.

existing law with comparatively unimportant changes. Further, though rarely, we may find a constitutional document which closely resembles the international treaty itself, for instance, Magna Carta.

It would not be suggested that all these differing private law transactions are governed by rules of universal or even of general application, and yet such is the underlying assumption of international lawyers in dealing with the only and sadly overworked instrument with which international society is equipped for the purpose of carrying out its multifarious transactions. Thus, if international society wishes to enact a fundamental, organic, constitutional law, such as the Covenant of the League of Nations was intended to be and in large measure is in fact, it employs the treaty. If two states wish to put on record their adherence to the principle of the three-mile limit of territorial waters, as in the first article of the Anglo-American Liquor Convention of 1924, they use a treaty. If further they wish to enter into a bargain which derogates from that principle, again they use a treaty. If Denmark wishes to sell to the United States of America her West Indian possessions, as she did in 1916, or if Great Britain wishes to cede Heligoland to Germany in return for a recognition of certain British rights in Africa, as happened in 1890, they do so by treaty. Again, if the great European Powers are engaged upon one of their periodic resettlements and determine upon certain permanent dispositions to which they wish to give the force of "the public law of Europe," they must do it by treaty. And if it is desired to create an international organization such as the International Union for the Protection of Works of Art and Literature, which resembles the corporation of private law, it is done by treaty.

Notes

The above extract serves to illustrate the variety of purposes for which treaties are used and to raise the question, with which the author was concerned, of the problems that result for the law of treaties in having a single body of rules that covers all types of treaties. The question is one that needs to be borne in mind when reading the materials in the remainder of this chapter.

VIENNA CONVENTION ON THE LAW OF TREATIES 1969

Loc. cit., p. 765, n. 3, above

Article 1

The present Convention applies to treaties between States.

Article 2

1. For the purposes of the present Convention:

(a) "treaty" means an international agreement concluded between States in written form and governed by international law, whether embodied in a single instrument or in two or more related instruments and whatever its particular designation; . . .

Article 3

The fact that the present Convention does not apply to international agreements concluded between States and other subjects of international law or between such other subjects of international law, or to international agreements not in written form, shall not affect:

(*a*) the legal force of such agreements;
(*b*) the application to them of any of the rules set forth in the present Convention to which they would be subject under international law independently of the Convention;
(*c*) the application of the Convention to the relations of States as between themselves under international agreements to which other subjects of international law are also parties.

Article 5

The present Convention applies to any treaty which is the constituent instrument of an international organization and to any treaty adopted within an international organization without prejudice to any relevant rules of the organization.

Article 6

Every State possesses capacity to conclude treaties.

Notes

1. *Capacity to make treaties.* The Convention reflects customary international law in providing that *states* may make treaties. Capacity to make treaties is, in fact, valuable evidence of statehood.[8] According to the International Law Commission's Commentary, the term "state" is used in Article 6 "with the same meaning as in the Charter of the United Nations, the Statute of the Court, the Geneva Convention on Diplomatic Relations; *i.e.* it means a State for the purposes of international law."[9]

The International Law Commission's Draft Articles contained a second paragraph to Article 6 concerning *federal states* which read as follows:

States members of a federal union may possess a capacity to conclude treaties if such capacity is admitted by the federal constitution and within the limits there laid down.[10]

[8] See above, p. 101 *et seq.*
[9] Y.B.I.L.C., 1966, II, p. 192.
[10] Y.B.I.L.C., 1966, II, p. 191. See on federal states, Di Marzo (1978) 16 C.Y.I.L. For an example of a "federal clause" in a treaty which limits the responsibility of the federal government for the action of units within the federation, see the 1969 American Convention on Human Rights, Art. 28.

The Commentary to it reads:

> More frequently, the treaty-making capacity is vested exclusively in the federal government, but there is no rule of international law which precludes the component States from being invested with the power to conclude treaties with third States. Questions may arise in some cases as to whether the component State concludes the treaty as an organ of the federal State or in its own right. But on this point also the solution must be sought in the provisions of the federal constitution.[11]

An example of a federal state in which units within the federation have the power to make treaties is Germany.[12] The final text of the Vienna Convention omitted this paragraph. The difficulty it presented, which was mentioned by several delegations from federal states, was that the Vienna Convention had been limited to treaties made by "states" and had excluded those made by other subjects of international law. It was therefore, it was thought, inconsistent to include a provision concerning units within a federal state which "even if the law conferred upon them a certain capacity to conclude international agreements . . . could not be assimilated in general to States . . . ."[13]

Occasionally *colonial and similar territories* on their way to independence have been recognised as having treaty-making powers. Some former British colonies have been in this position.[14] Thus Australia, Canada, India, New Zealand and South Africa were invited to participate in the Peace Conference at Paris in 1919 and became parties to the Treaty of Versailles and founder members of the League of Nations.

The decision not to extend the Vienna Convention to treaties to which *public international organisations* are parties was explained by the International Law Commission in its Commentary as follows:

> Treaties concluded by international organisations have many special characteristics; and the Commission considered that it would both unduly complicate and delay the drafting of the present articles if it were to attempt to include in them satisfactory provisions concerning treaties of international organisations.[15]

The 1986 Convention on the Law of Treaties between States and International Organisations or between International Organisations[16] confirms that international organisations have the capacity to enter into treaties in accordance with the

---

[11] *ibid.* p. 192.

[12] Art. 32(3) of the Bonn Constitution reads: "Insofar as the *Länder* have power to legislate, they may, with the consent of the Federal Government, conclude treaties with foreign states." Thus, for example the *Länder* of Baden-Wurttemberg and Bavaria are parties with Austria and Switzerland to a "Convention for the Protection of Lake Constance against Pollution of 27th October, 1960," printed as Appendix 7 in *Fresh Water Pollution Control,* Council of Europe, 1966.

[13] Mr Groepper (West Germany), *Treaty Conference Records,* 1969, p. 8. See the discussion generally, *ibid.* pp. 6–15.

[14] See Fawcett, *The British Commonwealth in International Law* (1963), pp. 144. *et seq.*

[15] Y.B.I.L.C., 1966, II, p. 187. See also Chiu, *The Capacity of International Organisations to Conclude Treaties* (1966). And see the *Reparation Case,* above, p. 132.

[16] Misc. 11 (1987), Cm. 244; (1986) 25 I.L.M. 543. Not in force. 35 parties required; 23 at present, including the U.K. The Convention contains a detailed legal regime modelled closely upon the 1969 Vienna Convention on the Law of Treaties. See Gaja (1987) 58 B.Y.I.L. 253; Isak and Loibl (1987) 38 O.Z.O.R.V. 49; Menon *The Law of Treaties Between States and International Organisations* (1992).

rules of the organisation, *i.e.* the "constituent instruments, decisions and resolutions adopted in accordance with them, and established practice of the organisation" (Article 6). In most cases, the capacity will derive from implied powers based upon "established practice."

Article 3 of the Vienna Convention, however, recognises that at customary international law entities other than states may have the international personality necessary to allow them to make treaties.

Individuals have never been recognised as having the capacity to make treaties, whether with states, or with other international persons with treaty-making capacity. The question has in recent years been discussed in the context of agreements between large municipal law companies and states, particularly agreements for the exploitation of oil. The nearest that the International Court of Justice has come to considering the question was in the *Anglo-Iranian Oil Company* case[17] in which it rejected an argument to the effect that a contract between Iran and the Anglo-Iranian Oil Company, a British company, was a treaty because of the part played by the United Kingdom Government in its negotiations. The Court stated:

> It is nothing more than a concessionary contract between a government and a foreign corporation.[18]

The Mandate for South West Africa was "an international agreement having the character of a treaty."[19] Are declarations accepting the compulsory jurisdiction of the International Court of Justice?[20]

2. *Intention to create legal relations.* This requirement, which is found in the law of contract in municipal law, is not mentioned in the Vienna Convention. The International Law Commission's Fourth Special Rapporteur stated that:

> in so far as this [requirement] may be relevant in any case, the element of intention is embraced in the phrase "governed by international law."[21]

States not infrequently wish to reach an agreement without going to the extent of making it enforceable at law. The Final Act of the Helsinki Conference on Security and Co-operation in Europe 1975[22] is an example.[23] The Act was stated to be "not eligible for registration under Article 102 of the Charter of the United Nations."[24] It was understood during the Conference that the Act would not be binding in law.[25]

---

[17] I.C.J. Rep. 1952, p. 93.
[18] *ibid.* p. 112. See further on such contracts, above, p. 573 *et seq.*
[19] *South Africa (Preliminary Objections)* cases, I.C.J. Rep. 1962 at p. 330.
[20] See below, p. 1004.
[21] Fourth Report on the Law of Treaties, Y.B.I.L.C., 1965, II, p. 12. On the law governing a treaty, see below, p. 771.
[22] (1975) 14 I.L.M. 1292.
[23] Note, however, the I.C.J.'s reliance on the Final Act in the *Nicaragua (Merits)* cases, below, p. 871. Other examples are the 1977 Gleneagles Agreement on Sporting Contacts with South Africa, *Kessing's Archives*, p. 28507 (text), and the 1978 Bonn Declaration on International Terrorism, *loc. cit.*, at p. 299, n. 24, above. See Aust (1986) 35 I.C.L.Q. 788; Busuttil (1982) 31 *ibid.* 474; and Johnson (1959) 35 B.Y.I.L. 1. Such agreement form a part of "soft" international law, as to which see above, p. 65.
[24] Final (unnumbered) clauses.
[25] Russell (1977) 70 A.J.I.L. 242 at 246. And see Schachter (1978) 71 *ibid.* p. 296.

On the question whether intention to create legal relations is to be presumed when agreements are made between states, contrast the views of Fawcett[26] and Mann.[27]

3. *"Governed by international law."* The International Law Commission's Fourth Special Rapporteur stated in his First Report.[28]

> ... The Commission felt in 1959 that the element of subjection to international law is so essential a part of an international agreement that it should be expressly mentioned in the definition. There may be agreements between States, such as agreements for the acquisition of premises for a diplomatic mission or for some purely commercial transaction, the incidents of which are regulated by the local law of one of the parties or by a private law system determined by reference to conflict of laws principles. Whether in such cases the two States are internationally accountable to each other at all may be a nice question; but even if that were held to be so, it would not follow that the basis of their international accountability was a treaty obligation. At any rate, the Commission was clear that it ought to confine the notion of an "international agreement" for the purposes of the law of treaties to one the whole formation and execution of which (as well as the obligation to execute) is governed by international law.

Article 2 of the Vienna Convention does not indicate the test to be used in determining whether an agreement between states is governed by international law. What should be the test? The intention of the parties? The subject-matter of the agreement? Should there be a presumption that an inter-state agreement which is intended to create legal relations is governed by international law?[29]

4. *Nomenclature.* The Vienna Convention adopts the term "treaty," not the term "agreement," as the generic term. In practice, a whole host of terms are used interchangeably with no legal significance turning upon the choice of one or another. The International Law Commission's Commentary reads:

> Thus, in addition to "treaty," "convention" and "protocol," one not infrequently finds titles such as "declaration," "charter," "covenant," "pact," "act," "statute," "agreement," "concordat," whilst names like "declaration," "agreement" and "modus vivendi" may well be found given both to formal and less formal types of agreements. As to the latter, their nomenclature is almost illimitable, even if some names such as "agreement," "exchange of notes," "exchange of letters," "memorandum of agreement," or "agreed minute" may be more common than others. It is true that some types of instruments are used more frequently for some purposes rather than others; it is also true that some titles are more frequently attached to some types of transaction rather than to others. But there is no exclusive or systematic use of nomenclature for particular types of transaction.[30]

"Exchange of notes" and "Exchange of letters" take the form of an exchange of correspondence between States and often read not unlike the offer and acceptance letters familiar to any student of the law of contract. A treaty may also take the

---

[26] (1953) 30 B.Y.I.L. 381 at pp. 385–400 (no presumption).

[27] (1957) 33 B.Y.I.L. 20 at pp. 30–32 (there is a presumption). See also Widdows (1979) 50 B.Y.I.L. 117.

[28] Y.B.I.L.C., 1962, II, p. 32.

[29] See Mann (1944) 21 B.Y.I.L. 11 at 22–28; *ibid.* (1974) 68 A.J.I.L. 490; and Widdows, *loc. cit.*, n. 27 above.

[30] Y.B.I.L.C., 1966 II, 188. On the "memorandum of understanding", see McNeill (1994) 88 A.J.I.L. 821.

form of a joint communiqué issued by Government Ministers to the press at the end of a meeting, provided the necessary intention to enter into legal relations is present.[31]

5. *Consideration.* Treaties do not require consideration in the sense of the common law of contract. Territory, for example, can be ceded by treaty without consideration.

LEGAL STATUS OF EASTERN GREENLAND

Denmark *v.* Norway (1933)

P.C.I.J. Reports, Series A/B, No. 53

In addition to claiming sovereignty over Greenland in this case on the basis of occupation (see the summary above, p. 203), Denmark also argued that Norway had recognised Danish sovereignty over the island by the "Ihlen Declaration." M. Ihlen was the Norwegian Foreign Minister. In conversations on July 14, 1919, with the Danish Minister accredited to Norway, the latter suggested to M. Ihlen that Denmark would raise no objection to any claim Norway might want to make at the Paris Peace Conference to Spitzbergen if Norway would not oppose the claim that Denmark was to make at the same Conference to the whole of Greenland. On July 22, 1919, M. Ihlen, in the course of further conversations with the Danish Minister, declared that "the Norwegian Government would not make any difficulty" concerning the Danish claim. These were the terms used as they were minuted by M. Ihlen for his Government's own purposes. Denmark argued before the Court that this undertaking was binding upon Norway. Judge Anzilotti agreed with the Court on this point.

Judgment of the Court

This declaration by M. Ihlen has been relied on by Counsel for Denmark as a recognition of an existing Danish sovereignty in Greenland. The Court is unable to accept this point of view. A careful examination of the words used and of the circumstances in which they were used, as well as of the subsequent developments, shows that M. Ihlen cannot have meant to be giving then and there a definitive recognition of Danish sovereignty over Greenland, and shows also that he cannot have been understood by the Danish Government at the time as having done so. In the text of M. Ihlen's minute, submitted by the Norwegian Government, which has not been disputed by the Danish Government, the phrase used by M. Ihlen is couched in the future tense: "ne fera pas de difficultés"; he had been informed that it was at the Peace Conference that the Danish Government intended to bring up the question: and two years later —when assurances had been received from the Principal Allied Powers —the Danish Government made a further application to the Norwegian Government to obtain the recognition which they desired of Danish sovereignty over all Greenland.

---

[31] *Aegean Sea* case, I.C.J. Rep. 1978, p. 39. It does not matter that, as in that case, the communiqué is not signed or initialled.

Nevertheless, the point which must now be considered is whether the Ihlen declaration—even if not constituting a definitive recognition of Danish sovereignty—did not constitute an engagement obliging Norway to refrain from occupying any part of Greenland.

... It is clear from the relevant Danish documents which preceded the Danish Minister's démarche at Christiania on July 14th, 1919, that the Danish attitude in the Spitzbergen question and the Norwegian attitude in the Greenland question were regarded in Denmark as interdependent, and this interdependence appears to be reflected also in M. Ihlen's minute of the interview. Even if this interdependence—which, in view of the affirmative reply of the Norwegian Government, in whose name the Minister for Foreign Affairs was speaking, would have created a bilateral engagement—is not held to have been established, it can hardly be denied that what Denmark was asking of Norway ("not to make any difficulties in the settlement of the [Greenland] question") was equivalent to what she was indicating her readiness to concede in the Spitzbergen question (to refrain from opposing "the wishes of Norway in regard to the settlement of this question"). What Denmark desired to obtain from Norway was that the latter should do nothing to obstruct the Danish plans in regard to Greenland. The declaration which the Minister for Foreign Affairs gave on July 22nd, 1919, on behalf of the Norwegian Government, was definitely affirmative: "I told the Danish Minister today that the Norwegian Government would not make any difficulty in the settlement of this question."

The Court considers it beyond all dispute that a reply of this nature given by the Minister of Foreign Affairs on behalf of his Government in response to request by the diplomatic representative of a foreign Power, in regard to a question falling within his province, is binding upon the country to which the Minister belongs. ...

It follows that, as a result of the undertaking involved in the Ihlen declaration of July 22, 1919, Norway is under an obligation to refrain from contesting Danish sovereignty over Greenland as a whole, and *a fortiori* to refrain from occupying a part of Greenland.

DISSENTING OPINION OF JUDGE ANZILOTTI. No arbitral or judicial decision relating to the international competence of a Minister for Foreign Affairs has been brought to the knowledge of the Court; nor has this question been exhaustively treated by legal authorities. In my opinion, it must be recognised that the constant and general practice of States has been to invest the Minister for Foreign Affairs—the direct agent of the chief of the State—with authority to make statements on current affairs to foreign diplomatic representatives, and in particular to inform them as to the attitude which the government, in whose name he speaks, will adopt in a given question. Declarations of this kind are binding upon the State.

As regards the question whether Norwegian constitutional law author-ised the Minister for Foreign Affairs to make the declaration, that is a point which, in my opinion, does not concern the Danish Government: it was M. Ihlen's duty to refrain from giving his reply until he had obtained any assent that might be requisite under the Norwegian laws.

Notes

1. Was there an oral treaty in the *Eastern Greenland* case?[32] If not, why was M. Ihlen's declaration binding?

2. The minutes of a Tripartite Committee established by three states to negotiate the referral of a dispute to the I.C.J. were "diplomatic documents recording the state of progress of the negotiations", but "possessed no legally binding force".[33]

3. The Vienna Convention was limited to written treaties "in the interest of clarity and simplicity."[34] The International Law Commission's Commentary reads: "The restriction of the use of the term "treaty" in the draft articles to international agreements expressed in writing is not intended to deny the legal force of oral agreements under international law or to imply that some of the principles contained in later parts of the Commission's draft articles . . . may not have relevance in regard to oral agreements."[35]

4. On the relevance of non-compliance with municipal law requirements, see below, p. 827.

NUCLEAR TEST CASES

Australia *v.* France; New Zealand *v.* France

I.C.J. Reports 1974, pp. 253, 457

For the facts, see above, p. 422. The Court found, by nine votes to six,[36] that "the claim of Australia no longer has any object and that the Court is therefore not called upon to given a decision thereon." The Court reached this conclusion because France had indicated its intention not to hold any further tests in the atmosphere in the South Pacific after its 1974 series of tests. It gave this undertaking by way of a series of unilateral public announcements in that year. The Court considered the legal significance of these statements in the following passage in the judgment in the Australian case. The companion case brought by New Zealand against France resulted in a similar ruling.

Judgment of the Court

34. . . . The first statement is contained in the communiqué issued by the Office of the President of the French Republic on June 8, 1974 . . .

---

[32] See Garner (1933) 27 A.J.I.L. 493; Hambro, *Festschrift Spiropoulos* (1957), p. 227; McNair, *Treaties*, p. 10. On statements by heads of state, etc., see Watts (1994–II) 247 Hague Recueil 9.

[33] *Maritime Delimitation and Territorial Questions Case (Qatar v. Bahrain)*, I.C.J. Rep. 1995, p. 6 at p. 16.

[34] Y.B.I.L.C., p. 10.

[35] *ibid.*

[36] The judges in the majority were President Lachs; Judges Forster, Gros, Bengzon, Petrén, Ignacio-Pinto, Morozov, Nagendra Singh, and Ruda. The dissenting judges were Judges Onyeama, Dillard, de Castro, Jiménez de Aréchaga, Sir Humphrey Waldock; Judge *ad hoc* Sir Garfield Barwick.

The Office of the President of the Republic takes this opportunity of stating that in view of the stage reached in carrying out the French nuclear defence programme France will be in a position to pass on to the stage of underground explosions as soon as the series of tests planned for this summer is completed.

A copy of the communiqué was transmitted with a Note dated June 11, 1974 from the French Embassy in Canberra to the Australian Department of Foreign Affairs . . .

35. . . . At the hearing of July 10, 1974 in [. . . the New Zealand] case, the Attorney-General of New Zealand . . . stated that on June 10, 1974 the French Embassy in Wellington sent a Note to the New Zealand Ministry of Foreign Affairs, containing a [similar] passage . . .

37. The next statement to be considered . . . will be that made on July 25, at a press conference given by the President of the Republic, when he said:

. . . on this question of nuclear tests, you know that the Prime Minister has publicly expressed himself in the National Assembly in his speech introducing the Government's programme. He had indicated that French nuclear testing would continue. I had myself made it clear that this round of atmospheric tests would be the last, and so the members of the Government were completely informed of our intentions in this respect . . .

39. On September 25, 1974, the French Minister for Foreign Affairs, addressing the United Nations General Assembly, said:

We have now reached a stage in our nuclear technology that makes it possible for us to continue our programme by underground testing, and we have taken steps to do so as early as next year.

The French Minister of Defence made similar statements on French television and at a press conference.

43. It is well recognised that declarations made by way of unilateral acts, concerning legal or factual situations, may have the effect of creating legal obligations. Declarations of this kind may be, and often are, very specific. When it is the intention of the State making the declaration that it should become bound according to its terms, that intention confers on the declaration the character of a legal undertaking, the State being thenceforth legally required to follow a course of conduct consistent with the declaration. An undertaking of this kind, if given publicly, and with an intent to be bound, even though not made within the context of

international negotiations, is binding. In these circumstances, nothing in the nature of a *quid pro quo* nor any subsequent acceptance of the declaration, nor even any reply or reaction from other States, is required for the declaration to take effect, since such a requirement would be inconsistent with the strictly unilateral nature of the juridical act by which the pronouncement by the State was made.

44. Of course, not all unilateral acts imply obligation; but a State may choose to take up a certain position in relation to a particular matter with the intention of being bound—the intention is to be ascertained by interpretation of the act. When States make statements by which their freedom of action is to be limited, a restrictive interpretation is called for.

45. With regard to the question of form, it should be observed that this is not a domain in which international law imposes any special or strict requirements. Whether a statement is made orally or in writing makes no essential difference, for such statements made in particular circumstances may create commitments in international law, which does not require that they should be couched in written form . . .

46. One of the basic principles governing the creation and performance of legal obligations, whatever their source, is the principle of good faith. Trust and confidence are inherent in international co-operation, in particular in an age when this co-operation in many fields is becoming increasingly essential. Just as the very rule of *pacta sunt servanda* in the law of treaties is based on good faith, so also is the binding character of an international obligation assumed by unilateral declaration. Thus interested States may take cognizance of unilateral declarations and place confidence in them, and are entitled to require that the obligation thus created be respected . . .

49. Of the statements by the French Government now before the Court, the most essential are clearly those made by the President of the Republic. There can be no doubt, in view of his function, that his public communications or statements, oral or written, as Head of State, are in international relations acts of the French State. His statements, and those of members of the French Government acting under his authority . . . constitute a whole. Thus, in whatever form these statements were expressed, they must be held to constitute an engagement of the State, having regard to their intention and to the circumstances in which they were made . . .

51. In announcing that the 1974 series of atmospheric tests would be the last, the French Government conveyed to the world at large, including the Applicant, its intention effectively to terminate these tests. It was bound to assume that other States might take note of these statements and rely on their being effective. The validity of these statements and their legal consequences must be considered within the general framework of the security of international intercourse, and the confidence and trust which are so essential in the relations among States. It is from the actual substance of these statements, and from the circumstances attending their

making, that the legal implications of the unilateral act must be deduced. The objects of these statements are clear and they were addressed to the international community as a whole, and the Court holds that they constitute an undertaking possessing legal effect.... It is true that the French Government has consistently maintained, for example in a Note dated February 7, 1973 from the French Ambassador in Canberra to the Prime Minister and Minister for Foreign Affairs of Australia, that it "has the conviction that its nuclear experiments have not violated any rule of international law," nor did France recognise that it was bound by any rule of international law to terminate its tests, but this does not affect the legal consequences of the statements examined above. The Court finds that the unilateral undertaking resulting from these statements cannot be interpreted as having been made in implicit reliance on an arbitrary power of reconsideration. The Court finds further that the French Government has undertaken an obligation the precise nature and limits of which must be understood in accordance with the actual terms in which they have been publicly expressed.

DISSENTING OPINION OF JUDGE SIR GARFIELD BARWICK.... Nothing is found as to the duration of the obligation although nothing said in the Judgment would suggest that it is of a temporary nature. There are apparently no qualifications of it related to changes in circumstances or to the varying needs of French security....

... The Judgment finds an intention to enter into a binding legal obligation after giving the warning that statements limiting a State's freedom of action should receive a restrictive interpretation ... I regret to say that I am unable to do so. There seems to be nothing, either in the language used or in the circumstances of its employment, which in my opinion would warrant, and certainly nothing to compel, the conclusion that those making the statements were intending to enter into a solemn and far-reaching international obligation.... I would have thought myself that the more natural conclusion to draw from the various statements was that they were statements of policy....

Notes

Although the undertaking in the *Nuclear Tests* cases could not by any stretch of the imagination be seen as other than unilateral, the cases are most conveniently dealt with in conjunction with the law of treaties. The undertakings were quite different from that in the *Eastern Greenland* case in being made in public, not in the context of negotiations, and without a *quid pro quo*. There seems little evidence to support the rule stated by the Court whereby a state may be bound by a unilateral public pronouncement intended by it to be binding without more.[37] If there is

---

[37] See Rubin (1977) 71 A.J.I.L. 1. See also Franck (1975) 69 A.J.I.L. 612. In the *Frontier Dispute* case, I.C.J. Rep. 1986, p. 554 at p. 573, the Court applied the *Nuclear Tests* case, confirming that intention was crucial.

such a rule, it is submitted that further by way of evidence of intent should be required than was present on the facts of the *Nuclear Tests* cases.

3. THE MAKING OF TREATIES[38]

(i) NOTE ON THE TREATY-MAKING POWER IN MUNICIPAL LAW[39]

Each state is left free by international law to make its own constitutional arrangements for the exercise of its treaty-making power. In the *United Kingdom*, the making of treaties is a prerogative power of the Crown.[40] It is the Crown which issues full powers or other authority to negotiate and sign treaties and which ratifies treaties if this is called for. Approval by Parliament is not required.[41] British practice since 1890 concerning treaties of cession comes close to establishing an exception to this rule. McNair concludes from this practice that:

> it is unlikely that the Crown will agree to cede any territory without being sure that Parliament would approve, or, if in doubt, without inserting a clause making the cession dependent upon Parliamentary approval.[42]

The Crown will occasionally, in its discretion, insert provisions in treaties making their entry into force conditional upon Parliamentary approval.[43] In 1924, the British Government announced the "Ponsonby Rule," as follows:

> It is the intention of His Majesty's Government to lay on the Table of both Houses of Parliament every Treaty, when signed, for a period of 21 days, after which the Treaty will be ratified and published and circulated in the Treaty Series. In the case of important Treaties, the Government will, of course, take an opportunity of submitting them to the House for discussion within this period. . . . But this means secret Treaties and secret clauses of Treaties will be rendered impossible. . . . There are, of course, international conventions of a purely technical character which are not subject to ratification, and there is no reason to alter the procedure with regard to them.[44]

The rule does not affect the position in law. The laying of a treaty before Parliament before ratification is only "to enable Parliament to discuss treaties requiring ratification before ratification [occurs]," it is not legally required. The Rule was discontinued after a change of government in the same year. It was re-introduced in 1929 and has normally applied ever since. It was not complied with in the case of the 1939 Treaty of Mutual Assistance between France, Turkey and the United Kingdom.[45] The Prime Minister explained:

---

[38] See generally, Blix, *Treaty-Making Power* (1960); Holloway, *Modern Trends in Treaty Law* (1967); Jones, *Full Powers and Ratification* (1949). See also Leigh and Blakeslee, *National Treaty Law and Practice* (1995).

[39] On the status of treaties in municipal law, see above, Chap. 3.

[40] See *R. v. Secretary of State, ex p. Rees-Mogg* [1994] 1 All E.R. 457, CA.

[41] On the need, however, for parliamentary legislation if a treaty binding upon the U.K. in international law is to have effect in the municipal law of the U.K. see above, p. 83.

[42] McNair, *Treaties*, p. 97.

[43] See the examples given by McNair, *ibid.* pp. 97–98.

[44] *Hansard*, H.C., Vol. 171, cols. 2003–2004, April 1, 1924.

[45] U.K.T.S. (1940), Cmd. 6165; 213 B.F.S.P. 200; 200 L.N.T.S. 173.

... in view of the exceptional circumstances of the present case, it is desired that the Anglo-French-Turkish Treaty should be ratified as soon as possible.[46]

The Rule has not been applied to the Declaration made by the United Kingdom accepting the compulsory jurisdiction of the International Court of Justice because there is no requirement of ratification.[47]

As of 1997, treaties laid before Parliament under the Ponsonby Rule have been accompanied by an explanatory memorandum which indicates the subject matter of the treaty, the reasons for becoming a party, the financial implications, any implementing legislation that will be required and what consultation has occurred and includes the text of any declarations and reservations made upon signature. Depending on their detail, explanatory memoranda may be relevant in the interpretation of a treaty.[48]

In 1996, a bill proposed by Lord Lester that would have required the approval of Parliament before the United Kingdom could become a party to a treaty was not supported by the Government and failed. Would such approval, which is required in many states and would be democratic, be desirable? Or might it slow down or prevent the United Kingdom becoming a party to some treaties? Note that the United States Senate has refused its consent for the ratification of some human rights treaties submitted to it by the President.

The United States Constitution, Article II, Section 2, states that the President "shall have power by and with the advice and consent of the Senate to make treaties, provided two-thirds of the Senators present concur.... "Distinct from "treaties" are "executive agreements." These are treaties in an international law sense but differ from "treaties" in United States constitutional law in that they are made by the President alone; they are not subject to approval by the United States Senate. There is no express provision for executive agreements in the Constitution; the power to make them is implied.[49]

(ii) THE TREATY-MAKING POWER IN INTERNATIONAL LAW[50]

McNAIR, THE LAW OF TREATIES

2nd ed., 1961, pp. 15–21. Some footnotes omitted

The following are the forms in which treaties are usually cast ...

(a) *Treaties in the form of agreements between states.* Instances of this practice can be found in ... the Treaty of Versailles and other Peace Treaties which concluded the First World War ...

(b) *Treaties in the form of agreements between heads of state,* which may perhaps be described as historically the oldest, and, in practice, the most orthodox, form in the case of treaties of an important character ...

(c) *Agreements in the form of inter-governmental agreements.* This form is now becoming increasingly common, as a perusal of the United Nations Treaty Series will show. It is in keeping with the general tendency

---

[46] *Hansard,* H.C., Vol. 352, col. 1407, October 25, 1939.
[47] *Hansard,* H.C., Vol. 578, cols. 1145–1146, November 27, 1957.
[48] Dr Fox, Minister of State, F.C.O., *Hansard,* H.L. Vol. XX, W.A. 430. December 16, 1996.
[49] On the definition of executive agreements, see [1973] U.S. D.I.L. 185.
[50] See Parry (1950) 36 Trans.Grot.Soc. 149.

towards informality. For the United Kingdom it means that no intervention on the part of Her Majesty is required and no use of the Great Seal, and Full Powers are issued by the Secretary of State for Foreign Affairs under his own signature and seal of office. It has become the regular form for agreements made between the Commonwealth countries; its convenience in such cases is manifest. . . .

Most Exchanges of Notes, now very common, fall into the category of inter-governmental agreements.

It is broadly true to say that the United Kingdom Government prefers to reserve the inter-governmental form for agreements of secondary importance or of a non-political character, but that is becoming increasingly difficult. . . .

(d) *Agreements expressed as made between Departments, or ministers, or other subordinate organs or agencies of Governments.* The following extract from the *Laws and Practices concerning the Conclusions of Treaties*[51] states the practice of the United Kingdom in this matter:

6. As regards inter-departmental agreements (*i.e.* agreements concluded directly between the Government Departments of different States) these agreements are, generally speaking, arrangements which concern matters of private law rather than matters of an international legal character (*e.g.* arrangements for, or in connection with, the purchase of goods, or for the sale on a commercial basis of materials or supplies) and are not such as would be normally registrable under Article 102 of the Charter of the United Nations. An example of such an agreement is the Agreement of 29 August 1949 between the United Kingdom Minister of Food and the Norwegian Director of Fisheries regarding the landing of fresh white fish in the United Kingdom from Norwegian fishing vessels. This Agreement was signed, on the one part, by an Assistant Secretary to the Ministry of Food on behalf of the Minister of Food and, on the other part, by the Norwegian Director of Fisheries.

What is important, is that this practice must not be allowed to obscure the fact that the real contracting parties are States. . . .

It is, however, necessary in view of the complexity and variety of organs, central or local, through which functions of government (including sometimes commercial activities) are discharged in the modern State, to be alert to the difference between an organ or agency of the central Government and capable of binding it, on the one hand, and, on the other, an organ, whether local or not, which possesses a legal personality distinct from the State itself and has no such capacity. It is believed that it is true only of an organ or agency of the central Government to say that its agreements bind the State; but the precise relation of certain departments to the central Government varies greatly in different States, and every case requires separate consideration upon its facts.

---

[51] UN Doc. ST/LEG/SER.B/3, p. 121.

VIENNA CONVENTION ON THE LAW OF TREATIES 1969

Loc. cit., p. 765, n. 3, above

Article 7

1. A person is considered as representing a State for the purpose of adopting or authenticating the text of a treaty or for the purpose of expressing the consent of the State to be bound by a treaty if:

(a) he produces appropriate full powers[52]; or
(b) it appears from the practice of the States concerned or from other circumstances that their intention was to consider that person as representing the State for such purposes and to dispense with full powers.

2. In virtue of their functions and without having to produce full powers, the following are considered as representing their State:

(a) Heads of States, Heads of Government and Ministers for Foreign Affairs,[53] for the purpose of performing all acts relating to the conclusion of a treaty;
(b) heads of diplomatic missions, for the purpose of adopting the text of a treaty between the accrediting State and the State to which they are accredited;
(c) representatives accredited by States to an international conference or to an international organisation or one of its organs, for the purpose of adopting the text of a treaty in that conference, organisation or organ.

Notes
The International Law Commission's Commentary reads:

> ... the production of full powers is the fundamental safeguard to the representatives of the States concerned of each other's qualifications to represent their State for the purpose of performing the particular act in question;
> ... it is for the States to decide whether they may safely dispense with the production of full powers. In earlier times the production of full powers was almost invariably requested; and it is still common in the conclusion of more formal types of treaty. But a considerable proportion of modern treaties are

---

[52] *Ed*. The term "full powers" is defined in Art. 2(1)(c) of the Convention as "a document emanating from the competent authority of a State designating a person or persons to represent the State for negotiating, adopting or authenticating the text of a treaty, for expressing the consent of the State to be bound by a treaty, or for accomplishing any other act with respect to a treaty."
[53] *Ed*. See the *Eastern Greenland* case, above p. 772.

concluded in simplified form, when more often than not the production of full powers is not required.[54]

Article 8

An act relating to the conclusion of a treaty performed by a person who cannot be considered under Article 7 as authorised to represent a State for that purpose is without legal effect unless afterwards confirmed by that State.

Notes
The International Law Commissions's Commentary reads:

Such cases [of acting without authority] are not, of course, likely to happen frequently, but instances have occurred. . . . In 1951 a convention concerning the naming of cheeses concluded at Stresa was signed by a delegate on behalf of Norway and Sweden, whereas it appears that he had authority to do so only from the former country. In both these instances the treaty was subject to ratification and was in fact ratified. A further case, in which the same question may arise, and one more likely to occur in practice, is where an agent has authority to enter into a particular treaty, but goes beyond his full powers by accepting unauthorised extensions or modifications of it. An instance of such a case was Persia's attempt, in discussions in the Council of the League, to disavow the Treaty of Erzerum of 1847 on the ground that the Persian representative had gone beyond his authority in accepting a certain explanatory note when exchanging ratifications.
. . . Where there is no authority to enter into a treaty, it seems clear, on principle, that the State must be entitled to disavow the act of its representative, and the article so provides. On the other hand, it seems equally clear that, notwithstanding the representative's original lack of authority, the State may afterwards endorse his act and thereby establish its consent to be bound by the treaty. It will also be held to have done so by implication if it invokes the provisions of the treaty or otherwise acts in such a way as to appear to treat the act of its representative as effective.[55]

Article 9

1. The adoption of the text of a treaty takes place by the consent of all the States participating in its drawing up except as provided in paragraph 2.
2. The adoption of the text of a treaty at an international conference takes place by the vote of two-thirds of the States present and voting, unless by the same majority they shall decide to apply a different rule.

Notes
The International Law Commission's Commentary reads:

In former times the adoption of the text of a treaty almost always took place by the agreement of all the States participating in the negotiations and unanimity

---

[54] Y.B.I.L.C., 1966. II, p. 193.
[55] *ibid*. p. 194. See also Art. 46, below, p. 827.

could be said to be the general rule. The growth of the practice of drawing up treaties in large international conferences or within international organisations has, however, led to so normal a use of the procedure of majority vote that, in the opinion of the Commission, it would be unrealistic to lay down unanimity as the general rule for the adoption of the texts of treaties drawn up at conferences or within organisations. Unanimity remains the general rule for bilateral treaties and for treaties drawn up between few States. But for other multilateral treaties a different general rule must be specified, although, of course, it will always be open to the States concerned to apply the rule of unanimity in a particular case if they should so decide. . . .

The Commission considered the further case of treaties like the Genocide Convention or the Convention on the Political Rights of Women, which are actually drawn up within an international organisation. Here, the voting rule for adopting the text of the treaty must clearly be the voting rule applicable in the particular organ in which the treaty is adopted. This case is, however, covered by the general provision in . . . [Art. 5, Vienna Convention] regarding the application of the rules of an international organisation, and need not receive mention in the present article.[56]

On the attempt to adopt the 1982 Law of the Sea Convention by consensus, see above, p. 370.

Article 11

The consent of a State to be bound by a treaty may be expressed by signature, exchange of instruments constituting a treaty, ratification, acceptance, approval or accession, or by any other means if so agreed.[57]

Article 12

1. The consent of a State to be bound by a treaty is expressed by the signature of its representative when:

(*a*) the treaty provides that signature shall have that effect;
(*b*) it is otherwise established that the negotiating States[58] were agreed that signature should have that effect; or
(*c*) the intention of the State to give that effect to the signature appears from the full powers of its representative or was expressed during the negotiation.

2. For the purposes of paragraph 1:

(*a*) the initialling of a text constitutes a signature of the treaty when it is established that the negotiating States so agreed;

---

[56] *ibid*.
[57] *Ed*. Art. 2(1)(*b*) reads: " 'ratification,' 'acceptance,' 'approval' and 'accession' mean in each case the international act so named whereby a State establishes on the international plane its consent to be bound by a treaty."
[58] *Ed*. Art. 2(1)(*e*) reads: " 'negotiating State' means a State which took part in the drawing up and adoption of the text of the treaty."

(b) the signature *ad referendum* of a treaty by a representative, if confirmed by his State, constitutes a full signature of the treaty.

Article 13

The consent of States to be bound by a treaty constituted by instruments exchanged between them is expressed by that exchange when:

(a) the instruments provide that their exchange shall have that effect; or
(b) it is otherwise established that those States were agreed that the exchange of instruments should have that effect.[59]

Article 14

1. The consent of a State to be bound by the treaty is expressed by ratification when:

(a) the treaty provides for such consent to be expressed by means of ratification;
(b) it is otherwise established that the negotiating States were agreed that ratification should be required;
(c) the representative of the State has signed the treaty subject to ratification; or
(d) the intention of the State to sign the treaty subject to ratification appears from the full powers of its representative or was expressed during the negotiation.

2. The consent of a State to be bound by a treaty is expressed by acceptance or approval under conditions similar to those which apply to ratification.

Notes
The International Law Commission's Commentary reads:

The modern institution of ratification[60] in international law developed in the course of the nineteenth century. Earlier, ratification had been an essentially formal and limited act by which, after a treaty had been drawn up, a sovereign confirmed, or finally verified, the full powers previously issued to his representative to negotiate the treaty. It was then not an approval of the treaty itself but a confirmation that the representative had been invested with authority to negotiate it and, that being so, there was an obligation upon the sovereign to ratify his representative's full powers, if these had been in order. Ratification came, however, to be used in the majority of cases as the means of submitting the treaty-making power of the executive to parliamentary control, and ultimately the doctrine of ratification underwent a fundamental change. It was

[59] *Ed.* See Weinstein (1952) 29 B.Y.I.L. 205.
[60] *Ed.* On ratification, see Blix (1953) 30 B.Y.I.L. 352.

established that the treaty itself was subject to subsequent ratification by the State before it became binding. Furthermore, this development took place at a time when the great majority of international agreements were formal treaties. Not unnaturally, therefore, it came to be the opinion that the general rule is that ratification is necessary to render a treaty binding.

. . . Meanwhile, however, the expansion of intercourse between States, especially in economic and technical fields, led to an ever-increasing use of less formal types of international agreements, amongst which were exchanges of notes, and these agreements are usually intended by the parties to become binding by signature alone. On the other hand, an exchange of notes or other informal agreement, though employed for its ease and convenience, has sometimes expressly been made subject to ratification because of constitutional requirements in one or the other of the contracting States.

. . . The general result of these developments had been to complicate the law concerning the conditions under which treaties need ratification in order to make them binding. The controversy which surrounds the subject is, however, largely theoretical. The more formal types of instrument include, almost without exception, express provisions on the subject of ratification, and occasionally this is so even in the case of exchanges of notes or other instruments in simplified form. Moreover, whether they are of a formal or informal type, treaties normally either provide that the instrument shall be ratified or, by laying down that the treaty shall enter into force upon signature or upon a specified date or event, dispense with ratification. Total silence on the subject is exceptional, and the number of cases that remain to be covered by a general rule is very small. But, if the general rule is taken to be that ratification is necessary unless it is expressly or impliedly excluded, large exceptions qualifying a rule have to be inserted in order to bring it into accord with modern practice, with the result that the number of cases calling for the operation of the general rule is small. Indeed, the practical effect of choosing either that version of the general rule, or the opposite rule that ratification is unnecessary unless expressly agreed upon by the parties, is not very substantial . . .

. . . Acceptance has become established in treaty practice during the past twenty years as a new procedure for becoming a party to treaties[61] . . . on the international plane, "acceptance" is an innovation which is more one of terminology than of method. If a treaty provides that it shall be open for signature "subject to acceptance," the process on the international plane is like "signature subject to ratification" . . .

. . . "Signature subject to acceptance" was introduced into treaty practice principally in order to provide a simplified form of "ratification" which would allow the government a further opportunity to examine the treaty when it is not necessarily obliged to submit it to a State's constitutional procedure for obtaining ratification. . . .

. . . The observations in the preceding paragraph apply *mutatis mutandis* to "approval," whose introduction into the terminology of treaty-making is even more recent than that of "acceptance."[62]

Article 15

The consent of a State to be bound by a treaty is expressed by accession when:

---

[61] *Ed.* See Liang (1950) 44 A.J.I.L. 342.
[62] Y.B.I.L.C., 1966, II, pp. 197–198.

(*a*) the treaty provides that such consent may be expressed by that State by means of accession;

(*b*) it is otherwise established that the negotiating States were agreed that such consent may be expressed by that State by means of accession; or

(*c*) all the parties have subsequently agreed that such consent may be expressed by that State by means of accession.

Notes

The International Law Commission's Commentary reads:

Accession is the traditional method by which a State, in certain circumstances, becomes a party to a treaty of which it is not a signatory...

Divergent opinions have been expressed in the past as to whether it is legally possible to accede to a treaty which is not yet in force and there is some support for the view that it is not possible. However, an examination of the most recent treaty practice shows that in practically all modern treaties which contain accession clauses the right to accede is made independent of the entry into force of the treaty, either expressly by allowing accession to take place before the date fixed for the entry into force of the treaty, or impliedly by making the entry into force of the treaty conditional on the deposit, *inter alia*, of instruments of accession.[63]

Article 16

Unless the treaty otherwise provides, instruments of ratification, acceptance, approval or accession establish the consent of a State to be bound by a treaty upon:

(*a*) their exchange between the contracting States;

(*b*) their deposit with the depositary; or

(*c*) their notification to the contracting States or to the depositary, if so agreed.

Notes

The International Law Commission's Commentary reads:

The point of importance is the moment at which the consent to be bound is established and in operation with respect to contracting States. In the case of exchange of instruments there is no problem; it is the moment of exchange. In the case of the deposit of an instrument with a depositary, the problem arises whether the deposit by itself establishes the legal nexus between the depositing State and other contracting States or whether the legal nexus arises only upon their being informed by the depositary. The Commission considered that the existing general rule clearly is that the act of deposit by itself establishes the legal nexus.[64]

[63] *ibid*. p. 199.
[64] *ibid*. p. 201.

Article 18

A State is obliged to refrain from acts which would defeat the object and purpose of a treaty when:

(a) it has signed the treaty or has exchanged instruments constituting the treaty subject to ratification, acceptance or approval, until it shall have made its intention clear not to become a party to the treaty; or

(b) it has expressed its consent to be bound by the treaty, pending the entry into force of the treaty and provided that such entry into force is not unduly delayed.

Notes
The International Law Commission's Commentary reads:

That an obligation of good faith to refrain from acts calculated to frustrate the object of the treaty attaches to a State which has signed a treaty subject to ratification appears to be generally accepted.[65]

(iii) RESERVATIONS[66]

VIENNA CONVENTION ON THE LAW OF TREATIES 1969

Loc. cit., p. 765, n. 3, above

Article 2

1. . . . (d) "Reservation" means a unilateral statement, however phrased or named, made by a State, when signing, ratifying, accepting, approving or acceding to a treaty, where it purports to exclude or to modify the legal effect of certain provisions of the treaty in their application to that State.

Article 19

A State may, when signing, ratifying, accepting, approving, or acceding to a treaty, formulate a reservation unless:

(a) the reservation is prohibited by the treaty;

[65] *ibid.* p. 202. On Art. 18, see Charme (1991) 25 Geo. Wash. J.I.L.E. 71, and Rogoff (1980) 32 Maine L.R. 263.
[66] See Anderson (1964) 13 I.C.L.Q. 450; Bishop, (1961–II) 103 Hague Recueil 245; Bowett (1976–7) 48 B.Y.I.L. 67; Fitzmaurice (1953) 2 I.C.L.Q. 1; Gamble (1980) 74 A.J.I.L. 372; Horn, *Reservations and Interpretative Declarations to Multilateral Treaties* (1988); Piper (1985) 71 Iowa L.R. 295; Redgwell (1993) 64 B.Y.I.L. 245; Ruda (1975–III) 146 Hague Recueil 95; Tomuschat (1967) 27 Z.A.O.R.V. 463; Zemanek, in Makarczyk, ed., *Essays in International Law in Honour of Judge Lachs* (1984), p. 323.

(*b*) the treaty provides that only specified reservations, which do not include the reservation in question, may be made; or

(*c*) in cases not falling under sub-paragraphs (*a*) and (*b*), the reservation is incompatible with the object and purpose of the treaty.

Article 20

1. A reservation expressly authorised by a treaty does not require any subsequent acceptance by the other contracting States unless the treaty so provides.

2. When it appears from the limited number of the negotiating States and the object and purpose of a treaty that the application of the treaty in its entirety between all the parties is an essential condition of the consent of each one to be bound by the treaty, a reservation requires acceptance by all the parties.

3. When a treaty is a constituent instrument of an international organisation and unless it otherwise provides, a reservation requires the acceptance of the competent organ of that organisation.

4. In cases not falling under the preceding paragraphs and unless the treaty otherwise provides:

(*a*) acceptance by another contracting State of a reservation constitutes the reserving State a party to the treaty in relation to that other State if or when the treaty is in force for those States;

(*b*) an objection by another contracting State to a reservation does not preclude the entry into force of the treaty as between the objecting and reserving States unless a contrary intention is definitely expressed by the objecting State;

(*c*) an act expressing a State's consent to be bound by the treaty and containing a reservation is effective as soon as at least one other contracting State has accepted the reservation.

5. For the purposes of paragraphs 2 and 4 and unless the treaty otherwise provides, a reservation is considered to have been accepted by a State if it shall have raised no objection to the reservation by the end of a period of twelve months after it was notified of the reservation or by the date on which it expressed its consent to be bound by the treaty, whichever is later.

Article 21

1. A reservation established with regard to another party in accordance with articles 19, 20 and 23:

(*a*) modifies for the reserving State in its relations with that other party the provisions of the treaty to which the reservation relates to the extent of the reservation; and (*b*) modifies those provisions to the same extent for that other party in its relations with the reserving State.

2. The reservation does not modify the provisions of the treaty for the other parties to the treaty *inter se.*

3. When a State objecting to a reservation has not opposed the entry into force of the treaty between itself and the reserving State, the provisions to which the reservation relates do not apply as between the two States to the extent of the reservation.

Article 22

1. Unless the treaty otherwise provides, a reservation may be withdrawn at any time and the consent of a State which has accepted the reservation is not required for its withdrawal.

2. Unless the treaty otherwise provides, an objection to a reservation may be withdrawn at any time.

3. Unless the treaty otherwise provides, or it is otherwise agreed:

(*a*) the withdrawal of a reservation becomes operative in relation to another contracting State only when notice of it has been received by that State;

(*b*) the withdrawal of an objection to a reservation becomes operative only when notice of it has been received by the State which formulated the reservation.

Article 23

1. A reservation, an express acceptance of a reservation and an objection to a reservation must be formulated in writing and communicated to the contracting States and other States entitled to become parties to the treaty.

2. If formulated when signing the treaty subject to ratification, acceptance or approval, a reservation must be formally confirmed by the reserving State when expressing its consent to be bound by the treaty. In such a case the reservation shall be considered as having been made on the date of its confirmation.

3. An express acceptance of, or an objection to, a reservation made previously to confirmation of the reservation does not itself require confirmation.

4. The withdrawal of a reservation or of an objection to a reservation must be formulated in writing.

Notes

1. The problems tackled in Articles 19–23, Vienna Convention, concern only multilateral treaties. In the case of a bilateral treaty, a proposed reservation is, in effect, a counter offer which the other party can accept or reject. With regard to

multilateral treaties, questions that have become more important as the size of the international community has increased are whether a reservation has to be accepted by all of the parties to be valid and, if not, what is the treaty relationship between a party that makes a reservation and one that objects to it.

With regard to these questions, in 1927 the League of Nations adopted the following approach:

> In order that any reservation whatever may be validly made in regard to a clause of the treaty, it is essential that this reservation should be accepted by all the contracting parties, as would have been the case if it had been put forward in the course of the negotiations. If not, the reservation, like the signature to which it is attached, is null and void.[67]

In contrast, in 1932 the Pan-American Union proposed a different approach:

> With respect to the juridical status of treaties ratified with reservations, which have not been accepted, the Governing Board of the Pan American Union understands that:
>   1. The treaty shall be in force, in the form in which it was signed, as between those countries which ratify it without reservations, in the terms in which it was originally drafted and signed.
>   2. It shall be in force as between the Governments which ratify it with reservations and the signatory States which accept the reservations in the form in which the treaty may be modified by said reservations.
>   3. It shall not be in force between a Government which may have ratified with reservations and another which may have already ratified, and which does not accept such reservations.[68]

In a case that addressed these questions, in the *Reservations to the Convention on Genocide* case,[69] the I.C.J. advised as follows:

> the Court is of opinion,
>   in so far as concerns the Convention on the Prevention and Punishment of the Crime of Genocide, in the event of a State ratifying or acceding to the Convention subject to a reservation made either on ratification or on accession, or on signature followed by ratification,
> *On Question I:*
>   by seven votes to five,
>   that a State which has made and maintained a reservation which has been objected to by one or more of the parties to the Convention but not by others, can be regarded as being a party to the Convention if the reservation is compatible with the object and purpose of the Convention; otherwise, that State cannot be regarded as being a party to the Convention.
> *On Question II:*
>   by seven votes to five,
>   (*a*) that if a party to the Convention objects to a reservation which it considers to be incompatible with the object and purpose of the Convention, it

---

[67] Report of the L.N. Committee of Experts for the Progressive Codification of International Law (1927) 8 L.N.O.J. 880 at 881.

[68] *Reservations to Multilateral Conventions*, UN Doc. A/1372, p. 11. The 1932 P.A.U. approach has been changed by a new set of O.A.S. standards in line with the Vienna Convention on the Law of Treaties: [1973] U.S. D.I.L. 179.

[69] I.C.J. Rep. 1951, p. 15. Advisory Opinion.

can in fact consider that the reserving State is not a party to the Convention[70];

(b) that if, on the other hand, a party accepts the reservation as being compatible with the object and purpose of the Convention, it can in fact consider that the reserving State is a party to the Convention.

On Question III:

by seven votes to five,

(a) that an objection to a reservation made by a signatory State which has not yet ratified the Convention can have the legal effect indicated in the reply to Question I only upon ratification. Until that moment it merely serves as a notice to the other State of the eventual attitude of the signatory State;

(b) that an objection to a reservation made by a State which is entitled to sign or accede but which has not yet done so, is without legal effect.

Clearly the Court preferred the Pan-American Union approach. In a joint dissenting judgment, Judges Guerrero, Sir Arnold McNair, Read and Hsu Mo considered that the League of Nations approach was consistent with customary international law.

2. Basically, the Vienna Convention also follows the Pan-American Union approach. More immediately, it substantially incorporates the International Law Commission's Draft Articles, except for Article 20(4)(b), Vienna Convention. The Commission had proposed, partly to discourage reservations, that an objection would preclude entry into force of a treaty between the two states concerned unless a contrary intention were expressed by the objecting state.[71] At the suggestion of the USSR, which argued for complete freedom for states to make reservations, the contrary approach was adopted at Vienna.[72] The United Kingdom Government regards the Convention rules as stating custom.[73]

3. In its Commentary to its Draft Articles, the International Law Commission stated:

The majority of reservations relate to the particular point which a particular State for one reason or another finds difficult to accept, and the effect of the reservation on the general integrity of the treaty is often minimal; and the same is true even if the reservation in question relates to a comparatively important provision of the treaty, so long as the reservation is not made by more than a few States. In short, the integrity of the treaty would only be materially affected if a reservation of a somewhat substantial kind were to be formulated by a number of States. This might, no doubt, happen; but even then the treaty itself would remain the master agreement between the other participating States. What is essential to ensure both the effectiveness and the integrity of the treaty is that a sufficient number of States should become parties to it, accepting the great bulk of its provisions. . . . But when today the number of the negotiating States may be upwards of one hundred States with very diverse cultural, economic and political conditions, it seems necessary to assume that the power to make reservations without the risk of being totally excluded by the objection of one or even of a few States may be a factor in promoting a

---

[70] *Ed.* Note that the Genocide Convention has no reservation clause.

[71] Draft Articles. Art. 17(4)(b).

[72] See *Treaty Conference Records*, 1969, pp. 30–35.

[73] Dept. of Trade Memorandum to the House of Commons Select Committee on European Legislation 1978, printed in U.K.M.I.L. 1978, (1978) 49 B.Y.I.L. 378. The European Commission on Human Rights takes the same view: *Temeltasch Case* (1983) 5 E.H.R.R. 417 at 432.

more general acceptance of multilateral treaties. Moreover, the failure of negotiating States to take the necessary steps to become parties to multilateral
treaties appears a greater obstacle to the development of international law
through the medium of treaties than the possibility that the integrity of such
treaties may be unduly weakened by the liberal admission of reserving States
as parties to them. The Commission also considered that, in the present era of
change and of challenge to traditional concepts, the rule calculated to promote
the widest possible acceptance of whatever measure of common agreement
can be achieved and expressed in a multilateral treaty may be the one most
suited to the immediate needs of the international community.[74]

4. The concept of the "object and purpose" of a treaty is used in both Articles
19 and 20. What different role does it serve in each?

5. For an example of a treaty provision prohibiting a certain kind of reservation,
see Article 64 of the European Convention on Human Rights 1950.[75] An unusual
example of a treaty provision that expressly authorises a certain kind of reservation (Article 20(1)) is Article 75, American Convention on Human Rights 1969,
which provides that the Convention "shall be subject to reservations only in
conformity with" the Vienna Convention on the Law of Treaties. In the *Effect of
Reservations* case,[76] it was concluded that Article 75 incorporated by reference
Article 19(c), Vienna Convention and thereby expressly permitted reservations
that are not "incompatible with the object and purpose" of the American Convention. Note also the "mathematical" test used in Article 20 of the Racial Discrimination Convention for determining whether a reservation is incompatible with its
"object and purpose."[77]

6. In the *Restrictions to the Death Penalty* case,[78] Guatemala had made a reservation to the guarantee of the right to life in the American Convention on Human
Rights 1969, Article 4, by which it did not accept that guarantee's prohibition of
the death penalty for "common crimes" (*e.g.* robbery) related to political offences.
This raised the question whether a reservation to a non-derogable human rights
treaty provision was permissible. On the question whether such a reservation was
impermissible as being contrary to the "object and purpose" of the Convention,
the American Court of Human Rights stated:

> Article 27 of the Convention allows the States Parties to suspend, in time of
> war, public danger, or other emergency that threatens their independence or
> security, the obligations they assumed by ratifying the Convention, provided
> that in doing so they do not suspend or derogate from certain basic or essential
> rights, among them the right to life guaranteed by Article 4. It would follow
> therefrom that a reservation which was designed to enable a State to suspend
> any of the non-derogable fundamental rights must be deemed to be incompat-
> ible with the object and purpose of the Convention and, consequently, not
> permitted by it. The situation would be different if the reservation sought
> merely to restrict certain aspects of a non-derogable right without depriving
> the right as a whole of its basic purpose. Since the reservation referred to by the
> Commission in its submission does not appear to be of a type that is designed
> to deny the right to life as such, the Court concludes that to that extent it can

---

[74] Y.B.I.L.C., 1966, II, pp. 205–206. See Boyle (1980) 29 I.C.L.Q. 498.

[75] See the *Belilos* case, below, p. 794.

[76] (1981) 22 I.L.M. 37 at 44.

[77] Art. 20 states that a reservation is "incompatible" if at least two-thirds of the contracting
parties object to it. This is a requirement that is unlikely to be met.

[78] (1984) 23 I.L.M. 320 at 341.

be considered, in principle, as not being incompatible with the object and purpose of the Convention.

On the rules governing the interpretation of reservations, the Court stated that since reservations became "an integral part" of a treaty by modifying or excluding its effect, they "must of necessity therefore also be interpreted by reference to relevant principles of general international law and the special rules set out in the Convention itself."[79]

7. In the *English Channel Arbitration*,[80] France had made reservations to Article 6, Continental Shelf Convention 1958 to which the United Kingdom had objected. As to the effect of these reservations and objections on the treaty relations under the Convention between the two parties, the Court of Arbitration stated:

> 61. . . . the effect of the rejection [by the U.K.] may properly, in the view of the Court, be said to render the reservations non-opposable to the United Kingdom. Just as the effect of the French reservations is to prevent the United Kingdom from invoking the provisions of Article 6 except on the basis of the conditions stated in the reservations, so the effect of their rejection is to prevent the French Republic from imposing the reservations on the United Kingdom for the purpose of invoking against it as binding a delimitation made on the basis of the conditions contained in the reservations. Thus, the combined effect of the French reservations and their rejection by the United Kingdom is neither to render Article 6 inapplicable *in toto*, as the French Republic contends, nor to render it applicable *in toto*, as the United Kingdom primarily contends. It is to render the Article inapplicable as between the two countries to the extent, but only to the extent, of the reservations; and this is precisely the effect envisaged in such cases by Article 21, paragraph 3 of the Vienna Convention on the Law of Treaties and the effect indicated by the principle of mutuality of consent.
>
> 62. The fact that Article 6 is not applicable as between the Parties to the extent that it is excluded by the French reservations does not mean that there are no legal rules to govern the delimitation of the boundary in areas where the reservation operates. On the contrary, as the International Court of Justice observed in the *North Sea Continental Shelf* cases, "there are still rules and principles of law to be applied" (I.C.J. Reports 1969, paragraph 83); and these are the rules and principles governing delimitation of the continental shelf in general international law.

8. An example of the operation of the principle of reciprocity in Article 21(1), Vienna Convention is found in the facts of the *Libyan People's Bureau Incident*[81] in respect of the Libyan reservation to the Vienna Convention on Diplomatic Relations permitting it to open a diplomatic bag if it entertained strong doubts as to the legitimacy of its contents. In accordance with Article 21(1)(*b*), Vienna Convention, the obligation in the Diplomatic Relations Convention not to open another state's diplomatic bag was modified to the extent of the reservation and would not have prevented the United Kingdom opening the Libyan bag. Thus Sir John Freeland explained to the Foreign Affairs Committee[82]:

> The fact of the matter is that the Law of Treaties Convention, which in this respect reflects customary international law, provides that where a State has established a reservation against another party, and that was the case with

---

[79] *ibid.* p. 341.
[80] (1979) 18 I.L.M. 397 at 419.
[81] Above, p. 353.
[82] Foreign Affairs Committee Report, *op. cit.*, p. 345, n. 2, above p. xxxi.

Libya as against the United Kingdom since we did not object, that reservation qualifies the obligation to which it is addressed for both of them. So, without more ado, we would have had the ability to respond.

9. Probably the most controversial reservations to the Genocide Convention that led to the *Reservations Case* are those made by a number of states not accepting Article IX of the Convention which provides for the compulsory juris-diction of the International Court of Justice in disputes arising under the Conven-tion.[83] Objections to them have been registered by a number of states.[84] What would be the effect of such reservations under the Vienna Convention?

10. Suppose that states A, B and C make a treaty by which they undertake to develop a new aeroplane and the treaty provides that "development costs will be shared by the contracting parties equally." The treaty has no provision on reserva-tions. D accedes to the treaty but makes its accession subject to the reservation that it will not regard itself as bound if its share of the costs of the venture rises above a stated level. A objects to this reservation but does not say that the treaty has no effect between A and D; B expressly accepts the reservation; C makes no response. Is D a party to the treaty according to the Vienna Convention? If so, what are its relations with A, B and C? Who decides these questions?

BELILOS v. SWITZERLAND[85]

Eur. Court H.R., Series A, Vol. 132. Judgment of April 20, 1988

The applicant claimed that she had not been given a fair trial in accordance with Article 6, European Convention on Human Rights when she was convicted of a criminal offence by a municipal Police Board in Switzerland. Switzerland entered a preliminary objection to the effect that the case fell within the scope of an "interpretative declaration" concerning Article 6 which it had made upon ratifica-tion and which, in its view, was a valid reservation under Article 64 of the Convention. On ratification, Switzerland had made what it described as two "interpretative declarations," including the one in issue, and two "reservations." In the following extract, the Court considered whether the Article 6 "inter-pretative declaration"[86] was, despite its title, a reservation to which Article 64 could apply.[87]

Judgment of the Court

41. The Commission . . . reached the conclusion that the declaration was a mere interpretative declaration which did not have the effect of a reservation; it based its view both on the wording of the declaration and

---

[83] UN Doc. ST/LEG/SER.E/15, pp. 86 *et seq.*
[84] *ibid.*
[85] See Bourguignon (1989) 29 Virg. J.I.L. 347; Cameron and Horn (1990) 33 G.Y.I.L. 69; McDonald (1988) 21 R.B.D.I. 429; Marks (1990) 39 I.C.L.Q. 300. See also the *Temeltasch* case *loc. cit.*, p. 791, n. 73, above.
[86] The "interpretative declaration" read: "The Swiss Federal Council considers that the guarantee of fair trial in Article 6(1) of the Convention, in the determination of civil rights and obligations or any criminal charge against the person in question is intended solely to ensure ultimate control by the judiciary over the acts or decisions of the public authorities relating to such rights or obligations or the determination of such a charge."
[87] Art. 64(1) permits reservations other than those "of a general character."

on the preparatory work. . . . More generally, the Commission considered that if a State made both reservations and interpretative declarations at the same time, the latter could only exceptionally be equated with the former.

42. In the Government's submission, on the other hand, the declaration was a "qualified" interpretative declaration. It consequently was in the nature of a reservation within the meaning of Article 2(1)(d) of the Vienna Convention on the Law of Treaties . . .

The Court considered a number of Government arguments in support of this submission, including the following:

44. Another factor, in the Government's submission, was the wording used in the declaration which clearly had a restrictive character.

The Court acknowledges that the wording of the original French text of the declaration, though not altogether clear, can be understood as constituting a reservation. . . .

47. The Government derived an additional argument from the fact that there had been no reaction from the Secretary General of the Council of Europe or from the States Parties to the Convention. . . . The Swiss Government inferred that it could in good faith take the declaration as having been tacitly accepted for the purposes of Article 64.

The Court does not agree with that analysis. The silence of the depository and the Contracting States does not deprive the Convention institutions of the power to make their own assessment. . . .

48. . . . Like the Commission and the Government, the Court recognises that it is necessary to ascertain the original intention of those who drafted the declaration. In its view, the documents show that Switzerland originally contemplated making a formal reservation but subsequently opted for the term "declaration." Although the documents do not make the reasons for the change of nomenclature entirely clear, they do show that the Federal Council has always been concerned to avoid the consequences which a broad view of the right of access to the courts . . . would have for the system of public administration and of justice in the cantons and consequently to put forward the declaration as qualifying Switzerland's consent to be bound by the Convention.

49. The question whether a declaration described as "interpretative" must be regarded as a "reservation" is a difficult one, particularly—in the instant case—because the Swiss Government has made both "reservations" and "interpretative declarations" in the same instrument of ratification. More generally, the Court recognises the great importance, rightly emphasised by the Government, of the legal rules applicable to reservations and interpretative declarations made by States Parties to the Convention. Only reservations are mentioned in the Convention, but several States have also (or only) made interpretative declarations, without always making a clear distinction between the two.

In order to establish the legal character of such a declaration, one must look behind the title given to it and seek to determine the substantive content. In the present case, it appears that Switzerland meant to remove certain categories of proceedings from the ambit of Article 6(1) and to secure itself against an interpretation of that Article which it considered to be too broad. However, the Court must see to it that the obligations arising under the Convention are not subject to restrictions which would not satisfy the requirements of Article 64 as regards reservations. Accordingly, it will examine the validity of the interpretative declaration in question, as in the case of a reservation, in the context of this provision.

The Court then held that the Swiss reservation was invalid because (i) it was a reservation of a "general character" (*i.e.* one that was "couched in terms that are too vague or broad for it to be possible to determine their exact scope or meaning") and so prohibited by Article 64(1) and (ii) it had not been accompanied by a "brief statement of the laws concerned" (*i.e.* those that were incompatible with the Convention necessitating the reservation) as required by Article 64(2), this being "not a purely formal requirement but a condition of substance."

60. In short, the declaration in question does not satisfy two of the requirements of Article 64 of the Convention, with the result that it must be held to be invalid. At the same time, it is beyond doubt that Switzerland is, and regards itself as, bound by the Convention irrespective of the validity of the declaration. Moreover, the Swiss Government recognised the Court's competence to determine the latter issue, which it argued before it. The Government's preliminary objection must therefore be rejected.

The Court upheld the applicant's claim that Article 6 had been infringed on the facts of the case.

Notes

1. The *Belilos* case mainly concerned the distinction between reservations and interpretative declarations. As to the latter, the Court adopted McRae's classification of "mere interpretative declarations" and "qualified interpretative declarations." McRae states[88]:

> The legal effect of an interpretative declaration depends initially upon whether the declarant seeks only to offer an interpretation of the treaty that may be found subsequently to be incorrect (a "mere interpretative declaration"), or whether the declarant purports to make its acceptance of the provision in question conditional upon acquiescence in that interpretation (a "qualified interpretative declaration"). The significance of the former lies in the effect it may have in subsequent proceedings to interpret the treaty, and this significance will vary according to whether the declaration has been accepted, ignored or objected to by other contracting parties. The latter type of

---

[88] (1978) 49 B.Y.I.L. 155 at 172–173.

interpretative declaration, on the other hand, must be assimilated to a reservation, for by asserting that its interpretation overrides any contrary interpretation the declarant has purported to exclude or to modify the terms of the treaty. Hence the legal consequences that attach to reservations ought to apply to "qualified interpretative declarations". . . .

The safest course for a State that is opposed to an interpretative declaration attached to another contracting party's instrument of acceptance is formally to object to it. The objecting State is protected should the declaration turn out to be a "qualified interpretative declaration," and the objection serves to diminish the effect the declaration might have, as a "mere interpretative declaration," upon the interpretation of the treaty.

The Court's approach underlines the wisdom of McRae's suggestion that a state opposed to an "interpretative declaration" should object to it in case it proves to be a reservation. Is it consistent with the need for certainty in international relations that a state may submit at the same time texts described as "interpretative declarations" and "reservations" and later be able to claim that one of the former is really a "reservation" after all? Note that under Article 2(1)(d), a statement may be a reservation "however phrased or named", but that for an "interpretative declaration" to qualify as a reservation it must be made on one of the occasions specified in Article 2(1)(d).

2. Another aspect of the case was the legal effect of the Court's determination that the Swiss reservation, as the "interpretative declaration" was inconsistent with Article 64 and hence invalid. The Court took the view that Switzerland was fully bound by the Convention without the benefit of the reservation. It did not draw an analogy with the situation where a valid reservation is subject to an objection and Article 21(3), Vienna Convention, above, p. 789 applies, so that Switzerland would not have been bound by Article 6 to the extent of its reservation. Another approach might have been prompted by Judge Lauterpacht's judgment in the *Norwegian Loans* case; below, p. 1010, in respect of invalid reservations to optional clause declarations. The Court might, that is, have considered whether the reservation was fundamental to Switzerland's acceptance of the Convention: if it was, the reservation would not have been severed and Switzerland's ratification of the Convention as a whole would have been invalid. Is the Court's judgment consistent with the I.C.J.'s response to Question I in the *Reservations* case, above, p. 790?[89] Is the Court's decision limited to the situation where, as on the facts (see judgment, para. 60), the state concerned does not question the continued application of the treaty in the absence of the reservation?

GENERAL COMMENT 24 ON RESERVATIONS TO THE INTERNATIONAL COVENANT ON CIVIL AND POLITICAL RIGHTS[90]

Human Rights Committee, 1994. (1995) 15 H.R.L.J. 464;
(1995) 2 I.H.R.R. 10

1. As of 1 November 1994, 46 of the 127 States parties to the International Covenant on Civil and Political Rights had, between them, entered 150 reservations of varying significance to their acceptance of the

---

[89] On this and the effect of invalidity generally, see Marks, *loc. cit.*, p. 794, n. 85, above. In *Loizidou v. Turkey*, E. Court. H.R.Rep. A310 (1995) a reservation to a declaration accepting jurisdiction was severed.

[90] See Redgwell (1997) 46 I.C.L.Q. 97.

obligations of the Covenant. . . . The number of reservations, their content and their scope may undermine the effective implementation of the Covenant and tend to weaken respect for the obligations of States parties. It is important for States parties to know exactly what obligations they, and other States parties, have in fact undertaken. . . . This will require a determination as to whether a unilateral statement is a reservation or an interpretative declaration and a determination of its acceptability and effects. . . .

4. The possibility of entering reservations may encourage States which consider that they have difficulties in guaranteeing all the rights in the Covenant nonetheless to accept the generality of obligations in that instrument. Reservations may serve a useful function to enable States to adapt specific elements in their laws to the inherent rights of each person as articulated in the Covenant. However, it is desirable in principle that States accept the full range of obligations, because the human rights norms are the legal expression of the essential rights that every person is entitled to as a human being.

5. The Covenant neither prohibits reservations nor mentions any type of permitted reservation. The same is true of the first Optional Protocol. . . .

6. The absence of a prohibition on reservations does not mean that any reservation is permitted. . . . Article 19(3) of the Vienna Convention on the Law of Treaties provides relevant guidance.[91] It stipulates that where a reservation is not prohibited by the treaty or falls within the specified permitted categories, a State may make a reservation provided it is not incompatible with the object and purpose of the treaty. . . .

7. In an instrument which articulates very many civil and political rights, each of the many articles, and indeed their interplay, secures the objectives of the Covenant. The object and purpose of the Covenant is to create legally binding standards for human rights by defining certain civil and political rights and placing them in a framework of obligations which are legally binding for those States which ratify; and to provide an efficacious supervisory machinery for the obligations undertaken.

8. Reservations that offend peremptory norms would not be compatible with the object and purpose of the Covenant. Although treaties that are mere exchanges of obligations between States allow them to reserve *inter se* application of rules of general international law, it is otherwise in human rights treaties, which are for the benefit of persons within their jurisdiction. Accordingly, provisions in the Covenant that represent customary international law (and *a fortiori* when they have the character of peremptory norms) may not be the subject of reservations. Accordingly, a State may not reserve the right to engage in slavery, to torture, to subject

---

[91] Although the Vienna Convention on the Law of Treaties was concluded in 1969 and entered into force in 1980—*i.e.* after the entry into force of the Covenant—its terms reflect the general international law on this matter as had already been affirmed by the International Court of Justice in *The Reservations to the Genocide Convention* case of 1951.

person to cruel, inhuman or degrading treatment or punishment, to arbitrarily deprive persons of their lives, to arbitrarily arrest and detain persons, to deny freedom of thought, conscience and religion, to presume a person guilty unless he proves his innocence, to execute pregnant women or children, to permit the advocacy of national, racial or religious hatred, to deny to persons of marriageable age the right to marry, or to deny to minorities the right to enjoy their own culture, profess their own religion, or use their own language. And while reservations to particular clauses of Article 14 may be acceptable, a general reservation to the right to a fair trial would not be.

9. Applying more generally the object and purpose test to the Covenant, the Committee notes that, for example, a reservation to Article 1 denying peoples the right to determine their own political status and to pursue their economic, social and cultural development, would be incompatible with the object and purpose of the Covenant. Equally, a reservation to the obligation to respect and ensure the rights, and to do so on a non-discriminatory basis (Article 2(1)) would not be acceptable. Nor may a State reserve an entitlement not to take the necessary steps at the domestic level to give effect to the rights of the Covenant (Article 2(2)).

10. ... it falls for consideration as to whether reservations to the non-derogable provisions of the Covenant are compatible with its object and purpose. While there is no hierarchy of importance of rights under the Covenant, the operation of certain rights may not be suspended, even in times of national emergency. This underlines the great importance of non-derogable rights. But not all rights of profound importance, such as Articles 9 and 27 of the Covenant, have in fact been made non-derogable. One reason for certain rights being made non-derogable is because their suspension is irrelevant to the legitimate control of the state of national emergency (for example, no imprisonment for debt, in Article 11). Another reason is that derogation may indeed be impossible (as, for example, freedom of conscience). At the same time, some provisions are non-derogable exactly because without them there would be no rule of law. A reservation to the provisions of Article 4 itself, which precisely stipulates the balance to be struck between the interests of the State and the rights of the individual in times of emergency, would fall in this category. And some non-derogable rights, which in any event cannot be reserved because of their status as peremptory norms, are also of this character—the prohibition of torture and arbitrary deprivation of life are examples.[92] While there is no automatic correlation between reservations to non-derogable provisions, and reservations which offend against the object and purpose of the Covenant, a State has a heavy onus to justify such a reservation.

---

[92] Reservations have been entered to both Art. 6 and Art. 7, but not in terms which reserve a right to torture or arbitrarily to deprive of life.

11. The Covenant consists not just of the specified rights, but of important supportive guarantees. These guarantees provide the necessary framework for securing the rights in the Covenant and are thus essential to its object and purpose. ... Reservations designed to remove these guarantees are thus not acceptable. Thus, a State could not make a reservation to Article 2, paragraph 3, of the Covenant, indicating that it intends to provide no remedies for human rights violations. ... A State may not reserve the right not to present a report and have it considered by the Committee. The Committee's role under the Covenant, whether under Article 40 or under the Optional Protocols, necessarily entails interpreting the provisions of the Covenant and the development of a jurisprudence. Accordingly, a reservation that rejects the Committee's competence to interpret the requirements of any provisions of the Covenant would also be contrary to the object and purpose of that treaty.

12. ... Domestic laws may need to be altered properly to reflect the requirements of the Covenant; and mechanisms at the domestic level will be needed to allow the Covenant rights to be enforceable at the local level. Reservations often reveal a tendency of States not to want to change a particular law. ... Of particular concern are widely formulated reservations which essentially render ineffective all Covenant rights which would require any change in national law to ensure compliance with Covenant obligations. No real international rights or obligations have thus been accepted. And when there is an absence of provisions to ensure that Covenant rights may be sued on in domestic courts, and, further, a failure to allow individual complaints to be brought to the Committee under the first Optional Protocol, all the essential elements of the Covenant guarantees have been removed.

13. ... A reservation [to the obligation to respect and ensure a Covenant right] cannot be made to the Covenant through the vehicle of the Optional Protocol but such a reservation would operate to ensure that the State's compliance with that obligation may not be tested by the Committee under the first Optional Protocol. ...

14. The Committee considers that reservations relating to the required procedures under the first Optional Protocol would not be compatible with its object and purpose. The Committee must control its own procedures as specified by the Optional Protocol and its rules of procedure. ...

16. The Committee finds it important to address which body has the legal authority to make determinations as to whether specific reservations are compatible with the object and purpose of the Covenant. As for international treaties in general, the International Court of Justice has indicated in the *Reservations to the Genocide Convention* case (1951) that a State which objected to a reservation on the grounds of incompatibility with the object and purpose of a treaty could, through objecting, regard the treaty as not in effect as between itself and the reserving State. Article 20, paragraph 4, of the Vienna Convention on the Law of Treaties 1969

contains provisions most relevant to the present case on acceptance of and objection to reservations. This provides for the possibility of a State to object to a reservation made by another State. Article 21 deals with the legal effects of objections by States to reservations made by other States. Essentially, a reservation precludes the operation, as between the reserving and other States, of the provision reserved; and an objection thereto leads to the reservation being in operation as between the reserving and objecting State only to the extent that it has not been objected to.

17. . . . the Committee believes that . . . [the Vienna Convention's] provisions on the role of State objections in relation to reservations are inappropriate to address the problem of reservations to human rights treaties. Such treaties, and the Covenant specifically, are not a web of inter-State exchanges of mutual obligations. They concern the endowment of individuals with rights. The principle of inter-State reciprocity has no place, save perhaps in the limited context of reservations to declarations on the Committee's competence under Article 41. And because the operation of the classic rules on reservations is so inadequate for the Covenant, States have often not seen any legal interest in or need to object to reservations. The absence of protest by States cannot imply that a reservation is either compatible or incompatible with the object and purpose of the Covenant. Objections have been occasional, made by some States but not others, and on grounds not always specified; when an objection is made, it often does not specify a legal consequence, or sometimes even indicates that the objecting party nonetheless does not regard the Covenant as not in effect as between the parties concerned. In short, the pattern is so unclear that it is not safe to assume that a non-objecting State thinks that a particular reservation is acceptable. In the view of the Committee, because of the special characteristics of the Covenant as a human rights treaty, it is open to question what effect objections have between States *inter se*. However, an objection to a reservation made by States may provide some guidance to the Committee in its interpretation as to its compatibility with the object and purpose of the Covenant.

18. It necessarily falls to the Committee to determine whether a specific reservation is compatible with the object and purpose of the Covenant. This is in part because, as indicated above, it is an inappropriate task for States parties in relation to human rights treaties, and in part because it is a task that the Committee cannot avoid in the performance of its functions. In order to know the scope of its duty to examine a State's compliance under Article 40 or a communication under the first Optional Protocol, the Committee has necessarily to take a view on the compatibility of a reservation with the object and purpose of the Covenant and with general international law. Because of the special character of a human rights treaty, the compatibility of a reservation with the object and purpose of the Covenant must be established objectively, by reference to legal principles, and the Committee is particularly well placed to perform this

task. The normal consequence of an unacceptable reservation is not that the Covenant will not be in effect at all for a reserving party. Rather, such a reservation will generally be severable, in the sense that the Covenant will be operative for the reserving party without benefit of the reservation.

19. Reservations must be specific and transparent, so that the Committee, those under the jurisdiction of the reserving State and other States parties may be clear as to what obligations of human rights compliance have or have not been undertaken. Reservations may thus not be general, but must refer to a particular provision of the Covenant and indicate in precise terms its scope in relation thereto. When considering the compatibility of possible reservations with the object and purpose of the Covenant, States should also take into consideration the overall effect of a group of reservations, as well as the effect of each reservation on the integrity of the Covenant, which remains an essential consideration. States should not enter so many reservations that they are in effect accepting a limited number of human rights obligations, and not the Covenant as such. So that reservations do not lead to a perpetual non-attainment of international human rights standards, reservations should not systematically reduce the obligations undertaken only to the presently existing in less demanding standards of domestic law. Nor should interpretive declarations or reservations seek to remove an autonomous meaning to Covenant obligations, by pronouncing them to be identical, or to be accepted only insofar as they are identical, with existing provisions of domestic law. States should not seek through reservations or interpretative declarations to determine that the meaning of a provision of the Covenant is the same as that given by an organ of any other international treaty body.

Notes

1. As the Human Rights Committee indicates (para. 18), it had no choice but to take a stand on the matter of reservations in order to assess whether a state was complying with its international obligations. Unfortunately, the Committee finds itself at odds with some contracting parties[93] on certain key points. Thus, the United Kingdom Observations on the General Comment read in part:

> 4. The modern law of reservations to multilateral treaties . . . owes it origin to the Advisory Opinion of the International Court of Justice of 28 May 1951 on Reservations to the Genocide Convention. The Genocide Convention is itself (in the Committee's phrase) a human rights treaty concluded for the benefit of persons within the jurisdiction of the States Parties to it. As the International Court observed, the Genocide Convention is of a type in which "the Contracting States do not have any interests of their own; they merely have, one and all, a common interest, namely the accomplishment of those high purposes which are the *raison d'être* of the Convention". It was in the light precisely of those

[93] See the Observations on General Comment 24 by France, the U.K. and the U.S.: (1997) 4 I.H.R.R. 6; (1996) 3 I.H.R.R. 261; (1996) 16 H.R.L. Gy. 424; and (1996) 3 I.H.R.R. 265; (1996) 16 H.R.L.J. 422, respectively.

characteristics of the Genocide Convention, and in the light of the desirability of widespread adherence to it, that the Court set out its approach towards reservations. The United Kingdom does not accordingly believe that rules different from those foreshadowed by the International Court and in due course embodied in the Vienna Convention on the Law of Treaties are required to enable the international community to cope with reservations to human rights treaties. The correct approach is rather to apply the general rules relating to reservations laid down in the Vienna Convention in a manner which takes full account of the particular characteristics of the treaty in question. . . .

13. The Committee correctly identifies Articles 20 and 21 of the Vienna Convention on the Law of Treaties as containing the rules which, taken together, regulate the legal effect of reservations to multilateral treaties. The United Kingdom wonders however whether the Committee is right to assume their applicability to incompatible reservations. The rules cited clearly do apply to reservations which are fully compatible with the object and purpose but remain open for acceptance or objection (see paragraph 9 above). It is questionable however whether they were intended also to cover reservations which are inadmissible *in limine*. For example, it seems highly improbable that a reservation expressly *prohibited* by the treaty (the case in Article 19(a) of the Vienna Convention) is open to acceptance by another Contracting State. And if so, there is no clear reason why the same should not apply to the other cases enumerated in Article 19, including incompatibility with the object and purpose under 19(c). The *Genocide Convention* Advisory Opinion did indeed deal directly with the matter, by stating that acceptance of a reservation as being *compatible* with the object and purpose entitles a party to consider the reserving State to be party to the treaty. In the converse case (*i.e.* the case where the reservation is *not* compatible with the object and purpose) the Court states plainly, "that State cannot be regarded as being a party to the Convention".[94] This is the approach which the United Kingdom has consistently followed in its own treaty practice.

14. The General Comment suggests, *per contra*, that an "unacceptable" reservation will generally be severable, in the sense that the Covenant will be operative for the reserving party as if the reservation had not been entered. . . .

15. The United Kingdom believes that the only sound approach is . . . that adopted by the International Court of Justice: a State which purports to ratify a human rights treaty subject to a reservation which is fundamentally incompatible with participation in the treaty régime cannot be regarded as having become a party at all—unless it withdraws the reservation. The test of incompatibility is and should be an objective one, in which the views of competent third parties would carry weight. Ultimately however it is a matter for the treaty Parties themselves and, while the presence or absence of individual State "objections" should not be decisive in relation to an objective standard, it would be surprising to find a reservation validly stigmatised as incompatible, with the object and purpose of the Covenant if none of the Parties had taken exception to it on that ground. For all other reservations the rules laid down in the Vienna Convention do and should apply—except to the extent that the treaty regulates such matters by its own terms.

The U.S. observations on the General Comment read in part:

It is clear that a State cannot exempt itself from a peremptory norm of international law by making a reservation to the Covenant. It is not at all clear

[94] I.C.J. Rep. 1951, p. 29.

that a State cannot choose to exclude one means of enforcement of particular norms by reserving against inclusion of those norms in its Covenant obligations.

The proposition that any reservation which contravenes a norm of customary international law is *per se* incompatible with the object and purpose of this or any other convention, however, is a much more significant and sweeping premise. It is, moreover, wholly unsupported by and is in fact contrary to international law. As recognized in the paragraph 10 analysis of non-derogable rights, an "object and purpose" analysis by its nature requires consideration of the particular treaty, right, and reservation in question. . . .

The precise specification of what is contrary to customary international law, moreover, is a much more substantial question than indicated by the Comment. Even where a rule is generally established in customary international law, the exact contours and meaning of the customary law principle may need to be considered.

Paragraph 8, however, asserts in a wholly conclusory fashion that a number of propositions are customary international law which, to speak plainly, are not. It cannot be established on the basis of practice or other authority, for example, that the mere expression (albeit deplorable) of national, racial or religious hatred (unaccompanied by any overt action or preparation) is prohibited by customary international law. The Committee seems to be suggesting here that the reservations which a large number of States Parties have submitted to Article 20 are *per se* invalid. Similarly, while many are opposed to the death penalty in general and the juvenile death penalty in particular, the practice of States demonstrates that there is currently no blanket prohibition in customary international law. Such a cavalier approach to international law by itself would raise serious concerns about the methodology of the Committee as well as its authority.

Another point worthy of clarification is whether the Committee really intends that, in the many areas which it mentions in paragraphs 8–11, any reservation whatsoever is impermissible, or only those which wholly vitiate the right in question. At the end of paragraph 8, for example, it is suggested that while reservations to particular clauses of Article 14 may be acceptable, a general reservation could not be taken to the article as a whole. Presumably, the same must also be true for many of the other subjects mentioned. For example, even where there is a reservation to Article 20, one would not expect such a reservation to apply to advocacy of racial hatred which constitutes incitement to murder or other crime. . . .

The reservations contained in the United States' instrument of ratification are integral parts of its consent to be bound by the Covenant and are not severable. If it were to be determined that any one or more of them were ineffective, the ratification as a whole could thereby be nullified.

The general view of the academic literature is that reservations are an essential part of the State's consent to be bound. They cannot simply be erased. This reflects the fundamental principle of the law of treaties: obligation is based on consent. A State which does not consent to a treaty is not bound by that treaty. A State which expressly withholds its consent from a provision cannot be presumed, on the basis of some legal fiction, to be bound by it. It is regrettable that General Comment 24 appears to suggest to the contrary.

2. Which view of the rules on reservations to human rights treaties is preferable? That of the Human Rights Committee or that of the United Kingdom and the United States indicated above? Is the Committee ambitious in its listing of the categories of derogations that would be contrary to the Covenant's object and purpose? Where should the balance be struck between the integrity of the treaty

and the need to get as many states as possible on board? Is the Committee's view on the severance of invalid reservations comparable to that in the *Belilos* case, above, p. 794, or was that case different because Switzerland did not appear to object to remaining bound by the ECHR without its reservation?

3. The International Law Commission has the question of reservations to treaties under consideration, with a view to clarifying or supplementing (not amending) the rules in Articles 19–23, Vienna Convention.[95] The matter of reservations to human rights treaties is regarded by the Commission, and others, as particularly urgent, given both the large number of reservations that have been made to some UN human rights treaties[96] and the view of the Human Rights Committee that (i) the Vienna Convention rules concerning objections to reservations do not apply to human rights treaties and (ii) the effect of invalidity of a reservation is severance.

(iv) Entry into Force

VIENNA CONVENTION ON THE LAW OF TREATIES 1969

Loc. cit., p. 765, n. 3, above

Article 24

1. A treaty enters into force in such a manner and upon such date as it may provide or as the negotiating States may agree.

2. Failing any such provision or agreement, a treaty enters into force as soon as consent to be bound by the treaty has been established for all the negotiating States.

3. When the consent of a State to be bound by a treaty is established on a date after the treaty has come into force, the treaty enters into force for that State on that date, unless the treaty otherwise provides.

4. The provisions of a treaty regulating the authentication of its text, the establishment of the consent of States to be bound by the treaty, the manner or date of its entry into force, reservations, the functions of the depositary and other matters arising necessarily before the entry into force of the treaty apply from the time of the adoption of its text.

Notes

The Vienna Convention provides that for its purposes "contracting State" means "a State which has consented to be bound by the treaty, whether or not the treaty has entered into force" (Article 2(1)(f)) and that "party" means "a State

---

[95] See the First and Second Reports on Reservations by the Special Rapporteur (M. Pellet), UN Docs. A/CN.4/470 and A/CN.4/1477 and Add 1. The Second Report is on human rights treaties.

[96] See Clark (1991) 85 A.J.I.L. 281, on the many reservations to the Women's Rights Convention.

which has consented to be bound by the treaty and for which the treaty is in force" (Article 2(1)(g)).

4. Observance and Application of Treaties

(i) Pacta Sunt Servanda

VIENNA CONVENTION ON THE LAW OF TREATIES 1969

Loc. cit., p. 765, n. 3, above

Article 26

Every treaty in force is binding upon the parties to it and must be performed by them in good faith.

Notes

The International Law Commission's Commentary reads:

> *Pacta sunt servanda*—the rule that treaties are binding on the parties and must be performed in good faith—is the fundamental principle of the law of treaties. There is much authority in the jurisprudence of international tribunals for the proposition that in the present context the principle of good faith is a legal principle which forms an integral part of the rule *pacta sunt servanda*. Thus, speaking of certain valuations to be made under Articles 95 and 96 of the Act of Algeciras, the Court said in the case concerning *Rights of Nationals of the United States of America in Morocco* (Judgment of August 27 1952)[97]: "The power of making the valuation rests with the Customs authorities, but it is a power which must be exercised reasonably and in good faith." Similarly, the Permanent Court of International Justice, in applying treaty clauses prohibiting discrimination against minorities, insisted in a number of cases, that the clauses must be so applied as to ensure the absence of discrimination in fact as well as in law; in other words, the obligation must not be evaded by a merely literal application of the clauses. Numerous precedents could also be found in the jurisprudence of arbitral tribunals. To give only one example, in the *North Atlantic Coast Fisheries Arbitration* the Tribunal, dealing with Great Britain's right to regulate fisheries in Canadian waters in which she had granted certain fishing rights to United States nationals by the Treaty of Ghent, said[98]: " . . . from the Treaty results an obligatory relation whereby the right of Great Britain to exercise its right of sovereignty by making regulations is limited to such regulations as are made in good faith, and are not in violation of the Treaty."[99]

[97] *Ed*. I.C.J. Rep. 1952, p. 212.
[98] (1910) Reports of International Arbitral Awards, Vol. XI, p. 188.
[99] Y.B.I.L.C., 1966, II, p. 211.

(ii) Relation with Internal Law

VIENNA CONVENTION ON THE LAW OF TREATIES 1969

Loc. cit., p. 765, n. 3, above

Article 27

A party may not invoke the provisions of its internal law as justification for its failure to perform a treaty. This rule is without prejudice to Article 46.[1]

Note
See to the same effect the 1949 Draft Declaration on Rights and Duties of States, above, p. 71.

(iii) Non-retroactivity

VIENNA CONVENTION ON THE LAW OF TREATIES 1969

Loc. cit., p. 765, n. 3, above

Article 28

Unless a different intention appears from the treaty or is otherwise established, its provisions do not bind a party in relation to any act or fact which took place or any situation which ceased to exist before the date of the entry into force of the treaty with respect to that party.

Notes
In the *De Becker* case,[2] the applicant alleged a violation by Belgium of Article 10 of the European Convention on Human Rights. He had been convicted in 1947 of a criminal offence and sentenced to life imprisonment and to the forfeiture for life of certain civil rights in accordance with the Belgian Penal Code (Article 123 sexies) including the right to participate in the running of a newspaper. The European Commission of Human Rights rejected the argument put by Belgium that the application was inadmissible *ratione temporis* because the sentence had been imposed before Belgium became a party to the Convention. It stated:

> whereas it should be pointed out in the first place that the judgment of the Brussels Military Court ... was delivered prior to 14th June, 1955, on which date the Convention came into force in respect of Belgium; whereas, moreover, the subsequent entry into force of the Convention cannot have invalidated retrospectively the forfeiture of rights complained of for all the preceding period, since the Convention, according to the generally recognised rules of international law, did not take effect retrospectively; whereas it follows that the

[1] See below, p. 827.
[2] (1958–59) 2 Y.B.E.C.H.R. 214.

Applicant cannot legally claim, for the period in question, to have been the victim of a violation of the rights guaranteed by the Convention, even if the state of affairs complained of is of a permanent nature; whereas it should nevertheless be noted that any person to whom the provisions of Article 123 sexies of the Belgian Penal Code are applied, is, in accordance with the very terms of that Article, deprived *ipso facto* and for life of the rights in question; that De Becker thus finds himself permanently deprived of the rights enumerated in Article 123 sexies and, in the event of an infringement of the provisions of the said Article, he may at any time be convicted under Article 123 non-ies; . . . Whereas it therefore appears that the Applicant finds himself in a continuing situation in respect of which he claims to be the victim of a violation of the right to freedom of expression guaranteed by Article 10 of the Convention and that the Application, insofar as it concerns this continuing situation extending after June 14, 1955, is consequently not inadmissible *ratione temporis*[3];

Article 28 of the Vienna Convention is consistent with such a ruling since the applicant's "situation" continued to exist after 1955.

What if a national of State A has his property confiscated by State B the day before a treaty between A and B comes into effect which makes such a confiscation illegal? Is State B liable under the treaty?

(iv) Territorial Application

VIENNA CONVENTION ON THE LAW OF TREATIES 1969

Loc. cit., p. 765, n. 3, above

Article 29

Unless a different intention appears from the treaty or is otherwise established, a treaty is binding upon each party in respect of its entire territory.

Notes

A question arises as to the territorial application of treaties made by a state with overseas possessions and other territories for whose international affairs it is responsible. The International Law Commission's Fourth Special Rapporteur on the Law of Treaties reported that "the general understanding today clearly is that, in the absence of any territorial clause or other indication of a contrary intention, a treaty is presumed to apply to all the territories for which the contracting States are internationally responsible."[4] Thus treaties made by the British Government apply to overseas territories for which the United Kingdom is internationally responsible unless the treaty indicates otherwise. For an example of a "territorial clause," see Article 63, European Convention on Human Rights 1950.[5]

---

[3] *ibid*. pp. 233–234.
[4] Third Report, Y.B.I.L.C., 1964, II, p. 15.
[5] As to units within a federal state, see above, p. 768.

(v) INCONSISTENT TREATIES

VIENNA CONVENTION ON THE LAW OF TREATIES 1969

Loc. cit., p. 765, n. 3, above

Article 30[6]

1. Subject to Article 103 of the Charter of the United Nations,[7] the rights and obligations of States parties to successive treaties relating to the same subject-matter shall be determined in accordance with the following paragraphs.

2. When a treaty specifies that it is subject to, or that it is not to be considered as incompatible with, an earlier or later treaty, the provisions of that other treaty prevail.

3. When all the parties to the earlier treaty are parties also to the later treaty but the earlier treaty is not terminated or suspended in operation under Article 59,[8] the earlier treaty applies only to the extent that its provisions are compatible with those of the later treaty.

4. When the parties to the later treaty do not include all the parties to the earlier one:

(*a*) as between States parties to both treaties the same rule applies as in paragraph 3;

(*b*) as between a State party to both treaties and a State party to only one of the treaties, the treaty to which both States are parties governs their mutual rights and obligations.

5. Paragraph 4 is without prejudice to Article 41,[9] or to any question of the termination or suspension of the operation of a treaty under Article 60[10] or to any question of responsibility which may arise for a State from the conclusion or application of a treaty the provisions of which are incompatible with its obligations towards another State under another treaty.

Notes

1. Imagine that States A and B make a treaty in which each undertakes not to allow any foreign military bases on its territory. States B and C make a treaty the following year in which B agrees that C shall establish a foreign base on B's territory. A learns of the treaty between B and C and protests, whereupon B refuses to allow C to establish the promised base. Has C a good claim against B to reparation under Article 30 of the Vienna Convention? What if B had ignored

---

[6] See Vierdag (1988) 59 B.Y.I.L. 75.
[7] *Ed*. Below, Appendix I.
[8] *Ed*. See below, p. 839.
[9] *Ed*. See below, p. 827.
[10] *Ed*. See below, p. 839.

the protest? Would A then have had a good claim for reparation against B? Could either A or C insist upon specific performance?[11]

2. Suppose that States D, E, and F agree by treaty to apply certain conservation measures when fishing for halibut and cod on the high seas. Later, D and E, but not F, become parties with a large number of other states, including G, to a halibut treaty by which fishing practices aimed at the conservation of halibut are agreed upon which are less strict than those in the earlier treaty between D, E, and F. Which rules as to the conservation of halibut and cod apply in the relations between D and E and D and F under Article 30? Which rules concerning halibut apply in the relations between D and G under Article 30?

3. Imagine that the Security Council, acting under Articles 41 and 25 of the United Nations Charter,[12] imposed in 1990 upon the members of the United Nations a legally binding obligation to refrain from supplying military weapons to State B, a United Nations member. State A, a United Nations member, has a treaty with State B that entered into force in 1975 that requires each state to supply the other with military weapons on request. State B now makes a request under the treaty. What is State A's legal position under the Vienna Convention? Would it matter if the treaty had entered into force in 1985? Or if State B was not a member of the United Nations?

5. TREATY INTERPRETATION[13]

FITZMAURICE, THE LAW AND PROCEDURE OF THE INTERNATIONAL COURT OF JUSTICE: TREATY INTERPRETATION AND CERTAIN OTHER TREATY POINTS

(1951) 28 B.Y.I.L. 1. Some footnotes omitted

. . . There are today three main schools of thought on the subject, which could conveniently be called the "intentions of the parties" or "founding fathers" school; the "textual" or "ordinary meaning of the words" school; and the "teleological" or "aims and objects" school. The ideas of these three schools are not necessarily exclusive of one another, and theories of treaty interpretation can be constructed (and are indeed normally held) compounded of all three. However, each tends to confer the primacy on one particular aspect of treaty interpretation, if not to the exclusion, certainly to the subordination of the others. . . . For the "intentions" school, the prime, indeed the only legitimate, object is to ascertain and give effect to the intentions, or presumed intentions, of the parties. . . . For

---

[11] It seems likely that specific performance is a "general principle of law" in the sense of Art. 38(1)(c), Statute of the I.C.J, below, Appendix I. On its extensive use in civil law systems, see Schlesinger, *Comparative Law* (5th ed., 1988), pp. 633 *et seq.*

[12] Below, Appendix I.

[13] See Bos (1980) 27 N.I.L.R. 3; Fitzmaurice (1957) 33 B.Y.I.L. 203; Lauterpacht (1949) 26 B.Y.I.L. 48; McDougal (1967) 61 A.J.I.L. 992; McDougal, Lasswell and Miller, *The Interpretation of Agreements and World Public Order* (1967; reprinted with additions, 1994); Maluwa (1990) 37 N.I.L.R. 330; Merrills (1968–69) A.Y.I.L. 55; Rosenne (1966) 5 Col. J.T.L. 205; Stone (1953–55) 1 Sydney L.R. 344; Vagts (1993) 4 E.J.I.L. 472; and Yambrusic, *Treaty Interpretation: Theory and Reality* (1987).

the "meaning of the text" school, the prime object is to establish what the text means according to the ordinary or apparent signification of its terms: the approach is therefore through the study and analysis of the text. For the "aims and objects" school, it is the general purpose of the treaty itself that counts, considered to some extent as having, or as having come to have, an existence of its own, independent of the original intentions of the framers. The main object is to establish this general purpose, and construe the particular clauses in the light of it: hence it is such matters as the general tenor and atmosphere of the treaty, the circumstances in which it was made, the place it has come to have in international life, which for this school indicate the approach to interpretation. It should be added that this last, the teleological, approach has its sphere of operation almost entirely in the field of general multilateral conventions, particularly those of the social, humanitarian, and law-making type.[14] All three approaches are capable, in a given case, of producing the same result in practice; but equally (even though the differences may, on analysis, prove to be more of emphasis and methodology than principle) they are capable of leading to radically divergent results.

INTERPRETATION OF PEACE TREATIES CASE (SECOND PHASE)

Advisory Opinion. I.C.J. Reports 1950, p. 221

The three 1947 Peace Treaties between the Allied Powers, on the one hand, and Bulgaria, Hungary and Romania, on the other, provided for commissions to hear disputes concerning the "interpretation or execution of the treaty" where they could not be resolved by negotiation. The commissions were to consist of three members. The two parties to the dispute were to appoint a member each; the parties were then to agree upon a third. If they could not agree, the third member was to be appointed by the Secretary-General of the United Nations. Disputes arose over the human rights guarantees in the treaties which could not, the United Kingdom and the United States claimed, be settled by negotiation. Bulgaria, Hungary and Romania refused to appoint members to the commissions. The General Assembly asked the Court whether the Secretary-General could appoint the third member of a commission when one party had failed to appoint its member and, if so, whether a commission consisting of the third member and the appointee of the other party could hear a dispute. The Court answered the first

---

[14] It may be useful to state briefly the main drawback of each method, if employed in isolation or pushed to an extreme. In the case of the "intentions" method, it is the element of unreality or fictitiousness frequently involved. There are so many cases in which the dispute has arisen precisely because the parties had no intentions on the point, or none that were genuinely common. To make the issue dependent on them involves either an abortive search or an artificial construction that does *not* in fact represent their intentions. The "textual" method suffers from the subjective elements involved in the notions of "clear" or "ordinary" meaning, which may be differently understood and applied according to the point of view of the individual judge. There may also be cases where the parties intended a term to be understood in a specialised sense, different from its ordinary one, but failed to make this clear on the face of the text. The teleological method, finally, is always in danger of "spilling over" into judicial legislation; it may amount, not to interpreting but, in effect, to amending an instrument in order to make it conform better with what the judge regards as its true purposes.

question in the negative, so that the second question did not arise. In the course of its opinion, the Court made the following comments on treaty interpretation.

Opinion of the Court

... the Governments of Bulgaria, Hungary and Romania are under an obligation to appoint their representatives to the Treaty Commissions, and it is clear that refusal to fulfil a treaty obligation involves international responsibility. Nevertheless, such a refusal cannot alter the conditions contemplated in the Treaties for the exercise by the Secretary-General of his power of appointment. These conditions are not present in this case, and their absence is not made good by the fact that it is due to the breach of a treaty obligation. The failure of machinery for settling disputes by reason of the practical impossibility of creating the Commission provided for in the Treaties is one thing[15]; international responsibility is another. The breach of a treaty obligation cannot be remedied by creating a Commission which is not the kind of Commission contemplated by the Treaties. It is the duty of the Court to interpret the Treaties, not to revise them.

The principle of interpretation expressed in the maxim: *Ut res magis valeat quam pereat*, often referred to as the rule of effectiveness, cannot justify the Court in attributing to the provisions for the settlement of disputes in the Peace Treaties a meaning which, as stated above, would be contrary to their letter and spirit.

Notes

1. The Court thus refused to apply the principle of effectiveness, according to which a treaty should be interpreted to give effect to its object and purpose, in such a way as to override the clear meaning of the text. At this point it parted company from the teleological approach.

2. The principle has been applied by the Court in a less extreme form in several cases. In the *Ambatielos* case,[16] Greece and the United Kingdom had replaced one bilateral commercial treaty between them by another. A Declaration accompanying the new treaty provided for the arbitration of "claims based upon the provisions of the [old treaty]. "The question arose whether, as argued by Greece, the Declaration applied to claims arising during the currency of the old treaty which were brought after the new treaty had been made as well as to such claims brought before it had been made. The Court ruled in favour of Greece:

> If the United Kingdom Government's interpretation were accepted, claims based on the Treaty of 1886, but brought after the conclusion of the Treaty of 1926 would be left without solution. They would not be subject to arbitration under either Treaty, although the provision on whose breach the claim was based might appear in both and might thus have been in force without a break since 1886. The Court cannot accept an interpretation which would have a

---

[15] *Ed*. For an example of a procedure for establishing a commission that would have avoided the difficulty in this case, see the Annex to the Vienna Convention on the Law of Treaties, below, p. 855.

[16] I.C.J. Rep. 1952, p. 28.

result obviously contrary to the language of the Declaration and to the continuous will of both Parties to submit all differences to arbitration of one kind or another.[17]

The principle has also been used where the meaning of the text is unclear to prefer an interpretation that gives some effect to a provision over one that does not. In the *Corfu Channel* case,[18] the Special Agreement by which the case was referred to the Court asked, *inter alia*, "is there any duty to pay compensation?" Albania argued that this question required only an answer "yes" or "no"; it did not require the Court to assess the amount of compensation due. The Court rejected this argument. It noted that it had, in any event, in answer to another question in the Special Agreement, to say whether international responsibility existed. Since international responsibility carried with it under customary international law an obligation to compensate and since there was no obligation to compensate in the absence of international responsibility, on Albania's interpretation of the question, the answer to it would add nothing to what the parties would otherwise know. The British argument, that the question required the Court to assess compensation, was preferred in order to give the question meaning. The Court said:

> It would indeed be incompatible with the generally accepted rules of interpretation to admit that a provision of this sort occurring in a special agreement should be devoid of purport or effect.[19]

The principle has been most strikingly applied by the Court in the specialised field of the constitutional law of international organisations to infer powers which are not expressly given to the organisation concerned but which are consistent with its purposes. See, in particular, the *Reparation*[20] and *Certain Expenses*[21] cases. See also the *South-West Africa* cases.[22]

VIENNA CONVENTION ON THE LAW OF TREATIES 1969

Loc. cit., p. 765, n. 3, above

Article 31

1. A treaty shall be interpreted in good faith in accordance with the ordinary meaning to be given to the terms of the treaty in their context and in the light of its object and purpose.

2. The context for the purpose of the interpretation of a treaty shall comprise in addition to the text, including its preamble and annexes:

(a) any agreement relating to the treaty which was made between all the parties in connexion with the conclusion of the treaty;

---

[17] *ibid.* p. 45.
[18] I.C.J. Rep. 1949, p. 4.
[19] *ibid.* p. 24.
[20] See above, p. 132.
[21] See below, p. 975.
[22] I.C.J. Rep. 1966, p. 6.

(*b*) any instrument which was made by one or more parties in connexion with the conclusion of the treaty and accepted by the other
parties as an instrument related to the treaty.

3. There shall be taken into account, together with the context:

(*a*) any subsequent agreement between the parties regarding the interpretation of the treaty or the application of its provisions;
(*b*) any subsequent practice in the application of the treaty which establishes the agreement of the parties regarding its interpretation;
(*c*) any relevant rules of international law applicable in the relations
between the parties.

4. A special meaning shall be given to a term if it is established that the
parties so intended.

Notes

1. The Vienna Convention rules on treaty interpretation are now regularly
applied by the I.C.J. as custom.[23] Which of the three approaches discussed by
Fitzmaurice[24] is adopted in the Vienna Convention, which can be taken to state
the customary law on the interpretation of treaties?[25] Note that the "object and
purpose" of a treaty is to be referred to in determining the meaning of the "terms
of the treaty" and not as an independent basis for interpretation.

2. On the *principle of effectiveness*, the International Law Commission's Commentary reads:

> The Commission, however, took the view that, in so far as the maxim *ut res
> magis valeat quam pereat* reflects a true general rule of interpretation, it is
> embodied in [Article 31, Vienna Convention] . . . When a treaty is open to two
> interpretations one of which does and the other does not enable the treaty to
> have appropriate effects, good faith and the objects and purposes of the treaty
> demand that the former interpretation should be adopted.[26]

The Commission clearly thought that the text as it stands permits the use of the
principle in the way it has been used by the World Court.[27]

3. *The Textual* or *"plain meaning" approach*. As stated by the International Law
Commission in its Commentary, "the jurisprudence of the International Court
contains many pronouncements from which it is permissible to conclude that the
textual approach to treaty interpretation is regarded by it as established law."[28]
See, for example, the *Admissions* case[29] and the *Competence* case.[30] On the limits to

---

[23] See, *e.g.* the *Maritime Delimitation and Territorial Questions* case *(Qatar v. Bahrain)*, I.C.J. Rep.
1995, p. 6 at p. 18.
[24] See above, p. 810.
[25] See the British Law Officers opinion, above, p. 766, n. 7; the *Restrictions to the Death Penalty
Case*, *loc. cit.*, p. 792, n. 78, above; and the *Wemhoff* case, Eur Court HR, Series A, vol. 7
(1968).
[26] Y.B.I.L.C., 1966, II, p. 219.
[27] See above, p. 811.
[28] Y.B.I.L.C., 1966, II, p. 220.
[29] I.C.J. Rep. 1948, p. 57.
[30] I.C.J. Rep. 1950, p. 4.

a "purely grammatical" approach, see the *Aegean Sea Continental Shelf* case, I.C.J. Rep. 1978, p. 23.

4. Would the Optional Protocol of Signature concerning the Compulsory Settlement of Disputes[31] adopted at the 1958 Geneva Conference on the Law of the Sea relating to disputes arising under the four Conventions adopted at the Conference constitute part of the "context" that could be used in interpreting any of those Conventions under Article 31(2)? Would the Resolution on Nuclear Tests on the High Seas[32] adopted at the same Conference? Could the definition of "warship" in the High Seas Convention be used to interpret the same term in the Territorial Sea Convention?[33]

5. *Subsequent Practice*. Fitzmaurice[34] states that:

> ... recourse to the subsequent conduct and practice of the parties in relation to the treaty is permissible, and may be desirable, as affording the best and most reliable evidence ... as to what its correct interpretation is.

The role of such practice is demonstrated by the following extract from the *Competence of the I.L.O. with respect to Agricultural Labour* case[35]:

> If there were any ambiguity, the Court might, for the purpose of arriving at the true meaning, consider the action which has been taken under the Treaty. The Treaty was signed in June 1919, and it was not until October 1921, that any of the Contracting Parties raised the question whether agricultural labour fell within the competence of the International Labour Organisation. During the intervening period the subject of agriculture had repeatedly been discussed and had been dealt with in one form and another.

What if both or all of the parties to a treaty act upon it in a way that is contrary to the clear meaning of the text over a lengthy period of time before such action is challenged by one of their number? Has the treaty, in effect, been revised informally?[36]

There would seem to be no reason to distinguish between subsequent practice by both or all of the parties jointly and such practice by both or all of them separately that is to the same effect. The value of practice showing the interpretation of just one or some of the parties, however, is less certain. The International Law Commission thought that only practice establishing the understanding of "the parties as a whole"[37] should be used. The phrase "agreement of the parties" in Article 31(3)(b) can probably be taken as reinforcing this view. Presumably, however, acquiescence is relevant so that the practice of one party of which the other parties have or can be deemed to have knowledge can, through lack of protest, establish the common interpretation of the parties. In the *Anglo-Iranian Oil Co.* case,[38] the International Court of Justice relied, in interpreting the Iranian declaration accepting the compulsory jurisdiction of the Court, upon an Iranian law approving the declaration some months after it was signed and some months before it was ratified. The Court said:

---

[31] U.K.T.S. 60 (1963), Cmnd. 2112; 450 U.N.T.S. 169.

[32] See above, p. 421.

[33] The definition originated in the I.L.C. Draft Articles, from which both Conventions derive.

[34] *loc. cit.*, p. 810, n. 13, above, p. 210.

[35] P.C.I.J. Rep., Series B, No. 2, pp. 39–40 (1922). Subsequent practice was also relied upon in the *Land, Island and Maritime Frontier Dispute* case, I.C.J. Rep. 1992, p. 351 at p. 586 and the *Jan Mayen* case, I.C.J. Rep. 1993, p. 38 at p. 51. See also the *Tadic* case, above, p. 753.

[36] See Fitzmaurice (1957) 33 B.Y.I.L. 203 at 225.

[37] Commentary, Y.B.I.L.C., 1966, II, p. 222.

[38] I.C.J. Rep. 1952, p. 92.

This clause . . . is . . . a decisive confirmation of the intention of the Government of Iran at the time when it accepted the compulsory jurisdiction of the
Court. . . . It is contended that this evidence as to the intention of the Government of Iran should be rejected as inadmissible and that this Iranian law is a
purely domestic instrument, unknown to other governments. The law is
described as "a private document written only in the Persian language which
was not communicated to the League or to any of the other States which had
made declarations. "The Court is unable to see why it should be prevented
from taking this piece of evidence into consideration. The law was published
in the Corpus of Iranian law voted and ratified during the period from January
15, 1931, to January 15, 1933. It has thus been available for the examination of
other governments during a period of about twenty years. The law was filed
for the sole purpose of throwing light on a disputed question of fact, namely,
the intention of the Government of Iran at the time when it signed the
Declaration.[39]

Clearly, the burden of watchfulness placed by the Court's approach upon other
parties to a treaty, particularly as their numbers grow, is a very great one.[40]

When France acceded to the Geneva Convention on the Continental Shelf 1958,
it declared its understanding of the meaning of Articles 1 and 2 of the Convention,[41] to which no reservations are permitted. Such an "understanding" may
qualify as an "instrument" in the sense of Article 31(2)(b), Vienna Convention. As
such it would be a factor to be taken into account when interpreting the Convention but would not by itself be conclusive.[42]

There may be a difference between action by a party accepting an obligation
and other action. Referring to declarations made by South Africa on its obligations under the Mandate for South-West Africa, the International Court of Justice
in the *South West Africa* case (1950)[43] said:

Interpretations placed upon legal instruments by the parties to them, though
not conclusive as to their meaning, have considerable probative value when
they contain recognition by a party of its own obligations under an instrument.

6. As to the establishment of a *"special meaning"* of a term (Article 31(4)),
Norway unsuccessfully argued in the *Eastern Greenland* case[44] that "in the legislative and administrative acts of the XVIIIth century on which Denmark relies . . .
the word 'Greenland' is used not in the geographical sense, but means only the
colonies of the colonised area on the West coast." The Court stated:

The geographical meaning of the word "Greenland" . . . must be regarded as
the ordinary meaning of the word. If it is alleged by one of the Parties that
some unusual or exceptional meaning is to be attributed to it, it lies on that
Party to establish its contention.

---

[39] *ibid.* p. 107. On the juridical nature of declarations accepting the compulsory jurisdiction
of the Court, see below, p. 1004.

[40] *cf.* above, p. 43.

[41] See above, p. 462, n. 28, on the Declaration concerning Art. 2. The U.S. noted the
declarations "without prejudice": UN Doc. ST.LEG/SER.D/15, p. 817.

[42] On "interpretative declarations" generally, see above, p. 796.

[43] I.C.J. Rep. 1950, p. 135.

[44] P.C.I.J. Rep., Series A, No. 53, p. 49.

7. *Particular rules and maxims.* McNair[45] states:

> From the time of Grotius onwards, if not before, successive generations of
> writers and, more recently, of arbitrators and judges, have elaborated rules for
> the interpretation of treaties, borrowing mainly from the private law of con-
> tract. One result ... is that today for many of the so-called rules of inter-
> pretation that one party may invoke before a tribunal the adverse party can
> often ... find another. ... The many maxims and phrases ... are merely prima
> facie guides to the intention of the parties and must always give way to
> contrary evidence of the intention of the parties in a particular case.

The Vienna Convention, adopting the scepticism voiced by McNair, refrains from
attempting to codify the numerous rules and maxims of interpretation, many of
which are familiar from municipal law, that undoubtedly exist. It remains true,
however, that some of the rules and maxims thus frowned upon will be of help
in many cases. This is true, for example, of the maxim *inclusio unius est exclusio
alterius*, which was stated in the *Life Insurance Claims*[46] to be "a rule of both law
and logic and applicable to the construction of treaties as well as municipal
statutes and contracts." The comment on it by Lopes L.J. in *Colquhoun v. Brooks*[47]
is, however, worth noting:

> The exclusion is often the result of inadvertence or accident, and the maxim
> ought not to be applied, when its application, having regard to the subject
> matter to which it is to be applied, leads to inconsistency or injustice.

An example of a somewhat questionable principle is the principle of restrictive
interpretation, whereby limitations upon a State's sovereignty are not to be
presumed, which was relied on by the P.C.I.J. in the *Wimbledon* case.[48] McNair
states:

> It is believed to be now of declining importance and the time may not be far
> distant when it will disappear from the books. It dates from an age in which
> treaties were interpreted not by legal tribunals, and not even much by lawyers
> but by statesmen and diplomats. ...
>   It is difficult to defend the rule on a basis of logic. Every treaty obligation
> limits the sovereign powers of a State. With rare exceptions a treaty imposes
> obligations on both parties ... if a so-called rule of interpretation is applied to
> restrict the obligations of one party, a sovereign State, it reduces the reciprocal
> benefit or "consideration" due to the other party, also a sovereign State, which
> seems to me to be absurd.[49]

It may, on occasions, contradict the principle of effectiveness.[50] It could have been
used, for example, in opposition to the Greek contention in the *Ambatielos*
case.[51]

---

[45] *Treaties*, pp. 364–366.
[46] *U.S. v. Germany* (1924) 7 R.I.A.A. 91 at 111.
[47] (1888) 21 Q.B.D. 52 at 65. See McNair, *Treaties*, p. 400.
[48] See above, p. 260.
[49] *Symbolae Verzijl*, p. 222 at pp. 235–236; reprinted in McNair, *Treaties* Appendix A, p. 754 at
p. 765.
[50] See above, p. 812.
[51] See above, p. 617.

VIENNA CONVENTION ON THE LAW OF TREATIES 1969

Loc. cit., p. 765, n. 3, above

Article 32

Recourse may be had to supplementary means of interpretation, including the preparatory work of the treaty and the circumstances of its conclusion, in order to confirm the meaning resulting from the application of Article 31, or to determine the meaning when the interpretation according to Article 31:

(a) leaves the meaning ambiguous or obscure; or
(b) leads to a result which is manifestly absurd or unreasonable.

Notes

1. The preparatory work, or *travaux préparatoires*, of a treaty is purposely not defined in the Vienna Convention. The International Law Commission thought that "to do so might only lead to the possible exclusion of relevant evidence."[52] In general terms, it is the record of the drafting of a treaty. It includes records of negotiations between the states that participate in the drafting and, in some cases, records of the work of independent bodies of experts, such as the International Law Commission and the United Nations Commission on Human Rights.[53] On a wide interpretation, it also includes such materials as unilateral statements by government spokesmen made prior to or at the time of the negotiations but not as a part of them. McNair[54] argues however, that evidence coming within this wider interpretation should not be admitted before international courts and tribunals: "Surely whatever value there may be in preparatory work is that it may afford evidence of the common intention of the parties."

At the Vienna Conference, the United States argued forcefully, but unsuccessfully, for a rule permitting the use of the preparatory work equally with the text in determining the parties' intention and not just as the supplementary aid proposed by the International Law Commission. It argued in part:

> . . . the restrictions upon the use of preparatory works expressed in Article 28 [Art. 32, Convention] do not, any more than the restrictions imposed upon the use of other circumstances, represent established practice . . . . Even in the *Lotus Case*,[55] which perhaps contains the most famous exposition of the alleged rule that "there is no occasion to have regard to preparatory work if the text of a convention is sufficiently clear in itself," the Court did in fact look at the *travaux*. . . . The habitual use of preparatory work by foreign offices needs no emphasis here.[56]

---

[52] Commentary, Y.B.I.L.C., 1966, II, p. 223.
[53] In *Read v. Secretary of State for the Home Dept.* [1989] A.C. 1014, HL, the explanatory report published with a Council of Europe convention was treated as a part of the *travaux*.
[54] *Treaties*, p. 421.
[55] P.C.I.J. Rep., Series A, No. 10 at p. 16 (1927).
[56] (1968) 62 A.J.I.L. 1021. This U.S. statement is also reported in *Treaty Conference Records*, 1968, p. 167. For another view favouring the use of preparatory work, see Lauterpacht (1935) 48 Harv.L.R. 549 and *ibid. Development*, Chap. 7.

Opposition to this proposal, based upon doubt about the value of preparation work, was voiced by the British delegate:

> ... preparation work was almost invariably confusing, unequal and partial: confusing because it commonly consisted of the summary records of statements made during the process of negotiations, and early statements on the positions of delegations might express the intention of the delegation at that stage, but bear no relation to the ultimate text of the treaty; unequal, because not all delegations spoke on any particular issue; and partial because it excluded the informal meetings between heads of delegations at which final compromises were reached and which were often the most significant feature of any negotiation.[57]

The French delegate also preferred the Commission's textual approach:

> It was much less hazardous and much more equitable when ascertaining the intention of the parties to rely on what they had agreed in writing, rather than to seek outside the text elements of intent which were far more unreliable, scattered as they were through incomplete or unilateral documents.[58]

Is it a good argument for the textual approach that "[t]he text adopted by the signatories is, with rare exceptions, the only and the most recent expression of their common intent?"[59] Is it a good argument in favour of allowing recourse to preparatory work in all cases to say that it does no harm to look at whatever evidence is available, and that, occasionally, it may help? It will be evident that much use is made of preparatory work in this case book. What impression do you have of its value for treaty interpretation from its use here? Is it helpful, for example, in deciding whether warships have a right of innocent passage through a foreign territorial sea under the 1982 Convention?[60] Or whether the conduct of scientific studies of the high seas is permitted by Article 87, 1982 Convention?[61] If the United States delegate is correct in his assertion as to the "habitual use of preparatory work by foreign offices," is that use evidence of state practice which is relevant in looking for a rule of customary international law?

In the *Employment of Women* case,[62] the Court referred to the preparatory work of a treaty to confirm the clear meaning of its text. Could it do this under the Vienna Convention? What would a court do if the preparatory work, resorted to for purposes of confirmation, contradicts the clear meaning of the text?

In the *Territorial Jurisdiction of the International Commission of the River Oder* case,[63] the Permanent Court of International Justice ruled that part of the preparatory work of the Treaty of Versailles 1919—the minutes of the Conference Committee on Ports, Waterways and Railways—could not be admitted in evidence before it for the purpose of interpreting the Treaty because not all of the parties to the case had participated in the drafting of the Treaty. The Court stated:

> ... three of the Parties concerned in the present case did not take part in the work of the Conference which prepared the Treaty of Versailles; ... accordingly, the record of this work cannot be used to determine, in so far as they are

---

[57] *Treaty Conference Records*, 1968, p. 178. On the use of preparatory work by the British Courts, see *Fothergill v. Monarch Airlines*, above, p. 94.

[58] *ibid.* p. 176.

[59] Huber, *Annuaire de l'Institut de Droit International* (1952), I, p. 199, Translation.

[60] See above, p. 406.

[61] See above, p. 419.

[62] P.C.I.J. Rep., Series A/B, No. 50 (1932). *cf.* the *Maritime Delimitation and Territorial Questions* case (Qatar v. Bahrain), I.C.J. Rep. 1995, p. 6 at p. 21.

[63] P.C.I.J. Rep., Series A, No. 23 (1929).

concerned, the import of the Treaty; . . . this consideration applies with equal force in regard to the passages previously published from this record and to the passages which have been reproduced for the first time in the written documents relating to the present case . . .

It thus refused to accept the distinction argued for by Poland in this case between preparatory work that had already been made public before presentation in the written proceedings in a case, which Poland thought should be admitted, and other preparatory work. The Vienna Convention contains no express limitation upon the use of the preparatory work in the sense of the ruling in the *Oder* case and the International Law Commission's Commentary shows that none was intended:

> The Commission doubted, however, whether this ruling reflected . . . actual practice . . . in the case of multilateral treaties. . . . Moreover, . . . [a] State acceding to a treaty . . . is perfectly entitled to request to see the *travaux préparatoires*, if it wishes, before acceding.[64]

How acceptable would the rule in the *Oder* case be in interpreting the United Nations Charter the number of parties to which is more than twice the original fifty who participated in its drafting?

2. Note that "the circumstances of" the "conclusion" of a treaty (Article 32) are, like the preparatory work, only a "supplementary means of interpretation." They were understood by the International Law Commission's Fourth Special Rapporteur as being "both the contemporary circumstances and the historical context in which the treaty was concluded."[65] An example of reliance upon background circumstances is found in the *Anglo-Iranian Oil Co.* case[66] where the International Court of Justice had to decide whether "treaties and conventions" in the Iranian declaration accepting the compulsory jurisdiction of the Court referred to treaties and conventions made before the declaration came into force as well as to those made afterwards. The Court noted:

> At the time when the Declaration was signed in October 1930 the Government of Iran considered all capitulatory treaties[67] as no longer binding, but was uncertain as to the legal effect of its unilateral denunciations. It is unlikely that the Government of Iran in such circumstances, should have been willing, on its own initiative, to agree that disputes relating to such treaties might be submitted for adjudication . . . by virtue of a general clause in the Declaration.[68]

VIENNA CONVENTION ON THE LAW OF TREATIES 1969

Loc. cit., p. 765, n. 3, above

Article 33

1. When a treaty has been authenticated in two or more languages, the text is equally authoritative in each language, unless the treaty provides

---

[64] Y.B.I.L.C., 1966, II, p. 223. See also Lauterpacht, *Development*, p. 137, and Rosenne (1963) 12 I.C.L.Q. 1378.
[65] Y.B.I.L.C., 1966, II, p. 59.
[66] I.C.J. Rep. 1952, p. 93.
[67] *Ed.* On capitulatory regimes, see above, p. 16, n. 54.
[68] I.C.J. Rep. 1952, p. 105.

or the parties agree that, in case of divergence, a particular text shall prevail.

2. A version of the treaty in a language other than one of those in which the text was authenticated shall be considered an authentic text if the treaty so provides or the parties so agree.

3. The terms of the Treaty are presumed to have the same meaning in each authentic text.

4. Except where a particular text prevails in accordance with paragraph 1, when a comparison of the authentic texts discloses a difference of meaning which the application of Articles 31 and 32 does not remove, the meaning which best reconciles the texts, having regard to the object and purpose of the treaty, shall be adopted.

Notes[69]

1. The International Law Commission's Commentary reads:

> The phenomenon of treaties drawn up in two or more languages has become extremely common and, with the advent of the United Nations, general multi-lateral treaties drawn up, or finally expressed, in five different languages have become quite numerous. When a treaty is plurilingual, there may or may not be a difference in the status of the different language versions for the purpose of interpretation. Each of the versions may have the status of an authentic text of the treaty; or one or more of them may be merely an "official text," that is text which has been signed by the negotiating states but not accepted as authoritative; or one or more of them may be merely an "official translation," that is a translation prepared by the parties or an individual government or by an organ of an international organisation. Today the majority of more formal treaties contain an express provision determining the status of the different language versions. If there is no such provision, it seems to be generally accepted that each of the versions in which the text of the treaty was "drawn" up is to be considered authentic, and therefore authoritative for purpose of interpretation. Few plurilingual treaties containing more than one or two articles are without some discrepancy between the texts. The different genius of the languages, the absence of a complete consensus *ad idem*, or lack of sufficient time to co-ordinate the texts may result in minor or even major discrepancies in the meaning of the texts. In that event the plurality of the texts may be a serious additional source of ambiguity or obscurity in the terms of the treaty. On the other hand, when the meaning of terms is ambiguous or obscure in one language but it is clear and convincing as to the intentions of the parties in another, the plurilingual character of the treaty facilitates inter-pretations of the text the meaning of which is doubtful.[70]

2. In the *Mavrommatis Palestine Concessions* case,[71] the Court had to interpret the phrases "public control" and *"contrôle public"* in the equally authentic English and French texts of the Palestine Mandate. The Court stated its approach as follows:

---

[69] See Hardy (1961) 37 B.Y.I.L. 72; Kuner (1991) 40 I.C.L.Q. 953; and Shelton (1997) 20 Hastings I.C.L.R. 611.

[70] Y.B.I.L.C., 1966, II, p. 224–225.

[71] P.C.I.J. Rep., Series A, No. 2 (1926).

... where two versions possessing equal authority exist one of which appears to have a wider bearing than the other, it is bound to adopt the more limited interpretation which can be made to harmonise with both versions and which, as far as it goes, is doubtless in accordance with the common intention of the Parties. In the present case this conclusion is indicated with especial force because the question concerns an instrument laying down the obligations of Great Britain in her capacity as Mandatory for Palestine and because the original draft of this instrument was probably made in English.[72]

Is the *Wemhoff Case* consistent with this?[73] In the *Standard Oil Company Tankers* case,[74] the Tribunal stated in interpreting a provision of the Treaty of Versailles 1919, of which the English and French texts are equally authentic, " ... there is a notable discrepancy in these texts, for while the English stipulates that due regard shall be had to any "legal or equitable interests," which corresponds to very clear and well-known conceptions of English and American law, of which equity is a form, the French employs the infinitely vaguer phrase of "droits et intérêts légitimes," which corresponds to no definite legal idea ... therefore everything points to the conclusion that the French phrase is merely the translation of the English, in which alone the expression employed has legal sense, and which makes clear the general tenor of the articles." The Tribunal then applied the English text.[75]

6. THIRD STATES[76]

FREE ZONES OF UPPER SAVOY AND THE DISTRICT OF GEX CASE

France *v.* Switzerland (1932)

P.C.I.J. Reports, Series A/B, No. 46

The facts of this case were nothing if not complicated. One of the many territorial problems that had to be dealt with at the Congress of Vienna in 1815 after the defeat of Napoleon was the future of Switzerland. On March 20, 1815, the powers participating in the Congress, who included France but not Switzerland, made a Declaration stating that if Switzerland "acceded to the stipulations contained in the present instrument, an Act shall be prepared containing the acknowledgment and the guarantee, on the part of all the Powers, of the perpetual neutrality of Switzerland in her new frontiers." One of the "stipulations" was that territory in the District of Gex on the French side of the proposed border between France and Switzerland and in the immediate vicinity of Geneva, which was to be just on the Swiss side of the border, should be linked with Geneva as a single economic unit. This was thought necessary partly because of the dependence of Geneva upon the District of Gex for food and other supplies. To this end, the Declaration stated, France would not levy customs duties upon goods crossing into Switzerland from

[72] *ibid.* p. 19.
[73] E. Court H.R. Rep. A 7 (1968) (the text that better achieves the purpose of a law-making treaty preferred).
[74] *U.S. v. Reparation Commission* (1926) 2 R.I.A.A. 777 at 792.
[75] See also the *German Reparations Case* (1924) 1 R.I.A.A. 429 at 439.
[76] See Chinkin, *Third Parties in International Law* (1993); Jiménez de Aréchaga (1956) 50 A.J.I.L. 338; Rosakis (1975) 35 Z.A.Ö.R.V. 1; and Schweisfurth (1985) 45 *ibid.* 653.

the District of Gex. Switzerland acceded to the Declaration, whereupon a second Declaration was made by the same Powers at Vienna on November 20, 1815, acknowledging the "perpetual neutrality of Switzerland." Somewhat similar arrangements were also made concerning territory in the District of Savoy, which was then in the State of Sardinia and later in France. The areas on the French and, originally, the Sardinian sides of the border with Switzerland in which these arrangements applied were known as the free zones.

As a result of changed circumstances, the justification for the zones had, arguably, disappeared by the time of the First World War. France wanted to end them and, on its initiative, Article 435 of the Treaty of Versailles 1919 provided that the parties to the Treaty, who included France, but not Switzerland, agreed that the zones were "no longer consistent with present conditions, and that it is for France and Switzerland to come to an agreement together with a view to settling between themselves the status of these territories . . . " Subsequently, the two states negotiated a treaty on the question which, although approved by the Swiss Diet, failed because it was rejected by a plebiscite of the Swiss people. Thereupon, France purported to abolish the zones unilaterally. In the present case, the Court was asked to decide whether Article 435 had abrogated the zones or had created for Switzerland an obligation to abrogate them. The Court by six votes to five ruled, as a matter of construction of Article 435, that it had done neither. It also made the following comments on the question of third state rights and duties. The zones are still in existence.

Judgment of the Court

It follows from the foregoing that Article 435, paragraph 2, as such, does not involve the abolition of the free zones. But, even were it otherwise, it is certain that in any case, Article 435 of the Treaty of Versailles is not binding upon Switzerland, who is not a Party to that Treaty, except to the extent to which that country accepted it. The extent is determined by the note of the Federal Council of May 5, 1919, an extract from which constitutes Annex I of the said Article. It is by that instrument, and by it alone, that Switzerland has acquiesced in the provision of Article 435; and she did so under certain conditions and reservations, set out in the said note, which state, *inter alia*: "The Federal Council would not wish that its acceptance of the above wording [*scil.* Article 435, paragraph 2, of the Treaty of Versailles] should lead to the conclusion that it would agree to the suppression of a system intended to give neighbouring territory the benefit of a special régime which is appropriate to the geographical and economical situation and which has been well tested" . . .

On the question of the legal effect of the two Declarations of 1815 the Court stated:

It follows from all the foregoing that the creation of the Gex zone forms part of a territorial arrangement in favour of Switzerland, made as a result of an agreement between that country and the Powers, including France, which agreement confers on this zone the character of a contract to which Switzerland is a Party.

It also follows that no accession by Switzerland to the Declaration of November 20th was necessary and, in fact, no such accession was sought:

it has never been contended that this Declaration is not binding owing to the absence of any accession by Switzerland.

The Court, having reached this conclusion simply on the basis of an examination of the situation of fact in regard to this case, need not consider the legal nature of the Gex zone from the point of view of whether it constitutes a stipulation in favour of a third Party.

But were the matter also to be envisaged from this aspect, the following observations should be made:

It cannot be lightly presumed that stipulations favourable to a third State have been adopted with the object of creating an actual right in its favour. There is however nothing to prevent the will of sovereign States from having this object and this effect. The question of the existence of a right acquired under an instrument drawn between other States is therefore one to be decided in each particular case: it must be ascertained whether the States which have stipulated in favour of a third State meant to create for that State an actual right which the latter has accepted as such.

VIENNA CONVENTION ON THE LAW OF TREATIES 1969

Loc. cit., p. 765, n. 3, above

Article 34

A treaty does not create either obligations or rights for a third State without its consent.

Article 35

An obligation arises for a third State from a provision of a treaty if the parties to the treaty intend the provision to be the means of establishing the obligation and the third State expressly accepts that obligation in writing.

Article 36

1. A right arises for a third State from a provision of a treaty if the parties to the treaty intend the provision to accord that right either to the third State, or to a group of States to which it belongs, or to all States, and the third State assents thereto. Its assent shall be presumed so long as the contrary is not indicated, unless the treaty otherwise provides.

2. A State exercising a right in accordance with paragraph 1 shall comply with the conditions for its exercise provided for in the treaty or established in conformity with the treaty.

Article 37

1. When an obligation has arisen for a third State in conformity with Article 35, the obligation may be revoked or modified only with the consent of the parties to the treaty and of the third State, unless it is established that they had otherwise agreed.

2. When a right has arisen for a third State in conformity with Article 36, the right may not be revoked or modified by the parties if it is established that the right was intended not to be revocable or subject to modification without the consent of the third State.

Article 38

Nothing in Articles 34 to 37 precludes a rule set forth in a treaty from becoming binding upon a third State as a customary rule of international law, recognised as such.

Notes

1. The general rule in Article 34 of the Vienna Convention, which is known by the maxim *pacta tertiis nec nocent nec prosunt*, undoubtedly reflects customary international law.

2. Commenting upon its Draft Article concerning *obligations* that, in substance, became Article 35 of the Vienna Convention, the International Law Commission acknowledged that the requirements in it are so strict that when they are met "there is, in effect, a second collateral agreement between the parties to the treaty, on the one hand, and the third state on the other; and that the juridical basis of the latter's obligation is not the treaty itself but the collateral agreement."[77]

3. Examples of third party rights are in the treaty provisions guaranteeing freedom of passage for ships through the Suez and Kiel Canals.[78] Note that in the case of the Hay-Pauncefote Treaty 1901 concerning the Panama Canal, in 1924 the United States Secretary of State took the position that "other nations . . . not being parties to the treaty have no rights under it."[79]

4. Some writers have suggested that certain types of treaties affecting third parties, including the international canal treaties referred to in the previous note, should be seen not as contracts having effect for third parties but rather as instruments intending to establish, and accepted by the international community as being able to establish, legal changes valid *erga omnes*. Thus McNair[80] distinguishes "the predominantly contractual type of treaty whose main object is to create obligations (both rights and duties) *in personam*," on the one hand, from "dispositive or 'real' treaties" and "constitutive or semi-legislative treaties," on the other. "Dispositive" treaties are "treaties creating or affecting territorial rights, and resembling the conveyance of English and American private law. . . . " McNair gives as examples treaties of cession, boundary treaties and mandate. As to "constitutive" treaties, he has in mind international settlements or arrangements such as those neutralising Switzerland and guaranteeing passage through the Suez Canal, as well as treaties creating states, *e.g.* Belgium, or other entities, *e.g.* the United Nations, and endowing them with legal personality valid *erga*

[77] Y.B.I.L.C., 1966, II, p. 227.
[78] See above, pp. 261–263.
[79] 5 Hackworth 222.
[80] *Treaties*, p. 256.

omnes. McNair suggests that the effect of "dispositive" and "constitutive" treaties is best explained not in terms of contract but of "some inherent and distinctive juridical element in those treaties."[81] The International Law Commission decided against adopting such a distinction:

> It considered that the provision in . . . [Article 36, Vienna Convention], regarding treaties intended to create rights in favour of States generally, together with the process mentioned in the present article, furnish a legal basis for the establishment of treaty obligations and rights valid *erga omnes*, which goes as far as is at present possible. Accordingly, it decided not to propose any special provision on treaties creating so-called objective régimes.[82]

5. What is the effect of Article 2(6) of the United Nations Charter[83] for states not members of the United Nations?[84]

7. AMENDMENT AND MODIFICATION

VIENNA CONVENTION ON THE LAW OF TREATIES 1969

Loc. cit., p. 765, n. 3, above

Article 39

A treaty may be amended by agreement between the parties. The rules laid down in Part II apply to such an agreement except in so far as the treaty may otherwise provide.

Article 40

1. Unless the treaty otherwise provides, the amendment of multilateral treaties shall be governed by the following paragraphs.

2. Any proposal to amend a multilateral treaty as between all the parties must be notified to all the contracting States, each one of which shall have the right to take part in:

(a) the decision as to the action to be taken in regard to such proposals;
(b) the negotiation and conclusion of any agreement for the amendment of the treaty.

3. Every State entitled to become a party to the treaty shall also be entitled to become a party to the treaty as amended.

---

[81] *ibid.* p. 255.
[82] Y.B.I.L.C., 1966, II, p. 231.
[83] Below, Appendix I.
[84] Contrast the views of Kelsen, *The Law of the United Nations* (1950), pp. 106–110, and Kunz (1947) 41 A.J.I.L. 119.

4. The amending agreement does not bind any State already a party to the treaty which does not become a party to the amending agreement; Article 30, paragraph 4(*b*) [above, p. 809], applies in relation to such State.

5. Any State which becomes a party to the treaty after the entry into force of the amending agreement shall, failing an expression of a different intention by that State:

(*a*) be considered as a party to the treaty as amended; and
(*b*) be considered as a party to the unamended treaty in relation to any party to the treaty not bound by the amending agreement.

Article 41

1. Two or more of the parties to a multilateral treaty may conclude an agreement to modify the treaty as between themselves alone if:

(*a*) the possibility of such a modification is provided for by the treaty; or
(*b*) the modification in question is not prohibited by the treaty and,

(i) does not affect the enjoyment by the other parties of their rights under the treaty or the performance of their obligations;
(ii) does not relate to a provision, derogation from which is incompatible with the effective execution of the object and purpose of the treaty as a whole.

2. Unless in a case falling under paragraph 1(*a*) the treaty otherwise provides, the parties in question shall notify the other parties of their intention to conclude the agreement and of the modification to the treaty for which it provides.

8. VALIDITY OF TREATIES[85]

(i) NON-COMPLIANCE WITH MUNICIPAL LAW REQUIREMENTS

VIENNA CONVENTION ON THE LAW OF TREATIES 1969

Loc. cit., p. 765, n. 3, above

Article 46

1. A state may not invoke the fact that its consent to be bound by a treaty has been expressed in violation of a provision of its internal law

---

[85] See Nahlik (1971) 65 A.J.I.L. 736. Note that Art. 42(1) of the Vienna Convention reads: The validity of a treaty or of the consent of a State to be bound by a treaty may be impeached only through the application of the present Convention.

regarding competence to conclude treaties as invalidating its consent unless that violation was manifest and concerned a rule of its internal law of fundamental importance.

2. A violation is manifest if it would be objectively evident to any State conducting itself in the matter in accordance with normal practice and in good faith.

Article 47

If the authority of a representative to express the consent of a State to be bound by a particular treaty has been made subject to a specific restriction, his omission to observe that restriction may not be invoked as invalidating the consent expressed by him unless the restriction was notified to the other negotiating States prior to his expressing such consent.

Notes

1. Opinion has been divided on the question whether non-compliance with a requirement of municipal law concerning competence to make a treaty affects the validity of a State's consent. The International Law Commission's Commentary summarises the three different approaches as follows:

> Some jurists maintain that international law leaves it to the internal laws of each State to determine the organs and procedures by which the will of a State to be bound by a treaty shall be formed and expressed.... On this view, internal laws limiting the power of State organs to enter into treaties are to be considered part of international law so as to avoid, or at least render voidable, any consent to a treaty given on the international plane in disregard of a constitutional limitation.... If this view were to be accepted, it would follow that other States would not be entitled to rely on the authority to commit the State ostensibly possessed by a Head of State, Prime Minister, Foreign Minister, etc., under [Article 7, Vienna Convention]... they would have to satisfy themselves in each case that the provisions of the State's constitution are not infringed or take the risk of subsequently finding the treaty void.... Other jurists, while basing themselves on the incorporation of constitutional limitations into international law, recognise that some qualification of that doctrine is essential if it is not to undermine the security of treaties.... On this view, a State contesting the validity of a treaty, on constitutional grounds may invoke only those provisions of the constitution which are notorious.... A third group of jurists considers that international law leaves to each State the determination of the organs and procedures by which its will to conclude treaties is formed, and is itself concerned exclusively with the external manifestations of this will on the international plane.... In consequence, if an agent, competent under international law to commit the State, expresses the consent of the State to a treaty through one of the established procedures, the State is held bound by the treaty in international law.... Some of these writers modify the stringency of the rule in cases where the other State is actually aware of the failure to comply with internal law or where the lack of constitutional authority is so manifest that the other State must be deemed to have been aware of it.[86]

[86] Y.B.I.L.C., 1966, II, p. 240–241. See also Meron (1978) 49 B.Y.I.L 772.

2. In the *Eastern Greenland* case,[87] Norway argued[88] that M. Ihlen was not competent under Norway's constitution to bind it on a matter such as that covered by the Ihlen declaration. Clearly the Court thought this to be irrelevant as far as international law was concerned. Similarly, in his report in the *Spanish Zones of Morocco Claims*,[89] M. Huber rejected a Spanish contention in respect of one of the claims—the *Rio-Martin* claim—that a treaty was not binding upon Spain because it had not been approved in a manner required by Moroccan law:

> The *Rapporteur* finds it unnecessary to elucidate this point of Moroccan constitutional law. It is enough to point out that the aforementioned exchange of letters between the authorised agents of the two Governments manifestly establishes their shared desire to transfer to a house at Tetuan rights that the British Government held in respect of the house at Martin by the terms of a treaty still valid for the point at issue.

3. The Government of the Isle of Man has no treaty-making power; treaties affecting the Isle of Man are made by the United Kingdom Government. Imagine that the Government of the Isle of Man were to purport to make a treaty with state A for the purchase of wheat. Could the United Kingdom avoid the treaty under Article 46? Could state A?

4. The International Law Commission's Commentary reads:

> ... [Article 47] is confined to cases in which the defect of authority relates to the execution of an act by which a representative purports *finally* to establish his state's consent to be bound.[90]

Where a treaty signed by a representative in excess of his authority requires ratification, if the state ratifies it "it will necessarily be held to have endorsed the unauthorised act of its representative and, by doing so, to have cured the original defect of authority."[91]

(ii) ERROR

VIENNA CONVENTION ON THE LAW OF TREATIES 1969

Loc. cit., p. 765, n. 3, above

Article 48

1. A State may invoke an error in a treaty as invalidating its consent to be bound by the treaty if the error relates to a fact or situation which was assumed by that State to exist at the time when the treaty was concluded and formed an essential basis of its consent to be bound by the treaty.

2. Paragraph 1 shall not apply if the State in question contributed by its own conduct to the error or if the circumstances were such as to put that State on notice of a possible error.

3. An error relating only to the wording of the text of a treaty does not affect its validity; Article 79 then applies.

---

[87] P.C.I.J. Rep., Ser. A/B, No. 53 (1933). For the Ihlen Declaration, see above, p. 772.
[88] P.C.I.J. Rep., Ser. C, No. 62, pp. 566–568.
[89] *Great Britain v. Spain* (1925) 2 R.I.A.A. 615 at 724. Translation.
[90] Y.B.I.L.C., 1966, II, p. 243.
[91] *ibid.*

Notes

1. Error, or mistake, plays a much less important part in the law of treaties in international law than it does in the law of contract in municipal law. The considerable care generally attendant upon the conclusion of treaties, together with, in some cases, the publicity and political scrutiny afforded to their drafting help to make this so. In practice, the International Law Commission points out, almost all the recorded instances in which errors of substance have been alleged, "concern geographical errors, and most of them concern errors in maps."[92]

2. Does Article 45 distinguish between mutual and unilateral error? Or between error of fact and of law?

3. In the *Temple* case,[93] the International Court of Justice was asked to rule that Cambodia, and not Thailand, had sovereignty over the Temple of Preah Vihear and that Thailand should both remove the armed guards and other persons it had placed in the Temple since 1954 and return sculptures and other objects it had taken therefrom. In 1904, the boundary between Cambodia (then a protectorate of France) and Thailand (then Siam) in the wild, remote and sparsely populated area of Preah Vihear was determined by a treaty between France and Siam. The treaty stated that it was to follow the watershed line and provided for the details to be worked out by a Mixed Franco-Siamese Commission. Surveys were conducted by technical experts for the Commission on the basis of which a map [the Annex I map] was prepared. This clearly placed the Temple in Cambodia. The map was never approved by the Commission which did not meet again after the map had been made. Cambodia relied upon the map. Thailand argued, *inter alia*, that the map embodied a material error because it did not follow the watershed line as required by the treaty. It argued this even though, as the Court found, the Siamese had received and accepted the map. The Court rejected Thailand's argument as follows:

> It is an established rule of law that the plea of error cannot be allowed as an element vitiating consent if the party advancing it contributed by its own conduct to the error, or could have avoided it, or if the circumstances were such as to put that party on notice of a possible error. The Court considers that the character and qualifications of the persons who saw the Annex I map on the Siamese side would alone make it difficult for Thailand to plead error in law. These persons included the members of the very Commission of Delimitation within whose competence this sector of the frontier had lain. . . . [94]

(iii) FRAUD AND CORRUPTION

VIENNA CONVENTION ON THE LAW OF TREATIES 1969

Loc. cit., p. 765, n. 3, above

Article 49

If a State has been induced to conclude a treaty by the fraudulent conduct of another negotiating State, the State may invoke fraud as invalidating its consent to be bound by the treaty.

[92] *ibid.*
[93] I.C.J. Rep. 1962, p. 6.
[94] *ibid.* p. 26.

Article 50

If the expression of a State's consent to be bound by a treaty has been procured through the corruption of its representative directly or indirectly by another negotiating State, the State may invoke such corruption as invalidating its consent to be bound by the treaty.

Notes

Fraud and corruption, like error, are not very important in practice in the law of treaties. As to *fraud*, the International Law Commission stated:

> Fraud is a concept found in most systems of law, but the scope of the concept is not the same in all systems. In International law, the paucity of precedents means that there is little guidance to be found either in practice or in the jurisprudence of international tribunals as to the scope to be given to the concept. In these circumstances, the Commission considered whether it should attempt to define fraud in the law of treaties. The Commission concluded, however, that it would suffice to formulate the general concept of fraud applicable in the law of treaties and to leave its precise scope to be worked out in practice and in the decisions of international tribunals.[95]

As to *corruption of a representative*, it stated:

> The strong term "corruption" is used expressly in order to indicate that only acts calculated to exercise a substantial influence on the disposition of the representative to conclude the treaty may be invoked as invalidating the expression of consent which he has purported to give on behalf of his state. The Commission did not mean to imply that under the present article a small courtesy or favour shown to a representative in connection with the conclusion of a treaty may be invoked as a pretext for invalidating the treaty.[96]

(iv) Coercion[97]

VIENNA CONVENTION ON THE LAW OF TREATIES 1969

Loc. cit., p. 765, n. 3, above

Article 51

The expression of a State's consent to be bound by a treaty which has been procured by the coercion of its representative through acts or threats directed against him shall be without any legal effect.

Article 52

A treaty is void if its conclusion has been procured by the threat or use of force in violation of the principles of international law embodied in the Charter of the United Nations.

[95] Y.B.I.L.C., 1966, II, p. 244.
[96] *ibid.* p. 245.
[97] See De Jong (1984) 15 N.Y.I.L. 209.

Notes

1. Coercion of a representative of a state is rare. Article 51 is directed at coercion of a representative personally and not at coercion of him through a threat of action against his state. An example of the exercise of both is reported to have occurred when President Hacha of Czechoslovakia signed a treaty with Germany establishing a German protectorate over Bohemia and Moravia in Berlin at 2.00 a.m. on March 15, 1939. According to one report

> The German ministers [Goering and Ribbentrop] were pitiless. . . . They literally hunted Dr. Hacha and M. Chvalkovsky round the table on which the documents were lying, thrusting them continually before them, pushing pens into their hands, incessantly repeating that if they continued in their refusal, half of Prague would lie in ruins from bombing within two hours, and that this would be only the beginning.[98]

Consent obtained contrary to Article 51 is of no legal effect; the state whose representative has been coerced cannot regard it as otherwise. The International Law Commission thought

> that the use of coercion against the representative of a state for the purpose of procuring the conclusion of a treaty would be a matter of such gravity that the article should provide for the absolute nullity of a consent to a treaty so obtained.[99]

2. As to coercion of a state, the International Law Commission's Commentary reads:

> The traditional doctrine prior to the Covenant of the League of Nations was that the validity of a treaty was not affected by the fact that it had been brought about by the threat or use of force. However, this doctrine was simply a reflection of the general attitude of international law during that era towards the legality of the use of force for the settlement of international disputes. With the Covenant and the Pact of Paris there began to develop a strong body of opinion which held that such treaties should no longer be recognised as legally valid. The endorsement of the criminality of aggressive war in the Charters of Allied Military Tribunals for the trial of the Axis war criminals, the clear-cut prohibition of the threat or use of force in Article 2(4) of the Charter of the United Nations, together with the practice of the United Nations itself, have reinforced and consolidated this development in the law. The Commission considers that these developments justify the conclusion that the invalidity of a treaty procured by the illegal threat or use of force is a principle which is *lex lata* in the international law of today. . . . Some members of the Commission expressed the view that any other forms of pressure, such as a threat to strangle the economy of a country, ought to be stated in the article as falling within the concept of coercion. The Commission, however, decided to define coercion in terms of a "threat or use of force in violation of the principles of the Charter,"[1] and considered that the precise scope of the acts covered by this definition should be left to be determined in practice by interpretation of the

---

[98] Dispatch by M. Coulondre, the French Ambassador to Berlin, quoted in Shirer, *The Rise and Fall of the Third Reich* (Pan Books Edition, 1964), p. 545.

[99] Y.B.I.L.C., 1966, II, p. 246.

[1] *Ed.* Note that in Art. 52 this wording was changed to "in violation of the principles of *international law embodied* in the Charter. . . . " Italics added.

relevant provisions of the Charter . . . the phrase "violation of the principles of the Charter" has been chosen rather than "violation of the Charter," in order that the article should not appear to be confined in its application to Members of the United Nations. The Commission further considered that a treaty procured by a threat or use of force in violation of the principles of the Charter must be characterised as void, rather than as voidable at the instance of the injured party. Even if it were conceivable that after being liberated from the influence of a threat or of a use of force a state might wish to allow a treaty procured from it by such means, the Commission considered it essential that the treaty should be regarded in law as void *ab initio*. This would enable the state concerned to take its decision in regard to the maintenance of the treaty in a position of full legal equality with the other state. If, therefore, the treaty were maintained in force, it would in effect be by the conclusion of a new treaty and not by the recognition of the validity of a treaty procured by means contrary to the most fundamental principles of the Charter of the United Nations.[2]

3. In the *Fisheries Jurisdiction (Jurisdiction)* case,[3] the International Court of Justice stated:

The letter of May 29, 1972 addressed to the Registrar by the Minister for Foreign Affairs of Iceland contains the following statement: "The 1961 Exchange of Notes took place under extremely difficult circumstances, when the British Royal Navy had been using force to oppose the 12-mile fishery limit established by the Icelandic Government in 1958."

This statement could be interpreted as a veiled charge of duress purportedly rendering the Exchange of Notes void *ab initio*, and it was dealt with as such by the United Kingdom in its Memorial. There can be little doubt, as is implied in the Charter of the United Nations and recognised in Article 52 of the Vienna Convention on the Law of Treaties, that under contemporary international law an agreement concluded under the threat or use of force is void. It is equally clear that a court cannot consider an accusation of this serious nature on the basis of a vague general charge unfortified by evidence in its support. The history of the negotiations which led up to the 1961 Exchange of Notes reveals that these instruments were freely negotiated by the interested parties on the basis of perfect equality and freedom of decision on both sides. No fact has been brought to the attention of the Court from any quarter suggesting the slightest doubt on this matter.

4. If state A were to attack state B and to be utterly defeated by it, would a peace treaty between the two states by which A agreed (i) to cede to B territory belonging to A and (ii) to pay compensation for injuries suffered by the population of B during the fighting be void because of coercion? Is Article 75 of the Vienna Convention applicable? This reads:

The provisions of the present Convention are without prejudice to any obligation in relation to a treaty which may arise for an aggressor State in

---

[2] *ibid.* pp. 246–247.
[3] *U.K. v. Iceland* I.C.J. Rep. 1973, p. 14. On the claim of duress in respect of the U.S.-Iranian Hostages Settlement, *see* Redwine (1981) 14 Vand. J.T.L. 847.

consequence of measures taken in conformity with the Charter of the United Nations with reference to that State's aggression.

On the present validity of title to territory based upon treaties that were made before the rule stated in Article 52 was established, see above, pp. 199, 229. Note that it is the acceptance of the treaty that must be coerced. A treaty, such as the 1979 Egyptian-Israeli Treaty of Peace, see above, p. 225, that is signed as a matter of choice is not invalid under Article 52, even though its terms may have been dictated or influenced by a prior use of force.

5. During the time of the USSR, Soviet writers used to support a doctrine of "unequal treaties".[4] The Soviet International Law textbook[5] stated:

> The principle that international treaties must be observed does not extend to treaties which are imposed by force,[6] and which are unequal in character . . .
> Equal treaties are treaties concluded on the basis of the equality of the parties; unequal treaties are those which do not fulfil this elementary requirement. Unequal treaties are not legally binding; . . .
> Treaties must be based upon the sovereign equality of the contracting parties.

Krylov[7] cites as examples of "unequal treaties" those establishing capitulatory regimes "by which an imperialist power imposes its will upon a weaker state . . ."[8] and the Munich Agreement of 1938,[9] by which France, Italy and the United Kingdom agreed to the cession to Germany of Sudeten German territory in Czechoslovakia. The Soviet International Law textbook gave the Anglo-Egyptian Treaty of Alliance of 1936[10] as a further example because it "violated the elementary sovereign rights of the Egyptian people."[11] Article 52 does not incorporate the Soviet doctrine. The "fundamental change of circumstances" rule[12] or the "clean slate" approach to state succession to treaties[13] might, however, be applicable in some cases. The Soviet doctrine has also received support from other writers.[14] At the Vienna Treaty Conference a Declaration on the Prohibition of Military, Political or Economic Coercion in the Conclusion of Treaties[15] was adopted by which the Conference:

> *Solemnly condemns* the threat or use of pressure in any form, whether military, political, or economic, by any state in order to coerce another State to perform any act relating to the conclusion of a treaty in violation of the principles of the sovereign equality of States and freedom of consent.

---

[4] On "unequal treaties", see Caflisch (1992) 35 G.Y.I.L. 52.
[5] Kozhevnikov, ed., *International Law* (1961), p. 248.
[6] On the meaning of "force" in Art. 2(4) of the UN Charter, see below, p. 863.
[7] (1947–I) 70 Hague Recueil 407.
[8] *ibid.* p. 434. Translation. On capitulatory regimes, see above, p. 16, n. 54.
[9] Misc. No. 8 (1938), Cmd. 5848.
[10] U.K.T.S. 6 (1937), Cmd. 5360.
[11] *op. cit.*, n. 5, above, p. 28.
[12] See below, p. 845.
[13] By this, a new state is not bound by the treaties made by its predecessor.
[14] For a statement typical of several made by Asian writers, see Sinha (1965) 14 I.C.L.Q. 121.
[15] *Treaty Conference Records*, 1969, p. 168.

(v) Ius Cogens[16]

VIENNA CONVENTION ON THE LAW OF TREATIES 1969

Loc. cit., p. 765, n. 3, above

Article 53

A treaty is void, if, at the time of its conclusion, it conflicts with a peremptory norm of general international law. For the purposes of the present Convention, a peremptory norm of general international law is a norm accepted and recognised by the international community of States as a whole as a norm from which no derogation is permitted and which can be modified only by a subsequent norm of general international law having the same character.

Article 64[17]

If a new peremptory norm of general international law emerges, any existing treaty which is in conflict with that norm becomes void and terminates.

Notes
1. The International Law Commission's Commentary reads:

The view that in the last analysis there is no rule of international law from which states cannot at their own free will contract out has become increasingly difficult to sustain, although some jurists deny the existence of any rules of *ius cogens* in international law, since in their view even the most general rules still fall short of being universal. The Commission pointed out that the law of the Charter concerning the prohibition of the use of force in itself constitutes a conspicuous example of a rule in international law having the character of *ius cogens*. Moreover, if some governments in their comments have expressed doubts as to the advisability of this article unless it is accompanied by provision for independent adjudication, only one questioned the existence of rules of *ius cogens* in the international law of today. Accordingly the Commission concluded that in codifying the law of treaties it must start from the basis that today there are certain rules from which states are not competent to derogate at all by a treaty arrangement, and which may be changed only by another rule of the same character. . . . The emergence of rules having the character of *ius cogens* is comparatively recent, while international law is in process of rapid development. The Commission considered the right course to be to provide in general terms that a treaty is void if it conflicts with a rule of *ius cogens* and to leave the full content of this rule to be worked out in state practice and in the

---

[16] See Mangallona (1976) 51 Phil. L.J. 521; Rozakis, *The Concept of Ius Cogens in the Law of Treaties* (1976); Scheuner (1967) 27 Z.A.O.R.V. 520 and 29 *ibid.* p. 28 (1969); Schwarzenberger (1965) 43 Texas L.R. 456, a shorter version of which is printed in (1965) 18 C.L.P. 191; Schwelb (1967) 61 A.J.I.L. 946; Sztucki, *Ius Cogens and the Vienna Convention of the Law of Treaties* (1974); Verdross (1966) 60 A.J.I.L. 55.

[17] Art. 64, which really contains a rule on termination, is included here for convenience.

jurisprudence of international tribunals. Some members of the Commission felt that there might be advantage in specifying, by way of illustration, some of the most obvious and best settled rules of *ius cogens* in order to indicate by these examples the general nature and scope of the rule contained in the article. Examples suggested included (a) a treaty contemplating an unlawful use of force contrary to the principles of the Charter,[18] (b) a treaty contemplating the performance of any other act criminal under international law, and (c) a treaty contemplating or conniving at the commission of acts, such as trade in slaves,[19] piracy or genocide, in the suppression of which every state is called upon to co-operate. Other members expressed the view that, if examples were given, it would be undesirable to appear to limit the scope of the articles to cases involving acts which constitute crimes under international law; treaties violating human rights, the equality of states or the principle of self determination were mentioned as other possible examples.[20]

The Commission eventually decided against including any examples of rules of *ius cogens* in Article 63 partly because "the mention of some cases ... might, even with the most careful drafting, lead to misunderstanding as to the position concerning other cases. ... "[21]

2. Can the International Court of Justice's reference to *ius cogens* in the *North Sea Continental Shelf* cases[22] be read as acceptance by the Court that there is such a concept in international law? How can a rule of *ius cogens* be changed? Rules of *ius cogens* are sometimes contrasted with rules of *ius dispositivum*, from which derogations are permitted by treaty. They are comparable with rules of public policy in municipal law.

3. Commenting upon the Vienna Conference, Sinclair states:

> Even before the Conference began, ... it was clear that the vast majority of international lawyers from the developing countries and from the Eastern European countries attached the highest importance to the concept that a treaty concluded in violation of an existing or new rule of *ius cogens* should be regarded as void and of no effect. ... On the other hand, the majority of Western European governments had, in their written and other comments on the Commission's proposals, expressed considerable doubts about the desirability of introducing *de lege ferenda* such a vague, indeterminate and undefined ground of invalidity; and some, including the United Kingdom Government, had stressed in addition that the application of the *ius cogens* articles must be made subject to independent adjudication.[23]

It was partly because of doubt about the provisions on *ius cogens* that France voted against the adoption of the Convention:

> It was no doubt a lofty concept but it was liable to jeopardise the stability of treaty law, which was a necessary safeguard in inter-State relations. On that point, even ... recourse to the International Court of Justice, could not make up for the lack of precision in the drafting of the texts. In consequence, the

---

[18] See In the *Nicaragua* case, below, pp. 871–872.
[19] In the *Aloeboetoe* case (1994) 1–2 I.H.R.R. 208, the Inter-American Court of Human Rights ruled that a 1762 treaty that imposed an obligation to sell prisoners as slaves "would today be null and void because it contradicts the norms of *ius cogens superveniens*."
[20] Y.B.I.L.C., 1966, II, pp. 247–248.
[21] *ibid.* p. 248.
[22] See above, p. 29.
[23] *loc. cit.*, p. 765, n. 1, above, p. 66.

judge would be given such wide discretion that he would become an international legislature and that was not his proper function.[24]

4. The concept of rules of *ius cogens* has similarities with that of obligations *erga omnes* that was spelt out in the *Barcelona Traction Case,* above, p. 604, and with that of the criminal responsibility of states which is found in the International Law Commission's Draft Article on State Responsibility, above, p. 487.[25] Of the three concepts, those of rules of *ius cogens* and obligations *erga omnes* have a strong claim to be customary international law, whereas that of the criminal responsibility of states is much more controversial. To a large extent, the three concepts are used to proscribe much the same kind of conduct. Thus a treaty to commit genocide would be invalid as contrary to *ius cogens,* and acts of genocide by a state would both be in breach of an obligation owed to all other states *erga omnes* and engage the criminal responsibility of the state. To judge from the examples given by the I.C.J. and the International Law Commission in their accounts of the three concepts, similar, though not quite such perfect coincidences, exist in the cases of resort to armed force and acts of aggression; slavery and the slave trade; and apartheid. The list of kinds of state conduct that is regarded as so fundamentally unacceptable by the international society of states as to be contrary to rules of *ius cogens* and obligations *erga omnes* can be seen to be growing and to overlap substantially with the catalogue of acts prohibited by the customary international law of human rights. For example, it must now be that a treaty between two states that provided for the prolonged arbitrary detention of a group of individuals would be contrary to *ius cogens* and any such detention would engage responsibility under the customary international law of human rights in an *erga omnes,* *Barcelona Traction* case, sense.

9. TERMINATION OF, SUSPENSION OF AND WITHDRAWAL FROM TREATIES[26]

(i) IN ACCORDANCE WITH THE TREATY OR OTHERWISE BY CONSENT

VIENNA CONVENTION ON THE LAW OF TREATIES 1969

Loc. cit., p. 765, n. 3, above

Article 54

The termination of a treaty or the withdrawal of a party may take place:

(*a*) in conformity with the provisions of the treaty; or

---

[24] M. Hubert (France), *Treaty Conference Records 1969,* p. 203.

[25] On the relationship between the three concepts, see Ganji, in Weiler, Cassese and Spinedi, eds., *International Crimes of State: A Critical Analysis of the I.L.C.'s Draft Article on State Responsibility* (1989), p. 151.

[26] See Kontou, *The Termination and Revision of Treaties in the Light of Customary International Law* (1994). Note generally that Art. 42(2) of the Vienna Convention reads: "The termination of a treaty, its denunciation or the withdrawal of a party, may take place only as a result of the application of the provisions of the treaty or of the present Convention. The same rule applies to suspension of the operation of a treaty."

(b) at any time by consent of all the parties after consultation with the other contracting States.

Article 55

Unless the treaty otherwise provides, a multilateral treaty does not terminate by reason only of the fact that the number of the parties falls below the number necessary for its entry into force.

Article 56[27]

1. A treaty which contains no provision regarding its termination and which does not provide for denunciation or withdrawal is not subject to denunciation or withdrawal unless:

(a) it is established that the parties intended to admit the possibility of denunciation or withdrawal; or
(b) a right of denunciation or withdrawal may be implied by the nature of the treaty.

2. A party shall not give less than twelve months' notice of its intention to denounce or withdraw from a treaty under paragraph 1.[28]

Article 57

The operation of a treaty in regard to all the parties or to a particular party may be suspended:

(a) in conformity with the provisions of the treaty; or
(b) at any time by consent of all the parties after consultation with the other contracting States.

Article 58

1. Two or more parties to a multilateral treaty may conclude an agreement to suspend the operation of provisions of the treaty, temporarily and as between themselves alone, if:

(a) the possibility of such a suspension is provided for by the treaty; or
(b) the suspension in question is not prohibited by the treaty and:

---

[27] See Widdows (1982) 53 B.Y.I.L 83.
[28] *Ed.* Art. 56(2) is based on "an obligation to act in good faith and have reasonable regard to the interests of the other party": *Agreement between WHO and Egypt Case*, I.C.J. Rep. 1980, p. 73 at p. 95. Advisory Opinion.

  (i) does not affect the enjoyment by the other parties of their rights
      under the treaty or the performance of their obligations;
 (ii) is not incompatible with the object and purpose of the treaty.

2. Unless in a case falling under paragraph 1(*a*) the treaty otherwise
provides, the parties in question shall notify the other parties of their
intention to conclude the agreement and of those provisions of the treaty
the operation of which they intend to suspend.

Article 59

A treaty shall be considered as terminated if all the parties to it conclude a later treaty relating to the same subject-matter and:

(*a*) it appears from the later treaty or is otherwise established that the
     parties intended that the matter should be governed by that treaty;
     or
(*b*) the provisions of the later treaty are so far incompatible with those
     of the earlier one that the two treaties are not capable of being
     applied at the same time.

2. The earlier treaty shall be considered as only suspended in operation
if it appears from the later treaty or is otherwise established that such was
the intention of the parties.

Notes
  The United Nations Charter is probably a treaty that allows the possibility of
withdrawal under Article 56(1)(*a*).[29] A treaty of political alliance would, probably
be a treaty covered by Article 56(1)(*b*).

(ii) MATERIAL BREACH[30]

VIENNA CONVENTION ON THE LAW OF TREATIES 1969

Loc. cit., p. 765, n. 3, above

Article 60

1. A material breach of a bilateral treaty by one of the parties entitles the
other to invoke the breach as a ground for terminating the treaty or
suspending its operation in whole or in part.

---

[29] See 7 U.N.C.I.O., *Documents*, p. 324.
[30] See Chinkin (1982) 17 T.I.L.J. 387; Hutchinson (1988) 59 B.Y.I.L. 151; Kirgis (1989) 22
   Cornell I.L.J. 549; Rosenne, *Breach of Treaty* (1985); Schwelb (1967) 7 Ind. J.I.L 309; Simma
   (1970) 20 O.Z.O.R.V.5. Sinha, *Unilateral Denunciation of Treaty because of Prior Violations of
   Obligations by Other Party* (1966).

2. A material breach of a multilateral treaty by one of the parties entitles:

(*a*) the other parties by unanimous agreement to suspend the operation of the treaty in whole or in part or to terminate it either:

    (i) in the relations between themselves and the defaulting State or
    (ii) as between all parties;

(*b*) a party specially affected by the breach to invoke it as a ground for suspending the operation of the treaty in whole or in part in the relations between itself and the defaulting State;

(*c*) any party other than the defaulting State to invoke the breach as a ground for suspending the operation of the treaty in whole or in part with respect to itself if the treaty is of such a character that a material breach of its provisions by one party radically changes the position of every party with respect to the further performance of its obligations under the treaty.

3. A material breach of a treaty, for the purposes of this article, consists in:

(*a*) a repudiation of the treaty not sanctioned by the present Convention; or

(*b*) the violation of a provision essential to the accomplishment of the object or purpose of the treaty.

4. The foregoing paragraphs are without prejudice to any provision in the treaty applicable in the event of a breach.

5. Paragraphs 1 to 3 do not apply to provisions relating to the protection of the human person contained in treaties of a humanitarian character, in particular to provisions prohibiting any form of reprisals against persons protected by such treaties.

Notes

1. The International Law Commission's Commentary reads:

> The great majority of jurists recognise that a violation of a treaty by one party may give rise to a right in the other party to abrogate the treaty or to suspend the performance of its own obligations under the treaty.... Opinion differs, however, as to the extent of the right to abrogate the treaty and the conditions under which it may be exercised.... State practice does not give great assistance in determining the true extent of this right or the proper conditions for its exercise. In many cases, the denouncing State has decided for quite other reasons to put an end to the treaty and, having alleged the violation primarily to provide a pretext for its action, has not been prepared to enter into a serious discussion of the legal principles involved. The other party has usually contested the denunciation primarily on the basis of the facts; and, if it has

sometimes used language appearing to deny that unilateral denunciation is ever justified, this has usually appeared rather to be a protest against the one-sided and arbitrary pronouncements of the denouncing State than a rejection of the right to denounce when serious violations are established.... The Commission was agreed that a breach of a treaty, however serious, does not *ipso facto* put an end to the treaty, and also that it is not open to a State simply to allege a violation of the treaty and pronounce that treaty at an end. On the other hand, it considered that within certain limits and subject to certain safeguards the right of a party to invoke the breach of a treaty as a ground for terminating it or suspending its operation must be recognised.... Some authorities have in the past seemed to assume that any breach of any provision would suffice to justify the denunciation of the treaty. The Commission, how-ever, was unanimous that the right to terminate or suspend must be limited to cases where the breach is of a serious character. It preferred the term "mate-rial" to "fundamental" to express the kind of breach which is required. The word "fundamental" might be understood as meaning that only the violation of a provision directly touching the central purposes of the treaty can ever justify the other party in terminating the treaty. But other provisions con-sidered by a party to be essential to the effective execution of the treaty may have been very material in inducing it to enter into the treaty at all, even although these provisions may be of an ancillary character.[31]

Note, however, that although Article 60 is available only in the case of a material breach, the general customary international law of countermeasures permits proportionate retaliation in the case of minor breaches of a treaty, as of any international law obligation.[32]

2. Support for the view that only a material, as opposed to any, breach justifies the termination or suspension of a treaty under the law of treaties is found in the *Tacna-Arica Arbitration*.[33] By Article 3 of the 1883 Treaty of Ancon between Chile and Peru it was provided that the Peruvian provinces of Tacna and Arica, sovereignty over which was sought by both parties, were to remain in the possession of Chile, which had obtained possession of them by armed force, for ten years and that after that time a plebiscite would be held to determine their future. In 1922, after the parties had been unable to agree upon arrangements for the plebiscite, the question whether the plebiscite had still to be held was referred to arbitration. Peru alleged, *inter alia*, that "Chile by preventing the performance of Article 3 has discharged Peru from her obligations thereunder, and hence that a plebiscite should not now be held and that Chile should be regarded as a trespasser in the territory now in question since the year 1894."[34] Chile had prevented the holding of the plebiscite as envisaged in Article 3, Peru argued, by her policy of "Chileanization" of the provinces by the introduction of Chilean nationals and by measures discriminating against Peruvians. The Arbitrator (President Coolidge, U.S.) rejected this argument on the facts:

The Arbitrator is far from approving the course of Chilean administration and condoning the acts committed against Peruvians to which reference has been made, but finds no reason to conclude that a fair plebiscite in the present circumstances cannot be held under proper conditions or that a plebiscite should not be had.... It is manifest that if abuses of administration could have the effect of terminating such an agreement, it would be necessary to establish

---

[31] Y.B.I.L.C., 1966, II, pp. 253–255.
[32] See above, p. 12.
[33] *Chile v. Peru* (1925) 2 R.I.A.A. 921.
[34] *ibid.* p. 929.

such serious conditions as the consequence of administrative wrongs as would operate to frustrate the purpose of the agreement, and, in the opinion of the Arbitrator, a situation of such gravity has not been shown.[35]

3. When is there a material breach under Article 60(3) (*b*) in the case of a law-making treaty with a number of provisions of roughly equal importance? Would, for example, a breach of Article 97 of the 1982 Law of the Sea Convention concerning criminal jurisdiction in respect of collisions on the high seas[36] be one?

4. In the case of some treaties, the International Law Commission stated in its Commentary, "a breach by one party tends to undermine the whole regime of the treaty as between all the parties."[37] The Commission gave disarmament treaties as examples of such treaties and explained:

> In the case of a material breach of such a treaty the interests of an individual party may not be adequately protected by the rules contained in paragraphs 2(*a*) and (*b*). It could not suspend the performance of its own obligations under the treaty *vis-à-vis* the defaulting State without at the same time violating its obligations to the other parties. Yet, unless it does so, it may be unable to protect itself against the threat resulting from the arming of the defaulting State. In these cases, where a material breach of the treaty by one party radically changes the position of every party with respect to the further performance of its obligations, the Commission considered that any party must be permitted without first obtaining the agreement of the other parties to suspend the operation of the treaty with respect to itself generally in its relations with all the other parties. Paragraph 2(*c*) accordingly so provides.[38]

Would the Nuclear Test Ban Treaty 1963,[39] or a treaty limiting the number of whales that may be caught annually be other examples of such treaties? Would Article 60(2)(*c*) be available in respect of a material breach of the 1948 Genocide Convention?[40] (Would Article 60(2)(*b*) be available in the same case?) What is the effect for the other innocent parties if one innocent party acts under Article 60(2)(*c*)? On the question of suspension of the Vienna Convention on Diplomatic Relations in the context of the *Libyan People's Bureau Incident*, see above, p. 351.

5. Paragraph 5 of Article 60 was added at Vienna. The provisions in the 1949 Geneva Red Cross Conventions[41] prohibiting reprisals against the persons protected by the Conventions were mentioned as coming within it.[42] Reference was also made to conventions concerning refugees, slavery, genocide, and human rights generally, although these do not contain provisions prohibiting reprisals in cases of breach.[43]

---

[35] *ibid.* pp. 943–944.
[36] See above, p. 427.
[37] Y.B.I.L.C., 1966, II, p. 255.
[38] *ibid.*
[39] See above, p. 421. See on this question, Schwelb (1964) 58 A.J.I.L. 642 at 663–669.
[40] For the Convention, see above, p. 745.
[41] See, *e.g.* Art. 46 of the Geneva Convention for the Amelioration of the Condition of the Wounded and Sick in Armed Forces in the Field, U.K.T.S. 39 (1958), Cmnd. 550; 75 U.N.T.S. 3: "Reprisals against the wounded, sick, personnel, buildings, or equipment protected by the Convention are prohibited."
[42] Mr Ruegger (Switzerland), introducing the amendment: *Treaty Conference Records*, 1969, p. 112.
[43] *ibid.*

LEGAL CONSEQUENCES FOR STATES OF THE CONTINUED PRESENCE OF SOUTH AFRICA IN NAMIBIA (SOUTH WEST AFRICA) NOTWITHSTANDING SECURITY COUNCIL RESOLUTION 276 (1970)

Advisory Opinion. I.C.J. Reports 1971, p. 16

By Resolution 2145, the United Nations General Assembly, exercising the supervisory functions which the United Nations had taken over from the League of Nations, terminated the mandate in respect of Namibia/South West Africa conferred by the League on the United Kingdom and exercised on its behalf by South Africa. It did so because South Africa had "failed to fulfil its obligations" under the mandate and had, "in fact, disavowed the mandate." In the following extract, the Court, when it considered the legal consequences of South Africa's continued presence in Namibia/South West Africa despite the General Assembly's action, considered and applied the rules as to "material breach" of a treaty, which the mandate was. The Court was of the opinion that the mandate had been validly terminated.

Opinion of the Court

91. One of the fundamental principles governing the international relationship thus established is that a party which disowns or does not fulfil its own obligations cannot be recognised as retaining the rights which it claims to derive from the relationship.

94. In examining this action [resolution 2145] of the General Assembly it is appropriate to have regard to the general principles of international law regulating termination of a treaty relationship on account of breach. . . . The rules laid down by the Vienna Convention on the Law of Treaties concerning termination of a treaty relationship on account of breach (adopted without a dissenting vote) may in many respects be considered as a codification of existing customary law on the subject. In the light of these rules [see Article 60(3)], only a material breach of a treaty justifies termination. . . .

95. General Assembly resolution 2145 (XXI) determines that both forms of material breach [in Article 60(3)] had occurred in this case. By stressing that South Africa "has in fact, disavowed the Mandate," the General Assembly declared in fact that it had repudiated it. The resolution in question is therefore to be viewed as the exercise of the right to terminate a relationship in case of a deliberate and persistent violation of obligations which destroys the very object and purpose of that relationship.

96. It has been contended that the Covenant of the League of Nations did not confer on the Council of the League power to terminate a mandate for misconduct of the mandatory and that no such power could therefore be exercised by the United Nations, since it could not derive from the League greater powers than the latter itself had. For this objection to prevail it would be necessary to show that the mandates system, as established under the League, excluded the application of the general

principle of law that a right of termination on account of breach must be presumed to exist in respect of all treaties, except as regards provisions relating to the protection of the human person contained in treaties of a humanitarian character (as indicated in Art. 60, para. 5, of the Vienna Convention). The silence of a treaty as to the existence of such a right cannot be interpreted as implying the exclusion of a right which has its source outside of the treaty, in general international law, and is dependent on the occurrence of circumstances which are not normally envisaged when a treaty is concluded.

Notes

Note that the Court treated Article 60 as stating customary international law. "in many [unidentified] respects"[44]

(iii) SUPERVENING IMPOSSIBILITY OF PERFORMANCE

VIENNA CONVENTION ON THE LAW OF TREATIES 1969

Loc. cit., p. 765, n. 3, above

Article 61

1. A party may invoke the impossibility of performing a treaty as a ground for terminating or withdrawing from it if the impossibility results from the permanent disappearance or destruction of an object indispensible for the execution of the treaty. If the impossibility is temporary, it may be invoked only as a ground for suspending the operation of the treaty.

2. Impossibility of performance may not be invoked by a party as a ground for terminating, withdrawing from or suspending the operation of a treaty if the impossibility, is the result of a breach by that party either of an obligation under the treaty or of any other international obligation owed to any other party to the treaty.

Notes

The International Law Commission's Commentary reads:

> State practice furnishes few examples of the termination of a treaty on this ground. But the types of cases envisaged . . . [include] the submergence of an island, the drying up of a river or the destruction of a dam or hydro-electric installation indispensable for the execution of a treaty.[45]

The law of state succession applies where a state party to a treaty ceases to exist: see above, p. 128.

[44] See also the reference to Art. 60 in the *Appeal relating to the Jurisdiction of the I.C.A.O. Council* case, I.C.J. Rep. 1972, p. 46, at p. 67. For commentary see Briggs (1974) 68 A.J.I.L. 51.

[45] Y.B.I.L.C., 1966, II, p. 256.

(iv) FUNDAMENTAL CHANGE OF CIRCUMSTANCES[46]

VIENNA CONVENTION ON THE LAW OF TREATIES 1969

Loc. cit., p. 765, n. 3, above

Article 62

1. A fundamental change of circumstances which has occurred with regard to those existing at the time of the conclusion of a treaty, and which was not foreseen by the parties, may not be invoked as a ground for terminating or withdrawing from the treaty unless:

(a) the existence of those circumstances constituted an essential basis of the consent of the parties to be bound by the treaty; and
(b) the effect of the change is radically to transform the extent of obligations still to be performed under the treaty.

2. A fundamental change of circumstances may not be invoked as a ground for terminating or withdrawing from a treaty:

(a) if the treaty establishes a boundary; or
(b) if the fundamental change is the result of a breach by the party invoking it either of an obligation under the treaty or of any other international obligation owed to any other party to the treaty.

3. If, under the foregoing paragraphs, a party may invoke a fundamental change of circumstances as a ground for terminating or withdrawing from a treaty it may also invoke the change as a ground for suspending the operation of the treaty.

Notes
1. The International Law Commission's Commentary reads:

> Almost all modern jurists, however reluctantly, admit the existence in international law of the principle with which this article is concerned and which is commonly spoken of as the doctrine of *rebus sic stantibus*.[47] Just as many systems of municipal law recognise that, quite apart from any actual impossibility of performance, contracts may become inapplicable through a fundamental change of circumstances, so also treaties may become inapplicable for the same reason. Most jurists, however, at the same time enter a strong caveat

---

[46] See Haraszti, (1975–III) 146 Hague Recueil 1; Lissitzyn (1967) 61 A.J.I.L. 895; Schwelb (1969) 29 Z.A.O.R.V. 39; Toth, 1974 Jur. Rev. 56, 147, 263.
[47] *Ed.* The term *rebus sic stantibus* means literally "things remaining as they are." Reference is often made to the *clausula rebus sic stantibus, i.e.* to an express or implied clause in a treaty conditioning its validity upon the continuance of the circumstances existing at the time when it is made.

as to the need to confine the scope of the doctrine within narrow limits and to regulate strictly the conditions under which it may be invoked; for the risks to the security of treaties which this doctrine presents in the absence of any general system of compulsory jurisdiction are obvious. The circumstances of international life are always changing and it is easy to allege that the changes render the treaty inapplicable. The evidence of the principle in customary law is considerable, but the International Court has not yet committed itself on the point. . . . The principle of *rebus sic stantibus* has not infrequently been invoked in State practice either *eo nomine* or in the form of a reference to a general principle claimed to justify the termination or modification of treaty obligations by reason of changed circumstances. Broadly speaking, it shows a wide acceptance of the view that a fundamental change of circumstances may justify a demand for the termination or revision of a treaty, but also shows a strong disposition to question the right of a party to denounce a treaty unilaterally on this ground.[48]

The Commission rejected the view that the rule should be limited to "so-called perpetual treaties", *i.e.* "treaties not making any provision for their termination."[49] Although cases of "supervening impossibility of performance," dealt with under Article 61, could be brought within Article 62, the International Law Commission "considered that juridically 'impossibility of performance' and 'fundamental change of circumstances' are distinct grounds for regarding a treaty as having been terminated, and should be kept separate."[50]

2. On the juridical basis of the rule, the International Law Commission's Commentary reads:

> In the past the principle has almost always been presented in the guise of a tacit condition implied in every "perpetual" treaty that would dissolve it in the event of a fundamental change of circumstances. The Commission noted, however, that the tendency today was to regard the implied term as only a fiction by which it was attempted to reconcile the principle of the dissolution of treaties in consequence of a fundamental change of circumstances with the rule *pacta sunt servanda*. In most cases the parties gave no thought to the possibility of a change of circumstances and, if they had done so, would probably have provided for it in a different manner. Furthermore, the Commission considered the fiction to be an undesirable one since it increased the risk of subjective interpretations and abuse. For this reason, the Commission was agreed that the theory of an implied term must be rejected and the doctrine formulated as an objective rule of law by which, on grounds of equity and justice, a fundamental change of circumstances may, under certain conditions, be invoked by a party as a ground for terminating the treaty.[51]

How does the rule compare with that of frustration in the common law of contract? What does the Commission mean when it refers to an "objective rule of law?" Is the test in Article 62 one of reasonable foreseeability, or what was actually forseen? Is it the foresight of *all* of the parties?

---

[48] Y.B.I.L.C., 1966, II, p. 257 *et seq.*
[49] *ibid.* p. 259.
[50] *ibid.* p. 256.
[51] *ibid.* p. 258.

FISHERIES JURISDICTION CASE (JURISDICTION)

United Kingdom *v.* Iceland

I.C.J. Reports 1974, p. 3

For the facts, see above, p. 447. The treaty which Iceland sought to have terminated *rebus sic stantibus* was the 1961 exchange of notes with the United Kingdom by which either party could refer a dispute concerning Iceland's extension of its fishing zone to the I.C.J., as the United Kingdom had done in this case.

Judgment of the Court

35. In his letter of May 29, 1972, to the Registrar, the Minister of Foreign Affairs of Iceland refers to "the changed circumstances resulting from the ever-increasing exploitation of the fishery resources in the seas surrounding Iceland."

36. . . . the Government of Iceland is basing itself on the principle of termination of a treaty by reason of change of circumstances. International law admits that a fundamental change in the circumstances which determined the parties to accept a treaty, if it has resulted in a radical transformation of the extent of the obligations imposed by it, may, under certain conditions, afford the party affected a ground for invoking the termination or suspension of the treaty. This principle, and the conditions and exceptions to which it is subject, have been embodied in Article 62 of the Vienna Convention on the Law of Treaties, which may in many respects be considered as a codification of existing customary law on the subject of the termination of a treaty relationship on account of change of circumstances.

37. One of the basic requirements embodied in that Article is that the change of circumstances must have been a fundamental one. In this respect the Government of Iceland has, with regard to developments in fishing techniques, referred . . . to the increased exploitation of the fishery resources in the seas surrounding Iceland and to the danger of still further exploitation because of an increase in the catching capacity of fishing fleets. The Icelandic statements recall the exceptional dependence of that country on its fishing for its existence and economic development. . . .

38. The invocation by Iceland of its "vital interests," which were not made the subject of an express reservation to the acceptance of the jurisdictional obligation under the 1961 Exchange of Notes, must be interpreted, in the context of the assertion of changed circumstances, as an indication by Iceland of the reason why it regards as fundamental the changes which in its view have taken place in previously existing fishing techniques. This interpretation would correspond to the traditional view

that the changes of circumstances which must be regarded as fundamental or vital are those which imperil the existence of vital development of one of the parties. . . .

If, as contended by Iceland, there have been any fundamental changes in fishing techniques in the waters around Iceland, those changes might be relevant for the decision on the merits of the dispute. . . . But the alleged changes could not affect in the least the obligation to submit to the Court's jurisdiction, which is the only issue at the present stage of the proceedings. It follows that the apprehended dangers for the vital interests of Iceland, resulting from changes in fishing techniques, cannot constitute a fundamental change with respect to the lapse or subsistence of the compromissory clause establishing the Court's jurisdiction. . . .

43. Moreover, in order that a change of circumstances may give rise to a ground for invoking the termination of a treaty it is also necessary that it should have resulted in a radical transformation of the extent of the obligations still to be performed. The change must have increased the burden of the obligations to be executed to the extent of rendering the performance something essentially different from that originally undertaken. In respect of the obligation with which the Court is here concerned, this condition is wholly unsatisfied; the change of circumstances alleged by Iceland cannot be said to have transformed radically the extent of the jurisdictional obligation which is imposed in the 1961 Exchange of Notes. . . . The present dispute is exactly of the character anticipated in the compromissory clause of the Exchange of Notes. Not only has the jurisdictional obligation not been radically transformed in its extent; it has remained precisely what it was in 1961.

44. In the United Kingdom Memorial it is asserted that there is a flaw in the Icelandic contention of circumstances: that the doctrine never operates so as to extinguish a treaty automatically or to allow an unchallengeable unilateral denunciation by one party; it only operates to confer a right to call for termination and, if that call is disputed, to submit the dispute to some organ or body with power to determine whether the conditions for the operation of the doctrine are present. In this connection the Applicant alludes to Articles 65 and 66 of the Vienna Convention on the Law of Treaties.

45. In the present case, the procedural complement to the doctrine of changed circumstances is already provided for in the 1961 Exchange of Notes, which specifically calls upon the parties to have recourse to the Court in the event of a dispute relating to Iceland's extension of fisheries jurisdiction. . . .

SEPARATE OPINION OF JUDGE SIR GERALD FITZMAURICE. With regard to the question of "changed circumstances" I have nothing to add to what is stated in paragraphs 35–43 of the Court's Judgment, except to emphasise that in my opinion the only change that could possibly be relevant (if at all) would be some change relating directly to the, so to speak, operability of the jurisdictional clause itself[52]—not to such things as developments in fishery techniques or in Iceland's situation relative to fisheries. These would indeed be matters that would militate for, not against, adjudication. But as regards the jurisdictional clause itself, the only "change" that has occurred is the purported extension of Icelandic fishery limits. This however is the absolute *reverse* of the type of change to which the doctrine of "changed circumstances" relates, namely one never contemplated by the Parties: it is in fact the actual change they did contemplate, and specified as the one that would give rise to the obligation to have recourse to adjudication.

Notes

See also the *Free Zones* case, above, p. 822.

(v) Severance of Diplomatic or Consular Relations

VIENNA CONVENTION ON THE LAW OF TREATIES 1969

Loc. cit., p. 765, n. 3, above

Article 63

The severence of diplomatic or consular relations between parties to a treaty does not affect the legal relations established between them by the treaty except in so far as the existence of diplomatic or consular relations is indispensable for the application of the treaty.

Notes

The International Law Commission noted in its Commentary that:

> the use of third states and even of direct channels as means for making necessary communications in case of severance of diplomatic relations are so common that the absence of the normal channels ought not to be recognised as a disappearance of a "means" or of an "object" indispensable for the execution of a treaty.[53]

Article 63 of the Vienna Convention differs from the Commission's Draft Article by the inclusion of the words "except in so far as" onwards. The severance of consular relations by the two parties to a treaty providing for a right of consular access to a detained national would presumably come within the stated exception.

(vi) Ius Cogens

See Article 64 of the Vienna Convention.[54]

---

[52] For instance if the character of the International Court itself had changed in the meantime so that it was no longer the entity the Parties had had in mind, *e.g.* if owing to developments in the United Nations, the Court had been converted into a tribunal of mixed law and conciliation, proceeding on a basis other than a purely juridical one.

[53] Y.B.I.L.C., 1966, II, p. 261.

[54] Above, p. 835.

10. General Provisions on the Invalidity, Termination and
Suspension of Treaties

(i) Consequences of Invalidity, Termination or Suspension

VIENNA CONVENTION ON THE LAW OF TREATIES 1969

Loc. cit., p. 765, n. 3, above

Article 69

1. A treaty the invalidity of which is established under the present convention is void. The provisions of a void treaty has no legal force.
2. If acts have nevertheless been performed in reliance on such a treaty:

(a) each party may require any other party to establish as far as possible in their mutual relations the position that would have existed if the acts had not been performed;
(b) acts performed in good faith before the invalidity was invoked are not rendered unlawful by reason only of the invalidity of the treaty.

3. In cases falling under articles 49, 50, 51 or 52, paragraph 2 does not apply with respect to the party to which the fraud, the act of corruption or the coercion is imputable.
4. In the case of the invalidity of a particular State's consent to be bound by multilateral treaty, the foregoing rules apply in the relations between that State and the parties to the treaty.

Article 70

1. Unless the treaty otherwise provides or the parties otherwise agree, the termination of a treaty under its provisions or in accordance with the present Convention:

(a) releases the parties from any obligation further to perform the treaty;
(b) does not affect any right, obligation or legal situation of the parties created through the execution of the treaty prior to its termination.

2. If a State denounces or withdraws from a multilateral treaty, paragraph 1 applies in the relations between that state and each of the other parties to the treaty from the date when such denunciation or withdrawal takes effect.

Article 71

1. In the case of a treaty which is void under Article 53 the parties shall:

(*a*) eliminate as far as possible the consequences of any act performed in reliance on any provision which conflicts with the peremptory norm of general international law; and

(*b*) bring their mutual relations into conformity with the peremptory norm of general international law.

2. In the case of a treaty which becomes void and terminates under Article 64, the termination of the treaty:

(*a*) releases the parties from any obligation further to perform the treaty;

(*b*) does not affect any right, obligation or legal situation of the parties created through the execution of the treaty prior to its termination; provided that those rights, obligations or situations may thereafter be maintained only to the extent that their maintenance is not in itself in conflict with the new peremptory norm of general international law.

Article 72

1. Unless the treaty otherwise provides or the parties otherwise agree, the suspension of the operation of a treaty under its provisions or in accordance with the present Convention:

(*a*) releases the parties between which the operation of the treaty is suspended from the obligation to perform the treaty in their mutual relations during the period of the suspension;

(*b*) does not otherwise affect the legal relations between the parties established by the treaty.

2. During the period of the suspension the parties shall refrain from acts tending to obstruct the resumption of the operation of the treaty.

Notes

The International Law Commission's Commentary reads:

The Commission considered that the establishment of the nullity of a treaty on any of the grounds set forth in ... [Articles 46–53 of the Vienna Convention] would mean that the treaty was void *ab initio* and not merely from the date when the ground was invoked. Only in the case of the treaty's becoming void and terminating under . . . [Article 64 of the Vienna Convention[55]] would the treaty not be invalid as from the very moment of its purported conclusion.[56]

This view is reflected in Article 69 of the Vienna Convention, as is the Commission's view that

> where neither party was to be regarded as a wrongdoer in relation to the cause of nullity (*i.e.* where no fraud, corruption or coercion was imputable to either party), the legal position should be determined on the basis of taking account both of the invalidity of the treaty *ab initio* and of the good faith of the parties.[57]

Invalidity because of a rule of *ius cogens* is treated separately in Article 71.

(ii) SEPARABILITY OF TREATY PROVISIONS

VIENNA CONVENTION ON THE LAW OF TREATIES 1969

Loc. cit., p. 765, n. 3, above

Article 44

1. A right of a party, provided for in a treaty or arising under Article 56, to denounce, withdraw from or suspend the operation of the treaty may be exercised only with respect to the whole treaty unless the treaty otherwise provides or the parties otherwise agree.

2. A ground for invalidating, terminating, withdrawing from or suspending the operation of a treaty recognised in the present Convention may be invoked only with respect to the whole treaty except as provided in the following paragraphs or in Article 60.

3. If the ground relates solely to particular clauses, it may be invoked only with respect to those clauses where:

(*a*) the said clauses are separable from the remainder of the treaty with regard to their application;

(*b*) it appears from the treaty or is otherwise established that acceptance of those clauses was not an essential basis of the consent of the other party or parties to be bound by the treaty as a whole; and

(*c*) continued performance of the remainder of the treaty would not be unjust.

4. In cases falling under Articles 49 and 50 the State entitled to invoke the fraud or corruption may do so with respect either to the whole treaty or, subject to paragraph 3, to the particular clauses alone.

---

[55] On *ius cogens*, see above, p. 835.
[56] Y.B.I.L.C., 1966, II, pp. 264–265.
[57] *ibid.*

5. In cases falling under Articles 51, 52 and 53, no separation of the provision of the treaty is permitted.

Notes

1. There would seem to be little evidence in state practice or in judicial or arbitral decisions to indicate whether in the application of the rules concerning the invalidity, termination and suspension of treaties, the treaty must be regarded as a whole, so that if one provision of the treaty is found to be invalid the treaty as a whole is invalid, or whether the provision in question may be separated from the remainder, so that the validity or continued operation of the latter is not affected. One of the few pronouncements upon the subject is that by Judge Lauterpacht in his individual opinion in the *Norwegian Loans* case.[58] The International Law Commission, whose view is reflected in Article 44 of the Vienna Convention, thought it was desirable to permit severance in appropriate cases, but that it was

> inappropriate that treaties between sovereign states should be capable of being invalidated, terminated or suspended in operation in their entirety even in cases where the ground of invalidity, termination or suspension may relate to quite secondary provisions in the treaty.[59]

2. Article 44(3)(c) was added at Vienna to "ensure that the rule of separability laid down in [Article 44] . . . would not create the very kind of international friction which the Commission sought to avoid"[60] by it.

(iii) LOSS OF THE RIGHT TO INVOKE A GROUND FOR INVALIDATING, ETC., A TREATY

VIENNA CONVENTION ON THE LAW OF TREATIES 1969

Loc. cit., p. 765, n. 3, above

Article 45

A State may no longer invoke a ground for invalidating, terminating, withdrawing from or suspending the operation of a treaty under Articles 46 to 50 or Articles 60 to 62 if, after becoming aware of the facts:

(a) it shall have expressly agreed that the treaty is valid or remains in force or continues in operation, as the case may be; or
(b) it must by reason of its conduct be considered as having acquiesced in the validity of the treaty or in its maintenance in force or in operation, as the case may be.

---

[58] See below, p. 1010. On invalid reservations, see above, p. 797.
[59] Commentary, Y.B.I.L.C., 1966, II, p. 238.
[60] Mr Kearney (U.S.), introducing the amendment, *Treaty Conference Records*, 1968, p. 230.

(iv) Settlement of Disputes

VIENNA CONVENTION ON THE LAW OF TREATIES 1969

Loc. cit., p. 765, n. 3, above

Article 65

1. A party which, under the provisions of the present Convention, invokes either a defect in its consent to be bound by a treaty or a ground for impeaching the validity of a treaty, terminating it, withdrawing from it or suspending its operation, must notify the other parties of its claim. The notification shall indicate the measure proposed to be taken with respect to the treaty and the reasons therefor.

2. If, after the expiry of a period which, except in cases of special urgency, shall not be less than three months after the receipt of the notification, no party has raised any objection, the party making the notification may carry out in the manner provided in Article 67 the measure which it has proposed.

3. If, however, objection has been raised by any other party, the parties shall seek a solution through the means indicated in Article 33 of the Charter of the United Nations.[61]

4. Nothing in the foregoing paragraphs shall affect the rights or obligations of the parties under any provisions in force binding the parties with regard to the settlement of disputes.

5. Without prejudice to Article 45,[62] the fact that a State has not previously made the notification prescribed in paragraph 1 shall not prevent it from making such notification in answer to another party claiming performance of the treaty or alleging its violation.

Article 66

If, under paragraph 3, of Article 65, no solution has been reached within a period of 12 months following the date on which the objection was raised, the following procedures shall be followed:

(a) any one of the parties to a dispute concerning the application or the interpretation of Article 53[63] or 64[64] may, by a written application, submit it to the International Court of Justice for a decision unless the parties by common consent agree to submit the dispute to arbitration;

---

[61] *Ed.* Below, Appendix I.
[62] *Ed.* Above, p. 853.
[63] *Ed.* Above, p. 835.
[64] *Ed.* Above, p. 835.

(b) any one of the parties to a dispute concerning the application or the interpretation of any of the other articles in Part V[65] of the present Convention may set in motion the procedure specified in the Annex to the Convention by submitting a request to that effect to the Secretary-General of the United Nations.

Annex to the Convention

1. A list of conciliators consisting of qualified jurists shall be drawn up and maintained by the Secretary-General of the United Nations. To this end, every state which is a Member of the United Nations or a party to the present Convention shall be invited to nominate two conciliators, and the names of the persons so nominated shall constitute the list. . . .

2. When a request has been made to the Secretary-General under Article 66, the Secretary-General shall bring the dispute before a conciliation commission constituted as follows:

The state or states constituting one of the parties to the dispute shall appoint:

(a) one conciliator of the nationality of that state or of one of those states, who may or may not be chosen from the list referred to in paragraph 1; and

(b) one conciliator not of the nationality of that state or of any of those states, who shall be chosen from the list.

The state or states constituting the other party to the dispute shall appoint two conciliators in the same way. The four conciliators chosen by the parties shall be appointed within sixty days following the date on which the Secretary-General receives the request.

The four conciliators shall, within sixty days following the date of the last of their own appointments, appoint a fifth conciliator chosen from the list, who shall be chairman.

If the appointment of the chairman or of any of the other conciliators has not been made within the period prescribed above for such appointment, it shall be made by the Secretary-General within sixty days following the expiry of that period. . . .

3. . . . Decisions and recommendations of the Commission shall be made by a majority vote of the five members.

4. The Commission may draw the attention of the parties to the dispute to any measures which might facilitate an amicable settlement.

5. The Commission shall hear the parties, examine the claims and objections, and make proposals to the parties with a view to reaching an amicable settlement of the dispute.

---

[65] *Ed.* Arts. 42–72.

6. The Commission shall report within twelve months of its constitution. Its report shall be deposited with the Secretary-General and transmitted to the parties to the dispute. The report of the Commission, including any conclusions stated therein regarding the facts or questions of law, shall not be binding upon the parties and it shall have no other character than that of recommendations submitted for the consideration of the parties in order to facilitate an amicable settlement of the dispute . . .

Notes
There was considerable debate at the Vienna Conference on the question of the procedure to be established for the settlement of disputes arising under the Convention. Certain states, including the United Kingdom, wanted provision for compulsory judicial settlement. It was felt that the rules in the Convention on invalidity, termination and suspension could easily be abused in the absence of compulsory and binding settlement procedures. This feeling was particularly strong with regard to the questions of *ius cogens* and fraud. Other states, including the USSR, with its then fundamental opposition to binding international settlement procedures independent of the control of the disputing parties, disagreed.[66] Eventually, "at the eleventh hour and in circumstances of high drama not fully revealed in the drab official records of the Conference,"[67] the compromise in Articles 65 and 66 and the Annex to the Convention was adopted. How satisfactory a guarantee against abuse of the Convention is it?[68] What if, in cases other than ones concerning *ius cogens*, the parties cannot agree upon a solution after exhausting the procedure provided for in Articles 65(3) and 66 and in the Annex? Has the claim invoking a defect in the claimant's consent, etc., failed?

11. REGISTRATION OF TREATIES[69]

See Article 102, United Nations Charter.[70]

VIENNA CONVENTION ON THE LAW OF TREATIES 1969

Loc. cit., p. 765, n. 3, above

Article 80

1. Treaties shall, after their entry into force, be transmitted to the Secretariat of the United Nations for registration or filing and recording, as the case may be, and for publication. . . .

---

[66] See, *e.g.* Mr Khlestov (USSR), in *Treaty Conference Records*, 1969, pp. 302–303. For a statement of the case for compulsory and binding settlement procedures, see Briggs (1967) 64 A.J.I.L. 976 at 983–988.

[67] Sinclair, *loc. cit.*, p. 765, n. 1 above, pp. 68–69.

[68] Note that France and Australia were influenced by the inadequacy—in their view— of the procedures for settlement when voting against the adoption of the Convention and abstaining respectively: *Treaty Conference Records*, 1969, pp. 203–209.

[69] See Brandon (1952) 29 B.Y.I.L. 186; Brandon (1953) 47 A.J.I.L. 49; Higgins, *The Development of International Law by the Political Organs of the United Nations* (1963), pp. 328–336; Lillich (1971) 65 A.J.I.L. 771; Hutchinson (1993) 46 C.L.P. 257; Tabory (1982) 76 A.J.I.L. 350.

[70] See Below, Appendix I.

Notes

1. By virtue of Article 102, only treaties registered with the UN may be invoked before the I.C.J. An unregistered treaty nonetheless remains legally binding between the parties.[71] The purpose of Article 102 of the United Nations Charter, like that of its predecessor, Article 18 of the League of Nations Covenant,[72] is to give publicity to treaty relations and avoid secret treaties. This has, to a large extent,[73] been achieved. Treaties registered under Article 102 are published in the United Nations Treaty Series, of which there are well over 1,000 volumes.

2. The terms "treaty" and "international agreement" in Article 102 have purposely been left undefined, "it being recognised that experience and practice will in themselves aid in giving definition to the terms of the Charter."[74] The Final Act of the Helsinki Conference on Security and Co-operation in Europe 1975, for example, was understood as not being eligible for registration since it was not binding in law.[75] At San Francisco it was thought that the word "agreement" must be understood as including "unilateral engagements of an international character which have been accepted by the state in whose favour such an engagement has been entered into."[76] On the basis of this interpretation, the Secretariat has, on its own initiative and with the approval of the General Assembly Sixth Committee, arranged[77] for the registration, *inter alia*, of declarations by new members of the United Nations accepting membership and declarations made under the "Optional Clause."[78] In respect of instruments submitted to it by Members, the Secretariat has taken the following position:

> ... the Secretariat ... follows the principle that it acts in accordance with the position of the Member State submitting an instrument for registration that so far as that party is concerned the instrument is a treaty or an international agreement within the meaning of Article 102. Registration of an instrument submitted by a Member State, therefore, does not imply a judgment by the Secretariat on the nature of the instrument, the status of a party, or any similar question. It is the understanding of the Secretariat that its action does not confer on the instrument the status of a treaty or an international agreement if it does not already have that status and does not confer on a party a status which it would not otherwise have.[79]

Thus, when, in 1957, Egypt submitted for registration a unilateral "Declaration on the Suez Canal and Agreements for its Operation,"[80] the Secretary-General replied that it would be registered on the understanding that Egypt thought that it came within Article 102. The Secretariat has, however, had occasion to indicate its views with regard to certain types of instrument and has suggested, for example, that "postal agreements (even though concluded for example, between

---

[71] *Maritime and Territorial Questions* case *(Qatar v. Bahrain)*, I.C.J. Rep. 1994, p. 112 at p. 122.

[72] Art. 18 read: "Every treaty or international engagement entered into hereafter by any Member of the League shall be forthwith registered with the Secretariat and shall as soon as possible be published by it. No such treaty or international engagement shall be binding until so registered."

[73] It is known, however, that some treaties are not registered. This is true, for example, of a Franco-United States Agreement of September 6, 1960, on NATO Nuclear Weapons.

[74] G.A.O.R., 1st Sess., Part II, Plenary, Annex 91, p. 1586.

[75] See Russell, *loc. cit.*, p. 625, n. 15, above, p. 246.

[76] 13 U.N.C.I.O., *Documents*, p. 705.

[77] 5 *U.N. Repertory of Practice* 293.

[78] *ibid.*

[79] UN Doc. ST/LEG/SER./A/105, November 1955, Prefatory Note.

[80] 265 U.N.T.S. 299.

the respective postmaster-general)" are within Article 102, but that agreements to which non-governmental international organisations (*e.g.* the International Patents Institute) are parties are not.[81] Clearly treaties between United Nations Members, on the one hand, and non-member states or public international organisations with treaty-making capacity, on the other, are covered. The International Law Commission's Commentary reads:

> Although the Charter obligation is limited to Member States, non-member States have in practice "registered" their treaties habitually with the Secretariat of the United Nations. Under Article 10 of the Regulations concerning the Registration and Publication of Treaties and International Agreements adopted by the General Assembly, the term used instead of "registration" when no Member of the United Nations is party to the agreement is "filing and recording," but in substance this is a form of voluntary registration.[82]

3. Could an unregistered treaty to which a member of the United Nations was a party be invoked by another party not a member of the United Nations before the International Court of Justice or an ad hoc arbitral tribunal?

---

[81] 5 *U.N. Repertory of Practice* 295–296.
[82] Y.B.I.L.C., 1966, II, p. 273.

CHAPTER 11

THE USE OF FORCE BY STATES[1]

1. THE UNILATERAL USE OF FORCE BY STATES

(i) THE LAW BEFORE 1945

BRIERLY, INTERNATIONAL LAW AND RESORT TO ARMED FORCE

(1932) 4 Cam.L.J. 308

THE relation of war to the international system was stated by W. E. Hall in a well-known passage of his treatise in these words: "International law has no alternative but to accept war, independently of the justice of its origin, as a relation which the parties to it may set up if they choose, and to busy itself only in regulating the effects of the relation."[2] This view, which came to be more or less generally accepted by international lawyers in the course of the nineteenth century, marked the definite abandonment of the claim of the classical jurists to distinguish between *bellum iustum* and *bellum iniustum*, and it was in a sense an admission that international law had so far failed in the primary task of all legal systems, that of establishing and maintaining a distinction between the legal and the illegal use of force. But it had the great merit of candour, and it brought the theory of the law into accord with what had always been and still remained the facts of international practice.

Notes
1. Brierly is here stating the position as it stood at the beginning of this century. Paradoxically, at the same time that international law condoned war it controlled

---

[1] See Arend and Beck, *International Law and the Use of Force* (1993); Bowett, *Self-Defence in International Law* (1958); Brownlie, *International Law and the Use of Force by States* (1963); Cassese, ed., *The Current Regulation of the Use of Force* (1986); Dinstein, *War, Aggression and Self-Defence* (2nd ed., 1994); Falk, *Legal Order in a Violent World* (1968); Higgins, *The Development of International Law through the Political Organs of the UN* (1963), pp. 167–239; McCoubrey and White, *International Law and Armed Conflict* (1992); McDougal and Feliciano, *Law and Minimum World Order: Legal Regulation of International Coercion* (1961); Schachter (1984) 82 Mich.L.R. 1620; Stone, *Legal Controls of International Conflict* (2nd ed., 1959); Waldock (1952-II) 81 Hague Recueil 451 (1952-II); and Colloquy papers in (1984–5) 10 Yale J.I.L. 261–94.
[2] *Ed. International Law* (8th ed.), p. 82.

resort to armed force short of war by the law of reprisals[3] and governed its conduct by the laws of war.[4]

2. On the question what amounts to war, McNair and Watts[5] state:

> War may begin, first, by a declaration of war... In the second place, a state of war will arise upon the commission of an act of force, under the authority of a State, which is done *animo belligerendi*, or which, being done *sine animo belligerendi*, the State against which it is directed expressly or impliedly elects to regard as creating a state of war... repelling force by force, while raising a presumption that the attacked State elects to regard war as having broken out, does not necessarily amount to such an election. So serious a matter as the existence of a state of war is not lightly to be implied. Furthermore, where leading political figures of a country engaged in hostilities refer to their country being "at war," caution must be exercised... since such references may prove to be more of emotional and political significance than legal.
>
> It will be apparent that the existence of a state of war depends upon the determination of the parties to the conflict, and can arise where only one of the parties to the conflict asserts the existence of a state of war, even if the other denies it or keeps silence. State practice has by and large accepted that for war to exist one at least of the contenders must so assert. Such a view... has enabled conflicts, even if militarily extensive as between the parties, to stay essentially limited rather than to entail the overall dislocation... which would accompany the escalation of those conflicts into a state of war. That so fundamental a concept of international law as war should depend upon the view of the parties involved—even of one of them alone—has been a principal reason for criticism and for the attraction of other, more objective, concepts such as the "threat or use of force" adopted in the Charter.

3. Although the question whether a state of war exists remains of significance in international law (*e.g.* the law of neutrality) and municipal law (*e.g.* concerning the status of aliens[6]), it is now exceptional for the parties to hostilities to regard themselves as legally at war.[7] The importance of the question has also been reduced by the fact that (i) the United Nations Charter rule on the use of force (Art.2(4)), draws no distinction between war and armed force short of war and (ii) the 1949 Geneva Red Cross Conventions and the 1977 Protocols[8] apply to "all cases of declared war or of any other armed conflict which may arise between two or more of the High Contracting Parties, even if the state of war is not recognised by one of them."[9]

---

[3] See above p. 12 and below p. 914.

[4] See mainly the Hague Conventions of 1899 and 1907, printed in Schindler, *The Laws of Armed Conflicts* (1973) (on the conduct of hostilities generally); the four 1949 Geneva Red Cross Conventions, *loc. cit.*, p. 289, n. 83, above (on the treatment of the injured, prisoners of war and civilians); and the two 1977 Protocols to the 1949 Conventions, *loc. cit.*, p. 625, n. 14, above (supplementing and revising the 1949 Conventions in their application to international conflicts (Protocol I) and extending the protection afforded to victims in non-international conflicts (Protocol II)). See generally, Green, *The Contemporary Law of Armed Conflict* (1993); McCoubrey and White, *International Law and Armed Conflict* (1992); and the literature cited, p. 625, n. 14, above.

[5] *The Legal Effects of War* (4th ed., 1966), pp. 7–8. Footnotes omitted. In the Falkland Islands "War," the U.K. studiously avoided any statement indicating that it regarded the conflict as war, and Argentina made no formal proclamation of war. *cf. Hansard*, H.L., Vol. 459, col. 646, January 30, 1985.

[6] See, *e.g. R. v. Bottrill, ex p. Kuechenmeister* [1947] K.B. 41.

[7] See Greenwood, (1987) 36 I.C.L.Q. 283.

[8] See above, n. 4.

[9] Art. 2, common to the four 1949 Conventions. See also Art. 1, Protocols I and II.

GENERAL TREATY FOR THE RENUNCIATION OF WAR 1928[10]

U.K.T.S. 29 (1929), Cmnd. 3410; 94 L.N.T.S. 57

The Signatory States . . .

Persuaded that the time has come when a frank renunciation of war as an instrument of national policy should be made to the end that the peaceful and friendly relations now existing between their peoples may be perpetuated;

Convinced that all changes in their relations with one another should be sought only by pacific means and be the result of a peaceful and orderly process, and that any signatory Power which shall hereafter seek to promote its national interests by resort to war should be denied the benefits furnished by this Treaty. . . .

Have decided to conclude a Treaty. . . .

Article I

The High Contracting Parties solemnly declare in the names of their respective peoples that they condemn recourse to war for the solution of international controversies, and renounce it as an instrument of national policy in their relations with one another.

Article II

The High Contracting Parties agree that the settlement or solution of all disputes or conflicts of whatever nature or of whatever origin they may be, which may arise among them, shall never be sought except by pacific means.

Notes

1. After the First World War, the League of Nations Covenant[11] imposed some limitations upon "resort to war." It was not until the General Treaty of 1928, however, that a comprehensive prohibition of war as an instrument of national policy was achieved. Somewhat ironically, 63 states, *i.e.* virtually the whole of the international community at that time, were parties to the Treaty when the Second World War started in 1939. The Treaty has never been terminated.[12] For practical purposes, it has been superseded by Article 2(4) of the United Nations Charter.

2. It has never been clear whether the Treaty prohibits armed force short of war as well as war. Thus, on the one hand, Bowett[13] states that the Pact only prohibits war "for under accepted terminology of international law (and without defending that terminology) measures involving the use of force but falling short of war are

[10] The Treaty is sometimes known as the Pact of Paris or the Briand-Kellogg Pact (after the French Foreign Minister and U.S. Secretary of State respectively).
[11] Articles 15 and 16, U.K.T.S. 4 (1919), Cmd. 153.
[12] There are now 67 parties.
[13] *op. cit.*, p. 859, n. 1, above, p. 136.

characterised as pacific; in this case Article 2 cannot be invoked as a reason for departing from the plain meaning of the terms of Article 1." Brownlie,[14] on the other hand, suggests that "the best guide to the meaning of the Pact is to be found by recourse to the subsequent practice of the parties" and concludes that this "leaves little room for doubt that it was understood to prohibit any substantial use of armed force." In 1934, the International Law Association resolved as follows:

> A signatory state which threatens to resort to armed force for the solution of an international dispute or conflict is guilty of a violation of the Pact.[15]

In 1935, it was emphasised in the House of Lords by the Lord Chancellor (Viscount Sankey) that the members of the Association "were expressing . . . their own views: they did not necessarily represent the opinions of lawyers in all their own countries, still less the opinions of their Governments."[16]

3. The treaty does not mention self-defence. In a reply to a communication from a United States spokesman during the drafting of the treaty, the British Foreign Secretary stated:

> I am entirely in accord with the views expressed by Mr. Kellogg in his speech of April 28 that the proposed treaty does not restrict or impair in any way the right of self-defence. . . . [17]

(ii) THE LAW AS OF 1945

(a) *The Use of Force*

ARTICLE 2(4) UNITED NATIONS CHARTER

4. All Members shall refrain in their international relations from the threat or use of force against the territorial integrity or political independence of any state, or in any other manner inconsistent with the Purposes of the United Nations.

Notes

1. Although phrased in terms of "members" of the United Nations, Article 2(4) is, as confirmed in the *Nicaragua* (*Merits*) case, below, p. 866, a rule of customary international law applying to all states.

2. The extent of the prohibition in Article 2(4) is not clear from the text. The Security Council and the General Assembly, being political rather than judicial bodies, have not spent much time debating the niceties of international law in particular cases so that there is not a great deal to be found in their practice on the meaning of Article 2(4). This is particularly so since the attention of representatives has usually been focused on questions of jurisdiction under Article 39 (Is there a breach of the peace, etc.?) and not upon questions of compliance with Article 2(4). Some more precise meaning has been given to Article 2(4) by the Section on the Principle of the Use of Force of the 1970 General Assembly

---

[14] *op. cit.*, p. 859, n. 1, above p. 87.
[15] *Report of the 38th Conference of the International Law Association*, Budapest (1934), p. 67.
[16] *Hansard*, H.L., 5th Series, Vol. 95, col. 1043, February 20, 1935.
[17] Cmd. 3153, p. 10.

Declaration on Principles of International Laws concerning Friendly Relations and Co-operation among States, below, Appendix III, although that too is vaguely worded in places,[18] and by the *Nicaragua (Merits)* case. The Declaration was adopted by consensus and can be taken to reflect the views of the United Nations membership as a whole on the legal meaning of the principles in the Charter upon which it elaborates.[19] In a controversial text, the Draft Articles on State Responsibility of the International Law Commission, as adopted on first reading, regard serious breaches of the rules on international peace and security, such as that in Article 2(4), as giving rise to the criminal responsibility of states in international law.[20]

3. *Force.* Article 2(4) prohibits the use of armed force, whether amounting to war or not. It probably does not prohibit political pressure (*e.g.* the refusal to ratify a treaty or the severance of diplomatic relations) or economic pressure (*e.g.* a trade boycott or the blocking of a bank account). As far as the latter is concerned, a proposal by Brazil during the drafting of Article 2(4) that states should be required to refrain from "economic measures" was rejected.[21] It is not wholly clear, however, whether this was because it was intended not to prohibit economic force or because the term "force" in Article 2(4) was thought sufficient to cover it without specific mention. In the opinion of Goodrich, Hambro and Simons,[22]

> It seems reasonable to conclude that while various forms of economic and political coercion may be treated as threats to the peace, as contrary to certain of the declared purposes and principles of the Organisation, or as violating agreements entered into or recognised principles of international law, they are not to be regarded as coming necessarily under the prohibition of Article 2(4), which is to be understood as directed against the use of armed force.

The matter was purposely not clarified in the 1970 Declaration. This just refers to "force" in the Section on the Principle of the Use of Force because of disagreement between mainly Western states, who argued that only armed force was prohibited, and Soviet bloc European and most (but not all) developing states, who claimed that "all forms of pressure, including those of a political and economic character, which have the effect of threatening the territorial integrity or political independence of any state" were prohibited.[23] The Western states were, however, prepared to admit, presciently in the light of the Arab oil boycott of 1973/74,[24] "that this was not to say that all forms of economic and political

---

[18] On the Declaration generally, see Arangio-Ruiz, *The UN Declaration on Friendly Relations and the System of Sources of International Law* (1979) and Rosenstock (1971) 65 A.J.I.L. 713. On its drafting, see Hazard (1964) 58 A.J.I.L. 952; Houben (1967) 61 *ibid.* 703; Lee (1965) 14 I.C.L.Q. 1296 and McWhinney (1966) 60 A.J.I.L. 1. The Section on the Principle on the Use of Force is reinforced by the 1987 UN Declaration on the Enhancement of the Effectiveness of the Principle of Refraining from the Threat or Use of Force in International Relations, G.A. Resn 42/22, G.A.O.R., 42nd Sess., Supp. 49, p. 287 (1987). Both Declarations were adopted by consensus.

[19] *cf.* the *Nicaragua (Merits)* case, judgment, para. 188, below, p. 866.

[20] See Art. 19(3), Draft Articles on State Responsibility, above, p. 487.

[21] 6 U.N.C.I.O., *Documents* 335.

[22] *Charter of the United Nations* (3rd ed., 1969), p. 49.

[23] UN Doc. A/AC.125/SR.114 (1970).

[24] In late 1973 (just after the *Yom Kippur War*) and early 1974, the Arab oil-producing states, led by Saudi Arabia, imposed an embargo on the supply of oil to the U.S. and other states (including all of the EEC countries) which they claimed were supporting Israel. The purpose was to cause those states to change their Middle East policies. For differing views on the legality of the embargo, which had a devastating economic effect, see the essays in Lillich, ed., *Economic Coercion and the New International Economic Order* (1976), and Paust and Blaustein, ed., *The Arab Oil Weapon* (1977).

pressure which threatened the territorial integrity and political independence of another state were permissible; they might well constitute illegal intervention."[25] The Section of the 1970 Declaration on Principles of International Law on the Principle of Non-Intervention, which is distinct from the Section on the Principle of the Use of Force, prohibits economic coercion (but without defining it). In the *Nicaragua (Merits)* case (judgment, para. 245), the I.C.J. found that the United States economic sanctions complained of by Nicaragua were not in breach of the principle of non-intervention.[26]

A use of armed force by State A against State D is clearly a breach of Article 2(4). If State T intervenes by armed force to assist State A, it too is directly in breach of Article 2(4). If it intervenes in the same way to assist State D, the right of collective self defence, below, p. 899, may justify its conduct. If State T assists State A in its attack upon State D by providing it with military or other equipment, training facilities, land bases, etc., then State T is probably indirectly engaged in the "use of force" contrary to Article 2(4).[27]

4. *Threat of force.*[28] The ultimatum issued by France and the United Kingdom to Egypt and Israel in 1956 demanding a ceasefire within 12 hours would be a "threat of force." On the question whether a "signalled intention to use" nuclear weapons (or other kinds of force) or the possession of nuclear weapons is a threat of force contrary to Article 2(4), see the *Nuclear Weapons* case, opinion, paras 47–48, below, pp. 925–926. Would another be the threat made by the Soviet Premier, Mr Khruschchev, in 1960 after the *U-2 Incident*, when he reportedly stated:

> Those countries that have bases on their territories should note most carefully the following: if they allow others to fly from their base to our territory we shall hit at those bases.[29]

United States military manoeuvres near the Nicaraguan border were held not to be a "threat to force" in the *Nicaragua Case (Merits)*.[30] But when, in 1994, "Iraqi artillery and tanks were deployed in positions pointing towards and within range of Kuwait, with ammunition at the ready" on the Iraqi side of the border, this was stated by the United Kingdom to be a "threat to Kuwait and a breach of the provisions of the Charter".[31]

---

[25] U.K. representative (Mr Sinclair), UN Doc. A/AC.125/SR.25 (1966).

[26] On the legality of U.S. economic sanctions against Nicaragua, see Henderson (1983) 43 Wash. & Lee L.R. 167. On the legality of economic sanctions generally, see Acevedo (1984) 78 A.J.I.L. 323; Barrie (1988) 82 A.J.I.L. 311; Delanis (1979) 12 Vand. J.T.L. 101; Farer (1985) 79 A.J.I.L. 405; Neff (1988) 59 B.Y.I.L. 113; and Parry, Blum, Lillich and Bilder (1977) 12 T.I.L.J. 1, 5, 17 and 41 respectively.

[27] This last situation is not specifically mentioned in the 1970 Declaration. The Section in the Declaration on the Principle on the Use of Force, paras 8 and 9, prohibits intervention in a *civil war* to assist rebels, by such "indirect aggression"; it would seem that assistance of the same sort to state A using armed force against state D is as much the "use of force" as this and is otherwise a breach of Art. 2(4). In any event, such assistance to state A is contrary to the Principle of Non-Intervention in the 1970 Declaration. On the limited UN practice concerning aid to a state using armed force against another state, see Higgins, *op. cit.*, p. 859, n. 1, above, p. 189.

[28] See Sadurska (1988) 82 A.J.I.L. 239.

[29] 5 Whiteman 714. On the *U-2 Incident*, see above, p. 241. See also on "threats of force," UN Secretary-General *Report on the Question of Defining Aggression*, UN Doc. A/2211, p. 52: "... the threat to use force is not always made in so crude and open a form [as an ultimatum]. There are sometimes veiled threats which may be very effective, but are difficult to detect."

[30] Judgment, para. 227, below, p. 877.

[31] Sir David Hannay, Security Council debate, October 16, 1994, S/PV. 3431, pp. 11–12.

5. *Against the territorial integrity or political independence of any state or in any manner, etc.* Article 2(4) prohibits the use of armed force by State A against State D that *either* deprives State D of the whole or a part of its territory (see, *e.g.* the invasion of Poland by Germany in 1939 and of Manchuria (a part of China) by Japan in 1931, p. 109, above, respectively) *or* brings State D under State A's political control (see *e.g.* the *Afghanistan* case, below, p. 891). A claim to sovereignty by State A over territory occupied by State D cannot be pursued by armed force[32] (see, *e.g.* the *Falkland Islands* case, below, p. 902, and the Iraq-Iran war[33]), but armed force can be used against an occupier by way of self-defence (see, again, the *Falkland Islands* case). The use of armed force by one state against another in furtherance of the principle of self-determination is not permitted, despite the emphasis placed upon that principle in recent years.[34]

The words "territorial integrity" (and "political independence") could be read as words of limitation, with a distinction being drawn between "integrity" (to do with annexation or permanent occupation or control) and "inviolability" (to do with trespass). Bowett[35] supports this limited reading on the basis in part that "the phrase having been included, it must be given its plain meaning." It was relied upon in the *Corfu Channel* case by the United Kingdom when it argued that *Operation Retail*, in which the Corfu Channel in Albanian territorial waters was mineswept by the United Kingdom after British ships had been damaged by mines in it, was not contrary to Article 2(4):

> But our action ... threatened neither the territorial integrity nor the political independence of Albania. Albania suffered thereby neither territorial loss nor [loss to] any part of its political independence.[36]

Although this argument was not specifically considered in the judgment, the Court's condemnation of *Operation Retail* is not in sympathy with it.[37] Brownlie[38] argues convincingly against such a limited interpretation as follows:

> The conclusion warranted by the *travaux préparatoires* is that the phrase under discussion was not intended to be restrictive but, on the contrary, to give more specific guarantees to small states and that it cannot be interpreted as having a qualifying effect.
>
> ... The phrase "political independence and territorial integrity" has been used on many occasions to epitomize the *total* of legal rights which a state has.

---

[32] See Feinberg (1980) 15 Israel L.R. 160, who takes the view expressed above. See, however, Jennings, *op. cit.*, p. 190, n. 1, p. 72, who argues that force can be used to recover territory if the claim to sovereignty of the state using force is justified. In that case, there is no use of force against the "territorial integrity" of another state.

[33] The Iran–Iraq war began in 1980, when Iraq attacked Iran in order to regain territory in the area of the Shatt al-Arab waterway which it had conceded to Iran by a 1975 treaty of reconciliation between the two states. See Amin (1982) 31 I.C.L.Q. 167.

[34] On the *Invasion of Goa* case in which India, not the inhabitants of Goa, took the initiative to incorporate Goa into India, see above, p. 220. On the disagreement among states on the question whether a state can help a "people" that has engaged in its own war of national liberation, see below, p. 886.

[35] *loc. cit.*, p. 859, n. 1, p. 152. The same author also points out (pp. 150–151) that Article 2(4) can be interpreted as requiring *either* a "specific intent," so that "the use or threat of force contravenes this obligation only where intended to jeopardise the political independence or territorial integrity of another state," *or* only that armed force must not be intentionally used with this result. The latter interpretation is the one that would appear to be followed in practice.

[36] *Corfu Channel* case, Pleadings, Vol. III, p. 296.

[37] See the passage from the judgment, above, p. 391.

[38] *op. cit.*, p. 859, n. 1 above, pp. 267–268.

Moreover, it is difficult to accept a "plain meaning" which permits evasion of obligations by means of a verbal profession that there is no intention to infringe territorial integrity and which was not intended by the many delegations which approved the text. Lastly, if there is an ambiguity the principle of effectiveness should be applied.

See also the 1970 Declaration, 4th and 5th paragraphs of the Section on the Principle on the Use of Force, which support this wider interpretation. Even if the words "territorial integrity" were to be read restrictively, the final phrase of Article 2(4) nonetheless indicates that the paragraph, taken as a whole, contains a general prohibition on the use of armed force as "an instrument of national policy" (in the words of the Briand-Kellogg Pact). One of the "purposes of the United Nations" is to "maintain international peace and security" (Charter, Art.1(1)). The use of armed force in international relations by way of reprisal,[39] humanitarian intervention[40] or otherwise (*e.g.* to persuade a state to a certain course of conduct) is contrary to this "purpose." This is so whether the armed force is used in the territory of another state (see the facts of the *Harib Fort* case, below, p. 916) or not (*e.g.* the use of force against a ship or aircraft[41] outside the state of registration). The only justification for the use of armed force by one state against another under the legal regime of the Charter is self-defence, see below, p. 894; participation in United Nations enforcement action, see below, p. 951 *et seq.*; or, seemingly, in some cases of humanitarian intervention.[42] Otherwise the interest in international peace and security prevails.

NICARAGUA CASE (MERITS)[43]

Nicaragua *v.* United States

I.C.J. Reports 1986, p. 14

In 1979, the right-wing Somoza Government in Nicaragua was overthrown by revolution by the left-wing Sandinista Government. In 1981, President Reagan terminated economic aid to Nicaragua on the ground that it had aided guerrillas fighting against the El Salvador Government, which enjoyed good relations with the United States, by allowing USSR arms to pass through its ports and territory en route for El Salvador. In this case, Nicaragua claimed, *inter alia*, that the United States had, contrary to customary international law, (i) used direct armed force against it by laying mines in Nicaraguan internal and territorial waters, causing damage to Nicaraguan and foreign merchant ships, and attacking and damaging Nicaraguan ports, oil installations and a naval base and (ii) given assistance to the *contras*, Nicaraguan guerrillas fighting to overthrow the Sandinista Government. Nicaragua also claimed that the United States had acted in breach of the bilateral

---

[39] On reprisals, see above, p. 12.
[40] On humanitarian intervention, see below, p. 917.
[41] These would presumably not be "territory" for the purposes of Art. 2(4). *cf.* the facts of the *Gulf of Tonkin Incident*, below, p. 901. In that case, the retaliation was justified as self-defence.
[42] See below, p. 917.
[43] The full name of the case is *Case Concerning Military and Paramilitary Activities in and against Nicaragua.* See Bernheim (1985) 11 Yale J.I.L. 104; Briggs *et al.* (1987) 81 A.J.I.L. 78–183; Gill (1988) 1 Hague Y.I.L. 30; Hohmann and de Waart (1987) 34 N.I.L.R. 162; McDonald (1986) 24 C.Y.I.L. 127; Modabber (1988) 10 Loyola L.A.I.C.L.J. 449; Turner (1987) 20 Vand. J.T.L. 53; White (1989) 9 Int. Rel. 535.

1956 U.S.-Nicaraguan Treaty of Friendship, Commerce and Navigation.[44] In the following extracts, the Court considered first whether it had jurisdiction in respect of claims by Nicaragua based on customary rules that paralleled rules in the UN Charter even though the United States had made a reservation to its acceptance of jurisdiction under Article 36(2), I.C.J. Statute excluding "disputes arising under a multilateral treaty". Having found that it did, the Court went on to consider whether the United States had infringed customary international law; it found itself unable to decide whether the United States had infringed Article 2(4), UN Charter or any other multilateral treaty provisions because of the United States reservation.

Judgment of the Court

175. The Court does not consider that, in the areas of law relevant to the present dispute, it can be claimed that all the customary rules which may be invoked have a content exactly identical to that of the rules contained in the treaties which cannot be applied by virtue of the United States reservation. On a number of points, the areas governed by the two sources of law do not exactly overlap, and the substantive rules in which they are framed are not identical in content. But in addition, even if a treaty norm and a customary norm relevant to the present dispute were to have exactly the same content, this would not be a reason for the Court to take the view that the operation of the treaty process must necessarily deprive the customary norm of its separate applicability. Nor can the multilateral treaty reservation be interpreted as meaning that, once applicable to a given dispute, it would exclude the application of any rule of customary international law the content of which was the same as, or analogous to, that of the treaty-law rule which had caused the reservation to become effective.

176. As regards the suggestion that the areas covered by the two sources of law are identical, the Court observes that the United Nations Charter, the convention to which most of the United States argument is directed, by no means covers the whole area of the regulation of the use of force in international relations. On one essential point, this treaty itself refers to pre-existing customary international law; this reference to customary law is contained in the actual text of Article 51, which mentions the "inherent right" (in the French text the "droit naturel") of individual or collective self-defence, which "nothing in the present Charter shall impair" and which applies in the event of an armed attack. The Court therefore finds that Article 51 of the Charter is only meaningful on the basis that there is a "natural" or "inherent" right of self-defence, and it is hard to see how this can be other than of a customary nature, even if its present content has been confirmed and influenced by the Charter. Moreover the Charter, having itself recognized the existence of this right, does not go on to regulate directly all aspects of its content. For example, it does not contain any specific rule whereby self-defence would warrant

[44] 9 U.S.T. 449.

only measures which are proportional to the armed attack and necessary to respond to it,[45] a rule well established in customary international law. Moreover, a definition of the "armed attack" which, if found to exist, authorizes the exercise of the "inherent right" of self-defence, is not provided in the Charter, and is not part of treaty law. It cannot therefore be held that Article 51 is a provision which "subsumes and supervenes" customary international law. It rather demonstrates that in the field in question, the importance of which for the present dispute need hardly be stressed, customary international law continues to exist alongside treaty law. The areas governed by the two sources of law thus do not overlap exactly, and the rules do not have the same content. This could also be demonstrated for other subjects, in particular for the principle of non-intervention.

177. But as observed above (paragraph 175), even if the customary norm and the treaty norm were to have exactly the same content, this would not be a reason for the Court to hold that the incorporation of the customary norm into treaty-law must deprive the customary norm of its applicability as distinct from that of the treaty norm. The existence of identical rules in international treaty law and customary law has been clearly recognized by the Court in the *North Sea Continental Shelf* cases. To a large extent, those cases turned on the question whether a rule enshrined in a treaty also existed as a customary rule, either because the treaty had merely codified the custom, or caused it to "crystallize", or because it had influenced its subsequent adoption. The Court found that this identity of content in treaty law and in customary international law did not exist in the case of the rule invoked, which appeared in one article of the treaty, but did not suggest that such identity was debarred as a matter of principle: on the contrary, it considered it to be clear that certain other articles of the treaty in question "were . . . regarded as reflecting, or as crystallizing, received or at least emergent rules of customary international law" (*I.C.J. Reports 1969*, p. 39, para. 63). More generally, there are no grounds for holding that when customary international law is comprised of rules identical to those of treaty law, the latter "supervenes" the former, so that the customary international law has no further existence of its own.

178. There are a number of reasons for considering that, even if two norms belonging to two sources of international law appear identical in content, and even if the States in question are bound by these rules both on the level of treaty-law and on that of customary international law, these norms retain a separate existence. This is so from the standpoint of their applicability. In a legal dispute affecting two States, one of them may argue that the applicability of a treaty rule to its own conduct depends on

---

[45] *Ed.* As Judge Higgins pointed out in her opinion, para. 5, in the *Nuclear Weapons* case, below, p. 934, the Court here understands proportionality as referring to "what is proportionate to repelling the attack, not a requirement of symmetry between the mode of the initial attack and the mode of response".

the other State's conduct in respect of the application of other rules, on other subjects, also included in the same treaty. For example, if a State exercises its right to terminate or suspend the operation of a treaty on the ground of the violation by the other party of a "provision essential to the accomplishment of the object or purpose of the treaty" (in the words of Art. 60, para. 3 *(b)*, of the Vienna Convention on the Law of Treaties), it is exempted, vis-à-vis the other State, from a rule of treaty-law because of the breach by that other State of a different rule of treaty-law. But if the two rules in question also exist as rules of customary international law, the failure of the one State to apply the one rule does not justify the other State in declining to apply the other rule. Rules which are identical in treaty law and in customary international law are also distinguishable by reference to the methods of interpretation and application. A State may accept a rule contained in a treaty not simply because it favours the application of the rule itself, but also because the treaty establishes what that State regards as desirable institutions or mechanisms to ensure implementation of the rule. Thus, if that rule parallels a rule of customary international law, two rules of the same content are subject to separate treatment as regards the organs competent to verify their implementation, depending on whether they are customary rules or treaty rules. The present dispute illustrates this point.

183. ... the Court has next to consider what are the rules of customary international law applicable to the present dispute. For this purpose, it has to direct its attention to the practice and *opinio juris* of States; as the Court recently observed.

> It is of course axiomatic that the material of customary international law is to be looked for primarily in the actual practice and *opinio juris* of States, even though multilateral conventions may have an important role to play in recording and defining rules deriving from custom, or indeed in developing them. (*Continental Shelf (Libyan Arab Jamahiriya Malta), I.C.J. Reports 1985*, pp. 29–30, para. 27.)

In this respect the Court must not lose sight of the Charter of the United Nations and that of the Organization of American States, notwithstanding the operation of the multilateral treaty reservation. Although the Court has no jurisdiction to determine whether the conduct of the United States constitutes a breach of those conventions, it can and must take them into account in ascertaining the content of the customary international law which the United States is also alleged to have infringed.

184. The Court notes that there is in fact evidence, to be examined below, of a considerable degree of agreement between the Parties as to the content of the customary international law relating to the non-use of force and non-intervention. This concurrence of their views does not however dispense the Court from having itself to ascertain what rules of customary international law are applicable. The mere fact that States declare

their recognition of certain rules is not sufficient for the Court to consider these as being part of customary international law, and as applicable as such to those States. Bound as it is by Article 38 of its Statute to apply, *inter alia*, international custom "as evidence of a general practice accepted as law", the Court may not disregard the essential role played by general practice. Where two States agree to incorporate a particular rule in a treaty, their agreement suffices to make that rule a legal one, binding upon them; but in the field of customary international law, the shared view of the Parties as to the content of what they regard as the rule is not enough. The Court must satisfy itself that the existence of the rule in the *opinio juris* of States is confirmed by practice.

185. In the present dispute, the Court, while exercising its jurisdiction only in respect of the application of the customary rules of non-use of force and non-intervention, cannot disregard the fact that the Parties are bound by these rules as a matter of treaty law and of customary international law. Furthermore, in the present case, apart from the treaty commitments binding the Parties to the rules in question, there are various instances of their having expressed recognition of the validity thereof as customary international law in other ways. It is therefore in the light of this "subjective element"—the expression used by the Court in its 1969 Judgment in the *North Sea Continental Shelf* cases (*I.C.J. Reports 1969*, p. 44)—that the Court has to appraise the relevant practice.

186. It is not to be expected that in the practice of States the application of the rules in question should have been perfect, in the sense that States should have refrained, with complete consistency, from the use of force or from intervention in each other's internal affairs. The Court does not consider that, for a rule to be established as customary, the corresponding practice must be in absolutely rigourous conformity with the rule. In order to deduce the existence of customary rules, the Court deems it sufficient that the conduct of States should, in general, be consistent with such rules, and that instances of State conduct inconsistent with a given rule should generally have been treated as breaches of that rule, not as indications of the recognition of a new rule. If a State acts in a way prima facie incompatible with a recognized rule, but defends its conduct by appealing to exceptions or justifications contained within the rule itself, then whether or not the State's conduct is in fact justifiable on that basis, the significance of that attitude is to confirm rather than to weaken the rule. ...

188. The Court thus finds that both Parties [in their pleadings] take the view that the principles as to the use of force incorporated in the United Nations Charter correspond, in essentials, to those found in customary international law. ... The Court has however to be satisfied that there exists in customary international law an *opinio juris* [as to the binding character of these principles] ... This *opinio juris* may, though with all due caution, be deduced from, *inter alia*, the attitude of the Parties and the attitude of States towards certain General Assembly resolutions, and

particularly resolution 2625 (XXV).[46] The effect of consent to the text of such resolutions . . . may be understood as an acceptance of the validity of the rule or set of rules declared by the resolution by themselves. The principle of non-use of force, for example, may thus be regarded as a principle of customary international law, not as such conditioned by provisions relating to collective security, or to the facilities or armed contingents to be provided under Article 43 of the Charter. It would therefore seem apparent that the attitude referred to expresses an *opinio juris* respecting such rule (or set of rules), to be thenceforth treated separately from the provisions, especially those of an institutional kind, to which it is subject on the treaty-law plane of the Charter.

189. As regards the United States in particular, the weight of an expression of *opinio juris* can similarly be attached to its support of the resolution of the Sixth International Conference of American States condemning aggression (18 February 1928) and ratification of the Montevideo Convention on Rights and Duties of States (26 December 1933), Article 11 of which imposes the obligation not to recognize territorial acquisitions or special advantages which have been obtained by force. Also significant is United States acceptance of the principle of the prohibition of the use of force which is contained in the declaration on principles governing the mutual relations of States participating in the Conference on Security and Co-operation in Europe (Helsinki, 1 August 1975), whereby the participating States undertake to "refrain in their mutual relations, *as well as in their international relations in general*," (emphasis added) from the threat or use of force. Acceptance of a text in these terms confirms the existence of an *opinio juris* of the participating States prohibiting the use of force in international relations.

190. A further confirmation of the validity as customary international law of the principle of the prohibition of the use of force expressed in Article 2, paragraph 4, of the Charter of the United Nations may be found in the fact that it is frequently referred to in statements by State representatives as being not only a principle of customary international law but also a fundamental or cardinal principle of such law. The International Law Commission, in the course of its work on the codification of the law of treaties, expressed the view that "the law of the Charter concerning the prohibition of the use of force in itself constitutes a conspicuous example of a rule in international law having the character of *jus cogens*."[47] Nicaragua in its Memorial on the Merits submitted in the present case states that the principle prohibiting the use of force embodied in Article 2, paragraph 4, of the Charter of the United Nations "has come to be recognized as *jus cogens*". The United States, in its Counter-Memorial on the questions of jurisdiction and admissibility, found it material to quote the views of scholars that this principle is a "universal

---

[46] *Ed.* Below, Appendix III.
[47] *Ed.* Y.B.I.L.C. 1966, II, p. 247.

norm", a "universal international law", a "universally recognized principle of international law", and a "principle of *jus cogens*".

191. As regards certain particular aspects of the principle in question it will be necessary to distinguish the most grave forms of the use of force (those constituting an armed attack) from other less grave forms. In determining the legal rule which applies to these latter forms, the Court can again draw on the formulations contained in . . . General Assembly resolution 2625 (XXV). . . .

193. The general rule prohibiting force allows for certain exceptions . . . the Court must express a view on the content of the right of self-defence, and more particularly the right of collective self-defence. First, with regard to the existence of this right, it notes that in the language of Article 51 of the United Nations Charter, the inherent right (or "droit naturel") which any State possesses in the event of an armed attack, covers both collective and individual self-defence. Thus, the Charter itself testifies to the existence of the right of collective self-defence in customary international law. Moreover . . . [in resolution 2625 (XXV)] the reference to the prohibition of force is followed by a paragraph stating that:

"nothing in the foregoing paragraphs shall be construed as enlarging or diminishing in any way the scope of the provisions of the Charter concerning cases in which the use of force is lawful.

This resolution demonstrates that the States represented in the General Assembly regard the exception to the prohibition of force constituted by the right of individual or collective self-defence as already a matter of customary international law.

194. With regard to the characteristics governing the right of self-defence, . . . reliance is placed by the Parties only on the right of self-defence in the case of an armed attack which has already occurred, and the issue of the lawfulness of a response to the imminent threat of armed attack has not been raised. Accordingly the Court expresses no view on that issue. The Parties also agree in holding that whether the response to the attack is lawful depends on observance of the criteria of the necessity and the proportionality of the measures taken in self-defence. . . .

195. In the case of individual self-defence, the exercise of this right is subject to the State concerned having been the victim of an armed attack. Reliance on collective self-defence of course does not remove the need for this. There appears now to be general agreement on the nature of the acts which can be treated as constituting armed attacks. In particular, it may be considered to be agreed that an armed attack must be understood as including not merely action by regular armed forces across an international border, but also "the sending by or on behalf of a State of armed bands, groups, irregulars or mercenaries, which carry out acts of armed force against another State of such gravity as to amount to" (*inter alia*) an actual armed attack conducted by regular forces, "or its substantial

involvement therein." This description, contained in Article 3, paragraph (g), of the Definition of Aggression annexed to General Assembly resolution 3314 (XXIX),[48] may be taken to reflect customary international law. The Court sees no reason to deny that, in customary law, the prohibition of armed attacks may apply to the sending by a State of armed bands to the territory of another State, if such an operation, because of its scale and effects, would have been classified as an armed attack rather than as a mere frontier incident had it been carried out by regular armed forces. But the Court does not believe that the concept of "armed attack" includes not only acts by armed bands where such acts occur on a significant scale but also assistance to rebels in the form of the provision of weapons or logistical or other support. Such assistance may be regarded as a threat or use of force, or amount to intervention in the internal or external affairs of other States. It is also clear that it is the State which is the victim of an armed attack which must form and declare the view that it has been so attacked. There is no rule in customary international law permitting its own assessment of the situation. . . .

199. . . . the Court [also] finds that in customary international law, whether of a general kind or that particular to the inter-American legal system,[49] there is no rule permitting the exercise of collective self-defence in the absence of a request by the State which regards itself as the victim of an armed attack. The Court concludes that the requirement of a request by the State which is the victim of the alleged attack is additional to the requirement that such a State should have declared itself to have been attacked.

200. . . . . Article 51 of the United Nations Charter requires that measures taken by States in exercise of this right of self-defence must be "immediately reported" to the Security Council. As the Court has observed above (paragraph . . . 188), a principle enshrined in a treaty, if reflected in customary international law, may well be so unencumbered with the conditions and modalities surrounding it in the treaty. Whatever influence the Charter may have had on customary international law in these matters, it is clear that in customary international law it is not a condition of the lawfulness of the use of force in self-defence that a procedure so closely dependent on the content of a treaty commitment and of the institutions established by it, should have been followed. On the other hand, if self-defence is advanced as a justification for measures which would otherwise be in breach both of the principle of customary international law and of that contained in the Charter, it is to be expected that the conditions of the Charter should be respected. Thus for the purpose of enquiry into the customary law position, the absence of a report may

---

[48] *Ed.* below, p. 945.
[49] *Ed.* The Court relied on the request requirement in the regional 1947 Rio Treaty, 21 U.N.T.S. 77. It cited no evidence in support of a request requirement in *general* custom.

be one of the factors indicating whether the State in question was itself convinced that it was acting in self-defence. . . .

202. The principle of non-intervention involves the right of every sovereign State to conduct its affairs without outside interference; though examples of trespass against this principle are not infrequent, the Court considers that it is part and parcel of customary international law. As the Court has observed [in the *Corfu Channel Case*]: "Between independent States, respect for territorial sovereignty is an essential foundation of international relations" (*I.C.J. Reports 1949*, p. 35), and international law requires political integrity also to be respected. . . . This principle [of non-intervention] is not, as such, spelt out in the Charter. But it was never intended that the Charter should embody written confirmation of every essential principle of international law in force. The existence in the *opinio juris* of States of the principle of non-intervention is backed by established and substantial practice. It has moreover been presented as a corollary of the principle of the sovereign equality of States. . . .

203. The principle has since been reflected in numerous declarations adopted by international organisations and conferences in which the United States and Nicaragua have participated, *e.g.*, General Assembly resolution 2131 (XX).[50] It is true that the United States, while it voted in favour of General Assembly resolution 2131 (XX), also declared at the time of its adoption in the First Committee that it considered the declaration in that resolution to be "only a statement of political intention and not a formulation of law." . . . However, the essentials of resolution 2131 (XX) are repeated in the Declaration approved by resolution 2625 (XXV), which set out principles which the General Assembly declared to be "basic principles" of international law, and on the adoption of which no analogous statement was made by the United States representative.

204. . . . In a different context, the United States expressly accepted the principles set forth in the declaration, to which reference has already been made, appearing in the Final Act of the Conference on Security and Co-operation in Europe (Helsinki, 1 August 1975),[51] including an elaborate statement of the principle of non-intervention; while these principles were presented as applying to the mutual relations among the participating States, it can be inferred that the text testifies to the existence, and the acceptance by the United States, of a customary principle which has universal application.

205. . . . As regards the . . . content of the principle of non-intervention—the Court will define only those aspects of the principle which appear to be relevant to the resolution of the dispute. In this respect it notes that, in view of the generally accepted formulations, the principle forbids all States or groups of States to intervene directly or indirectly in internal or external affairs of other States. A prohibited intervention must

---

[50] *Ed.* Below, p. 889.
[51] *Ed.* See above, p. 625.

accordingly be one bearing on matters in which each State is permitted, by the principle of State sovereignty, to decide freely. One of these is the choice of a political, economic, social and cultural system, and the formulation of foreign policy. Intervention is wrongful when it uses methods of coercion in regard to such choices, which must remain free ones. The element of coercion, which defines, and indeed forms the very essence of, prohibited intervention, is particularly obvious in the case of an intervention which uses force, either in the direct form of military action, or in the indirect form of support for subversive or terrorist armed activities within another State. . . . General Assembly resolution 2625 (XXV) equates assistance of this kind with the use of force by the assisting State when the acts committed in another State "involve a threat or use of force." These forms of action are therefore wrongful in the light of both the principle of non-use of force, and that of non-intervention. . . .

206. However, before reaching a conclusion on the nature of prohibited intervention, the Court must be satisfied that State practice justifies it. There have been in recent years a number of instances of foreign intervention for the benefit of forces opposed to the government of another State. The Court is not here concerned with the process of decolonisation; this question is not in issue in the present case. It has to consider whether there might be indications of a practice illustrative of belief in a kind of general right for States to intervene, directly or indirectly, with or without armed force, in support of an internal opposition in another State, whose cause appeared particularly worthy by reason of the political and moral values with which it was identified. For such a general right to come into existence would involve a fundamental modification of the customary law principle of non-intervention.

207. In considering the instances of the conduct above described, the Court has to emphasise that, as was observed in the *North Sea Continental Shelf* cases, for a new customary rule to be formed, not only must the acts concerned "amount to a settled practice," but they must be accompanied by the *opinio juris sive necessitatis*. Either the States taking such action or other States in a position to react to it, must have behaved so that their conduct is

"evidence of a belief that this practice is rendered obligatory by the existence of a rule of law requiring it. The need for such a belief, i.e., the existence of a subjective element, is implicit in the very notion of the *opinio juris sive necessitatis*." (*I.C.J. Reports 1969*, p. 44, para. 77.) . . .

The significance for the Court of cases of State conduct prima facie inconsistent with the principle of non-intervention lies in the nature of the ground offered as justification. Reliance by a State on a novel right or any unprecedented exception to the principle might, if shared in principle by other States, tend towards a modification of customary international law.

In fact however, the Court finds that States have not justified their conduct by reference to a new right of intervention or a new exception to the principle of its prohibition. The United States authorities have on some occasions clearly stated their grounds for intervening in the affairs of a foreign State for reasons connected with, for example, the domestic policies of that country, its ideology, the level of its armaments, or the direction of its foreign policy. But these were statements of international policy, and not an assertion of rules of existing international law.

209. The Court therefore finds that no such general right of intervention in support of an opposition within another State, exists in contemporary international law. The Court concludes that acts constituting a breach of the customary principle of non-intervention will also, if they directly or indirectly involve the use of force, constitute a breach of the principle of non-use of force in international relations.

210. When dealing with the rule of the prohibition of the use of force, the Court considered the exception to it constituted by the exercise of the right of collective self-defence in the event of armed attack. Similarly, it must now consider the following question: if one State acts towards another State in breach of the principle of non-intervention, may a third State lawfully take such action by way of counter-measures against the first State as would otherwise constitute an intervention in its internal affairs? A right to act in this way in the case of intervention would be analogous to the right of collective self-defence in the case of an armed attack, but both the act which gives rise to the reaction, and that reaction itself, would in principle be less grave. Since the Court is here dealing with a dispute in which a wrongful use of force is alleged, it has primarily to consider whether a State has a right to respond to intervention with intervention going so far as to justify a use of force in reaction to measures which do not constitute an armed attack but may nevertheless involve a use of force. The question is itself undeniably relevant from the theoretical viewpoint. However, since the Court is bound to confine its decision to those points of law which are essential to the settlement of the dispute before it, it is not for the Court here to determine what direct reactions are lawfully open to a State which considers itself the victim of another State's act of intervention, possibly involving the use of force. Hence it has not to determine whether, in the event of Nicaragua's having committed any such acts against El Salvador, the latter was lawfully entitled to take any particular counter-measure. It might however be suggested that, in such a situation, the United States might have been permitted to intervene in Nicaragua in the exercise of some right analogous to the right of collective self-defence, one which might be resorted to in a case of intervention short of armed attack.

211. The Court has recalled above (paragraphs 193 to 195) that for one State to use force against another, on the ground that that State has committed a wrongful act of force against a third State, is regarded as lawful, by way of exception, only when the wrongful act provoking the

response was an armed attack. Thus the lawfulness of the use of force by a State in response to a wrongful act of which it has not itself been the victim is not admitted when this wrongful act is not an armed attack. In the view of the Court, under international law in force today—whether customary international law or that of the United Nations system—States do not have a right of "collective" armed response to acts which do not constitute an "armed attack." ...

The Court considered the principles of state sovereignty, freedom of commerce and navigation and international humanitarian law and concluded that they were all infringed by a state that mines another state's ports. It then began to apply the customary international law that it had stated to the facts of the case.

227. The Court will first appraise the facts in the light of the principle of the non-use of force. ... For the most part, the complaints by Nicaragua are of the actual use of force against it by the United States. Of the acts which the Court has found imputable to the Government of the United States, the following are relevant in this respect:

— the laying of mines in Nicaraguan internal or territorial waters in early 1984 ... ;
— certain attacks in Nicaraguan ports, oil installations and a naval base.[52] ...

These activities constitute infringements of the principle of the prohibition of the use of force, defined earlier, unless they are justified by circumstances which exclude their unlawfulness, a question now to be examined. The Court has also found ... the existence of military manoeuvres held by the United States near the Nicaraguan borders; and Nicaragua has made some suggestion that this constituted a "threat of force," which is equally forbidden by the principle of non-use of force. The Court is however not satisfied that the manoeuvres complained of, in the circumstances in which they were held, constituted on the part of the United States a breach, as against Nicaragua, of the principle forbidding recourse to the threat or use of force. ...

228. As to the claim that United States activities in relation to the *contras* constitute a breach of the customary international law principle of the non-use of force, the Court finds that ... the United States has committed a prima facie violation of that principle by its assistance to the *contras* in Nicaragua, by "organising or encouraging the organisation of irregular forces or armed bands ... for incursion into the territory of another

---

[52] *Ed.* The Court found that the mining was effected not by the *contras* but by persons, probably "UCLAs" ["Unilaterally Controlled Latino Assets" in CIA vocabulary], "in the pay and acting on the instructions of ... [the CIA], under the supervision and with the logistic support of United States agents;" the attacks on ports, etc., were similarly executed by " 'UCLAs,' while United States nationals participated in the planning, direction and support": I.C.J.Rep. 1986, pp. 48–51.

State," and "participating in acts of civil strife . . . in another State," in the terms of General Assembly resolution 2625 (XXV). According to that resolution, participation of this kind is contrary to the principle of the prohibition of the use of force when the facts of civil strife referred to "involve a threat or use of force." In the view of the Court, while the arming and training of the *contras* can certainly be said to involve the threat or use of force against Nicaragua, this is not necessarily so in respect of all the assistance given by the United States Government.[53] In particular the Court considers that the mere supply of funds to the *contras*, while undoubtedly an act of intervention in the internal affairs of Nicaragua, as will be explained below, does not in itself amount to a use of force."

229. The Court must thus consider whether . . . the acts in question of the United States are justified by the exercise of its right of collective self-defence against an armed attack. . . . For the Court to conclude that the United States was lawfully exercising its right of collective self-defence, it must first find that Nicaragua engaged in an armed attack against El Salvador, Honduras or Costa Rica.

230. As regards El Salvador, the Court has found . . . that it is satisfied that between July 1979 and the early months of 1981, an intermittent flow of arms was routed via the territory of Nicaragua to the armed opposition in that country. The Court was not however satisfied that assistance has reached the Salvadorian armed opposition, on a scale of any significance, since the early months of 1981, or that the Government of Nicaragua was responsible for any flow of arms at either period. Even assuming that the supply of arms to the opposition in El Salvador could be treated as imputable to the Government of Nicaragua, to justify invocation of the right of collective self-defence in customary international law, it would have to be equated with an armed attack by Nicaragua on El Salvador. As stated above [para. 195], the Court is unable to consider that, in customary international law, the provision of arms to the opposition in another State constitutes an armed attack on that State. Even at a time when the arms flow was at its peak, and again assuming the participation of the Nicaraguan Government, that would not constitute such armed attack.

231. Turning to Honduras and Costa Rica, the Court has also stated . . . that it should find established that certain trans-border incursions into the

---

[53] *Ed.* On the nature and extent of U.S. involvement in *contra* activities, the Court stated (I.C.J. Rep. 1986, pp. 61–62): " . . . the financial support given by the United States to . . . the *contras* . . . is a fully established fact. . . . [However], the Court has not been able to satisfy itself that the respondent State 'created' the *contra* force . . . Nor does the evidence warrant a finding that the United States gave 'direct and critical combat support,' at least if that form of words is taken to mean that this support was tantamount to direct intervention by the United States combat forces, or that all *contra* operations reflected strategy and tactics wholly devised by the United States. On the other hand, the Court holds it established that the United States authorities largely financed, trained, equipped, armed and organized the FDN".

territory of those two States, in 1982, 1983 and 1984, were imputable to the Government of Nicaragua. Very little information is however available to the Court as to the circumstances of these incursions or their possible motivations, which renders it difficult to decide whether they may be treated for legal purposes as amounting, singly or collectively, to an "armed attack" by Nicaragua on either or both States.... There are however other considerations which justify the Court in finding that neither these incursions, nor the alleged supply of arms to the opposition in El Salvador, may be relied on as justifying the exercise of the right of collective self-defence.

232. The exercise of the right of collective self-defence presupposes that an armed attack has occurred; and it is evident that it is the victim State, being the most directly aware of that fact, which is likely to draw general attention to its plight. It is also evident that if the victim State wishes another State to come to its help in the exercise of the right of collective self-defence, it will normally make an express request to that effect. Thus in the present instance, the Court is entitled to take account, in judging the asserted justification of the exercise of collective self-defence by the United States, of the actual conduct of El Salvador, Honduras and Costa Rica at the relevant time, as indicative of a belief by the State in question that it was the victim of an armed attack by Nicaragua, and of the making of a request by the victim State to the United States for help in the exercise of collective self-defence.

233. The Court has seen no evidence that the conduct of those States was consistent with such a situation, either at the time when the United States first embarked on the activities which were allegedly justified by self-defence, or indeed for a long period subsequently....

235. There is also an aspect of the conduct of the United States which the Court is entitled to take into account.... At no time, up to the present, has the United States Government addressed to the Security Council ... the report which is required by Article 51 of the United Nations Charter in respect of measures which a State believes itself bound to take when it exercises the right of individual or collective self-defence. The Court, whose decision has to be made on the basis of customary international law, has already observed that in the context of that law, the reporting obligation enshrined in Article 51 of the Charter of the United Nations does not exist.... But the Court is justified in observing that this conduct of the United States hardly conforms with the latter's avowed conviction that it was acting in the context of collective self-defence as consecrated by Article 51 of the Charter. This fact is all the more noteworthy because, in the Security Council, the United States has itself taken the view that failure to observe the requirement to make a report contradicted a State's claim to be acting on the basis of collective self-defence (S/PV.2187).

236. Similarly, while no strict legal conclusion may be drawn from the date of El Salvador's announcement that it was the victim of an armed attack, and the date of its official request addressed to the United States

concerning the exercise of collective self-defence, those dates have a
significance as evidence of El Salvador's view of the situation. The declaration and the request of El Salvador, made publicly for the first time in
August 1984, do not support the contention that in 1981 there was an
armed attack capable of serving as a legal foundation for United States
activities which began in the second half of that year. ...

237. Since the Court has found that the condition *sine qua non* required
for the exercise of the right of collective self-defence by the United States
is not fulfilled in this case ... even if the United States activities in
question had been carried on in strict compliance with the canons of
necessity and proportionality, they would not thereby become lawful. If
however they were not, this may constitute an additional ground of
wrongfulness. On the question of necessity, the Court observes that the
United States measures taken in December 1981 ... cannot be said to
correspond to a "necessity" justifying the United States action against
Nicaragua on the basis of assistance given by Nicaragua to the armed
opposition in El Salvador. First, these measures were only taken, and
began to produce their effects, several months after the major offensive of
the armed opposition against the Government of El Salvador had been
completely repulsed (January 1981), and the actions of the opposition
considerably reduced in consequence. Thus it was possible to eliminate
the main danger to the Salvadorian Government without the United
States embarking on activities in and against Nicaragua. ... Whether or
not the assistance to the *contras* might meet the criterion of proportionality, the Court cannot regard the United States activities ... relating to
the mining of the Nicaraguan ports and the attacks on ports, oil installations, etc., as satisfying that criterion. Whatever uncertainty may exist as
to the exact scale of the aid received by the Salvadorian armed opposition
from Nicaragua, it is clear that these latter United States activities in
question could not have been proportionate to that aid. Finally on this
point, the Court must also observe that the reaction of the United States
in the context of what it regarded as self-defence was continued long after
the period in which any presumed armed attack by Nicaragua could
reasonably be contemplated.

238. Accordingly, the Court concludes that the plea of collective self-
defence against an alleged armed attack on El Salvador, Honduras or
Costa Rica, advanced by the United States to justify its conduct toward
Nicaragua, cannot be upheld; and accordingly that the United States has
violated the principle prohibiting recourse to the threat or use of force by
the acts listed in paragraph 227 above, and by its assistance to the *contras*
to the extent that this assistance "involve[s] a threat or use of force". ...

239. The Court comes now to the application in this case of the principle of non-intervention in the internal affairs of States ...

241. The Court ... does not consider it necessary to seek to establish
whether the intention of the United States to secure a change of governmental policies in Nicaragua went so far as to be equated with an

endeavour to overthrow the Nicaraguan Government. It appears to the Court to be clearly established first, that the United States intended, by its support of the *contras*, to coerce the Government of Nicaragua in respect of matters in which each State is permitted, by the principle of State sovereignty, to decide freely (see paragraph 205 above); and secondly that the intention of the *contras* themselves was to overthrow the present Government of Nicaragua. . . . The Court considers that in international law, if one State, with a view to the coercion of another State, supports and assists armed bands in that State whose purpose is to overthrow the government of that State, that amounts to an intervention by the one State in the internal affairs of the other, whether or not the political objective of the State giving such support and assistance is equally far-reaching. It is for this reason that the Court has only examined the intentions of the United States Government so far as they bear on the question of self-defence.

242. The Court therefore finds that the support given by the United States, up to the end of September 1984, to the military and paramilitary activities of the *contras* in Nicaragua, by financial support, training, supply of weapons, intelligence and logistic support, constitutes a clear breach of the principle of non-intervention. The Court has however taken note that, with effect from the beginning of the United States governmental financial year 1985, namely 1 October 1984, the United States Congress has restricted the use of the funds appropriated for assistance to the *contras* to "humanitarian assistance." . . . There can be no doubt that the provision of strictly humanitarian aid to persons or forces in another country, whatever their political affiliations or objectives, cannot be regarded as unlawful intervention, or as in any other way contrary to international law. . . .

243. An essential feature of truly humanitarian aid is that it is given "without discrimination" of any kind. In the view of the Court, if the provision of "humanitarian assistance" is to escape condemnation as an intervention in the internal affairs of Nicaragua, not only must it be limited to the purposes hallowed in the practice of the Red Cross, namely "to prevent and alleviate human suffering," and "to protect life and health and to ensure respect for the human being"; it must also, and above all, be given without discrimination to all in need in Nicaragua, not merely to the *contras* and their dependents.

244. As already noted, Nicaragua has also asserted that the United States is responsible for an "indirect" form of intervention in its internal affairs inasmuch as it has taken, to Nicaragua's disadvantage, certain action of an economic nature. The Court's attention has been drawn in particular to the cessation of economic aid in April 1981; the 90 per cent reduction in the sugar quota for United States imports from Nicaragua in April 1981; and the trade embargo adopted on 1 May 1985. While admitting in principle that some of these actions were not unlawful in themselves, counsel for Nicaragua argued that these measures of economic

constraint add up to a systematic violation of the principle of non-intervention.

245. The Court ... is unable to regard such action on the economic plane as is here complained of as a breach of the customary-law principle of non-intervention.

246. Having concluded that the activities of the United States in relation to the activities of the *contras* in Nicaragua constitute prima facie acts of intervention, the Court must next consider whether they may nevertheless be justified on some legal ground. As the Court has stated, the principle of non-intervention derives from customary international law. It would certainly lose its effectiveness as a principle of law if intervention were to be justified by a mere request for assistance made by an opposition group in another State—supposing such a request to have actually been made by an opposition to the régime in Nicaragua in this instance. Indeed, it is difficult to see what would remain of the principle of non-intervention in international law if intervention, which is already allowable at the request of the government of a State, were also to be allowed at the request of the opposition. This would permit any State to intervene at any moment in the internal affairs of another State, whether at the request of the government or at the request of its opposition. Such a situation does not in the Court's view correspond to the present state of international law.

247. The Court has already indicated (paragraph 238) its conclusion that the conduct of the United States towards Nicaragua cannot be justified by the right of collective self-defence in response to an alleged armed attack on one or other of Nicaragua's neighbours. So far as regards the allegations of supply of arms by Nicaragua to the armed opposition in El Salvador, the Court has indicated that while the concept of an armed attack includes the despatch by one State of armed bands into the territory of another State, the supply of arms and other support to such bands cannot be equated with armed attack. Nevertheless, such activities may well constitute a breach of the principle of the non-use of force and an intervention in the internal affairs of a State, that is, a form of conduct which is certainly wrongful, but is of lesser gravity than an armed attack. The Court must therefore enquire now whether the activities of the United States towards Nicaragua might be justified as a response to an intervention by that State in the internal affairs of another State in Central America. . . .

249. On the legal level the Court cannot regard response to an intervention by Nicaragua as such a justification. While an armed attack would give rise to an entitlement to collective self-defence, a use of force of a lesser degree of gravity cannot, as the Court has already observed . . ., produce any entitlement to take collective counter-measures involving the use of force. The acts of which Nicaragua is accused, even assuming them to have been established and imputable to that State, could only have justified proportionate counter-measures on the part of the State

which had been the victim of these acts, namely El Salvador, Honduras or Costa Rica. They could not justify counter-measures taken by a third State, the United States, and particularly could not justify intervention involving the use of force.

267. The Court also notes that Nicaragua is accused by the 1985 finding of the United States Congress of violating human rights. . . .

268. . . . while the United States might form its own appraisal of the situation as to respect for human rights in Nicaragua, the use of force could not be the appropriate method to monitor or ensure such respect. With regard to the steps actually taken, the protection of human rights, a strictly humanitarian objective, cannot be compatible with the mining of ports, the destruction of oil installations, or again with the training, arming and equipping of the *contras*. The Court concludes that the argument derived from the preservation of human rights in Nicaragua cannot afford a legal justification for the conduct of the United States, and cannot in any event be reconciled with the legal strategy of the respondent State, which is based on the right of collective self-defence.

Continuing to apply custom, the Court also found that the United States had infringed Nicaragua's sovereignty and freedom of maritime commerce and international humanitarian law by the conduct indicated in paragraphs (5) and (6) of the *dispositif* (below). The Court also found breaches of the 1956 Treaty of Friendship.

292. For these reasons

THE COURT . . .

(2) By twelve votes to three,[54]

Rejects the justification of collective self-defence maintained by the United States of America in connection with the military and paramilitary activities in and against Nicaragua the subject of this case;

(3) By twelve votes to three,[55]

Decides that the United States of America, by training, arming, equipping, financing and supplying the *contra* forces or otherwise encouraging, supporting and aiding military and paramilitary activities in and against Nicaragua, has acted, against the Republic of Nicaragua, in breach of its obligation under customary international law not to *intervene* in the affairs of another State;

---

[54] *Ed.* The Judges in the majority were President Nagendra Singh; Vice-President de Lacharrière; Judges Lachs, Ruda, Elia, Ago, Sette-Camara, Mbaye, Bedjaoui, Ni and Evensen; Judge *ad hoc* Colliard. Judges Oda, Schwebel and Sir Robert Jennings dissented.

[55] *Ed.* Judges Oda, Schwebel and Sir Robert Jennings dissented.

(4) By twelve votes to three,[55a]

Decides that the United States of America, by certain attacks in Nicaraguan territory in 1983–1984 . . . and further by those acts of intervention referred to in subparagraph (3) hereof which involve the use of force, has acted, against the Republic of Nicaragua, in breach of its obligation under customary international law not to use force against another State;

(5) By twelve votes to three,[55b]

Decides that the United States of America, by directing or authorising overflights of Nicaraguan territory, and by the acts imputable to the United States referred to in subparagraph (4) hereof, has acted, against the Republic of Nicaragua, in breach of its obligation under customary international law not to violate the sovereignty of another State;

(6) By twelve votes to three,[55c]

Decides that, by laying mines in the internal or territorial waters of the Republic of Nicaragua during the first months of 1984, the United States of America has acted, against the Republic of Nicaragua, in breach of its obligations under customary international law not to use force against another State, not to intervene in its affairs, not to violate its sovereignty and not to interrupt peaceful maritime commerce;

(7) By fourteen votes to one,[56]

Decides that, by the acts referred to in subparagraph (6) hereof, the United States of America has acted, against the Republic of Nicaragua, in breach of its obligations under Article XIX of the [1956] Treaty of Friendship, Commerce and Navigation . . . ;

(8) By fourteen votes to one,[57]

Decides that the United States of America, by failing to make known the existence and location of the mines laid by it, referred to in subparagraph (6) hereof, has acted in breach of its obligations under customary international law in this respect;

(9) By fourteen votes to one,[58]

[55a] *ibid.*
[55b] *ibid.*
[55c] *ibid.*
[56] *Ed.* Judge Schwebel dissented.
[57] *Ed.* Judge Oda dissented.
[58] *Ed.* Judge Oda dissented.

Finds that the United States of America, by producing in 1983 a manual entitled *Operaciones sicológicas en guerra de guerrillas*, and disseminating it to *contra* forces, has encouraged the commission by them of acts contrary to general principles of humanitarian law; but does not find a basis for concluding that any such acts which may have been committed are imputable to the United States of America as acts of the United States of America;

(10) By twelve votes to three,[59]

Decides that the United States of America, by the attacks on Nicaraguan territory referred to in subparagraph (4) hereof, and by declaring a general embargo on trade with Nicaragua on 1 May 1985, has committed acts calculated to deprive of its object and purpose the [1956] Treaty of Friendship, Commerce and Navigation . . . ;

(11) By twelve votes to three,[59a]

Decides that the United States of America, by the attacks on Nicaraguan territory referred to in subparagraph (4) hereof, and by declaring a general embargo on trade with Nicaragua on 1 May 1985, has acted in breach of its obligations under Article XIX of the [1956] Treaty of Friendship, Commerce and Navigation . . . .

Notes
1. Much to the delight of international lawyers and the chagrin of the defendant state, the *Nicaragua (Merits)* case gave the I.C.J. an unprecedented opportunity to explore the law governing the use of armed force *ante bellum* and intervention by states and to do so in the area in which it was most in need of clarification, namely that in which state A gives assistance to rebels seeking to overthrow the government of state D or, conversely, to the government of state D to defeat the rebels against it.[60]

2. *Indirect Use of Force*. The *Nicaragua (Merits)* case confirms that the giving of assistance to rebels may be an indirect use of force contrary to customary international law. Everything turns upon the kind of assistance. The Court held that the U.S. had infringed the rule prohibiting the threat or use of force by "the arming and training of the *contras*," but that it had not done so by "the mere supply of funds."[61] Since the whole of the Section on the Principle on the Use of

---

[59] *Ed.* Judges Oda, Schwebel and Sir Robert Jennings dissented.
[59a] *ibid.*
[60] On the international law on intervention in civil wars generally, see Falk, ed., *The International Law of Civil War* (1971); Farer (1974–III) 142 Hague Recueil 291 (1974–II); Little, *Intervention* (1975); Luard, ed., *The International Regulation of Civil War* (1972); Moore, ed., *Law and Civil War in the Modern World* (1974); Tanca, *Foreign Armed Intervention in Internal Conflict* (1993).
[61] Judgment, para. 228. The distinction between these two forms of assistance, which is supportable on the basis that financial assistance, for example, to buy arms is more indirect or remote than giving the arms themselves, echoes the different wording of the 1965 *Non-Intervention* Declaration, below, p. 889, which expressly prohibits financial assistance, and the section on the Principle of the Use of Force of the 1970 Declaration, Appendix III, below, which does not.

Force in the 1970 Declaration was accepted by the Court as amplifying the customary rule, other forms of assistance within that Section's very general language[62] can probably be taken to have been understood by it as involving the illegal use of force too. Thus the establishment, organisation or control[63] of a rebel force or the giving of material support (*e.g.* logistic support, bases) would also qualify. Whereas financial assistance is not an indirect use of force, it is nonetheless contrary to international law as intervention in another state's affairs.[64] Humanitarian assistance, however, whether financial or otherwise (blankets, food, etc.), is perfectly lawful—provided that it is given equally to rebels and others in the community in need.[65]

There is disagreement on the question whether, exceptionally, a state may intervene to assist a "people" fighting a war of national liberation, *i.e.* one to realise their right to self-determination.[66] Developing states take the view that the use of force by a colonial power to repress such action by a "people" is a breach of the rule prohibiting the use of force so that a state may intervene to give "material" (troops, equipment, etc.) as well as "moral" assistance to the rebels.[67] Western states deny that the prohibition of the use of force applies to action taken to repress an internal rebellion and argue that the Principle of Non-Intervention prohibits "material assistance." The Section on the Principle of Self-Determination in the 1970 Declaration intentionally avoids the issue by simply stating (para. 6) that "such peoples are entitled to seek and receive support" (undefined). *cf.* the similarly equivocal wording of the 1974 General Assembly Resolution on the Definition of Aggression, Article 7, below p. 947. The question was purposely not considered in the *Nicaragua* (*Merits*) case (judgment, para. 206).

In the *Nicaragua* (*Merits*) case, the Court did consider and reject (judgment, para. 206) the idea that there was a right of intervention (to the level of the use of force) to support the "political or moral values" of a rebellion. The prohibition on intervention is ideologically neutral; in particular, intervention is not permitted to assist a rebellion to protect democracy or human rights.[68]

3. *Assistance to governments.*[69] Like assistance by a state to rebels seeking to overthrow the government of another state, assistance to a government attempting to suppress a rebellion has been a common feature of international relations since the Second World War. The legality of assistance to a government *where the rebels are assisted by a third state* was considered by the I.C.J. in the *Nicaragua* case

---

[62] See paras 8 and 9.

[63] There comes a point where the intervening state's control over a rebel force is so complete that the latter becomes an arm of the former so that its acts are imputable to that state. On this aspect of the *Nicaragua Case* (*Merits*), see above, p. 878, n. 53.

[64] On intervention, see below, p. 889.

[65] *Nicaragua Case* (*Merits*), judgment, paras 242–243. The Court refrained from ruling on the legality of the humanitarian assistance given by the U.S. for lack of information as to its use.

[66] See Wilson, *International Law and the Use of Force by National Liberation Movements* (1988).

[67] A number of General Assembly resolutions support the latter part of this view. See, *e.g.* G.A.Resn 2908, G.A.O.R., 27th Sess., Supp. 30, p. 2 (1972), which "urges all states . . . to provide moral and material assistance to all peoples struggling for their freedom and independence in the colonial Territories and to those living under alien domination—in particular to the national liberation movements of the Territories of Africa. . . . " The resolution was adopted by 99 votes to five (France, Portugal, South Africa, U.K., and the U.S.), with 23 abstentions.

[68] *cf.* Schachter (1984) 78 A.J.I.L. 650 who argues against Reisman's claim, *ibid.* p. 642, of a right to intervene "to increase the probability of the free choice of peoples' about their government." But there comes a point where humanitarian intervention is permitted; see below, p. 917.

[69] See Doswald-Beck (1985) 56 B.Y.I.L. 189.

(*Merits*) in the light of the U.S. claim that its challenged action would be justified as assistance to the governments of El Salvador, Honduras and Costa Rica in the form of collective self defence against Nicaragua which was assisting rebels against them. The Court held that the right of self defence,[70] whether individual or collective, is only available in response to an "armed attack" and that the Nicaraguan assistance to rebels complained of did not constitute such an attack. The Court's definition of an "armed attack" (judgment, para. 195), with its requirement of the sending of armed bands "by or on behalf of" the aggressor state to conduct an operation that meets the Court's "scale and effects" test, must mean that most cases of the indirect use of force contrary to customary international law by a state by the giving of assistance to rebels will not generate the right of self defence against that state.[71] A less restrictive meaning of "armed attack" was suggested by Judge Sir Robert Jennings in his dissenting opinion[72]:

> It may readily be agreed that the mere provision of arms cannot be said to amount to an armed attack. But the provision of arms may, nevertheless, be a very important element in what might be thought to amount to armed attack, where it is coupled with other kinds of involvement. Accordingly, it seems to me that to say that the provision of arms, coupled with "logistical or other support" is not armed attack is going much too far. Logistical support may itself be crucial.... If there is added to all this "other support," it becomes difficult to understand what it is, short of direct attack by a State's own forces, that may not be done apparently without a lawful response in the form of collective self-defence....
>
> This looks to me neither realistic nor just in the world where power struggles are in every continent carried on by destabilisation, interference in civil strife, comfort, aid and encouragement to rebels, and the like. The original scheme of the United Nations Charter, whereby force would be deployed by the United Nations itself, ... has never come into effect.... In this situation it seems dangerous to define unnecessarily strictly the conditions for lawful self-defence, so as to leave a large area where both a forcible response to force is forbidden....

The approach suggested by Judge Sir Robert Jennings is in line with that of Western states. The text of the 1974 Resolution on the Definition of Aggression[73] which the Court relied upon for its definition of an "armed attack" was a compromise between the views of Western and developing states.

The Court indicated that, although it has no right of self-defence (that would permit the use of armed force), a state faced with intervention by another state assisting rebels against it at a level not amounting to an "armed attack" may take "proportionate countermeasures" against the intervening state. These would include economic and political sanctions; the Court left unanswered (see judgment, paras 210, 249) the question whether armed force (*e.g.* by cross border raids to pursue guerrillas or to destroy their supply routes or bases) is also permitted. The Court was emphatic, however, that intervention below the level of an "armed attack" "could not justify countermeasures taken by a third state" (judgment,

---

[70] On the right of self-defence generally, see below, p. 894.

[71] But see, exceptionally, Renamo, the Mozambique rebel force, which conducted guerrilla warfare against the Mozambique Government in the 1980s: see White, *loc. cit.*, p. 866, n. 43, above, p. 549. Renamo was controlled by South Africa and could be said to have been "sent by or on behalf of it"—not just assisted by South Africa—and conducted operations that probably met the Court's "scale and effects" requirement, thus justifying individual and collective self-defence against South Africa.

[72] I.C.J. Rep. 1986, p. 543.

[73] Art. 3(*g*), below, p. 946.

para. 249) against a state assisting rebels. Thus, El Salvador, but not the U.S., could have taken them against Nicaragua. Intervention by a third state is "allowable at the request of the government of a state" (judgment, para. 246), but only, by inference, against the rebels themselves and within the limits imposed by territorial sovereignty. El Salvador, for example, could have invited the U.S. to send troops or provide arms to help it fight against the rebels on El Salvadoran territory, but the U.S. could not have effected countermeasures against Nicaragua. Note that if the Court were, in an appropriate case, to decide that a victim state may react to unlawful intervention below the level of an armed attack by way of forcible countermeasures, it would be supposing a second and surprising exception (additional to self defence) to the rule that armed force is illegal in international relations—an exception that would significantly limit the present clear rule that reprisals are illegal. Might a better approach have been a wider definition of an "armed attack" (justifying self defence) along the lines suggested by Judge Sir Robert Jennings?

On the legality of assistance to the constitutional government to suppress *a rebellion that is not externally supported*, Wright[74] wrote in 1960 that international law

> does not permit the use of force in the territory of another state on invitation either of the recognised or the insurgent government in times of rebellion, insurrection, or civil war. Since international law recognises the right of revolution, it cannot permit other states to intervene to prevent it.

This statement is consistent with the "broad principle" in the 1965 and 1970 Declarations "that internal conflicts within the state are the concern of that State alone"[75] and with the wish underlying the *Nicaragua* judgment to minimalise the internationalisation of conflict in the interest of international peace and security.[76] The United Kingdom supports a rule of non-intervention, save in the case of "temporary difficulties":

> Nevertheless, the United Kingdom did not consider that that rule in any way prejudiced the right of a legally constituted and internationally recognised Government to seek and receive from a friendly State assistance in preserving or restoring internal law and order. Of course, any Government which responded to such a request for assistance would have to satisfy itself that the response was proper, and it would have to expect its actions to come under the closest scrutiny of the international community. His Government believed, however, that it would be wrong to suggest by an unduly broad definition of "civil strife" that there were no circumstances in which a Government in temporary difficulties could seek and receive assistance from a friendly State which it trusted to render aid with full respect for the territorial integrity and political independence of the recipient State.[77]

---

[74] (1960) 54 A.J.I.L. 521 at 529.

[75] Bowett, in Moore, ed., *op. cit.*, p. 885, n. 60, above, at p. 41.

[76] See White, *loc. cit.*, p. 866, n. 43, above, at p. 536. The lawfulness of intervention not involving the use of armed force to assist a government was recognised in the *Nicaragua* case, judgment, para. 246, above, p. 882.

[77] U.K. representative (Mr Sinclair) in the 1967 Special Committee on Principles of International Law, etc., UN Doc. A/AC.125/SR.57, p. 5; 1967 B.P.I.L. 36. *cf.* the 1986 Foreign Office Policy Document No. 148, paras II.6–9, reprinted in U.K.M.I.L. 1986 (1986) 57 B.Y.I.L. 614.

(b) *Intervention*

DECLARATION ON THE INADMISSIBILITY OF INTERVENTION IN THE DOMESTIC AFFAIRS OF STATES AND THE PROTECTION OF THEIR INDEPENDENCE AND SOVEREIGNTY 1965[78]

G.A. Resolution. 2131 (XX). December 21, 1965. G.A.O.R., 20th Sess., Supp. 14, p. 11; (1966) 60 A.J.I.L. 662

The General Assembly... solemnly declares:...

1. No state has the right to intervene, directly or indirectly, for any reason whatever, in the internal or external affairs of any other state. Consequently, armed intervention and all other forms of interference or attempted threats against the personality of the state or against its political, economic and cultural elements, are condemned.

2. No state may use or encourage the use of economic, political or any other type of measures to coerce another state in order to obtain from it the subordination of the exercise of its sovereign rights or to secure from it advantages of any kind. Also, no state shall organise, assist, foment, finance, incite or tolerate subversive, terrorist or armed activities directed towards the violent overthrow of the régime of another state, or interfere in civil strife in another state.

3. The use of force to deprive peoples of their national identity constitutes a violation of their inalienable rights and of the principle of non-intervention.

4. The strict observance of these obligations is an essential condition to ensure that nations live together in peace with one another, since the practice of any form of intervention not only violates the spirit and letter of the Charter of the United Nations but also leads to the creation of situations which threaten international peace and security.

5. Every state has an inalienable right to choose its political, economic, social and cultural systems, without interference in any form by another State.

Notes

1. Paragraphs 1, 2, 3, and 5 of the 1965 Declaration were incorporated almost verbatim into the Section on the Principle of Non-Intervention in the 1970 Declaration on Principles of International Law, below, Appendix III. Both were regarded as stating the customary international law on intervention in the *Nicaragua* case (judgment, para. 203).

---

[78] The Resolution was adopted by 109 to 0, with one abstention. The one abstaining state was the U.K., which accepted the "fundamental propositions set out in the resolution" but objected to the manner in which that resolution had been evolved and the imprecision of some of its language": 1967 B.P.I.L. 35, 36.

2. Although a state's interference in another state's affairs may not amount to the use of force, it may nonetheless be contrary to international law as intervention. Thus, in the *Nicaragua* case, the funding of the *contras*, although not an unlawful use of force, was illegal intervention (judgment, para. 228). The prohibition upon intervention in civil wars (the sole subject of this section) is just one aspect of a more general prohibition the limits of which have always been uncertain and are not well defined in the vague language of the 1965 and 1970 Declarations. Intervention is defined by Oppenheim as "forcible or dictatorial interference by a State in the affairs of another State, calculated to impose certain conduct or consequences on that other State."[79] In the Nineteenth Century, it was often darkly associated with the armed intervention, on humanitarian or other grounds, by powerful European states in the affairs of their weaker brethren.[80] As the 1965 Declaration indicates, it also includes other, more subtle, forms of influence or control.[81] For example, intervention in the "external affairs" of another state (paragraph 1) may include a case in which "State A sought to persuade State B by threats or by other measures amounting to economic coercion not to enter an association with other States."[82] The Principle of Non-Intervention in the 1965 and 1970 Declarations overlaps with that on the Use of Force in Article 2(4) and the 1970 Declaration. An armed attack upon another State annexing its territory is the ultimate form of intervention. Certain kinds of assistance to rebels in a civil war is within both principles also: see the *Nicaragua Case (Merits)* (judgment, para. 205).

The following notes contain accounts of instances of intervention by force in the affairs of other states. The justifications given by the intervening state vary from the request of the constitutional government, to the maintenance or exclusion of socialism or communism within or from a region, to the defence of nationals, to the existence of a treaty right of intervention. Are any of these cases ones in which the intervention, mostly by one superpower or another, can properly be justified on these grounds or otherwise in accordance with the rules as to the use of force and intervention?

3. *The Hungarian Uprising*.[83] On October 23, 1956, demonstrations took place in Budapest against the Hungarian Government calling, *inter alia*, for Mr Nagy to be brought into the Government. Fighting broke out and, at 2 a.m. on October 24, Russian tanks appeared in Budapest. Nonetheless, at 8.13 a.m., it was announced that a new Government was to be formed under Mr Nagy. At 9 a.m., it was announced that "the Government had applied for help to the Soviet formations stationed in Hungary [under the Warsaw Pact]." It is not clear when and by whom the application was made.[84] On November 1, Hungary denounced the Warsaw Pact after Mr Nagy had unsuccessfully demanded the withdrawal of new Soviet troops known to be entering Hungary. On the same day, Mr Nagy broadcast a declaration of Hungarian neutrality and called for the assistance of other states to defend it. On November 4, Soviet troops again entered Budapest and overcame resistance in a few days. On the same day, Mr Kadar announced that he had formed a Government in place of that of Mr Nagy and that he had requested the second intervention of Soviet troops. Thereafter the uprising petered out. The United Nations Special Committee on the Problem of Hungary, which was not allowed into Hungary to investigate, found it impossible to reach any conclusion

---

[79] Oppenheim, Vol. I, p. 430.

[80] *cf.* the passage in the *Corfu Channel* case judgment, above, p. 395.

[81] See Damrosch (1989) 83 A.J.I.L. 1.

[82] U.K. representative (Mr Sinclair) in the 1967 Special Committee on Principles of International Law, etc., UN Doc. A/AC.125/SR.73, p. 22; 1967 B.P.I.L. 39.

[83] The following summary is based on the Report of the UN Special Committee on the Problem of Hungary, G.A.O.R., 11th Sess., Supp. 18 (1957).

[84] It is not known when Mr Nagy's Government actually took office.

on the question whether any request for aid had been made at the beginning; it rejected the Soviet argument[85] that what the committee called a "spontaneous national uprising" had been fomented by ex-Nazi leaders and Western powers who had sent in arms. The case demonstrates one of the weaknesses of allowing intervention at the request of the constitutional government, namely that of determining which is the constitutional government (if any can be found in the middle of a revolution) and whether it in fact made a request.

4. *The Czechoslovak* case. In 1968, with the arrival of Mr Dubcek and other new leaders in power by lawful means, the still communist Government of Czechoslovakia introduced certain reforms resulting, *inter alia*, in increased freedom of speech, that were significantly at variance with Czechoslovakia's previous policies. In August 1968, troops from the USSR and other East European communist states entered Czechoslovakia. With the assistance of Soviet advisers, the policies and composition of the Czech Government thereafter gradually changed, with the movement towards liberalisation being reversed. The USSR first claimed that the Czech Government had requested the intervention, but this was strenuously denied by that Government. Later the intervention was explained by Mr Brezhnev, in a speech in Poland, as follows:

> ... It is well known, comrades, that there are common natural laws of socialist construction, deviation from which could lead from socialism as such. And when external and internal forces hostile to socialism try to turn the development of a given socialist country in the direction of restoration of the capitalist system ... this is no longer merely a problem for the country's people, but a common problem, the concern of all socialist countries.
>
> It is quite clear that an action such as military assistance to a fraternal country to end a threat to the socialist system is an extraordinary measure, dictated by necessity; it can be called forth only by the overt actions of enemies of socialism within the country and beyond its boundaries, actions that create a threat to the common interests of the socialist camp.[86]

This doctrine of limited sovereignty, now abandoned, became known as the "Brezhnev Doctrine."[87]

5. *The Afghanistan* case.[88] In 1978, the non-aligned Daud Government was ousted by force by the more left-wing Taraki (later Amin) Government, which established closer links with the USSR. In 1979, this Government was overthrown by a new USSR backed Government led by President Karmal, an Afghanistan politician flown to Afghanistan to take office by the USSR from virtual exile in Eastern Europe. The change of government was accompanied by an airlift into Kabul of 4000 USSR troops. The USSR claimed that the Afghanistan Government had requested USSR intervention under a 1978 bilateral treaty of friendship[89] to protect Afghanistan from "armed incursions and provocations from outside." USSR troops, thought to number 100,000, were then brought into Afghanistan, assisting the Afghan army in fighting guerilla opponents of the Karmal (and later Najibullah) Government. A Security Council draft resolution which deplored the USSR intervention and called for the withdrawal of USSR troops was vetoed by

---

[85] G.A.O.R., 11th Sess., Special Political Committee, 41st Meeting, p. 189 (1957).

[86] 20 *Current Digest of the Soviet Press*, No. 46, pp. 3–4; December 4, 1968.

[87] See Moore and Turner, *International Law and the Brezhnev Doctrine* (1987).

[88] See *Keesing's Archives*, p. 30229.

[89] For the terms of this treaty see, *ibid.* p. 29459. It provides for the parties to "consult each other and take by agreement appropriate measures to ensure the security, independence and territorial integrity of their countries."

the USSR.[90] A General Assembly resolution of January 14, 1980[91] re-affirmed that "respect for the sovereignty, territorial integrity and political independence of every state is a fundamental principle of the Charter" and strongly deplored "the recent armed intervention in Afghanistan which is inconsistent with that principle." The resolution appealed to all states "to refrain from any interference in the internal affairs of that country" and called for the "immediate, unconditional and total withdrawal of the foreign troops from Afghanistan." The General Assembly resolution was phrased in the terms of both the Use of Force and Non-Intervention Principles in the 1970 Declaration. By the 1988 Geneva Accords[92] between Afghanistan, Pakistan, the US and the USSR, the USSR agreed to withdraw its troops. Was the USSR intervention lawful?

6. *The Dominican Republic* case.[93] On April 24, 1965, a revolution occurred against the Cabral Government. It was led by young military officers and members of the Dominican Revolutionary Party. Fighting broke out and the situation deteriorated to the point where the military junta which had replaced the Cabral Government in opposition to the rebels informed the United States Embassy that it was not able to guarantee the safety of United States nationals. In response to the request from the junta,[94] 400 United States marines were landed in the Republic on April 28 in order, President Johnson stated, to protect United States and other foreign nationals. This figure was later increased to over 20,000 troops. On May 2, President Johnson gave a different reason for the United States involvement, which anticipates the Brezhnev Doctrine:

> ... what began as a popular democratic revolution ... very shortly ... was taken over ... by a band of communist conspirators ... The American nation cannot ... permit the establishment of another Communist Government in the Western Hemisphere ... This was the unanimous view of all the American nations when, in January 1962, they declared ... 'The Principles of communism are incompatible with the principles of the inter-American system.' ... This is and this will be the common action and common purpose of the democratic forces of the hemisphere."[95]

7. *Bangladesh.* Until 1971, Pakistan consisted of East and West Pakistan, with India between the two parts. On March 26, 1971, East Pakistan declared itself independent under the name of Bangladesh. The Pakistan army was initially successful in suppressing the rebellion, but in November 1971 rebel guerrilla forces launched a general offensive with considerable success. There was evidence to suggest that India, which by then had taken into its territory about one million refugees from East Pakistan, had given the guerrillas military assistance and Pakistani and Indian troops clashed in the border area. On December 3, 1971, Pakistan attacked India in the west. War was declared on both sides and fighting began in earnest in east and west. By December 17, 1971, Pakistan had surrendered on both fronts. Bangladesh has since received general recognition (including that of Pakistan) as an independent state. Was India entitled in law to give

---

[90] The vote, on January 7, 1980, was by 13 to 2 (GDR, USSR).

[91] GA Resn. ES-6/2; G.A.O.R., 6th Emerg. Sp. Sess., Supp. 1, p. 2 (1980). The vote was by 104 votes to 18, with 18 abstentions.

[92] (1988) 27 I.L.M. 577.

[93] See Friedmann (1965) 59 A.J.I.L. 857, at pp. 866–868; Meeker, 53 *US Dept. of State Bull.* 60 (1965); and Thomas and Thomas, *The Dominican Republic Crisis 1965* (1967).

[94] According to one U.S. source, the request was solicited by the U.S. Government: see Thomas and Thomas, *loc. cit.*, n. 93 above, pp. 75, n. 10, and 94.

[95] 52 *US Dept. of State Bull.* 745–746 (1965).

military assistance to the Bangladeshi guerrillas? Was its refugee problem relevant? Was Pakistan entitled to attack India on December 3?[96]

8. *The Grenada* case.[97] In 1979, Maurice Bishop became Prime Minister of a new revolutionary Government of Grenada, a small Caribbean state, formerly a U.K. colony. The new Government, which, unlike its elected predecessor, had communist leanings, established links with Cuba and the USSR. In October 1983, disagreement within Bishop's party led to his Government being ousted by a more radical left-wing Government. On October 19th, Bishop and some of his supporters were executed and 17 civilians, on some accounts possibly many more, were killed when government forces fired on the crowd. A curfew was ordered, with forces empowered to shoot on sight. On October 23rd, the U.S. sent troops to Grenada, supported by troops from several other Caribbean states, who quickly took control of the island after fighting with Grenada forces. U.S. troops were evacuated in December 1983 and a centre right Government was democratically elected in 1984. The U.S. justified its intervention on three grounds: the protection of U.S. nationals; a request to intervene from the Organisation of Eastern Caribbean States (OECS), of which Grenada was a member; and a request from the Governor-General of Grenada. These justifications have been doubted. Although there were US nationals in Grenada, all accounts suggest that they were not at risk. The competence of the OECS to request a non-member state to intervene in the absence of external aggression and by the procedure followed is questionable, and the Governor-General was probably not constitutionally competent to request assistance. A draft Security Council resolution condemning the U.S. intervention as illegal was vetoed by the U.S.[98] A General Assembly resolution deploring the U.S. action was adopted by 108 votes to 9, with 27 abstentions.[99]

9. *The Panama* case.[1] On December 20th, 1989 the U.S. invaded Panama, sending troops to supplement others already based there, to overthrow the government of General Noriega. After some resistance by Noriega forces, the invasion was successful, with General Noriega surrendering to the U.S. authorities, after initially taking refuge in the papal nuncio's residence. He was then flown to the U.S. to face drugs charges. The invasion took place shortly after General Noriega, who had annulled the results of an election which he was believed to have lost, had been proclaimed the Panamanian Head of State, with wide ranging powers, and had declared war on the U.S. President Bush stated that he had ordered U.S. intervention to protect U.S. nationals (on December 16th a U.S. soldier had been killed by Panamanian security forces); to restore democracy; to protect the Panama Canal; and to prosecute General Noriega for drug-related offences. The UN General Assembly deplored the U.S. intervention as "a flagrant violation of international law."[2] The matter was discussed by the Security Council, but a draft resolution calling for the immediate cessation of U.S. intervention was vetoed.[3] Note that there were no rebels against the Noriega Government when the U.S.

---

[96] On self defence, see below, p. 894.

[97] See Beck (1993) 33 Virg. J.I.L. 765; Davidson, *Grenada* (1987); Doswald-Beck (1984) 31 N.I.L.R. 355; Gilmore, The *Grenada Intervention* (1984); Joyner (1984) 78 A.J.I.L. 131; Moore, *ibid.*, 145; Quigley (1986–7) 18 Inter-American L.R. 271; Vagts (1984) 78 A.J.I.L. 169. As in other intervention cases, the existence and timing of the claimed requests for assistance are difficult to establish.

[98] S.C.O.R., 2491st Meeting. October 27, 1983.

[99] G.A. Resn. 38/7, G.A.O.R., 38th Sess., Supp. 47, p. 19 (1983).

[1] See Henkin, Sofaer and Wedgwood (1991) 29 Col. J.T.L. 293, 281, 609; Hilaire (1990) 68 R.D. I. 241; Nanda, Farer and D'Amato (1990) 84 A.J.I.L. 494, 503, 516 respectively.

[2] G.A. Resn. 44/240, UN Press Release GA/7977, p. 91. The vote was 75 to 20, with 40 abstentions.

[3] The vote was 10 to 4; France, the U.K. and the U.S. voted against: 26 *UN Chronicle*, No.1, 1990, p. 67.

intervened; nor, of course, was there any government request for intervention. Was this just a classic case of a superpower imposing its will on a client state?

10. *The Cyprus* case.[4] Cyprus has a population which is four-fifths Greek Cypriot and one-fifth Turkish Cypriot. The United Nations Force in Cyprus (UNFICYP) was established there in 1964[5] to help keep the peace between the two communities. Following the overthrow of the Makarios Government in 1974 by a coup supported by Greece and resulting in the establishment of a Greek Cypriot junta, Turkey invaded the island in the same month. The Security Council called upon "all states to respect the sovereignty, independence and territorial integrity of Cyprus" and demanded "an immediate end to foreign military intervention" in Cyprus that was contrary to such respect.[6] In 1983, an independent state called the Turkish Republic of Northern Cyprus was declared to have been established.[7] Turkey claimed that its intervention in 1974 was justified under the Treaty of Guarantee[8] made between Cyprus, Greece, Turkey, and the United Kingdom in 1959 when Cypriot independence was agreed. By this treaty, Cyprus undertook to "ensure the maintenance of its independence, territorial integrity and security, as well as respect for its constitution." (Article 1). The three guaranteeing powers, who undertook to recognise and guarantee the independence, territorial integrity and security of Cyprus (Article 2), agreed in the event of a breach of the treaty to consult to determine what representations or measures were necessary. Insofar as concerted action proved impossible, each of them reserved "the right to take action with the sole aim of establishing the state of affairs created" by the treaty (Article 4). Could Turkey rely upon the treaty (supposing "action" includes the use of force and that tripartite consultation occurred (it had not)) to justify its intervention in the face of Article 2(4) of the Charter or the Principle of Non-Intervention in the 1970 Declaration? Would Article 103 of the United Nations Charter, below, Appendix I, be relevant?

(c) *The Right of Self-Defence*

THE CAROLINE CASE[9]

29 B.F.S.P. 1137–1138; 30 B.F.S.P. 195–196

The case arose out of the Canadian Rebellion of 1837. The rebel leaders, despite steps taken by United States authorities to prevent assistance being given to them, managed on December 13, 1837, to enlist at Buffalo in the United States the support of a large number of American nationals. The resulting force established itself on Navy Island in Canadian waters from which it raided the Canadian shore and attacked passing British ships. The force was supplied from the United States shore by an American ship, the *Caroline*. On the night of December 29–30, the British seized the *Caroline*, which was then in the American port of Schlosser, fired her and sent her over Niagara Falls. Two United States nationals were killed. The legality of the British acts was discussed in detail in correspondence in 1841–1842 when Great Britain sought the release of a British subject, McLeod, who had been

---

[4] See Polyviou, *Cyprus: The Tragedy and the Challenge* (1975), and Necatigil, *The Cyprus Question and the Turkish Position in International Law* (2nd ed., 1993).
[5] See below, p. 974.
[6] S.C. Resn. 353 (1974), S.C.O.R., 29th Year, *Resolutions and Decisions*, p. 7. See, most recently, S.C. Resn. 440 (1978), S.C.O.R., 29th Year, *ibid.* p. 11.
[7] See above, p. 112.
[8] Cmnd. 1093.
[9] See Jennings (1938) 32 A.J.I.L. 82 and Rogoff and Collins (1990) 16 Brooklyn J.I.L. 493.

arrested in the United States on charges of murder and arson arising out of the incident.

MR. WEBSTER TO MR. FOX (April 24, 1841). It will be for ... [Her Majesty's] Government to show a necessity of self-defence, instant, overwhelming, leaving no choice of means, and no moment for deliberation. It will be for it to show, also, that the local authorities of Canada, even supposing the necessity of the moment authorised them to enter the territories of The United States at all, did nothing unreasonable or excessive; since the act, justified by the necessity of self-defence, must be limited by that necessity, and kept clearly within it. It must be shown that admonition or remonstrance to the person on board the *Caroline* was impracticable, or would have been unavailing; it must be shown that day-light could not be waited for; that there could be no attempt at discrimination between the innocent and the guilty; that it would not have been enough to seize and detain the vessel; but that there was a necessity, present and inevitable, for attacking her in the darkness of the night, while moored to the shore, and while unarmed men were asleep on board, killing some and wounding others, and then drawing her into the current, above the cataract, setting her on fire, and, careless to know whether there might not be in her the innocent with the guilty, or the living with the dead, committing her to a fate which fills the imagination with horror. A necessity for all this, the Government of The United States cannot believe to have existed.

LORD ASHBURTON TO MR. WEBSTER (July 28, 1842). It is so far satisfactory to perceive that we are perfectly agreed as to the general principles of international law applicable to this unfortunate case. Respect for the inviolable character of the territory of independent nations is the most essential foundation of civilisation. ...

Notes

1. In his reply, Lord Ashburton made a remarkably good attempt at justifying the British action in accordance with the test formulated by Webster, which has commonly been accepted as indicating when the pre-UN Charter, customary international law right of self-defence could be exercised.

2. *Anticipatory self-defence.* It was not doubted in the *Caroline* case that the British Government was entitled to anticipate further attacks. It was argued before the International Military Tribunal at Nuremberg that the German invasion of Norway in 1940 was an act of self-defence in the face of an imminent Allied landing there. The Tribunal recalled that preventive action in foreign territory is justified only in the circumstances cited by Webster in the *Caroline* case and found on the facts that there was no imminent threat of an Allied landing in Norway.[10]

3. *Proportionality.* A Report made to the League of Nations in 1927 said:

---

[10] (1947) 41 A.J.I.L. 205. *cf.* the I.M.T. for the Far East, judgment, pp. 994–995, quoted in Horwitz, *The Tokyo Trial*, Int.Conc. No. 465 (1950), p. 560.

Legitimate defence implies the adoption of measures proportionate to the seriousness of the attack and justified by the seriousness of the danger.[11]

See Article 51, United Nations Charter.[12]

Notes

1. It is generally accepted that, as the *Nicaragua* (*Merits*) case, judgment, para. 176, above, p. 867, confirms, in customary international law action taken as self-defence remains subject to the *Caroline* requirements of necessity and proportionality. Article 51 has not caused custom to change in these respects and, as Advisory Opinion in the *Nuclear Weapons* case[13] states, Article 51 itself imposes the same requirements as a matter of treaty obligation. There is, however, uncertainty as to the effect of Article 51 on the customary international law right of self-defence in other respects. Kelsen[14] reads Article 51 as meaning that for United Nations members the right of self-defence "has no other content than the one determined by Article 51." The significance of this interpretation is that Article 51 can be read as excluding the right of anticipatory self-defence and the right to defend nationals abroad. Bowett,[15] however, argues that Article 51 was not intended to limit the pre-1945 customary international law right, as evidenced by the use of the word "inherent" and the *travaux préparatoires*, so that it remains fully intact. He states:

It is . . . fallacious to assume that members have only those rights which the Charter accords to them; on the contrary they have those rights which general international law accords to them except in so far as they have surrendered them under the Charter . . .

Now the relevant obligation assumed by members is, *prima facie*, that contained in Art. 2(4) . . . As we have seen, the view of Committee I at San Francisco was that this prohibition left the right of self-defence unimpaired.[16]

There is evidence in the *travaux préparatoires* to support the view that the purpose of Article 51 was to reassure regional organisations (particularly the OAS) that their arrangements for collective security were not prejudiced by the UN system through the Security Council, with the text of Article 51 being drafted with this in mind rather than with any intention to set the exact limits of the full right to self-defence. Thus the official British Government Commentary on the Charter reads:

It was considered at the Dumbarton Oaks Conference that the right of self-defence was inherent in the proposals and did not need explicit mention in the Charter. But self-defence may be undertaken by more than one state at a time,

---

[11] L.N.Doc. A. 14, 1927. V.V. Legal 1927. V. 14, pp. 60, 69; quoted in Brownlie, *op. cit.*, p. 859, n. 1, p. 261.

[12] Below, Appendix I. On Art. 51, see Greig (1991) 40 I.C.L.Q. 366; Penna (1991) 20 Denver J.I.L.P. 41; and Plofchan (1992) 13 Mich. J.I.L. 336.

[13] Opinion, para. 41, below, p. 925.

[14] *The Law of the United Nations* (1950), p. 914.

[15] *op. cit.*, p. 859, n. 1, p. 185.

[16] Committee I [of Commission I], commenting upon Art. 2(4), reported that "the use of arms in legitimate self-defence remains admitted and unimpaired." 6 U.N.C.I.O., Documents 459.

and the existence of regional organisations made this right of special importance to some states, while special treaties of defence made its explicit recognition important to others. Accordingly the right is given to individual states or to combinations of states to act until the Security Council itself has taken the necessary measures.[17]

In terms of customary international law, what matters now is not the intention of the fifty states that participated in the drafting of the Charter in 1945, but the development of state practice since then. Unfortunately, there is much divergence of practice, with Western states claiming a wider right of self-defence than developing states are prepared to concede. Even so, it is clear that state practice does not support a totally unreconstructed pre-1945 right of self-defence. It is also evident that whatever right of self-defence is to be found in Articles 2(4) and 51 exists as customary, as well as treaty, law and accordingly applies equally to UN members and non-members alike.

2. *Anticipatory self-defence.* If, despite its drafting history,[18] Article 51 is understood by states as indicating the full extent of the current right of self-defence, there must be considerable doubt as to whether the right of anticipatory self-defence survives. The argument for saying that it does not is based upon the use of the phrase "an armed attack occurs" in Article 51. Brownlie[19] states, for example, that "the ordinary meaning of the phrase precludes action which is preventative in character." In contrast, Bowett[20] argues:

> The history of Art. 51 suggests . . . that the article should safeguard the right of self-defence, not restrict it . . . furthermore, it is a restriction [no right of anticipation] which bears no relation to the realities of a situation which may arise prior to an actual attack and call for self-defence immediately if it is to be of any avail at all. No state can be expected to await an initial attack which, in the present state of armaments, may well destroy the state's capacity for further resistance and so jeopardise its very existence.

Henkin[21] argues against a right of anticipatory self-defence as follows:

> Nothing in . . . its drafting . . . suggests that the framers of the Charter intended something broader than the language implied . . . It was that mild, old-fashioned Second World War which persuaded all nations that for the future national interests will have to be vindicated, or necessary change achieved, as well as can be by political means, but not by war and military self-help. They recognised the exception of self-defence in emergency, but limited to actual armed attack, which is clear, unambiguous, subject to proof, and not easily open to misinterpretation or fabrication. . . . It is precisely in the age of the major deterrent that nations should not be encouraged to strike first under pretext of prevention or pre-emption.

When does an armed attack begin to "occur"? Before soldiers, aircraft or missiles cross the border? From the time that troops are massed or ships set sail? The wider the meaning, the less the divergence between the two views.

[17] Misc. 9 (1945), Cmd. 6666, p. 9.
[18] See McCormack (1991) 25 Israel L.R. 1.
[19] *op. cit.*, p. 859, n. 1, above, p. 275.
[20] *op. cit.*, p. 859, n. 1, above, pp. 188–192. *cf.* Greenwood (1987) 89 W.Virg. L.R. 933 at 943.
[21] *How Nations Behave* (2nd ed., 1979), pp. 141–142. *cf.* Brownlie *(1989)* 26 Coexistence 17.

The difference between the two views would also be diminished if the "cumulation of events" theory of self-defence were adopted. According to this theory, which is followed in their practice by such states as Israel,[22] the U.S.[23] the United Kingdom[24] and South Africa[25] and which has great attractions for states faced with constant cross-border guerrilla raids, a series of attacks should be viewed as a whole, so that action taken to prevent future attacks in the series can be seen not as anticipatory self-defence but as self-defence against one attack that continues to occur. However, as Bowett[26] notes, the Security Council has, in cases such as the *Harib Fort* case, consistently rejected such an approach, regarding such action, despite its primary purpose (defence, not retaliation), as reprisals. Pre-emptive strikes, therefore, can only be justified on the basis of a right of anticipatory self-defence, which, if it continues to exist, supposes a reasonable belief that a particular attack, or raid, is imminent. Note, however, that the limited definition of an "armed attack" (justifying self–defence) in the *Nicaragua* case considerably limits any self defence claim.

As to the requirement of imminence, in 1981, Israel attacked and destroyed a nuclear reactor nearing completion in Iraq, justifying its conduct on the ground of anticipatory self-defence: the reactor would be used to manufacture weapons that would be used against Israel.[27] The Israeli action was unanimously condemned by the Security Council as a "clear violation" of Article 2(4). Could the threat posed by the reactor have been regarded as sufficiently "imminent" for the purposes of any right of anticipatory self-defence?

In the *Nicaragua* case (judgment, para. 194), the Court left open the question whether there is a right of anticipatory self-defence.

The United Kingdom justifies its arms sales abroad under Article 51[28]:

> Our policy on arms sales to Indonesia is based on the principle that all sovereign states enjoy the right, under article 51 of the United Nations charter, to defend themselves. This is a right we claim for ourselves and it would be inconsistent and discriminatory to deny it to others. ... A ban on arms sales to Indonesia would not in our view bring about a change in the circumstances of East Timor.

3. *Armed attack.* The meaning of "armed attack" was considered in the *Nicaragua* (*Merits*) case judgment, para. 195, and is discussed above, p. 887. In so far as the cross-border use of force by "regular armed forces" is concerned, does the Court suppose that any such use of force is an "armed attack," or must its "scale and effects" be such that it can be said to be significant? Note the references to self-defence in connection with the *Korean Airliner Flight 007 Incident*, above, p. 242, the

---

[22] See, *e.g.* the Israeli raid on Beirut airport, below, p. 915, n. 79.

[23] See, *e.g.* the *Libyan Air raid*, below, p. 913.

[24] *ibid.* and the *Harib Fort* case, below, p. 916.

[25] South Africa has regularly made cross border raids into neighbouring African states to attack ANC bases on a "cumulation of events" basis, the ANC being perceived as posing a security threat to South Africa by its terrorist attacks: see Kwakwa (1987) 12 Yale J.I.L. 421 (1987). South Africa has been consistently condemned by the Security Council for such incursions: see *e.g.* S.C.Resn 568 (1984), S.C.O.R., 40th Year, *Resolutions and Decisions*, p. 20 (attack on Botswana "an act of aggression").

[26] Below. p. 914.

[27] S.C. Resn 487 (1981), S.C.O.R., 36th Year, *Resolutions and Decisions*, p. 10. For the Security Council debate, see S/PV.2280, June 12 1981, reprinted in (1981) 20 I.L.M. 965. See D'Amato (1983) 77 A.J.I.L. 584 and Mallinson and Mallinson (1982) 15 Vand. J.I.L. 417.

[28] Minister of State, FCO, *Hansard*, H.C., Vol. 237 W.A. 122, February 8, 1994; U.K.M.I.L. 1994; (1994) 65 B.Y.I.L. 691.

Gulf of Tonkin Incident, below. p. 901, and the *Libyan People's Bureau Incident*, above, p. 351. Did they all involve "armed attacks"?

On the defence of nationals abroad, see the *Entebbe* case, below, p. 909.

4. *Collective Self-defence.* The customary international law right of collective self-defence was examined in the *Nicaragua (Merits)* case (judgment, paras 199–200, 232–8). Before state T may embark upon collective self-defence, state D must declare itself a victim of an armed attack and request state T's assistance.[29] There need not, however, be any threat to state T's security for it to be entitled to respond. In his dissenting opinion, Judge Sir Robert Jennings criticised this last aspect of the Court's judgment as follows[30]:

> The assisting State surely must, by going to the victim State's assistance, be also, and in *addition* to other requirements, in some measure defending itself. There should even in "collective self-defence" be some real element of self involved with the notion of defence. This is presumably also the philosophy which underlies mutual security arrangements, such as the system of the Organisation of American States, for which indeed Article 51 was specifically designed.

Note also the Court's reliance upon the absence of any report by the United States to the Security Council on the steps taken by it against Nicaragua when assessing whether the United States was, as it claimed, acting in collective self-defence.

5. *Interference with vessels beyond the territorial sea.* There is a long-established right on the part of a state engaged in armed conflict to stop and search a vessel flying another's state flag where it is reasonably suspected of carrying weapons to another party to the conflict.[31] Following the Iranian searching of the *Barber Perseus*, a United Kingdom merchant vessel, in the Persian Gulf during the Iran-Iraq War, a Foreign Office Minister stated[32]:

> The U.K. upholds the general principle of freedom of navigation of the high seas. However, under Article 51 of the UN Charter, a State such as Iran actively engaged in an armed conflict, is entitled to exercise its inherent right of self-defence to stop and search a foreign merchant ship on the high seas if there are reasonable grounds for suspecting that the ship is taking arms to the other side for use in the conflict. This is an exceptional right: if the suspicions prove to be unfounded and if the ship has not committed acts calculated to give rise to suspicion, then the ship's owners have a good claim for compensation for loss caused by the delay.

---

[29] Does the Court suppose that state D has to request or approve the particular form that the assistance takes?

[30] I.C.J. Rep. 1986, p. 545. Footnote omitted. Judge Sir Robert Jennings also questioned whether the requirements of "some sort of formal declaration and request might sometimes be unrealistic": *ibid.*

[31] See the correspondence respecting the capture of the *Virginius*, Parl. Papers, LXXVI, 1874, p. 85, Spain No. 3 (1874), p. 85. Some of the crew members were British subjects.

[32] *Hansard*, H.C., Vol. 90, col. 428, January 28, 1986; U.K.M.I.L. 1986; (1986) 57 B.Y.I.L. 583. In contrast, when Iran fired on the *Gentle Breeze*, a U.K. merchant ship, in the Gulf in 1987, the U.K. protested at a "flagrant violation of international law": U.K.M.I.L. 1987; (1987) 58 B.Y.I.L. 603. The Foreign Office chose to treat the *Barber Perseus* case under the law of peace; if the Iran-Iraq War came within the law of war, Iran was exercising a belligerent's right to stop and search neutral shipping: see Lowe (1986) 10 Mar. Pol. 171 at 183.

In the Algerian emergency 1956–62, France stopped and searched several thousand foreign vessels on the high seas for weapons destined for rebel forces, claiming the right of self-defence.[33]

The Cuban Quarantine concerned the shipment of equipment that threatened the United States in the future, not in the context of existing hostilities. On October 22, 1962, President Kennedy announced the United States intention to impose a "strict quarantine on all offensive military equipment under shipment to Cuba."[34] The United States decided upon this policy after discovering that the USSR was sending to Cuba missiles and other weapons and materials which could be seen as a threat to United States security. On October 23, at the suggestion of the United States, the Security Council met and discussed the proposed quarantine but took no action.[35] On the same day, the Council of the Organisation of American States adopted a resolution[36] recommending that

> member states, in accordance with Articles 6 and 8 of the Inter-American Treaty of Reciprocal Assistance[37] take all measures, individually and collectively, including the use of armed force, which they may deem necessary to ensure that the Government of Cuba cannot continue to receive from the Sino-Soviet powers military material and related supplies which may threaten the peace and security of the Continent and to prevent the missiles in Cuba with offensive capability from ever becoming an active threat to the peace and security of the Continent.

Following this, also on October 23, the United States President issued a Proclamation which in part gave the following authorisation:

> Any vessel or craft which may be proceeding toward Cuba may be intercepted and may be directed to identify itself, its cargo, equipment and stores and its ports of call, to stop, to lie to, to submit to visit and search, or to proceed as directed. Any vessel which fails or refuses to respond to or to comply with directions shall be subject to being taken into custody.

It was intended that these powers would be exercised "within a reasonable distance of Cuba."[38] During the course of the "quarantine," a Lebanese ship under charter to the USSR was boarded but allowed to proceed and a Soviet tanker was cleared after visual checking from alongside. Both incidents occurred on the high seas. Other ships heading for Cuba changed course of their own accord.[39] The operation was ended on November 21, 1962. Meeker (United States Deputy Legal Adviser) justified the United States action as follows:

> The quarantine was based on a collective judgment and recommendation of the American Republics made under the Rio Treaty. It was considered not to contravene Article 2, paragraph 4, because it was a measure adopted by a regional organisation in conformity with the provisions of Chapter VIII of the Charter.[40] The purposes of the Organisation and its activities were considered to be consistent with the purposes and principles of the United Nations as provided in Article 52. This being the case, the quarantine would no more

[33] 4 Whiteman 513–5. See Van Zwanenberg (1961) 10 I.C.L.Q. 785.
[34] *Keesings Archives*, p. 19061.
[35] S.C.O.R., 17th Year, 1022nd-1025th Meetings.
[36] 47 *US Dept. of State Bull.* 723.
[37] *Ed.* The "Rio Treaty," signed at Rio de Janeiro on September 2, 1947: 21 U.N.T.S. 77.
[38] Proclamation 3504 (1963) 57 A.J.I.L. 512.
[39] See Christol & Davis (1963) 57 A.J.I.L. 525 at 530.
[40] *Ed.* Below, Appendix I.

violate Article 2, paragraph 4, than measures voted for by the Council under Chapter VII, by the General Assembly under Articles 10 and 11, or taken by United Nations members in conformity with Article 51.[41]

Did the United States have a good case on this ground?[42] Note that Meeker does not justify the quarantine on the basis of "self-defence."[43] Could he have done so? Note also the following comment by Dean Acheson, a former United States Secretary of State for Foreign Affairs:

> I must conclude that the propriety of the Cuban quarantine is not a legal issue. The power, position and prestige of the United States has been challenged by another state; and law simply does not deal with such questions of ultimate power—power that comes close to the source of sovereignty. I cannot believe that there are principles of law that say we must accept destruction of our way of life. . . . The survival of states is not a matter of law.[44]

The 1982 Law of the Sea Convention, Article 110(1), makes no provision for jurisdiction over vessels on the high seas on the basis of self-defence.[45]

6. On August 2 and 4, 1964, in the context of the Vietnam war, North Vietnamese torpedo-boats attacked United States warships in the Gulf of Tonkin, but were beaten off. The attacks occurred on the high seas. In retaliation, on August 5, the United States bombed the base from which the torpedo-boats operated and an oil storage depot to great effect. The retaliatory measures were justified by the United States in terms of freedom of the high seas and the right of self-defence. The British representative to the Security Council supported this view:

> The latest attacks on the United States ships took place, according to the information we have been given, some sixty-five miles from land. It seems to my delegation in these circumstances that, having regard to the repeated nature of these attacks and their mounting scale, the United States Government has a right in accordance with international law, to take action directed to prevent the recurrence of such attacks on its ships. Preventive action in accordance with that aim is an essential right which is embraced by any definition of that principle of self-defence. It therefore seems to my delegation that the action taken by the United States Government is fully consistent with Article 51 of the Charter.[46]

The USSR representative characterised the measures as an "act of aggression." No resolution was voted upon or adopted. Is the case any different from the *Harib Fort* case?[47]

7. *The Role of Security Council.* The right of self-defence is a temporary one in the scheme of Article 51, existing only until the Security Council acts. In practice, of course, such is the power of the "veto," the Security Council may never act

[41] (1963) 57 A.J.I.L. 515.

[42] See article cited in n. 39 above and Wright (1963) 57 A.J.I.L. 546.

[43] Note, however, the following passage in the President's broadcast on October 22: "We no longer live in a world where only the actual firing of weapons represents a sufficient challenge to a nation's security to constitute a maximum peril. Nuclear weapons are so destructive, and ballistic missiles so swift, that any substantially increased possibility of their use or any sudden change in their deployment may well be regarded as a threat to the peace." *Keesing's Archives*, p. 19060.

[44] (1963) 57 Proc. A.S.I.L. 14.

[45] See above, p. 431.

[46] 1964 B.P.I.L. 268.

[47] Below, p. 916.

and the right of self-defence will be of unlimited duration. Who is to judge when the Council "has taken the measures necessary . . . [etc.]"? The British Commentary on the Charter reads:

> It will be for the Security Council to decide whether these measures have been taken and whether they are adequate for the purpose. In the event of the Security Council failing to take any action, or if such action as it does take is clearly inadequate, the right of self-defence could be invoked by any Member or group of Members as justifying any action they thought fit to take.[48]

Is there an obligation placed upon a Member of the United Nations exercising the right of self-defence to inform the Security Council *before* it does so? See further, the *Falkland Islands War*, below.

THE FALKLAND ISLANDS WAR[49]

UN Doc. S/PV. 2346, p. 7; S/PV. 2360, pp. 21–23, 37–38;
S/PV. 1362, pp. 103–107

On April 2, 1982, Argentine forces invaded the Falkland Islands. On the following day Argentina took possession by force of the island of South Georgia, some 800 miles to the east of the Falklands. The small British military garrison on the Falklands and the few troops sent to South Georgia surrendered on April 2 and 3 respectively after some fighting. Both Argentine actions were taken in pursuit of claims of sovereignty over these islands, as to which see above, p. 213. On April 1, the President of the Security Council, acting for the Council, had called upon Argentina and the United Kingdom "to refrain from the use or threat of force in the region."[50] On April 3, following the Argentine action the Security Council adopted Resolution 502,[51] which reads:

> The Security Council,
> Recalling the statement made by the President of the Security Council at the 2345th meeting of the Security Council on 1 April 1982 calling on the Governments of Argentina and the United Kingdom of Great Britain and Northern Ireland to refrain from the use or threat of force in the region of the Falkland Islands,
> Deeply disturbed at reports of an invasion on 2 April 1982 by armed forces of Argentina,
> Determining that there exists a breach of the peace in the region of the Falkland Islands (Islas Malvinas),
> 1. Demands an immediate cessation of hostilities;
> 2. Demands an immediate withdrawal of all Argentine forces from the Falkland Islands (Islas Malvinas);

---

[48] *loc. cit.*, p. 897, n. 17, above, p. 9.
[49] See Coll and Arend, *The Falklands War* (1985) and Franck (1983) 77 A.J.I.L. 109. See also, p. 213, n. 49. On the background and for accounts of the invasion, see Calvert, *The Falkland Islands Crisis: the Rights and Wrongs* (1982); Hastings and Jenkins, *The Battle for The Falklands* (1983); Honeywell and Pearce, *Falkland Islands/Malvinas: Whose Crisis?* (1982); Sunday Times Insight Team, *The Falklands War* (1982).
[50] UN Doc.S/PV.2345, p. 33.
[51] UN Doc.S/PV.2346, p. 6 (text). The resolution was adopted by 10 votes (France, Guyana, Ireland, Japan, Jordan, Togo, Uganda, U.K., U.S., Zaire) to one (Panama), with four abstentions (China, Poland, Spain, USSR).

3. Calls on the Governments of Argentina and the United Kingdom to seek a diplomatic solution to their differences and to respect fully the purposes and principles of the Charter of the United Nations.

On April 5, a British military expedition (the Task Force) sailed for the South Atlantic, Economic sanctions were imposed against Argentina by the United Kingdom and the European Communities. The United States gave the United Kingdom logistical assistance. The Organisation of American States resolved that its members should support Argentina. On April 25, British troops recovered South Georgia by force. After diplomatic efforts to achieve a peaceful solution had failed, the Task Force landed on the Falklands on May 21. The Argentine garrison surrendered on June 14, 1982. The following extracts are from the debates in the Security Council in which arguments on the legality of the Argentinian action and the British response were put.

2346th Meeting on April 2

MR. ROCA (ARGENTINA). I wish to inform the Council that today the Government of Argentina has proclaimed the recovery of its national sovereignty over the territories of the Malvinas Islands, South Georgia Islands and South Sandwich Islands, in an act which responds to a just Argentine claim, an act of self-defence in response to the acts of aggression by the United Kingdom.[52]

2350th Meeting on April 3

MR. COSTA MENDEZ (ARGENTINA). Some delegations here have stated that my Government acted hastily. . . . [i]t seems difficult to describe my country as acting hastily when, with the greatest respect for peaceful solutions, it has borne with a situation of continued usurpation of its territory by a colonial Power for 150 years. Argentina has wisely, patiently and imaginatively negotiated on its long-standing claim but the United Kingdom has not given the slightest indication of being flexible nor made a single just proposal. Furthermore, we have been accused in this chamber of violating Article 2(3) and (4) of the United Nations Charter. No provision of the Charter can be taken to mean the legitimisation of situations which have their origin in wrongful acts, in acts carried out before the Charter was adopted and which subsisted during its prevailing force. Today, in 1982, the purposes of the Organisation cannot be invoked

---

[52] *Ed.* By "acts of aggression," Mr Roca may have been referring to the events of 1833 or to an incident on South Georgia in which, in March 1982, employees of an Argentine company landed on the island to recover scrap metal under a commercial contract. The Commander of the British Antarctic Survey base at Grytviken lowered an Argentine flag which the men had raised and insisted that they obtain official landing permission. *H.M.S. Endurance,* a lightly armed ice-patrol vessel, was dispatched to the area. The Argentine Government denied the need for permission to land on Argentine territory, whereupon the British Government indicated that the men would be removed, by force if necessary, if such permission were not obtained. The matter was unresolved on April 2.

to justify acts carried out in the last century in flagrant violation of principles that are today embodied in international law.

... It speaks volumes that the terms [of the U.K. draft resolution] are absolutely identical to those put forward more than 22 years ago in this same chamber in the case of Goa, when Portugal was hanging on to its colonial power, which consumed it and gave rise to a new Portugal. That resolution sought to deny India its territorial rights, just as an attempt is being made here to deny my country its proper rights. That draft resolution was thrown out by the Council because it was merely a defence, an expression of continuing colonialism.

Sir Anthony Parsons (U.K.) The Foreign Minister of Argentina ... referred to our manoeuvres, our evasive tactics, our procrastinations [in negotiations] over the years. Of course, I cannot accept these charges.

... I [also] understood him to say that ... Article 2, paragraphs 3 and 4 ... were not necessarily applicable to situations which arose before the Charter was adopted.

... this is an extremely dangerous doctrine. The world is distressingly full of crisis situations, which have from time to time exploded into hostility in every continent on the globe. A large number of those situations have their origins years, decades, centuries before the United Nations Charter was adopted in 1945. If the proposition were to be accepted that the use of force was valid for situations which originated before the Charter was adopted, by heaven I believe the world would be an infinitely more dangerous and flammable place than it already is. ...

The Foreign Minister of Argentina argued that the people of the Falkland Islands are not a population in international law. Those 1,800 or 1,900 people are not recent arrivals in the Islands. The vast majority of them were born there to families which had been settled there for four, five, six generations since the first half of the nineteenth century. In the judgment of my Government, whether they are 1,800 or 18 million, they are still entitled to the protection of international law and they are entitled to have their freely expressed wishes respected.

These have been the only objectives of my Government in that area for a very long time. I cannot believe that the international community takes the view that Britain in the 1980s has a "colonialist" or "imperialist" ambition in the South Atlantic.

Finally, it has also been argued that this was not an invasion because the Islands belong to Argentina, a proposition which of course my Government contests. But the fact is that the United Kingdom has been accepted by the United Nations—by the General Assembly, by the Committee of 24—as the Administering Authority. It therefore flies in the face of the facts and in the face of reason to suggest that this was not an armed invasion.

2360th Meeting on May 21

MR. ROS (ARGENTINA). It is known that under Article 51 of the Charter ... [t]here is a legal obligation to suspend self-defence once the Security Council "has taken measures necessary to maintain international peace and security." The determination of whether such measures have been effective must be reached objectively and cannot be left to the arbitrary judgment of the Government of the United Kingdom itself ...

The exercise of self-defence which the United Kingdom is alleging could only have taken place in the absence of a resolution by the Security Council. But now the resolution has been adopted, and the response of the United Kingdom to the Council has been the reiterated violation of that resolution, which demands the cessation of hostilities. ...

Self-defence can be used only to repel imminent and grave danger. In the existing circumstances, the United Kingdom could not allege any imminent and grave danger. Argentina had complied in regard to the cessation of hostilities and had not threatened the United Kingdom. ...

The United Kingdom cannot claim self-defence of territorial integrity to justify its acts of aggression. It is Argentine territorial integrity which has been violated. ...

SIR ANTHONY PARSONS (U.K.) The Argentine invasion was carried out by the use of force against the entirely peaceful population of the Falkland Islands, people who had threatened no one at any time. There was no question of self-defence by Argentina. It is clear, therefore, that the Argentine action was also contrary to the fourth paragraph of Article 2 of the Charter [as well as Article 2(3)]. This is the obligation to:

"refrain ... from the ... use of force ... in any ... manner inconsistent with the Purposes of the United Nations."

I need hardly remind this Council that the very first purpose of the United Nations is:

" ... to bring about by peaceful means ... settlement of international disputes ... " (Art. 1(1)). ...

Indeed, by its first use of armed force, Argentina committed an act of aggression within the meaning of the definition suggested by the General Assembly in resolution 3314 (XXIX).[53] ...

Having established that the Argentine use of force was illegal, it follows that the military occupation of the Falkland Islands was and is also

---

[53] *Ed.* Below, p. 945.

illegal. This was made clear by the Declaration on Friendly Relations,[54] which was adopted by way of consensus in 1970 and which includes the following proposition:

"The territory of a State shall not be the object of military occupation resulting from the use of force in contravention of the provisions of the Charter."

As if that were not enough, the continued Argentine occupation is also clearly contrary to operative paragraph 2 of Security Council resolution 502 (1982).

A word on self-defence. . . . British territory has been invaded by Argentine armed forces. British nationals are being subjected to both military occupation and military government against their freely expressed wishes. Argentina is using force day by day to occupy British territory and to subjugate the Falkland Islanders. Resolution 502 (1982) has proved insufficient to bring about withdrawal. Nothing could be clearer against that background than that the United Kingdom is fully entitled to take measures in exercise of its inherent right of self-defence, recognised by Article 51 of the Charter. If the Charter were otherwise, it would be a licence for the aggressor and a trap for the victim of aggression. The first use of force to settle disputes, to seize territory and to subjugate peoples is something which the Charter was intended to prevent.

2362nd Meeting on May 22

SIR ANTHONY PARSONS (U.K.) Under-Secretary Ros also argued that there is an obligation to suspend self-defence once the Security Council "has taken measures necessary to maintain international peace and security." . . .

The United Kingdom accepts that the determination, [whether such measures have been taken] must be an objective one. It must be reached in the light of all the relevant circumstances. . . .

By resolution 502 (1982) the Security Council demanded the immediate withdrawal of all Argentine forces from the Falkland Islands. Argentina did not withdraw any of its forces: it did quite the opposite . . . The resolution determined that there was a breach of the peace as a result of the Argentine invasion . . . The results of that invasion were Argentine occupation. Accordingly, the breach of the peace still subsisted despite the adoption of the resolution. How, then, can it seriously be maintained that

---

[54] *Ed.* Below, Appendix II.

resolution 502 (1982) amounted to a measure "necessary to maintain international peace and security"?

In my letter to the President of the Security Council dated 30 April I pointed out that the reference in Article 51 to measures necessary to maintain international peace could

" . . . only be taken to refer to measures which are actually effective to bring about the stated objective. Clearly, the Security Council's decision in its resolution 502 (1982) has not proved effective. The United Kingdom's inherent right of self-defence is thus unimpaired."[55]

The argument of Under-Secretary Ros that the exercise of self-defence is not available because the Security Council adopted resolution 502 (1982) would lead to absurd results. A State which has committed an act of aggression is told to stop its aggression and to withdraw by the Security Council. That State does not heed the demand. The victim, according to Mr Ros, would then be obliged to fold his arms and allow the aggressor to continue his aggression and to digest its fruits.

A further argument of the Under-Secretary was that "the United Kingdom could not allege any imminent and grave danger." The Argentine invasion of 2 April not only posed an imminent and grave danger but it was determined by the Security Council to have caused an actual breach of the peace. It flies in the face of reason that there was no imminent and grave danger. There was an actual and grave danger to the people of the Falkland Islands: that they would continue for ever to be governed by an alien régime which they most decidedly and unanimously did not want. . . .

Finally, the Under-Secretary argued that the United Kingdom had violated resolution 502 (1982) by dispatching the Royal Navy. He argued that this was contrary to operative paragraph 1 of the resolution 502 (1982) which demanded a cessation of hostilities. The resolution has to be read as a whole. The preamble makes clear that there had been an invasion of the Falklands on 2 April by armed forces of Argentina which had caused a breach of peace. It was to these hostilities by Argentina that operative paragraph 1 was directed. The Falkland Islands had been at peace before 2 April and had never threatened Argentina. We maintained only the smallest of garrisons there. Had Argentina complied with operative paragraph 1 by ceasing its hostilities against the people of the Falkland Islands on 3 April and had Argentina complied with the demand for the immediate withdrawal of all Argentine forces there would have been no need for the Royal Navy to exercise the United

---

[55] The U.K. representative had earlier stated that, in compliance with Art. 51, the U.K. "have meticulously informed the President of the Council of every step we are taking in this regard": UN Doc. S/PV.2360, p. 36.

Kingdom's right of self-defence when it arrived off the Falkland Islands.

Notes

1. Resolution 502, which was drafted by the United Kingdom representative on the Council, was adopted under Article 40. This point was agreed when the question was raised whether the United Kingdom was eligible to vote upon it.[56] It would not have been eligible to do so if the resolution had been adopted under Chapter VI or Article 52(3) of the Charter instead of Chapter VII; see Article 27(3), Charter. Argentina, which happened not to be a member of the Security Council at the time, was allowed, in accordance with normal practice, to participate in the debate, but it had no vote. As a permanent member, the United Kingdom had not only the right to vote, but also had the advantage of the power of veto, which it exercised on June 4 to veto a draft resolution calling for a cease-fire in the fighting then occurring in the Falklands.[57]

2. The Argentine argument justifying the invasion despite Article 2(3) (4) is not convincing. The whole object of the Charter regime is to prohibit the unilateral use of armed force in the resolution of international disputes, not to approve it. *cf.* the reasoning in the *Corfu Channel* case, above, p. 391, in favour of the Albanian counter-claim. In the context of territorial disputes, a state must use peaceful means to achieve possession, however good its claim to title. The one exception is the right of self-defence. It is interesting that the British response would have been too late to have been regarded as self-defence in United Kingdom criminal law. If, for example D were to learn that squatters had broken into and were occupying his country cottage, and he were to go and eject them the next day (*i.e.* as soon as he could), this would not be an act of self-defence. Were the objections by Argentina in the Security Council to the British use of force couched in these terms? Or was the argument instead largely that the right to self-defence terminated once resolution 502 had been adopted and, therefore, the Security Council had taken the necessary "measures"? The Council debates support the view that there is a customary right of self-defence even though an attack is complete (in this case the garrison had surrendered) provided that the response is immediate and continuous. There is therefore no need to resort to general principles of law. Why did the United Kingdom emphasise the "purposes of the United Nations" rather than the "territorial integrity" part of Article 2(4) when condemning Argentina's action? How does the Falkland Islands situation differ from that of Goa, as to which, see above, p. 220?

3. On May 2, 1982, a British submarine sank an Argentine Cruiser, the *General Belgrano*, with much loss of life, when it was just outside the 200-mile exclusion zone which the United Kingdom had declared around the Falkland Islands. The Ministry of Defence statement proclaiming the zone indicated that "these measures are without prejudice to the right of the United Kingdom to take additional measures which may be needed in the exercise of its right of self-defence under Article 51 of the UN Charter."[58] The cruiser was judged to be posing a threat to British warships in the area.

---

[56] UN Doc. S/PV. 2350, pp. 81–85. The U.K. representative later referred to it as "a mandatory resolution under Article 40" which "it was not open to Argentina to purport to reject": UN Doc. S/PV. 2360, p. 36.

[57] UN Doc. S/PV. 2373, p. 16. The vote was nine to two (U.K. and U.S.), with four abstentions (France, Guyana, Jordan, Togo).

[58] *Keesing's Archives*, p. 31709. On maritime security zones, see Leiner (1984) 24 Virg. J.I.L. 967 and Subedi, *Land and Maritime Zones of Peace in International Law* (1996).

THE ENTEBBE INCIDENT[59]

UN Doc. S/PV. 1939, pp. 27, 51–59, 92 and UN Doc. S/PV. 1941, pp. 31–32.
Reprinted in (1976) 15 I.L.M. 1224

On June 27, 1976, an Air France airliner bound for Paris from Tel Aviv was hijacked over Greece after leaving Athens airport. Two of the hijackers appear to have been West German nationals; the other two held Arab passports. The airliner was diverted to Entebbe airport in Uganda where the Jewish passengers (about 100) were separated from the others and the latter released. The hijackers demanded the release of about 50 Palestinian terrorists imprisoned in various countries. The evidence seems to suggest that Uganda did not take such steps as it might have done against the hijackers and, indeed, helped them, although Uganda denied this. On July 3, 1976, Israel flew transport aircraft and soldiers to Entebbe and rescued the hostages by force. The hijackers were killed during the operation, as were some Ugandan and Israeli soldiers. There was also extensive damage to Ugandan aircraft and the airport. The following is an extract from the Security Council debate on the matter in July 1976.

Lt. Col. Juma Oris Abdullah (Uganda). Uganda gave all the help and hospitality it was capable of giving to all the hostages. The response to this humanitarian gesture by Zionist Israel—the vehicle of imperialism—was to invade Uganda, once again living up to its record of barbarism and banditry. . . .

We call upon this Council unreservedly to condemn in the strongest possible terms Israel's barbaric, unprovoked and unwarranted aggression against the sovereign Republic of Uganda. Uganda demands full compensation from Israel for the damage to life and property caused during its invasion. . . .

Mr. Herzog (Israel). Uganda violated a basic tenet of international law in failing to protect foreign nationals on its territory. Furthermore, it behaved in a manner which constituted a gross violation of the 1970 Hague Convention on the Suppression or Unlawful Seizure of Aircraft.[60] This Convention had been ratified by both Israel and Uganda. . . .

The right of a State to take military action to protect its nationals in mortal danger is recognised by all legal authorities in international law. In *Self Defence in International Law*, Professor Bowett states, on page 87, that the right of the State to intervene by the use or threat of force for the protection of its nationals suffering injuries within the territory of another State is generally admitted, both in the writings of jurists and in the practice of States. In the arbitration between Great Britain and Spain in 1925, one of the series known as the Spanish Moroccan claims[61] Judge Huber, as Rapporteur of the Commission, stated:

---

[59] See Akehurst (1977) 5 Int. Rel. 3; Boyle (1982) 29 N.I.L.R. 32; Krift (1977) 4 Brooklyn J.I.L. 43; and Margo (1977) 94 S.A.L.J. 306. For a full account of the incident, see Stevenson, *90 Minutes at Entebbe* (1976).
[60] *Ed.* See Article 6, above, p. 295.
[61] *Ed. loc. cit.*, p. 57, n. 36, above.

However, it cannot be denied that at a certain point the interest of a State in exercising protection over its nationals and their property can take precedence over territorial sovereignty, despite the absence of any conventional provisions.... It presupposes the inadequacy of any other means of protection against some injury, actual or imminent, to the persons or property of nationals and, moreover, an injury which results either from the acts of the territorial State and its authorities or from the acts of individuals or groups of individuals which the territorial State is unable, or unwilling, to prevent.

In the *Law of Nations*, 6th edition, p. 427, Brierly states as follows:

Every effort must be made to get the United Nations to act. But, if the United Nations is not in a position to move in time and the need for instant action is manifest, it would be difficult to deny the legitimacy of action in defence of nationals which every responsible Government would feel bound to take if it had the means to do so; this is, of course, on the basis that the action was strictly limited to securing the safe removal of the threatened nationals.[62] ...

The right of self-defence is enshrined in international law and in the Charter of the United Nations and can be applied on the basis of the classic formulation, as was done in the well-known Caroline Case, permitting such action where there is a

necessity of self-defence, instant, overwhelming, leaving no choice of means and no moment for deliberation.

That was exactly the situation which faced the Government of Israel.

Mr. OYONO (CAMEROON). The Security Council, which is responsible for international peace and security, must vigorously condemn this barbaric act which constitutes a flagrant violation of the norms of international law and flouts the spirit and letter of the United Nations Charter, Article 2, paragraph 4....

In the spirit of the Charter, that prohibition means that Member States have an obligation to settle their international disputes by peaceful means in order to maintain international peace and security. I need hardly remind you that our Organisation is not dedicated to anarchy or to the notion that might makes right, but is an organised community whose mutually accepted principles and rules must be scrupulously respected, and their violation adequately punished.

---

[62] Ed. O'Connell, *International Law* (2nd ed.) Vol. I, p. 303 is quoted to the same effect.

It is the corner-stone of our Organisation that there can be no justification for the use of force against the sovereignty, independence or territorial integrity of a State, unless we wish to imperil international co-operation in its present form and indeed the very existence of States that do not yet possess modern, sophisticated systems of detection and deterrence.

MR. SCRANTON (UNITED STATES). Israel's action in rescuing the hostages necessarily involved a temporary breach of the territorial integrity of Uganda. Normally, such a breach would be impermissible under the Charter of the United Nations. However, there is a well established right to use limited force for the protection of one's own nationals from any imminent threat of injury or death in a situation where the State in whose territory they are located is either unwilling or unable to protect them. The right, flowing from the right of self-defence, is limited to such use of force as is necessary and appropriate to protect threatened nationals from injury.

The requirements of this right to protect nationals were clearly met in the Entebbe case. Israel had good reason to believe that at the time it acted Israeli nationals were in imminent danger of execution by the hijackers. Moreover, the actions necessary to release the Israeli nationals or to prevent substantial loss of Israeli lives had not been taken by the Government of Uganda, nor was there a reasonable expectation such actions would be taken. In fact, there is substantial evidence that the Government of Uganda co-operated with and aided the hijackers. A number of the released hostages have publicly related how the Ugandan authorities allowed several additional terrorists to reinforce the original group after the plane landed, permitted them to receive additional arms and additional explosives, participated in guarding the hostages and according to some accounts, even took over sole custody of some or all of the passengers to allow the hijackers to rest. The ease and success of the Israeli effort to free the hostages further suggests that the Ugandan authorities could have overpowered the hijackers and released the hostages if they had really had the desire to do so. . . .

That Israel might have secured the release of its nationals by complying with the terrorists' demands does not alter these conclusions. No State is required to yield control over persons in lawful custody in its territory under criminal charges. Moreover, it would be a self-defeating and dangerous policy to release prisoners, convicted in some cases of earlier acts of terrorism, in order to accede to the demands of terrorists.

It should be emphasised that this assessment of the legality of Israeli actions depends heavily on the unusual circumstances of this specific case. In particular, the evidence is strong that, given the attitude of Ugandan authorities, co-operation with or reliance on them in rescuing the passengers and crew was impracticable.

Notes

1. No resolution was adopted at the end of the debate. A United Kingdom/United States draft resolution[63] which limited itself to condemning hijacking and did not comment on the conduct of the parties did not receive the necessary votes for adoption and a draft resolution[64] proposed by Benin/Libya/Tanzania condemning Israel was not put to the vote.

2. By no means all writers agree with those quoted by the Israeli representative in the debate on a post-1945[65] right to defend nationals abroad. Brownlie, for example, states:

> ... it is very doubtful if the present form of intervention has any basis in the modern law. The instances in which states have purported to exercise it, and the terms in which it is delimited, show that it provides infinite opportunities for abuse.[66] Forcible intervention is now unlawful. It is true that the protection of nationals presents particular difficulties and that a government faced with a deliberate massacre of a considerable number of nationals in a foreign state would have cogent reasons of humanity for acting, and would also be under very great political pressure. The possible risks of denying the legality of action in a case of such urgency, an exceptional circumstance, must be weighed against the more calculable dangers of providing legal pretexts for the commission of breaches of the peace in the pursuit of national rather than humanitarian interests.[67]

3. Does the part of the Court's judgment in the *Corfu Channel* case on intervention (above, p. 391), support Brownlie? If there is a right to protect nationals abroad, how serious does the threat to their person have to be for it to arise? Is there any support for a right to intervene to protect the property of nationals abroad?[68] On humanitarian intervention, see below, p. 917.

4. On the United States attempt to rescue the hostages in Iran, see the *U.S. Diplomatic and Consular Staff* case, above, p. 358. The United States justified its action, in a report to the Security Council pursuant to Article 51, Charter, as being "in exercise of its inherent right of self-defence with the aim of extricating American nationals who are and remain the victims of the Iranian armed attack on our Embassy."[69] The Court did not rule upon legality of the rescue attempt.[70]

5. The facts of the *Nicaragua* case may both explain why the Court did not in that case address the question of the forcible protection of nationals abroad and why the wording of the judgment could be read by implication as excluding it. It is noticeable, however, that the Court did not *expressly* reserve this question

---

[63] UN Doc. S/12138; (1976) 15 I.L.M. 1226.

[64] UN Doc. S/12139; (1976) 15 I.L.M. 1227.

[65] For state practice evidencing the right before then, see Bowett, *op. cit.*, p. 859, n. 1, above, pp. 96–105.

[66] *Ed.* Might the *Dominican Republic* case, above, p. 845, the *Grenada* case, above, p. 893, and the *Panama* case, above, p. 893, support this view?

[67] *op. cit.*, p. 859, n. 1 above p. 301. See generally Ronzitti, *Rescuing Nationals Abroad through Military Coercion and Intervention on Grounds of Humanity* (1985). On the 1990 Liberian Incident, see Lillich (1992) 35 G.Y.I.L. 205.

[68] See the Lord Chancellor's statement justifying the 1956 Anglo-French invasion of Suez to protect Suez Canal installations: *Hansard*, H.L., Vol. 199, cols 1348 *et seq.*, November 1, 1956.

[69] I.C.J. Reports 1979, at p. 18. See D'Angelo (1981) 21 Virg.J.I.L. 485. *cf.* the *Mayaguez* case (rescue by U.S. troops by force of a U.S. merchant ship and its crew captured by Cambodia; justified as self-defence of nationals): [1975] U.S.D.I.L. 777. See Paust (1975–1976) 85 Yale L.J. 774.

[70] Judges Morozov and Tarazi concluded that it was not justified by Art. 51, Charter: I.C.J. Rep. 1980, at pp. 57, 64, respectively.

(contrast its treatment of anticipatory self-defence) and that the thrust of the judgment is to minimise the opportunities for the lawful use of force in international relations.

6. *United States air raid on Libya.*[71] On April 15, 1986 United States military aircraft based in the United Kingdom and on United States aircraft carriers in the Mediterranean bombed military targets in Libya, hitting most of the targets successfully but killing, it was estimated, approximately 100 civilians as well. The air strike was in response to what the United States was sure was a series of Libyan conducted or supported terrorist acts against United States nationals and property, including the April 9 bombing of a Berlin nightclub in which a United States soldier was killed and 50 other soldiers were injured.[72] President Reagan characterised the mission as being "fully consistent with Article 51 of the UN Charter"; it was "pre-emptive action" that would "not only diminish Col. Kadhafi's capacity to export terror" but also "provide him with incentives and reasons to change his criminal behaviour." A draft Security Council resolution condemning the air strike received the required majority (11 to four votes), but was vetoed by the United States and the United Kingdom.[73] Speaking in support of the legality of the United States action, and of the United Kingdom participation in it, the British representative on the Security Council stated[74]:

> The United States has, as any of us do, the inherent right of self-defence, as reaffirmed in Article 51 of the Charter.
> ... the right of self-defence is not an entirely passive right. It plainly includes the right to destroy or weaken the capacity of one's assailant, to reduce his resources, and to weaken his will so as to discourage and prevent further violence.
> At the same time, the right of self-defence should be used in a proportionate way. That is why when President Reagan told Mrs Thatcher last week that the United States intended to take action, she concentrated on the principle of self-defence and the consequent need to limit the action and to relate the selection of targets clearly to terrorism.

7. A similar incident occurred on June 26, 1993 when the United States destroyed the Iraqi intelligence headquarters in Baghdad by missiles fired from United States aircraft carriers. The attack caused the loss of six or more civilian lives as some missiles went astray. The attack followed the uncovering of an unexecuted Iraqi plan to kill President Bush in Kuwait in April 1993. The United States justified its attack under Article 51 and reported it to the Security Council, as that provision required. The United States stated[75]:

> Our response has been proportionate and aimed at a target directly linked to the operation against President Bush. It was designed to damage the terrorist infrastructure of the Iraqi regime, reduce its ability to promote terrorism and deter further acts of aggression against the United States.

The United Kingdom supported the United States attack ("proper and proportionate"), as did the Russian Federation; France "fully understands" the reason

---

[71] See Greenwood (1987) 89 W.Virg.L.R. 933.
[72] U.S. nationals died in terrorist attacks in 1985: Greenwood, above, citing Falk, in Thompson, ed., *Mad Dogs* (1986), p. 124.
[73] S/PV. 2682, April 21, 1986, France, U.K. and U.S. vetoes.
[74] S/PV. 2679, pp. 27–28, U.K.M.I.L. 1986 (1986) 57 B.Y.I.L. 641.
[75] UN Doc. S/PV. 3245, p. 6. On the incident, see Baker (1994) 24 Ga.J.I.C.L. 99; Quigley (1994) 17 Hastings I.C.L.R. 241; Reisman (1994) 5 E.J.I.L. 120.

for the attack; China and other states indicated their concern.[76] Was this a case of self defence or a reprisal?[77]

(d) *Reprisals involving the Use of Force*

BOWETT, REPRISALS INVOLVING RECOURSE TO ARMED FORCE

(1972) 66 A.J.I.L. 1. Some footnotes omitted

... Not surprisingly, as states have grown increasingly disillusioned about the capacity of the Security Council to afford them protection against what they would regard as illegal and highly injurious conduct directed against them, they have resorted to self-help in the form of reprisals and have acquired the confidence that, in so doing, they will not incur anything more than a formal censure from the Security Council. The law on reprisals is, because of its divorce from actual practice, rapidly degenerating to a stage where its normative character is in question.

... To take what is now perhaps the classic case, let us suppose that guerrilla activity from State A, directed against State B, eventually leads to a military action within State A's territory by which State B hopes to destroy the guerrilla bases from which the previous attacks have come and to discourage further attacks. Clearly, this military action cannot strictly be regarded as self-defence in the context of the previous guerrilla activities: they are past, whatever damage has occurred as a result cannot now be prevented and no new military action by State B can really be regarded as a defence against attacks in the past. But if one broadens the context and looks at the whole situation between these two states, cannot it be said that the destruction of the guerrilla bases represents a proper, proportionate means of defence—for the security of the state *is* involved —against future and (given the whole context of past activities) certain attacks? The reply that this constitutes an argument of "anticipatory" self-defence which is no longer permitted under the Charter, since Article 51 requires an actual "armed attack," is scarcely adequate. It was never the intention of the Charter to prohibit anticipatory self-defence and the traditional right certainly existed in relation to an "imminent" attack. Moreover, the rejection of an anticipatory right is, in this day and age, totally unrealistic and inconsistent with general state practice.[78]

---

[76] UN Doc. S/PV. 3245, pp. 13 *et seq. Keesings Archives*, p. 39531.

[77] See Gray (1994) 65 B.Y.I.L. 135 at 170.

[78] Pakistan justified the entry of her troops into Kashmir in 1948 on this basis before the Security Council, an argument opposed only by India. Israel's invasion of Sinai in October 1956 and June 1967 rested on the same argument. The O.A.S. has used the same argument in relation to the blockade of Cuba during the 1962 missile crisis. Several states have expressed the same argument in the Sixth Committee in connection with the definition of aggression and the UN itself invoked the principle of anticipatory self-defence to justify action by O.N.U.C. in Katanga in December 1961, and December 1963. Following the invasion of Czechoslovakia by the USSR in 1968, it is permissible to assume that the USSR now shares this view for there certainly existed no "armed attack."

In fact, the records of the Security Council are replete with cases where states have invoked self-defence in this broader sense but where the majority of the Council have rejected this classification and regarded their action as unlawful reprisals. . . .

Weighing the advantages against the disadvantages . . . it would seem that the approach of the Security Council in assessing whether a case for lawful self-defence has been made out has been somewhat unrealistic. To confine this assessment to the incident and its immediate "cause," without regard to the broader context of the past relations between the parties and events arising therefrom, is to ignore the difficulties in which states may be placed, especially in relation to guerrilla activities. . . .

Recent practice, particularly in the context of the Arab-Israel confrontation, suggests that not only have states like Israel, the United States and the United Kingdom not abandoned their wider view of self-defence —based upon the "accumulation of events" theory—despite the Security Council's rejection of the theory, but, even more striking, Israel has relied less and less on a self-defence argument and has taken action which is openly admitted to be a reprisal. The Beirut raid of December 28, 1968,[79] is the obvious example of an action not really defended on the basis of self-defence at all. Indeed, even as a reprisal, the motivation for reprisals seems to have shifted from that of punishment for previous acts to deterrence of future possible acts.[80] . . . It cannot be expected that the Security Council will ever accept this justification. But there is clearly some evidence that certain reprisals will, even if not accepted as justified, at least avoid condemnation. . . . Obviously, if this trend continues, we shall achieve a position in which, while reprisals remain illegal *de jure*, they become accepted *de facto*. Indeed, it may be that the more relevant distinction today is not between self-defence and reprisals but between

---

[79] *Ed.* 13 civil airplanes valued at over $40 million were destroyed while on the ground at Beirut airport in Lebanon by Israeli commandos. There was no loss of life. The raid was in retaliation for an attack on December 26 on an El Al airplane at Athens airport by Palestine guerrillas. The airplane was damaged and a passenger—an Israeli—killed. The Security Council condemned Israel "for its premeditated military action in violation of its obligations under the Charter" and considered that Lebanon was entitled to "appropriate redress for the destruction it has suffered": S.C. Resn. 262 (1968), S.C.O.R., 23rd Year, *Resolutions and Decisions*, p. 12. Adopted unanimously. See Falk (1969) 63 A.J.I.L. 415 and Blum (1970) 64 *ibid.* 73.

[80] The Israeli Chief of Staff, General Yetzhak Bar Lev, was reported to have stated the purpose as being "to make clear to the other side that the price they must pay for terrorist activities can be very high"; see *New York Times*, January 5, 1969, Sec. 4, p. 1. However, Ambassador Rosenne, in the Security Council, did raise the justification of self-defence (see Doc. S/PV. 1460, pp. 22–23). *Ed.* The 1982 Israeli invasion of the Lebanon, leading to the departure of P.L.O. forces that had been attacking Israel from Lebanese bases, is yet another "accumulation of events" case. See Gross (1983) 13 Cal. W.I.L.J. 458. *cf.* the 1985 Israeli bombing of the PLO headquarters in Tunisia, killing between 45 to 70 people, following the killing of Israeli tourists in Cyprus by Palestinian guerrillas. The bombing was condemned by the Security Council as "an act of armed aggression . . . in flagrant violation of . . . international law": S.C.Resn. 573 (1985), S.C.O.R., 40th Year, *Resolutions and Decisions*, p. 23. The resolution was adopted by 14 votes to 0, with the U.S. abstaining.

reprisals which are likely to be condemned and those which, because they satisfy some concept of "reasonableness," are not.

Notes

1. On reprisals in international law, see above, p. 12. As Bowett accepts, armed reprisals remain contrary to international law: see the 1970 Declaration on Principles of International Law, Section on the Principle on the Use of Force, para. 6, which expressly prohibits them.[81] One of the cases to which Bowett refers in which the Security Council rejected a claim of self-defence in the "broader sense" was the *Harib Fort Incident*.[82] In 1964, the Yemen brought a complaint against the United Kingdom before the Security Council resulting from the following situation. In 1963 and 1964, the British Government had complained to the Security Council of a large number of shooting incidents on the Yemeni-South Arabian border and of aerial raids in South Arabian territory from the Yemen. In three raids in March 1964, bedouin and their flocks had been attacked from the air. Thereupon, on March 28, 1964, British military aircraft bombed Harib Fort in the Yemen after having first dropped leaflets advising people to leave the area. The Yemen claimed that 25 people were killed, but this figure was disputed. The British representative justified this action as follows:

> 26. There is, in existing law, a clear distinction to be drawn between two forms of self-help. One, which is of a retributive or punitive nature, is termed "retaliation" or "reprisals"; the other, which is expressly contemplated and authorised by the Charter, is self-defence against armed attack.... It is clear that the use of armed force to repel or prevent an attack—that is, legitimate action of a defensive nature—may sometimes have to take the form of a counter-attack....
>
> 28. The fact that some of these aggressive acts from the Yemen have fortunately, in recent weeks, not resulted in loss of life or very serious damage is quite beside the point.[83] In the past lives have been lost as the result of these actions, and far inside Federation territory. This naturally causes great alarm among the people concerned.
>
> 29.... It indeed would be a strange legal doctrine which deprived the people of the Federation [of South Arabia] of any right to be defended, or deprived those responsible for defending them from taking appropriate measures of a preventive nature.[84]
>
> 30. It is therefore necessary to emphasise once more that the fort at Harib was not merely a military installation, but was known to be a centre for aggressive action against the Federation. To destroy the fort with the minimum use of force was therefore a defensive measure which was proportionate and confined to the necessities of the case.
>
> 31. It has no parallel with acts of retaliation or reprisals, which have as an essential element the purposes of vengeance or retribution. It is this latter use of force which is condemned by the Charter, and not the use of force for defensive purposes such as warding off future attacks.[85]

The Security Council adopted a resolution in which it:

---

[81] *cf.* the *Nuclear Weapons* case, Opinion, para. 46, below, p. 925.

[82] S.C.O.R., 19th Year, 1106th–1111th Meetings, April 2nd–8th, 1964. *cf.* the *Gulf of Tonkin Incident* discussed above, p. 901, under self-defence.

[83] *Ed.* Two camels were killed and two tents were burnt: UN Doc. S/5618.

[84] *Ed.* The U.K. was acting under a treaty of protection with the Federation.

[85] S.C.O.R., 19th Year, 1106th Meeting, April 2, 1964.

1. *Condemns* reprisals as incompatible with the purposes and principles of the United Nations;
2. *Deplores* the British military action at Harib on 28 March 1964;
3. *Deplores* all attacks and incidents which have occurred in the area.[86]

2. Bowett lists as factors which the practice of the Security Council suggests are relevant to the question whether a reprisal is "reasonable" and hence unlikely to be condemned, the proportionality between the reprisal and the earlier illegal act that causes it; whether the reprisal is against civilians or the armed forces; whether it is one against human life or property; whether the state against which it is taken has provoked the reprisal; whether the reprisal jeopardises the chances of a peaceful settlement by its timing; and whether, at least in the guerrilla context, the state taking the reprisal has exhausted all practical measures for the defence of its territory within its own borders.[87]

(e) Humanitarian Intervention[88]

U.K. FOREIGN OFFICE POLICY DOCUMENT No. 148

U.K.M.I.L. 1986, (1986) 57 B.Y.I.L. 614

II.18. The final, and by far the most controversial, category of exceptions to the general prohibition on intervention is that on humanitarian grounds. This should be distinguished from action to protect a state's own nationals abroad . . . The vast literature on this subject in the past and present century has wrestled with the difficulty of reconciling a state's supposedly absolute sovereignty with even more fundamental human rights which may be held to justify intervention on behalf of oppressed nationals of another state.

II.20. . . . Lauterpacht's rationale for humanitarian intervention is that 'ultimately, peace is more endangered by tyrannical contempt for human rights than by attempts to assert, through intervention, the sanctity of human personality.'[89] A substantial body of opinion and of practice has thus supported the view that when a state commits cruelties against and persecution of its nationals in such a way as to deny their fundamental human rights and to shock the conscience of mankind, intervention in the interest of humanity is legally permissible.

[86] *ibid.* 1111th Meeting, April 9. The resolution adopted by 9 votes to 0, with 2 abstentions.

[87] See also the guidelines suggested by Falk, *loc. cit.*, p. 915, n. 79, above, at pp. 439–440, which are discussed by Bowett.

[88] On the question whether there is a right of humanitarian intervention, see the contrasting views in Lillich, ed., *Humanitarian Intervention and the United Nations* (1973) and Moore, ed., *Law and Civil War in the Modern World* (1974) (articles by Brownlie and Lillich). See also Akehurst, in Bull, ed., *Intervention in World Politics* (1984), p. 95; Benjamin 1992–1993 16 Fordham I.L.J. 120; Franck and Rodley (1973) 67 A.J.I.L. 275; Lillich (1993) 53 Z.A.O.R.V. 557; Nanda (1991–1992) 20 Denver J.I.L.P. 305; Rodley, ed., *To Loose the Bonds of Wickedness* (1992); Ronzitti, *op. cit.*, p. 912, n. 67; Simon (1993) 24 Cal. W.I.L.J. 117; Teson, *Humanitarian Intervention* (2nd ed., 1997); Tyagi (1995) 16 Mich. J.I.L. 883; Verwey (1985) 32 N.I.L.R. 357.

[89] *International Law and Human Rights*, p. 32.

II.21. The state practice to which advocates of the right of humanitarian intervention have appealed provides an uncertain basis on which to rest such a right. Not least this is because history has shown that humanitarian ends are almost always mixed with other less laudable motives for intervening, and because often the 'humanitarian' benefits of an intervention are either not claimed by the intervening state or are only put forward as an *ex post facto* justification of the intervention. In the nineteenth century, interventions by the Western Powers to protect the Christian and other minorities in the Ottoman Empire, such as the Maronites on Mount Lebanon,[90] are those most often said to have been for humanitarian ends. The two most discussed instances of alleged humanitarian intervention since 1945 are the Indian invasion of Bangladesh in 1971[91] and Tanzania's 'humanitarian' invasion of Uganda in 1979.[92] But, although both did result in unquestionable benefits for, respectively, the peoples of East Bengal and Uganda, India and Tanzania were reluctant to use humanitarian ends to justify their invasion of a neighbour's territory. Both preferred to quote the right to self-defence under Article 51. And in each case the self-interest of the invading state was clearly involved.

II.22. In fact, the best case that can be made in support of humanitarian intervention is that it cannot be said to be unambiguously illegal. . . . But the overwhelming majority of contemporary legal opinion comes down against the existence of a right of humanitarian intervention, for three main reasons: first, the UN Charter and the corpus of modern international law do not seem specifically to incorporate such a right; secondly, state practice in the past two centuries, and especially since 1945, at best provides only a handful of genuine cases of humanitarian intervention, and, on most assessments, none at all; and finally, on prudential grounds, that the scope for abusing such a right argues strongly against its creation. . . . In essence, therefore, the case against making humanitarian intervention an exception to the principle of non-intervention is that its doubtful benefits would be heavily outweighed by its costs in terms of respect for international law.

---

[90] *Ed.* In 1860, in events erupting from the same religious tension that affected Lebanon during the 1975–1990 civil war, some 5,000 Christians were killed by Moslems. By treaty, Turkey, which then held the Lebanon as a part of its Empire, agreed with the major Western powers that action should be taken to end the killings and a French force was sent on behalf of the European powers. See Pogany (1986) 35 I.C.L.Q. 182.

[91] *Ed.* See above, p. 892.

[92] *Ed.* After Uganda had illegally occupied a part of Tanzania by armed force, Tanzania used armed force to eject the Ugandan troops and continued on into Uganda. Together with Ugandan rebels, Tanzanian forces defeated President Amin's forces, causing President Amin to flee and the replacement of his government, which had been responsible for atrocious human rights violations, with an estimated 300,000 deaths. Although Tanzania did not unequivocally justify its invasion of Uganda on grounds of humanitarian intervention, commentators have suggested that this was the only possible legal basis: see, *e.g.* Teson, *op. cit.*, p. 917, n. 88, above, pp. 179–195.

Notes

Another case relied upon as evidence of a right to humanitarian intervention is the 1964 intervention in the Congo by Belgium, with United States and United Kingdom logistical assistance, after 30 or more European and other aliens had been killed by revolutionaries and many others held hostage were at risk. However, the rescue operation, by which 2,000 people of many nationalities were evacuated by Belgian paratroopers, was undertaken with the consent of the Congolese Government and hence was not dependent upon any right to humanitarian intervention. Like all of the cases cited in United Kingdom Foreign Office Policy Document No. 148 as examples of humanitarian intervention, the Congo case involved large-scale violations of the right to life. If a right of humanitarian intervention at least in such circumstances did exist before 1945, the reluctance of states to invoke it in the post-war period prior to 1991[93] suggested that it has not survived Article 2(4), UN Charter. But the end of the Cold War and the arrival of President Saddam Hussein have proved catalysts for change, as the following materials show.

SECURITY COUNCIL RESOLUTION 688 (1991)

April 3, 1991. S.C.O.R., 46th Year, Resolutions and Decisions, p. 31

The Security Council ...

Recalling Article 2, paragraph 7, of the Charter of the United Nations,

Gravely concerned by the repression of the Iraqi civilian population in many parts of Iraq, including most recently in Kurdish populated areas which led to a massive flow of refugees towards and across international frontiers and to cross border incursions, which threaten international peace and security in the region,

Deeply disturbed by the magnitude of the human suffering involved ...

Reaffirming the commitment of all Member States to the sovereignty, territorial integrity and political independence of Iraq and of all States in the area ...

1. *Condemns* the repression of the Iraqi civilian population in many parts of Iraq, including most recently in Kurdish populated areas, the consequences of which threaten international peace and security in the region;

2. *Demands* that Iraq, as a contribution to removing the threat to international peace and security in the region, immediately end this repression and expresses the hope in the same context that an open dialogue will

---

[93] *cf.* the *Nicaragua (Merits)* case, judgment, para. 268, above, p. 883.

take place to ensure that the human and political rights of all Iraqi citizens are respected;

3. *Insists* that Iraq allow immediate access by international human-itarian organizations to all those in need of assistance in all parts of Iraq and to make available all necessary facilities for their operations; . . .

5. *Requests further* the Secretary-General to use all the resources at his disposal, including those of the relevant United Nations agencies, to address urgently the critical needs of the refugees and displaced Iraqi population;

6. *Appeals* to all Member States and to all humanitarian organizations to contribute to these humanitarian relief efforts . . .

Notes

1. After the Iraqi army occupying Kuwait was defeated[94] rebellions against President Saddam Hussein's rule occurred in both northern and southern Iraq. These were put down with brutal ferocity by the still strong Iraqi army causing a flood of refugees. In northern Iraq well over 1 million Kurdish refugees fled to the Turkish and Iranian borders where they received some Western aid, although many died.[95] Resolution 688 was a response to this situation.[96] It was adopted by 10 votes to three (Cuba, Yemen, Zimbabwe), with two absentions (China and India). The resolution was heavily criticised by those states voting against and abstaining as being concerned with a domestic issue.[97] How should one interpret Article 2(7) in the light of Resolution 688?[98]

2. Following the adoption of Resolution 688, in April 1991, United States, United Kingdom and French land forces established, despite initial Iraqi objec-tions, "safe havens" in northern Iraq for the Kurds, providing them with a secure place in which to live and receive food and other humanitarian assistance.[99] The coalition forces left in July 1991 and were replaced, with Iraqi consent, by UN guards. The coalition states also established "no fly zones", from which Iraqi aircraft were excluded, in Iraq north of the 38th parallel (as of April 1991) and south of the 32nd parallel (as of August 1991) in order to protect the Kurds and the Shiite/Marsh Arab population respectively from Iraqi attack.

3. Do these initiatives fall within the "humanitarian aid" dicta in the *Nicaragua (Merits)* case, judgment, para. 242, above, p. 881? The United Kingdom is clear that they were not taken under Resolution 688, and certainly its terms do not provide for them. The United Kingdom, which had been doubtful about the legality and merits of humanitarian intervention by individual states in Foreign Office Policy Document No. 148, above p. 917, was prepared to recognise an evolution in the law concerning humanitarian intervention in a case such as Iraq, by states acting through the UN or by themselves. In a memorandum[1] to the HC Foreign Affairs Committee in 1992, the FCO stated:

[94] On the Kuwait war, see below, p. 956.
[95] See the Report of the Secretary-General, UN Doc. S/22454, March 28, 1991.
[96] On Resolution 688, see Gallant (1991) 7 Am. U.J.I.L.P. 681.
[97] See UN Doc. S/PV. 1982.
[98] By its terms, the domestic jurisdiction limitation in Art. 2(7) does not apply to Chapter VII enforcement action. Resolution 688 was not made under Chapter VII, and hence was subject to Art. 2(7).
[99] On the "safe havens", see Freedman and Boren, in Rodley, ed., *To Loose the Bonds of Wickedness* (1995), Chap. 3, and Malanczuk (1991) 2 E.J.I.L. 114.
[1] U.K.P.I.L. 1992, (1992) 63 B.Y.I.L. 825.

The principle of provision of relief by the UN in areas of internal conflict is well established. The UN is increasingly acting upon that principle. We support both the principle of such intervention in cases of extreme humanitarian need, and the relief operations of this type in which the UN is involved. In former Yugoslavia the UNHCR has been delivering relief to areas affected by internal conflict in Bosnia-Herzegovina since the middle of this year—first by airlift to Sarajevo and more recently in a large scale road convoy operation. Such relief operations can (for example: in former Yugoslavia, Somalia[2]) be supported by units of UN troops mandated to provide protection. Elsewhere (for example: Afghanistan) the UN humanitarian agencies are operating in conflict areas *without* military protection. We have demonstrated our support for such UN operations by financial assistance and, in the case of military protected operations, by our provision of British troops for protection duties, (for example: Iraq, former Yugoslavia). . . .

We believe that international intervention *without* the invitation of the government of the country concerned can be justified in cases of extreme humanitarian need. This is why we were prepared to commit British forces to Operation Haven, mounted by the Coalition in response to the refugee crisis involving the Iraqi Kurds. The deployment of these forces was entirely consistent with the objectives of SCR 688. . . .

In the course of questioning before the [Foreign Affairs] Committee, Mr Aust, FCO, Legal Counselor, gave the following answers that relate to humanitarian intervention generally and the Iraqi case in particular[3]:

> . . . Resolution 688, which applies not only to northern Iraq but to the whole of Iraq, was not made under Chapter VII. Resolution 688 recognized that there was a severe human rights and humanitarian situation in Iraq and, in particular, northern Iraq; but the intervention in northern Iraq "Provide Comfort" was in fact, not specifically mandated by the United Nations, but the states taking action in northern Iraq did so in exercise of the customary international law principle of humanitarian intervention.
>
> . . . the practice of states does show over a long period that it is generally accepted that in extreme circumstances a state can intervene in another state for humanitarian reasons. I think before doing so though a state would have to ask itself several questions. First of all, whether there was a compelling and an urgent situation of extreme humanitarian distress which demanded immediate relief. It would have to ask itself whether the other state was itself able or willing to meet that distress and deal with it. Also whether there was any other practical alternative to intervening in order to relieve the stress, and also whether the action could be limited in time and scope. . . .
>
> . . . Resolution 688 did not actually authorize it but it did recognize there was a very serious situation in Iraq, particularly in North Iraq. Most of the precedents before that relate perhaps more to intervention in order to protect one's own nationals who are being mistreated or neglected by the territorial state. But international law in this field develops to meet new situations and that is what we are seeing now in the case of Iraq.

Is the development being referred to in the above extract one that covers intervention to provide humanitarian aid to persons who lack food, shelter, etc., only? Or does it extend also to the more familiar situation historically of large scale killings by the territorial state? Consider whether the UN actions in Bosnia and

---

[2] *Ed.* The U.K. did not provide troops in Somalia.
[3] Parliamentary Papers, 1992–1993, H.C., Paper 235–iii, pp. 85, 92.

Herzegovina, Somalia and Rwanda suppose UN competence to take enforcement action under Chapter VII in both of the above situations too?

3. *Bosnia and Herzegovina.* Following the humanitarian action taken in Iraq, the Security Council, in the post–Cold War era, found itself able to act, despite the doubts of some of its members, for at least partly humanitarian reasons in a number of situations of internal conflict.[4] Although the facts of these situations vary, in all of them, in contrast with the Iraqi situation, the action was (i) clearly UN action, at least in the sense that named UN forces were used,[5] and (ii) taken under Chapter VII, on a generous reading of a "threat to the peace" basis for jurisdiction in Article 39.[6]

The first of these cases was Bosnia and Herzegovina. Here the Security Council acted through a number of resolutions to secure the provision of humanitarian aid and the protection of civilians during the civil war in that state and to exclude intervention in the war by Serbia and Montenegro. By Resolution 770,[7] which was adopted in August 1992, the Council

> Recognising that the situation in Bosnia and Herzegovina constitutes a threat to international peace and security and that the provision of humanitarian assistance in Bosnia and Herzegovina is an important element in the Council's efforts to restore international peace and security ...
> Acting under Chapter VII ...
> 2. Calls upon states to take nationally or through regional agencies or arrangements all measures necessary to facilitate in coordination with the United Nations the delivery by relevant United Nations humanitarian organisations and others of humanitarian assistance to Sarajevo and wherever needed in other parts of Bosnia and Herzegovina ...

By Resolution 776,[8] paragraph 2 of Resolution 770 was eventually implemented through UNPROFOR.[9] Later Security Council resolutions, again made under Chapter VII, took matters further by authorising the United States to intercept shipping to enforce UN sanctions against the FRY[10]; establishing a no fly zone over Bosnia and Herzegovina[11]; and establishing safe areas in Bosnia and Herzegovina for Muslims which UNPROFOR would protect.[12]

4. *Somalia.*[13] In December 1992, the UN Security Council authorised intervention to provide humanitarian aid in the context of the civil war in Somalia.[14] By then, the fighting between the warring factions had developed to such a point that the relief agencies were being prevented from providing the humanitarian

---

[4] See Farer, in Damrosch, ed., *Enforcing Restraint: Collective Intervention in Internal Conflicts* (1993), Chap. 8, and Freudenschuss (1994) 5 E.J.I.L. 492.

[5] The Somalian and Rwandan operations were dominated by the U.S. and France respectively. *cf.* the U.S. controlled Haitian intervention, below, p. 943.

[6] See below, p. 942.

[7] S.C.O.R., *Resolutions and Decisions*, 1992, p. 24. Adopted by 12 votes to 0, with three abstentions (China, India, Zimbabwe).

[8] *ibid.* p. 33.

[9] As to which, see above, p. 150.

[10] Resolution 787, *id.*, p. 29. In 1991, an arms embargo was imposed in the territory of the former Yugoslavia generally, S.C. Resolution 713, *id.*, 1991, p. 42, and in 1992 sanctions were imposed against Serbia and Montenegro, S.C. Resolution 757, *id.*, 1992, p. 13.

[11] S.C. Resolution 816, *id.*, 1993, p. 4.

[12] S.C. Resolution 819, 824, 836, 844, S.C.O.R., *Resolutions and Decisions* 1993, pp. 6, 8, 13, 15.

[13] See Hutchinson (1993) 34 Harv. I.L.J. 624, and Makinda, *Seeking Peace from Chaos: Humanitarian Intervention in Somalia* (1993).

[14] See further on the civil war, above, p. 104.

aid urgently needed by one million or so persons facing starvation. Resolution 794 read in part[15]:

> The Security Council . . .
> Recognising the unique character of the present situation in Somalia . . .
> Determining that the magnitude of the human tragedy caused by the conflict in Somalia, further exacerbated by the obstacles being created to the distribution of humanitarian assistance, constitutes a threat to international peace and security . . .
> 10. Acting under Chapter VII[16] of the Charter of the United Nations, authorises the Secretary-General and Member states . . . to use all necessary means to establish as soon as possible a secure environment for humanitarian relief operations in Somalia.

The resolution called on "all Member States which are in a position to do so to provide military forces" under the unified command of the United States. The result was the establishment of UNITAF, a multi-national force, consisting mostly of United States troops. However, although the distribution of humanitarian relief was improved, matters did not go well. In the face of armed opposition against UNITAF from the warring factions, the Security Council decided by Resolution 814[17] to establish UNOSOM II with a mandate to take enforcement action involving the forcible disarmament of all local factions, including General Aidid's forces. UNOSOM II was not under United States command, the United States withdrawing most of its forces. Following attacks by General Aidid's forces resulting in serious UNOSOM II casualties, the Security Council adopted Resolution 837[18] authorising "all necessary measures against all those responsible for the armed attacks . . . to establish the effective authority of UNOSOM II throughout Somalia", including their arrest, trial and punishment. General Aidid evaded capture and UNOSOM II military operations were gradually scaled down, with all troops having left by the end of 1995. The Somalia case is an important precedent for UN action under Chapter VII for the provision of humanitarian aid in a purely civil war situation in the absence of government consent, although the operation itself is generally deemed to have been largely a failure in the face of opposition by the competing warlords.

6. *Rwanda.* The Rwandan population is composed largely of members of the Hutu (85 per cent) and Tutsi tribes. Between April and July 1994, approximately half a million Tutsis were killed in genocidal acts organised by an interim government of extremist Hutus, and over a million other Tutsis fled into neighbouring states. When the scale of the killings became known, the Security Council, acting under Chapter VII, adopted Resolution 929.[19] This authorised member states in co-operation with the Secretary-General and using "all necessary means" to conduct an operation with the object of (i) contributing, impartially, to the security and protection of displaced persons, refugees and civilians at risk, *inter alia,* by establishing secure humanitarian areas and (ii) supporting the distribution of relief supplies. To this end, UNAMUR II was established under French command and with mostly French and African personnel. UNAMUR II remained in being until 1996.

[15] S.C.O.R., *Resolutions and Decisions,* 1992, p. 63. Adopted unanimously.
[16] By finding a threat to the peace and hence being able to act under Chapter VII, the Security Council avoided any limitation that might be argued for under Art. 2(7), Charter.
[17] S.C.O.R., *Resolutions and Decisions,* 1993, p. 80.
[18] *ibid.* p. 83. Adopted unanimously.
[19] S.C.O.R., *Resolutions and Decisions,* 1994, p. 62. Adopted by 10 votes to 0, with five abstentions (New Zealand, China, Brazil, Pakistan and Nigeria).

7. In its resolutions, the Security Council stated that the UN actions in Bosnia and Herzegovina, Somalia and Rwanda were all taken under Chapter VII, but without specifying which Article was being used. Was it acting by way of recommendation under Article 39? Since the UN was taking enforcement action under Chapter VII, the consent of the state upon whose territory the UN forces operated was not needed, as is the case in UN peace-keeping operations: see below, p. 974. In what other ways did the three UN forces differ from peace-keeping forces? Did the role of any of them shade into peace-keeping? In the light of the Iraqi Safe Havens precedent, could individual states have exercised a right of humanitarian intervention under international law independently of the UN in the Bosnia and Herzegovina, Somalia or Rwanda cases?

(f) *Legality of Nuclear Weapons*[20]

LEGALITY OF THE THREAT OR USE OF NUCLEAR WEAPONS CASE

Advisory Opinion. (1997) 35 I.L.M. 809 and 1343

By G.A. Resolution 49/75K, the UN General Assembly requested an opinion on the following question: "Is the threat or use of nuclear weapons in any circumstances permitted under international law?" After ruling that it had jurisdiction to give the opinion, see below, p. 1036, the Court responded as follows:

Opinion of the Court

36 . . . in order correctly to apply to the present case the Charter law on the use of force and the law applicable in armed conflict, in particular humanitarian law, it is imperative for the Court to take account of the unique characteristics of nuclear weapons, and in particular their destructive capacity, their capacity to cause untold human suffering, and their ability to cause damage to generations to come.

37. The Court will now address the question of the legality or illegality of recourse to nuclear weapons in the light of the provisions of the Charter relating to the threat or use of force.

38. The . . . prohibition of the use of force [in Article 2(4)] is to be considered in the light of other relevant provisions of the Charter. In Article 51, the Charter recognizes the inherent right of individual or collective self-defence if an armed attack occurs. A further lawful use of force is envisaged in Article 42, whereby the Security Council may take military enforcement measures in conformity with Chapter VII of the Charter.

39. These provisions do not refer to specific weapons. They apply to any use of force, regardless of the weapons employed. The Charter

---

[20] On the Advisory Opinion, see Bekker (1997) 91 A.J.I.L. 126; Clark (1996) 7 Crim. L.F. 265; Falk (1997) 91 A.J.I.L. 64. See earlier, Green (1988–1989) 17 Den. J.I.L.P. 1; Pogany, ed., *Nuclear Weapons and International Law* (1987); Schwarzenberger, *The Legality of Nuclear Weapons* (1958); Weston (1983) 28 McGill L.J. 542.

neither expressly prohibits, nor permits, the use of any specific weapon, including nuclear weapons. A weapon that is already unlawful *per se*, whether by treaty or custom, does not become lawful by reason of its being used for a legitimate purpose under the Charter.

40. The entitlement to resort to self-defence under Article 51 is subject to certain constraints. Some of these constraints are inherent in the very concept of self defence. Other requirements are specified in Article 51.

41. The submission of the exercise of the right of self-defence to the conditions of necessity and proportionality is a rule of customary international law. As the Court stated in the [Nicaragua Case, para. 176, above, p. 867] ... : "there is a specific rule whereby self-defence would warrant only measures which are proportional to the armed attack and necessary to respond to it, a rule well established in customary international law". This dual condition applies equally to Article 51 of the Charter, whatever the means of force employed.

42. The proportionality principle may thus not in itself exclude the use of nuclear weapons in self-defence in all circumstances. But at the same time, a use of force that is proportionate under the law of self-defence, must, in order to be lawful, also meet the requirements of the law applicable in armed conflict which comprise in particular the principles and rules of humanitarian law.

43. Certain States have in their written and oral pleadings suggested that ... the very nature of nuclear weapons, and the high probability of an escalation of nuclear exchanges, mean that there is an extremely strong risk of devastation. The risk factor is said to negate the possibility of the condition of proportionality being complied with. The Court does not find it necessary to embark upon the quantification of such risks; nor does it need to enquire into the question whether tactical nuclear weapons exist which are sufficiently precise to limit those risks: it suffices for the Court to note that the very nature of all nuclear weapons and the profound risks associated therewith are further considerations to be borne in mind by States believing they can exercise a nuclear response in self-defence in accordance with the requirements of proportionality. ...

46. Certain States asserted that the use of nuclear weapons in the conduct of reprisals would be lawful. The Court does not have to examine, in this context, the question of armed reprisals in time of peace, which are considered to be unlawful. Nor does it have to pronounce on the question of belligerent reprisals save to observe that in any case any right of recourse to such reprisals would, like self-defence, be governed *inter alia* by the principle of proportionality.

47. In order to lessen or eliminate the risk of unlawful attack, States sometimes signal that they possess certain weapons to use in self-defence against any State violating their territorial integrity or political independence. Whether a signalled intention to use force if certain events occur is or is not a "threat" within Article 2, paragraph 4, of the Charter depends upon various factors. If the envisaged use of force is itself unlawful, the

stated readiness to use it would be a threat prohibited under Article 2, paragraph 4. Thus it would be illegal for a State to threaten force to secure territory from another State, or to cause it to follow or not follow certain political or economic paths. The notions of "threat" and "use" of force under Article 2, paragraph 4, of the Charter stand together in the sense that if the use of force itself in a given case is illegal—for whatever reason—the threat to use such force will likewise be illegal. In short, if it is to be lawful, the declared readiness of a State to use force must be a use of force that is in conformity with the Charter. For the rest, no State —whether or not it defended the policy of deterrence—suggested to the Court that it would be lawful to threaten to use force if the use of force contemplated would be illegal.

48. Some States put forward the argument that possession of nuclear weapons is itself an unlawful threat to use force. Possession of nuclear weapons may indeed justify an inference of preparedness to use them. In order to be effective, the policy of deterrence, by which those States possessing or under the umbrella of nuclear weapons seek to discourage military aggression by demonstrating that it will serve no purpose, necessitates that the intention to use nuclear weapons be credible. Whether this is a "threat" contrary to Article 2, paragraph 4, depends upon whether the particular use of force envisaged would be directed against the territorial integrity or political independence of a State, or against the Purposes of the United Nations or whether, in the event that it were intended as a means of defence, it would necessarily violate the principles of necessity and proportionality. In any of these circumstances the use of force, and the threat to use it, would be unlawful under the law of the Charter.

49. Moreover, the Security Council may take enforcement measures under Chapter VII of the Charter. From the statements presented to it the Court does not consider it necessary to address questions which might, in a given case, arise from the application of Chapter VII.

50. The terms of the question put to the Court by the General Assembly in resolution 49/75K could in principle also cover a threat or use of nuclear weapons by a State within its own boundaries. However, this particular aspect has not been dealt with by any of the States which addressed the Court orally or in writing in these proceedings. The Court finds that it is not called upon to deal with an internal use of nuclear weapons.

51. Having dealt with the Charter provisions relating to the threat or use of force, the Court will now turn to the law applicable in situations of armed conflict. It will first address the question whether there are specific rules in international law regulating the legality or illegality of recourse to nuclear weapons *per se*; it will then examine the question put to it in the light of the law applicable in armed conflict proper, i.e. the principles and rules of humanitarian law applicable in armed conflict, and the law of neutrality.

52. The Court notes by way of introduction that international customary and treaty law does not contain any specific prescription authorizing the threat or use of nuclear weapons or any other weapon in general or in certain circumstances, in particular those of the exercise of legitimate self-defence. Nor, however, is there any principle or rule of international law which would make the legality of the threat or use of nuclear weapons or of any other weapons dependent on a specific authorization. State practice shows that the illegality of the use of certain weapons as such does not result from an absence of authorization but, on the contrary, is formulated in terms of prohibition.

53. The Court must therefore now examine whether there is any prohibition of recourse to nuclear weapons as such; it will first ascertain whether there is a conventional prescription to this effect. ...

57. The pattern until now has been for weapons of mass destruction to be declared illegal by specific instruments. The most recent such instruments are the Convention of 10 April 1972 on the Prohibition of the Development, Production and Stockpiling of Bacteriological (Biological) and Toxic Weapons and on their Destruction[21]—which prohibits the possession of bacteriological and toxic weapons and reinforces the prohibition of their use—and the Convention of 13 January 1993 on the Prohibition of the Development, Production, Stockpiling and Use of Chemical Weapons and on Their Destruction[22]—which prohibits all use of chemical weapons and requires the destruction of existing stocks. Each of these instruments has been negotiated and adopted in its own context and for its own reasons. The Court does not find any specific prohibition of recourse to nuclear weapons in treaties expressly prohibiting the use of certain weapons of mass destruction.

58. In the last two decades, a great many negotiations have been conducted regarding nuclear weapons; they have not resulted in a treaty of general prohibition of the same kind as for bacteriological and chemical weapons. However, a number of specific treaties have been concluded in order to limit:

(a) the acquisition, manufacture and possession of nuclear weapons.[23] ...

(b) the deployment of nuclear weapons.[24] ...

(c) the testing of nuclear weapons.[25] ...

---

[21] *Ed.* 1015 U.N.T.S. 163; U.K.T.S. 11 (1976), Cmnd. 6397.

[22] *Ed.* Misc. 21 (1993), Cm. 2331; (1993) 32 I.L.M. 800.

[23] *Ed.* The Court cited, *inter alia*, the Tlatelolco Treaty, 634 U.N.T.S. 326; U.K.T.S. 54 (1970), Cmnd. 4409; the Rarotonga Treaty (1985) 24 I.L.M. 1442; and the 1990 German Settlement Treaty, U.K.T.S. 88 (1991), Cm. 1756; (1990) 29 I.L.M. 1186. The first two of these made Latin America and the South Pacific respectively nuclear free zones.

[24] *Ed.* The Court cited, *inter alia*, the Tlatelolco and Rarotonga Treaties, above, and the Antarctica Treaty, above, p. 231.

[25] *Ed.* The Court cited, *inter alia*, the Tlatelolco and Rarotonga Treaties, above, and the Nuclear Test Ban Treaty, above, p. 421.

59. Recourse to nuclear weapons is directly addressed by two of these Conventions [the Tlatelolco and Rarotonga Treaties] and also in connection with the indefinite extension of the Treaty on the Non-Proliferation of Nuclear Weapons of 1968[26] . . .

62. The Court notes that the treaties dealing exclusively with acquisition, manufacture, possession, deployment and testing of nuclear weapons, without specifically addressing their threat or use, certainly point to an increasing concern in the international community with these weapons; the Court concludes from this that these treaties could therefore be seen as foreshadowing a future general prohibition of the use of such weapons, but they do not constitute such a prohibition by themselves. As to the treaties of Tlatelolco and Rarotonga and their Protocols, and also the declarations made in connection with the indefinite extension of the Treaty on the Non-Proliferation of Nuclear Weapons, it emerges from these instruments that:

(a) a number of States have undertaken not to use nuclear weapons in specific zones (Latin America; the South Pacific) or against certain other States (non-nuclear-weapon States which are parties to the Treaty on the Non-Proliferation of Nuclear Weapons);

(b) nevertheless, even within this framework, the nuclear-weapon States have reserved the right to use nuclear weapons in certain circumstances; and

(c) these reservations met with no objection from the parties to the Tlatelolco or Rarotonga Treaties or from the Security Council.

63. These two treaties, the security assurances given in 1995 by the nuclear-weapon States and the fact that the Security Council took note of them with satisfaction, testify to a growing awareness of the need to liberate the community of States and the international public from the dangers resulting from the existence of nuclear weapons. The Court moreover notes the signing, even more recently, on 15 December 1995, at Bangkok, of a Treaty on the Southeast Asia Nuclear-Weapon-Free Zone, and on 11 April 1996, at Cairo, of a treaty on the creation of a nuclear-weapons-free zone in Africa. It does not, however, view these elements as amounting to a comprehensive and universal conventional prohibition on the use, or the threat of use, of those weapons as such.

64. The Court will now turn to an examination of customary international law to determine whether a prohibition of the threat or use of nuclear weapons as such flows from that source of law. As the Court has stated, the substance of that law must be "looked for primarily in the

---

[26] *Ed.* 788 U.N.T.S. 169; U.K.T.S. 96 (1970), Cmnd. 4503.

actual practice and *opinio juris* of States" (*Continental Shelf (Libyan Arab Jamahiriya/Malta), Judgment, I.C.J. Reports 1985*, p. 29, para. 27).

65. States which hold the view that the use of nuclear weapons is illegal ... refer to a consistent practice of non-utilization of nuclear weapons by States since 1945 and they would see in that practice the expression of an *opinio juris* on the part of those who possess such weapons.

66. Some other States, which assert the legality of the threat and use of nuclear weapons in certain circumstances, invoked the doctrine and practice of deterrence in support of their argument. They recall that they have always, in concert with certain other States, reserved the right to use those weapons in the exercise of the right to self-defence against an armed attack threatening their vital security interests. In their view, if nuclear weapons have not been used since 1945, it is not on account of an existing or nascent custom but merely because circumstances that might justify their use have fortunately not arisen.

67. The Court does not intend to pronounce here upon the practice known as the "policy of deterrence". It notes that it is a fact that a number of States adhered to that practice during the greater part of the Cold War and continue to adhere to it. Furthermore, the Members of the inter-national community are profoundly divided on the matter of whether non-recourse to nuclear weapons over the past fifty years constitutes the expression of an *opinio juris*. Under these circumstances the Court does not consider itself able to find that there is such an *opinio juris* ...

70. The Court notes that General Assembly resolutions, even if they are not binding, may sometimes have normative value. They can, in certain circumstances, provide evidence important for establishing the existence of a rule or the emergence of an *opinio juris*. To establish whether this is true of a given General Assembly resolution, it is necessary to look at its content and the conditions of its adoption; it is also necessary to see whether an *opinio juris* exists as to its normative character. Or a series of resolutions may show the gradual evolution of the *opinio juris* required for the establishment of a new rule.

71. Examined in their totality, the General Assembly resolutions put before the Court declare that the use of nuclear weapons would be "a direct violation of the Charter of the United Nations"; and in certain formulations that such use "should be prohibited". The focus of these resolutions has sometimes shifted to diverse related matters; however, several of the resolutions under consideration in the present case have been adopted with substantial numbers of negative votes and absten-tions; thus, although those resolutions are a clear sign of deep concern regarding the problem of nuclear weapons, they still fall short of estab-lishing the existence of an *opinio juris* on the illegality of the use of such weapons.

72. The Court further notes that the first of the resolutions of the General Assembly expressly proclaiming the illegality of the use of nuclear weapons, resolution 1653 (XVI) of 24 November 1961 (mentioned

in subsequent resolutions), after referring to certain international declarations and binding agreements, from the Declaration of St. Petersburg of 1868 to the Geneva Protocol of 1925, proceeded to qualify the legal nature of nuclear weapons, determine their effects, and apply general rules of customary international law to nuclear weapons in particular. That application by the General Assembly of general rules of customary law to the particular case of nuclear weapons indicates that, in its view, there was no specific rule of customary law which prohibited the use of nuclear weapons; if such a rule had existed, the General Assembly could simply have referred to it and would not have needed to undertake such an exercise of legal qualification.

73. Having said this, the Court points out that the adoption each year by the General Assembly, by a large majority, of resolutions recalling the content of resolution 1653 (XVI), and requesting the member States to conclude a convention prohibiting the use of nuclear weapons in any circumstance, reveals the desire of a very large section of the international community to take, by a specific and express prohibition of the use of nuclear weapons, a significant step forward along the road to complete nuclear disarmament. The emergence, as *lex lata*, of a customary rule specifically prohibiting the use of nuclear weapons as such is hampered by the continuing tensions between the nascent *opinio juris* on the one hand, and the still strong adherence to the practice of deterrence on the other.

The Court then considered whether the use of nuclear weapons was consistent with international humanitarian law and the law of neutrality.

90. Although the applicability of the principles and rules of humanitarian law and of the principle of neutrality to nuclear weapons is hardly disputed, the conclusions to be drawn from this applicability are, on the other hand, controversial.

91. According to one point of view, the fact that recourse to nuclear weapons is subject to and regulated by the law of armed conflict does not necessarily mean that such recourse is as such prohibited. As one State put it to the Court: ...

the legality of the use of nuclear weapons must therefore be assessed in the light of the applicable principles of international law regarding the use of force and the conduct of hostilities, as is the case with other methods and means of warfare (United Kingdom, Written Statement, p. 75, para. 4.2(3)); and

The reality ... is that nuclear weapons might be used in a wide variety of circumstances with very different results in terms of likely civilian casualties. In some cases, such as the use of a low yield nuclear weapon against warships on the High Seas or troops in sparsely populated areas, it is possible to envisage a nuclear attack which caused comparatively few civilian casualties. It is by no means the case that every use of nuclear weapons against a military objective would inevitably cause very great collateral civilian casualties. (United Kingdom, Written Statement, p. 53, para. 3.70; see also United States of America, Oral Statement, CR 95/34, pp. 89–90.)

92. Another view holds that recourse to nuclear weapons could never be compatible with the principles and rules of humanitarian law and is therefore prohibited. In the event of their use, nuclear weapons would in all circumstances be unable to draw any distinction between the civilian population and combatants, or between civilian objects and military objectives, and their effects, largely uncontrollable, could not be restricted, either in time or in space, to lawful military targets. Such weapons would kill and destroy in a necessarily indiscriminate manner, on account of the blast, heat and radiation occasioned by the nuclear explosion and the effects induced; and the number of casualties which would ensue would be enormous. The use of nuclear weapons would therefore be prohibited in any circumstance, notwithstanding the absence of any explicit conventional prohibition. That view lay at the basis of the assertions by certain States before the Court that nuclear weapons are by their nature illegal under customary international law, by virtue of the fundamental principle of humanity. . . .

94. The Court would observe that none of the States advocating the legality of the use of nuclear weapons under certain circumstances, including the "clean" use of smaller, low yield, tactical nuclear weapons, has indicated what, supposing such limited use were feasible, would be the precise circumstances justifying such use; nor whether such limited use would not tend to escalate into the all-out use of high yield nuclear weapons. This being so, the Court does not consider that it has a sufficient basis for a determination on the validity of this view.

95. Nor can the Court make a determination on the validity of the view that the recourse to nuclear weapons would be illegal in any circumstance owing to their inherent and total incompatibility with the law applicable in armed conflict. Certainly, as the Court has already indicated, the principles and rules of law applicable in armed conflict—at the heart of which is the overriding consideration of humanity—make the conduct of armed hostilities subject to a number of strict requirements. Thus, methods and means of warfare, which would preclude any distinction between civilian and military targets, or which would result in unnecessary suffering to combatants are prohibited. In view of the unique characteristics of nuclear weapons, to which the Court has referred above, the use of such weapons in fact seems scarcely reconcilable with respect for such requirements. Nevertheless, the Court considers that it does not have sufficient elements to enable it to conclude with certainty that the

use of nuclear weapons would necessarily be at variance with the principles and rules of law applicable in armed conflict in any circumstance.

96. Furthermore, the Court cannot lose sight of the fundamental right of every State to survival, and thus its right to resort to self-defence, in accordance with Article 51 of the Charter, when its survival is at stake.

Nor can it ignore the practice referred to as "policy of deterrence", to which an appreciable section of the international community adhered for many years. The Court also notes the reservations which certain nuclear-weapon States have appended to the undertakings they have given, notably under the Protocols to the Treaties of Tlatelolco and Rarotonga, and also under the declarations made by them in connection with the extension of the Treaty on the Non-Proliferation of Nuclear Weapons, not to resort to such weapons.

97. Accordingly, in view of the present state of international law viewed as a whole, as examined above by the Court, and of the elements of fact at its disposal, the Court is led to observe that it cannot reach a definitive conclusion as to the legality or illegality of the use of nuclear weapons by a State in an extreme circumstance of self-defence, in which its very survival would be at stake.

98. ...international law, and with it the stability of the international order which it is intended to govern, are bound to suffer from the continuing difference of views with regard to the legal status of weapons as deadly as nuclear weapons. It is consequently important to put an end to this state of affairs: the long-promised complete nuclear disarmament appears to be the most appropriate means of achieving that result. ...

99. In these circumstances, the Court appreciates the full importance of the recognition by Article VI of the Treaty on the Non-Proliferation of Nuclear Weapons of an obligation to negotiate in good faith a nuclear disarmament. ... The legal import of that obligation goes beyond that of a mere obligation of conduct; the obligation involved here is an obligation to achieve a precise result—nuclear disarmament in all its aspects—by adopting a particular course of conduct, namely, the pursuit of negotiations on the matter in good faith.

100. ...In the view of the Court, [its fulfilment] remains without any doubt an objective of vital importance to the whole of the international community today. ...

105. For these reasons,

THE COURT ...

(2) *Replies* in the following manner to the question put by the General Assembly:

A. Unanimously,

There is in neither customary nor conventional international law any specific authorization of the threat or use of nuclear weapons;

B. By eleven votes to three,[27]

There is in neither customary nor conventional international law any comprehensive and universal prohibition of the threat or use of nuclear weapons as such; ...

C. Unanimously,

A threat or use of force by means of nuclear weapons that is contrary to Article 2, paragraph 4, of the United Nations Charter and that fails to meet all the requirements of Article 51 is unlawful;

D. Unanimously,

A threat or use of nuclear weapons should also be compatible with the requirements of the international law applicable in armed conflict, particularly those of the principles and rules of international humanitarian law, as well as with specific obligations under treaties and other undertakings which expressly deal with nuclear weapons;

E. By seven votes to seven, by the President's casting vote,[28]

It follows from the above-mentioned requirements that the threat or use of nuclear weapons would generally be contrary to the rules of international law applicable in armed conflict, and in particular the principles and rules of humanitarian law;

However, in view of the current state of international law, and of the elements of fact at its disposal, the Court cannot conclude definitively whether the threat or use of nuclear weapons would be lawful or unlawful in an extreme circumstance of self-defence, in which the very survival of a State would be at stake;

F. Unanimously,

There exists an obligation to pursue in good faith and bring to a conclusion negotiations leading to nuclear disarmament in all its aspects under strict and effective international control.

---

[27] Judges Shahabuddeen, Weeramantry and Koroma dissented.
[28] In favour: President Bedjaoui; Judges Ranjeva, Herczegh, Shi, Fleischhauer, Vereschetin, Ferrari Bravo. Against: Vice-President Schwebel; Judges Oda, Guillaume, Shahabuddeen, Weeramantry, Koroma, Higgins.

Dissenting Opinion of Judge Higgins

7. I have not been able to vote for these findings [in paragraph 2E of the *dispositif*] for several reasons. It is an essential requirement of the judicial process that a court should show the steps by which it reaches its conclusions. I believe the Court has not done so in respect of the first part of paragraph 2E. The findings in a judicial *dispositif* should be clear. I believe paragraph 2E is unclear in its meaning (and one may suspect that this lack of clarity is perhaps regarded as a virtue). I greatly regret the *non liquet* offered in the second part of paragraph 2E. ...

8. After finding that the threat or use of nuclear weapons is not prohibited *per se* by reference to the Charter or treaty law, the Court moves to see if it is prohibited *per se* by reference to the law of armed conflict (and especially humanitarian law).

9. It is not sufficient, to answer the question put to it, for the Court merely briefly to state the requirements of the law of armed conflict (including humanitarian law) and then simply to move to the conclusion that the threat or use of nuclear weapons is generally unlawful by reference to these principles and norms. The Court limits itself to affirming that the principles and rules of humanitarian law apply to nuclear weapons. It finds in paragraph 95, by reference to "the unique characteristics of nuclear weapons", that their use is "scarcely reconcilable" with the requirements of humanitarian law and "would generally be contrary" to humanitarian law (*dispositif*, para. 2E). At no point in its Opinion does the Court engage in the task that is surely at the heart of the question asked: the systematic application of the relevant law to the use or threat of nuclear weapons. It reaches its conclusions without the benefit of detailed analysis. An essential step in the judicial process–that of legal reasoning—has been omitted. ...

25. I do not consider it juridically meaningful to say that the use of nuclear weapons is "generally contrary to the rules of international law applicable in armed conflict, and in particular the principles and rules of humanitarian law". What does the term "generally" mean? Is it a numerical allusion, or is it a reference to different types of nuclear weapons, or is it a suggestion that the rules of humanitarian law cannot be met save for exceptions? If so, where is the Court's analysis of these rules, properly understood, and their application to nuclear weapons? And what are any exceptions to be read into the term "generally"? Are they to be linked to an exceptional ability to comply with humanitarian law? Or does the term "generally", especially in the light of paragraph 96, suggest that if a use of nuclear weapons in extreme circumstances of self-defence were lawful, that might *of itself* exceptionally make such a use compatible with the humanitarian law? The phraseology of paragraph 2E of the *dispositif* raises all these questions and answers none of them. ...

27. The meaning of the second sentence of paragraph 2E of the *dispositif*, and thus what the two sentences of paragraph 2E of the *dispositif*

mean when taken together, is unclear. The second sentence is presumably not referring to self-defence in those exceptional circumstances, implied by the word "generally", that might allow a threat or use of nuclear weapons to be compatible with humanitarian law. If, as the Court has indicated in paragraph 42 (and operative paragraph 2C), the Charter law does not *per se* make a use of nuclear weapons illegal, and if a specific use complied with the provisions of Article 51 *and* was also compatible with humanitarian law, the Court can hardly be saying in the second sentence of paragraph 2E that it knows not whether such a use would be lawful or unlawful.

28. Therefore it seems the Court is addressing the "general" circumstances that it envisages—namely that a threat or use of nuclear weapons violates humanitarian law—and that it is addressing whether in *those* circumstances a use of force *in extremis* and in conformity with Article 51° of the Charter, might nonetheless be regarded as be lawful, or not. The Court answers that it does not know.

29. What the Court has done is reach a conclusion of "incompatibility in general" with humanitarian law; and then effectively pronounce a *non liquet* on whether a use of nuclear weapons in self-defence when the survival of a State is at issue might still be lawful, even were the particular use to be contrary to humanitarian law. Through this formula of non-pronouncement the Court necessarily leaves open the possibility that a use of nuclear weapons contrary to humanitarian law might nonetheless be lawful. This goes beyond anything that was claimed by the nuclear weapons States appearing before the Court, who fully accepted that any lawful threat or use of nuclear weapons would have to comply with both the *jus ad bellum* and the *jus in bello* (see para. 86). . . .

32. Can the reference to "the current state of international law" [in paragraph 2E] possibly refer to humanitarian law? . . . [H]umanitarian law . . . is very well-developed. The fact that its principles are broadly stated and often raise further questions that require a response can be no ground for a *non liquet*. It is exactly the judicial function to take principles of general application, to elaborate their meaning and to apply them to specific situations. This is precisely the role of the International Court, whether in contentious proceedings or in its advisory function.

33. Perhaps the reference to "the current state of international law" is a reference to perceived tensions between the widespread acceptance of the possession of nuclear weapons (and thus, it may be presumed, of the legality of their use in certain circumstances) as mentioned by the Court in paragraphs 67 and 96 on the one hand, and the requirements of humanitarian law on the other. If so, I believe this to be a false dichotomy. The pursuit of deterrence, the shielding under the nuclear umbrella, the silent acceptance of reservations and declarations by the nuclear powers to treaties prohibiting the use of nuclear weapons in certain regions, the seeking of possible security assurances—all this points to a significant international practice which is surely relevant not only to the law of self-

defence but also to humanitarian law. If a substantial number of States in the international community believe that the use of nuclear weapons might *in extremis* be compatible with their duties under the Charter (whether as nuclear powers or as beneficiaries of "the umbrella" or security assurances) they presumably *also* believe that they would not be violating their duties under humanitarian law.

34. Nothing in relevant statements made suggests that those States giving nuclear assurances or receiving them believed that they would be violating humanitarian law,—but decided nonetheless to act in disregard of such violation. In sum, such weight as may be given to the State practice just referred to has a relevance for our understanding of the complex provisions of humanitarian law as much as for the provisions of the Charter law of self-defence.

35. For all of these reasons, I am unable to see why the Court resorts to the answer it does in the second part of paragraph 2E of the *dispositif*.

36. It is also, I think, an important and well-established principle that the concept of *non liquet*—for that is what we have here—is no part of the Court's jurisprudence. . . .

38. This unwelcome formulation ignores sixty-five years of proud judicial history and also the convictions of those who went before us. Former President of the International Court, Judge Elias, reminds us that there are what he terms "useful devices" to assist if there are difficulties in applying the usual sources of international law. In his view these "preclude the Court from pleading *non liquet* in any given case" (Elias, *The International Court of Justice and Some Contemporary Problems.* 1983, p. 14).

39. The learned editors of the 9th Edition of *Oppenheim's International Law* remind us:

> there is [not] always a clear and specific legal rule readily applicable to every international situation, but that every international situation is capable of being determined *as a matter of law* (Jennings and Watts, Vol. 1, p. 13). . . .

41. . . .The judicial lodestar, whether in difficult questions of interpretation of humanitarian law, or in resolving claimed tensions between competing norms, must be those values that international law seeks to promote and protect. In the present case, it is the physical survival of peoples that we must constantly have in view. We live in a decentralized world order, in which some States are known to possess nuclear weapons but choose to remain outside of the non-proliferation treaty system; while other such non-parties have declared their intention to obtain nuclear weapons; and yet other States are believed clandestinely to possess, or to be working shortly to possess nuclear weapons (some of whom indeed may be party to the NPT). It is not clear to me that either a pronouncement of illegality in all circumstances of the use of nuclear weapons or the

answers formulated by the Court in paragraph 2E best serve to protect mankind against that unimaginable suffering that we all fear.

Dissenting Opinion of Vice-President Schwebel

More than any case in the history of the Court, this proceeding presents a titanic tension between State practice and legal principle. It is accordingly the more important not to confuse the international law we have with the international law we need. ...

The essence of the problem is this. Fifty years of the practice of States does not debar, and to that extent supports, the legality of the threat or use of nuclear weapons in certain circumstances. At the same time, principles of international humanitarian law which antedate that practice govern the use of all weapons including nuclear weapons, and it is extraordinarily difficult to reconcile the use—at any rate, some uses—of nuclear weapons with the application of those principles. ...

State practice demonstrates that nuclear weapons have been manufactured and deployed by States for some 50 years; that in that deployment inheres a threat of possible use; and that the international community, by treaty and through action of the United Nations Security Council, has, far from proscribing the threat or use of nuclear weapons in all circumstances, recognized in effect or in terms that in certain circumstances nuclear weapons may be used or their use threatened.

No only have the nuclear Powers avowedly and for decades, with vast effort and expense, manufactured, maintained and deployed nuclear weapons. They have affirmed that they are legally entitled to use nuclear weapons in certain circumstances and to threaten their use. They have threatened their use by the hard facts and inexorable implications of the possession and deployment of nuclear weapons; by a posture of readiness to launch nuclear weapons 365 days a year, 24 hours of every day; by the military plans, strategic and tactical, developed and sometimes publicly revealed by them; and, in a very few international crises, by threatening the use of nuclear weapons. In the very doctrine and practice of deterrence, the threat of the possible use of nuclear weapons inheres.

This nuclear practice is not a practice of a lone and secondary persistent objector. This is not a practice of a pariah Government crying out in the wilderness of otherwise adverse international opinion. This is the practice of five of the world's major Powers, of the permanent Members of the Security Council, significantly supported for almost 50 years by their allies and other States sheltering under their nuclear umbrellas. That is to say, it is the practice of States—and a practice supported by a large and weighty number of other States—that together represent the bulk of the world's military and economic and financial and technological power and a very large proportion of its population. This practice has been recognized, accommodated and in some measure accepted by the international community. That measure of acceptance is ambiguous but not meaningless. It is obvious that the alliance structures that have been predicated upon the deployment of nuclear weapons accept the legality of their use in certain circumstances. But what may be less obvious is the effect of the Non-Proliferation Treaty and the structure of negative and positive security assurances extended by the nuclear Powers and accepted by the Security Council in pursuance of that Treaty, as well as of reservations by nuclear Powers adhering to regional treaties that govern the possession, deployment and use of nuclear weapons. . . .

While it is not difficult to conclude that the principles of international humanitarian law—above all, proportionality in the application of force, and discrimination between military and civilian targets—govern the use of nuclear weapons, it does not follow that the application of those principles to the threat or use of nuclear weapons "in any circumstance" is easy. Cases at the extremes are relatively clear; cases closer to the centre of the spectrum of possible uses are less so.

At one extreme is the use of strategic nuclear weapons in quantities against enemy cities and industries. This so-called "countervalue" use (as contrasted with "counterforce" used directly only against enemy nuclear forces and installations) could cause an enormous number of deaths and injuries, running in some cases into the millions; and, in addition to those immediately affected by the heat and blast of those weapons, vast numbers could be affected, many fatally, by spreading radiation. Large-scale "exchanges" of such nuclear weaponry could destroy not only cities but countries, and render continents, perhaps the whole of the earth, uninhabitable, if not at once then through longer-range effects of nuclear fallout. It cannot be accepted that the use of nuclear weapons on a scale which would—or could—result in the deaths of many millions in indiscriminate inferno and by far-reaching fallout, have profoundly pernicious effects in space and time, and render uninhabitable much or all of the earth, could be lawful.

At the other extreme is the use of tactical nuclear weapons against discrete military or naval targets so situated that substantial civilian casualties would not ensue. For example, the use of a nuclear depth-charge to destroy a nuclear submarine that is about to fire nuclear missiles, or has fired one or more of a number of its nuclear missiles, might well be lawful. By the circumstance of its use, the nuclear depth-charge would not give rise to immediate civilian casualties. It would easily meet the test of proportionality; the damage that the submarine's missiles could inflict on the population and territory of the target State would infinitely outweigh that entailed in the destruction of the submarine and its crew. The submarine's destruction by a nuclear weapon would produce radiation in the sea, but far less than the radiation that firing of its missiles would produce on and over land. Nor is it as certain that the use of a conventional depth-charge would discharge the mission successfully; the far greater force of a nuclear weapon could ensure destruction of the submarine whereas a conventional depth-charge might not.

An intermediate case would be the use of nuclear weapons to destroy an enemy army situated in a desert. In certain circumstances, such a use of nuclear weapons might meet the tests of discrimination and proportionality; in others not. The argument that the use of nuclear weapons is inevitably disproportionate raises troubling questions, which the British Attorney General addressed in the Court's oral proceedings in these terms:

> If one is to speak of "disproportionality", the question arises: disproportionate to what? The answer must be "to the threat posed to the victim State". It is by reference to that threat that proportionality must be measured. So one has to look at all the circumstances, in particular the scale, kind and location of the threat. To assume that any defensive use of nuclear weapons must be disproportionate, no matter how serious the threat to the safety and the very survival of the State resorting to such use, is wholly unfounded. Moreover, it suggests an overbearing assumption by the critics of nuclear weapons that they can determine in advance that no threat, including a nuclear, chemical or biological threat, is ever worth the use of any nuclear weapon. It cannot be right to say that if an aggressor hits hard enough, his victim loses the right to take the only measure by which he can defend himself and reverse the aggression. That would not be the rule of law. It would be an aggressor's charter.

Referring then to paragraph 2E of the *dispositif*, Judge Schwebel continued:

> This is an astounding conclusion to be reached by the International Court of Justice. Despite the fact that its Statute "forms an integral part" of the United Nations Charter, and despite the comprehensive and categorical terms of Article 2, paragraph 4, and Article 51 of that Charter, the Court concludes on the supreme issue of the threat or use of force of our age that it has no opinion. In "an extreme circumstance of self-defence, in which the very survival of a State would be at stake" the Court finds that international law and hence the Court have nothing to say. After many months of agonizing appraisal of the law, the Court discovers that there is none. When it comes to the supreme interests of State, the Court discards the legal progress of the Twentieth Century, put aside the provisions of the Charter of the United Nations of which it is "the principal judicial organ", and proclaims, in terms redolent of *Realpolitik*, its ambivalence about the most important provisions of modern international law. If this was to be its ultimate holding, the Court would have done better to have drawn on its undoubted discretion not to render an Opinion at all.

. . .

Notes

1. Was it an abdication of responsibility for the Court not to express an opinion (see para. 2E, *dispositif*) on the question whether the threat or use of nuclear

weapons "would be lawful or unlawful in an extreme circumstance of self-defence"? If the leading world powers take the view, as they do, that they may lawfully use nuclear weapons in self-defence as a last resort, can this be contrary to customary international law? Nuclear weapons were used at Hiroshima, *inter alia*, to bring the Second World War with Japan to an end without the loss of military lives that further conventional armed force would entail. Would such a use now be illegal?

2. The request for the above advisory opinion by the UN General Assembly had been preceded by a similar request for an advisory opinion by the General Assembly of the World Health Organisation (WHO). The Court declined to give an opinion in respect of the WHO request for jurisdictional reasons: see below, p. 1036.

2. COLLECTIVE MEASURES THROUGH THE UNITED NATIONS[29]

(i) ACTION UNDER CHAPTER VI

See Chapter VI, United Nations Charter, below Appendix I.

Note

Who can seise the Security Council of a situation or dispute under Chapter VI? What powers of action has the Security Council under Chapter VI?[30] Can it take decisions binding upon member states?

(ii) SECURITY COUNCIL ACTION UNDER CHAPTER VII: JURISDICTION

See Article 39, United Nations Charter, below, Appendix I.

THE SPANISH QUESTION

S.C.O.R., 1st Year, 1st Series, 47th Meeting, pp. 370–376, June 18, 1946

In April 1946, the representative of Poland in the Security Council, invoking Article 2(6), 34 and 35 of the Charter, raised before the Council the situation in Spain and submitted a draft resolution asking the Council to declare "that the existence and activities of the Franco régime in Spain have led to international friction and endangered international peace and security" and asking it to call upon, "in accordance with Articles 39 and 41 of the Charter, all Members of the United Nations who maintain diplomatic relations with the Franco Government to sever such relations immediately."

A Sub-Committee, which was appointed to determine whether the Franco régime had the effect attributed to it in the draft resolution, concluded: " . . . although the activities of the Franco régime do not at present constitute an existing threat to the peace within the meaning of Article 39 of the Charter and

---

[29] See Murphy, *The United Nations and the Control of International Violence* (1983); White, *Keeping the Peace* (1993).
[30] For commentaries on the key UN Charter Articles, see Goodrich, Hambro and Simons, *op. cit.*, p. 863, n. 22, above, and Simma, ed., *The Charter of the United Nations* (1994).

therefore the Security Council has no jurisdiction to direct or authorise enforcement measures under Article 40 or 42, nevertheless such activities do constitute a situation "likely to endanger the maintenance of international peace and security," within the meaning of Article 34 of the Charter. . . . The Security Council is therefore empowered by paragraph 1 of Article 36 to recommend procedures or methods of adjustment in order to improve the situation mentioned. . . . [31] The representative of Poland, Mr Lange on the Sub-Committee filed a reservation concerning this conclusion.[32] The question was discussed in the Security Council when the report was presented to it.

MR. LANGE (POLAND). The report of the Sub-Committee makes a distinction between a potential and an actual threat to peace, and then interprets Article 39 to mean that the term "threat to the peace" used there refers only to an actual threat and not to a potential threat. I find it impossible to make sense of such a distinction. Any threat to the peace is potential by nature. It may mature tomorrow, after tomorrow, or in five years. It is a question of time. If the threat to the peace is no longer potential, then we have to do with actual aggression.

. . . Under this narrow interpretation of Article 39, namely, that it does not cover a potential threat to the peace, the Security Council would be unable to act in such cases as that of Fascist Italy prior to the actual invasion of Ethiopia, or Nazi Germany prior to the actual dropping of bombs on Polish cities.

It would seem, moreover, that the sanctions enumerated in Article 41 clearly indicate that when Article 39 speaks of a threat to peace, it refers not only to an act of aggression which has already been committed or to a threat which might materialise in a few weeks or months, but to any threat, however potential. Otherwise such sanctions as the interruption of postal, telegraphic, radio and other means of communication and the severance of diplomatic relations would have no meaning. If the threat to the peace is so immediate that it is about to materialise into actual warfare, the only sanctions which have any meaning are military sanctions. Article 41, however, clearly sets out weaker forms of sanctions, and I think we have to keep this in mind in our interpretation of Article 39.

THE PRESIDENT (MR. PARODI, FRANCE). . . . [The representative of Poland's] reservation places a special interpretation on the recommendation contained in the report; he takes the recommendation to imply that the Security Council has no direct jurisdiction to act in cases where the threats to peace are only potential. Article 39 of the Charter contains the word "threat"; by itself, this word seems to me to imply necessarily a state of affairs which is no more than a virtual possibility. So long as there is no act of aggression and so long as there is only a threat, such a threat

---

[31] Report of the Sub-Committee on the Spanish Question, S.C.O.R., 1st Year, 1st Ser., Sp. Supp., p. 5. The Sub-Committee was composed of representatives of Australia, Brazil, China, France and Poland.

[32] *ibid.* p. 6.

is perforce contingent, latent or, in other words, "potential." The French text of Article 34 of the Charter, however, contains the words "si . . . cette situation semble devoir menacer le maintien de la paix," and the English text speaks of a situation "likely to endanger . . . peace." Consequently Article 34 of the Charter also refers to a threatening or dangerous situation.

If the two articles of the Charter referred to are compared, it seems to me that the report merely meant to say that we ought to rely on Article 39 or Article 34, according to whether the threat is more or less remote, or more or less imminent. The report relies on Article 34, because of its estimate of the facts and as a result of assessing the more or less imminent nature of the threat.

Notes

1. The Polish draft resolution failed to obtain a majority. The proposal to consider the matter under Chapter VI obtained a majority but was vetoed by the USSR. Consequently the Spanish Question was not debated.

2. Often the Security Council acts under Chapter VII without discussing the question of jurisdiction under Article 39 at all, let alone deciding upon which part of Article 39—"breach of the peace," etc.—its jurisdiction is founded. In so far as the Security Council does discuss or decide these questions, it is difficult to rationalise its practice because of the influence of political considerations.

3. *Threat to the peace.* This requires a threat to *international* peace, although this limitation was reduced in significance by the Security Council's practice in respect of Southern Africa, in which it characterised two essentially internal situations—those in Southern Rhodesia and South Africa—as threatening international peace and security because of the potential for international conflict resulting from the existence and policies of racist régimes surrounded or bordered by black Africa.[33] In the case of Southern Rhodesia, in its first resolution[34] on November 12, 1965, no mention was made by the Security Council of a threat to the peace. In the second,[35] on November 20, 1965, the Council "[d]etermines that the situation resulting from the proclamation of independence by the illegal authorities in Southern Rhodesia is extremely grave . . . and that its continuance in time constitutes a threat to international peace and security." In the third,[36] on April 9, 1966, the Council, having noted in the preamble that there had developed a real threat of substantial supplies of oil reaching the illegal Government of Southern Rhodesia, thereby encouraging it and prolonging its life," "[d]etermines that the resulting situation constitutes a threat to the peace." In the fourth[37] on December 16, 1966, the Council "[a]cting in accordance with Articles 39 and 41 of the United Nations Charter, 1. *Determines* that the present situation in Southern Rhodesia constitutes a threat to international peace and security." *cf.* the similar development in the resolutions leading to the imposition of mandatory economic sanctions against South Africa, see below, p. 966. Bearing in mind the *Spanish*

---

[33] Note also that the civil war situation in the Congo in 1960–61 was found to be a "threat to international peace and security": S.C. Resn. 161, S.C.O.R., *Resolutions and Decisions*, p. 2 (1961). White, *op. cit.*, p. 940, n. 29, above, p. 36, states that "the civil war could suck in outside forces including the superpowers, and that was why . . . [it] was a threat to international peace."

[34] Resn 216, see below, p. 963.

[35] Resn 217, see below, p. 963.

[36] Resn 221, see below, p. 965.

[37] Resn 232, see below, p. 966.

Question case, above, how imminent was the threat to the peace in either the Southern Rhodesian or South African cases? How far can the precedents they establish[38] be applied to other internal situations? To any government that provokes its neighbours, intentionally or otherwise? To any civil conflict that has repercussions for a neighbour (*e.g.* the *Bangladesh* case, see above, p. 892)? Note that the Southern Rhodesian and South African cases indicate that jurisdiction under Article 39 is not co-terminous with a breach of Article 2(4). Note also that whereas all "acts of aggression" (at least under the General Assembly definition, see below) and "breaches of the peace" will be a breach of Article 2(4), a "threat to the peace" of the Southern Rhodesian or South African kind will not.[39] It has been suggested that economic or political coercion could amount to a "threat to the peace."[40]

Other more recent cases have confirmed this wide reading of the concept of a threat to international peace. Thus the situations in Bosnia and Herezegovina, above, p. 922, Somalia, above, p. 922 and Rwanda above, p, 923 were regarded as a threat to the peace because of the possible effects of the conflict beyond the state's borders. Two other cases that push the Security Council's Chapter VII jurisdiction to its limits are the *Haiti* and *Lockerbie* cases, below.[41]

Haiti. In 1991, a military coup overthrew the democratically elected government of President Aristide, who went into exile in the United States. After OAS initiatives and sanctions had failed, in 1993 sanctions were imposed by the Security Council, acting under Chapter VII, that were aimed at restoring the legitimate government.[42] In October 1993, by Resolution 875,[43] having determined that the situation in Haiti constituted a "threat to the peace", the Security Council:

> *Calls upon* Member States, acting nationally or through regional agencies or arrangements, cooperating with the legitimate Government of Haiti, to use *such measures commensurate with the specific circumstances as may be necessary* under the authority of the Security Council to ensure strict implementation of the provisions of Resolution 841 and 873 relating to the supply of petroleum or petroleum products or arms and related material of all types, and in particular to halt inward maritime shipping as necessary in order to inspect and verify their cargoes and destinations.

On the day of the adoption of Resolution 875, United States warships were put on station off Haiti to impose a maritime embargo. The UN sanctions, not having proved immediately effective, in May 1994, the Security Council, still acting under Chapter VII, adopted Resolution 940.[44] By this, the Council

> *authorized* Member States to form a multilateral force under unified command and control and, in this framework, *to use all necessary means* to facilitate the departure from Haiti of the military leadership . . . , the prompt return to the legitimately elected president and the restoration of the legitimate authorities of the Government of Haiti, and to establish and maintain a secure and stable

---

[38] For doubts as to their constitutionality, see Gross (1978) 49 B.Y.I.L. 223, 228.

[39] Other more immediate threats of the use of armed force (*e.g.* an ultimatum) will be.

[40] See Broms, *loc. cit.*, p. 948, n. 52, p. 386 (economic coercion) and Goodrich, Hambro and Simons, in the passage quoted above, p. 863 (economic and political coercion). Broms also suggests that economic coercion could be a breach of the peace.

[41] On the Security Council's jurisdiction to establish the International Criminal Tribunal for the Former Yugoslavia, see above, p. 753.

[42] See S.C. Resolutions 841 and 873, S.C.O.R., *Resolutions and Decisions*, 1993, pp. 119, 125.

[43] *ibid.* p. 125.

[44] S.C.O.R., *Resolutions and Decisions*, 1994, p. 77. Adopted by 12 votes to 0, with 2 abstentions (China and Brazil; Rwanda did not participate).

environment that will permit the implementation of the Governors Island Agreement [to restore the legitimate Government] . . .

On the basis of Resolution 940, in September 1994, a UN multi-national force, that was United States led and composed entirely of United States troops, was sent to Haiti. In October, the President Aristide returned to Haiti on a United States plane to replace the revolutionary government.

What was the threat to international peace in the Haitian case?[45]

Lockerbie. The facts of the *Lockerbie* and *Niger* air sabotage cases are explained above, p. 306. As noted there, when Libya did not respond to requests to return the two Libyan accused for trial, the United States, the United Kingdom and France took the matter to the Security Council. On January 21, 1992, in Resolution 731,[46] the Council:

> 1. *Condemns* the destruction of Pan Am flight 103 and Union de transports aériens flight 772 and the resultant loss of hundreds of lives;
> 2. *Strongly deplores* the fact that the Libyan Government has not yet responded effectively to the above requests to cooperate fully in establishing responsibility for the terrorist acts referred to above against Pan Am flight 103 and *Union de transports aériens* flight 772;
> 3. *Urges* the Libyan Government immediately to provide a full and effective response to those requests so as to contribute to the elimination of international terrorism;
> 4. *Requests* the Secretary-General to seek the cooperation of the Libyan Government to provide a full and effective response to those requests;
> 5. *Urges* all States individually and collectively to encourage the Libyan Government to respond fully and effectively to those requests;

On March 3, 1993, Libya took the case to the I.C.J. claiming a breach of the Montreal Convention, see below, p. 1041, and sought interim measures of protection. Thereupon, between the oral arguments and the decision of the Court, the three western states took the case again to the Security Council, which adopted Resolution 748[47] in their favour. By it the Council

> *Acting* under Chapter VII of the Charter,
> 1. *Decides* that the Libyan Government must now comply without any further delay with paragraph 3 of resolution 731 (1992) regarding the requests addressed to the Libyan authorities by France, the United Kingdom of Great Britain and Northern Ireland, and the United States of America,
> 2. *Decides also* that the Libyan Government must commit itself definitively to cease all forms of terrorist action and all assistance to terrorist groups and that it must promptly, by concrete actions, demonstrate its renunciation of terrorism;

Resolution 748 also imposed certain sanctions on Libya, for example by requiring all states to deny permission for aircraft to fly from their territory to Libya and to prohibit the supply of arms to Libya. Resolution 748 was made under Chapter VII on the basis that the failure of Libya "to demonstrate by concrete actions its

---

[45] See Reisman (1995) 89 A.J.I.L. 82. See also Freudenschuss, *loc. cit.*, p. 922, n. 4, above, p. 520, who notes that a number of Latin American states questioned Resolution 940, partly on jurisdictional grounds. On the *Haitian* case generally, see Weller, ed., *The Haitian Crisis in International Law* (1995).

[46] S.C.O.R., *Resolutions and Decisions*, 1992, p. 51. Adopted unanimously.

[47] *ibid.* p. 52.

renunciation of terrorism and in particular its continued failure to respond fully and effectively to the requests in Resolution 731 (1992) constitute a threat to international peace and security" (preamble).[47a]

In view of Resolution 748, the I.C.J. did not make an order for interim measures for the following reasons:

> 39. Whereas both Libya and the United Kingdom, as Members of the United Nations, are obliged to accept and carry out the decisions of the Security Council in accordance with Article 25 of the Charter; whereas the Court, which is at the stage of proceedings on provisional measures, considers that prima facie this obligation extends to the decision contained in resolution 748 (1992); and whereas, in accordance with Article 103 of the Charter, the obligations of the Parties in that respect prevail over their obligations under any other international agreement, including the Montreal Convention;
>
> 40. Whereas the Court, while thus not at this stage called upon to determine definitively the legal effect of Security Council resolution 748 (1992), considers that, whatever the situation previous to the adoption of that resolution, the rights claimed by Libya under the Montreal Convention cannot now be regarded as appropriate for protection by the indication of provisional measures;
>
> 41. Whereas, furthermore, an indication of the measures requested by Libya would be likely to impair the rights which appear prima facie to be enjoyed by the United Kingdom by virtue of Security Council resolution 748 (1992)

On the question of the competence of the I.C.J. to review decisions of the Security Council, which was raised by the *Lockerbie* case and by the general growth and range of activity of the Security Council following the end of the Cold War, see below, p. 1041.

4. *Breach of the peace.* A breach of the peace, which would seem to include any use of armed force, has, despite the evidence of much world conflict since 1945, rarely been found to have occurred. The only cases are the *Korean* case, below, p. 882; the *Falkland Islands War*, below, p. 855; the *Iran–Iraq War*[48] and the *Kuwait* case, below, p. 956.

RESOLUTION ON THE DEFINITION OF AGGRESSION 1974

G.A.Resolution. 3314 (XXIX). 14 December 1974. G.A.O.R. 29th Sess., Supp. 31, p. 142; (1975) 69 A.J.I.L. 480

The General Assembly adopts the following definition of Aggression:

Article 1

Aggression is the use of armed force by a State against the sovereignty, territorial integrity or political independence of another State, or in any

---

[47a] *cf.* S.C. Resns 1044, 1054 and 1070 (1996), UN Doc SC/6315, pp. 13 *et seq.*, imposing sanctions on Sudan for failure to extradite terrorists suspected of attempting to assassinate the Egyptian President.

[48] S.C. Resn 598 (1987), S.C.O.R., 42nd Year., *Resolutions and Decisions*, p. 5; (1987) 26 I.L.M. 1479.

other manner inconsistent with the Charter of the United Nations, as set out in this Definition.

Explanatory note: In this Definition the term "State":

    (*a*) Is used without prejudice to questions of recognition or to whether a State is a Member of the United Nations;

    (*b*) includes the concept of a "group of States" where appropriate.

Article 2

The first use of armed force by a State in contravention of the Charter shall constitute *prima facie* evidence of an act of aggression although the Security Council may, in conformity with the Charter, conclude that a determination that an act of aggression has been committed would not be justified in the light of other relevant circumstances, including the fact that the acts concerned or their consequences are not of sufficient gravity.

Article 3

Any of the following acts, regardless of a declaration of war, shall, subject to and in accordance with the provisions of Article 2, qualify as an act of aggression:

    (*a*) The invasion or attack by the armed forces of a State of the territory of another State, or any military occupation, however temporary, resulting from such invasion or attack, or an annexation by the use of force of the territory of another State or part thereof;

    (*b*) Bombardment by the armed forces of a State against the territory of another State or the use of any weapons by a State against the territory of another State;

    (*c*) The blockade of the ports or coasts of a State by the armed forces of another State; . . .

    (*e*) The use of armed forces of one State which are within the territory of another State with the agreement of the receiving State, in contravention of the conditions provided for in the agreement or any extension of their presence in such territory beyond the termination of the agreement;

    (*f*) The action of a State in allowing its territory, which it has placed at the disposal of another State, to be used by that other State for perpetrating an act of aggression against a third State[49]

    (*g*) The sending by or on behalf of a State of armed bands, groups, irregulars or mercenaries, which carry out acts of armed force against

---

[49] *Ed.* See the U.K. assistance to the U.S. in the *Libyan Air Raid* case: above, p. 913.

another State of such gravity as to amount to the acts listed above, or its substantial involvement therein.

Article 4

The acts enumerated above are not exhaustive and the Security Council may determine that other acts constitute aggression under the provisions of the Charter.

Article 5

1. No consideration of whatever nature, whether political, economic, military or otherwise, may serve as a justification for aggression.

2. A war of aggression is a crime against international peace. Aggression gives rise to international responsibility.

3. No territorial acquisition or special advantage resulting from aggression is or shall be recognized as lawful.

Article 6

Nothing in this Definition shall be construed as in any way enlarging or diminishing the scope of the Charter including its provisions concerning cases in which the use of force is lawful.

Article 7

Nothing in this Definition, and in particular Article 3, could in any way prejudice the right to self-determination, freedom and independence, as derived from the Charter, of peoples forcibly deprived of that right and referred to in the Declaration on Principles of International Law concerning Friendly Relations and Co-operation among States in accordance with the Charter of the United Nations, particularly peoples under colonial and racist régimes or other forms of alien domination; nor the right of these peoples to struggle to that end and to seek and receive support, in accordance with the principles of the Charter and in conformity with the above-mentioned Declaration.

Notes

1. The Resolution also refers to the following explanatory notes in the Report of the Special Committee on the Question of Defining Aggression[50]:

1. With reference to Article 3, paragraph (b), the Special Committee agreed that the expression "any weapons" is used without making a distinction between conventional weapons, weapons of mass destruction and any other kind of weapon.

2. With reference to Article 5, paragraph 1, the Committee had in mind, in particular, the principle contained in the Declaration on Principles of International Law concerning Friendly Relations and Co-operation among States in

[50] G.A.O.R., 29th Sess., Supp. 19 (1974).

accordance with the Charter of the United Nations according to which "No State or group of States has the right to intervene, directly, for any reason whatever, in the internal or external affairs of any other State."

3. With reference to Article 5, paragraph 2, the words "international responsibility" are used without prejudice to the scope of this term.

4. With reference to Article 5, paragraph 3, the Committee states that this paragraph should not be construed so as to prejudice the established principles of international law relating to the inadmissibility of territorial acquisition resulting from the threat or use of force.

2. The question of the definition of aggression was the subject of debate within the United Nations for over 20 years. After a long period during which the Special Committee on the Question of Defining Aggression seemed to be doing no more than going through the motions, the spirit of détente of the early 1970s led to the adoption of the present definition by the Committee and then by the General Assembly. In both cases adoption was by consensus, *i.e.* without a vote.[51] The definition has had a mixed reception.[52] It glosses over or avoids many disputed points in the interest of agreement.

3. The 1974 text contains elements of each of the two approaches to the definition of aggression that had been championed over the years of debate: the enumerative approach, by which all of the acts that constitute aggression are listed, and the general definition approach. The general definition in Article 1 follows the pattern of Article 2(4), Charter. Like Article 2(4), it is limited to armed force; despite the doubts of a number of states, it excludes economic aggression.[53] "The economic, ideological and other modes of aggression were carefully considered . . . but the result was an interpretation that they did not fall within the term 'aggression' as it had been used in the Charter."[54] Article 1 differs from Article 2(4) in that it does not control the *threat* of armed force. It seems unlikely that "sovereignty" adds anything to "political independence" in the definition. The reference to "recognition" in the explanatory note to Article 1 is intended to protect entities such as North and South Korea whose status is disputed. Article 2 is a compromise between the priority principle preferred by some states (*e.g.* the USSR) and an approach emphasising the intent and purpose of the alleged aggressor supported by others (*e.g.* the United Kingdom). "Other relevant circumstances" in Article 2 would include the intention of the state resorting to force, which might be to engage in individual or collective self-defence. To safeguard the interests of landlocked states, it was agreed that nothing in Article 3(c) "shall be construed as justification for a State to block, contrary to international law, the routes of free access of a landlocked country to and from the sea.[55] It was also agreed that nothing in Article 3(d) "shall be construed as in any way prejudicing or diminishing the authority of a coastal state to enforce its national legislation in maritime zones within the limits of its national jurisdiction provided such exercise is not inconsistent with the Charter of the United Nations."[56] This makes it clear that a coastal state is not committing aggression when, for example, it takes

---

[51] On consensus, see above, p. 18.
[52] See Broms (1977–I) 154 Hague Recueil 299; Brown-John (1977) 15 C.Y.I.L. 301; Cassin *et al.*, (1975) 16 H.I.L.J. 589; Ferencz, *Defining International Aggression* (1975) 2 Vols.; Garvey (1977) 17 Virg. J.J.I.L. 177; Stone (1977) 71 A.J.I.L. 224; *ibid. Conflict through Consensus: UN Approaches to Aggression*, (1977).
[53] See, however, Stone, n. 52 above, p. 230.
[54] Broms, *loc. cit.*, n. 52, above, p. 386.
[55] Report of the Sixth Committee of the General Assembly on the Question of Defining Aggression, December 6, 1974, UN Doc. A/9890, para. 9.
[56] *ibid.* para. 10.

action in the enforcement of an exclusive fishing zone.[57] Article 3(f)(g) covers indirect aggression, but is not as extensive as the equivalent provision in the 1970 Declaration on Principles of International Law.[58] However, Article 4 indicates that the list in Article 3 is not exhaustive. Article 5(2) distinguishes between a *"war* of aggression" and "aggression" generally and characterises only the former as criminal. The understanding would seem to have been that a war of aggression results in individual criminal responsibility under international law (as at Nuremberg) but that other, lesser forms of aggression give rise only to state responsibility of a civil kind, with an obligation only to make reparation.[59] Article 6 has in mind, but carefully avoids defining, the right to self-defence.

4. The Resolution is intended to assist the General Assembly and the Security Council by clarifying a key concept (see its use in Articles 1 and 39, Charter) in the United Nations scheme for the maintenance of international peace and security and which (like many others) is left undefined in the text of the Charter. Although a General Assembly resolution is not binding upon the Security Council, the definition has had an effect upon Security Council practice; the concept has since been referred to frequently in draft resolutions and debate and has generally "gained more substance than before."[60] The first finding by the Security Council that "aggression" had occurred was made in 1976, after the adoption of the 1974 definition, when South Africa was condemned for its "aggression" against Angola.[61]

(iii) SECURITY COUNCIL ACTION UNDER CHAPTER VII: POWERS

(a) *The Original Scheme*

See Articles 40–50, United Nations Charter, below, Appendix I.

Notes

It was originally intended that action under Chapter VII involving use of armed force, *i.e.* action under Article 42, would be effected by armed forces provided by member states in accordance with bilateral agreements between each of them and the Security Council under Article 43. With a view to arranging for such agreements, on April 30, 1947, the Military Staff Committee, having been requested by the Security Council "to examine from a military point of view the provisions contained in Article 43 of the Charter, and to submit the results of the Study and any recommendations to the Council in due course,"[62] presented a report in the form of the texts and, where agreement on one text had not proved possible, alternative texts of 41 numbered Articles, entitled "General Principles Governing

---

[57] See above, p. 446.
[58] See below, Appendix III. There is no equivalent to para. 9 of the Section on the Principle on the Use of Force.
[59] See Ferencz, *op. cit.,* p. 948, n. 52, above, Vol. II, p. 43. On the more recent ILC proposals for criminal responsibility, see above, p. 487.
[60] Broms, *loc. cit.,* p. 948, n. 52, above, p. 383. The Resolution (para. 4) "calls the attention of the Security Council to the definition it contains and recommends its use under Article 39." The possibility of formally adopting the definition was considered within the Security Council but not pursued: *ibid.* p. 397, n. 137.
[61] S.C. Resn 387 (1976), S.C.O.R., 20th year, *Resolutions and Decisions,* p. 11. Several findings of aggression have since been made against South Africa (see, *e.g.* S.C.Resn 568, above, p. 898, n. 25) and Israel (see, *e.g.* S.C.Resn 573, above, p. 915, n. 80). The General Assembly had not been so reticent, see *e.g.* the General Assembly finding of aggression against Communist China in the Korean War, see below, p. 885.
[62] S.C.O.R., 1st Year, 1st Series, 23rd Meeting (February 16, 1946), p. 369.

the Organisation of the Armed Forces made available to the Security Council by Member Nations of the United Nations."[63] The report, although showing some common ground among the five permanent members, disclosed disagreements on a number of crucial matters. Most notably, there was disagreement as to the size of the total force to be made available by Members to the Council (the United States sought a much larger force than the USSR and, to a lesser extent, China, France and United Kingdom), the contribution of each of the permanent members (China, France, the United Kingdom and the United States favoured contributions that would be in proportion in size and content to each member's national strength; the USSR wanted all contributions to be equal in size and content, although exceptions might be permitted), the location of the force when not in the service of the Council (China, France, the United Kingdom and the United States proposed that it should be based anywhere it was permitted to stay; the USSR wanted national contingents to return to their own territory), and the provision of bases, rights of passage and other facilities and assistance (China, France, the United Kingdom and the United States sought the negotiation of general guarantees in such matters; the USSR was of the opinion that they should be left for separate negotiations in respect of individual agreements under Article 43). The Security Council adopted, with amendments, the Articles on which agreement had been reached. It failed to reconcile the differences reflected in the report on the question of contributions by the permanent members and at that point terminated its discussion of the report. No further attempt at implementing Article 43 has occurred. No state has made an agreement with the Security Council under it.

As a result, what is left to the Security Council in accordance with the original plan is action (subject to the power of veto) under Articles 29, 40 and 41. It may make recommendations under Article 39, which are not binding. It may "call upon" the parties to comply with "provisional measures" (*e.g.* a cease fire) under Article 40. On the question whether measures under Article 40 are binding, Goodrich, Hambro and Simons[64] state:

> There would appear to be considerable agreement that the parties concerned are obligated to comply with resolutions specifically adopted under Article 40 . . .
> There is considerably less agreement as to whether these obligations are applicable, if the Council fails to cite Article 40 and/or fails to make a formal determination under Article 39 that a threat to the peace, [etc.] . . . exists.

Measures not involving the use of armed force may be required of members by a decision (binding under Article 25) under Article 41 (see the economic sanctions imposed on Southern Rhodesia and South Africa, below, pp. 963, 966). A non-binding recommendation for voluntary measures of the same sort may be made, presumably (since Article 41 is expressed in wholly mandatory terms) under Article 39; measures involving the use of armed force cannot be taken under Article 42 in the absence of Article 43 agreements.[65] The *Southern Rhodesian* case, below, however, seems to establish that the Security Council can *authorise* a member state to use force that would otherwise be illegal in order to assist the international community in maintaining international peace and security. Action

---

[63] S.C.O.R., 2nd Year, Sp. Supp. No. 1, p. 1.
[64] *op. cit.*, p. 863, n. 22, above, p. 306.
[65] Note, however, the sugestions made by Schachter, below, p. 961, n. 22, in the context of UN action in the Gulf War.

in accordance with the Korean precedent, below, although unlikely to occur again, demonstrates another way in which, if the political will is present, the United Nations may act to maintain international peace and security, namely by recommendation under Article 39 on the basis of implied powers.

(b) *The Korean Question*[66]

Notes

Korea became part of Japan in 1910. In 1943, the Allied Powers agreed that it would become an independent state when the Second World War ended. In 1945, Japanese troops in Korea surrendered to the USSR north of the 38th Parallel and to the United States south of it. As agreed at the Moscow Conference of December 1945, a Joint Commission composed of USSR and United States representatives was then established to assist in the formation of a provisional Korean Government and, ultimately, of a Korean state. The Joint Commission soon found itself at loggerheads, and in September 1947, the question of Korea was submitted to the General Assembly by the United States. The USSR denied the United Nations' competence to act on the ground that arrangements for Korea's future had been set in train by other means. Despite this, the General Assembly discussed the question and resolved that elections for a Korean national assembly should be held under supervision of the United Nations Temporary Commission on Korea which was established for this purpose. The Commission was not allowed into North Korea (*i.e.* north of the 38th Parallel) but it supervised and approved elections held in the South. A South Korean Government was established and, on December 12, 1948, approved by the General Assembly.

On June 25, 1950, North Korean armed forces crossed the 38th Parallel into South Korea and fighting broke out. The resulting crisis was immediately debated by the Security Council which adopted the following series of resolutions.

SECURITY COUNCIL RESOLUTION OF JUNE 25, 1950

S.C.O.R., 5th Year, Resolutions and Decisions, pp. 4–5

The Security Council,

Recalling the finding of the General Assembly in its resolution of 21st October 1949 that the Government of the Republic of Korea is a lawfully established government having effective control and jurisdiction over that part of Korea where the United Nations Temporary Commission on Korea was able to observe and consult and in which the great majority of the people of Korea reside; and that this Government is based on elections which were a valid expression of the free will of the electorate of that part of Korea and which were observed by the Temporary Commission; and that this is the only such Government in Korea;

---

[66] See Bowett, *United Nations Forces* (1964); Chap. 3; Kelsen, *Recent Trends in the Law of the United Nations* (1950), a supplement to the same author's *The Law of the United Nations*, Chap. 2; Kunz (1951) 45 A.J.I.L. 137; Stone, *op. cit.*, p. 859, n. 1, above, pp. 228–237.

Mindful of the concern expressed by the General Assembly in its resolutions of 12 December 1948 and 21 October 1949 of the consequences which might follow unless Member States refrained from acts derogatory to the results sought to be achieved by the United Nations in bringing about the complete independence and unity of Korea; and the concern expressed that the situation described by the United Nations Commission on Korea in its report menaces the safety and well-being of the Republic of Korea and of the people of Korea and might lead to open military conflict there;

Noting with grave concern the armed attack upon the Republic of Korea by forces from North Korea,

Determines that this action constitutes a breach of the peace,

I. Calls for the immediate cessation of hostilities; and calls upon the authorities of North Korea to withdraw forthwith their armed forces to the 38th parallel; . . .

III. Calls upon all Members to render every assistance to the United Nations in the execution of this resolution and to refrain from giving assistance to the North Korean authorities.[67]

SECURITY COUNCIL RESOLUTION OF JUNE 27, 1950

S.C.O.R., 5th Year, Resolutions and Decisions, p. 5

The Security Council . . .

Having noted from the report of the United Nations Commission for Korea that the authorities in North Korea have neither ceased hostilities nor withdrawn their armed forces to the 38th parallel, and that urgent military measures are required to restore international peace and security; and

Having noted the appeal from the Republic of Korea to the United Nations for immediate and effective steps to secure peace and security.

Recommends that the Members of the United Nations furnish such assistance to the Republic of Korea as may be necessary to repel the armed attack and to restore international peace and security in the area.[68]

---

[67] Adopted by nine votes (China, Cuba, Ecuador, Egypt, France, India, Norway, U.K., U.S.) to 0 with one abstention (Yugoslavia). The USSR was absent.

[68] Adopted by seven votes (China, Cuba, Ecuador, France, Norway, U.K., U.S.) to one (Yugoslavia), with two members abstaining (Egypt, India). The USSR was absent. India later accepted the resolution.

SECURITY COUNCIL RESOLUTION OF JULY 7, 1950

S.C.O.R., 5th Year, Resolutions and Decisions, p. 5

The Security Council . . .

1. Welcomes the prompt and vigorous support which governments and peoples of the United Nations have given to its Resolutions of 25 and 27 June 1950 to assist the Republic of Korea in defending itself against armed attack and thus to restore international peace and security in the area;

2. Notes that Members of the United Nations have transmitted to the United Nations offers of assistance for the Republic of Korea;

3. Recommends that all Members providing military forces and other assistance pursuant to the aforesaid Security Council resolutions make such forces and other assistance available to a unified command under the United States;

4. Requests the United States to designate the commander of such forces;

5. Authorizes the unified command at its discretion to use the United Nations flag in the course of operations against North Korean forces concurrently with flags of the various nations participating;

6. Requests the United States to provide the Security Council with reports as appropriate on the course of action taken under the unified command.[69]

Notes

1. The Secretary-General asked member states what assistance, if any, each would give to the Republic of Korea in accordance with the June 27 Resolution and received 53 replies which were interpreted by the Secretary-General as indicating support for the Resolution. "By the end of 1950, personnel, transport, commodities, supplies, funds, facilities and other assistance had been offered . . . by 39 Member States of the United Nations in accordance with the Security Council's resolution of 27 June 1950, by one non-member State [Italy] and by nine organisations."[70] Sixteen member states finally sent armed forces to Korea.[71]

2. The Security Council ceased to play an active part in the conduct of the war after the representative of the USSR resumed his seat on August 1, 1950. By early October the United Nations force had pushed North Korean forces back to the 38th Parallel and the question was whether it should cross it. On October 7, the General Assembly, acting on a report from the UN Commission in Korea, passed a resolution[72] which, by implication, authorised it to do so. By late October, troops from mainland China had entered the war and in mid-November they achieved considerable success against the United Nations force. After the USSR had vetoed

---

[69] Adopted by seven votes (China, Cuba, Ecuador, France, Norway, U.K., U.S.) to 0 with three abstentions (Egypt, India, Yugoslavia). The USSR was absent.

[70] *Yearbook of the United Nations* (1950), p. 226.

[71] Australia, Belgium, Canada, Colombia, Ethiopia, France, Greece, Luxembourg, Netherlands, New Zealand, Philippines, Thailand, Turkey, South Africa, U.K. and U.S.

[72] Resn 376, G.A.O.R., 5th Sess., Supp. 20, pp. 9–10 (1950).

a draft resolution condemning the Chinese action on November 30[73] the General Assembly became the organ effectively seised of the question. Wary of expanding the war unduly, the Assembly postponed consideration of a draft resolution[74] along the lines of that vetoed in the Security Council and instead, on December 14, 1950, appointed a committee of three to "determine the basis on which a satisfactory cease-fire in Korea can be arranged".[75] After the committee had unsuccessfully made overtures to the Peking Government, a resolution[76] was adopted on February 1, 1951, finding that Communist China "by giving direct aid and assistance to those who were already committing aggression in Korea and by engaging in hostilities against United Nations forces" was "itself engaged in aggression" in Korea and calling upon it to "cause its forces and nationals in Korea to cease hostilities against the United Nations forces and to withdraw from Korea." The resolution also established an Additional Measures Committee "as a matter of urgency to consider additional measures to be employed to meet [the] aggression [in Korea] . . . " and a Good Offices Committee to continue to work for a cease-fire. In the absence of satisfactory progress by the latter, the former presented a report in accordance with which the Assembly recommended on May 18. 1951,[77] that "every State: (a) apply an embargo on the shipment to areas under the control of the Central People's Government of the People's Republic of China and of the North Korean authorities of . . . [war material] . . . " "By June 30th 1951, . . . [t]he Governments of thirty-one Member states and three non-member States reported that they had implemented the resolution."[78] Truce negotiations between the United Nations Command and a Chinese-North Korean delegation were begun in July 1951. Neither the General Assembly nor the Security Council were involved except that on December 3, 1952, the Assembly adopted a resolution[79] relating to the repatriation of war prisoners when that question had brought negotiations almost to a halt. "In actual fact, the armistice negotiations were conducted by the United Nations Command under instructions which in the final analysis were given by the United States government in Washington."[80] An armistice in Korea come into effect on July 27, 1953. Attempts at a political settlement of the Korean Question at the Geneva Conference in 1954 were unsuccessful.

3. In proposing the Security Council resolution of July 7, 1950, the representative of the United Kingdom said: "It is clear to all concerned that unified command is essential if confusion is to be avoided . . . Had the Charter come fully into force and had the agreement provided for in Article 43 of the Charter been concluded, we should, of course, have proceeded differently, and the action to be taken by the Security Council to repel the armed attack would no doubt have been founded on Article 42. As it is, however, the Council can naturally act only under Article 39, which enables the Security Council to recommend what measures should be taken to restore international peace and security. The necessary recommendations were duly made in the resolutions of 25 and 27 June, but in the nature of things they could only be recommendations to individual Members of the United Nations. It could not therefore be the United Nations or the Security

---

[73] See S.C.O.R., 5th Year, 530th Meeting, p. 25 (1950).
[74] See G.A.O.R., 5th Sess., Annexes, Agenda Item 76, p. 4.
[75] Resn 384, G.A.O.R., 5th Sess., Supp. 20, p. 15 (1950).
[76] Resn 498, G.A.O.R., 5th Sess., Supp. 20A, p. 1 (1951).
[77] Resn 500, G.A.O.R., 5th Sess., Supp. 20A, p. 2 (1951).
[78] Annual Report of the Secretary-General on the work of the Organisation, July 1, 1950—June 30, 1951, G.A.O.R., 5th Sess., Supp. No. 1, p. 53 (1950).
[79] Resn 610 G.A.O.R., 7th Sess., Supp. No. 20, p. 3 (1953).
[80] Goodrich, *Collective Measures against Aggression*, (1953) Int. Conc. No. 494, p. 178.

Council which themselves appointed a United Nations commander. All the Security Council can do is to recommend that one of its members should designate the commander of the forces which individual members have now made available."[81]

4. The constitutionality of the Security Council resolutions of June–July 1950 is uncertain.[82] Is it relevant that neither North nor South Korea were members of the United Nations or that, arguably, neither were states? Does it matter that the USSR was absent when they were adopted? On this last question, note that whereas there is a well established practice accepted by all the permanent members of the Security Council by which abstention by a permanent member does not "veto" a resolution[83] there is no such practice with regard to absence and the USSR has consistently maintained that the Korean resolutions were invalid because of its absence. Although the USSR was in violation of Article 28 in absenting itself from the Council, this would not justify the Security Council in acting in the USSR's absence even if the violation were regarded as a "material breach."[84] The "veto" power was given to permanent members because of their primary responsibility in fact to maintain international peace and security.[85] Could it have been intended that the Security Council should adopt resolutions such as the Korean ones without the participation of all the permanent members? Arguing from the text of the Charter, if Article 27 meant *all* the permanent members, should it not have said so, like the Article 108? On the other hand, if it meant all the permanent members *present*, should it not have said that (compare Article 18(3))?[86] Of what significance is the fact that the Security Council has no quorum rule?[87] Would the Council be able to act in the absence of all the permanent members?

5. On the question whether the force in Korea was a United Nations force, note the conclusion of Bowett.[88]

There can be no doubt that, in practice, the overwhelming majority of States involved in the Korean action were fully prepared to regard it as a United Nations action involving United Nations Forces.

Bowett refers to a number of facts indicating acceptance of this view of the nature of the force, including the use of the United Nations flag and the adoption of General Assembly Resolution 483(V)[89] authorising the award of a "distinguishing ribbon or other insignia for personnel which had participated in Korea in the defence of the principles of the Charter of the United Nations." An alternative view, which avoids the problem of the constitutionality of the Security Council resolutions, is that the force was an exercise of the customary international law right of collective self-defence.[90]

---

[81] S.C.O.R., 5th Year, 476th Meeting, pp. 3–4 (1950).
[82] See p. 951, n. 66, above.
[83] The I.C.J. stated in the *Legal Consequences* case, I.C.J.Rep. 1971, p. 22, that the practice "has been generally accepted by Members of the United Nations and evidences a general practice of that Organisation."
[84] On "material breach" in the law of treaties, see above, p. 839.
[85] See the Four Power Statement, June 7, 1945, 11 U.N.C.I.O., *Documents* 711.
[86] See Kelsen, *Law of the United Nations* (1950), pp. 240–244.
[87] See *ibid.* p. 244.
[88] *op. cit.*, p. 951, n. 66, above, p. 47.
[89] G.A.O.R., 5th Sess., Supp. No. 20, p. 76 (1950).
[90] See Stone, *op. cit.*, p. 859, n. 1, above, pp. 234–237.

(c) *The Invasion of Kuwait*[91]

The thaw in relations between the superpowers starting in the late 1980s resulted in a revitalised Security Council which, when faced with an armed aggression by Iraq against Kuwait on August 2, 1990, reacted in the following unprecedented manner.

SECURITY COUNCIL RESOLUTION 660 (1990)

August 2, 1990. S.C.O.R., 45th Year, Resolutions and Decisions, p. 19;
(1990) 29 I.L.M. 1325

The Security Council . . .

Determining that there exists a breach of international peace and security as regards the Iraqi invasion of Kuwait,

Acting under Articles 39 and 40 of the Charter of the United Nations,

1. Condemns the Iraqi invasion of Kuwait;

2. Demands that Iraq withdraw immediately and unconditionally all its forces to the positions in which they were located on 1 August 1990;

3. Calls upon Iraq and Kuwait to begin immediately intensive negotiations for the resolution of their differences and supports all efforts in this regard, and especially those of the League of Arab States . . . [92]

Notes

Resolution 660 placed the Security Council within the confines of Chapter VII within hours of the Iraqi invasion, following which Iraqi forces quickly obtained control over all Kuwait's territory. The parallels with the initial reaction of the Security Council to the invasion of South Korea in 1950[93] are strong except that on this occasion all of the permanent members voted for the resolution. As in the Korean episode, the Security Council preferred to use the more neutral term "breach of the peace," rather than "act of aggression," although it is clear that Iraq had committed large scale armed aggression without legal justification.[94] Iraq initially justified its invasion by stating that its troops had been invited in to Kuwait by an opposition group to restore order to the country[95] but it soon

---

[91] See Franck and Patel (1991) 85 A.J.I.L. 63; Gray (1994) 65 B.Y.I.L. 135; Greenwood (1992) 55 M.L.R. 153; Joyner (1991) 32 Virg. J.I.L. 1; Kaikobad (1992) 63 B.Y.I.L. 299; Khadduri (1994) 15 Mich. J.I.L. 847; Khan (1993) 45 Stan.L.R. 425; Lavalle (1992) 23 N.Y.I.L. 3; Moore, *Crisis in the Gulf: Enforcing the Rule of Law* (1992); Roberts (1993) 25 N.Y.U.J.I.L.P. 687; Rostow (1991) 85 A.J.I.L. 506; Rowe, *The Gulf War 1990–1 in International Law and English Law* (1993); Schachter (1991) 85 A.J.I.L. 452; Warbrick (1991) 40 I.C.L.Q. 482; Weller (1991) 3 A.J.I.C.L. 1; White and McCoubrey (1991) 10 Int. Rel. 347. For documents, see Lauterpacht, Greenwood, Weller and Bethlehem, *The Kuwait Crisis: Basic Documents* (1991), Vol. 1. See also *The United Nations and the Iraq–Kuwait Conflict 1990–6, UN Blue Book Series No. 9* (1996).

[92] Adopted by 14 votes to 0, with no abstentions. Yemen did not participate in the vote.

[93] S.C. Resn. of June 25, 1950, above p. 951.

[94] "Invasion" is the principal type of armed aggression listed in the General Assembly's Definition of Aggression, see above, p. 945.

[95] UN Doc. S/PV. 2932, p. 11.

became clear that Iraq's intention was to incorporate Kuwait into Iraq by force. Iraq appears to have no claim to Kuwait in the light of the 1963 agreement between Iraq and Kuwait whereby the boundary between the two countries was formally recognised.[96] Annexation by force is declared to be unlawful in the General Assembly's 1970 Declaration on Principles of International Law.

SECURITY COUNCIL RESOLUTION 661 (1990)

August 6, 1990. S.C.O.R., 45th Year, Resolutions and Decisions, p. 19;
(1990) 29 I.L.M. 1325

The Security Council ...

Deeply concerned that ... resolution [660] has not been implemented ...

Affirming the inherent right of individual or collective self-defence, in response to the armed attack by Iraq against Kuwait, in accordance with Article 51 of the Charter,

Acting, under Chapter VII of the Charter ...

2. Decides ... to take the following measures to secure compliance of Iraq with paragraph 2 of resolution 660 ... and to restore the authority of the legitimate government of Kuwait;

3. Decides that all States shall prevent:

(a) The import into their territories of all commodities and products originating in Iraq or Kuwait or exported therefrom after the date of the present resolution;

(b) Any activities by their nationals or in their territories which would promote ... the export ... of any commodities or products from Iraq or Kuwait; ...

(c) The sale or supply by their nationals or from their territories ... of any commodities or products, including weapons or any other military equipment ... but not including supplies intended strictly for medical purposes, and, in humanitarian circumstances, foodstuffs, to any person or body in Iraq or Kuwait ...

4. Decides that all States shall not make available to the Government of Iraq ... any funds ...

5. Calls upon all States, including States non-members of the United Nations, to act strictly in accordance with the provisions of the present resolution notwithstanding any contract entered into or licence granted before the present resolution;

6. Decides to establish ... a Committee of the Security Council consisting of all the members of the Council, to undertake the following tasks. ..

(a) To examine the reports on the progress of the implementation of the present resolution which will be submitted by the Secretary General;

[96] 485 U.N.T.S. 321.

(b) To seek from all States further information regarding the action taken by them concerning the effective implementation of the provisions laid down in the present resolution . . . [97]

Notes

1. As with most of the resolutions adopted in the Gulf crisis, the discussion leading up to the adoption of Resolution 661 was very brief, agreement having been hammered out before the public meeting. One result of this was that the ambiguities in the resolution were not often clarified by any of the representatives' statements. One problem that arose regarding Resolution 661, in which the Security Council impliedly acted under Article 41 to impose sanctions, concerned the mechanism by which foodstuffs would be allowed into Iraq and Kuwait. This was clarified to a certain extent by Security Council Resolution 666[98] adopted on September 13, 1990, which authorised the Secretary General to report to the Sanctions Committee on the food needs of the people of Iraq and Kuwait with particular attention to children, expectant mothers, the sick and the elderly and to report on how those needs would best be met.[99] Resolution 661 contained Security Council "decisions" that were legally binding under Article 25, Charter. It applies to "all states", including non-UN members.

2. As well as resolutions fine tuning the embargo,[1] the Security Council also adopted a series of resolutions in the period prior to the authorization of full scale force against Iraq which were more in the nature of declarations or judgments on certain Iraqi actions.[2] On August 9, 1990, the Security Council unanimously adopted Resolution 662[3] which decided that the Iraqi "merger" of Kuwait into Iraq was "null and void" and called upon states not to recognise the annexation. Resolution 664,[4] unanimously adopted on August 18, 1990, demanded that Iraq release foreign nationals held hostage in Iraq and Kuwait. Resolution 667[5] of September 16, 1990, unanimously condemned Iraq for its "aggressive acts" against diplomatic premises and personnel in Kuwait and demanded that Iraq comply with the Vienna Conventions on diplomatic and consular relations (as to which, see above, pp. 340 *et seq.*). Resolution 674,[6] of October 29, 1990 reminded Iraq "that under international law it is liable for any loss, damage or injury arising in regard to Kuwait and third States, and their nationals and corporations, as a result of the invasion and illegal occupation of Kuwait by Iraq" and invited those States, etc., to compile information regarding claims to be made against Iraq. Resolution 677,[7] adopted unanimously on November 28, 1990, condemned Iraqi attempts to alter the demographic composition of Kuwait by deporting thousands

---

[97] Adopted by 13 votes to 0, with two abstentions (Cuba and Yemen).

[98] S.C.O.R. 45th Year, *Resolutions and Decisions*, p. 22; (1990) 29 I.L.M. 1330. Adopted by 13 votes to 2 (Cuba, Yemen).

[99] See also S.C. Resn 670, September 25, 1990, *ibid.* p. 24; (1990) 29 I.L.M. 1334. Adopted by 14 votes to one (Cuba). This made it clear that the sanctions extended to air traffic.

[1] See also S.C. Resn 669, September 24, 1990, *ibid.* p. 24; (1990) 29 I.L.M. 1333, which entrusted the Sanctions Committee established under Resn 661 to examine requests for economic assistance under the provisions of Art. 50, Charter, made by states other than Iraq suffering loss as a result of the imposition of the sanctions.

[2] On the judicial role of the Security Council see Schachter (1964) 58 A.J.I.L. 960 and Higgins (1970) 64 A.J.I.L. 1.

[3] S.C.O.R., 45th Year, *Resolutions and Decisions*, p. 20; (1990) 29 I.L.M. 1327.

[4] *ibid.* p. 21; (1990) 29 I.L.M. 1328.

[5] *ibid.* p. 23; (1990) 29 I.L.M. 1332.

[6] *ibid.* p. 25. Adopted by 13 votes to 0, with two abstentions (Cuba and Yemen).

[7] *ibid.* p. 27. Adopted unanimously.

of Kuwaiti citizens to Iraq.[8] All but Resolution 662 were expressly adopted under Chapter VII of the Charter.[9] Is there a specific provision in Chapter VII which allows for the adoption of such resolutions?

SECURITY COUNCIL RESOLUTION 665 (1990)

August 25, 1990. S.C.O.R., 45th Year, Resolutions and Decisions, p. 21;
(1990) 29 I.L.M. 1329

The Security Council . . .
Having decided to impose economic sanctions under Chapter VII of the Charter . . .
Gravely alarmed that Iraq continues to refuse to comply with resolutions [660, 661, 662, and 664] and in particular at the conduct of the government of Iraq in using Iraqi flag vessels to export oil,

1. Calls upon those Member States co-operating with the Government of Kuwait which are deploying maritime forces to the area to use such measures commensurate to the specific circumstances as may be necessary under the authority of the Security Council to halt all inward and outward maritime shipping in order to inspect and verify their cargoes and destinations and to ensure strict implementation of . . . resolution 661
. . .
4. Further requests the States concerned to co-ordinate their actions . . . using as appropriate mechanisms of the Military Staff Committee . . .[10]

Notes

1. This resolution allowed the predominantly Western naval forces in the Gulf to stop and search vessels suspected of trading with Iraq or sailing from Iraq and to use minimum force for this purpose. The exact power upon which such an authorization is based is unclear, although there is a "precedent" for it in the authorization to the United Kingdom to use force to stop oil reaching the port of Beira in 1966.[11] Some members felt uneasy that force was being authorised without the agreements necessary under Article 43.[12] This was perhaps the reason why the resolution referred to the Military Staff Committee although there was no evidence of any formal control of the operation by this Committee.[13] Is this perhaps another example of an implied power under Article 39 of the Charter?

2. In the period before the Security Council authorised the use of force against Iraq, the United States and the United Kingdom asserted that the growing

---

[8] The Security Council also discussed the atrocities carried out by Iraqi forces in Kuwait at the meeting at which this resolution was adopted: UN Doc. S/PV. 2962.
[9] Resn 662 appeared to be treated as a binding decision of the Security Council by the members of the Council voting for it: UN Doc. S/PV. 2934. The resolution referred to S.C. Resns 660 and 661 which were expressly adopted under Chap. VII.
[10] Adopted by 13 votes to 0, with two abstentions (Cuba and Yemen).
[11] S.C. Resn 221 (1966), below, p. 965.
[12] See UN Doc. S/PV. 2938, p. 11 (Cuba) and p. 21 (Colombia). See also the objections by Iraq: *ibid.* p. 66.
[13] On the Committee and the use of force under Art. 42, see above p. 949.

military presence in the Gulf[14] was not only at the request of the Saudi government to protect Saudi Arabia from further Iraqi expansion but also could take the
form of collective self-defence of Kuwait at the request of the deposed Kuwaiti
government if Iraq failed to withdraw.[15] In voting for Resolution 665, both states
reserved the right to act in collective self-defence of Kuwait without the need for
Security Council authorization, and stated that authorization was sought on this
occasion for political rather than legal reasons.[16]

3. The Prime Minister, Mrs Thatcher, in her House of Commons speech of
September 6, 1990 made clear the British position:

> Resolution 661, which called for comprehensive economic sanctions
> expressly affirms the inherent right of individual or collective self-defence, in
> response to an armed attack by Iraq against Kuwait, in accordance with article
> 51 of the United Nations Charter. We hope that economic sanctions will prove
> to be sufficient. That is why they must be strictly enforced. But we are not
> precluded by reason of any Security Council resolution from exercising the
> inherent right of collective-self defence in accordance with the rules of inter-
> national law.[17]

Resolution 661 refers to Article 51 which preserves the inherent right of self-
defence "until the Security Council has taken measures necessary to maintain
international peace and security". Could it be argued that comprehensive mandatory sanctions are such measures and that once the Council has adopted them
any right to use force outside the framework of the United Nations is lost or
suspended until the Security Council terminates the sanctions? In the Falklands
War debate, Sir Anthony Parsons, the British representative, suggested that the
measures must be effective before they can impair the right of self-defence.[18]

SECURITY COUNCIL RESOLUTION 678 (1990)

*1990. S.C.O.R., 45th Year, Resolutions and Decisions, p. 27;
(1990) 29 I.L.M. 1565*

The Security Council,
Recalling and reaffirming [all its previous resolutions on the Gulf]
. . .

---

[14] By the end of 1990, 29 countries had contributed to the U.S. inspired response to the Iraqi
invasion. Argentina, Australia, Bahrain, Bangladesh, Belgium, Canada, Czechoslovakia,
Denmark, Egypt, France, Germany, Greece, Italy, Kuwait, Morocco, Netherlands, New
Zealand, Niger, Norway, Oman, Pakistan, Qatar, Saudi Arabia, Senegal, Spain, Syria, the
United Arab Emirates, the U.K. and the U.S. At this time 750,000 "allied" or "coalition"
troops faced 500,000 Iraqi troops. The U.S. commanded the coalition forces and contributed 500,000 troops. *Keesing's Archives,* pp. 37935–36.

[15] See *Keesing's Archives*, p. 37638.

[16] See UN Doc. S/PV. 2938, p. 26 (U.S.) and p. 47 (U.K.). No such reservations were
expressed at the adoption of Resn 678, below, which authorised the full scale use of force
against Iraq on November 29, 1990, S/PV. 2963, p. 78 (U.K.) and p. 101 (U.S.). No other
member made such a reservation. Indeed, some expressed the view that the use of force
could only be authorised by the Security Council: see, *e.g.,* p. 74 (Malaysia).

[17] *Hansard*, H.C., Vol. 177, col. 737.

[18] See above, p. 902. The effectiveness of sanctions against Iraq have yet to be fully assessed
but they certainly appear more watertight than those imposed against Southern Rhodesia
and South Africa. For some materials see Lauterpacht *et al., op. cit.,* p. 956, n. 91, above, pp.
197–243.

Acting under Chapter VII of the Charter . . .

1. Demands that Iraq comply fully with resolution 660 (1990) and all subsequent resolutions and decides, while maintaining all its decisions, to allow Iraq one final opportunity, as a pause of goodwill, to do so;

2. Authorises Member States co-operating with the Government of Kuwait, unless Iraq on or before January 15, 1991 fully implements, as set forth in paragraph 1 above, the foregoing resolutions, to use all necessary means to uphold and implement Security Council resolution 660 (1990) and all subsequent relevant resolutions and to restore international peace and security in the area;

3. Requests all States to provide appropriate support for the actions undertaken in pursuance of paragraph 2 of this resolution;

4. Requests the States concerned to keep the Council regularly informed on the progress of actions undertaken pursuant to paragraphs 2 and 3 of this resolution . . . [19]

Notes

1. By this Resolution, the Security Council decided that sanctions alone were insufficient to make Iraq withdraw from Kuwait, and so authorised member states, which in practice meant the coalition forces already gathered in the Gulf, commanded by the United States, to use "all necessary means" including armed force to enforce the decisions of the Security Council. Iraq objected to the Resolution, stating, *inter alia*, that it was only under Articles 42 and 43 of the Charter that force could be sanctioned by the Security Council.[20] It is interesting to note that this resolution did not mention the Military Staff Committee and that the only obligation imposed on the states contributing to the coalition forces was to report periodically to the Security Council. In fact once Resolution 678 had been adopted no further resolution emerged from the Security Council on the Gulf until the cease-fire. In the Korean operation, Article 39 was stated to be the source of the authorization to use force.[21] There is some doubt in the Iraqi case as to the Charter basis for Resolution 678. Presumably, in the absence of any agreements under Article 43 and of provision for Military Staff Committee involvement, it was not made under Article 42.[22] The more likely basis for it is Article 39, although no mention was made of it or of Korea as a precedent during the adoption of Resolution 678.[23] Bearing in mind the arguments made against the constitutionality of the Korean operation,[24] are there any doubts about that of Resolution 678?

---

[19] Adopted by 12 votes to two (Cuba and Yemen), with one abstention (China).
[20] UN Doc. S/PV. 2963, pp. 19–20.
[21] See above, p. 951 *et seq.*
[22] On the intended link between the use of force under Art. 42, Art. 43 agreements and Military Staff Commitee involvement, see above, p. 949. In the Iraqi case, there was also no express finding that measures under Art. 41 had proved inadequate. Although this might be implied, it could be argued that such an important finding would normally be stated expressly. In support of the argument that Art. 42 was the basis for Resolution 678, Schachter suggests, *loc. cit.*, p. 956, n. 91 above, p. 464, that Art. 42 may be read as permitting the authorisation of the *voluntary* use of force by member states.
[23] UN Doc. S/PV. 2963.
[24] See above, p. 955.

Another, and more convincing, interpretation is that the action of the coalition states throughout was not UN action but an exercise of the right of collective self defence, and the "authorisation" in Resolution 678 was of political rather than legal significance.[25]

2. It was upon the basis of Resolution 678 that the coalition forces gathered in the Gulf started their air campaign on January 16, 1991 soon after the deadline had run out without any concrete signs of an Iraqi withdrawal. The ground offensive for the liberation of Kuwait started on February 24, 1991 and was successful in its objective of removing the Iraqi army from Kuwait within five days. As with the resolution authorising the use of force in Korea,[26] Resolution 678 included the unambiguous phrase authorising the use of force "to restore international peace and security in the region". The coalition, however, appeared to interpret Resolution 678 as only authorising the enforcement of the previous 12 Security Council resolutions directed to remove Iraq out of Kuwait, rather than interpreting the resolution in a wider sense. Coalition forces did enter Iraq and forcefully occupied parts of southern Iraq for several weeks following the cease-fire, and the coalition air forces did mount continuous attacks on military targets throughout Iraq as well as Kuwait, but the coalition did not attempt to remove the Iraqi regime of Saddam Hussein. Do you think that the decision not to try to inflict total defeat on Iraq was a political one rather than being based on the principle of non-intervention? Or would such further action have been illegal under international law? Does the fact that President Saddam Hussein appeared guilty of a crime against peace within the Nuremberg Principles[27] affect your answer?

3. A temporary cease-fire was detailed in Security Council Resolution 686 of March 2, 1991[28] by which Iraq, *inter alia*, accepted liability for any damage caused by the invasion and agreed to rescind its annexation of Kuwait. A formal cease-fire was established by Security Council Resolution 687 of April 3, 1991.[29] This very detailed resolution contained many provisions which further punished Iraq by requiring it, *inter alia*, to

(i) permit the destruction of Iraqi chemical and biological weapons and all ballistic missiles with a range greater than 150 kilometres[30];

(iii) submit to on-site inspections of weapon making facilities;

(iv) to provide details of locations and amounts of weaponry and undertake not to use, acquire, etc., weapons of mass destruction;

(v) to return all Kuwaiti property that had been seized during the invasion; and

---

[25] Schachter, *loc. cit.*, p. 961, n. 91, above, p. 460, n. 24, notes that Resolution 678 was "probably of decisive importance in obtaining U.S. congressional approval." He also quotes, *id.*, p. 461, n. 28, Mr Fleischhauer, a Legal Counsel to the U.N. Secretary-General, stating that *Resolution 678* was not adopted under Art. 42 because it did not provide for "a collective enforcement action by the United Nations, let alone under its command." In contrast with Korea, there was no provision for a UN command structure, force title or flag: *id.*, pp. 459–60.

[26] S.C. Resn of June 27, 1950, above, p. 951.

[27] See above, p. 745.

[28] S.C.O.R., 46th Year, *Resolutions and Decisions*, p. 8. Adopted by 11 votes to one (Cuba), with three abstentions (China, India, Yemen).

[29] *ibid.* p. 11; (1991) 30 I.L.M. 846. Adopted by 12 votes to one (Cuba), with two abstentions (Yemen, Ecuador).

[30] During the War, Iraq launched several SCUD missile attacks against Saudi Arabia and Israel.

(vi) to compensate those who suffered loss or injury because of the invasion.

The resolution created a Special Commission to monitor compliance and to ensure that Iraq did not develop such military capability in the future. With regard to the duty to compensate, a Compensation Commission and a Compensation Fund, to be financed out of Iraqi oil sales, were established by the Security Council.[31] The Commission has begun making recommendations for payment. The resolution did not immediately lift the sanctions imposed against Iraq by Resolution 661, and in particular a strict arms embargo was maintained.[32] By Resolution 689[33] of April 9, 1991, the Security Council unanimously agreed to establish a 1,400 strong observer force, the UN Iraq–Kuwait observer Mission (UNIKOM), along the Iraq–Kuwait border to replace coalition forces.[34]

Iraq has failed to cooperate fully with UN weapons inspectors and to meet all of its other obligations under Resolution 687. As a result, UN sanctions remain in place. In 1996, however, a "food for oil" deal was agreed, by which Iraq was permitted to sell a limited amount of oil to buy food, medicines and other humanitarian goods.[35]

4. On coalition states humanitarian intervention after the Gulf War, see above, p. 919.

(d) *The Southern Rhodesian Question*[36]

SECURITY COUNCIL DEBATE

S.C.O.R., 21st Year, 1276th Meeting, pp. 5 et seq., April 9, 1966

On November 12, 1965, the day after Southern Rhodesia's unilateral declaration of independence, the Security Council decided, in Resolution 216 (1965), "to condemn the unilateral declaration of independence made by the racist minority in Southern Rhodesia" and "to call upon all states not to recognise this illegal racist minority régime in Southern Rhodesia and to refrain from rendering any assistance" to it.[37] On November 20, it adopted Resolution 217 (1965) in which it called upon "all States to refrain from any action which would assist and encourage the illegal régime and, in particular, to desist from providing it with arms, equipment, and military materials, and to do their utmost in order to break all economic relations with Southern Rhodesia, including an embargo on oil and petroleum products."[38] In the following debate the United Kingdom sought further Security Council action.

---

[31] S.C. Resn 692 (1991), S.C.O.R., 46th Year, *Resolutions and Decisions*, p. 18.

[32] Both Resns 686 and 687 were adopted under Chapter VII and were accepted unconditionally by Iraq.

[33] S.C.O.R., 46th Year, *Resolutions and Decisions*, p. 15.

[34] See UN Doc. S/22454, April 5, 1991, Report of the Secretary General.

[35] See *Keesing's Archives*, p. 41424.

[36] See Fawcett (1965–66) 41 B.Y.I.L. 103; Fenwick (1967) 61 A.J.I.L. 753; Howell (1969) 63 A.J.I.L. 771; McDougal and Reisman (1968) 62 A.J.I.L. 1.

[37] Resn 216 (1965) S.C.O.R., 20th Year, *Resolutions and Decisions*, p. 8. Adopted by 10 votes (Bolivia, China, Ivory Coast, Jordan, Malaysia, Netherlands, USSR, U.K., U.S., Uruguay) to 0, with one abstention (France).

[38] Resn 217 (1965), S.C.O.R., 20th Year, *Resolutions and Decisions*, p. 8. Adopted by the same votes as Resn 216 (1965), above.

19. [LORD CARADON (UNITED KINGDOM)] On November 20, 1965, in resolution 217 (1965), the Council called for an oil embargo against Rhodesia. My Government has taken action in response to that call. But as we meet here today an oil tanker, called the *Joanna V*, with a full cargo of oil, rides at anchor in the port of Beira. Another tanker, also with a full cargo of oil, called the *Manuela*, has recently been close to Beira—and I have a message about that ship to which I shall presently refer. The *Manuela* could still put in to Beira very soon. But it is not merely a matter of one or two ships. Other tankers may follow, and will surely do so unless we act now. If the oil carried by such ships is pumped through the pipeline to the refinery at Umtali, which has been closed since last December, then the normal system of supply of petroleum products to Rhodesia will start again. If the oil from these tankers, and others to follow, reaches Rhodesia, the oil embargo for which this Council called will be severely prejudiced, the illegal regime in Salisbury will be encouraged, the purposes so clearly stated and so widely accepted here in the United Nations will be most seriously frustrated.

20. I come therefore to this Council to seek your help and your authority to stop this happening. . . .

21. Without that authority, the United Kingdom Government has to face the defiance of the United Nations with its hands tied. The Royal Navy undoubtedly had the physical power to prevent the *Joanna V*, for instance, from entering Beira. But in this matter my Government has been anxious that at all times its actions should be lawful actions and that it should not risk acting in breach of the law of nations. One of the very purposes of the action we are, at considerable sacrifice to ourselves, taking against the illegal regime in Southern Rhodesia is to assert the rule of law and principles of the United Nations Charter. I therefore ask the Council now, by adopting the draft resolution [Resolution 221 (1966), below] I propose, to enable the United Kingdom to carry out without fear of illegality the responsibilities which in the Rhodesian situation are ours. I ask the Council, in furtherance of our common cause, and to meet the threat which I have described, to enable the United Kingdom Government to take within the law all steps, including the use of force as the situation may demand, to stop the arrival at Beira of ships taking oil to the rebel regime. . . .

69. MR. GOLDBERG (UNITED STATES OF AMERICA). . . . The question of intercepting vessels on the high seas, the question of arresting and detaining them, is a matter that has a long history in the field of international law. . . . We are asked in the Security Council, and it should be a matter of deep consideration and concern for all of us, to put our sanction upon what will be a rule of international law—that when this Council acts vessels on the high seas can be arrested and detained in the interest of the international law which we will be making here today, if we adopt the draft resolution as I hope we will do.

SECURITY COUNCIL RESOLUTION 221 (1966)

S.C.O.R., 21st Year, Resolutions and Decisions, p. 5

The Security Council,

Recalling its resolutions Nos. 216 of November 12, 1965 and 217 of November 20, 1965 and in particular its call to all States to do their utmost to break off economic relations with Southern Rhodesia, including an embargo on oil and petroleum products,

Gravely concerned at reports that substantial supplies of oil may reach Rhodesia as the result of an oil tanker having arrived at Beira and the approach of a further tanker which may lead to the resumption of pumping through the CPMR pipeline with the acquiescence of the Portuguese authorities,

Considering that such supplies will afford great assistance and encouragement to the illegal regime in Southern Rhodesia, thereby enabling it to remain longer in being,

1. Determines that the resulting situation constitutes a threat to the peace;

2. Calls upon the Portuguese Government not to permit oil to be pumped through the pipeline from Beira to Rhodesia;

3. Calls upon the Portuguese Government not to receive at Beira oil destined for Rhodesia;

4. Calls upon all States to ensure the diversion of any of their vessels reasonably believed to be carrying oil destined for Rhodesia which may be en route for Beira;

5. Calls upon the Government of the United Kingdom to prevent by the use of force if necessary the arrival at Beira of vessels reasonably believed to be carrying oil destined for Rhodesia, and empowers the United Kingdom to arrest and detain tanker known as the Joanna V upon her departure from Beira in the event her oil cargo is discharged there.[39]

Notes

1. "At 0720 hours G.M.T. on the morning of April 10, *H.M.S. Berwick* made contact with the tanker *Manuela* which was then 180 miles south of Beira. As the tanker made no reply to signal instructions, at 0802 hours G.M.T. a British naval officer with escort was put on board the tanker with written instructions to its master to divert from his course to Beira, and was followed by a British armed naval party. The ship's master reported that his instructions were to proceed to Beira to make good engine defects. He was then informed in writing that, in view of the United Nations resolution, the tanker could not be allowed to proceed to Beira and that the British Government had authority, if necessary, to use force to prevent this. . . . The master . . . agreed to proceed to Lourenco Marques."[40] The

[39] Adopted by 10 votes (Argentina, China, Japan, Jordan, Netherlands, New Zealand, Nigeria, Uganda, U.K., U.S.), to 0, with five abstentions (Bulgaria, France, Mali, USSR, Uruguay).

[40] Letter from the permanent representative of the U.K. to the Secretary-General, April 11, 1966, S.C.O.R., 21st Year, Supp. for April-June 1966, p. 34.

Joanna V left Beira without discharging oil. The *Joanna V* had been registered as a Greek ship, but its registration was cancelled by Greece on April 6.[41] Was the boarding of the Manuela (of Greek registration) lawful in international law? What effect has Article 110, 1982 Law of the Sea Convention.[42] The "Beira patrol" was maintained by British warships until 1975.

2. On December 16, 1966, the Security Council imposed selective mandatory economic sanctions on Southern Rhodesia under Article 41 of the Charter and reminded Members that failure to implement them would give rise to a violation of Article 25 of the Charter.[43] On May 29, 1968, the Council, "[g]ravely concerned that the measures taken by the Security Council have not been complied with by all States and that some States, contrary to resolution 232 (1966) of the Security Council and to their obligations under Article 25 of the Charter, have failed to prevent trade with the illegal régime in Southern Rhodesia. . . . Acting under Chapter VII of the United Nations Charter" imposed comprehensive and mandatory economic sanctions upon Southern Rhodesia.[44]

3. In 1979, the Security Council terminated its sanctions against Southern Rhodesia in the light of the agreement for Zimbabwe's independence.[45]

(e) *Economic sanctions against South Africa*

SECURITY COUNCIL RESOLUTION 418 (1977)

S.C.O.R., 32nd Year, Resolutions and Decisions, p. 5

The Security Council,

Recalling its resolution 392 (1976) of June 19, 1976, strongly condemning the South African Government for its resort to massive violence against and killings of the African people, including school children and students and others opposing racial discrimination, and calling upon that Government urgently to end violence against the African people and to take urgent steps to eliminate *apartheid* and racial discrimination,

Recognising that the military build-up by South Africa and its persistent acts of aggression against the neighbouring States seriously disturb the security of those States. . . .

Gravely concerned that South Africa is at the threshold of producing nuclear weapons,

Recalling its resolution 181 (1963) of August 7, 1963 and other resolutions concerning a voluntary arms embargo against South Africa,

Convinced that a mandatory arms embargo needs to be universally applied against South Africa in the first instance,

Acting therefore under Chapter VII of the Charter of the United Nations,

---

[41] *Keesings Archives*, p. 21418. It was given provisional registration by Panama but this was withdrawn on April 12.

[42] See above, p. 430.

[43] Resn 232 (1966), S.C.O.R., 21st Year, *Resolutions and Decisions*, p. 7. Adopted by 11 votes to 0, with four abstentions (Bulgaria, France, Mali, USSR).

[44] Resn 253 (1968), S.C.O.R., 23rd Year, *Resolutions and Decisions*. Adopted unanimously.

[45] S.C. Resn 460 (1979), S.C.O.R., 34th Year, *Resolutions and Decisions*, p. 15.

1. Determines, having regard to the policies and acts of the South African Government, that the acquisition by South Africa of arms and related *matériel* constitutes a threat to the maintenance of international peace and security;

2. Decides that all States shall cease forthwith any provision to South Africa of arms and related *matériel* of all types, including the sale or transfer of weapons and ammunition, military vehicles and equipment, para-military police equipment, and spare parts for the aforementioned and shall cease as well the provision of all types of equipment and supplies and grants of licensing arrangements for the manufacture or maintenance of the aforementioned;

3. Calls upon all States to review, having regard to the objectives of the present resolution, all existing contractual arrangements with and licences granted to South Africa relating to the manufacture and maintenance of arms, ammunition of all types and military equipment and vehicles, with a view to terminating them;

4. Further decides that all States shall refrain from any co-operation with South Africa in the manufacture and development of nuclear weapons; . . .

Notes

In 1963, "convinced that the situation in South Africa [of conflict resulting from the policy of apartheid contrary to the principles of the Charter] is seriously disturbing international peace and security," the Security Council had "solemnly call[ed] upon all States to cease forthwith the shipment of arms, ammunition of all types, and military vehicles to South Africa.[46] In 1970, "convinced . . . that the . . . continued application of the policies of apartheid and the constant build-up of the South African military and police forces . . . constitutes a potential threat to international peace and security, the Council strengthened (no training of or co-operation with South African forces, no technical assistance, etc.) the 1963 voluntary arms embargo. In 1975 and 1976, the Western permanent members of the Council vetoed attempts to make the embargo mandatory under Chapter VII on the ground that there was no threat to the peace in the sense of Article 39. Strong action taken by the South African authorities against black opposition (the banning of black organisations, the arrest of their leaders and the closing of black newspapers) caused them to accept resolution 418 (1977). Like the more general sanctions imposed earlier against Southern Rhodesia see above, p. 888, these were adopted under Article 41 of the Charter. Resolution 418 (like the Southern Rhodesian resolution previously) had been implemented in the United Kingdom by Orders in Council made under the United Nations Act 1946.[47] In 1995, following the changes in South Africa, the embargo imposed by Resolution 418 and all other UN measures against South Africa were terminated and the Security Council ceased to be seized of the question of South Africa.[48]

---

[46] S.C. Resn 181 (1963), S.C.O.R., 18th Year, *Resolutions and Decisions*, p. 9.
[47] See the Export of Goods (Control) Order 1987, (S.I. 1987 No. 2070).
[48] S.C. Resns 919 and 930, UN Doc SC/5974, pp. 48, 64.

(iv) THE ROLE OF THE GENERAL ASSEMBLY

See Articles 10–14, United Nations Charter, below, Appendix I.

UNITING FOR PEACE RESOLUTION[49]

G.A. Resolution. 377 (V), November 3, 1950; G.A.O.R., 5th Sess.,
Supp. 20, p. 10

The General Assembly

Reaffirming the importance of the exercise by the Security Council of its primary responsibility for the maintenance of international peace and security, and the duty of the permanent members to seek unanimity and to exercise restraint in the use of the veto,

Reaffirming that the initiative in negotiating the agreements for armed forces provided for in Article 43 of the Charter belongs to the Security Council, and desiring to ensure that, pending the conclusion of such agreements, the United Nations has at its disposal means for maintaining international peace and security,

Conscious that failure of the Security Council to discharge its responsibilities on behalf of all the Member States, particularly those responsibilities referred to in the two preceding paragraphs, does not relieve Member States of their obligations or the United Nations of its responsibility under the Charter to maintain international peace and security,

Recognising in particular that such failure does not deprive the General Assembly of its rights or relieve it of its responsibilities under the Charter in regard to the maintenance of international peace and security,

Recognising that discharge by the General Assembly of its responsibilities in these respects calls for possibilities of observation which would ascertain the facts and expose aggressors; for the existence of armed forces which could be used collectively; and for the possibility of timely recommendation by the General Assembly to Members of the United Nations for collective action which, to be effective, should be prompt,

1. Resolves that if the Security Council, because of lack of unanimity of the permanent members, fails to exercise its primary responsibility for the maintenance of international peace and security in any case where there appears to be a threat to the peace, breach of the peace, or act of aggression, the General Assembly shall consider the matter immediately with a view to making appropriate recommendations to Members for collective measures, including in the case of a breach of the peace or act of aggression the use of armed force when necessary, to maintain or restore

---

[49] See Andrassy (1956) 50 A.J.I.L. 563; Reicher (1981) 20 Col.J.T.L. 1; and Woolsey (1951) 45 A.J.I.L. 129.

international peace and security. If not in session at the time, the General Assembly may meet in emergency special session within twenty-four hours of the request therefor. Such emergency special session shall be called if requested by the Security Council on the vote of any seven[50] members, or by a majority of the Members of the United Nations. . . .

7. Invites each Member of the United Nations to survey its resources in order to determine the nature and scope of the assistance it may be in a position to render in support of any recommendations of the Security Council or of the General Assembly for the restoration of international peace and security.

8. Recommends to the State Members of the United Nations that each Member maintain within its national armed forces elements so trained, organised and equipped that they could promptly be made available, in accordance with its constitutional processes, for service as a United Nations unit or units, upon recommendations by the Security Council or the General Assembly, without prejudice to the use of such elements in exercise of the right of individual or collective self-defence recognised in Article 51 of the Charter. . . .

Notes

1. The resolution was adopted by 52 votes to five with two abstentions.

2. The resolution established (i) a Peace Observation Commission with representatives of 14 Member States, "which could observe and report on the situation in any area where there exists international tension the continuance of which is likely to endanger the maintenance of international peace and security" at the instance of the General Assembly or the Security Council and subject to the consent of the state whose territory is to be entered and (ii) a Collective Measures Committee "to study and make a report to the Security Council and the General Assembly . . . on methods, including those in Section C[51] of the present resolution which might be used to maintain and strengthen international peace and security . . . " A Balkan Sub-Commission of the Peace Observation Commission was established in 1952 which sent observers to Northern border areas of Greece at the request of Greece. Apart from this, the Peace Observation Commission has not been used. The Collective Measures Committee submitted three Reports in the period 1951–54. Both bodies are still formally in existence.

3. Introducing the resolution in the First Committee of the General Assembly the representative of the United States is reported as saying:

> . . . the authors of the joint draft resolution (A/C.1/576), of which his country was one, had been inspired by the United Nations action in Korea, which had proved that the Organisation could be an effective instrument for suppressing aggression. Nevertheless, if aggressors were to be deterred by fear of the United Nations, certain organisational weaknesses would have to be remedied. . . .
>
> Five years had elapsed and, while the Security Council had in many respects served admirably the purposes for which it had been set up, experience had

---

[50] *Ed.* Now nine.
[51] See paras 7 and 8 of the Resolution.

shown that it was impossible to rely solely on the Council. . . . The right of veto had already been used nearly fifty times; the Security Council had not established an adequate system of observation; it had not taken the initiative required of it in virtue of Article 43.[52]

The representative of the USSR is reported as saying:

> . . . it could be contended that the veto was no good; that it was an obstruction; that it doomed the Security Council to a palsied state, that it prevented the Council or the United Nations from taking measures to discharge their responsibilities. If that were so, however, common sense and elementary good faith would require, in accordance with Article 109 of the Charter, that steps be taken to abolish such a provision. But the sponsors of the joint proposal avoided that course, although they attached considerable significance to speeches attacking the principle of unanimity in the Security Council, which was said to be the source of all the sorrows, failures and fiascos which the United Nations had experienced. . . . The principal questions relating to implementation of measures for the maintenance of peace and security had remained unsolved, not because of the veto, but because of the position taken in the Security Council by the Anglo-American bloc, which had consistently tried to foist decisions designed for its own benefit, on the Security Council, decisions which consistently failed to take into consideration the interests of the United Nations and were designed to favour the American monopolists. That had been done by dint of the Anglo-American bloc's majority in the Security Council. There was no use in the veto if a majority could always be commanded. The advantage was always on the side of the majority, particularly when it had reached an understanding and had set forth an objective to which all members of the majority must submit, though perhaps not all of them sympathised with it.[53]

4. The General Assembly has acted under the Resolution on a number of occasions, including Korea (1950),[54] the Suez Question (1956), the Hungarian Uprising (1956), Lebanon and Jordan (1958), the Congo Question (1960), the Middle East (1967), the Pakistan Civil War (Bangladesh) (1972), Afghanistan (1980), the Palestine Situation (1980, 1982), Namibia (1981) and the Question of Occupied Arab Territories (1982). In nearly all of these cases, an emergency special session, in accordance with paragraph 1, was necessary.

5. See further on the role of the General Assembly under Articles 11–14, Charter, the *Certain Expenses* case, below, p. 975.

(v) THE DOMESTIC JURISDICTION LIMITATION[55]

See Article 2(7), United Nations Charter, below, Appendix I.

---

[52] G.A.O.R., 5th Sess.; 1st Committee, 354th Meeting (October 9, 1950), p. 63.

[53] *ibid.* 357th Meeting (October 10, 1950), p. 82.

[54] But see Petersen (1959) 13 Int.Org. 219, who concludes that the Assembly did not act under the Resolution in the *Korean* case.

[55] See Gilmour (1967) 16 I.C.L.Q. 330; Goodrich, Hambro and Simons, *op. cit.*, p. 863, n. 22, above, pp. 60–73; Higgins, *op. cit.*, p. 859, n. 1, above, pp. 58–130.

THE SPANISH QUESTION

S.C.O.R., 1st Year, 1st Series, 44th Meeting, pp. 317–319

For the background to this case, see above, p. 940.

MR. EVATT (AUSTRALIA). At the San Francisco Conference, together with other colleagues sitting at this Council with me today, I had some share in the final drafting of Article 2, paragraph 7, and I should like to quote from the memorandum presented by my delegation to the First Committee of Commission I at that Conference:

"Once a matter is recognised as one of legitimate international concern, no exception to the general rule is needed to bring it within the powers of the Organisation. The general rule itself ceases to apply as soon as the matter ceases to be one of domestic jurisdiction."

Therefore, the Security Council must determine that point. The Security Council has to look at the facts of this particular situation and ask itself whether the situation is essentially within the domestic jurisdiction of Spain.

What are the facts? The facts are that there is a situation the continuance of which, in the finding of the Sub-Committee, is likely to endanger the maintenance of international peace and security. That situation has already led to strong expression of concern and disapproval by various Governments and to the closing of a frontier. There is a record of past participation in the Second World War and of recent action hindering the victorious Allies in removing vestiges of Nazism. Various Governments, Members of the United Nations, have already broken off diplomatic relations and recognised a rival Government. All this is a matter of vital international concern. The situation, I submit, is the complete antithesis of an essentially domestic situation.

Then, as to the action proposed, the recommended measures are the breaking off of diplomatic relations by all Members of the United Nations. This is a form of action completely within the control of the various nations as it is within their sole discretion to adopt this measure. The matter of diplomatic relations with other countries belongs to the sphere of external and international relationships. Further, the termination of diplomatic relations is the normal action taken by nations to express their disapproval or to make their protest against the international actions of another nation. Again, the proposed action follows directly from the decision taken in the course of international deliberations during the past year seeking to exclude Franco's Spain from membership in the United Nations. Inasmuch as the United Nations, which is the organised family of nations, has already denied membership to Franco's Spain, it is completely logical and consequential for it not to maintain diplomatic relations with a regime, which according to the

United Nations' own decision can never become a member of that Organisation.

Then, I turn to the purpose of the action in order to demonstrate that this matter is not essentially one of domestic concern. The object is to remove a danger to international peace and a cause of international friction. It is true that this international objective may be served by a withdrawal of the Franco regime, but how that change is to be brought about is entirely a matter for the Spanish Government and people. The United Kingdom, the United States of America and France, in favouring such a change last March, expressed the hope that Franco himself would peacefully withdraw. So long as he remains, there is likely to be an international situation of concern to the United Nations because in the view of the Sub-Committee it is one likely to endanger the maintenance of international peace and security. . . .

The argument, therefore, that the United Nations and the Security Council, or any other Members of the United Nations, cannot touch this matter because it only affects internal affairs in Spain is unsubstantiated and should be rejected.

Notes

1. The provision equivalent to Article 2(7) in the League of Nations Covenant was Article 15(8) which read:

> If the dispute between the parties is claimed by one of them, and is found by the Council, to arise out of a matter which by international law is solely within the domestic jurisdiction of that party, the Council shall so report, and shall make no recommendations as to its settlement.

In its Advisory Opinion in the *Nationality Decrees issued in Tunis and Morocco* case[56] the P.C.I.J. was asked whether questions concerning the application to British subjects of nationality decrees made in Tunis and Morocco by France were matters of domestic jurisdiction in the sense of Article 15(8). The Court replied in the negative. It stated:

> The question whether a certain matter is or is not solely within the jurisdiction of a state is an essentially relative question; it depends upon the development of international relations. Thus, in the present state of international law, questions of nationality are, in the opinion of the Court, in principle within this reserved domain.
>
> For the purpose of the present opinion, it is enough to observe that it may well happen that, in a matter which, like that of nationality, is not, in principle, regulated by international law, the right of a state to use its discretion is nevertheless restricted by obligations which it may have undertaken towards other states. In such a case, jurisdiction which, in principle, belongs solely to the state, is limited by rules of international law. Article 15, paragraph 8, then ceases to apply as regards those states which are entitled to invoke such rules, and the dispute as to the question whether a state has or has not the right to

[56] P.C.I.J.Rep., Ser. B, No. 4 (1923).

take certain measures becomes in these circumstances a dispute of an international character and falls outside the scope of the exception contained in this paragraph.[57]

2. Article 2(7) was inserted at the instance of the four sponsoring powers. Mr Dulles (U.S.), speaking for them, explained:

> ... the four power amendment dealt with domestic jurisdiction as a basic principle, and not, as had been the case in the original Dumbarton Oaks Proposals and in Article 15 of the Covenant of the League of Nations, as a technical and legalistic formula designed to deal with the settlement of disputes by the Security Council. This change in concept had been caused, he explained, by the change in the character of the Organisation as planned in the discussions at San Francisco. The scope of the Organisation was now broadened to include functions which would enable the Organisation to eradicate the underlying causes of war as well as to deal with crises leading to war. Under the Social and Economic Council the Organisation would deal with economic and social problems. This broadening of the scope of the Organisation constituted a great advance, but it also engendered special problems.
>
> For instance, the question had been raised as to what would be the basic relation of the Organisation to member states: would the Organisation deal with the governments of the member states, or would the Organisation penetrate directly into the domestic life and social economy of the member states? As provided in the amendment of the sponsoring governments, Mr. Dulles pointed out that this principle would require the Organisation to deal with the governments. . . .
>
> In reply to the contention that domestic jurisdiction should be determined in accordance with international law, Mr. Dulles again pointed out that international law was subject to constant change and therefore escaped definition. It would, in any case, be difficult to define whether or not a given situation came within the domestic jurisdiction of a state. In this era the whole internal life of a country was affected by foreign conditions.[58]

3. Objections to United Nations jurisdiction based upon Article 2(7) have been raised in connection with such subjects as the character or internal activities of national governments (including respect for human rights) and the administration and future of non-self-governing territories. When the General Assembly has decided to take jurisdiction in respect of a question despite the protests of the state concerned, that state has, on occasions, walked out. South Africa walked out during discussion of *apartheid*; France did so when Algeria was discussed; and the United Kingdom was not present when voting on a matter concerning Southern Rhodesia occurred (before 1965). On the narrow reading of Article 2(7) in a humanitarian context, see the *Iraqi Safe Havens* case, above, p. 920.

4. Goodrich, Hambro and Simon[59] comment upon practice concerning Article 2(7) as follows:

> Ambiguity results from the fact that a permissive view with respect to what the Organisation *may* do can be the result either of a restrictive definition of intervention or a restrictive interpretation of "essentially within the domestic jurisdiction." United Nations practice is conclusive, however, on one point, namely, that placing a matter on the agenda for discussion does not constitute

---

[57] *ibid.* p. 24.
[58] 5 U.N.C.I.O., *Documents* 507.
[59] *op. cit.*, p. 863, n. 22, above pp. 67–68. See also Watson (1977) 71 A.J.I.L. 60.

intervention. With regard to discussion, the same would appear to be true, although some members have taken an opposing view. The argument for not regarding discussion as intervention is that only after discussion can a decision be taken as to the competence of the organ. But in practice it is difficult, if not impossible, to prevent discussion of substance at this preliminary stage, and it has not generally been done. On the question whether steps taken beyond discussion, such as establishing a commission of inquiry or making recommendations to the parties, constitute intervention, the record is not clear since the attitude adopted on this issue cannot usually be separated from the assessment made of the degree of international concern. It has been suggested, however, that a distinction can be made between a recommendation of a general nature addressed to all members and one that is directed to a particular state.

Generally speaking, fears expressed at San Francisco that Article 2(7) would be a serious limitation on the work of the United Nations have not been justified in practice.

(vi) Peace-Keeping Forces[60]

Notes

It soon became apparent that the United Nations needed not only the capacity to conduct enforcement action against an aggressor, but also a peace-keeping, or policing, competence. In a situation in which tension is running high between adjoining states or where law and order has broken down within a state, a neutral United Nations police presence can be of great help in maintaining or restoring the peace. The first United Nations force of this kind was the UN Emergency Force (UNEF). This was established by the General Assembly in 1956 to supervise the cease-fire in the Middle East after the Suez Invasion.[61] In 1960, the UN Force in the Congo (ONUC) was formed by the Security Council at the request of the Republic of the Congo to help restore peace in its territory after civil war had broken out shortly after its independence.[62] Both of these forces have since been disbanded, as have the more recent UN operation in Somalia (UNOSOM II)[63] and the UN Protection Force in Yugoslavia (UNPROFOR)[64] United Nations peace-keeping forces now in operation are the UN Force in Cyprus (UNFICYP), which was established by the Security Council in 1964 after fighting had broken out between Greek and Turkish Cypriots[65]; the UN Disengagement Observation

---

[60] See Bowett, *op. cit.*, p. 951, n. 66, above; Cassese, ed., *United Nations Peace-Keeping: Legal Essays* (1978); Higgins, *United Nations Peace-Keeping: Documents and Commentary*, 4 vols. (1969–81); McCoubrey and White, *The Blue Helmets: Legal Regulation of United Nations Military Operations* (1996); Ratner, *The New UN Peacekeeping* (1995); Seyersted, *United Nations Forces in the Law of Peace and War* (1966).

[61] For a discussion of the legal aspects of UNEF, see the UN Secretary-General's Report on UNEF, 1958, UN Doc. A/3943, G.A.O.R., 13th Sess., Annexes, Agenda Item 65. See also Lauterpacht (1957) 22 Int. Org. 413 and Rosner, *The United Nations Emergency Force* (1963).

[62] See Miller (1961) 55 A.J.I.L. 1.

[63] On UNOSOM, see above, p. 923.

[64] On UNPROFOR, see above, p. 150. The UN peace-keeping operations now in the Balkans are the UN Preventive Deployment Force (UNPREDEP); the UN Mission in Bosnia and Herzegovina (UNMIBH); the UN Transitional Administration for Eastern Slavonia, Baranja and Western Sirmium (UNTAES); and the UN Mission of Observers in Previaka (UNMOP).

[65] See Stegenga, *The United Nations Force in Cyprus* (1968) and Theodorides (1982) 31 I.C.L.Q. 765.

Force (UNDOF), which patrols the buffer zone between Israel and Syria[66]; the UN Interim Force in the Lebanon (UNIFIL), which polices the Israeli-Lebanese border[67]; and the UN Support Mission in Haiti (UNSMIH). The present practice is for the mandate of these forces to be renewed for a period of up to six months at a time. The creation of such forces has become a matter for the Security Council, to the exclusion of the General Assembly, with the Secretary-General being delegated considerable powers in respect of their functioning.

Such forces may only operate on the territory of a state with its consent. For example, UNEF operated only on Egyptian soil; it was refused permission to enter Israel. When, just prior to the Six Day War in 1967, Egypt withdrew its consent, UNEF was withdrawn from the Middle East.[68] Peace-keeping forces are composed of military contingents of armed troops voluntarily made available by member states and acting under United Nations Command. UNEF consisted, at its peak, of about 6,000 men from the armed forces of ten states. United Nations peace-keeping forces are required to remain impartial and to avoid action that may affect the claims of opposing parties. They may only use their arms in self-defence.

Although the line between peace-keeping operation and Chapter VII enforcement action is clear in theory, in practice some UN forces have been given functions that are, to some extent, mixed. See, in particular, ONUC, UNOSOM II and UNPROFOR.

There is no Article in the United Nations Charter which expressly provides for peace-keeping forces. Their constitutionality was confirmed in the *Certain Expenses* Case, below.

CERTAIN EXPENSES OF THE UNITED NATIONS CASE[69]

Advisory Opinion. I.C.J. Reports 1962, p. 151

Certain members of the United Nations fell seriously behind in the payment of the financial contributions assessed to them by the General Assembly under Article 17 of the Charter because of their refusal to accept these assessments so far as they related to the financing of UNEF and ONUC on the ground that both of these forces were unconstitutional. The General Assembly requested the advice of the I.C.J. The Court's opinion comments upon the relationship of the General

---

[66] See above, p. 225.
[67] Established by the Security Council in 1978, S.C. Resn. 425 (1978), S.C.O.R., 33rd Year, *Resolutions and Decisions*, p. 5. In addition to the above peace-keeping forces, there are also several UN observer missions—the UN Truce Supervision Organisation (UNTSO) in the Middle East; the UN Military Observer Group in India and Pakistan (UNMOGIP); the UN Iraq–Kuwait Observer Mission (UNIKOM); the UN Observer Mission in Georgia (UNIMIG); the UN Observer Mission in Liberia (UNIMIL); the UN Mission of Observers in Tajikstan (UNMOT); and the UN Verification Mission in Guatemala (MINUGUA); the UN Angola Verification Mission (UNAVEM III); these missions are usually unarmed and limited to observing and reporting; they do not intervene to maintain the peace. There is also the UN Mission for the Referendum in Western Sahara (MINURSO), which has the task its name indicates.
[68] UNEF was re-established by the Security Council in 1973 to supervise the cease-fire after the *Yom Kippur* War. Plans by which it would have supervised the 1979 Egyptian-Israeli Peace Treaty arrangements were not pursued in the face of USSR opposition. It ceased to exist when its mandate expired in 1979.
[69] UN Doc. S/5653; (1964) 3 I.L.M. 545.

Assembly and the Security Council in the maintenance of peace as well as upon constitutionality of the two peace-keeping forces concerned.

Opinion of the Court

The question on which the Court is asked to give its opinion is whether certain expenditures which were authorised by the General Assembly to cover the costs of the United Nations operations in the Congo (hereinafter referred to as ONUC) and of the operations of the United Nations Emergency Force in the Middle East (hereinafter referred to as UNEF), "constitute 'expenses of the Organisation' within the meaning of Article 17, paragraph 2, of the Charter of the United Nations."

... On the previous occasions when the Court had to interpret the Charter of the United Nations, it has followed the principles and rules applicable in general to the interpretation of treaties, since it has recognised that the Charter is a multilateral treaty, albeit a treaty having certain special characteristics. In interpreting Article 4 of the Charter, the Court was led to consider "the structure of the Charter" and "the relations established by it between the General Assembly and the Security Council"; a comparable problem confronts the Court in the instant matter. The Court sustained its interpretation of Article 4 by considering the manner in which the organs concerned "have consistently interpreted the text" in their practice (*Competence of the General Assembly for the Admission of a State to the United Nations, I.C.J. Reports* 1950, pp. 8—9). . . .

Turning to paragraph 2 of Article 17, the Court observes that, on its face, the term "expenses of the Organisation" means all the expenses and not just certain types of expenses which might be referred to as "regular expenses." An examination of other parts of the Charter shows the variety of expenses which must inevitably be included within the "expenses of the Organisation" just as much as the salaries of staff or the maintenance of buildings. . . .

... it has been argued before the Court that one type of expenses, namely those resulting from operations from the maintenance of international peace and security, are not "expenses of the Organisation" within the meaning of Article 17, paragraph 2, of the Charter, inasmuch as they fail to be dealt with exclusively by the Security Council, and more especially through agreements negotiated in accordance with Article 43 of the Charter.

The argument rests in part upon the view that when the maintenance of international peace and security is involved, it is only the Security Council which is authorised to decide on any action relative thereto. It is argued further that since the General Assembly's power is limited to discussing, considering, studying and recommending, it cannot impose an obligation to pay the expenses which result from the implementation of its recommendations. This argument leads to an examination of the respective functions of the General Assembly and of the Security Council under the Charter, particularly with respect to the maintenance of international peace and security. . . .

The responsibility conferred [by Art. 24] is "primary," not exclusive. This primary responsibility is conferred upon the Security Council, as stated in Article 24, "in order to ensure prompt and effective action." To this end, it is the Security Council which is given a power to impose an explicit obligation of compliance if for example it issues an order or command to an aggressor under Chapter VII. It is only the Security Council which can require enforcement by coercive action against an aggressor.

The Charter makes it abundantly clear, however, that the General Assembly is also to be concerned with international peace and security. . . . The word "measures" [in Art. 14] implies some kind of action, and the only limitation which Article 14 imposes on the General Assembly is the restriction found in Article 12, namely, that the Assembly should not recommend measures while the Security Council is dealing with the same matter unless the Council requests it to do so. Thus while it is the Security Council which, exclusively, may order coercive action, the functions and powers conferred by the Charter on the General Assembly are not confined to discussion, consideration, the initiation of studies and the making of recommendations; they are not merely hortatory. Article 18 deals with *"decisions"* of the General Assembly "on important questions." These "decisions" do indeed include certain recommendations, but others have dispositive force and effect. Among these latter decisions, Article 18 includes suspension of rights and privileges of membership, expulsion of Members "and budgetary questions." In connection with the suspension of rights and privileges of membership and expulsion from membership under Articles 5 and 6, it is the Security Council which has only the power to recommend and it is the General Assembly which decides and whose decision determines status; but there is a close collaboration between the two organs. Moreover, these powers of decision of the General Assembly under Articles 5 and 6 are specifically related to preventive or enforcement measures. . . .

The argument supporting a limitation on the budgetary authority of the General Assembly with respect to the maintenance of international peace and security relies especially on the reference to "action" in the last sentence of Article 11, paragraph 2. . . .

The Court considers that the kind of action referred to in Article 11, paragraph 2, is coercive or enforcement action. This paragraph, which applies not merely to general questions relating to peace and security, but also to specific cases brought before the General Assembly by a State under Article 35, in its first sentence empowers the General Assembly, by means of recommendations to States or to the Security Council, or to both, to organise peace-keeping operations, at the request, or with the consent, of the States concerned. This power of the General Assembly is a special power which in no way derogates from its general powers under

Article 10 or Article 14 except as limited by the last sentence of Article 11, paragraph 2. This last sentence says that when "action" is necessary the General Assembly shall refer the question to the Security Council. The word "action" must mean such action as is solely within the province of the Security Council. It cannot refer to recommendations which the Security Council might make, as for instance under Article 38, because the General Assembly under Article 11 has a comparable power. The "action" which is solely within the province of the Security Council is that which is indicated by the title of Chapter VII of the Charter, namely "Action with respect to threats to the peace, breaches of the peace, and acts of aggression." If the word "action" in Article 11, paragraph 2, were interpreted to mean that the General Assembly could make recommendations only of a general character affecting peace and security in the abstract, and not in relation to specific cases, the paragraph would not have provided that the General Assembly may make recommendations on questions brought before it by States or by the Security Council. Accordingly, the last sentence of Article 11, paragraph 2, has no application where the necessary action is not enforcement action.

The practice of the Organisation throughout its history bears out the foregoing elucidation of the term "action" in the last sentence of Article 11, paragraph 2. Whether the General Assembly proceeds under Article 11, or under Article 14, the implementation of its recommendations for setting up commissions or other bodies involves organisational activity—action—in connection with the maintenance of international peace and security. Such implementation is a normal feature of the functioning of the United Nations. . . .

The Court accordingly finds that the argument which seeks, by reference to Article 11, paragraph 2, to limit the budgetary authority of the General Assembly in respect of the maintenance of international peace and security, is unfounded.

It has further been argued before the Court that Article 43 of the Charter constitutes a particular rule, a *lex specialis*, which derogates from the general rule in Article 17, whenever an expenditure for the maintenance of international peace and security is involved. . . .

With reference to this argument, the Court will state at the outset that, for reasons fully expounded later in this Opinion, the operations known as UNEF and ONOC were not *enforcement* actions within the compass of Chapter VII of the Charter and that therefore Article 43 could not have any applicability to the cases with which the Court is here concerned. However, even if Article 43 were applicable, the Court could not accept this interpretation of its text for the following reasons.

There is nothing in the text of Article 43 which would limit the discretion of the Security Council in negotiating such agreements. It cannot be assumed that in every such agreement the Security Council would insist, or that any Member State would be bound to agree, that such State would bear the entire cost of the "assistance" which it would make available including, for example, transport of forces to the point of operation, complete logistical maintenance in the field, supplies, arms and ammunition, etc. If, during negotiations under the terms of Article 43, a Member State would be entitled (as it would be) to insist, and the Security Council would be entitled (as it would be) to agree, that some part of the expense should be borne by the Organisation then such expense would form part of the expenses of the Organisation and would fall to be apportioned by the General Assembly under Article 17. . . .

Moreover, an argument which insists that all measures taken for the maintenance of international peace and security must be financed through agreements concluded under Article 43, would seem to exclude the possibility that the Security Council might act under some other Article of the Charter. The Court cannot accept so limited a view of the powers of the Security Council under the Charter. It cannot be said that the Charter has left the Security Council impotent in the face of an emergency situation when agreements under Article 43 have not been concluded.

Articles of Chapter VII of the Charter speak of "situations" as well as disputes, and it must lie within the power of the Security Council to police a situation even though it does not resort to enforcement action against a State. The costs of actions which the Security Council is authorised to take constitute "expenses of the Organisation within the meaning of Article 17, paragraph 2."

. . . In determining whether the actual expenditures authorised constitute "expenses of the Organisation within the meaning of Article 17, paragraph 2, of the Charter," the Court agrees that such expenditures must be tested by their relationship to the purposes of the United Nations in the sense that if an expenditure were made for the purpose which is not one of the purposes of the United Nations, it could not be considered an "expense of the Organisation."

The purposes of the United Nations are set forth in Article I of the Charter. . . .

. . . These purposes are broad indeed, but neither they nor the powers conferred to effectuate them are unlimited. Save as they have entrusted the Organisation with the attainment of these common ends, the Member States retain their freedom of action. But when the Organisation takes action which warrants the assertion that it was appropriate for the fulfilment of one of the stated purposes of the United Nations, the presumption is that such an action is not *ultra vires* the Organisation.

If it is agreed that the action in question is within the scope of the function of the Organisation but it is alleged that it has been initiated or carried out in a manner not in conformity with the division of functions among the several organs which the Charter prescribes, one moves to the internal plane, to the internal structure of the Organisation. If the action was taken by the wrong organ, it was irregular as a matter of that internal structure, but this would not necessarily mean that the expense incurred was not an expense of the Organisation. Both national and international law contemplate cases in which the body corporate or politic may be bound, as to third parties, by an *ultra vires* act of an agent.

In the legal systems of States, there is often some procedure for determining the validity of even a legislative or governmental act, but no analogous procedure is to be found in the structure of the United Nations. Proposals made during the drafting of the Charter to place the ultimate authority to interpret the Charter in the International Court of Justice were not accepted; the opinion which the Court is in course of rendering is an *advisory* opinion. As anticipated in 1945, therefore, each organ must, in the first place at least, determine its own jurisdiction. If the Security Council, for example, adopts a resolution purportedly for the maintenance of international peace and security and if, in accordance with a mandate or authorisation in such resolution, the Secretary-General incurs financial obligations, these amounts must be presumed to constitute "expenses of the Organisation."

In considering the operations in the Middle East, the Court must analyse the functions of UNEF as set forth in resolutions of the General Assembly. Resolution 998 (ES-I) of November 4, 1956 requested the Secretary-General to submit a plan "for the setting up, with the consent of the nations concerned, of an emergency international United Nations Force to secure and supervise the cessation of hostilities in accordance with all the terms of" the General Assembly's previous resolution 997 (ES-I) of November 2, 1956. The verb "secure" as applied to such matters as halting the movement of military forces and arms into the area and the conclusion of a cease-fire, might suggest measures of enforcement, were it not that the Force was to be set up "with the consent of the nations concerned."

In his first report on the plan for an emergency international Force the Secretary-General used the language of resolution 998 (ES-I) in submitting his proposals. The same terms are used in General Assembly resolution 1000 (ES-I) of November 5, in which operative paragraph 1 reads:

> "*Establishes* a United Nations Command for an emergency international Force to secure and supervise the cessation of hostilities in accordance with all the terms of General Assembly resolution 997 (ES-I) of November 2, 1956."

This resolution was adopted without a dissenting vote. In his second and final report on the plan for an emergency international Force of November 6, the Secretary-General, in paragraphs 9 and 10, stated:

> "While the General Assembly is enabled to *establish* the Force with the consent of those parties which contribute units to the Force, it could not request the Force to be *stationed* or *operate* on the territory of

a given country without the consent of the Government of that country. This does not exclude the possibility that the Security Council could use such a Force within the wider margins provided under Chapter VII of the United Nations Charter. I would not for the present consider it necessary to elaborate this point further, since no use of the Force under Chapter VII, with the rights in relation to Member States that this would entail, has been envisaged.

10. The point just made permits the conclusion that the setting up of the Force should not be guided by the needs which would have existed had the measure been considered as part of an enforcement action directed against a Member country. There is an obvious difference between establishing the Force in order to secure the cessation of hostilities, with a withdrawal of forces, and establishing such a Force with a view to enforcing a withdrawal of forces."

Paragraph 12 of the Report is particularly important because in resolution 1001 (ES-I) the General Assembly, again without a dissenting vote, "*Concurs* in the definition of the functions of the Force as stated in paragraph 12 of the Secretary-General's report." Paragraph 12 reads in part as follows:

"the functions of the United Nations Force would be, when a cease-fire is being established, to enter Egyptian territory with the consent of the Egyptian Government, in order to help maintain quiet during and after the withdrawal of non-Egyptian troops, and to secure compliance with the other terms established in the resolution of November 2, 1956. The Force obviously should have no rights other than those necessary for the execution of its functions, in co-operation with local authorities. It would be more than an observers' corps, but in no way a military force temporarily controlling the territory in which it is stationed; nor, moreover, should the Force have military functions exceeding those necessary to secure peaceful conditions on the assumption that the parties to the conflict take all necessary steps for compliance with the recommendations of the General Assembly."

It is not possible to find in this description of the functions of UNEF . . . any evidence that the Force was to be used for purposes of enforcement. Nor can such evidence be found in the subsequent operations of the Force, operations which did not exceed the scope of the functions ascribed to it.

It could not therefore have been patent on the face of the resolution that the establishment of UNEF was in effect "enforcement action" under Chapter VII which, in accordance with the Charter, could be authorised only by the Secretary Council.

On the other hand, it is apparent that the operations were undertaken to fulfil a prime purpose of the United Nations, that is, to promote and to maintain a peaceful settlement of the situation. This being true, the Secretary-General properly exercised the authority given him to incur financial obligations of the Organisation and expenses resulting from such obligations must be considered "expenses of the Organisation within the meaning of Article 17, paragraph 2."

Apropos what has already been said about the meaning of the word "action" in Article 11 of the Charter, attention may be called to the fact that resolution 997 (ES-I), which is chronologically the first of the resolutions concerning the operations in the Middle East mentioned in the request for the advisory opinion, provides in paragraph 5:

> "*Requests* the Secretary-General to observe and report promptly on the compliance with the present resolution to the Security Council *and* to the General Assembly, for such further *action as they may deem appropriate in accordance with the Charter.*" . . .

The Court notes that these "actions" may be considered "measures" recommended under Article 14, rather than "action" recommended under Article 11. The powers of the General Assembly stated in Article 14 are not made subject to the provisions of Article 11, but only of Article 12. Furthermore, as the Court has already noted, the word "measures" implies some kind of action. So far as concerns the nature of the situations in the Middle East in 1956, they could be described as "likely to impair . . . friendly relations among nations," just as well as they could be considered to involve "the maintenance of international peace and security." Since the resolutions of the General Assembly in question do not mention upon which article they are based, and since the language used in most of them imply reference to either Article 14 or Article 11, it cannot be excluded that they were based upon the former rather than the latter article. . . .

The Court concludes that, from year to year, the expenses of UNEF have been treated by the General Assembly as expenses of the Organisation within the meaning of Article 17, paragraph 2, of the Charter.

The operations in the Congo were initially authorised by the Security Council in the resolution of July 14, 1960 which was adopted without a dissenting vote. The resolution, in the light of the appeal from the Government of the Congo, the report of the Secretary-General and the debate in the Security Council, was clearly adopted with a view to maintaining international peace and security. However, it is argued that that resolution has been implemented, in violation of provisions of the Charter inasmuch as under the Charter it is the Security Council that determines which States are to participate in carrying out decisions involving the maintenance of international peace and security, whereas in the case of the Congo the Secretary-General himself determined which States were to participate with their armed forces or otherwise. . . .

The Court then considered the subsequent Security Council resolutions authorising and supporting the Secretary-General's action.

In the light of such a record or reiterated consideration, confirmation, approval and ratification by the Security Council and by the General Assembly of the actions of the Secretary-General in implementing the resolution of July 14, 1960, it is impossible to reach the conclusion that the operations in question usurped or impinged upon the prerogatives conferred by the Charter on the Security Council. The Charter does not forbid the Security Council to act through instruments of its own choice: under Article 29 it "may establish such subsidiary organs as it deems necessary for the performance of its functions"; under Article 98 it may entrust "other functions" to the Secretary-General.

It is not necessary for the Court to express an opinion as to which article or articles of the Charter were the basis for the resolutions of the Security Council, but it can be said that the operations of ONUC did not include a use of armed force against a State which the Security Council, under Article 39, determined to have committed an act of aggression or to have breached the peace. The armed forces which were utilised in the Congo were not authorised to take military action against any State. The operation did not involve "preventive or enforcement measures" against any State under Chapter VII and therefore did not constitute "action" as that term is used in Article 11.

For the reasons stated, financial obligations which, in accordance with the clear and reiterated authority of both the Security Council and the General Assembly, the Secretary-General incurred on behalf of the United Nations, constitute obligations of the Organisation for which the General Assembly was entitled to make provision under the authority of Article 17....

For these reasons, the Court is of opinion, by nine votes to five,[70] that the expenditures authorised [by the General Assembly related to operations of UNEF and ONUC] ... constitute "expenses of the Organisation" within the meaning of Article 17, paragraph 2, of the Charter of the United Nations.

Notes

1. Although the General Assembly adopted the Court's opinion,[71] a number of states, particularly France and the USSR, refused to pay their contributions and became subject to the suspension of voting rights in the General Assembly under Article 19. By the expedient of not dealing with matters that could not be disposed of without objection, the General Assembly survived the whole of the 19th Session (1964–65) without putting the matter to the test. Then, the United States which had, with good reason in law, been pressing for the application of Article

---

[70] The judges in the majority were Vice-President Alfaro; Judges Badawi, Wellington Koo, Spiropoulos, Sir Percy Spender, Sir Gerald Fitzmaurice, Tanaka, Jessup, Morelli. President Winiarski and Judges Basdevant, Moreno Quintana, Koretsky and Bustamante y Rivero dissented.

[71] G.A. Resn 1854, G.A.O.R., 17th Sess, Supp. 17, p. 54 (1962).

19, gave way and accepted that Article 19 would not be enforced in the existing situation. There seems little doubt that this was a serious setback to the authority of the United Nations over its members. Under arrangements adopted in 1973, contributions are assessed not on the basis used for ordinary contributions to the United Nations budget, but on the basis that increases the amount paid by permanent members of the Security Council and developed states.[72] A number of states remain in default of their payments in respect of particular forces.

2. How widely did the Court apply the doctrine of implied powers? Did it look to see what was essential for the execution of the United Nations function or what was consistent with them? Compare the *Reparation* case, above, p. 132.

---

[72] G.A. Resn 3101 (1973).

CHAPTER 12

ARBITRATION AND JUDICIAL SETTLEMENT OF DISPUTES[1]

1. INTRODUCTORY NOTE

It is a principle of international law that states "shall settle their international disputes by peaceful means"[2] and not by resort to force. This principle is reinforced by Article 33, UN Charter[3] and the 1982 Manila Declaration on the Peaceful Settlement of International Disputes.[4] In international relations, most disputes are settled through negotiation between the parties or by third-party assistance in the form of good offices, conciliation or the conduct of fact-finding inquiries.[5]

As in municipal law, litigation in international law is very much a matter of last resort. The possible worsening of relations by unilateral recourse to law, the uncertainty of the outcome of legal proceedings,[6] and the embarrassment and finality of an adverse ruling by a body beyond one's control are considerations common to both systems which conspire to make this so.[7] If the cost of legal proceedings sometimes deters the plaintiff at the national level, the absence in most cases of compulsory jurisdiction is an even greater weapon for the defendant in international law. This chapter is limited to the machinery for the settle-

---

[1] See Anand, *International Courts and Contemporary Conflicts* (1974); *ibid. Studies in International Adjudication* (1969); Bilder, in Damrosch, *loc. cit.*, p. 988, n. 24, below, p. 155; Gillis Wetter, *The International Arbitral Process: Public and Private*, 5 Vols. (1979); Grieves, *Supranationalism and International Adjudication* (1969); Janis, ed., *International Courts for the Twenty-First Century* (1992); Jenks, *The Prospects of International Adjudication* (1964); Lauterpacht, *Aspects of the Administration of International Justice* (1991); Merrills, *International Dispute Settlement* (2nd ed., 1991); Mosler and Bernhardt, ed., *Judicial Settlement of Disputes*, (1974); and Simpson and Fox, *International Arbitration* (1959). See also Katz, *The Relevance of International Adjudication* (1968).

[2] Art. 2(3), UN Charter, below, Appendix I. See Hutchinson (1992) 14 A.Y.I.L. 1. Although Art. 2(3) is expressed in terms of UN "members," it can be taken to state customary international law.

[3] Appendix I, below.

[4] G.A. Resn 37/10, G.A.O.R., 37th Sess., Supp. 51, p. 261 (1982).

[5] See Bar-Yaacov; *The Handling of International Disputes by Means of Inquiry* (1974); Cot, *International Conciliation* (1968), Eng. trans. (by Myers) (1972); David Davies Memorial Institute of International Studies, *Report of a Study Group on the Peaceful Settlement of International Disputes* (1966); Lall, *Modern International Negotiations* (1966); Northedge and Donelan, *International Disputes* (1971); UN Office of Legal Affairs, *Handbook on the Peaceful Settlement of Disputes between States* (1992); Vallat, in *Cambridge Essays in International Law* (1965), p. 155. For an example of a fact-finding commission of inquiry, see the *Red Crusader Case*, above, p. 442. For an example of conciliation, see the *Jan Mayen Case*, above, p. 389.

[6] Paradoxically, some of the uncertainty of international law is, as Gross points out (in Gross, ed., *The Future of the International Court of Justice* (1976) Vol. II, p. 727 at p. 746), because so few cases are taken to court.

[7] *cf.* Fitzmaurice in *The Future of the International Court, loc. cit.*, n. 6, above, pp. 463–470.

ment of disputes upon a basis of law, whether by arbitration or judicial settlement. This is so for reasons of space and because arbitral tribunals and courts apply international law so that their functioning is of particular interest to lawyers.

2. ARBITRATION[8]

INTERPRETATION OF ARTICLE 3, PARAGRAPH 2, OF THE TREATY OF LAUSANNE

Advisory Opinion, P.C.I.J. Reports, Series B, No. 12, at p. 26 (1925)

Opinion of the Court

If the word "arbitration" is taken in a wide sense, characterised simply by the binding force of the pronouncement made by a third Party to whom the interested Parties have had recourse, it may well be said that the decision in question is an "arbitral award."

This term, on the other hand, would hardly be the right one, if the intention were to convey a common and more limited conception of arbitration, namely, that which has for its object the settlement of differences between States by *judges* of their own choice and *on the basis of respect for law* (Hague Convention for the pacific settlement of international disputes, dated October 18th, 1907, Article 37). It appears, in fact, that according to the arguments put forward on both sides before the Council, the settlement of the dispute in question depends, at all events for the most part, on consideration not of a legal character; moreover, it is impossible, properly speaking, to regard the Council, acting in its capacity of an organ of the League of Nations . . . as a tribunal of arbitrators.

Notes

1. Arbitration was defined by the International Law Commission as "a procedure for the settlement of disputes between States by a binding award on the basis of law and as a result of an undertaking voluntarily accepted."[9] Schwarzenberger states: "The only difference between arbitration and *judicial settlement* lies in the method of selecting the members of these judicial organs. While, in arbitration proceedings, this is done by agreement between the parties, judicial settlement presupposes the existence of a standing tribunal with its own bench of judges and its own rules of procedure which parties to a dispute must accept."[10]

2. Arbitration in recent times dates from the mixed claims commissions estab-

---

[8] See Sohn, (1963–I) 108 Hague Recueil 1; Soons, ed., *International Arbitration: Past and Prospects* (1990); Stuyt, *Survey of International Arbitrations 1794–1989* (1990). See also the I.L.C.'s Model Rules on Arbitral Procedure, Y.B.I.L.C., 1958, II, p. 83.

[9] Y.B.I.L.C., 1953, II, p. 202.

[10] *Manual of International Law* (6th ed., 1976), p. 195.

lished under the Jay Treaty[11] of 1794 between Great Britain and the United States. One well known and successful instance of its use in the nineteenth century was the *Alabama Claims Arbitration*[12] of 1872, also between Great Britain and the United States. Resort to arbitration still occurs,[13] although it has in recent years been to a large extent replaced by the "lump-sum settlement agreement" in the important area of state responsibility for the treatment of aliens.[14] Note also the procedure for the arbitration of investment disputes between states and foreign companies introduced by the 1965 ICSID Convention.[15]

3. Arbitration tribunals may consist of a single arbitrator or they may be collegiate bodies.[16] Where the former is the case, the arbitrator is sometimes a dignitary (*e.g.* a Head of State) who may delegate his responsibilities to a person knowledgeable in international law[17] In the *Rainbow Warrior* case[18] the UN Secretary-General was called upon to arbitrate for the first time. If the tribunal is a collegiate body, it will usually be a mixed commission,[19] *i.e.* one upon which sit two or more arbitrators (commissioners, etc.) appointed in equal numbers by each of the parties separately plus an Umpire (or Presiding Commissioner, etc.) appointed jointly by the parties or by the arbitrators appointed by them.

4. *The Permanent Court of Arbitration.*[20] This was established in 1900 in accordance with the 1899 Hague Convention for the Pacific Settlement of International Disputes[21] and, later, the 1907 Convention of the same name.[22] Each party to either Convention selects up to four persons "of known competence in questions of international law" and "of the highest moral competence" to serve for a renewable period of six years as members of the Court.[23] Should the parties to a dispute decide to refer a case to the Court, under the 1907 Convention they appoint a tribunal from the members of the Court of any size and composition upon which they agree; in the absence of agreement to the contrary, the tribunal is established according to a prescribed formula. Twenty-eight cases have been referred to the Court or conducted with the cooperation of its Bureau. Of these, only four have been decided since 1945, despite efforts to encourage the Court's use.

---

[11] 1 Malloy 590.

[12] Moore, 1 *Int. Arb.* 495.

[13] Examples are the *Air Services Agreement* case, above, p. 11, and the *Anglo-French Continental Shelf* case, see above, p. 467.

[14] See above, p. 585. But note that the Iran-U.S. Claims Tribunal was established in 1981 to consider claims by the U.S. and its nationals against Iran and *vice versa*, as well as inter-state claims. In the case of small claims, the national state was authorised to bring the claim on behalf of its national; in the case of large claims, nationals, usually companies, were permitted to act for themselves. Aldrich, *The Jurisprudence of the Iran-U.S. Claims Tribunal* (1996); Avanessian, *Iran-U.S. Claims Tribunal in Action* (1993); Mapp, *The Iran-U.S. Claims Tribunal* (1993). In 1990, the remaining small claims were settled by lump sum settlement agreement: see 25 Iran-U.S. C.T.R. 327 (1990–II).

[15] See above, p. 586.

[16] See Johnson (1953) 30 B.Y.I.L. 53.

[17] See, *e.g.* the *Clipperton Island* case, above, p. 200.

[18] *loc cit.*, p. 502, n. 49, above.

[19] See, *e.g.* the Mexican Claims Commission by which several of the cases in Chap. 8 were decided.

[20] On the Court, see Lillich, (1978–III) 161 Hague Receuil 358; Schwarzenberger (1980) 34 Y.B.W.A. 329; Shifman (1995) 8 L.J.I.L. 203; and the special issue on the Court in (1993) 6 L.J.I.L. 199.

[21] U.K.T.S. 9 (1901), Cd. 798. The Convention entered into force in 1900.

[22] U.K.T.S. 6 (1971), Cmnd. 4575. 82 parties, including the U.K., to one or both Conventions. The 1907 Convention revised the 1899 Convention in the light of the experience of the Court in its early cases.

[23] Art. 23, 1899 Convention; Art. 44, 1907 Convention.

3. The World Court[24]

The state of health of the World Court has improved remarkably in recent times. Whereas there were years in the 1960s to the 1980s when the Court had very little to do, the Court's list in the 1990s has been full. If there used to be concern over its uncertain future,[25] the worry now is whether it can cope with all of the cases referred to it.[26] The main reason[27] for this change is an increase in confidence in the Court. In the years after the *South-West Africa* cases,[28] the Court's reputation plummeted among developing states, who saw the Court as wedded to western attitudes and approaches to international law.[29] The *Nicaragua* case marked a change of perception on their part and the Court now has cases to which states from many regions of the world are parties.[30]

At the same time, it has yet to be established that two other problems with which the Court has been confronted have been resolved. In several cases in the 1970s and 1980s, the Court experienced the phenomenon of the "non-appearing" defendant.[31] Iceland boycotted the proceedings in the *Fisheries Jurisdiction* cases and in five cases since then the defendant state has not appeared.[32] This can, as in the *Nicaragua* case, present difficulties in ensuring that the Court has all of the evidence it needs in order to decide a case.

The other problem is part of the more general weakness of effectiveness that international law faces. Whereas the judgments and orders of the P.C.I.J. in contentious litigation were all complied with, the record of the I.C.J. since the Second World War has been less satisfactory. The judgments in the *Corfu Channel* case, the *Fisheries Jurisdiction* cases, the *U.S. Diplomatic and Consular Staff in Tehran* case, and the *Nicaragua* case, were not respected,[32a] and nearly all the orders for

---

[24] See Damrosch, ed., *The International Court of Justice at a Crossroads* (1987); Lowe and Fitzmaurice, eds., *Fifty Years of the International Court of Justice* (1996); McWhinney, *The International Court of Justice and the Western Tradition of International Law* (1987); *ibid. Judicial Settlement of International Disputes* (1991); Rosenne, *The Law and Practice of the International Court* (2nd rev. ed., 1985); *ibid. The World Court* (5th rev. ed., 1995); Singh, *The Role and Record of the International Court of Justice* (1989).

[25] See Gross, ed., *The Future of the International Court of Justice* (3 vols., 1976).

[26] See the Study Group Report, *op. cit.*, p. 995, n. 39, below.

[27] There has also been a large increase in the 1990s in the number of states who are the Court's potential clients in contentious litigation.

[28] I.C.J. Rep. 1966, p. 6. Having earlier held that it had jurisdiction in the cases, the Court in effect reversed this decision by ruling that Liberia and Ethiopia, the claimant states, lacked the necessary "legal right or interest" to bring these cases alleging that South Africa had not complied with its obligations under the mandate for South-West Africa/Namibia. The Court's judgment angered a majority of the General Assembly to the point where its Fourth Committee refused to approve a financial appropriation for the Court.

[29] One reason for the establishment of a new International Tribunal on the Law of the Sea, see above, p. 476, by UNCLOS III was a lack of confidence in the Hague Court.

[30] In early 1997, the Court had eight cases on its list, the parties to which were *Hungary v. Slovakia, Botswana v. Namibia, Spain v. Canada, Bosnia/Herzegovina v. the FRY, Qatar v. Bahrain, Cameroon v. Nigeria, Iran v. U.S., Libya v. U.K.* and *Libya v. U.S.*

[31] See Elkind, *Non-Appearance before the International Court of Justice* (1984); Fitzmaurice (1980) 51 B.Y.I.L. 89; Sinclair (1981) 31 I.C.L.Q. 338; and Thirlway, *Non-Appearance before the International Court of Justice* (1985).

[32] The *Nuclear Test* cases above, p. 422; the *Pakistani Prisoners of War Case*, I.C.J. Rep. 1973, pp. 328, 347; the *Aegean Sea Continental Shelf* case, I.C.J. Rep. 1978, p. 3; the *U.S. Diplomatic and Consular Staff* case above, p. 358; the *Nicaragua* case, above, p. 358. For the *Fisheries Jurisdiction* cases, see above, p. 447.

[32a] But, after many years of stalemate, in 1992, as a part of a general settlement of claims between the two states, the U.K. approved the delivery to Albania of the gold that had

interim measures have not been followed.[33] The judgment in the *Right of Passage* case, above, p. 257, was soon negated by the Indian invasion of Goa. On the power, as yet unexercised, of the Security Council to enforce decisions of the Court, see Article 94(2) of the Charter.[34] In 1986, the U.S. vetoed a draft Security Council resolution calling for "full and immediate compliance" with the *Nicaragua* case judgment.[35]

(i) ORGANISATION

See Articles 2–33, Statute of the International Court of Justice.[36]

Notes

1. The World Court, which is by far the most important international court,[37] is the name commonly given to the Permanent Court of International Justice and the present International Court of Justice. The Permanent Court of International Justice was established in 1920 under the auspices of the League of Nations. In 1946, it was replaced by the International Court of Justice, which was made "the principal judicial organ of the United Nations" by Article 92 of the United Nations Charter. The International Court of Justice is organised in accordance with the Statute of the International Court of Justice which is a part of the United Nations Charter and which in most respects is identical with the Statute of its predecessor. The World Court has always had its seat at The Hague.

2. The members of the Court, with the states of which they are nationals, are: President Schwebel (United States of America); Vice-President Weeramantry (Sri Lanka); Judges Oda (Japan), Bedjaoui (Algeria), Guillaume (France), Ranjeva (Madagascar), Herczegh (Hungary), Jiuyong (China), Fleischhauer (Germany), Koroma (Sierra Leone), Vereshchetin (Russian Federation), Higgins (United Kingdom), Parra-Aranguren (Venezuela), Kooijmans (Netherlands), Rezek (Brazil).

3. Judges are elected by the Security Council and the General Assembly according to a complicated procedure (Statute, Arts. 4–14) in which a lot of political infighting occurs. In recent years, the balance of nationalities represented on the Court has changed with the nature of the international community.[38] The under-

---

been the subject matter of the *Monetary Gold* case, see below, p. 1029, and Albania paid the U.K. £2 million in respect of all British claims against it. Following this, the Corfu Channel Incident was regarded as closed; (1992) 63 B.Y.I.L. 781.

[33] On provisional measures, see below, p. 1030.

[34] Below, Appendix II. See Kerley, in *The Future of the International Court of Justice, loc. cit.* at p. 988, n. 25, above, p. 276.

[35] UN Inf. Centre London *Newsletter* November 6, 1986.

[36] See Appendix I, below. The present I.C.J. Rules of Court were adopted in 1978.

[37] On the International Tribunal for the Law of the Sea, see above, p. 476. On the International Criminal Tribunal for the Former Yugoslavia, see above, p. 748. The only other international courts are regional as well as limited in jurisdiction. See the Inter-American Court of Human Rights, the European Court of Human Rights, the European Court of Justice, the European Nuclear Energy Tribunal, the European Tribunal in Matters of State Immunity and the Court of Justice of the Cartegena Agreement. For details, see the UN *Handbook, op. cit.*, p. 985, n. 5, above, pp. 69–70.

[38] In 1920, there were 10 Judges from western Europe; two from Asia; two from South America; and one from the U.S. In the period immediately after the Second World War, Latin American representation rose to four; it has since fallen as Afro-Asian representation has increased. The number of western European judges has also declined, although it is still substantial. See Schwarzenberger (1982) 36 Y.B.W.A. 241. See on the election process generally, Rosenne, in the *The Future of the International Court of Justice, loc cit.*, p. 988, n. 25, above. On the "cultural" balance of the Court; see McWhinney (1987) 65 Wash. U.L.R. 873 and Prott, *The Latent Power of Culture and the International Judge* (1979).

standing now is that the 15 seats on the Court are distributed (in terms of nationalities and power blocs) as follows: nationals of five western states; three African states (one francophonic civil law, one anglophonic common law and one Arab); three Asian states; two East European states[39]; and two Latin American states.[40] It is also the convention that there should be a national of each of the five permanent members of the Security Council. This has been the case since 1945 save that there was no Chinese judge (nationalist or communist) between 1967 and 1985 when no candidate was put forward.

4. The Court normally sits as a full court of 15 judges, although since 1982 several cases have been referred to a Chamber.[41] The Court gives a single, collegiate judgment. Individual judges in the majority may add their own separate opinions. Individual dissenting judges may give dissenting opinions.[42] The Court's judgments are in English and French, with the authentic text printed on the left hand page.

ROSENNE, THE COMPOSITION OF THE COURT

in The Future of the International Court of Justice, loc. cit., p. 988, n. 25, above, Vol. I, pp. 388–390

Provision for the recusal of judges in cases in which they have an interest is made in Articles 17 and 24, Statute of the Court.[43] The following extract concerns the particular problem that arises from the fact that Court members have increasingly had experience within the United Nations as representatives of their governments or in some other capacity and have thereby been involved in cases which later come to the Court.

This type of *ad hoc* disqualification is not based on personal interests which lead to personal bias in the exercise of the judicial function. . . . The problem is to avoid the suspicion of obvious political bias. . . .

The first indication of this problem occurred in *Anglo-Iranian Oil Co.* Here Sir Benegal Rau, who had been elected to the Court in 1951, had previously been the representative of India on the Security Council when that body had been seised of the United Kingdom's complaint of failure

---

[39] Although there are, in a Cold War sense, still two East European judges, this category is out of date.

[40] See Lee and McWhinney (1987) 25 C.Y.I.L. 187.

[41] The *Gulf of Maine* case, above, p. 466, was the first such case. This new departure follows a change in the Rules of the Court which allows the parties to a case "a decisive influence in the composition of ad hoc Chambers": Jiménez de Aréchaga (1973) 67 A.J.I.L. 1 at 2. Thus the composition of the *Gulf of Maine* Chamber, which consisted entirely of North American and West European judges, was "entirely in accordance with the latent wishes of the parties": Judge Oda, *Gulf of Maine (Order)* case, I.C.J. Rep. 1982, p. 10. Judge Oda was one of several judges who were critical of the litigants' influence in the *Gulf of Maine* case as being inconsistent with the Court's sovereignty and prejudicing the universal quality of its jurisprudence. The three chambers established since then have generally been more balanced. The Court also has an Environmental Chamber for environmental cases. See Schwebel (1986) 61 Wash L.R. 1061 at 1070. On Chambers, see Art. 26, Statute, below, Appendix III. See generally, Mosler, in Dinstein, ed., *International Law in a Time of Perplexity: Essays in Honour of Shabtai Rosenne* (1989); Oda (1988) 82 A.J.I.L. 556; Ostrihansky (1988) 37 I.C.L.Q. 30; Schwebel (1987) 81 A.J.I.L. 831.

[42] See Hussain, *Dissenting and Separate Opinions at the World Court* (1984).

[43] See below, Appendix I.

by the Iranian Government to comply with the provisional measures indicated by the Court. Sir Benegal thought that he ought not to sit in this case, and the Court agreed with him. . . .

The next formal indication occurred in 1965, in *South West Africa*, when South Africa made an application concerning the composition of the Court as it existed after the election of 1963. After listening to the contentions of the parties in closed hearings the Court, by eight votes to six (the two judges *ad hoc* taking part), decided not to accede to that application. The assumption at the time that this application referred at least in part to Judge Padilla Nervo, elected in 1963, was subsequently confirmed in *Namibia*. Prior to his election he had twice been permanent representative of Mexico to the United Nations; he had also been the representative of Mexico on the Trusteeship Council (where the affairs of South West Africa had been discussed) as well as President of the General Assembly.

A third indication, and one of extreme gravity, occurred in *Namibia*. Here the written statement of South Africa contained a broad (and public) challenge to the participation in this case of the President, Sir Zafrulla Khan, and Judges Padilla Nervo and Morozov, on the basis of their previous involvement in the affairs of South West Africa as members of their countries' delegations to the United Nations. The President has also been President of the General Assembly, and Judge Morozov had been one of his country's representatives on the Security Council when it had discussed South West Africa, and had played an active part in drawing up some resolutions directly relevant in the advisory case. In a series of three separate orders, unanimous in the cases of the President and Judge Padilla Nervo, and adopted by 10 votes to four in the case of Judge Morozov (the recused judges not taking part), these challenges were all rejected. No hearings took place on those challenges. In 1965 the order was unreasoned, and no indication was given of how the Court divided on the challenge. In 1971 these orders, too, were unreasoned, but the advisory opinion itself gives the reasons; and the third indicates how the Court divided regarding Judge Morozov. In this respect, the greater frankness of the 1971 process, by implication also extending to the 1965 decision as regards Judge Padilla Nervo, is to be welcomed and is certainly less maladroit. . . .

The Court reached the general conclusion that the previous activity of each of its three members in his former capacity of representative of his Government, did not attract the disqualification imposed by Article 17, paragraph 2, of the Statute. In the case of Judge Padilla Nervo, the Court found no reason to depart from its decision in 1965 after hearing the same contentions. In the other two cases, the Court found that the activities in United Nations organs of the Judges concerned prior to their election to the Court did not furnish grounds for treating them differently from Judge Padilla Nervo. In the case of Judge Morozov the Court also took into consideration his participation in the formulation of a certain Security Council resolution concerning the Pretoria trial of some South West

Africans: this participation in the work of the United Nations as representative of his Government did not justify any different conclusions.

In these instances, the decision was reached by the Court after due deliberation. Another case is far less satisfactory. It relates to the non-participation of Judge Sir Zafrulla Khan (re-elected in 1964) in the second phase of *South West Africa*. This has never been satisfactorily explained. The various inspired newspaper accounts of this incident give rise to the most serious misgivings, and these have become magnified by the 1971 decision on the participation of that judge in *Namibia*.

Namibia confirms that in this respect there need be no difference between contentious and advisory proceedings, although doubtless in course of time characteristic and conceptual differences could make their presence felt.

GROSS, THE INTERNATIONAL COURT OF JUSTICE: CONSIDERATION OF REQUIREMENTS FOR ENHANCING ITS ROLE IN THE INTERNATIONAL LEGAL ORDER

in The Future of the International Court of Justice, loc. cit., p. 988, n. 25, above, Vol. I, pp. 61–64. Some footnotes omitted

The institution of judges *ad hoc* in contentious cases [under Article 31, Statute of the Court] and in advisory proceedings under Articles 68 of the Statute and . . . [Article 102(3)] of the [revised] Rules of the Court has been a matter of controversy between those who would suppress it for the sake of enhancing the impartiality of the Court[44] and those who, for a variety of reasons, would maintain it.[45] There are also those who, occupying a middle ground, assert that the abolition of judges *ad hoc* should be combined with the exclusion of "national" judges from the bench, that is, judges who are [members of the Court and] nationals of one or both parties before the Court.[46] In this view, the essential objective is equality between the parties; this can be achieved either by adding to the bench a judge *ad hoc* or by excluding the "national judge." . . .

Fitzmaurice [has] attacked the system . . . arguing in particular two points: First, those who advocate its retention on the ground that it increases confidence in the Court argue from an impermissible premises that judges, particularly *ad hoc* judges, will necessarily espouse the view of their government. Secondly, once a case is terminated, a judge *ad hoc* may feel himself free of every obligation of confidence and may reveal to his government what had been said in the deliberations of the Court. This could have harmful consequences for the independence of judges, partic-

---

[44] For a recent view, see F. L. Grieves, *Supranationalism and International Adjudication*, (1969), p. 180.

[45] [Rosenne, *The Law and Practice of the International Court* (1965), pp. 202–205.]

[46] Erik Castrén, "Revision de la Charte des Nations Unies," 7 Revue Hellénique de Droit International 20–34, at 32 (1954).

ularly if such revelations occurred shortly before elections to the Court.[47] ...

The fact of the matter is that in every case where the majority of the Court gave a favourable judgment for the appointing state, the judge *ad hoc* concurred, and he dissented in nearly every case where the judgment went against it. Such voting alignments, even if the *ad hoc* judge is the only dissenting judge, as was the case in the recent *Barcelona Traction*[48] judgment, do not necessarily reflect on the independence of the judges concerned. Even the majority of 14 in that case could be wrong, and, despite concurrence in the result, there was wide disparity in the actual reasoning of the various judges. ...

It has often been observed that where two parties appoint judges *ad hoc*, their votes cancel each other out. In litigation where only one party appoints a judge *ad hoc*, the other party having a national as a titular judge, his vote could make a difference in marginal cases, but there have been no such cases.

The most constructive view on the role of judges *ad hoc* has been expressed in two forms. According to one, such judges, while not representing their own countries, "fulfil a useful function in supplying local knowledge and a national point of view."[49] The other sees the task of an *ad hoc* judge not so much in his influence upon the judgment as upon its formulation. It rests with such judges "to represent their countries' interests in the whole process through which the decision is produced and the reasons formulated. If the role of the judges *ad hoc* could be more accurately designated as that of assessors, the grant to them of the status of judge (with the right to vote) represents a concession to diplomatic susceptibilities."[50]

It is recognised on all sides that diplomatic susceptibilities and politico-psychological considerations are involved, and if one takes them seriously, then the system of judges *ad hoc* should be left alone. To the purist it will remain objectionable as a survival of the basic idea of arbitration in the system of international adjudication. ...

Perhaps the system of judges *ad hoc* is dying a quiet death anyhow. And if states continue to select qualified persons who are not their nationals as judges *ad hoc* then the main argument against the system, that in some fashion such judges represent "their" governments on the Court, would lose much of its persuasiveness.

(ii) Access in Contentious Litigation

See Articles 34–35, Statute of the International Court of Justice and Article 93 of the United Nations Charter.[51]

---

[47] *Ed.* 45 *Annuaire de l'Institute de droit international*, II, p. 444 (1954).
[48] *Ed.* Above, p. 604.
[49] Informal Inter-Allied Committee, Report, para. 39; (1945) 39 A.J.I.L. Supp. 1 at 11. ...
[50] [Rosenne, *op. cit.*, p. 203, n. 45.]
[51] See below, Appendix I.

Notes

1. Two states that are not members of the United Nations—Nauru and Switzerland—are currently parties to the Statute of the Court under Article 93(2) of the Charter. The conditions set by the Security Council and the General Assembly for Switzerland were:

    (a) Acceptance of the provisions of the Statute of the International Court of Justice;

    (b) Acceptance of all the obligations of a Member of the United Nations under Article 94 of the Charter;

    (c) An undertaking to contribute to the expenses of the Court such equitable amount as the General Assembly shall assess from time to time after consultation with the Swiss Government.[52]

2. As far as access to the Court for states not parties to the Statute is concerned, the Security Council, acting under Article 35(2), has resolved:

> 1. The International Court of Justice shall be open to a State which is not a party to the Statute of the International Court of Justice, upon the following condition, namely, that such State shall previously have deposited with the Registrar of the Court a declaration by which it accepts the jurisdiction of the Court, in accordance with the Charter of the United Nations and with the terms and subject to the conditions of the Statute and Rules of the Court, and undertakes to comply in good faith with the decision or decisions of the Court and to accept all the obligations of a Member of the United Nations under Article 94 of the Charter;
>
> 2. Such declaration may be either particular or general. A particular declaration is one accepting the jurisdiction of the Court in respect only of a particular dispute or disputes which have already arisen. A general declaration is one accepting the jurisdiction generally in respect of all disputes or of a particular class or classes of disputes which have already arisen or which may arise in the future. A State, in making such a general declaration, may, in accordance with Article 36, paragraph 2, of the Statute, recognise as compulsory, *ipso facto* and without special agreement, the jurisdiction of the Court, provided, however, that such acceptance may not, without explicit agreement, be relied upon *vis-à-vis* States parties to the Statute of the International Court of Justice.[53]

Particular declarations in the sense of this resolution were filed by Albania as respondent in the *Corfu Channel* case[54] and Italy as claimant in the *Monetary Gold* case.[55] A number of general declarations have been filed in the past[56] but there are none in operation now. Before becoming a member of the United Nations, West Germany was a party to the *North Sea Continental Shelf* cases on the basis of such a declaration.[57] In those cases, the question of the status of West Germany as a state was not raised by the other parties. Apparently for this reason the Court did not find it necessary to consider it (although presumably it would have done if one of the parties, with the agreement of the other, had been, for example, a company).[58]

---

[52] G.A.Resn 91 (I), December 11, 1946.

[53] S.C. Resn 9 (1946), S.C.O.R., 1st Sess., *Resolutions and Decisions*, p. 18.

[54] See below, p. 996.

[55] I.C.J. Rep. 1954, p. 19.

[56] See I.C.J. *Yearbook* 1994–1995, p. 67.

[57] *Pleadings*, Vol. I, pp. 6, 8.

[58] The Security Council Resolution states that "all questions as to the validity or the effect of a declaration" made in accordance with it are questions for decision by the Court.

Article 34, Statute, limits access to the Court to states. On the question whether access should be opened to public international organisations or to individuals or companies, a Study Group on the Court reported[59]:

80 The principle reflected in Article 34 of the Court's Statute—that only States may appear before the Court in contentious cases—is long established and it has not been a main focus of criticism. Yet, since neither international personality nor the capacity to bring claims is restricted to States, as the Court itself affirmed in the *Reparations* case, the logic of excluding the United Nations and specialised agencies from using the Court as parties is not self-evident. These organisations are compelled to use arbitration in their disputes with States, or else use the device of the "binding" advisory opinion.[60] From the perspective of the rules of law, this device is evidently inadequate. It is a significant gap in institutional arrangements that public international organisations cannot be held legally accountable to States in the principal judicial organ of the international community, nor can States be held legally accountable to such organisations. This is the more odd in that, in substance, public international organisations are nothing other than States acting collectively.

81 On the other hand, there seems to be little demand for direct standing from the organisations themselves, and there is the difficulty that such a change would require an amendment of Article 34 of the Statute. If disputes between States and international organisations were to go to the ICJ, they would, of course, add to the pressure on the Court's list, and so make it all the more important that the "core" problem identified above [*i.e.* the pressure of work of the Court] be effectively addressed . . .

84 Although, in the past, academic criticism of the "only States" provision in Article 34 has sometimes ventured to suggest that individuals should be given *locus standi*,[61] there is no strong support for this idea in current thinking. Indeed, if the contemporary concern is over how the Court can cope with inter-State disputes, it would be counterproductive to compound the problem by opening up the Court to individuals—and there are in any case other fora in which human rights cases by individuals can be pursued.

(iii) JURISDICTION IN CONTENTIOUS LITIGATION

See Article 36–37, Statute of the International Court of Justice.[62]

(a) *Jurisdiction under Article 36(1)*

ROSENNE, THE LAW AND PRACTICE OF THE INTERNATIONAL COURT

1965, Vol. I, pp. 333–334. Footnotes omitted

In practice, two generic types of agreement for referring a matter to the Court can be discerned. The classic method by which the parties refer a

---

[59] Report of the Study Group on the International Court of Justice established by the British Institute of International and Comparative Law (1996) 45 I.C.L.Q. Supp. pp. 24–25.

[60] *Ed.* See below, p. 1036.

[61] *Ed.* See further Rosenne, *The Law and Practice of the International Court* (2nd rev. ed., 1985), p. 291.

[62] See below, Appendix I.

case to the Court is by a *special agreement* (*compromis*). This is an agreement whereby two or more States agree to refer a particular and defined matter to the Court for a decision. The distinguishing feature of the special agreement as a title of jurisdiction is that jurisdiction is conferred and the Court is seised of the defined issues of the concrete case by the mere notification to the Court of the agreement. Only if an agreement has that double effect can it be regarded as a true special agreement, as that expression is used in the Statute and Rules of Court, so as to lead to the application of the special procedure, reminiscent of the procedure of classical international arbitration, which those texts specify. During the period of the Permanent Court, eleven cases were instituted by special agreement. Since 1947, the *Minquiers and Ecrehos and Frontier Land* cases were instituted in this way; and in the *Corfu Channel* case the subsequent special agreement replaced the Court's prorogated jurisdiction.[63]

The more usual method of conferring jurisdiction under this head is by a compromissory clause in a multilateral or bilateral treaty.[64] The treaty may be one providing for the reference of a given dispute to the Court, a general treaty of peaceful settlement of disputes, or a treaty regulating some other topic and containing a compromissory clause. The effect of such a provision is to establish the jurisdiction of the Court, as between the parties, to the extent specified in the compromissory clause. This device also had its origin in arbitration, but the permanence of the International Court since 1922 has enabled it to make great headway, and there are now hundreds of sets of jurisdictional obligations of this character—bilateral and multilateral—in force between States.

CORFU CHANNEL CASE (PRELIMINARY OBJECTION)[65]

U.K. *v.* Albania

I.C.J. Reports 1948, p. 15

On May 22, 1947, the United Kingdom brought a claim against Albania before the Court by unilateral application in accordance with Article 40(1)[66] of the Statute and Article 32(2)[67] of the Rules of the Court. The United Kingdom argued that the Court had jurisdiction "under Article 36(1) of its Statute as being a matter, which

---

[63] *Ed.* Recent cases include the *Land, Island and Maritime Frontier Dispute* case (*El Salvador v. Honduras*), I.C.J. Rep. 1990, p. 92, and the *Gabcikovo-Nagymaros Project* case (*Hungary v. Slovakia*) (pending). On compromissory clauses, see Charney (1987) 81 A.J.I.L 855.

[64] *Ed.* See, *e.g.* the *U.S. Diplomatic and Consular Staff in Tehran* case, above, p. 358, and the *Genocide Convention* case, below, p. 1030. On the current status of the 1928 General Act of Arbitration, see Merrills (1980) 39 C.L.J. 137.

[65] See Waldock (1948) 2 I.L.Q. 377.

[66] See below, Appendix I.

[67] This is now Art. 35(2), Statute. It reads: "When a case is brought before the Court by means of an application, the application must, as laid down in Art. 40, para. 1, of the Statute, indicate the party making it, the party against whom the claim is brought and the subject of the dispute. It must also, as far as possible, specify the provision on which the applicant founds the jurisdiction of the Court, state the precise nature of the claim and give a succinct statement of the facts and grounds on which the claim is based . . . "

is one specially provided for in the Charter of the United Nations, on the grounds: (a) that the Security Council of the United Nations, at the conclusion of proceedings in which it dealt with the dispute under Article 36 of the Charter, by a Resolution, decided to recommend both the Government of the United Kingdom and the Albanian Government to refer the present dispute to the International Court of Justice; (b) that the Albanian Government accepted the invitation of the Security Council under Article 32 of the Charter to participate in the discussion of the dispute and accepted the condition laid down by the Security Council, when conveying the invitation, that Albania accepts in the present case all the obligations which a Member of the United Nations would have to assume in a similar case; (c) that Article 25 of the Charter provides that the Members of the United Nations agree to accept and carry out the decisions of the Security Council in accordance with the present Charter."[68] Albania was informed of the application by the Court Registry and responded by a letter of July 2, 1947, the relevant terms of which are indicated in the following extract from the Court's judgment. Later, when steps had been taken for the hearing of the case by the Court, Albania filed a document raising a preliminary objection to the jurisdiction of the Court.

Judgment of the Court

In support of its application, the Government of the United Kingdom invoked certain provisions of the Charter of the United Nations and of the Statute of the Court to establish the existence of a case of compulsory jurisdiction. The Court does not consider that it needs to express an opinion on this point, since, as will be pointed out, the letter of July 2, 1947, addressed by the Albanian Government to the Court, constitutes a voluntary acceptance of its jurisdiction.

The letter of July 2, 1947 . . . removes all difficulties concerning the question of the admissibility of the Application and the question of the jurisdiction of the Court.

With respect to the first point, the Albanian Government, while declaring on the one hand that it "would be within its rights in holding that the Government of the United Kingdom was not entitled to bring the case before the International Court by unilateral application, without first concluding a special agreement with the Albanian Government," states on the other hand, that "it is prepared notwithstanding this irregularity in the action taken by the Government of the United Kingdom, to appear before the Court." This language used by the Albanian Government cannot be understood otherwise than as a waiver of the right subsequently to raise an objection directed against the admissibility of the Application founded on the alleged procedural irregularity of that instrument.

The letter of July 2, 1947, is no less decisive as regards the question of the Court's jurisdiction. Not only does the Albanian Government, which had already certain obligations towards the Security Council by its telegram of January 24, 1947,[69] declare in that letter that it "fully accepts the

---

[68] I.C.J. Rep. 1948, p. 17.
[69] *Ed.* It was in this telegram that Albania accepted the invitation of the Security Council under Art. 32 of the Charter to participate in its discussions of the dispute.

recommendation of the Security Council" to the effect that the dispute should be referred to the Court in accordance with the provisions of the Court's Statute, but, after stating that it is "profoundly convinced of the justice of its case," it accepts in precise terms "the jurisdiction of the Court for this case." The letter of July 2, therefore, in the opinion of the Court, constitutes a voluntary and indisputable acceptance of the Court's jurisdiction.

While the consent of the parties confers jurisdiction on the Court, neither the Statute nor the Rules require that this consent should be expressed in any particular form.

The Albanian contention that the Application cannot be entertained because it has been filed contrary to the provisions of Article 40, paragraph 1, and of Article 36, paragraph 1, of the Court's Statute, is essentially founded on the assumption that the institution of proceedings by application is only possible where compulsory jurisdiction exists and that, where it does not, proceedings can only be instituted by special agreement.

This is a mere assertion which is not justified by either of the texts cited. Article 32, paragraph 2, of the Rules[70] does not require the Applicant, as an absolute necessity, but only "as far as possible," to specify in the application the provision on which he founds the jurisdiction of the Court. It clearly implies, both by its actual terms and by the reasons underlying it, that the institution of proceedings by application is not exclusively reserved for the domain of compulsory jurisdiction.

In submitting the case by means of an Application, the Government of the United Kingdom gave the Albanian Government the opportunity of accepting the jurisdiction of the Court. This acceptance was given in the Albanian Government's letter of July 2, 1947.

Besides, separate action of this kind was in keeping with the respective position of the parties in proceedings where there is in fact a claimant, the United Kingdom, and a defendant, Albania. . . .

For these reasons . . . the Court, by 15 votes against 1,[71] rejects the Preliminary Objection submitted by the Albanian Government.

SEPARATE OPINION BY JUDGES BASDEVANT, ALVAREZ, WINIARSKI, ZORIČIĆ, DE VISSCHER, BADAWI AND KRYLOV. Whilst concurring in the judgment of the Court, we feel obliged to state that we should have wished the Court to have passed upon the merits of the claim of the Government of the United Kingdom to treat the present case as one falling within the compulsory jurisdiction of the Court . . . Under the regime of the Charter, the rule holds good that the jurisdiction of the International Court of Justice, as of the Permanent Court of International Justice before it,

---

[70] *Ed.* Now Rules of Court, Art. 35(2).
[71] The judges in the majority were President Guerrero; Vice-President Basdevant; Judges Alvarez, Fabela, Hackworth, Winiarski, Zoričić, de Visscher, Sir Arnold McNair, Klaestad, Badawi Pasha, Krylov, Read, Hsu Mo and Asevedo. Judge *ad hoc* Daxner dissented.

depends on the consent of the States parties to a dispute. But Article 36 of the Charter had made it possible for the Security Council to recommend the parties to refer their dispute to the International Court of Justice in accordance with the provisions of the Court's Statute. The Security Council, for the first time, availed itself of this power on April 9, 1947. . . .

The arguments presented on behalf of the United Kingdom to establish that this was a new case of compulsory jurisdiction—which arguments the Agent and Counsel for the Albanian Government sought to refute——have not convinced us. In particular, having regard (1) to the normal meaning of the word recommendation, a meaning which this word has retained in diplomatic language, as is borne out by the practice of the Pan-American Conference, of the League of Nations, of the International Labour Organisation, etc., (2) to the general structure of the Charter and of the Statute which founds the jurisdiction of the Court on the consent of States, and (3) to the terms used in Article 36, paragraph 3, of the Charter and to its object which is to remind the Security Council that legal disputes should normally be decided by judicial methods, it appears impossible to us to accept an interpretation according to which this Article, without explicitly saying so, has introduced more or less surreptitiously, a new case of compulsory jurisdiction. . . .

Notes

1. Just prior to the Court's ruling, the parties announced that they had reached agreement to submit the case to the Court by special agreement.

2. The doctrine relied upon by the Court to found its jurisdiction in this case is that of the *forum prorogatum*. By this, the Court has jurisdiction where the parties have given their consent by separate acts expressly or impliedly accepting it, one of those acts being the making of a unilateral application under Article 40(1) of the Court's Statute. In other terms, *forum prorogatum* "is the possibility that if State A commences proceedings against State B on a non-existent or defective jurisdictional basis, State B can remedy the situation by conduct amounting to an acceptance of the jurisdiction of the Court."[72] In the *Mavromattis (Merits)* case, brought by Greece against the United Kingdom, the United Kingdom replied in its written argument to an issue raised by Greece that was not within the jurisdiction of the Court under the mandate for Palestine under which the case had been brought, thus impliedly accepting the Court's jurisdiction on the issue. The Court decided that it had jurisdiction in respect of the issue "in consequence of an agreement between the parties resulting from the written proceedings . . ."[73] In the *Rights of Minorities in Polish Upper Silesia* case, in which Poland had first raised objections to jurisdiction in its second written pleadings (its rejoinder) after having argued the case on its merits in its first written pleadings (its countermemorial), the Court said: "And there seems to be no doubt that the consent of a State to the submission of a dispute to the Court may not only result from an express declaration, but may also be inferred from acts conclusively establishing it. It seems hard to deny that the submission of arguments on the merits, without making reservations in regard to the question of jurisdiction, must be regarded as .

[72] Judge *ad hoc* Lauterpacht Individual Opinion, para. 24, in the *Genocide Convention* case *(Further Requests for Provisional Measures)*, I.C.J. Rep. 1993, p. 325.
[73] P.C.I.J. Rep., Ser. A, No. 5, p. 27 (1925).

an unequivocal indication of the desire of a State to obtain a decision on the merits of a suit. . . . If, in a special case, the Respondent has, by an express declaration, indicated his desire to obtain a decision on the merits and his intention to abstain from raising the question of jurisdiction, it seems clear that he cannot, later on in the proceedings, go back upon that declaration."[74]

In the 1930s, in the course of revision of the Rules of Court by the judges of the Permanent Court of International Justice, a proposal put forward by some of the Judges requiring an applicant state to indicate the basis for the Court's jurisdiction in its application was not adopted. Opposing the proposal, Judge Shücking is reported as saying: "It was not desirable to insist on the application containing a reference to the treaty clause upon which it was based. The institution of the *forum prorogatum* had been introduced into the procedure by the Court's practice, in particular in Judgment No. 12 [*Rights of Minorities* case] and it was in the interests of the good administration of justice. If they now made it a necessary condition for the admissibility of an application that it must specify the treaty clause, and if, in a given case, the applicant was unable to specify it, because no such clause existed, the Court would be compelled to reject the application *a limine*. But that would amount to abolishing the institution of the *forum prorogatum*. . . ."[75] The revised text of the Rules of Court required that the basis for the Court's jurisdiction should be specified "as far as possible."[76]

3. In the *Anglo-Iranian Oil Co.* case, brought by the United Kingdom against Iran, the United Kingdom, having first based the Court's jurisdiction on the Iranian declaration under Article 36(2), continued: "Alternatively, whether or not the Court has the right to exercise jurisdiction in this case by virtue of the . . . declaration of the Imperial Government of Persia [under Article 36(2) of the Statute], the Government of the United Kingdom expect that Iran, as a Member of the United Nations, one of the purposes of which is 'to bring about by peaceful means and in conformity with the principles of justice and international law, adjustment or settlement of international disputes or situations which might lead to a breach of the peace' . . . and mindful of the principle that 'legal disputes should as a general rule be referred . . . to the . . . Court . . . ' will agree to appear before the Court voluntarily in order to hear and answer on their merits the arguments of the Government of the United Kingdom. (*Forum prorogatum*; *Corfu Channel* case (Preliminary Objection) . . .)."[77] Iran declined to accept this invitation and objected to the Court's jurisdiction generally. Despite this, the Court, before giving judgment on Iran's objections to its jurisdiction, made an order at the request of the United Kingdom for interim measures of protection. When the Court later sustained Iran's objections to its jurisdiction, it stated that the order "ceases to be operative upon the delivery of this judgment" and "that the provisional measures lapse at the same time."[78]

4. In the *Monetary Gold* case, the respondent states—France, the United Kingdom and the United States—indicated their willingness in the Washington Statement of April 25, 1951, to be brought before the Court by either Albania or Italy. In response, Italy filed an application with the Court but then challenged the Court's jurisdiction. Rejecting Italy's objections, the Court stated, *inter alia*: "The Governments of France, the United Kingdom and the United States of America, and the Government of Italy, by their separate and successive acts—the adoption of the Washington Statement, in the one case, and in the other case, the deposit on

---

[74] *ibid.* No. 15, pp. 24–25 (1928). See also the *Chorzów Factory (Indemnity) (Merits)* case, *ibid.* No. 17, p. 37 (1928).

[75] P.C.I.J. Rep., Ser. D, 2, Add. 3, p. 69.

[76] Now Rules of the Court of the I.C.J., Art. 35(2), above, p. 997, n. 67.

[77] I.C.J. *Pleadings, Anglo-Iranian Oil Co.* case, p. 17.

[78] I.C.J. Rep. 1952, p. 114.

May 19, 1953, of the Declaration of acceptance of the jurisdiction of the Court and the filing of the Application—have referred a case to the Court within the meaning of Article 36(1) of its Statute. They have thus conferred jurisdiction on the Court to deal with the questions submitted in the Application of the Italian Government."[79]

5. Applications relying on *forum prorogatum* have since been made in the *Treatment in Hungary of Aircraft of the U.S.A.* cases[80] (applications by the United States against Hungary and the USSR respectively), in three *Aerial Incident* cases[81] (the United States against Czechoslovakia and the USSR respectively) and the *Antarctica* cases[82] (the United Kingdom *v.* Argentina and Chile respectively). In all of these cases, no basis for jurisdiction other than *forum prorogatum* was available. In each case the respondent state took no positive action and eventually the case was struck off the Court's list.

To avoid this kind of "fishing" for jurisdiction, the Rules of Court, Article 38(5), now provide:

> Where the applicant state proposes to found the jurisdiction of the Court upon a consent thereto yet to be given or manifested by the state against which such application is made, the application shall be transmitted to that state. It shall not however be entered in the General List, nor any action be taken in the proceedings, unless and until the state against which such application is made consents to the Court's jurisdiction for the purpose of the case.

On the basis of Article 38(5), a unilateral application by Hungary in 1992 concerning the Gabcikovo-Nagymaros Project was transmitted to Slovakia but not registered on the Court's list when Slovakia did not respond. Later, jurisdiction was conferred in the case of that name by special agreement between the two states.

Bosnia and Herzegovina sought unsuccessfully to establish jurisdiction *forum prorogatum* as an additional ground for jurisdiction in the *Genocide Convention* case[83] on the basis of a letter by the Presidents of Serbia and Montenegro to the President of the Arbitration Commission of the International Conference for Peace in Yugoslavia. The I.C.J. considered that it "was by no means clear to the Court whether the letter . . . was intended as an 'immediate commitment' by the two Presidents, binding on Yugoslavia, to accept unconditionally the unilateral submission to the Court" of one or more legal questions, or "as no more than the enunciation of a general policy of favouring judicial settlement, which did not embody an offer or commitment."

6. The wording "all matters specially provided for in the Charter of the United Nations" in Article 36(1) would seem to have no meaning; it was included at a time when it was hoped that the Charter would provide for the Court to have compulsory jurisdiction. There is no provision in the Charter as it was finally drafted to which the wording could be taken to refer, apart from Article 36(3) of

---

[79] *ibid.* 1954, p. 19, at p. 31. The Court declined to hear the case because it lacked jurisdiction on another ground (Albania was not a party to the proceedings): see below, p. 1029.

[80] *ibid.* pp. 99, 103.

[81] *ibid.* 1956, pp. 6, 9; *ibid.* 1959, p. 276.

[82] *ibid.* 1956, pp. 12, 15.

[83] *loc. cit.,* p. 1030, below, p. 16. The statement in the letter read: "FR Yugoslavia proposes that in the event that agreement is not reached among the participants in the Conference, these questions should be adjudicated by the International Court of Justice in accordance with its Statute." The argument was repeated unsuccessfully in the *Genocide Convention* case (*Further Provisional Measures*), I.C.J. Rep. 1993, p. 325. See the individual opinion of Judge *ad hoc* Lauterpacht, *ibid.* p. 416.

the Charter, as to which see the Separate Opinion in the *Corfu Channel* case, above.

(b) *Jurisdiction under Article 36(2)*[84]

UNITED KINGDOM DECLARATION ACCEPTING THE COMPULSORY JURISDICTION OF THE COURT

Misc. No. 4 (1969), Cmnd. 3872

I have the honour, by direction of Her Majesty's Principal Secretary of State for Foreign and Commonwealth Affairs, to declare on behalf of the Government of the United Kingdom of Great Britain and Northern Ireland that they accept as compulsory *ipso facto* and without special convention, on condition of reciprocity, the jurisdiction of the International Court of Justice, in conformity with paragraph 2 of Article 36 of the Statute of the Court, until such time as notice may be given to terminate the acceptance, over all disputes arising after 24th October 1945, with regard to situations or facts subsequent to the same date, other than:

(i) any dispute which the United Kingdom

    (a) has agreed with the other Party or Parties thereto to settle by some other method of peaceful settlement; or

    (b) has already submitted to arbitration by agreement with any States which had not at the time of submission accepted the compulsory jurisdiction of the International Court of Justice:

(ii) disputes with the Government of any other country which is a member of the Commonwealth with regard to situations or facts existing before January 1, 1969:

(iii) disputes in respect of which any other Party to the dispute has accepted the compulsory jurisdiction of the International Court of Justice only in relation to or for the purposes of the dispute; or where the acceptance of the Court's compulsory jurisdiction on behalf of any other Party to the dispute was deposited or ratified less than twelve months prior to the filing of the application bringing the dispute before the Court.

... The Government of the United Kingdom also reserve the right at any time, by means of a notification addressed to the Secretary-General of

[84] See Briggs, (1958–I) 93 *Hague Recueil* 224; Gross, in Damrosch, *op. cit.*, p. 988, n. 24, above, p. 19; Kelly (1987) 12 Yale J.I.L. 342; Merrills (1979) 50 B.Y.I.L. 87 and *ibid.* (1993) 64 B.Y.I.L. 197; Oda (1988) 59 B.Y.I.L. 1; Szafarz, *The Compulsory Jurisdiction of the International Court of Justice* (1993), Chap. 3. Waldock (1955–56) 32 B.Y.I.L. 244.

the United Nations, and with effect as from the moment of such notification, either to add to, amend or withdraw any of the foregoing reservations, or any that may hereafter be added. . . . "

Notes

1. The current United Kingdom Declaration under Article 36(2) (the "Optional Clause"), which came into force on January 1, 1969, contains several reservations. Reservation (i)(b) was added "specifically to avoid an application over its dispute with Saudi Arabia over the Buraimi Oasis".[85]

2. Reservations (i)–(iii) in the United Kingdom declaration are not expressly permitted by Article 36. In practice, however, the Court has accepted that states may attach reservations to their declarations in addition to the conditions which it may attach in accordance with Article 36(3).[86]

3. Reservation (iii) in the British declaration applies to the Egyptian declaration, by which the jurisdiction of the Court is accepted by Egypt solely in connection with certain disputes concerning the Suez Canal.[87] Note also that the same reservation would have prevented Portugal bringing a case against the United Kingdom in the way that it brought the *Right of Passage* case[88] against India. Portugal made its declaration, which was valid for one year and then became terminable upon notice (which has not yet been given), on December 19, 1955. It brought its application on December 22, 1955.

4. "On condition of reciprocity" in the United Kingdom declaration refers to the *principle of reciprocity* which follows from the wording "in relation to any other state accepting the same obligation" in Article 36(2).[89] According to this principle, a state accepts the Court's jurisdiction *vis-à-vis* any other state only in so far as that state has accepted it also. If state A makes a declaration subject to reservation X and state B makes one subject to reservation Y, the Court has jurisdiction to hear disputes between these two states only in so far as they are not covered by reservations X or Y. In other words, "jurisdiction is conferred on the Court only to the extent to which the two declarations coincide in conferring it."[90] See further on the principle of reciprocity, the extracts from the three cases immediately below these notes.[91] The "reciprocity" condition in Article 36(3) is quite distinct from the principle of reciprocity in Article 36(2) and was introduced to cover the case where a state might only want to be bound by the Court's jurisdiction if a worthwhile number of other states were bound or if a state whose acceptance was particularly important to it was bound.

5. *Juridical character of a declaration.* In the *Nicaragua* case *(Jurisdiction and Admissibility)*,[92] the Court referred to optional clause declarations as "unilateral acts" establishing "a series of bilateral engagements." In his separate opinion Judge Sir Robert Jennings regarded them as *sui generis*, although allowing that "some parts

---

[85] *Per* Judge Sir Robert Jennings, *Nicaragua (Jurisdiction and Admissibility)* case, I.C.J. Rep. 1984, at p. 551.

[86] On reservations generally, see Alexandrov, *Reservations in Unilateral Declarations accepting the Compulsory Jurisdiction of the International Court of Justice* (1995).

[87] See above, p. 263.

[88] I.C.J. Rep. 1957, p. 125.

[89] See Weiss, in Damrosch, ed., *op. cit.*, p. 988, n. 24, above, p. 82.

[90] *Anglo-Iranian Oil Co.* case, I.C.J. Rep. 1952, p. 93, at p. 103.

[91] The principle was also invoked successfully as it applied under the 1928 General Act in the *Aegean Sea Continental Shelf* case, I.C.J. Rep. 1978, p. 37. Turkey was allowed to rely upon a Greek reservation to the Act to exclude the Court's jurisdiction.

[92] Judgment, para. 60, below, p. 1021. See also the *Nuclear Tests* case, judgment, para. 43, above, p. 775.

of the law of treaties may be applied by useful analogy."[93] As to the interpretation of declarations, in the *Anglo-Iranian Oil Co. (Jurisdiction)* case,[94] the Court stated:

> The Government of the United Kingdom has further argued that the Declaration would contain some superfluous words if it is interpreted as contended by Iran. It asserts that a legal text should be interpreted in such a way that a reason and a meaning can be attributed to every word in the text. It may be said that this principle should in general be applied when interpreting the text of a treaty. But the text of the Iranian Declaration is not a treaty text resulting from negotiations between two or more States. It is the result of unilateral drafting by the Government of Iran, which appears to have shown a particular degree of caution when drafting the text of the Declaration. It appears to have inserted *ex abundanti cautela* words which, strictly speaking, may seem to have been superfluous.

6. There are 62 declarations under the "Optional Clause" in force.[95] France terminated its declaration in 1974 as a result of the *Nuclear Tests* cases.[96] The U.S. terminated its declaration in 1985 because of the *Nicaragua* case.[97] The U.K. is now the only Security Council permanent member that is bound by the Optional Clause. 27 of the above declarations are terminable upon notice[98]; ten are terminable upon six months' or one year's notice; seven are valid for five-year periods which are automatically renewed in the absence of notice to the contrary before their expiry; one is valid for five years; and one is now valid for one-year periods in the absence of notice of termination. 16 contain no time limit (and no provision for notice). In the *Nicaragua (Jurisdiction and Admissibility)* case, judgment, para. 63, p. 1022, below, the Court stated that a declaration (*e.g.* the Nicaraguan one: text below, p. 1015, n. 27) for an indefinite period of time was terminable on "reasonable" notice. A Declaration terminable upon notice is one that is made for a "certain time" (Statute, Art. 36(3))[99]

In the *Nicaragua (Jurisdiction and Admissibility)* case[1] the Court held that the principle of reciprocity only applies to "the scope and substance of the commitments entered into"; it does not extend to the "formal conditions of their creation, duration or extinction". Accordingly, in that case, the U.S. was not permitted to rely upon the "terminable upon notice" limitation in the Nicaraguan declaration. The 1990 Spanish "Optional Clause" declaration provides:

---

[93] *cf.* Judge Schwebel in the same case: I.C.J. Rep. 1984, p. 620. In the *Fisheries Jurisdiction Cases (Jurisdiction)*, I.C.J. Rep. 1973, p. 16, the I.C.J. referred to "optional clause" declarations as "treaty provisions."

[94] I.C.J. Rep. 1952, p. 105.

[95] They are those of Australia, Austria, Barbados, Belgium, Botswana, Bulgaria, Cambodia, Cameroon, Canada, Colombia, Costa Rica, Cyprus, Denmark, Dominican Republic, Egypt, El Salvador, Estonia, Finland, Gambia, Georgia, Greece, Guinea-Bissau, Haiti, Honduras, Hungary, India, Japan, Kenya, Liberia, Liechtenstein, Luxembourg, Madagascar, Malawi, Malta, Mauritius, Mexico, Nauru, Netherlands, New Zealand, Nicaragua, Nigeria, Norway, Pakistan, Palau, Panama, Paraguay, Philippines, Poland, Portugal, Senegal, Somalia, Spain, Sudan, Suriname, Swaziland, Sweden, Switzerland, Togo, Uganda, U.K., Uruguay, Zaire. Is there any discernible pattern of states?

[96] As to which see above, p. 774.

[97] Above, p. 866.

[98] Some of these had originally been valid for a certain number of years (usually 5) after which they were stated to be terminable upon notice.

[99] *Right of Passage* case (*Preliminary Objections*), I.C.J. Rep. 1957, p. 125.

[1] Judgment, para. 62, below, p. 1022.

The withdrawal of [this] ... Declaration shall become effective after a period of six months has elapsed from the date of receipt by the Secretary-General of the United Nations of the relevant notification by the Spanish Government. However, in respect of States which have established a period of less than six months between notification of the withdrawal of their Declaration and in becoming effective, the withdrawal of the Spanish Declaration shall become effective after such shorter period has elapsed.

Would this achieve the result that the U.S. unsuccessfully sought to achieve on the basis of the principle of reciprocity in the *Nicaragua* case?

7. The value for the state making it of a declaration terminable upon notice was demonstrated in 1954 when Australia withdrew its declaration of 1940, which had been valid for five years and then became terminable upon notice, and made a new one adding a reservation in respect of disputes concerning pearl fishing off the Australian coast. At the time it seemed likely that Japan might bring a claim against Australia with this subject-matter before the Court under the "Optional Clause." Note also the reservation made by Canada in 1970 (and since withdrawn). In view of its 1970 legislation on arctic waters, which controversially extended its jurisdiction to control pollution in those waters and which brought an immediate protest from the United States, Canada terminated its declaration and made a new one with a new reservation excluding disputes about the legislation. Canada explained that its "new reservation ... does not in any way reflect lack of confidence in the court but takes into account the limitations within which the court must operate and the deficiencies of the law which it must interpret and apply."[2] See also the U.K. reservation added to avoid an application arising out of a dispute with Saudi Arabia.[3]

8. The fact that a case comes within a reservation to an "Optional Clause" declaration so that the Court lacks jurisdiction under Article 36(2) does not affect the possibility of the Court having jurisdiction on some other basis (*e.g.* a jurisdiction clause in a treaty between the parties): *Appeal Relating to the Jurisdiction of the I.C.A.O. Council* case.[4]

9. One measure of the utility of the "Optional Clause" as a basis for the Court's jurisdiction is the fact that since 1945 the Court has decided on their merits seven cases resulting from applications under the "optional clause".[5] Preliminary objections to jurisdiction or admissibility been upheld or the case has been settled in the other 11 such cases.

INTERHANDEL CASE

Switzerland *v.* U.S.

I.C.J. Reports 1959, p. 6

Switzerland brought this claim against the United States for the restitution of the assets of Interhandel, a Swiss company, in the United States. The property had been taken by the United States in 1942 on the ground that Interhandel was German, and so enemy, controlled. Switzerland disputed this and, after several

---

[2] 9 I.L.M. 612 (1970). See MacDonald (1970) 8 C.Y.I.L. 3 (1970).
[3] See above, p. 1002.
[4] I.C.J. Rep. 1972, p. 46, p. 53.
[5] The *Anglo-Norwegian Fisheries* case, above, p. 375; the *U.S. Nationals in Morocco* case, I.C.J. Rep., p. 176; the *Right of Passage* case, above, p. 257; the *Temple* case, I.C.J. Rep. 1962, p. 6; the *Nicaragua* case above, p. 966; the *Arbitral Award of 1989* case, I.C.J. Rep. 1991, p. 53; and the *Jan Mayen* case, I.C.J. Rep. 1993, p. 38.

years of negotiation, etc., in 1948 asked the United States to return Interhandel's property. On July 26, 1948, the United States refused to do so. After unsuccessful court proceedings in the United States, in 1957 Switzerland instituted proceedings under the Optional Clause.

Judgment of the Court

According to [the United States Second Preliminary Objection to the Court's jurisdiction] . . . the present dispute, even if it is subsequent to the date of the Declaration of the United States, arose before July 28, 1948, the date of the entry into force of the Swiss Declaration. The argument set out in the Preliminary Objections is as follows:

> The United States Declaration, which was effective August 26th, 1946, contained the clause limiting the Court's jurisdiction to disputes "hereafter arising," while no such qualifying clause is contained in the Swiss Declaration which was effective July 28th, 1948. But the reciprocity principle . . . requires that as between the United States and Switzerland the Court's jurisdiction be limited to disputes arising after July 28th, 1948. . . . Otherwise, retroactive effect would be given to the compulsory jurisdiction of the Court.

In particular, it was contended with regard to disputes arising after August 26th, 1946, but before July 28th, 1948, that "Switzerland, as a Respondent, could have invoked the principle of reciprocity and claimed that, in the same way as the United States is not bound to accept the Court's jurisdiction with respect to disputes arising before its acceptance, Switzerland, too, could not be required to accept the Court's jurisdiction in relation to disputes arising before its acceptance."

Reciprocity in the case of Declarations accepting the compulsory jurisdiction of the Court enables a Party to invoke a reservation to that acceptance which it has not expressed in its own Declaration but which the other Party has expressed in its Declaration. For example, Switzerland, which has not expressed in its Declaration any reservation *ratione temporis*, while the United States has accepted the compulsory jurisdiction of the Court only in respect of disputes to August 26th, 1946, might, if in the position of Respondent, invoke by virtue of reciprocity against the United States the American reservation if the United States attempted to refer to the Court a dispute with Switzerland which had arisen before August 26th, 1946. This is the effect of reciprocity in this connection. Reciprocity enables the State which has made the wider acceptance of the jurisdiction of the Court to rely upon the reservations to the acceptance laid down by the other Party. There the effect of reciprocity ends. It cannot justify a State in this instance, the United States in relying upon a restriction which the other Party, Switzerland, has not included in its own Declaration.

The Second Preliminary Objection must therefore be rejected. . . .

Notes

1. A reservation of the sort in issue here is a reservation *ratione temporis*. What if the declaration made by Switzerland had contained a reservation limiting that state's acceptance of the Court's jurisdiction to disputes arising after its declaration came into force on July 28, 1948? Assuming that the dispute in the case arose subsequent to the date of the United States declaration but before July 28, 1948, could the United States then have relied on the principle of reciprocity to better effect than it was able to do on the facts of the case as they actually were?

2. The United States also objected unsuccessfully to jurisdiction on the ground that the dispute had arisen before the United States acceptance of the Court's jurisdiction in 1946 in respect of "disputes arising hereafter." Although the United States had taken Interhandel's assets in 1942 and although the United States and Switzerland had disagreed over the enemy or non-enemy character of Interhandel before 1946, in the Court's opinion the dispute itself only arose when the United States refused Switzerland's request to return Interhandel's assets on July 26, 1948. Applying the United States *ratione temporis* reservation, the Court noted that "the facts and situation which have led to a dispute must not be confused with the dispute itself."[6] The United Kingdom declaration, above, p. 1002, applies to disputes arising as of 1945, "with regard to situations or facts subsequent to the same date." Would such a formula have helped the United States in the *Interhandel* case.[7]

A "situations or facts" limitation, which can be difficult to apply, was in issue in the *Right of Passage (Merits)* case.[8] There the Indian declaration extended to "all disputes arising after February 5th, 1930, with regard to situations or facts subsequent to the same date." The Court held that the "dispute" in the case arose in 1954, when India contested the exercise of a right of passage over Indian territory. As to the date of the "situation or facts", the Court stated:

> The facts or situations to which regard must be had in this connection are those with regard to which the dispute has arisen or, in other words, as was said by the Permanent Court in the case concerning the *Electricity Company of Sofia and Bulgaria*, only "those which must be considered as being the source of the dispute", those which are its "real cause". The Permanent Court, in this connection, was unwilling to regard as such an earlier arbitral award which was the source of the rights claimed by one of the Parties, but which had given rise to no difficulty prior to the facts constituting the subject of the dispute. "It is true", it said, "that a dispute may presuppose the existence of some prior situation or fact, but it does not follow that the dispute arises in regard to that situation or fact." (Series A/B, No. 77, p. 82.) The Permanent Court thus drew a distinction between the situations or facts which constitute the source of the rights claimed by one of the Parties and the situations or facts which are the source of the dispute. Only the latter are to be taken into account for the purpose of applying the Declaration accepting the jurisdiction of the Court.
>
> The dispute submitted to the Court is one with regard to a situation and, at the same time, with regard to certain facts: on the one hand there is the situation of the Portuguese enclaves within the territory of India, which gave rise to the need for a right of passage for Portugal and to its claim to such a right; on the other hand there are the facts of 1954 which Portugal advances as showing the failure of India to comply with its obligations, infringements of that right.

[6] I.C.J. Rep. 1959, p. 22.
[7] See Greig, *International Law* (2nd ed., 1976), pp. 657–61.
[8] I.C.J. Rep. 1960, p. 6 at p. 35. For the facts of this case, see above, p. 257.

Up to 1954 the situation of those territories may have given rise to a few minor incidents, but passage had been effected without any controversy as to the title under which it was effected. It was only in 1954 that such a controversy arose and the dispute relates both to the existence of a right of passage to go into the enclaved territories and to India's failure to comply with obligations which, according to Portugal, were binding upon it in this connection. It was from all of this that the dispute referred to the Court arose; it is with regard to all of this that the dispute exists. This whole, whatever may have been the earlier origin of one of its parts, came into existence only after 5 February 1930. The time-condition to which acceptance of the jurisdiction of the Court was made subject by the Declaration of India is therefore complied with.

3. On the "self-judging" or "automatic" reservation aspect of the *Interhandel* case, see below, p. 1013. The Court finally declined jurisdiction in the case because local remedies had not been *fully* exhausted.

NORWEGIAN LOANS CASE[9]

France *v.* Norway

I.C.J. Reports 1957, p. 9

France brought this claim against Norway under the "Optional Clause" on behalf of French holders of Norwegian bonds. Norway objected to the Court's jurisdiction on several grounds, including that discussed in the following extract from its judgment. Judge Lauterpacht reached the same decision as the Court, but for different reasons.

Judgment of the Court

The Court will at the outset direct its attention to the Preliminary Objections of the Norwegian Government. . . .

It will be recalled that the French Declaration accepting the compulsory jurisdiction of the Court contains the following reservation:

This declaration does not apply to differences relating to matters which are essentially within the national jurisdiction as understood by the Government of the French Republic.

In the Preliminary Objections filed by the Norwegian Government it is stated:

The Norwegian Government did not insert any such reservation in its own Declaration. But is has the right to rely upon the restrictions placed by France upon her own undertakings.

Convinced that the dispute which has been brought before the Court by the Application of July 6, 1955, is within the domestic jurisdiction,

[9] See Jennings (1958) 7 I.C.L.Q. 349. On "automatic" reservations, see Crawford (1979) 50 B.Y.I.L. 63.

the Norwegian Government considers itself fully entitled to rely on this right. Accordingly, it requests the Court to decline, on grounds that it lacks jurisdiction, the function which the French Government would have it assume.

... in the present case the jurisdiction of the Court depends upon the Declarations made by the Parties in accordance with Article 36, paragraph 2, of the Statute on condition of reciprocity; and that, since two unilateral declarations are involved, such jurisdiction is conferred upon the Court only to the extent to which the Declarations coincide in conferring it. A comparison between the two Declarations shows that the French Declaration accepts the Court's jurisdiction within narrower limits than the Norwegian Declaration; consequently the common will of the Parties, which is the basis of the Court's jurisdiction, exists within these narrower limits indicated by the French reservation. ...

In accordance with the condition of reciprocity to which acceptance of the compulsory jurisdiction is made subject in both Declarations and which is provided for in Article 36, paragraph 3, of the Statute, Norway, equally with France, is entitled to except from the compulsory jurisdiction of the Court disputes understood by Norway to be essentially within its national jurisdiction. ...

The Court does not consider that it should examine whether the French reservation is consistent with the undertaking of a legal obligation and is compatible with Article 36, paragraph 6, of the Statute which provides. ...

The validity of the reservation has not been questioned by the Parties. It is clear that France fully maintains its Declarations, including the reservation, and that Norway relies upon the reservation. ...

The Court considers that the Norwegian Government is entitled, by virtue of the condition of reciprocity, to invoke the reservation contained in the French Declaration of March 1, 1949; that this reservation excludes from the jurisdiction of the Court the dispute which has been referred to it by the Application of the French Government; that consequently the Court is without jurisdiction to entertain the Application. ...

For these reasons, the Court, by 12 votes to three,[10] finds that it is without jurisdiction to adjudicate upon the dispute which has been brought before it by the Application of the Government of the French Republic of July 6, 1955.

INDIVIDUAL OPINION OF JUDGE LAUTERPACHT. ... I consider that as the French Declaration of Acceptance excludes from the jurisdiction of the Court, "matters which are essentially within the national jurisdiction as

[10] The judges in the majority were President Hackworth; Vice-President Badawi; Judges Winiarski, Zoričić, Klaestad, Armand-Ugon, Kojevnikov, Sir Muhammad Zafrulla Khan, Sir Hersch Lauterpacht, Moreno Quintana, Córdova and Wellington Koo. Judges Guerrero, Basdevant and Read dissented.

understood by the Government of the French Republic"—it is for the reason of that latter qualification an instrument incapable of producing legal effects before this Court and of establishing its jurisdiction. This is so for the double reason that: (a) it is contrary to the Statute of the Court; (b) the existence of the obligation being dependent upon the determination by the Government accepting the Optional Clause, the Acceptance does not constitute a legal obligation. That Declaration of Acceptance cannot, accordingly, provide a basis for the jurisdiction of the Court. . . .

If that type of reservation is valid, then the Court is not in the position to exercise the power conferred upon it—in fact, the duty imposed upon it—under paragraph 6 of Article 36 of its Statute. . . . The French reservation lays down that if, with regard to that particular question, there is a dispute between the Parties as to whether the Court has jurisdiction, the matter shall be settled by a decision of the French Government. The French reservation is thus not only contrary to one of the most fundamental principles of international—and national—jurisprudence according to which it is within the inherent power of a tribunal to interpret the text establishing its jurisdiction. It is also contrary to a clear specific provision of the Statute of the Court as well as to the general Articles I and 92 of the Statute and of the Charter, respectively, which require the Court to function in accordance with its Statute.

Now what is the result of the fact that a reservation or part of it are contrary to the provisions of the Statute of the Court? The result is that that reservation or that part of it is invalid. Some examples may usefully illustrate that aspect of the question: What would be the position if in accepting—or purporting to accept—the obligations of Article 36 of the Statute, a State were to exclude the operation of paragraph 6 of that Article not only with regard to one reservation but with regard to all reservations or, generally, with regard to any disputed question of the jurisdiction of the Court?

What would be the position if the Declaration were to make it a condition that the oral proceedings of the Court shall be secret; or that its Judgment shall not be binding unless given by unanimity; or that it should contain no reasons; or that Dissenting Opinion shall be attached; or that Judges of certain nationality or nationalities shall be excluded; or that, contrary to what is said in Article 38 of its Statute, the Court shall apply only treaties and custom in the sense that it shall not be authorised to apply general principles of law as recognised by civilised States and that if it is unable to base its decision on treaty or custom it shall pronounce a *non liquet*? . . .

In accepting the jurisdiction of the Court Governments are free to limit its jurisdiction in a drastic manner. As a result there may be little left in the Acceptance which is subject to the jurisdiction of the Court. This the Governments, as trustees of the interests entrusted to them, are fully entitled to do. Their right to append reservations which are not inconsistent with the Statute is no longer in question. But the question whether that little that is left is or is not subject to the jurisdiction of the Court must be determined by the Court itself. . . .

I arrive at the same conclusion on the second—and different—ground, namely, that having regard to the formulation of the reservation of national jurisdiction on the part of the French Government the Acceptance embodying the 'automatic reservation" is invalid as lacking in an essential condition of validity of a legal instrument. . . . An instrument in which a party is entitled to determine the existence of its obligation is not a valid and enforceable legal instrument of which a court of law can take cognizance. It is not a legal instrument. It is a declaration of a political principle and purpose. . . .

If the clause of the Acceptance reserving to the declaring Government the right of unilateral determination is invalid, then there are only two alternatives open to the Court: it may either treat as invalid that particular part of the reservation or it may consider the entire Acceptance to be tainted with invalidity. (There is a third possibility—which has only to be mentioned in order to be dismissed—namely, that the clause in question invalidates not the Acceptance as a whole but the particular reservation. This would mean that the entire reservation of matters of national jurisdiction would be treated as invalid while the Declaration of Acceptance as such would be treated as fully in force).

International practice on the subject is not sufficiently abundant to permit a confident attempt at generalisation and some help may justifiably be sought in applicable general principles of law as developed in municipal law. That general principle of law is that it is legitimate—and perhaps obligatory—to sever an invalid condition from the rest of the [contract or other legal] instrument and to treat the latter as valid provided that having regard to the intention of the parties and the nature of the instrument the condition in question does not constitute an essential part of the instrument. *Utile non debet per inutile vitiari.* The same applies also to provisions and reservations relating to the jurisdiction of the Court. It would be consistent with the previous practice of the Court that it should, if only possible, uphold its jurisdiction when such a course is compatible with the intention of the parties and that it should not allow its jurisdiction to be defeated as the result of remediable defects of expression which are not of an essential character. If that principle were applied to the case now before the Court this would mean that, while the French acceptance as a whole would remain valid, the limitation expressed in the words "as understood by the Government of the French Republic" would be treated as invalid and non-existent with the further result that Norway could not rely on it. The outcome of the interpretation thus adopted would be somewhat startling inasmuch as it would, in the present case, favour the very State which originally made that reservation and defeat the objection of the defendant State—an aspect of the question commented upon in another part of this Opinion. That fact need not necessarily be a decisive reason against the adoption of any such interpretation.

However, I consider that it is not open to the Court in the present case to sever the invalid condition from the Acceptance as a whole. For the principle of severance applies only to provisions and conditions which are not of the essence of the undertaking. Now an examination of the history of this particular form of the reservation of national jurisdiction shows that the unilateral right of determining whether the dispute is essentially within domestic jurisdiction has been regarded by the declaring State as one of the crucial limitations—perhaps the crucial limitation—of the obligation undertaken by the acceptance of the Optional Clause of Article 36 of the Statute. As is well known, that particular limitation is, substantially, a repetition of the formula adopted, after considerable discussion, by the Senate of the United States of America in giving its consent and advice to the acceptance, in 1946, of the Optional Clause by that country. That instrument is not before the Court and it would not be proper for me to comment upon it except to the extent of noting that the reservation in question was included therein having regard to the decisive importance attached to it and notwithstanding the doubts, expressed in various quarters, as to its consistency with the Statute. It will also be noted that some governments, such as those of India and the Union of South Africa, have attributed so much importance to that particular formation of the reservation that they cancelled their previous acceptance of the Optional Clause in order to insert, in a substituted Declaration of Acceptance, a clause reserving for themselves the right of unilateral determination. To ignore that clause and to maintain the binding force of the Declaration as a whole would be to ignore an essential and deliberate condition of the Acceptance.

Notes

1. Note that Norway was entitled to rely on France's reservation as if it read "as understood by the *Norwegian* Government." Since France had excluded cases concerning *its* domestic jurisdiction, Norway could do likewise. How did the Court manage to avoid ruling on the validity of the reservation? Could the Court have done so if France had been relying on it?

2. Judge Guerrero, who was the only other judge in the *Norwegian Loans* case to express an opinion on the validity of the French Declaration, stated in his dissenting opinion: "By the fact that France reserves her right to determine herself the limit between her own national jurisdiction and the jurisdiction of the Court, France renders void her main undertaking, for the latter ceases to be compulsory if it is France and not the Court that holds the power to determine the limit between their respective jurisdictions. The reservation conflicts also with paragraph 6 of Article 36. . . . "[11] He did not "agree that the Court is without jurisdiction when its lack of jurisdiction is founded on the terms of a unilateral instrument which I consider to be contrary to the spirit and to the letter of the Statute and which, in my view, is, for that reason, null and void."[12]

---

[11] I.C.J. Rep. 1957, p. 68. See Shihata, *The Power of the International Court to Determine its own Jurisdiction* (1965).
[12] *ibid.* p. 70.

3. In the *Interhandel* case, brought by Switzerland against the United States, the Court was confronted with the same form of "domestic jurisdiction" reservation in the United States Declaration.[13] It did not, however, either when deciding not to order certain interim measures[14] or when upholding the United States objections to its jurisdiction,[15] find it necessary to comment on the validity of the reservation or the Declaration containing it even though the reservation was invoked by the United States at both stages. In deciding that it lacked jurisdiction, the Court ruled instead that Switzerland had not exhausted local remedies, thus making it unnecessary for the Court to consider the objection to its jurisdiction presented by the United States (and challenged by Switzerland) relying upon the reservation.

Several judges in their separate opinions at the Preliminary Objection stage did, however, consider the questions that the objection raised. In his opinion, Judge Lauterpacht elaborated upon the position he had taken in the *Norwegian Loans* case.[16] Judge Spender reached the same conclusions as Judge Lauterpacht. Judge Klaestad, the President of the Court, agreed that the reservation was contrary to Article 36(6). As to the effect of this, he stated:

> It appears from the debate in the United States Senate concerning the acceptance of the compulsory jurisdiction of the Court ... that fear was expressed lest the Court might assume jurisdiction in matters which are essentially within the domestic jurisdiction of the United States, particularly in matters of immigration and the regulation of tariffs and duties and similar matters. The navigation of the Panama Canal was also referred to. Such were the considerations underlying the acceptance of Reservation (b). It may be doubted whether the Senate was fully aware of the possibility that this Reservation might entail the nullity of the whole Declaration of Acceptance, leaving the United States in the same legal situation with regard to the Court as States which have filed no such Declarations. Would the Senate have accepted this Reservation if it had been thought that the United States would thereby place themselves in such a situation, taking back by means of the Reservation what was otherwise given by the acceptance of the Declaration? The debate in the Senate does not appear to afford sufficient ground for such a supposition.
>
> For my part, I am satisfied that it was the true intention of the competent authorities of the United States to issue a real and effective Declaration accepting the compulsory jurisdiction of the Court, though—it is true—with far-reaching exceptions. That this view is not unfounded appears to be shown by the subsequent attitude of the United States Government. . . .
>
> These considerations have led me to the conclusion that the Court, both by its Statute and by the Charter, is prevented from acting upon that part of the Reservation which is in conflict with Article 36, paragraph 6, of the Statute, but that this circumstance does not necessarily imply that it is impossible for the Court to give effect to the other parts of the Declaration of Acceptance which are in conformity with the Statute. Part (a) of the Fourth Preliminary Objection should therefore in my view be rejected.[17]

---

[13] See on the case, Briggs (1959) 53 A.J.I.L. 301 and *ibid.* p. 547.

[14] I.C.J. Rep. 1957, p. 105.

[15] *ibid.* 1959, p. 6.

[16] In the *Nicaragua* case, Judge Schwebel saw "great force" in Judge Lauterpacht's argument, although "since declarations incorporating self-judging provisions apparently have been treated as valid, certainly by the declarants, for many years, the passage of time may have rendered Judge Lauterpacht's analysis less compelling today... ": I.C.J. Rep. 1984, pp. 601–602.

[17] *ibid.* 1959, pp. 77–78.

Judge *ad hoc* Carry stated that he agreed "generally" with Judge Klaestad's Opinion; he did not give a full judgment of his own. Judge Armand-Ugon reached the same conclusion as Judge Klaestad. As to the effect of the reservation's invalidity, he was of the opinion that it "does not imply that the acceptance of the Court's jurisdiction, given in the American Declaration, is altogether without value and to be considered as null and void in its entirety. . . . The way in which this Declaration was employed by the Government of the United States in . . . cases [which the U.S. has submitted to the Court] shows that the reservation . . . was not a determining factor at the time of its formulation and submission."[18] In his judgment with respect to interim measures, Judge Wellington Koo considered that the reservation was applicable at that stage and was valid.[19]

4. In the *Aerial Incident of July 27, 1955*, case,[20] which was brought by the United States against Bulgaria, Bulgaria invoked the United States domestic jurisdiction reservation. The United States withdrew the case before the Court made any ruling on its jurisdiction.

5. There are five declarations in force with "domestic jurisdiction" reservations of the "self-judging" or "automatic" kind: those of Liberia, Malawi, Mexico, Philippines and Sudan.[21] A number of declarations[22] have reservations excluding "disputes with regard to questions which by international law fall exclusively within the jurisdiction of [the state making it]" or differently worded reservations to that effect. Some of them omit any reference to international law but, at the same time, do not add "self-judging" words. Are such reservations open to challenge too? Do they serve any purpose? The 1957 Declaration made by the United Kingdom, contained a reservation in respect of " . . . any question which, in the opinion of the Government of the United Kingdom, affects the national security of the United Kingdom or any of its dependent territories."[23] Was this open to the same objections as those raised against the French and United States domestic jurisdiction reservations?

Might reliance by a state upon a "self judging" reservation in a case to which no state acting in good faith or reasonably would have concluded it did apply founder on the "principle of good faith" to which the Court refers in the *Nicaragua* case (judgment, para. 60, below, p. 1021) or the administrative law doctrine of "abuse of power," which might claim to be a general principle of law?[24]

NICARAGUA CASE (JURISDICTION AND ADMISSIBILITY)[25]

Nicaragua *v.* U.S.

I.C.J. Reports 1984, p. 392

Nicaragua made a unilateral application under Article 40, I.C.J. Statute claiming that the U.S. had acted in breach of its international law obligations by the use of

---

[18] *ibid.* p. 93.

[19] *ibid.* 1957, pp. 113–114.

[20] *ibid.* 1960, p. 146.

[21] The French and U.S. declarations containing such reservations have been withdrawn. The Philippines reservation was added in 1972.

[22] *e.g.* the Canadian declaration.

[23] The reservation was omitted in a revised declaration in 1958.

[24] Note that the U.S., quite properly, did not rely upon its self-judging reservation in the *Nicaragua* case. Had it done so, would the Court have had occasion to consider its validity? See the *Norwegian Loans* case, where neither side challenged the validity of the comparable French reservation.

[25] See Briggs (1979) 85 A.J.I.L. 373; Cutler (1985) 25 Virg.J.I.L. 437; Franck (1979) 85 A.J.I.L. 379; Greig (1991) 62 B.Y.I.L. 119; Highet (1987) 21 Int. Lawyer 1083; Kirgis (1979) 85 A.J.I.L. 652; Ostrihansky (1988) 1 Hague.Y.I.L. 3; Reisman (1980) 86 A.J.I.L. 128.

force against Nicaragua and otherwise intervening in Nicaraguan affairs in support of guerrillas fighting to overthrow the Nicaraguan Government.[26] Nicaragua argued that the Court had jurisdiction to hear the case under the Optional Clause and under the 1956 U.S.-Nicaraguan Treaty of Friendship. With regard to the Optional Clause, Nicaragua relied upon its 1929 Declaration[27] and the U.S. 1946 Declaration accepting the Court's compulsory jurisdiction. There was, however, a problem with the Nicaraguan 1929 Declaration. Although a signatory to the P.C.I.J. Statute, and hence competent to make an Optional Clause declaration under it, Nicaragua had never completed the ratification process.[28] Consequently, the Statute, and so the Declaration made under it, were never in force for Nicaragua. Under Article 36(5), I.C.J. Statute, provision is made for optional clause declarations under the P.C.I.J. Statute "which are still in force" to remain in force, giving the I.C.J. compulsory jurisdiction under them. In this case, the U.S. argued that, not having been in force, the Nicaraguan Declaration could not be "still in force" so that it did not come within Article 36(5). In the present judgment, the Court disagreed.

Judgment of the Court

26. The Court notes that Nicaragua, having failed to deposit its instrument of ratification of the Protocol of Signature of the Statute of the Permanent Court, was not a party to that treaty. Consequently the Declaration made by Nicaragua in 1929 had not acquired binding force prior to such effect as Article 36, paragraph 5, of the Statute of the International Court of Justice might produce.

27. However, while the declaration had not acquired binding force, it is not disputed that it could have done so ... at any time between the making of Nicaragua's declaration and the day on which the new Court came into existence, if not later, ratification of the Protocol of Signature would have sufficed to transform the content of the 1929 Declaration into a binding commitment; no one would have asked Nicaragua to make a new declaration. ... In sum, Nicaragua's 1929 Declaration was valid at the moment when Nicaragua became a party to the Statute of the new Court; it had retained its potential effect. ...

28. The characteristics of Nicaragua's declaration have now to be compared with the conditions of applicability of Article 36, paragraph 5, as laid down in that provision. ... [one] condition which declarations have to fulfil is that they should be "still in force" (in English) or "faites pour une durée qui n'est pas encore expirée" (in French).

---

[26] See further the *Nicaragua* (*Merits*) case, above, p. 866.

[27] The Nicaraguan Declaration reads: "On behalf of the Republic of Nicaragua I recognise as compulsory unconditionally the jurisdiction of the Permanent Court of International Justice." There are no reservations.

[28] In 1939 the Nicaraguan Foreign Minister sent a telegram to the League of Nations as depository, saying that the Statute had been ratified according to Nicaraguan consitutional law and that the instrument of ratification would be deposited. In 1942, the League wrote to Nicaragua noting that the instrument had not been received. During proceedings in the case, Nicaragua acknowledged that the process of ratification had not been completed and raised the possibility that the instrument might have been lost in wartime transit at sea.

30.... it does not appear possible to reconcile the two [language] versions of Article 36, paragraph 5, by considering that both versions refer to binding declarations.... According to the *travaux préparatoires* the word "binding" was never suggested; and if it had been suggested for the English text, there is no doubt that the drafters would never have let the French text stand as finally worded. Furthermore, the Court does not consider the French text to imply that *la durée non expirée* (the unexpired period) is that of a commitment of a binding character. It may be granted that, for a period to continue or expire, it is necessary for some legal effect to have come into existence. But this effect does not necessarily have to be of a binding nature. A declaration validly made under Article 36 of the Statute of the Permanent Court had a certain validity which could be preserved or destroyed, and it is perfectly possible to read the French text as implying only this validity.

31.... the Court cannot but be struck by the fact that the French Delegation at the San Francisco Conference called for the expression "still in force" to be translated, not by "encore en vigueur" but by the term: "pour une durée qui n'est pas encore expirée." In view of the excellent equivalence of the expressions "encore en vigueur" and "still in force," the deliberate choice of the expression "pour une durée qui n'est pas encore expirée" seems to denote an intention to widen the scope of Article 36, paragraph 5, so as to cover declarations which have not acquired binding force.... It is therefore the Court's opinion that the English version in no way expressly excludes a valid declaration of unexpired duration, made by a State not party to the Protocol of Signature of the Statute of the Permanent Court, and therefore not of a binding character....

36. This finding as regards the interpretation of Article 36, paragraph 5, must, finally, be compared to the conduct of States and international organisations in regard to this interpretation. In that respect, particular weight must be ascribed to certain official publications, namely the *I.C.J. Yearbook* (since 1946–1947), the *Reports* of the Court to the General Assembly of the United Nations (since 1968) and the annually published collection of *Signatures, Ratifications, Acceptances, Accessions, etc.,* concerning the Multilateral Conventions and Agreements in respect of which the Secretary-General acts as Depositary. The Court notes that, ever since they first appeared, all these publications have regularly placed Nicaragua on the list of those States that have recognised the compulsory jurisdiction of the Court by virtue of Article 36, paragraph 5, of the Statute. Even if the *I.C.J. Yearbook* has, in the issue for 1946–1947 and as from the issue for 1955–1956 onwards, contained a note[29] recalling certain facts concerning Nicaragua's ratification of the Protocol of Signature of the Statute of the Permanent Court of International Justice, this publication has never modified the classification of Nicaragua or the binding character attributed to

---

[29] *Ed.* The note recalled, *inter alia*, that no instrument of ratification had been received.

its 1929 Declaration—indeed the *Yearbooks* list Nicaragua among the States "still bound by" their declarations under Article 36 of the Statute of the Permanent Court. . . .

37. The Court has no intention of assigning these publications any role that would be contrary to their nature but will content itself with noting that they attest a certain interpretation of Article 36, paragraph 5 (whereby that provision would cover the declaration of Nicaragua), and the rejection of an opposite interpretation (which would refuse to classify Nicaragua among the States covered by that Article). . . . the inclusion of Nicaragua in the "List of States which have recognised the compulsory jurisdiction of the International Court of Justice, or which are still bound by their acceptance of the Optional Clause of the Statute of the Permanent Court of International Justice," as from the appearance of the first *I.C.J. Yearbook* (1946–1947), contrasts with its exclusion from the list in the last Report of the Permanent Court of International Justice of "States bound by the [optional] clause." It is therefore difficult to escape the conclusion that the basis of this innovation was to be found in the possibility that a declaration which, though not of binding character, was still valid, and was so for a period that had not yet expired, permitted the application of Article 36, paragraph 5, so long as the State in question, by ratifying the Statute of the International Court of Justice, provided it with the institutional foundation that it had hitherto lacked. From that moment on, Nicaragua would have become "bound" by its 1929 Declaration, and could, for practical purposes, appropriately be included in the same *Yearbook* list as the States which have been bound even prior to the coming into force of the post-war Statute.

38. The importance of this lies in the significance to be attached to the conduct of the States concerned, which is dependent on the testimony thus furnished by these publications. The point is not that the Court in its administrative capacity took a decision as to Nicaragua's status which would be binding upon it in its judicial capacity, since this clearly could not be so. It is that the listing found appropriate for Nicaragua amounted over the years to a series of attestations which were entirely official and public, and extremely numerous, and ranged over a period of nearly 40 years; and that hence the States concerned—first and foremost, Nicaragua—had every opportunity of accepting or rejecting the thus-proclaimed applicability of Article 36, paragraph 5, to the Nicaraguan Declaration of 1929.

39. . . . Having regard to the public and unchanging nature of the official statements concerning Nicaragua's commitment under the Optional-Clause system, the silence of its Government can only be interpreted as an acceptance of the classification thus assigned to it. It cannot be supposed that that Government could have believed that its silence could be tantamount to anything other than acquiescence. Besides, the Court would remark that if proceedings had been instituted against Nicaragua at any time in these recent years, and it had sought to deny

that, by the operation of Article 36, paragraph 5, it had recognised the compulsory jurisdiction of the Court, the Court would probably have rejected that argument.... If the Court considers that it would have decided that Nicaragua would have been bound in a case in which it was the Respondent, it must conclude that its jurisdiction is identically established in a case where Nicaragua is the Applicant.

40. As for States other than Nicaragua, including those which could be supposed to have the closest interest in that State's legal situation in regard to the Court's jurisdiction, they have never challenged the interpretation to which the publications of the United Nations bear witness and whereby the case of Nicaragua is covered by Article 36, paragraph 5. Such States as themselves publish lists of States bound by the compulsory jurisdiction of the Court have placed Nicaragua on their lists. Of course, the Court is well aware that such national publications simply reproduce those of the United Nations, where that particular point is concerned. Nevertheless, it would be difficult to interpret the fact of such reproduction as signifying an objection to the interpretation thus given; on the contrary, this reproduction contributes to the generality of the opinion which appears to have been cherished by States parties to the Statute as regards the applicability to Nicaragua of Article 36, paragraph 5.

41. Finally, what States believe regarding the legal situation of Nicaragua so far as the compulsory jurisdiction of the Court is concerned may emerge from the conclusions drawn by certain governments as regards the possibility of obliging Nicaragua to appear before the Court or of escaping any proceedings it may institute. The Court would therefore recall that in the case concerning the *Arbitral Award Made by the King of Spain on December 23 1906*[30] Honduras founded its application both on a special agreement, the Washington Agreement, and on Nicaragua's Optional-Clause declaration. It is also difficult for the Court not to consider that the United States letter of April 6, 1984[31] implies that at that date the United States, like other States, believed that Nicaragua was bound by the Court's jurisdiction in accordance with the terms of its 1929 Declaration.

42. The Court thus finds that the interpretation whereby the provisions of Article 36, paragraph 5, cover the case of Nicaragua has been confirmed by the subsequent conduct of the parties to the treaty in question, the Statute of the Court. However, the conduct of States which has been considered has been in relation to publications of the Court and of the United Nations Secretariat which ... do not indicate the legal reasoning leading to the conclusion that Nicaragua fell within the category of States to whose declarations Article 36, paragraph 5, applied. The view might have been taken that that paragraph applied because the Nicaraguan telegram of November 29, 1939 in itself constituted ratification of the

[30] *Ed*. I.C.J. Rep. 1960, p. 192.
[31] *Ed*. The Schultz letter. See below, p. 1021.

Protocol of Signature. It should therefore be observed that the conduct of Nicaragua in relation to the publications in question also supports a finding of jurisdiction under Article 36, paragraph 2, of the Statute independently of the interpretation and effect of paragraph 5 of that Article.

43. Nicaragua has in fact also contended that the validity of Nicaragua's recognition of the compulsory jurisdiction of the Court finds an independent basis in the conduct of the Parties. . . .

44. The United States however objects that this contention of Nicaragua is flatly inconsistent with the Statute of the Court, which provides only for consent to jurisdiction to be manifested in specified ways; an "independent title of jurisdiction, as Nicaragua calls it, is an impossibility.". . .

46. . . . The question is therefore whether, even if the consent of Nicaragua is real, the Court can decide that it has been given valid expression even on the hypothesis that the 1929 Declaration was without validity, and given that no other declaration has been deposited by Nicaragua since it became a party to the Statute of the International Court of Justice. In this connection the Court notes that Nicaragua's situation has been wholly unique, in that it was the publications of the Court itself . . . which affirmed (and still affirm today, for that matter) that Nicaragua had accomplished the formality in question. Hence, if the Court were to object that Nicaragua ought to have made a declaration under Article 36, paragraph 2, it would be penalising Nicaragua for having attached undue weight to the information given on that point by the Court and the Secretary-General of the United Nations and, in sum, having (on account of the authority of their sponsors) regarded them as more reliable than they really were.

47. . . . The Court finds that this exceptional situation cannot be without effect on the requirements obtaining as regards the formalities that are indispensable for the consent of a State to its compulsory jurisdiction to have been validly given. It considers therefore that, having regard to the origin and generality of the statements to the effect that Nicaragua was bound by its 1929 Declaration, it is right to conclude that the constant acquiescence of that State in those affirmations constitutes a valid mode of manifestation of its intent to recognise the compulsory jurisdiction of the Court under Article 36, paragraph 2, of the Statute, and that accordingly Nicaragua is, vis-à-vis the United States, a State accepting "the same obligation" under that Article.

48. The United States, however, further contends that even if Nicaragua is otherwise entitled to invoke against the United States the jurisdiction of the Court under Article 36, paragraphs 2 and 5, of the Statute, Nicaragua's conduct in relation to the United States over the course of many years estops Nicaragua from doing so. The United States asserts that since 1943 Nicaragua has consistently represented to the United States of America that Nicaragua was not bound by the Optional Clause, and

when the occasion arose that this was material to the United States diplomatic activities, the United States relied upon those Nicaraguan representations. . . .

49. In 1943, the United States ambassador to Nicaragua consulted the Nicaraguan Foreign Minister on the question whether the Protocol of Signature of the Statute of the Permanent Court had been ratified by Nicaragua. According to a despatch from the Ambassador to Washington, a decree of July 1935 signed by the President of Nicaragua, mentioning the approval of the ratification by the Senate and Chamber of Deputies, was traced, as was a copy of the telegram to the Secretariat of the League of Nations dated 29 November 1939 . . . The decree stated that it was to become effective on the date of its publication in *La Gaceta*. The Ambassador informed his Government that:

> "The Foreign Minister informs me that the decree was never published in *La Gaceta*. He also declared that there is no record to the instrument of ratification having been transmitted to Geneva. It would appear that, while appropriate legislative action was taken in Nicaragua to approve adherence to the Protocol, Nicaragua is not legally bound thereby, in as much as it did not deposit its official document of ratification with the League of Nations." . . .

According to the United States, the United States and Nicaragua could only have understood at that point in time that Nicaragua was not bound by the Optional Clause, and that understanding never changed.

50. . . . in 1955–1958 there was diplomatic contact between Honduras, Nicaragua and the United States over the dispute which was eventually determined by the Court as the case of the *Arbitral Award Made by the King of Spain on 23 December 1906* (I.C.J. Reports 1960, p. 192). One of the questions then under examination was whether Honduras would be entitled to institute proceedings against Nicaragua in reliance upon the 1929 Declaration and Article 36, paragraph 5, of the Statute, and in this connection . . . the [Nicaraguan] Ambassador is alleged to have observed [to U.S. officials] that there was

> "some doubt as to whether Nicaragua would be officially obligated to submit to the International Court because an instrument of ratification of the Court's jurisdiction was never sent" . . .

51. . . . the Court does not need to deal at length with the contention based on estoppel. The Court has found that the conduct of Nicaragua, having regard to the very particular circumstances in which it was placed, was such as to evince its consent to be bound in such a way as to constitute a valid mode of acceptance of jurisdiction (paragraph 47, above). It is thus evident that the Court cannot regard the information

obtained by the United States in 1943, or the doubts expressed in diplomatic contacts in 1955, as sufficient to overturn that conclusion, let alone to support an estoppel. Nicaragua's contention that since 1946 it has consistently maintained that it is subject to the jurisdiction of the Court, is supported by substantial evidence.

Having established that the Nicaraguan Optional Clause Declaration could give it jurisdiction, the Court then considered the effect of the 1984 Schultz letter sent by the U.S. to the UN purporting to modify its 1946 Declaration by excluding for two years "disputes with any Central American state or arising out of or related to events in Central America." The letter stated that "notwithstanding the terms of the . . . [1946] declaration, this proviso shall take effect immediately."

59. Declarations of acceptance of the compulsory jurisdiction of the Court are facultative, unilateral engagements, that States are absolutely free to make or not to make. In making the declaration a State is equally free either to do so unconditionally and without limit of time for its duration, or to qualify it with conditions or reservations. In particular, it may limit its effect to disputes arising after a certain date; or it may specify how long the declaration itself shall remain in force, or what notice (if any) will be required to terminate it. However, the unilateral nature of declarations does not signify that the State making the declaration is free to amend the scope and the contents of its solemn commitments as it pleases.[32] . . .

60. . . . the declarations, even though they are unilateral acts, establish a series of bilateral engagements with other States accepting the same obligation of compulsory jurisdiction, in which the conditions, reservations and time-limit clauses are taken into consideration. In the establishment of this network of engagements, which constitutes the Optional-Clause system, the principle of good faith plays an important role, . . .

61. The most important question relating to the effect of the 1984 notification is whether the United States was free to disregard the clause of six months' notice which, freely and by its own choice it had appended to its 1946 Declaration. In so doing the United States entered into an obligation which is binding upon it *vis-à-vis* other States parties to the Optional-Clause system. Although the United States retained the right to modify the contents of the 1946 Declaration or to terminate it, a power which is inherent in any unilateral act of a State, it has, nevertheless assumed an inescapable obligation towards other States accepting the Optional Clause, by stating formally and solemnly that any such change should take effect only after six months have elapsed as from the date of notice.

62. The United States has argued that the Nicaraguan 1929 Declaration, being of undefined duration, is liable to immediate termination, without

[32] *Ed.* The Court quoted the *Nuclear Tests* case, judgment, para. 43, above, p. 775.

previous notice, and that therefore Nicaragua has not accepted "the same obligation" as itself for the purposes of Article 36, paragraph 2, and consequently may not rely on the six months' notice proviso against the United States. The Court does not however consider that this argument entitles the United States validly to act in non-application of the time-limit proviso included in the 1946 Declaration. The notion of reciprocity is concerned with the scope and substance of the commitments entered into, including reservations, and not with the formal conditions of their creation, duration or extinction. It appears clearly that reciprocity cannot be invoked in order to excuse departure from the terms of a State's own declaration, whatever its scope, limitations or conditions. . . .

63. Moreover, since the United States purported to act on April 6, 1984 in such a way as to modify its 1946 Declaration with sufficiently immediate effect to bar an Application filed on April 9, 1984, it would be necessary, if reciprocity is to be relied on, for the Nicaraguan Declaration to be terminable with immediate effect. But the right of immediate termination of declarations with indefinite duration is far from established. It appears from the requirements of good faith that they should be treated, by analogy, according to the law of treaties, which requires a reasonable time for withdrawal from or termination of treaties that contain no provision regarding the duration of their validity. Since Nicaragua has in fact not manifested any intention to withdraw its own declaration, the question of what reasonable period of notice would legally be required does not need to be further examined: it need only be observed that from 6 to 9 April would not amount to a "reasonable time."

64. The Court would also recall that in previous cases in which it has had to examine the reciprocal effect of declarations made under the Optional Clause, it has determined whether or not the "same obligation" was in existence at the moment of seising of the Court, by comparing the effect of the provisions, in particular the reservations, of the two declarations at that moment. The Court is not convinced that it would be appropriate, or possible, to try to determine whether a State against which proceedings had not yet been instituted could rely on a provision in another State's declaration to terminate or modify its obligations before the Court was seised. . . .

65. In sum, the six months' notice clause forms an important integral part of the United States Declaration and it is a condition that must be complied with in case of either termination or modification. Consequently, the 1984 notification, in the present case, cannot override the obligation of the United States to submit to the compulsory jurisdiction of the Court *vis-à-vis* Nicaragua, a State accepting the same obligation.

67. The question remains to be resolved whether the United States Declaration of 1946, though not suspended in its effects vis-à-vis Nicaragua by the 1984 notification, constitutes the necessary consent of the United States to the jurisdiction of the Court in the present case, taking into account the reservations which were attached to the declaration.

Specifically, the United States has invoked proviso *(c)* to that declaration, which provides that the United States acceptance of the Court's compulsory jurisdiction shall not extend to "disputes arising under a multilateral treaty, unless (1) all parties to the treaty affected by the decision are also parties to the case before the Court, or (2) the United States of America specially agrees to jurisdiction." . . .

73. It may first be noted that the multilateral treaty reservation could not bar adjudication by the Court of all Nicaragua's claims, because Nicaragua, in its Application, does not confine those claims only to violations of the four multilateral conventions referred to.[33] . . . On the contrary, Nicaragua invokes a number of principles of customary and general international law that, according to the Application, have been violated by the United States. The Court cannot dismiss the claims of Nicaragua under principles of customary and general international law, simply because such principles have been enshrined in the texts of the conventions relied upon by Nicaragua. The fact that the above-mentioned principles, recognised as such, have been codified or embodied in multilateral conventions does not mean that they cease to exist and to apply as principles of customary law, even as regards countries that are parties to such conventions. Principles such as those of the non-use of force, non-intervention, respect for the independence and territorial integrity of States, and the freedom of navigation, continue to be binding as part of customary international law, despite the operation of provisions of conventional law in which they have been incorporated. Therefore, since the claim before the Court in this case is not confined to violation of the multilateral conventional provisions invoked, it would not in any event be barred by the multilateral treaty reservation in the United States 1946 Declaration.

The Court then held that it also had jurisdiction under the dispute settlement provision of the 1956 U.S.-Nicaraguan Treaty of Friendship, there being a dispute arising in respect of the treaty's provisions guaranteeing freedom of commerce and navigation.

113. For these reasons,

THE COURT,

(1)(a) *finds*, by 11 votes to five,[34] that it has jurisdiction to entertain the Application filed by the Republic of Nicaragua on April 9, 1984, on the basis of Article 36, paragraphs 2 and 5, of the Statute of the Court;

(b) *finds*, by 14 votes to two,[35] that it has jurisdiction to entertain the Application filed by the Republic of Nicaragua on April 9, 1984, in so far as that Application relates to a dispute concerning the interpretation or

---

[33] *Ed.* These were the UN Charter and three Inter-American treaties.
[34] Judges Mosler, Oda, Ago, Schwebel and Sir Robert Jennings dissented.
[35] Judges Ruda and Schwebel dissented.

application of the Treaty of Friendship, Commerce and Navigation between the United States of America and the Republic of Nicaragua signed at Managua on January 21, 1956, on the basis of Article XXIV of that Treaty;

(c) *finds*, by 15 votes to one,[36] that it has jurisdiction to entertain the case.

Separate Opinion of Judge Sir Robert Jennings

The question ... is whether Article 36, paragraph 5, of the present Court's Statute had the effect of transferring to the new Court, Nicaragua's subscription to the Optional Clause of the Protocol of Signature and the Statute of the Permanent Court, which entire instrument required ratification; but which was never ratified, with the admitted consequence that Nicaragua never became obligated by the compulsory jurisdiction of the Permanent Court?

The answer would seem to be placed beyond doubt according to the English text of Article 36, paragraph 5, ...

One can do no more than speculate on the purpose of the change in the French text [from *en vigueur*], for the records are sparse. So one is left with the rule that if there be, which I doubt, material difference between the meaning of the texts, the one which best reconciles the different language versions, all five of them that is to say, is to be preferred. For the present case at least there is no great difficulty in doing that. A declaration of acceptance of compulsory jurisdiction, which declaration never came into operation under the old Statute, certainly cannot be said, under the new Statute, to be "still in force," which is the language used in four of the versions of the Statute; and is the meaning consonant with what was said to be the purpose of the provision, namely the carry over to the new Court of obligations created in respect of the old Court.

There is no difficulty in collecting the same meaning in the French formula: *pour une durée qui n'est pas encore expirée*. What is referred to by that formula is surely a declaration by which the compulsory jurisdiction of the Permanent Court was actually established. A declaration to which, owing to failure to ratify the Protocol, no date of commencement of the obligation in respect of the Permanent Court could be assigned, cannot be said to be *pour une durée qui n'est pas encore expirée*. That which never began cannot be said to have had a duration at all.

... The judgment of the Court ... regards the *Yearbooks* and other publications as a factor confirming its interpretation of the effect of Article 36, paragraph 5; if not an independent source of jurisdiction for the Court. In my view, thus to allow considerable, and even decisive, effect, to statements in the Court's *Yearbook* is mistaken in general principle; ...

... the Court should always distinguish between its administrative

---

[36] Judge Schwebel dissented.

functions—including the compilation of the *Yearbook* by the Registrar on the Court's instructions—and its judicial functions. When there is a dispute between States as to the Court's jurisdiction, that dispute may be, as in the present case, submitted to the Court for determination in its judicial capacity. To hold, after the exchange of voluminous written pleadings and after two rounds of oral proceedings, that the matter was, before all this, virtually settled as a result of the action of the Registrar acting on behalf of the Court in its administrative capacity, and without benefit of judicial argument and procedure, is not free from an element of absurdity.

But even apart from the objections of principle, the *Yearbooks* do not at all yield any certain message on the status of the Nicaraguan declaration; on the contrary they consistently—each one of them—alert the attentive reader to the existence of doubts.

Notes

1. Finding that the Court's decision that it had jurisdiction in the case to be "contrary to law and fact,"[37] the U.S. decided not to participate further in the case and did not present evidence or arguments on the merits.[38] In 1985, the U.S. terminated its optional clause declaration.[39] Having read the Court's judgment as to jurisdiction, would you agree with the U.S. Government's position that the Court was "determined to find in favour of Nicaragua,"[40] or with Franck, who, although critical of the Court's reasoning, suggests that "it would be hard for a fair-minded reader of the majority's reasoned opinion to conclude that this result could not be reached by a dedicated and impartial judge?"[41]

2. As well as finding that it had jurisdiction, the Court also rejected, unanimously, U.S. objections as to admissibility,[42] including objections to the effect that the dispute concerned a matter that should be resolved by the political organs of the United Nations rather than its Court and that the Court should not involve itself in a situation that concerned an ongoing armed conflict.[43] On the propriety of Nicaragua's reference of the case to the Court, the 1982 Manila Declaration on the Peaceful Settlement of International Disputes,[44] reads:

[37] (1985) 24 I.L.M. 246.

[38] For criticism of this action, see Franck, *loc cit.*, p. 1015, n. 25, above. Supporting it, see Almond (1987) 17 Cal. W.I.L.J. 146.

[39] For criticism of the U.S. termination, see Gardner (1985) 24 Col J.T.L 421. See generally, Arend, ed., *The U.S. and the Compulsory Jurisdiction of the International Court of Justice* (1986).

[40] (1985) 24 I.L.M. 248.

[41] *loc. cit.*, p. 1015, n. 25, above, p. 382.

[42] The distinction between objections as to jurisdiction and as to admissibility is explained by Fitzmaurice (1958) 34 B.Y.I.L 12–13, as follows: "The latter is a plea that the tribunal should rule the claim to be inadmissible on some ground other than its ultimate merits: the former is a plea that the tribunal itself is incompetent to give any rulings at all as to the merits or the admissibility of the claim." Examples of objections as to admissibility are objections based on the rules on the nationality of claims or the exhaustion of local remedies.

[43] On this aspect of the case and the related question of the distinction between "legal" and "political" disputes (see the text of Art. 36(2)), see Almond, *loc. cit.*, p. 1025, n. 38, above; Gordon, in Damrosch, *op. cit.*, p. 988, n. 24, above; Merrills (1987) 24 Coexistence 169. See also on the Court and the Security Council below, p. 1041. The fact that negotiations are being actively pursued is also not a bar to recourse to judicial settlement or arbitration: *Aegean Sea Continental Shelf* case I.C.J. Rep. 1978, p. 13.

[44] *loc. cit.*, p. 985, n. 4, above.

Recourse to judicial settlement of legal disputes, particularly referral to the International Court of Justice, should not be considered an unfriendly act between States.

(iv) Third States in Contentious Litigation[45]

EAST TIMOR CASE

Portugal *v.* Australia

I.C.J. Reports 1995, p. 90

Portugal brought an application instituting proceedings against Australia under Article 36(2), I.C.J. Statute. Portugal claimed that Australia had failed to respect the rights of Portugal as the administering power of East Timor, and the right of the people of East Timor to self-determination, by entering into a 1989 treaty with Indonesia, which had occupied by force and illegally claimed title to East Timor. The treaty delimited the continental shelf between East Timor and Australia. In the following extract, the Court considered Australia's objection to the Court's jurisdiction in the case on the ground that it would be required to determine Indonesia's rights and duties without that state's consent. On the legality of Indonesia's claim to East Timor, see above, p. 119.

Judgment of the Court

26. The Court recalls in this respect that one of the fundamental principles of its Statute is that it cannot decide a dispute between States without the consent of those States to its jurisdiction. This principle was reaffirmed in the Judgment given by the Court in the case concerning *Monetary Gold Removed from Rome in 1943* and confirmed in several of its subsequent decisions . . .

27. The Court notes that Portugal's claim . . . is based on the assertion that Portugal alone in its capacity as administering Power, had the power to enter into the Treaty on behalf of East Timor, that Australia disregarded this exclusive power, and, in so doing, violated its obligations to respect the status of Portugal and that of East Timor.

The Court also observes that Australia, for its part, rejects Portugal's claim to the exclusive power to conclude treaties on behalf of East Timor, and the very fact that it entered into the 1989 Treaty with Indonesia shows that it considered that Indonesia had that power. Australia in substance argues that even if Portugal had retained that power, on whatever basis, after withdrawing from East Timor, the possibility existed that the power could later pass to another State under general international law, and that it did so pass to Indonesia; Australia affirms moreover that, if the power in question did pass to Indonesia, it was acting in conformity with international law in entering into the 1989 Treaty with that State, and

---

[45] See Chinkin, *Third Parties in International Law* (1993), Chaps 7 and 8.

could not have violated any of the obligations Portugal attributes to it. Thus, for Australia, the fundamental question in the present case is ultimately whether, in 1989, the power to conclude a treaty on behalf of East Timor in relation to its continental shelf lay with Portugal or with Indonesia.

28. The Court has carefully considered the argument advanced by Portugal which seeks to separate Australia's behaviour from that of Indonesia. However, in the view of the Court, Australia's behaviour cannot be assessed without first entering into the question why it is that Indonesia could not lawfully have concluded the 1989 Treaty, while Portugal allegedly could have done so; the very subject-matter of the Court's decision would necessarily be a determination whether, having regard to the circumstances in which Indonesia entered and remained in East Timor, it could or could not have acquired the power to enter into treaties on behalf of East Timor relating to the resources of its continental shelf. The Court could not make such a determination in the absence of the consent of Indonesia.

29. However, Portugal puts forward an additional argument aiming to show that the principle formulated by the Court in the case concerning *Monetary Gold Removed from Rome in 1943* is not applicable in the present case. It maintains, in effect, that the rights which Australia allegedly breached were rights *erga omnes* and that accordingly Portugal could require it, individually, to respect them regardless of whether or not another State had conducted itself in a similarly unlawful manner.

In the Court's view, Portugal's assertion that the right of peoples to self-determination, as it evolved from the Charter and from United Nations practice, has an *erga omnes* character, is irreproachable. The principle of self-determination of peoples has been recognized by the United Nations Charter and in the jurisprudence of the Court (see *Legal Consequences for States of the Continued Presence of South Africa in Namibia (South West Africa) notwithstanding Security Council Resolution 276 (1970), Advisory Opinion, I.C.J. Reports 1971*, pp. 31–32, paras. 52–53; *Western Sahara, Advisory Opinion, I.C.J. Reports 1975*, pp. 31–33, paras. 54–59); it is one of the essential principles of contemporary international law. However, the Court considers that the *erga omnes* character of a norm and the rule of consent to jurisdiction are two different things. Whatever the nature of the obligations invoked, the Court could not rule on the lawfulness of the conduct of a State when its judgment would imply an evaluation of the lawfulness of the conduct of another State which is not a party to the case. Where this is so, the Court cannot act, even if the right in question is a right *erga omnes*.

The Court then rejected an argument by Portugal that the Court would not have to decide who had the capacity to act for East Timor because the General Assembly and the Security Council had determined that Portugal was the administering power, see the resolutions cited above, p. 119, which determinations the Court would accept as "givens". In the Court's view, the resolutions did not establish that third states should deal exclusively with Portugal in respect of East Timor's continental shelf.

34. The Court emphasizes that it is not necessarily prevented from adjudicating when the judgment it is asked to give might affect the legal interests of a State which is not a party to the case. Thus, in the case concerning *Certain Phosphate Lands in Nauru (Nauru v. Australia)*, it stated, *inter alia*, as follows:

> In the present case, the interests of New Zealand and the United Kingdom do not constitute the very subject-matter of the judgment to be rendered on the merits of Nauru's Application . . . In the present case, the determination of the responsibility of New Zealand or the United Kingdom is not a prerequisite for the determination of the responsibility of Australia, the only object of Nauru's claim . . . In the present case, a finding by the Court regarding the existence or the content of the responsibility attributed to Australia by Nauru might well have implications for the legal situation of the two other States concerned, but no finding in respect of that legal situation will be needed as a basis for the Court's decision on Nauru's claims against Australia. Accordingly, the Court cannot decline to exercise its jurisdiction. (*I.C.J. Reports 1992*, pp. 261–261, para. 55).

However, in this case, the effects of the judgment requested by Portugal would amount to a determination that Indonesia's entry into and continued presence in East Timor are unlawful and that, as a consequence, it does not have the treaty-making power in matters relating to the continental shelf resources of East Timor. Indonesia's rights and obligations would thus constitute the very subject-matter of such a judgment made in the absence of that State's consent. Such a judgment would run directly counter to the "well-established principle of international law embodied in the Court's Statute, namely, that the Court can only exercise jurisdiction over a State with its consent" (*Monetary Gold Removed from Rome in 1943, Judgment, I.C.J. Reports 1954*, p. 32).

38. For these reasons,

THE COURT,

By fourteen votes to two,[46]

Finds that it cannot in the present case exercise the jurisdiction conferred upon it by the declarations made by the Parties under Article 36, paragraph 2, of its Statute to adjudicate upon the dispute referred to it by the Application of the Portuguese Republic.

---

[46] In favour: President Bedjaoui; Vice-President Schwebel; Judges Oda, Sir Robert Jennings, Guillaume, Shahabuddeen, Aguilar-Mawdsley, Ranjeva, Herczegh, Shi, Fleischhauer, Koroma, Vereshchetin; Judge *ad hoc* Sir Ninian Stephen. Judge Weeramantry and Judge *ad hoc* Skubiszewski dissented.

Notes

1. In the *East Timor* case, Indonesia had no wish to become a party to the case and, unlike Australia, could not be brought before the Court under Article 36(2), as it had not made an "optional clause" declaration.

2. The *Monetary Gold* case[47] concerned gold belonging to the National Bank of Albania that had been seized by Germany from a bank in Rome during the Second World War. It had since fallen into the hands of the allied forces and was to be distributed by a Tripartite Commission, consisting of France, the United Kingdom and the United States. Following an arbitral decision against it, and acting under an agreement that gave the Court jurisdiction in the matter, Italy instituted proceedings before the Court, against the three allied powers claiming the gold, but Albania, in whose favour the arbitrator had decided, declined to be a party to the case before the I.C.J. The Court decided that it did not have jurisdiction because "Albania's legal interests would not only be affected by a decision, but would form the very subject-matter of the decision."

3. A different situation from that in the *East Timor* case is that in which a third state wishes to participate in a case without becoming a party to it.[48] It may become a party with the consent of the other party or parties, which may have been given earlier by treaty[49] or under Article 36(2), or may be given *ad hoc* by special agreement. Otherwise, there is the possibility of intervention, as a third party, under Articles 62 or 63, I.C.J. Statute, below, Appendix III.

4. The Court gave Nicaragua permission to intervene under Article 62 in the *Land, Island and Maritime Frontier Dispute* case (El Salvador v. Honduras),[50] although only in respect of the legal regime of the Gulf of Fonseca; the application was refused in respect of other matters before the Court. The Court stated:

> 72. ... the fact is that El Salvador now claims that the waters of the Gulf are subject to a condominium of the coastal States, and has indeed suggested that that régime "would in any case have been applicable to the Gulf under customary international law". Nicaragua has referred to the fact that Nicaragua plainly has rights in the Gulf of Fonseca, the existence of which is undisputed, and contends that "The condominium, if it is declared to be applicable, would by its very nature involve three riparians, and not only the parties to the Special Agreement." In the opinion of the Chamber, this is a sufficient demonstration by Nicaragua that it has an interest of a legal nature in the determination whether or not this is the régime governing the waters of the Gulf: the very definition of a condominium points to this conclusion. Furthermore, a decision in favour of some of the Honduran theses would equally be such as may affect legal interests of Nicaragua.

The *Land, Island and Maritime Frontier Dispute* case is the only one in which an application to intervene under Article 62 has been successful.[51] Intervention under Article 62 is a matter for the Court; there is no right to intervene and the parties to the case may only seek to persuade the Court to adopt any view that they have. The burden of proof is on the state seeking to intervene.[52] A state may

---

[47] I.C.J. Rep. 1954, p. 19 at p. 32.

[48] On intervention by a third state, see Grieg (1992) 32 Virg.J.I.L. 285; Macdonald and Hughes (1993) 5 A.J.I.C.L. 1; Ruda, in Lowe and Fitzmaurice, *op. cit.*, p. 988, n. 24, above, Chap. 26; Rosenne, *Intervention in the International Court of Justice* (1993).

[49] In the *Monetary Gold* case, Albania could have seized the Court under the agreement on the basis of which Italy did so.

[50] I.C.J. Rep. 1990, p. 92 at p. 121.

[51] On the Court's historically restrictive approach, see Chinkin (1986) 80 A.J.I.L. 495 and McGinley (1985) 34 I.C.L.Q. 671.

[52] *Land, Island and Maritime Frontier Dispute* case, I.C.J. Rep. 1990, p. 117.

be permitted to intervene even though there is no "jurisdictional link" between the intervening state and the parties to the case.[53] Since it is not a party to the case, an intervening state is not bound by the Court's judgment: see Article 59, I.C.J. Statute.

5. Intervention under Article 63, which applies in cases where a state is a party to a treaty that is being interpreted by the Court, has been permitted in two cases: the *Wimbledon* case[54] and the *Haya de la Torre* case.[55] Although a third state has a right to intervene under Article 63, the Court must first decide whether it qualifies.[56]

(v) Provisional Measures in Contentious Litigation[57]

See Article 41(1), Statute of the International Court of Justice.[58]

CASE CONCERNING APPLICATION OF THE GENOCIDE CONVENTION[59]

Bosnia and Herzegovina *v.* Yugoslavia (Serbia and Montenegro)

I.C.J. Reports 1993, p. 3

Bosnia and Herzegovina brought an application instituting proceedings under Article IX, Genocide Convention alleging breaches of that Convention by Yugoslavia (Serbia and Montenegro), *i.e.* the Federal Republic of Yugoslavia (FRY). Immediately after bringing the application, Bosnia and Herzegovina requested an indication of provisional measures by the Court under Article 41, I.C.J. Statute. In the following extract from its Order, the Court considered whether it had jurisdiction to act and the measures that should be indicated.

Order of the Court

14. Whereas on a request for provisional measures the Court need not, before deciding whether or not to indicate them, finally satisfy itself that it has jurisdiction on the merits of the case, yet it ought not to indicate such measures unless the provisions invoked by the Applicant or found in the Statute appear, prima facie, to afford a basis on which the jurisdiction of the Court might be established; whereas this consideration embraces jurisdiction both *ratione personae* and *ratione materiae*, even though, inasmuch as almost all States are today parties to the Statute of

---

[53] *ibid.* p. 135.
[54] See above, p. 260 (Poland intervened).
[55] I.C.J. Rep. 1951, p. 71.
[56] On the Court's refusal to permit El Salvador to intervene under Art. 63 in the *Nicaragua* case, see Damrosch, *op. cit.*, p. 988, n. 24, above, p. 376.
[57] See Dumbauld, *Interim Measures of Protection in International Controversies* (1932); Elkind, *Interim Measures; a Functional Approach* (1981); Greig (1991) 11 A.Y.I.L. 108; Mendelson ((1972–3) 46 B.Y.I.L. 259; Merrills (1995) 44 I.C.L.Q. 90; Oda, in Lowe and Fitzmaurice, *op. cit.*, p. 988, n. 24, above, Chap. 29; Sztucki, *Interim Measures in the Hague Court* (1983).
[58] See below, Appendix I. See also Rule 66 of Rules of Court.
[59] See Gaffikin (1995) 17 Sydney L.R. 458 and Warbrick (1993) 52 C.L.J. 367.

the Court, it is in general only the latter which requires to be considered; . . .

On the question of *jurisdiction personae*, the Court noted that under Article 35(1), Statute of the Court, it was "open to the States parties to the present Statute", which included all UN member states. It then reviewed Security Council Resolution 777 and General Assembly Resolution 47/1, as to which, see above, p. 129, by which it was decided that the FRY did not succeed to the UN membership of Yugoslavia (SFRY) and would have to apply for membership. The Court continued:

18. Whereas, while the solution adopted is not free from legal difficulties, the question whether or not Yugoslavia is a Member of the United Nations and as such a party to the Statute of the Court is one which the Court does not need to determine definitively at the present stage of the proceedings;

19. Whereas Article 35 of the Statute, after providing that the Court shall be open to the parties to the Statute, continues:

2. The conditions under which the Court shall be open to other States shall, subject to the special provisions contained in treaties in force, be laid down by the Security Council, but in no case shall such conditions place the parties in a position of inequality before the Court;

whereas the Court therefore considers that proceedings may validly be instituted by a State against a State which is a party to such a special provision in a treaty in force, but is not party to the Statute, and independently of the conditions laid down by the Security Council in its resolution 9 of 1946 (cf. *S.S. "Wimbledon", 1923, P.C.I.J., Series A, No. 1*, p. 6); whereas a compromissory clause in a multilateral convention, such as Article IX of the Genocide Convention relied on by Bosnia-Herzegovina in the present case, could, in the view of the Court, be regarded prima facie as a special provision contained in a treaty in force; whereas accordingly if Bosnia-Herzegovina and Yugoslavia are both parties to the Genocide Convention, disputes to which Article IX applies are in any event prima facie within the jurisdiction *ratione personae* of the Court;

20. Whereas the Court must therefore now consider its jurisdiction *ratione materiae*; whereas Article IX of the Genocide Convention, upon which Bosnia-Herzegovina in its Application claims to found the jurisdiction of the Court, provides that

Disputes between the Contracting Parties relating to the interpretation, application or fulfilment of the present Convention, including those relating to the responsibility of a State for genocide or for any of the other acts enumerated in article III, shall be submitted to the International Court of Justice at the request of any of the parties to the dispute;

The Court noted that the SFRY had ratified the Genocide Convention in 1950 and that in December 1993 Bosnia-Herzegovina had sent a note to the UN Secretary-General indicating its wish to succeed to the Convention with effect from the date of its independence in March 1992, which had been accepted in those terms by the Secretary-General. The Court then ruled that even if Bosnia-Herzegovina's note was to be treated as one indicating accession (rather than succession), as the FRY argued, it still had jurisdiction under Article 41 to issue provisional measures. The Court concluded:

26. Whereas Article IX of the Genocide Convention, to which both Bosnia-Herzegovina and Yugoslavia are parties, thus appears to the Court to afford a basis on which the jurisdiction of the Court might be founded to the extent that the subject-matter of the dispute relates to "the interpretation, application or fulfilment" of the Convention, including disputes "relating to the responsibility of a State for genocide or for any of the other acts enumerated in article III" of the Convention; . . .

34. Whereas the power of the Court to indicate provisional measures under Article 41 of the Statute of the Court has as its object to preserve the respective rights of the parties pending the decision of the Court, and pre-supposes that irreparable prejudice shall not be caused to rights which are the subject of dispute in judicial proceedings; and whereas it follows that the Court must be concerned to preserve by such measures the rights which may subsequently be adjudged by the Court to belong either to the Applicant or to the Respondent;

35. Whereas the Court, having established the existence of a basis on which its jurisdiction might be founded, ought not to indicate measures for the protection of any disputed rights other than those which might ultimately form the basis of a judgment in the exercise of that jurisdiction; whereas accordingly the Court will confine its examination of the measures requested, and of the grounds asserted for the request for such measures, to those which fall within the scope of the Genocide Convention; . . .

45. Whereas . . . all parties to the Convention have thus undertaken "to prevent and to punish" the crime of genocide; whereas in the view of the Court, in the circumstances brought to its attention and outlined above in which there is a grave risk of acts of genocide being committed, Yugoslavia and Bosnia-Herzegovina, whether or not any such acts in the past may be legally imputable to them, are under a clear obligation to do all in their power to prevent the commission of any such acts in the future;

46. Whereas the Court is not called upon, for the purpose of its decision on the present request for the indication of provisional measures, now to establish the existence of breaches of the Genocide Convention by either Party, but to determine whether the circumstances require the indication of provisional measures to be taken by the Parties for the protection of rights under the Genocide Convention; and whereas the Court is satisfied, taking into account the obligation imposed by Article I

of the Genocide Convention, that the indication of measures is required for the protection of such rights; ...

48. Whereas in its request for the indication of provisional measures Bosnia-Herzegovina has also maintained that the Court should exercise its power to indicate provisional measures with a view to preventing the aggravation or extension of the dispute whenever it considers that circumstances so require; whereas from the information available to the Court it is satisfied that there is a grave risk of action being taken which may aggravate or extend the existing dispute over the prevention or punishment of the crime of genocide, or render it more difficult of solution; ...

51. Whereas the decision given in the present proceedings in no way prejudges the question of the jurisdiction of the Court to deal with the merits of the case, or any questions relating to the admissibility of the Application, or relating to the merits themselves, and leaves unaffected the right of the Governments of Bosnia-Herzegovina and Yugoslavia to submit arguments in respect of those questions;

52. For these reasons,

THE COURT

Indicates, pending its final decision in the proceedings instituted on 20 March 1993 by the Republic of Bosnia and Herzegovina against the Federal Republic of Yugoslavia (Serbia and Montenegro), the following provisional measures:

A. (1) Unanimously,

The Government of the Federal Republic of Yugoslavia (Serbia and Montenegro) should immediately, in pursuance of its undertaking in the Convention on the Prevention and Punishment of the Crime of Genocide of 9 December 1948, take all measures within its power to prevent commission of the crime of genocide;
(2) By 13 votes to 1,[60]
The Government of the Federal Republic of Yugoslavia (Serbia and Montenegro) should in particular ensure that any military, paramilitary or irregular armed units which may be directed or supported by it, as well as any organizations and persons which may be subject to its control, direction or influence, do not commit any acts of genocide, of conspiracy to commit genocide, of direct and public incitement to commit genocide, or of complicity in genocide, whether directed against the Muslim population of Bosnia and Herzegovina or against any other national, ethnical, racial or religious group;

[60] In favour: President Sir Robert Jennings; Vice-President Oda; Judges Ago, Schwebel, Bedjaoui, Ni, Evensen, Guillaume, Shahabuddeen, Aguilar-Mawdsley, Weeramantry, Ranjeva, Ajibola. Judge Tarassov dissented.

B. Unanimously,

The Government of the Federal Republic of Yugoslavia (Serbia and Montenegro) and the Government of the Republic of Bosnia and Herzegovina should not take any action and should ensure that no action is taken which may aggravate or extend the existing dispute over the prevention or punishment of the crime of genocide, or render it more difficult of solution.

Notes

1. The main problem which has arisen in respect of the Court's power to indicate provisional measures has been to identify the circumstances in which they can be indicated before the Court's jurisdiction has been established to hear the merits of a case. The difficulty has been to find a rule that properly takes account both of the fact that the Court may ultimately decide that it lacks jurisdiction to hear the case and of the fact that the parties' rights may be irreparably damaged before a decision as to jurisdiction is taken. After some uncertainty in earlier cases,[61] the Court has now settled on a *prima facie* jurisdiction test: see para. 14, Order.

2. In the *Genocide Convention* case, Bosnia and Herzegovina came back to the Court with a request for further provisional measures.[62] The Court declined this request because the proposed measures did not fall within Article IX, Genocide Convention, which was the basis for the Court's *prima facie* jurisdiction in the case. However, the Court did reaffirm the measures it had ordered earlier. It noted "the persistence of conflicts on the territory of Bosnia-Herzegovina and the commission of heinous acts in the course of those conflicts" and concluded that the "present perilous situation demands . . . an immediate implementation of those measures".[63]

3. The Court's Statute does not make it clear whether provisional measures are binding in law and the Court has never stated its view. The word "order" suggests that they are binding, as might the fact that notice of them has to be given to the Security Council (Article 41(2), Statute), but the word "indicate" hints otherwise. Sztucki states[64]:

> It is inherent in the provisional nature of orders concerning interim protection that they lack the quality of *res judicata*, as this notion has been defined by the Court—*i.e.* they do not embody the concurrent characteristics of being "binding" (Art. 59) and "final" (Art. 60).
>
> At present it also appears to be generally accepted that orders indicating interim measures are not enforceable under Article 94(2) of the UN Charter, by extensive interpretation of that provision which explicitly envisages "judgments."

4. Generally, states have not respected provisional measures that are indicated against them. This was true in the *Anglo-Iranian Oil Co.* case, the *Fisheries Jurisdiction* cases, the *Nuclear Tests* cases and the *U.S. Diplomatic and Consular Staff in Tehran* case and there would not appear to have been full compliance in the

---

[61] See the *Anglo-Iranian Oil Co.* case (*Interim Measures*), I.C.J. Rep. 1951, p. 89, and the *Nuclear Tests Cases (Interim Protection)*, I.C.J. Rep. 1973, p. 99.

[62] *Genocide Convention* case (*Further Requests for Provisional Measures*), I.C.J. Rep. 1993, p. 325.

[63] *ibid.* p. 349.

[64] *op. cit.*, p. 1030, n. 57, p. 262. Footnotes omitted.

Nicaragua case. A current judge on the Court, Judge Oda, has written[65]: "It is not going too far to state that the provisional measures indicated by the Court have had hardly any practical effect in most cases of a highly charged political nature."

(vi) ADVISORY JURISDICTION[66]

See Article 96, United Nations Charter and Articles 65–68, Statute of the International Court of Justice.[67]

Notes

In addition to its jurisdiction to decide cases brought by states under Article 36 of its Statute, the World Court

> may give an advisory opinion on any legal question at the request of whatever body may be authorised by or in accordance with the Charter of the United Nations to make such a request.[68]

The General Assembly and the Security Council are authorised "by" the Charter[69] to request opinions. ECOSOC and the Trusteeship Council have been authorised "in accordance with" the Charter,[70] as have 15 of the 17 United Nations specialised agencies (the exceptions are the Universal Postal Union and the Multilateral Investment Guarantee Agency), the International Atomic Energy Agency (which is not a specialised agency), the Interim Committee of the General Assembly and the Committee on Applications for Review of Administrative Tribunal Judgments.

Although advisory opinions are not binding in law upon the requesting body, they have over the years usually been accepted and acted upon by it and by any state concerned. Whereas the record of formal acceptance of opinions remains good, that of compliance in fact has not been perfect. Striking examples were the failure of the General Assembly to enforce the opinion given to it in the *Certain Expenses* case[71] and the steadfast refusal of the old South Africa over many years to fall in line with the opinions on South West Africa/Namibia.[72]

Occasionally, provision is made in advance for an opinion to be binding. The 1946 General Convention on the Privileges and Immunities of the United Nations provides that if a difference arises between the United Nations and a member a request for an advisory opinion should be made by an organ of the United Nations and that the opinion rendered by the Court "shall be accepted as decisive by the parties."[73]

---

[65] Lowe and Fitzmaurice, *op. cit.*, p. 988, n. 24, above, p. 557.
[66] See Keith, *The Extent of the Advisory Jurisdiction of the International Court of Justice* (1971); Pomerance, *The Advisory Function of the International Court in the League and UN Eras* (1973); Pratap, *The Advisory Jurisdiction of the International Court* (1972); Szasz, in *The Future of the International Court of Justice, loc. cit.*, p. 988, n. 25, above, Vol. II, p. 499.
[67] Below, Appendix I.
[68] Statute of the Court, Art. 65(1).
[69] UN Charter, Art. 96(1).
[70] UN Charter, Art. 96(2). The UN Secretary-General has proposed that he be allowed to request advisory opinions. For differing views on the matter, see Schwebel (1984) 78 A.J.I.L. 869 and Higgins, in Lowe and Fitzmaurice, *op. cit.*, p. 988, n. 24, Chap. 31.
[71] See above, p. 975.
[72] See above, p. 132.
[73] Art. 30, U.K.T.S. 10 (1950), Cmnd. 7891. *cf.* Article XII, Statute of the I.L.O. Administrative Tribunal. See Ago (1991) 85 A.J.I.L. 439.

States may not request advisory opinions, but they are permitted, along with international organisations, to participate in proceedings before the Court.[74] Individuals and other entities have no *locus standi*.

Recourse to the Court for advisory opinions has declined since 1945. Whereas the Permanent Court of International Justice gave 27 opinions in 18 years, the International Court of Justice has so far given only 21. Requests have concerned constitutional questions about the functioning of the requesting body,[75] points of law relevant to a dispute between states[76] or abstract questions of law.[77]

LEGALITY OF THE THREAT OR USE OF NUCLEAR WEAPONS CASE

Advisory Opinion. (1997) 35 I.L.M. 809 and 1343.

For the question put to the Court by the UN General Assembly in this case, see the extract above, p. 924. In the following extract, the Court considered whether it had jurisdiction to respond.

Opinion of the Court

13. The Court must furthermore satisfy itself that the advisory opinion requested does indeed relate to a "legal question" within the meaning of [Article 65 of] its Statute and the United Nations Charter. . . .

The question put to the Court by the General Assembly is indeed a legal one, since the Court is asked to rule on the compatibility of the threat or use of nuclear weapons with the relevant principles and rules of international law. To do this, the Court must identify the existing principles and rules, interpret them and apply them to the threat or use of nuclear weapons, thus offering a reply to the question posed based on law.

The fact that this question also has political aspects, as, in the nature of things, is the case with so many questions which arise in international life, does not suffice to deprive it of its character as a "legal question" and to "deprive the Court of a competence expressly conferred on it by its Statute" (*Application for Review of Judgement No. 158 of the United Nations Administrative Tribunal, Advisory Opinion, I.C.J. Reports 1973*, p. 172, para. 14). Whatever its political aspects, the Court cannot refuse to admit the legal character of a question which invites it to discharge an essentially judicial task, namely, an assessment of the legality of the possible conduct of States with regard to the obligations imposed upon them by international law (cf. *Conditions of Admission of a State to Membership in the United Nations (Article 4 of the Charter), Advisory Opinion, I.C.J. Reports 1947–1948*, pp. 61–62; . . .

---

[74] Art. 66, Statute of the Court. Over 20 states made written and/or oral statements to the Court in the *Nuclear Weapons* case, above, p. 924.

[75] *e.g.* the *Certain Expenses* case, above, p. 975.

[76] *e.g.* the *Western Sahara* case, above, p. 115.

[77] *e.g.* the *Nuclear Weapons* case, above, p. 924.

Furthermore, as the Court said in the Opinion it gave in 1980 concerning the *Interpretation of the Agreement of 25 March 1951 between the WHO and Egypt;*

> Indeed, in situations in which political considerations are prominent it may be particularly necessary for an international organization to obtain an advisory opinion from the Court as to the legal principles applicable with respect to the matter under debate . . . " (*Interpretation of the Agreement of 25 March 1951 between the WHO and Egypt, Advisory Opinion, I.C.J. Reports 1980,* p. 87, para. 33).

The Court moreover considers that the political nature of the motives which may be said to have inspired the request and the political implications that the opinion given might have are of no relevance in the establishment of its jurisdiction to give such an opinion.

14. Article 65, paragraph 1, of the Statute provides: "The Court *may* give an advisory opinion . . . " (Emphasis added.) This is more than an enabling provision. As the Court has repeatedly emphasized, the Statute leaves a discretion as to whether or not it will give an advisory opinion that has been requested of it, once it has established its competence to do so. In this context, the Court has previously noted as follows:

> The Court's Opinion is given not to the States, but to the organ which is entitled to request it; the reply of the Court, itself an 'organ of the United Nations', represents its participation in the activities of the Organization, and, in principle, should not be refused." (*Interpretation of Peace Treaties with Bulgaria, Hungary and Romania, First Phase, Advisory Opinion, I.C.J. Reports 1950,* p. 71;

The Court has constantly been mindful of its responsibilities as "the principal judicial organ of the United Nations" (Charter, Art. 92). When considering each request, it is mindful that it should not, in principle refuse to give an advisory opinion. In accordance with the consistent jurisprudence of the Court, only "compelling reasons" could lead it to such a refusal (. . . *Western Sahara, Advisory Opinion, I.C.J. Reports 1975,* p. 21 . . .). There has been no refusal, based on the discretionary power of the Court, to act upon a request for advisory opinion in the history of the present Court; in the case concerning the *Legality of the Use by a State of Nuclear Weapons in Armed Conflict,* the refusal to give the World Health Organization the advisory opinion requested by it was justified by the Court's lack of jurisdiction in that case. The Permanent Court of International Justice took the view on only one occasion that it could not reply to a question put to it, having regard to the very particular circumstances of the case, among which were that the question directly concerned an already existing dispute, one of the States parties to which was neither a party to the Statute of the Permanent Court nor a Member of the League of Nations, objected to the proceedings, and refused to take part in any way (*Status of Eastern Carelia, P.C.I.J., Series B, No. 5*).

15. Most of the reasons adduced in these proceedings in order to persuade the Court that in the exercise of its discretionary power it should decline to render the opinion requested by General Assembly resolution 49/75K were summarized in the following statement made by one State in the written proceedings:

> The question presented is vague and abstract, addressing complex issues which are the subject of consideration among interested States and within other bodies of the United Nations which have an express mandate to address these matters. An opinion by the Court in regard to the question presented would provide no practical assistance to the General Assembly in carrying out its functions under the Charter. Such an opinion has the potential of undermining progress already made or being made on this sensitive subject and, therefore, is contrary to the interest of the United Nations Organization." (United States of America, Written Statement, pp. 1–2; ...)

In contending that the question put to the Court is vague and abstract, some States appeared to mean by this that there exists no specific dispute on the subject-matter of the question. In order to respond to this argument, it is necessary to distinguish between requirements governing contentious procedure and those applicable to advisory opinions. The purpose of the advisory function is not to settle—at least directly—disputes between States, but to offer legal advice to the organs and institutions requesting the opinion (cf. *Interpretation of Peace Treaties I.C.J. Reports 1950*, p. 71). The fact that the question put to the Court does not relate to a specific dispute should consequently not lead the Court to decline to give the opinion requested.

Moreover, it is the clear position of the Court that to contend that it should not deal with a question couched in abstract terms is "a mere affirmation devoid of any justification", and that "the Court may give an advisory opinion on any legal question, abstract or otherwise" (*Conditions of Admission of a State to Membership in the United Nations (Article 4 of the Charter), Advisory Opinion, 1948, I.C.J. Reports 1947–1948*, p. 61 ...).

Certain States have however expressed the fear that the abstract nature of the question might lead the Court to make hypothetical or speculative declarations outside the scope of its judicial function. The Court does not consider that, in giving an advisory opinion in the present case, it would necessarily have to write "scenarios", to study various types of nuclear weapons and to evaluate highly complex and controversial technological, strategic and scientific information. The Court will simply address the issues arising in all their aspects by applying the legal rules relevant to the situation.

16. Certain States have observed that the General Assembly has not explained to the Court for what precise purposes it seeks the advisory opinion. Nevertheless, it is not for the Court itself to purport to decide whether or not an advisory opinion is needed by the Assembly for the performance of its functions. The General Assembly has the right to decide for itself on the usefulness of an opinion in the light of its own needs.

Equally, once the Assembly has asked, by adopting a resolution, for an advisory opinion on a legal question, the Court, in determining whether there are any compelling reasons for it to refuse to give such an opinion, will not have regard to the origins or to the political history of the request or to the distribution of votes in respect of the adopted resolution.

17. It has also been submitted that a reply from the Court in this case might adversely affect disarmament negotiations and would, therefore, be contrary to the interest of the United Nations. The Court is aware that, no matter what might be its conclusions in any opinion it might give, they would have relevance for the continuing debate on the matter in the General Assembly and would present an additional element in the nego-tiations on the matter. Beyond that, the effect of the opinion is a matter of appreciation. The Court has heard contrary positions advanced and there are no evident criteria by which it can prefer one assessment to another. That being so, the Court cannot regard this factor as a compelling reason to decline to exercise its jurisdiction.

18. Finally, it has been contended by some States that in answering the question posed, the Court would be going beyond its judicial role and would be taking upon itself a law-making capacity. It is clear that the Court cannot legislate, and, in the circumstances of the present case, it is not called upon to do so. Rather its task is to engage in its normal judicial function of ascertaining the existence or otherwise of legal principles and rules applicable to the threat or use of nuclear weapons. The contention that the giving of an answer to the question posed would require the Court to legislate is based on a supposition that the present *corpus juris* is devoid of relevant rules in this matter. The Court could not accede to this argument; it states the existing law and does not legislate. This is so even if, in stating and applying the law, the Court necessarily has to specify its scope and sometimes note its general trend.

19. In view of what is stated above, the Court concludes that it has the authority to deliver an opinion on the question posed by the General Assembly, and that there exist no "compelling reasons" which would lead the Court to exercise its discretion not to do so.

An entirely different question is whether the Court, under the con-straints placed upon its as a judicial organ, will be able to give a complete answer to the question asked of it. However, that is a different matter from a refusal to answer at all.

Notes

1. As the Court notes, Opinion, para. 14, the *Eastern Carelia* case is the only one in which the World Court has declined, in the exercise of its discretion, to give an opinion that fell within its jurisdiction. In that case, Russia had refused to participate in the proceedings. The opinion sought concerned the interpretation of a peace treaty between Russia and Finland that bore upon a dispute between them on the status of Eastern Carelia. The Court was concerned that it would, in effect, be deciding the dispute without the consent of one of the parties and without its account of the facts.

2. The refusal to give an opinion in the *Legality of the Use by a State of Nuclear Weapons in Armed Conflict* case (the *WHO Nuclear Weapons* case), was different from the *Eastern Carelia* case in that it was based on jurisdictional grounds. The question put to the Court by the WHO General Assembly in that case, in a decision of 3 September 1993, was:

> In view of the health and environmental effects, would the use of nuclear weapons by a state in war or other armed conflict be a breach of its obligations under international law including the WHO Constitution?

The Court held, by 11 votes to three, that the question did not fall within the scope of WHO's "activities", as is required by Article 96(2), Charter, when a question is put to the Court by an authorised specialised agency. The Court interpreted the WHO Constitution, Article 2, as giving WHO the competence to deal with the effects on health of the use of nuclear weapons and to act preventively to protect people from these effects. But the question put to the Court concerned the legality, rather than the effects, of the use of nuclear weapons, which was a matter that did not fall within WHO's remit.

The above two cases are the only ones in which the World Court has not given a requested opinion.

(vii) THE WORLD COURT AND THE SECURITY COUNCIL[78]

CASE CONCERNING QUESTIONS OF INTERPRETATION AND APPLICATION OF THE MONTREAL CONVENTION ARISING OUT OF THE AERIAL INCIDENT AT LOCKERBIE (PROVISIONAL MEASURES)

Libya *v.* U.K.

I.C.J. Reports 1992, p. 3

At the request of the U.S., the U.K. and France, on January 21, 1992, the Security Council adopted Resolution 731, which "urged" Libya, *inter alia*, to respond to the request of those three states to extradite two Libyan nationals for trial in Scotland. On March 3, 1993, Libya instituted proceedings against the U.S.[79] and the U.K. before the I.C.J. under Article 14, Montreal Convention for the Suppression of

---

[78] See Akande (1997) 46 I.C.L.Q. 309; Alvarez (1996) 90 A.J.I.L. 1; Bedjaoui, *The New World Order and the Security Council* (1994); Brownlie, *Essays in Honour of Wang Tieya* (1994); Franck (1992) 86 A.J.I.L. 519; Gill (1995) 26 N.Y.I.L. 33; Gowlland-Debbas (1994) 88 A.J.I.L. 643; Macdonald (1993) 31 C.Y.I.L. 3; Reisman (1993) 87 A.J.I.L. 83; Skubiszewski, in Lowe and Fitzmaurice, *op. cit.*, p. 988, n. 24, above, Chap. 33; Watson (1993) 34 Harv.I.L.J. 1.

[79] For the case brought by Libya against the U.S., see I.C.J. Rep. 1992, p. 234.

Unlawful Acts Against the Safety of Civil Aviation.[80] Libya asked the Court to declare that (i) it had complied with its obligations under the Montreal Convention by taking the required steps to investigate the case and prosecute the two Libyans[81] and (ii) the U.K. had breached the Convention by seeking to force Libya to return the alleged offenders and by not providing assistance for the Libyan proceedings.

Also on March 3, 1993, Libya applied to the Court for provisional measures. After the oral hearing of this application, the Security Council, at the request of the same three states, adopted Resolution 748, under Chapter VII of the Charter, requiring Libya to return the alleged offenders and imposing sanctions against it for not doing so. The Council acted on the basis that Libya had been engaged in international terrorism, which was a "threat to the peace" under Article 39, Charter. For the texts of the resolutions and further details of the case, see above, p. 944.

As noted above, p. 945, the request for interim measures was rejected because of Resolution 748. The case is still pending before the Court on its merits. At that stage, it might be, depending upon the arguments put, that the Court would be called upon to consider the legality of Security Council Resolutions 731 and 748, the latter of which imposes an obligation upon Libya to extradite the alleged offenders whereas the Montreal Convention allows Libya a choice. The Court found it unnecessary to consider this question when ruling on Libya's provisional measures request. However, several judges, including Judge Weeramantry, did reflect upon the Court's competence to review the legality of Security Council resolutions and related matters in their individual opinions.

Dissenting Opinion of Judge Weeramantry

This case has raised as perhaps no case has done in the past, certain questions of importance and interest concerning the respective functions of this Court and the Security Council. . . .

In the United Nations system, the sphere of [the Security Council and the Court] . . . is laid down in the Charter, as within a domestic jurisdiction it may be laid down in a constitution. However, unlike in many domestic systems where the judicial arm may sit in review over the actions of the executive arm, subjecting those acts to the test of legality under the Constitution, in the United Nations system the International Court of Justice is not vested with the review or appellate jurisdiction often given to the highest courts within a domestic framework (. . . *Legal Consequences . . . I.C.J. Reports 1971*, p. 16). At the same time, it is the principal judicial organ of the United Nations, charged with the task, *inter alia*, of deciding in accordance with international law such disputes as are submitted to it (Art. 38 of the Statute of the Court). . . .

---

[80] Art. 14 provides that a Convention party may unilaterally request the reference of a dispute concerning the interpretation or application of the Convention to arbitration; if agreement on a tribunal is not possible within six months of the request, it may unilaterally refer the case to the I.C.J. Libya did not wait six months.

[81] The Montreal Convention requires a party, in its discretion, to prosecute or extradite an alleged offender: see above, p. 300. Libya decided to prosecute. In any event there was also no extradition treaty between Libya and the U.K. and Libya, like many states, does not extradite its own nationals.

As a judicial organ, it will be the Court's duty from time to time to examine and determine from a strictly legal point of view matters which may at the same time be the subject of determination from an executive or political point of view by another principal organ of the United Nations. . . . The concepts it uses are juridical concepts, its criteria are standards of legality, its method is that of legal proof. Its tests of validity and the bases of its decisions are naturally not the same as they would be before a political or executive organ of the United Nations.

Yet this much they have in common—that all organs alike exercise their authority under and in terms of the Charter. There can never truly be a question of opposition of one organ to another but rather a common subjection of all organs to the Charter. The interpretation of Charter provisions is primarily a matter of law, and such questions of law may in appropriate circumstances come before the Court for judicial determination. When this does occur, the Court acts as guardian of the Charter and of international law for, in the international arena, there is no higher body charged with judicial functions and with the determination of questions of interpretation and application of international law. Anchored to the Charter in particular and to international law in general, the Court considers such legal matters as are properly brought before it and the fact that its judicial decision based upon the law may have political consequences is not a factor that would deflect it from discharging its duties under the Charter of the United Nations and the Statute of the Court. . . .

It is clear . . . that the Court must at all times preserve its independence in performing the functions which the Charter has committed to it as the United Nations' principal judicial organ. It is clear also that in many an instance the performance of those independent functions will lead the Court to a result in total consonance with the conclusions of the Security Council. But it by no means follows from these propositions that the Court when properly seised of a legal dispute should co-operate with the Security Council to the extent of desisting from exercising its independent judgment on matters of law properly before it. . . .

There have indeed been prior instances where the same matter has come up for consideration before both the Security Council and the Court. Mention may be made in this connection of the following cases where the jurisdiction of both the Court and the Security Council was invoked in one and the same matter: *Aegean Sea Continental Shelf, Interim Protection* (I.C.J. Reports 1976, p. 3); *United States Diplomatic and Consular Staff in Tehran, Provisional Measures* (I.C.J. Reports 1979, p. 7); *Military and Paramilitary Activities in and against Nicaragua, Provisional Measures* (I.C.J. Reports 1984, p. 169).

In all these cases, however, the Court and the Council were approached by the same party, seeking before these different organs the relief appropriate to the nature and function of each. . . .

In the present case, the Court and the Council have been approached by opposite parties to the dispute, each claiming a form of relief consistent with its own position. It is this situation which gives special importance to the current case. . . .

In the *United States Diplomatic and Consular Staff in Tehran* case, the Court observed that:

> it does not seem to have occurred to any member of the Council that there was or could be anything irregular in the simultaneous exercise of their respective functions by the Court and the Security Council. Nor is there in this any cause for surprise. (*I.C.J. Reports 1980*, p. 21, para. 40.)

The role of the Court was made even clearer when the Court observed:

> Whereas Article 12 of the Charter expressly forbids the General Assembly to make any recommendation with regard to a dispute or situation while the Security Council is exercising its functions in respect of that dispute or situation, no such restriction is placed on the functioning of the Court by any provision of either the Charter or the Statute of the Court. The reasons are clear. It is for the Court, the principal judicial organ of the United Nations, to resolve any legal questions that may be in issue between parties to the dispute; and the resolution of such legal questions by the Court may be an important and sometimes decisive, factor in promoting the peaceful settlement of the dispute. (*Ibid.*, p. 22, para. 40; see also *Military and Paramilitary Activities in and against Nicaragua, I.C.J. Reports 1984*, pp. 433–434, para. 93.) . . .

The submission before us relating to the exercise of Security Council powers in adopting resolution 731 (1992) [above, p. 944] calls for a brief examination of those powers from a strictly legal point of view. . . .

The Security Council] is charged under Article 24 with the primary responsibility for the maintenance of international peace and security and has a mandate from all Member States to act on their behalf in this regard. By Article 25, all Members agree to accept and carry out its decisions.

Chapter VI entrusts it with powers and responsibilities in regard to settlement of disputes, and Chapter VII gives it very special powers when it determines the existence of any threat to the peace, breach of the peace or act of aggression. Such determination is a matter entirely within its discretion.

With these provisions should be read Article 103 of the Charter which states that in the event of a conflict between the obligations of the Members of the United Nations under the Charter and their obligations under any international agreement, their obligations under the Charter shall prevail. Seeing that Security Council decisions are to be accepted and carried out by all Member States, the obligations thus created are given priority by Article 103 over obligations under any other agreement.

All this amounts to enormous power indeed and international law as embodied in the Charter requires all States to recognize this power and act according to the directions issuing from it.

But does this mean that the Security Council discharges its variegated functions free of all limitations, or is there a circumscribing boundary of norms of principles within which its responsibilities are to be discharged?

Article 24 itself offers us an immediate signpost to such a circumscribing boundary when it provides in Article 24(2) that the Security Council, in discharging its duties under Article 24(1), "*shall* act in accordance with the Purposes and Principles of the United Nations". The duty is imperative and the limits are categorically stated.

Judge Weeramantry then reviewed the *travaux préparatoires* of the UN Charter and continued:

The history of the United Nations Charter thus corroborates the view that a clear limitation on the plenitude of the Security Council's powers is that those powers must be exercised in accordance with the well-established principles of international law. It is true this limitation must be restrictively interpreted and is confined only to the principles and objects which appear in Chapter I of the Charter... The restriction nevertheless exists and constitutes an important principle of law in the interpretation of the United Nations Charter.

The obligation of the Court, as one of the principal organs of the United Nations, to "co-operate in the attainment of the aims of the Organization and strive to give effect to the decisions of other principal organs, and not achieve results which would render them nugatory" (Rosenne, *The Law and Practice of the International Court*, p. 70) should be read in the light of this clear limitation.

Notes

1. As Judge Weeramantry demonstrates, it is well understood that the Court and the Security Council may both exercise jurisdiction in a case or matter at the same time. What is also clear, is that the Court has no power of judicial review or appeal in respect of Security Council action: there is no remedy available before the I.C.J. that is comparable to those available before national courts, such as an application for *certiorari* before the U.K. courts, by which a state or other international legal person might challenge the legality of Security Council action directly.

2. At the same time, the Security Council does not have unlimited jurisdiction and if the extent of its powers or the legality of its acts are called in question in proceedings before the I.C.J., the latter has competence, within as yet not wholly defined limits, to pronounce upon the questions raised. The occasions for doing so may occur in the exercise by the Court of its advisory jurisdiction, as in the *Certain Expenses* case, above, p. 975, and the *Legal Consequences* case, see below, or in the course of the contentious litigation, as on the facts of the *Lockerbie* case.

3. The limits to the powers of the Security Council and the legality of its acts were matters raised in argument before the Court in the *Legal Consequences* case.[82] In Resolution 2145 the General Assembly declared that South Africa had failed to fulfil its obligations under the mandate for South West Africa/Namibia and decided that the mandate had, as a result, been terminated. When South Africa failed to withdraw from South West Africa/Namibia, as called upon to do by Security Council Resolutions 264 and 269, the Council, in Resolution 276, declared the continued presence of South Africa in South West Africa/Namibia to be illegal. In the *Legal Consequences* case, the Council asked the Court: "What are the legal consequences for states of the continued presence of South Africa in Namibia?" A key issue was whether the Security Council resolutions, which were not adopted under Chapter VII, were decisions that were legally binding upon member states under Article 25, Charter. The Court determined that they were. In his dissenting opinion, Judge Fitzmaurice considered the general question of the limits to the Security Council's powers as follows:

> If the effect of [Article 24, Charter] were automatically to make *all* decisions of the Security Council binding, then the words "in accordance with the present Charter" [in Article 25] would be quite superfluous. They would add nothing to the preceding and only other phrase in the Article, namely "The Members of the United Nations agree to accept and carry out the decisions of the Security Council", which they are clearly intended to qualify. They effectively do so only if the decisions referred to are those which *are* duly binding "in accordance with the present Charter" . . .
>
> 115. There is more. *Even when acting under Chapter VII of the Charter itself*, the Security Council has no power to abrogate or alter territorial rights, whether of sovereignty or administration. Even a war-time occupation of a country or territory cannot operate to do that. It must await the peace settlement. This is a principle of international law that is as well-established as any there can be,—and the Security Council is as much subject to it (for the United Nations is itself a subject of international law) as any of its individual member States are. The Security Council might, after making the necessary determinations under Article 39 of the Charter, order the occupation of a country or piece of territory *in order to restore peace and security*, but it could not thereby, or as part of that operation, abrogate or alter territorial rights,—and the right to administer a mandated territory is a territorial right without which the territory could not be governed or the mandate be operated. It was to keep the peace, not to change the world order, that the Security Council was set up.
>
> 116. These limitations on the powers of the Security Council are necessary because of the all too great ease with which any acutely controversial international situation can be represented as involving a latent threat to peace and security, even where it is really too remote genuinely to constitute one. Without these limitations, the functions of the Security Council could be used for purposes never originally intended. . . . [where there was] no threat to peace and security other than such as might be artificially created as a pretext for the realization of ulterior purposes.

4. The question of the competence of the Court to decide whether the Security Council has exceeded the limits of its powers that are found to exist was also in

---

[82] I.C.J. Rep. 1971, p. 16. As the case demonstrated, many of the same considerations as apply to the Court's competence to review the powers and acts of the Security Council apply also to its competence *vis.-à-vis* the General Assembly, although the powers and political sensitivity of the acts of the Council are clearly greater.

issue in the *Legal Consequences* case.[83] Responding to French Government objections that the General Assembly Resolution 2145 terminating the mandate was *ultra vires*, the Court stated;

> 89. Undoubtedly, the Court does not possess powers of judicial review or appeal in respect of the decision taken by the United Nations organs concerned. The question of the validity or conformity with the Charter of General Assembly resolution 2145 (XXI) or of related Security Council resolutions does not form the subject of the request for advisory opinion. However, in the exercise of its judicial function and since objections have been advanced the Court, in the course of its reasoning, will consider these objections before determining any legal consequences arising from those resolutions.

Having then examined the constitutional basis for Resolution 2145 and the related Security Council resolutions, the Court concluded that they were valid. In so doing, as Judge *ad hoc* El-Kosheri stated in his dissenting opinion in the *Lockerbie* case,[84] "the Court implied that it was perfectly conceivable that it could reach a negative conclusion, were it to detect any violation of the Charter or departure from the Charter's purposes and principles." Such an approach is almost inevitable for a judicial body. As Judge Petrén stated in his separate opinion in the *Legal Consequences* case[85]:

> So long as the validity of the resolutions upon which resolution 276 (1970) is based has not been established, it is clearly impossible for the Court to pronounce on the legal consequences of resolution 276 (1970), for there can be no such legal consequences if the basic resolutions are illegal, and to give a finding as though there were such would be incompatible with the role of a court. It seems to me that the majority should have expressed itself on this point more precisely and firmly, but I note that it likewise considered that the opinion must include an examination of the validity of the resolutions in question.

5. The question then is how broad is the Court's power of review. In particular, would it be open to the Court to rule that the Security Council's interpretation of what might constitute a threat to the peace,[86] was incorrect as a matter of law?[87] Could it go further and exercise a power of judicial review over a decision on the facts in a particular case as to whether there was a threat to the peace or act of aggression? Or over a decision to adopt a particular response (economic sanctions, the establishment of a war crimes tribunal?[88]) to a threat to the peace? Later in his opinion, Judge Weeramantry suggested that the Court could not question Security Council action under Chapter VII:

> . . . once we enter the sphere of Chapter VII, the matter takes on a different complexion, for the determination under Article 39 of the existence of any threat to the peace, breach of the peace or act of aggression, is one entirely

[83] I.C.J. Rep. 1971, p. 45.
[84] *ibid*. 1992, pp. 102–103.
[85] *ibid*. p. 131.
[86] International terrorism? The likely reaction of other states to an internal conflict or humanitarian need? See on threats to the peace generally, above, pp. 942 *et seq.*
[87] The doctrine of "subsequent practice" in the interpretation of treaties, above, p. 815, suggests that the Security Council's interpretation of its powers should be respected if it is accepted and followed by UN members generally. *cf.* the Yugoslav Tribunal's judgment in the *Tadic* case, above, p. 753.
[88] On the Yugoslav Tribunal's judgment in the *Tadic* case on this point, see above, p. 753.

within the discretion of the Council. It would appear that the Council and no other is the judge of the existence of the state of affairs which brings Chapter VII into operation. That decision is taken by the Security Council in its own judgment and in the exercise of the full discretion given to it by Article 39. Once taken, the door is opened to the various decisions the Council may make under that Chapter.

CHARTER OF THE UNITED NATIONS

WE THE PEOPLES OF THE UNITED NATIONS DETERMINED to save succeeding generations from the scourge of war, which twice in our lifetime has brought untold sorrow to mankind, and to reaffirm faith in fundamental human rights, in the dignity and worth of the human person, in the equal rights of men and women and of nations large and small, and to establish conditions under which justice and respect for the obligations arising from treaties and other sources of international law can be maintained, and to promote social progress and better standards of life in larger freedom,

AND FOR THESE ENDS to practise tolerance and live together in peace with one another as good neighbours, and to unite our strength to maintain international peace and security, and to ensure, by the acceptance of principles and the institution of methods, that armed force shall not be used, save in the common interest, and to employ international machinery for the promotion of the economic and social advancement of all peoples.

HAVE RESOLVED TO COMBINE OUR EFFORTS TO ACCOMPLISH THESE AIMS. Accordingly, our respective Governments, through representatives assembled in the city of San Francisco, who have exhibited their full powers found to be in good and due form, have agreed to the present Charter of the United Nations and do hereby establish an international organisation to be known as the United Nations.

Chapter 1

PURPOSES AND PRINCIPLES

Article 1

The Purposes of the United Nations are:

1. To maintain international peace and security, and to that end: to take effective collective measures for the prevention and removal of threats to the peace, and for the suppression of acts of aggression or other breaches of the peace, and to bring about by peaceful means, and in conformity with the principles of justice and international law, adjustment or settlement of international disputes or situations which might lead to a breach of the peace;

2. To develop friendly relations among nations based on respect for the principles of equal rights and self-determination of peoples, and to take other appropriate measures to strengthen universal peace;

3. To achieve international co-operation in solving international problems of an economic, social, cultural, or humanitarian character, and in promoting and encouraging respect for human rights and for fundamental freedom for all without distinction as to race, sex, language, or religion; and

4. To be a centre for harmonising the actions in the attainment of these common ends.

Article 2

The Organisation and its Members, in pursuit of the Purposes stated in Article 1, shall act in accordance with the following Principles.

1. The Organisation is based on the principle of the sovereign equality of all its Members.

2. All Members, in order to ensure to all of them the rights and benefits resulting from membership, shall fulfil in good faith the obligations assumed by them in accordance with the present Charter.

3. All Members shall settle their international disputes by peaceful means in such a manner that international peace and security, and justice, are not endangered.

4. All Members shall refrain in their international relations from the threat or use of force against the territorial integrity or political independence of any state, or in any other manner inconsistent with the Purposes of the United Nations.

5. All Members shall give the United Nations every assistance in any action it takes in accordance with the present Charter, and shall refrain from giving assistance to any state against which the United Nations is taking preventive or enforcement action.

6. The Organisation shall ensure that states which are not Members of the United Nations act in accordance with these Principles so far as may be necessary for the maintenance of peace and security.

7. Nothing contained in the present Charter shall authorise the United Nations to intervene in matters which are essentially within the domestic jurisdiction of any state or shall require the Members to submit such matters to settlement under the present Charter; but this principle shall not prejudice the application of enforcement measures under Chapter VII.

CHAPTER 2

MEMBERSHIP

Article 3

The original Members of the United Nations shall be the states which, having participated in the United Nations Conference on International Organisation at San Francisco, or having previously signed the Declaration by United Nations on

January 1, 1942, sign the present Charter and ratify it in accordance with Article 110.

Article 4

1. Membership in the United Nations is open to all other peace-loving states which accept the obligations contained in the present Charter and, in the judgment of the Organisation, are able and willing to carry out these obligations.

2. The admission of any such state to membership in the United Nations will be effected by a decision of the General Assembly upon the recommendation of the Security Council.

Article 5

A Member of the United Nations against which preventive or enforcement action has been taken by the Security Council may be suspended from the exercise of the rights and privileges of membership by the General Assembly upon the recommendation of the Security Council. The exercise of these rights and privileges may be restored by the Security Council.

Article 6

A Member of the United Nations which has persistently violated the Principles contained in the present Charter may be expelled from the Organisation by the General Assembly upon the recommendation of the Security Council.

CHAPTER 3

ORGANS

Article 7

1. There are established as the principal organs of the United Nations: a General Assembly, a Security Council, a Economic and Social Council, a Trusteeship Council, an International Court of Justice, and a Secretariat.

2. Such subsidiary organs as may be found necessary may be established in accordance with the present Charter.

Article 8

The United Nations shall place no restrictions on the eligibility of men and women to participate in any capacity and under conditions of equality in its principal and subsidiary organs.

CHAPTER 4

THE GENERAL ASSEMBLY

Composition

Article 9

1. The General Assembly shall consist of all the Members of the United Nations.

2. Each Member shall have not more than five representatives in the General Assembly.

Functions and Powers

Article 10

The General Assembly may discuss any questions or any matters within the scope of the present Charter or relating to the powers and functions of any organs provided for in the present Charter, and, except as provided in Article 12, may make recommendations to the Members of the United Nations or to the Security Council or to both on any such questions or matters.

Article 11

1. The General Assembly may consider the general principles of co-operation in the maintenance of international peace and security, including the principles governing disarmament and the regulations of armaments, and may make recommendations with regard to such principles to the Members or to the Security Council or to both.

2. The General Assembly may discuss any questions relating to the maintenance of international peace and security brought before it by any Member of the United Nations, or by the Security Council, or by a state which is not a Member of the United Nations in accordance with Article 35, paragraph 2, and, except as provided in Article 12, may make recommendations with regard to any such questions to the state or states concerned or to the Security Council or to both. Any such question on which action is necessary shall be referred to the Security Council by the General Assembly either before or after discussion.

3. The General Assembly may call the attention of the Security Council to situations which are likely to endanger international peace and security.

4. The powers of the General Assembly set forth in this Article shall not limit the general scope of Article 10.

Article 12

1. While the Security Council is exercising in respect of any dispute or situation the functions assigned to it in the present Charter, the General Assembly shall not

make any recommendation with regard to that dispute or situation unless the Security Council so requests.

2. The Secretary-General, with the consent of the Security Council, shall notify the General Assembly at each session of any matters relative to the maintenance of international peace and security which are being dealt with by the Security Council and shall similarly notify the General Assembly, or the Members of the United Nations if the General Assembly is not in session, immediately the Security Council ceases to deal with such matters.

Article 13

1. The General Assembly shall initiate studies and make recommendations for the purpose of:

   a. promoting international co-operation in the political field and encouraging the progressive development of international law and its codification;
   b. promoting international co-operation in the economic, social, cultural, educational, and health fields, and assisting in the realisation of human rights and fundamental freedoms for all without distinction as to race, sex, language, or religion.

2. The further responsibilities, functions and powers of the General Assembly with respect to matters mentioned in paragraph 1(b) above are set forth in Chapters IX and X.

Article 14

Subject to the provisions of Article 12, the General Assembly may recommend measures for the peaceful adjustment of any situation, regardless of origin, which it deems likely to impair the general welfare or friendly relations among nations, including situations resulting from the violation of the provisions of the present Charter setting forth the Purposes and Principles of the United Nations.

Article 15

1. The General Assembly shall receive and consider annual and special reports from the Security Council; these reports shall include an account of the measures that the Security Council has decided upon or taken to maintain international peace and security.

2. The General Assembly shall receive and consider reports from the other organs of the United Nations.

Article 16

The General Assembly shall perform such functions with respect to the international trusteeship system as are assigned to it under Chapter XII and XIII, including the approval of the trusteeship agreements for areas not designated as strategic.

Article 17

1. The General Assembly shall consider and approve the budget of the Organisation.

2. The expenses of the Organisation shall be borne by the Members as apportioned by the General Assembly.

3. The General Assembly shall consider and approve any financial and budgetary arrangements with specialised agencies referred to in Article 57 and shall examine the administrative budgets of such specialised agencies with a view to making recommendations to the agencies concerned.

Voting

Article 18

1. Each member of the General Assembly shall have one vote.

2. Decisions of the General Assembly on important questions shall be made by a two-thirds majority of the members present and voting. These questions shall include: recommendations with respect to the maintenance of international peace and security, the election of the non-permanent members of the Security Council, the election of the members of the Economic and Social Council, the election of members of the Trusteeship Council in accordance with paragraph 1(c) of Article 86, the admission of new Members to the United Nations, the suspension of the rights and privileges of membership, the expulsion of Members, questions relating to the operation of the trusteeship system, and budgetary questions.

3. Decisions on other questions, including the determination of additional categories of questions to be decided by a two-thirds majority, shall be made by a majority of the members present and voting.

Article 19

A Member of the United Nations which is in arrears in the payment of its financial contributions to the Organisation shall have no vote in the General Assembly if the amount of its arrears equals or exceeds the amount of the contributions due from it for the preceding two full years. The General Assembly may, nevertheless, permit such a Member to vote if it is satisfied that the failure to pay is due to conditions beyond the control of the Member.

Article 20

The General Assembly shall meet in regular annual sessions and in such special sessions as occasion may require. Special sessions shall be convoked by the Secretary-General at the request of the Security Council or of a majority of the Members of the United Nations.

Article 21

The General Assembly shall adopt its own rules of procedure. It shall elect its President for each session.

Article 22

The General Assembly may establish such subsidiary organs as it deems necessary for the performance of its functions.

CHAPTER 5

THE SECURITY COUNCIL

Composition

Article 23[1]

1. The Security Council shall consist of fifteen[2] Members of the United Nations. The Republic of China, France, the Union of Soviet Socialist Republics, the United Kingdom of Great Britain and Northern Ireland, and the United States of America shall be permanent members of the Security Council. The General Assembly shall elect ten other Members of the United Nations to be non-permanent members of the Security Council, due regard being specially paid, in the first instance to the contribution of Members of the United Nations to the maintenance of international peace and security and to the other purposes of the Organisation, and also to equitable geographical distribution.

2. The non-permanent members of the Security Council shall be elected for a term of two years. In the first election of the non-permanent members after the increase of the membership of the Security Council from eleven to fifteen, two of the four additional members shall be chosen for a term of one year. A retiring member shall not be eligible for immediate re-election.

3. Each member of the Security Council shall have one representative.

Functions and Powers

Article 24

1. In order to ensure prompt and effective action by the United Nations, its Members confer on the Security Council primary responsibility for the maintenance of international peace and security, and agree that in carrying out its duties under this responsibility the Security Council acts on their behalf.

2. In discharging these duties the Security Council shall act in accordance with the Purposes and Principles of the United Nations. The specific powers granted to the Security Council for the discharge of these duties are laid down in Chapters VI, VII, VIII and XII.

3. The Security Council shall submit annual and, when necessary, special reports to the General Assembly for its consideration.

[1] As amended in 1965.
[2] Formerly 11.

Article 25

The Members of the United Nations agree to accept and carry out the decisions of the Security Council in accordance with the present Charter.

Article 26

In order to promote the establishment and maintenance of international peace and security with the least diversion for armaments of the world's human and economic resources, the Security Council shall be responsible for formulating, with the assistance of the Military Staff Committee referred to in Article 47, plans to be submitted to the Members of the United Nations for the establishment of a system for the regulation of armaments.

Voting

Article 27[3]

1. Each member of the Security Council shall have one vote.

2. Decisions of the Security Council on procedural matters shall be made by an affirmative vote of nine[4] members.

3. Decisions of the Security Council on all other matters shall be made by an affirmative vote of nine[4] members including the concurring votes of the permanent members; provided that, in decisions under Chapter VI, and under paragraph 3 of Article 52, a party to a dispute shall abstain from voting.

Procedure

Article 28

1. The Security Council shall be so organised as to be able to function continuously. Each member of the Security Council shall for this purpose be represented at all times at the seat of the Organisation.

2. The Security Council shall hold periodical meetings at which each of its members may, if it so desires, be represented by a member of the government or by some other specially designated representative.

3. The Security Council may hold meetings at such places other than the seat of the Organisation as in its judgment will best facilitate its work.

Article 29

The Security Council may establish such subsidiary organs as it deems necessary for the performance of its functions.

---

[3] As amended in 1965.
[4] Formerly seven.

Article 30

The Security Council shall adopt its own rules of procedure, including the method of selecting its President.

Article 31

Any Member of the United Nations which is not a member of the Security Council may participate, without vote, in the discussion of any question brought before the Security Council whenever the latter considers that the interests of that Member are specially affected.

Article 32

Any Member of the United Nations which is not a member of the Security Council or any state which is not a Member of the United Nations, if it is a party to a dispute under consideration by the Security Council, shall be invited to participate, without vote, in the discussion relating to the dispute. The Security Council shall lay down such conditions as it deems just for the participation of a state which is not a Member of the United Nations.

CHAPTER 6

PACIFIC SETTLEMENT OF DISPUTES

Article 33

1. The parties to any dispute, the continuance of which is likely to endanger the maintenance of international peace and security, shall, first of all, seek a solution by negotiation, enquiry, mediation, conciliation, arbitration, judicial settlement, resort to regional agencies or arrangements, or other peaceful means of their own choice.

2. The Security Council shall, when it deems necessary, call upon the parties to settle their dispute by such means.

Article 34

The Security Council may investigate any dispute, or any situation which might lead to international friction or give rise to a dispute, in order to determine whether the continuance of the dispute or situation is likely to endanger the maintenance of international peace and security.

Article 35

1. Any Member of the United Nations may bring any dispute, or any situation of the nature referred to in Article 34, to the attention of the Security Council or of the General Assembly.

2. A state which is not a Member of the United Nations may bring to the attention of the Security Council or of the General Assembly any dispute to which

it is a party if it accepts in advance, for the purposes of the dispute, the obligations of pacific settlement provided in the present Charter.

3. The proceedings of the General Assembly in respect of matters brought to its attention under this Article will be subject to the provisions of Articles 11 and 12.

Article 36

1. The Security Council may, at any stage of a dispute of the nature referred to in Article 33 or of a situation of like nature, recommend appropriate procedures or methods of adjustment.

2. The Security Council should take into consideration any procedures for the settlement of the dispute which have already been adopted by the parties.

3. In making recommendations under this Article the Security Council should also take into consideration that legal disputes should as a general rule be referred by the parties to the International Court of Justice in accordance with the provisions of the Statute of the Court.

Article 37

1. Should the parties to a dispute of the nature referred to in Article 33 fail to settle it by the means indicated in that Article, they shall refer it to the Security Council.

2. If the Security Council deems that the continuance of the dispute is in fact likely to endanger the maintenance of international peace and security, it shall decide whether to take action under Article 36 or to recommend such terms of settlement as it may consider appropriate.

Article 38

Without prejudice to the provisions of Articles 33 to 37, the Security Council may, if all the parties to any dispute so request, make recommendations to the parties with a view to a pacific settlement of the dispute.

CHAPTER 7

ACTION WITH RESPECT TO THREATS TO THE PEACE, BREACHES OF THE PEACE, AND ACTS OF AGGRESSION

Article 39

The Security Council shall determine the existence of any threat to the peace, breach of the peace, or act of aggression and shall make recommendations, or decide what measures shall be taken in accordance with Article 41 and 42, to maintain or restore international peace and security.

Article 40

In order to prevent an aggravation of the situation, the Security Council may, before making the recommendations or deciding upon the measures provided for in Article 39, call upon the parties concerned to comply with such provisional measures as it deems necessary or desirable. Such provisional measures shall be without prejudice to the rights, claims, or position of the parties concerned. The Security Council shall duly take account of failure to comply with such provisional measures.

Article 41

The Security Council may decide what measures not involving the use of armed force are to be employed to give effect to its decisions, and it may call upon the Members of the United Nations to apply such measures. These may include complete or partial interruption of economic relations and of rail, sea, air, postal, telegraphic, radio, and other means of communication, and the severance of diplomatic relations.

Article 42

Should the Security Council consider that measures provided for in Article 41 would be inadequate or have proved to be inadequate, it may take such action by air, sea or land forces as may be necessary to maintain or restore international peace and security. Such action may include demonstrations, blockade, and other operations by air, sea, or land forces of Members of the United Nations.

Article 43

1. All Members of the United Nations, in order to contribute to the maintenance of international peace and security, undertake to make available to the Security Council, on its call and in accordance with a special agreement or agreements, armed forces, assistance, and facilities, including rights of passage, necessary for the purpose of maintaining international peace and security.

2. Such agreement or agreements shall govern the numbers and types of forces, their degree of readiness and general location, and the nature of the facilities and assistance to be provided.

3. The agreement or agreements shall be negotiated as soon as possible on the initiative of the Security Council. They shall be concluded between the Security Council and Members or between the Security Council and groups of Members and shall be subject to ratification by the signatory states in accordance with their respective constitutional processes.

Article 44

When the Security Council has decided to use force it shall, before calling upon a Member not represented on it to provide armed forces in fulfilment of the obligations assumed under Article 43, invite that Member, if the Member so desires, to participate in the decisions of the Security Council concerning the employment of contingents of that Member's armed forces.

Article 45

In order to enable the United Nations to take urgent military measures, Members shall hold immediately available national airforce contingents for combined international enforcement action. The strength and degree of readiness of these contingents and plans for their combined action shall be determined, within the limits laid down in the special agreement or agreements referred to in Article 43, by the Security Council with the assistance of the Military Staff Committee.

Article 46

Plans for the application of armed force shall be made by the Security Council with the assistance of the Military Staff Committee.

Article 47

1. There shall be established a Military Staff Committee to advise and assist the Security Council on all questions relating to the Security Council's military requirements for the maintenance of international peace and security, the employment and command of forces placed at its disposal, the regulation of armaments, and possible disarmament.

2. The Military Staff Committee shall consist of the Chiefs of Staff of the permanent members of the Security Council or their representatives. Any Member of the United Nations not permanently represented on the Committee shall be invited by the Committee to be associated with it when the efficient discharge of the Committee's responsibilities requires the participation of that Member in its work.

3. The Military Staff Committee, shall be responsible under the Security Council for the strategic direction of any armed forces placed at the disposal of the Security Council. Questions relating to the command of such forces shall be worked out subsequently.

4. The Military Staff Committee with the authorisation of the Security Council and after consultation with appropriate regional agencies, may establish regional sub-committees.

Article 48

1. The action required to carry out the decisions of the Security Council for the maintenance of international peace and security shall be taken by all the Members of the United Nations or by some of them, as the Security Council may determine.

2. Such decisions shall be carried out by the Members of the United Nations directly and through their action in the appropriate international agencies of which they are members.

Article 49

The Members of the United Nations shall join in affording mutual assistance in carrying out the measures decided upon by the Security Council.

Article 50

If preventive or enforcement measures against any state are taken by the Security Council, any other state, whether a Member of the United Nations or not, which finds itself confronted with special economic problems arising from the carrying out of those measures shall have the right to consult the Security Council with regard to a solution of those problems.

Article 51

Nothing in the present Charter shall impair the inherent right of individual or collective self-defence if an armed attack occurs against a Member of the United Nations, until the Security Council has taken measures necessary to maintain international peace and security. Measures taken by Members in the exercise of this right of self-defence shall be immediately reported to the Security Council and shall not in any way affect the authority and responsibility of the Security Council under the present Charter to take at any time such action as it deems necessary in order to maintain or restore international peace and security.

CHAPTER 8

REGIONAL ARRANGEMENTS

Article 52

1. Nothing in the present Charter precludes the existence of regional arrangements or agencies for dealing with such matters relating to the maintenance of international peace and security as are appropriate for regional action, provided that such arrangements or agencies and their activities are consistent with the Purposes and Principles of the United Nations.

2. The Members of the United Nations entering into such arrangements or constituting such agencies shall make every effort to achieve pacific settlement of local disputes through such regional arrangements or by such regional agencies before referring them to the Security Council.

3. The Security Council shall encourage the development of pacific settlement of local disputes through such regional arrangements or by such regional agencies either on the initiative of the state concerned or by reference from the Security Council.

4. This Article in no way impairs the application of Articles 34 and 35.

Article 53

1. The Security Council shall, where appropriate, utilize such regional arrangements or agencies for enforcement action under its authority. But no enforcement action shall be taken under regional arrangements or by regional agencies without the authorisation of the Security Council, with the exception of measures against any enemy state, as defined in paragraph 2 of this Article, provided for pursuant to Article 107 or in regional arrangements directed against renewal of

aggressive policy on the part of any such state, until such time as the Organisation may, on request of the Governments concerned, be charged with the responsibility for preventing further aggression by such a state.

2. The term enemy state as used in paragraph 1 of this Article applies to any state which during the Second World War has been an enemy of any signatory of the present Charter.

Article 54

The Security Council shall at all times be kept fully informed of activities undertaken or in contemplation under regional arrangements or by regional agencies for the maintenance of international peace and security.

CHAPTER 9

INTERNATIONAL ECONOMIC AND SOCIAL CO-OPERATION

Article 55

With a view to the creation of conditions of stability and well-being which are necessary for peaceful and friendly relations among nations based on respect for the principle of equal rights and self-determination of peoples, the United Nations shall promote:

    a. higher standards of living, full employment, and conditions of economic and social progress and development;
    b. solutions of international economic, social, health, and related problems; and international cultural and educational co-operation; and
    c. universal respect for, and observance of, human rights and fundamental freedoms for all without distinction as to race, sex, language, or religion.

Article 56

All Members pledge themselves to take joint and separate action in co-operation with the Organisation for the achievement of the purposes set forth in Article 55.

CHAPTER 10

THE ECONOMIC AND SOCIAL COUNCIL

Composition

Article 61[5]

1. The Economic and Social Council shall consist of fifty-four[6] Members of the United Nations elected by the General Assembly.

[5] As amended in 1973.
[6] Originally 18.

2. Subject to the provisions of paragraph 3, eighteen[7] members of the Economic and Social Council shall be elected each year for a term for a three years. A retiring member shall be eligible for immediate re-election.

3. At the first election after the increase in the membership of the Economic and Social Council from twenty-seven to fifty-four members, in addition to the members elected in place of the nine[7] members whose term of office expires at the end of that year, twenty-seven additional members shall be elected. Of these twenty-seven additional members, the term of office of nine[7] members so elected shall expire at the end of one year, and of nine[7] other members at the end of two years, in accordance with arrangements made by the General Assembly.

4. Each member of the Economic and Social Council shall have one representative.

Functions and Powers

Article 62

1. The Economic and Social Council may make or initiate studies and reports with respect to international economic, social, cultural, educational, health, and related matters and may make recommendations with respect to any such matters to the General Assembly, to the Members of the United Nations, and to the specialized agencies concerned.

2. It may make recommendations for the purpose of promoting respect for, and observance of, human rights and fundamental freedoms for all.

3. It may prepare draft conversions for submission to the General Assembly, with respect to matters falling within its competence.

4. It may, call, in accordance with the rules prescribed by the United Nations, international conferences on matters falling within its competence.

Article 68

The Economic and Social Council shall set up commissions in economic and social fields and for the promotion of human rights, and such other commissions as may be required for the performance of its functions.

CHAPTER 11

DECLARATION REGARDING NON-SELF-GOVERNING TERRITORIES

Article 73

Members of the United Nations which have or assume responsibilities for the administration of territories whose peoples have not yet attained a full measure

[7] Originally six.

of self-government recognise the principle that the interests of the inhabitants of these territories are paramount, and accept as a sacred trust the obligation to promote to the utmost, within the system of international peace and security established by the present Charter, the well-being of the inhabitants of these territories, and, to this end:

a. to ensure, with due respect for the culture of the peoples concerned, their political, economic, social, and educational advancement, their just treatment, and their protection against abuses;
b. to develop self-government, to take due account of the political aspirations of the peoples, and to assist them in the progressive development of their free political institutions, according to the particular circumstances of each territory and its peoples and their varying stages of advancement;
c. to further international peace and security;
d. to promote constructive measures of development, to encourage research, and to co-operate with one another and, when and where appropriate, with specialized international bodies with a view to the practical achievement of the social, economic, and scientific purposes set forth in this Article; and
e. to transmit regularly to the Secretary-General for information purposes, subject to such limitation as security and constitutional considerations may require, statistical and other information of a technical nature relating to economic, social, and educational conditions in the territories for which they are respectively responsible other than those territories to which Chapters XII and XIII apply.

Article 74

Members of the United Nations also agree that their policy in respect of the territories to which this Chapter applies, no less than in respect of their metropolitan areas, must be based on the general principle of good neighbourliness, due account being taken of the interests and well-being of the rest of the world, in social, economic, and commercial matters.

CHAPTER 14

THE INTERNATIONAL COURT OF JUSTICE

Article 92

The International Court of Justice shall be the principal judicial organ of the United Nations. It shall function in accordance with the annexed Statute, which is based upon the Statute of the Permanent Court of International Justice and forms an integral part of the present Charter.

Article 93

1. All Members of the United Nations are *ipso facto* parties to the Statute of the International Court of Justice.

2. A state which is not a Member of the United Nations may become a party to the Statute of the International Court of Justice on conditions to be determined in

each case by the General Assembly upon the recommendation of the Security Council.

Article 94

1. Each Member of the United Nations undertakes to comply with the decision of the International Court of Justice in any case to which it is a party.

2. If any party to a case fails to perform the obligations incumbent upon it under a judgment rendered by the Court, the other party may have recourse to the Security Council, which may, if it deems necessary, make recommendations or decide upon measures to be taken to give effect to the judgment.

Article 95

Nothing in the present Charter shall prevent Members of the United Nations from entrusting the solution of their differences to other tribunals by virtue of agreements already in existence or which may be concluded in the future.

Article 96

1. The General Assembly or the Security Council may request the International Court of Justice to give an advisory opinion on any legal question.

2. Other organs of the United Nations and specialized agencies, which may at any time be so authorized by the General Assembly, may also request advisory opinions of the Court on legal questions arising within the scope of their activities.

CHAPTER 15

THE SECRETARIAT

Article 97

The Secretariat shall comprise a Secretary-General and such staff as the Organization may require. The Secretary-General shall be appointed by the General Assembly upon the recommendation of the Security Council. He shall be the chief administrative officer of the Organization.

Article 98

The Secretary-General shall act in that capacity in all meetings of the General Assembly, of the Security Council, of the Economic and Social Council, and of the Trusteeship Council, and shall perform such other functions as are entrusted to him by these organs. The Secretary-General shall make an annual report to the General Assembly on the work of the Organisation.

Article 99

The Secretary-General may bring to the attention of the Security Council any matter which in his opinion may threaten the maintenance of international peace and security.

Article 100

1. In the performance of their duties the Secretary-General and the staff shall not seek or receive instructions from any government or from any other authority external to the Organization. They shall refrain from any action which might reflect on their position as international officials responsible only to the Organization.

2. Each Member of the United Nations undertakes to respect the exclusively international character of the responsibilities of the Secretary-General and the staff and not to seek to influence them in the discharge of their responsibilities.

Article 101

1. The staff shall be appointed by the Secretary-General under regulations established by the General Assembly.

2. Appropriate staffs shall be permanently assigned to the Economic and Social Council, the Trusteeship Council, and, as required, to other organs of the United Nations. The staffs shall form a part of the Secretariat.

3. The paramount consideration in the employment of the staff and in the determination of the conditions of service shall be the necessity of securing the highest standards of efficiency, competence, and integrity. Due regard shall be paid to the importance of recruiting the staff on as wide a geographical basis as possible.

CHAPTER 16

MISCELLANEOUS PROVISIONS

Article 102

1. Every treaty and every international agreement entered into by any Member of the United Nations after the present Charter comes into force shall as soon as possible be registered with the Secretariat and published by it.

2. No party to any such treaty or international agreement which has not been registered in accordance with the provisions of paragraph 1 of this Article may invoke that treaty or agreement before any organ of the United Nations.

Article 103

In the event of a conflict between the obligations of the Members of the United Nations under the present Charter and their obligations under any other international agreement, their obligations under the present Charter shall prevail.

Article 104

The Organization shall enjoy in the territory of each of its Members such legal capacity as may be necessary for the exercise of its functions and the fulfilment of its purposes.

Article 105

1. The Organization shall enjoy in the territory of each of its Members such privileges and immunities as are necessary for the fulfilment of its purposes.

2. Representatives of the Members of the United Nations and officials of the Organization shall similarly enjoy such privileges and immunities as are necessary for the independent exercise of their functions in connexion with the Organization.

3. The General Assembly may make recommendations with a view to determining the details of the application of paragraphs 1 and 2 of this Article or may propose conventions to the Members of the United Nations for this purpose.

CHAPTER 18

AMENDMENTS

Article 108

Amendments to the present Charter shall come into force for all Members of the United Nations when they have been adopted by a vote of two-thirds of the members of the General Assembly and ratified in accordance with their respective constitutional processes by two-thirds of the Members of the United Nations, including all the permanent members of the Security Council.

Article 109[8]

1. A General Conference of the Members of the United Nations for the purpose of reviewing the present Charter may be held at a date and place to be fixed by a two-thirds vote of the members of the General Assembly and by a vote of any ten[9] members of the Security Council. Each Member of the United Nations shall have one vote in the conference.

2. Any alteration of the present Charter recommended by a two-thirds vote of the conference shall take effect when ratified in accordance with their respective constitutional processes by two-thirds of the Members of the United Nations including all the permanent members of the Security Council.

3. If such a conference has not been held before the tenth annual session of the General Assembly following the coming into force of the present Charter, the proposal to call such a conference shall be placed on the agenda of that session of the General Assembly, and the conference shall be held if so decided by a majority vote of the members of the General Assembly and by a vote of any seven members of the Security Council.

---

[8] As amended in 1968.
[9] Formerly seven.

CHAPTER 19

RATIFICATION AND SIGNATURE

Article 111

The present Charter, of which the Chinese, French, Russian, English, and Spanish texts are equally authentic, shall remain deposited in the archives of the Government of the United States of America. . . .

STATUTE OF THE INTERNATIONAL COURT OF JUSTICE

Article 1

THE INTERNATIONAL COURT OF JUSTICE established by the Charter of the United Nations as the principal judicial organ of the United Nations shall be constituted and shall function in accordance with the provisions of the present Statute.

CHAPTER 1

ORGANIZATION OF THE COURT

Article 2

The Court shall be composed of a body of independent judges, elected regardless of their nationality from among persons of high moral character, who possess the qualifications required in their respective countries for appointment to the highest judicial offices, or are jurisconsults of recognized competence in international law.

Article 3

1. The Court shall consist of fifteen members, no two of whom may be nationals of the same state.

2. A person who for the purposes of membership in the Court could be regarded as a national of more than one state shall be deemed to be a national of the one in which he ordinarily exercises civil and political rights.

Article 4

1. The members of the Court shall be elected by the General Assembly and by the Security Council from a list of persons nominated by the national groups in the Permanent Court of Arbitration, in accordance with the following provisions.

2. In the case of Members of the United Nations not represented in the Permanent Court of Arbitration, candidates shall be nominated by the national groups appointed for this purpose by their governments under the same conditions as those prescribed for members of the Permanent Court of Arbitration by Article 44

of the Convention of The Hague of 1907 for the pacific settlement of international disputes.

3. The conditions under which a state which is a party to the present Statute but is not a Member of the United Nations may participate in electing the members of the Court shall, in the absence of a special agreement, be laid down by the General Assembly upon recommendation of the Security Council.

Article 5

1. At least three months before the date of the election, the Secretary-General of the United Nations shall address a written request to the members of the Permanent Court of Arbitration belonging to the states which are parties to the present Statute, and to the members of the national groups appointed under Article 4, paragraph 2, inviting them to undertake, within a given time, by national groups, the nomination of persons in a position to accept the duties of a member of the Court.

2. No group may nominate more than four persons, not more than two of whom shall be of their own nationality. In no case may the number of candidates nominated by a group be more than double the number of seats to be filled.

Article 6

Before making these nominations, each national group is recommended to consult its highest court of justice, its legal faculties and schools of law, and its national academies and national sections of international academies devoted to the study of law.

Article 7

1. The Secretary-General shall prepare a list in alphabetical order of all the persons thus nominated. Save as provided in Article 12, paragraph 2, these shall be the only persons eligible.

2. The Secretary-General shall submit this list to the General Assembly and to the Security Council.

Article 8

The General Assembly and the Security Council shall proceed independently of one another to elect the members of the Court.

Article 9

At every election, the electors shall bear in mind not only that the persons to be elected should individually possess the qualifications required, but also that in the body as a whole the representation of the main forms of civilization and of the principal legal systems of the world should be assured.

Article 10

1. Those candidates who obtain an absolute majority of votes in the General Assembly and in the Security Council shall be considered as elected.

2. Any vote of the Security Council, whether for the election of judges or for the appointment of members of the conference envisaged in Article 12, shall be taken without any distinction between permanent and non-permanent members of the Security Council.

3. In the event of more than one national of the same state obtaining an absolute majority of the votes both of the General Assembly and of the Security Council, the eldest of these only shall be considered as elected.

Article 11

If, after the first meeting held for the purpose of the election, one or more seats remain to be filled, a second and, if necessary, a third meeting shall take place.

Article 12

1. If, after the third meeting, one or more seats still remain unfilled, a joint conference consisting of six members, three appointed by the General Assembly and three by the Security Council, may be formed at any time at the request of either the General Assembly or the Security Council, for the purpose of choosing by the vote of an absolute majority one name for each seat still vacant, to submit to the General Assembly and the Security Council for their respective acceptance.

2. If the joint conference is unanimously agreed upon any person who fulfills the required conditions, he may be included in its list, even though he was not included in the list of nominations referred to in Article 7.

3. If the joint conference is satisfied that it will not be successful in procuring an election, those members of the Court who have already been elected shall, within a period to be fixed by the Security Council, proceed to fill the vacant seats by selection from among those candidates who have obtained votes either in the General Assembly or in the Security Council.

4. In the event of an equality of votes among the judges, the eldest judge shall have a casting vote.

Article 13

1. The members of the Court shall be elected for nine years and may be re-elected; provided, however, that of the judges elected at the first election, the terms of five judges shall expire at the end of three years and the terms of five more judges shall expire at the end of six years.

2. The judges whose terms are to expire at the end of above-mentioned initial periods of three and six years shall be chosen by lot to be drawn by the Secretary-General immediately after the first election has been completed.

3. The members of the Court shall continue to discharge their duties until their places have been filled. Though replaced, they shall finish any cases which they may have begun.

4. In the case of the resignation of a member of the Court, the resignation shall be addressed to the President of the Court for transmission to the Secretary-General. This last notification makes the place vacant.

Article 14

Vacancies shall be filled by the same method as that laid down for the first election, subject to the following provision: the Secretary-General shall, within one month of the occurrence of the vacancy, proceed to issue the invitations provided for in Article 5, and the date of the election shall be fixed by the Security Council.

Article 15

A member of the Court elected to replace a member whose term of office has not expired shall hold office for the remainder of his predecessor's term.

Article 16

1. No member of the Court may exercise any political or administrative function, or engage in any other occupation of a professional nature.

2. Any doubt on this point shall be settled by the decision of the Court.

Article 17

1. No member of the Court may act as agent, counsel, or advocate in any case.

2. No member may participate in the decision of any case in which he has previously taken part as agent, counsel, or advocate for one of the parties, or as a member of a national or international court, or of a commission of enquiry, or in any other capacity.

3. Any doubt on this point shall be settled by the decision of the Court.

Article 18

1. No member of the Court can be dismissed unless, in the unanimous opinion of the other members, he has ceased to fulfil the required conditions.

2. Formal notification thereof shall be made to the Secretary-General by the Registrar.

3. This notification makes the place vacant.

Article 19

The members of the Court, when engaged on the business of the Court, shall enjoy diplomatic privileges and immunities.

Article 20

Every member of the Court shall, before taking up his duties, make a solemn declaration in open court that he will exercise his powers impartially and conscientiously.

Article 21

1. The Court shall elect its President and Vice-President for three years; they may be re-elected. . . .

Article 22

1. The seat of the Court shall be established at The Hague. This, however, shall not prevent the Court from sitting and exercising its functions elsewhere whenever the Court considers it desirable. . . .

Article 23

1. The Court shall remain permanently in session, except during the judicial vacations, the dates and duration of which shall be fixed by the Court. . . .

3. Members of the Court shall be bound, unless they are on leave or prevented from attending by illness or other serious reasons duly explained to the President, to hold themselves permanently at the disposal of the Court.

Article 24

1. If, for some special reason, a member of the Court considers that he should not take part in the decision of a particular case, he shall so inform the President.

2. If the President considers that for some special reason one of the members of the Court should not sit in a particular case, he shall give him notice accordingly.

3. If in any such case the member of the Court and the President disagree, the matter shall be settled by the decision of the Court.

Article 25

1. The full Court shall sit except when it is expressly provided otherwise in the present Statute.

2. Subject to the condition that the number of judges available to constitute the Court is not thereby reduced below eleven, the Rules of the Court may provide for allowing one or more judges, according to circumstances and in rotation, to be dispensed from sitting.

3. A quorum of nine judges shall suffice to constitute the Court.

Article 26

1. The Court may from time to time form one or more chambers, composed of three or more judges as the Court may determine, for dealing with particular categories of cases; for example, labour cases and cases relating to transit and communications.

2. The Court may at any time form a chamber for dealing with a particular case. The number of judges to constitute such a chamber shall be determined by the Court with the approval of the parties.

3. Cases shall be heard and determined by the chambers provided for in this Article if the parties so request.

Article 27

A judgment given by any of the chambers provided for in Articles 26 and 29 shall be considered as rendered by the Court.

Article 28

The chambers provided for in Articles 26 and 29 may, with the consent of the parties, sit and exercise their functions elsewhere than at The Hague.

Article 29

With a view to the speedy dispatch of business, the Court shall form annually a chamber composed of five judges which, at the request of the parties, may hear and determine cases by summary procedure. In addition, two judges shall be selected for the purpose of replacing judges who find it impossible to sit.

Article 30

1. The Court shall frame rules for carrying out its functions. In particular, it shall lay down rules of procedure.

2. The Rules of the Court may provide for assessors to sit with the Court or with any of its chambers, without the right to vote.

Article 31

1. Judges of the nationality of each of the parties shall retain their right to sit in the case before the Court.

2. If the Court includes upon the Bench a judge of the nationality of one of the parties, any other party may choose a person to sit as judge. Such person shall be chosen preferably from among those persons who have been nominated as candidates as provided in Articles 4 and 5.

3. If the Court includes upon the Bench no judge of the nationality of the parties, each of these parties may proceed to choose a judge as provided in paragraph 2 of this Article.

4. The provisions of this Article shall apply to the case of Articles 26 and 29. In such cases, the President shall request one or, if necessary, two of the members of the Court forming the chamber to give place to the members of the Court of the nationality of the parties concerned, and, failing such, or if they are unable to be present, to the judges specially chosen by the parties.

5. Should there be several parties in the same interest, they shall, for the purpose of the preceding provisions, be reckoned as one party only. Any doubt upon this point shall be settled by the decision of the Court.

6. Judges chosen as laid down in paragraphs 2, 3, and 4 of this Article shall fulfil the conditions required by Articles 2, 17 (paragraph 2), 20, and 24 of the present Statute. They shall take part in the decision on terms of complete equality with their colleagues.

Article 32

1. Each member of the Court shall receive an annual salary.

2. The President shall receive a special annual allowance.

3. The Vice-President shall receive a special allowance for every day on which he acts as President.

4. The judges chosen under Article 31, other than members of the Court, shall receive compensation for each day on which they exercise their functions.

5. These salaries, allowances, and compensation shall be fixed by the General Assembly. They may not be decreased during the term of office.

8. The above salaries, allowances, and compensation shall be free of all taxation.

Article 33

The expenses of the Court shall be borne by the United Nations in such a manner as shall be decided by the General Assembly.

CHAPTER 2

COMPETENCE OF THE COURT

Article 34

1. Only states may be parties in cases before the Court.

2. The Court, subject to and in conformity with its Rules, may request of public international organisations information relevant to cases before it, and shall receive such information presented by such organisations on their own initiative.

3. Whenever the construction of the constituent instrument of a public international organisation or of an international convention adopted thereunder is in question in a case before the Court, the Registrar shall so notify the public international organisation concerned and shall communicate to it copies of all the written proceedings.

Article 35

1. The Court shall be open to the states parties to the present Statute.

2. The conditions under which the Court shall be open to other states shall, subject to the special provisions contained in treaties in force, be laid down by the Security Council, but in no case shall such conditions place the parties in a position of inequality before the Court.

3. When a state which is not a Member of the United Nations is a party to a case, the Court shall fix the amount which that party is to contribute towards the expenses of the Court. This provision shall not apply if such state is bearing a share of the expenses of the Court.

Article 36

1. The jurisdiction of the Court comprises all cases which the parties refer to it and all matters specially provided for in the Charter of the United Nations or in treaties and conventions in force.

2. The states parties to the present Statute may at any time declare that they recognise as compulsory *ipso facto* and without special agreement, in relation to any other states accepting the same obligation, the jurisdiction of the Court in all legal disputes concerning:

  a. the interpretation of a treaty;
  b. any question of international law;
  c. the existence of any fact which, if established, would constitute a breach of an international obligation;
  d. the nature or extent of the reparation to be made for the breach of an international obligation.

3. The declarations referred to above may be made unconditionally or on condition of reciprocity on the part of several or certain states, or for a certain time.

4. Such declarations shall be deposited with the Secretary-General of the United Nations, who shall transmit copies thereof to the parties to the Statute and to the Registrar of the Court.

5. Declarations made under Article 36 of the Statute of the Permanent Court of International Justice and which are still in force shall be deemed, as between the parties to the present Statute, to be acceptance of the compulsory jurisdiction of the International Court of Justice for the period which they still have to run and in accordance with their terms.

6. In the event of a dispute as to whether the Court has jurisdiction, the matter shall be settled by the decision of the Court.

Article 37

Whenever a treaty or convention in force provides for reference of a matter to a tribunal to have been instituted by the League of Nations, or to the Permanent Court of International Justice, the matter shall, as between the parties to the present Statute, be referred to the International Court of Justice.

Article 38

1. The Court, whose function is to decide in accordance with international law such disputes as are submitted to it, shall apply:

   a. international conventions, whether general or particular, establishing rules expressly recognised by the contesting states;
   b. international custom, as evidence of a general practice accepted as law;
   c. the general principles of law recognised by civilised nations;
   d. subject to the provisions of Article 59, judicial decisions and the teachings of the most highly qualified publicists of the various nations, as subsidiary means for the determination of rules of law.

2. This provision shall not prejudice the power of the Court to decide a case *ex aequo et bono*, if the parties agree thereon.

CHAPTER 3

PROCEDURE

Article 39

1. The official languages of the Court shall be French and English. If the parties agree that the case shall be conducted in French, the judgment shall be delivered in French. If the parties agree that the case shall be conducted in English, the judgment shall be delivered in English.

2. In the absence of an agreement as to which language shall be employed each party may, in the pleadings, use the language which it prefers; the decision of the Court shall be given in French and English. In this case the Court shall at the same time determine which of the two texts shall be considered as authoritative.

3. The Court shall, at the request of any party, authorise a language other than French or English to be used by that party.

Article 40

1. Cases are brought before the Court, as the case may be, either by the notification of the special agreement or by a written application addressed to the Registrar. In either case the subject of the dispute and the parties shall be indicated.

2. The Registrar shall forthwith communicate the application to all concerned.

3. He shall also notify the Members of the United Nations through the Secretary-General, and also any other states entitled to appear before the Court.

Article 41

1. The Court shall have the power to indicate, if it considers that circumstances so require, any provisional measures which ought to be taken to preserve the respective rights of either party.

2. Pending the final decision, notice of the measures suggested shall forthwith be given to the parties and to the Security Council.

Article 53

1. Whenever one of the parties does not appear before the Court, or fails to defend its case, the other party may call upon the Court to decide in favour of its claim.

2. The Court must, before doing so, satisfy itself, not only that it has jurisdiction in accordance with Articles 36 and 37, but also that the claim is well founded in fact and law.

Article 55

1. All questions shall be decided by a majority of the judges present.

2. In the event of an equality of votes, the President or the judge who acts in his place shall have a casting vote.

Article 56

1. The judgment shall state the reasons on which it is based.

2. It shall contain the names of the judges who have taken part in the decision.

Article 57

If the judgment does not represent in whole or in part the unanimous opinion of the judges, any judge shall be entitled to deliver a separate opinion.

Article 58

The judgment shall be signed by the President and by the Registrar. It shall be read in open court, due notice having been given to the agents.

Article 59

The decision of the Court has no binding force except between the parties and in respect of that particular case.

Article 60

The judgment is final and without appeal. In the event of dispute as to the meaning or scope of the judgment, the Court shall construe it upon the request of any party.

Article 61

1. An application for revision of a judgment may be made only when it is based upon the discovery of some fact of such a nature as to be a decisive factor, which fact was, when the judgment was given, unknown to the Court and also to the party claiming revision, always provided that such ignorance was not due to negligence.

2. The proceedings for revision shall be opened by a judgment of the Court expressly recording the existence of the new fact, recognising that it has such a character as to lay the case open to revision, and declaring the application admissible on this ground.

3. The Court may require previous compliance with the terms of the judgment before it admits proceedings in revision.

4. The application for revision must be made at latest within six months of the discovery of the new fact.

5. No application for revision may be made after the lapse of ten years from the date of the judgment.

Article 62

1. Should a state consider that it has an interest of a legal nature which may be affected by the decision in the case, it may submit a request to the Court to be permitted to intervene.

2. It shall be for the Court to decide upon this request.

Article 63

1. Whenever the construction of a convention to which states other than those concerned in the case are parties is in question, the Registrar shall notify all such states forthwith.

2. Every state so notified has the right to intervene in the proceedings; but if it uses this right, the construction given by the judgment will be equally binding upon it.

Article 64

Unless otherwise decided by the Court, each party shall bear its own costs.

CHAPTER 4

ADVISORY OPINIONS

Article 65

1. The Court may give an advisory opinion on any legal question at the request of whatever body may be authorised by or in accordance with the Charter of the United Nations to make such a request.

2. Questions upon which the advisory opinion of the Court is asked shall be laid before the Court by means of a written request containing an exact statement of the question upon which an opinion is required, and accompanied by all documents likely to throw light upon the question.

Article 66

The Registrar shall forthwith give notice of the request for an advisory opinion to all states entitled to appear before the Court.

2. The Registrar shall also, by means of a special and direct communication, notify any state entitled to appear before the Court or international organisation considered by the Court, or, should it not be sitting, by the President, as likely to be able to furnish information on the question, that the Court will be prepared to receive, within a time limit to be fixed by the President, written statements, or to hear, at a public sitting to be held for the purpose, oral statements relating to the question.

3. Should any such state entitled to appear before the Court have failed to receive the special communication referred to in paragraph 2 of this Article, such state may express a desire to submit a written statement or to be heard; and the Court will decide.

4. States and organisations having presented written or oral statement or both shall be permitted to comment on the statements made by other states or organisations in the form, to the extent, and within the time limits which the Court, or, should it not be sitting, the President, shall decide in each particular case. Accordingly, the Registrar shall in due time communicate any such written statements to states and organisations having submitted similar statements.

Article 67

The Court shall deliver its advisory opinion in open court, notice having been given to the Secretary-General and to the representatives of Members of the United Nations, of other states and of international organisations immediately concerned.

Article 68

In the exercise of its advisory functions the Court shall further be guided by the provisions of the present Statute which apply in contentious cases to the extent to which it recognises them to be applicable.

CHAPTER 5

AMENDMENT

Article 69

Amendments to the present Statute shall be effected by the same procedure as is provided by the Charter of the United Nations for amendments to that Charter, subject however to any provisions which the General Assembly upon recommendation of the Security Council may adopt concerning the participation of states which are parties to the present Statute but are not Members of the United Nations.

Article 70

The Court shall have power to propose such amendments to the present statute as it may deem necessary, through written communications to the Secretary-General, for consideration in conformity with the provisions of Article 69.

APPENDIX II

MEMBERS OF THE UNITED NATIONS

There are 185 members. The date indicates the year of admission; no date is given for the 51 original members.

Afghanistan (1946)
Albania (1955)
Algeria (1962)
Andorra (1993)
Angola (1976)
Antigua and Barbuda (1981)
Argentina
Armenia (1992)
Australia
Austria (1955)
Azerbaijan (1992)
Bahamas (1973)
Bahrain (1971)
Bangladesh (1974)
Barbados (1966)
Belarus (formerly Byelorussian SSR)
Belgium
Belize (1981)
Benin (formerly Dahomey) (1960)
Bhutan (1971)
Bolivia
Bosnia and Herzegovina (1992)
Botswana (1966)
Brazil
Brunei Darussalam (1984)
Bulgaria (1955)
Burkino Faso (formerly Upper Volta) (1960)
Burundi (1962)
Cambodia (1955)
Cameroon (1960)
Canada
Cape Verde (1975)
Central African Republic (1960)
Chad (1960)
Chile
China[1]

Colombia
Comoros (1975)
Congo (1960)
Congo, Democratic Republic of (formerly Zaire) (1960)
Costa Rica
Côte D'Ivoire (1960)
Croatia (1992)
Cuba
Cyprus (1960)
Czech Rep. (1993)
Denmark
Djibouti (1977)
Dominica (1978)
Dominican Republic
Ecuador
Egypt[2]
El Salvador
Equatorial Guinea (1968)
Eritrea (1993)
Estonia (1991)
Ethiopia
Fiji (1970)
Finland (1955)
France
Gabon (1960)
Gambia (1965)
Georgia (1992)
Germany (1973)[3]
Ghana (1957)
Greece
Grenada (1974)
Guatemala
Guinea (1958)
Guinea-Bissau (1974)
Guyana (1966)
Haiti
Honduras
Hungary (1955)
Iceland (1946)
India
Indonesia (1950)

Iran
Iraq
Ireland (1955)
Israel (1949)
Italy (1955)
Jamaica (1962)
Japan (1956)
Jordan (1955)
Kazakhstan (1992)
Kenya (1963)
Korea, Democratic People's Republic (1991)
Korea, Republic of (1991)
Kuwait (1963)
Kyrgyz Rep. (1992)
Lao People's Democratic Republic (1955)
Latvia (1991)
Lebanon
Lesotho (1966)
Liberia
Libya (1955)
Liechtenstein (1990)
Lithuania (1991)
Luxembourg
Macedonia, Former Yugoslav Republic of (1993)
Madagascar (1960)
Malawi (1964)
Malaysia (1957)[4]
Maldives (1965)
Mali (1960)
Malta (1964)
Marshall Islands (1990)
Mauritania (1961)
Mauritius (1968)
Mexico
Micronesia, Federated States of (1991)
Moldova, Rep. of (1992)
Monaco (1993)

1080

Mongolia (1961)
Morocco (1956)
Mozambique (1975)
Myanmar (formerly Burma) (1948)
Namibia (1990)
Nepal (1955)
Netherlands
New Zealand
Nicaragua
Niger (1960)
Nigeria (1960)
Norway
Oman (1971)
Pakistan (1947)
Palau (1994)
Panama
Papua New Guinea (1975)
Paraguay
Peru
Philippines
Poland
Portugal (1955)
Qatar (1971)
Romania (1955)
Russian Federation

Rwanda (1962)
St Kitts and Nevis (1983)
St Lucia (1979)
St Vincent and the Grenadines (1980)
Samoa (1976)
San Marino (1992)
Sao Tomé and Principe (1975)
Saudi Arabia
Senegal (1960)
Seychelles (1976)
Sierra Leone (1961)
Singapore (1965)[5]
Slovak Rep. (1993)
Slovenia (1992)
Solomon Is. (1978)
Somalia (1960)
South Africa
Spain (1955)
Sri Lanka (1955)
Sudan (1956)
Suriname (1975)
Swaziland (1963)
Sweden (1946)
Syria (1945)[6]
Tajikistan (1992)

Thailand (1946)
Togo (1960)
Trinidad and Tobago (1962)
Tunisia (1956)
Turkey
Turkmenistan (1992)
Uganda (1962)
Ukraine (formerly Ukranian SSR)
United Arab Emirates (1971)
United Kingdom
United Republic of Tanzania (1961)[7]
United States
Uruguay
Uzbekistan (1992)
Vanuatu (1981)
Venezuela
Viet Nam (1977)
Yemen (1947)[8]
Yugoslavia[9]
Zaire (1960)
Zambia (1964)
Zimbabwe (1980)

---

[1] Following the 1949 revolution in China, the defeated Chiang Kai-shek Government, which had withdrawn to Taiwan, continued to be recognised as the Government of China in the UN. By resolution 2758 (XXVI) of October 25, 1971, the General Assembly decided "to restore all its rights to the People's Republic of China and to recognize the representatives of its Government as the only legitimate representatives of China to the United Nations, and to expel forthwith the representatives of Chiang Kai-shek from the place they unlawfully occupy at the United Nations and in all the organizations related to it".

[2] In 1958, Egypt and Syria united as the one state of the United Arab Republic, which replaced its predecessors as a single UN member. In 1961, Egypt and Syria resumed their separate membership when the union was dissolved.

[3] In 1990, the German Democratic Republic, a UN member (1973), united with the Federal Republic of Germany.

[4] The Federation of Malaya (1957) changed its name to Malaysia in 1963, when Singapore and other territories joined. Singapore became an independent state and UN member, both in 1964.

[5] See n. 4 above.

[6] See n. 2 above.

[7] Tanganyika (1961) and Zanzibar (1963) were UN members. They united as the United Republic of Tanzania and became a single UN member, both in 1964.

[8] Yemen (1947) and Democratic Yemen (1967) were UN members. They united to become the Republic of Yemen and a single UN member, both in 1990.

[9] On the position concerning Yugoslavia, see above, p. 129.

GENERAL ASSEMBLY DECLARATION ON PRINCIPLES OF INTERNATIONAL LAW CONCERNING FRIENDLY RELATIONS AND CO-OPERATION AMONG STATES IN ACCORDANCE WITH THE CHARTER OF THE UNITED NATIONS 1970[1]

The General Assembly . . .

1. *Solemnly proclaims* the following principles:

The principle that States shall refrain in their international relations from the threat or use of force against the territorial integrity or political independence of any State, or in any other manner inconsistent with the purposes of the United Nations.

Every State has the duty to refrain in its international relations from the threat or use of force against the territorial integrity or political independence of any State, or in any other manner inconsistent with the purposes of the United Nations. Such a threat or use of force constitutes a violation of international law and the Charter of the United Nations and shall never be employed as a means of settling international issues.

A war of aggression constitutes a crime against the peace for which there is responsibility under international law.

In accordance with the purposes and principles of the United Nations, States have the duty to refrain from propaganda for wars of aggression.

Every State has the duty to refrain from the threat or use of force to violate the existing international boundaries of another State or as a means of solving international disputes, including territorial disputes and problems concerning frontiers of States.

Every State likewise has the duty to refrain from the threat or use of force to violate international lines of demarcation, such as armistice lines, established by or pursuant to an international agreement to which it is a party or which it is otherwise bound to respect. Nothing in the foregoing shall be construed as prejudicing the positions of the parties concerned with regard to the status and effects of such lines under their special régimes or as affecting their temporary character.

States have a duty to refrain from acts of reprisal involving the use of force.

Every State has the duty to refrain from any forcible action which deprives peoples referred to in the elaboration of the principle of equal rights and self-determination of their right to self-determination and freedom and independence.

Every State has the duty to refrain from organising or encouraging the organisation of irregular forces or armed bands, including mercenaries, for incursion into the territory of another State.

---

[1] G.A. Resn 2625 (XXV), October 24, 1970. The resolution was adopted by the General Assembly without a vote.

Every State has the duty to refrain from organising, instigating, assisting or participating in acts of civil strife or terrorist acts in another State or acquiescing in organised activities within its territory directed towards the commission of such acts, when the acts referred to in the present paragraph involve a threat or use of force.

The territory of a State shall not be the object of military occupation resulting from the use of force in contravention of the provisions of the Charter. The territory of a State shall not be the object of acquisition by another State resulting from the threat or use of force. No territorial acquisition resulting from the threat or use of force shall be recognised as legal. Nothing in the foregoing shall be construed as affecting:

(a) Provisions of the Charter or any international agreement prior to the Charter régime and valid under international law; or
(b) The powers of the Security Council under the Charter.

All States shall pursue in good faith negotiations for the early conclusion of a universal treaty on general and complete disarmament under effective international control and strive to adopt appropriate measures to reduce international tensions and strengthen confidence among States.

All States shall comply in good faith with their obligations under the generally recognised principles and rules of international law with respect to the maintenance of international peace and security, and shall endeavour to make the United Nations security system based upon the Charter more effective.

Nothing in the foregoing paragraphs shall be construed as enlarging or diminishing in any way the scope of the provisions of the Charter concerning cases in which the use of force is lawful.

The principle that States shall settle their international disputes by peaceful means in such a manner that international peace and security and justice are not endangered

Every State shall settle its international disputes with other States by peaceful means, in such a manner that international peace and security, and justice, are not endangered.

Every State shall accordingly seek early and just settlement of their international disputes by negotiation, inquiry, mediation, conciliation, arbitration, judicial settlement, resort to regional agencies or arrangements or other peaceful means of their choice. In seeking such a settlement, the parties shall agree upon such peaceful means as may be appropriate to the circumstances and nature of the dispute.

The parties to a dispute have the duty, in the event of failure to reach a solution by any one of the above peaceful means, to continue to seek a settlement of the dispute by other peaceful means agreed upon by them.

States parties to an international dispute, as well as other States, shall refrain from any action which may aggravate the situation so as to endanger the maintenance of international peace and security, and shall act in accordance with the purposes and principles of the United Nations.

International disputes shall be settled on the basis of the sovereign equality of States and in accordance with the principle of free choice of means. Recourse to, or acceptance of, a settlement procedure freely agreed to by States with regard to existing or future disputes to which they are parties shall not be regarded as incompatible with sovereign equality.

Nothing in the foregoing paragraphs prejudices or derogates from the applicable provisions of the Charter, in particular those relating to the pacific settlement of international disputes.

The principle concerning the duty not to intervene in matters within the domestic jurisdiction of any State, in accordance with the Charter

No State or group of States has the right to intervene, directly or indirectly, for any reason whatever, in the international or external affairs of any other State. Consequently, armed intervention and all other forms of interference or attempted threats against the personality of the State or against its political, economic and cultural elements, are in violation of international law.

No State may use or encourage the use of economic, political or any other type of measures to coerce another State in order to obtain from it the subordination of the exercise of its sovereign rights and to secure from it advantages of any kind. Also, no State shall organise, assist, foment, finance, incite or tolerate subversive, terrorist or armed activities directed towards the violent overthrow of the régime of another State, or interfere in civil strife in another State.

The use of force to deprive peoples of their national identity constitutes a violation of their inalienable rights and of the principle of non-intervention.

Every State has an inalienable right to choose its political, economic, social and cultural systems, without interference in any form by another State.

Nothing in the foregoing paragraphs shall be construed as affecting the relevant provisions of the Charter relating to the maintenance of international peace and security.

The duty of States to co-operate with one another in accordance with the Charter

States have the duty to co-operate with one another, irrespective of the differences in their political, economic and social systems, in the various spheres of international relations, in order to maintain international peace and security and to promote international economic stability and progress, the general welfare of nations and international co-operation free from discrimination based on such differences.

To this end:

(*a*) States shall co-operate with other States in the maintenance of international peace and security;

(*b*) States shall co-operate in the promotion of universal respect for and observance of human rights and fundamental freedoms for all, and in the elimination of all forms of racial discrimination and all forms of religious intolerance;

(*c*) States shall conduct their international relations in the economic, social, cultural, technical and trade fields in accordance with the principles of sovereign equality and non-intervention;

(*d*) States Members of the United Nations have the duty to take joint and separate action in co-operation with the United Nations in accordance with the relevant provisions of the Charter.

States should co-operate in the economic, social and cultural fields as well as in the field of science and technology and for the promotion of international cultural and educational progress. States should co-operate in the promotion of economic growth throughout the world, especially that of the developing countries.

The principle of equal rights and self-determination of peoples

By virtue of the principle of equal rights and self-determination of peoples enshrined in the Charter, all peoples have the right freely to determine, without external interference, their political status and to pursue their economic, social and cultural development, and every State has the duty to respect this right in accordance with the provisions of the Charter.

Every State has the duty to promote, through joint and separate action, the realisation of the principle of equal rights and self-determination of peoples, in accordance with the provisions of the Charter, and to render assistance to the United Nations in carrying out the responsibilities entrusted to it by the Charter regarding the implementation of the principle in order:

(a) To promote friendly relations and co-operation among States; and
(b) To bring a speedy end to colonialism, having regard to the freely expressed will of the peoples concerned;

and bearing in mind that subjection of peoples to alien subjugation, domination and exploitation constitutes a violation of the principle, as well as a denial of fundamental human rights, and is contrary to the Charter of the United Nations.

Every State has the duty to promote through joint and separate action universal respect for the observance of human rights and fundamental freedoms in accordance with the Charter.

The establishment of a sovereign and independent State, the free association or integration with an independent State or the emergence into any other political status freely determined by a people constitute modes of implementing the right of self-determination by that people.

Every State has the duty to refrain from any forcible action which deprives peoples referred to above in the elaboration of the present principle of their right to self-determination and freedom and independence. In their actions against and resistance to such forcible action in pursuit of the exercise of their right to self-determination, such peoples are entitled to seek and to receive support in accordance with the purposes and principles of the Charter of the United Nations.

The territory of a colony or other non-governing territory has, under the Charter of the United Nations, a status separate and distinct from the territory of the State administering it; and such separate and distinct status under the Charter shall exist until the people of the colony or non-self-governing territory have exercised their right of self-determination in accordance with the Charter, and particularly its purposes and principles.

Nothing in the foregoing paragraphs shall be construed as authorizing or encouraging any action which would dismember or impair, totally or in part, the territorial integrity or political unity of sovereign and independent States conducting themselves in compliance with the principle of equal rights and self-determination of peoples as described above and thus possessed of a government representing the whole people belonging to the territory without distinction as to race, creed or colour.

Every State shall refrain from any action aimed at the partial or total disruption of the national unity and territorial integrity of any other State or country.

The principle of sovereign equality of States

All States enjoy sovereign equality. They have equal rights and duties and are equal members of the international community, notwithstanding differences of an economic, social political or other nature.

In particular, sovereign equality includes the following elements:

(a) States are juridically equal;
(b) Each State enjoys the rights inherent in full sovereignty;
(c) Each State has the duty to respect the personality of other States;

(d) The territorial integrity and political independence of the State are inviolable;

(e) Each State has the right freely to choose and develop its political, social, economic and cultural systems;

(f) Each State has the duty to comply fully and in good faith with its international obligations and to live in peace with other States.

The principle that States shall fulfil in good faith the obligations assumed by them in accordance with the Charter

Every State has the duty to fulfil in good faith the obligations assumed by it in accordance with the Charter of the United Nations.

Every State has the duty to fulfil in good faith its obligations under the generally recognized principles and rules of international law.

Every State has the duty to fulfil in good faith its obligations under international agreements valid under the generally recognized principles and rules of international law.

Where obligations arising under international agreements are in conflict with the obligations of Members of the United Nations under the Charter of the United Nations, the obligations under the Charter shall prevail.

2. *Declares* that:

In their interpretation and application the above principles are interrelated and each principle should be construed in the context of the other principles.

Nothing in this Declaration shall be construed as prejudicing in any manner the provisions of the Charter or the rights and duties of Member States under the Charter or the rights of peoples under the Charter taking into account the elaboration of these rights in this Declaration.

3. *Declares further* that:

The principles of the Charter which are embodied in this Declaration constitute basic principles of international law, and consequently appeals to all States to be guided by these principles in their international conduct and to develop their mutual relations on the basis of their strict observance.

INDEX